### Frank A. Beach (1911–1988)

*Grant money comes from taxes; taxes come from a lot of folks who don't have much money. Spend that money wisely.*

*To what degree should my choice of research work be governed by human needs, by social imperatives, and how am I going to justify spending all of my energies on any research that does not bear directly on pressing human problems? . . . The solution, or rationalization, that I have finally come up with is that it is a perfectly worthwhile way of spending one's life to do your level best to increase human knowledge, and it is not necessary nor is it always even desirable to be constrained by possible applicability of what you find to immediate problems. This may sound very peculiar to some young people, but it is a value judgment which I myself have made and which I can live with.*

### John Garcia

*I always use anthropomorphism and teleology to predict animal behavior because this works better than most learning theories. I could rationalize this heresy by pointing to our common neurosensory systems or to convergent evolutionary forces. But, in truth, I merely put myself in the animal's place. I cannot think in the cryptic jargon of learning.*

### Walter B. Cannon (1871–1945)

*As a matter of routine I have long trusted unconscious processes to serve me. . . . [One] example I may cite was the interpretation of the significance of bodily changes which occur in great emotional excitement, such as fear and rage. These changes—the more rapid pulse, the deeper breathing, the increase of sugar in the blood, the secretion from the adrenal glands—were very diverse and seemed unrelated. Then, one wakeful night, after a considerable collection of these changes had been disclosed, the idea flashed through my mind that they could be nicely integrated if conceived as bodily preparations for supreme effort in flight or in fighting.*

### Susan S. Schiffman

*I have learned as much from outside academia as from within. Many industrial firms have great research equipment and the money to apply to a problem. For instance, for some of my odor studies I needed extremely pure, highly expensive chemicals. The cost would be prohibitive in a university laboratory, even with a large research grant. But industrial firms are willing to support the research if the information might help develop products that they can market.*

### Luigi Valzelli (1927–1989)

*I am also convinced that psychology and psychiatry may both be assumed at the key of understanding history, philosophy, and the evolution of man . . . perhaps the "essence" of man.*

# Biological Psychology

## ABOUT THE AUTHOR

James W. Kalat (rhymes with ballot), born in 1946, received an A.B. degree summa cum laude from Duke University in 1968 and a Ph.D. in psychology in 1971 from the University of Pennsylvania, where he worked with Paul Rozin. He was a faculty member at Duke University from 1971 to 1977 and has been at North Carolina State University since 1977. He is also the author of *Introduction to Psychology*. (The second edition was published by Wadsworth in 1990.)

# Biological
# Psychology

## FOURTH EDITION

**JAMES W. KALAT**

*North Carolina State University*

**Brooks/Cole Publishing Company**
Pacific Grove, California

*Psychology Editor:* Kenneth King

*Development Editor:* Mary Arbogast

*Assistant Editor:* Julie Johnson

*Editorial Assistant:* Cynthia Campbell

*Production Editor:* Sandra Craig

*Designer:* Carolyn Deacy

*Print Buyer:* Karen Hunt

*Art Editor:* Kelly Murphy

*Permissions Editor, Photo Researcher:* Marion Hansen

*Copy Editor:* Pat Tompkins

*Technical Illustrations:* Darwen and Vally Hennings, Joel Ito, Carlyn Iversen, Precision Graphics, Nadine Sokol, John and Judy Waller

*Cover Illustration:* Tomo Narashima

*Composition and prepress services:* Interactive Composition Corporation

*Printer:* Arcata Graphics/Hawkins

4  5  6  7  8  9  10

Library of Congress Cataloging-in-Publication Data

Kalat, James, W.
    Biological psychology / James W. Kalat. — 4th ed.
        p.  cm.
    Includes bibliographical references and indexes.
    ISBN 0-534-16254-1 (alk. paper)
    1. Neuropsychology.  2. Psychobiology.  I. Title.
    [DNLM:
1. Neurophysiology.  2. Psychophysiology.  WL 103 K14b]
    QP360.K33  1992
    612.8 — dc20
    DNLM/DLC
    for Library of Congress                                  91–24288

TO MY BROTHER ED AND HIS FAMILY

# Brief Contents

# Contents

briefly. "But that is only the first part of our work. The second is to be as cruel to you as possible. To humiliate and confuse you . . . to destroy your will. To reduce you to a state of helpless bewilderment so you will agree to cooperate with us. And I won't deceive you, Cathy—if I thought we could get your cooperation that way, I would have carried out my instructions."

"What cooperation?" Cathy asked intently.

"How well I know you, Cathy!" he exclaimed, and once again she heard the old remembered tenderness in Carl's voice. "I never forgot you. I loved you. And I understand you. Beneath your soft exterior you have an iron will of your own. I told my superiors about you. Cruelty would be counterproductive. We could destroy you but never compel you to do what you feel is wrong. I tried to explain this. They refused to listen." He gave a tight laugh. "I am afraid we KGB have too often found that brutality works."

He glanced at his watch again with obvious anxiety, then took hold of her hand. "Cathy, I haven't much time!" In his eyes she saw all the urgency and fear of a man under intolerable stress. "I am disobeying my instructions. Instead of threatening you, I am imploring, *begging* you. Help me to stop a monstrous crime. I need your cooperation."

"What crime . . . what cooperation?" Cathy's voice was hushed.

Carl went to a briefcase and took out a sheaf of papers. He gave them to her. "Read, and you will understand what is threatening all of us," he said.

Cathy began to read. Slowly at first, taking care over each word. But as the meaning of what she was reading penetrated, she turned the pages more rapidly, unable to believe their contents. The whole thing was incredible. Unbelievable! Terrifying!

At last she put the papers down with a shaking hand. Carl was looking at her. "It's a speech, isn't it?" she said.

"Every word of it is true."

"Who is supposed to give this speech?"

Carl's eyes were fixed on Cathy's. "You are."

"Me! . . . Why? I have no such authority."

"You are the President's wife. Your people will trust you. They will know it isn't a hoax."

"What about my husband, the President, and all the other . . ."

"They will not be available," Carl answered calmly.

"What do you mean . . . not available?"

# Preface

## TO THE INSTRUCTOR (Students can read it too.)

Biological psychology is the most interesting topic in the world. I am sure every professor and every textbook author feels that way about his or her own topic. But the others are wrong; this really *is* the most interesting topic. It deals with the fundamental questions of what the human mind is, what its relationship with the brain is, how it works, and why we are the way we are.

My primary goal in writing this text has been to engage readers' interest. I have tried to focus on the biological mechanisms that are most relevant to key issues in psychology—topics such as the mind-body problem, the development of language and learning, sexual behavior, alcoholism, psychosomatic illnesses, anxiety, aggressive behavior, recovery from brain damage, depression, and schizophrenia. I hope that by the end of the book readers will clearly see what the study of the brain has to do with "real psychology" and that they will be interested in learning more.

Every chapter in this text has been revised. The most substantial revisions are in Chapters 1 (Global Issues), 7 (Vision), and 14 ( The Biology of Learning and Memory). The organization of the fourth edition differs from that of the third in these ways:

- Chapter 6 (Sensory Systems) now covers the sensory systems other than vision, with all material on vision deferred to Chapter 7, except for material on development of the visual system, which is in Chapter 8.
- Chapter 8, Development of the Brain and Brain-Behavior Relationships, is new, although it incorporates some material previously discussed in the chapters on anatomy and the visual system.
- The chapters on depression and schizophrenia, previously separate, have been combined into Chapter 16, Biology of Mood Disorders, Schizophrenia, and Autism.
- The BioSketches have been deleted, but a number of noted investigators are pictured and quoted on the inside covers.
- All chapters except Chapter 1 are divided into modules, each beginning with its own introduction and finishing with its own summary and questions. This organization makes it easier for instructors to assign part of a chapter per day instead of assigning a whole chapter per week. Parts of chapters can also be covered in a different order.

- The most noticeable change in the fourth edition is the use of four-color illustrations throughout the text. I hope this adds to both the clarity and the enjoyment.

Instructors adopting this text for class use may obtain from the publisher a copy of the Instructor's Manual, written by Thomas Stonebraker of Greenville College. Contained in the manual are nearly two thousand multiple-choice test items, which are also available on diskette for IBM and Macintosh computers. Additionally, there is a set of overhead transparencies. A Study Guide, written by Elaine Hull of SUNY-Buffalo, is available for student purchase. I am grateful for the excellent work of Stonebraker and Hull.

I have received helpful comments and suggestions from many students and colleagues, including Stephen Black, Bartley Hoebel, Elaine Hull, William Moorcroft, Duane Rumbaugh, Thomas Stonebraker, and Thomas Wason. My special thanks to Dana Copeland for a large number of color photos of human brains. I appreciate the helpful comments provided by the following reviewers: Elizabeth Adkins-Regan, Cornell University; Peter Brunjes, University of Virginia, Charlottesville; Carl Erickson, Duke University; Dennis Feeney, University of New Mexico; Earl Hagstrom, University of New Hampshire; and Seth Sharpless, University of Colorado, Boulder. Jeffrey Willner, University of North Carolina, Chapel Hill, made a final check of a preliminary draft of this edition and provided detailed and extremely helpful recommendations. Early drafts of the illustrations were reviewed by Francisco Gonzalez-Lima, Robert Graham, and Robert Lansing. I thank them for their excellent suggestions.

Thanks also to the staffs of the libraries at North Carolina State University and at the Marine Biological Laboratory of Woods Hole, Massachusetts, for helping me locate various obscure materials.

In preparing this text I have been most fortunate to work with Mary Arbogast on the writing and organization, and with Sandra Craig on the production. Both have offered excellent judgment and many good ideas; both have voluntarily put in far more effort than I could possibly have asked. I have also been fortunate to work with Kelly Murphy and Marion Hansen on the art program and with Julie Johnson on supplements. Carolyn Deacy designed the text and cover. Pat Tompkins did a thorough job of copy editing the manuscript. The artwork was prepared by Darwen and Vally Hennings, Joel Ito, Carlyn Iverson, Precision Graphics, Nadine Sokol, and John and Judy Waller. I appreciate the splendid help these people provided.

I also thank Ken King, the best psychology editor in the business and a great friend. Thanks to my wife, Ann, and my children, David, Sam, and Robin, who listened every time I wanted to talk about the latest thing I had read. And thanks to my department head, Paul Thayer, for being consistently supportive and encouraging.

I welcome correspondence from both students and faculty. Write: James W. Kalat, Department of Psychology, Box 7801, North Carolina State University, Raleigh, NC 27695-7801, U.S.A.

# TO THE STUDENT (Instructors can read it too.)

A college education serves many purposes: to prepare you for a job or for post-graduate education; to provide a background useful to such nonoccupational roles as citizen and parent; to develop your ability to analyze an issue, assemble the relevant information, reach a conclusion, and apply the conclusion; and to satisfy intellectual curiosity and generate new intellectual curiosity.

Yet another goal that we don't always talk about may be even more important: to help you develop a philosophy of life — a coherent set of beliefs about the nature of the universe, the nature of life, and the purposes of your own life; a philosophy to help you organize future thinking and determine priorities and values.

A college education promotes the formation of a philosophy of life by bringing together a wide variety of people from diverse backgrounds, with different views and values. Course work in philosophy, literature, religion, history, and the like introduce you to the views of some great thinkers. Science courses contribute by addressing the questions of what the universe is all about. Consider: The scientific theories we generally regard as the greatest include Copernicus's theory that the earth goes around the sun and Darwin's theory of evolution by natural selection. We identify these theories as great because they affect our basic beliefs about the place of human beings in the universe, not because they contribute directly to our standard of living.

Some philosophies of life can be stated briefly:

- Do unto others as you would have others do unto you.
- From each according to ability, to each according to need.
- Eat, drink, and be merry, for tomorrow we die.
- My country, right or wrong. I only regret that I have but one life to lose for my country.

My own philosophy of life — well, one of my philosophies of life — is that life is a game in which the players do not know the rules. The game starts without warning or preparation (birth); we do not know when it will end (death). We do not know the object of the game, how the scorekeeper (if any) keeps score, or what rewards or penalties might be based on one's score. Initially we play by the rules given by our parents, until at maturity we realize that our parents have no claim to ultimate authority. We must then decide for ourselves the rules by which we shall live.

To make an intelligent decision, we need to understand as much as we can about the universe and especially about ourselves. What are we? How did we come to be the way we are? Why are we conscious?

Biological psychology provides at least a few tentative answers and certainly helps to clarify the questions. This book will, I hope, provoke you to think about what we mean when we say that the brain controls behavior. We all (I presume) know that is true, and yet most of us find this fact difficult to reconcile with our experience of making conscious decisions. What is the relationship between mind and brain? If they are in some sense the same thing, what does it mean to say they are the same thing?

In this textbook you will learn a great deal of detailed information, as is necessary in any field. The point is not to learn those details for their own sake but to apply them to the overall issues of mind and brain and the fundamental questions of what we are and what our relationship to the universe is.

# Biological Psychology

# CHAPTER ONE

# The Global Issues of Biological Psychology

## MAIN IDEAS

**1.** Biological psychologists seek to explain behavior in terms of its physiology, its development, its evolution, and its function.

**2.** Mind and brain are closely related, but we do not know the exact nature of their relationship or what mind really is. Both philosophers and scientists would like to know whether minds could exist independently of brains, whether brains could function equally well if they did not give rise to minds, and what aspects of brain activity are responsible for conscious experience.

**3.** Direct electrical stimulation of the brain can induce behavioral changes and subjective experiences. Studies of electrical stimulation of the brain provide strong evidence that the brain is responsible for mental activity.

**4.** Many experiments in biological psychology use animal subjects. Some of those experiments inflict pain or distress. The ethics of such experiments has become controversial.

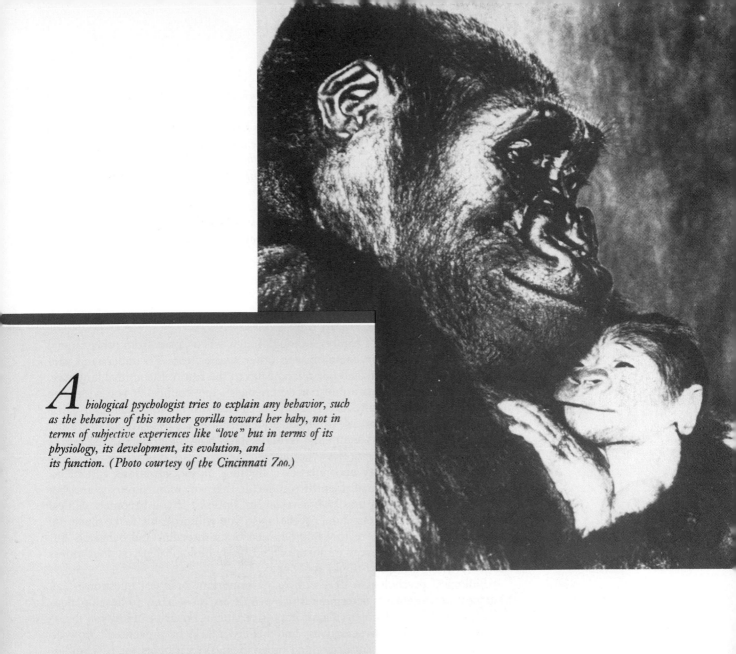

*A* biological psychologist tries to explain any behavior, such as the behavior of this mother gorilla toward her baby, not in terms of subjective experiences like "love" but in terms of its physiology, its development, its evolution, and its function. (Photo courtesy of the Cincinnati Zoo.)

*I*t is often said that Man is unique among animals. It is worth looking at this term "unique" before we discuss our subject proper. The word may in this context have two slightly different meanings. It may mean: Man is strikingly different—he is not identical with any animal. This is of course true. It is true also of all other animals: Each species, even each individual is unique in this sense. But the term is also often used in a more absolute sense: Man is so different, so "essentially" different (whatever that means) that the gap between him and animals cannot possibly be bridged—he is something altogether new. Used in this absolute sense the term is scientifically meaningless. Its use also reveals and may reinforce conceit, and it leads to complacency and defeatism because it assumes that it will be futile even to search for animal roots. It is prejudging the issue.

*Niko Tinbergen (1973)*

Human beings are part of nature. Although much sets us apart from other animal species, we have much in common with other species, too. To understand who we are, we need to understand our relationship to the rest of the animal kingdom.

To understand the nature of our experiences—our "minds" if you wish—we need to understand the physical structure that is responsible for them. Our experience, our behavior, our sense of personal identity—all are products of the brain. **Biological psychology** is an attempt to understand how the brain and the rest of the nervous system generate those products.

Biological psychology encompasses a number of specializations and fields; Table 1.1 describes some of them. If you decide that you want to pursue a career in any of these specializations, you have several options. If you become a clinical psychologist, counselor, or school psychologist, you will probably make much use of information about the relationship between brain disorders and behavior. But even if you choose a career in an unrelated field, biological psychology offers much worth knowing and thinking about.

Biological psychologists deal with many important practical questions: Can biological measurements determine which people are most likely to develop alcoholism, depression, schizophrenia, or impulsive violent behavior? How can disorders such as insomnia, hyperactivity, and anxiety attacks be prevented? How do tranquilizers, antidepressant drugs, and other medical treatments for psychological disorders work? Is it possible to promote behavioral recovery following brain damage?

In addition to the practical questions, biological psychologists wrestle with broad philosophical issues: What is the relationship between the mind and the brain? Could a mind exist independently of a brain? If not, then what is it about the physical structure and functioning of the brain that gives rise to the mind?

How does heredity influence behavior? Our capacity for behavior is a product of our evolutionary history. But did that evolutionary history leave us with genes that *force* us to think and act in certain ways? Did it leave us with genes that make it easier for us to develop certain behaviors instead of others? Or did it leave us with genes that are completely adaptable to the influences of the environment, so that our thinking and behavior are entirely a product of the way we were brought up?

And what about our sense of personal identity? Each of us has a feeling that "I am a single individual," with one mind and one personality. Yet we know that

## Table 1.1  Some of the Major Specializations in Biological Psychology

| | |
|---|---|
| Physiological psychologist<br>Psychobiologist<br>Biopsychologist<br>Behavioral neuroscientist | Graduate degree: Ph.D., probably in psychology, behavioral science, or other related field. May hold position in a research institution, but more likely in a college or university department of psychology or behavioral science. Conducts research on how behavior relates to the physiology of the brain and other organs of the body. |
| Comparative psychologist | Graduate degree: Ph.D. in psychology. Conducts research on animal behavior, concentrating on its development, evolution, and function. (Called a comparative psychologist because he or she compares different animal species to one another.) |
| Ethologist | Graduate degree: Ph.D. in zoology. Conducts research on animal behavior, usually under natural or seminatural conditions, concentrating on its development, evolution, and function. Similar to comparative psychologist except for training. Comparative psychologists tend to be more interested in learned behaviors, and ethologists are more interested in unlearned, species-specific behaviors. |
| Neuroscientist | Graduate degree: Ph.D. or M.D. A general term referring to anyone who conducts research on the nervous system, including any area from brain anatomy to behavior. |
| Neuroanatomist | A neuroscientist who studies the anatomy of the nervous system. |
| Neurophysiologist | A neuroscientist who studies the functioning of the nervous system. |
| Developmental neurobiologist | A neuroscientist who studies the development of the nervous system. |
| Neurochemist | A neuroscientist who studies the chemistry of the nervous system. |
| Psychiatrist | Graduate degree: M.D. plus specialization in psychiatry (medical treatment of psychological disorders). Generally holds position in hospital or in private practice. Vast majority of psychiatrists treat patients; some also conduct research on the effects of drugs and other medical treatments on human behavior. |
| Neurologist | Graduate degree: M.D. plus specialization in neurology (medical treatment of brain damage). Usually holds position in hospital or in private practice. Vast majority of neurologists treat patients; some also collect and publish data about the effects of brain damage on humans. |
| Psychopharmacologist | Graduate degree: Ph.D. in psychology, biology, or related field, and/or M.D. May hold position in a college or university or in a hospital or other medical institution. Conducts research on the effects of drugs on behavior, working with either humans or nonhuman animals. |
| Neuropsychologist | Graduate degree: Ph.D. in psychology, probably also taking selected courses at a medical school. May hold position in a college or university or in a hospital or other medical institution. Occupied primarily with testing the learning, memory, sensation and perception, motor coordination, language, and other behavioral capacities of people believed to be brain damaged. Generally works with psychiatrists and neurologists to help diagnose a patient's problems. |
| Psychophysiologist | Graduate degree: Ph.D. in psychology or biology. Studies relationship of behavior and experience to changes in heart rate, brain waves, and other body measurements. |

the brain is composed of billions of cells communicating with one another by paths that are sometimes long and indirect. Under certain circumstances, one part of the brain may fail to communicate with another part of the brain. How, then, does our sense of an undivided personal identity arise? And is it an illusion?

Biological psychologists do not have firm answers to any of these questions, but most of them are motivated by curiosity about such questions. Although our scientific investigations may not directly answer the great philosophical questions, they may improve the quality of our speculations.

In this chapter, we focus on the global issues of biological psychology. First we consider examples of biological explanations of behavior and the philosophical issues related to such explanations. Then we turn to the ethics of experimentation on animals. In later chapters we shall examine numerous biological explanations in more detail.

## BIOLOGICAL EXPLANATIONS OF BEHAVIOR

Psychologists try to explain behavior. Biological psychologists try to explain behavior in biological terms. For example, consider how various kinds of psychologists try to explain human language: Cognitive psychologists study the relationship between what is said and the meaning behind it. Developmental psychologists study how children's language capacities increase as the children grow older. Social psychologists explore the relationship between language and culture and how social pressures influence speech. Learning researchers examine the ways in which reinforcements and punishments influence the frequency and content of speech. Biological psychologists try to determine what goes on in the brain that makes speech possible.

The explanations that biological psychologists seek are not necessarily restricted to brain activity, however. Tinbergen (1951) distinguished four types of biological explanations: physiological, ontogenetic, evolutionary, and functional.

A **physiological explanation** relates an activity to how the brain and other organs function, even at the cellular and chemical levels. The body is a machine and, like any other machine, it converts one kind of energy into another kind of energy. Among other things, the body converts chemical energy into various kinds of brain activity and into the movement of various parts of the body. We can try to understand the "why" of behavior by a detailed study of the brain's machinery.

The term *ontogenetic* comes from Greek roots meaning "to be" and "origin" (or genesis). Thus an **ontogenetic explanation** describes how a structure or a behavior develops. When possible, it begins with the genes and traces how those genes combine with the influence of the environment to produce the final outcome.

An **evolutionary explanation** relates a structure or a behavior to the evolutionary history of a species. For example, humans have tiny hair follicles on most of our skin. Most of these hairs are too short to be of any real use; they are a remnant of the longer hairs that our remote apelike ancestors had. Similarly, our capacities for behavior are evolutionarily modified from the capacities that other mammals exhibit. (Appendix A describes the principles of evolution.)

A **functional explanation** describes *why* a structure or behavior evolved as it did. Suppose individuals with gene G are slightly more successful at finding mates and reproducing than are individuals with gene g. In the next generation, the percentage of individuals having gene G will increase and the percentage of individuals having gene g will decrease. (That is what the theory of evolution is all about.) We can reverse this reasoning: If gene G has become widespread in the population, then individuals having this gene must have been more successful than other individuals were in reproducing. A functional explanation demonstrates how a particular gene increased reproductive success.

---

# AN EXAMPLE: BIRD SONG

---

Let us consider how these four types of biological explanation apply to a specific example of behavior. The example is bird song and the question is, Why do birds sing? But we can make the question more specific. Not all birds sing. Even among songbirds, adult males generally do most of the singing. Depending on the species, females and immature males may sing less or not at all. The adult males sing vigorously in spring and early summer (the mating season); in most species they become silent or sing only an occasional fragment of a song during the fall and winter. So the question becomes, Why do particular kinds of birds sing at the particular times they do?

First, let us note what is *not* an explanation: We cannot explain bird song by saying that it is an "instinct." The term *instinct* is—at best—a label for a category of behaviors depending more on species membership than on individual experience. But labeling a behavior "instinctive" does not tell us *how* the behavior developed or *why* the species evolved the set of genes promoting this behavior. It is too easy to say that birds sing because they have an instinct to sing, that mother squirrels take care of their babies because they have a maternal instinct, or that cats attack mice because they have a hunting instinct. In each of these cases, people may believe they have explained the behavior, but they have only named it. For this reason, many investigators of animal behavior avoid the term *instinct* altogether.

## A Physiological Explanation of Bird Song

Bird song depends on two areas of the brain (known as the caudal nucleus of the hyperstriatum ventrale and the robust nucleus of the archistriatum). These areas are well developed in songbirds, such as sparrows and finches; they are small or absent in birds with only simple vocalizations, such as chickens and pigeons. In the songbirds, the relevant brain areas are larger in males than they are in females (Arnold, 1980). (See Figure 1.1.)

The size of these brain areas depends on testosterone, a hormone generally occurring in higher levels in males than in females. At the start of the breeding season, testosterone levels rise in males, causing the brain areas responsible for bird song to increase in size. When those areas grow large enough, the bird begins to sing. If the testes are surgically removed from a male songbird, his testosterone level drops, the brain areas responsible for song decrease in size, and he does not sing.

What do you suppose happens if an experimenter injects large amounts of testosterone into a female? The relevant areas of her brain grow and she begins to sing—even in species such as canaries in which females ordinarily never sing! This evidence indicates that both the size of the brain areas and the ability to sing depend on testosterone, not on being a genetic male (Nottebohm, 1980a). (It also indicates that at least a few brain areas can change their size in adult vertebrates.)

**Figure 1.1**

*In songbirds, certain areas of the brain are larger in males (left) than in females (right). Generally, only the males sing. (Photos courtesy of Arthur P. Arnold.)*

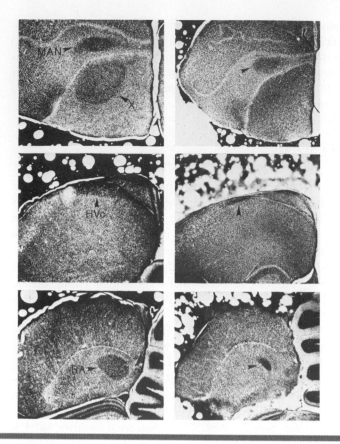

In short, the physiological explanation states that testosterone causes the growth of certain brain areas necessary for song and that this mechanism stimulates song mostly in males during the breeding season. Note that this explanation is incomplete: It does not specify how the brain areas control the muscles to produce song. The answer to that question is known to some extent (Arnold, 1982), though not completely. As is usually the case in science, answering one question leads to other, more detailed questions.

## An Ontogenetic Explanation of Bird Song

As mentioned, certain areas of the brain make it possible for a bird to sing. But how does it know *what* to sing? The answer is more complicated for some species than it is for others (Nottebohm, 1980b).

Pigeons, doves, chickens, and turkeys make only simple coos and cackles, which ornithologists (bird biologists) do not classify as "songs." These species do not need to learn their calls. In fact, even if they are deafened early in life, they develop normal calls. (Note that these observations do not explain how pigeons and the others acquire their calls. They merely indicate that we should look for the answers in the embryology of the nervous system, not in the individual's experience.)

In other species, however, each bird has to learn its song by listening to others of its species. For example, in several sparrow species, a male reared in isolation from the sounds of its own species will develop a distinctly abnormal song. To develop a normal song, a male must hear the song of its own species, either from adult males or from tape recordings (Marler & Peters, 1977). It can learn the song from a tape recording only during a **sensitive period** early in life. The sensitive period varies from species to species; in song sparrows it lasts from about age 20 days to about age 60 days. Exposure to that recording before age 20 days or after age 60 days has little effect (Marler & Peters, 1987, 1988). However, a bird can learn its song from a live tutor either during the sensitive period or at a later age (Baptista, 1985; Baptista & Petrinovich, 1984).

*A song sparrow learns its song by imitating others of its species. (Ed Reschke.)*

This is a most unusual type of learning. A male sparrow that learns its song during the first two months or so of life cannot begin to practice the song until it reaches sexual maturity the following spring—more than half a year later! As spring approaches, the young sparrow begins to sing. At first its song is like the babbling of a human infant, a disorganized mixture of many sounds. As time passes, the sparrow eliminates some of its sounds and rearranges the others into an order that comes closer and closer to matching what it heard the previous summer. For example, male song sparrows at first produce songs of six or more notes at a time before eventually settling on the three-note call that is typical of their species (Marler & Peters, 1981, 1982).

What about the female? In nature, females do not sing, but they do learn their song. A female that is injected with enough testosterone will sing her species' song, if she was exposed to it during the sensitive period (Marler, 1970). Like a male, she sings an abnormal song if she never heard her species' song.

In short, sparrows (and numerous other songbirds) ordinarily hear their song early in life. During that time they form a **template** (or model) of what their song should sound like. Later, if and when their testosterone levels are high enough to enable them to sing, they engage in an apparent trial-and-error process to match their own song to the template. They may also be able to perfect that template by listening to other live birds. (Tape recordings have no effect after the sensitive period ends.)

## An Evolutionary Explanation of Bird Song

Through natural selection, each species evolves adaptations that distinguish it from other species. But because such changes are mostly slow and gradual, we can see in each species certain remnant characteristics of its ancestors. In some cases we can roughly reconstruct how a particular feature may have evolved.

For example, two species of birds that appear to be closely related (based on their anatomy) generally produce similar vocalizations. To the trained ear, the song of each species of sparrow is recognizable and the song of each species of warbler is recognizable. Yet it is also possible to hear an unfamiliar species and say, "That's probably some kind of sparrow," or "That sounds like a warbler of some sort." Even though each species has evolved a unique song, it also retains general features characteristic of its ancestors.

In certain cases biologists can use bird calls and songs to infer something about the evolutionary relationship among various species. For example, the many species of sandpipers emit similar calls, presumably because they share a common ancestor. Two species—dunlins and Baird's sandpipers—give their calls in distinct pulses. (Other sandpipers do not.) This resemblance implies that these two species are more closely related than the others, that they share a recent evolutionary link (Kroodsma & Miller, 1982).

*The similarity of this dunlin's song to that of a Baird's sandpiper suggests that the two species are closely related. (Russell Fieber/FPG International Corp.)*

### A Functional Explanation of Bird Song

If a bird species has genes that enable it to learn its song and to sing it at the appropriate time (spring), then natural selection must have favored those genes for certain reasons. What might those reasons be?

The song of a male bird serves two functions. First, it attracts females of the species and primes them to engage in reproductive behaviors. For example, a female canary that hears a large number and variety of canary songs is quick to respond to a male sexually, quick to lay eggs, and likely to lay a large number of eggs (Kroodsma, 1976). Second, a male's song alerts other males to his presence and announces that he is defending that territory. In this way he may deter competition for his nesting site and the female with which he mates.

Given these principles, we can understand why males sing frequently during the breeding season and rarely during fall and winter. They sing only when they are defending a territory and seeking a mate. We can also see why each species sings its own song: A male song sparrow, for example, gains an advantage by attracting female song sparrows and by driving away other male song sparrows. He would gain no advantage if his song were easily confused with those of other species (Miller, 1982).

Finally, a functional explanation can apply to some of the physical characteristics of bird songs. A singing bird gains an advantage by being heard throughout the territory he can defend. A song heard more widely offers no advantage; it might even be harmful if it attracts cats and other predators. For this reason, most birds produce songs with notes ranging from 1 kHz (kilohertz) upward — frequencies that do not carry well over long distances in a forest (Konishi, 1969).

Note the relationship between evolution and physiology. The bird has the physiology that it does because evolution has favored that physiology. Note also that we do not have to assume that the bird *knows* why it sings at all, much less why it sings at a particular time and place. Evolution has equipped it with the tendency to sing in certain ways and at certain times, but we need not assume that the bird knows its evolutionary history or the purposes its song may serve.

## BIOLOGICAL EXPLANATIONS OF HUMAN BEHAVIOR

Most of us raise no objection to a biological explanation of bird song. We may feel differently about a similar explanation of human behavior, however. Suppose a biological psychologist told you that the anger you experience merely reflects a pattern of activity in one area of your brain, which has been heightened by certain hormones, and that the romantic attraction you feel toward someone is the result of activity in another area of the brain, also heightened by hormones. Moreover, your brain was programmed by natural selection to enable these experiences to develop. Would you resist these explanations?

Such explanations raise difficult philosophical questions, but before we pursue them, we need to distinquish between two types of biological explanation: biological factors that *force* a behavior to occur and biological factors that *enable* a behavior to occur.

Sometimes, the properties of the brain or the rest of the body force certain behaviors to occur. Some human examples: People sweat when they become too hot. The pupil of the eye constricts in the presence of bright light. The leg jerks upward when the knee is tapped in a certain place (the knee-jerk reflex). The flow of saliva increases when we drink unsweetened lemon juice. These behaviors are sure to occur in almost all people under almost all circumstances.

In other cases, a biological influence may make a behavior possible but not absolutely necessary. For example, although a pattern of activity in certain areas of your brain may increase the likelihood of your engaging in aggressive behavior, you may or may not attack someone, depending on the activity in certain other brain areas—the areas that assess the probable consequences of your behavior. An increase in the levels of sex hormones in your blood may increase your sexual motivation, but your actual behavior will depend on your past experiences, the current social setting, and other, possibly competing, motivations.

The full explanation of your behavior is still biological. Your past experiences exert their effects by means of your brain. Your perception of the current situation is a brain activity. So are your competing motivations. The point is that behavior, especially human behavior, is the product of many forces. For the sake of simplicity, I shall not always point this out, but you should always bear it in mind when you listen to any biological explanation of behavior.

## THE MIND-BRAIN RELATIONSHIP

A moment ago I suggested that many of us feel uncomfortable with the idea that our thoughts and actions are the result of physical processes in the brain. Why? Because we have been taught since early childhood that each of us has a "mind" that is separate from the body but capable of interacting with it in some way. For example, it seems to me that I make a conscious decision to do something and then I do it.

How can that be, if my action is governed by a series of chemical processes in the brain? Somehow there must be a close relationship between mind and brain, but what is the nature of that relationship? This is the **mind-body problem,** or **mind-brain problem.**

### The Difficulty of the Problem

Let us consider four basic interpretations of the relationship between the mind and the brain, along with the strengths and weaknesses of each.

According to the **materialist position,** the brain is a machine and consciousness is irrelevant to its functioning. *Strengths:* The brain is indeed a machine, and so far as we can tell it follows the same physical and chemical principles as any other machine. Investigators find no evidence for any mysterious force that acts on the brain from the outside. *Weaknesses:* As the French philosopher René Descartes pointed out, it is impossible to doubt the existence of one's own mind. (As he put it, "I think, therefore I am.") Similarly, each of us has the distinct impression that our conscious minds make decisions affecting our actions. If that is just an illusion, it is certainly a strong and persistent one. Finally, if consciousness has no influence at all over the brain and behavior, how can we talk about consciousness? (When we talk about consciousness, that indicates that our consciousness has influenced our vocal muscles, if nothing else.)

According to the **dualist position,** the mind exists independently of the brain and exerts some control over it. *Strength:* This view fits with our commonsense notion of what the mind is and does. *Weaknesses:* If we believe that the universe is composed solely of matter and energy (as most scientists do), then what is the mind? If it is not a type of matter or energy, how could it possibly alter the electrical and chemical activities of the brain?

The dualist position is no doubt the most popular position with the general public, but most brain investigators find it the least acceptable. Roger Sperry (1988), a distinguished brain researcher, has proposed a modified version of the dualist view, in which brain activity produces a conscious mind, which in turn acts on the brain. However, this rather vague proposal does not explain what the mind is or how it alters brain functioning. Moreover, although Sperry believes that the mind can affect the brain, he also insists that the mind cannot exist independently of the brain.

According to the **identity position,** the mind is the same thing as brain activity, just described in different terms. For example, we could describe Michelangelo's statue *David* as a piece of marble with such-and-so dimensions. This physical description would sound very different from a description of the same object as a work of art. The identity position implies that a conscious mind cannot exist without brain functioning, but it also implies that the brain cannot function independently of a conscious mind. *Strengths:* This view accepts the idea that the mind exists and yet describes it as part of the physical universe. Many scientists find this an appealing theory. *Weaknesses:* This view is so vague. Why and how does the brain give rise to conscious experience? And why are we conscious of some activities that take place in the nervous system (such as vision) but not of others (such as spinal reflexes)?

The emergent property position is a modified version of the identity position. According to the **emergent property position,** consciousness is not a property of all brain activity; it emerges when the brain is organized in certain ways. *Strengths:* This view acknowledges that some kinds of brain activity are conscious while others (such as spinal reflexes) are not. It also allows the possibility that the brains of different animal species, being organized in somewhat different ways, could produce different kinds of mental experience. *Weaknesses:* Again the problem is vagueness. What kind of brain organization produces consciousness, and why and how?

Table 1.2 outlines these four positions on the mind-brain problem and several others. At this point, no interpretation seems fully satisfactory.

The mind-brain relationship is exceedingly difficult to investigate scientifically. The main reason for this difficulty is that although each of us is directly aware of his or her own conscious mind, we cannot observe anyone else's mind. (Indeed, none of us can be certain that any other person is conscious at all. If you insisted that you are the only conscious being in the universe, what could anyone else say or do to convince you otherwise?)

Although it is hard to imagine scientific evidence that would solve the mind-body problem, it is nevertheless possible to collect scientific evidence that bears on some related questions: Does losing part of the brain mean losing part of the mind? (As we shall see throughout this book, the answer is yes.) And does stimulation of part of the brain elicit behaviors and experiences? Let us deal with that question now.

## Control of Behavior by Electrical Stimulation of the Brain

In 1870, Gustav Fritsch and Eduard Hitzig reported that mild, nondestructive electrical stimulation of portions of a dog's cerebral cortex could cause muscle movements. At low intensities, the electrical current stimulated discrete, limited movements—always on the side of the body opposite the stimulation. Depending

## Table 1.2 Philosophical Positions on the Mind-Body (or Mind-Brain) Problem

| Position | Explanation |
|---|---|
| *Dualism* | Holds that mind and brain are fundamentally different and that each can exist independently of the other. |
| *Interactionism* | A type of dualism based on the writings of the French philosopher René Descartes. It holds that mind and brain interact with each other and influence each other. (*How* they might do so has always been unclear.) |
| *Parallelism* | A type of dualism originally proposed by the Dutch philosopher Baruch Spinoza. It maintains that mind and brain exist separately and do not affect each other. Activities of mind and brain nevertheless agree, much as two accurate clocks may always give the same time, even though neither one influences the other. |
| *Monism* | Holds that only one kind of "substance" exists in the universe. Different versions of monism disagree on the nature of that substance. |
| *Materialism* | A version of monism holding that only the material world exists; minds either do not exist at all or at least do not exist independently. |
| *Mentalism* (or immaterialism) | Based on the writings of the Irish philosopher George Berkeley, this version of monism holds that the physical world exists only in one's mind or only in the mind of God. That is, the material world could not exist independently of a conscious subject to perceive it. |
| *Epiphenomenalism* | A version of monism maintaining that the conscious mind is an accidental byproduct of brain activity, just as a lawn mower accidentally produces noise. The mind does not influence brain activity or behavior any more than noise influences the functioning of the lawn mower. (An epiphenomenon is a secondary phenomenon or aftereffect.) |
| *Identity position* | A version of monism holding that mind and brain are two ways of talking about the same thing. Only one kind of substance exists; that substance is neither *mind* nor *material* but *mind-material*. |
| *Panprotopsychic identism* | A variant of the identity position championed by Bernhard Rensch (1971). It holds that consciousness is present in a primitive, potential form in all matter. (*Panprotopsychic* comes from *pan* = universal, *proto* = primitive, and *psychic* = mental.) |
| *Emergent property position* | View that mind is not a property of matter itself, including brain matter, but that it emerges as a new property when the matter is organized in a particular way. For analogy, the properties of water emerge when hydrogen and oxygen are combined, even though neither hydrogen nor oxygen by itself has those properties. |

on the exact point stimulated, the dog would move its neck, back, abdomen, tail, leg, or some other part of its body. Repeated stimulation of the same point consistently elicited the same response. Later experiments yielded similar results for many species.

Electrical activity occurs naturally in the brain at all times. Ordinarily, nerves carrying messages from the sense organs cause this electrical activity. Their impulses combine with the electrical activity already present in certain areas of the brain to produce activity in other areas, which then activate still other areas. Eventually, the areas of the brain that control movement generate activity. Fritsch and Hitzig had directly stimulated the movement-controlling areas, bypassing all the preliminary stages.

The Mind-Brain Relationship

**Electrical Stimulation of Complex Behaviors** Electrical stimulation of the brain can evoke not only simple muscle movements but also more complex sequences of behavior, particularly if the animal is awake during the stimulation and free to move about. Working with chickens, Erich von Holst and Ursula von St. Paul (1960) implanted electrodes permanently into lower parts of the brain and cemented the electrodes on the skull to hold them in place. Later they attached wires to the exposed electrodes and passed a weak electrical current to the chicken's brain while it was awake and moving about.

Stimulation of various areas elicited such behaviors as feeding, drinking, cackling, grooming, turning the body to one side, sitting down, sleeping, escape flight, and aggressive attack (Figure 1.2). Similarly, W. R. Hess (1944) found that electrical stimulation of certain brain areas could induce an animal to fall asleep suddenly. The behavior elicited depends on the exact location of the electrode and the intensity of the stimulation. (Stronger current can stimulate more distant cells.)

The elicited behavior also varied depending on environmental stimuli. For instance, in experiments with rats, stimulation at a specific point caused eating if only food were present and drinking if only water were present (Coons, Levak, & Miller, 1965; Valenstein, Cox, & Kakolewski, 1970).

**Electrical Stimulation of the Human Brain** We cannot, of course, experiment on human brains just for research purposes. However, a variety of medical purposes allow us to investigate the electrical stimulation of human brains.

Electrical stimulation has most often been used with humans in attempts to identify the part of a person's brain responsible for **epilepsy,** a syndrome caused by abnormal repetitive activity of nerve cells in the brain. This abnormal activity originates in a damaged or malfunctioning area of the brain called the **focus** of the epilepsy. The focus is located in different places for different individuals. The abnormal repetitive activity spreads outward from the focus until a large portion of the cerebral cortex is involved, causing uncontrollable convulsions in some people. Epilepsy is usually treated with drugs; however, some people have frequent major seizures that do not respond to drug therapy. In such cases surgeons sometimes remove the focus area.

The first step is to find the focus. Because the brain has no pain receptors, it can be explored by anesthetizing only the scalp, leaving the brain itself awake and alert during the surgery. The surgeon exposes part of the brain and then applies an electrode to stimulate small areas of the cortex, one after another. Eventually, as the surgeon stimulates some point, the patient says, "That makes me feel the way I feel when I'm about to have a seizure." This point is identified as the focus of the epilepsy and can be surgically removed. Ordinarily, the surgery greatly reduces or eliminates the epileptic seizures, and the effects of losing a small piece of brain are usually not serious (Penfield & Roberts, 1959).

While trying to find the focus, the surgeon can note the effects of stimulating other parts of the patient's brain. As in nonhuman brains, stimulation of some points produces motor responses. For instance, in one person stimulation caused a series of hand movements; if the man was holding a newspaper at the time, he would fold it and rotate it or feel around its edge, as long as the stimulation continued (Bickford, Dodge, & Uihlein, 1960). The evoked movement was, in general, not subject to voluntary control.

Some years ago, a few people were given electrical stimulation of the so-called pleasure areas of the brain, in an attempt to provide them with relief from severe pain or depression. R. G. Heath (1964) described a patient whose septal area was stimulated (without his knowledge) by remote control during a psychi-

**Figure 1.2**
*Before stimulation (**a**) the rooster ignores the stuffed polecat. With low-level stimulation (**b**) of some points in the brain (not identified), the rooster orients toward the model but does not attack. With stronger stimulation (**c, d**), he attacks the model. At the end of the attack, after the stimulation is turned off (**e**), he makes a triumphant call (**f**). (From von Holst & von St. Paul, 1960.)*

atric interview. Before the stimulation, he was on the verge of tears as he described his father's illness and his own imagined responsibility for it. Within 15 seconds after the stimulation, he suddenly grinned and started discussing a plan to seduce his girlfriend.

Because electrical stimulation of the brain can elicit not only sensations and movements but also emotional changes, it appears that brain activity is responsible for what we call mind. This is, to be sure, not a new conclusion, but the results of brain stimulation provide particularly strong evidence for it.

## WHY INVESTIGATORS STUDY ANIMALS, AND THE ETHICS OF ANIMAL RESEARCH

Although studies of animals account for only 7 or 8 percent of all published research in psychology as a whole (Gallup & Suarez, 1980), they account for a much higher percentage of the studies in biological psychology. About 95 percent of the animals used are rats, mice, or birds. Their brains and behavior are not identical to those of humans, but chemically, anatomically, and functionally their nervous systems are organized in a similar manner (see Figure 1.3).

Given that the underlying goal of most biological psychologists is to understand the human brain and human behavior, why do they study nonhuman animals? Here are five reasons:

1. *The underlying mechanisms of behavior are similar across species and sometimes are easier to study in a nonhuman species.* If you wanted to understand how a complex machine works, you might begin by examining a smaller, simpler machine that operates on the same principle. The same is true for studying brain-behavior relationships. For example, much of the early research on

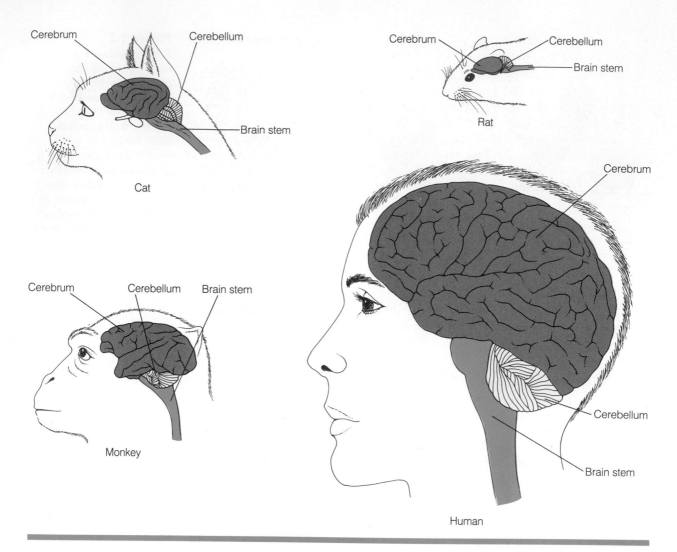

**Figure 1.3**
**Brains of several species**

*The general plan and organization of the brain are similar for all mammals, even though the size varies from species to species.*

nerve cells was conducted on squid nerves, which are similar to human nerves but thicker and therefore easier to study. Or if we wanted to study how certain behaviors change from infancy to old age, we might use mice or rats, which have a life expectancy of two to three years, instead of humans, who live eighty years or more.

2. *Sometimes a certain process is highlighted or exaggerated in animals and therefore is easier to notice than it is in humans.* Consider, for example, the sensitive period for bird-song learning. The evidence shows that certain experiences have a stronger effect at an early age than they do at a later age. The same principle may or may not be true of humans, but once we have seen it clearly in nonhumans, we at least have a good idea of what to look for in humans.

3. *We are interested in animals for their own sake.* Humans are by nature curious. We would like to understand why birds sing, why the Druids built Stonehenge, where the moon came from, and how the rings of Saturn formed, re-

gardless of whether or not such information turns out to be useful for anything other than satisfying our curiosity.

4. *What we learn about animals sheds light on human evolution.* What is the place of humans in nature? How did we come to be the kinds of beings that we are? One way to approach such questions is to examine other species. Can we find some trace of language capacity in chimpanzees and other nonhuman species? How much intelligence do monkeys, rats, and other species show? Humans did not evolve from chimpanzees, monkeys, or rats, but we do share common ancestors with these modern animals, and comparing the structure and function of various animal nervous systems with our own provides important clues to our evolution.

5. Finally, *certain experiments are impossible with humans because of legal or ethical restrictions.* For example, investigators sometimes insert electrodes into the brain cells of rats or other animals to determine the relationship between brain activity and behavior. Such experiments answer questions that investigators cannot address with human studies.

Let us focus on the fourth and fifth reasons in more detail: the relationship of animal studies to an understanding of human evolution and the ethics of experimenting with animals.

## Evolutionary Relationships Among Species

The basic concept of evolution is well established in biology, partly because the fossil evidence shows that species change, but also partly because what we know of genetics makes evolution a logical necessity. (See Appendix A.) Still, it remains difficult to specify several important details about evolutionary history. For example, biologists are confident that humans and chimpanzees evolved from a common ancestor, but they are less certain about exactly when the two species separated and are still less certain about how our common ancestor may have looked or acted.

The basic line of inference goes like this: Humans are more similar to chimpanzees than they are to any other species, in a wide variety of details including the specific chemical structure of our proteins and our chromosomes. Those similarities point to the probability of a common ancestor from which both humans and chimpanzees inherited most of their genes. As we trace back the fossils of humans and chimpanzees, they become more and more alike, until eventually we cannot distinguish one from the other. Both humans and chimpanzees are more like monkeys than they are like rats and other rodents, more like rats than they are like opossums, and more like opossums than they are like platypuses. Therefore, the common ancestors of the primates (humans, apes, and monkeys) probably separated from the common ancestors of the rodents somewhat more recently than they separated from the ancestors of the opossums. Using similar reasoning, evolutionary biologists have constructed an "evolutionary tree" that shows the relationships among various species (see Figure 1.4).

Evolutionary relationships guide investigators' choice of experimental animals to some extent. A researcher interested in the mechanisms of human memory and intelligence generally chooses a species closely related to humans, one that presumably has highly similar brain mechanisms. However, someone who is studying the structure and chemistry of nerve cells could select any convenient species because the most basic principles vary little from one species to another. Researchers also consider the ease of conducting the experiment. For example,

EVOLUTIONARY TREE

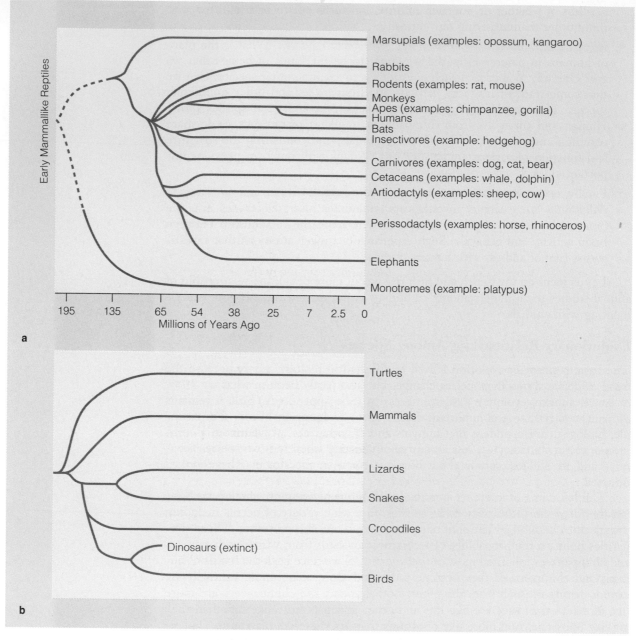

**Figure 1.4**
*(a) Evolutionary relationships among various species of mammals. (b) Evolutionary relationships among mammals, birds, and several kinds of reptiles. The relationships more remote in time (toward the left side of the figure) are less well established.*

for a study of olfaction (smell), an investigator might find it easy to work with rats, which guide much of their normal behavior by following odors. But rats would be a poor choice for a study of color vision.

## Ethical Issues in Animal Research

In this book you will read about experiments in which animals were subjected to electrical shocks, brain damage, surgery, brain stimulation, injections of drugs or hormones, and other treatments that could not be given to human beings. Some people equate such animal experimentation with cruelty to animals, and heated controversy has arisen about the ethics of using animals in biological and psychological experiments. If it is wrong to perform such experiments on humans, they ask, why is it not also wrong to perform them on animals?

This is indeed a difficult question. On the one hand, it is undeniable that laboratory animals sometimes undergo painful or debilitating procedures that are *not* intended for their own benefit. Anyone with a conscience (including scientists) is bothered by this fact. On the other hand, experimentation with animals is essential for learning more about both human and animal physiology (American Medical Association, 1988). Animal experimentation was an essential step in the medical research that led to our ability to prevent or treat polio, diabetes, measles, smallpox, massive burns, heart disease, and other conditions. The majority of Nobel Prizes in physiology or medicine have been awarded for research conducted on nonhuman animals. The hope to find methods of treating or preventing AIDS and various brain diseases (such as Alzheimer's disease) rests largely with animal research. In biological psychology, when dealing with certain questions about brain functioning, our only choice is between conducting research on animals or not answering the questions at all.

The ethical issue has much in common with other ethical dilemmas. For example, should a woman have the option of aborting an unwanted pregnancy? If we focus on the welfare of the fetus, then we come to one answer; if we focus on the welfare of the woman, then we come to the other answer. Likewise, we can reach different conclusions about animal research depending on whether we focus on the interests of the animals themselves or on the interests of the people who may benefit from the research.

As with the abortion debate, some people have taken firm and often heated positions on animal research (see Figure 1.5). Some animal-rights advocates have taken extreme measures, even breaking into research labs, stealing animals, vandalizing property, and threatening researchers.

In this debate people often fail to notice the substantial government regulation of animal research. In the United States, for example, laws require all animal laboratories to meet certain standards of cleanliness and animal care. Professional organizations such as the Society for Neuroscience publish guidelines for the use of animals in research (see Appendix C). All colleges and other research institutions that receive federal funds are required to have Laboratory Animal Care Committees that evaluate proposed experiments to ensure that they are designed to minimize pain and discomfort. Such committees, which include veterinarians and community representatives as well as scientists, can prohibit experiments that are more likely to inflict great pain than they are to gain great knowledge.

Still, some opponents of animal research remain unsatisfied and uncompromising. Some, the "minimalists," would like to reduce animal research to a minimum, to just those experiments that are clearly worthwhile and that inflict little if any pain. Others, the "abolitionists," wish to prohibit all animal experimentation

**Figure 1.5**

*For many years opponents of animal research have been protesting against experimentation with animals. This ad represents a reply by supporters of such research. (Courtesy of the Foundation for Biomedical Research.)*

without exception. According to one opponent of animal research, "We have no moral option but to bring this research to a halt. Completely. . . . We will not be satisfied until every cage is empty" (Regan, 1986, pp. 39–40). For abolitionists, animal research is always wrong, whether or not the animals are treated well and regardless of how valuable the results may be. Such people maintain that all life is equally valuable and that any animal has the same rights as any human. Keeping an animal (presumably even a pet) in a cage is slavery. Killing an animal to eat it, to use its fur, or to gain scientific knowledge is murder. Most biological scientists support animal *welfare* and work toward improving conditions for laboratory animals, but they deny that animals have the same *rights* as humans (Johnson, 1990).

If society takes the equal-rights-for-animals position, it has a price to pay. For example, the best current treatment for people with a defective heart valve is to transplant a valve from a pig's heart. If we decide that a pig's life has the same value as a human's life, then it is unethical to kill a pig to save a human, and people with defective heart valves will have to settle for some treatment with a lower chance of success. Similarly, if the value of a rat's life or a monkey's life is the same as that of a human's life, then we will have to tell people suffering from AIDS, spinal cord damage, and other incurable diseases and handicaps, "Sorry.

We must greatly slow down the progress toward a treatment for your condition." Many victims of incurable diseases have organized to oppose animal-rights groups and to support animal research (Feeney, 1987).

Biological psychologists believe that many of the claims made by abolitionists are exaggerated, unfair, and in some cases simply untrue. A few examples:

*Claim: Laboratory animals are given intense, repeated, inescapable shocks until they can no longer even scream in pain. They are left to die of hunger and thirst. Extreme pain and stress are inflicted upon them in attempts to drive them insane.*

*Reply: Caroline Coile and Neal Miller (1984) examined the psychological studies published over five years and could not find a single example to support any of these charges. Even over the whole history of psychology, experiments that inflicted severe pain on animals have been rare.*

*Claim: Research on animals leads to no useful discoveries.*

*Reply: Nearly all of our progress in medicine and in biological psychology is traceable in part to pioneering studies conducted on animals. While it is undeniable that much research on animals leads to little of practical value—and the same is true of research in any field—animal research has led to the development of antianxiety drugs, new methods of treating pain and depression, an awareness of how certain drugs can impair fetal development, an understanding of the effects of old age on memory, methods to help people overcome neuromuscular disorders, and numerous other advances (N. E. Miller, 1985).*

*Claim: Psychologists have been remiss in failing to consider alternative research methods that do not require animals, such as studying embryos, plants, tissue cultures, and computer simulations.*

*Reply: That criticism is simply puzzling (Gallup & Suarez, 1985). Embryos, plants, and tissue cultures do not behave in ways that would make them suitable subjects for psychological experiments. It is impossible to program a computer to simulate a behavior until after one understands the behavior. Although computer simulations may be suitable for classroom demonstrations, they are no substitute for using real animals in research.*

However, even if we disregard the exaggerated claims made by the opponents of animal research, a legitimate moral question remains: Under what circumstances, if any, is it justifiable to conduct research on animals (which, after all, did not volunteer for the studies) and sometimes to inflict varying degrees of distress upon them? Even ardent defenders of animal research agree to the need for limits and guidelines.

Most investigators wish to conduct research on animals only if the expected value of the results is greater than whatever suffering the animals might experience. However, applying that principle in practice can be difficult. Many apparently promising experiments produce inconclusive results, and a less promising experiment sometimes leads to unexpected and important results (Gallistel, 1981). Further, we have no standard measurement of animal suffering. Even if we did, we have no reasonable formula to compare the value of results to the expected suffering. In general, investigators are less disturbed about performing potentially painful procedures on insects than on rats and less disturbed about using rats than about using monkeys. But even that kind of distinction rests on loose, vague judgments. In short, investigators try to balance the value of the expected results against the cost to the animals, but in specific cases there is much room for disagreement.

## SUMMARY

1. Biological psychology encompasses the work of many kinds of specialists, including psychologists, biologists, and medical doctors. (p. 2)

2. Biological psychologists try to answer four types of questions about any given behavior: How does it relate to the physiology of the brain and other organs? How does it develop within the individual? How did the capacity for the behavior evolve? And why did the capacity for this behavior evolve? (That is, what function does it serve?) (p. 4)

3. For example: Birds sing because of activity in certain brain areas that enlarge under the influence of the hormone testosterone. Many birds learn to sing their song by hearing it early in life, even though they cannot practice it until the following year. Many species have songs that roughly resemble those of related species, presumably because both species evolved from a common ancestor. In most species, males sing more than females do and males sing mostly during the breeding season; available evidence indicates that the song's function is to attract and stimulate a mate and to deter rival males. (p. 5)

4. Biological psychologists' attempts to explain human behavior and experience in biological terms seem to conflict with our impression that a conscious mind controls behavior. (p. 8)

5. Both philosophers and scientists try to understand the relationship between mind and brain. Various people have proposed that the brain is a machine, that the mind is independent of the brain, or that the mind and brain are identical. Although the results of brain research are more compatible with some proposals than with others, no theory seems fully satisfactory at present. (p. 9)

6. One line of investigation relevant to the mind-brain question involves studies of how electrical stimulation affects the brain. Such stimulation can directly evoke a variety of behaviors. (p. 10)

7. The ethics of using animals in research is controversial. Some research does inflict stress or pain on animals; however, many research questions can be investigated only through animal research. (p. 13)

## REVIEW QUESTIONS

1. What is the difference between an evolutionary explanation and a functional explanation? (p. 4)

2. Give a physiological explanation of why male birds sing more than females do. Give a functional explanation also. (pp. 5, 8)

3. What is meant by the "sensitive period" for learning bird song? In what way do certain birds learn a song from a live tutor differently from how they learn it from a tape recording? (p. 7)

4. What is the "mind-brain problem"? Describe the pros and cons of some major positions on this question. (p. 9)

5. Describe one type of evidence that seems relevant to the mind-brain problem. (p. 10)

6. Describe at least one reason why biological psychologists sometimes conduct their research on nonhuman animals. (p. 13)

## THOUGHT QUESTIONS

1. Marler (1970) found that white-crowned sparrows have "dialects"—that is, their song varies noticeably from one part of the country to another. How might such dialects develop? Would pigeons and chickens be more likely or less likely than sparrows to have dialects?

2. Suppose a philosopher asks you what findings about the brain and its control of behavior philosophers should know about. That is, what scientific information is relevant to the mind-body problem? What would you answer? (Keep this question in mind as you read this book; see what relevant information you can find.)

## SUGGESTIONS FOR FURTHER READING

**Fodor, J. A.** (1981, January). The mind-body problem. *Scientific American, 244* (1), 114–123. A brief discussion of major philosophical positions on the mind-body problem.

**Konishi, M.** (1985). Birdsong: From behavior to neuron. *Annual Review of Neuroscience, 8,* 125–170. A thorough review of research on the factors that control bird song.

**Rensch, B.** (1971). *Biophilosophy.* New York: Columbia University Press. A biologist turned psychologist turned philosopher attempts to deal with the mind-body problem and other philosophical issues from a scientific standpoint.

**Valenstein, E.** (1973). *Brain control.* New York: Wiley-Interscience. A critical treatment of electrical brain stimulation and psychosurgery.

# GLOSSARY

**biological psychology** study of the biological principles underlying behavior

**dualist position** belief that the mind exists independent of the brain and exerts some control over it

**emergent property position** theory that the mind emerges as a new property when matter is organized in a particular way

**epilepsy** a syndrome caused by abnormal repetitive activity of the nerve cells in the brain

**epiphenomenalism** theory that the conscious mind is an accidental spin-off of brain activity

**evolutionary explanation** hypothesis that relates a structure or a behavior to the evolutionary history of a species

**focus** a damaged or malfunctioning area of the brain from which an epileptic seizure originates

**functional explanation** description of why a structure or behavior evolved as it did

**identity position** belief that the mind is the same thing as brain activity, described in different terms

**interactionism** theory that the mind and the brain are separate but interact with each other and influence each other

**materialist position** belief that the brain is a machine and that consciousness is irrelevant to its functioning

**mentalism** theory that the physical world exists only if a conscious mind perceives it

**mind-body problem** or **mind-brain problem** question of how the mind is related to the brain

**monism** theory that only one kind of substance exists in the universe (not separate physical and mental substances)

**ontogenetic explanation** description of how a structure or a behavior develops

**panprotopsychic identism** theory that consciousness is present in a primitive, potential form in all matter

**parallelism** theory that mind and brain exist separately but do not affect each other

**physiological explanation** concept that relates an activity to how the brain and other organs of the body function

**sensitive period** a time (generally early in life) when a particular type of experience has an especially strong and long-lasting effect on the development of behavior

**template** a model that an individual attempts to match or to copy

# CHAPTER TWO

# Nerve Cells and Nerve Impulses

## MAIN IDEAS

**1.** Two kinds of cells compose the nervous system: neurons and glia. Only the neurons transmit impulses from one location to another.

**2.** Many molecules in the bloodstream that are free to enter other body organs are unable to enter the brain.

**3.** The structure of a neuron is somewhat plastic throughout life. The fibers of a neuron can increase or decrease their branching pattern as a function of experience, age, and chemical influences.

**4.** The nerve impulse, known as an action potential, is an electrical change across the membrane of a neuron, caused by the sudden flow of sodium ions into the neuron followed by a flow of potassium ions out of the neuron.

**5.** Myelin is an insulating sheath that increases the velocity of transmission in certain vertebrate neurons.

**6.** Many small neurons convey information without action potentials, through graded electrical potentials that vary in intensity.

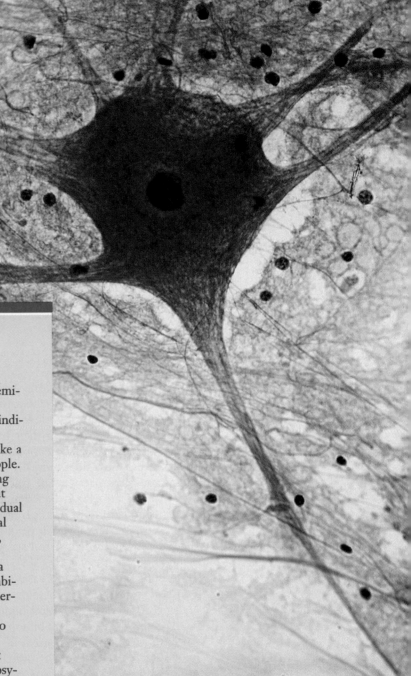

A society is composed of many people. A chemical compound is composed of two or more atoms. Similarly, a nervous system is composed of many individual cells.

The nervous system is in many regards more like a chemical compound than it is like a society of people. Although we sometimes speak of a society as taking collective action, the individuals who compose that society never entirely lose their capacity for individual action. The nervous system is more like a chemical compound: When oxygen and hydrogen combine, they lose the properties ordinarily associated with oxygen and hydrogen and form water, which has a very different set of properties. Similarly, the combination of many cells in a nervous system has properties very different from those of a single cell.

Although we cannot understand what people do and why by studying a single cell, it is the logical place to begin. Just as a chemist must know about atoms to make sense of compounds, a biological psychologist must know about cells of the nervous system to understand how the nervous system works. (Advice: Parts of this chapter and the next deal with chemistry. You might want to refresh your memory of basic chemistry by reading Appendix B.)

*(Ed Reschke.)*

# The Cells of the
# Nervous System

Until the late 1800s, the best available microscopic views of the nervous system revealed little detail about the organization of the brain. Brain cells are small and generally colorless; before the discovery of staining techniques, they were hard to distinguish from their background. Long, thin fibers were observed between one nerve cell and another. Several of the most respected authorities maintained that these fibers actually merged one cell into another; that is, they denied that any gap separated one cell from the next.

In the late 1800s, Santiago Ramón y Cajal demonstrated that a single nerve cell, or *neuron*, does not merge with its neighbors. Each cell is distinct; a small gap separates it from each neighboring cell.

Philosophically, we can see some appeal in the old concept that one neuron might merge into another. We each experience our conscious awareness as a single thing, not as a combination of many. In a way it seems right that all the cells in the brain should join together physically as a single unit. Yet we now know that they do not. The adult human brain contains a great many neurons (Figure 2.1)—approximately 100 billion, according to one estimate (Williams & Herrup, 1988). (Because certain areas of the brain contain a large number of very small cells, an accurate count is difficult.) Those billions of cells combine to produce both unified experience and coordinated, organized behavior. Before we can begin to contemplate how they act together, we need to know a little about the properties of the individual cell.

## NEURONS AND GLIA

In this chapter we shall deal with some detailed information about neuron structure and function. At times it may not be obvious why a student of psychology needs to know such things. However, to theorize about how the brain controls behavior, a psychologist needs to know a little about what neurons can and cannot do. Moreover, certain interesting points about behavior can be related directly to what we know about the individual neuron. For example, a kind of memory loss called Korsakoff's syndrome (see p. 491) is caused by a deficiency in

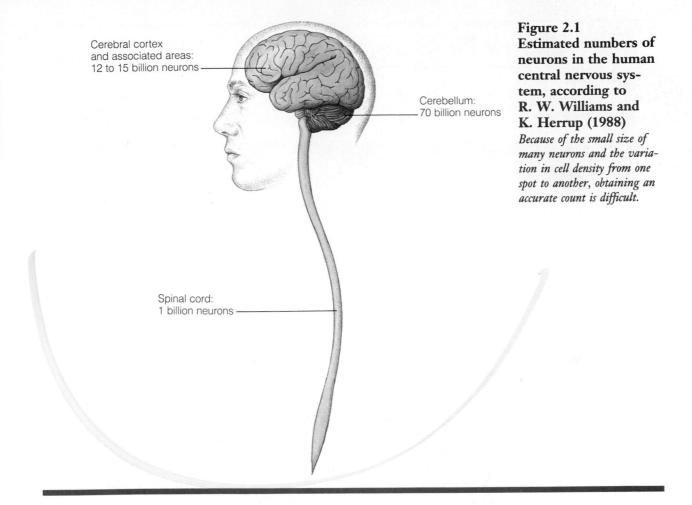

**Figure 2.1**
**Estimated numbers of neurons in the human central nervous system, according to R. W. Williams and K. Herrup (1988)**
*Because of the small size of many neurons and the variation in cell density from one spot to another, obtaining an accurate count is difficult.*

Cerebral cortex
and associated areas:
12 to 15 billion neurons

Cerebellum:
70 billion neurons

Spinal cord:
1 billion neurons

the nutrition of neurons; alcohol exerts some of its long-term effects by changing the structure of neurons; anesthetic drugs prevent the transmission of information by neurons. To understand these and other examples, we need a basic understanding of what neurons are, what they do, and how they do it.

The nervous system consists of two kinds of cells, neurons and glia. **Neurons** are cells that receive information and transmit it to other cells by conducting electrochemical impulses; they are the cells people usually mean when they refer to "nerve cells." The various types of glia and their functions will be described later.

Neurons resemble other body cells in certain basic properties, so we shall begin with some information common to all animal cells.

## The Structures Within an Animal Cell

Figure 2.2 illustrates a cell from a rat's liver, which contains the same basic structures as most other animal cells. Cells differ, of course, in the exact size, shape, arrangement, and abundance of these structures. The structures illustrated in Figure 2.2 are not the only structures found in animal cells, but they are among the most important.

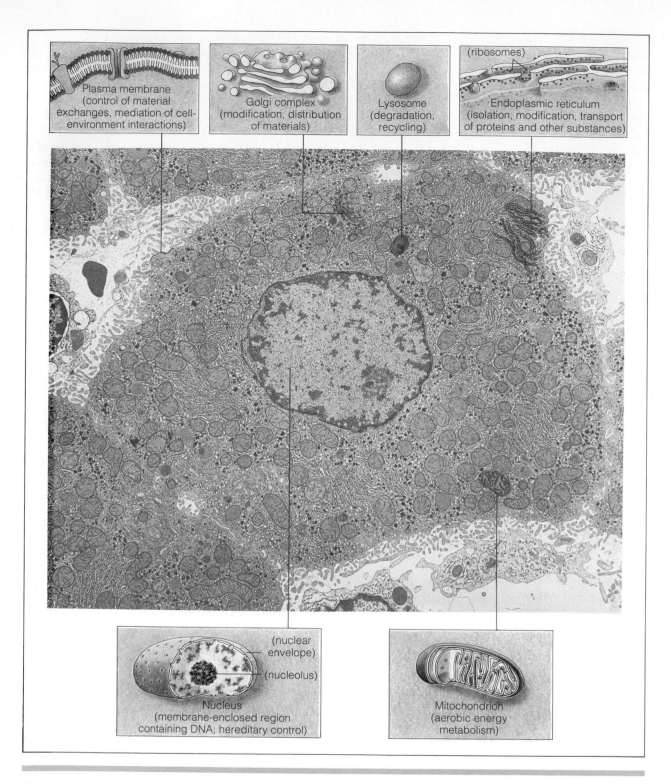

**Figure 2.2**
**A liver cell from a rat, magnified × 15,000**
*The nucleus, membrane, and other structures are characteristic of most animal cells. (Micrograph courtesy of G. L. Decker.)*

Every cell is surrounded by a **membrane** (often called a *plasma membrane*), a structure composed of two layers of fat molecules, which are free to flow around one another. (Figure 2.12 shows this arrangement in more detail.) The membrane controls the flow of materials between the inside of the cell and the outside environment. A few chemicals, such as water, oxygen, carbon dioxide, and many fat-soluble molecules, move fairly freely across the membrane, while other chemicals move poorly or not at all. The fluid inside the cell membrane is the **cytoplasm.**

All animal cells (except red blood cells) contain a **nucleus,** the structure that contains the chromosomes. A **mitochondrion** (plural: mitochondria) is the site where the cell performs metabolic activities, which provide the energy the cell requires for all its other activities. Mitochondria require fuel and oxygen to function. **Ribosomes** are the sites at which the cell synthesizes new protein molecules. Proteins provide building materials for the cell and facilitate various chemical reactions. Some ribosomes float freely within the cell; others are attached to the **endoplasmic reticulum,** a network of thin tubes transporting newly synthesized proteins to other locations. **Lysosomes** contain enzymes that break down many chemicals into their component parts so they can be recycled for other uses. The **Golgi complex** is a network of vesicles preparing hormones and other products for secretion.

## The Structure of a Neuron

A neuron (Figure 2.3) contains a nucleus, a membrane, mitochondria, ribosomes, and the other structures typical of animal cells. What sets a neuron apart from other cells is its shape. From the central body of the neuron, many small, thin fibers may emanate. Some of those fibers extend great distances; some branch widely. The size and shape of neurons vary almost endlessly. The distinctive shape of a given neuron determines its connections with other neurons and thereby determines how it will contribute to the overall functioning of the nervous system. For example, certain neurons send axon branches to wide areas of the brain, transmitting the same message to a great many cells. Other neurons have widely branching dendrites, which enable them to receive and compare input from many sources. Still other neurons with shorter axons and dendrites exchange information with fewer sources.

Figure 2.4 shows one example of a neuron, a motor neuron that has its cell body in the spinal cord and one fiber extending to a muscle. It would be misleading to call this a "typical" neuron; neurons vary so widely in their shape that no one neuron is typical of all others any more than an artichoke is typical of all vegetables. Nevertheless, the motor neuron contains all the parts found in other neurons.

Most neurons have three major components: the cell body, dendrites, and an axon. The **cell body,** or **soma** (Latin for *body*), contains the nucleus, some ribosomes and mitochondria, and other structures found in most cells. Much of the metabolic work of the neuron occurs here. Cell bodies of neurons range in diameter from 0.005 mm to 0.1 mm in mammals and up to a full millimeter in certain invertebrates, such as the squid.

The **dendrites** are thin, widely branching fibers that get narrower as they get farther from the cell body. (The term *dendrite* comes from a Greek root word meaning *tree*; a dendrite's shape resembles that of a tree.) The dendrite's surface is lined with specialized junctions at which the dendrite receives information from

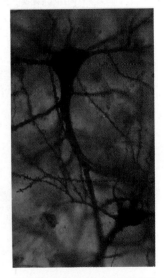

**Figure 2.3
Neurons, stained to appear dark**
*The distinctive characteristic of each neuron is its shape. Because neurons differ greatly in their branching patterns, some pool information from many sources and some send their output over great distances. Other neurons have a much more restricted region of input and output. (McCoy/Scheilbel/Rainbow.)*

27

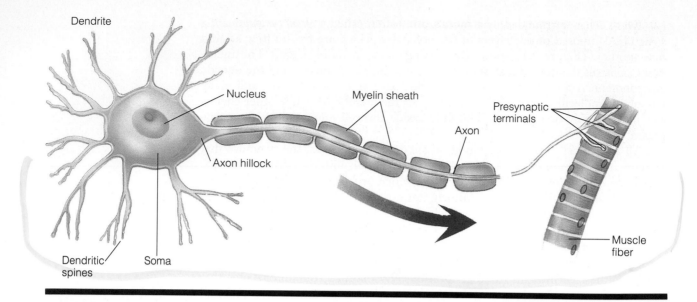

**Figure 2.4**
**The components of a motor neuron**

*The cell body of a motor neuron is located in the spinal cord. The various parts are not drawn to scale; in particular, a real axon is much longer in proportion to the size of the soma.*

other neurons. Thus, the greater the surface area of a dendrite, the more information it can receive. **Dendritic spines,** short outgrowths along the dendrites, expand the surface area of many dendrites.

The **axon** is a single fiber thicker and longer than the dendrites. (The term *axon* comes from a Greek word meaning *axis;* in some ways it resembles a long axis extending from one pole of the neuron.) Mature neurons have either one axon or none. In contrast, a neuron may have any number of dendrites. However, an axon may have many branches. In most cases the branches form near the tip, remote from the cell body.

In large neurons, the point where the axon begins is marked by a swelling of the soma known as the **axon hillock.** The axon maintains a constant diameter along its entire length. Generally, an axon carries an impulse from the cell body toward other cells. Some axons are a meter or more in length — for example, the axons going from the spinal cord to the feet of a giraffe. A neuron without an axon can convey information only to other neurons immediately adjacent to it.

The axon of a motor neuron is covered with an insulating material called a **myelin sheath.** Myelin covers some but not all vertebrate axons. Invertebrate axons do not have myelin sheaths.

Each branch of an axon swells at its tip, forming a **presynaptic terminal,** or *end bulb.* This is the point from which the axon releases chemicals that cross through the *synapse* (the junction between one neuron and the next) and influence the next cell. The release of these chemicals requires considerable energy; consequently the presynaptic terminals have many mitochondria. We shall discuss synapses in detail in Chapter 3.

Table 2.1 lists the anatomical distinctions between dendrites and axons. Occasionally, however, we encounter a structure that strains the definitions. For example, certain neurons, including all the sensory neurons, have cell bodies located on a stalk (see Figure 2.7c). One long fiber conveys impulses from the sensory receptor toward the cell body. Because it conveys information toward the cell body, it functions as a dendrite. Yet its structure is that of an axon. In some cases, investigators may disagree on whether something is a dendrite or an axon.

## Table 2.1 Anatomical Distinctions Between Dendrites and Axons

| Dendrites | Axons |
|---|---|
| A neuron may have many dendrites, each with many branches. | A neuron may have one axon or none. An axon may have many branches. |
| Usually shorter than the axon. Some neurons have a long "apical" dendrite with branches (see Figure 2.7d). | May be any length, in some cases up to 1 meter or longer. |
| Diameter usually tapers toward the periphery of the dendrite. | Diameter usually constant over the length of the axon until the presynaptic terminal. |
| No hillock. | Relatively large axons join the cell body at a distinct swelling called the axon hillock. |
| Usually branch at acute angles. | Usually branch perpendicular to the main trunk of the axon. |
| Seldom covered with myelin (an insulating sheath). | Often covered with myelin (among vertebrates only). |
| Usually have ribosomes. | Usually have few ribosomes or none. |

You will note in Table 2.1 the frequent use of the word *usually*. The structure of neurons varies enormously, and there are exceptions to practically any rule about dendrites and axons. Many neurons, especially the smaller ones, violate the rule that dendrites receive information and axons conduct it to other cells. In some cases dendrites and cell bodies transmit information directly to the dendrites and cell bodies of another neuron, without the intervention of an axon.

## Variations Among Neurons

For some purposes it is useful to distinguish among three types of neurons: receptor neurons, motor neurons, and interneurons. A **receptor** or **sensory neuron** (Figure 2.5) is specialized to be highly sensitive to a particular type of stimulation, such as light, sound waves, touch, or certain chemicals. As a rule, each receptor is highly sensitive to one kind of stimulus and relatively insensitive to most others. For example, a few molecules of an airborne chemical can excite the olfactory receptors in the nose but not the receptors in the eye. A single photon of light can affect receptors in the eye but not the olfactory receptors. However, the selectivity is not absolute; all receptors can be stimulated by electricity and other intense stimuli.

A **motor neuron** (Figure 2.4) receives excitation from other neurons and conducts impulses from its soma in the spinal cord to muscle or gland cells. **Interneurons** (Figure 2.7b) receive information from other neurons (either receptor neurons or interneurons) and send it to either motor neurons or interneurons. Many interneurons connect only to other interneurons, not to receptor or motor neurons. Most of the neurons in the human nervous system are interneurons.

Some other terms you may encounter are *efferent*, *afferent*, and *intrinsic*. An **efferent axon** carries information away from a structure; an **afferent axon** brings

The Cells of the
Nervous System

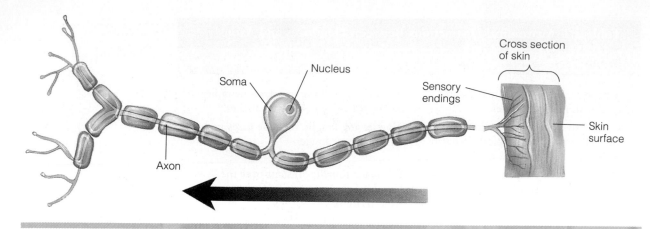

**Figure 2.5**
**A sensory neuron**

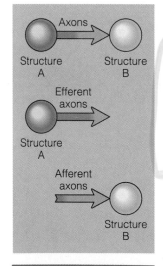

**Figure 2.6**
*It all depends on the point of view. An axon from A to B is an* efferent *axon from A; it is an* afferent *axon to B.*

information into a structure. Every axon that is efferent *from* one structure is afferent *to* some other structure, as Figure 2.6 shows. An **intrinsic neuron** is one whose axons and dendrites are all confined within a given structure. For example, an intrinsic neuron of the cerebral cortex has no dendrites or axons that extend beyond the borders of the cortex.

The shape of neurons varies greatly, as Figure 2.7 illustrates. The function of a neuron depends on its shape (Palay & Chan-Palay, 1977). The dendrites of the Purkinje cell of the cerebellum (the neuron in Figure 2.7a) have about 100,000 specialized sites (synapses) for receiving transmissions from other neurons; it contributes to the precise timing of movements. The neurons in Figure 2.7d and f also have widely branching dendrites that receive and integrate information from many sources. The neuron in Figure 2.7b, an interneuron, has an axon and dendrites that branch diffusely but only within a small radius. It is well suited to exchange information with many other cells and to engage in extensive feedback, influencing some of the same cells that influence it.

The neurons in Figure 2.7c are the sensory neurons of the spinal cord. They receive information from touch receptors at the periphery of the body and convey it over a long axon that does not branch until it reaches the spinal cord. The neuron in Figure 2.7e, a bipolar cell of the retina in the eye, conveys information about excitation of the visual receptors. Note that the dendrites of the bipolar cell branch over a limited area and that its axon is short, with only a few branches. If either its dendrites or its axon branched widely, vision would be blurry because information from different parts of the retina would not remain distinct.

## Glia

Besides neurons, the other major components of the nervous system are **glia** (or *neuroglia*). The term *glia* is derived from a Greek word meaning *glue*. Originally investigators believed that glia were like glue or putty that held the neurons together (Somjen, 1988). Although that concept is obsolete, the term remains.

On the average, a glial cell is about one-tenth the size of a neuron. Glia are about ten times more numerous than neurons in the human brain, somewhat less in the brains of most other species. Thus, in the human brain, glia occupy about the same total space as the neurons (see Figure 2.8).

Glia do not transmit information to other cells. They show electrical activity, but it is a passive activity, driven by the neurons around them. Several anatomical

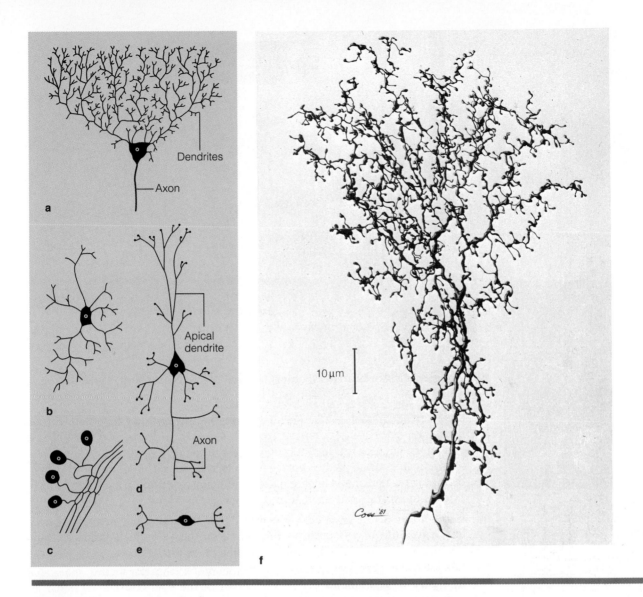

**Figure 2.7**
**The diverse shapes of neurons**

*(a) Purkinje cell, a cell type found only in the cerebellum; (b) interneuron of the spinal cord; (c) sensory neurons from skin to spinal cord; (d) pyramidal cell of the motor area of the cerebral cortex; (e) bipolar cell of retina of the eye; (f) Kenyon cell, from a honey-bee. [Part (f) courtesy of R. G. Goss.]*

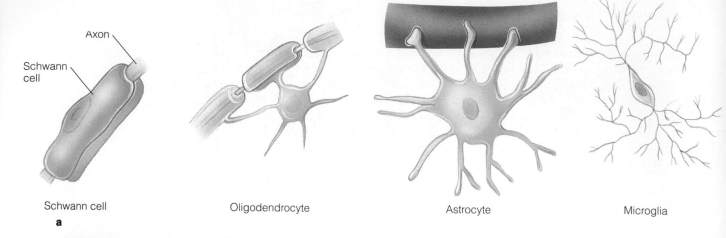

Axon

Schwann
cell

Schwann cell

Oligodendrocyte

Astrocyte

Microglia

**a**

**b**

**Figure 2.8**

*(a) Shapes of some glia cells. Glia, also known as neuroglia, perform a number of important roles in the nervous system even though they do not communicate information on their own. Among other functions, they guide the growth and migration of neurons, produce the myelin sheaths that insulate certain vertebrate axons, and remove waste products from the brain. (b) Astrocytes, stained black. (Manfred Kage/Peter Arnold, Inc.)*

types of glia perform various functions (Kimelberg & Norenberg, 1989; Varon & Somjen, 1979):

1. Two kinds of glia build the myelin sheaths that surround and insulate certain vertebrate axons: **oligodendrocytes** (OL-i-go-DEN-druh-sites) in the brain and spinal cord and **Schwann cells** in the periphery of the body. Even the unmyelinated axons of the central nervous system are in contact with oligodendrocytes. For unmyelinated axons, the main function of the oligodendrocytes is to separate one axon from another.

2. Glia remove waste material, particularly that created when neurons die. At least two kinds of glia perform this function: the very small **microglia** and the larger, star-shaped **astrocytes,** also known as astroglia.

3. Where neurons die, glia, especially astrocytes, fill up the vacant space and sometimes form scar tissue.

4. One type of astrocyte, called **radial glia,** guide the migration of neurons and the growth of their axons and dendrites during embryonic development. Schwann cells perform a related function after damage to axons in the periphery, guiding a regenerating axon to the appropriate target. After the brain is mature, biologists believe that radial glia transform into other forms of astrocytes, which provide structural support to help axons and dendrites hold their shape and position.

5. Astrocytes remove chemicals that the neurons have released and later return those chemicals or their derivatives either to the neurons or to the blood.

Glia probably perform other functions besides those just listed, such as modifying the communication between one neuron and another, releasing chemicals that promote neuronal growth, promoting immune reactions in the brain, and providing a reservoir of nutrients. These and other possibilities require further investigation (Kimelberg & Norenberg, 1989; Somjen, 1988).

## THE BLOOD-BRAIN BARRIER

Have you ever wondered why certain chemicals produce greater effects on the brain than others do—for example, why heroin produces greater effects and stronger addictions than morphine does? (Heroin and morphine are chemically very similar to each other.) Or why some chemical injections have no direct effect on the brain? An important part of the answer is that some chemicals enter the brain faster than others do. For example, heroin enters the brain faster than morphine does. And some chemicals, including most proteins, cannot enter the brain at all.

For all vertebrates and some invertebrates, the mechanism that keeps many chemicals out of the brain is known as the **blood-brain barrier** (Cserr & Bundgaard, 1986). Many chemicals, especially proteins and other large molecules, either cannot enter brain cells or do so very slowly. The blood-brain barrier protects the brain against a variety of potentially harmful substances.

The blood-brain barrier depends on the arrangement of endothelial cells along the capillaries (Bundgaard, 1986; Rapoport & Robinson, 1986). (Endothelial cells are the protective cells that line the blood vessels, the lymphatic vessels, and the heart.) In most parts of the body, such cells are separated by gaps large enough to allow the passage of large molecules. In the brain, the endothelial cells are tightly joined to one another. Many molecules simply cannot pass through those joints.

Some kinds of molecules do cross the blood-brain barrier. Oxygen, carbon dioxide, and a few other small, uncharged molecules pass freely back and forth. Because heroin, nicotine, and cannabinol (the active substance in marijuana) are soluble in fats, they can dissolve in the fats of the capillary walls and cross. Heroin crosses more freely and therefore produces stronger effects on the brain than morphine does. A mechanism called an active transport system pumps into the brain certain important chemicals that would not be able to pass through the barrier otherwise. For example, one transport system pumps glucose into the brain; another pumps in certain large amino acids. Figure 2.9 illustrates the blood-brain barrier.

Because of variation in the structure of the blood-brain barrier, certain chemicals enter one part of the brain and not others. For example, the blood-brain barrier excludes sex hormones (such as estradiol and testosterone) from areas of the brain that are unrelated to sexual behavior (Nicholson & Rice, 1986).

Astrocytes surround most of the endothelial cells along the capillaries, especially in areas where the blood-brain barrier is strong. In ways not yet understood, the astrocytes strengthen the barrier; when they are absent, the blood-brain barrier is generally weak (Anders, Dorovini-Zis, & Brightman, 1980; Bradbury, 1979).

## THE NOURISHMENT OF VERTEBRATE NEURONS

Most of the cells in the body use a wide variety of fuels. Not the neurons. Vertebrate neurons derive the vast majority of their nutrition from **glucose,** a simple sugar. (Cancer cells and the testis cells that make sperm also rely overwhelmingly

## Figure 2.9
## The blood-brain barrier

*Most large molecules and electrically charged molecules cannot cross from the blood to the brain. A few small, uncharged molecules such as $O_2$ and $CO_2$ can cross; so can certain fat-soluble molecules. Active transport systems pump glucose and certain amino acids across the membrane.*

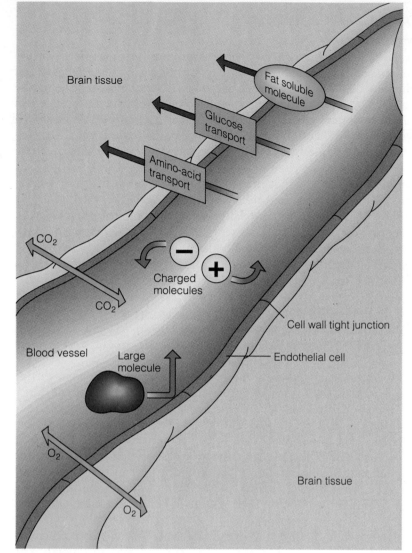

on glucose.) The metabolic pathway that uses glucose requires oxygen; consequently, the neurons—especially their dendrites—consume an enormous amount of oxygen compared to other organs of the body (Wong-Riley, 1989).

Glia cells, on the other hand, derive most of their energy from glycogen, a carbohydrate molecule that is metabolized without use of oxygen. Glycogen is at most a minor source of energy for neurons (Coopersmith & Leon, 1987; Cummins, Lust, & Passonneau, 1983).

Why do neurons depend so heavily on glucose? Apparently it is not because they are incapable of using anything else. Neurons have the enzymes necessary to metabolize certain other sugars, plus lactate and the ketone fats acetoacetate and 3-hydroxybutyrate. The infant brain does, in fact, use these alternative fuels. In most parts of the adult vertebrate brain, however, these other nutrients cannot cross the blood-brain barrier in significant amounts (Gjedde, 1984). But areas of the brain with a relatively weak blood-brain barrier can and do use ketone fats and certain sugars for part of their nutrition (Hawkins & Biebuyck, 1979). When the amount of ketone fats in the diet increases, the use of those fats by neurons increases also (Lavau, Fornari, & Hashim, 1978).

For neurons that depend exclusively on glucose, a shortage of glucose is rarely a problem. The liver can convert many carbohydrates, proteins, and fats into glucose; except in diabetes and other disease states, the glucose level in the blood is always sufficient to meet the brain's needs. An inability to *use* glucose can be a problem, however. To use glucose, the body needs vitamin $B_1$, **thiamine.** If a person's diet is low in thiamine over several weeks, the neurons will have increasing difficulty in using glucose.

## CHANGES IN THE STRUCTURE OF NEURONS AND GLIA

Skin cells and cells in many other parts of the body can divide at any time during life to replace cells that have died. However, most areas of the adult vertebrate brain cannot replace lost neurons.

Neuroscientists once believed that adult vertebrates were incapable of generating any new neurons at all. Gradually, a list of exceptions has emerged. The olfactory receptors undergo steady turnover throughout life as old receptors die and new ones take their place (Graziadei & deHan, 1973; Graziadei & Monti Graziadei, 1985). Within the brain itself, additional neurons form throughout life in certain limited areas, at least in the rat brain (Bayer, 1985; Kaplan, 1985). These new neurons are apparently small to moderate in size, without the long axons that link one part of the rat's brain with another. It has not been possible to demonstrate the development of new neurons in the mature primate brain (Rakic, 1985).

Although some new neurons do originate in the adult brain, the great majority of mature neurons cannot divide. Cancer is an abnormal proliferation of cells. Because most neurons cannot proliferate, brain cancers are generally—maybe always—limited to glial cells, which can and do divide throughout life.

Even without the development of new neurons, the structure of the brain can change in two ways: New glia can form, and the dendritic branches of neurons can grow or retract. As a rule, dendrites branch more widely in larger animals than in smaller animals (Purves & Lichtman, 1985); they also branch more widely in certain members of the species than in others. For example, if rats are kept for one month or longer in large cages, in groups of ten to twelve per cage, with a constantly changing variety of objects for them to explore, they develop more glial cells and a wider pattern of dendritic branches than do rats kept in individual cages (Greenough, 1975; Uphouse, 1980). The anatomical changes are known to last at least a month, and probably much longer, after the animals have been removed from the enriched environment (Camel, Withers, & Greenough, 1986). Similar results have been reported for Jewel fish (Coss & Globus, 1979) and honeybees (Coss, Brandon, & Globus, 1980). (See Figure 2.10.)

Dendrites apparently change their structure from time to time in practically all individuals. Dale Purves and R. D. Hadley (1985) developed a method of injecting dye into a neuron that enabled them to examine the structure of a living neuron at two times, days to weeks apart. They found that dendritic patterns gradually change. Some branches grow and extend while others retract. Some

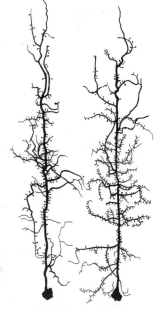

**Figure 2.10
Comparison of structures of neurons from the brains of Jewel fish reared in isolation (*left*) and reared with others of their own species (*right*)**
*Note the richer branching pattern in the neuron on the right. (Photo courtesy of Richard Coss.)*

**Figure 2.11
Dendritic trees of two
neurons, each viewed
at two times**
*During a month, some
branches elongated and others
retracted. The shape of the
neuron is in flux even during
adulthood. (From Purves &
Hadley, 1985.)*

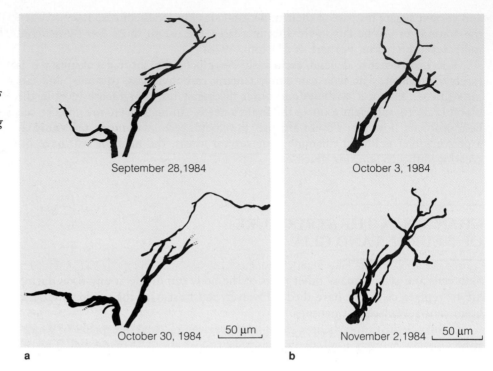

September 28,1984

October 3, 1984

October 30, 1984    50 μm

November 2,1984    50 μm

a

b

new dendrites grow and old ones disappear altogether (see Figure 2.11). Evidently, the anatomy of the brain is in constant flux at the microscopic level as neurons change their connections with other neurons.

Alcohol can impair the dendritic branching of neurons. Pregnant rats that are forced to drink large amounts of alcohol give birth to offspring with abnormal patterns of dendritic branching (West, Hodges, & Black, 1981). The dendritic branches of mice retract after the mice are exposed to alcohol, even in adulthood (Riley & Walker, 1978).

People over age 70 may have either wider or narrower dendritic branches than middle-aged people do. When S. J. Buell and P. D. Coleman (1981) examined the cortices of people who had died at various ages, they found that normal, alert old people had lost a certain number of neurons. However, the dendrites of their remaining neurons had compensated for the loss by growing longer and branching more widely, thereby increasing their contact with other neurons. Among the elderly who had grown senile, the dendrites of the surviving neurons had failed to compensate for the loss of other neurons. In fact, the dendrites were slightly shorter and less branched than the dendrites of middle-aged people.

## SUMMARY

1. Santiago Ramón y Cajal used newly discovered staining techniques in the late 1800s to establish that the nervous system is composed of separate cells, now known as neurons. (p. 24)

2. Neurons receive information from, and transmit information to, other cells. The nervous system also contains *glia*, cells that do not exchange information with other cells. (pp. 25, 30)

3. Neurons include four major parts: dendrites, a cell body, an axon, and presynaptic terminals. Neuron

shape varies greatly, depending on the function of the neuron and the connections it makes with other cells. (p. 27)

4. Because of a set of mechanisms known as the blood-brain barrier, many molecules, especially large molecules, cannot enter the brain. The blood-brain barrier prevents fuels other than glucose from entering most areas of the brain. For this reason, neurons rely heavily on glucose for their nutrition. (pp. 33, 34)

5. Certain areas of the brain can generate new neurons even after the brain has reached maturity. (p. 35)

6. Neurons can alter their shape even after maturity. An enriched environment can lead to longer and more widely branched dendrites. Alcohol can lead to a shrinkage of dendrites. Healthy, alert old people have an increased proliferation of dendritic branches, whereas senile people have slightly shrunken dendrites. (p. 35)

## REVIEW QUESTIONS

1. Identify nucleus, mitochondrion, ribosomes. (p. 27)

2. Suppose you were looking at a small fiber in the brain; how could you tell whether it was a dendrite or an axon? (p. 27)

3. Distinguish among receptor neurons, motor neurons, and interneurons. Distinguish between afferent and efferent. (p. 29)

4. Describe an example of how a neuron's shape relates to its function. (p. 30)

5. What are the functions of the glia? (p. 32)

6. What mechanisms cause the blood-brain barrier? Under what circumstances is the barrier weakened? (p. 33)

7. What is the primary fuel of neurons in the adult vertebrate brain? Why do most brain neurons use very little of other fuels? (p. 33)

8. Which vitamin is necessary for neurons to use their primary fuel? (p. 35)

9. What is the current belief about whether new neurons can form in an adult vertebrate brain? (p. 35)

10. What environmental influences can increase or decrease the branching patterns of dendrites? How does the brain differ between alert and senile old people? (p. 35)

## THOUGHT QUESTION

1. Fetal alcohol syndrome is a condition in which the babies of alcoholic mothers are born with a variety of physical deformities and behavioral abnormalities. What abnormalities would you expect to find in the brain structure of such children?

## SUGGESTIONS FOR FURTHER READING

**Kimelberg, H. K., & Norenberg, M. D.** (1989, April). Astrocytes. *Scientific American, 260* (4), 66–76. An overview of the functions of glia.

*Science*, November 4, 1988. A special issue devoted to neurons and the nervous system.

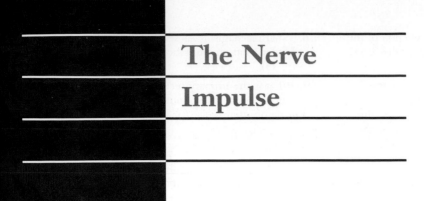

# The Nerve
# Impulse

Touch your desk with your finger. Pay attention to exactly when you feel the sensation of touch. Do you feel the sensation as soon as your finger contacts the desk? Or is there a delay while you wait for the sensation to travel from your finger to your brain?

It probably seems to you that you feel the sensation instantly. (For that reason, people once believed that the sensation actually took place in the finger itself.) We now know that there is a delay between the time your finger contacts the surface and the time you become aware of it. The delay is short—less than a tenth of a second—and it will probably never inconvenience you. It nevertheless exists, and its existence indicates that your perception of touch takes place in your brain, not in your finger. (See Digression 2.1.) It also indicates that axons transmit information at a finite, measurable velocity.

Given that axons must convey information to the brain before the information is perceived, here is something else to think about: What if sensory information faded as it was transported over a distance? That is, suppose the longer it took for information to reach your brain, the weaker the signal became. In that case, you might feel a pinch on your upper arm more clearly than you felt a similar pinch on your finger. A pinch on the tip of your toes would feel even weaker. Short people would feel a pinch on their toes more clearly than tall people would.

Fortunately, your axons are specialized to transmit sensory information over a distance without any loss of intensity or clarity. It takes you a bit longer to feel a pinch on your toes than to feel a pinch on your shoulder, but you do not feel it any less clearly or distinctly. The rest of this chapter explains how axons manage to transmit information over a distance.

## THE RESTING POTENTIAL OF THE NEURON

The membrane of a neuron is specialized to control the exchange of chemicals between the inside and outside of the cell; it also maintains an electrical gradient necessary for neural signaling. All parts of a neuron are covered by a membrane about 8 nanometers (nm) thick (just less than 0.00001 mm), composed of two lay-

## How to Determine the Delay Between Finger Contact and the Perception of Touch

You were asked to touch your desk with your finger and to pay attention to exactly when you perceived the touch. Although there actually is a short delay between finger contact and the sensation of it, you are not aware of it. Why not?

The delay is simply too short. Try tapping yourself on the shoulder. Because your shoulder is closer to your brain than your finger is, theoretically you should feel the touch on your shoulder before you feel it on your finger. However, the two sensations arrive at your brain only a couple hundredths of a second apart, and you are not aware of any delay between them. (Vision and hearing are sensitive to very short time delays; touch is not.)

Although you do not notice a delay yourself, an experimenter can measure the delay. Suppose an experimenter taps you sometimes on the shoulder and sometimes on the finger—or better yet, sometimes on the shoulder and sometimes on the ankle. You respond, perhaps by pressing a button, as soon as you feel the touch. Your response time will be longer for a touch on the finger or on the ankle than for a touch

on the shoulder, because your shoulder is closer to your brain. The extra delay indicates how long it takes for the touch information to travel the extra distance.

Still, for this experiment to produce meaningful results, the experimenter must be able to measure your response time to the hundredth of a second. Here is a way to make an approximate measurement without fancy equipment: First arrange a group of about 20 people in a row, with each person holding the ankle of the next person. Pinch the first person's ankle and start timing. As soon as each person feels a pinch, he or she pinches the next person. When the last person feels the pinch, he or she says "Now," and you measure how much time has passed since the first pinch. (Repeat this procedure a few times until you get consistent results.) Then repeat the procedure, but this time have everyone grab the next person's shoulder. You will find that the pinch travels down the line faster when people are pinching shoulders than when they are pinching ankles. (Rozin & Jonides, 1977).

ers of fat molecules with protein molecules embedded in the fats (see Figure 2.12). Each of the fat molecules has a water-soluble end and a water-insoluble end. The water-soluble ends point outward (toward the exterior of the cell on one side and the interior on the other), while the water-insoluble ends point toward one another. This structure provides the membrane with a good combination of flexibility and firmness while retarding the flow of chemicals across the membrane.

In the absence of any outside disturbance, the membrane undergoes electrical **polarization;** that is, the neuron inside the membrane has a slightly negative electrical potential with respect to the outside. In a resting neuron, this electrical potential, or difference in voltage, is called the **resting potential.** It is produced by the unequal distribution of ions between the inside and outside of the neuron.

When the neuron is at its resting potential, sodium, potassium, and other common ions are distributed unequally across the membrane. The difference in distribution is called a **concentration gradient.** Table 2.2 gives typical concentrations for human neurons (Guyton, 1974).

Researchers can measure the resting potential by inserting a very thin **microelectrode** into the cell body, as Figure 2.13 shows. The diameter of the electrode must be as small as possible so that it can enter the cell without causing

The Nerve Impulse

**Figure 2.12
The membrane
of a neuron**

*Embedded in it are protein
channels that permit certain
ions to cross through the
membrane at a controlled
rate. Each membrane
molecule has a water-seeking
"head" and two fatty water-
avoiding "tails."*

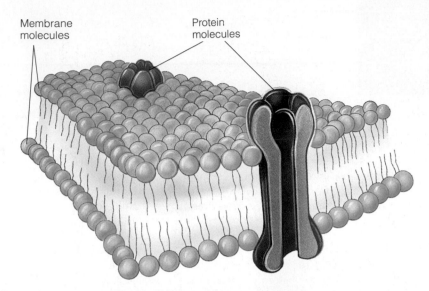

Membrane
molecules

Protein
molecules

damage. By far the most common electrode is a fine glass tube filled with a concentrated salt solution, such as 2 to 3 molar (M) potassium chloride, and tapering to a tip diameter of 0.0005 mm or less. This electrode, inserted into the neuron, is connected to recording equipment. A reference electrode placed somewhere outside the cell completes the circuit. Connecting the electrodes to a voltmeter, we find that the neuron's interior has a potential somewhere in the range of $-30$ to $-90$ millivolts (mV) relative to its exterior.

## The Forces Behind the Resting Potential

One mechanism that maintains the resting potential is the selective permeability of the neuron membrane to the passage of chemicals. **Selective permeability** means that some molecules pass much more freely through the membrane than others do. Oxygen, carbon dioxide, urea, and water cross directly through the membrane in either direction at all times. However, most molecules, especially

### Table 2.2 Average Ion Concentrations Inside and Outside Neurons

| Ion | Concentration inside neuron, M* | Concentration outside neuron, M* |
|---|---|---|
| $Na^+$ (sodium) | 0.010 | 0.142 |
| $K^+$ (potassium) | 0.141 | 0.005 |
| $Cl^-$ (chloride) | 0.004 | 0.103 |
| $HCO_3^-$ (bicarbonate) | 0.010 | 0.028 |

*M = molar, a measure of the concentration of a substance in water solution.

2 / Nerve Cells and
Nerve Impulses

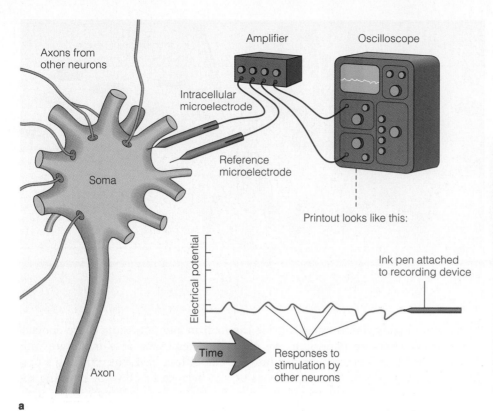

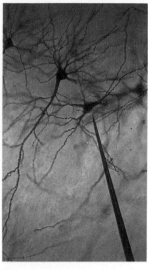

**a**

**b**

**Figure 2.13**
(*a*) *Diagram of the apparatus for recording a neuron's response to stimulation.* (*b*) *A microelectrode and neurons, magnified hundreds of times by a light microscope. Brain tissue has been sliced and stained to make the neurons easy to see. In a living organism, microelectrodes like this one can record the electrical activity of a neuron.* (Fritz Goro.)

large ones, can seldom if ever cross the membrane. A few important ions, such as potassium, chloride, and sodium, cross the membrane through gates (or pores) in specialized proteins embedded in the membrane. Each of these ions travels through a different kind of gate, and the gates control the rate at which their ions pass. When the membrane is at rest, the potassium and chloride gates permit potassium and chloride ions to pass at a moderate rate, but the sodium gates are closed. An occasional sodium ion sneaks through one of the potassium gates, but the total flow of sodium ions is greatly restricted. Figure 2.14 illustrates these gates. As we shall see later, certain kinds of stimulation can open the sodium gates.

How did sodium ions become so much more concentrated outside the neuron than inside it? The ultimate driving force is a protein complex called the **sodium-potassium pump.** This pump transports sodium ions out of the cell while simultaneously drawing potassium ions into the cell. To be precise, the pump ejects three sodium ions for every two potassium ions it brings in. Since both sodium and potassium ions carry a +1 electrical charge, the result is a net movement of positive ions out of the cell. The sodium-potassium pump is an **active transport** (one that requires energy) as opposed to the passive flow of ions through open gates in the membrane.

By itself the sodium-potassium pump would establish only a small difference in charge across the membrane. The selective permeability of the membrane greatly increases the size of the effect. The action of the sodium-potassium pump establishes the concentration gradients for sodium and potassium, with sodium

**Figure 2.14**
**Ion gates in the membrane of a neuron**
*When a gate opens, it permits one kind of ion to cross the membrane. When it closes, it prevents passage of that ion.*

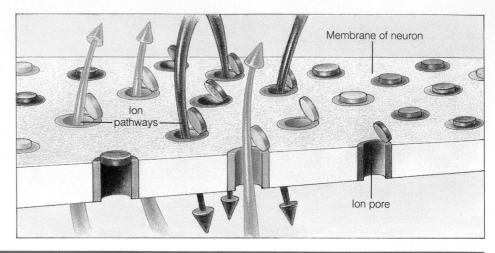

Membrane of neuron

Ion pathways

Ion pore

being more highly concentrated outside the neuron and potassium more concentrated inside. Because potassium can cross the membrane at a moderate rate, many of the potassium ions pumped into the cell diffuse back out, carrying a positive charge with them. The sodium ions do not balance this flow by entering the cell, because they cross the membrane at a much slower rate. Figure 2.15a illustrates this process.

The concentration of potassium is the result of an equilibrium of competing forces. The sodium-potassium pump actively moves potassium into the neuron. (That is, it expends energy.) The potassium ions then flow passively from their area of greater concentration to the area of lesser concentration. The **electrical gradient** also plays a part: Because the inside of the cell is negatively charged with respect to the outside, potassium ions are attracted into the neuron and thus remain more abundant there than they would be if the concentration gradient were the only influence.

Similarly, the concentration gradient of sodium ions is the result of the sodium-potassium pump, which actively moves sodium out of the cell, and the very slow passive diffusion of sodium into the cell, driven by both a concentration gradient and an electrical gradient.

**Figure 2.15 (opposite)**
*(a) The role of the sodium-potassium pump. The pump brings potassium ions ($K^+$) into the cell and takes sodium ions ($Na^+$) out. Because potassium leaks out much faster than sodium leaks in, the net effect is an abundance of positive charges outside the cell and a negative charge inside it. (b) Competing forces acting on $Na^+$ and $K^+$ ions when the neuron is at rest. The sodium-potassium pump has pushed most of the $Na^+$ out of the cell and most of the $K^+$ ions in. Because ions tend to move from an area of greater concentration to an area of lesser concentration, the concentration gradient tends to push $Na^+$ ions into the cell and $K^+$ ions out. Because the total positive charge is greater outside the cell than inside, the electrical gradient tends to push both $Na^+$ and $K^+$ ions into the cell. For $K^+$ ions the two gradients virtually cancel each other out. For $Na^+$ ions both gradients push in the same direction; sodium stays outside the cell only because the sodium gates are closed.*

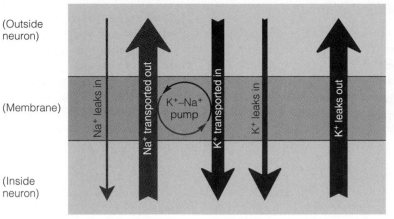

a

**Concentration Gradient**

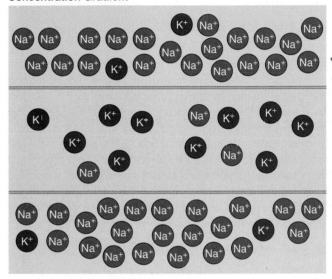

**Electrical Gradient**

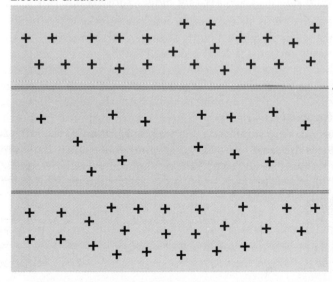

b

### Why a Resting Potential?

Presumably, evolution could have equipped us with neurons that were electrically neutral at rest. The sodium-potassium pump does not expend much energy; still, there must be some advantage to justify even a slight energy expense.

The advantage of the resting potential is that it prepares the neuron to respond rapidly to a stimulus. As we shall see in the next section, an excitation of the neuron opens the sodium gates, enabling sodium to enter the cell explosively. Because the membrane did its work in advance by maintaining the concentration gradient for sodium, the cell is prepared to respond strongly and rapidly to a stimulus.

The resting potential of a neuron can be compared to a poised bow and arrow: An archer who pulls the bow in advance and then waits is ready to fire as soon as the appropriate moment comes. Evolution has applied the same strategy to the neuron.

## THE ACTION POTENTIAL

The resting potential can remain stable as long as the animal remains healthy and the neuron is not stimulated. In nature, stimulation of the neuron takes place at the synapse. We shall consider the synapse in Chapter 3.

Figure 2.16 shows the measured electrical potential inside an axon as a function of time. We can measure the potential using the apparatus shown in Figure 2.13b, with the addition of an extra electrode to stimulate the axon. The extra electrode is placed on the membrane surface close to the intracellular electrode.

Time 0 shows the resting potential, before any stimulus is applied to the neuron. At time 1, we stimulate the neuron by applying a negative charge through the additional electrode, which further increases the negative charge inside the neuron. The change is called **hyperpolarization,** meaning increased polarization. As soon as the artificial stimulation ceases, the cell's charge returns to its original resting level (time 2).

Now, let us apply currents for **depolarization** of the neuron—that is, reduction of its polarization toward zero. We apply a small depolarizing current at time 3 and a slightly larger current at time 4. The cell's potential decreases by just a few millivolts and returns to the resting level as soon as the stimulation ceases. However, when we apply just a slightly stronger current at time 5, the cell's potential shoots well beyond the level produced by the current itself (time 6). The cell has reached its **threshold,** a point at which a brief stimulation triggers a rapid, massive flow of ions across the membrane. Although it varies from cell to cell, the threshold is generally about 15 mV above the resting potential.

Any subthreshold stimulation produces a small response proportional to the amount of current. Any stimulation beyond the threshold, regardless of *how far* beyond, produces the same response seen at time 6 in Figure 2.16. This response is referred to variously as an **action potential,** an impulse, or a spike. Action potentials occur in axons. As a rule, dendrites produce potentials proportional to the magnitude of the stimulation.

Within a given cell, all action potentials are approximately equal in size and shape (amplitude) under normal circumstances. This is the **all-or-none law:** *The size and shape of the action potential are independent of the intensity of the stimulus that initiated it.*

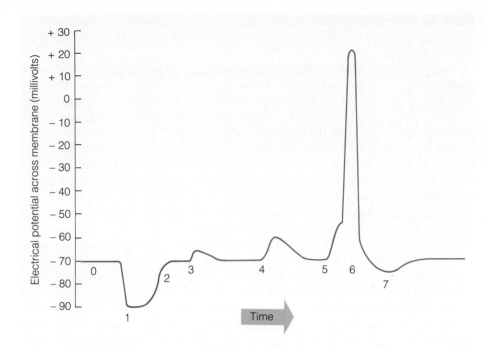

**Figure 2.16**
**Electrical potentials**
**across a neuron mem-**
**brane during artificial**
**stimulation**
*Time 1 is a hyperpolariza-*
*tion; 3, 4, and 5 are three*
*degrees of depolarization. See*
*text for a further explanation.*

As a consequence of this law, a neuron's messages are analogous to those of a telegraph. A neuron cannot send larger action potentials any more than a telegraph operator could send louder dots and dashes. In both cases, the message is conveyed by the time sequence of impulses and pauses. For instance, a neuron might signal "dim light" by a low frequency of action potentials and "brighter light" by a higher frequency. It is also possible that impulses in clusters, such as

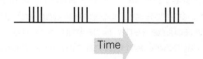

might signal something different from the same number of impulses evenly distributed:

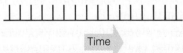

## Molecular Basis of the Action Potential

The action potential can be related to the distribution of ions across the membrane of an axon. Remember that the sodium concentration is much higher outside the neuron than inside. In addition to this concentration gradient, sodium ions are attracted to the inside of the neuron by an electrical gradient, because of the negative charge inside the neuron. If sodium ions were free to flow across the membrane, they would diffuse rapidly into the cell. Ordinarily, the membrane is almost impermeable to sodium, but during the action potential, its permeability increases sharply.

The membrane proteins that form the sodium gates are **voltage-activated gates;** that is, their permeability to sodium depends on the voltage difference across the membrane. As the membrane of the neuron becomes even slightly depolarized, the sodium gates begin to open and sodium flows more freely. If the depolarization is less than the threshold, the increased entry of sodium ions is balanced by an increased exit of potassium ions. (Potassium ions leave the cell at this time primarily because the electrical gradient that had held them inside the cell has been weakened. Also, depolarization of the membrane opens the potassium gates wider as well as the sodium gates.)

When the potential across the membrane reaches threshold, the sodium gates open wide enough that sodium enters the cell faster than potassium can exit. The entering sodium ions depolarize the cell still further, opening the sodium gates even wider. Sodium ions rush into the neuron until the electrical potential across the membrane passes beyond zero to a reversed polarity (point 6 on Figure 2.16).

Compared to the total number of sodium and potassium ions in and around the axon, only a small percentage cross the membrane during an action potential. Even at the peak of the action potential, sodium ions continue to be far more concentrated outside the neuron than inside. An action potential increases the sodium concentration inside a neuron by less than 1 percent in most cases. Because of the persisting concentration gradient, sodium ions should still tend to diffuse into the cell. However, they are no longer attracted into the cell by an electrical gradient; in fact, the interior of the neuron has become temporarily positive with respect to the outside. This reversed electrical gradient blocks the further entry of sodium.

Moreover, at about the peak of the action potential, the sodium gates begin to close, while the potassium gates remain wider open than usual. Sodium ions no longer enter the neuron in significant numbers, but potassium ions rapidly leave because they are much more concentrated inside and because they are no longer attracted by a negative charge. As potassium ions depart, the charge across the membrane returns toward the resting level. Because of the increased permeability to potassium, enough ions may leave to drive the potential beyond the normal resting level to a temporary hyperpolarization (time 7 in Figure 2.16).

Figure 2.17 summarizes the movements of ions during an action potential. At the end of this process, the membrane has returned to its resting potential. The inside of the neuron has slightly more sodium ions and slightly fewer potassium ions than before the action potential. After a rapid series of action potentials, still more sodium ions accumulate within the axon. Eventually, however, the sodium-potassium pump restores the original distribution.

For the neuron to function properly, sodium and potassium must flow across the membrane at just the right pace. At the peak of the action potential, sodium ions must stop entering the cell and potassium ions must exit to return the membrane to its resting potential. Scorpion venom attacks the nervous system by keeping sodium channels open and closing potassium channels (Pappone & Cahalan, 1987; Strichartz, Rando, & Wang, 1987). As a result, the membrane goes into a prolonged depolarization that makes it useless for conveying information.

**Local anesthetic** drugs such as Novocain and Xylocaine attach to the sodium gates of the membrane, preventing sodium ions from entering (K. W. Miller, 1985). In doing so, such drugs block action potentials in the affected area.

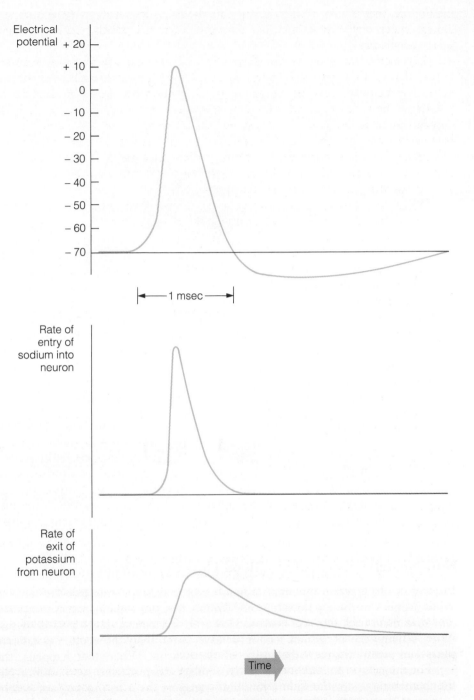

Electrical potential
+ 20
+ 10
0
− 10
− 20
− 30
− 40
− 50
− 60
− 70

|← 1 msec →|

Rate of entry of sodium into neuron

Rate of exit of potassium from neuron

Time

**Figure 2.17**
**The movement of sodium and potassium ions during an action potential**
*Note that sodium ions cross during the peak of the action potential and that potassium ions cross later in the opposite direction, returning the membrane to its original polarization.*

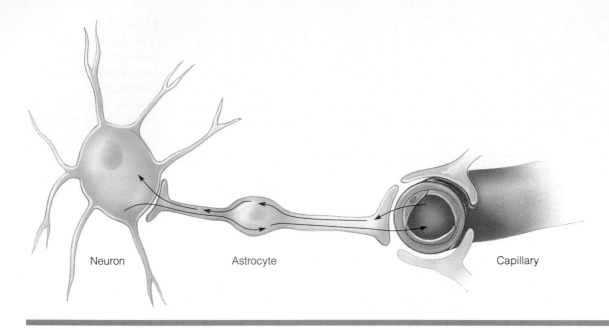

Neuron          Astrocyte          Capillary

**Figure 2.18**

*When a neuron is highly active, it extrudes potassium ions faster than the sodium-potassium pump can return them to the cell. The astrocytes then pump the excess potassium to the nearest arteries. The additional potassium dilates the walls of the arteries and therefore promotes increased blood flow to this area of the brain.*

If anesthetics are applied to sensory nerves, such as nerves carrying pain messages, they block the messages in those nerves from reaching the brain.

**General anesthetics,** such as ether and chloroform, decrease brain activity in a different way. They open the potassium gates, promoting the flow of potassium ions out of the neuron. Therefore they hyperpolarize the neuron and decrease the probability of an action potential (Nicoll & Madison, 1982). Because the neurons fire few action potentials, the nervous system becomes unresponsive to most stimuli.

### How Neural Activity Affects Blood Flow to the Brain

As a result of an action potential, a number of potassium ions exit the neuron. What happens to these potassium ions? Eventually, the sodium-potassium pump can drive them back into the neuron. However, if a neuron has a period of sustained activity, the potassium ions may leave faster than the sodium-potassium pump can return them to the inside of the neuron. When that happens, the potassium ions are not permitted to accumulate. Instead, the surrounding glia cells absorb the excess potassium ions and transport them to the walls of nearby arteries (Figure 2.18). The potassium ions dilate (expand) the artery walls and thereby increase the flow of blood to that part of the brain (Paulson & Newman, 1987). *This is why blood flow increases to the most active areas of the brain.*

### The Refractory Period

While the electrical potential across the membrane is returning from its peak toward the resting point, it is still above the threshold. Why does the cell not produce another action potential during this period? Evidently, there is a brief period when the cell is resistant to reexcitation. During a period of 1 or more milliseconds (msec) after an action potential, the cell is in such a **refractory period.** During the first part of this period, called the **absolute refractory period,** the membrane cannot produce an action potential in response to stimulation of any intensity. During the second part, the **relative refractory period,** a stimulus must exceed the usual threshold to produce an action potential. Throughout the total refractory period, permeability to sodium ions is low and permeability to potassium ions is higher than normal.

The refractory period sets a maximum on the firing frequency of a neuron. If the absolute refractory period were 1 msec, for example, no stimulus could produce more than 1,000 action potentials per second. Stimuli that were weaker than the maximum would produce lower frequencies, depending on the relative refractory period.

## PROPAGATION OF THE ACTION POTENTIAL

Up to this point, we have dealt with the action potential as it occurs at one location along the axon. It is now time to consider how it moves down the axon toward some other cell.

Generally, an action potential begins on the axon hillock. It cannot be conducted any great distance down the axon in the manner that electricity is conducted in a wire, because the axon is a poor conductor of electricity. Rather, each point along the membrane regenerates the action potential in much the same way that it was generated initially.

At the time of the action potential, sodium ions enter one point along the axon, bearing positive charges. That location temporarily is positively charged with respect to neighboring areas along the axon. The positive charge flows both down the axon and across the membrane, as Figure 2.19 shows. If the resistance to electrical flow is great across the membrane and relatively low inside the axon, the charge will flow relatively far along the axon. If, on the other hand, the resistance is slight across the membrane and greater inside the axon—as it is in the thinnest axons—the charge will flow only a short distance along the axon before crossing the membrane.

As the charge passes down the axon, it slightly depolarizes the adjacent areas of the membrane. The areas closest to the action potential are depolarized enough to reach their threshold and to generate an action potential of their own. In this manner the action potential is regenerated. The action potential passes as a wave along the axon. If we could record simultaneously the electrical potentials from all points along the axon, the result would resemble Figure 2.20.

The **propagation of the action potential** refers to the transmission of an action potential down an axon. The propagation of an animal species is the production of babies; in a sense the action potential gives birth to a new action potential at each point along the axon. In this manner, the action potential can be just as strong at the end of the axon as it was at the beginning. The action potential is much slower than electrical conduction because it requires the diffusion of sodium ions at successive points along the axon. The thinnest axons are the slowest; their action potentials travel at a velocity of less than 1 meter per second (m/sec). In the thickest unmyelinated axons, action potentials reach a velocity of about 10 m/sec. In axons surrounded by myelin, which we shall discuss in the next section, the velocity may reach or exceed 100 m/sec. In comparison, electricity travels at 300 million m/sec.

## Figure 2.19

*Current that enters an axon at the point of the action potential flows down the axon, thereby depolarizing adjacent areas of the membrane. The current flows more easily through relatively thick axons. Behind the area of sodium entry, potassium ions exit.*

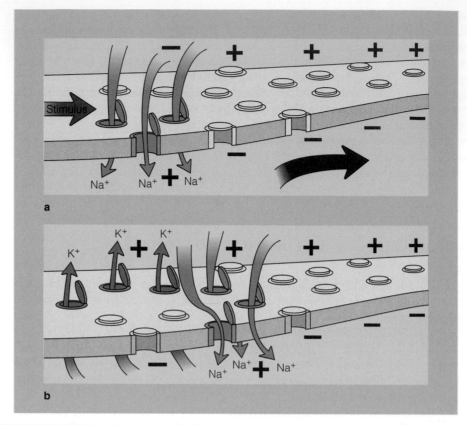

Let us reexamine Figure 2.19 for a moment. What is to prevent the electrical charge from flowing in the other direction, opposite the direction that the action potential is traveling? Nothing. In fact, the electrical charge does flow in both directions. In that case, what prevents the action potential from traveling in both directions? The answer is the refractory period. Normally, an action potential begins at the axon hillock and flows to adjacent areas of the axon. From then on, the action potential can flow in one direction only—away from the axon hillock—because the area behind the action potential is in its refractory period.

## THE MYELIN SHEATH AND SALTATORY CONDUCTION

As just noted, the maximum velocity of action potentials in the thickest unmyelinated axons of vertebrates is about 10 m/sec. At that speed, an impulse from a giraffe's foot would take about a second to reach the brain. Even in smaller animals, a speed of 10 m/sec is too slow for the coordination of certain rapid responses. Myelin sheaths increase speed to make such coordination possible.

Before we discuss how myelin sheaths accelerate action potentials, consider the following analogy. Suppose it were my job to carry written messages over a distance of 3 kilometers (km), without using any mechanical device. One solution

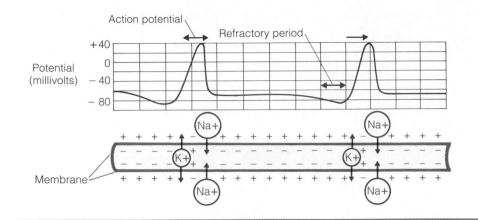

**Figure 2.20**
**Two action potentials
as waves traveling
along the axon**
*Note that they are depicted
here as a function of location
on the axon rather than as a
function of time.*

would be for me to run with the message over the 3 km. That would be analogous to the propagation of the action potential along an unmyelinated axon; it would get the job done but not very rapidly. An alternative would be for me to tie the message to a baseball and throw it. The problem with that approach is that I cannot throw a ball even close to a distance of 3 km. The ideal compromise would be to station people at moderate distances along the 3 km and to throw the message-bearing ball from person to person until it reaches its destination.

The principle behind **myelinated axons** (axons covered with myelin) is the same. Many vertebrate axons are covered with a myelin sheath, a coating made up largely of fats. The myelin sheath is interrupted at intervals of approximately 1 mm by short unmyelinated sections of axon called **nodes of Ranvier** (RAHN-vee-ay). (See Figure 2.21.)

Suppose an action potential is initiated at the axon hillock. It is propagated along the axon until it reaches the first myelin segment. The action potential cannot regenerate along the membrane between one node and the next for two reasons: First, the myelin sheath increases the resistance to electrical transmission at every point between the nodes. Second, sodium gates are located in abundance at the nodes but are virtually absent in the myelinated areas between nodes (Catterall, 1984). Thus, sodium and potassium ions cannot cross the membrane between one node and the next. After an action potential occurs at a node, positively charged ions flow through the interior of the axon, carrying enough electrical charge to depolarize the membrane at the next node and regenerate the action potential (see Figure 2.22). This flow of ions is considerably faster than the regeneration of an action potential at each point along the axon; consequently the transmission of impulses is faster in myelinated axons than in axons without myelin—in some cases as fast as 120 meters per second. The alternation of action potentials at nodes and a rapid flow of ions between nodes is referred to as **saltatory conduction,** from the Latin word *saltare* meaning *to jump.*

Some diseases, such as multiple sclerosis, destroy myelin sheaths. The result is at least to slow down action potentials and in many cases to stop them altogether. An axon that has lost its myelin is not the same as one that has never had any myelin; it still lacks sodium gates in the areas previously covered with myelin. Therefore, when the membrane is depolarized in those areas, an action potential cannot arise.

**Figure 2.21
An axon surrounded by
a myelin sheath and
interrupted by nodes
of Ranvier**
*The lower part shows a cross
section through both the axon
and the myelin sheath.
Magnification × 30,000
(approximately).*

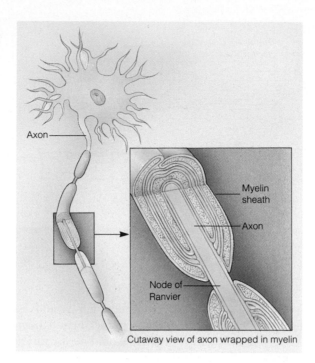

Axon

Myelin
sheath

Axon

Node of
Ranvier

Cutaway view of axon wrapped in myelin

## SIGNALING WITHOUT ACTION POTENTIALS

What we have just discussed concerning action potentials pertains to the axons of many but not all neurons. Dendrites do not produce action potentials, and very small neurons do not produce action potentials in any of their parts. Investigators who insert an electrode into a cell body or an axon are likely to enter relatively large neurons, simply because it is difficult to insert an electrode into a small cell without damaging it. A disproportionate amount of our knowledge, therefore, has come from large neurons.

Large neurons with long axons are specialized to transmit messages over long distances, such as from the spinal cord to the muscles, or from one part of the brain to another. A small neuron with a short axon (or no axon at all) communicates over shorter distances, and it differs from the larger neurons in several ways (Bullock, 1979; Pearson, 1979).

A **local neuron**—a small neuron with no more than a short axon—exchanges information only with other neurons in its own vicinity. Local neurons do not produce action potentials. Rather, they produce **graded potentials,** membrane potentials that vary in magnitude. Graded potentials do not follow the all-or-none law. When a local neuron is stimulated, it depolarizes (or in some cases hyperpolarizes) in proportion to the intensity of the stimulus. The change in membrane potential is conducted to adjacent areas of the cell. Unlike action potentials, graded potentials decay in intensity as they pass along the cell.

Actually, all neurons have graded potentials, at least in their dendrites. The distinctive feature of a local neuron is that it has *only* graded potentials; no part of

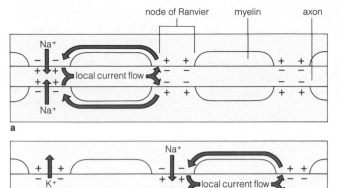

**Figure 2.22**
**Saltatory conduction in a myelinated axon**
*An action potential at the node triggers flow of current to the next node, where the membrane regenerates the action potential.*

the cell produces action potentials. Its graded potentials are sufficient to convey information to other cells.

In a large neuron with a long axon, the dendrites receive information on one end of the cell and the axon transmits information to its target at the other end. Local neurons do not have such a polarity between one end and the other; they can receive information at various points along their membrane and transmit the information in either direction. Various areas of a local neuron may receive information and other areas (some of them immediately adjacent) transmit the information to other neurons. In many cases the dendrites of a local neuron pass information directly to the dendrites of another neuron.

This chapter has concentrated on what happens within a neuron, as if each neuron acted independently. That is a bit like studying the telephone system by examining what happens in a single telephone: Although that is a reasonable place to start, a telephone would be useless if it were not connected to a network of other telephones. Similarly, a neuron contributes to behavior only because of its connections within a vast network. In Chapter 3 we examine what happens at those connections.

## SUMMARY

1. At rest, the inside of a neuron has a negative charge with respect to the outside. Sodium ions are actively pumped out of the neuron, while potassium ions are pumped in. Potassium ions are moderately free to flow across the membrane of the neuron, while the flow of sodium ions is greatly restricted. (p. 39)

2. When the charge across the membrane is reduced, sodium ions can flow more freely across the membrane. If the change in membrane potential is sufficient to reach the threshold of the neuron, then sodium ions enter explosively and the charge across the membrane is suddenly reduced and reversed. This event is known as the action potential. (p. 44)

3. The magnitude of the action potential is independent of the size of the stimulus that initiated it; this is the all-or-none law. (p. 44)

4. Immediately after an action potential, the membrane enters a refractory period, during which it is resistant to starting another action potential. (p. 48)

5. The action potential is regenerated at successive points along the axon by a combination of electrical flow through the axon and the diffusion of sodium ions across the membrane. The action potential maintains a constant magnitude as it passes along the axon. (p. 49)

6. In axons that are covered with myelin, action potentials form only in the nodes between myelinated seg-

53

ments. Between the nodes, ions flow faster than the action potential propagates in axons without myelin. (p. 50)

7. Many small local neurons transmit messages over relatively short distances by graded potentials that decay over time and space, instead of by action potentials. (p. 52)

## REVIEW QUESTIONS

1. What is the difference between a hyperpolarization and a depolarization? What is an action potential? (p. 44)

2. State the all-or-none law of the action potential. (p. 44)

3. Explain the ion movements responsible for the action potential and the return to the resting potential. (p. 45)

4. Distinguish between the absolute refractory period and the relative refractory period. (p. 49)

5. How does the refractory period limit the maximum frequency of action potentials in an axon? (p. 49)

6. How does an action potential propagate along an axon? (p. 49)

7. How does myelin increase the velocity of the action potential? Why does loss of myelin severely impair the ability of an axon to conduct action potentials? (p. 50)

8. What is a graded potential? How does a local neuron differ from a neuron with a long axon? (p. 52)

## THOUGHT QUESTIONS

1. Suppose the threshold for some neuron were the same as that neuron's resting potential. What would happen? At what frequency would the cell produce action potentials?

2. In the laboratory, researchers can apply an electrical stimulus at any point along the axon and thereby set up action potentials traveling in both directions from the point of stimulation. An action potential traveling in the usual direction, away from the axon hillock, is said to be traveling in the *orthodromic* direction. An action potential traveling toward the axon hillock is traveling in the *antidromic* direction. If we started an orthodromic action potential at the axon hillock and an antidromic action potential at the opposite end of the axon, what would happen when they met at the center? Why? Can you imagine any research that might make use of antidromic impulses?

## SUGGESTION FOR FURTHER READING

**Shepherd, G. M.** (1983). *Neurobiology*. New York: Oxford University Press. The first seven chapters provide additional details about neurons, the membrane, and the action potential.

## GLOSSARY

**absolute refractory period** time immediately after an action potential, when the membrane cannot produce an action potential in response to stimulation of any intensity

**action potential** depolarization of an axon produced by a stimulation beyond the threshold

**active transport** transfer of chemicals across a membrane by expenditure of energy as opposed to passive diffusion

**afferent axon** a neuron that brings information into a structure

**all-or-none law** principle that the size and shape of the action potential are independent of the intensity of the stimulus that initiated it

**astrocyte** (astroglia) a relatively large, star-shaped glia cell

**axon** a single fiber that extends from a neuron

**axon hillock** a swelling of the soma, the point where the axon begins

**blood-brain barrier** the mechanism that keeps many chemicals out of the brain

**cell body** structure of a cell that contains the nucleus

**concentration gradient** difference in concentration of a solute across some distance

**cytoplasm** fluid inside the cell membrane

**dendrite** thin, widely branching fiber that emanates from a neuron

**dendritic spine** short outgrowth along the dendrites

**depolarization** reduction in the level of polarization across a membrane

**efferent axon** a neuron that carries information away from a structure

**electrical gradient** difference in electrical potential across some distance

**endoplasmic reticulum** a network of thin tubes within a cell that transport newly synthesized proteins to other locations

**general anesthetic** chemical that depresses brain activity as a whole

**glia** a type of cell in the nervous system that (unlike neurons) does not conduct impulses to other cells

**glucose** a simple sugar, the main fuel of vertebrate neurons

**Golgi complex** a network of vesicles within a cell that prepare hormones and other products for secretion

**graded potential** membrane potential that varies in magnitude

**hyperpolarization** increased polarization across a membrane

**interneuron** a neuron that receives information from other neurons and sends it to either motor neurons or interneurons

**intrinsic neuron** a neuron whose axons and dendrites are all confined within a given structure

**local anesthetic** drugs that block action potentials in the nerves in a particular area where the drug is applied

**local neuron** a small neuron with no more than a short axon

**lysosome** structure within a cell that contains enzymes that break down many chemicals into their component parts

**membrane** structure that surrounds a cell

**microelectrode** a very thin electrode, generally made of glass and filled with an electrolyte solution

**microglia** a very small type of glia cell that removes waste material in the brain

**mitochondrion** (plural: **mitochondria**) the structure where the cell performs the metabolic activities that provide energy

**motor neuron** a neuron that receives excitation from other neurons and conducts impulses from its soma in the spinal cord to muscle or gland cells

**myelinated axon** axon covered with myelin

**myelin sheath** an insulating material that covers many vertebrate axons

**neuron** cell that receives information and transmits it to other cells by conducting electrochemical impulses

**node of Ranvier** short unmyelinated section of axon between segments of myelin

**nucleus** structure within a cell that contains the chromosomes

**oligodendrocyte** glia cell that surrounds and insulates certain axons in the vertebrate brain and spinal cord

**polarization** an electrical gradient across a membran

**presynaptic terminal** the tip of an axon, the point from which the axon releases chemicals

**propagation of the action potential** transmission of an action potential down an axon

**radial glia** a type of glia cells that guides the migration of neurons and the growth of their axons and dendrites during embryological development

**receptor** a neuron specialized to be highly sensitive to a specific type of stimulation

**refractory period** brief period following an action potential, when the cell resists reexcitation

**relative refractory period** time after an action potential, when a stimulus must exceed the usual threshold to produce an action potential

**resting potential** electrical potential across a membrane when a neuron is at rest

**ribosome** the site at which the cell synthesizes new protein molecules

**saltatory conduction** alternation between action potentials at nodes and a more rapid conduction by the flow of ions between nodes

**Schwann cell** glia cell that surrounds and insulates certain axons in the periphery of the vertebrate body

**selective permeability** tendency to permit certain chemicals but not others to cross a membrane

**sensory neuron** a neuron specialized to be highly sensitive to a specific type of stimulation

**sodium-potassium pump** mechanism that actively transports sodium ions out of the cell while simultaneously drawing potassium ions in

**soma** structure of a cell that contains the nucleus

**thiamine** (vitamin B₁) a chemical necessary for the metabolism of glucose

**threshold** level of depolarization at which a brief stimulation triggers a rapid, massive electrical change by the membrane

**voltage-activated gate** gate in the neuronal membrane that opens as the membrane becomes depolarized

# CHAPTER THREE

# Synapses and Drugs

## MAIN IDEAS

**1.** At a synapse, one neuron releases a chemical known as a neurotransmitter that excites or inhibits another cell.

**2.** A single release of neurotransmitter produces only a subthreshold response in the receiving cell. This response summates with other subthreshold responses to determine whether or not the cell will produce an action potential. The synapses are a major site for the integration of incoming information.

**3.** Because different neurotransmitters contribute in different ways to the control of behavior, many behavioral abnormalities can be traced to the excess or deficit of transmission at a particular type of synapse.

**4.** Many of the drugs that affect behavior and experience do so by altering activity at synapses, through various mechanisms.

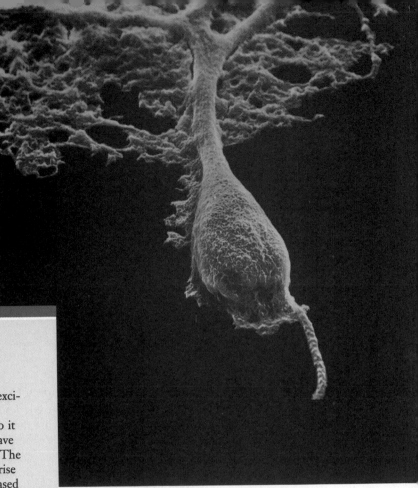

(*Lennart Nilsson*.)

Chapter 2 described what happens during the excitation or inhibition of a neuron. We did not discuss where this excitation comes from or what happens to it when it reaches the end of an axon. As you might have guessed, these two questions have the same answer: The death of an impulse at the end of one neuron gives rise to the birth of a new response in another neuron, based on activity at specialized junctions between the neurons, called *synapses*. The synapses are central to all comparison and integration of information in the brain.

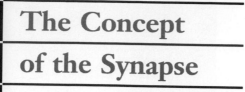

# The Concept
# of the Synapse

In the late 1800s, Ramón y Cajal's observations demonstrated that neurons do not physically merge into one another; a narrow gap separates one neuron from the next. No one knew what takes place at that gap. As far as anyone knew, information might be transmitted across the gap in the same way that it was transmitted along an axon.

Then, in 1906, Charles Scott Sherrington inferred that a specialized type of communication occurs at this gap between neurons. He labeled the point of communication between neurons the **synapse** and predicted most of the major properties of the synapse. What makes Sherrington's accomplishment particularly impressive is that he based his conclusions almost entirely on behavioral data. Decades later, when techniques became available to measure and record the processes that Sherrington had inferred, most of his predictions turned out to be correct.

## THE PROPERTIES OF SYNAPSES

Sherrington conducted most of his experiments on **reflexes,** automatic responses to stimuli. In a simple reflex, receptors excite interneurons, which excite effector neurons, which excite muscles, as Figure 3.1 shows. This circuit is called a **reflex arc.** Because a reflex depends on communication from one neuron to another—not just on the transmission of action potentials along an axon—Sherrington reasoned that the properties of a reflex might reveal some of the special properties of synapses.

In a typical experiment, a dog was strapped into a harness suspended above the ground. Sherrington pinched one of the dog's feet; after a short delay, the dog *flexed* (raised) the pinched leg and *extended* the others. Both the flexion and the extension were reflexive movements—automatic reactions to the stimulus. Furthermore, Sherrington found the same movements after he made a cut that disconnected the spinal cord from the brain; evidently, the flexion and extension were controlled by the spinal cord itself. In an intact animal, the brain could modify the reflexive movements but was not necessary for their occurrence.

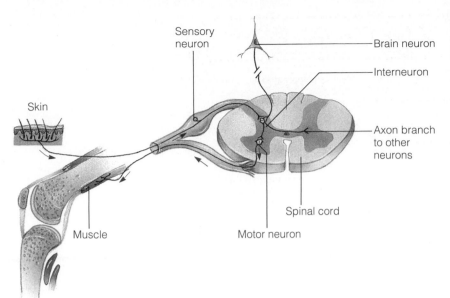

Figure 3.1
A reflex arc through
the spinal cord, sim-
plified to show the
relationship among
sensory neuron, inter-
neuron, and motor
neuron

Sherrington observed several properties of reflexes suggesting that some special process must occur at the junctions between neurons: (1) Reflexes are slower than conduction along an axon; consequently, there must be some delay at the synapses. (2) Several weak stimuli presented at slightly different times or slightly different locations produce a stronger reflex than a single stimulus does. Therefore, the synapse must be able to *summate* different stimuli. (3) When one set of muscles becomes excited, a different set becomes relaxed. Evidently, synapses are connected so that the excitation of one leads to a decreased excitation, or even an inhibition, of others. We shall consider each of these points in some detail.

## Speed of a Reflex and Delay of Transmission at the Synapse

When Sherrington pinched a dog's foot, the dog flexed that leg after a short delay. During the delay, an impulse had to travel up an axon from a skin receptor to the spinal cord, then an impulse had to travel from the spinal cord back down the leg to a muscle. Sherrington measured the total distance that the impulse traveled from skin receptor to spinal cord to muscle and calculated the speed at which the impulse must have traveled to produce a muscle response after the measured delay. He found that the overall speed of conduction through the reflex arc was significantly slower than the known speed of conduction along an axon. Therefore, he deduced, transmission between one neuron and another at the synapse must be slower than transmission along an axon (see Figure 3.2).

## Temporal Summation

Sherrington's work with reflex arcs suggested that repeated stimuli occurring within a brief time can have a cumulative effect. He referred to this phenomenon as **temporal summation.** When Sherrington pinched a dog's foot very lightly, the leg did not move. After the same light pinch was repeated several times in rapid succession, however, the leg flexed slightly. The more rapid the series of

**Figure 3.2
Sherrington's evidence
for synaptic delay**
*An impulse traveling through
a synapse in the spinal cord is
slower than one traveling
through a similar distance
along an uninterrupted axon.*

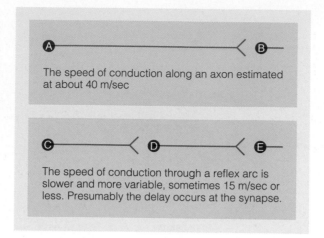

pinches, the greater the response. Sherrington surmised that a single pinch produced a weak synaptic transmission but not enough to produce an action potential in the next cell. That is, the excitation would be less than the threshold of the second cell, the **postsynaptic neuron.** (The neuron that delivers the synaptic transmission is the **presynaptic neuron.**) Sherrington suggested that this subthreshold excitation begins to decay within a fraction of a second but is capable of combining with a second small excitation that quickly follows it. A rapid succession of pinches produces a series of weak activations at the synapse, each adding its effect to what was left of the previous excitations. If the excitations occur rapidly enough, they can combine to exceed the threshold and therefore produce an action potential in the postsynaptic neuron.

Decades after Sherrington's work, it became possible to measure some of the single-cell properties he had inferred. To record the activity evoked in a neuron by synaptic input, researchers insert a microelectrode into the neuron and measure changes in the electrical potential across the membrane. Using this method, John Eccles (1964) was able to demonstrate temporal summation in single cells. He attached stimulating electrodes to some of the axons that formed synapses onto a neuron. He then recorded from the neuron while stimulating one or more of those axons. For example, after he had briefly stimulated an axon, Eccles recorded a slight depolarization of the membrane of the postsynaptic cell (point 1 in Figure 3.3).

Note that this partial depolarization is a graded potential. Unlike action potentials, which are always depolarizations, graded potentials may be either depolarizations (excitatory) or hyperpolarizations (inhibitory). A graded depolarization is known as an **excitatory postsynaptic potential,** abbreviated **EPSP.** Like an action potential, an EPSP results from the entry of sodium ions into the cell (see Chapter 2). The synaptic activation opens some number of sodium gates and increases the entry of sodium ions across the membrane. However, transmission at a single synapse does not open enough sodium gates to provoke an action potential. Unlike an action potential, an EPSP is a subthreshold event that decays over time and space. That is, its magnitude decreases as it travels along the membrane.

When Eccles stimulated the axon twice in close succession, two consecutive EPSPs were recorded in the postsynaptic cell. If the delay between EPSPs was

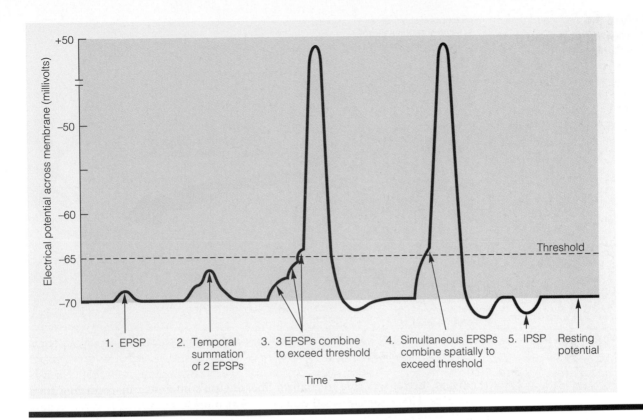

1. EPSP  2. Temporal summation of 2 EPSPs  3. 3 EPSPs combine to exceed threshold  4. Simultaneous EPSPs combine spatially to exceed threshold  5. IPSP  Resting potential

short enough, temporal summation occurred; that is, the second EPSP added to what was left of the first one (point 2 in Figure 3.3). The summation of two EPSPs might or might not be enough to exceed the threshold of the postsynaptic cell, depending on the size of the EPSP, on the time between the two, and on the threshold of the postsynaptic cell. In Figure 3.3 at point 3, three consecutive EPSPs combine to exceed the threshold and produce an action potential.

## Spatial Summation

Sherrington's work with reflex arcs also suggested that **spatial summation** is a property of synapses: Several synaptic inputs originating from separate locations can exert a cumulative effect on a neuron. To study this phenomenon, Sherrington again began with a pinch that was too weak to elicit a response. But this time, instead of repeating the pinch, he gave the dog simultaneous pinches at two points on the foot. Although neither pinch alone would elicit a movement, the two together did elicit a response. Sherrington's interpretation was that pinching two points on the foot activated two sensory neurons, each of which sent an axon to the same interneuron. Excitation from either axon alone would excite a synapse on the interneuron, but one excitation would be insufficient for an action potential. When both excitations were present at the same time, however, their combined effect exceeded the threshold for producing an action potential (see Figure 3.4).

**Figure 3.3**
**Recording from a postsynaptic neuron during synaptic activation, showing (1) an EPSP, (2) subthreshold temporal summation of EPSPs, (3) summation of EPSPs leading to an action potential, (4) spatial summation of simultaneous EPSPs leading to an action potential, and (5) an IPSP**

The Concept of the Synapse

**Figure 3.4
Temporal and spatial
summation**

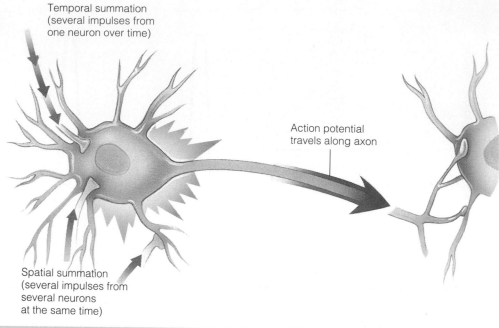

Temporal summation
(several impulses from
one neuron over time)

Action potential
travels along axon

Spatial summation
(several impulses from
several neurons
at the same time)

Again, Eccles was able to confirm Sherrington's inference by recording from single cells. He demonstrated the spatial summation of EPSPs: If two axons have excitatory synapses onto a neuron and either one can produce an EPSP, then activating both simultaneously produces a larger EPSP. If the combination exceeds the threshold of the cell, an action potential will begin (point 4 in Figure 3.3). Note that temporal summation and spatial summation produce the same result: Either one generates an action potential in the postsynaptic cell.

## Inhibitory Synapses

When Sherrington vigorously pinched a dog's foot, the dog contracted the flexor muscles of that leg and the extensor muscles of the other three legs (see Figure 3.5). At the same time, the dog relaxed the extensor muscles of the stimulated leg and the flexor muscles of the other legs. Sherrington's explanation for this series of coordinated and adaptive movements depended, again, on the synapses and in particular on the connections among neurons in the spinal cord: A pinch on the foot sends a message along a sensory neuron to an interneuron in the spinal cord, which in turn excites the motor neurons connected to the flexor muscles of that leg. Sherrington surmised that the interneuron also sends a message that decreases excitation of motor neurons connected to the extensor muscles in the same leg. He did not know whether the interneuron actually formed an inhibitory synapse onto the motor neuron to the extensor muscles or whether it simply decreased the amount of excitation. In either case, the result was to prevent the flexor and extensor muscles of the leg from contracting at the same time.

Eccles and other later researchers demonstrated that the interneuron actually has an inhibitory synapse onto the motor neuron of the extensor muscle. At these synapses, input from the axon hyperpolarizes the postsynaptic cell, increasing the cell's negative charge and decreasing the probability of an action potential by moving the potential further from the threshold (point 5 in Figure 3.3). This temporary hyperpolarization—called an **inhibitory postsynaptic potential**, or

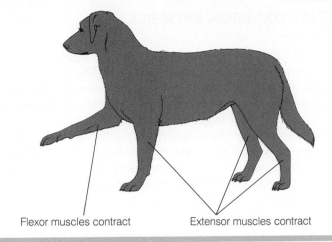

Flexor muscles contract          Extensor muscles contract

**Figure 3.5**
**Flexor muscles (which draw an extremity toward the trunk of the body) and extensor muscles (which move an extremity away from the body)**
*Flexor muscles are antagonists of extensor muscles.*

**IPSP**—resembles an EPSP except that it changes in the opposite direction. An IPSP occurs when synaptic input selectively opens the gates for potassium ions to leave the cell (carrying a positive charge with them) or for chloride ions to enter the cell (carrying a negative charge).

Inhibition is more than just the absence of excitation; it is an active "brake" that can suppress irrelevant or competing responses. If the inhibition is strong enough, it can cancel the simultaneous excitation at other synapses of the same postsynaptic cell.

## RELATIONSHIP AMONG EPSP, IPSP, AND ACTION POTENTIAL

Under normal circumstances, it would be rare for any neuron to be exposed to a single EPSP or IPSP at a time. A neuron may have thousands of synapses along its surface, some that excite the neuron and others that inhibit it. Any number and combination of synapses may be active at any time, giving rise to a continuing combination of temporal and spatial summation. The momentary balance between EPSPs and IPSPs determines whether the neuron reaches its threshold and produces an action potential. The greater the number of EPSPs, the greater the probability of an action potential; the greater the number of IPSPs, the lower the probability of an action potential.

Moreover, some synapses have more influence than others do because of their locations. EPSPs and IPSPs are graded potentials; they decrease in strength as they flow from their point of origin toward other parts of the neuron. For that reason, a synapse located close to the axon hillock, where action potentials originate, has a greater influence than a synapse near the far end of a dendrite.

In many neurons, the EPSPs and IPSPs merely modify the frequency of action potentials that the neuron would fire spontaneously. That is, many neurons have a **spontaneous firing rate,** producing many action potentials per second even without synaptic input. EPSPs increase the frequency of action potentials in these neurons, while IPSPs decrease it. For example, if the neuron's spontaneous firing rate were 10 per second, a steady stream of EPSPs might increase the rate to 15 or 20 or more, whereas a steady stream of IPSPs might decrease the rate to 5 or fewer action potentials per second.

The Concept
of the Synapse

# THE NEURONAL DECISION PROCESS

The neuron can be compared to a thermostat, a smoke detector, or any other device that detects something and triggers a response: The area of the neuron that receives synaptic input is analogous to the sensor. When input reaches a certain level, the neuron triggers an action potential, just as the thermostat turns on the furnace or the smoke detector triggers a fire alarm.

That is, the synapses enable the postsynaptic neuron to integrate information. They provide for the convergence and comparison of messages from different cells at different times. For instance, a given neuron may be stimulated simultaneously at both synapses that produce EPSPs and synapses that produce IPSPs. The EPSPs compete against IPSPs, and the net result is a complicated, not exactly algebraic summation of the two effects. We could regard the summation of EPSPs and IPSPs as a "decision"; that is, the postsynaptic cell "decides" to fire or not based on the combination of "information" (EPSPs and IPSPs) that it receives.

Although we may think of a neuron as "deciding" whether to fire action potentials, we should not imagine that any neuron decides between eggs and toast for breakfast. A great many neurons are involved in any behavior, and behavior depends on a whole network, not a single neuron. The translation between activity of a neuron and activity of the whole animal is complex. We cannot even assume, for instance, that an inhibitory synapse tends to inhibit behavior. In many cases, one cell has an inhibitory synapse onto a second cell, which in turn inhibits a third cell. The first synapse, by inhibiting an inhibitor, has the net effect of increasing the excitation of the third cell. This principle of double negatives, or inhibition of inhibition, is common in the nervous system.

## SUMMARY

1. The synapse is the point of communication between two neurons. Charles S. Sherrington first inferred the properties of synapses, based on his observations of reflexes. (p. 58)

2. Because transmission through a reflex arc is slower than transmission through an equivalent length of axon, Sherrington inferred that there is a delay of transmission at the synapse. (p. 59)

3. Graded potentials (EPSPs and IPSPs) summate their effects. The summation of graded potentials from stimuli at different times is temporal summation. The summation of graded potentials from different locations is spatial summation. (p. 59)

4. A single stimulation at a synapse produces a brief graded potential in the postsynaptic cell. An excitatory graded potential (depolarizing) is an EPSP. An inhibitory graded potential (hyperpolarizing) is an IPSP. (pp. 60, 62)

5. An EPSP occurs when sodium gates open in the membrane; an IPSP occurs when potassium or chloride gates open. (pp. 60, 62)

6. At any time the EPSPs on a neuron compete with the IPSPs; the balance between the two determines the rate of firing of the neuron. (p. 63)

## REVIEW QUESTIONS

1. What evidence did Sherrington use to support his conclusion that transmission at a synapse is different from transmission along an axon? (p. 59)

2. What is the difference between temporal summation and spatial summation? What evidence did Sherrington have for their existence? (p. 59)

3. What evidence did Sherrington have for inhibition in the nervous system? (p. 62)

4. What ion gates in the membrane open during EPSPs? What gates open during IPSPs? (pp. 60, 62)

5. What does the phrase spontaneous firing rate mean in a neuron? (p. 63)

## THOUGHT QUESTIONS

1. When Sherrington measured the reaction time of a reflex (that is, the delay between stimulus and response), he found that the response occurred faster after a strong stimulus than after a weak one. How could you explain this finding? Remember that all action potentials—whether produced by strong or weak stimuli—travel at the same speed along a given axon.

2. A pinch on an animal's right hind foot leads to excitation of an interneuron that excites the motor neurons connected to the flexor muscles of that leg; the interneuron also inhibits the motor neurons connected to the extensor muscles of the leg. In addition, this interneuron sends impulses that reach the motor neuron connected to the extensor muscles of the left hind leg. Would you expect the interneuron to excite or inhibit that motor neuron? (Hint: The connections are adaptive. When an animal lifts one leg it must put additional weight on the other legs to maintain balance.)

3. Neuron X has a synapse onto neuron Y, and Y has a synapse onto Z. Presume here that no other neurons or synapses are present. An experimenter finds that excitation of neuron X causes an action potential in neuron Z after a short delay. However, she determines that the synapse of X onto Y is inhibitory. Explain how the stimulation of X might produce excitation of Z.

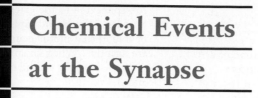

# Chemical Events at the Synapse

Although Charles Sherrington accurately inferred many properties of the synapse, he reached one major incorrect conclusion: He thought that synaptic transmission relied on an electrical impulse, believing that it occurred too quickly to be a chemical reaction. Later research found that in the vast majority of cases, synaptic transmission relies on chemical processes that are much faster than Sherrington thought possible and far more versatile than anyone would have guessed.

## THE DISCOVERY THAT MOST SYNAPTIC TRANSMISSION IS CHEMICAL

In 1905, a young British scientist, T. R. Elliott, demonstrated that the hormone *adrenaline* closely mimics the effects of the sympathetic nervous system, a set of nerves that control the internal organs (see Chapter 4). For example, stimulation of the sympathetic nerves accelerates the heartbeat, relaxes the stomach muscles, and dilates the pupils of the eyes. Applying adrenaline directly to the surface of the heart, the stomach, and the pupils produces those same effects. Elliott therefore suggested that the sympathetic nerves stimulate muscles by releasing adrenaline or something similar. This suggestion implied that synapses in general may operate by releasing chemicals. Elliott's evidence was not decisive, however; perhaps adrenaline merely mimicked certain effects ordinarily produced by electrical stimulation. Sherrington's prestige was so great that most scientists ignored Elliott's results and continued to assume that synapses transmitted information by electrical impulses.

Otto Loewi, a German physiologist, was also attracted to the idea that synapses operate by releasing chemicals, although he did not see how he could test the theory decisively. So for almost twenty years he set it aside. Then in 1920, he aroused from sleep with a sudden idea. He wrote himself a note and then went back to sleep. Unfortunately, the next morning he could not read his own note. The following night at 3 A.M., when he awoke with the same idea, he rushed to the laboratory and performed the experiment at once.

He repeatedly stimulated the vagus nerve to a frog's heart, causing the heart rate to decrease. He then collected fluid from that heart, transferred it to a sec-

66

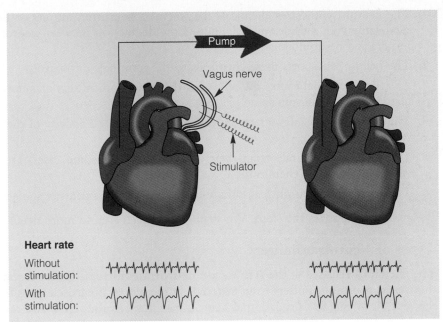

**Figure 3.6
Loewi's experiment
demonstrating that
nerves send messages
by releasing chemicals**
*He stimulated the vagus
nerve to one heart, decreasing
the heartbeat. Then he transferred fluid surrounding that
heart to another heart, decreasing its heartbeat too.*

ond frog's heart, and found that the second heart also decreased its rate of beat-ing. (This experiment is diagrammed in Figure 3.6.) In a later experiment, he stimulated the accelerator nerve to the first frog's heart, causing the heart rate to increase. When he collected fluid from that heart and transferred it to the second heart, this fluid caused the heart rate to increase. That is, stimulating one nerve to the heart released something that inhibited heart rate, and stimulating a differ-ent nerve released something else that increased heart rate. Those "somethings" had to be chemicals. (The fluids that Loewi transferred could not have held loose electricity!) Therefore, Loewi concluded that nerves send messages by releasing chemicals.

Loewi later remarked that if he had thought of this experiment in the light of day, he probably never would have tried it (Loewi, 1960). Even if synapses did re-lease chemicals, his daytime reasoning went, there was little chance that they would release enough of the chemicals to make collecting them easy. Fortunately, by the time he realized the experiment was unlikely to work, he had already com-pleted the research, for which he later won the Nobel Prize.

Although we now know that most synapses operate by transmitting chemi-cals, a few electrical synapses do exist. They occur mostly in situations where it is important for two neurons to synchronize their activities exactly, such as synapses controlling rapid escape movements in certain fish and invertebrates.

## THE SEQUENCE OF CHEMICAL
## EVENTS AT A SYNAPSE

A great many medical conditions and drugs that affect behavior do so by altering neurotransmission. Consequently, an understanding of the chemical events oc-curring at a synapse is fundamental to much of current research in biological psy-chology. The events at a synapse, in summary form, are as follows:

1. The neuron synthesizes chemicals that serve as neurotransmitters or neuro-modulators. (In a while we shall address the distinction between neurotransmitters and neuromodulators.)

2. The neuron transports these chemicals to the terminals of its axons.

3. An action potential causes the release of the neurotransmitters or neuromodulators from the terminals.

4. The released molecules attach to receptors and alter the activity of the postsynaptic neuron.

5. The molecules separate from their receptors and (in some cases) are converted into inactive chemicals.

6. The presynaptic neuron reabsorbs some of the neurotransmitter molecules.

Figure 3.7 summarizes the steps. We shall discuss each step in more detail.

## Types of Neurotransmitters

The chemicals released at the synapse are **neurotransmitters.** Each neuron synthesizes its neurotransmitters from materials in the blood. Neuroscientists believe that dozens of chemicals function as neurotransmitters in the brain, and research has been gradually adding to the list of known or suspected neurotransmitters (S. H. Snyder, 1984). Three major categories of neurotransmitters are **biogenic amines** (containing an $NH_2$ group), amino acids, and peptides. We shall consider some of these in more detail later; for now, you can familiarize yourself with some of their names (see Table 3.1).

## Synthesis of Transmitters

Every cell in the body builds some of the materials it needs by chemical reactions, converting substances provided by the diet into other chemicals necessary for normal functioning. The neuron is no exception. Each neuron synthesizes its neurotransmitters from precursor molecules that reach the cell by way of the blood, derived originally from foods the individual ate. Many neurotransmitters can be synthesized both in the cell body and in the terminal, close to their point of release. The peptide neurotransmitters, however, are synthesized only in the cell body. Under normal circumstances, the brain maintains fairly constant levels of each neurotransmitter even during periods of fasting. Nevertheless, if the diet has a high or low concentration of the precursors necessary for making a particular neurotransmitter, the brain may produce a slightly higher or lower than usual amount of that neurotransmitter (R. J. Wurtman, 1982, 1983; Wurtman, Hefti, & Melamed, 1981).

Figure 3.8 illustrates the chemical steps in the synthesis of acetylcholine, serotonin, dopamine, epinephrine, and norepinephrine. Note the relationship among epinephrine, norepinephrine, and dopamine—three closely related compounds known as **catecholamines.** Some neurons synthesize dopamine; others have an additional enzyme that converts dopamine to norepinephrine; still others can convert norepinephrine to epinephrine.

Each pathway in Figure 3.8 begins with substances found in the diet. Acetylcholine, for example, is synthesized from choline, which is abundant in cauliflower and milk. The body can also make choline from lecithin, a component of egg yolks, liver, soybeans, butter, peanuts, and several other foods. The amino acids phenylalanine and tyrosine, constituents of most proteins, are precursors of dopamine, norepinephrine, and epinephrine.

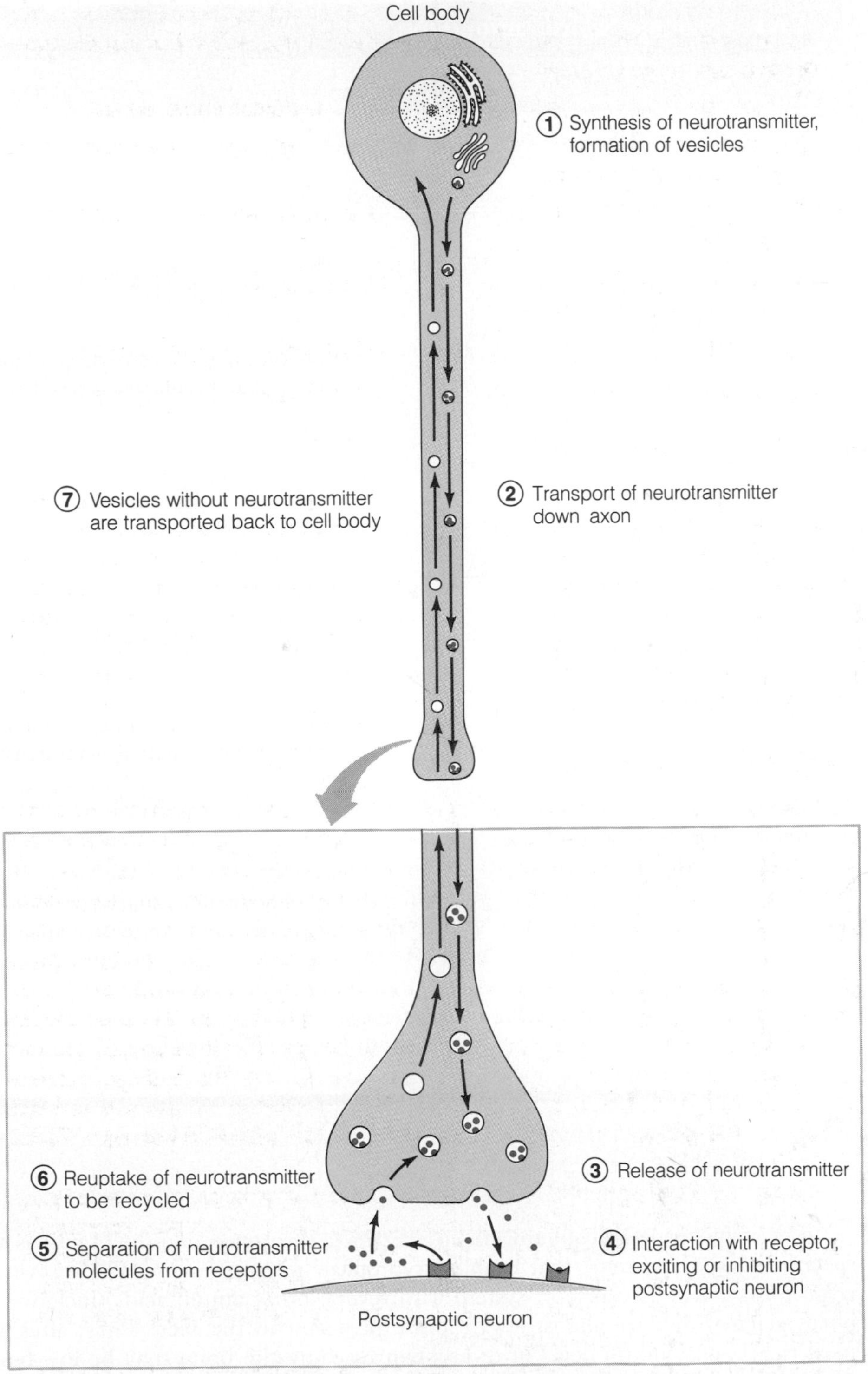

Cell body

① Synthesis of neurotransmitter, formation of vesicles

② Transport of neurotransmitter down axon

⑦ Vesicles without neurotransmitter are transported back to cell body

⑥ Reuptake of neurotransmitter to be recycled

⑤ Separation of neurotransmitter molecules from receptors

③ Release of neurotransmitter

④ Interaction with receptor, exciting or inhibiting postsynaptic neuron

Postsynaptic neuron

**Figure 3.7
The major events
in transmission at
a synapse**

## Table 3.1 Some Neurotransmitters

| Name and Pronunciation | Abbreviation | Comment |
|---|---|---|
| **The Biogenic Amines (or Monoamines)** (each contains an NH$_2$ group) | | |
| **Acetylcholine** (ah-SET-il-KO-leen or ASS-uh-teel-KO-leen) | ACh | The transmitter released from nerves onto skeletal muscles; also used in the brain. |
| **Serotonin** (sehr-oh-TO-nin) | 5-HT | Also known as 5-hydroxytrypt-amine, from which its abbreviation is derived. |
| **Histamine** (HISS-tuh-meen) | | |
| *Catecholamines* (biogenic amines that also contain a ) | | |
| **Dopamine** (DO-puh-meen) | DA | |
| **Norepinephrine** (NOR-ep-uh-NEFF-rin) | NE | Also known as noradrenaline. |
| **Epinephrine** (ep-uh-NEFF-rin) | | Also known as adrenaline; an important hormone as well as neurotransmitter. |
| *Amino Acids* (the building blocks of proteins) | | |
| **Glutamate** (GLOO-tuh-mate) | | Probably the most abundant neurotransmitter in the vertebrate brain. |
| **Glycine** (GLY-seen) | | |
| **Aspartate** (uh-SPAR-tate) | | |

The amino acid **tryptophan** is the precursor to serotonin, and the brain has a special "transport system" that enables tryptophan to enter neurons. However, tryptophan shares its transport system with several other amino acids (including phenylalanine) that are almost always more prevalent in the diet. Thus, after a meal rich in protein, the level of tryptophan reaching the brain may be low because of competition from the other amino acids. One way to increase the amount of tryptophan entering the brain is to eat carbohydrates with the protein. Carbohydrates increase release of the hormone **insulin,** which takes a number of competing amino acids out of the bloodstream and into cells throughout the body, thus decreasing the competition against tryptophan for entry into the brain (J. J. Wurtman, 1985).

| Name and Pronunciation | Abbreviation | Comment |
|---|---|---|
| **Gamma-amino-butyric acid** (GAH-buh) | GABA | |
| *Peptide Neurotransmitters* (chains of amino acids) | | |
| **Leu-enkephalin** (loo-in-KEF-uh-lin) | | Has effects that resemble opiate drugs such as morphine and heroin. |
| **Met-enkephalin** (met-in-KEF-uh-lin) | | Has effects that resemble opiate drugs. |
| **β-endorphin** (bayt-uh-en-DOR-fin) | | Has effects that resemble opiate drugs. |
| **Substance P** | | Released by nerves that report pain. |
| **Cholecystokinin** (ko-leh-SIS-to-KINE-in) | CCK | |
| **Vasopressin** | | |
| **Vasoactive intestinal protein** | VIP | |
| **Gastrin** | | |
| **Galanin** | | |
| **Neuropeptide Y** | | |
| **Oxytocin** | | |
| **Somatostatin** | | |
| and more than 30 other peptides | | |
| *Other Neurotransmitters* | | |
| **Adenosine** | | |
| **ATP** | | Released at some nerve-muscle junctions onto smooth muscle. |

## Transport of Transmitters

Much of the synthesis of neurotransmitter molecules takes place in the cell body. From there the neurotransmitter is transported down the axon to the terminal, where it can be released. The speed of transport varies from only 1 millimeter per day to more than 100 mm per day, depending on the type of chemical and the diameter of the axon.

Even at the highest speeds, transport from cell body to terminal may take hours, sometimes days, in certain neurons. For example, an axon from the spinal cord to the muscles may extend a meter or so in large animals such as giraffes. Neurons do not completely depend on these transport processes, however; they

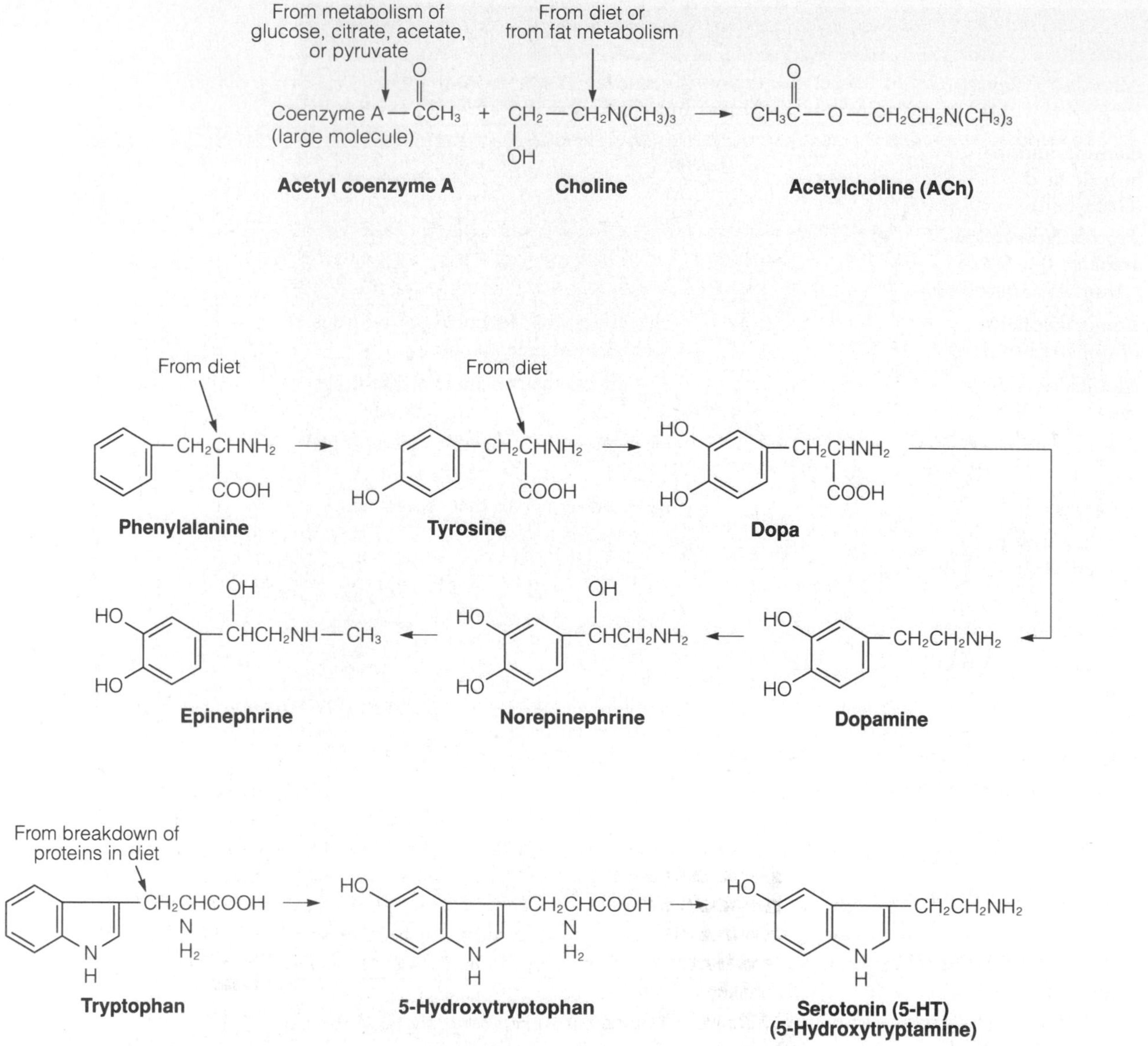

**Figure 3.8**
**Steps in the synthesis of acetylcholine, serotonin, dopamine, norepinephrine, and epinephrine**

*Arrows represent chemical reactions.*

can synthesize certain neurotransmitters (including acetylcholine and the catecholamines) in the terminals themselves. But because peptide transmitters can be synthesized only in the cell body, neurons take a long time to replenish their supply of peptides after releasing them. Neurons can release acetylcholine repeatedly within a short time; they release peptide neurotransmitters less frequently.

## Release and Diffusion of Transmitters

The terminal of an axon has voltage-dependent calcium gates. When the membrane is at rest, these gates are closed and calcium stays outside the cell. However, when an action potential reaches the end of an axon, the depolarization changes the voltage across the membrane and opens the calcium gates. Through a mechanism not yet clearly understood, the increased calcium concentration inside the presynaptic cell causes the cell to release a certain amount of its neurotransmitter during the next 1 or 2 milliseconds. The depolarization by itself does not release the neurotransmitter; it promotes the release only indirectly, by increasing the calcium concentration within the cell (Augustine, Charlton, & Smith, 1987).

A presynaptic neuron occasionally releases a small amount of neurotransmitter into the synaptic cleft even if the neuron has not been stimulated. If we record from the postsynaptic cell, then we see evidence of this release in periodic EPSPs or IPSPs. Such potentials have a minimum size, known as a **quantum.** The size of the quantum may vary from one synapse to another, but it is constant for a given synapse from one time to another.

If we examine either the spontaneous EPSPs or those evoked by stimulation, we find that the size of the EPSP varies but that all EPSPs are integral multiples of the quantum. That is, an EPSP may be 30 times the quantum or 31, but never 30.5.

Why are neurotransmitters always released in quanta? The answer is not clear. We do know that most terminals contain a large number of **vesicles,** tiny near-spherical packets filled with neurotransmitter (Figure 3.9). For many years investigators assumed that the vesicle was the anatomical basis for the quantum—that is, they assumed that an action potential caused some number of vesicles to spill their contents into the synaptic cleft. However, later evidence suggested that the terminal often releases neurotransmitter molecules stored *outside* the vesicles. Much doubt remains about what percentage of neurotransmitter release comes from the vesicles (Tauc, 1982). Consequently, we do not know why terminals release transmitter in quantum units.

After the presynaptic cell releases the neurotransmitter, the chemical diffuses across the synaptic cleft to the postsynaptic membrane, where it attaches to a receptor. The cleft is only 0.02 to 0.05 microns wide, and the neurotransmitter takes no more than 10 microseconds to diffuse across the cleft. The total delay in transmission across the synapse, including the time it takes for the presynaptic cell to release the neurotransmitter, is 0.5 to 2 milliseconds (Martin, 1977; Takeuchi, 1977).

The brain as a whole uses dozens of neurotransmitters, but no single neuron releases them all. For many years investigators believed that each neuron released just one neurotransmitter. We now know that most neurons release two or three transmitters; some may release as many as five or six. However, according to the available evidence, a neuron releases the *same* combination of transmitters from all branches of its axon. For example, if one branch of the axon releases norepinephrine and enkephalin, then all its branches release norepinephrine and enkephalin (Eccles, 1986).

This principle makes sense if we assume that the nucleus of the neuron controls the metabolism of the entire cell and sends the same chemicals to all parts of the cell. However, various branches of an axon may release different proportions of its transmitters. It is also possible that the entire neuron may release mostly one transmitter at one time and mostly another transmitter at another time (Black, Adler, & LaGamma, 1986; Changeux, 1986).

Why does a neuron release a combination of transmitters instead of just one transmitter? Investigators are not certain, but a combination of transmitters probably enables the neuron to send a more complex message. One transmitter might excite or inhibit the postsynaptic neuron while another prolongs or limits the effects of the first (Hökfelt et al., 1986).

**Figure 3.9**

*(a)* Diagram of a synapse. The end of the presynaptic axon swells to form the terminal, which releases the neurotransmitter. *(b)* An electron micrograph, showing a synapse magnified thousands of times. The small round structures in the middle cell are vesicles. The thick, dark area at the bottom of this cell is the synapse. (D. D. Kunkel, University of Washington/BPS.) *(c)* Electron micrograph showing axon terminals onto the soma of a neuron. Magnified × 11,000. (From Lewis et al., 1969.)

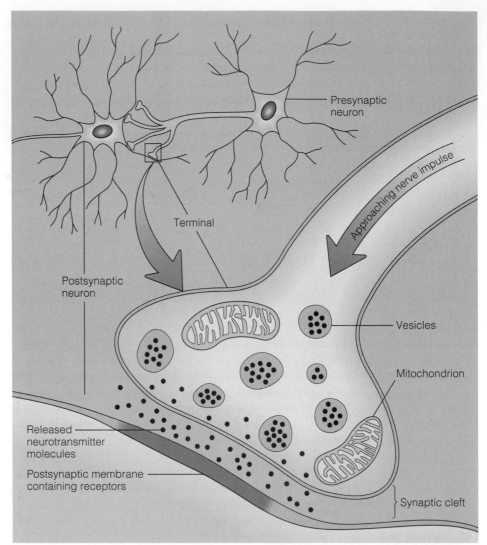

Presynaptic neuron

Approaching nerve impulse

Terminal

Postsynaptic neuron

Vesicles

Mitochondrion

Released neurotransmitter molecules

Postsynaptic membrane containing receptors

Synaptic cleft

a

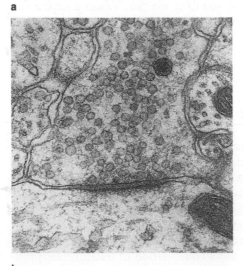

b

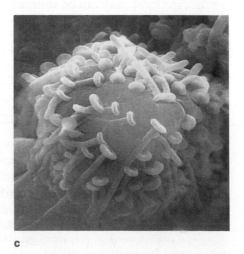

c

Although a neuron releases only a limited number of neurotransmitters, it may receive and respond to a number of different neurotransmitters at various synapses. For example, it might respond to acetylcholine released at one synapse, serotonin at another synapse, GABA at still another, and so on. Although the neuron produces only a few types of neurotransmitters, it can apparently produce enough types of receptors to respond to a great variety of incoming neurotransmitters.

## Activation of Receptors of the Postsynaptic Cell

In English, the term *fern* refers to a small plant. In German, *fern* means far away. In French, it means nothing at all. The meaning of any word depends on who hears it or reads it. The same is true of neurotransmitters. The meaning of a neurotransmitter depends on the receptor that receives it. For example, the neurotransmitter acetylcholine may have a rapid but brief effect on one neuron, a slow but prolonged effect on another neuron, and no effect at all on still another, depending on the receptors of the postsynaptic neurons.

Neurotransmitters can affect other neurons in many ways. For convenience, we distinguish three major types of effects: ionotropic, metabotropic, and modulatory.

**Ionotropic Effects** Some neurotransmitters exert **ionotropic effects** on the postsynaptic neuron. This means that the neurotransmitter attaches to a receptor on the membrane and thereby opens the gates for some type of ion (see Figure 3.10). For example, the neurotransmitter *glutamate* opens sodium gates, thereby enabling sodium ions to enter the postsynaptic cell. The sodium ions, bringing with them a positive charge, partially depolarize the membrane. Consequently, glutamate is an *excitatory* neurotransmitter.

GABA is another neurotransmitter that exerts ionotropic effects, but its effects are *inhibitory*. When GABA attaches to its receptors on the membrane, it opens chloride gates, enabling chloride ions, with their negative charge, to cross the membrane into the cell more rapidly than usual.

Acetylcholine exerts ionotropic effects at some synapses but not at others. The synapses at which it produces ionotropic effects are known as *nicotinic* synapses because they can be stimulated by the drug *nicotine*. When acetylcholine attaches to one of its nicotinic receptors, the membrane-bound proteins shown in Figure 3.11, it opens the gates for sodium ions to cross the membrane for about 1 to 3 msec (Changeux, Devillers-Thiéry, & Chemouilli, 1984; Giraudat & Changeux, 1981). Ionic effects at synapses are rapid but short-lived. Typically the neurotransmitter opens the ion channels within 10 msec after its release and keeps them open for about 10 to 20 msec (North, 1989; Westbrook & Jahr, 1989). Ionotropic synapses are therefore useful for conveying information about visual and auditory stimulation, muscle movements, and other events that change rapidly.

**Metabotropic Effects and "Second Messenger" Systems** At certain other synapses, neurotransmitters exert **metabotropic effects.** These effects take place through a sequence of metabolic reactions; they are slower, longer lasting, and more complicated than the ionic effects. The effects emerge about 30 msec after the release of the transmitter (North, 1989); they may last seconds or longer—in some cases, much longer.

Figure 3.12 shows a receptor molecule for epinephrine, a neurotransmitter that exerts metabotropic effects. This receptor is a protein (a long chain of amino

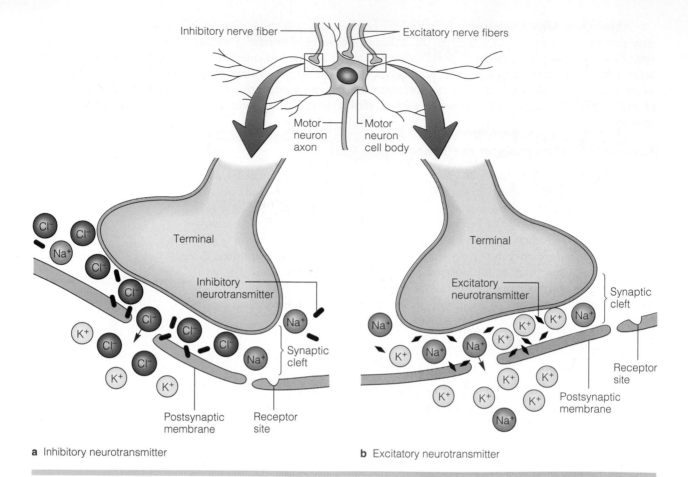

a Inhibitory neurotransmitter

b Excitatory neurotransmitter

**Figure 3.10**
**Ionotropic synapses**

*At an ionotropic synapse, a neurotransmitter (**a**) may open chloride gates, hyperpolarizing the membrane, or (**b**) may open sodium gates, depolarizing the membrane.*

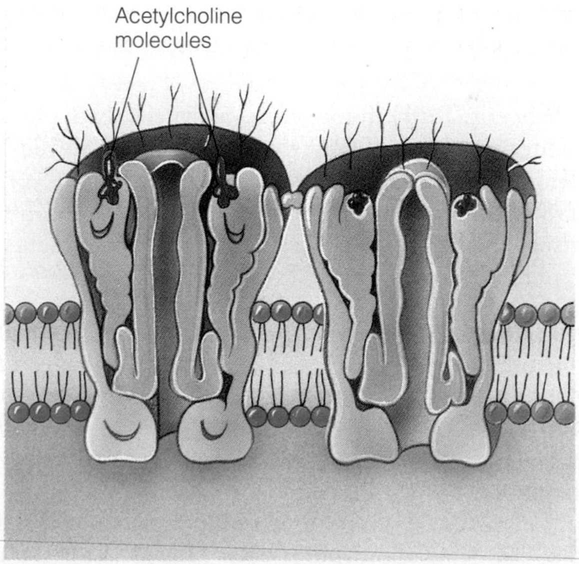

**Figure 3.11**
**Acetylcholine receptors embedded in a membrane**

*The receptors on the left have acetylcholine molecules attached to them; consequently, their ion pores are open.*
*(From Lindstrom, 1979.)*

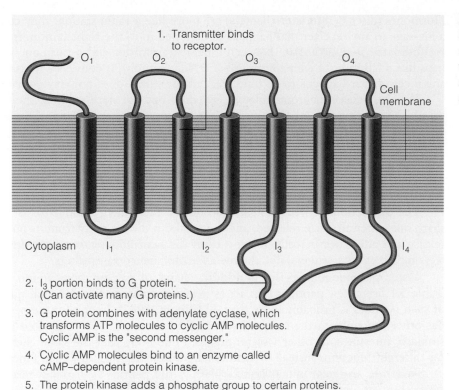

**Figure 3.12**
**Sequence of events at a metabolic synapse, using a second messenger within the postsynaptic neuron**

1. Transmitter binds to receptor.

$O_1$   $O_2$   $O_3$   $O_4$

Cell membrane

Cytoplasm   $I_1$   $I_2$   $I_3$   $I_4$

2. $I_3$ portion binds to G protein.
   (Can activate many G proteins.)

3. G protein combines with adenylate cyclase, which transforms ATP molecules to cyclic AMP molecules. Cyclic AMP is the "second messenger."

4. Cyclic AMP molecules bind to an enzyme called cAMP–dependent protein kinase.

5. The protein kinase adds a phosphate group to certain proteins.

6. The phosphorylated proteins either open or close some type of ion gate, alter the structure of the cell, or change the metabolism of the cell. These changes are slow but long lasting.

acids) that winds back and forth across the membrane. When an epinephrine molecule attaches to its receptor, it alters the configuration of the rest of the protein—but exactly how it alters the protein is not yet understood. The altered protein enables a portion of the protein inside the neuron to react with other molecules, as described in Figure 3.12 (Levitzki, 1988; O'Dowd, Lefkowitz, & Caron, 1989).

The chemical steps in Figure 3.12 are difficult to remember. Here are the main points: A series of chemical steps produces an increased concentration of **cyclic AMP** inside the neuron. Cyclic AMP (adenosine monophosphate) is a versatile and important compound. It is described as a **second messenger:** Just as the "first messenger" (the neurotransmitter) carries a message to the postsynaptic cell, the second messenger carries a message to several areas within the postsynaptic cell. Cyclic AMP provides the energy to alter certain proteins. Exactly which proteins are altered, and how they are altered, varies from one cell to another. In some cases the altered proteins open or close one type of ion gate in the membrane. In other cases the proteins alter the structure of the cell or change its metabolic activity. The changes are relatively slow and long lasting compared to the effects of ionotropic synapses.

**Neuromodulators, Including Peptides**  A neurotransmitter is like a telephone line; it conveys a message directly and exclusively from the sender to the receiver.

Chemical Events
at the Synapse

Hormones (discussed in later chapters) are more like a radio station; they convey a message to any receiver that happens to be tuned in to the right station. A **neuromodulator** is intermediate between a neurotransmitter and a hormone—perhaps like a CB radio. Like a hormone (or a radio station), it conveys a message to any receiver that happens to be tuned in, but the signal does not travel very far.

Neurons release neuromodulators generally but not necessarily at their terminals. They diffuse to other neurons in their region, perhaps even to the neuron that released them. They affect all those nearby cells that have receptors for them—that is, all the cells "tuned to the right station" (Vizi, 1984). Just as the strength of a CB radio signal fades rapidly over a mile or two, the effect of a neuromodulator is greatest for nearby cells. As the modulator diffuses to greater distances, its concentration decreases.

The distinction between a neurotransmitter and a neuromodulator is not a sharp one. After all, once released, any chemical can diffuse away from its point of release and affect nearby cells. In most cases the neuromodulators exert their effects by second messengers, like the metabotropic neurotransmitters.

Many neuromodulators are **peptides**—chains of two or more amino acids. Table 3.1 lists a few peptides that act as neuromodulators, but the total number of such peptides is probably more than 40 (Bloom, 1987). Each of these peptides has other functions in the body as well; in fact, most of them originated in the stomach, intestines, or other visceral organs. (The body uses the same chemicals for different functions instead of synthesizing a new chemical for each function.)

As a rule, the neuromodulators, especially the peptide neuromodulators, by themselves produce little effect on a neuron. This is why they are called "modulators"; they modulate (alter) the effect of neurotransmitters (Millhorn et al., 1989). For example, certain neuromodulators prolong or limit the effect of a neurotransmitter. Such neuromodulators are said to have a "conditional" effect; they produce an effect only when the neurotransmitter is present. Other neuromodulators have other effects, such as limiting the release of neurotransmitter from the presynaptic neuron. Table 3.2 highlights some differences between neurotransmitters and peptide neuromodulators.

Recall that most neurons release two or more chemicals from their terminals. In many cases one of them is a neurotransmitter such as acetylcholine and the other is a peptide neuromodulator. Such a combination can have highly adaptive effects. For example, stimulation at one set of synapses leads to salivation. Acetylcholine starts the salivation; a peptide neuromodulator released with it causes the salivation to continue. The effect of acetylcholine by itself would be too brief, and the effect of the peptide by itself would be too weak and too slow. In other cases, a peptide may reduce or halt the effect of acetylcholine (Crawley, 1990).

## Presynaptic Receptors

In one special kind of synapse, the receptor is located on the terminal at the tip of an axon. Such a receptor is known as a **presynaptic receptor.** At most sites, activation of a presynaptic receptor inhibits the later release of neurotransmitter from the terminal; in some cases, however, it facilitates release.

In many cases a receptor on the presynaptic neuron is sensitive to some neurotransmitter other than the one the neuron itself releases (Starke, 1981). In many other cases the presynaptic neuron has receptors sensitive to the same neurotransmitter that the neuron releases (Dubocovich, 1984; Roth, 1984). A presynaptic receptor that responds to the neuron's own neurotransmitter is known as an **autoreceptor.** Many investigators believe that autoreceptors provide negative

## Table 3.2 Differences Between Neurotransmitters and Peptide Neuromodulators

| | Neurotransmitters | Peptide Neuromodulators |
|---|---|---|
| Location of synthesis | Partly in cell body but mostly in the terminal, near point of release. | Entirely in cell body. |
| Potential for repeated release | Many molecules recycled; others synthesized near point of release. Can be released at high frequency. | Generally not recycled; newly synthesized molecules may take hours to reach the terminal. Can be released only at a low frequency. |
| Location of effects | Generally limited to the postsynaptic neuron. | In some cases may diffuse to nearby cells. |
| Type of effects | Ionotropic: open gates in membrane for some type of ion. | Prolong or limit the effects of a neurotransmitter. Effects are slow but long lasting. |
| | Metabotropic: more slowly open ion gates or alter the metabolism or structure of the neuron. | |
| Onset of effects | Ionotropic: less than 10 msec. | Slower than neurotransmitters. |
| | Metabotropic: 30 msec. | |
| Duration of effects | Ionotropic: 10–20 msec. | Seconds, maybe minutes, maybe hours? |
| | Metabotropic: less than a second to a few seconds, maybe longer. | |

Based on Bloom, 1987; Carlsson, 1987; Millhorn et al., 1989; Shepherd, 1988; Vizi, 1984.

feedback. That is, after the terminal releases the neurotransmitter, some transmitter molecules return to the presynaptic neuron where they activate autoreceptors, which in turn inhibit further release of the neurotransmitter (see Figure 3.13). However, the evidence to support this view is only indirect and not entirely conclusive (Kalsner, 1990). Therefore, some investigators consider that the role of the autoreceptors is still uncertain.

### Inactivation and Reuptake of Neurotransmitters

A neurotransmitter does not normally linger at the postsynaptic membrane for long. If it did, it might continue exciting or inhibiting the postsynaptic neuron indefinitely. Various neurotransmitters are inactivated in different ways.

After acetylcholine activates a receptor, it is broken down by the enzyme **acetylcholinesterase** (a-SEE-til-ko-lih-NES-teh-raze) into two fragments, acetate and choline. Acetate by itself cannot stimulate the receptor, and choline

**Figure 3.13**
**Two types of presynaptic receptors**
*(a) A norepinephrine synapse with an inhibitory receptor, probably sensitive to some other neurotransmitter. (b) A norepinephrine synapse with an autoreceptor, sensitive to norepinephrine. Autoreceptors may contribute to negative feedback, although the evidence for this function is not yet solid.*

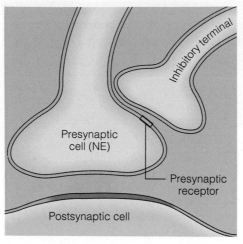

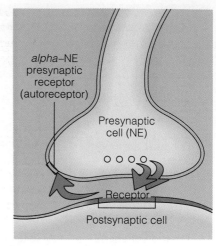

a          b

does so only weakly (Krnjević & Reinhardt, 1979). The choline diffuses back to the presynaptic neuron, which takes it up and reconnects it with acetate already in the cell to form acetylcholine again. That is, the brain recycles its choline. The process is highly efficient but not perfect; after a rapid series of transmissions at a synapse, the number of quanta released per transmission declines—presumably because the cell has used up its acetylcholine faster than it can reassemble it.

If the enzyme acetylcholinesterase is not present in adequate amounts, acetylcholine may remain at the synapse for an abnormally long time and continue to excite it. This leads to a strategy in some drug therapies: Certain disorders, such as myasthenia gravis, are associated with a deficit of transmission at acetylcholine synapses. One way to elevate someone's acetylcholine transmission is to give drugs that inhibit acetylcholinesterase.

Serotonin and the catecholamines (DA, NE, and epinephrine) are not broken down into inactive fragments at the postsynaptic membrane. They simply detach from the membrane. The presynaptic neuron takes up most of these neurotransmitter molecules intact and reuses them. This process is called **reuptake**.

Some of the serotonin and catecholamine molecules, either before or after being reabsorbed, are converted into inactive chemicals that cannot stimulate the receptor. The enzymes that convert catecholamine transmitters into inactive chemicals are **COMT** (catechol-o-methyltransferase) and **MAO** (monoamine oxidase, which affects serotonin as well as catecholamines). We shall encounter MAO again later; certain antidepressant drugs act by inhibiting MAO.

## NEUROTRANSMITTERS AND BEHAVIOR

The brain uses a great many chemicals as neurotransmitters and neuromodulators. Adding to the complexity, each of the widely investigated neurotransmitters has more than one type of receptor. For example, acetylcholine has at least four types of nicotinic receptors and five types of muscarinic receptors (McCormick, 1989). Norepinephrine has several types of alpha and beta receptors (Surprenant,

1989); serotonin has receptors known as type $1_A$, $1_B$, $1_C$, type 2, and type 3 (Pierce & Peroutka, 1989). GABA has some receptors that respond to the benzodiazepine tranquilizers such as Valium and Xanax, and other receptors that do not (Stephenson & Dolphin, 1989). Apparently, every transmitter has several types of receptors to which it can attach.

Why so many neurotransmitters and so many types of receptors? It is probably for the same reason that our alphabet has more than just three or four letters. The nervous system needs a large number of elements that can be combined in different ways if it is to produce complex behavior. To be more specific: Different neurotransmitters control different aspects of behavior. Stimulation of type 2 serotonin receptors may promote one type of behavior or experience while stimulation of type $1_A$ receptors facilitates another and stimulation of muscarinic acetylcholine receptors leads to yet another. The nervous system is complex and full of redundant pathways, so we should not imagine that a given neurotransmitter has only one function or that a given behavior depends on a single neurotransmitter. Still, a given type of synapse seems to be more important for some functions than for others. Consequently, an excess or deficit of activity at a particular type of synapse may produce altered behavior, even abnormal behavior. And a drug or other treatment that facilitates or blocks a particular type of synapse may be useful in treating certain behavioral abnormalities. We shall return to this point repeatedly in later chapters.

## SUMMARY

1. Most synapses operate by the transmission of a chemical, the neurotransmitter, from the presynaptic cell to the postsynaptic cell. (p. 66)

2. Many chemicals are used as neurotransmitters. As far as we know, each neuron releases the same combination of neurotransmitters from all branches of its axon. (p. 68)

3. It is possible to increase or decrease the production of a given neurotransmitter, at least briefly, by consuming food with a high or low concentration of the precursors to that neurotransmitter. (p. 68)

4. At certain synapses, a neurotransmitter exerts its effects by attaching to a receptor that opens the gates to allow a particular ion, such as sodium, to cross the membrane more readily. At other synapses, a neurotransmitter may lead to slower but longer-lasting changes inside the postsynaptic cell. (p. 75)

5. Presynaptic receptors are on the terminal of an axon. Activation of such receptors may inhibit or facilitate the release of a neurotransmitter from that axon. (p. 78)

6. After a neurotransmitter has activated its receptor, some of the transmitter molecules are reabsorbed by the presynaptic cell. Other molecules are metabolized into inactive chemicals and eventually excreted. (p. 79)

7. Different neurotransmitters contribute to behavior in different ways. Certain behavioral abnormalities can be traced to an excess or deficit of chemical activity at particular types of synapses. (p. 80)

## REVIEW QUESTIONS

1. What evidence did Loewi offer to show that transmission at a synapse depends on the release of chemicals? (p. 66)

2. How can changes in diet modify the levels of certain neurotransmitters in the brain? (p. 68)

3. What is a "quantum" of neurotransmitter? (p. 72)

4. Distinguish between ionotropic and metabotropic effects at synapses. (p. 75)

5. What does a "second messenger" do? (p. 77)

6. List differences between neurotransmitters and neuromodulators. (p. 79)

7. What is an autoreceptor and how does it contribute to negative feedback? (p. 78)

8. After acetylcholine excites its receptor and then detaches from it, what prevents it from attaching and exciting the receptor again? (p. 79)

## THOUGHT QUESTION

1. Suppose axon A enters a ganglion (a cluster of neurons) and axon B leaves on the other side. An experimenter who stimulates A can shortly thereafter record an impulse traveling down B. We would like to know whether B is just an extension of axon A, or whether A formed an excitatory synapse on some neuron in the ganglion, whose axon is axon B. How could an experimenter determine the answer? You should be able to think of more than one good method. Presume that the anatomy within the ganglion is so complex that you cannot simply trace the course of an axon through it.

## SUGGESTION FOR FURTHER READING

**Millhorn, D. E., Bayliss, D. A., Erickson, J. T., Gallman, E. A., Szymeczek, C. L., Czyzyk-Krzeska, M., & Dean, J. B.** (1989). Cellular and molecular mechanisms of chemical synaptic transmission. *American Journal of Physiology, 257* (6, Part 1), L289–L310. A thorough review of research on the chemistry of the synapse.

# Synapses, Drugs, and Behavior

Drugs that affect behavior have become an important part of our society. Medical doctors prescribe tranquilizers for people with severe anxiety, antidepressant drugs for depressed people, and still other drugs for people with schizophrenia, attention-deficit disorder, and other psychological disorders. Meanwhile, thousands of people take illegal drugs to go through new experiences or to "get high."

In many cases, people discovered the effects of a drug first, mostly by accident, and investigators later determined how the drug affects the brain (see Digression 3.1). Drugs can affect the brain in a wide variety of ways. However, a majority of drugs with potent effects on the brain—both medically prescribed drugs and illegal, abused drugs—exert their effects by altering the transmission at synapses.

It would be pointless to try to memorize the names of all the drugs and all their effects. Certain drugs will become more familiar as we discuss their effects in later chapters. At this point, let us simply consider a few of the ways in which drugs can affect synapses. We shall look at drugs prescribed for medical purposes (such as antidepressants), drugs used and abused for recreational purposes (such as cocaine), and drugs used primarily as research tools (such as AMPT, alpha-methyl-para-tyrosine).

## HOW DRUGS CAN AFFECT SYNAPSES

A drug can mimic or increase the effects of a given neurotransmitter, or it can block those effects. A drug that blocks the effects is called an **antagonist,** meaning *enemy*. A drug that mimics or increases the effects is called an **agonist.** (*Antagonist* is sometimes used in everyday speech, while *agonist* is seldom used except in discussions of drug effects. The term *agonist* is derived from a Greek word meaning *contestant*; an antagonist is an "anti-agonist," or member of the opposing team.)

Investigators say that a particular drug has an **affinity** for a particular type of receptor, meaning that it has a tendency to attach to that receptor. The stronger

# Accidental Discoveries of Psychiatric Drugs

We like to think that basic science comes first and that applied science or technology comes later, taking the discoveries of basic science and applying them in rational ways to solve practical problems. Yet the history of drug therapies, particularly in psychiatry, includes many examples of the reverse, in which useful drugs were stumbled upon by accident and basic researchers then had to search for an explanation for their success.

Disulfiram, for example, was originally used in the manufacture of rubber. Someone noticed that workers in a certain rubber factory developed a distaste for alcohol (Levitt, 1975). Now better known by the trade name Antabuse, disulfiram is used to help alcoholics quit drinking alcohol.

Iproniazid was originally marketed as rocket fuel. Eventually someone discovered that it was useful therapy for tuberculosis. Later, while experimenting on its effects in treating tuberculosis, someone discovered that it was an effective antidepressant (Klerman, 1975).

The use of bromides to control epilepsy was originally based on a theory, but the theory was all wrong (Friedlander, 1986; Levitt, 1975). In the 1800s it was believed that epilepsy was caused by masturbation. It was also believed that bromides reduced sexual drive. Therefore, the reasoning went, bromides should reduce epilepsy. It turns out that bromides do relieve epilepsy, but they do so for altogether different reasons.

---

the drug's affinity for a receptor, the more powerful the drug is likely to be as an agonist or antagonist.

Drugs that affect synapses can act as agonists or antagonists in a multitude of ways, which we will group into three categories: Drugs can alter the release of transmitter from the presynaptic neuron, they can alter reception by the postsynaptic neuron, and they can alter the events that occur after transmission is complete.

## Effects of Drugs on the Presynaptic Neuron

A drug can affect the presynaptic neuron by altering the synthesis of the transmitter or the amount of transmitter that is released. For example, the drug AMPT blocks the synthesis of dopamine, norepinephrine, and epinephrine. As shown in Figure 3.14, tyrosine from the diet is ordinarily converted into dopa, which is the precursor to dopamine, norepinephrine, and epinephrine. AMPT is similar enough to tyrosine that it attaches to the same enzyme. When it does so, it blocks the enzyme from attaching to tyrosine; as a result, very little tyrosine is converted to dopa.

A drug can also stimulate the release of a neurotransmitter from its storage in presynaptic neurons. Amphetamine, for example, increases the release of norepinephrine and dopamine. If the supplies of norepinephrine and dopamine are lower than normal (because of previous treatment with AMPT, for example), then amphetamine has little or no effect on the brain or on behavior. It exerts its effects only by releasing stored norepinephrine and dopamine.

By releasing norepinephrine and dopamine, amphetamine increases alertness and arousal. Consequently, we conclude that norepinephrine and dopamine synapses have something to do with alertness and arousal. A few hours after a large dose of amphetamine, however, a person may enter a rebound state of depression, probably because the brain cannot resynthesize new norepinephrine fast enough to replace all that was suddenly released (Pincus & Tucker, 1978).

Drugs can affect the presynaptic neuron in yet another way. Recall that many neurons have presynaptic receptors—receptors on the presynaptic terminal that facilitate or inhibit the release of transmitter. Some drugs act on these presynaptic receptors. For example, the neurotransmitter *adenosine* acts at many presynaptic receptors to inhibit the release of excitatory transmitters such as glutamate. Caffeine blocks the effects of adenosine. Note that by blocking the effects of adenosine (which inhibits release of glutamate), caffeine increases the release of glutamate (Silinsky, 1989). This is the main route by which caffeine stimulates the nervous system.

## Effects of Drugs on the Postsynaptic Receptors

A number of drugs exert their effects by attaching directly to the receptors on the postsynaptic neuron, presumably because they have a structure so similar to the neurotransmitter that they fit into the same receptor site. For example, recall that acetylcholine has certain synapses referred to as nicotinic synapses because the drug nicotine stimulates them. Nicotine simply attaches directly to those receptors and stimulates them much the way acetylcholine does. That is, nicotine is an acetylcholine agonist. As a result, nicotine increases heart rate and arouses parts of the cerebral cortex.

A number of other drugs attach to a receptor on the postsynaptic neuron but fail to stimulate it—something like a key that fits into a lock but will not turn. The neurotransmitter itself cannot attach to the receptor because the drug is in the way. Haloperidol, used in the treatment of schizophrenia, blocks dopamine synapses. It is a dopamine antagonist. (The effectiveness of haloperidol against schizophrenia is often taken as evidence that schizophrenia reflects an excess of dopamine activity. More on this in Chapter 16.)

In some cases investigators began by discovering a receptor sensitive to a particular drug and later discovered a neurotransmitter that stimulates the receptor. For example, Candace Pert and Solomon Snyder found that morphine and other opiate drugs attach to specific receptors in the brain (p. 210); within a few years other investigators discovered *endorphins*, neurotransmitters that stimulate the same receptors. For years investigators could not explain the effects of marijuana on the brain. Many believed that it had only general effects on the membranes. Then, investigators localized specific receptors for cannabinoids, the psychoactive chemicals in marijuana (Devane, Dysarz, Johnson, Melvin, & Howlett, 1988). Those receptors are coupled with G-proteins; presumably they are the receptors for some as-yet undiscovered neurotransmitter (Matsuda, Lolait, Brownstein, Young, & Bonne, 1990).

There is one more way for a drug to affect the postsynaptic receptors: A drug can attach to a receptor that modifies the sensitivity of a neighboring receptor. For example, benzodiazepine tranquilizers (the most common anxiety-reducing drugs) attach to receptors adjacent to GABA receptors; in the process they increase the sensitivity of the GABA receptors. (More on this in Chapter 13.)

## Effects of Drugs on the Events Following Transmission

Ordinarily, after a neurotransmitter stimulates its receptor and then detaches from it, its job is finished. It may be reabsorbed by the presynaptic neuron for later use or it may be metabolized into other chemicals that do not excite the receptor. One way or another, the neurotransmitter is inactivated.

**Figure 3.14**
**Events at a norepinephrine synapse and the drugs that can inhibit each step**

*AMPT blocks the conversion of tyrosine to dopa. Reserpine causes leakage from the vesicles that store norepinephrine. Amphetamine increases the release. Clonidine stimulates the presynaptic receptors that inhibit release of nonrepinephrine. Tricyclic antidepressants block reuptake. Pargyline blocks MAO (monoamine oxidase), an enzyme that breaks down norepinephrine and similar transmitters.*

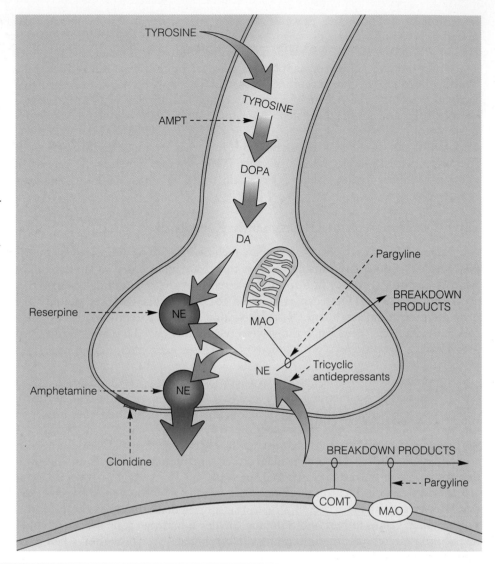

Some drugs, however, interfere with this inactivation. For example, a class of drugs called *tricyclic antidepressants* prevents the presynaptic neurons from reabsorbing dopamine, norepinephrine, and serotonin (see Figure 3.14). Thus, after a neuron releases one of those neurotransmitters, the molecules remain for a long time in the synaptic cleft, where they may excite their receptors repeatedly.

Cocaine also blocks the reuptake of norepinephrine and dopamine. (Do you see why cocaine produces effects similar to those of amphetamine?) In addition to blocking reuptake of these neurotransmitters, cocaine decreases the total amount of brain activity (London et al., 1990). (See Figure 3.15.) (Cocaine is chemically related to Novocain and Xylocaine; in fact, cocaine is sometimes used as a local anesthetic, especially in eye surgery.)

Other drugs interfere with an enzyme that inactivates a neurotransmitter after it stimulates postsynaptic receptors. For example, the enzyme acetylcholinesterase breaks down acetylcholine into acetate and choline. Physostigmine blocks the enzyme acetylcholinesterase, prolonging the effects of acetylcholine at

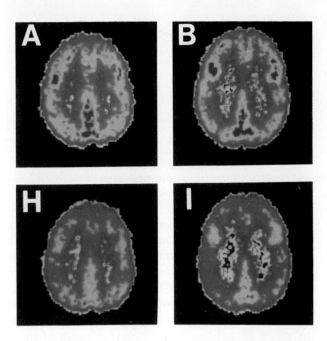

**Figure 3.15**
*Sometimes "your brain on drugs" is not like throwing something onto a frying pan; it is more like throwing it into the refrigerator. As these PET scans show, the brain has lower metabolism and lower overall activity under the influence of cocaine than it has ordinarily. Red indicates highest activity, followed by yellow, green, and blue. A and B represent brain activity under normal conditions; H and I show activity after a cocaine injection. (From London et al., 1990.)*

its synapse. Drugs similar to physostigmine are sometimes prescribed for myasthenia gravis, a disease caused by a loss of acetylcholine synapses at the nerve-muscle junctions (a type of synapse).

## Some Complications

The preceding discussion has oversimplified matters in a couple of ways that you should be aware of. First, a given neurotransmitter may stimulate more than one type of receptor. Consequently, two drugs that both stimulate, say, serotonin synapses might produce very different effects on behavior because one drug stimulates one type of serotonin receptor and the other drug stimulates a different type of serotonin receptor.

Second, we commonly talk about a drug's effect, yet just about every drug has multiple effects. When we talk about the effect of amphetamine, for example, we generally refer to its most pronounced biochemical effects, stimulation of norepinephrine and dopamine synapses. However, amphetamine has many other, generally less pronounced effects on serotonin synapses, acetylcholine synapses, and perhaps still other types of synapses. Because the intensity of such secondary effects varies widely from one person to another, it is hard to predict how a given individual will react to a given drug.

## HALLUCINOGENIC DRUGS

Certain drugs of abuse, including LSD, closely resemble certain neurotransmitters, especially serotonin (see Figure 3.16). Because of this resemblance, LSD can attach to a serotonin receptor and act as an agonist. Contrast this mode of action to that of amphetamine: Amphetamine acts by releasing norepinephrine and dopamine from the presynaptic neurons; if the neurons have a low supply of these neurotransmitters, amphetamine is ineffective. In contrast, even after the complete removal of the presynaptic neurons that release serotonin, LSD still exerts

Synapses, Drugs, and
Behavior

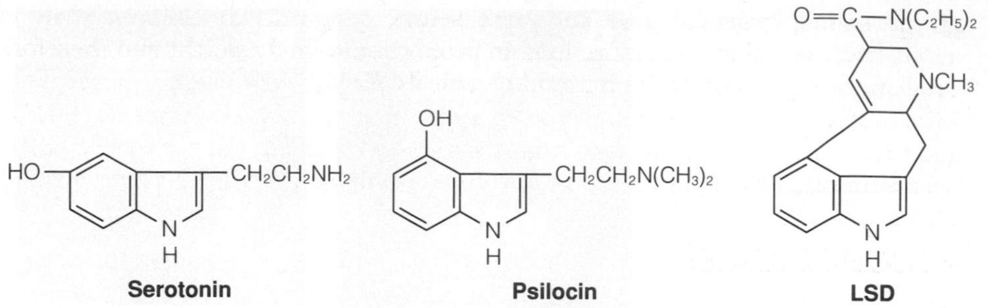

**Figure 3.16
Resemblance of the
neurotransmitter sero-
tonin to two chemicals
with hallucinogenic
effects**

Serotonin　　　　Psilocin　　　　LSD

its full effect. It may even produce a greater than normal effect: After the removal of the serotonin-containing neurons, the postsynaptic neuron may develop an increased number of serotonin receptors as a kind of "compensation." The increased number of receptors makes LSD more effective (Jacobs, 1987).

Serotonin (5-HT) has several types of receptors, each with slightly different properties and no doubt different roles in behavior. LSD, it turns out, has a strong affinity for only one of these types, the 5-HT$_2$ receptor (Jacobs, 1987). Receptors of that type are abundant in much of the brain.

Does this account of LSD explain its effects on behavior? Only in part. We know what LSD does chemically but not how it produces hallucinations and other changes in experience. Presumably the 5-HT$_2$ receptors contribute in some way to perception, and an abnormal pattern of stimulation of those receptors leads to abnormal perceptions. But in contrast to our knowledge of the chemistry, our understanding of how synaptic activity relates to experience is sketchy.

We also have only a meager understanding of LSD "flashbacks." LSD stimulates serotonin synapses for a few hours; a large dose can decrease the number of receptors for a few days. But some LSD users report flashbacks—spontaneous visual or emotional experiences—months, even years, later (Abraham, 1983). The drug would have washed out of the body long before then, and the synapses presumably should have returned to normal. Evidently either the synapses or something else in the neurons has been altered almost permanently.

Hallucinogenic chemicals may have played a role in the Salem witchcraft trials of 1692. In Salem Village, Massachusetts, a number of people, mostly children and teenagers, reported bizarre symptoms, including convulsions, prickling sensations on the skin, visual hallucinations, pain, nausea, and periods of blindness and deafness. They blamed their symptoms on other members of the community, whom they accused of being witches. About twenty people were convicted of witchcraft and hanged.

The reported symptoms were long assumed to be hysterical or imaginary, but they may have been more than that. First, the symptoms showed up in a number of infants and cows, who could hardly be accused of pretending or imagining them or of being victims of suggestion. Second, at least three people reportedly died of the symptoms.

Linnda Caporael (1976) and Mary Matossian (1982) have argued that the symptoms were real and that they were caused by **ergot** poisoning. Ergot is a substance produced by a fungus that sometimes grows on rye. The climate in Massachusetts at the time was probably conducive to the growth of ergot. Ergot poisoning produces convulsions, a sensation in the skin as if ants were crawling inside, pain, nausea, and other symptoms similar to those reported at Salem. Ergot poisoning generally produces more severe symptoms in children than in adults because children eat more food in proportion to body weight and therefore consume a larger dose of the harmful chemicals. Ergot is the natural source from which LSD is manufactured; in nature ergot may spontaneously produce LSD and similar chemicals. Thus, the supposed victims of witchcraft may have actually been suffering from a combination of food poisoning and an LSD experience.

# ALCOHOL ABUSE

The most widely abused drug is alcohol. Alcohol inhibits the flow of sodium across the membrane, expands the surface of all membranes, and generally interferes with nervous system activity. In addition to this nonspecific effect on neurons throughout the brain, alcohol alters one type of GABA receptor, the $GABA_A$ receptor, making it more responsive. As a result, the neurotransmitter GABA has greater effects than usual. Because GABA transmission leads to relaxation and decreased anxiety, alcohol promotes calmness.

Alcohol abuse is a peculiarly human phenomenon. Although it is possible to get rats and other species to drink alcohol under certain circumstances, sometimes even in large quantities, only humans spontaneously develop an alcohol habit that grossly interferes with normal living. Even among humans, only a minority of drinkers develop a serious problem. Why do certain people develop an alcohol problem, while others continue to drink in moderation?

## The Effects of Alcohol on the Body and on Behavior

Alcohol by itself does not make people feel happy. Rather, it increases people's susceptibility to social influences. That is, although you are unlikely to elevate your mood much by drinking alone, drinking at a party may reduce your inhibitions and help you enjoy the party more. Alcohol also helps people to forget their tension, anxiety, and other problems (Cowan, 1983).

Chronic problem drinkers have bouts of drinking that go far beyond social facilitation. Many, especially the older ones, suffer a variety of cognitive deficits, including reasoning impairments and impaired retrieval of memories (see, for example, Nelson, McSpadden, Fromme, & Marlatt, 1986). Problem drinkers who abstain from alcohol will gradually improve in performance of cognitive tasks, especially if they quit drinking before age 40 (Goldman, 1983). Prolonged, severe alcohol abuse may lead to vitamin $B_1$ deficiency, which in turn leads to *Korsakoff's syndrome*, characterized by a permanent memory impairment (see Chapter 14).

## Antabuse, a Drug Treatment for Alcohol Abuse

After a person drinks ethyl alcohol, enzymes in the liver metabolize it to **acetaldehyde,** a poisonous substance. The enzyme **acetaldehyde dehydrogenase** then converts acetaldehyde to **acetic acid,** which the body can use as a source of energy:

$$\text{Ethyl alcohol} \longrightarrow \text{Acetaldehyde} \xrightarrow{\text{Acetaldehyde dehydrogenase}} \text{Acetic acid}$$

Over a long time, acetaldehyde can cause cirrhosis of the liver and damage to other organs. Even in the short term, it can cause illness if its concentration in an organ is high enough. It can be fatal in large doses, especially if combined with tranquilizers.

Synapses, Drugs, and Behavior

Individuals vary in their levels of the enzyme acetaldehyde dehydrogenase, and these variations relate to tolerance for alcohol. For example, most mice have relatively low levels of the enzyme; they cannot drink alcohol without becoming ill. One genetic strain, however, the C57 strain, has high levels of acetaldehyde dehydrogenase (Horowitz & Whitney, 1975). These mice quickly convert acetaldehyde to harmless acetic acid. Unlike other mice, they will drink large quantities of alcohol. Most humans have ample amounts of acetaldehyde dehydrogenase, but about half of all Asians have low amounts (Harada et al., 1982; Reed, 1985). For this reason, many people of Asian ancestry feel ill, or at least experience intense flushing in the face, after drinking alcohol (Helzer et al., 1990). Not surprisingly, alcohol abuse is less common among Chinese and Japanese people than it is among people of European or African ancestry.

The drug *disulfiram*, which goes by the trade name **Antabuse,** decreases a person's levels of acetaldehyde dehydrogenase. Antabuse inactivates all copper-containing enzymes, including acetaldehyde dehydrogenase. For about 24 hours after taking an Antabuse pill, people must avoid all contact with alcohol, at the risk of grave illness. They must even avoid shampoos that contain alcohol because alcohol absorbed through the scalp can be dangerous, too.

Antabuse is sometimes used to help people stop abusing alcohol (Peachey & Naranjo, 1983). The idea is that such a person will learn an aversion to the taste of alcohol because of the illness that follows. In fact, however, the drug may be effective mostly because of its threat value. Many of the people who take Antabuse abstain from drinking completely, never experiencing the illness that alcohol would cause them (Fuller & Roth, 1979). Those who drink in spite of taking the pill do get ill, but they are as likely to stop taking the pill as to stop drinking alcohol. Evidently, Antabuse functions mostly as a way for an alcoholic to make a daily reaffirmation of the decision to abstain from alcohol.

## Possible Biological Predispositions to Alcohol Abuse

At this point, no one can predict with much accuracy who will become a severe alcohol abuser and who will not. We can identify certain risk factors, however. First, the risk of alcoholism is greater for those who grow up in a culture or subculture that tolerates public drunkenness and for individuals who are victims of child abuse or witnesses to hostility between their parents. Environmental influences of this type are certainly important. Our interest here, however, is to identify possible biological influences.

A predisposition toward alcoholism can, it appears, be inherited. According to one long-term study of adopted boys in Boston, boys who were close biological relatives of alcoholics had an increased probability of eventually becoming alcoholics themselves, even if they were adopted by nonalcoholics (Vaillant & Milofsky, 1982).

Still, not all children of alcoholics become alcoholics, and it is not obvious how the genes predisposing to alcohol abuse might exert their effects. The design of several studies has been to compare young adults who have an alcoholic father with young adults who are not closely related to any alcoholic. (Children of alcoholic mothers are excluded because of the potential effects of alcohol during pregnancy.) Most studies have used sons instead of daughters, simply because alcohol abuse is more common in men than it is in women. The assumption behind such studies is that a fair number of the sons of alcoholics are at risk of becoming alcoholics themselves; they might be considered prealcoholics. Fewer of the sons

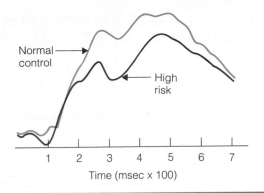

**Figure 3.17**
**P300 waves evoked
from two groups of
young men in response
to a visual stimulus**
*(Based on Begleiter et al.,
1984.)*

Normal control

High risk

Time (msec x 100)

of nonalcoholics will become alcoholics themselves. Therefore, any observable differences between the sons of alcoholics and the sons of nonalcoholics are probably also differences between people likely to become alcoholics and people not likely to become alcoholics. Here are the major conclusions from those studies.

First, sons of alcoholics tend to underestimate how intoxicated they are. After drinking various mixtures of vodka and water, sons of alcoholics rate themselves as less intoxicated than do the sons of nonalcoholics, even though they were actually just as impaired if not more so (O'Malley & Maisto, 1985; Schuckit, 1984). Presumably, sons of alcoholics continue drinking until they recognize that they are tipsy, but because they are slow to recognize their intoxication, they may have already impaired their judgment by the time they reach that point.

Second, alcohol provides some relief from stress for almost everyone, but it provides more relief for the sons of alcoholics than it does for the sons of nonalcoholics. When confronted with a stressful situation (such as an impending electric shock or delivering a speech to a large audience), most people feel tense and experience increased heart rate. Alcohol lowers the tension and the heart rate for everyone, but especially for sons of alcoholics. Perhaps they are predisposed to alcohol abuse because of the positive effects they experience (Levenson, Oyama, & Meek, 1987).

Third, sons of alcoholics show a weaker brain response to meaningful stimuli than do the sons of nonalcoholics. In general, a new or meaningful stimulus evokes a distinctive brain wave called a **P300 wave,** a positive wave occurring about 300 msec after the stimulus. The P300 wave is weaker in alcoholic men than in nonalcoholic men; furthermore, it is weaker in the 7- to 13-year-old sons of alcoholic men than in the sons of nonalcoholics (Begleiter, Porjesz, Bihari, & Kissin, 1984). (See Figure 3.17.) How a weak P300 wave relates to alcoholism is hardly obvious, but it may indicate a biological difference that emerges early in life.

Note the advantage of studying sons (or daughters) of alcoholics instead of alcoholics themselves: When investigators find a difference between alcoholics and nonalcoholics, they do not know whether the difference relates to some predisposition to alcohol abuse or whether it is the result of years of drinking. By studying alcoholics' children who have not yet become alcoholics themselves, investigators can get closer to the predisposing factors.

Synapses, Drugs, and
Behavior

## SUMMARY

1. Many drugs affect behavior by altering the activity at particular types of synapses. They exert their effects by altering the release of neurotransmitter, by stimulating or blocking receptors, or by blocking the processes that usually inactivate neurotransmitters after they detach from their receptors. (p. 83)

2. Drugs can alter release of a neurotransmitter either by interfering with the synthesis of the transmitter, by directly provoking release of the transmitter, or by altering the sensitivity of the autoreceptors that ordinarily regulate release of the transmitter. (p. 84)

3. Drugs can directly stimulate postsynaptic receptors, occupy them without stimulating them (and therefore prevent neurotransmitters from stimulating them), or attach to sites that alter the structure of the receptor. (p. 85)

4. Drugs can block the reuptake of a used transmitter into the presynaptic neuron and therefore prolong the effect of the transmitter on its receptors; they can also block the enzymes that break down the transmitter into inactive molecules. (p. 86)

5. The drug LSD acts by directly stimulating type-2 serotonin receptors (5-HT$_2$). How this stimulation leads to hallucinations is not known. (p. 87)

6. Antabuse blocks one step in the breakdown of alcohol and thereby leads to a buildup of toxic acetaldehyde. It is sometimes used to help people break an alcohol habit. (p. 89)

7. A hereditary tendency exists for alcohol abuse. One way in which that tendency is manifested is apparently that people at risk for alcoholism feel less intoxication than normal when drinking moderate amounts of alcohol. (p. 91)

## REVIEW QUESTIONS

1. What is the difference between an agonist drug and an antagonist drug? (p. 83)

2. How does amphetamine exert its effects on the brain? Why is amphetamine less effective if it is preceded by AMPT? (p. 84)

3. How does haloperidol affect synapses? (p. 85)

4. How do tricyclic antidepressants affect the synapses? (p. 86)

5. How does LSD affect synapses? (p. 87)

6. What biological explanation may account for the symptoms attributed to witchcraft in Salem in 1692? (p. 88)

7. What are the steps in metabolic breakdown of ethyl alcohol by the liver? (p. 89)

8. What is a biological explanation for why many people of Asian ancestry are unlikely to become alcohol abusers? (p. 90)

9. How does Antabuse help people break a habit of alcohol abuse? (p. 90)

10. How could someone try to identify people at greater than average risk of alcoholism? (p. 91)

## THOUGHT QUESTIONS

1. Every prescription drug has side effects—unintended and generally undesirable effects—in addition to the effects the physician hopes to achieve. Both the nature and the intensity of the side effects vary substantially from one patient to another. Why?

2. Suppose haloperidol, which blocks dopamine synapses, is found to suppress the symptoms of the newly discovered disease X. One possible explanation of its effectiveness is that disease X is caused by supersensitive dopamine receptors. What other explanations are possible?

## SUGGESTIONS FOR FURTHER READING

**Hamilton, L. W., & Timmons, C. R.** (1990). *Principles of behavioral pharmacology.* Englewood Cliffs, NJ: Prentice-Hall. An excellent description of the ways in which drugs can affect behavior.

**Snyder, S. H.** (1986). *Drugs and the brain.* New York: Freeman. A description of the effects of tranquilizers, antidepressants, antischizophrenic drugs, and illegal drugs.

**Vaillant, G. E.** (1983). *The natural history of alcoholism.* Cambridge, MA: Harvard University Press. Report of a long-term study of alcoholic men.

# GLOSSARY

**acetaldehyde** toxic substance produced in the metabolism of alcohol

**acetaldehyde dehydrogenase** enzyme that converts acetaldehyde to acetic acid

**acetic acid** chemical that the body uses as a source of energy

**acetylcholinesterase** enzyme that breaks acetylcholine into acetate and choline

**affinity** tendency of a drug to bind to a particular type of receptor

**agonist** drug that mimics or increases the effects of a drug

**Antabuse** trade name for disulfiram, a drug that helps people break an alcohol habit by changing the way they metabolize it

**antagonist** drug that blocks the effects of a drug

**autoreceptor** presynaptic receptor that responds to its own neurotransmitter

**biogenic amine** neurotransmitter containing an amine group (—NH$_2$)

**catecholamine** compound such as dopamine, norepinephrine, and epinephrine that contains both catechol and an amine (—NH$_2$)

**COMT** catechol-o-methyltransferase, an enzyme that metabolizes catecholamines

**cyclic AMP** cyclic adenosine monophosphate, a chemical that serves as a second messenger within many neurons

**ergot** product of a fungus that sometimes grows on grains

**excitatory postsynaptic potential (EPSP)** graded depolarization of a neuron

**inhibitory postsynaptic potential (IPSP)** temporary hyperpolarization of a membrane

**insulin** hormone that increases the conversion of glucose into stored fat and facilitates the transfer of glucose across the cell membrane

**ionotropic effect** synaptic effect that depends on the rapid opening of some kind of gate in the membrane

**MAO** monoamine oxidase, enzyme that converts catecholamines and serotonin into synaptically inactive forms

**metabotropic effect** effect at a synapse that produces a relatively slow but long-lasting effect through metabolic reactions

**neuromodulator** chemical that has properties intermediate between those of a neurotransmitter and those of a hormone

**neurotransmitter** chemical released at a synapse

**peptide** chemical compound composed of two or more amino acids

**postsynaptic neuron** neuron on the receiving end of a synapse

**presynaptic neuron** neuron on the releasing end of a synapse

**presynaptic receptor** receptor located on the terminal at the tip of an axon

**P300 wave** positive wave occurring about 300 msec after a novel or meaningful stimulus

**quantum** the minimum size of an EPSP or IPSP in a postsynaptic neuron

**reflex** automatic response to a stimulus

**reflex arc** circuit of neurons and their connections that is responsible for producing a reflex

**reuptake** reabsorption of a neurotransmitter by the presynaptic terminal

**second messenger** chemical activated by a neurotransmitter, which in turn initiates processes that carry messages to several areas within the neuron

**spatial summation** combination of effects of activity from two or more synapses onto a single neuron

**spontaneous firing rate** speed of action potentials that a neuron produces in the absence of synaptic input

**synapse** point of communication between two neurons or between a neuron and a muscle

**temporal summation** combination of effects of more than one synaptic input at different times

**tryptophan** amino acid that serves as the precursor to serotonin

**vesicle** tiny, nearly spherical packet near the axon terminals filled with the neurotransmitter

# CHAPTER FOUR

# Anatomy of the Nervous System and Methods of Investigation

## MAIN IDEAS

**1.** Each part of the nervous system has specialized functions, although the parts must work together to produce behavior. Damage in different areas leads to different types of behavioral deficits.

**2.** The cerebral cortex, the largest structure in the mammalian brain, performs elaborate processing of sensory information and provides for fine control of movement.

**3.** A variety of investigative techniques can determine how the functioning of various brain areas relates to behavior.

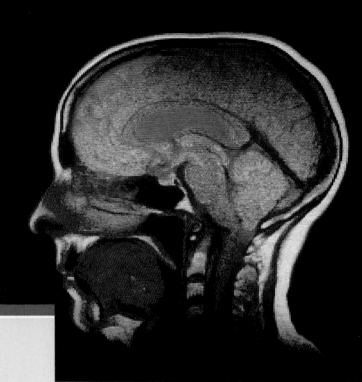

**T**rying to learn **neuroanatomy** (the anatomy of
the nervous system) from a book is much like trying
to learn geography from a road map. A map can tell
you that Mystic, Georgia, is about 40 km north of
Enigma, Georgia, and that the two cities are connected by a combination of roads, including U.S.
Route 129. Similarly, a book can tell you that the
habenula is about 4.6 mm from the interpeduncular
nucleus in a rat's brain (slightly farther in a human
brain) and that the two structures are connected by a
set of axons known as the habenulopeduncular tract,
also sometimes known as the fasciculus retroflexus.
But these two little gems of information are likely to
seem both mysterious and enigmatic unless you have
some interest in that part of Georgia or in that area
of the brain.

This chapter does not try to provide a detailed
road map of the brain. It is more like a world globe,
describing the large, basic structures (analogous to the
continents) and a few distinctive features of each. The
chapter also describes the most important methods
used to study the role of various brain structures in
the control of behavior. Later chapters fill in some
additional detail on specific parts of the brain as
they become relevant in the discussion of particular
behaviors.

# Basic Subdivisions of the Vertebrate Nervous System

A little animal called a eugnot lives in the jaws of a great monster. The teeth of that monster are sharp and its jaw muscles are ferocious. The monster chews up all sorts of other animals that are nearly the same size, shape, and flavor as the eugnot. But it hardly ever bites the eugnot; even when it does, the bites are almost always gentle. The eugnot seems fearless; it ventures right up to the teeth, and sometimes right between the upper and lower teeth. But before the jaws bite down hard, it manages to get out of the way. What do you suppose accounts for the charmed life of this little animal?

That little "animal" is your tongue. (*Eugnot* is *tongue* spelled backward.) It lives in your jaws, an extremely vulnerable place, and yet your teeth do not bite it. Not often, anyway. The reason is the central nervous system, a mechanism that coordinates the actions of each part of the body with the actions of all the others.

Not all species have such a well-developed central nervous system. The zoologist Jakob von Uexküll (1934/1957) described the nervous system of sea urchins (Figure 4.1) as a "reflex republic": Each neuron acts almost independently of the others, and therefore each muscle acts almost independently of the others. A certain number of muscles move one direction, and another set of muscles moves another direction. When the animal eventually moves in one direction or another, it is almost like the outcome of a "vote" in which "the majority rules."

Sea urchins are **invertebrates,** animals without backbones. Shellfish, worms, insects, crustaceans, and the like are also invertebrates, which have no spinal cord and generally no single group of neurons numerous enough to call a brain.

The nervous system of vertebrates — animals with a backbone (fish, amphibians, reptiles, birds, and mammals) — has a well-developed central coordination. The neurons that control your jaw muscles stay in close contact with the neurons that control your tongue muscles, generally preventing you from biting your own tongue. The neurons that control your left hand communicate with those that control your right hand, enabling you to play a piano, thread a needle, and perform other tasks that require close coordination of the hands. Still, no single "monarch" area of the nervous system governs all the others. The coordinated

**Figure 4.1**
**Sea urchin and its nervous system**
*(N. G. McDaniel/Photo Researchers, Inc.)*

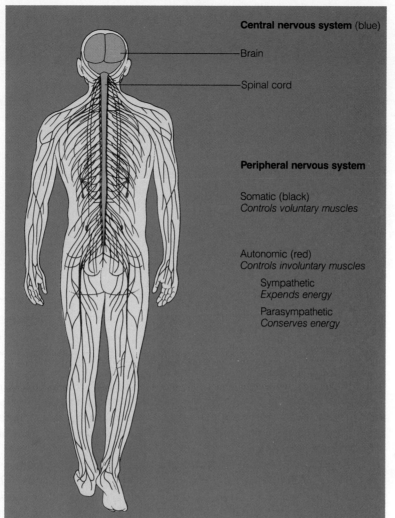

**Figure 4.2**
*The human nervous system consists of the central nervous system and the peripheral nervous system. Each of these divisions has the major subdivisions shown.*

**Central nervous system** (blue)

Brain

Spinal cord

**Peripheral nervous system**

Somatic (black)
*Controls voluntary muscles*

Autonomic (red)
*Controls involuntary muscles*

　Sympathetic
　*Expends energy*

　Parasympathetic
　*Conserves energy*

behavior of the nervous system as a whole emerges from the communication among various areas, not from a single dominant area.

Invertebrate neurons operate by the same basic principles as vertebrate neurons, and we can learn much from them about nerve conduction, synaptic transmission, and even the possible single-cell mechanisms of learning (Chapter 14). However, their organization into a structural whole differs substantially from that of vertebrates, and in this book we deal almost exclusively with vertebrates.

The vertebrate nervous system consists of two major divisions: the central nervous system and the peripheral nervous system (see Figure 4.2). The **central nervous system (CNS)** contains the spinal cord and the brain (forebrain, midbrain, and hindbrain). The **peripheral nervous system (PNS)** has two divisions: the autonomic nervous system and the somatic nervous system. The **somatic**

Basic Subdivisions of
the Vertebrate
Nervous System

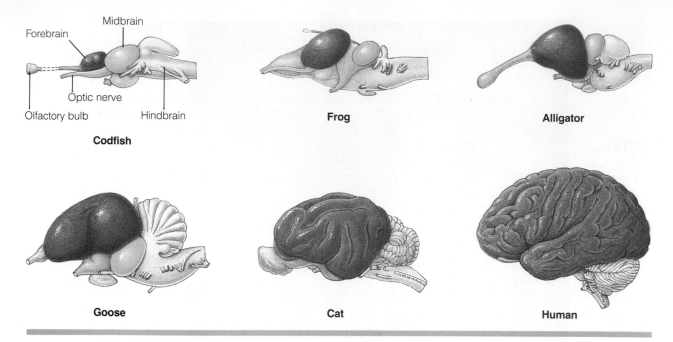

Codfish

Forebrain
Midbrain
Optic nerve
Olfactory bulb
Hindbrain

Frog

Alligator

Goose

Cat

Human

**Figure 4.3**
**The brains of six vertebrates (not drawn to the same scale)**
*The human forebrain surrounds the midbrain and part of the hindbrain. (After Romer, 1962.)*

**nervous system** consists of the nerves that convey messages from the sense organs to the CNS and from the CNS to the muscles and glands. The **autonomic nervous system** is a set of neurons that control the heart, the intestines, and other organs.

The structure of the vertebrate nervous system is largely the same from one species to another. Consequently, we can learn a great deal about how the human nervous system works by studying the nervous system of other species. Figure 4.3 illustrates the brains of five vertebrate species. In all five we can distinguish three major areas: the *forebrain*, the *midbrain*, and the *hindbrain*. Note that the forebrain forms a larger proportion of the brain in mammals, such as rats and humans, than in fish, amphibians, and reptiles. In fact, the mammalian forebrain surrounds the entire midbrain and part of the hindbrain.

## SOME TERMINOLOGY

If you were trying to learn the road map of a state or country, you would have to memorize many names of places. The same is true in learning about the brain: You will have to memorize a great many terms. Furthermore, the directional terms for a state are simple: north, south, east, west. Because the brain is a three-dimensional structure, however, we need a greater variety of directional terms. Table 4.1 and Figure 4.4 present some of the basic terms people use to describe the anatomy of the brain.

In Figure 4.4, note that the terms *dorsal* and *ventral* mean toward the back and toward the stomach. In a four-legged animal, the top of the brain (with re-

4 / Anatomy of the
Nervous System
and Methods
of Investigation

## Table 4.1 Anatomical Terms Referring to Directions

| Term | Definition |
|------|------------|
| **Dorsal** | Toward the back, away from the ventral (stomach) side. The top of the brain is considered dorsal because that is its position in four-legged animals. |
| **Ventral** | Toward the stomach, away from the dorsal (back) side. (*Venter* is the Latin word for *belly*. It also shows up in the word *ventriloquist*, literally meaning *stomach-talker*.) |
| **Anterior** | Toward the front end. |
| **Posterior** | Toward the rear end. In humans, the ventral spinal cord is sometimes called *anterior* and the dorsal cord is called *posterior*. |
| **Rostral** | Toward the head. |
| **Caudal** | Toward the rear, away from the head. |
| **Superior** | Above another part. |
| **Inferior** | Below another part. |
| **Lateral** | Toward the side, away from the midline. |
| **Medial** | Toward the midline, away from the side. |
| **Proximal** | Located close (*approximate*) to the point of origin or attachment. |
| **Distal** | Located farther (more *distant*) from the point of origin or attachment. |
| **Ipsilateral** | On the same side of the body (left or right). |
| **Contralateral** | On the opposite side of the body (left or right). |
| **Coronal plane** (or frontal plane) | A plane that shows brain structures as they would be seen from the front. |
| **Sagittal plane** | A plane that shows brain structures as they would be seen from the side. |
| **Horizontal plane** (or transverse plane) | A plane that shows brain structures as they would be seen from above. |

spect to gravity) is dorsal (on the same side as the animal's back) and the bottom of the brain is ventral (on the stomach side). Because humans assume an upright posture, the dorsal side of the human brain is at right angles to the dorsal side of the spinal cord, and the ventral side of the brain is at right angles to the ventral side of the spinal cord. We maintain this terminology because it is convenient: The terms *dorsal* and *ventral* always have the same meaning in the brain, regardless of the species of animal under consideration.

Table 4.2 introduces some additional terminology that relates to clusters of neurons and anatomical structures of the brain. Such technical terms, or jargon, enable investigators to communicate with one another with precision and with a minimum of ambiguity.

Basic Subdivisions of
the Vertebrate
Nervous System

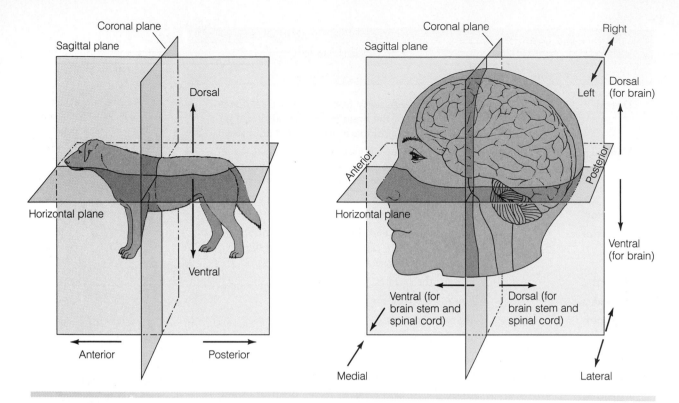

**Figure 4.4**
**Terms describing anatomical directions in the nervous system**

*In four-legged animals, dorsal and ventral point in the same direction for the head as they do for the rest of the body. However, humans' upright posture has tilted the head relative to the spinal cord, so the dorsal and ventral directions of the head are not parallel to the dorsal and ventral directions of the spinal cord.*

| Table 4.2  Terms Referring to Parts of the Nervous System | |
|---|---|
| *Term* | *Definition* |
| Lamina | A row or layer of cell bodies separated from other cell bodies by a layer of axons and dendrites. |
| Column | A set of cells perpendicular to the surface of the cortex, having similar properties. |
| Tract | A set of axons within the CNS, also known as a *projection*. If axons extend from cell bodies in structure A to synapses onto B, we say that the fibers "project" from A onto B. |
| Nerve | A set of axons in the periphery, either from the CNS to a muscle or gland, or from a sensory organ to the CNS. |
| Nucleus | A cluster of neuron cell bodies within the CNS. |
| Ganglion | A cluster of neuron cell bodies, usually outside the CNS (as in the sympathetic nervous system), or any cluster of neurons in an invertebrate species. |
| Gyrus (plural: gyri) | A protuberance on the surface of the brain. |
| Sulcus (plural: sulci) | A fold or groove that separates one gyrus from another. |
| Fissure | A long, deep sulcus. |

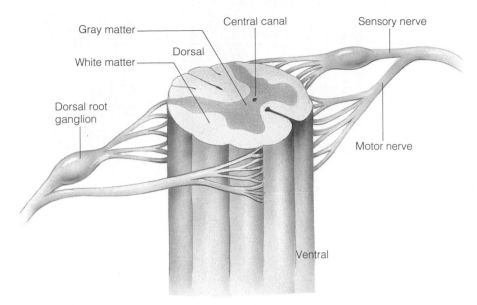

**Figure 4.5**
**Diagram of a cross section through the spinal cord**
*The dorsal root on each side conveys sensory information to the spinal cord; the ventral root conveys motor commands to the muscles.*

Gray matter

Central canal

Sensory nerve

White matter

Dorsal

Dorsal root ganglion

Motor nerve

Ventral

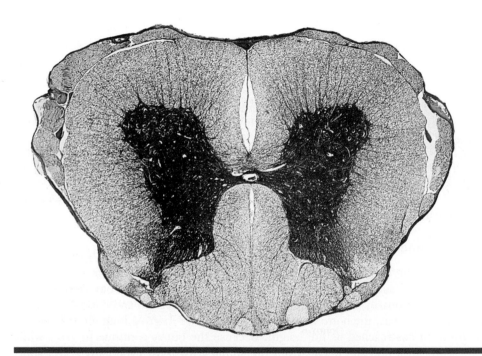

**Figure 4.6**
**Photo of a cross section through the spinal cord**
*The H-shaped structures in the center are gray matter, composed largely of cell bodies. The surrounding white matter is composed of axons. The axons are organized in tracts; some carry information from the brain and higher levels of the spinal cord downward, while others carry information from lower levels upward. (Manfred Kage/Peter Arnold, Inc.)*

## THE SPINAL CORD AND ITS COMMUNICATION WITH THE PERIPHERY

The **spinal cord** is the part of the CNS that communicates with the sense organs and muscles below the level of the head. It is a segmented structure, with each segment having both a sensory nerve and a motor nerve on its left and right sides, as Figures 4.5 and 4.6 show. The sensory nerves enter the spinal cord on the dorsal (back) side; the axons of the motor nerves leave on the ventral (stomach) side.

Basic Subdivisions of
the Vertebrate
Nervous System

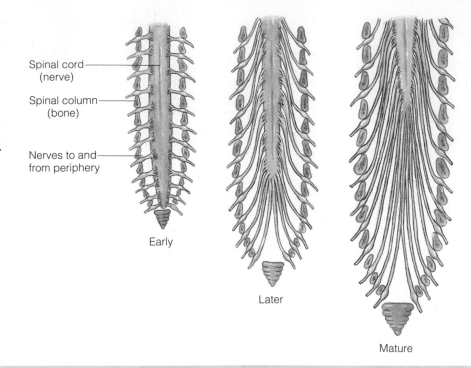

**Figure 4.7
Relationship of the
spinal cord to the
vertebral column
during development**
*The neural part of the
column reaches its full size
early, but the surrounding
column continues to expand.*

Spinal cord
(nerve)

Spinal column
(bone)

Nerves to and
from periphery

Early

Later

Mature

The **Bell-Magendie Law** refers to the observation that the dorsal roots of the spinal cord carry sensory information and the ventral roots carry motor information to the muscles and glands. It was named after the English scientist Charles Bell and the French scientist François Magendie, who independently contributed to this conclusion early in the nineteenth century. The cell bodies of the sensory neurons are located outside the cord in the **dorsal root ganglia.** (A ganglion is a cluster of neurons outside the CNS.) Cell bodies of the motor neurons are located within the spinal cord.

### Development of the Spinal Cord

Early in embryonic development, the bones of the spinal column form around the nerve cord in such a way that the sensory and motor nerves from each segment exit through nearby holes in the spinal column. As prenatal and childhood development proceeds, the bony spinal column continues to grow long after the spinal cord itself has reached its full length. Because the bones continue to grow while the cord does not, the nerves from the spinal cord must eventually travel some distance down the spinal column before they exit (Figure 4.7).

### Segments of the Spinal Cord

The spinal cord has 31 segments and therefore 31 sets of sensory and motor nerves, the **spinal nerves** (see Figure 4.8). Beginning at the top, we distinguish 8 cervical nerves, 12 thoracic nerves, 5 lumbar nerves, 5 sacral nerves, and 1 coccygeal nerve.

Each spinal nerve innervates a limited area of the body. The skin area innervated by a sensory spinal nerve is called a **dermatome.** Figure 4.9 shows the locations of the dermatomes. For example, the third thoracic nerve (T3) innervates a strip of skin just above the nipples on the chest plus the underarm area. But the

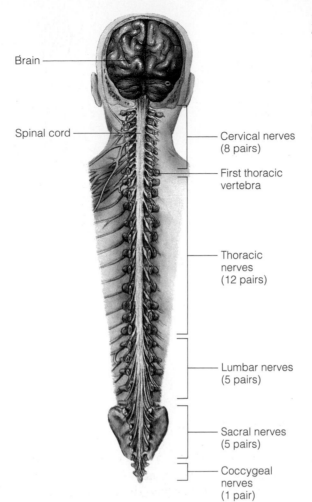

**Figure 4.8**
**The human central**
**nervous system (CNS)**
*Spinal nerves from each segment of the spinal cord exit through the correspondingly numbered opening between vertebrae. (From Starr & Taggart, 1989.)*

Brain

Spinal cord

Cervical nerves
(8 pairs)

First thoracic
vertebra

Thoracic
nerves
(12 pairs)

Lumbar nerves
(5 pairs)

Sacral nerves
(5 pairs)

Coccygeal
nerves
(1 pair)

borders between dermatomes are not so distinct as Figure 4.9 implies; there is actually one-third to one-half overlap between adjacent pairs.

The thickness of a segment of the spinal cord depends on the density of muscles and receptors in the dermatome attached to it. For example, the cervical segments of the spinal cord, which attach to the forelimbs, are very large in strong flying birds with large wings (Sarnat & Netsky, 1981). The thoracic segments of the cord are extremely thin in turtles, which have almost no muscles in the corresponding dermatomes.

## Spinal Pathways

The sensory nerves that enter a segment of the spinal cord make synapses with interneurons within the spinal cord. These in turn make synapses with other interneurons and with motor neurons. In the cross section through the spinal cord shown in Figure 4.10, the H-shaped **gray matter** in the center of the cord is densely packed with cell bodies and dendrites, with few myelinated axons. Many

Basic Subdivisions of
the Vertebrate
Nervous System

**Figure 4.9**
**Dermatomes inner-**
**vated by the 31 sen-**
**sory spinal nerves**
*Areas I, II, and III of the face*
*are not innervated by the*
*spinal nerves, but instead by*
*three branches of the fifth*
*cranial nerve (discussed later*
*in this chapter). Although this*
*figure shows distinct borders*
*between dermatomes, the der-*
*matomes actually overlap one*
*another up to about one-third*
*of their width.*

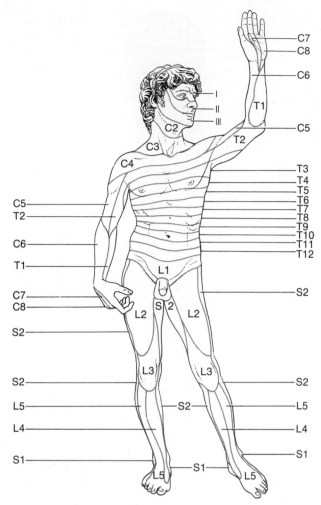

of the interneurons' axons form branches that leave the gray matter and travel toward the brain in the **white matter.** The white matter is composed mostly of myelinated axons, which are white. Likewise, the gray matter of the brain contains many cell bodies and dendrites; the white matter of the brain consists mostly of myelinated axons.

Each segment of the spinal cord contains neurons that communicate with a particular dermatome of the body; it also contains spinal paths conveying messages between the brain and the lower segments of the spinal cord. If the spinal cord is cut, the brain loses sensation from and control over all parts of the body served by the spinal cord below the cut.

## THE AUTONOMIC NERVOUS SYSTEM

The autonomic nervous system is a set of neurons that receives information from and sends commands to the heart, intestines, and other organs. It is composed of two parts: the sympathetic and parasympathetic nervous systems (see Figure

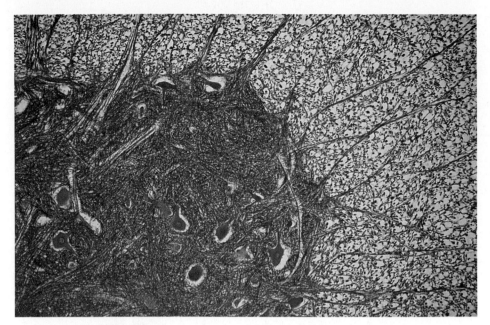

**Figure 4.10**
**A section of gray matter of the spinal cord (lower left) and white matter surrounding it**
*Note that axons enter the gray matter from the white matter and extend from the gray matter into the white matter. (Manfred Kage/Peter Arnold, Inc.)*

4.11). The **sympathetic nervous system** consists of two paired chains of **ganglia** (collections of neuron cell bodies) lying just to the left and right of the spinal cord in its central regions (the thoracic and lumbar areas) and connected by axons to those spinal cord regions. Axons also extend from the sympathetic ganglia to the body's organs. The sympathetic nervous system prepares the body for "fight or flight" activities: It increases the heart rate and breathing rate and it decreases digestive activity. Because all the sympathetic ganglia are closely linked, they tend to act as a single system. That is, they act "in sympathy" with one another.

The term *para* means *beside* or *related to*; the **parasympathetic nervous system** has functions that are related to, and generally opposite to, those of the sympathetic nervous system. Although the sympathetic and parasympathetic systems act in opposition to one another, they are usually both active at the same time. However, the relative balance of activity may tilt more toward one system at one time and more toward the other at another time.

The parasympathetic nervous system is sometimes also known as the craniosacral system because its nerves originate from the cranial nerves and the sacral spinal cord (Figure 4.11). Unlike the ganglia in the sympathetic system, the parasympathetic ganglia are not arranged in a chain near the spinal cord. Rather, long axons extend from the spinal cord to parasympathetic ganglia close to each internal organ; shorter fibers then extend from the parasympathetic ganglia into the organs themselves. Because the parasympathetic ganglia are not linked to one another, they sometimes act more independently than the sympathetic ganglia do. Activity of the parasympathetic system decreases heart rate, increases digestive rate, and in general promotes energy-conserving, nonemergency functions.

The sweat glands, the adrenal glands, the muscles that constrict blood vessels, and the muscles that erect the hairs of the skin have sympathetic input only. (See Digression 4.1.) Other organs are controlled by both the sympathetic and parasympathetic systems, but generally in opposite directions. For example, the sympathetic nervous system increases heart rate; the parasympathetic nervous sys-

Basic Subdivisions of
the Vertebrate
Nervous System

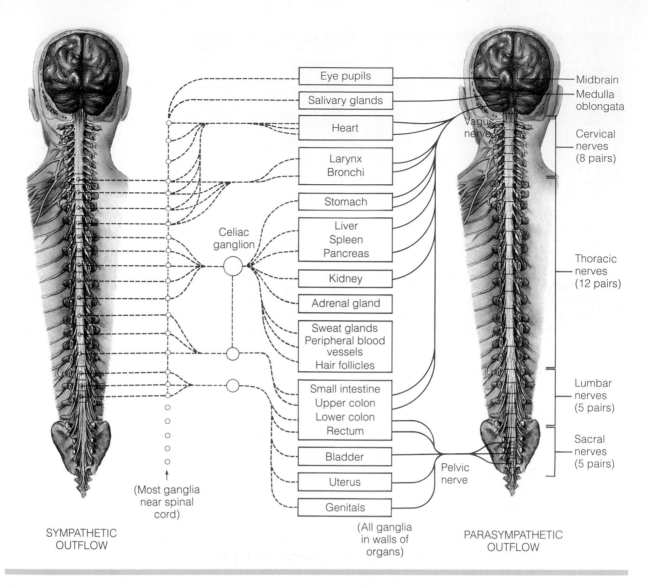

| | |
|---|---|
| Eye pupils | Midbrain |
| Salivary glands | Medulla oblongata |
| Heart | Cervical nerves (8 pairs) |
| Larynx Bronchi | |
| Stomach | |
| Liver Spleen Pancreas | Thoracic nerves (12 pairs) |
| Kidney | |
| Adrenal gland | |
| Sweat glands Peripheral blood vessels Hair follicles | |
| Small intestine Upper colon Lower colon Rectum | Lumbar nerves (5 pairs) |
| Bladder | Sacral nerves (5 pairs) |
| Uterus | |
| Genitals | |

Vagus nerve

Celiac ganglion

(Most ganglia near spinal cord)

Pelvic nerve

SYMPATHETIC OUTFLOW

(All ganglia in walls of organs)

PARASYMPATHETIC OUTFLOW

**Figure 4.11
The sympathetic nervous system (dashed lines) and parasympathetic nervous system (solid lines)**
*(From Starr & Taggart, 1989.)*

tem decreases it. The parasympathetic nervous system increases digestive activity; the sympathetic nervous system decreases it.

The final synapses of the parasympathetic nervous system onto any organ use the neurotransmitter acetylcholine. Most of the final synapses of the sympathetic nervous system use norepinephrine, although a few, such as the ones that control the sweat glands, use acetylcholine. Because the two systems use different transmitters, certain drugs may excite or inhibit one system or the other. For example, over-the-counter cold remedies exert their effects largely by blocking parasympathetic activity or by increasing sympathetic activity (which in turn competes with parasympathetic activity). This action is useful because the flow of sinus fluids is a parasympathetic response; thus, drugs that block the parasympathetic system inhibit sinus flow. The common side effects of cold remedies also stem from their tendency to decrease parasympathetic activities: The drugs inhibit salivation and digestion and increase heart rate.

## "Gooseflesh"

Erection of the hairs, known as "gooseflesh" or "goose bumps," is controlled by the sympathetic nervous system. What does this response have to do with the "fight or flight" functions that are usually associated with the sympathetic nervous system?

Human body hairs are so short that erecting them accomplishes nothing of importance; the response is an evolutionary relic from ancient ancestors with furrier bodies. Erecting the hairs helps nonhuman mammals to conserve their body warmth in a cold environment by increasing their insulation. It also serves several species as a defense against enemies in fight or flight situations. Consider, for example, the Halloween cat, or any other frightened, cornered animal; by erecting its hairs, it looks larger and may thereby deter its opponent.

The porcupine's quills, which are an effective defense against potential predators, are actually modified body hairs. In a fight or flight situation, sympathetic nervous system activity leads to erection of the quills, just as it leads to erection of the hairs in other mammals (Richter & Langworthy, 1933). The behavior that makes the quills so useful, their erection in response to fear, evidently evolved before the quills themselves did.

## THE HINDBRAIN

The brain itself (as distinct from the spinal cord) consists of three major divisions: the hindbrain, the midbrain, and the forebrain. (See Table 4.3.) Brain investigators—unfortunately, perhaps—use a variety of terms synonymously. For example, instead of the English terms *hindbrain*, *midbrain*, and *forebrain*, some people prefer words with Greek roots: rhombencephalon, mesencephalon, and prosencephalon. In this text we shall use the words with English roots, but you may encounter the Greek terms in other reading.

The **hindbrain** (the most posterior part of the brain) consists of the medulla, the pons, and the cerebellum. The medulla and pons plus the midbrain and certain central structures of the forebrain constitute the **brain stem** (see Figure 4.12).

The **medulla,** or medulla oblongata, is a structure just above the spinal cord; in many ways it might be regarded as an enlarged, elaborated extension of the spinal cord, although it is located in the skull rather than in the spine. The medulla controls a number of vital reflexes—such as breathing, heart rate, vomiting, salivation, coughing, and sneezing—through the **cranial nerves.** Damage to the medulla is frequently fatal. A large dose of morphine or other opiates, cocaine, or amphetamine can interrupt breathing or heartbeat because of the drug's effects on the medulla. However, marijuana affects many receptors elsewhere in the brain but few in the medulla (Herkenham et al., 1990). Consequently, even a huge dose of marijuana is unlikely to stop someone's breathing or heartbeat.

Just as the lower parts of the body are connected to the spinal cord via sensory and motor nerves, the skin and muscles of the head and the internal organs are connected to the brain by twelve pairs (one right and one left) of cranial

Basic Subdivisions of
the Vertebrate
Nervous System

**Table 4.3 Major Divisions of the Brain**

| Area | Also Known As | Structures |
|------|---------------|-----------|
| Hindbrain | Rhombencephalon (literally, parallelogram-brain) | Medulla, pons, cerebellum |
| Midbrain | Mesencephalon (literally, middle-brain) | Tectum, tegmentum, superior colliculus, inferior colliculus, substantia nigra |
| Forebrain | Prosencephalon (literally, forward-brain) | Includes diencephalon and telencephalon |
| | Diencephalon (literally, between-brain) | Thalamus, hypothalamus |
| | Telencephalon (literally, end-brain) | Cerebral cortex, hippocampus, basal ganglia, and other subcortical structures |

nerves. Most cranial nerves include both sensory and motor components, although some include just one or the other (see Table 4.4). Each cranial nerve originates in a **nucleus** (a cluster of neurons within the CNS) that integrates the sensory information and regulates the motor output. The cranial nerve nuclei for nerves 5 through 12 are located in the medulla and pons of the hindbrain. Those for cranial nerves 1 through 4 are located in the midbrain and forebrain (see Figure 4.13).

The **pons** lies anterior to the medulla; like the medulla, it contains the nuclei for several cranial nerves. The term *pons* is Latin for *bridge;* the name reflects the fact that many nerve fibers cross between left and right at the level of the pons. These fibers are principally axons from neurons in the pons that are going to the cerebellum.

The medulla and pons also contain the **reticular formation** and the **raphe system.** These two systems send axons diffusely throughout the forebrain. They have a lot to do with arousal and sleep, as we shall see in Chapter 10.

The **cerebellum** is a large hindbrain structure with a great many deep folds. It is best known for its contributions to the control of movement, which will be discussed in Chapter 9. In addition, the lateral parts of the cerebellum contribute to the speed and skill of acquiring language and cognition (Leiner, Leiner, & Dow, 1989). That is, individuals with cerebellar damage sometimes have memory problems or have trouble finding the right word. Learning-disabled children often have damaged cerebellums.

## THE MIDBRAIN

The **midbrain** starts in the middle of the brain, although in mammals it is eventually dwarfed and surrounded by the forebrain. In birds, reptiles, amphibians, and fish, the midbrain is proportionately much larger than it is in mammals. The roof of the midbrain is called the **tectum.** (*Tectum* is the Latin word for *roof.*) The two swellings on each side of the tectum are the **superior colliculus** and the **inferior colliculus** (see Figures 4.12 and 4.13), both part of important routes for sensory information.

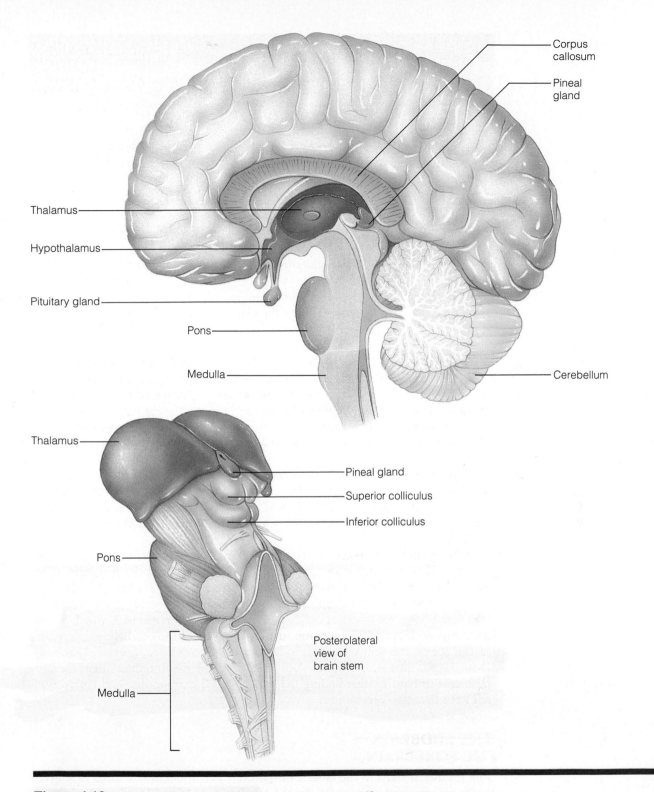

Corpus callosum

Pineal gland

Thalamus

Hypothalamus

Pituitary gland

Pons

Medulla

Cerebellum

Thalamus

Pineal gland

Superior colliculus

Inferior colliculus

Pons

Posterolateral view of brain stem

Medulla

**Figure 4.12**
**Midline structures of the human brain, with a separate drawing of the brain stem**

## Table 4.4 The Cranial Nerves

| Number and Name | Function of Sensory Component | Function of Motor Component |
|---|---|---|
| 1. Olfactory | Smell | (no motor nerve) |
| 2. Optic | Vision | (no motor nerve) |
| 3. Oculomotor | Sensations from eye muscles | Eye movements, pupil constriction |
| 4. Trochlear | Sensations from eye muscles | Eye movements |
| 5. Trigeminal | Sensations from skin of face, nose, and mouth | Chewing, swallowing |
| 6. Abducens | Sensations from eye muscles | Eye movements |
| 7. Facial | Taste from the anterior two-thirds of the tongue, visceral sensations from the head | Facial expressions, crying, salivation, and dilation of blood vessels in the head |
| 8. Statoacoustic | Hearing, equilibrium | (no motor nerve) |
| 9. Glossopharyngeal | Taste and other sensations from throat and posterior third of tongue | Swallowing, salivation, dilation of blood vessels |
| 10. Vagus | Taste and sensations from neck, thorax, and abdomen | Swallowing, control of larynx, parasympathetic nerves to heart and viscera |
| 11. Accessory | (no sensory nerve) | Movements of shoulders and head; parasympathetic to viscera |
| 12. Hypoglossal | Sensation from tongue muscles | Movement of tongue |

Under the tectum is the **tegmentum,** the dorsal part of the midbrain. (In Latin, *tegmentum* means a covering, such as a rug on the floor.) The tegmentum includes the nuclei for the third and fourth cranial nerves, parts of the reticular formation, and extensions of the pathways between the forebrain and the spinal cord or hindbrain. Another midbrain structure is the **substantia nigra,** an area that gives rise to a dopamine-containing pathway that deteriorates in Parkinson's disease (see Chapter 9).

## THE FOREBRAIN

The **forebrain** is the most anterior and most prominent portion of the mammalian brain. The outer portion is the cerebral cortex. (*Cerebrum* means *brain;* *cortex* means *covering.*) Under the cerebral cortex lie other forebrain structures, including the thalamus, which provides the main source of input to the cerebral cortex. A set of structures known as the basal ganglia plays a major role in certain

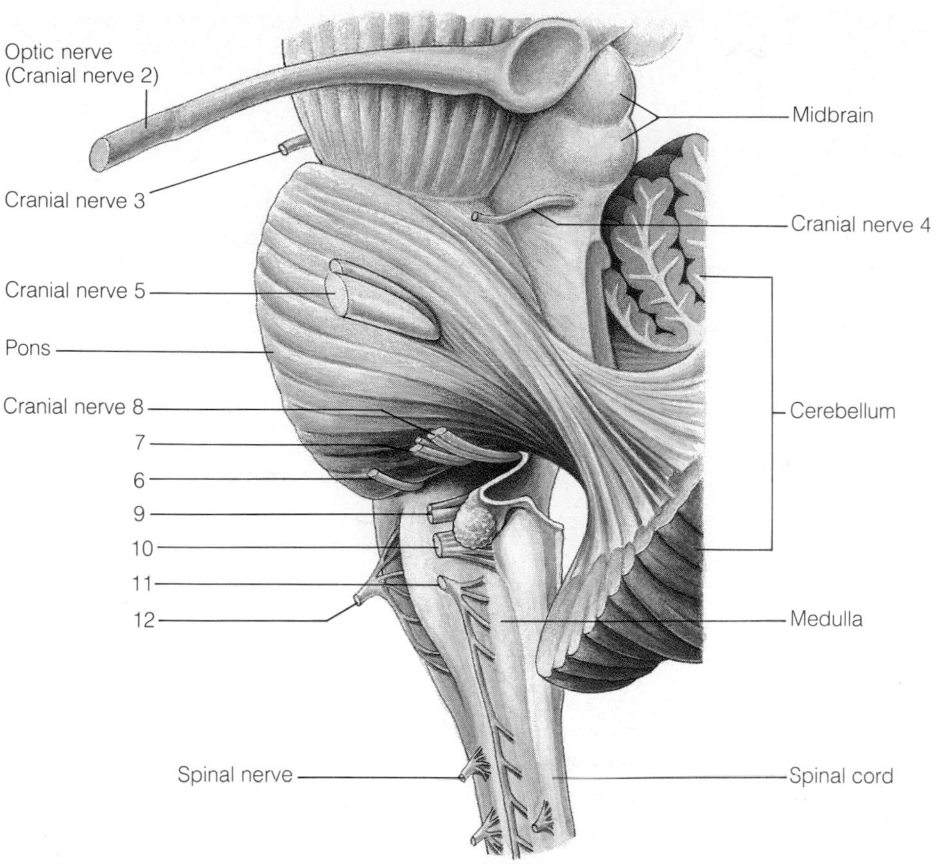

**Figure 4.13
Cranial nerves 3
through 12**
*(After Nieuwenhuys et al., 1988.)*

Labels:
Optic nerve (Cranial nerve 2)
Cranial nerve 3
Cranial nerve 5
Pons
Cranial nerve 8
7
6
9
10
11
12
Spinal nerve
Midbrain
Cranial nerve 4
Cerebellum
Medulla
Spinal cord

aspects of movement. A number of other structures, known as the **limbic system**, form a border (or limbus) around the brain stem. These structures, heavily linked with one another, are particularly important for motivated and emotional behaviors, such as eating, drinking, sexual behavior, anxiety, and aggressive behavior. The larger structures of the limbic system are the olfactory bulb, hypothalamus, hippocampus, amygdala, and cingulate gyrus of the cerebral cortex. Figure 4.14 shows the positions of these structures in a three-dimensional perspective. Figures 4.15 and 4.16 show coronal and sagittal sections through the human brain. Figure 4.15 also includes a view of the ventral surface of the brain.

In describing the forebrain we shall begin with the subcortical areas and then examine the cerebral cortex in greater detail. Later chapters return to each of these areas.

## Hypothalamus

The **hypothalamus** is a small area located near the base of the brain just ventral to the thalamus (see Figures 4.12 and 4.16). It has widespread connections with the rest of the forebrain and the midbrain. The hypothalamus contains a number of distinct nuclei. Damage to one of the hypothalamic nuclei leads to abnormalities in one or more motivated behaviors, such as feeding, drinking, temperature regulation, sexual behavior, fighting, or activity level.

Basic Subdivisions of
the Vertebrate
Nervous System

**Figure 4.14
The limbic system, a
set of subcortical
structures that form a
border (or limbus)
around the brain stem**

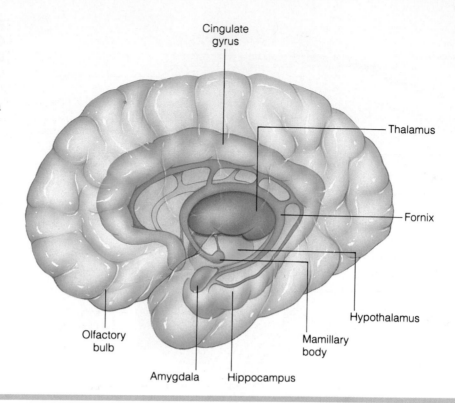

Cingulate
gyrus

Thalamus

Fornix

Hypothalamus

Mamillary
body

Olfactory
bulb

Amygdala

Hippocampus

The hypothalamus also regulates the secretion of hormones through its effects on the pituitary gland. The hypothalamus conveys messages to the pituitary gland, partly through nerves and partly through hypothalamic hormones, to alter the release of hormones by the pituitary.

## Pituitary Gland

The **pituitary gland** is an **endocrine** (hormone-producing) **gland** attached to the base of the hypothalamus by a stalk that contains neurons, blood vessels, and connective tissue (see Figure 4.16). In response to messages from the hypothalamus, the pituitary synthesizes and releases hormones into the bloodstream, which carries them to other organs. The pituitary is sometimes called the "master gland" of the body because its secretions control the timing and amount of hormone secretion by the other endocrine organs, such as the thyroid, the adrenal glands, and the ovaries or testes.

## Basal Ganglia

The **basal ganglia,** a group of subcortical structures left and right of the thalamus, include three major structures: the caudate nucleus, the putamen, and the globus pallidus (see Figure 4.17). Some authorities include several other structures as well.

4 / Anatomy of the
Nervous System and
Methods of
Investigation

112

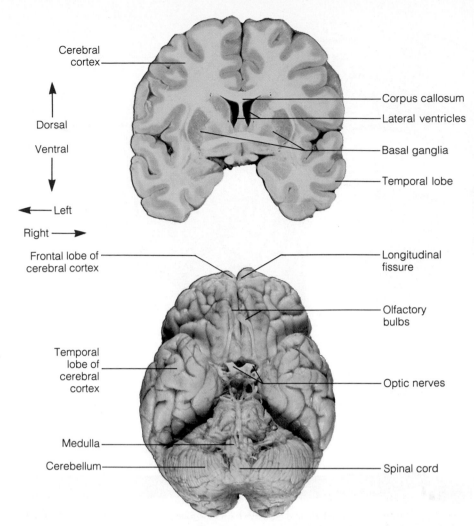

Figure 4.15
Views of the
human brain
*(Top) Coronal section.
(Bottom) Ventral surface.
The optic nerves are the
nerves from the eyes to the
brain. (Photos at left courtesy
of Dr. Dana Copeland; photo
below Dan McCoy/Rainbow.)*

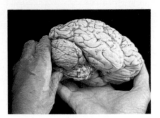

Cerebral cortex

Dorsal

Ventral

Left

Right

Corpus callosum

Lateral ventricles

Basal ganglia

Temporal lobe

Frontal lobe of cerebral cortex

Temporal lobe of cerebral cortex

Medulla

Cerebellum

Longitudinal fissure

Olfactory bulbs

Optic nerves

Spinal cord

The basal ganglia are damaged in Parkinson's disease, Huntington's disease, and other conditions that impair the control of movement. The basal ganglia do not control movement directly, however; they send no axons directly to the medulla or spinal cord. Rather, they send messages to the thalamus and the midbrain, which relay information to the cerebral cortex, which in turn sends messages to the medulla or spinal cord. The basal ganglia also contribute to speech and other complex behaviors (Damasio, 1983).

## Hippocampus

The **hippocampus** (from a Latin word meaning *sea horse*) is a large structure between the thalamus and the cerebral cortex, mostly toward the posterior of the forebrain, as shown in Figure 4.14. Two major axon tracts, the **fornix** and the

Basic Subdivisions of
the Vertebrate
Nervous System

113

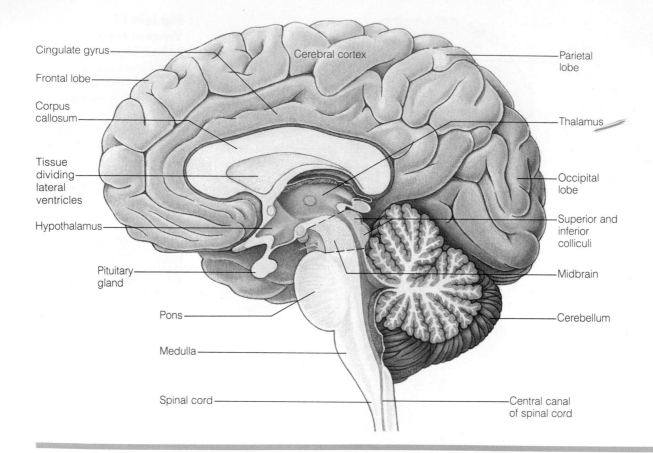

Labels on figure:
Cingulate gyrus
Frontal lobe
Corpus callosum
Tissue dividing lateral ventricles
Hypothalamus
Pituitary gland
Pons
Medulla
Spinal cord
Cerebral cortex
Parietal lobe
Thalamus
Occipital lobe
Superior and inferior colliculi
Midbrain
Cerebellum
Central canal of spinal cord

**Figure 4.16**
**A sagittal section through the human brain**
(*After Nieuwenhuys et al., 1988.*)

**fimbria,** link the hippocampus with the hypothalamus and several other structures. (The fornix was named after an ancient Roman arch that was a famous gathering place for prostitutes. That arch also gave us the word *fornication.*) We shall consider the role of the hippocampus in memory in Chapter 14.

## Thalamus

The **thalamus** resembles two footballs joined side by side. The term *thalamus* was derived from a Greek word meaning *anteroom, inner chamber,* or *bridal bed* (Jones, 1985). One nucleus of the thalamus is called the *pulvinar,* meaning *pillow;* it is shaped a little like a pillow on the bridal bed.

The thalamus is the main source of input to the cerebral cortex and almost the only source of sensory information. A few other subcortical areas send axons to the cortex, but most of their information controls arousal and attention rather than sensation (Foote & Morrison, 1987).

Some investigators have described the thalamus as a way station for information going to the cerebral cortex. It is much more than just a passive relay, however. The sensory information has been processed through other synapses before it reaches the thalamus, and it is processed again in the thalamus before being sent to the cortex.

Each nucleus of the thalamus sends its axons to, and receives axons from, a particular part of the cerebral cortex. Figure 4.18 diagrams the routes of axons from five of the many thalamic nuclei. We shall consider the cerebral cortex in more detail because of its great size and importance in the human brain.

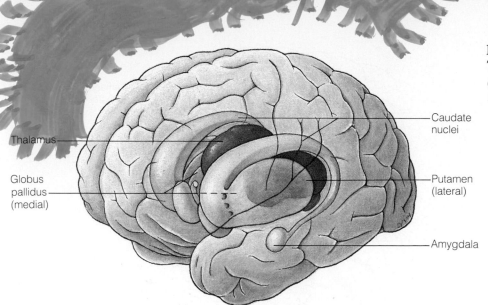

**Figure 4.17**
**The basal ganglia**
*(After Nieuwenhuys et al., 1988.)*

Thalamus

Globus
pallidus
(medial)

Caudate
nuclei

Putamen
(lateral)

Amygdala

## THE VENTRICLES

The cerebral **ventricles** are fluid-filled cavities within the brain. The nervous system begins its development as a tube surrounding a fluid canal. The canal persists into adulthood as the **central canal** of the spinal cord and, with much expansion, as the ventricles of the brain. Two large lateral ventricles are located within the two hemispheres of the forebrain (see Figure 4.19). Toward the posterior they connect to the third ventricle, which connects to the fourth ventricle in the medulla.

The ventricles and the central canal of the spinal cord contain **cerebrospinal fluid (CSF),** a clear fluid similar to blood plasma. CSF is formed by cells lining the four ventricles. It flows from the lateral ventricles to the third and then to the fourth ventricle. From the fourth ventricle, part flows into the central canal of the spinal cord, but the larger part goes through an opening into the thin **subarachnoid space,** between the brain and one of the thin membranes that surround it. From the subarachnoid space, CSF is gradually reabsorbed into the blood vessels of the brain.

Cerebrospinal fluid cushions the brain against mechanical shock when the head moves. It also provides buoyancy; just as a person weighs less in water than on land, the cerebrospinal fluid helps to support the weight of the brain. The CSF also provides a reservoir of hormones and nutrition for the brain and spinal cord.

Sometimes the flow of CSF is obstructed and it accumulates within the ventricles or in the subarachnoid space, thus increasing the pressure on the brain. When this occurs in infants, the skull bones may spread, causing an overgrown head. This condition, known as **hydrocephalus** (HI-dro-SEFF-ah-luss), is usually associated with mental retardation.

Basic Subdivisions of
the Vertebrate
Nervous System

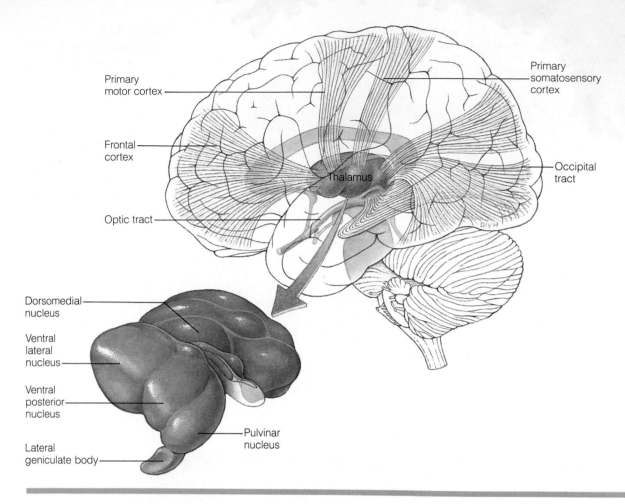

Labels on the figure:
- Primary motor cortex
- Frontal cortex
- Optic tract
- Thalamus
- Primary somatosensory cortex
- Occipital tract
- Dorsomedial nucleus
- Ventral lateral nucleus
- Ventral posterior nucleus
- Lateral geniculate body
- Pulvinar nucleus

**Figure 4.18**
**Routes of information from some specific nuclei of the thalamus to limited areas of the cerebral cortex**
*(After Nieuwenhuys et al., 1988.)*

## SUMMARY

1. The main divisions of the vertebrate nervous system are the central nervous system and the peripheral nervous system. The central nervous system consists of the spinal cord, the hindbrain, the midbrain, and the forebrain. (p. 97)

2. Each segment of the spinal cord has a sensory nerve on each side and a motor nerve on each side. Several spinal pathways convey information to the brain. (p. 102)

3. The sympathetic nervous system (one of the two divisions of the autonomic nervous system) activates the body's internal organs for vigorous activities. The parasympathetic system promotes digestion and other nonemergency processes. (p. 104)

4. The hindbrain consists of the medulla, pons, and cerebellum. The medulla and pons control breathing, heart rate, and other vital functions through the cranial nerves. The cerebellum contributes to movement. (p. 107)

5. The subcortical areas of the forebrain include the hypothalamus, pituitary gland, basal ganglia, hippocampus, and thalamus. (p. 110)

6. Each area of the cerebral cortex receives input from a nucleus of the thalamus. The thalamus processes that information before sending it to the cortex. (p. 114)

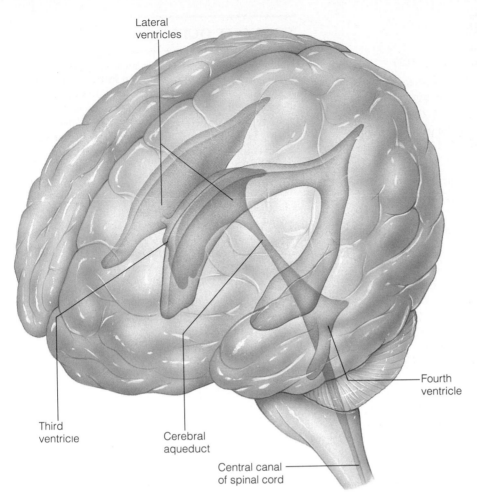

Lateral
ventricles

Third
ventricle

Cerebral
aqueduct

Central canal
of spinal cord

Fourth
ventricle

**Figure 4.19**
**The cerebral ventricles**
*(Top) Diagram showing
positions of the four ventricles.
(Bottom) Photo of a human
brain, viewed from above,
with a horizontal cut through
one hemisphere to show the
position of the lateral ventricle. Note that the two parts of
this figure are seen from different angles. (Photo courtesy
of Dr. Dana Copeland.)*

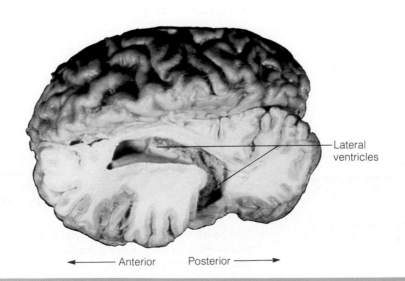

Lateral
ventricles

◀— Anterior    Posterior —▶

117

## REVIEW QUESTIONS

1. What is the Bell-Magendie Law? (p. 102)

2. Why do nerves from the adult spinal cord travel down within the bones of the spinal column before they exit to the periphery? (p. 102)

3. What are the functions of the sympathetic and parasympathetic nervous systems? Where are their ganglia located? (p. 105)

4. Why do certain drugs excite either the sympathetic or the parasympathetic nervous system but not the other? (p. 106)

5. Name the principal structures of the hindbrain and the midbrain. (p. 107)

6. What do the cranial nerves do? (p. 107)

7. Cover the labels in Figures 4.14 through 4.18 and identify the structures shown. (p. 112)

8. Which subcortical area is the main source of input to the cerebral cortex? (p. 114)

9. What do the ventricles contain? (p. 115)

## THOUGHT QUESTION

1. The drug phenylephrine is sometimes prescribed for people suffering from a sudden loss of blood pressure and for other medical disorders. It acts by stimulating norepinephrine synapses, including those that constrict blood vessels. One common side effect of this drug is gooseflesh. Explain why. What other side effects might the person expect to experience?

## SUGGESTIONS FOR FURTHER READING

**Blakemore, C.** (1977). *Mechanics of the mind.* New York: Cambridge University Press. An interesting, highly readable introduction to brain functioning.

**Goldberg, S.** (1979). *Clinical neuroanatomy made ridiculously simple.* Miami: Medmaster. A short paperback reviewing features of the human CNS that are most important in medicine.

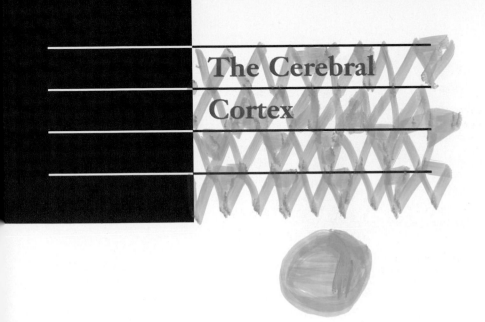

# The Cerebral Cortex

The **cerebral cortex,** the outer surface of the forebrain, consists of two hemi-spheres, one on the left side and one on the right, covering all the other forebrain structures (Figure 4.20). Each hemisphere is organized to receive sensory infor-mation mostly from the contralateral (opposite) side of the body and to control muscles mostly on the contralateral side through axons to the spinal cord and the cranial nerve nuclei.

The cerebral cortex is gray matter, consisting largely of cell bodies. Large numbers of axons extend inward from the cortex, forming the white matter (Fig-ure 4.15). Neurons in each hemisphere communicate with neurons in the corre-sponding part of the other hemisphere by two bundles of axons, the **corpus cal-losum** (Figures 4.15, 4.16, and 4.19) and the smaller **anterior commissure** (Figure 4.15). (Several other commissures link subcortical structures.)

## ORGANIZATION OF THE CEREBRAL CORTEX

The microscopic structure of the cells of the cerebral cortex varies substantially from one cortical area to another. These differences in appearance relate to dif-ferences in function. Much of the research on the cerebral cortex has been di-rected toward understanding the relationship between structure and function.

### Laminae and Columns of the Cerebral Cortex

The cerebral cortex of humans and most other mammals contains up to six dis-tinct **laminae,** layers of cell bodies parallel to the surface of the cortex and sepa-rated from each other by fiber layers (see Figure 4.21). The laminae vary in thick-ness and prominence from one area of the cortex to another, and a given lamina may be absent from certain parts of the cortex. Lamina V, which sends long axons to the spinal cord and other distant areas, is thickest in the motor cortex, the area with the greatest control of the muscles. Lamina IV, which receives axons from the various sensory nuclei of the thalamus, is prominent in the visual cortex and the auditory cortex, but absent from the motor cortex. Anecdotal reports have

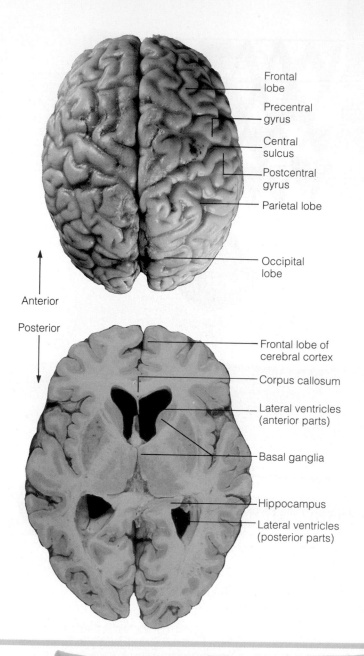

Frontal
lobe

Precentral
gyrus

Central
sulcus

Postcentral
gyrus

Parietal lobe

Occipital
lobe

Anterior

Posterior

Frontal lobe of
cerebral cortex

Corpus callosum

Lateral ventricles
(anterior parts)

Basal ganglia

Hippocampus

Lateral ventricles
(posterior parts)

**Figure 4.20
Dorsal view of the
surface of the brain
and a horizontal
section through the
brain**
*(Photos courtesy of Dr. Dana
Copeland.)*

found lamina IV to be even thicker than normal in the visual cortex of a person with "photographic memory" and in the auditory cortex of a musician with "perfect pitch" (Scheibel, 1984).

The cells of the cortex are also organized into **columns** of cells perpendicular to the laminae (Mountcastle, 1957). (See Figure 4.22.) The cells within a given column have the same properties. For example, if one cell in a given column responds to touch on the palm of the left hand, then all the cells in that column respond to touch on the palm of the left hand. If one cell responds to a particular pattern of light at a particular location in the retina, then all cells in that column respond to the same pattern of light in the same location. The evolution of the cerebral cortex has largely been the addition of more columns. A column of cells contains about the same number of neurons in one mammalian species as in another; the difference among species is in how many columns they have (Killackey, 1990).

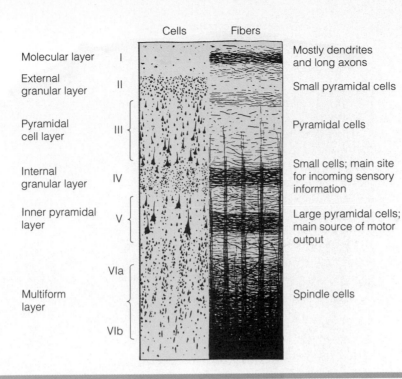

| Cells | | Fibers | |
|---|---|---|---|
| Molecular layer | I | | Mostly dendrites and long axons |
| External granular layer | II | | Small pyramidal cells |
| Pyramidal cell layer | III | | Pyramidal cells |
| Internal granular layer | IV | | Small cells; main site for incoming sensory information |
| Inner pyramidal layer | V | | Large pyramidal cells; main source of motor output |
| Multiform layer | VIa | | Spindle cells |
| | VIb | | |

**Figure 4.21**
**The six laminae of the human cerebral cortex**
*(Adapted from Ranson & Clark, 1959.)*

## Sensory, Motor, and Association Areas of Cortex

Many authorities divide the cerebral cortex into three types of areas: sensory areas, motor areas, and association areas. That distinction provides a convenient shorthand description, although it implies a more absolute division of labor than is generally the case.

Brain investigators once believed that the sensory nuclei of the thalamus sent their input to the sensory areas of the cortex, which in turn sent their input to the association areas, which in turn sent input to the motor areas. Finally, the motor areas sent messages that controlled the muscles.

This sequential idea was appealing. It implied that association areas received all their information from other cortical areas and then "thought" about it. The idea of association areas coincided with the idea of a unified consciousness, a single self aware of all sensory experiences. Besides, the association areas form a larger percentage of the human brain than of the brains of most other species. Apparently we had a physical explanation for why humans are, at least in our own opinion, so much smarter than other species.

By the 1940s this idea had to be amended. The association areas of the cortex receive much of their input directly from the thalamus, not just from other cortical areas. J. E. Rose and C. N. Woolsey (1949) proposed a theory to rescue the concept of association areas. The association areas, they conceded, receive input from the thalamus, but that input comes from what they called *intrinsic* nuclei of the thalamus—thalamic nuclei that received their own input from other thalamic nuclei, not directly from sensory pathways. In other words, the intrinsic nuclei were association areas of the thalamus, and the cortical areas to which they sent messages were therefore association areas, too.

Later work with more advanced techniques found that the intrinsic nuclei are not entirely associational either (I. T. Diamond, 1979, 1983). They receive their

The Cerebral Cortex

**121**

**Figure 4.22
Columns in the
cerebral cortex**

*Each column extends through
several laminae. Neurons
within a given column have
similar properties. For example, in the somatosensory cortex, all the neurons within a
given column respond to stimulation of the same area of
skin.*

Surface of cortex

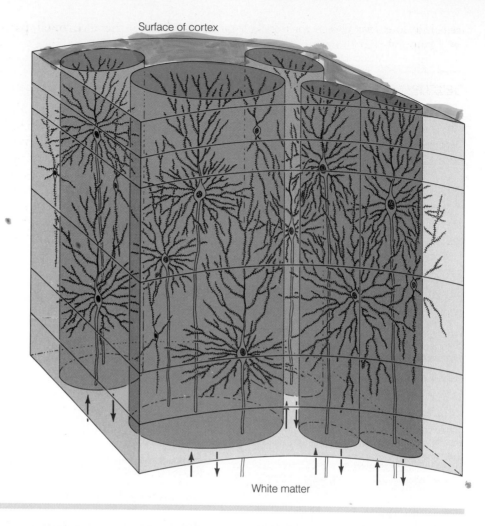

White matter

input from sensory pathways or from the reticular formation (a diffuse set of neurons that activate other neurons throughout the cortex); they receive little input
from other thalamic nuclei (E. G. Jones, 1985). Thus, the intrinsic areas of the
thalamus and the association areas of the cortex are specialized sensory areas
rather than areas set aside for processing a special kind of "associational" information.

Most areas of the cerebral cortex receive some sensory input from the thalamus; they also receive input from other areas of the cortex, and they send output
that controls the muscles. The difference between motor areas, sensory areas, and
association areas is a matter of degree (I. T. Diamond, 1979). For example, some
areas have a high level of sensory input and little motor output, while others have
little sensory input and a great deal of motor output. Some areas are heavily controlled by input from other cortical areas; other areas are less influenced by cortical information. Still, most areas of the cortex perform some combination of sensory, associational, and motor functions.

We can distinguish fifty or more areas of the cerebral cortex, based on differences in the thickness of the six laminae and on the appearance of cells and fibers
within each lamina. For convenience of discussion, however, we shall group these

4 / Anatomy of the
Nervous System and
Methods of
Investigation

areas into four *lobes* named for the skull bones that lie over them: occipital, parietal, temporal, and frontal.

## OCCIPITAL LOBE

The **occipital lobe,** located at the posterior (caudal) end of the cortex (Figure 4.23), is the main target for axons from the thalamic nuclei that receive input from the visual pathways. The very posterior pole of the occipital lobe is known as the *primary visual cortex* or as the *striate cortex* because of its striped appearance in cross section. Destruction of any part of the striate cortex causes loss of vision in part of the visual field. The location of the damage determines which part of the visual field will become blind. For example, extensive damage to the striate cortex of the right hemisphere causes blindness in the left visual field (the left side

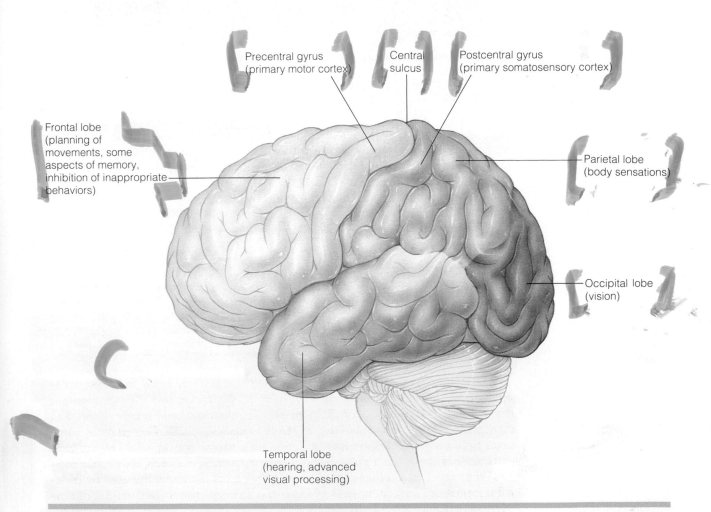

Precentral gyrus
(primary motor cortex)

Central
sulcus

Postcentral gyrus
(primary somatosensory cortex)

Frontal lobe
(planning of
movements, some
aspects of memory,
inhibition of inappropriate
behaviors)

Parietal lobe
(body sensations)

Occipital lobe
(vision)

Temporal lobe
(hearing, advanced
visual processing)

**Figure 4.23**
**Some major subdivisions of the human cerebral cortex, with indications of a few of their primary functions**

**Figure 4.24
Organization of (a)
sensory areas of the
postcentral gyrus and
(b) motor areas of the
precentral gyrus**
*Each location along either
gyrus is primarily involved in
sensations or motor control for
one area in the opposite half
of the body. The drawing of
the somatosensory cortex shows
just one of four bands; the
others are located in planes
parallel to the one shown.
(After Penfield & Rasmussen,
1950.)*

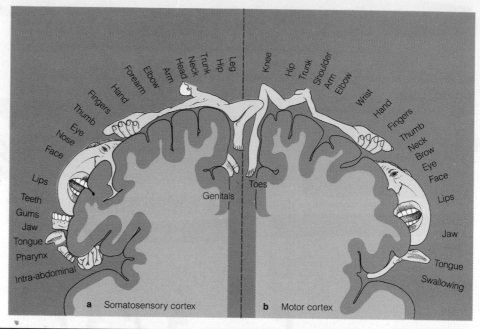

a   Somatosensory cortex          b   Motor cortex

of the world from the viewer's perspective). Blindness from occipital lobe damage
is called *cortical blindness*. A person with cortical blindness has normal eyes, normal pupillary reflexes, and some eye movements. However, the person gains no
information from the eyes.

Vision is not the only function of the occipital lobe. Karl Lashley (1929)
found that occipital lobe damage impaired the maze-learning ability of rats that
were already blind. Evidently, the occipital cortex contributes something important even in blind rats.

## PARIETAL LOBE

The **parietal lobe** lies between the occipital lobe and the **central sulcus,** one of
the deepest grooves in the surface of the cortex (see Figure 4.23). The parietal
lobe is specialized primarily for dealing with body information, including touch,
muscle-stretch receptors, and joint receptors.

The area just posterior to the central sulcus, called the **postcentral gyrus** or
the *primary somatosensory cortex*, is the primary target for touch sensations and
other skin and muscle information. Direct electrical stimulation of the postcentral
gyrus evokes sensations on the opposite side of the body, often described as tingling or not quite natural sensations.

The postcentral gyrus includes four bands of cells running parallel to the
central sulcus. Along each band are separate areas that receive information from
different parts of the body, as Figure 4.24a shows. Two of the bands receive
mostly light-touch information, one receives deep-pressure information, and one
receives a combination of both (Kaas, Nelson, Sur, Lin, & Merzenich, 1979).
That is, the postcentral gyrus contains four separate representations of the body.

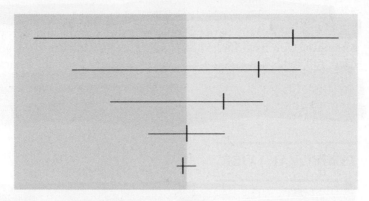

**Figure 4.25
Results when a patient with right parietal lobe damage attempts to bisect a line**
*Note that when the line is relatively long, the patient ignores most of the line at the left. When the line is shorter, the patient may bisect the line accurately or may even err in the opposite direction.*

The representation of the body in the postcentral gyrus varies from one species to another and even from one individual to another (Cusick, Wall, & Kaas, 1986). The representation of the paws is unusually large in raccoons; the representation of the snout is unusually large in rats. The pattern for bats, which use their feet to hang upside down and which use their forelimbs as wings instead of legs, is quite distorted compared to the one shown in Figure 4.24 (Calford, Graydon, Huerta, Kaas, & Pettigrew, 1985).

Following damage to the parietal lobe, people do not completely lose the sense of touch, or the muscle and joint senses, at least not permanently. Rather, they suffer a variety of symptoms that suggest difficulty in interpreting such information and in using it to control movement (J. C. Lynch, 1980). Some common symptoms include:

1. Impairment of ability to identify objects by touch. For example, a blind person who suffers damage to the parietal lobe loses the ability to read Braille (Gloning, Gloning, Weingarten, & Berner, 1954).

2. Clumsiness on the side of the body opposite the damage.

3. Neglect of the opposite side of the body, especially neglect of the left side after right-hemisphere parietal lobe damage (Bisiach & Luzzatti, 1978; Levine, Warach, Benowitz, & Calvanio, 1986). People with such damage may fail to dress the left side of the body, read only the right side of a page, and describe from memory only the right side of a familiar scene. When asked to draw an object, they generally draw only its right side. When asked to draw a mark to divide a line in half, they draw the mark well to the right side of the line (ignoring or distorting the left side), unless the line is very short (Marshall & Halligan, 1990). (See Figure 4.25.)

4. Distortion of body image. One young man suffered damage to his parietal lobe in an automobile accident. After recovering from the immediate effects of the injury, he began to complain about sensations from his left eye. In fact, both eyes were normal and both had 20/20 vision. He nevertheless demanded surgical removal of the eye, threatened suicide when surgeons refused to remove it, and eventually tried (unsuccessfully) to remove the eye himself with a pellet gun (Dalby, Arboleda-Florez, & Seland, 1989).

5. Inability to draw and follow maps, describe how to get somewhere, or say what something might look like when viewed from a different angle.

The parietal cortex is also important for relating visual information to spatial information. Certain parietal cells may be responsible for your knowing that something you have looked at is still the same object after you have tilted your head and looked at it from a different angle (Andersen, Essick, & Siegel, 1985). After parietal lobe damage, a person may find it necessary to focus directly on an object with the center of the retina to identify it (J. C. Lynch, 1980). To recognize a group of objects, such a person must look at the objects one at a time.

## TEMPORAL LOBE

The **temporal lobe** is located laterally in each hemisphere, near the temples (see Figure 4.23). It is the primary cortical target for information originating in the ears and the vestibular organs (which deal with balance and equilibrium). When a person performs a task requiring attention to sound, activity increases in the temporal cortex (Cohen et al., 1988).

The temporal lobe also contributes to some of the more complex aspects of vision, including perception of complex patterns such as faces. A tumor in the temporal lobe may give rise to elaborate visual hallucinations, whereas a tumor in the occipital lobe ordinarily evokes only simple sensations, such as flashes of light. In humans, the left temporal lobe and part of the parietal lobe also contain *Wernicke's area* (see Chapter 5), which is critical for the comprehension of language.

The temporal lobes also play a part in emotional and motivational behaviors. Temporal lobe damage can lead to a set of behaviors known as the **Klüver-Bucy syndrome** (named for the investigators who first described it). Monkeys with damaged temporal lobes fail to display normal fears and anxieties (Klüver & Bucy, 1939). Previously wild and aggressive monkeys can be handled easily after such surgery. They put almost anything they find into their mouths. They attempt to pick up snakes and lighted matches (which intact monkeys consistently avoid). It is hard to determine how much of this behavior results from an emotional change and how much from a visual deficit. For example, a monkey might handle a snake because it was no longer afraid of snakes or because it did not recognize what the snake was.

## FRONTAL LOBE

The **frontal lobe** (which contains the motor cortex and the prefrontal cortex) extends from the central sulcus to the anterior limit of the brain (see Figure 4.23). The posterior portion of the frontal lobe is the **precentral gyrus,** which is specialized for the control of fine movements, such as moving one finger at a time. It has separate areas responsible for different parts of the body (Figure 4.24), mostly on the contralateral side of the body but with slight control of the ipsilateral side, too.

The most anterior portion of the frontal lobe, the **prefrontal cortex,** is a fairly large structure, especially in species with a large brain overall, such as humans (Figure 4.26). It is not the primary target for any single sensory system, but it receives information from all the sensory systems, including sensations from the interior of the body. The prefrontal cortex is the only cortical area known to receive input from all sensory modalities (Stuss & Benson, 1984).

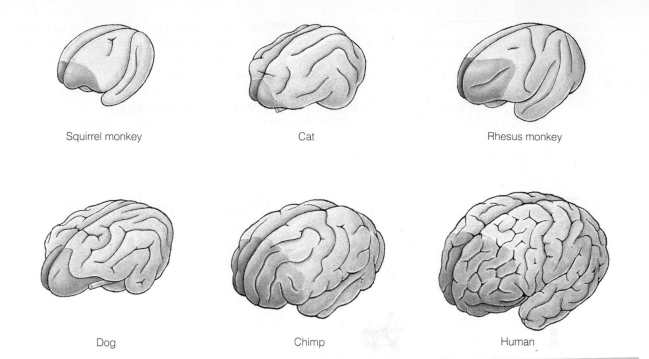

Squirrel monkey

Cat

Rhesus monkey

Dog

Chimp

Human

**Figure 4.26**
**The prefrontal cortex**
**(shaded area) in the**
**brain of six species**
*Note that the prefrontal*
*cortex constitutes a larger*
*proportion of the human*
*brain than of the brains*
*of these other species.*
*(After Fuster, 1989.)*

The prefrontal cortex was the target of *prefrontal lobotomies*, an infamous type of brain surgery conducted in attempts to control certain types of psychological disorder (see Digression 4.2). As a consequence of the surgery, people generally lost their initiative and failed to inhibit socially unacceptable impulses. They also showed impairments in certain aspects of memory and in their facial expressions of emotion.

However, the results of prefrontal lobotomies provided only a superficial understanding of what the prefrontal lobes do and how they do it. The work of Patricia Goldman-Rakic and others has led to a more advanced understanding. According to Goldman-Rakic (1988), the prefrontal cortex is particularly important for behaviors guided by an "internal representation" of the world. For example, a monkey without its prefrontal cortex is fully capable of learning always to go toward the green light to find food and never to go toward a blue light. That task does not require an internal representation of the world; it requires only a response to stimuli present at the time. The same monkey is greatly impaired on **delayed-response tasks,** in which it must remember, for example, where it saw a green light last and go toward it 30 seconds after it was turned off. There are many versions of the delayed-response task, but the basic procedure is always to provide a signal indicating the correct response, turn off the signal, impose a delay, and then test whether the animal can still make the correct response. A correct response to a delayed-response task requires an internal representation of past stimuli. Goldman-Rakic's research indicates that the prefrontal cortex includes a great many separate circuits representing past stimuli of different types—visual, auditory, and so forth.

Research on the prefrontal cortex has led to a biological explanation of a well-known observation in developmental psychology. Remember Jean Piaget's

The Cerebral Cortex

# The Rise and Fall of Prefrontal Lobotomies

In the late 1940s and early 1950s, about 40,000 **prefrontal lobotomies** were performed in the United States (Shutts, 1982). The operation consists of damaging the prefrontal cortex or cutting the connections between the prefrontal cortex and the rest of the cortex. The impetus to performing this operation was a report that damage to the prefrontal cortex of primates in the laboratory had made them tamer without impairing their sensory or motor capacities in any striking way. It was reasoned that the same operation might help people suffering from severe and otherwise untreatable psychiatric disorders.

The largest number of lobotomies in the United States was performed by Walter Freeman, a medical doctor who had never been trained in surgery. His techniques were amazingly crude, even by the standards of the 1940s. He performed many of the operations in his office or in other sites outside the hospital. (Freeman carried his equipment, such as it was, around with him in his car, which he called his "lobotomobile.")

Freeman and others became increasingly casual about deciding who should get a lobotomy. At first, the technique was used only in cases of severe, untreatable schizophrenia. Lobotomy did calm some schizophrenic people, but the effects were often disappointing, even to Freeman and others who performed the operations. (We now know that the frontal lobes of many severe schizophrenics are partly shrunken and less active than normal; lobotomy was therefore damaging a structure that had already been impaired.) As time went on, Freeman tried lobotomy for people with an assortment of other major and minor disorders. Some would, in fact, be considered normal by today's standards.

After antischizophrenic and antidepressive drugs became available in the mid-1950s, the use of lobotomy declined sharply. Freeman, who had been praised by some of his colleagues and barely tolerated by others, lost his privilege to practice at most hospitals and

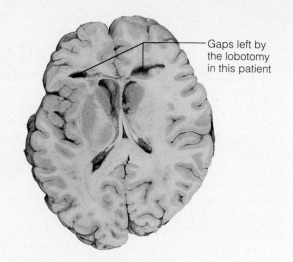

Gaps left by the lobotomy in this patient

*A horizontal section of the brain of a person who had a prefrontal lobotomy many years previously. The two holes in the frontal cortex are the visible results of the operation. (Photo courtesy of Dr. Dana Copeland.)*

faded into the same obscurity as lobotomy itself. Lobotomy has been an exceedingly rare operation since the mid-1950s (Lesse, 1984; Tippin & Henn, 1982).

Among the common consequences of prefrontal lobotomy were apathy, a loss of planning and initiative, memory disorders (Chapter 14), distractibility, generally blunted emotions, and a loss of facial expression (Stuss & Benson, 1984). People with such damage lose their social inhibitions; they behave in a tactless, callous manner and ignore the rules of polite, civilized conduct. If the damage is extensive, people have trouble suppressing one behavior and substituting another (Damasio, 1979). For example, after they have learned to sort a set of cards by color, it is difficult for them to shift to sorting them by the numbers or patterns on the cards.

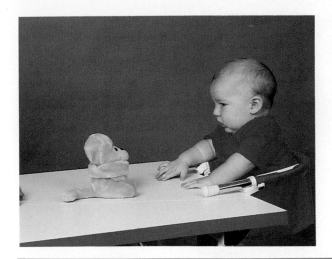

Figure 4.27
Piaget's object
permanence task

*An infant sees a toy, then an investigator places a barrier in front of the toy. Infants younger than about 9 months old fail to reach for the hidden toy. This task is similar to the delayed-response task, which infant monkeys cannot master until their prefrontal cortex matures. (Doug Goodman/Monkmeyer Press.)*

concept of *object permanence* from your study of introductory psychology or developmental psychology? In the object permanence task, an observer shows a toy to an infant, places the toy behind a barrier, and then watches whether the child reaches for it. Generally, a child less than 9 months old does not reach for it (Figure 4.27). Goldman-Rakic (1987) noted the similarity between this task and the delayed-response task: In both cases, the individual must respond to a signal that was once present but is now gone.

Monkeys, it turns out, fail the delayed-response task until they are about 2 to 4 months old. Most of the synapses in the monkey's prefrontal cortex develop between ages 2 and 4 months. Presumably, the monkeys become capable of responding correctly on the delayed-response task at 2 to 4 months *because* the synapses of the prefrontal cortex develop at that time.

In humans as in monkeys, the prefrontal cortex is one of the last cortical structures to mature (Figure 4.28). Massive numbers of synapses develop in the human brain between ages $7\frac{1}{2}$ and 12 months. Perhaps infants fail the object permanence task before about age 9 months because this task requires activity in the prefrontal cortex, and the necessary synapses are not present until about age 9 months (Goldman-Rakic, 1987).

## EVOLUTION OF THE BRAIN AND THE CEREBRAL CORTEX

How did the human brain come to be the way it is? It is difficult to reconstruct the evolution of the brain, because brains do not fossilize. However, we can draw a few inferences by comparing the brains of species alive today. From the fossil record we infer that the earliest mammals were small animals similar in some ways to the hedgehogs of today. Certainly humans did not evolve from hedgehogs, but we apparently evolved from animals that hedgehogs resemble to some extent.

The Cerebral Cortex

**Figure 4.28**
**Approximate order in which areas of the human cortex mature**

*The brown areas mature first, as indicated by the formation of myelin. The gold areas mature later, and the beige areas mature last. In this drawing the temporal cortex has been pulled back to reveal some midline structures not usually visible from this angle. (Based on von Bonin, 1950.)*

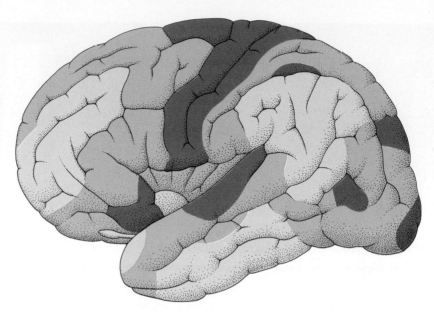

One reason why humans have larger brains than the earliest mammals did is simply that the human body is larger than that of the early mammals. As a rule, the size of an animal's brain is closely related to its body size. As Figure 4.29 illustrates, the logarithm of body weight is an accurate predictor of the logarithm of brain weight (Jerison, 1985). However, we should not take this relationship too literally; weight fluctuates when an animal's diet or health changes. Furthermore, the weight of an elephant includes a greater percentage of bone than does the weight of a smaller land mammal, such as a mouse, or an oceanic mammal, such as a whale. Weight may simply be a convenient index of some other, more important variable (Harvey & Krebs, 1990). Still, the principle is that animals with larger bodies generally have larger brains.

But that principle by itself is not a sufficient explanation for the large brains of humans. As Figure 4.29 indicates, primates (humans, apes, and monkeys) have a higher brain-to-body ratio than most other species. Primates also have extensive folding (gyri and sulci) in their cerebral cortex. The folds provide for more surface area and consequently a greater number of neurons. In general, the larger a species' brain, the more folding occurs, but primates have an even greater degree of folding than one would predict from the overall volume of their brains (Zilles, Armstrong, Moser, Schleicher, & Stephan, 1989). In short, primates have an enlarged surface of their cerebral cortex in comparison to their body size. Exactly *why* this is true is uncertain; we can say that primates have relied more heavily on brain development than other species have, but that is more a restatement of what we are trying to explain than a real explanation.

The evolution of the brain apparently has proceeded mainly by adding new areas, instead of just expanding the old areas (Killackey, 1990; Rakic, 1988). For example, the primary visual cortex does not vary much from one mammalian species to another. Naturally, it is larger in humans than it is in mice and other small mammals, but it is not proportionately larger, compared to the total volume of the human cortex. Similarly, the primary auditory cortex and the primary so-

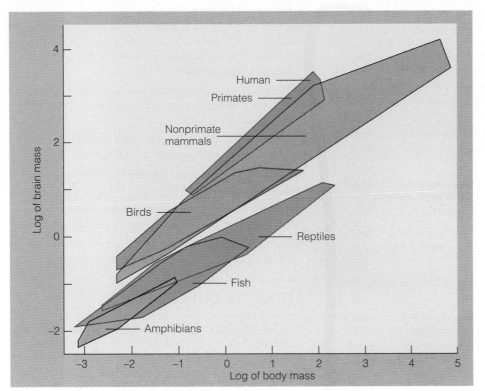

**Figure 4.29
Relationship between
brain mass and body
mass across species**
*Each species is one point
within one of the polygonal
areas. Note that primates in
general and humans in
particular have a high ratio
of brain mass to body mass.
(Based on Jerison, 1985.)*

matosensory cortex have not expanded proportionately as the human brain as a whole expanded. Instead, new sensory areas have been added—for example, second, third, and fourth visual areas that process the same visual information in different ways, enabling us to identify multiple relationships among visual stimuli. In addition, we have evolved multiple auditory and somatosensory areas, plus the large "multisensory" prefrontal cortex.

It is tempting to assume that the size of an animal's brain is proportional to the animal's intelligence, but things are not that simple. First, measuring animal intelligence is extremely difficult (Thomas, 1980). Apparent differences in intelligence sometimes result from sensory differences, motivational differences, or differences in training techniques. The difficulties of comparing intelligence across species are so great that one authority has argued that all nonhuman vertebrates may be equal in intelligence (MacPhail, 1985). While few other psychologists agree, we have no simple or convincing way to refute this position.

Second, brain size is not a very informative indicator of what the brain does. Two animal brains with the same overall size may differ in organization. For example, gorillas and humans, which rely heavily on vision, have well-developed visual areas. Structures essential for localizing sounds are unusually large in dolphins and bats, which find their way about by echolocation (Harrison & Irving, 1966). Raccoons, whose sense of touch is very precise, have an unusually large area of the cerebral cortex devoted to touch (Rensch & Dücker, 1963). In short, the relative size of various brain areas has something to do with the behavioral abilities and deficits of an animal, but it is problematical and perhaps meaningless to talk about the relationship between total brain size and the animal's intelligence.

The Cerebral Cortex

## SUMMARY

1. The cerebral cortex is composed of six laminae (layers) of neurons. A given lamina may be absent from certain parts of the cortex. The cortex is organized into columns of cells arranged perpendicular to the laminae. (p. 119)

2. Almost every cortical area has sensory, associational, and motor functions, although the degree of each varies. (p. 121)

3. The occipital lobe of the cortex is primarily responsible for vision. Damage to part of the occipital lobe leads to blindness in part of the visual field. (p. 123)

4. The parietal lobe deals with body sensations. The postcentral gyrus contains four separate representations of the body. (p. 124)

5. The temporal lobe contributes to hearing and to complex aspects of vision. (p. 126)

6. The frontal lobe includes the precentral gyrus, which controls fine movements. It also includes the prefrontal cortex, which is essential for behaviors guided by an internal representation of the world. The prefrontal cortex receives information from each of the sensory systems. (p. 126)

7. The size of the vertebrate brain is closely related to body size. Humans and other primates have a higher than usual brain-to-body ratio. The relationship of brain size to intelligence is uncertain. (p. 129)

## REVIEW QUESTIONS

1. In what way do the neurons within a given column resemble one another? (p. 120)

2. Why is it an overstatement to divide the cerebral cortex into distinct sensory, associational, and motor areas? (p. 121)

3. How does cortical blindness differ from blindness caused by damage to the eyes? (p. 124)

4. What kind of brain damage leads to sensory neglect of the left half of the body? (p. 124)

5. What is the Klüver-Bucy syndrome? What kind of brain damage is associated with it? (p. 126)

6. Give a biological explanation of why 9-month-old children fail Piaget's object permanence task. (p. 127)

## THOUGHT QUESTION

1. When monkeys with Klüver-Bucy syndrome pick up lighted matches and snakes, it is not obvious whether they are displaying a deficit in emotional response or a difficulty identifying what the object is. What kind of research might help to answer this question?

## SUGGESTIONS FOR FURTHER READING

**Klawans, H. L.** (1988). *Toscanini's fumble and other tales of clinical neurology.* Chicago: Contemporary Books. Fascinating description of cases of human brain damage and other neurological conditions.

**Valenstein, E. S.** (1986). *Great and desperate cures.* New York: Basic Books. Account of the rise and fall of prefrontal lobotomies.

# Methods of Investigating How the Brain Controls Behavior

In the nineteenth century, Franz Joseph Gall observed (or so he thought) that people with an excellent verbal memory had bulging, protruding eyes. He drew the inference that verbal memory depended on a part of the brain immediately behind the eyes and that overdevelopment of this part of the brain pushed the eyes forward. If this were so, Gall reasoned, bulges and depressions elsewhere on the skull might also reflect overdevelopment or underdevelopment of the underlying brain areas. Thus, by comparing skull features among people and relating them to those people's behavior, it should be possible to identify the activities conducted by each part of the brain. And after identifying the functions of all brain areas in this manner, one should be able to determine the personality of an unknown person by feeling bumps and depressions on his or her head. These were the basic premises of the "science" of phrenology. Figure 4.30 shows a typical phrenologist's map of the human skull.

The phrenologists' methods were a classic example of pseudoscience. In many cases phrenologists identified an area on their map of the brain by observing only one or two people. Moreover, they ignored discrepancies when someone's behavior did not fit the theory.

Nevertheless, researchers today maintain one of the phrenologists' basic assumptions: Different parts of the brain do control different aspects of behavior. If brain area A controls behavior X, then individuals with a deficiency of behavior X should have some deficiency in brain area A. Individuals with a greater than normal amount of behavior X should have an excess of activity in area A; area A may even be larger than normal in such individuals (Scheibel, 1984).

Current research differs from phrenology in several major respects, however. Psychologists no longer attempt to localize such personality traits as self-esteem, reverence, and "marvellousness." Rather, we attempt to understand how the brain produces such biological functions as vision, control of finger movements, and temperature regulation. We consider not only localized brain areas but also diffuse systems of neurons that may not be confined to one region. And we examine the electrical and chemical activity of brain areas and systems, not just their size. That is, a behavior may be deficient because some brain area is inactive, not just

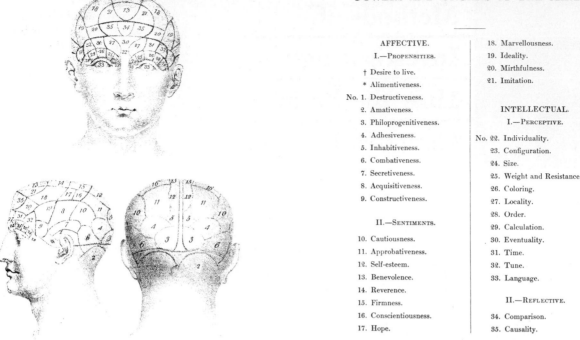

AFFECTIVE.

I.—PROPENSITIES.

† Desire to live.
* Alimentiveness.
No. 1. Destructiveness.
2. Amativeness.
3. Philoprogenitiveness.
4. Adhesiveness.
5. Inhabitiveness.
6. Combativeness.
7. Secretiveness.
8. Acquisitiveness.
9. Constructiveness.

II.—SENTIMENTS.

10. Cautiousness.
11. Approbativeness.
12. Self-esteem.
13. Benevolence.
14. Reverence.
15. Firmness.
16. Conscientiousness.
17. Hope.

18. Marvellousness.
19. Ideality.
20. Mirthfulness.
21. Imitation.

INTELLECTUAL.

I.—PERCEPTIVE.

No. 22. Individuality.
23. Configuration.
24. Size.
25. Weight and Resistance.
26. Coloring.
27. Locality.
28. Order.
29. Calculation.
30. Eventuality.
31. Time.
32. Tune.
33. Language.

II.—REFLECTIVE.

34. Comparison.
35. Causality.

**Figure 4.30**
**A phrenologist's map**
**of brain areas**
*(From Spuzheim, 1908.)*

because that brain area is small or damaged. Still, a major goal of current research is to determine what functions differentiate one area of the brain from other areas. A number of techniques have been developed in pursuit of this goal; a few of the most common are described here.

## THE STEREOTAXIC INSTRUMENT

Investigators sometimes wish to study the effects of stimulating or damaging a small area buried deep in an animal's brain, or they wish to record the activity of such an area. To do so, they use a **stereotaxic instrument**. Figure 4.31 shows a stereotaxic instrument for a rat, by far the most commonly used animal in research of this type. The rat is anesthetized and then positioned in the stereotaxic instrument. Ear bars and a clamp around the nose and mouth hold the head in place. Any part of the brain can be located fairly accurately from the position of two landmarks on the head: the ear bars and **bregma** (the point where the frontal and parietal skull bones join, as shown in Figure 4.32).

To calculate the position, the researcher refers to a **stereotaxic atlas** (or map) of the animal's brain areas in relation to the external landmarks. Such atlases have been published for the brains of many species. Figure 4.33, from Pellegrino and Cushman's (1967) atlas, illustrates one slice through the brain of an adult rat. The scale at the bottom indicates distances in millimeters left or right from the center of the skull. The scales at the left and right indicate distances dorsal and ventral from the top surface of the brain and from the ear bars, respectively. The notations in the upper corners indicate that this slice is 6.0 mm anterior to the ear bars and 0.2-mm anterior to bregma. Other pages of the atlas present slices at 0.2-mm intervals.

**Figure 4.31**
**A stereotaxic instrument for locating brain areas in small animals**

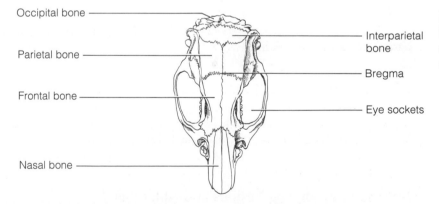

Occipital bone

Parietal bone

Frontal bone

Nasal bone

Interparietal bone

Bregma

Eye sockets

**Figure 4.32**
**Skull bones of a rat and the position of bregma**

An experimenter who wants to insert an electrode into the ventromedial hypothalamus (VMH in Figure 4.33) places the anesthetized animal in the stereotaxic instrument, cuts back the skin over the skull, dries the skull, and marks points directly above the ventromedial hypothalamus, one on each side of the brain, using measurements from the brain atlas. The experimenter then drills small holes at those points, inserts a thin metal electrode insulated except at the tip, and lowers the electrode to the level of the target. An investigator who wishes to make a lesion then applies a DC electrical current (typically 0.1 to 0.2 milliampere for 10 to 20 seconds) or a radio-frequency current to destroy a small amount of brain tissue near the tip of the electrode. An investigator who wishes

Methods of Investigating How the Brain Controls Behavior

135

**Figure 4.33
A typical page from a
stereotaxic atlas of the
rat brain showing a
coronal section 6.0 mm
anterior to the ear bars**
*The surrounding unlabeled
area is the cerebral cortex.
Abbreviations refer to various
areas of the brain; for example, CC = corpus callosum.
(From Pellegrino et al.,
1979.)*

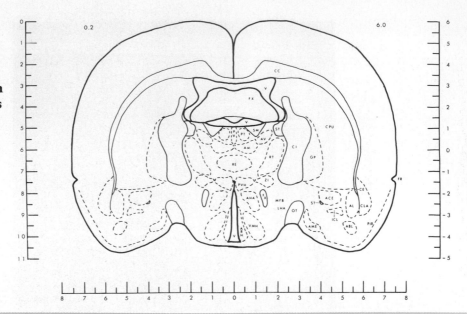

to stimulate cells without destroying them applies a weaker current for a shorter time. To record spontaneous activity, the investigator would simply attach one end of a wire to the electrode and the other end to a recording device.

## LESIONS AND ABLATIONS

A **lesion** is destruction or functional disruption of an area of the brain. An **ablation** is removal of part of the brain. Lesions and ablations can be produced intentionally by experimenters with laboratory animals, or they can occur naturally, as when a person has a stroke or a head wound. When a lesion or ablation leads to a deficit in some behavior, it is assumed that the damaged area had some role in the control of that behavior, although its exact role is often difficult to determine. The lesion technique has been widely used throughout the history of biological psychology.

### Methods of Producing Lesions and Ablations

Lesions and ablations can be produced in experimental animals in several ways. To remove a large area on the external surface of the brain, an experimenter can cut back a flap of skull and then remove the desired brain tissue with a knife or with vacuum suction. To make smaller lesions, especially lesions beneath the surface of the brain, the investigator inserts an electrode using the stereotaxic device and then applies a current.

The electrode inevitably kills a few cells on the way to the target. To find out the effects of such accidental damage and to separate them from the effects of the lesion itself, an experimenter produces a **sham lesion** in a control group. That is, the experimenter goes through all the same procedures but does not apply the electrical current. Any behavioral difference between the lesioned group and the sham-lesion group must result from the lesion itself and not from damage caused by inserting the electrode.

## Histological Techniques

Suppose an investigator has made a lesion in a rat's brain and then has tested the behavioral effects of the lesion. When the experiment is over, the investigator usually examines the rat's brain to determine the size and the exact location of the lesion.

The rat is deeply anesthetized, then perfused with chemicals that preserve the tissues. Then the brain is removed and stained. Without some special treatment, brain tissue looks fairly uniform; it is difficult to identify even the major nuclei and tracts. Therefore, investigators use various histological procedures to highlight the kinds of brain tissue they wish to examine. (*Histology* is the branch of biology that deals with the structure of tissues.)

First, investigators harden the brain tissue either by freezing it or by forcing a chemical into it that hardens it. (Using such a chemical is called "embedding" the tissue.) Then the brain is divided into slices just a few microns thick by means of a device called a microtome. Finally, the tissue is stained with chemicals that attach selectively either to cell bodies or to axons or to some other structures. The stains enable investigators to see the differences between one part of the nervous system and another. Table 4.5 lists a few of the histological stains frequently used in the study of the brain. The photomicrographs in this book show tissues treated this way.

## Difficulties of Interpreting the Results of Lesion Experiments

The results of lesion experiments can be hard to interpret. As an analogy, suppose no one understood how a television works. To find out, an investigator explodes a small firecracker inside the set, damaging nearby structures, and then examines the effects on the set and tries to characterize any loss to the picture and sound. Later, someone performs an autopsy on the set to determine exactly what physical damage was associated with the impaired functioning.

You can see the problems. With luck, an investigator might find that a firecracker in one area destroys the sound and a firecracker in another area destroys the picture. But that would not tell us *how* either area controlled the picture or sound. Moreover, the loss of sound or picture might not be due to the destruction of a structure in the area but to the interruption of wires that happened to be passing through.

Investigating a brain by making lesions presents similar difficulties, although they are not insurmountable. One of the greatest difficulties is to describe the behavioral deficit after a lesion. To say that a lesion interfered with maze learning would be insufficient. We would want to know *how* it interfered. For example, in one study, four monkeys learned a maze that could be solved either by attending to visual cues or by memorizing a pattern of left and right turns (Traverse & Latto, 1986). In fact, different monkeys solved the maze in different ways. Some of the monkeys attended to left and right; subsequent lesions in the posterior parietal cortex, an area sensitive to body location, greatly impaired their maze performance. Other monkeys attended to visual cues; later damage to their posterior parietal cortex had little effect on their maze performance. An experimenter who had not previously analyzed *how* the monkeys had learned the maze might easily have been confused by the fact that the same lesion impaired performance in some monkeys and not others.

After researchers think they know what deficit is associated with a given lesion, a good way to verify their interpretation is to look for a **double dissociation of function:** a demonstration that lesion 1 impairs behavior A more than behavior B, while lesion 2 impairs behavior B more than behavior A. Such results

| **Table 4.5 Some Common Histological Stains and Methods** | |
| --- | --- |
| *Method* | *Description* |
| Rapid Golgi stain | A slice of tissue is immersed first in a solution of osmium tetroxide and potassium dichromate and then in a dilute silver nitrate solution. The silver nitrate invades a few neurons, generally less than 10 percent, apparently at random. When it invades a neuron, however, it diffuses through the entire cell, including all branches of the axon and dendrites, staining them dark brown. The investigator can then see the entire neuron. |
| Procion yellow or Procion brown stain | Like the Golgi stain, these stains diffuse through the entire neuron, producing a bright fluorescence. A common procedure is to use a glass electrode to record from a neuron and then inject one of the Procion dyes through the same electrode, marking the cell for later identification. |
| Nissl stains | Several Nissl stains are in common use, including cresylviolet and toluidine blue. The investigator stains a brain slice with one of these chemicals and then bathes it in chloroform, which removes the stain from myelinated fibers. The result is a violet staining of cell bodies. |
| Weigert stain | Hematoxylin solution and chromium salts are used to stain axons blue to black. Staining alternate sections with Nissl and Weigert stains lets the investigator see both cell bodies and fibers. |
| Nauta method | The investigator freezes brain sections, permeates them with silver pyridine solution, ammoniacal silver nitrate, and then with a mixture of formaldehyde, alcohol, and citric acid. Degenerating axons take on a dark stain. (An axon degenerates when it has been cut off from its cell body.) This method can be used to trace the course of axons originating in the brain. |
| Horseradish peroxidase method | Horseradish peroxidase (HRP) is injected into a specific area of a living brain, where it is absorbed by axon terminals and transported back to their cell bodies. Later the animal is killed; the brain is sliced and treated with a benzidine derivative, which reacts with HRP to form granules. This technique is useful for tracing a set of axons back to their origin. |

help researchers ascertain that the behavioral deficits are not simply the product of overall inactivity, blindness, or some other general disorder that should affect both behaviors.

## STIMULATION OF AND RECORDING FROM THE BRAIN

The lesion methods determine what behaviors occur when certain areas of the brain are damaged. Alternative ways to study brain functioning are to insert electrodes into the brain and briefly stimulate certain areas (to see how increased activity of those areas affects behavior) and to use the electrodes to record spontaneous brain activity (to determine what behaviors accompany that activity).

Researchers always feel more confidence in a conclusion if they can support it through different types of experiments. For example, lesion experiments have shown that damage to the lateral hypothalamus causes an animal to stop eating, while experiments with implanted electrodes have demonstrated that stimulating the same area increases eating. Recording of neurons in this area has revealed that spontaneous activity is high around the time of a meal. All these lines of evidence indicate that the lateral hypothalamus has something to do with eating. (Yet the results do not tell us *how* the lateral hypothalamus contributes to eating.)

## LABELING BRAIN ACTIVITY

Several methods adopt the strategy of labeling certain chemicals in the brain so that investigators can observe their distribution. Two such methods are autoradiography and immunohistochemistry.

### Autoradiography

An autograph is a person's signature. An autoradiograph is a signal produced radioactively by a chemical. **Autoradiography** is a method of determining where a chemical is located in the brain.

To conduct autoradiography, an investigator begins by injecting a radioactively labeled chemical, such as radioactively labeled glucose, amino acids, or drugs into a laboratory rat. After the injection, the investigator waits a few minutes for the chemicals to reach the brain and then kills the rat and slices its brain into thin sections. The investigator then places each section against a piece of X-ray film, which records all the radioactivity that the labeled chemicals emit. In that manner it creates a map of the relative amounts of radioactivity in different parts of the rat's brain.

For example, an investigator might inject radioactively labeled glucose or 2-deoxy-D-glucose, which neurons take up when they absorb glucose. (The advantage of 2-deoxy-D-glucose is that it is metabolized much more slowly than glucose and so remains in the cell longer.) The most active neurons take up more glucose than less active neurons do; consequently, the autoradiography provides a map of relative activity levels in the brain (Hibbard, McGlone, Davis, & Hawkins, 1987). By the same logic, researchers can inject radioactive amino acids and later look for the brain areas that incorporated them into radioactive proteins or inject radioactively labeled drugs to find the receptors to which they attach.

### Immunohistochemistry

The term *immunohistochemistry* is a combination of *immuno-*, referring to the immune system, *histo-*, meaning tissues, and *chemistry*. **Immunohistochemistry**, therefore, is a method of using the immune system to label particular types of tissues.

First, investigators purify a protein or peptide in which they are interested. Then they inject it into an animal, whose immune system will form antibodies to it. They collect the antibodies from the animal's blood, chemically attach them to dyes, and inject the combination into another animal. The antibodies, carrying the dye with them, circulate through the blood until they attach to proteins or peptides like the original ones.

This method eventually stains a particular protein or peptide everywhere it occurs in the brain, providing a means of mapping the distribution of that chemical in the brain. For example, if the investigators began by isolating acetylcholine receptors, they would eventually produce a set of slides in which dye was attached to acetylcholine receptors.

# STUDIES THAT USE THE NATURAL DEVELOPMENT OF THE BRAIN

Sometimes an investigator wishes to study a set of cells that is intermingled thoroughly with other cells, making it impossible to stimulate or damage one set of cells without equally affecting the others. Investigators cannot make the surgical manipulations themselves, but they may be able to let nature do the work for them. For example, certain individuals may lack one type of cell or another for genetic reasons. And because different parts of the brain mature at different rates, an individual may lack certain types of cells at one age but have those cells at a later age.

## Genetic Lesions and Arrested Development

Sometimes an investigator wants to explore the function of a particular type of cell that is distributed widely and interspersed with other types of cells. One way to study such cells is to take advantage of a genetic mutation. For example, one mutation prevents granule cells from developing in the cerebellum of mice. Such mice have great difficulty maintaining their balance. Their legs tremble constantly, and they can hardly take a step without falling over. Such evidence is at least a start toward understanding the role of the granule cells (Sidman, Green, & Appel, 1965).

Another way to remove a particular type of cell is to interfere with brain maturation at a particular stage. Different cell types mature at different times. If experimenters expose the brain to X rays or to the neurotoxin MAM (methylazoxymethanol acetate), they can destroy the cells that are dividing and developing at that time, while sparing mature cells (Anderson & Altman, 1972; Sanberg, Pevsner, Autuono, & Coyle, 1985). When the researchers repeat the experiment at different ages, they can examine the contributions of different populations of cells.

## Correlation of Developing Brain with Developing Behavior

Suppose a certain structure or system in the brain and a certain behavior both reach maturity fairly suddenly at the same time. With caution we can use this as evidence that the structure is responsible for the behavior.

For example, the retina of a frog contains four anatomical types of cells known as constricted tree, E-tree, H-tree, and broad tree, according to their shape. Physiological recordings from cells in the retina reveal that different cells respond best to four different stimuli: edges, convex edges, moving contrast, and dimness. Each of the four anatomical types of cells probably responds best to a different stimulus. But which is which? The question is not easy to answer because the physiological responses of cells can be recorded only when they are alive, and their anatomy can be determined only by staining them after they are dead.

Pomeranz and Chung (1970) were able to relate two of the anatomical types to visual responses by studying the retinas of tadpoles (baby frogs) (see Figure 4.34). They noted that tadpoles lack the constricted tree cells and have no cells that respond best to edges. They therefore inferred that constricted tree cells respond to edges. Moreover, E-tree cells could be found only in the center of the tadpole's retina, and cells responsive to convex edges could be recorded only in the center of the retina. Thus, E-trees are apparently responsive to convex edges. The researchers were unable to pair up the other two types of cell, however.

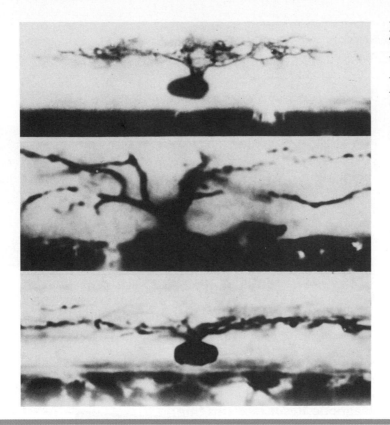

**Figure 4.34**
**Three cell types in the tadpole retina**
*From top to bottom, E-tree, H-tree, and broad tree. (From Pomeranz & Chung, 1970.)*

## STUDIES OF THE STRUCTURE OF LIVING HUMAN BRAINS

Suppose we want to investigate whether a given person has any kind of brain abnormality. Experimenters could hardly insert electrodes into that person's brain. To study the brains of living people, investigators turn to other methods, sometimes called "noninvasive" or "less invasive" methods because they do not require surgical invasion into the brain. We begin with methods of examining the structure of living brains.

### Computerized Axial Tomography

Is Alzheimer's disease associated with any loss of brain tissue? Is schizophrenia? One way to find out is to use **computerized axial tomography**, better known as a **CT scan** or **CAT scan** (Andreasen, 1988). A CT scan makes use of X rays, but X rays generally reveal very little contrast between one part of the brain and another. To increase the contrast, a physician begins by injecting a dye into the blood. The physician then places the person's head into a CT scanner like the one shown in Figure 4.35a. X rays are passed through the head and recorded by detectors on the opposite side. The CT scanner is rotated 1 degree at a time and the procedure is repeated until a measurement has been taken at each angle over 180 degrees. From the 180 measurements, a computer can reconstruct images of the brain. Figure 4.35b shows a CT scan of a normal brain; CT scans also show

Methods of
Investigating How
the Brain Controls
Behavior

**141**

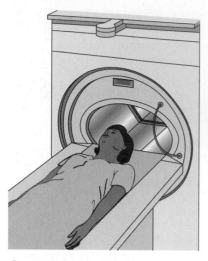

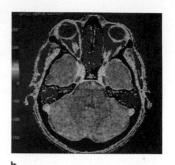

a

b

**Figure 4.35**
*(a) CT scanner. A person's head is placed into the device and then a rapidly rotating source sends X rays through the head while detectors on the opposite side make photographs. A computer then constructs an image of the brain. (b) A view of a normal human brain generated by computerized axial tomography (CT scanning). (Dan McCoy/Rainbow.)*

that the cortex is atrophied (shrunken) in patients with Alzheimer's disease and that the cerebral ventricles are enlarged in certain people with schizophrenia.

## Magnetic Resonance Imaging

A second method of examining brain anatomy in a living person is **magnetic resonance imaging** (MRI), also known as **nuclear magnetic resonance** (NMR). Magnetic resonance imaging can produce images with a high degree of resolution without exposing the brain to any radiation at all (Moonen, van Zijl, Frank, LeBihan, & Becker, 1990). The method uses the fact that any atom with an odd atomic weight—such as hydrogen—has an inherent rotation. Ordinarily, each atom's axis of rotation points in a random direction, but an outside magnetic field can align the axes of rotation. A radio frequency field can then make all these atoms move like tiny gyros. When the radio frequency field is turned off, the atomic nuclei release electromagnetic energy as they relax. By measuring that energy, MRI devices form an image of the brain, such as the one in Figure 4.36. Like CT scans, an MRI image can reveal structural defects such as an enlarged ventricle or an atrophied cortex.

## MEASUREMENT OF HUMAN BRAIN ACTIVITY

At any moment, certain areas of the brain are more active than others. For example, the visual cortex becomes more active during visual stimulation, and the olfactory bulb becomes more active during olfactory stimulation. Investigators have developed several noninvasive ways to measure changes in brain activity.

### The Electroencephalograph

A device called the **electroencephalograph (EEG)** records electrical activity of the brain via electrodes attached to the scalp. It enables investigators to make gross determinations of brain activity in humans and other animals without actually cutting into the skull. Electrodes, generally eight or fewer, are attached with glue or other adhesive to various locations on the surface of the scalp. The output of those electrodes is then amplified and recorded. From an examination of EEG records, an investigator can determine whether the person is asleep, dreaming, awake, or excited. Abnormalities in the EEG record may also suggest the presence of epilepsy, a tumor, or other medical problems located in a brain region under a particular electrode.

With the **evoked potential** method, experimenters use the EEG apparatus to record the brain's activity in response to sensory stimuli. Any sensory stimulus evokes electrical activity with a very short latency (delay) over a limited area of the cerebral cortex. If the individual reacts to the stimulus as meaningful and attention getting, another electrical response appears with a latency of about 0.3 second. Digression 4.3 describes a fascinating attempt to develop this method to communicate with totally paralyzed people (see also Figure 4.37).

## Regional Cerebral Blood Flow

When an area of the brain becomes more active, its blood supply, its use of glucose, and its synthesis of proteins increase. Researchers can capitalize on this fact by administering small amounts of certain radioactive chemicals and then monitoring these chemicals to measure the relative activity of various areas of the brain. We already encountered this strategy in autoradiography. With a few changes in procedure, it can be applied to a living human brain.

In the **regional cerebral blood flow** method (rCBF), an investigator uses a chemical that dissolves in the blood. One such substance is xenon ($^{133}$Xe), a radioactive gas. After a person inhales xenon, it enters the bloodstream. Because it does not react chemically with anything in the body, the xenon goes wherever the blood goes. Thus, the radioactivity recorded from a particular part of the brain will be proportional to the amount of blood flow to it. The investigator places the person's head in a device that records the release of radioactivity (see Figure 4.38). A computer then uses that information to construct an image of the brain in full color, like those in Figure 4.39. Areas with a great deal of radioactivity appear red. Areas of decreasing activity appear orange, yellow, green, blue, and violet. The areas that appear red are the most active; blue or violet areas are the least active.

A typical way of using the rCBF method is to ask a person to engage in a series of tasks, such as listening to music, solving a problem, and moving the fingers in a certain way. The investigator then uses the rCBF results to compare the type of brain activity that occurs during the various tasks (Andreasen, 1988). This method can be used to detect possible brain abnormalities in people with psychological disorders. For example, when most people sort cards according to a complex set of rules, activity in the prefrontal cortex increases. When people with schizophrenia perform the same task, many of them fail to show that increase (Berman, Zec, & Weinberger, 1986). Those who fail to show increased blood flow to the prefrontal cortex generally perform poorly on the task.

## PET Scans

**Positron-emission tomography** (PET) provides a high-resolution image of brain activity. PET scans rely on the fact that the radioactive decay of certain elements emits a positron. A positron is an antimatter particle with the same mass as an electron but an opposite charge.

First, the person receives an injection of glucose or some other chemical with a radioactive label of $^{11}$C, $^{18}$F, or $^{15}$O. (These chemicals have half-lives ranging from 110 minutes for $^{18}$F to 2 minutes for $^{15}$O. Because their half-lives are so

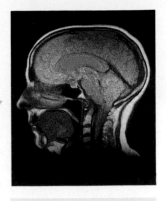

**Figure 4.36**
**A view of a living brain generated by magnetic resonance imaging**
*Any atom with an odd atomic weight (such as hydrogen) has an inherent rotation. An outside magnetic field can align the axes of rotation. A radio frequency field can then make all these atoms move like tiny gyros. When the radio frequency field is turned off, the atomic nuclei release electromagnetic energy as they relax. By measuring that energy, we can obtain an image of a structure such as the brain without damaging it. (Dan McCoy/Rainbow.)*

Methods of
Investigating How
the Brain Controls
Behavior

## Evoked Potentials as a Means of Communication

Suppose you became completely paralyzed. You cannot move your lips to talk; you cannot move your hands or feet to write. But you can still hear, see, and feel; you would like to be able to communicate with others. (If nothing else, you want to tell your physician where you hurt.) Would there be any way for you to communicate?

Maybe. If you can see, your brain will exhibit evoked responses to visual stimuli. When people see anything that is especially meaningful to them, they produce a special kind of evoked response called a *P300 wave*. It is called "P300" because it is positive (P) and occurs about 300 milliseconds following a stimulus. The P300 wave is generally considered an indication of attention or interest.

L. A. Farwell & E. Donchin (1988) set up a device that uses the P300 response. Suppose you are thinking of the word *neck* (because you want to tell someone that your neck hurts). The investigator shows you a display like the one in Figure 4.37 and asks you to pay special attention to the first letter of your word (*n*) and to silently count all the times it is highlighted. Various rows and columns are highlighted in a random order. If all goes according to plan, you show a clear P300 wave whenever the third column or the second row is lit, because they include the letter *n*. The information from your brain waves feeds to a computer which eventually determines that you are thinking of the letter *n*. You then go on to the letter *e*, and so forth. If your P300 waves are not entirely reliable, the computer may make a mistake—for example, it may say you were thinking of *d* when you were really thinking of *e*. You would then think of "*bksp*" (backspace) for your next letter, erasing the *d*.

This technology is a bit awkward, at least in its current stage of development. At best, it enables people to spell out 2 or 3 letters per minute. So it might take you 10 or 15 minutes to say "GIVE ME MORE PAIN MEDICINE." Still, the method enables people who cannot move any muscles at all to communicate.

Could this method be used to "read someone's mind"? Fortunately or unfortunately, it cannot read the mind of someone who does not want his or her mind to be read. The method works only if the person cooperates.

short, the investigators must make them in a cyclotron near the PET scanner. Cyclotrons are very large and very expensive. Consequently, PET scans are available only at the largest research hospitals.) The chemical chosen for injection depends on the nature of the research question. For example, glucose goes to the most active areas of the brain and is suitable for finding which areas of the brain are most active at a given moment. Drugs have affinities for particular receptors and are suitable for studies of the relative abundance of various types of synaptic receptors. When a radioactive label decays, releasing a positron, the positron immediately collides with a nearby electron. When a positron and an electron collide, they emit two gamma rays in exactly opposite directions. The person's head is surrounded by a set of gamma ray detectors. When the detectors record two gamma rays at the same time, they identify a spot halfway between those two detectors as the point of origin of the gamma rays. Using this information, a computer can determine how many gamma rays are coming from each spot in the brain—and, therefore, how much of the radioactively labeled chemical is located in each area (Phelps & Mazziotta, 1985). Figure 4.40 includes several examples of PET scans of the human brain.

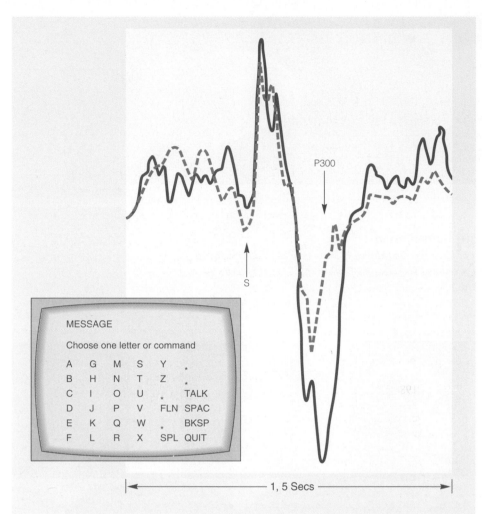

**MESSAGE**

Choose one letter or command

| A | G | M | S | Y | * | |
|---|---|---|---|---|---|---|
| B | H | N | T | Z | * | |
| C | I | O | U | * | TALK |
| D | J | P | V | FLN | SPAC |
| E | K | Q | W | * | BKSP |
| F | L | R | X | SPL | QUIT |

|← —————— 1, 5 Secs —————— →|

P300

S

**Figure 4.37**
**A computer display that enables people to communicate through brain waves**
*One row or column at a time is highlighted at random. The viewer who is trying to communicate one letter counts the number of times that letter is highlighted. Doing so makes that letter especially meaning ful and causes a P300 wave. (From Donchin, 1975.) The computer determines which letter most reliably causes a P300 wave and thereby determines which letter the person is thinking about. The extra symbols: SPAC = space, BKSP = backspace (delete previous letter), FLN = file name (used to store a message on a disk or call up a message already stored on a disk), SPL = special (a preprogrammed special message). The asterisks ( * ) are placeholders were additional options or messages can be added later. (From Farwell and Donchin, 1988.)*

**Figure 4.38**
*No, it's not a state-of-the-art hairdo. A person engages in a congnitive task while attached to an apparatus that records regional cerebral blood flow in the brain to determine which areas become more active, and by how much. (Burt Glinn/ Magnum.)*

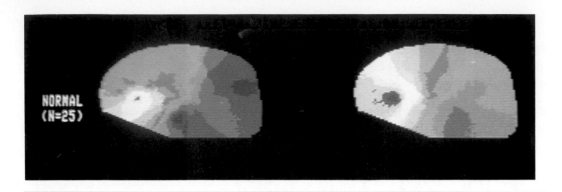

**Figure 4.39**
**An rCBF image of a normal human brain**
*Red indicates the greatest amount of blood flow and therefore brain activity. Yellow shows the next greatest amount, followed by green and blue. (Karen Berman and Daniel Weinberger, National Institute of Mental Health.)*

**Figure 4.40**
**PET scans of normal people, showing differences during various tasks**
*Red indicates the greatest level of brain activity; blue indicates the least.* **Left column:** *Brain activity with no special stimulation and during passive exposure to visual and auditory stimuli.* **Center column:** *Activity while listening to music, language, or both.* **Right column:** *Activity during performance of a cognitive task, an auditory memory task, and a task of moving fingers of the right hand in a fixed sequence. Arrows indicate regions of greatest activity. (Courtesy of Michael E. Phelps and John C. Mazziotta, University of California, Los Angeles, School of Medicine.)*

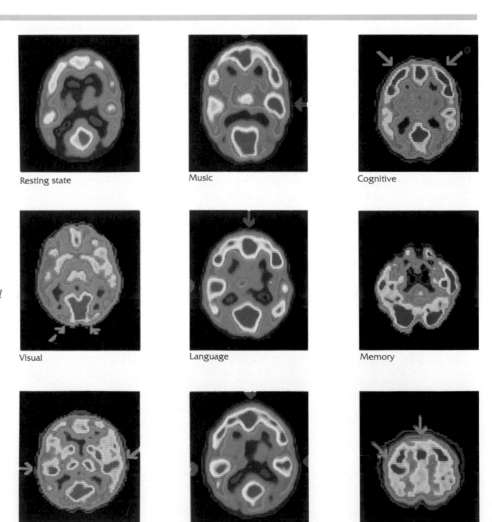

Resting state

Music

Cognitive

Visual

Language

Memory

Auditory

Language and music

Motor

PET scans enable physicians to localize tumors, certain types of epilepsy, and other disorders that alter the metabolic rate of a given brain area. They also enable researchers to answer some questions that could not be answered any other way. For example, Harry Chugani and Michael Phelps (1986) performed PET scans on infant brains to determine when various brain structures become active. They found that the thalamus and brain stem showed fairly high rates of activity by age 5 weeks. Most of the cerebral cortex and the outer part of the cerebellum were immature at 5 weeks but much more advanced by 3 months. The frontal lobes of the cerebral cortex showed little sign of activity until the age of $7\frac{1}{2}$ months.

The brain is a complex structure. You have encountered a great deal of terminology and many facts in this chapter. Do not become discouraged if you cannot remember everything. It will help to refer back to this chapter to review the anatomy of certain structures as you encounter their functions again in later chapters. Gradually, the material will become more familiar.

## SUMMARY

1. A stereotaxic device can enable an investigator to implant electrodes deep in the brain to make lesions or to stimulate neurons or record from them. (p. 134)

2. One of the most common methods of studying brain functioning is by examining the effects of lesions (brain damage). (p. 136)

3. Lesion studies help to locate the brain areas most critical to a particular behavioral function, but they do not indicate *how* that area controls behavior. (p. 137)

4. Autoradiography is a way of measuring the activity of various brain areas at a given time. Histochemistry is a method of identifying the distribution of a particular chemical in various parts of the brain. (p. 139)

5. To study the role of a particular type of cell, investigators examine individuals whose brain developed abnormally or they compare the behaviors of individuals at various stages of development. (p. 140)

6. CT scans and MRI images can reveal the structure of the brain in a living person. (p. 141)

7. Electroencephalographs, PET scans, and rCBF images can indicate the activity taking place in various parts of a human brain at a given time. (p. 142)

## REVIEW QUESTIONS

1. Describe the method for inserting an electrode into an area of an animal's brain that cannot be seen from the surface. (p. 134)

2. What are some of the difficulties in interpreting the results of a lesion experiment? (p. 137)

3. Describe methods used to study the structure of a living human brain. (p. 141)

4. Describe methods used to study the functioning of a living human brain. (p. 142)

## THOUGHT QUESTIONS

1. One of the many kinds of cells in the cerebral cortex is the stellate cell, which is an unusually small neuron. Stellate cells are more numerous in adults than in children and more numerous in humans than in other species. How might one determine what special role, if any, stellate cells have in the control of behavior? Describe at least three possibilities. (For one attempt to answer this question, see Scheibel & Scheibel, 1963.)

2. Multiple sclerosis destroys the myelin sheaths of axons. Why should we expect that evoked potentials would have longer than normal latencies in people with this disease?

## SUGGESTION FOR FURTHER READING

**Morihisa, J. M.** (1984). *Brain imaging in psychiatry*. Washington, DC: American Psychiatric Press. Provides more information on PET scans and similar methods.

## GLOSSARY

**ablation** removal of a structure

**anterior commissure** set of axons connecting the two cerebral hemispheres; smaller than the corpus callosum

**autonomic nervous system** set of neurons that regulates functioning of the internal organs

**autoradiography** method of injecting a radioactively labeled chemical and then mapping the distribution of radiation in the brain

**basal ganglia** set of subcortical forebrain structures including the caudate nucleus, putamen, and globus pallidus

**Bell-Magendie Law** observation that the dorsal roots of the spinal cord carry sensory information and that the ventral roots carry motor information toward the muscles and glands

**brain stem** the hindbrain, midbrain, and posterior central structures of the forebrain

**bregma** a point on the skull where the frontal and parietal bones join

**central canal** fluid-filled channel in the center of the spinal cord

**central nervous system (CNS)** the brain and the spinal cord

**central sulcus** a large groove in the surface of the primate cerebral cortex, separating frontal from parietal cortex

**cerebellum** a large, highly convoluted structure in the hindbrain

**cerebral cortex** outer layer of the mammalian forebrain

**cerebrospinal fluid (CSF)** liquid similar to blood serum, found in the ventricles of the brain and in the central canal of the spinal cord

**column** collection of cells having similar properties, arranged perpendicular to the laminae

**computerized axial tomography (CT scan, CAT scan)** method of visualizing a living brain by injecting a dye into the blood and then passing X rays through the head and recording them by detectors on the other side

**corpus callosum** large set of axons that connects the two hemispheres of the cerebral cortex

**cranial nerve** part of a set of nerves controlling sensory and motor information of the head, connecting to nuclei in the medulla, pons, midbrain, or forebrain

**delayed-response task** assignment in which an animal must respond on the basis of a signal it remembers but which is no longer present

**dermatome** area of skin connected to a particular spinal nerve

**dorsal root ganglion** set of sensory neuron somas on the dorsal side of the spinal cord

**double dissociation of function** demonstration that one lesion impairs behavior A more than it impairs behavior B, while a second lesion impairs behavior B more than it impairs behavior A

**electroencephalograph (EEG)** device that records the electrical activity of the brain through electrodes on the scalp

**endocrine gland** gland that releases hormones

**evoked potential** electrical activity recorded from the brain, usually via electrodes on the scalp, in response to sensory stimuli

**fimbria** band of axons along the medial surface of the hippocampus

**forebrain** the most anterior part of the brain, including the cerebral cortex and other structures

**fornix** tract of axons connecting the hippocampus with the hypothalamus and other areas

**frontal lobe** one of the lobes of the cerebral cortex

**ganglion** (plural: **ganglia**) a cluster of neuron cell bodies

**gray matter** areas of the nervous system with a high density of cell bodies and dendrites, with few myelinated axons

**hindbrain** most posterior part of the brain, including the medulla, pons, and cerebellum

**hippocampus** large forebrain structure between the thalamus and cortex

**hydrocephalus** accumulation of excessive fluid in the head

**hypothalamus** forebrain structure located just ventral to the thalamus

**immunohistochemistry** method of using the immune system to label particular types of tissues

**inferior colliculus** part of the auditory system located in the midbrain

**invertebrate** animal lacking a backbone

**Klüver-Bucy syndrome** condition in which monkeys with damaged temporal lobes fail to display normal fears and anxieties

**lamina** (plural: **laminae**) a layer of cells

**lesion** damage to a structure

**limbic system** interconnected set of subcortical structures in the forebrain, including the hypothalamus, hippocampus, amygdala, olfactory bulb, septum, other small structures, and parts of the thalamus and cerebral cortex

**magnetic resonance imaging** method of imaging a living brain by using a magnetic field and a radio frequency field to make atoms with odd atomic weights all rotate in the same direction and then removing those fields and measuring the energy the atoms release

**medulla** hindbrain structure located just above the spinal cord

**midbrain** middle part of the brain, including superior colliculus, inferior colliculus, tectum, and tegmentum

**neuroanatomy** the anatomy of the nervous system

**nuclear magnetic resonance** method of imaging a living brain by using a magnetic field and a radio frequency field to make atoms with odd atomic weights all rotate in the same direction and then removing those fields and measuring the energy the atoms release

**nucleus** a cluster of neurons within the central nervous system

**occipital lobe** one of the four lobes of the cerebral cortex

**parasympathetic nervous system** system of nerves innervating the internal organs, tending to conserve energy

**parietal lobe** one of the lobes of the cerebral cortex

**peripheral nervous system (PNS)** nerves outside the brain and spinal cord

**phrenology** nineteenth-century theory that personality types are related to bumps on the skull

**pituitary gland** endocrine gland whose secretions regulate the activity of many other hormonal glands

**pons** hindbrain structure, anterior or ventral to the medulla

**positron-emission tomography** a method of mapping activity in a living brain by recording the emission of radioactivity from injected chemicals

**postcentral gyrus** gyrus of the cerebral cortex just posterior to the central gyrus; a primary projection site for touch and other body sensations

**precentral gyrus** gyrus of cerebral cortex just anterior to the central sulcus; a primary point of origin for axons of the pyramidal system of motor control

**prefrontal cortex** the most anterior portion of the frontal lobe of the cerebral cortex

**prefrontal lobotomy** surgical disconnection of the prefrontal cortex from the rest of the brain

**raphe system** group of neurons in the pons and medulla whose axons extend throughout much of the forebrain

**regional cerebral blood flow** method of estimating activity of different areas of the brain by dissolving radioactive xenon in the blood and measuring radioactivity from different brain areas

**reticular formation** network of neurons in the medulla and higher brain areas, important for behavioral arousal

**sham lesion** control procedure for an experiment, in which an investigator inserts an electrode into a brain but does not pass a current

**somatic nervous system** nerves that convey messages from the sense organs to the CNS and from the CNS to muscles and glands

**spinal cord** portion of the central nervous system found within the spinal column

**spinal nerve** nerve that conveys information between the spinal cord and either sensory receptors or muscles in the periphery

**stereotaxic atlas** an atlas of the location of brain areas relative to external landmarks

**stereotaxic instrument** device for the precise placement of electrodes in the head

**subarachnoid space** area beneath the arachnoid membrane that surrounds the nervous system

**substantia nigra** midbrain area that gives rise to a dopamine-containing pathway

**superior colliculus** midbrain structure active in vision, visuomotor coordination, and other processes

**sympathetic nervous system** network of nerves innervating the internal organs that prepare the body for vigorous activity

**tectum** roof of the midbrain

**tegmentum** dorsal part of the midbrain

**temporal lobe** one of the lobes of the cerebral cortex

**thalamus** structure in the center of the forebrain

**ventricle** any of the four fluid-filled cavities in the brain

**white matter** area of the nervous system consisting mostly of myelinated axons

# CHAPTER FIVE

# Lateralization, Language, and Brain Disconnection Syndromes

## MAIN IDEAS

**1.** The left and right hemispheres of the brain communicate through the corpus callosum. After damage to the corpus callosum, each hemisphere has access to information only from the opposite half of the body and the opposite visual field.

**2.** In most people the left hemisphere is specialized for language and "analytical" processing. The right hemisphere is specialized for certain complex visual-spatial tasks and "synthetic" processing.

**3.** Damage in the left hemisphere can lead to two major kinds of language impairment. People with Broca's aphasia have difficulty speaking and have trouble using and understanding prepositions and other grammatical connectives. People with Wernicke's aphasia have trouble understanding language and recalling the names of objects, although they can still pronounce words fluently and string them together grammatically. Brain damage can also lead to more specialized language deficits.

*(Photo courtesy of Irene Pepperberg.)*

The human brain consists of neurons numbering in at least the tens of billions. Each of those neurons contributes to behavior and experience in its own specialized way. Yet each of us experiences the self as a unity, not a conglomerate of separate voices. Although your brain parts are many, your consciousness is one.

That unity of consciousness comes about through the connections between various brain parts. What happens if major connections are broken? In that case, although different parts of the brain continue their activities, they become unable to communicate with one another. One part of the brain does not know what another part of the brain is doing. When such disconnections occur in humans, they offer fascinating clues about how the brain operates and they raise equally fascinating unanswered questions.

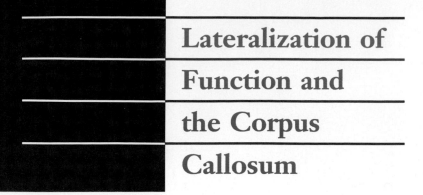

# Lateralization of Function and the Corpus Callosum

The left hemisphere of the cerebral cortex is connected to skin receptors mainly in the right half of the body, and it has the main control of muscles on the right side of the body. It sees only the right half of the world. The right hemisphere is connected to sensory receptors mainly on the left half of the body and controls muscles on the left side. It sees only the left half of the world. Each hemisphere has limited sensory input and motor control on its own side of the body. The degree of ipsilateral control (control of the same side of the body) varies from one individual to another. *Why* humans and all other vertebrates evolved so that each hemisphere controls the contralateral side of the body, instead of the ipsilateral side, no one knows.

Ordinarily, the left and right hemispheres exchange information through a set of axons called the **corpus callosum** (Figure 5.1; see also Figures 4.15 and 4.16) and through the smaller anterior commissure and hippocampal commissure. Each hemisphere has access to the information that passed initially to the opposite hemisphere within 7 to 13 milliseconds (Saron & Davidson, 1989).

The two hemispheres are not simply mirror images of each other. In most humans, the left hemisphere is specialized for the control of language. The right hemisphere has some functions that are more difficult to summarize, as we shall see later in this chapter. Such division of labor between the two hemispheres is known as **lateralization.** If it were not for the corpus callosum, your left hemisphere could talk only about the information from the right side of your body, and your right hemisphere could perform its functions only on the information from the left side of your body. Because of the corpus callosum, however, each hemisphere deals with the information from both sides of the body, although it may deal with information from one side slightly faster than the other. Only after damage to the corpus callosum (or to one hemisphere or the other) do we fully recognize the effects of lateralization.

Before we can discuss lateralization in any detail, we must consider some background material concerning the connections from the eyes to the brain. The connections from the left and right eyes to the left and right hemispheres are more complex than you might expect.

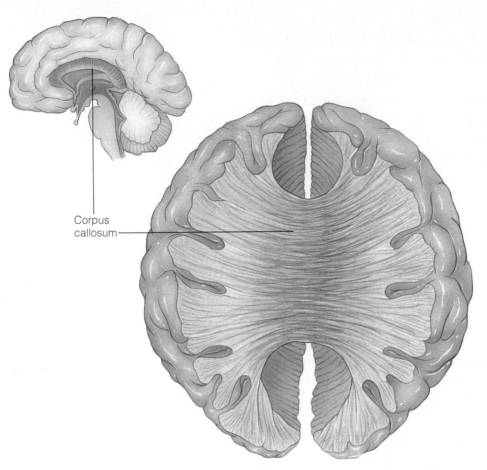

Figure 5.1
**Two views of the cor-
pus callosum, a large
set of axons conveying
information between
the two hemispheres**
*(Left) A sagittal section
through the human brain.
(Right) A dissection (viewed
from above) in which gray
matter has been removed to
expose the corpus callosum.*

Corpus
callosum

## CONNECTIONS OF THE EYES TO THE
## BRAIN'S LEFT AND RIGHT HEMISPHERES

Each hemisphere is also connected to the eyes in such a way that it gets input
from the opposite half of the visual world—that is, the left hemisphere sees the
right side of the world and the right hemisphere sees the left side of the world.
For rabbits and other species that have the left eye facing the left side of the
world and the right eye facing the right side of the world, the connections from
eye to brain are easy to describe: The left eye connects to the right hemisphere
and the right eye connects to the left hemisphere. *Your eyes are not connected to the
brain in that way.* Both of your eyes face forward. You can see the left side of the
world almost as well with your right eye as you can with your left eye.

Imagine how the eyes would be connected to the brain in a cyclops—the
mythical giant with just one eye, located in the middle of its forehead. Presume
that, like all other vertebrates, its left hemisphere sees the right half of the world
and its right hemisphere sees the left half of the world. In Figure 5.2, note that
light from the left half of the world passes through the pupil to strike the right
half of the cyclops's eye and that light from the right half of the world strikes the
left half of the cyclops's eye. Then the information goes from the left half of the

Lateralization
of Function and
the Corpus
Callosum

153

**Figure 5.2
Connections from
the eye to the brain
in a mythical being,
the cyclops**

*Notice that the left half of the
eye sees the right half of the
world and sends its information to the left half of the
brain. The right half of the
eye sees the left half of the
world and sends its information to the right half of the
brain. Human eyes are connected to the brain in this
same manner, except that we
have two such eyes.*

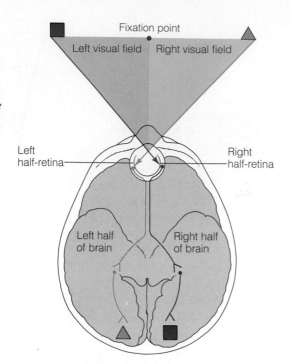

retina to the left half of the brain and from the right half of the retina to the right half of the brain.

Each human eye is located in front of the head, like the eye of a cyclops. Each of your eyes sends its information to the brain in the same way that the cyclops's eye does. That is, you have two cyclopean eyes.

Figure 5.3 illustrates the connections from the eyes to the human brain. Vision starts with stimulation of the receptors that line the *retina* on the back of each eye. Light from the **visual field**—the part of the world visible to the eyes at a particular moment—enters the eyes; light from the right visual field shines onto the left half of both retinas, and light from the left visual field shines onto the right half of both retinas. The left half of *each* retina connects to the left hemisphere; thus, the left hemisphere sees the right visual field. Similarly, the right half of each retina connects to the right hemisphere, which sees the left visual field. (If you have trouble remembering all this, recall that each human eye connects the same way as the cyclops's eye.) A small vertical strip down the center of each retina, covering about 5 degrees of visual arc, connects to both hemispheres (Innocenti, 1980). In Figure 5.3, note how half of the axons from each eye cross to the opposite side of the brain at the **optic chiasm** (literally, the "optic cross").

Information about each visual field projects to just one side of the cerebral cortex. The auditory system handles information differently. Although each ear receives sound waves from just one side of the head, it sends input to both sides of the brain, though somewhat more strongly to the opposite side. (The reason for this is that people locate sounds in space by comparing the input from the two ears. Any part of the brain that contributes to localizing sounds must receive input from both ears.)

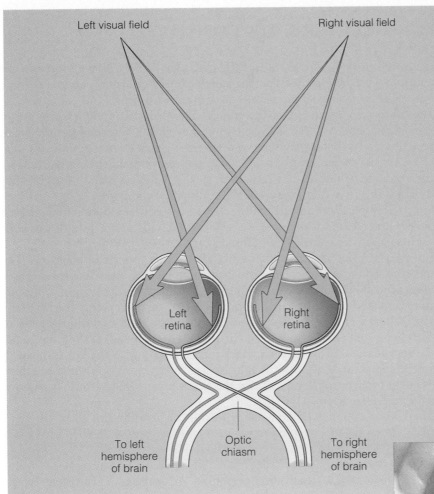

Left visual field

Right visual field

Left retina

Right retina

To left hemisphere of brain

Optic chiasm

To right hemisphere of brain

a

**Figure 5.3**

*(a) Route of visual input to the two hemispheres of the brain. Note that the left hemisphere is connected to the left half of each retina and thus gets visual input from the right half of the world, while the opposite occurs with the right hemisphere. (b) Close-up of olfactory bulbs and the optic chiasm. At the optic chiasm, axons from the right half of the left retina cross to the right hemisphere, and axons from the left half of the right retina cross to the left hemisphere. (Photo courtesy of Dr. Dana Copeland.)*

Olfactory bulbs

Optic nerves (cut)

Optic chiasm

Blood vessels

b

# EFFECTS OF CUTTING THE CORPUS CALLOSUM

Damage to the corpus callosum blocks the exchange of information between the two hemispheres. A few people have had their corpus callosum cut as a therapy for severe epilepsy. Epilepsy can usually be treated with drugs, but some rare individuals fail to respond to any of the antiepileptic drugs. If their seizures are so severe and so frequent as to be incapacitating, they and their attending physicians may be willing to try almost anything to relieve the epilepsy. In certain cases, surgeons have cut the corpus callosum. The idea is to prevent epileptic seizures from crossing from one hemisphere to the other, so that when seizures do occur, they should be less severe because they will affect only half the body.

In fact, the operation has generally relieved the epilepsy better than anyone had initially expected. Not only are the seizures limited to one side of the body but they also occur less often than before the operation.

How does severing the corpus callosum affect other aspects of behavior? The surgeons who conducted the operations had some idea of what to expect, based on studies with nonhuman animals. Following damage to the corpus callosum, laboratory animals show normal sensation, control of movement, learning and memory, and motivated behaviors. Their responses are abnormal only when sensory stimuli are limited to one side of the body. For example, if they see something in the left visual field, they can reach out to it only with the left forepaw. If they learn to do something with the left forepaw, they cannot do the same thing with the right forepaw, unless they learn the skill all over again with that paw and the left hemisphere (Sperry, 1961).

People who have undergone damage to the corpus callosum show the same tendencies. They can still walk, swim, and carry on other motor activities that use both sides of the body, although their coordination is sometimes slow and awkward (Zaidel & Sperry, 1977). They suffer little or no impairment of overall intellectual performance, motivation, emotion, or language. However, careful experiments by Roger Sperry and his students (Nebes, 1974) revealed subtle behavioral effects when stimuli were limited to one side of the body or the other.

In one typical experiment, a split-brain patient stared straight ahead as pictures were flashed on the left side of a screen (see Figure 5.4). When the corpus callosum is destroyed, any information that enters one hemisphere cannot pass to the other. Thus, the information went only to the right hemisphere. The picture stayed on the screen long enough for the person to see it clearly in the left visual field but not long enough for the person to move his or her eyes to bring the picture into the other visual field. The experimenter then told the person (both hemispheres could hear the instructions) to put one hand behind a cloth curtain, to feel the ten or so objects behind the curtain, and to hold up the object that had just been shown on the screen. Split-brain patients consistently performed correctly if permitted to use their left hand (controlled by the right hemisphere, which saw the display on the screen). But if they were told to use their right hand, accuracy fell to the chance level. When the experimenter flashed the display on the right side of the screen, the right hand performed correctly and the left hand failed.

For most people, the ability to speak depends on the left hemisphere of the cerebral cortex. In split-brain people, when a display was flashed in the right visual field, thus going to the left hemisphere, the person could name the object easily. But when it was flashed in the left visual field, thus going to the right hemisphere, the person could not name or describe the object, although he or she

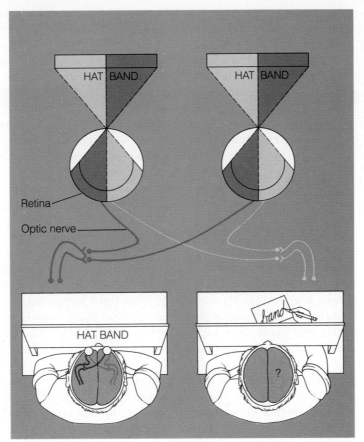

**Figure 5.4**
**Demonstration of the effects of damage to the corpus callosum**
*When the word* hatband *is flashed on a screen, a woman with a split brain can report only what her left hemisphere saw,* band. *However, with her left hand she can point to a hat, which is what the right hemisphere saw.*

was able to point to it with the left hand. The person could even say, "I don't know what it is," while simultaneously pointing to the correct choice with the left hand. (Of course, a split-brain person who *watched* the left hand pick up an object in the center or right visual field could then name the object.)

## Do Split-Brain People Have Two Minds or One?

The two hemispheres of a split-brain person can process information and answer questions independently of each other. Indeed, they seem at times to act as if they are separate people sharing one body. One person sometimes found himself buttoning his shirt with one hand while unbuttoning it with the other hand. Another person would pick up a newspaper with the right hand, only to have the left hand (controlled by the less verbal hemisphere) put it down. Repeatedly the right hand picked it up; an equal number of times the left hand put it down, until finally the left hand threw it to the floor (Preilowski, 1975).

One split-brain person described his experience—or, rather, his left hemisphere described his experience—as follows (Dimond, 1979): "If I'm reading I can hold the book in my right hand; it's a lot easier to sit on my left hand, than to hold it with both hands. . . . You tell your hand—I'm going to turn so many pages in a book—turn three pages—then somehow the left hand will pick up two

Lateralization
of Function and
the Corpus
Callosum

pages and you're at page 5, or whatever. It's better to let it go, pick it up with the right hand, and then turn to the right page. With your right hand you correct what the left has done."

Such conflicts are reported to be more common in the first months after surgery than they are later. The corpus callosum does not grow back (Bogen, Schultz, & Vogel, 1988). However, the brain learns to use certain subcortical connections between the left and right halves of the brain (Myers & Sperry, 1985). Also, the hemispheres gradually find ways to cooperate with each other, sometimes in surprising ways. One person who was being tested with the standard apparatus shown in Figure 5.4 suddenly seemed able to name what he saw in either visual field. However, the right hemisphere could answer correctly only when the answers were restricted to two possibilities (such as yes/no or true/false) and only when the subject was allowed to correct himself immediately after making a guess. Suppose something was flashed in the left visual field. The experimenter might ask, "Was it a letter of the alphabet?" The left (speaking) hemisphere would take a guess: "Yes." If that was correct, the person would get credit for a correct answer. But if the left hemisphere guessed incorrectly, the right hemisphere, which saw the display on the screen and heard the left hemisphere's guess, knew the guess was wrong. The right hemisphere would then make the face frown. (Both hemispheres can control facial muscles on both sides of the face.) The left hemisphere, feeling the frown, would say, "Oh, I'm sorry, I meant no." If such corrections are permitted, split-brain patients can guess the correct answers consistently.

In certain cases the two hemispheres have been able to exchange information so quickly that some psychologists suspect the hemispheres may be passing information through the anterior commissure or the hippocampal commissure, which were not divided when the corpus callosum was cut. For example, when subjects focus on a dot on a screen while a red or green patch is flashed on each side of the screen, they cannot say whether the two patches were the same color. They can, however, press a button to indicate that at least one patch was green and a different button to indicate that neither patch was green (Sergent, 1986).

As a rule, having a split brain confers a disadvantage on some aspects of behavior and has no apparent effect on other aspects. Under unusual conditions, however, it yields an advantage by enabling the two halves of the brain to pay attention to different things at the same time. In one experiment, subjects were asked to watch a screen while a dot flashed about among four points in the left visual field and another dot simultaneously flashed about among four different points in the right visual field, as Figure 5.5 shows. Then another dot was flashed about among four points in one visual field or the other and the subject was asked whether it traced the same pattern as the dot previously seen in the same visual field. For a normal person, this is a nearly impossible task because the unified brain becomes confused between what has been presented in the two visual fields. Split-brain subjects get the correct answer about 75 percent of the time, however (Holtzman & Gazzaniga, 1985), because each hemisphere sees only one visual field and suffers no interference or confusion.

Does the split-brain person have one mind or two? Investigators are not in complete agreement, and the question is complicated by our inability to say exactly what we mean by *mind*. But apparently each hemisphere can answer certain questions on its own, and the two hemispheres sometimes exchange information by facial signals or other means that two separate people might use for communication. Thus, the two hemispheres of a split-brain person seem to be at least partly independent.

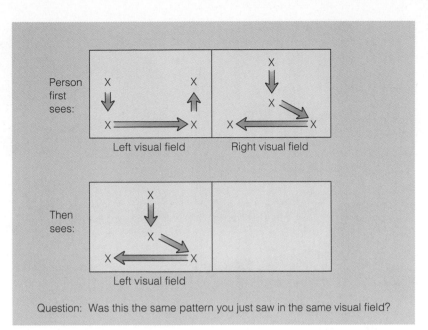

Person first sees:

Left visual field          Right visual field

Then sees:

Left visual field

Question: Was this the same pattern you just saw in the same visual field?

## Functions of the Right Hemisphere of the Cerebral Cortex

When investigators discovered that the left hemisphere controls speech, most ob-servers thought of the right hemisphere as something like a vice president. That is, it supported the "major" hemisphere in various ways but was definitely subor-dinate to it. Later studies, including some with split-brain patients, indicate that the right hemisphere is capable of more than researchers had assumed.

First, although it usually cannot control speech or writing, the right hemi-sphere does understand simple speech and can often make sense of a written word (Levy, 1983). A split-brain person who hears a verbal description of an object can feel some objects with the left hand (right hemisphere) and pick up the described object. Such a person can do the same after seeing the name of the object in only the left visual field. In a few split-brain patients, the left hand can write or can ar-range letter blocks to describe information known only by the right hemisphere (Gazzaniga, LeDoux, & Wilson, 1977; Levy, Nebes, & Sperry, 1971). Such peo-ple can do so even though their left hemisphere is in complete control of spoken language.

In people with an intact, healthy brain, the right hemisphere is less active than the left hemisphere during speech (Papanicolaou, Moore, Deutsch, Levin, & Eisenberg, 1988). However, it contributes to the emotional content of speech. People who have suffered damage to the right hemisphere speak with less than the normal amount of inflection and expression (Shapiro & Danly, 1985). They also have trouble interpreting the emotions that other people express through their tone of voice (Tucker, 1981). And they may fail to appreciate humor and irony in speech.

The right hemisphere may be more specialized for emotional expression in general than the left hemisphere is. After damage to the right hemisphere, people have some trouble both in producing facial expressions of emotion and in under-standing other people's facial expressions (Borod, Koff, Lorch, & Nicholas, 1986;

Lateralization
of Function and
the Corpus
Callosum

**Figure 5.6
Two faces made by
combining half of a
smiling face with half
of a neutral face**
*Which one looks happier to
you? Your answer may sug-
gest which hemisphere of your
brain is dominant for interpreting emotional expressions.
(From Levy et al., 1983.)*

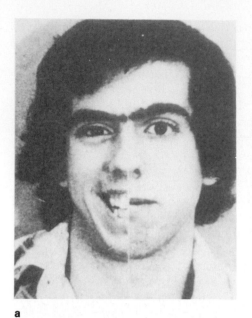 

a                                         b

Kolb & Taylor, 1981; Rinn, 1984). Moreover, according to the studies of Jerre
Levy and her colleagues on normal (brain-intact) people, when the left and right
hemispheres perceive different emotions in someone's face, the response of the
right hemisphere dominates. For example, examine the faces in Figure 5.6. Each
of these was made by combining half of a smiling face with half of a neutral face.
Which face looks happier to you, face A or face B? Most people choose face A,
the one with the smile on the viewer's left (Heller & Levy, 1981; Hoptman &
Levy, 1988). Similarly, a frown on the viewer's left looks sadder than a frown on
the viewer's right (Sackeim, Putz, Vingiano, Coleman, & McElhiney, 1988).

The right hemisphere also appears to be more adept than the left hemisphere
at recognizing and dealing with complex visual patterns. Neurologists have long
known that people who suffer damage to the right hemisphere have difficulty
finding their way between one place and another and have trouble recognizing
faces. Split-brain patients have given us additional information about these specialized functions of the right hemisphere.

For example, a split-brain person can arrange puzzle pieces more accurately
with the left hand than with the right. Although the person's right hand can write
words much better than the left, the left hand does better at drawing a box, a bicycle, and similar objects.

In one experiment, split-brain subjects were asked to feel a three-dimensional
object without looking at it (Levy-Agresti & Sperry, 1968). Then they were
shown two-dimensional representations of objects and were told to point to the
two-dimensional pattern corresponding to the object they felt. The subjects were
much more accurate when using the left hand for this task than when using the
right. Thus, the right hemisphere appears to be specialized for complex visual and
spatial tasks.

The right hemisphere is not necessary for *all* visual and spatial tasks, however. In one study, stroke patients who had suffered damage to the right hemisphere performed about as well as normal people did at estimating the positions

of nine major cities on an outline map of the United States. They were also as good as normal people were at estimating the distances between points on a sheet of paper. However, they were greatly impaired when they had to combine these tasks by imagining the positions of those same nine cities and estimating the distances between them (Morrow, Ratcliff, & Johnston, 1986). Evidently, the right hemisphere is more essential for tasks that require internal representations of visual and spatial information—imagination, we might say.

How can we best describe the difference in functions between the left and right hemispheres? It is partly but not entirely correct to say that the left hemisphere is specialized for language and the right hemisphere for complex visual functions, spatial functions, and certain aspects of emotions. For example, most people can identify a melody more easily when listening with the left ear (right hemisphere) than when listening with the right ear. Professional musicians, however, can identify melodies better when listening with the right ear, suggesting that they process the music primarily in the left hemisphere (Shanon, 1980). Evidently what the left hemisphere does best extends to some other tasks besides language. According to John Bradshaw and Norman Nettleton (1981), the left hemisphere is sequential, analytic, and time dependent. That is, regardless of whether it is dealing with speech, music, or other stimuli, the left hemisphere treats the stimuli as a sequence of units. The right hemisphere, in contrast, is "synthetic" and "holistic," by which Bradshaw and Nettleton mean that it deals with overall patterns instead of breaking them into units. Unfortunately, this description of the left and right hemispheres may be too vague to be useful (Zaidel, 1983). Describing exactly how the left and right hemispheres differ remains difficult.

## Evidence for Hemispheric Specializations in Intact People

Although the differences between the two hemispheres are more apparent after damage to the corpus callosum, certain differences can be demonstrated even in an intact person—that is, a person without brain damage. These differences are, however, generally so small and inconsistent that they emerge only as statistical trends with a large number of people.

For example, when left-hemisphere activity increases, the eyes tend to turn toward the right and the person is likely to move the right hand. (Conversely, when the right hemisphere is activated, the eyes move left and the person tends to move the left hand.) Here is a demonstration: When people are trying to answer a verbal question, such as "What does this proverb mean?"—a left-hemisphere task—they gaze to the right more often than they gaze to the left. When trying to answer a spatial question, such as "Imagine your home and try to count the number of windows," they are more likely to turn their eyes to the left (Kinsbourne, 1972). Similarly, when they try to arrange block letters to form as many words as possible, they make mostly right-hand movements; when they try to arrange puzzle pieces to make a picture, they make mostly left-hand movements (Hampson & Kimura, 1984). These results apply primarily to right-handers; left-handers give inconsistent results. Even in right-handers the effect is not dependable, however. People are more likely to gaze in the predicted direction if the experimenter stands behind them instead of in front of them (Ehrlichmann & Weinberger, 1978). When standing in front, the experimenter may distract people or inhibit their natural behaviors.

A related example: A person stares at a fixation point straight ahead and the experimenter flashes a simple stimulus either to the left or to the right of the fixation point. The stimulus (shown in Figure 5.7) is a horizontal line intersected

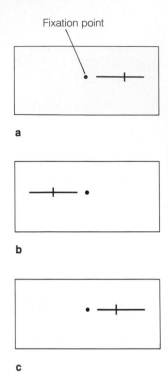
Fixation point

**a**

**b**

**c**

**Figure 5.7**

*An intact person who sees these displays only briefly in one visual field tends to neglect part of the line. For example, when the left hemisphere sees the top display, it attends mostly to the right half of the line, neglecting the left half. Consequently, the person says that the vertical line was in the center of the horizontal line.*

by a shorter vertical line. The person's task is to say whether the vertical line is in the left, right, or center of the horizontal line. Because the stimulus is visible for only 0.13 second, the task is difficult and people make many errors. When the line is in the right visual field, they tend to neglect the left half of the horizontal line, and when it is in the left visual field, they tend to neglect the right half of the line (Reuter-Lorenz, Kinsbourne, & Moscovitch, 1990). For example, a person who sees the display in Figure 5.7a is likely to say that the vertical line is in the middle of the horizontal line. Note the similarity between these results and the effects of damage to the parietal cortex, as discussed in Chapter 4 (p. 125): After damage to the right parietal cortex, people neglect the left side of a line. When a stimulus is flashed in the right visual field, sending information to the left hemisphere, the left hemisphere is highly active, the right hemisphere is not, and again the person tends to neglect the left side of the line.

Another example: Speaking triggers activity in the hand controlled by the hemisphere that controls speech. Most people use many hand gestures while speaking, often without being aware that they are doing so. Most right-handers move the right hand more actively while they speak; left-handers vary in which hand they move more actively (Kimura, 1973a, 1973b).

Here is a demonstration you can try yourself: Count how many times a child can tap the index finger of one hand within 1 minute; then repeat with the other hand. Now repeat the measurements while the child taps a finger and talks at the same time. For most right-handers, talking decreases the tapping rate with the right hand more than it does with the left hand (Kinsbourne & McMurray, 1975). Evidently, it is more difficult to do two things at once if both activities depend on the same hemisphere. (Adults may tap too fast for you to count the taps accurately. Have the person tap with a pencil on a piece of paper; later you can count the markings.)

Another demonstration: Find a stick that you can balance on one hand, but only with difficulty. See how long you can balance it with each hand while talking and compare it to the times without talking. Most right-handers find that talking interferes with their performance with the right hand but not with the left (Hicks, 1975). Again, left-handers are more variable.

## Hemispheric Differences and Cognitive Style

Occasionally you may hear someone say something like "I don't do well in science courses because those are left-brain courses and I am a right-brain person." That kind of statement is based on two reasonable scientific premises and one doubtful assumption. The scientific premises are that (1) the left hemisphere is specialized for verbal or analytic processing and the right hemisphere is specialized for nonverbal or synthetic processing and (2) certain tasks evoke greater activity in one hemisphere than in the other. The doubtful assumption is that a given individual relies consistently on one hemisphere or the other, regardless of the task or situation.

That assumption is at best a great overstatement, because anyone with an intact brain makes use of both hemispheres for every task. Granted, the left hemisphere may be more active for some tasks and the right hemisphere may be more active for other tasks, but on any task a normal person uses both hemispheres. Furthermore, the relative balance of activity varies from time to time and from task to task. A person will rely mostly on the right hemisphere at one time and mostly on the left hemisphere at another time.

Finally, what evidence do you suppose a person has for a statement like "I do poorly in science courses because I am a right-brain person"? Did the person undergo a CT scan or PET scan to determine that the right hemisphere was larger than the left, or that it had a higher metabolic rate? Not likely. Generally when people say "I am right-brained," all they mean is that they perform better on creative tasks than on logical tasks. Therefore the statement really boils down to "I do poorly in science courses because I do poorly in science courses."

# DEVELOPMENT OF LATERALIZATION AND ITS RELATIONSHIP TO HANDEDNESS

Because in most people language depends primarily on the left hemisphere, it is natural to ask whether the left hemisphere is anatomically different from the right. If so, is this difference present before speech develops, or is it a result of speech? What is the relationship between handedness and hemispheric dominance for speech?

## Anatomical Differences Between the Hemispheres

For many years biological psychologists believed that the left and right hemispheres were anatomically the same, in spite of their differences in action. Then Norman Geschwind and Walter Levitsky (1968) reported that one section of the temporal cortex, called the **planum temporale** (PLAY-num tem-poh-RAH-lee), is larger in the left than in the right hemisphere for 65 percent of people (Figure 5.8). The size is about equal for 24 percent and larger in the right hemisphere for 11 percent. The size differences for this area are reasonably large; in fact, they are visible to the naked eye if one knows where to look. The planum temporale includes areas important for language.

The planum temporale is evidently larger in the left than in the right hemisphere even before language develops. Sandra Witelson and Wazir Pallie (1973) examined the brains of fourteen infants who had died before the age of 3 months. In twelve of the fourteen, the planum temporale was larger in the left than in the right hemisphere—on the average, about twice as large. Children who suffer brain damage during their first 4 years of life show more language impairment after left-hemisphere damage than after right-hemisphere damage (Aram & Ekelman, 1986).

Indeed, hand preference, which is largely but imperfectly related to speech lateralization, begins to emerge at an earlier age than one might suppose. Most infants younger than 3 months old hold a rattle longer in their right hand than in their left hand before dropping it (Caplan & Kinsbourne, 1976). These are presumably the children who grow up to be right handed, although the investigators did not report a long-term follow-up on these children.

One convenient indicator of the size of the planum temporale is the length of the **Sylvian**, or **lateral, fissure** (one of the major fissures, or folds, on the side of the cortex). In humans, the Sylvian fissure is 14 percent larger on the left side than on the right, on the average. Figure 5.14, later in this chapter, shows this fissure (p. 175). In chimpanzees, the fissure is only 5 percent larger on the left side; in monkeys, the two sides are practically equal (Yeni-Komshian & Benson, 1976).

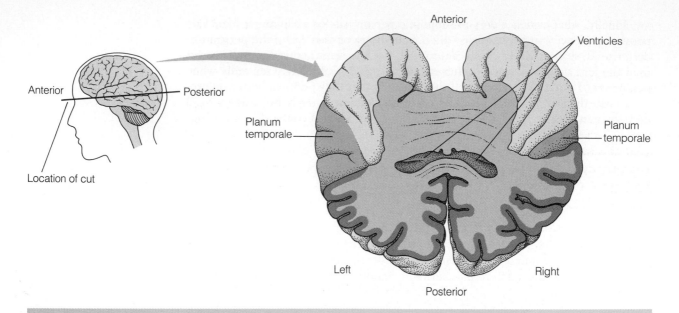

Anterior

Posterior

Anterior

Ventricles

Planum temporale

Planum temporale

Location of cut

Left

Right

Posterior

**Figure 5.8**
**Horizontal section through a human brain just above the surface of the temporal lobe**
*Note that the planum temporale, an area critical for speech comprehension, is substantially larger in the left hemisphere than in the right hemisphere. (From Geschwind & Levitsky, 1968.)*

## Maturation of the Corpus Callosum

The corpus callosum matures gradually over the first 5 to 10 years of human life, making it one of the last brain structures to reach full maturity (Trevarthen, 1974). The developmental process is not so much a matter of growing new axons, however, as it is of selecting certain axons and discarding others.

At an early stage of development, the brain generates far more axons in the corpus callosum than it will have at maturity (Ivy & Killackey, 1981; Killackey & Chalupa, 1986). The reason for this is that any two neurons connected via the corpus callosum need to have corresponding functions. For example, suppose a given neuron in the occipital cortex of the left hemisphere responds to light in the very center of the retina. It should be connected to a right-hemisphere neuron that responds to light in that same location. During early embryonic development, the genes cannot specify exactly where those two neurons will be. Therefore, a great many connections are made across the corpus callosum, but only those axons that happen to connect very similar cells survive (Innocenti & Caminiti, 1980).

But how does a neuron "know" that it is connected to another neuron with properties similar to its own? Apparently a neuron recognizes whether the input from the other neuron is synchronized with its own activity. Cats ordinarily have a certain number of connections across the corpus callosum to link the visual areas of the brain. If either or both eyelids are sewn shut for the first 3 months of life, they develop fewer than the normal number of axons across the corpus callosum. The same result occurs if their eye muscles are damaged early in life so they cannot focus both eyes in the same direction at the same time (Innocenti, Frost, & Illes, 1985). In other words, experience sharpens the selection of axons across the corpus callosum, enabling the right axons to survive. Abnormal experiences cause a reduction in the number of axons and other abnormalities.

Because the connections across the human corpus callosum take years to develop their mature adult pattern, the behavior of young children resembles that of split-brain adults in some situations. A 9-week-old infant who has one arm re-

5 / Lateralization, Language, and Brain Disconnection Syndromes

164

strained will never reach across the midline of the body to pick up a toy on the other side (Provine & Westerman, 1979). Apparently at that age each hemisphere has little access to the sensory information or motor control of the opposite hemisphere. By age 17 weeks, however, infants will reach across the midline to pick up a toy more often than not.

In one study, 3- and 5-year-old children were asked to feel two fabrics, either with the same hand or with the opposite hands, and say whether they were the same or different kinds of material. The 5-year-olds did equally well with one hand or with two. The 3-year-olds made 90 percent more errors with different hands than with the same hand (Galin, Johnstone, Nakell, & Herron, 1979). The likely interpretation is that the corpus callosum matures sufficiently between ages 3 and 5 to make the comparison of stimuli across the two hands much easier by age 5.

## Development Without a Corpus Callosum

Rarely, for unknown reasons, the corpus callosum fails to form. The problem may be genetic or perhaps a toxin to which the mother was exposed during pregnancy. Whatever the cause, a person born without a corpus callosum develops differently from other people and is in many ways different from a person who once had a corpus callosum and then lost it in split-brain surgery (Chiarello, 1980).

People born without a corpus callosum can perform some tasks that split-brain patients fail. They can verbally describe what they feel with either hand or what they see in either visual field; they can also feel one object with the left hand and another with the right hand and say whether they are the same or different (Bruyer et al., 1985; Sanders, 1989).

How do people born without a corpus callosum manage to perform tasks that usually require a corpus callosum? One possible explanation is that each hemisphere develops speech; thus the left hemisphere describes what the right hand feels and the right hemisphere describes what the left hand feels. However, the available evidence argues against any right-hemisphere speech in these people (Lassonde, Bryden, & Demers, 1990). A second possible explanation is that each hemisphere develops pathways connecting it to both sides of the body. Thus the left (speaking) hemisphere could feel both the left hand and the right hand. A third possibility is that people born without a corpus callosum develop larger-than-normal connections elsewhere in the brain. In addition to the corpus callosum, people have two other major axonal connections in the forebrain: The **anterior commissure** (Figure 4.15, p. 113) connects the hemispheres in the anterior part of the cerebral cortex, and the **hippocampal commissure** connects the left hippocampus to the right hippocampus (Figure 5.9). In most people these commissures do not convey enough information to enable the left hemisphere to describe what the right hemisphere sees or feels. But perhaps in people who lack a corpus callosum the other commissures develop beyond the usual level.

Although people born without a corpus callosum do not show the usual effects of split-brain surgery, they are nevertheless far from normal. For example, although they can coordinate the movements of their two hands to lace and tie their shoes, they do so very slowly (Sauerwein, Lassonde, Cardu, & Geoffroy, 1981). Their language abilities in general are impaired, even on tasks that have nothing to do with the left versus right sides of the body. The exact language impairment varies from one person to another, but may include difficulty thinking of words that rhyme with a particular word (Temple, Jeeves, & Vilarroya, 1989) or understanding passive sentences (Jeeves & Temple, 1987; Sanders, 1989). Evi-

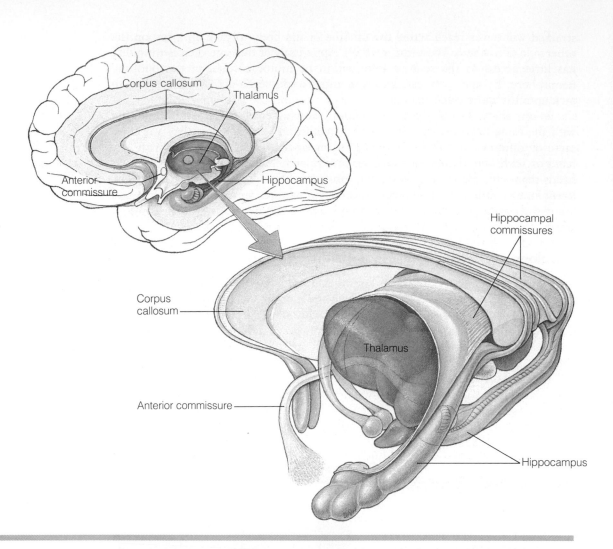

Corpus callosum

Thalamus

Anterior commissure

Hippocampus

Hippocampal commissures

Corpus callosum

Thalamus

Anterior commissure

Hippocampus

**Figure 5.9**
**Location of the anterior commissure and hippocampal commissures in three-dimensional perspective**

*These commissures exchange information between the two hemispheres, as does the larger corpus callosum. (Based on Nieuwenhuys, 1988, and others.)*

5 / Lateralization, Language, and Brain Disconnection Syndromes

**166**

dently the "cost" of reorganizing the brain without a corpus callosum is that the left hemisphere does not develop its full, normal language capacities.

Moreover, people born without a corpus callosum are slow and clumsy on many motor tasks. For example, when they reach out to pick up an object, they do not begin to mold their fingers and thumb into the correct position until they actually contact the object (Jeeves & Silver, 1988). Other people mold them into position while the hand is on the way to the object. A possible explanation is that in people who develop without a corpus callosum, each hand may constantly receive conflicting commands from the two hemispheres of the brain.

## Handedness and Its Relationship to Language Dominance

About 10 percent of all people are left handed or ambidextrous. (Here we shall consider ambidextrous people to be left handed. Indeed, most left-handers are partly ambidextrous.) Of all the surviving prehistoric drawings and paintings that show people using a tool with one hand or the other, more than 90 percent show them using the right hand (Coren & Porac, 1977). Thus, right-handedness appears to be part of our ancient heritage, not a recent development.

The brain of a left-handed person is different from that of a right-handed person, but it is not simply the reverse. For about 99 percent of right-handed people, the left hemisphere is strongly dominant for speech. The planum temporale and certain other areas are decidedly larger in the left hemisphere than in the right, and left-hemisphere damage greatly impairs language while right-hemisphere damage barely affects it. In only a very few left-handers is the right hemisphere as dominant as the left hemisphere is for right-handers. The right hemisphere is dominant for speech in an estimated 30 to 40 percent of left-handers, while the left hemisphere is dominant in the others (Levy, 1982). These figures may be misleading, however. Most left-handers, both those with left speech dominance and those with right speech dominance, have at least partial control of language by both hemispheres (Satz, 1979). Damage to either hemisphere impairs language. The corpus callosum is about 11 percent thicker in left-handers than in right-handers, presumably facilitating cross-hemisphere communication and bilateral representation of functions (Witelson, 1985).

Why are certain people left handed and others right handed? Genetics is a factor but not the only determinant. The chance of having a left-handed child is higher if both parents are left handed, but the family data on handedness do not suggest any simple Mendelian effects.

Norman Geschwind and Albert Galaburda (1985) proposed that handedness is under the control of unidentified biological factors, possibly hormones, that also modify the development of other parts of the body. They found that left-handers are more likely than right-handers to have neuronal abnormalities in the left hemisphere, dyslexia, childhood allergies, migraine headaches in adulthood, and disorders of the immune system. They are also more likely to stutter than right-handers are. Left-handers are not always at a disadvantage, however; more left-handers than right-handers excel at mathematics and architecture.

These observations do *not* mean that left-handedness causes migraine headaches, immune disorders, and so forth, any more than they mean that migraine headaches and immune disorders cause left-handedness. They do suggest that the factors leading to left-handedness *in some individuals* overlap the factors that lead to allergies, migraine headaches, and immune disorders.

But what might those factors be? Geschwind and Galaburda suggested the male hormone testosterone (see Figure 5.10). Left-handedness is more common in males than it is in females; so are allergies, immune disorders, stuttering, and the other related tendencies. According to Geschwind and Galaburda, high levels of testosterone may delay the maturation of the left hemisphere and may also retard the growth of the thymus gland and other structures of the immune system. The results could include a tendency toward left-handedness, well-developed right-hemisphere functions but less developed left-hemisphere functions, and increased vulnerability to a variety of disorders.

*— for presentation*

This hypothesis remains speculative. One problem is that it seems to imply a large difference between males and females in their hand preference, brain lateralization, and likelihood of developing various disorders. The sexes differ, to be sure, but the differences are not enormous. Although investigators can demonstrate certain differences between male brains and female brains *on the average*, the variations from one individual to another are much larger than the average differences between males and females (Byne, Bleier, & Houston, 1988).

Geschwind and Galaburda's hypothesis is a most provocative one. Perhaps further research will confirm that it is correct about the role of testosterone; if not, it will at least spur the search for some other underlying factor linking left-handedness and a variety of other conditions.

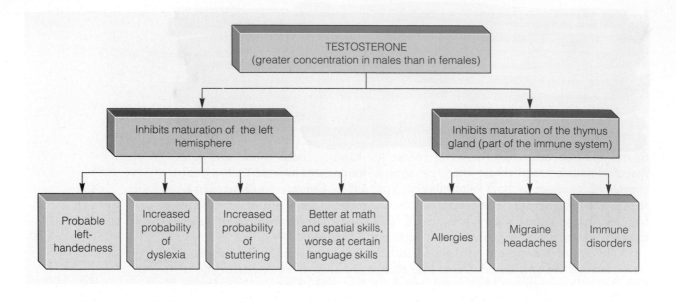

**Figure 5.10**
**Geschwind and Galaburda's hypothesis on the role of testosterone in brain development and medical disorders**

## SUMMARY

1. Visual information from each visual field crosses through the eyes to reach the opposite side of the retina. In humans, stimulation of the left half of each retina (from the right visual field) sends impulses to the left hemisphere of the brain. Stimulation of the right half of each retina (from the left visual field) sends impulses to the right half of the brain. (p. 153)

2. The corpus callosum, a set of axons connecting the two hemispheres, has been surgically cut in a small number of people to relieve severe, otherwise untreatable epilepsy. (p. 156)

3. After the corpus callosum is cut, the left hemisphere can answer questions verbally and can control the right hand. The right hemisphere can control the left hand. Each hemisphere sees the opposite side of the world and feels the opposite side of the body, but neither hemisphere has direct access to the knowledge of the other any longer. (p. 156)

4. Although the two hemispheres of a split-brain person are sometimes in conflict, they find many ways to cooperate and to cue each other. (p. 157)

5. The left hemisphere of most people is specialized for language or for "sequential, analytic" tasks. The right hemisphere is specialized for control of complex visual-spatial functions, especially those that require internal representations of visual and spatial information. It is also specialized for "synthetic, holistic" tasks. (p. 159)

6. People with an intact corpus callosum tend to look to the right when the left hemisphere is highly activated; they tend to look left when the right hemisphere is highly activated. When one hemisphere is more activated than the other, people tend to perform best at the tasks associated with the more activated hemisphere. (p. 161)

7. The left hemisphere differs anatomically from the right hemisphere even during infancy. Young children have some trouble comparing information from the left and right hands, because the corpus callosum is not fully mature. (p. 163)

8. In children born without a corpus callosum, the rest of the brain develops in unusual ways and the children fail to show the same deficits as adults who sustain damage to the corpus callosum. (p. 165)

9. The brain of a left-handed person is not simply the mirror image of the brain of a right-handed person. Left-handers are more likely to stutter and to have a variety of other medical and psychological anomalies, some of them advantages and others disadvantages. According to one hypothesis, all these effects may be exaggerations of the normal effects of testosterone on development. (p. 166)

10. A child born without a corpus callosum can name what he or she feels in the left hand, unlike an adult with a damaged corpus callosum. What is a likely explanation for this difference? (p. 165)

11. List some of the biological characteristics that are more prevalent among left-handers than among right-handers. According to Geschwind and Galaburda, what may account for these increased prevalences? (p. 166)

## REVIEW QUESTIONS

1. Why is the left hemisphere of the brain simply connected to the right eye in rabbits, but not in humans? (p. 153)

2. In the human eye, what part of each retina connects to the left hemisphere? To the right hemisphere? What part of the visual field does the left hemisphere see? What part does the right hemisphere see? (p. 154)

3. Can a split-brain person name something after feeling it with the left hand? With the right hand? Why? (p. 156)

4. Describe one way in which the two hemispheres of a split-brain person cooperate. (p. 158)

5. What kinds of tasks can the right hemisphere perform better than the left hemisphere? (p. 159)

6. Describe one task that apparently demonstrates differences between the left and right hemispheres in intact people. (p. 161)

7. What evidence do we have that the left hemisphere differs from the right hemisphere even before a child develops language? (p. 163)

8. How does experience affect the development of the corpus callosum? (p. 164)

9. In what way is the behavior of a young child similar to that of a split-brain person? (p. 165)

## THOUGHT QUESTIONS

1. As discussed on p. 158, certain split-brain patients can press a button with the right hand to answer a question about information presented to the left visual field. How does the left hemisphere (which controls the right hand) know what was in the left visual field? Sergent (1986) suggests that the information passes from the right hemisphere to the left hemisphere via other connections in the brain, such as the anterior commissure or the hippocampal commissure. Can you imagine any other possible explanation? If so, how could you test whether your hypothesis is plausible?

2. People born without a corpus callosum show one peculiarity not typical of split-brain patients: Whenever they move the fingers of one hand, they involuntarily move the fingers of the other hand, too. What possible explanation can you suggest?

## SUGGESTION FOR FURTHER READING

**Springer, S. P., & Deutsch, G.** (1989). *Left brain, right brain* (3rd ed.). New York: W. H. Freeman. Discusses the split-brain phenomenon and the specializations of the two hemispheres evident in normal people.

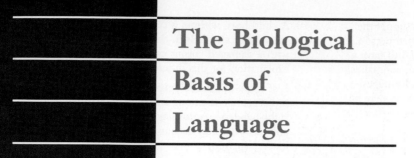

# The Biological Basis of Language

$S$uppose your physician has just told you that you have a brain tumor. It causes you little hardship now, but it will become life threatening in a year or two if a surgeon does not remove it. After the operation—if you agree to it—you will have a normal life expectancy and you will be entirely healthy, except for one thing: Removal of the tumor requires removing some brain tissue. And because of the tumor's location, the operation will leave you virtually incapable of understanding language. In many ways you will still be able to carry on a normal life. You will understand the meanings of many symbols and signals, including smiles and frowns. But you will make no sense of anything you try to read, and you will understand only a little of what you hear other people say. Under these conditions, will you agree to have the surgery?

Some people say yes and some say no. Even those who say yes are generally hesitant. Most of us would willingly undergo a life-saving operation that would cost us the use of both arms or both legs, or one that would leave us blind or deaf. But to lose language comprehension is to lose an important part of what makes us human.

## NONHUMANS' ABILITIES TO ACQUIRE LANGUAGE

How do children learn to speak and to understand language? Is it entirely a matter of learning by observation and imitation, or do children somehow inherit a tendency to learn language and a predisposition to learn it in a particular way? One way to approach this question is to try to teach nonhuman animals to use language.

Many early attempts to teach chimpanzees to talk and to understand speech ended in failure (Premack, 1976). Differences between the chimpanzee and human vocal apparatus account for the chimps' failure to learn to speak (Bryan, 1963), although they do not explain the chimps' failure to understand speech.

The first success in teaching chimpanzees an approximation to human language was reported by Beatrice and Allen Gardner (1975), who trained a chimp named Washoe to use American Sign Language, the language of the American deaf. Washoe's trainers used a combination of imitation, reward, and occasionally putting Washoe's hands into the appropriate positions. After 51 months of training, her vocabulary had reached 132 words.

**Figure 5.11**
*One of the Premacks' chimps, Elizabeth, reacts to colored plastic chips that read "Not Elizabeth banana insert— Elizabeth apple wash." (Photo courtesy of Ann Premack.)*

At about the same time as the Gardners' experiment, Ann and David Premack (D. Premack, 1970; Premack & Premack, 1972) began training a chimp named Sarah to communicate using plastic chips. The Premacks taught Sarah (and later other chimpanzees) to interpret commands given by a column of chips and to use the chips to construct her own requests (see Figure 5.11). Each chip represented a word or concept. The Premacks' method allowed Sarah less spontaneity and creativity than Washoe had with sign language; however, it enabled Sarah to express more complicated concepts. Sarah eventually used correct word order, negatives, questions, the symbols for *same* and *different*, plurals, the expression *is the name of*, compound sentences, and *if-then* constructions.

In a still more elaborate project on chimpanzee language, chimps have been trained to punch buttons bearing symbols to type out messages on a computer (Rumbaugh, 1977). The computer creates a visual display of the typed message; it also responds appropriately to all meaningful requests. These chimps have learned to make requests of the computer (such as "Please machine give me apple" or "Please machine turn on movie"). They also have learned to type messages to communicate with other chimps ("Please share your chocolate with me").

Have such chimpanzees really learned a little human language, or have they just learned a complicated set of tricks to get rewards? That is, we humans may interpret a set of symbols as "Elizabeth apple wash," but do the symbols really mean the same thing to the chimpanzee? Many psychologists have been skeptical. They pointed out that the chimpanzees seldom combined symbols to make *original* sentences (as even very young children do), and that the chimpanzees use their symbols almost exclusively to request, not to describe (Terrace, Pettito, Sanders, & Bever, 1979). A chimp's comprehension seemed limited to symbols arranged in a familiar way; if the experimenter varied the word order a little, the chimpanzee seemed not to understand (Rumbaugh, 1990). In short, although

The Biological Basis of Language

chimpanzees learned the meanings of hundreds of symbols, they demonstrated little understanding of *syntax*, the rules for combining words to express new meanings.

That, at any rate, was the conclusion based on studies of the common chimpanzee, *Pan troglodytes*. More impressive results have emerged from studies of the rare and endangered species *Pan paniscus*, sometimes known as the pygmy chimpanzee (a misleading term because these animals are almost as large as common chimpanzees) and sometimes known as the bonobo (also a misleading term because it refers to a place in Africa where they do not live). *Pan paniscus* has a social order resembling that of humans in several regards. Males and females form strong, sometimes long-term personal attachments. They often copulate in a face-to-face position. The female is sexually responsive throughout the month and not just during her fertile period. Unlike most other primates, these males contribute significantly to infant care. Adults often share food with one another. They even stand comfortably on their hind legs. In short, they resemble humans more than any other primates do.

In the mid-1980s Sue Savage-Rumbaugh, Duane Rumbaugh, and their associates began trying to teach a female bonobo, Matata, to press symbols that light up when touched; each symbol represents a word (see Figure 5.12). She made very disappointing progress. However, her infant son Kanzi seemed to learn a great deal just by watching her attempts. When given a chance to use the symbol board, he quickly surpassed the performance of his mother and of all common chimps that had been tested—even though Kanzi had never received any formal training. Furthermore, it soon became clear that Kanzi understood a fair amount of spoken language. The experimenters first noticed that whenever anyone said the word "light" he would flip the light switch. By age $5\frac{1}{2}$ he understood about 150 English words and could respond to complex, unfamiliar spoken commands such as "throw your ball in the river," "go to the refrigerator and get out a tomato," and "let's chase to the A-frame" (Savage-Rumbaugh, 1990; Savage-Rumbaugh, Sevcik, Brakke, & Rumbaugh, in press). Kanzi has demonstrated language comprehension comparable to that of a 2- to $2\frac{1}{2}$-year-old child (Greenfield & Savage-Rumbaugh, 1990).

Kanzi and his younger sister Mulika understand far more language than they produce. Both have attempted to produce English sounds, although they continue to be limited mostly to pressing symbols on their symbol boards. Their productions exceed those of other chimpanzees in some important regards: First, they use the symbols to name and describe objects even when they are not requesting them. Second, they occasionally use the symbols to relate events of the past. One time Kanzi punched the symbols "Matata bite" to explain the cut he had received on his hand an hour previously. Third, Kanzi and Mulika frequently make original, creative requests. For example, after Kanzi had learned to press the symbols to ask someone to play "chase" with him, he asked one person to chase another person while he watched!

Why have Kanzi and Mulika been so much more successful than other chimpanzees? One reason probably pertains to species differences: Perhaps bonobos have greater language capacities than common chimpanzees, or perhaps they simply have a better ability to code and remember the kinds of sounds humans use in speech. A second reason is that Kanzi and Mulika began language training at an early age, unlike the chimpanzees in most other studies. A third reason may pertain to the method of training: Perhaps learning by observation and imitation promotes better understanding than the formal training methods of previous studies (Savage-Rumbaugh, Sevcik, Brakke, & Rumbaugh, in press).

**Figure 5.12**
*Kanzi, a bonobo, points to answers on a board in response to questions he hears through earphones. The experimenter with him does not know what the questions are or what answers are expected. (From Georgia State University's Language Research Center, operated with the Yerkes Primate Center of Emory. Photo courtesy of Duane Rumbaugh.)*

Can any nonprimate species learn any aspect of language? Maybe. Dolphins and sea lions have been trained to respond to visual and auditory cues with meanings such as "bottom hoop fetch surface" (go to the bottom, get the hoop, and fetch it to the surface) or "large ball mouth" (touch your mouth to the largest ball). However, these performances represent only a limited degree of language comprehension (Herman, Richards, & Wolz, 1984; Schusterman & Krieger, 1986).

Spectacular results have been reported for Alex, an African gray parrot (Figure 5.13). Parrots are, of course, famous for imitating human sounds; Irene Pepperberg was the first to argue that parrots can learn the meaning of each sound. She kept Alex in a stimulating environment and taught him to say a variety of words in conjunction with specific objects. First she and the other trainers would say a word many times, then they would offer rewards if Alex approximated the same sound. Here is an excerpt from a "conversation" with Alex early in training (Pepperberg, 1981):

> **Pepperberg:** Pasta! (*Takes pasta*) Pasta! (*Alex stretches from his perch, appears to reach for pasta.*)
> **Alex:** Pa!
> **Pepperberg:** Better . . . what is it?
> **Alex:** Pah-ah.
> **Pepperberg:** Better!
> **Alex:** Pah-ta.
> **Pepperberg:** Okay, here's the pasta. Good try.

Although this example concerns pasta, Pepperberg generally used toys for rewards. For example, if Alex said "paper," "wood," or "key," she would give him what he asked for. In no case did she reward him for saying "paper" or "wood" by giving him a piece of food.

The Biological Basis
of Language

**Figure 5.13**
*Alex, a gray parrot, has apparently learned to converse about toy objects in simple English—for example, giving the correct answer to "What color is the circle?" He receives no food rewards. (Photo from David Carter.)*

Alex made gradual progress, apparently learning to give spoken answers to spoken questions (Pepperberg, 1990)! He can answer such questions as "What color is the key?" (answer: "green") and "What object is gray?" (answer: "circle"). Is Alex really speaking English? Certainly we must await more research to establish exactly what this bird is doing and how he does it. If he really does understand and speak English, we will have to rethink some assumptions about what sort of brain development is necessary for language.

What do we learn about language from studies of nonhuman language abilities? At a practical level, we may gain some insights into how best to teach language to those who do not learn it easily. The methods we develop for teaching chimpanzees may be useful for brain-damaged people or autistic children (see, for example, Glass, Gazzaniga, & Premack, 1973). At a more theoretical level, we find out something about how special humans are—and are not. We learn that the brain structures necessary for language are not entirely limited to the human brain. Although humans undeniably develop language far more readily than any other species does, our language abilities are an elaboration of abilities found to some degree in other species. Finally, these studies call attention to the difficulty of defining *language*: The main reason we have such trouble deciding whether chimpanzees or parrots have language is that we have not specified exactly what we mean by the term.

## EFFECTS OF BRAIN DAMAGE ON HUMAN LANGUAGE

Biological psychologists have learned much about the brain mechanisms of vision, hearing, and muscle control by studying the brains of other species. With regard to language, their investigations must be based almost entirely on humans. Although bonobos and maybe even African gray parrots can learn a certain amount of language, language learning does not come as easily for them as it does for us. The human brain is specialized to facilitate language.

Most of our knowledge about the brain mechanisms of language has come from studies of brain-damaged people. Such information can be useful and sometimes fascinating. However, it is limited to telling us *where* in the brain language comprehension and production take place, not *how* they take place (Caramazza, 1988).

## Broca's Aphasia

Occasionally a person suddenly loses all ability to speak. In 1861, one patient who had been mute for 30 years was taken to the French surgeon Paul Broca because of gangrene. When the patient happened to die five days later, Broca did an autopsy on the man's brain and found a lesion restricted to a small part of the frontal lobe of the left cerebral cortex near the motor cortex (Boring, 1950; Schiller, 1979). In later years Broca examined the brains of other patients whose only problem had been a language impairment of sudden origin; in nearly all cases he found damage in that same area, which is now known as **Broca's area** (Figure 5.14). The usual cause of the damage was a stroke (an interruption of blood flow to part of the brain).

Later studies confirmed that Broca's area and surrounding areas are damaged in most patients who suffer **aphasia,** a loss of language because of brain damage.

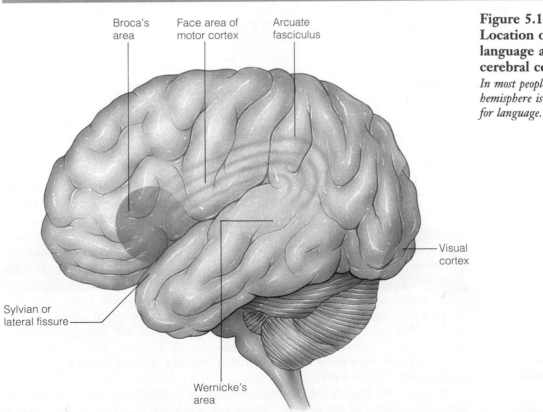

Broca's area · Face area of motor cortex · Arcuate fasciculus · Visual cortex · Wernicke's area · Sylvian or lateral fissure

**Figure 5.14**
**Location of the major language areas of the cerebral cortex**
*In most people, only the left hemisphere is specialized for language.*

175

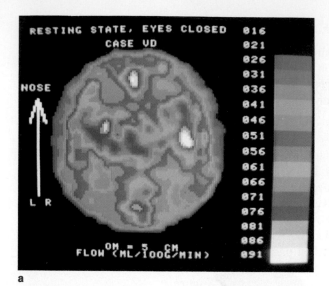

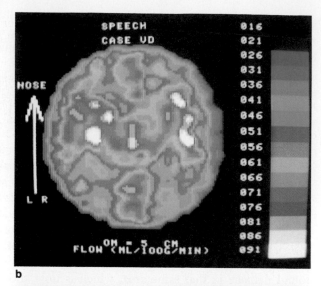

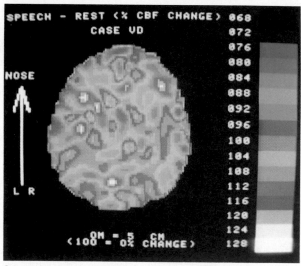

**Figure 5.15**
**Records showing rCBF for one normal adult subject**
*Red indicates the highest level of activity, followed by yellow, green, and blue. (**a**) Blood flow to the brain at rest. (**b**) Blood flow while subject describes a magazine story. (**c**) Difference between (b) and (a). The results in (c) indicate which brain areas increased their activity during language production. Note the increased activity in many areas of the brain, especially on the left side. (From Wallesch, Henriksen, Kornhuber, & Paulson, 1985.)*

The kind of aphasia typically associated with damage to Broca's area is sometimes known as *Broca's aphasia* or *nonfluent aphasia* because the person cannot speak fluently.

Damage limited just to Broca's area produces only a mild, temporary speech impairment. Long-lasting and severe loss of speech is more often associated with extensive damage that includes Broca's area, part of the left motor cortex, some areas farther posterior in the left cortex, and parts of the thalamus or basal ganglia (Alexander, Benson, & Stuss, 1989; Damasio & Geschwind, 1984). Furthermore, when normal people speak, they have increased cerebral blood flow in Broca's area, the motor cortex and surrounding areas, the left thalamus, and the basal ganglia (Wallesch, Henriksen, Kornhuber, & Paulson, 1985). Apparently speech depends on a fairly large circuit that includes all these areas and not just Broca's area (Figure 5.15).

People with Broca's aphasia have a variety of deficits, depending on the size and exact location of the damage. In general, there are four effects (Geschwind,

1970, 1972): difficulty in language production, telegraphic speech, difficulty with the phonetics of reading, and better language comprehension than language production.

**Difficulty in Language Production** Some people with Broca's aphasia cannot speak at all, although they may be able to make a variety of sounds and sometimes even hum or sing. Those with less extensive damage can speak, but with difficulty; words are spoken slowly and articulated poorly. They have trouble not only in producing sounds but also in copying simple mouth movements (Kimura & Watson, 1989). However, their problem is not just a lack of control of the throat; such people also have trouble with writing and with expressing themselves through gestures (Cicerone, Wapner, Foldi, Zurif, & Gardner, 1979). In addition, deaf people with damage in and around Broca's area find it difficult to produce sign language (Bellugi, Poizner, & Klima, 1983). They can make only a few brief signs, even though their ability to use their hands in other ways may be unimpaired.

**Telegraphic Speech** When someone with Broca's aphasia speaks at all, the speech is meaningful but it omits pronouns, prepositions, conjunctions, helper verbs, quantifiers, and tense and number endings. These omitted words and endings are sometimes known as the *closed* class of grammatical forms because a language rarely adds new prepositions, conjunctions, and the like. In contrast, new nouns and verbs enter the language every year. Someone with Broca's aphasia can speak nouns and verbs more easily than closed-class words.

The problem is not simply that Broca's aphasics want to minimize the labor of pronouncing a great many words. Such people find it difficult to repeat a phrase using many prepositions and conjunctions, such as "No ifs, ands, or buts," although they can successfully repeat "The general commands the army." Furthermore, patients who cannot read aloud "To be or not to be" can read "Two bee oar knot two bee" (Gardner & Zurif, 1975). Clearly, the trouble depends on the meanings of words, not just their pronunciation.

**Difficulty with the Phonetics of Reading** One patient with Broca's aphasia was unable to read aloud any pronounceable nonsense syllables, such as VIL or DUZ (Schweiger, Zaidel, Field, & Dobkin, 1989). When he tried to read a real word aloud, he often substituted a word of similar meaning but entirely different sound. For example, he read the word *frog* as *turtle*. That error indicates that some area of his brain was able to interpret the approximate meaning of the word but that his brain was insensitive to what the word should sound like.

**Better Language Comprehension Than Language Production** People with Broca's aphasia understand both spoken and written language better than they can produce it. They have occasional trouble hearing the articles (*a, an,* and *the*) in a stream of speech, although they can understand them if they hear them (M. Grossman, Carey, Zurif, & Diller, 1986). A more serious deficit is that they have trouble understanding the same word categories that they cannot say—prepositions, conjunctions, and other relational words. That deficit may or may not impair their language comprehension; sometimes the meaning of a sentence is clear enough without the relational words, and sometimes it depends heavily on those words, as Table 5.1 demonstrates.

In the process of guessing the meaning, Broca's aphasics sometimes change the meaning, especially if the sentence is strange or irregular. For example, when

**Table 5.1  What Language Might Sound Like to a Person with Broca's Aphasia**

In each case, prepositions, conjunctions, relative pronouns, articles, and word endings have been removed from a published text.

**Example 1** (Mostly understandable even after words have been removed):
James Baker made progress . . . Moscow last week. . . . U.S. secretary State wrap . . . several arms-control agreement, include sharp restriction . . . U.S. . . . Soviet chemical weapon. He said he had settle . . . "most vex . . . problem" . . . stand . . . way . . . strategic arms-reduction treaty (START). . . . them, official add, breakthrough . . . difficult issue . . . cruise missile. Baker also use his good office . . . encourage talk . . . Moscow . . . breakaway republic . . . Lithuania (follow . . . story). . . . groundwork almost guarantee . . . next week summit" . . . (*Newsweek*, May 28, 1990).

**Example 2** (More difficult):
Pigeon, dove, chicken, . . . turkey make . . . simple coo . . . cackle, . . . ornithologist (bird biologist) do not classify . . . "song." . . . species do not need . . . learn . . . call. . . . fact, . . . they are deaf . . . early . . . life, they develop normal call. (Note . . . observation do not explain . . . pigeon . . . other acquire . . . call. They merely indicate . . . we should look . . . answers . . . embryology . . . nervous system, not . . . individual experience.) (page 6 of this text).

**Example 3** (Almost incomprehensible): . . . other public building . . . certain town . . . many reason . . . will be prudent . . . refrain . . . mention . . . I will assign no fictitious name . . . boast . . . one . . . anciently common . . . most town, great . . . small . . . wit . . . workhouse . . . born . . . day . . . date . . . I need not trouble . . . myself . . . repeat . . . it can be . . . no possible consequence . . . reader . . . stage . . . business . . . event . . . item . . . mortality . . . name . . . prefix . . . head . . . chapter (*Oliver Twist*, by Charles Dickens, opening of Chapter 1).

they are asked to repeat an implausible sentence, they do not repeat it verbatim but instead change it to something more plausible. A Broca's aphasic may change "The bicycle is riding the boy" to "The bicycle is riding by the boy" (Ostrin & Schwartz, 1986).

People with Broca's aphasia have their greatest trouble understanding a sentence whose meaning depends on word order or other grammatical devices. For example, they have difficulty understanding the sentence "The girl that the boy is chasing is tall" (Zurif, 1980). They are not sure who is chasing whom and which one is tall.

## Wernicke's Aphasia

In 1874 Carl Wernicke (generally pronounced WER-nih-kee in the United States; the German pronunciation is VER-nih-keh), a 26-year-old junior assistant in a German hospital, discovered that damage in part of the left temporal cortex produced language impairment very different from what Broca had reported. Patients could produce language, but they had trouble comprehending the verbal and written communications of others. This brain area, now known as **Wernicke's area** (Figure 5.14), is located near the auditory part of the cerebral cortex. Damage in and around Wernicke's area produces *Wernicke's aphasia*, also sometimes known as *fluent aphasia* because the person can still speak smoothly. The typical symptoms are as follows:

1. *No difficulty with articulation*. In contrast to Broca's aphasics, Wernicke's aphasics speak rapidly, articulately, and fluently, except when they pause to try to think of the name of something.

2. *Poor language comprehension.* Wernicke's aphasics have great trouble understanding both spoken and written speech. When speaking to someone suffering from this condition, many people try to help the person by simply speaking very slowly, mostly by drawing out the vowels. That strategy does not help at all. It does help to pause at the boundaries between phrases—for example: "The truck (pause) chased the car (pause) that hit the bus" (Blumstein, Katz, Goodglass, Shrier, & Dworetsky, 1985).

3. *Difficulty finding the right word*. People suffering from Wernicke's aphasia have **anomia** (ay-NOME-ee-uh), a difficulty in recalling the names of objects and in constructing relative clauses. A typical result follows: "Yes, all the little, little pe-, ah, puh, ah, places the, the ah, big big of-fi-ces then have undergone this here ah, the, ah, the, ah, there and they're there, but they can't hear, hi, hi, can't see them because it's s-so-so big, other big buildings are there" (Martin & Blossom-Stach, 1986).

Although people with Wernicke's aphasia speak grammatically, what they say makes little sense. Even when they do manage to find some of the right words, they fail to arrange the words properly, saying, for example, "The Astros listened to the radio tonight" (instead of "I listened to the Astros on the radio tonight") or "The car was towntown for a photograph, to a friend on a bookstore, and a restaurant" (Martin & Blossom-Stach, 1986).

The following conversation is between a woman with Wernicke's aphasia and a speech therapist trying to teach her the names of some objects. Although her speech comprehension is better than that of many Wernicke's aphasics, she has a severe difficulty with naming. (The Duke University Department of Speech Pathology and Audiology provided this dialogue.)

**Therapist:** (*Holding picture of an apron*) Can you name that one?
**Woman:** Um . . . you see I can't, I can I can barely do; he would give me sort of umm . . . .
**T:** A clue?
**W:** That's right . . . just a like, just a . . . .
**T:** You mean, like, "You wear that when you wash dishes or when you cook a meal . . ."?
**W:** Yeah, something like that.
**T:** Okay, and what is it? You wear it around your waist, and you cook . . . .
**W:** Cook. Umm, umm, see I can't remember.
**T:** It's an apron.
**W:** Apron, apron, that's it, apron.
**T:** (*Holding another picture*) That you wear when you're getting ready for bed after a shower.
**W:** Oh, I think that he put under different, something different. We had something, you know, umm, you know.
**T:** A different way of doing it?
**W:** No, umm . . . umm . . . . (*Pause*)
**T:** It's actually a bathrobe.
**W:** Bathrobe. Uh, we didn't call it that, we called it something else.
**T:** Smoking jacket?
**W:** No, I think we called it, uh . . . .

T: Lounging . . . ?
W: No, no, something, in fact we called it just . . . . (*Pause*)
T: Robe?
W: Robe. Or something like that.

The conversation proceeded similarly through pictures of a bird, a thermos, a bride, an airplane, and an arm; the woman could not name any of them, although she seemed to recognize the names when she heard them. The therapist then began to review:

T: (*Apron picture*) The thing you wear when you're cooking.
W: (*Silence*)
T: Apron.
W: Apron.
T: (*Robe picture*) What's this?
W: Apron, umm, umm.
T: Robe.
W: Robe.
T: (*Apron picture*) What's this?
W: (*Silence*)
T: That's the apron again.
W: Apron, apron, apron.
T: (*Robe picture*) And this?
W: Apron.
T: That's the robe.
W: Robe. Robe, robe. Apron, robe, apron, robe.
T: (*Apron picture*) Now this one again.
W: Apron.
T: (*Robe picture*) Uh-huh.
W: Robe.
T: (*Bird picture*) Okay. Now this is . . . .
W: Apron, robe . . . .
T: Bird.
W: Bird. Bird.
T: (*Apron picture*) What's this first one again?
W: (*Sigh*)
T: That's the apron.
W: Apron, apron, apron, apron.
T: (*Bird picture*) And that's the . . . .
W: (*Silence*)

Unlike hearing people, deaf people who suffer damage to Wernicke's area do not lose their ability to understand sign language. Rather, they lose that ability after damage in the parietal lobe, the area responsible for touch and other body sensations (Bellugi, Poizner, & Klima, 1983).

## PET Scan Studies of Language Processing

For many years, the study of brain-damaged people was almost the only available method for determining how different parts of the brain contribute to language. The introduction of PET scans has enabled investigators to address some questions that they could not answer with observations on brain-damaged patients.

The procedure is this: First, a healthy (brain-intact) person looks at some printed words, while the investigators record brain activity with a PET scanner (see p. 144). Then the person stares at a blank card, while the investigators again record brain activity. Finally, a computer subtracts the brain activity on the second task from the activity on the first task; the difference is the activity specifically generated by reading the words.

Figure 5.16 shows the results of one study (Posner, Petersen, Fox, & Raichle, 1988). Note that reading enhanced brain activity in the occipital lobe only. Activity in the occipital lobe was to be expected; after all, the occipital lobe is the brain's primary visual area. The more surprising result was that this task did *not* activate the temporal lobe. We might have expected that a person would have to convert the written word into sound to read it. Certainly that is true for children who are just learning to read. These results suggest that experienced adult readers can process words directly in the visual areas of the brain, without necessarily converting them to sounds.

Next the investigators ask the person to read pairs of words and decide whether they rhyme with each other. Some pairs look similar and rhyme (such as *face* and *pace*), some look similar but do not rhyme (*pint* and *lint*), and some look different but rhyme anyway (*row* and *though*). So to answer the questions, the person must attend to the sounds and not just the appearances of the words. The computer compares the brain areas activated by this task with the brain areas activated by simply looking at words; the result is that this task leads to greater activity in the temporal lobes (Posner et al., 1988). That is, the person must convert the written word into a sound, using the part of the cortex specialized for hearing.

Now the investigators ask the person to read one object-word at a time on a screen and then to state a way to use the object. (For example, *hammer—pound*, or *cake—eat*). They also ask the person to listen to spoken words and to state a use for each. The brain areas activated by these tasks are compared to those activated by simply repeating the word after seeing it or hearing it. Stating uses for words activates much of the frontal cortex, including Broca's area and other nearby areas (Petersen, Fox, Posner, Mintun, & Raichle, 1988; Posner et al., 1988). Furthermore, reading a word and stating a use produces about the same results as listening to a word and stating a use. In short, the frontal cortex processes both spoken and written language in the same way (see Figure 5.17).

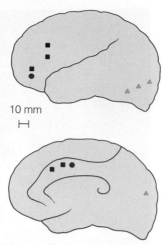

10 mm

**Figure 5.16
Brain areas activated
by certain tasks**
*Passively reading words activates areas in the occipital cortex more than they are activated when the person simply stares ahead (triangles).*
Reading the name of an object and thinking of a way to use the object activates the areas marked with squares. Listening to words and silently counting dangerous animals activates the areas marked with circles.
(From Posner et al., 1988.)

## Disconnection of Broca's Area from Wernicke's Area

Carl Wernicke suggested that the area we now call Wernicke's area, located near the auditory cortex in the temporal lobe, was involved in transferring sounds into language comprehension, and that Broca's area, located near the motor cortex in the frontal lobe, was involved in converting language representations into the muscle movements necessary for speech. Wernicke further argued that Wernicke's area must be connected to Broca's area and that at least one of the two areas must be connected to the visual and auditory areas of the cortex. If so, he reasoned, specific behavior deficits should result from any damage to one of those connections. This theory, expanded and repopularized by Norman Geschwind a century later (Geschwind, 1970, 1972), offers explanations for many specific impairments related to language.

One type of language impairment is known as **conduction aphasia** on the theory that the person has trouble "conducting" language information from Wernicke's area to Broca's area. People with this language impairment can pronounce words normally (suggesting that Broca's area is intact) and can understand language reasonably well (suggesting that Wernicke's area is intact). However, they have trouble repeating what others say and carrying on a conversation. When they speak, they may have trouble finding words, especially the names of objects. In that regard they resemble people with Wernicke's aphasia. One interpretation

The Biological Basis
of Language

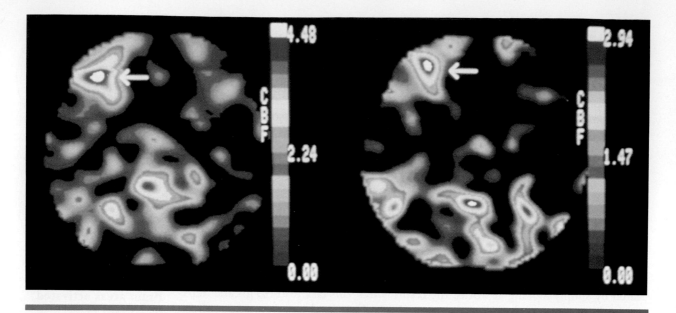

**Figure 5.17**
**PET scans indicating where brain activity increases when people state a use of a word (such as *cake — eat*) instead of simply repeating the word (such as *cake — cake*)** *In the PET scan on the left, people heard the word they were to respond to; in the scan on the right, they saw it. In both cases, activity increases markedly in the left anterior frontal cortex (marked with arrow). (From Petersen et al., 1988.)*

is that the information cannot get to Broca's area to be spoken, perhaps because of damage to the **arcuate fasciculus** (AR-kyoo-wait fuh-SIK-yoo-lus) (see Figure 5.14), a set of fibers that runs from Wernicke's area to Broca's area (Damasio & Damasio, 1980). However, most people with conduction aphasia have extensive brain damage that includes parts of the parietal and temporal cortex (Kempler et al., 1988), so conduction aphasia probably depends on much more than just damage to the arcuate fasciculus. Table 5.2 contrasts Broca's aphasia, Wernicke's aphasia, and conduction aphasia.

## Disconnections of Language Areas from Other Parts of the Brain

Discussions of the next two clinical syndromes begin with a behavioral description. After reading the first paragraph of each, try to guess where the brain damage might be before you read the neurological explanation.

**Word Blindness Despite Ability to Write** A person can suddenly lose the ability to read without losing any other language ability. Even writing ability is spared, although the person cannot read what he or she has just written. This condition is known as **word blindness,** or **alexia.** Vision is intact in the left visual field but is lost in the right visual field.

The cause? The left visual cortex has been destroyed (by stroke, perhaps), as has the posterior part of the corpus callosum, known as the *splenium*, which contains the fibers from the visual areas of the cortex. The person can see only with the right visual cortex (left visual field), and information in the right visual cortex cannot get to the language areas in the left hemisphere (Greenblatt, 1973; Hécaen & Kremin, 1976; Staller, Buchanan, Singer, Lappin, & Webb, 1978). Spontaneous writing is normal because vision is not necessary for writing; a normal person can, after all, write with his or her eyes closed. Reading is impaired, however, because it requires transfer of information from the vision to the language areas of the brain.

**Table 5.2 Three Types of Aphasia**

| Type | Pronunciation | Content of Speech | Comprehension |
|------|---------------|-------------------|---------------|
| Broca's aphasia | Very poor | Speaks mostly nouns and verbs; omits prepositions and other grammatical connectives | Has trouble only if understanding depends on prepositions, sentence grammar, or word order |
| Wernicke's aphasia | Unimpaired | Speech is grammatical but sometimes nonsensical; has trouble finding the right word, especially names of objects | Seriously impaired |
| Conduction aphasia | Unimpaired | Cannot repeat what others say; has trouble with names of objects | Slightly impaired in some cases |

Most people suffering from word blindness can name the objects they see in the left visual field. This may seem surprising, since the fibers that transmit visual information across the corpus callosum have been damaged. Geschwind (1970, 1972) has suggested that the right hemisphere may somehow convert the visual identification of an object into touch or other kinds of sensory representations that can be sent across the intact anterior corpus callosum. Because the right hemisphere cannot convert written words or letters into any nonvisual code, the left hemisphere has no access to them. For the same reason, most people with word blindness cannot name the colors they see.

Certain people have had their posterior corpus callosum cut for medical reasons. When they see something in the left visual field (right hemisphere), they can sometimes transfer enough information across the anterior corpus callosum for the left hemisphere to describe the object partially, but not necessarily to name it (Sidtis, Volpe, Holtzman, Wilson, & Gazzaniga, 1981). They often describe it as a "tip of the tongue" experience; a patient might say, "I saw an article of clothing . . . it's worn by men, mostly in fall. . . . Oh, it's a hunter's cap." It is as if the information is flowing piecemeal across the corpus callosum and the left hemisphere must infer what the object is, instead of seeing it directly.

**Ability to Follow Instructions Only with the Right Hand** Following a particular kind of brain damage, a person can follow someone's verbal instructions, such as "Comb your hair" or "Wave good-bye," with the right side of the body but not the left. The left hand is capable of the movements, however, and the person may make those movements spontaneously with the left hand. He or she can also use the left hand to imitate those movements when someone else makes them.

The problem here is simply damage to the corpus callosum (Geschwind, 1975). Verbal messages can get from the language areas in the left hemisphere to the motor cortex in the left hemisphere, which controls the right half of the body. The right motor cortex, controlling the left half of the body, is intact and can generate the movements either spontaneously or by imitation. Verbal information from the left hemisphere cannot reach the left side of the body, however.

A person with damage to the corpus callosum can nevertheless follow verbal instructions that require using muscles on both sides of the face, such as "Smile"

The Biological Basis
of Language

or "Raise your eyebrows." Each hemisphere has some control of the facial muscles on both sides of the face, especially the upper face, and many of the muscles near the midline of the body (Rinn, 1984).

### Therapy and Recovery from Aphasia

Aphasia resulting from brain damage may or may not be permanent. After either a stroke or a wound to the head, the resulting aphasia gradually decreases in many cases and disappears altogether in some (Mohr et al., 1980). Recovery is better after subcortical lesions that cause aphasia than after lesions of the cerebral cortex (Olsen, Bruhn, & Öberg, 1986). If the left hemisphere is damaged in early childhood, the right hemisphere assumes control of some of the left hemisphere's normal functions, at the expense of its own. Thus, after left-hemisphere damage, a child recovers language better than an adult would, but his or her visual-spatial abilities fail to develop as well as normal (Lansdell, 1969).

Speech therapists work with aphasic patients to get them to practice and improve whatever language skills they retain. Although it is generally agreed that patients improve more if they get therapy promptly, speech therapy is helpful even for patients who do not receive it until years after their stroke or injury (Helm-Estabrooks & Ramsberger, 1986). If the person regains no use of spoken language after severe brain damage, it is sometimes possible to teach him or her to use cutout colored paper symbols as words, in a manner similar to what the Premacks used with chimpanzees. Patients who cannot speak or understand speech can learn to arrange simple sentences, such as "Andrea give John water," and to use paper symbols for more complex concepts as well (Gardner, Zurif, Berry, & Baker, 1976; Glass, Gazzaniga, & Premack, 1973).

## SUMMARY

1. Chimpanzees can learn to communicate by sign language or by other nonvocal means. Although their productions are often impressive, they are less likely to make original sentences than are children with similar vocabularies. Bonobos (pygmy chimpanzees) are capable of learning to understand both symbols and spoken words. (p. 170)

2. After damage to areas in the left hemisphere, people lose some or all of their ability to understand and use language. (p. 174)

3. People with Broca's aphasia, generally associated with damage to the left frontal cortex, find it difficult to speak or write. They find it especially difficult to use prepositions, conjunctions, and other grammatical connectives. They also fail to understand speech when its meaning depends on grammatical connectives, sentence structure, or word order. (p. 175)

4. People with Wernicke's aphasia, generally associated with damage to the left temporal cortex, have trouble understanding speech and find it difficult to recall the names of objects. (p. 178)

5. Studies using PET scans indicate that reading without speaking depends on the occipital cortex. Reading tasks that require attention to sound activate the temporal cortex. (p. 181)

6. Other specialized problems, such as word blindness, arise if Wernicke's area and Broca's area are disconnected from other parts of the cerebral cortex, such as the visual area, the auditory area, or the motor-control area. (p. 181)

## REVIEW QUESTIONS

1. What is one reason why chimpanzees learn sign language better than spoken language? (p. 170)

2. How do the results of language training with bonobos (pygmy chimpanzees) differ from those with common chimpanzees? (p. 172)

3. Where are Broca's area and Wernicke's area? (p. 175)

4. In what ways is language impaired in Broca's aphasia? In what ways is it impaired in Wernicke's aphasia? (p. 175)

5. How can an investigator use a PET scan to determine which areas of the brain are especially activated when a person speaks? (p. 180)

6. Following brain damage, a person can still speak normally, can see, and can write, but cannot read. Where is the brain damage probably located? (p. 182)

7. If an aphasic patient fails to recover speech, what method can help the patient communicate? (p. 184)

## THOUGHT QUESTIONS

1. Most people with Broca's aphasia suffer from partial paralysis on the right side of the body. Most people with Wernicke's aphasia do not. Why?

2. In a syndrome called *word deafness*, a person cannot understand spoken language, although both language and hearing are normal in other respects. What would be a possible neurological explanation?

## SUGGESTIONS FOR FURTHER READING

**Aitchison, J.** (1983). *The articulate mammal: An introduction to psycholinguistics* (2nd ed.). New York: Universe Books. Discusses language and the biological specializations that make language possible.

**Geschwind, N.** (1979). Specializations of the human brain. *Scientific American, 241* (3), 180–199. Discusses the effects of brain damage on language.

**Rumbaugh, D. M.** (1990). Comparative psychology and the great apes: Their competence in learning, language, and numbers. *Psychological Record, 40*, 15–39. Description of research on the cognitive capacities of chimpanzees.

## GLOSSARY

**alexia** inability to read

**anomia** difficulty in recalling the names of objects

**anterior commissure** set of axons that connects the hemispheres in the anterior part of the cerebral cortex

**aphasia** lack of language abilities

**arcuate fasciculus** band of fibers running between Broca's area and Wernicke's area

**Broca's area** portion of the human left frontal lobe associated with speech production

**conduction aphasia** difficulty in repeating what others say and in carrying on a conversation

**corpus callosum** large set of axons that connects the two hemispheres of the cerebral cortex

**hippocampal commissure** set of axons that connects the left hippocampus to the right hippocampus

**lateral fissure** one of the major fissures, or folds, on the side of the cortex

**lateralization** division of labor or specializations between the two hemispheres of the brain

**optic chiasm** point at which parts of the optic nerves cross to the opposite side of the brain

**planum temporale** area of the temporal cortex that is larger in the left than in the right hemisphere for most people

**Sylvian fissure** one of the major fissures, or folds, on the side of the cortex

**visual field** the part of the world visible to the eyes at a particular moment

**Wernicke's area** portion of the human left temporal lobe associated with language comprehension

**word blindness** inability to read

# CHAPTER SIX

# Sensory Systems

## MAIN IDEAS

**1.** Our senses have evolved not to give us complete information about all the stimuli in the world but to give us the information most useful to us.

**2.** Each sensory nerve carries information about one type of sensation. Whenever a given nerve is excited, even if it is artificially excited by electricity, the brain's interpretation of its message is the same.

**3.** Each sensory system has receptors that are highly sensitive to a given type of energy. The receptors convert that energy into action potentials, which code the information in a manner that the brain can process.

According to an American Indian saying, "A pine needle fell. The eagle saw it. The deer heard it. The bear smelled it" (Herrero, 1985). Different species are sensitive to different information. Bees and many other insects can see short-wavelength (ultraviolet) light that is invisible to humans; conversely, humans see long-wavelength (red) light that these insects cannot see. Bats produce sonar waves at 20,000 to 100,000 hertz (cycles per second) and then localize insect prey by listening to the echoes. Most adult humans cannot hear any sounds in that range, although children may hear the lower part of the range (Griffin, Webster, & Michael, 1960).

Many animal species are sensitive to only a small range of stimuli, the stimuli most useful to their way of life. For example, a frog's eyes include cells that respond selectively to small, dark moving objects — such as insects (Lettvin, Maturana, McCulloch, & Pitts, 1959). The ears of the cricket frog, *Acris crepitans*, are highly sensitive to sounds around the frequencies 550 and 3,550 Hz — the frequencies found in the adult male's croak. The frog's ear is poorly sensitive to other sounds. In frog species in which the male produces other sounds, the ears are "tuned" to respond to the particular sounds those males make (Capranica & Frishkopf, 1966; Capranica,

Frishkopf, & Nevo, 1973). Similarly, 17-year locusts are highly sensitive to the songs produced by their own species and are virtually deaf to other sounds (Simmons, Wever, & Pylka, 1971).

We generally assume that human sensory systems simply reflect the physical world. Granted, human visual and auditory abilities are broader and less specialized than those of frogs and locusts, perhaps because a wider range of stimuli is biologically relevant to us than to them. However, humans have some important sensory specializations. For example, we can detect the sweet taste of certain nutritious substances and the bitter taste of poisons at low concentrations (Richter, 1950; Schiffman & Erickson, 1971). Conversely, we fail to taste many substances that are neither helpful nor harmful (for instance, sand and cellulose). Our olfactory systems are sensitive to a wide variety of gases but completely insensitive to others, including some that it would be useless for us to detect (nitrogen, for example). Thus, this chapter concerns not how our sensory systems enable us to perceive Reality with a capital R, but how they enable us to get biologically useful information.

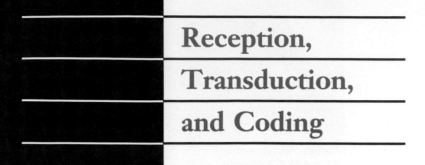

# Reception, Transduction, and Coding

When physical energy such as light or sound reaches the sense organs, it must be converted to a form that can be processed in the brain. That conversion has three steps: reception, transduction, and coding (see Figure 6.1). **Reception** is simply the absorption of physical energy. **Transduction** is the conversion of that physical energy to an electrochemical pattern in the neurons. **Coding** is the one-to-one correspondence between some aspect of the physical stimulus and some aspect of the nervous system activity. For example, molecules from a squeezed lemon strike receptors in the nose (reception); they lead to a chemical reaction that changes the polarization across the membrane of the receptor cell (transduction); and the resulting activity in that neuron and other neurons sends a distinctive message to the brain (coding).

## RECEPTION AND TRANSDUCTION

A receptor, like any other neuron, can produce electrical changes across its membrane that lead to action potentials. The difference is that a receptor is highly sensitive to one form of energy (Ashmore & Saibil, 1990). For example, certain touch receptors produce action potentials in response to very slight mechanical pressures that would fail to excite other neurons. Visual receptors can absorb and respond to as little as a single photon of light. Auditory receptors can detect air vibrations only slightly more intense than the vibrations produced by blood traveling through the vessels of the ear. Olfactory and taste receptors respond to chemicals that, first of all, would seldom be in a position to excite neurons anywhere else but in the nose or on the tongue and, second, would not excite other neurons even if they did reach them.

After the receptor absorbs energy from light, sound waves, or whatever, it transduces (converts) the received energy into nerve activity. The stimulation of a receptor produces a **generator potential,** a local depolarization or hyperpolarization of a neuron membrane. If the generator potential is intense enough, it may trigger an action potential.

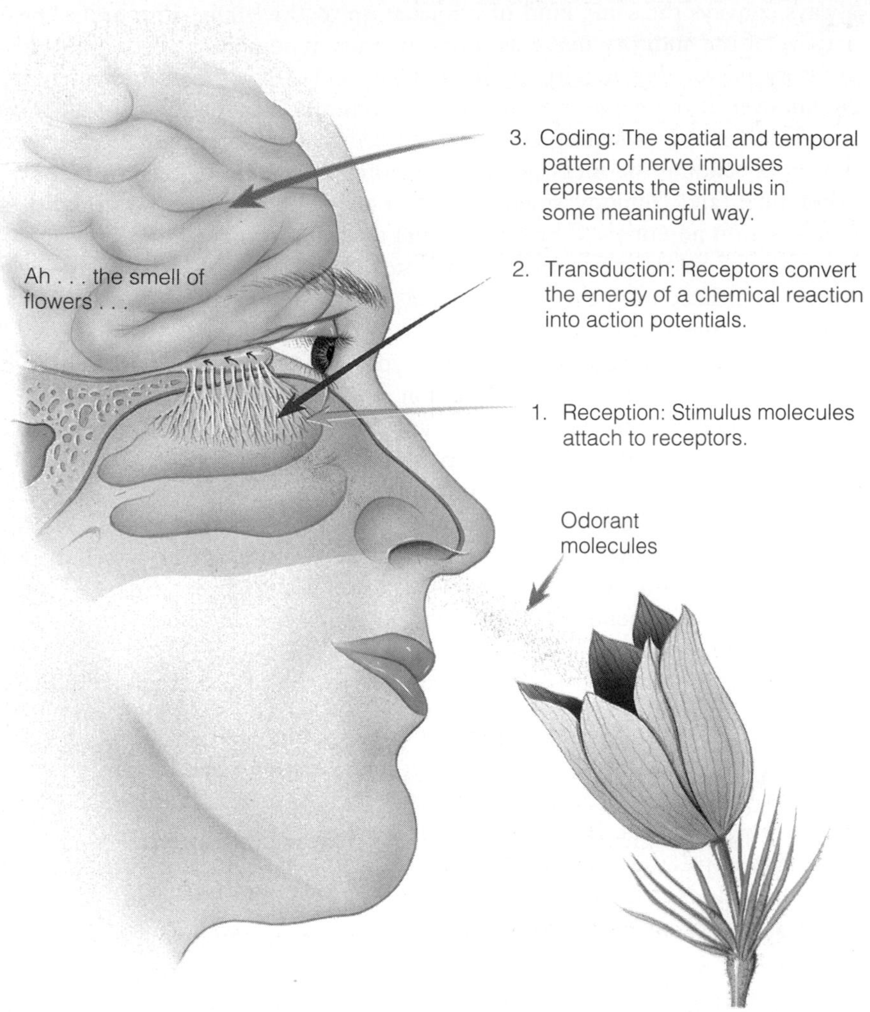

Figure 6.1
**Three steps in the sensation and perception of a stimulus**

3. Coding: The spatial and temporal pattern of nerve impulses represents the stimulus in some meaningful way.

2. Transduction: Receptors convert the energy of a chemical reaction into action potentials.

1. Reception: Stimulus molecules attach to receptors.

Ah . . . the smell of flowers . . .

Odorant molecules

# CODING

At one time people believed that the brain's representation of a physical stimulus would have to resemble the stimulus itself. That is, to see a table you would need a pattern of activity in a set of neurons that were arranged in the shape of a table. That view has long been discarded. The word *table* does not look like a table or sound like a table. A computer stores a record of the word *table* as a series of electromagnetic pulses that physically resemble neither actual tables nor *tables* as a spoken or written word. Similarly, the brain can store its representation for *table* in any code, provided only that a one-to-one relationship exists between the stimulus itself and the brain's code for it.

One important aspect of all sensory coding is *which* neurons are active. A given frequency of impulses may mean one thing when it occurs in one neuron and something quite different in another. In 1838, Johannes Müller described this basic insight as the **law of specific nerve energies**. Müller held that whatever excited a particular nerve established a special kind of "energy" unique to that nerve. In more modern terms, we could say that any activity by a particular nerve

Reception, Transduction, and Coding

always conveys the same kind of information to the brain. The brain "hears" the activity of the auditory nerve as sound because it somehow recognizes this as the auditory nerve. *Any* activity of the auditory nerve gives rise to an experience of sound, even if the nerve is stimulated by something other than sound waves.

Another way of stating the law of specific nerve energies: No nerve has the option of sending the message "high C note" at one time, "bright yellow" at another time, and "lemony smell" at yet another. It sends only one kind of message — action potentials. The brain somehow interprets the action potentials from the auditory nerve as sounds, the action potentials from the olfactory nerve as smells, and those from the optic nerve as light. (Admittedly, *somehow* glosses over a profound mystery.)

If you poke your eye or rub it hard, you may see spots or flashes of light even if the room is totally dark. The reason is that the mechanical pressure excites some receptors in the retina of the eye; anything that excites those receptors is perceived as light. (If you wish to try this experiment, press gently on your eyeball with your eye shut and without contact lenses on the eye.)

If it were possible to take the nerves from your eyes and ears and cross-transplant them so that the visual receptors were connected to the auditory nerve and vice versa, you would literally "see" sounds and "hear" lights. This implies that perceptions depend on which neurons are active and how active each one is at a given time.

Although the law of specific nerve energies is still considered fundamentally correct a century and a half after it was first stated, we must add some important qualifications. First, certain cells with a spontaneous rate of firing may signal one kind of stimulus by an increase in firing and a different kind by a decrease in firing. For instance, certain cells in the visual system increase their firing rate in response to red light and decrease below the spontaneous rate in response to green light. The same cell, therefore, may contribute to the perception of both red and green.

Second, it is possible that the "rhythm" of impulses may code certain kinds of information. For example, the following three records of impulses over time may convey different information, even though they represent the same mean frequency in the same cell:

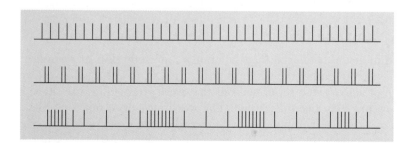

Third, although the law of specific nerve energies applies to the nerve as a whole, it may not apply equally well to individual axons within the nerve. The brain knows, for example, that activity in any of the taste nerves means taste, not light or sound. But does it also know that activity in one axon means salty taste, while activity in another axon means sweet taste? Or do all taste axons contribute to all tastes?

## LABELED-LINE CODING VERSUS CODING AS A PATTERN ACROSS FIBERS

Suppose you run a bakery and you need to send frequent messages to your supplier two blocks away. Suppose further that you can communicate only by ringing three large bells on the roof of your bakery. You would have to work out some sort of code.

One possibility would be to label the three bells: The high-pitched bell means "I need flour." The medium-pitched bell means "I need sugar." And the low-pitched bell means "I need eggs." Then you simply ring the right bell at the right moment. The more you need something, the faster you ring the bell. We shall call this the "labeled-line code," because each bell has a single, unchanging label.

Another possibility would be to set up a code that depends on a relationship among the three bells: Ringing the high and medium bells equally means that you need flour. The medium and low bells together call for sugar; the high and low bells together call for eggs. Ringing all three together means you need vanilla extract. Ringing mostly the high bell while ringing the other two bells slightly means you need hazelnuts. Ringing mostly the low bell, slightly less the high bell, and still less the medium bell means you need caraway seeds. And so forth. We call this the "across-fiber pattern code," because the meaning depends on the pattern across bells.

The across-fiber pattern code has the advantage of being more versatile; with just three bells you can call for all sorts of necessary ingredients. Its disadvantage is that it is complicated. If your supplier forgets the code or cannot hear your bells clearly, you may get a delivery of iodized salt after you asked for maple syrup.

Which kind of code does the vertebrate nervous system use? When you see, hear, taste, or smell something, the stimulus excites a great many receptors. Does each axon convey a single, unambiguous message, such as "green light" or "E-flat above high C"? Or does it send a message that means something only when it is part of a pattern composed of the activities of many axons?

According to the **labeled-line theory,** each receptor responds to a limited range of stimuli, and each receptor has a direct line to the brain. According to the **across-fiber pattern theory,** each receptor responds to a wider range of stimuli, and it contributes to the perception of every stimulus in its system (such as vision or hearing). In other words, a given level of response by a given sensory axon means little to the brain unless it knows what a number of other axons are doing at the same time.

Which theory is correct? It depends. The perception of pitch in hearing depends on a labeled-line system, at least for high-frequency tones. A given high-frequency tone excites only a small group of receptors. If something destroyed those receptors in your ear, you would no longer be able to hear that tone.

At the other extreme, color vision depends on a pattern across fibers. If you have full color vision, you can perceive red, red-orange, orange, orange-yellow, yellow, yellow-green. . . . You do not have a separate receptor type for each color you can distinguish. Instead, you have three types of receptors, and each color of light produces a distinctive pattern of responses by those three types of receptors. The response of a single color-sensitive neuron at a given time is ambiguous; the brain can interpret the message only by comparing it with the activity in other neurons.

With regard to taste and olfaction, as you will see, investigators are still not certain how the information is coded. Are there labeled lines from each receptor to the brain, or does the brain read a pattern across many types of neurons? This is just one of the basic unanswered questions about the physiology of sensation.

## SUMMARY

1. Each type of receptor transduces a particular kind of energy into a generator potential. (p. 188)

2. Sensory information is coded so that the brain can process it. The coded information bears no physical similarity to the stimuli being coded. (p. 189)

3. According to the law of specific nerve energies, the brain interprets any activity of a given sensory neuron as representing the kind of sensory information that neuron is tuned to. (p. 189)

4. Sensory information can be coded either in terms of a labeled-line system or in terms of an across-fiber pattern system. (p. 191)

## REVIEW QUESTIONS

1. What is the difference between transduction and coding? (p. 188)

2. What is the law of specific nerve energies, and how must it be modified in light of modern knowledge of the nervous system? (p. 190)

3. What is the difference between the labeled-line theory and the across-fiber pattern theory? (p. 191)

## SUGGESTIONS FOR FURTHER READING

**Goldstein, E. B.** (1989). *Sensation and perception* (3rd ed.). Belmont, CA: Wadsworth. A general textbook on the sensory systems, emphasizing vision and hearing.

**Marks, L. E.** (1978). *The unity of the senses.* New York: Academic Press. Interesting description of the general principles of sensation and perception, including similarities among sensory systems.

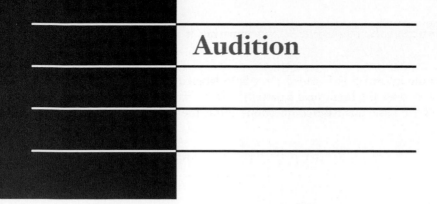

# Audition

If a tree falls in an uninhabited forest where no one is present to hear it, does it make a sound? The answer depends on what we mean by "sound." If we mean sound waves, then of course a tree falling in an uninhabited forest makes a sound. Sound waves, a physical phenomenon, are sure to occur when a falling tree hits the ground. But the term *sound* usually refers not to the sound waves themselves but to a perception, an experience. By that definition, not even a volcanic eruption or an atomic explosion would make a sound if no one were present to hear it.

The human auditory system enables us to hear not only falling trees but also the birds singing in the trees and the wind blowing through the leaves. Some blind people learn to walk down a hallway clicking their heels against the floor and listening to the echoes to localize the walls and other obstructions. Our auditory systems are amazingly well adapted for detecting and interpreting an enormous variety of information.

## SOUND

Sound waves are periodic compressions of air, water, or other media. When a tree hits the ground, both the tree and the ground vibrate, setting up sound waves in the air that strike someone's ears. If a similar object hit the ground on the moon, where there is no air, people would not hear it—unless, perhaps, they put an ear to the ground.

Sound waves vary in two ways, amplitude and frequency. The **amplitude** of a sound wave is its intensity. A very intense compression of air, such as that produced by a bolt of lightning, produces sound waves of great amplitude, which a listener hears as great loudness. **Loudness** is the perception of intensity; it is not the same thing as amplitude. If the amplitude of a sound doubles, its perceived loudness increases but it does not double.

The **frequency** of a sound is the number of compressions per second, measured in hertz (Hz, cycles per second). **Pitch** is a perception closely related to frequency. As a rule, the higher the frequency of a sound, the higher its pitch. Discrepancies can occur, however. For example, a person who listens to a

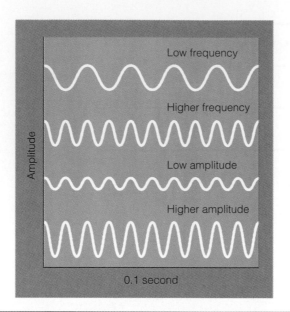

**Figure 6.2**
**Four sound waves**
*The period (time) between the peaks determines the frequency of the sound, which we experience as pitch. Here, the top line represents 5 sound waves in 0.1 second, or 50 Hz—a very low-frequency sound that we would experience as a very low pitch. The other three lines represent 100 Hz. The vertical extent of each line represents its amplitude or intensity, which we experience as loudness.*

Within the figure:
Low frequency

Higher frequency

Low amplitude

Higher amplitude

Amplitude

0.1 second

combination of sounds at frequencies 1,000 Hz, 1,500 Hz, 2,000 Hz, and 2,500 Hz—all even multiples of 500 Hz—will also hear a pitch corresponding to 500 Hz. (This is known as "perceptual restoration of the missing fundamental.")

Figure 6.2 illustrates the amplitude and frequency of sounds. In each part of the figure, the height of the waves corresponds to amplitude, and the number of waves per second corresponds to frequency.

The average adult human can hear air vibrations ranging from about 15 or 20 Hz to somewhat less than 20,000 Hz. Perception of high pitch decreases with age; preschool children are better than adults at hearing pitches of 20,000 Hz and above (B. A. Schneider, Trehub, Morrongiello, & Thorpe, 1986). For middle-aged adults, the upper limit for hearing decreases by about 80 Hz every six months (von Békésy, 1957). The upper limit drops even faster for those exposed to loud noises.

## STRUCTURES OF THE EAR

You may have heard of a "Rube Goldberg" device. Rube Goldberg (1883–1970) was a cartoonist who drew enormously complicated inventions to perform simple tasks. For example, a person's tread on the front doorstep would pull a string that raised a cat's tail, awakening the cat, which would then chase a bird that had been resting on a balance, which would swing up to strike a doorbell. The functioning of the ear may remind you a little of a Rube Goldberg device, since sound waves are transduced into action potentials through a many-step, roundabout process. Unlike Rube Goldberg's inventions, however, the ear actually works.

The first step in hearing is the entry of sound waves into the auditory canal, as Figure 6.3 shows. At the end of the auditory canal, vibrations strike the **tympanic membrane,** or eardrum, which vibrates at the same frequency as the sound waves that strike it. The tympanic membrane is attached to three bones in the middle ear that transmit the vibrations to the *oval window* of the inner ear. These bones are sometimes known by their English names—hammer, anvil, and stir-

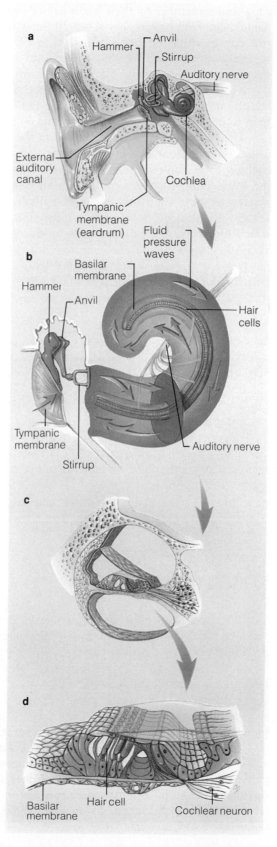

**Figure 6.3**
**Structures of the ear**
*When sound waves strike the tympanic membrane in (a), they cause it to vibrate three tiny bones—the hammer, anvil, and stirrup—that convert the sound waves into stronger vibrations in the fluid-filled cochlea (b). Those vibrations displace the hair cells along the basilar membrane in the cochlea. (c) A cross section through the cochlea. (d) A close-up of the hair cells.*

rup—and sometimes by their Latin names—malleus, incus, and stapes. The tympanic membrane has an area about 20 times larger than the footplate of the stirrup, connected to the oval window. As in a hydraulic pump, the vibrations of the tympanic membrane are transformed into more forceful vibrations when they reach the smaller stirrup. The net effect of the system is to convert the sound waves into waves of greater pressure on the small oval window. This is important because more force is required to move the viscous fluid inside the oval window than to move the eardrum, which has air on both sides of it.

The auditory receptors are located in the inner ear in a snail-shaped structure called the **cochlea** (KO-klee-uh, Latin for *snail*). A cross section through the cochlea, as in Figure 6.3c, shows that it contains three long fluid-filled tunnels, the scala vestibuli, scala media, and scala tympani. The stirrup contacts the oval window at the entrance to the scala vestibuli; from there vibrations are transmitted to the rest of the cochlea. When the vibrations reach the **basilar membrane,** which forms the floor of the scala media, they displace the **hair cells** that lie along the basilar membrane (Figure 6.3d). As the scala media is pushed up and down by the pressure waves, the hair cells are bent between the tectorial and basilar membranes. The hair cells respond within microseconds to a displacement as small as $10^{-10}$ meter (0.1 nanometer, about the diameter of one atom), thereby

**Figure 6.4**

*(a, b) Hair cells from a frog sacculus, an organ that detects ground-borne vibrations. (c) The cochlea of a cat. (d) The cochlea of a fence lizard. Kc = kinocilium, one of the components of a hair bundle. (From Hudspeth, 1985.)*

opening sodium channels in the membrane of the neuron (Fettiplace, 1990; Hudspeth, 1985). The axons of the hair cells form the auditory nerve, the eighth cranial nerve. Figure 6.4 shows electron micrographs of the hair cells of three different species.

## PITCH PERCEPTION

Our ability to understand speech or to enjoy music depends on our ability to differentiate among sounds of different pitches, even when the sounds are presented for brief periods in rapid succession. How do we do so?

According to one early theory, the **frequency theory,** the basilar membrane vibrates in synchrony with a sound and causes hair cells to produce action potentials at the same frequency. For example, a sound at 500 Hz would cause 500 action potentials per second in the auditory nerve. The downfall of this theory in its simplest form is that adults can distinguish pitches up to 20,000 Hz and children can hear even higher frequencies. The refractory period of neurons prevents them from maintaining such high rates of action potentials.

According to the **place theory,** an alternative proposed by Hermann von Helmholtz, the basilar membrane resembles the strings of a piano in that each area along the membrane is tuned to a specific pitch and vibrates whenever that pitch is present. Thus, according to this theory, a sound at any pitch activates the hair cells at only one place along the basilar membrane. The nervous system distinguishes among pitches on the basis of which neurons are activated. The downfall of this theory in its original form is that no portion of the basilar membrane has physical properties like those that cause a piano string to resonate to a tone. Moreover, the various parts of the basilar membrane are bound together, so no one part could resonate without carrying neighboring parts with it.

According to the currently prevalent theory (Corso, 1973; Gulick, 1971), the mechanism for discriminating pitch differs for low and high pitches. For low-pitched sounds (up to about 100 Hz), the frequency theory seems to apply. The basilar membrane vibrates in synchrony with the sound waves, and hair cells generate one action potential per wave. Weak sounds activate only a small number of hair cells, while stronger sounds activate greater numbers. Thus, at low pitches the frequency of impulses identifies the pitch, and the number of cells firing identifies the loudness.

For pitches near 100 Hz or higher, a given neuron cannot fire at the same rate as the frequency of the sound waves. A neuron may nevertheless produce action potentials phase-locked to the *peaks* of the sound waves (that is, always occurring at the same phase in the sound wave), as illustrated here:

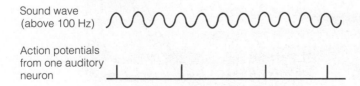

Sound wave
(above 100 Hz)

Action potentials
from one auditory
neuron

Additional auditory neurons also produce action potentials phase-locked with peaks of the sound wave but not necessarily in phase with the action potentials of the first neuron:

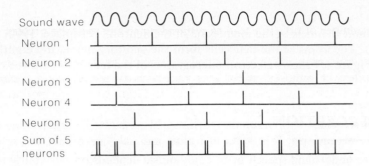

If we consider the auditory nerve as a whole, including a large number of individual fibers, we find that each sound wave of moderately high frequency produces a *volley* of impulses by various fibers; that is, at least a few neurons fire synchronously with each wave in, say, a 600 Hz tone. Although no individual fiber can produce impulses at a rate of 600 per second, the auditory nerve as a whole can have volleys of impulses at 600 per second. This is the **volley principle** of pitch discrimination (Rose, Brugge, Anderson, & Hind, 1967).

Do such volleys really contribute to pitch perception? Investigators have demonstrated that volleys of impulses do occur in the auditory nerve, and biological psychologists generally assume that the brain can use any information produced by neurons. In this case, however, we do not know how the brain uses the volleys, if it does. How does a structure somewhere in the brain "read" the impulses across many neurons to detect a volley? Note that if it does do so, this is an example of an across-fiber pattern code (see p. 191); the brain must detect a pat-

**Figure 6.5**
**The basilar membrane of the human cochlea**
*High-frequency sounds produce their maximum displacement near the base. Low-frequency sounds produce their maximum displacement near the apex.*

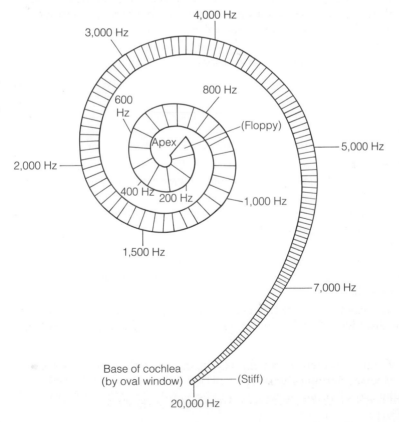

198

tern over a number of fibers instead of responding to any message present in just one.

At some tone near 5,000 Hz the volley principle becomes inadequate; even staggered volleys of impulses cannot keep pace with the sound waves. Before this point is reached, however, another mechanism comes into play, similar to the mechanism postulated by the place theory.

At its **base,** where the stirrup meets the cochlea, the basilar membrane is thin (about 0.15 mm) and stiff. It is wider (0.5 mm) and only one-hundredth as stiff at the other end of the cochlea, the **apex** (von Békésy, 1956; Yost & Nielsen, 1977). (See Figure 6.5.) You may be surprised that the basilar membrane is thinnest at the base, where the cochlea itself is widest. The difference is made up of a bony shelf that attaches to the basilar membrane. When a vibration strikes the basilar membrane, it sets up a *traveling wave.* As the wave travels along the membrane, it produces some displacement at all points, but the amount of displacement varies because of differences in the thickness and stiffness of the membrane.

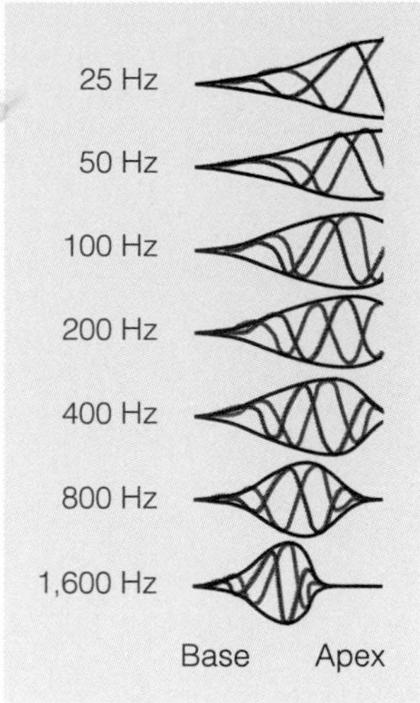

Vibrations at different frequencies set up traveling waves that peak at different points along the basilar membrane, as Figures 6.5 and 6.6 illustrate. The traveling wave for a low-frequency vibration peaks at or near the apex, where the membrane is large and floppy. For progressively higher frequencies, the point of maximum displacement gets closer to the base. In fact, the highest frequencies produce practically no displacement of the membrane near the apex. The waveforms in Figure 6.6 are drawn fairly broadly to be easily visible. In healthy tissues, however, the waves are sharply defined, falling rapidly on both sides of the maximum displacement (Zwislocki, 1981).

To summarize, we identify the lowest pitches by the frequency of impulses. We discriminate among high pitches in terms of the place along the basilar membrane at which the receptors show their greatest activity; the higher the pitch, the closer the maximum displacement to the base of the cochlea. We discriminate intermediate pitches (about 60 to 5,000 Hz) through a combination of frequency (perhaps aided by the volley principle) and place.

25 Hz
50 Hz
100 Hz
200 Hz
400 Hz
800 Hz
1,600 Hz

Base        Apex

**Figure 6.6
Traveling waves in the basilar membrane set up by different frequencies of sound**
*Note that the peak displacement is closer to the base of the cochlea for high frequencies and is toward the apex for lower frequencies. In reality, the peak of each wave is much narrower than shown here.*

## DEAFNESS

Complete deafness is rare. About 99 percent of deaf people can hear at least certain pitches if they are loud enough. We distinguish two categories of hearing impairment: nerve deafness and conductive deafness.

**Nerve deafness,** or **inner-ear deafness,** results from damage to the cochlea, the hair cells, or the auditory nerve. The damage can occur in any degree. It may be confined to one part of the cochlea or to neurons in one part of the cochlea. The result is an impairment in hearing pitches in one range of frequencies—most often the high frequencies. Although nerve deafness is permanent, hearing aids can compensate for the loss.

Nerve deafness can be inherited. It can also develop from a variety of prenatal problems or disorders of early childhood (Robillard & Gersdorff, 1986), including:

- Exposure of one's mother to rubella (German measles), syphilis, or other contagious diseases during pregnancy
- Exposure of one's mother to various toxins during pregnancy

Audition

- Inadequate activity of the thyroid gland
- Certain diseases, including multiple sclerosis

Prolonged exposure to loud noises is one of the most common causes of hearing loss in adults. Some degree of nerve deafness is also common in old age (Corso, 1985).

**Conductive deafness,** or **middle-ear deafness,** occurs if the bones of the middle ear fail to transmit sound waves properly to the cochlea. Such deafness can be caused by certain diseases and infections or by a tumorous growth of bones in and around the middle ear. Conductive deafness is sometimes temporary. If it persists, it can sometimes be corrected by surgery. Because people with conductive deafness have a normal cochlea and auditory nerve, they can hear sounds that bypass the middle ear. For example, they can hear their own voices, which can be conducted through the bones of the skull directly to the cochlea.

## LOCALIZATION OF SOUNDS

Determining the direction and distance of a sound is complicated. Unlike touch, for which receptors are spread over the whole body, or even vision, in which each eye has receptors focused on separate points in space, audition requires a comparison between the two ears—which are in effect just two points in space—to locate the sources of stimuli. And yet this system can be accurate enough for owls to hunt mice on dark nights, solely by their sounds, identifying not only the left-right direction of a sound source but its elevation as well (Knudsen & Konishi, 1978).

Information from the two ears progresses through several subcortical structures on its way to the auditory cortex, as Figure 6.7 illustrates. Virtually all aspects of the auditory system, from the external ear to the auditory cortex, show adaptations that facilitate the localization of sounds.

Two methods are used for sound localization (Yost & Nielsen, 1977). The first is the difference in loudness between the two ears. The head impedes the passage of sound waves, especially if the wavelength is shorter than the width of the head; that is, for short-wavelength (high-frequency) sounds, the head creates a *sound shadow* (Figure 6.8). Consequently, the sound is louder for the closer ear. In adults, this mechanism produces accurate sound localization for pitches above 3,000 Hz and progressively less accurate localization for lower pitches.

The second method of localization is the difference in *time of arrival* at the two ears. A sound coming from a source directly in front of a person reaches both ears at the same time. A sound coming directly from the left will reach the left ear about 600 microseconds ($600 \times 10^{-6}$ seconds) before it reaches the right ear. Sounds coming from intermediate locations will reach the two ears at times 0 to 600 microseconds apart.

The time of a sound's onset is useful for localizing sounds with a sharp onset, such as the sound of an object hitting the floor. It is less useful for localizing sounds with a gradual onset. When threatened by a predator, many birds give alarm calls that increase gradually in loudness; such calls are difficult for the predator to localize.

However, for low-frequency sound waves, even gradual-onset sounds can be localized. Any sound wave has phases, with two consecutive peaks 360 degrees apart. Figure 6.9 shows sound waves in phase and sound waves 45, 90, and 180 degrees out of phase. If a sound comes from one side of the head, the sound wave

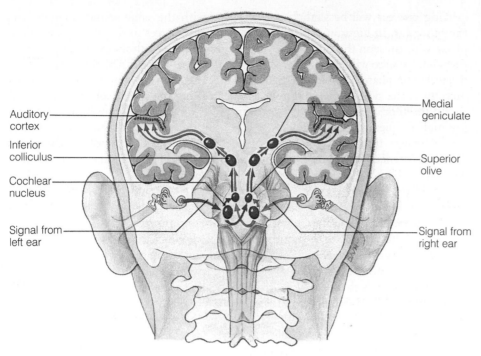

Auditory cortex

Inferior colliculus

Cochlear nucleus

Signal from left ear

Medial geniculate

Superior olive

Signal from right ear

**Figure 6.7**
**Route of auditory impulses from the receptors in the ear to the auditory cortex**
*The cochlear nucleus receives input from only the ipsilateral ear. All later stages have input originating from both ears.*

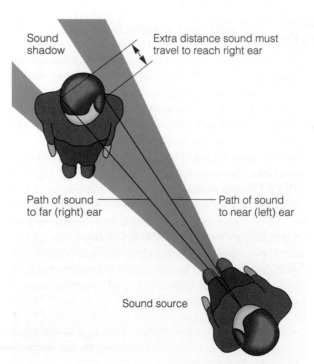

Sound shadow

Extra distance sound must travel to reach right ear

Path of sound to far (right) ear

Path of sound to near (left) ear

Sound source

**Figure 6.8**
**Differential loudness as a cue for sound localization**
*The sound shadow shown does not include the effects of diffraction, or "bending" of sound waves around the head. (After Lindsay & Norman, 1972.)*

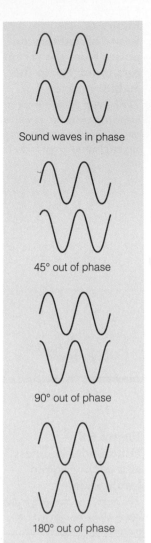

**Figure 6.9
What it means for
sound waves to be in
phase and out of phase**

Sound waves in phase

45° out of phase

90° out of phase

180° out of phase

striking one ear will be slightly out of phase with the same sound wave striking the other ear. In Figure 6.10a, note that the sound waves in the left ear are out of phase with those in the right ear. For each wave, the receptors in the ear closer to the sound source will fire slightly sooner than those in the farther ear will. A large difference in phase between the two ears indicates that the sound source is almost directly to the side; a small difference indicates that the sound source is either directly ahead or directly behind. However, phase differences are useless for localizing high-frequency sounds. As Figure 6.10b shows, with high-frequency sounds it would be easy to confuse the phase of one wave with the phase of another wave. Phase differences provide information useful for localizing sounds with frequencies up to about 1,500 Hz.

In short, humans localize low frequencies (up to 1,500 Hz) by differences in phase and time of onset. We localize high frequencies (above 3,000 Hz) by loudness differences. We are less accurate at localizing intermediate frequencies.

The usefulness of both methods of localization depends on the size of the head. For a small species such as the mouse, the ears are so close together that the animal cannot detect phase differences between sounds even at low frequencies. Small animals therefore have trouble localizing low-pitched tones. They also have some trouble localizing sounds of 3,000 Hz or so—sounds that humans easily localize by differences in loudness. High-frequency tones are louder to one ear than to the other because the head creates a "sound shadow." But the head creates a shadow only when the wavelength of the sound is less than the width of the head. A tone at 3,000 Hz has a short wavelength relative to the width of the human head, but not relative to a mouse's head. The smaller the animal, the higher the frequency must be before the animal can use loudness as a cue to direction. Thus, small-headed species such as mice cannot use phase differences for localization at all, and they can use loudness differences only for higher pitches than humans can.

During the course of evolution, each species seems to have evolved a sensitivity to those pitches that it can easily localize. Rodents and other small animals are less sensitive to low-pitched sounds than humans are, but they are more sensitive to higher pitches, up to 40,000, 60,000, or even 100,000 Hz. Vervets, a species of monkeys with relatively small heads, are more sensitive to high frequencies than other monkeys are but less sensitive to low frequencies (Owren, Hopp, Sinnott, & Petersen, 1988). The hearing range of larger mammals is shifted toward lower pitches. The upper limit for elephants is just 10,000 Hz (Heffner & Heffner, 1982). These findings underscore a point made at the beginning of this chapter: Each species is most sensitive to the information most useful to it.

The two methods of sound localization depend on different brain structures. Localization based on loudness depends on the lateral part of the superior olive (in the medulla); localization based on phase differences depends on the medial part. Small-headed species, such as the mouse, which cannot use phase differences to localize sound, have no medial superior olive at all; they have just the lateral superior olive (Masterton, 1974).

## SUMMARY

1. We detect the pitch of low-frequency sounds by the frequency of action potentials in the auditory system. We detect the pitch of high-frequency sounds by the area of greatest response along the basilar membrane. (p. 197)

2. Damage to the nerve cells or to the bones that conduct sounds to the nerve cells can cause deafness. (p. 199)

3. We localize high-frequency sounds on the basis of differences in loudness between the ears. We localize low-frequency sounds on the basis of differences in phase. (p. 200)

**Figure 6.10**
**Phase differences between the ears as a cue for sound localization**
*Note that a low-frequency tone (**a**) arrives at the ears slightly out of phase. The ear for which the receptors fire first (here, the person's left ear) is interpreted as being closer to the sound. If the difference in phase between the ears is small, then the sound source is close to the center of the body. However, with a high-frequency sound (**b**) the phase differences become ambiguous. The person cannot tell which sound wave in the left ear corresponds to which sound wave in the right ear.*

## REVIEW QUESTIONS

1. Differentiate among the frequency theory, the volley principle, and the place theory of pitch perception. (p. 197)

2. How do our mechanisms of pitch perception vary among low-, medium-, and high-pitched tones? (p. 197)

3. What are the two major categories of deafness, and what causes each? (p. 199)

4. What mechanisms enable an animal to localize sounds? How does the effectiveness of each method depend on the size of the animal's head? (p. 200)

## THOUGHT QUESTIONS

1. Why do you suppose the human auditory system evolved sensitivity to sounds in the range of 20 to 20,000 Hz instead of some other range of frequencies?

2. The text explains how we might distinguish loudness for low-pitched sounds on the basis of the frequency theory. How might we distinguish loudness for high-pitched sounds?

## SUGGESTION FOR FURTHER READING

**Zwislocki, J. J.** (1981). Sound analysis in the ear: A history of discoveries. *American Scientist, 69,* 184–192. An excellent review of transduction and coding of auditory information.

# The Mechanical
# Senses

The next time you turn on your radio or stereo set, place your hand on its surface and feel the vibrations. The vibrations you feel in your hand are the same vibrations you hear.

If you were to practice enough, could you learn to "hear" the vibrations with your fingers? No. You might improve your ability to recognize a particular pattern of vibrations, but they would still feel like vibrations, and the detectors in your skin would never become sensitive to the airborne vibrations we experience as sounds.

If a species with no ears had enough time, might its vibration detectors *evolve* into sound detectors? Yes! In fact, that is probably how our remote ancestors did evolve the ability to hear. Fish have no ears as such; they have a *lateral line system* consisting of a long row of touch receptors on each side of the body. Those touch receptors produce sensations that provide the equivalent of hearing for fish. (Snakes also lack ears and apparently do not detect airborne vibrations. Instead, they are able to detect vibrations in the ground.) Primitive vertebrates probably had a variety of touch receptors, perhaps somewhat like today's fish. From those touch receptors we ultimately evolved our organs of hearing. But we also evolved receptors responsive to mechanical stimulation — receptors that generally receive little attention in psychology, but whose importance is clear as soon as we contemplate what it would be like to live without them.

We categorize several senses as *mechanical senses* because they respond to pressure, bending, or other distortions of a receptor. These senses include touch, pain, and other body sensations, as well as vestibular sensation, a system specialized to detect the position and movement of the head. Audition could be regarded as a mechanical sense as well, because the hair cells are modified touch receptors. However, it is convenient to keep audition separate because it provides information about objects at a distance, while the other mechanical senses provide information about what is happening to one's own body.

# VESTIBULAR SENSATION

Try this demonstration: Attempt to read this text while you jiggle your head up and down, back and forth. It is a little inconvenient, you will find, but not too bad. Now hold your head steady and jiggle the book up and down, back and forth. Suddenly, reading becomes much more difficult. Why?

When you move your head, the **vestibular organ** adjacent to the cochlea monitors each movement and directs compensatory movements of your eyes. When your head moves left, your eyes move right; when your head moves right, your eyes move left. Almost effortlessly, you keep your eyes focused on what you want to see. When you move the page, however, the vestibular organ cannot help you keep your eyes on target. Vestibular sensations (sensations from the vestibular organ) detect the direction of tilt and the amount of acceleration of the head. These sensations seldom enter our conscious awareness; nevertheless, they contribute to the guidance of both eye movements and balance.

Figure 6.11 shows the anatomy of the vestibular organ. It consists of two otolith organs and three semicircular canals (D. E. Parker, 1980). Like the hearing receptors, the vestibular receptors are modified touch receptors. One **otolith organ** has a horizontal patch of hairs; the other has a vertical patch. Calcium carbonate particles called otoliths lie next to the hair cells in the otolith organs. When the head tilts in different directions, the otoliths push against different sets of hair cells and excite them.

The three **semicircular canals,** oriented in three different planes, are filled with a jellylike substance and lined with hair cells. An acceleration of the head in

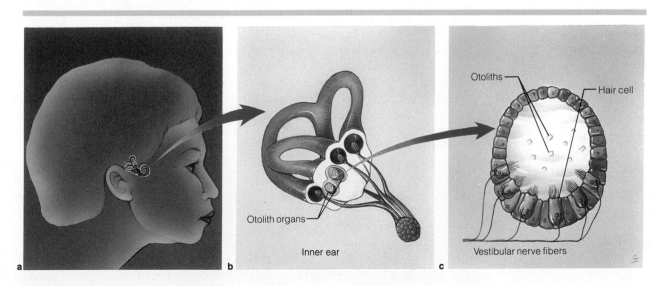

**Figure 6.11**
*(a) Location of the vestibular organs. (b) Structures of the vestibular organs. (c) Cross section through an otolith organ. Calcium carbonate particles, called otoliths, press against different hair cells depending on the direction of tilt and rate of acceleration of the head.*

any plane causes the jellylike substance in one of these canals to push against the hair cells. Action potentials initiated by cells of the vestibular system travel via part of the eighth cranial nerve to the brain stem and cerebellum.

## SOMATOSENSATION

The **somatosensory system,** the sensation of the body and its movements, is not one sense but many. We can distinguish discriminative touch (by which we identify the shape of an object), deep pressure, cold, warmth, pain, and the sense of position and movement of joints.

The skin is packed with a variety of touch receptors. Figure 6.12 shows some of the major receptor types found in mammalian skin, and Table 6.1 lists some of their probable functions (Iggo & Andres, 1982). Other receptors, which are not included on the list, respond to deep stimulation, movement of joints, and movement of muscles.

A touch receptor may consist of a simple bare ending (such as pain receptors), an elaborated neuron ending (Ruffini endings and Meissner's corpuscles), or a bare ending surrounded by nonneural cells that modify its function (Pacinian corpuscles). Some of the more sensitive areas of skin, such as the fingertips, have as many as 700 touch cells in 2 square millimeters of surface. Although different receptor types are apparently associated with different types of sensation, certain receptors are not yet well understood.

**Figure 6.12**
**Some sensory receptors found in the skin, the human body's largest organ**

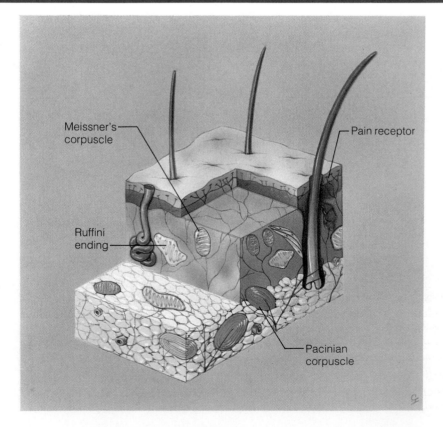

Meissner's corpuscle

Pain receptor

Ruffini ending

Pacinian corpuscle

## Table 6.1 Touch Receptors and Their Probable Functions

| Receptor | Location | Responds To | Rate of Adaptation to a Prolonged Stimulus |
|---|---|---|---|
| Free nerve ending (un-myelinated or thinly myelinated fibers) | Around base of hairs and elsewhere in skin | Pain, warmth, cold | Uncertain |
| Hair-follicle receptors | Hair-covered skin | Movement of hairs | Rapid |
| Meissner's corpuscles | Hairless areas | Sudden displacement of skin; low-frequency vibration (flutter) | Rapid (?) |
| Pacinian corpuscles | Both hairy and hairless skin | Sudden displacement of skin; high-frequency vibration | Very rapid |
| Merkel's disks | Both hairy and hairless skin | Indentation of skin | Slow |
| Ruffini endings | Both hairy and hairless skin | Stretch of skin | Slow |
| Krause end bulbs | Hairless areas, perhaps including genitals; maybe some hairy areas | Uncertain | Uncertain |

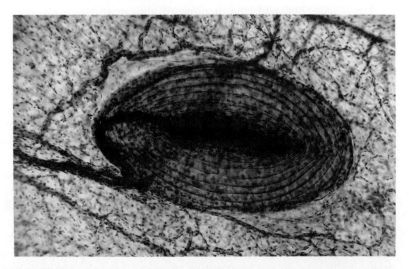

**Figure 6.13**
**A Pacinian corpuscle, a type of receptor that responds best to sudden displacement of the skin or to high-frequency vibrations**
*Pacinian corpuscles respond only briefly to steady pressure on the skin. The onionlike outer structure provides a mechanical support to the neuron inside it so that a sudden stimulus can bend it but a sustained stimulus cannot. (Ed Reschke.)*

One example of a receptor is the Pacinian corpuscle (Figure 6.13), which detects a sudden displacement of the skin or high-frequency vibration on the skin. Inside the onionlike surround is a neuron membrane. When mechanical pressure bends the membrane, its resistance to sodium flow decreases, and sodium ions enter, depolarizing the membrane (Loewenstein, 1960). The onionlike outer structure provides a mechanical support such that a gradual or constant pressure on the skin does not bend the neuron's membrane; only a sudden or vibrating stimulus can bend it.

Information from the various touch receptors enters the spinal cord and passes toward the brain. Figure 6.14 depicts two of the major somatosensory paths. The point of this figure is certainly not for you to try to memorize these paths but merely to demonstrate that different types of sensory information have different routes to the brain and that they project to different brain areas.

Information that travels up different routes in the spinal cord also reaches different parts of the thalamus and cerebral cortex. For example, one area of the ventral-posterior thalamus responds to activity of the Pacinian corpuscles. Within that area, different parts respond to different parts of the body. At least three other nearby areas of the thalamus respond to different receptors or combinations of receptors (Dykes, Sur, Merzenich, Kaas, & Nelson, 1981).

The various areas of the somatosensory thalamus send their impulses to different areas of the somatosensory cortex, located in the parietal lobe. The somatosensory cortex includes four parallel strips, each of which has its own representation of the entire body (see Chapter 4). Two of the strips respond mostly to touch on the skin; the other two respond mostly to deep pressure and movement of the joints and muscles (Kaas, 1983).

In short, various aspects of somatosensation remain at least partly separate from one another at all levels, from the receptors to the somatosensory area of the cerebral cortex.

## PAIN

Pain is a sensation evoked by a harmful stimulus, including cuts, diseases, chemical irritation, intense heat, and intense cold (LaMotte & Collins, 1982). Pain alerts us to danger or injury. Some people have a genetically determined inability to detect pain, hot, and cold, because of abnormalities of the nerves responsible for transmitting pain messages. Other people have a genetically determined *indifference* to pain; they can tell the difference between sharp and dull pain and between hot and cold, but none of those sensations bothers them (Comings & Amromin, 1974). (Curiously, these people also never complain about headaches or itching sensations.) People who are either insensitive or indifferent to pain are prone to frequent and sometimes serious injury. If they pick up a red-hot pan, they do not immediately put it down; if they step barefoot onto a tack or a piece of glass, they may continue to walk on the injured foot without realizing what has happened.

However, a person who is already aware of a hurt does not need constant reminders; extreme, prolonged pain interferes with behavior more than it directs it. People have a variety of physiological mechanisms that inhibit pain; because of these mechanisms, the intensity of pain varies from one person to another and from one situation to another for a given individual (Liebeskind & Paul, 1977). For example, some soldiers and athletes report little pain from serious injuries; occasionally they do not even notice an injury until the action is over.

To account for such variations in pain responsiveness, Ronald Melzack and P. D. Wall (1965) proposed a highly influential theory of pain known as the **gate theory.** According to this theory, certain areas of the spinal cord receive messages not only from pain receptors but also from other receptors in the skin and from axons descending from the brain. If these other inputs to the spinal cord are sufficiently active, they close the "gates" for the pain messages. In that case, the pain messages cannot get through to the brain.

Although Melzack and Wall's gate theory included certain details that turned out to be wrong, the general principle is valid: Various kinds of nonpain stimuli

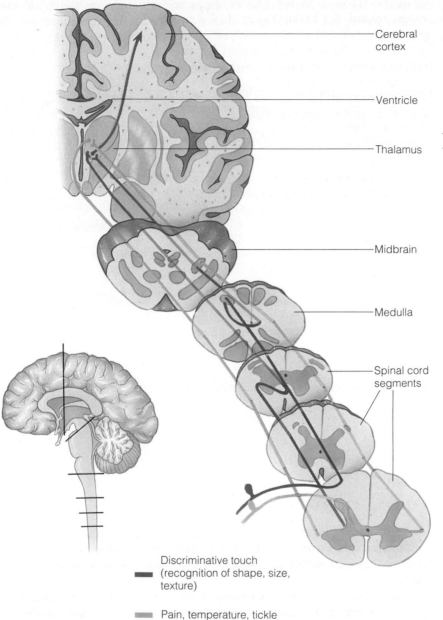

**Figure 6.14**
**Two major pathways
ascending the spinal
cord**
*Note that all sensory input
enters through the dorsal roots
of the spinal cord and that
different kinds of sensory information travel through different pathways.*

Cerebral
cortex

Ventricle

Thalamus

Midbrain

Medulla

Spinal cord
segments

Discriminative touch
(recognition of shape, size,
texture)

Pain, temperature, tickle

can modify the sensation of pain. We begin with the neurons and neurotransmitters that convey pain information, then we shall turn to the mechanisms that inhibit pain.

## Pain Neurons and Their Neurotransmitters

Unmyelinated axons and some thinly myelinated axons carry pain information to the spinal cord, releasing a neurotransmitter known as **substance P** to the neurons they contact in the spinal cord (Piercey, Schroeder, Folkers, Xu, & Horig, 1981). The spinal cord neurons in turn send their information to the ventrobasal nucleus of the thalamus (Tasker, 1976).

What effect would you expect if an investigator injected substance P into an animal's brain or spinal cord? The animal scratches, bites, and shows other indications of pain—not pain in the spinal cord itself, but pain felt in the part of the body that ordinarily sends information to that section of the spinal cord.

An animal also shows signs of pain and distress after a spinal injection of **capsaicin,** a chemical that causes neurons containing substance P to release it suddenly. An injection of capsaicin causes an animal to react about the same as it would after an injection of substance P itself for about 5 to 10 minutes. Afterward, however, because the neurons released substance P far faster than they could resynthesize it, they have less ability than usual to release it. Consequently, the animal becomes relatively insensitive to pain for a long time, sometimes months (Gamse, Leeman, Holzer, & Lembeck, 1981; Jancsó, Kiraly, & Jancsó-Gábor, 1977; Yarsh, Farb, Leeman, & Jessell, 1979).

Capsaicin occurs in nature in jalapeño peppers and other hot peppers. When you eat a hot pepper, the capsaicin in the pepper causes certain neurons in your tongue to release substance P, giving you a sensation of pain or heat. After the heat sensation wears off, you may experience a pleasant state of relief, probably accompanied by a decreased sensitivity to pain on your tongue. However, do not try to use jalapeño peppers as a home remedy for pain. Very little capsaicin from the diet is absorbed into the blood.

## Opiates and Endorphins

For centuries people have been using morphine and other opiate drugs to relieve pain, induce sleep, and stimulate pleasure, although no one knew how the drugs worked. A classic example of a nonexplanation came from an unknown physician who said that opium induces sleep "because of its dormitive properties." (*Dormitive* is just a fancy word for sleep inducing.) We can do better than that today, although we still cannot offer a complete explanation of how opiates affect behavior.

Beginning in the 1950s, investigators discovered that most drugs with behavioral effects interact with one or another of the synaptic receptors. It was natural, therefore, to look for some sort of receptor with which opiate drugs might interact. For years those presumed receptors remained elusive. Then Candace Pert and Solomon Snyder (1973) identified brain receptors that bind specifically to morphine and to other drugs with related effects. They also demonstrated that the opiate receptors are concentrated in certain areas of the brain—the same areas where substance P is concentrated (McLean, Skirboll, & Pert, 1985). Apparently, opiate receptors play an important role in inhibiting or limiting the pain-producing effects of substance P (Figure 6.15).

But presumably evolution did not equip us with receptors just to deal with drugs derived from the opium poppy. The discovery of opiate receptors implied

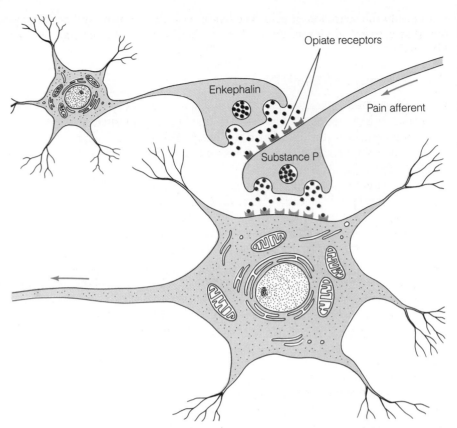

**Figure 6.15**
**Synapses responsible for pain and its inhibition**
*The pain afferent neuron releases substance P as its neurotransmitter. Another neuron releases enkephalin at presynaptic synapses; the enkephalin inhibits the release of substance P and therefore alleviates pain.*

Opiate receptors

Enkephalin

Pain afferent

Substance P

that the brain must have its own natural substances with opiatelike effects. Before long, those substances were discovered: The brain produces two peptide neurotransmitters, composed of five amino acids each—**met-enkephalin** and **leu-enkephalin** (Hughes et al., 1975)—that have opiatelike properties. (The term *enkephalin* refers to the fact that these chemicals were first found in the brain, or encephalon. The two enkephalins are the same except at one end, where met-enkephalin has methionine and leu-enkephalin has leucine.) Although the enkephalins have chemical structures very unlike morphine, they interact with the same receptors as morphine. In addition, the pituitary gland produces two hormones with opiate-type effects—*beta-endorphin* and *dynorphin*. These two chemicals also serve as neurotransmitters. Collectively, met-enkephalin, leu-enkephalin, beta-endorphin, and dynorphin are known as **endorphins,** a contraction of *endogenous morphines*. They are the brain's own morphines. Brain investigators use the term *endorphins* to refer to any or all of these chemicals; they use the term *enkephalins* to refer specifically to the two short peptides.

What is the role of endorphins in behavior? Like other neurotransmitters, they contribute to a variety of behaviors. They produce **analgesia** (relief from pain); they also promote positive reinforcement. The enkephalin synapses are concentrated mostly in the **periaqueductal gray** area of the brain stem and surrounding areas (Figure 6.16). Activity at these synapses probably blocks the release of substance P from pathways responsible for pain, both in the brain and in the spinal cord (Reichling, Kwiat, & Basbaum, 1988; Terman, Shavitt, Lewis,

The Mechanical
Senses

**Figure 6.16**
**The periaqueductal gray area, where electrical stimulation relieves pain**
Periaqueductal *means "around the aqueduct," a passageway of cerebrospinal fluid between the third and fourth ventricles.*

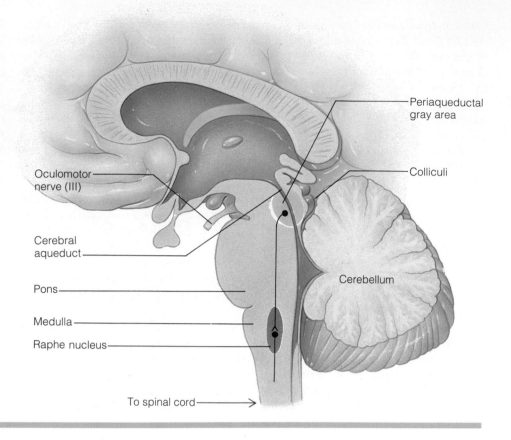

Oculomotor nerve (III)

Cerebral aqueduct

Pons

Medulla

Raphe nucleus

To spinal cord →

Periaqueductal gray area

Colliculi

Cerebellum

Cannon, & Liebeskind, 1984). (You may recognize this as the basic idea of Melzack and Wall's gate theory of pain.) For people suffering from severe pain, physicians have sometimes implanted electrodes and provided stimulation to the periaqueductal gray area. Up to 60 percent of people suffering from severe pain experience noticeable analgesia, which may last hours after the stimulation ends (Barbaro, 1988).

Either enkephalins or electrical stimulation of the periaqueductal gray area can yield analgesia, but neither one produces the nausea that people typically report after receiving morphine injections. Why not? Morphine injections produce effects not only in the brain but also in the digestive system (Bechara & van der Kooy, 1985). The enkephalins act only in the brain; hence they do not produce nausea.

## Stimuli That Produce Analgesia

The endorphins relieve pain, presumably at times when pain is more disruptive than informative. Under what circumstances would neurons release endorphins? That is, what stimuli or situations stimulate the release of endorphins?

One such stimulus is pain itself. After a person has already experienced pain, the pain has served its function of alerting and warning the person; continuous, intense pain is not necessary. For example, after an animal has received a shock to its feet, it becomes somewhat less responsive than usual to the next painful stimulus. The analgesia depends on the release of endorphins in some situations but not in others. Exposure to intermittent or low-intensity continuous shock produces analgesia in rats through the release of endorphins. We know that endorphins are necessary because the effect is blocked by **naloxone,** a drug that blocks opiate receptors. However, exposure to continuous, high-intensity shock also decreases pain sensitivity through a different, unidentified route that naloxone does not block (Terman & Liebeskind, 1986). We therefore conclude that this route does not require endorphins. It is also apparently independent of the cerebral cortex, as damage to the cerebral cortex does not impair this kind of analgesia (Meagher, Grau, & King, 1990).

Stressful situations can also release endorphins. The mere presence of a cat causes the release of endorphins by rats and thereby decreases their response to pain (Lester & Fanselow, 1985). In one experiment, morphine had stronger effects on hamsters that were exposed to loud noises than on hamsters that were not exposed to them. Evidently the noises themselves released endorphins, which then added to the effects of the morphine (Schnur, Martinez, & Hang, 1988).

Pleasant stimuli can release endorphins as well. For example, listening to "thrilling" music—the kind that sends a tingling sensation down your back or all over your body—also decreases pain (A. Goldstein, 1980). We believe it does so by releasing endorphins because naloxone blocks both the tingling sensation and the painkilling effects of the music.

Medical doctors and physical therapists sometimes try to control patients' pain by stimuli that release endorphins. Two examples are acupuncture, an ancient Chinese technique of gently twisting thin needles placed in the skin, and **transcutaneous electrical nerve stimulation** (TENS), the application of prolonged, mild electrical shock to the arms, legs, or back. TENS provides relief for more than half of people in pain, with almost none of the side effects or risks associated with painkilling drugs (Pomeranz, 1989).

## Possible Risks from Excessive Endorphin Activity

In controlled doses, morphine is a medically useful painkiller. Taken in larger doses as a recreational drug, it can make a person passive and unproductive. Similarly, the elicitation of endorphins can sometimes do harm as well as good.

A mouse defeated in a fight by another mouse releases large amounts of endorphins, which decrease its response to pain. The endorphin release depends not just on the pain or damage the mouse received in battle but on the fact that the mouse has "lost." A victorious mouse that has suffered equal injuries releases smaller amounts of endorphins. The defeated mouse adopts a submissive posture: It sits upright with limp forepaws, tilts its head to an angle, and retracts its ears. It turns away from its opponent and squeals when approached. This posture is apparently useful in deterring the victorious mouse from attacking again. Both the decreased response to pain and the submissive posture depend on the release of endorphins (Miczek, Thompson, & Shuster, 1986). A mouse or rat shows similar effects after enduring a series of inescapable shocks—which would also lead to an experience of "defeat."

So far, so good. But the defeated animal "gives up." It does not fight back against any opponent; it does not take simple steps to escape and avoid shock (Maier, Sherman, Lewis, Terman, & Liebeskind, 1983). Such animals also have a decreased immune response and decreased resistance to the growth of tumors (Shavit et al., 1985). In short, although endorphin secretion is ordinarily helpful in enabling an individual to cope with injuries and stress, excessive endorphins can interfere with normal, productive activity.

## SUMMARY

1. The vestibular system is a sensory system that detects the position and acceleration of the head and adjusts body posture and eye movements based on that information. (p. 205)

2. The somatosensory system depends on a variety of receptor types sensitive to different kinds of stimulation of the skin and internal tissues. The brain maintains several parallel somatosensory representations of the body. (p. 206)

3. A certain harmful stimulus may give rise to a greater or lesser degree of pain, depending on other current and recent stimuli. According to the gate theory of pain, other stimuli can close certain gates and block the transmission of pain. (p. 208)

4. Pain messages are transmitted in thin axons with no myelin or with thin myelin sheaths. They release substance P as a neurotransmitter. (p. 210)

5. Capsaicin induces the rapid release of substance P, thus producing a painful sensation. However, because it releases substance P faster than the neurons can resynthesize it, the individual will have a period of lower-than-usual sensitivity to pain. (p. 210)

6. Opiate drugs attach to a particular type of receptor in the brain. The brain produces its own opiate-type chemicals, including the neurotransmitters leu-enkephalin and met-enkephalin, and the hormones beta-endorphin and dynorphin. The enkephalins decrease pain sensations, probably by blocking the release of substance P. (p. 210)

7. Pain, stress, "thrilling" music, and other experiences can release endorphins and thereby decrease sensitivity to pain. (p. 212)

8. A mouse or rat that is defeated in battle, or one that endures repeated, inescapable shocks, releases large amounts of endorphins. As a result, it becomes insensitive to pain, adopts a submissive posture, and fails to fight back even when fighting back could be effective. (p. 213)

## REVIEW QUESTIONS

1. If a person suffers damage to the vestibular system, he or she has trouble reading street signs while walking. Why? (p. 205)

2. In what way is touch several senses instead of just one sense? (p. 206)

3. Which neurotransmitter do pain-receptor neurons release? (p. 210)

4. Why do jalapeño peppers taste hot? (p. 210)

5. What evidence do we have that mild foot shock produces analgesia by releasing endorphins while prolonged, intense shocks to the feet produce analgesia in some other manner? (p. 212)

6. What harm can result from a great release of endorphins? (p. 213)

## THOUGHT QUESTIONS

1. If you want to scare snakes away, is it more effective to kick the ground or to shout? Why?

2. Why is the vestibular sense generally useless under conditions of weightlessness?

## SUGGESTION FOR FURTHER READING

**Snyder, S.** (1989). *Brainstorming: The science and politics of opiate research.* Cambridge, MA: Harvard University Press. Fascinating "insider's" history of the discovery of endorphins.

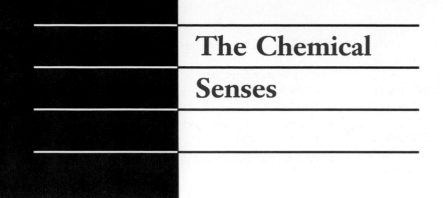

# The Chemical Senses

$S$uppose you had the godlike power to design a new species of animal. But you could equip it with only one sensory system. Which sense would you give it?

Your first impulse might be to choose either vision or hearing. After all, those senses are extremely versatile and valuable to humans. But an animal with only one sensory system is not going to be much like humans, is it? To have any chance of survival it will probably have to be small and rather slow, perhaps even a one-celled animal. What sense will be most useful to such an animal?

Most theorists believe that the first sensory system of the earliest animals was probably a chemical sensitivity (G. H. Parker, 1922). A chemical sense enables a small animal to cope with the basics of survival: finding food, distinguishing food from nonfood, identifying certain kinds of danger, and even locating mates.

Now, imagine that you as a human have to choose one of your senses to *lose*. Which one will it be? Most of us would prefer not to lose vision, hearing, or touch. Losing sensitivity to pain can be dangerous. You might choose to sacrifice your olfaction or taste.

Curious, isn't it? If an animal is going to survive with only one sense, that sense almost has to be a chemical sense, and yet if an animal such as ourselves has many other well-developed senses, the chemical senses seem dispensable. Perhaps we underestimate the importance of these senses.

## TASTE

When we talk about the "taste" of food, we generally mean a combination of taste and smell. The term *flavor* would be better for that purpose; *taste* should refer to the stimulation of the taste buds found mostly on the tongue and to some extent on the upper palate of the mouth.

We can describe most if not all tastes with the four terms *sweet*, *sour*, *salty*, and *bitter*. The simplicity of the description could mean either that the system is simple or that it is poorly understood. Perhaps we experience a greater variety of

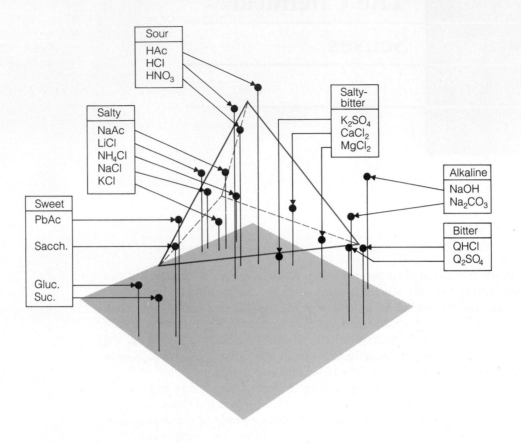

**Figure 6.17**
**Representation of taste stimuli based on judgments of similarity among tastes**

*The greater the distance between points is, the greater will be the difference in taste. (From Schiffman & Erickson, 1971.)*

tastes, but we have trouble describing them because of the lack of taste adjectives in our language.

To find out how people experience tastes without limiting them to English words, Susan Schiffman asked people to rate the similarities in taste between pairs of compounds. From the similarity ratings, a computer plotted a spatial representation of all the stimuli, such that the more similar the tastes of two stimuli, the closer they were to each other on the plot. Schiffman found the distribution shown in Figure 6.17. Note that sweet, sour, salty, and bitter substances fell at the four points of a tetrahedron. Two alkaline substances fell outside the tetrahedron, however. In later research, Schiffman found other substances that fell well outside the tetrahedron, including monosodium glutamate, sodium succinate, and certain amino acids and dipeptides (Schiffman & Erickson, 1980; Schiffman, McElroy, & Erickson, 1980). Many people reported difficulty finding words to describe those tastes. In short, *most* tastes can be described as sweet, sour, salty, or bitter, but a few defy those descriptions.

### Taste Receptors and Taste Paths to the Brain

The receptors for taste are not true neurons but modified skin cells. The relationship of taste receptors to skin cells is particularly evident in fish, which have taste

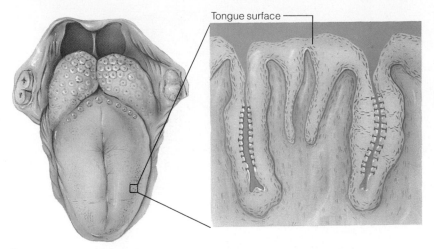

Tongue surface

**Figure 6.18**
**The organs of taste**
*(a) The tongue is covered with taste buds, especially at the tip and at the back. Taste buds are located in papillae. (b) Photo showing cross section of a taste bud. Each taste bud contains about fifty receptor cells. (SIU/Peter Arnold, Inc.)*

a

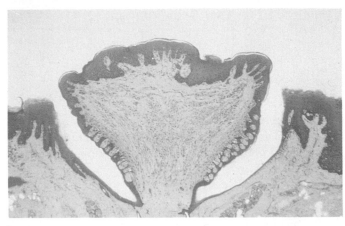

b

receptors scattered over their entire body surface, from nose to tail (Bardach & Villars, 1974). The modification is complete in most regards; the taste receptors have excitable membranes and they release neurotransmitters to excite neighboring neurons, which in turn transmit information to the brain. Like more typical skin cells, however, taste receptors are gradually sloughed off and replaced, each one lasting about 10 to 14 days (Kinnamon, 1987).

Mammalian taste receptors are located in **taste buds,** located in **papillae,** or folds on the surface of the tongue (Figure 6.18). A given papilla may contain any number of taste buds from none to ten or more (Arvidson & Friberg, 1980), and each taste bud contains about 50 receptor cells. Each of the neurons carrying impulses from the taste bud receives synaptic contacts from a number of receptors (Altner, 1978).

Information from the receptors in the anterior two-thirds of the tongue is carried to the brain along the chorda tympani, a branch of the seventh cranial nerve (the facial nerve). Taste information from the posterior tongue and the throat is carried along branches of the ninth and tenth cranial nerves. Those three nerves project to different parts of the **nucleus solitarius** in the medulla (Travers, Pfaffmann, & Norgren, 1986). From the nucleus solitarius, information branches out, reaching (among other areas) the pons, the lateral hypothalamus, the amygdala, the ventral-posterior thalamus, and two areas of the cerebral cor-

The Chemical Senses

**Figure 6.19**
**Major routes of impulses related to the sense of taste in the human brain**
*The thalamus and cerebral cortex receive impulses from both the left and the right sides of the tongue.*

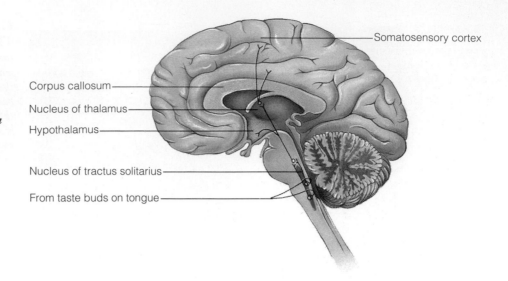

Somatosensory cortex

Corpus callosum

Nucleus of thalamus

Hypothalamus

Nucleus of tractus solitarius

From taste buds on tongue

tex, one of which is responsible for taste and one of which is responsible for the sense of touch on the tongue (Pritchard, Hamilton, Morse, & Norgren, 1986; Yamamoto, 1984). Figure 6.19 diagrams a few of these major connections.

## Types of Taste Receptors

How many types of taste receptors does the tongue have? At least four seem likely—one each for sweet, sour, salty, and bitter—although there could be more. In particular, the tongue may have more than one kind of sweet or bitter receptor. One way of identifying the types of receptors is to find procedures that affect one taste without affecting others. For example, certain chemicals can alter the response of sweetness receptors without affecting other taste receptors (see Digression 6.1). Therefore, we conclude that there must be a sweetness receptor, independent of receptors for other tastes. Similarly, we have reason to believe that sour, salty, and bitter receptors are independent of one another.

The receptors for salty tastes operate on a simple principle. Recall that a neuron produces an action potential when sodium ions cross its membrane. A saltiness receptor cell, which detects the presence of sodium, does not need a specialized membrane site sensitive to sodium. It simply permits sodium ions on the tongue to cross its membrane. The higher the concentration of sodium on the tongue, the greater the response of this receptor. Chemicals such as amiloride, which prevents sodium from crossing the membrane, reduce the intensity of salty tastes (Desimone, Heck, Mierson, & Desimone, 1984; Schiffman, Lockhead, & Maes, 1983). The chemical bretylium tosylate, which facilitates the passage of sodium across the membrane, intensifies salty tastes (Schiffman, Simon, Gill, & Beeker, 1986).

Sour receptors operate on a different principle. When an acid binds to the receptor, it closes potassium channels, preventing potassium from leaving the cell. The result is an increased accumulation of positive charges within the neuron and therefore a depolarization of the membrane (Shirley & Persaud, 1990).

## Miracle Berries and the Modification of Taste Receptors

Although the **miracle berry,** a plant native to West Africa, is practically tasteless, it temporarily changes the taste of other substances. Miracle berries contain a protein, **miraculin,** that modifies sweet receptors in such a way that they can be stimulated by acids (Bartoshuk, Gentile, Moskowitz, & Meiselman, 1974). If you ever get a chance to chew a miracle berry (and I do recommend it), for about the next half hour all acids (which are normally sour) will taste sweet. They will continue to taste sour as well.

Miraculin was, for a time, commercially available in the United States as a diet aid. The idea was that dieters could coat their tongue with a miraculin pill and then eat and drink unsweetened, slightly acidic substances. Such substances would taste sweet without providing many calories.

A colleague and I once spent an evening experimenting with miracle berries. We drank straight lemon juice, sauerkraut juice, even vinegar. All tasted extremely sweet. Somehow we forgot how acidic these substances are. We awoke the next day to find our mouths full of ulcers.

Other taste-modifying substances include an extract from the plant *Gymnema sylvestre*, which makes people temporarily insensitive to both sweet and bitter tastes (Bartoshuk et al., 1974), and the chemical theophylline, which reduces the bitterness of many substances (Kodama, Fukushima, & Sakata, 1978). After eating artichokes, some people report a sweet taste from water (Bartoshuk, Lee, & Scarpellino, 1972).

Have you ever tasted orange juice just after brushing your teeth? And did you wonder why something that usually tastes so good suddenly tasted so bad? Most toothpastes contain sodium lauryl sulfate, a chemical that intensifies bitter tastes while weakening sweet tastes (DeSimone, Heck, & Bartoshuk, 1980; Schiffman, 1983). Evidently it disrupts the membrane surfaces, preventing molecules from binding to sweetness receptors. Fortunately, the effect wears off in a few minutes.

Sweetness receptors apparently operate like metabotropic synapses (p. 76). After a molecule binds to the sweetness receptor, it activates a second messenger, cyclic AMP, within the cell, eventually opening sodium channels (Shirley & Persaud, 1990). Researchers remain uncertain whether we have just one kind of sweetness receptor or several. Several studies suggest that the receptor for sucrose (cane sugar) is different from the receptor for saccharin, which has both a sweet and a bitter taste. For example, preexposure to caffeine enhances both the sweetness and the bitterness of saccharin without affecting the purely sweet taste of sucrose. Preexposure to adenosine decreases both components of the saccharin taste, again without affecting sucrose (Schiffman, Diaz, & Beeker, 1986). Moreover, preexposure of the tongue to sucrose decreases its later response to other sweet tastes, and preexposure to quinine decreases its response to other bitter tastes, but neither one decreases the response to combined sweet-bitter substances such as saccharin (Birch & Mylvaganam, 1976). Evidently saccharin and similar chemicals excite a special sweet-bitter receptor that differs from the receptors excited by sucrose.

As yet, no one knows how bitter receptors operate. So many unrelated chemicals taste bitter that it seems unlikely that they could all excite the same receptor. About the only thing bitter substances have in common is that nearly all of them are harmful in some way.

The Chemical Senses

The strongest evidence for multiple bitter receptors comes from studies of the taste of PTC (phenylthiocarbamide) and similar substances. PTC and similar substances include an H—N—C=S chemical group. Most people find substances with this group bitter, but some people find them tasteless except at very high concentrations. The ability to taste PTC is controlled by a dominant gene. Those who cannot taste it also tend to be less sensitive than other people are to the bitterness of caffeine, but they are about as sensitive as others are to the bitterness of quinine (Hall, Bartoshuk, Cain, & Stevens, 1975). Apparently, we must have more than one type of bitterness receptor.

## The Coding of Taste Information

How do we perceive tastes? According to the simplest explanation, the labeled-line theory, each kind of receptor—sweet, sour, salty, bitter, possibly one or more others—has its own direct route to the brain. That is, each axon carries information about just one taste. This may seem self-evident, but it is not. A number of different receptor cells transmit synaptic messages to a cell whose axon goes to the brain, so a given axon might convey a mixture of messages. According to the alternative theory, the across-fiber pattern theory, various receptors combine their information such that each axon conveys a combination of information about various tastes, and the brain must examine the pattern of firing across many axons to distinguish one taste from another. In other words, a given level of response by a given cell means nothing except in the context of what other cells are doing, just as the meaning of the letter *h* depends on its context.

It might seem that we could settle this dispute by examining the activity of various taste axons, but the results are inconclusive. Each axon responds best to a particular taste—such as sweet or salty—but it responds somewhat to all types of taste stimuli (Pfaffmann, Frank, & Norgren, 1979; Scott & Perrotto, 1980; Smith, VanBuskirk, Travers, & Bieber, 1983a; Yamamoto, Yuyama, Kato, & Kawamura, 1985). Thus we may label an axon as "salt-best," for example, but we cannot be sure that it contributes only to the experience of salty tastes and not to other tastes as well.

Do the various axons at least fall into a limited number of types? To answer that, we have to find out, for example, whether all the axons that respond best to salt resemble one another in the ways they respond to sugars, acids, and bitter substances. The answer is, "Well, sort of." About two-thirds of all taste axons fall into three well-defined categories: one set that responds best to sweet tastes, one that responds well to both salty and bitter tastes, and one that responds well to both salty and sour tastes (Scott & Chang, 1984). All the axons in any one of those categories resemble all the others in its category. But that still leaves about one-third of all axons in a variety of miscellaneous categories or unclassified. The difference between the labeled-line theory and the across-fiber pattern theory boils down to these questions: (1) If a cell responds best to sweet substances, but somewhat to salty ones also, does its response to NaCl contribute in any way to the salty taste of NaCl? The labeled-line theory says no: Saltiness depends only on the response of salt-best cells. The across-fiber pattern theory says yes: All cells contribute to all tastes. (2) Are the cells that respond best to sweet substances absolutely necessary for identifying sweet tastes? The labeled-line theory says yes. The across-fiber pattern theory says no: Even without those axons the brain could identify sweet tastes based on a pattern of firing across the other axons.

If we could somehow remove all the sweet-best axons, we could test how that removal affected salty, sweet, and other tastes. No one can conduct that experiment surgically, but we can conduct it statistically: If we collect information on how each neuron responds to each substance, and then simply ignore all the information from the sweet-best cells, is there enough information left in the remaining cells to distinguish among all the possible tastes? The answer is no; the remaining cells can still distinguish among salty, sour, and bitter substances, but they cannot distinguish sweet substances from the others (Smith, VanBuskirk, Travers, & Bieber, 1983b). This result is exactly what the labeled-line theory predicts.

However, if we examine *only* the response of the sweet-best axons, we cannot tell the difference between sweet substances and any other substance (Scott, 1987). That is, a dilute sucrose solution might produce exactly the same response as a more concentrated solution of NaCl. This conforms to the across-fiber pattern theory: The brain has to compare the responses of many axons to interpret the response of any one axon.

If all this sounds a bit confusing, it is because it really is confusing. Perhaps taste perception relies on a scheme intermediate between the labeled-line theory and the across-fiber pattern theory: Each taste axon contributes to all tastes, as the across-fiber pattern theory holds, but it contributes more to the experience of one taste than it does to others, as the labeled-line theory holds (Scott & Chang, 1984).

## OLFACTION

**Olfaction,** the sense of smell, is the detection and recognition of chemicals in contact with the membranes inside the nose. In an ordinary day most of us pay little attention to what we smell, and an entire industry — the deodorant industry — is dedicated to removing one type of smell from our experience. But olfaction is important for our appreciation of food, for discriminating good wine from poor wine, for recognizing that old meat is rotting, and for detecting smoke. Natural gas companies put a strong odor into their gas so that people can smell a leak in the gas line. Most mammals, including humans to some extent, alter their social responses to one another because of odors (see Digression 6.2). Olfaction is more important than we sometimes realize. But we have few words to describe what we smell.

Suppose you have two bottles of clear liquid, differing only in their smell. You have labeled one of them A and the other B. You are on the telephone trying to explain to someone who has the same two bottles of liquid which one to label A and which to label B. So you have to describe the smells well enough for the other person to understand you. Could you do it?

You would soon discover that the English language has very few words to describe smells. You might describe the smell of bottle A as strong or weak, pleasant or unpleasant. If you recognized the smell, you might say it smells like coffee, or apples, or skunks, or whatever. But if the two bottles had similar smells, such as two flowers or two wines, you might find yourself unable to describe the difference.

With practice you would improve, however. In one study, adults tried to identify common objects just from their smell — such as bananas, popcorn,

# Pheromones

A **pheromone** is an odorous chemical released by one animal that affects the behavior of other members of the same species. Most mammalian species use pheromones in sexual attraction; they can determine from another animal's smell whether it is a male, a female in estrus, or a female not in estrus. Pheromones can also produce longer-lasting effects (Bronson, 1974): The odor of a group of female mice can stop another female mouse's estrous cycle, and the odor of a male can restore the estrous cycle. However, just after the female becomes pregnant, the odor of an unfamiliar male can cause her to abort.

Do humans secrete and respond to pheromones? Maybe. They definitely secrete a variety of odorous chemicals. If you were given two T-shirts, identical except that one had been worn by your brother or sister and the other had been worn by someone you do not know, could you identify which shirt was which, just by the smell? Most people can. In one study, 27 of 40 adults chose the correct shirt (Porter, Balogh, Cernoch, & Franchi, 1986).

In the same study, people were given two shirts, one that had been worn by a baby in their own family and one that had been worn by an unrelated baby. Nearly all the mothers as well as most of the fathers, grandmothers, and aunts were able to identify which was which, just by sniffing the two shirts. Some said, "This smells like our baby." Others said it smelled like the mother or the father and therefore probably belonged to a family member (Porter et al., 1986).

Do people's odors affect other people's sex-related behaviors, as pheromones do in other species? The clearest evidence relates to the timing of women's menstrual cycles. Many of the women who live together in a college dormitory gradually synchronize their menstrual cycles, unless they are taking birth control pills. (Why this happens, no one knows. Females of other species do not typically synchronize their cycles.) To test whether pheromones are responsible for the synchronization, researchers exposed volunteer women to the underarm odor of a donor woman who was selected because she had regular 28-day cycles and did not shave her underarms or use deodorants. A swab of her underarm secretions was applied to the upper lip of each recipient woman three times a week. Recipients were instructed not to wipe it off for at least three hours. As you might expect, this experiment had a high drop-out rate; six of the eleven volunteers quit the study. Of the five who completed it, four became synchronized to the donor woman's menstrual cycle (Russell, Switz, & Thompson, 1980).

cigarette butts, mothballs, and tuna. At first, most could identify only a few. After several hours of practice, they learned to identify 64 objects with greater than 90 percent accuracy (Desor & Beauchamp, 1974). Evidently human olfaction can identify a great many odors.

Olfaction can be impaired at least briefly by a number of medical conditions, including vitamin $B_{12}$ deficiency. A loss of olfaction is a common, if seldom reported, side effect of many drugs used in medicine (Schiffman, 1983).

## Olfactory Receptors

The neurons responsible for smell are the **olfactory cells,** which line the olfactory epithelium in the rear of the nasal air passages (see Figure 6.20). In mammals, each olfactory cell has cilia (threadlike structures) that extend from the cell body into the mucous surface of the nasal passage (Getchell, Margolis, & Getchell, 1985). The olfactory receptor sites are probably located on the cilia. Because odorant molecules must pass through a mucous fluid before they reach

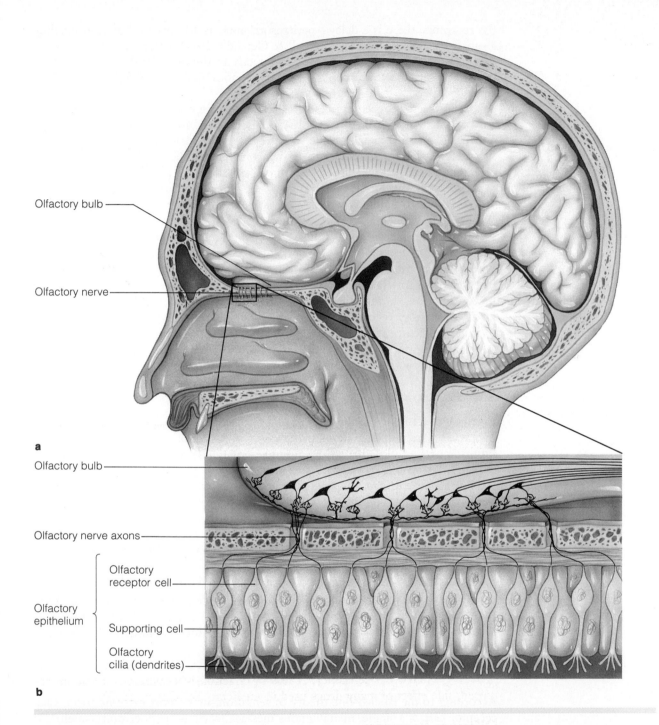

Olfactory bulb

Olfactory nerve

a

Olfactory bulb

Olfactory nerve axons

Olfactory epithelium {
  Olfactory receptor cell
  Supporting cell
  Olfactory cilia (dendrites)
}

b

**Figure 6.20**
**Olfactory receptors**
*(a) Location of receptors in nasal cavity. (b) Close-up of olfactory cells.*

the receptors, there is a delay—perhaps as much as 300 msec—between inhaling a substance and smelling it (Getchell & Getchell, 1987). After an olfactory cell is stimulated, its axon carries an impulse directly to the olfactory bulb, from which connections extend to the cerebral cortex, hippocampus, amygdala, and hypothalamus (Scalia & Winans, 1976).

The olfactory receptors resemble synaptic receptors in some important regards. Like synaptic receptors, olfactory receptors are proteins stimulated by chemicals. And like metabotropic synaptic receptors, olfactory receptors activate a second-messenger system within the neuron that enables a small amount of the odorant chemical to produce an enormous effect on the polarization of the neuron's membrane (Shirley & Persaud, 1990; Snyder, Sklar, Hwang, & Pevsner, 1989). However, unlike synaptic receptors, each olfactory receptor responds to a great variety of chemicals, not just one.

Investigators have not yet answered one of the most fundamental questions about olfactory receptors: How many kinds do we have? Do we have a separate type of receptor for every odor we can discriminate? Surely not; it hardly seems likely that we had special receptors waiting around for someone to invent each new perfume, each new chemical that we can distinguish. But do we have 2 or 3 kinds of olfactory receptors, or 20, or 2,000? The surest way to decide would be to isolate olfactory receptors chemically and count the number of types. No one has done that yet; in the meantime, we have other evidence about olfactory receptors and how they code information.

## Specific Anosmias

One way to estimate the minimum number of olfactory receptor types is to study people who are markedly insensitive to one type of odor. A general lack of olfaction is known as **anosmia;** an inability to smell one type of chemical is a **specific anosmia.** For example, about 2 to 3 percent of all people are insensitive to the smell of isobutyric acid, the smelly component of sweat (Amoore, 1967). (This is hardly a disabling handicap.) Because people can lose the ability to smell just this one chemical, there must be a receptor specific to isobutyric acid. A reasonable research strategy is to search for additional specific anosmias, on the theory that each specific anosmia represents the loss of a different type of receptor.

At least 5 other specific anosmias are known—musky, fishy, urinous, spermous, and malty—and less firm evidence suggests 26 other possible specific anosmias (Amoore, 1977). What should we conclude? One possibility is that the nose has many receptor types. Another possibility is that a specific anosmia has some other explanation and that it does not represent the loss of a particular type of receptor.

## The Receptive Properties of Olfactory Receptors

According to the labeled-line theory of sensation, in its most extreme form, each receptor carries a single, unambiguous message, such as "pepperminty smell." At least in that form, the labeled-line theory is incorrect for olfaction. Each olfactory receptor responds to many chemicals, and most chemicals excite large populations of olfactory receptors (Moulton, 1976; Tanabe, Iino, & Takagi, 1975). Identification of a particular odor probably depends on a pattern across a fair number of receptors, if not all of them.

Nevertheless, different odorant chemicals produce their maximum activation in different populations of receptors, apparently for two reasons (Kauer, 1987):

First, the nasal cavity acts to some extent like a gas chromatograph that separates molecules based on their molecular weight and other physical properties. Certain molecules penetrate the mucous lining in the lower part of the nose and excite receptors there, while other molecules rise to the farther areas of the nose before they excite receptors. In other words, the brain may distinguish among chemicals based on how far up the nose they go before they excite receptors. Second, olfactory receptors probably differ in the kinds of chemicals that excite them best. We could imagine each receptor as a "lock" that can be opened only by an odorant molecule shaped like the appropriate "key" (Amoore, 1963) — except that the olfactory receptors are loose locks that can be opened to varying degrees by a great variety of molecules.

Generally, similar receptors are grouped together in the nose. That is, receptors that respond strongly to a particular chemical tend to be surrounded by other receptors that also respond strongly to that chemical.

## SUMMARY

1. We can describe most but perhaps not all tastes as combinations of sweet, sour, salty, and bitter. (p. 215)

2. Taste receptors are modified skin cells located in taste buds in papillae on the tongue. (p. 216)

3. The tongue has at least four kinds of receptors, one each for sweet, sour, salty, and bitter. It may have more than one kind of receptor for sweet and bitter substances. (p. 218)

4. Salty receptors respond simply to sodium ions crossing the membrane. At sweet receptors, sucrose or other substances activate a second messenger within the neuron. (p. 218)

5. Several receptors may contribute to the response of a taste axon on the way to the brain. Each taste axon responds best to one kind of substance but also responds somewhat to other kinds. Investigators differ on whether the axon contributes only to one taste or to all tastes. (p. 220)

6. People are generally poor at describing odors, although they can improve greatly with practice. (p. 221)

7. Olfactory receptors are proteins, probably located on the cilia of olfactory cells in the nose. Investigators do not know how many kinds of receptors exist. (p. 222)

8. Each olfactory receptor responds to many odorant molecules, though it responds more vigorously to some than to others. (p. 224)

9. Identification of an odor probably depends on a combination of responses from many, if not all, olfactory cells. (p. 224)

## REVIEW QUESTIONS

1. What is the evidence that a few tastes are not simply combinations of sweet, sour, salty, and bitter? (p. 216)

2. How long does a taste receptor last before it is replaced? (p. 217)

3. How does amiloride block salty tastes? (p. 218)

4. What are the effects of miraculin and *Gymnema sylvestre* extract on sweetness receptors? (p. 219)

5. What evidence indicates that we have more than one kind of bitter receptor? (p. 220)

6. Describe the pros and cons of the labeled-line theory and the across-fiber pattern theory as they apply to taste. (p. 220)

7. What is a pheromone? (p. 222)

8. How do olfactory receptors resemble synaptic receptors? (p. 224)

9. What is a specific anosmia? (p. 224)

## THOUGHT QUESTION

1. Researchers have found that most olfactory receptors respond to a wide variety of odorant molecules and that most molecules stimulate a large population of receptors. Do these findings support or conflict with the theory that specific anosmias reveal odorant-specific receptors?

## SUGGESTION FOR FURTHER READING

**Finger, T. E., & Silver, W. L.** (Eds.). (1987). *Neurobiology of taste and smell.* New York: Wiley. A scholarly review of research on taste and smell.

# GLOSSARY

**across-fiber pattern theory** notion that each receptor responds to a wide range of stimuli and contributes to the perception of every stimulus in its system

**amplitude** the intensity of a sound or other stimulus

**analgesia** relief from pain

**anosmia** general lack of olfaction

**apex** one end of the cochlea, farthest from the point where the stirrup meets the cochlea

**base** (of tympanic membrane) point at which the stirrup meets the cochlea

**basilar membrane** floor of the scala media, within the cochlea

**capsaicin** a chemical that causes neurons containing substance P to release it suddenly

**cochlea** structure in the inner ear, containing auditory receptors

**coding** the one-to-one correspondence between some aspect of the physical stimulus and some aspect of the nervous system's activity

**conductive deafness** hearing loss that occurs if the bones of the middle ear fail to transmit sound waves properly to the cochlea

**endorphin** category of chemicals the body produces that stimulate the same receptors as opiates

**frequency** the number of sound waves per second

**frequency theory** concept that pitch perception depends on differences in frequency of action potentials by auditory neurons

**gate theory** assumption that stimulation of certain non-pain axons in the skin or in the brain can inhibit transmission of pain messages in the spinal cord

**generator potential** local depolarization or hyperpolarization of a neuron membrane

**hair cell** a type of sensory receptor shaped like a hair

**inner-ear deafness** hearing loss that results from damage to the cochlea, the hair cells, or the auditory nerve

**labeled-line theory** concept that each receptor responds to a limited range of stimuli and has a direct line to the brain

**law of specific nerve energies** principle that any activity by a particular nerve always conveys the same kind of information to the brain

**leu-enkephalin** a chain of five amino acids believed to function as a neurotransmitter that inhibits pain

**loudness** perception of the intensity of a sound

**met-enkephalin** a chain of five amino acids thought to act as a neurotransmitter that inhibits pain

**middle-ear deafness** hearing loss that occurs if the bones of the middle ear fail to transmit sound waves properly to the cochlea

**miracle berry** African berry that contains the protein miraculin

**miraculin** protein that alters taste buds so that acids taste sweet

**naloxone** drug that blocks opiate receptors

**nerve deafness** hearing loss that results from damage to the cochlea, hair cells, or auditory nerve

**nucleus solitarius** area in the medulla that receives input from taste receptors

**olfaction** sense of smell

**olfactory cell** neuron responsible for smell, located on the olfactory epithelium in the rear of the nasal air passages

**otolith organ** an organ responsible for vestibular sensation

**papilla** fold on the surface of the tongue

**periaqueductal gray area** area of the brain stem that is rich in enkephalin synapses

**pheromone** odorous chemical released by one animal that affects the behavior of other members of the same species

**pitch** the experience that corresponds to the frequency of a sound

**place theory** concept that pitch perception depends on which part of the inner ear has cells with the greatest activity level

**reception** the absorption of physical energy by a receptor

**semicircular canal** canal lined with hair cells and oriented in three planes, sensitive to the direction of tilt of the head

**somatosensory system** sensory network that monitors the surface of the body and its movements

**specific anosmia** inability to smell one type of chemical

**substance P** a neurotransmitter released by nerves sensitive to pain

**taste bud** structure on the tongue that contains taste receptors

**transcutaneous electrical nerve stimulation** method of relieving pain by applying prolonged, mild electrical shock to the arms, legs, or back

**transduction** the conversion of physical energy by a receptor into an electrochemical pattern in the neurons

**tympanic membrane** the eardrum

**vestibular organ** component in the inner ear that detects tilt of the head

**volley principle** tenet that a sound wave of a moderately high pitch may produce a volley of impulses by various fibers even if no individual fiber can produce impulses in synchrony with the sound waves

# CHAPTER SEVEN

# Vision

## MAIN IDEAS

**1.** Vertebrate vision depends on two kinds of receptors: cones, which contribute to color vision, and rods, which do not.

**2.** Three types of cones enable us to distinguish among colors. For genetic reasons, some people do not perceive colors in the same way as most people do. Color blindness has several types.

**3.** Within the retina, a process called lateral inhibition enhances the contrast between a brightly lit area and a neighboring dimmer area.

**4.** Information from the retina is transmitted to several areas of the brain, which process the information in different ways.

**5.** Certain cells in the visual cortex respond specifically to light patterns in a particular shape, such as bars and edges.

(Tom McHugh/The National Audubon Collection/PR.)

Some years ago, a graduate student was taking his final oral exam for the Ph.D. degree in psychology. He had answered without difficulty many questions, most of them about animal behavior, his specialty. Then one member of his committee asked, "How far can an ant see?" The student suddenly turned pale. He did not know the answer, and evidently he was supposed to know it. (Do you know the answer? Think about it for a minute before you read on.)

Quickly the poor graduate student mentally reviewed everything he had read about the compound eye of insects. He remembered reading about how insects can detect light and about their color vision and their ability to detect movement. But nothing about how *far* they can see. Finally he gave up and admitted he did not know.

With a sheepish grin, the professor told him, "Presumably an ant can see 93 million miles—the distance to the sun."

Yes, this was a trick question—a beaut, as trick questions go. But it illustrates an important point: How far an ant can see, or how far you or anyone else can see, depends on how far the light travels. Good eyes cannot see farther than bad eyes. We fall into a trap because we perceive the objects we see as being "out there," when in fact the stimulation is on the retinas of our eyes. This is just one of many ways in which our common sense about vision misleads us.

# Visual Coding and the Retinal Receptors

Imagine that you are a piece of iron. I admit, that's not easy to do. A piece of iron doesn't have a brain, and even if it did it would not have much experience. But try to imagine it anyway.

So there you are, sitting around doing nothing, as usual, when along comes a drop of water. What will be your perception, your experience, of the water?

You will have the experience of rust. From your point of view, water is above all else *rustish*.

Now return to your perspective as a human. You know that the property *rustish* is not really a property of water itself; it is a property of the way water interacts with iron.

The same is true of human perception. In vision, for example, when you look at the leaves of a tree, you perceive them as *green*. But green is no more a property of the leaves themselves than rustish is a property of water. The greenness is what happens when the light bouncing off the leaves interacts with the neurons in the back of your eye, and eventually with the neurons in your brain. That is, the greenness is really in us—just as the rust is really in the piece of iron. To understand how we perceive light and color, we begin with the receptors in the eyes.

## THE EYE AND ITS CONNECTIONS TO THE BRAIN

Figure 7.1 illustrates the basic structures of the eye. Light enters through an opening in the eyeball called the **pupil** and is focused by the cornea and lens onto the **retina** (Figure 7.1), which is the rear surface of the eye, lined with visual receptors—rods and cones. As in a camera, the light rays are focused so that the image is reversed. Light from the left side of the world strikes the right half of the retina and vice versa. Light from above strikes the bottom half of the retina; light from below strikes the top half of the retina.

Long ago, both scientists and philosophers worried about how the brain turns the image right side up again. That is a problem only if you imagine a little person in the head—a little right-side-up person—who looks at the pattern of brain activity on a screen somewhere.

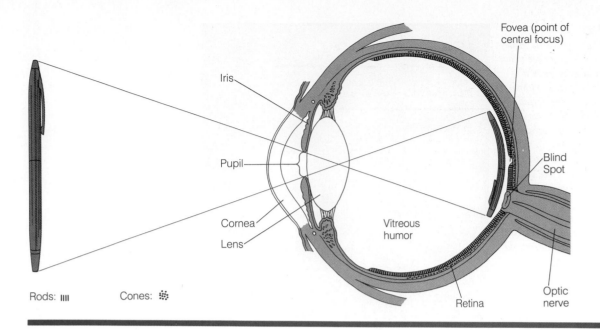

Rods: ||||    Cones: ⁂

**Figure 7.1**
**Diagrammatic cross section of the vertebrate eye, showing the projection of an image onto the retina**

Let's say this another way: A visual image does not need to be right side up on the retina, because the bottom part of the retina does not "know" that it is the bottom. The same is true of the brain. If a surgeon could somehow twist your entire brain 180 degrees, while leaving intact all the nerve connections between the brain and the sense organs, the world would not suddenly look upside down to you. In fact, it would not look different at all. Consider the computer analogy: When a computer stores instructions for what to write on the top and bottom of the page, the instructions for the top of the page need not be located physically above those for the bottom of the page.

## The Fovea

An area called the **fovea** (meaning *pit*) in the center of the retina is specialized for acute, detailed vision. Because blood vessels and ganglion cell axons are almost absent near the fovea, the fovea has the most unimpeded vision available in the eye. The tight packing of receptors further aids perception of detail.

You have heard the expression "eyes like a hawk." In many bird species the eyes occupy more than half the volume of the head, as compared to only 5 percent of the head in humans. Furthermore, many bird species have two foveas per eye. Each eye has one fovea pointing ahead and one pointing to the side (Wallman & Pettigrew, 1985). The two foveas enable such birds to perceive detail in their peripheral vision.

Hawks and other birds of prey have a greater density of visual receptors on the top half of their retinas (looking down) than they have on the bottom half of their retinas (looking up). That arrangement is highly adaptive, because predatory

**Figure 7.2**
*One owlet has turned its head almost upside down to see above itself. Birds of prey have a great density of receptors on the upper half of the retina, enabling them to see down in great detail during flight. But they see objects above themselves very poorly, unless they turn their heads. Take another look at the prairie falcon at the start of this chapter. It is not a one-eyed bird; it is a bird that has tilted its head. Do you now understand why? (Chase Swift.)*

birds spend most of their day soaring high in the air, looking down. However, it does pose a problem when the bird lands and needs to look up. To see above itself, the bird must turn its head, as Figure 7.2 shows, so that it can focus the light from above on the part of its retina that has the greatest density of receptors (Waldvogel, 1990).

## The Route of Visual Information to the Brain

Visual information goes through several levels of processing. When light enters the eye, it passes through several layers of cells before it strikes the retinal receptors. (However, those cells are so transparent that they distort vision minimally.)

The rods and cones in the retina send information to other neurons located toward the center of the eyeball, rather than directly to the brain, as one might suppose (Figure 7.3). The receptors make synaptic contact with **horizontal cells** and **bipolar cells** (Figure 7.4). (We shall consider these connections in more detail later in this chapter.) The bipolars make synapses onto **amacrine cells** (local neurons with no axon) and **ganglion cells,** also located in the eyeball.

The ganglion cell axons group together to form the **optic nerve** (or optic tract), which loops around to exit through the back of the eye. The point at which it leaves is called the **blind spot** because it has no receptors (Figure 7.1). Blood vessels also enter the eye through the blind spot. Curiously, people are never spontaneously aware of having a blind spot. In fact, even people with very large blind spots, caused by glaucoma or other eye diseases, are seldom aware of them.

Note that some ganglion cells are located much closer to the blind spot than other ganglion cells are. All other things being equal, the messages from the closer ganglion cells would reach the brain sooner—and the person would see events in different parts of the retina just slightly out of synchrony. But all other things are not equal: The axons from ganglion cells farther from the blind spot conduct their action potentials slightly faster (Stanford, 1987). Consequently,

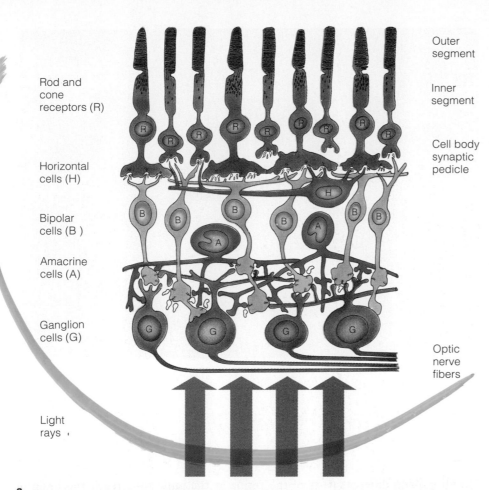

Rod and
cone
receptors (R)

Horizontal
cells (H)

Bipolar
cells (B)

Amacrine
cells (A)

Ganglion
cells (G)

Light
rays

Outer
segment

Inner
segment

Cell body
synaptic
pedicle

Optic
nerve
fibers

a

**Figure 7.3**
(*a*) *Diagram of the neurons
of the retina. The top of the
figure is the back of the
retina. All the optic nerve
fibers group together and then
turn around to exit through
the back of the retina, in the
"blind spot" of the eye.
(Adapted from Dowling &
Boycott, 1966.) (***b***) Photo of a
cross section through the
retina. (Ed Reschke.)*

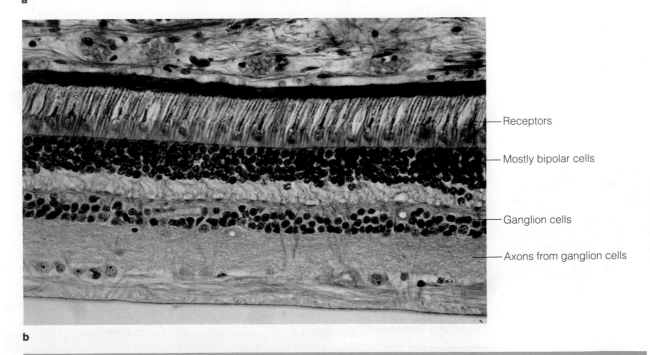

Receptors

Mostly bipolar cells

Ganglion cells

Axons from ganglion cells

b

Figure 7.4
**Figure 7.4**
**A bipolar cell from the retina of a carp, stained with Procion yellow**
*Bipolar cells get their name from the fact that a fibrous process is attached to each end (or pole) of the neuron. (From Dowling, 1987.)*

25 μm

stimuli striking different parts of the retina at the same time reach the brain at the same time.

After the optic nerve leaves the retina, it travels back on the lower surface of the brain. The optic nerve from the left eye and the optic nerve from the right eye meet at the optic chiasm (Figure 7.5), where half of the axons from each eye cross to the opposite side of the brain. Most of the axons in the optic nerve go to the lateral geniculate nucleus of the thalamus. Some axons go to the superior colliculus, and a smaller number go to several other areas. The occipital lobe of the cerebral cortex receives input from the lateral geniculate. Parts of the temporal lobe and parietal lobe receive input from the occipital lobe and from areas of the thalamus other than the lateral geniculate. Figure 7.5 outlines a few of the major connections. Each area processes visual information in different ways. Let's begin with the receptors in the retina.

## VISUAL RECEPTORS: RODS AND CONES

The retina contains two types of receptors: **rods** and **cones** (see Figure 7.6). The cones, which are specialized for color vision, are more sensitive to detail and are located near the center of the retina, whereas the rods are more sensitive to dim light and are found toward the periphery of the retina. Table 7.1 summarizes the functional distinctions between the two. These differences are reflected in several aspects of our experience. For detailed vision we try to focus an object on the fovea, where cones are concentrated and acuity is the greatest. To perceive the

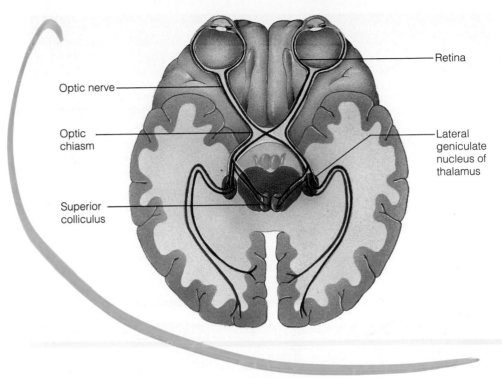

Retina

Optic nerve

Optic chiasm

Superior colliculus

Lateral geniculate nucleus of thalamus

**Figure 7.5**
**Major connections in the visual system of the brain**
*Part of the visual input goes to the thalamus and from there to the visual cortex. Another part of the visual input goes to the superior colliculus.*

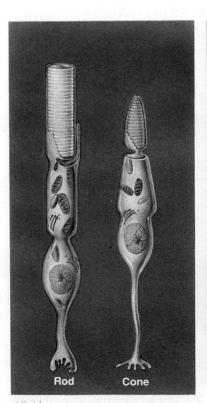

Rod

Cone

a

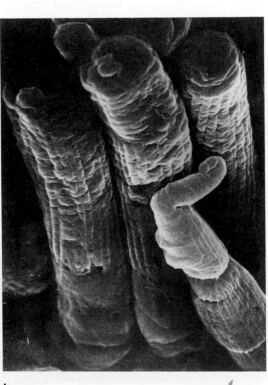

b

**Figure 7.6**
*(a) Diagram of a rod and a cone. (b) Photo of rods and a cone, produced with a scanning electron microscope and magnified × 7,000. (Micrograph courtesy of E. R. Lewis, F. S. Werblin, and Y. Y. Zeevi.)*

## Table 7.1 Functional Distinctions Between Rods and Cones

| Characteristic | Rods | Cones |
| --- | --- | --- |
| Location | Absent from fovea; increasingly common toward periphery | More common toward center of the retina |
| Sensitivity to detail (acuity) | Low because many rods funnel onto a single postsynaptic neuron | Greater because fewer cones funnel onto a single postsynaptic neuron |
| Sensitivity to dim light | Greater | Lesser |
| Contribute to color vision? | No | Yes |
| Species more abundant in | Rodents, other nocturnal animals | Birds, primates |

dimmest lights, such as faint stars in the night sky, we often find it better to look slightly to the side so that the light rays from the target fall outside the fovea.

### Differences Between Peripheral Vision and Foveal Vision

We can see dim lights better in the periphery of the retina for two reasons. One is simply that rods are more sensitive to light than cones are. The second is that near the fovea only a small number of receptors convey input to a given postsynaptic cell, but in the periphery great numbers of rods funnel their input into each postsynaptic cell. That is, in the periphery, the summation of many inputs increases detection of dim light, at the expense of perceiving details.

Because the number of cones decreases toward the periphery of the retina, we are color blind in the extreme periphery. You can demonstrate this for yourself as follows: Mix several colored pencils behind your back and pick one at random. Hold it behind your head and move it very slowly into your field of vision. If you have normal peripheral vision, you will be just able to detect the presence of the pencil and its brightness at a point where you cannot yet perceive its color.

### Chemical Basis for Receptor Excitation

Both rods and cones contain **photopigments,** chemicals that release energy when struck by light. Photopigments consist of 11-*cis*-retinal (a derivative of vitamin A) bound to proteins called *opsins*. The 11-*cis*-retinal is stable in the dark, but even a single photon of light can convert it to another form, all-*trans*-retinal. (The light is absorbed in this process; it does not continue to bounce around in the eye.) When the light converts 11-*cis*-retinal to all-*trans*-retinal, it triggers changes in the opsin, converting hundreds of second-messenger molecules to their active state, ultimately closing a number of ion channels in the cell membrane (Lamb & Pugh, 1990; Nathans, Thomas, & Hogness, 1986). This is similar to what happens at many inhibitory synapses in the brain; in fact, rhodopsin (the kind of opsin found in rods) is chemically related to many neurotransmitter receptors.

(Do not be confused by the fact that light inhibits the activity of the receptor cell. It is possible to convey just as much information by a decrease in a signal as by an increase.)

Although 11-*cis*-retinal is so sensitive that a single photon can activate it, it seldom discharges a false alarm in the dark. The average molecule of this chemical has about a 50 percent chance of a spontaneous activation within a thousand years. Because each rod has an estimated 200 billion of these molecules, however, the average rod cell has about one spontaneously active molecule per minute (Yau, Matthews, & Baylor, 1979).

The conversion of 11-*cis*-retinal to all-*trans*-retinal releases energy that decreases the permeability of the receptor's membrane to sodium. (This is the *transduction* process.) The result is a graded hyperpolarization of the receptor — not a depolarization: the greater the light, the greater the hyperpolarization. Ordinarily, even in the dark, the receptor is in a steady state of partial depolarization and is constantly sending inhibitory synaptic transmission to the *bipolar cells*, which are the next cells in the pathway of the visual system. When light hyperpolarizes the receptor, it slows the rate of inhibitory transmission to the bipolars and thereby leads to a net excitation of the bipolar cells.

## COLOR VISION

Color vision may have evolved independently more than once. Some insects can distinguish among different wavelengths of light, although their distinctions differ from ours. Fish, too, evolved color vision, perhaps because their survival requires them to perceive contrast in a range of environments. In bluish waters, one set of cones can detect dark but not light objects. In greenish waters, another set of cones can detect light but not dark objects. A combination of the two kinds of cones enables fish to perceive patterns under more varied conditions than they could with either type of cone alone (Levine & MacNichol, 1982).

Although the extent of color vision varies widely among vertebrates, at least rudimentary color vision is widespread. Species active during the day, including monkeys and most birds, have many cones and well-developed color vision. Cows, contrary to a somewhat popular opinion, also have good color vision (Dabrowska, Harmata, Lenkiewicz, Schiffer, & Wojtusiak, 1981). In fact, of all the vertebrates that researchers have tested, only one — the skate — has no cones at all (Dowling, 1987).

Color vision is based on differential responses of various receptors to light of different wavelengths. The shortest visible wavelengths, about 400 nm (1 nm = nanometer, or $10^{-9}$ m), are perceived as violet; progressively longer wavelengths are perceived as blue, green, yellow, orange, and red, near 700 nm (Figure 7.7). Discrimination among colors poses some special coding problems for the nervous system. A cell in the visual system, like any other neuron, can vary only its frequency of action potentials or, in a cell with graded potentials, its membrane polarization. If the cell's response indicates the brightness of the light, then it cannot simultaneously be a code for color. Conversely, if each response indicates a different color, the cell has no way to signal brightness. The inevitable conclusion is that no single neuron can simultaneously indicate brightness and color; our perceptions must depend on patterns of responses by a number of different neurons.

Figure 7.7
**Figure 7.7**
**A beam of light separated into its wavelengths**
*Although the wavelengths vary over a continuum, we perceive them as several distinct colors.*

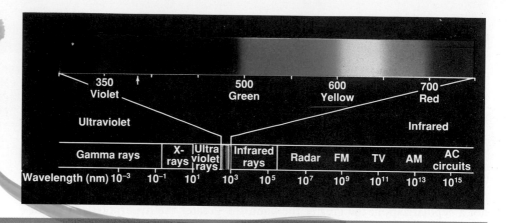

Three theories have been proposed to account for how all those neurons produce the experience of color: the trichromatic theory, the opponent-process theory, and the retinex theory. None of these theories by itself is satisfactory; combined, they account for the major phenomena of color vision.

### The Trichromatic (Young-Helmholtz) Theory

The **trichromatic theory** of color vision, also known as the **Young-Helmholtz theory,** was first proposed by Thomas Young and later modified by Hermann von Helmholtz, both in the nineteenth century. According to this theory, we perceive color through the relative rates of response by three kinds of cones, with each kind maximally sensitive to a different set of wavelengths. (*Trichromatic* means three colors.) Figure 7.8 shows wavelength-sensitivity functions for the three cone types, which we shall call *short-wavelength*, *medium-wavelength*, and *long-wavelength* cones. Note that each cone is sensitive to a broad range of wavelengths, not just to a narrow band, but is more responsive to some wavelengths than to others.

According to the trichromatic theory, we discriminate among wavelengths by the ratio of activity across the three types of cones. That is, light at 500 nm excites the medium-wavelength cone to about 65 percent of its maximum, the long-wavelength receptor to 40 percent of its maximum, and the short-wavelength receptor to 30 percent of its maximum. This ratio of responses among the three cones defines the color perception, in this case blue-green. More intense light would increase the activity of all three cones but would not greatly alter the ratio of responses. When all three types of cones are equally active, we see white (or gray).

Note that the trichromatic theory proposes an across-fiber pattern of coding (see p. 191). A given response rate by a given cone, say a middle-wavelength cone, is ambiguous. For example, a low response rate might indicate low-intensity 540 nm light, or brighter 500 nm light, or still brighter 460 nm light. Even a high response rate is ambiguous; it could equally well indicate bright light specifically at 540 nm or bright white light, which includes 540 nm. The nervous system can determine the color and brightness of the light only by comparing the responses of the three types of cones.

A degree of color vision would be possible with just two types of cones, but not with only one. Rats have just one kind of cone (Neitz & Jacobs, 1986). Al-

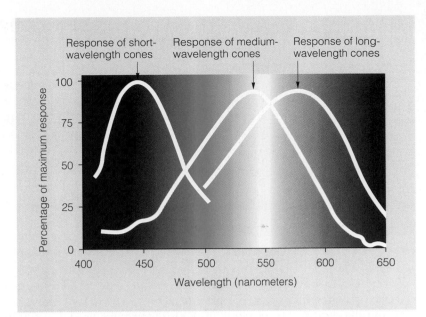

**Figure 7.8**
**Response of three kinds of cones to various wavelengths of light**
*Note that each kind responds somewhat to a wide range of wavelengths but best to wavelengths in a particular range.*

The figure shows three curves labeled "Response of short-wavelength cones," "Response of medium-wavelength cones," and "Response of long-wavelength cones." The y-axis is "Percentage of maximum response" (0 to 100), and the x-axis is "Wavelength (nanometers)" (400 to 650).

though their cones probably enable rats to see better during the day than they would if they had only rods, rats cannot discriminate between colors.

Originally, the Young-Helmholtz theory was based strictly on **psychophysical observations,** reports by human observers concerning their perceptions of various stimuli. For example, observers find that they can match any possible color by mixing appropriate amounts of just three wavelengths. So we conclude that three types of cones are sufficient to account for human color vision. Modern methods have clearly established physical differences among the three kinds of cones. Although all cones contain 11-*cis*-retinal, different opsins are bound to it in the three kinds of cones. The opsins modify the sensitivity of the photopigment to light to produce the three different peaks of wavelength absorption (Wald, 1968).

## The Opponent-Process Theory

The next neurons in the visual system after the cones are the bipolar cells. Each bipolar cell receives input from two or three types of cones. Therefore, the trichromatic theory does not apply at this level or beyond. We can identify a long-wavelength cone, but not a long-wavelength bipolar cell.

For example, one type of bipolar cell receives excitatory synapses from medium-wavelength cones and inhibitory synapses from long-wavelength cones. Its response rate increases when green light shines on the cones connected to it; red light causes it to decrease its response rate below its spontaneous firing rate. In the presence of yellow, blue, white, or gray light, this cell maintains a response rate close to its spontaneous firing level.

Note that the response rate of such a bipolar cell is *less* ambiguous about color than the response rate of any cone is. From the response rate of a given medium-wavelength cone, we cannot determine whether the cell is stimulated by green light, by white light, or even by bright red or blue light. But imagine a bipolar cell that increases its response rate in the presence of green light, de-

Visual Coding and
the Retinal Receptors

**Figure 7.9**
**Stimulus for demonstrating negative color afterimages**

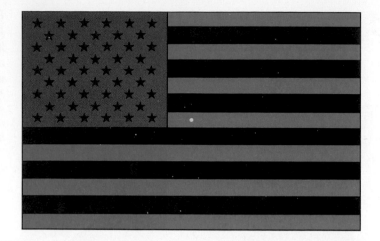

*Stare at the dot in the center of the flag under bright light for about a minute and then look at a white field. You should see a red, white, and blue flag.*

creases it in the presence of red light, and remains unchanged in the presence of white light. When that cell increases its response rate, the brain knows it is looking at something approximately green. It might be a very yellowish green or bluish green, but it cannot be red or white. In effect, the bipolar cell has subtracted the amount of red light from the amount of green light.

The **opponent-process theory** of Ewald Hering, a nineteenth-century rival of Helmholtz, describes this manner of coding color information. According to the opponent-process theory, we perceive color in terms of paired opposites: white versus black, red versus green, and blue versus yellow (Hurvich & Jameson, 1957). In modern terms, we have neurons that are excited by green and inhibited by red, or excited by red and inhibited by green, and so forth. Hering supported his view with psychophysical observations, such as the phenomenon of color afterimages: If you stare at something yellow for about a minute and then look at a white background, you see blue. Similarly, if you stare at blue, red, or green, you see a yellow, green, or red afterimage, respectively (Figure 7.9). These **negative afterimages** represent the results of fatiguing one or another kind of response by bipolar cells. For example, in the prolonged presence of green light, a particular bipolar cell may have undergone prolonged excitation. When the green light is removed, the cell's response drops below its usual level of spontaneous firing, and its output is perceived as red.

Beyond the level of the cones, color coding in many neurons of the visual system resembles Hering's opponent processes (DeValois & Jacobs, 1968). Many bipolar cells are excited by green light on the retina and inhibited by red light or are excited by red light and inhibited by green. Other bipolars are excited by yellow or blue and inhibited by the other. White-black bipolar cells are most strongly stimulated by a combination of all wavelengths (white). There is no such thing as black light. White-black bipolar cells are most effectively inhibited when the light shining on their cones is much fainter than the light shining on other cones surrounding them. (We shall return to this point later.)

Although we do not know exactly how the three kinds of cone connect to the bipolar cells, Figure 7.10 illustrates one possibility. Note that the activity of bipolar cell 1 depends on the ratio of activity between the medium-wavelength and long-wavelength cones. For example, red light, which excites the long-wavelength cone, excites bipolar cell 1. Green light excites the medium-wavelength cone and

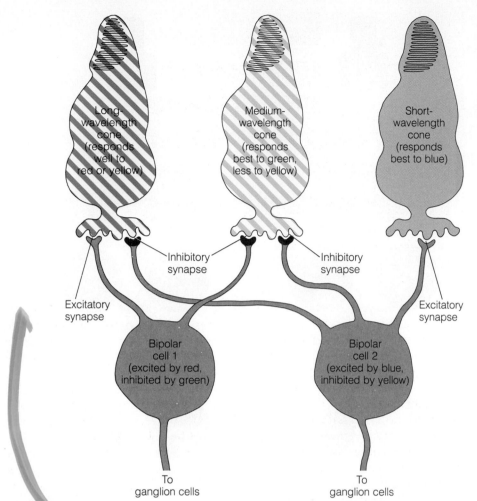

thus inhibits bipolar cell 1. Yellow light excites both the long-wavelength cone and the medium-wavelength cone and therefore produces little net effect on bipolar cell 1.

## The Retinex Theory

If a room is illuminated with bright red lights, or if you wear red-tinted glasses, your retina will receive mostly red light from all objects in the room. According to either the Young-Helmholtz theory or the opponent-process theory, you should perceive everything as various shades of red. In fact, however, you continue to perceive greens, yellows, blues—the entire range of colors. You have **color constancy,** the ability to perceive an object as the same color under different lights.

If you then focus on one of those green, yellow, or blue objects in isolation, shutting off all light from surrounding objects, something strange happens: It suddenly looks red! Evidently, color constancy depends on simultaneous contrast between an object and objects of other colors.

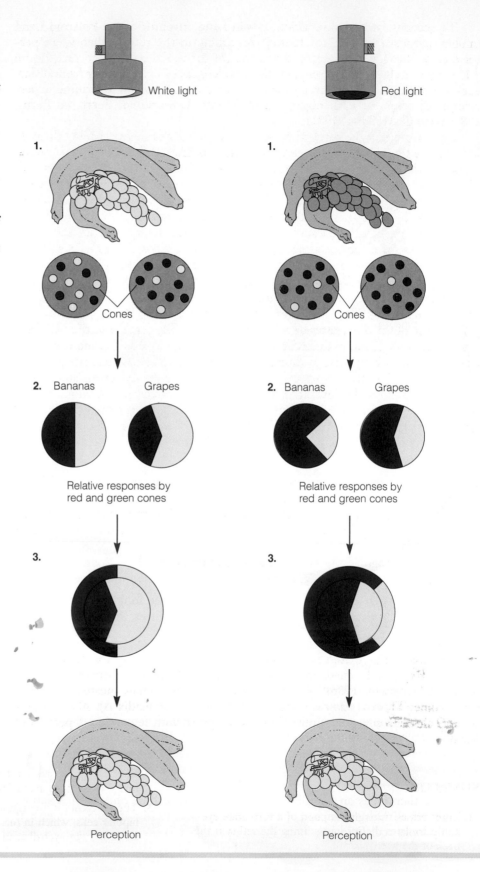

### Figure 7.11

*Bananas and grapes excite a particular ratio of short-, medium-, and long-wave-length cones under white light and a different ratio under red light. According to the retinex theory, the cortex examines the ratio of red to green in the bananas and the ratio of red to green in the grapes. It then compares one ratio to the other. From the comparison of ratios the cortex can nearly ignore the background colors and perceive the bananas as yellow and the grapes as green, despite the change in lighting.*

White light

Red light

1.

Cones

1.

Cones

2. Bananas    Grapes

Relative responses by
red and green cones

2. Bananas    Grapes

Relative responses by
red and green cones

3.

3.

Perception

Perception

To account for this observation, Edwin Land, inventor of the Polaroid Land camera, proposed the **retinex theory.** According to the retinex theory, we perceive color through the combined activities of the retina and the cortex (Figure 7.11). The cerebral cortex compares the wavelengths of light coming from different parts of the retina at a given time and from that comparison determines a perception of color for each object (Land, Hubel, Livingstone, Perry, & Burns, 1983; Land & McCann, 1971).

Certain areas of the cerebral cortex follow the retinex theory, while others do not. The occipital lobe of the cerebral cortex contains at least four visual areas, known as V1 through V4, as Figure 7.12 shows. Color-sensitive neurons in area **V1,** located at the extreme tip of the occipital cortex, change their response depending on the wavelength of light falling on certain parts of the retina. Those cells follow the opponent-process theory. But neurons in area V4, located in the anterior part of the occipital cortex, follow the retinex theory. Certain cells there respond to the presence of green objects, others to yellow objects, and so forth. Such cells continue to respond to those objects even if the light falling on the objects is, say, mostly red. The cells' activity depends on the contrast between one area of the retina and another, not just on the wavelengths coming from a given spot on the retina (Zeki, 1980, 1983).

Because of the differences between areas V1 and V4, damage to the two areas can impair color vision in different ways. After damage to area V1, monkeys have trouble distinguishing one color from another under any circumstances. After damage to area V4, they can learn to distinguish between, say, green and orange patches under normal white light. Having done so, however, the monkeys become confused if the overhead white light is changed to green or red (Wild, Butler, Carden, & Kulikowski, 1985). They have lost their color constancy.

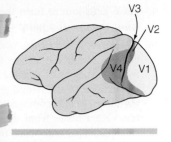

**Figure 7.12**
**Location of areas V1–V4 in monkey cortex**

## Color Blindness

You and I know that many people can see the shape, size, movement, and other features of an object without fully perceiving its color. But people have not always realized that such a thing is possible. Until the 1600s they took it for granted that color was part of an object; anyone who saw the object at all would see its color (Fletcher & Voke, 1985).

We now recognize the existence of several types of color blindness. For genetic reasons, some people lack the long-wavelength, medium-wavelength, or short-wavelength cones. Other people have low numbers or defective forms of one type of cone.

In the most common form of color blindness, red-green color blindness, people have trouble distinguishing red from green. Both reds and greens tend to look grayish yellow. The reason is an alteration of the genes coding for the opsins in both the long- and medium-wavelength cones (Nathans, Piantanida, Eddy, Shows, & Hogness, 1986). Those genes are recessive genes located on the X chromosome. That is, they are sex-linked genes (see Appendix A). About 8 percent of males are red-green color blind, as compared with fewer than 1 percent of females.

## SUMMARY

1. Light passes through the pupil of a vertebrate eye and stimulates the receptors lining the retina at the back of the eye. (p. 230)

2. Visual receptors are most densely packed in the fovea, the central area of the retina. (p. 231)

3. The receptors in the retina pass their information to bipolar cells, which in turn stimulate ganglion cells, all within the eyeball itself. The axons from the gan-

glion cells join to form the optic tract, which exits from the eye at a point called the blind spot. (p. 232)

4. The optic tracts of the two eyes join at the optic chiasm, where half of the axons from each eye cross to the opposite side of the brain. Most of the axons then travel to the lateral geniculate nucleus of the thalamus, which communicates with the visual cortex. Other axons from the optic tract go to the superior colliculus and other areas of the brain. (p. 234)

5. The retina has two kinds of receptors: rods and cones. Rods are more sensitive to dim light. Cones, which are located mostly near the center of the retina, are more sensitive to detail. Cones contribute to color vision; rods do not. (p. 234)

6. Light stimulates the receptors by triggering a change in molecules of 11-*cis*-retinal, which release energy, thereby activating second messengers within the cell. (p. 236)

7. Three theories account for color vision. According to the trichromatic theory (or Young-Helmholtz theory), color perception begins with the stimulation of three types of cones in the retina. Each wavelength of light stimulates a distinctive ratio of responses by the three types of cones. (p. 238)

8. According to the opponent-process theory of color vision, visual system neurons beyond the receptors themselves respond with an increase in activity to indicate one color of light and a decrease to indicate the opposite color. The three pairs of opposites are red-green, yellow-blue, and white-black. (p. 239)

9. According to the retinex theory, the cerebral cortex compares the wavelengths of light coming from different parts of the retina at a given time and from that comparison determines a perception of color for each object. (p. 241)

10. For genetic reasons, certain people are unable to distinguish one color from another in the same way that most people do. The most common type of color blindness is an inability to distinguish between red and green. (p. 243)

## REVIEW QUESTIONS

1. When light from the environment strikes the retina, it is reversed left-right and up-down. Does the nervous system turn the image right side up? If so, where and how? If not, does the reversal of the image cause any difficulties? (p. 230)

2. Why is perception of detail better in the fovea than it is toward the periphery of the retina? Why is perception of dim light better in the periphery? (pp. 231, 236)

3. What makes the blind spot of the retina blind? (p. 232)

4. Where in the brain do axons of the optic nerve go? (p. 234)

5. What are the differences between rods and cones? (p. 236)

6. How does 11-*cis*-retinal contribute to the detection of light? (p. 236)

7. Describe the Young-Helmholtz theory, the opponent-process theory, and the retinex theory. (p. 238)

8. Why is color blindness more common in men than in women? (p. 243)

## THOUGHT QUESTION

1. How could you test for the presence of color vision in a bee? Examining the retina will not help; invertebrate receptors resemble neither rods nor cones. It is possible to train bees to approach one visual stimulus and not another. The difficulty is that if you trained some bees to approach, say, a yellow card and not a green card, you would not know whether they solved the problem by color or by brightness. Because brightness is different from physical intensity, you cannot equalize brightness by any physical measurement, nor can you assume that two colors that are equally bright to humans are also equally bright to bees. How might you get around the problem of brightness to study the possibility of color vision in bees?

## SUGGESTIONS FOR FURTHER READING

**Dowling, J. E.** (1987). *The retina*. Cambridge, MA: Harvard University Press. Detailed, well-illustrated review of research on retinal receptors and their connections to other neurons within the eye.

**Lennie, P., & D'Zmura, M.** (1988). Mechanisms of color vision. *Critical Reviews in Neurobiology, 3,* 333–400. Thorough review of psychological and physiological research on color vision.

# Neural Basis of Visual Perception

$B$y looking at Figure 7.13 you can experience some optical illusions. They are called optical illusions because most people perceive something different from what is actually there. The various theories about these optical illusions, despite their disagreements, all agree that the causes are within the brain, not within the eyeballs. (If you look at one line of the Müller-Lyer illusion with one eye and the other line with the other eye, you will still see the illusion.)

A different kind of optical illusion does depend on processes within the eyeball, however. In Figure 7.14, you may see dark diamonds at the crossroads among the black squares. Cells within each eye are responsible for those perceptions.

The point of these demonstrations is simply that our perceptions are not the same thing as the stimuli that strike our receptors. When sensory information reaches the brain, the brain alters that information in ways that ordinarily make it more useful but in some cases distort it.

## MECHANISMS OF PROCESSING IN THE VISUAL SYSTEM

The human retina contains roughly 120 million rods and 6 million cones. If we were aware of the activity in every receptor, we would be flooded with information. We do not need or want information about 126 million points of light. We merely need to know what objects are out there and where they are. Imagine, as an analogy, that Senator Philip Buster receives thousands of letters from constituents on some issue. The senator directs staff members to summarize the information; for example, "55 percent of the letters were in favor of legalizing miracle berries for the following reasons . . . , and 45 percent were opposed for the following reasons. . . ." The summary digests sacks of mail into a single page. Although much detailed information has been lost, the important patterns have been emphasized.

## Figure 7.13
## Three optical illusions

*(a) Lines A and B are the same length. (b) B is the extension of A. (c) The lines are straight.*

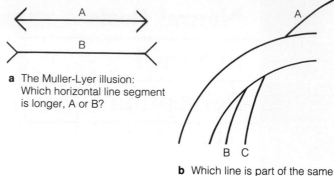

**a** The Muller-Lyer illusion: Which horizontal line segment is longer, A or B?

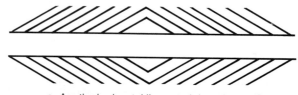

**b** Which line is part of the same circular arc as A?

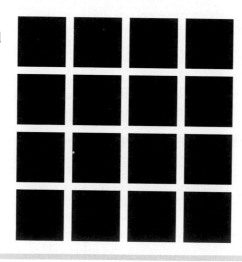

**c** Are the horizontal lines straight or bowed?

## Figure 7.14
## Another kind of optical illusion

*Do you see dark diamonds at the "crossroads"?*

The information provided by our visual receptors is analogous to the sacks of letters; much of it is repetitive. The brain needs to summarize the information—to highlight the important patterns, such as the borders between objects.

### Lateral Inhibition

**Lateral inhibition**—reduction of activity in one neuron by activity in a neighboring neuron—is a method of sharpening the contrast at borders and of enhancing the response of the nervous system to changes. It occurs in touch and hearing as well as in vision.

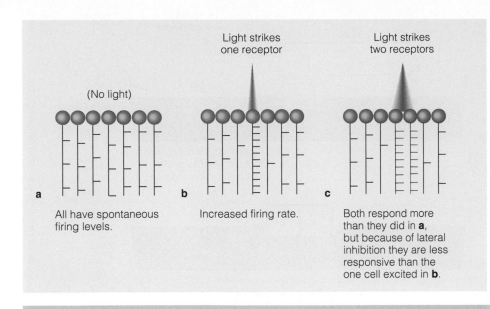

**Figure 7.15**
**Three representations of a set of receptors from the *Limulus* retina**
*Light shines on the receptors as shown. The short horizontal lines represent action potentials.*

Light strikes one receptor

Light strikes two receptors

(No light)

**a** All have spontaneous firing levels.

**b** Increased firing rate.

**c** Both respond more than they did in **a**, but because of lateral inhibition they are less responsive than the one cell excited in **b**.

Lateral inhibition was first discovered in studies of *Limulus*, the horseshoe crab (Hartline, 1949). When light shines on a visual receptor, activity in that receptor increases. If light is added onto neighboring receptors, activity in those receptors increases but activity in the first receptor decreases (Figure 7.15). That is, activity in any receptor decreases the activity of surrounding receptors. That decrease is the effect of lateral inhibition.

The vertebrate eye has a similar pattern of response, although the anatomy is quite different from that of *Limulus*. To understand the principle, let us consider an analogy: If I place a wooden block on a surface of gelatin, the block depresses the gelatin beneath it while raising the surrounding surface (Figure 7.16a). The depression is analogous to the excitation of a neuron; the rise in the surrounding gelatin is analogous to lateral inhibition of surrounding neurons. Then I place a second block next to the first. As the second block sinks into the gelatin, it raises the first (Figure 7.16b). Finally, I try placing a row of blocks on the gelatin. The blocks at the beginning and end of the row sink deeper than the others (Figure 7.16c). Why? Because each block in the interior of the row is subject to an upward pressure from both sides, while the blocks at the beginning and end of the row are subject to that pressure from one side only.

In the vertebrate retina, lateral inhibition is accomplished by the horizontal cells. Each receptor cell excites one or more bipolar cells, as Figure 7.17 shows. It also excites a large, widely branching horizontal cell (H), which *inhibits* the nearby bipolar cells. The bipolar cell that receives excitation from the receptor also receives inhibition via the horizontal cell. The net effect is excitation. However, the surrounding bipolar cells receive no excitation from the receptor; they receive only the inhibition. The result is excitation of a bipolar cell and inhibition of its neighbors—in other words, lateral inhibition.

Now let us consider the more complex and more realistic case in which light strikes a whole set of receptors, not just one. Anywhere in Figure 7.17, imagine a border between light and dark. Draw a line between two receptors and imagine

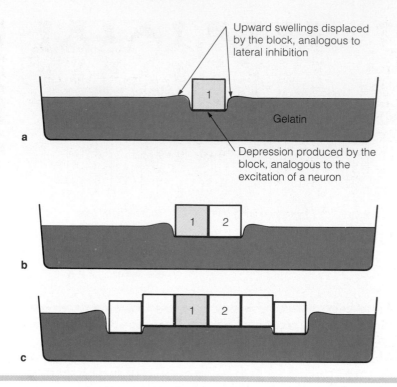

Upward swellings displaced by the block, analogous to lateral inhibition

Gelatin

Depression produced by the block, analogous to the excitation of a neuron

light striking all the receptors to the right of the line but none to the left of the line. All the bipolar cells to the right of that line receive the same amount of excitation from the receptors. However, they do not receive the same amount of inhibition from the horizontal cells. The bipolar cell just to the right of the light-dark border is inhibited by the stimulation of the receptor above it and the nearby receptors to the right. But the receptors to its left are not excited, and therefore they do not send inhibitory messages via the horizontal cells. Now consider a bipolar cell farther to the right. It is inhibited by horizontal cell input from both the left and the right. Consequently, the bipolar cells in the middle of an illuminated area are *less* active than those just inside the border of the illuminated area. They both receive the same excitation, but those surrounded by the larger area of excitation receive the greater amount of inhibition.

An important first step in the organism's summarizing of visual information and extracting meaning from it, lateral inhibition emphasizes the borders between light and dark, which are normally the edges of an object.

## Receptive Fields

In tracing what happens to visual information as it passes from the retina to various points in the brain, we must make extensive use of a concept known as the **receptive field.** The receptive field of a neuron is an area of the body in which stimulation of some kind excites or inhibits the cell, directly or indirectly. For a

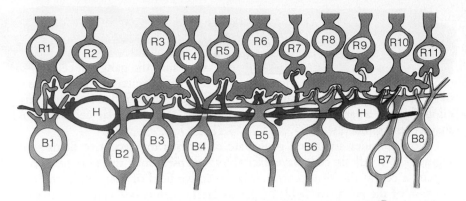

**Figure 7.17**
**Diagram of connections in the vertebrate retina**
*Receptors excite horizontal and bipolar cells; horizontal cells inhibit bipolars. (Based on Dowling & Boycott, 1966.)*

neuron in the visual system, the receptive field is an area of the retina. In other systems of the brain, a neuron's receptive field may be part of the basilar membrane, part of the skin, or part of any other receptive structure.

Examine cell B3 in Figure 7.17. Cell B3 can be excited when light strikes receptor R3. It is also connected to a horizontal cell that receives input from receptors R1 through R8; therefore, bipolar cell B3 is inhibited by excitation of any of those receptors. We say that receptors R1 through R8 constitute the receptive field of cell B3. That is, stimulation anywhere in that area affects the cell by either exciting or inhibiting it. Figure 7.17 shows cells along only one dimension. If we present the entire retina in two dimensions, the receptive field of a cell such as B3 looks like the drawing in Figure 7.18b. Other bipolar cells have the reverse receptive field, with an inhibitory region in the center and an excitatory field in the surround.

We can describe the receptive field of a visual cell in two ways. The first is to describe it as an area of the retina, as in Figure 7.18. The second is to describe it as an area of the visual field. Because every spot on the retina receives its input from one point in the visual field, the two ways are equivalent.

To map the receptive fields of neurons in the visual system, an investigator can shine light on specific receptors in the retina while recording from a cell in the brain. If light on a particular receptor either increases or decreases the firing rate of a brain cell, then that receptor is part of the cell's receptive field. If the light has no effect, the receptor is outside the receptive field.

Customarily, an investigator may say that a particular neuron in the visual system responds to a particular pattern of light—for example, "this cell in the cerebral cortex responds best to a green horizontal line." The investigator does *not* mean that light shining on the neuron excites it. Rather, the neuron is excited when that pattern of light shines on the neuron's receptive field in the retina.

## How Receptive Fields Are Built

A group of bipolar cells sends its output to ganglion cells; in turn, a group of ganglion cells sends its output to cells in the lateral geniculate, and so on. The neurons at each level have receptive fields made by combining the receptive fields of all incoming fibers.

Neural Basis of
Visual Perception

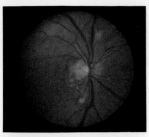

a

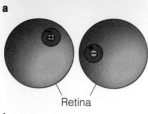

Retina

b

**Figure 7.18**
*(a) View of the retina through an ophthalmoscope. (Don Wong/Science Source/ PR.) (b) Diagrams of two typical receptive fields of bipolar cells (greatly magnified).*

For example, suppose seven bipolar cells have partly overlapping receptive fields on the retina, as Figure 7.19a illustrates. All seven of these bipolar cells have synapses onto a ganglion cell. The bipolar cell with receptive field *d* excites that ganglion cell; the other six inhibit it. As a result, the ganglion cell has the receptive field shown to the right of Figure 7.19a: It is excited by light in the center of its receptive field and inhibited by light in the surround. Note that this ganglion cell has a larger receptive field than any of the bipolar cells, although its shape is the same.

Now consider six lateral geniculate cells, with the receptive fields shown in Figure 7.19b. All six cells have excitatory synapses onto the next neuron in the system, a cell in the visual cortex. The receptive field of that cell in the cortex is the sum of the receptive fields of the six lateral geniculate cells—a bar shape, as shown to the right of Figure 7.19b.

## PARALLEL PATHWAYS IN THE VISUAL SYSTEM

Look out your window. Perhaps you see someone walking by. A perception so simple that you take it for granted is actually a combination of many kinds of visual information: shape, size, color, brightness, distance, movement. . . . How does your visual system keep track of such different kinds of information?

We could imagine that each neuron might be sensitive to all aspects. For example, one neuron somewhere in your brain might detect a long, thin, bright green, horizontal bar-shaped object 40 meters away from you, moving directly upward at 0.5 m/sec. Another neuron might be maximally responsive to a short, dull-blue, vertical bar-shaped stationary object 1 meter away from you. And so forth.

In fact our visual system is organized in a much different manner. We have three separate, partly independent pathways in the cerebral cortex—one responsible mostly for details of shape, one responsible for color and brightness, and one responsible for movement and certain aspects of distance (Livingstone, 1988; Livingstone & Hubel, 1988; Zeki & Shipp, 1988). When you see a person walking, one set of neurons identifies the shape, another set concentrates on the colors of skin and clothing, and another sees which direction the person is walking and how fast. At least that is true to some extent; the three pathways do communicate with one another. Some sort of communication among them would seem to be necessary for you to see that walking person as a single, unified entity (Kaas, 1989).

### Ganglion Cells and Lateral Geniculate Cells

The three visual pathways of the cerebral cortex begin with two major types of ganglion cells in the retina. Remember that the bipolar cells make contact onto ganglion cells, whose axons form the optic nerve. In cats, monkeys, and many other mammals, the receptive field of a ganglion cell is either excitatory or inhibitory in the center, and the opposite in the surrounding region (Kuffler, 1953).

Most of the ganglion cells fall into two major categories. The smaller cells, sometimes known as **X cells,** are located mostly in or near the fovea. The larger cells, sometimes known as **Y cells,** are distributed fairly evenly throughout the retina (Sherman & Spear, 1982; Fukuda, Hsiao, & Watanabe, 1985). A less numerous category, the **W cells,** are only weakly responsive to visual stimuli (Raczkowski, Hamos, & Sherman, 1988); their function is poorly understood and we shall not consider them further in this text.

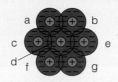

a

b

Receptive fields of 7 bipolar cells (a–g)

Receptive field of one ganglion cell, which is excited by the bipolar cell with receptive field d and inhibited by the other 6 bipolar cells.

Receptive fields of 6 lateral geniculate cells (1–6) cells

Receptive field of one cell in the visual cortex that is excited by the 6 lateral geniculate cells

**Figure 7.19**
(*a*) *The input from seven bipolar cells with the receptive fields shown on the left combines to give a ganglion cell the receptive field shown at the right.* (*b*) *One neuron in the visual cortex receives its input from six lateral geniculate cells, whose receptive fields line up in a row on the retina, as shown to the left. Consequently, this visual cortex cell has a bar-shaped receptive field.*

Most Y cells and apparently all X cells send their axons to the lateral geniculate nucleus of the thalamus. The lateral geniculate has six distinct laminae (layers). On each side of the brain, three of those laminae receive their input from the eye on the same side of the head; the other three receive their input from the opposite side. (No cell in the lateral geniculate has binocular vision.)

Of the six laminae, four are composed of **parvocellular** neurons and two are composed of **magnocellular** neurons. Parvocellular means *small celled*, from the Latin root *parv-*, meaning *small*. Magnocellular means *large celled*, from the Latin root *magn-*, meaning large. (The same root appears in *magnify* and *magnificent*.) The X cells make synapses onto parvocellular neurons and the Y cells make synapses onto magnocellular neurons.

The parvocellular neurons are sensitive to color. That is, each one is excited by light of one color (such as red) in its receptive field and inhibited by another color (such as green). The magnocellular neurons are color blind; they respond equally to light of any wavelength. The parvocellular neurons, which have smaller receptive fields, are better adapted to detect visual details; the magnocellular neurons detect the broader outlines of shapes. The magnocellular neurons respond rapidly but only briefly to a stimulus, while the parvocellular neurons give a sustained response to an unchanging stimulus. Consequently, the magnocellular neurons are well suited to detect movement; the parvocellular neurons are better suited to analyze a stationary object. Table 7.2 summarizes the differences between parvocellular and magnocellular neurons.

## Cerebral Cortex

When axons from the lateral geniculate reach the cerebral cortex, the two pathways (parvocellular and magnocellular) become three. The parvocellular neurons and magnocellular neurons make contact with cells in different parts of lamina 4C in the **primary visual cortex** (area V1, also known as the **striate cortex** because of its striped appearance). From there, the magnocellular system projects mostly to lamina 4B of area V1. The parvocellular pathway splits; it sends some of its information to clusters of neurons called **blobs** (because of the shape of the cluster) in laminae 2 and 3 and the rest to the area between blobs, known conveniently as **interblobs**. The magnocellular neurons also send information to some

Neural Basis of
Visual Perception

**Table 7.2 Distinctions Between Parvocellular and Magnocellular Neurons in the Lateral Geniculate**

|  | *Parvocellular Neurons* | *Magnocellular Neurons* |
|---|---|---|
| Input | X cells (small cell bodies) | Y cells (large cell bodies) |
| Cell bodies | Smaller | Larger |
| Receptive fields | Smaller | Larger |
| Color sensitive? | Yes | No |
| Response | Sustained response; adapted for detailed analysis of stationary objects | Fast, transient responses; adapted to detect movement and broad outlines of shape |

cells in the blobs but not the same cells as the parvocellular neurons. The blob cells that receive their input from the parvocellular neurons are highly sensitive to color—in most cases, excited by red and inhibited by green or excited by green and inhibited by red (Ts'o & Gilbert, 1988). The blob cells that receive their input from the magnocellular neurons are color blind but highly sensitive to changes in brightness.

So at this point we have three pathways: the magnocellular pathway (sensitive to movement and to broad outlines of shape), the blobs (most cells sensitive to color and the others sensitive to brightness), and the interblobs (sensitive to details of shape). These three pathways remain distinct in the next level of the visual system, the **secondary visual cortex (V2)**. Here the magnocellular path sends its information to the thick stripe areas, the interblobs relay their information to the pale stripes, and the blobs pass their information to the thin stripes.

The thick stripes (part of the magnocellular pathway) are highly sensitive to movement and to **stereoscopic depth perception**—the ability to detect depth by differences in what the two eyes see. To illustrate, hold a finger in front of your eyes and look at it, first with just the left eye and then with just the right eye. Try this again, holding your finger at different distances. Note that the two eyes see your finger differently and that the closer your finger is to your face, the greater the difference between the two views. The thick stripes in area V2 are highly sensitive to the amount of discrepancy between the two views; presumably the thick stripes are responsible for stereoscopic depth perception. (When you look at something with just one eye, the cells in your thick stripes are almost unresponsive.)

## Visual Processing at Higher Levels

The occipital cortex has four major visual areas: areas V1 and V2 that we have already considered, plus areas **V3** and **V4** (see Figure 7.20). Several areas in the temporal, parietal, and frontal cortex respond to visual information as well. In these "higher" levels of the visual system, the three pathways—from the thick stripes, thin stripes, and pale stripes—continue to remain mostly distinct from one another.

Form information—previously analyzed in the interblobs of area V1 and the pale stripes of V2—is further analyzed in the **inferior temporal cortex,** specialized for advanced analysis of visual patterns. Cells in this area have large receptive

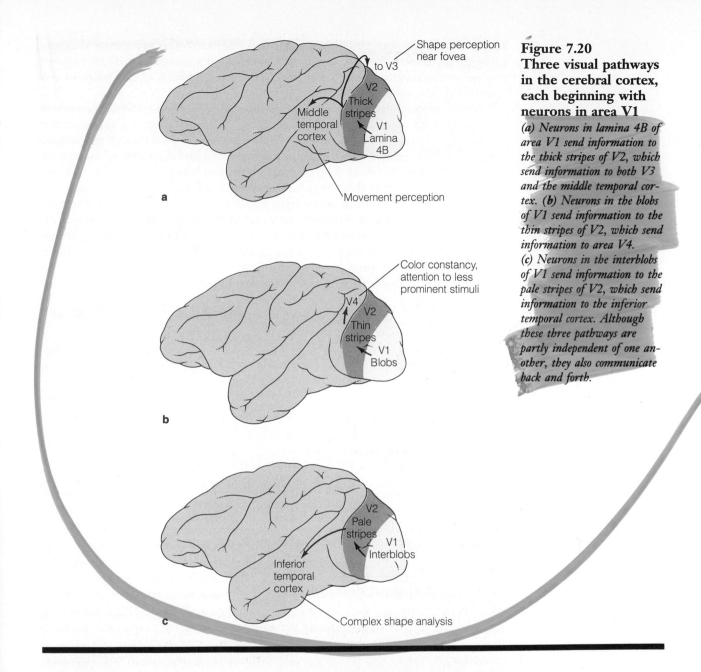

**Figure 7.20**
**Three visual pathways in the cerebral cortex, each beginning with neurons in area V1**

*(a) Neurons in lamina 4B of area V1 send information to the thick stripes of V2, which send information to both V3 and the middle temporal cortex. (b) Neurons in the blobs of V1 send information to the thin stripes of V2, which send information to area V4. (c) Neurons in the interblobs of V1 send information to the pale stripes of V2, which send information to the inferior temporal cortex. Although these three pathways are partly independent of one another, they also communicate back and forth.*

fields, with a median width of 26 degrees of the visual field, always including the fovea (Desimone & Gross, 1979). Although most of these cells respond at least moderately well to a wide variety of stimuli, a few respond preferentially to certain highly complex patterns. One study found two cells in macaque monkeys that responded more vigorously to the sight of a hand than to any other stimulus, and twenty cells that responded most vigorously to a face (Desimone, Albright, Gross, & Bruce, 1984). Later studies have found many cells that respond mostly to faces, though not specifically to a single face (Desimone, 1991).

The response of a cell in the inferior temporal cortex depends on the shape of the object in its visual field but is not much affected by changes in the object's size or location. Thus, in macaques face-sensitive cells respond both to profiles facing left and profiles facing right. This area of the brain may be essential for

Neural Basis of
Visual Perception

**shape constancy**—our ability to recognize an object as the same even as it approaches or retreats or rotates. As might be expected, damage in this area impairs the ability to recognize objects but does not cause blindness at any point in the visual field (Ungerleider & Pribram, 1977).

The magnocellular pathway continues in area V3 and the **middle temporal cortex.** Area V3 contributes to shape recognition, mostly near the center of the visual field (Gattass, Sousa, & Gross, 1988). The response of cells in the middle temporal cortex depends mostly on an object's speed and direction of movement (Bruce, Desimone, & Gross, 1981; Gross, Bruce, Desimone, Fleming, & Gattass, 1981; Saito et al., 1986). They may be responsible not only for our perception of whether the object is moving left or right but also of whether it is moving toward us or away. After damage limited to neurons in the middle temporal cortex, an animal can identify shapes as well as ever but has great trouble identifying which direction an object is moving (Newsome & Paré, 1988). The same kind of brain damage in humans is probably responsible for cortical "motion blindness," in which a brain-damaged patient sees stationary objects normally but cannot describe the direction and speed of moving objects.

The analysis of color, which depends on the blobs of area V1 and the thin stripes of V2, continues in a part of the occipital lobe known as area V4. Each cell in area V4 is selectively responsive to a particular color in its rather large receptive field (Zeki, 1980). Recall that according to the retinex theory of color vision, the cortex determines the color of an object by comparing what it sees of that object to what it sees of other objects. Evidently area V4 is responsible for this function. For example, monkeys with damage to area V4 can learn to pick up a yellow object to get food, but if the overhead lighting is changed from white to blue, the monkey can no longer find the yellow object (Wild, Butler, Carden, & Kulikowski, 1985). In short, area V4 seems to be responsible for **color constancy,** the ability to recognize the color of an object despite changes in the lighting. However, V4 also has other functions, including some relating to visual attention. Monkeys with damage in V4 have trouble learning to focus their eyes on the smaller, slower, or duller of two visual stimuli (Schiller & Lee, 1991). Figure 7.21 summarizes the three major visual pathways in the cerebral cortex.

## Relationship of the Three Visual Pathways to Human Perception

The separation of the three visual pathways has certain implications for human vision (Livingstone, 1988; Livingstone & Hubel, 1988). For example, consider Figure 7.22a, which has yellow-to-gray borders. Because the yellow and gray are about equally bright, the photo has very little brightness contrast. The parvocellular pathway, which is color sensitive, can detect the stimulus. However, the magnocellular pathway, which is highly sensitive to brightness contrast but not sensitive to color, detects this stimulus only weakly. The parvocellular pathway is more important for analysis of the details of form; if you focus on one point at a time, you can see each detail of the photo. However, the magnocellular pathway is more important for perceiving the overall pattern or outline of the object. Because the magnocellular system is poorly stimulated, we are slow to see the bicycle in the photo.

Similarly, Figure 7.22b stimulates the parvocellular pathway much more than it does the magnocellular pathway. If a pattern like this covering a television or computer screen steadily moves in one direction or the other, observers sometimes fail to perceive the movement.

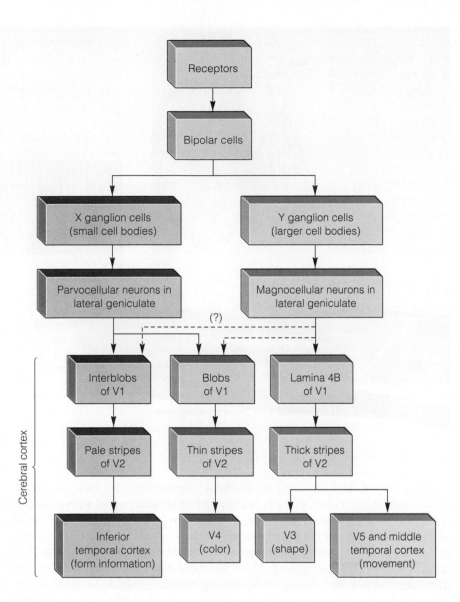

**Figure 7.21**
**Summary of the separate pathways responsible for vision in the primate brain**
*It is not critical to remember all the details of which set of cells sends its output exactly where. The important point is that the visual system maintains largely independent pathways that analyze different aspects of the stimulus.*

Finally, consider the painting in Figure 7.23. The artist has indicated shadows by distinct colors. The result is a painting that does not look entirely realistic, and yet the shadows enable us to perceive the illusion of depth about as well in the color version as in the black and white version. The reason is that the magnocellular pathway, which is more important for depth perception, is sensitive only to brightness, not to color.

In summary, the visual system of the cerebral cortex has three separate pathways: one responsible mostly for perception of color, one responsible mostly for perception of fine detail, and one responsible mostly for perception of movement and depth. Each pathway performs its functions somewhat independently of the others, although in some unknown way the brain combines the information in the three pathways to experience each stimulus as a unity.

Neural Basis of
Visual Perception

a                                                                                          b

## Figure 7.22

*(a) The left image can be seen only by color, because the yellows and grays are about equally bright. Therefore, seeing it depends on the parvocellular system, which is specialized for perceiving details but not overall form. Notice that you can perceive detail in this photo by looking at one spot at a time but that you have trouble seeing the bicycle as a whole. The image on the right excites your magnocellular system as well; note how easily you see the overall pattern of this bicycle. (From Livingstone & Hubel, 1988.) (b) A pattern of lines that stimulates the parvocellular pathway much more than the magnocellular pathway. Movement of such lines is difficult to detect because the magnocellular pathway is responsible for movement detection.*

Why do we have so many visual areas? Remember, we have not only the three major pathways but also a large number of separate areas within each pathway. Hedgehogs, generally regarded as relatively primitive mammals, get along with only a few visual areas in their brain. Somewhere in the evolutionary procession from primitive mammalian brains to monkey and human brains, a great many new visual areas developed. What do those extra areas enable us to see that hedgehogs cannot see? Surely it is nothing simple; hedgehogs respond to the shape, color, and movement of visual stimuli. Somehow these extra visual areas may facilitate subtle capacities such as color constancy, or they may simply increase the precision of the same capacities that hedgehogs have (Kaas, 1989). At this point, no one is sure.

## MECHANISMS OF SHAPE PERCEPTION

Now that we have described the basic organization of the three cortical pathways for vision, let's examine in more detail how the primary visual cortex processes shapes. The pioneering work in this area won a Nobel Prize for David Hubel and Torsten Wiesel before investigators recognized the distinction among the three major pathways.

Hubel and Wiesel found that most neurons in the primary visual cortex of cats and monkeys have **binocular** receptive fields. That is, they respond to por-

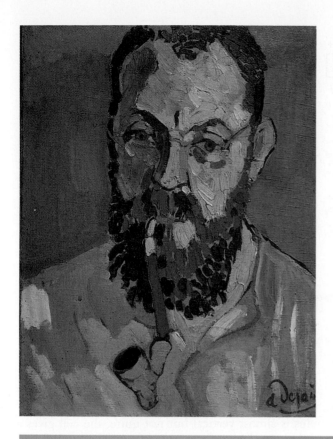 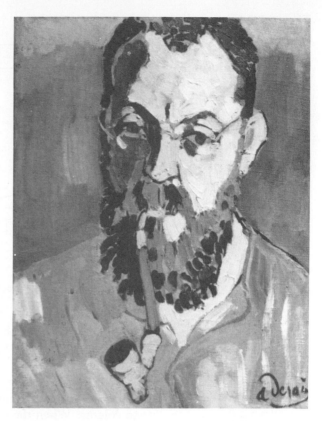

**Figure 7.23**
*The artist André Derain (1880–1954) has shown depth with colored shadows in this portrait of painter Henri Matisse (1905). Although the painting does not look realistic, we perceive the depth easily because the magnocellular pathway (responsible for depth perception) is color blind. Note that we perceive depth about equally well in the color painting and in the black and white version. (Tate Gallery, London/Art Resource, NY.)*

tions of both eyes. Moreover, most visual cortex cells have receptive fields shaped like a bar or an edge (Hubel & Wiesel, 1959). The cells may therefore serve as **feature detectors**—neurons whose responses indicate the presence of a particular feature. They distinguished three categories of neurons in the visual cortex: simple, complex, and hypercomplex cells.

## Simple Cells

The receptive fields shown in Figure 7.24 are typical of **simple cells,** which are found exclusively in the striate cortex. Each simple cell can be excited by a point of light anywhere in the excitatory part of its receptive field (pluses) and inhibited by light anywhere in the inhibitory part (minuses). Light covering the entire excitatory area produces more excitation than a single point of light does. For example, a cell with a receptive field like that depicted in Figure 7.24c is maximally responsive to a vertical bar of light in a specific location on the retina. The response of the cell decreases sharply if the bar of light is moved slightly to the left or right or if it is tilted even a few degrees from the vertical, because light then strikes the inhibitory regions as well. The receptive fields for different cortical cells have different orientations, which include vertical, horizontal, and intermediate angles. Most cells with receptive fields near the fovea respond best to vertical or horizontal lines; cells with receptive fields in the periphery may respond best to other angles (Schall, Vitek, & Leventhal, 1986).

Figure 7.25 illustrates how the orientation of a stimulus affects the response of a simple cell. The illustrated cell detects vertical lines in its receptive field. It

Neural Basis of
Visual Perception

**Figure 7.24**
**Typical receptive fields for simple visual cortex cells of cats and monkeys**
*(Based on Hubel & Wiesel, 1959.)*

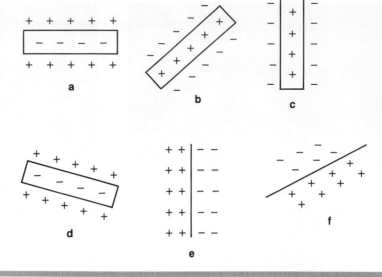

gives its greatest response when a vertical line is in the center of its receptive field, as in the fifth stimulus of the first column and the third stimulus of the second column. When the stimulus is almost vertical but not quite, the cell gives a less vigorous response. When the stimulus is closer to horizontal, the cell is unlikely to respond at all.

## Complex Cells

**Complex cells,** located in either area V1 or V2, have a larger receptive field than simple cells do. Unlike the receptive fields we have encountered up to this point, the receptive fields of complex cells cannot be mapped into fixed excitatory and inhibitory zones. A complex cell is practically unaffected by a small point of light in the retina. Instead, it responds to a pattern of light in a particular orientation (for instance, a vertical bar) preferably moving perpendicular to its axis. (For example, a vertical bar produces its greatest response if it is moving horizontally.) Any stimulus with the right orientation and movement within the large receptive field excites the cell, regardless of the exact location of the stimulus within that receptive field (see Figure 7.26).

We have two ways of determining whether a given cell in the visual cortex is a simple cell or a complex cell: (1) Find a bar of light to which the cell vigorously responds. Move the light slightly to one side or the other. If the cell responds only to light in one location, it is a simple cell. (2) Shine small spots of light instead of a bar. If any spot produces significant excitation or inhibition, the cell is a simple cell.

## Hypercomplex cells

**Hypercomplex cells** resemble complex cells with one additional feature: A hypercomplex cell has a strong inhibitory area at one end of its bar-shaped receptive field. The cell responds to a bar-shaped pattern of light anywhere in its broad re-

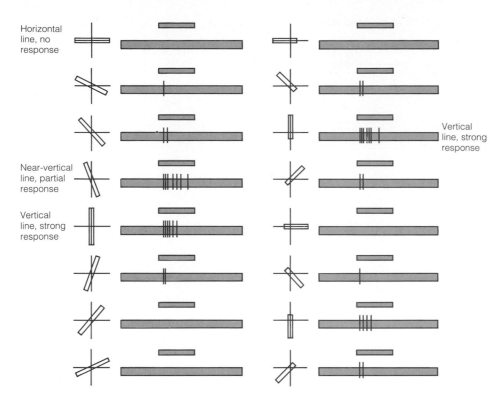

Horizontal line, no response

Near-vertical line, partial response

Vertical line, strong response

Vertical line, strong response

**Figure 7.25
Responses of a cat's cortical cell to a bar of light presented at varying angles**
*The short horizontal lines indicate the time when light is on. (From Hubel & Wiesel, 1959.)*

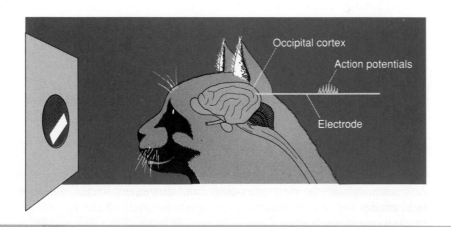

Occipital cortex

Action potentials

Electrode

**Figure 7.26**
**The receptive field of a complex cell in the visual cortex**

*It is like a simple cell in that its response depends on the angle of orientation of a bar of light. It is unlike a simple cell in that the complex cell's response is the same for a bar in any position within the receptive field.*

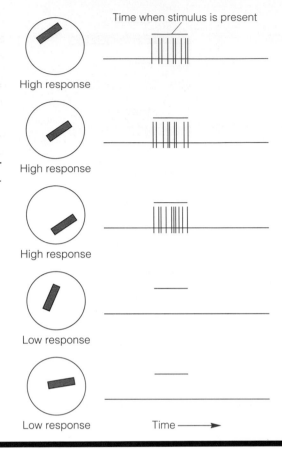

ceptive field, provided that the bar does not extend beyond a certain point (see Figure 7.27). Table 7.3 summarizes the properties of simple, complex, and hypercomplex cells.

## Feature Detectors and Human Vision

Each cell in the visual cortex responds vigorously to a bar of light with a particular orientation, in a particular location. But what does such a cell have to do with perception?

For one thing, it is possible to fatigue such a cell through repetitive stimulation. When it is fatigued, we are *less* able to see the stimuli it responds to than we are ordinarily. For example, consider Figure 7.28 (from Blakemore & Sutton, 1969): Cover the two stripe patterns on the right and stare at the little rectangle in the middle of the left half for a minute or so. As you do so, you fatigue a set of cortical neurons responding to wide stripes in the upper part of your visual field and another set responding to narrow stripes in the lower part of your visual field. Then look at the small square in the center of the right half of the figure. Note that the stripes in the upper set look narrower than those in the lower set. The reason is that you have fatigued two sets of neurons, which are now contributing less than usual to your perception. Your perception is now dominated by neurons

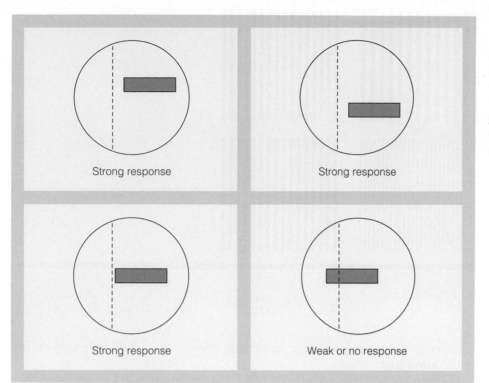

**Figure 7.27**
*The receptive field of a hyper-complex cell responds to a bar in a particular orientation (in this case, horizontal) any-where in its receptive field, provided that the bar does not extend into a strongly in-hibitory area.*

## Table 7.3 Summary of Cells in the Primary Visual Cortex

| Characteristic | Simple Cells | Complex Cells | Hypercomplex Cells |
|---|---|---|---|
| Location | V1 | V1 and V2 | V1 and V2 |
| Binocular input? | Yes | Yes | Yes |
| Size of receptive field | Smallest | Medium | Largest |
| Response to single point of light | Excited or inhibited, depending on location | No response | No response |
| Best stimulus | Bar of light in particular location | Bar of light anywhere in receptive field | Same as complex cells but with strong inhibitory field at one end |
| Sensitive to orientation of stimulus? | Yes | Yes | Yes |

**Figure 7.28**
**Stimulus for demonstrating width aftereffects**

*First stare at the little rectangle in the left half of the figure for a minute or so. Then look at the small square in the right half of the figure. Does one set of stripes look narrower than the other?*

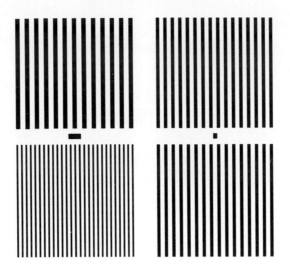

sensitive to narrow stripes in the upper part of your visual field and wide stripes in the lower part.

Similar phenomena demonstrate other feature detectors in human vision. For example, if you stare at a waterfall for a minute or more and then look away, the rocks and trees next to the waterfall appear to be flowing upward. This effect, termed the *waterfall illusion,* is caused by the fatigue of feature-detector neurons responsive to downward motion.

However, even if we grant that feature-detector neurons contribute to pattern perception, the question remains of how we perceive more complex patterns. Are other cells, at increasingly complex levels, responsible for recognizing your grandmother, identifying your psychology professor, and so on? Such specialization is unlikely for several reasons. One of the principal reasons is that no kind of brain damage prevents you from recognizing, say, your grandmother without also disrupting other visual perceptions. But if we do not have "grandmother cells," then how do we put together the information from various cells to recognize such complex patterns?

You may recognize this as basically the same question we encountered on page 250: How do we unify the perceptions based on three parallel and partly independent visual pathways? At a deeper level, we are reformulating the mind-brain question—what is the relationship between our conscious experience and the activity of countless cells in the brain?

At this point investigators do not have an answer. In fact, some are not convinced that feature-detector analysis is the best way to describe what happens in the brain. Maybe no individual cell is responsible for perceiving a particular visual stimulus. Digression 7.1 presents one alternative way of describing the functions of cells in the visual cortex.

## Columnar Organization of the Visual Cortex

Investigators have long known that the cerebral cortex is organized in laminae (see Figure 4.21). For example, the fourth lamina consists of cells that receive direct input from the lateral geniculate, and the fifth lamina consists of cells that

# Neurons in the Visual Cortex as Spatial Frequency Detectors

Most of the research on the visual cortex assumes that the neurons analyze a visual scene into its component bar-shaped lines. It would be possible to analyze the scene in an unlimited number of other ways. If we were designing a robot to analyze a visual scene, would we have it break the scene into lines? Perhaps, but perhaps not. From a mathematical standpoint, it is easier to describe a complex visual pattern as the sum of many sine waves. One branch of mathematics, Fourier analysis, has shown that by adding together a number of sine waves, we can approximate any graphical function whatsoever—even a square wave (see Figure 7.29).

Similarly, a complex visual scene can be described as the sum of a number of sine-wave gratings of light and dark. Any visual scene has a complex pattern of light and dark, going from top to bottom and from left to right. But that complex pattern is composed of a great many simple sine waves.

Suppose that each neuron in the visual cortex responds to a different sine-wave grating. For example,

one might be responsive to the sine-wave pattern in Figure 7.30a and another to the pattern in Figure 7.30b. In that case, the response of the total ensemble can reconstruct the original stimulus.

Do the cells in the visual cortex have these properties? Investigators who have shined sine-wave gratings on the retina have found that each neuron in the visual cortex responds better to one sine-wave pattern than to others and that different cells respond to different patterns (DeValois, Albrecht, & Thorell, 1982; Maffei & Fiorentini, 1973). At this point, we are not sure whether it is best to describe cells in the visual cortex as bar detectors, as sine-wave detectors, or as detectors of some other aspect of the stimulus.

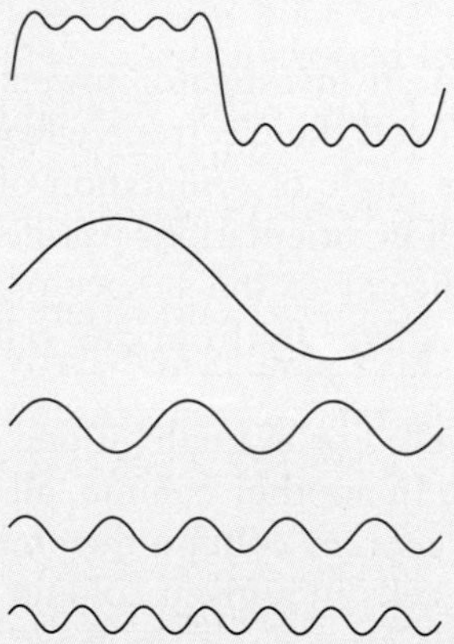

**Figure 7.30**
**Examples of sine-wave gratings**
*Going from left to right, the brightness repeatedly increases and decreases in a sine-wave pattern.*

**Figure 7.29**
*Fourier analysis reveals that the graph at the top is composed of the five sine waves below it.*

**Figure 7.31**
**Columns of neurons in the visual cortex**
*When an electrode passes perpendicular to the surface of the cortex, it encounters a sequence of neurons with parallel receptive fields. (The colored lines show the angle of orientation of the receptive field for each cell.) When an electrode passes at some other angle, it encounters neurons with a variety of receptive fields. (From Hubel, 1963.)*

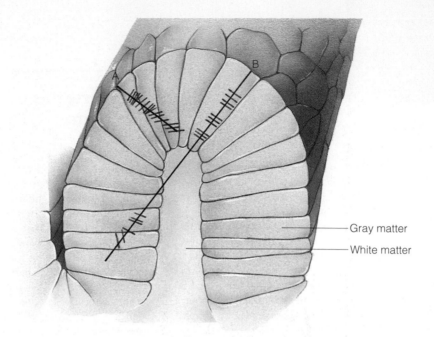

Gray matter
White matter

send axons to the medulla and spinal cord. In other words, if we take a layer of cells parallel to the surface of the cortex, we find that all these cells share certain properties.

The perpendicular groups of cortical cells called **columns** (see Figure 4.22) share common properties as well. When researchers insert an electrode perpendicular to the surface of the cortex and penetrate the cortex, they find that all the neurons in a column respond to similar aspects of the stimulus (Hubel & Wiesel, 1977). They have overlapping receptive fields and similar responses to similar stimuli.

For example, Figure 7.31 shows the results when an investigator lowers an electrode into the visual cortex and records from each cell the electrode encounters. Each red line represents a neuron and shows the angle of orientation of its receptive field. In electrode path B, the first 12 cells show orientations parallel to one another. Electrode path A is not exactly perpendicular to the surface of the cortex, and it encounters receptive fields that change gradually from one cell to the next.

The cells in a column share other properties as well. For example, if one cell is equally responsive to both eyes, the others are also. In another column, all the cells might be more responsive to the left eye; in still another column they might be more responsive to the right eye. As a rule, if the cells in a given column are sensitive to color, they are all maximally excited by the same color. In short, the cells within each column all deal with more or less the same information, although they may process it in somewhat different ways.

The same is true for other parts of the cortex, not just the visual system. In the auditory cortex, the somatosensory cortex, and other areas, each column of the cortex has cells with overlapping receptive fields and similar properties (Lynch, 1989). The stimulus that excites one cell most strongly is generally about the same as the stimulus that most strongly excites the other cells in the column.

Presumably this feature facilitates useful communication in the cortex. If a company has 20 workers trying to solve the same problem, it generally puts their desks close together so the workers can talk to one another. Evidently the brain uses the same strategy.

## ROLE OF THE SUPERIOR COLLICULUS

Throughout this section we have been discussing the fate of visual information from the lateral geniculate onward. Actually, not all of the optic tract goes to the lateral geniculate; some axons go to the superior colliculus (refer to Figure 7.5). To some extent, the superior colliculus duplicates the function of the lateral geniculate, contributing to pattern perception (Casagrande, Harting, Hall, Diamond, & Martin, 1972). It is also in a position, however, to take the same information that goes to the lateral geniculate (and eventually the visual cortex) and process it in a different way. Unlike the lateral geniculate, the superior colliculus is not purely a visual structure; especially in its deeper layers, it contains cells that respond to visual, auditory, and touch stimuli (Wurtz & Albano, 1980). For example, a given cell might respond to a visual stimulus 30 degrees to the right of the animal's center, to an auditory stimulus from the same direction, and to a whisker touch from the same direction (Drager & Hubel, 1975). The superior colliculus contributes to eye and head movements in response to each of those stimuli (Hikosaka & Wurtz, 1986).

Gerald Schneider (1969) demonstrated that lesions of the superior colliculus produce effects very different from lesions of the visual cortex. After damage to their visual cortex, hamsters failed to learn to discriminate between a speckled pattern and diagonal stripes (to approach one and not the other for reward). Hamsters with damage to the superior colliculus eventually succeeded in this task. They often walked almost to the wrong stimulus before turning around and wandering back to the right one—that is, they had difficulty orienting to the correct stimulus from a distance—but they did master the discrimination of pushing only the door with the correct stimulus on it. On the other hand, hamsters with damage to the superior colliculus seemed totally blind in the presence of a visible sunflower seed, failing to orient toward it and approach it directly. Although hamsters with visual cortex lesions had trouble with complicated visual discriminations, they had no trouble turning toward a seed and finding it.

To summarize: If a task requires an animal to determine *what* pattern it sees (for example, stripes versus dots), visual cortex lesions cause greater impairment than superior colliculus lesions do. If the task requires the animal to determine *where* the pattern is, then superior colliculus lesions cause greater impairment.

Humans who have suffered damage to part of the visual cortex seem completely blind—and describe themselves as completely blind—in the affected area of the visual field. Is their blindness in fact complete, or could the superior colliculus (or other subcortical visual areas) provide certain aspects of vision?

After damage to the right visual cortex, a person cannot describe an object in the left visual field in any way and cannot even say whether or not there is any light in that field. However, such a person who is told to guess *where* the object is can point toward it with surprising accuracy—surprising even to himself or herself (Perenin & Jeannerod, 1978; Weiskrantz, Warrington, Sanders, & Marshall, 1974). One person was able to point at targets in his blind area even though his unimpaired vision was limited to 9 degrees of the visual field (Bridgeman &

Staggs, 1982). With training such people can improve their accuracy in moving their eyes toward visual stimuli that they still claim not to see (Zihl, 1980). Even when they are making no effort to respond to the blind part of their visual field, light in that area alters, and sometimes interferes with, their eye movements toward targets in the intact visual field (Rafal, Smith, Krantz, Cohen, & Brennan, 1990).

The ability to point toward objects in a damaged area of the visual field is known as **blindsight.** Although a small part of the phenomenon may result from light that scatters from the blind part of the visual field into the intact part of the visual field (Campion, Latto, & Smith, 1983), most investigators believe that blindsight depends on contributions from the superior colliculus (Rafal et al., 1990). In short, the superior colliculus or neighboring areas can apparently respond to visual stimuli even when a person is not conscious of those stimuli.

## SUMMARY

1. Lateral inhibition is a mechanism by which stimulation in each area of the retina suppresses the responses in neighboring areas. It enhances the contrast at light-dark borders. (p. 246)

2. Each neuron in the visual system has a receptive field—an area of the retina to which it is connected. Light on some parts of the receptive field excites the cell, while light on other areas inhibits it. (p. 248)

3. Receptive fields of higher level neurons are built up by excitatory and inhibitory connections from lower level neurons. In the simplest case the receptive field of a higher level neuron is the sum of the receptive fields of all the lower level neurons connected to it. (p. 249)

4. The visual cortex has three more or less independent visual pathways. One pathway deals mostly with color; one deals mostly with details of shape; and one deals mostly with movement, depth, and broad outlines of shape. How the brain combines these three pathways to perceive an object as a unity is unclear. (p. 250)

5. The separation of the three pathways accounts for certain phenomena of human vision. For example, we have trouble perceiving the overall pattern in a scene that has color borders but no brightness contrast. The magnocellular pathway that is most important for perceiving overall borders is not sensitive to color. (p. 254)

6. In the primary visual cortex, most cells have a receptive field shaped like a bar or an edge. They are designated as feature-detector cells because they respond to particular features. A simple cell has a fixed excitatory area and a fixed inhibitory area; a complex cell responds equally to a given pattern in any location within its receptive field. (p. 257)

7. We can demonstrate the importance of feature-detector cells by fatiguing them. For example, after staring at a set of wide stripes, you have trouble seeing similar stripes. Stripes slightly narrower than the ones you have stared at will seem narrower than they really are. (p. 260)

8. The visual cortex has columns of cells perpendicular to the surface of the cortex. Cells within a given column have similar properties; the stimulus that excites one cell most strongly is likely to excite all the others in the column strongly as well. (p. 262)

9. The superior colliculus contributes to the perception of the location of an object. It also participates in eye movements and other movements directed toward a visual target. (p. 265)

## REVIEW QUESTIONS

1. Suppose light shines equally on all the receptors in a square area of the retina. In which part of the retina will the bipolar cells show the greatest activity? Why? (p. 247)

2. How does a horizontal cell produce lateral inhibition in the vertebrate eye? (p. 247)

3. Where is the receptive field of a cell in the visual cortex? (p. 249)

4. Visual cortex cells have bar-shaped receptive fields. How are those built up from the input from lateral geniculate cells that have circular receptive fields? (p. 249)

5. What are the differences between parvocellular neurons and magnocellular neurons? (p. 251)

6. What is the function of the pathway through the blobs of area V1 and the thin stripes of area V2? (p. 252)

7. What is the function of the pathway through the interblobs of area V1 and the pale stripes of area V2? (p. 252)

8. What is the function of the magnocellular pathway through lamina 4B of area V1 and the thick stripes of area V2? (p. 252)

9. What type of brain damage is probably responsible for motion blindness? (p. 254)

10. What is color constancy, and which brain area is most directly responsible for producing it? (p. 254)

11. If a repeating pattern of red and green lines (about equally bright) moves across a computer screen, why is it often difficult to perceive the movement? (p. 254)

12. A given cell in the visual cortex responds best to a vertical bar of light. How could you determine whether it is a simple cell, a complex cell, or a hypercomplex cell? (p. 258)

13. How do the properties of cells in the visual cortex enable us to understand the waterfall illusion? (p. 262)

14. What is the function of the superior colliculus? (p. 265)

## THOUGHT QUESTIONS

1. Explain the dark diamonds you see in Figure 7.14 in terms of lateral inhibition.

2. After a receptor cell is stimulated, the bipolar cell receiving input from it shows an immediate burst of response. A fraction of a second later, the bipolar's response rate decreases, even though the stimulation from the receptor cell remains constant. How can you account for that decrease? (Hint: What does the horizontal cell do?)

3. Cortical cells have receptive fields with preferred orientations of horizontal, vertical, and intermediate angles. Why would it be unsatisfactory for an animal to have only two kinds of cells, horizontal and vertical, without the intermediates? Note: Such an animal would not necessarily be blind to intermediate angles. Even a 45-degree line could give rise to a slight response by both cells. (Hint: How could the animal tell the difference between a line at a 5-degree angle and one at a 10-degree angle? Between a 45-degree angle and a 135-degree angle?)

## SUGGESTIONS FOR FURTHER READING

**Ali, M. A., & Klyne, M. A.** (1985). *Vision in vertebrates.* New York: Plenum. An overview of the research on the visual system.

**Livingstone, M. S.** (1988, January). Art, illusion and the visual system. *Scientific American, 258* (1), 78–85. Interesting discussion of the three pathways in the visual system of the cerebral cortex.

**Masland, R. H.** (1986, December). The functional architecture of the retina. *Scientific American, 255* (6), 102–111. Description of how bipolar cells, horizontal cells, and amacrine cells combine to produce the receptive fields of ganglion cells.

## GLOSSARY

**amacrine cell** local neuron within the eye having no axon

**areas V1–V4** (*see* **V1** through **V4**)

**binocular** responding to portions of both eyes

**bipolar cell** one of the cell types in the eye

**blindsight** ability to point toward objects in a damaged area of the visual field

**blind spot** point on the retina where the optic nerve exits, which therefore lacks receptors

**blob** cluster of neurons within the primary visual cortex, strongly responsive to the color of a visual stimulus

**color constancy** ability to recognize the color of an object despite changes in lighting

**column** collection of cortical neurons, arranged perpendicular to the surface of the cortex, all of which respond to similar aspects of the stimulus

**complex cell** cell type of the visual cortex that responds best to a light stimulus of a particular shape anywhere in its receptive field; its receptive field cannot be mapped into fixed excitatory and inhibitory zones

**cone** one type of receptor in the retina, specialized for color vision and detailed vision

**feature detector** neuron whose responses indicate the presence of a particular feature

**fovea** center of the retina, point at which receptors are most densely packed

**ganglion cell** type of neuron within the eye

**horizontal cell** a cell type in the vertebrate eye, responsible for lateral inhibition

**hypercomplex cell** cell of the visual cortex that responds best to stimuli of a precisely limited type, anywhere in a large receptive field, with a strong inhibitory field at one end of its field

**inferior temporal cortex** portion of the cortex where neurons are highly sensitive to complex aspects of the shape of visual stimuli within very large receptive fields

**interblob** area of the primary visual cortex between blobs, responsible for shape perception

**lateral inhibition** restraint of activity in one neuron by activity in a neighboring neuron

**magnocellular neuron** large-celled neuron of the visual system that is sensitive to changing or moving stimuli

**middle temporal cortex** portion of the cortex where neurons are highly sensitive to the speed and direction of movement of visual stimuli

**negative afterimage** temporary perception of one color—for example, red—as a result of prolonged viewing of its opposite color—for example, green

**opponent-process theory** notion that we perceive color in terms of paired opposites: white versus black, red versus green, and blue versus yellow

**optic nerve** band of axons from the ganglion cells of the retina to the brain

**parvocellular neuron** small-celled neuron of the visual system that is sensitive to color differences and visual details

**photopigment** chemical in the rods and cones that releases energy when struck by light

**primary visual cortex** area of the cortex responsible for the first stage of visual processing

**psychophysical observation** report by human observers concerning their perceptions of various stimuli

**pupil** opening in the eyeball through which light enters

**receptive field** region of the receptive surface (such as retina or skin) that can excite or inhibit a given neuron

**retina** rear surface of the eye, lined with visual receptors

**retinex theory** concept that the cerebral cortex compares the wavelengths of light coming from different parts of the retina at a given time and from that comparison determines a perception of color for each object

**rod** one type of receptor in the retina, specialized for vision in dim light

**secondary visual cortex** area of the visual cortex responsible for second stage of visual processing

**shape constancy** ability to perceive the shape of an object despite the movement or rotation of the object

**simple cell** type of visual cortex cell that can be excited by a point of light anywhere in the excitatory part of its receptive field and inhibited by light anywhere in the inhibitory part

**stereoscopic depth perception** ability to detect depth by differences in what the two eyes see

**striate cortex** area of the occipital cortex with distinctly striped appearance; synonymous with primary visual cortex, or V1

**trichromatic theory** theory that we perceive color by means of the relative rates of response by three kinds of cones, with each kind maximally sensitive to a different set of wavelengths

**V1** primary visual cortex, area responsible for the first stage of visual processing

**V2** secondary visual cortex, area responsible for the second stage of visual processing

**V3** area of the visual cortex responsible for detailed spatial perception, especially in and near the fovea

**V4** area of the visual cortex responsible for processing color information

**W cell** type of ganglion cell that is only weakly responsive to visual stimuli

**X cell** small ganglion cell, located mostly in or near the fovea

**Y cell** relatively large ganglion cell, distributed fairly evenly throughout the retina

**Young-Helmholtz theory** proposal that we perceive color by means of the relative rates of response by three kinds of cones, with each kind maximally sensitive to a different set of wavelengths

# CHAPTER EIGHT

# Development of the Brain and Brain-Behavior Relationships

## MAIN IDEAS

**1.** Axons find their way to their targets in a relatively specific way, not at random. To some extent, they identify appropriate target cells by chemical markers on those cells. To some extent, the postsynaptic cells select among the axons that attach to them. They accept synapses from some axons and reject others.

**2.** The properties of the neurons in the visual cortex are to a large degree molded by experience. Neurons become more responsive to common stimuli and less responsive to uncommon stimuli.

**3.** The human brain can develop improperly for various reasons, including genetics, head injury, exposure to toxic substances, and inadequate nutrition.

"Some assembly required." Have you ever bought a device with those ominous words on the package? Sometimes all you have to do is to attach two or three parts, maybe tighten a few bolts. But in other cases "some assembly required" means facing page after page of incomprehensible instructions. Incomprehensible, at least, to those of us who are not mechanically gifted. I remember putting together my daughter's bicycle and wondering how something that looked so simple could be so complicated.

The human nervous system comes with an enormous amount of assembly required. The instructions for assembling the nervous system are different from those for assembling, say, a bicycle. Instead of just saying, "Put this piece here and that piece there," the instructions for the brain say, "Put these axons here and those dendrites there, and then wait to see what happens. Keep the connections that seem to be working well, move some of the others around, throw away the rest, and then make some new ones similar to the ones you kept." Moreover, the brain continues moving connections around as long as it is alive and healthy. The assembly of the brain is never complete; it literally takes the rest of your life.

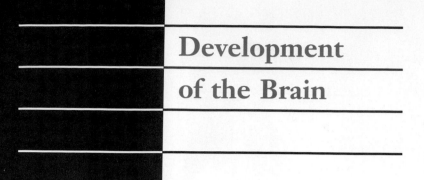

# Development
# of the Brain

As a college student, you can probably perform a number of feats today that you could not possibly have performed several years ago: solve calculus problems perhaps, or read a foreign language, or convincingly pretend that you understand James Joyce. Have you developed these new skills because your brain has grown? No. Your brain has no doubt moved a number of synapses around, but its overall size and gross structure are about the same as before.

Now think of all the things 2-year-old children can do that they could not do the day they were born: walk, talk, pick up small objects, draw simple pictures, control their bowel and bladder functions. Have they developed these new skills because of brain growth? To some extent, yes. The brain of a newborn cannot learn to walk and talk until it has grown and matured in many ways. But much of behavioral development in children depends on experience and on moving synapses around in much the same way an adult brain does.

Often it seems reasonable to distinguish between learning (which can occur at any age) and maturation (which is most prominent early in life). But, as we shall see, many of the processes of brain development depend on experience in complex ways that sometimes blur the distinction between learning and maturation.

## GROWTH AND DIFFERENTIATION OF THE VERTEBRATE BRAIN

The human central nervous system begins to form when the embryo is about two weeks old. First, the dorsal surface of the embryo thickens and then long thin lips rise and curl, merging to form a neural tube surrounding a fluid-filled cavity (see Figure 8.1). The tube sinks under the surface of the skin and continues to develop. The forward end enlarges and differentiates into the hindbrain, midbrain, and forebrain (see Figure 8.2); the rest becomes the spinal cord. The fluid-filled cavity within the neural tube becomes the central canal of the spinal cord and the four ventricles of the brain. The fluid inside the canal and ventricles is the cerebrospinal fluid (CSF). This same basic process occurs in all other vertebrates as

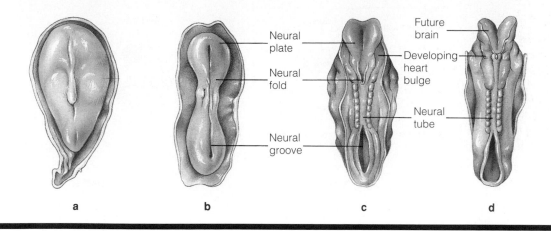

Neural plate

Neural fold

Neural groove

Future brain

Developing heart bulge

Neural tube

a      b      c      d

**Figure 8.1**
**Early development of the human central nervous system**
*The brain and spinal cord begin as folding lips surrounding a fluid-filled canal. Stages shown occur at approximately ages two to three weeks.*

well, varying mostly in speed. For example, the nervous system matures rapidly in mice, slowly in elephants.

At birth, the human brain weighs about 350 grams (g). Certain areas of the forebrain are immature for the first few weeks, as indicated by their low levels of glucose use. Development is rapid, however, and areas of the brain that are almost silent at birth approach adult patterns of activity within 7 to 8 months (Chugani & Phelps, 1986). At the end of the first year, the brain weighs 1,000 g, not much less than the adult weight of 1,200 to 1,400 g.

Animal species with larger bodies generally have larger brains. Within a single species, such as humans, the relationship between body size and brain size is much weaker. Although the brain is close to its adult size by age 1 year, the rest of the body continues to grow long after that. Some people grow much more than others do during adolescence; consequently, the ultimate size of the body has only a weak relationship to the size of the brain (Riska & Atchley, 1985).

As the brain grows, what happens at the microscopic level? Does the brain simply produce more neurons that do exactly what infant neurons were doing? Or do the new cells lead to some kind of reorganization of the brain's structure? Recall from Chapters 4 and 7 that the cerebral cortex is composed of columns and similar repeating units. The adult cortex has more columns than the infant cortex has, but the average size of columns is not enormously larger than it was in the infant.

Anthony-Samuel LaMantia and Dale Purves (1989) created a way to stain and photograph the living brain of an infant mouse and then to photograph the same section of brain later in development. They found that brain anatomy is stable over short periods of time. However, from age 4 to 6 days until two weeks later, the brain adds new units. The glomeruli of the olfactory bulb are analogous to the columns of the visual cortex. As Figure 8.3b shows, the glomeruli present in the first week of life are still present two weeks later, but some new glomeruli have also appeared. Evidently, the brain develops partly by the expansion of old units and partly by the addition of new units. A similar principle holds across species: Primate brains, which are larger than the brains of most other mammalian species, also have more columns and specialized subdivisions of the cortex (Kaas, 1989; Killackey, 1990).

Development of the Brain

**Figure 8.2**
**Human brain at five stages of development**
*The brain already shows the adult structure at birth, although it continues to grow for the first year or so. (The illustrations are not to scale.) (Photo courtesy of Dana Copeland.)*

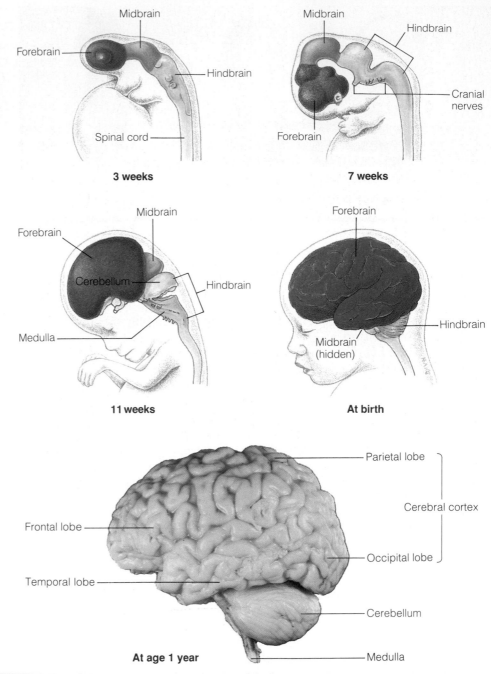

3 weeks

7 weeks

11 weeks

At birth

At age 1 year

## PATHFINDING BY AXONS

The development of the nervous system naturally entails the production and alteration of neurons. Neuroscientists distinguish four major stages in the development of neurons: proliferation, migration, differentiation, and myelination.

**Proliferation** is the production of new cells. Early in development, cells lining the ventricles of the brain divide to make new cells. Some of these new cells

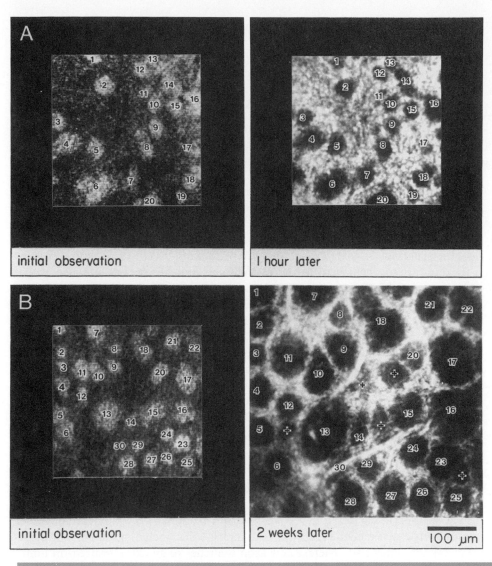

**Figure 8.3**
**Photos of sections of the olfactory bulbs of mice**
*The initial observations (left) were taken in mice 4 to 6 days old. The later observations (right) were taken an hour later or two weeks later, using a different staining procedure. In (a), note the consistency of appearance over one hour; each glomerulus is easily recognized and is in the same position. In (b), the 30 original glomeruli are still present two weeks later, but 5 new glomeruli have appeared. The brain develops partly by growth of old units and partly by addition of new units. (From LaMantia & Purves, 1989.)*

initial observation

I hour later

initial observation

2 weeks later

100 μm

remain where they are, continuing to divide and redivide. Others become primitive neurons and glia that **migrate** (move) toward their eventual destinations in the brain. The cerebral cortex develops from the inside out; that is, each arriving wave of new cells migrates beyond the previous cells.

In humans, most neuron proliferation occurs before birth. Migration is naturally a little slower, but it too becomes almost complete during infancy.

At first, primitive neurons look much like any other cell of the body. Gradually a neuron **differentiates**, forming the axon and dendrites that provide its distinctive shape. Generally the axon grows first; in fact, it may grow while the neuron is migrating. (Some neurons leave an axon growing behind them, somewhat like a long tail.) After the neuron reaches its final location, dendrites begin to form, very slowly at first. Most dendritic growth occurs at the time when incoming axons are due to arrive.

Finally, some axons myelinate, as glial cells produce the insulating sheaths that make rapid transmission possible. Neurons can be functional before they develop myelin, although the myelin certainly improves their function. In humans,

Development
of the Brain

myelin forms first in the spinal cord, and then in the hindbrain, midbrain, and forebrain.

For the nervous system to operate properly, axons must reach their proper targets, forming synapses with the correct neurons. How do they find their way?

## Basic Strategies for Directing an Axon to Its Target

Suppose you operate a U.S. government office in Washington, DC. You need to convey some secret messages—so secret that you cannot use telephones or the mail. You decide to install private telegraph cables to the places where you expect to send messages. You tell one of your employees, "Here, Carlos, take this cable and run it across the street to the Office of Bureaucratic Mismanagement." Because it is so near, you hardly give a thought as to how he is going to find the way. Then you tell another employee, "Here, Carla, take this very long cable and stretch it to the mayor's office in Truth or Consequences, New Mexico." (Carla got the tough job.) Now you definitely have to worry: Will Carla find a reasonably direct route from here to there? Will she find her way at all? You would have to make sure that she has a map and a compass and that she knows how to read street signs. Or, if some other employee had made the same trip last week and had carefully left a trail, you could just tell Carla to follow the purple arrows along the side of the road.

The developing nervous system faces a similar problem. It sends some of its axons over enormous distances. For example, the cerebral cortex sends certain axons all the way to the spinal cord, and the spinal cord sends motor axons to muscles in the arms, legs, and elsewhere. How do these axons find their way to the correct locations? And does the nervous system ever know that its axons have reached their targets?

## Chemical Pathfinding by Axons

A famous biologist, Paul Weiss (1924), once conducted an experiment in which he grafted an extra leg to a salamander and then waited for axons to grow into it. (Such an experiment could never work with a mammal. Salamanders and other amphibians can regenerate many parts of their bodies, including limbs, that mammals cannot. They also generate new axon branches to an extra, grafted-on limb.) After the axons reached the muscles, Weiss observed the animal's behavior. The extra leg, positioned right next to one of the hind legs, moved in perfect synchrony with the normal adjacent leg.

One possible interpretation of these results is that each axon to the normal limb had developed a branch that found its way to exactly the same muscle in the extra limb. Weiss dismissed that interpretation as unbelievable. He suggested instead that the nerves attached to muscles at random and then sent a variety of messages, each one "tuned" to a different muscle. In other words, it did not matter which axon was attached to which muscle. The muscles were like a series of radios, each tuned to a different station. They all received the same signals through the air, but each one responded only to the station to which it was tuned.

Weiss's theory has not stood the test of time. Later evidence supported the interpretation Weiss had dismissed as unbelievable: that the salamander's extra leg moved in synchrony with its neighbor because each axon had sent a branch to each leg and each branch had attached to exactly the same muscle. That is, a growing axon finds its way to the correct target.

Since the time of Weiss's work, most of the research on axon growth has dealt with how sensory axons find their way to the correct targets in the brain.

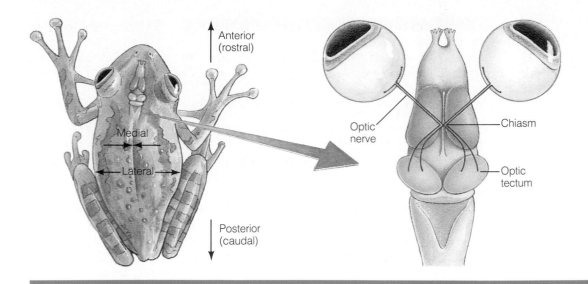

Figure 8.4
*The optic tectum is a large structure in fish, amphibians, reptiles, and birds. In location it corresponds to the midbrain of mammals, but its function is more elaborate, analogous to what the cerebral cortex does in mammals. (After Romer, 1962.)*

(The issues and difficulties are the same as those for axons finding their way to muscles in the periphery.) Roger Sperry, who was a student of Weiss, conducted much of the decisive research in this area. In one study, he cut the optic nerve of some newts. In amphibians, unlike mammals, a damaged optic nerve grows back and contacts the **tectum,** the main visual area of fish, amphibians, reptiles, and birds (see Figure 8.4). Sperry found that when the new synapses formed, the newt regained normal vision.

To discover how the axons find their targets, Sperry (1943) repeated the experiment, but this time after he cut each optic nerve, he rotated the eye by 180 degrees. When the axons grew back to the tectum, would the axons rotated to the dorsal side of the eye go where axons from the dorsal side ordinarily go, and would the axons now on the ventral side go where axons on the ventral side ordinarily go? Or would each axon ignore the fact that it was in a new position and find its way back to its *original* target, indicating that it "knew" where to go? Sperry found that the axons from what had originally been the dorsal side of the retina (which was now on the ventral side) grew back to their original target area of the tectum—the area responsible for vision in the dorsal side of the retina. Likewise, axons from what had once been the ventral side of the retina (now on the dorsal side) grew back to the tectal area responsible for vision on the ventral side of the retina. The newt now saw the world upside down and backward. It responded to stimuli in the sky as if they were on the ground, to stimuli on the left as if they were on the right (see Figure 8.5). Evidently each axon regenerated to the area of the tectum where it had originally been—the area where it "knew" it belonged.

In another experiment, Domenica Attardi and Roger Sperry (1963) damaged parts of the retina in a group of goldfish and cut their optic nerves. The optic nerve from the intact part of each retina grew back to the tectal area that it ordinarily innervated, as Figure 8.6 shows. Again, each axon found its appropriate target. The tectal areas originally innervated by the damaged parts of the retina now had vacant synapses, with no incoming axons. As with the previous experiment, these results suggested that each axon might be following a chemical trail to its destination, like a bloodhound sniffing its way through the forest.

Development
of the Brain

**Figure 8.5
Summary of Sperry's
experiment on nerve
connections in newts**

*After he cut the optic nerve
and inverted the eye, the optic
nerve axons grew back to
their original targets, not the
targets corresponding to the
eye's current position.*

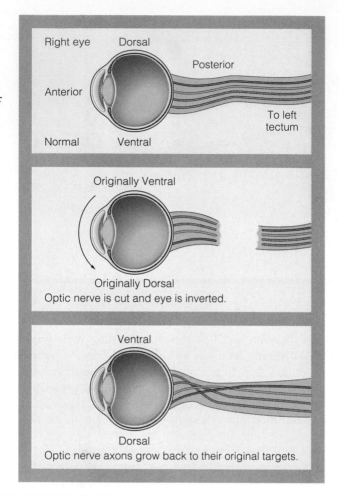

Right eye  Dorsal

Posterior

Anterior

To left
tectum

Normal  Ventral

Originally Ventral

Originally Dorsal
Optic nerve is cut and eye is inverted.

Ventral

Dorsal
Optic nerve axons grow back to their original targets.

The next question was how specific a target the axon might have. Did an axon from an amphibian's or goldfish's retina have to find the tectal cell with exactly the right chemical marker on its surface, like a key finding the right lock? Such a mechanism would be barely plausible. Just think of the billions of axons the nervous system has. Does the body have to synthesize a separate chemical marker for each one of them?

Later results indicated that an axon does not have to search for its one and only possible target. It follows a path of **cell adhesion molecules (CAMs),** glycoproteins on the surface of cells, that distinguish one type of cell from another (Edelman, 1987). That path leads an axon to its approximately correct target. But if that area has been damaged, does the axon simply die or does it make contact with some other cell? In two similar experiments, investigators removed the caudal half of the tectum of goldfish and cut the optic nerve. Ordinarily, axons from the anterior side of the retina make contact with the caudal tectum. When those axons reached the tectum, they formed synapses with the most caudal portion of what was left of the tectum (Figure 8.7). That is, the whole optic nerve made a compressed projection onto the now-small tectum (Gaze & Sharma, 1970; Yoon, 1971).

In a related experiment, investigators destroyed the anterior half of the retina of goldfish and then cut the optic nerve, letting the axon from the posterior half-

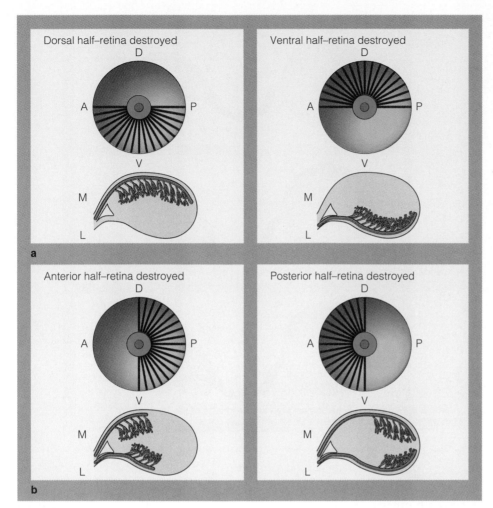

**Figure 8.6**

*After half of the goldfish retina is destroyed and the optic nerve from the other half is cut, the optic nerve grows back to just half of the optic tectum, the part that it ordinarily innervates. (**a**) After the destruction of the dorsal or ventral half-retina, axons from the remaining half-retina regenerate to the medial-dorsal or lateral-ventral half of the tectum, respectively. (**b**) After the destruction of the anterior or posterior half-retina, axons from the remaining half of the retina regenerate to the appropriate half of the tectum. (Based on Attardi & Sperry, 1963.)*

retina regenerate. Initially it connected only to its normal area, the rostral part of the tectum. Months later, however, some of the axons began creeping from the edge of the rostral tectum into the adjacent areas of the caudal tectum (Figure 8.8). This process continued until the axons had spread themselves evenly over the entire tectum (Schmidt, Cicerone, & Easter, 1977).

These experiments suggest an alternative interpretation of how axons attach to targets: Imagine the growing axons as males, and the target cells as females. Generally, the northernmost males mate with the northernmost females, and the southernmost males mate with the southernmost females. Similarly, the axons and cells have a gradient of preferences. The axons from the most anterior regions of the retina pair with the most caudal cells available, the axons from the most posterior retina pair with the most rostral cells, and the intermediate axons space themselves out as evenly as they can.

## Competition Among Axons

Let us continue with this analogy of axons as males pairing with target cells as females. In human dating, males are selective about which females they pursue, but females are just as selective, or more so, about which males they will accept as po-

**Figure 8.7**
**Results of experiments on regeneration of the goldfish optic nerve after damage to the optic tectum**

*Experimenters cut the optic nerve and destroyed the caudal part of the tectum. Then the axons that ordinarily innervate the caudal tectum grew back to the most caudal part of the remaining tectum. Other axons arranged themselves in the correct order as before, though not on the same target cells as before. (Based on results of Gaze & Sharma, 1970; Yoon, 1971.)*

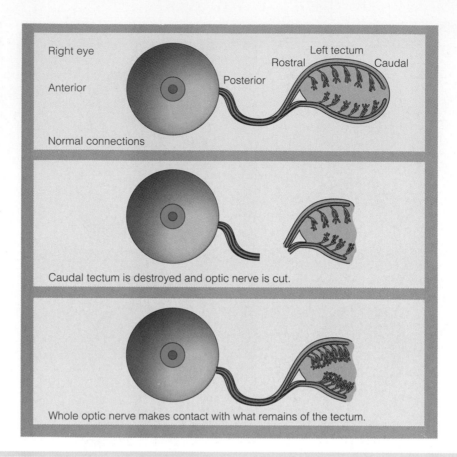

tential suitors. Axons show selectivity in that they grow toward certain targets and not toward others. Are those target cells also selective? That is, do they accept synapses from any and all axons, or do they accept some and reject others?

The answer: They do accept some and reject others; their selectivity plays an important part in the construction of the nervous system (Easter, Purves, Rakic, & Spitzer, 1985; Purves & Lichtman, 1980). In the early stages of embryonic development, the nervous system overproduces neurons and axons. Many parts of the CNS develop two or three times as many neurons as will actually survive into adulthood. Their axons then grow out toward their targets, following a path of cell adhesion molecules (CAMs), and establish more-or-less correct connections. At this point, each axon forms synapses onto a number of target cells, and each target cell receives synapses from a large number of axons. And then gradually certain synapses are eliminated. The postsynaptic cell develops a strong connection with some of those axons, but not all. In many cases, one cell accepts an axon that another cell rejects. Figure 8.9 summarizes the results: At first, axons and postsynaptic cells have many tentative connections with one another; later they develop fewer but stronger attachments. In humans, this process takes place mostly during prenatal development, although neurons continue to occasionally shift synapses throughout life.

As the postsynaptic cells favor some axons and reject others, each axon grows additional branches onto each postsynaptic cell that accepts it, while it withdraws from others. Many axons fail to form any lasting synapses at this time. Those axons and their cell bodies degenerate and die. Each part of the brain has a period

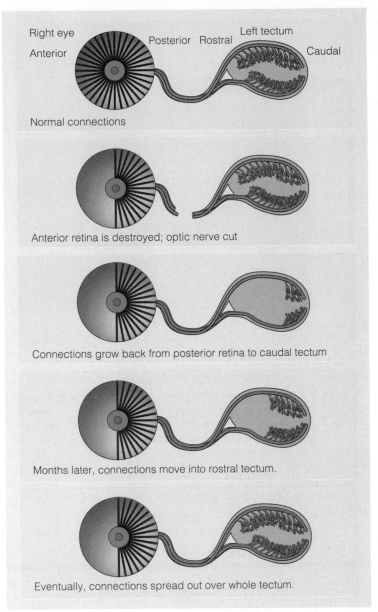

**Figure 8.8**
**Results of an experiment on regrowth of a goldfish's optic nerve after damage to half of the retina**
*Experimenters destroyed the anterior retina and cut the optic nerve. At first, axons from the posterior retina grew back to their original target cells in the caudal tectum (as they did in the earlier experiment by Attardi and Sperry). However, as months passed, connections moved into the vacant rostral portion of the tectum and eventually spread out over the whole tectum. (Based on results of Schmidt, Cicerone, & Easter, 1977.)*

Right eye
Anterior
Posterior    Rostral    Left tectum
Caudal

Normal connections

Anterior retina is destroyed; optic nerve cut

Connections grow back from posterior retina to caudal tectum

Months later, connections move into rostral tectum.

Eventually, connections spread out over whole tectum.

of massive cell death when it is littered with dead and dying cells (Figure 8.10). This does not indicate that something is wrong; it is a natural part of development (Finlay & Pallas, 1989).

How does a postsynaptic neuron "decide" which axon or axons to accept and which to reject? The mechanisms are still somewhat mysterious, but we can imagine several possibilities. First, just as axons approach some targets and not others because of their chemical markers, the postsynaptic cells may recognize chemical markers on the axons that identify them as more acceptable or less acceptable. Second, in many cases the postsynaptic cell is more likely to form synapses with combinations of axons that are simultaneously active, instead of combinations that send uncorrelated messages. Third, after an axon forms a

Development
of the Brain

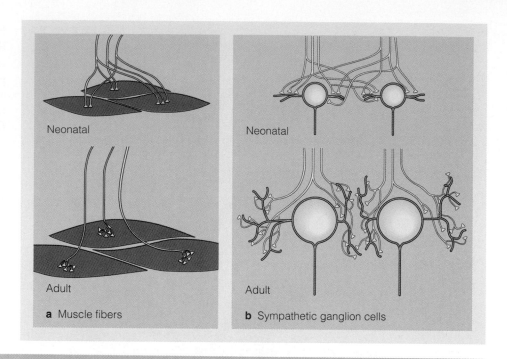

## Figure 8.9
## Development by elimination of synapses

*(a) Early in development, each muscle fiber receives synapses from branches of several motor axons. The muscle fiber gradually strengthens its synapse with one axon and rejects the others. (However, an axon can form synapses with many muscle fibers.) (b) Early in development, neurons in the ganglia of the sympathetic nervous system receive synapses from many axons. Later, each cell rejects the incoming axons from some neurons and accepts the axons from others. Although the cell as a whole may accept axons from numerous different neurons, typically each dendrite forms lasting synapses with only one axon. That axon may, however, form a great many branches and therefore a great many synapses onto that dendrite. (After Purves & Lichtman, 1980.)*

## Figure 8.10
## Mean number of motor neurons in the ventral spinal cord of human fetuses at ages 11 weeks to 32 weeks

*Note that the number of motor neurons is highest at 11 weeks and drops steadily until about 25 weeks. This is when motor neuron axons make synapses with muscles. Those that fail to make synapses die. (From Forger & Breedlove, 1987.)*

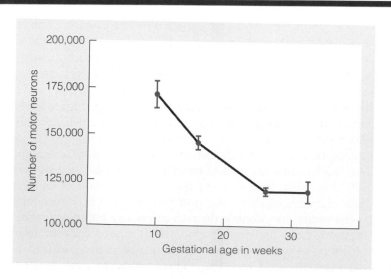

strong attachment to one cell, it may become less attractive to other cells because it is diverting more of its neurotransmitters in another direction.

Why does the CNS produce more neurons than it needs? There are at least two possibilities: (1) The extra neurons enable the postsynaptic cells to be selective. In a sense, overproduction of neurons followed by cell death provides an opportunity for "survival of the fittest." Perhaps each postsynaptic cell has a greater opportunity to find an acceptable axon if it can choose among many. (2) The extra neurons enable the CNS to compensate for unpredictable variations in body size. For example, when the motor neuron axons begin growing from the spinal cord toward the leg muscles, there is no way to predict exactly how large that leg will be or exactly how many muscle fibers it will have. The spinal cord sends out a great many axons; the larger the leg is, the more axons survive. In short, the death of excess axons enables the body to end up with just the necessary number.

## Chemical Mechanisms of Neuron Death and Neuron Survival

Exactly *how* does a postsynaptic cell accept some axons and reject others? Or to put it another way, how does a neuron know whether its axon has been accepted or rejected?

So far as we know, a postsynaptic cell has no special "rejection" message. But certain neurons do release a chemical that serves as an "acceptance" message. The neurons in the ganglia of the sympathetic nervous system send their axons to various organs of the body. When they form lasting synapses, the postsynaptic cell delivers a protein called **nerve growth factor** (NGF) that promotes the survival and growth of that axon. An axon that does not receive enough nerve growth factor degenerates, and its cell body dies. In other words, various axons in the sympathetic nervous system compete with one another for NGF, which they need for survival. This mechanism is particularly important during the embryonic stage when many neurons die, but it continues to operate throughout life; certain axons need nerve growth factor to survive and thrive. In its absence, about 85 percent of the neurons in the sympathetic nervous system die (Johnson, Gorin, Brandeis, & Pearson, 1980). Rita Levi-Montalcini won a Nobel Prize for her discovery of NGF and her research on its properties (Levi-Montalcini, 1987).

Nerve growth factor is a **trophic factor,** a chemical that promotes survival and activity. (The word *trophic* is derived from ancient Greek for *nourishment*.) It is just one of the body's trophic factors and is effective only for certain kinds of axons. Other trophic factors influence other types of axons. For example, **brain-derived neurotrophic factor,** a chemical related to NGF, promotes growth of certain populations of acetylcholine-containing axons in the hippocampus, amygdala, cerebral cortex, and olfactory areas of the brain (Phillips, Hains, Laramee, Rosenthal, & Winslow, 1990). Circumstantial evidence suggests that other trophic factors, not yet chemically identified, promote the growth of other kinds of axons (Barde, 1989; Oppenheim, Haverkamp, Prevette, McManaman, & Appel, 1988).

## PIONEER NEURONS

The development of connections to and from the cerebral cortex poses some special problems. The human cerebral cortex forms extensive connections with the thalamus and other subcortical structures that are fairly well developed and ready for synaptic contacts by the 35th day of embryonic development. But the cerebral cortex itself is slow to mature. The first cortical neurons appear during the 7th week of fetal development, and the others develop gradually until at least the 16th week (Rakic, 1978). So the subcortical areas are ready to form synapses with cortical cells before most of the cortical cells themselves are ready. And by the time the cortical cells are ready, the cortex has grown so large that these cells are far from the subcortical areas with which they must exchange connections. If the axons are to find their way from cortex to thalamus, or from thalamus to cortex, they will have to travel a substantial distance, past an enormous number of other cells and axons. How do they do so?

Earlier in this chapter I suggested that one way people could find their way from Washington, DC, to New Mexico would be to follow a path left by a previous traveler. The CNS uses that principle in connecting the cortex to subcortical structures. Early in embryonic development, when neurons in the cerebral cortex are all immature, the brain develops neurons called **subplate cells** just below where the cerebral cortex is developing. Axons from the thalamus and other subcortical areas synapse with these subplate cells; the subplate cells extend their axons back to the subcortical areas, to other subplate cells, and across the corpus callosum to the opposite hemisphere. The subplate cells maintain much neural activity, but they do so only temporarily. When the neurons of the cerebral cortex mature, they extend their axons down through the cortex to the subplate cells and then follow the axons of the subplate cells to their various targets, including the subcortical areas of the brain. Then the thalamic axons that had made contact with the subplate neurons extend their axons farther, making synapses in the cerebral cortex. After these new synapses are formed, the subplate neurons die. In this manner, the subplate neurons act as "pioneer neurons"; they survive only briefly themselves, but they establish paths to be used by later-developing, permanent neurons (McConnell, Ghosh, & Shatz, 1989).

## SUMMARY

1. In vertebrate embryos, the central nervous system begins as a tube surrounding a fluid-filled cavity. The human CNS grows to about one-fourth of adult size by birth and to almost adult size by age 1 year. (p. 272)

2. During development of the nervous system, growing axons manage to find their way to approximately the right locations. Over the years, investigators have discovered some of the mechanisms by which axons find their way. (p. 276)

3. In many nonmammalian species, a damaged optic nerve can regenerate. When it does so, the axons grow back to more or less their original targets, apparently identifying their target cells chemically. (p. 276)

4. Axons identify their targets relatively, not absolutely. For example, an axon that ordinarily connects to the

extreme caudal part of the tectum will, if deprived of its normal target, connect to the most caudal area available. (p. 278)

5. Initially, many axons attach to each postsynaptic cell. The postsynaptic cell selects one or more of these axons and delivers to them a trophic factor, a chemical that promotes survival and growth. Nerve growth factor is one trophic factor. (p. 279)

6. An axon that does not receive the trophic factor withdraws from that cell. Axons that do not establish a lasting synapse with any target cell degenerate, and their cell bodies die. (p. 283)

7. Development of the cerebral cortex poses special problems because its cells reach maturity far later than the neurons of the thalamus, with which they must make contact. To solve this problem, the thalamic cells form synapses with temporary "pioneer" neurons just below the developing cortex. When the cortical neurons become mature, their axons follow the paths of the pioneer cells' axons. (p. 283)

## REVIEW QUESTIONS

1. Why is brain size only weakly correlated with body size among a population of people? (p. 273)

2. How did Roger Sperry establish that each axon finds its way to a relatively specific target, instead of connecting at random? (p. 277)

3. Suppose the optic nerve of a fish or amphibian is cut and permitted to regenerate, but part of the tectum has been destroyed. What will happen to the axons that ordinarily make contact with the now-damaged area? (p. 278)

4. In what sense do axons compete with one another? (p. 279)

5. At what age does the nervous system have the largest number of neurons: during early embryonic development, during infancy, or during adulthood? (p. 280)

6. What is nerve growth factor and how does it contribute to the development of the nervous system? (p. 283)

7. Why does the brain need a population of temporary "pioneer" neurons, the subplate neurons? (p. 283)

## THOUGHT QUESTIONS

1. Biologists can develop antibodies against nerve growth factor (that is, molecules that inactivate nerve growth factor). What would happen if someone injected such antibodies into a developing nervous system?

2. Suppose the primary visual cortex (area V1) is destroyed in newborn kittens. Lateral geniculate cells no longer have target cells to which they can send their axons. What is likely to happen to the lateral geniculate cells? And what will happen to ganglion cells in the retina? Which kind of ganglion cell should show the greater effect — X cells or Y cells? (Recall from p. 251 that X cells send all their axons to the lateral geniculate, while Y cells send axons to the superior colliculus as well.) For published research on this question, see Tong, Spear, Kalil, and Callahan (1982).

## SUGGESTIONS FOR FURTHER READING

**Edelman, G.** (1987). *Neural Darwinism.* New York: Basic Books. Detailed theoretical treatment of how neurons and synapses are selected through competition with one another.

**Levi-Montalcini, R.** (1988). *In praise of imperfection.* New York: Basic Books. Autobiography by the discoverer of nerve growth factor.

**Purves, D.** (1988). *Body and brain.* Cambridge, MA: Harvard University Press. An excellent account of research on the growth of axons and the development of the vertebrate nervous system.

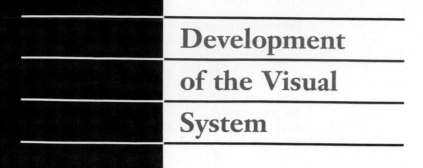

# Development of the Visual System

Remember Carla, who had to lay a cable from Washington, DC, to an office in New Mexico? Suppose we complicate her task a bit further. After she gets the cable to the right city, she has to take it to the office of "the person who knows the most about Southwestern plant life." Now it will not be sufficient to give her a map and compass or even to show her the path. Once she reaches her destination, she will have to ask questions. She will have to gain some experience to decide where to set up the cable connections.

Many of the connections in the nervous system are like that as well. Once axons get to approximately their correct targets, they form a large number of synapses, only some of which will survive. The selection of synapses depends partly on experience. The best illustrations of this principle come from the development of the visual system.

## INFANT VISION

When cartoonists want us to see a character as an infant, they draw the eyes large in proportion to the head. Infant eyes look large because they approach full size sooner than the rest of the head does and far sooner than the rest of the body. There is a good reason for this tendency: Infant eyes form an enormous number of complex attachments to the brain, as described in Chapter 7. If the eyes grew substantially after making those attachments and then sent new axons to the brain, the brain would have to reorganize its connections continually to use the additional information. One way to minimize this problem is to have the eyes reach full size early, as they do in mammals. In many fish, the eyes continue to grow long after they form their connections with the brain. Evolution found a different way to avoid massive reorganization of the brain in fish, as Digression 8.1 describes.

Although human infants at first have very little control of movement, they have surprisingly well-developed sensory capacities. Within the first day or two after birth, human infants spend more time looking at faces, circles, or stripes than they spend looking at a plain display with no pattern (see Figure 8.11).

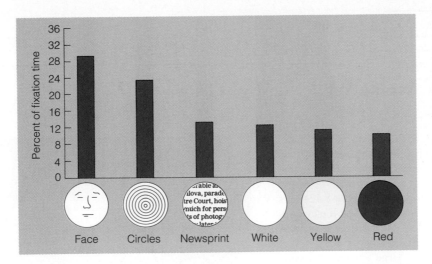

Figure 8.11
**Amount of time infants spend looking at various patterns**
*Even in the first two days after birth, they look more at faces and other complex patterns than at a plain color or at incomprehensible newsprint. (Based on Fantz, 1963.)*

However, the receptors in and around the fovea are immature at birth (Abramov et al., 1982). Therefore, infants, unlike older children and adults, see better in the periphery than they do in the center of vision.

Connections from the retina to the brain are only partly mature at birth. For example, studies of both humans and nonhumans indicate that cortical neurons with horizontal or vertical receptive fields develop earlier than those with diagonal receptive fields. Consequently, infants less than 3 months old have trouble seeing narrow diagonal lines. Infants stare at broad diagonal stripes as much as they do at broad horizontal or vertical stripes. But although they stare at narrow horizontal or vertical stripes (see Figure 8.14), they treat narrow diagonal stripes as if they were looking at a plain gray area (Leehy, Moskowitz-Cook, Brill, & Held, 1975). In short, the infant is capable of a fair amount of vision at birth, and yet there is much room for fine-tuning of the system based on experience.

To answer detailed questions about the development of the visual system, investigators need to insert electrodes into cells of the visual cortex to record the activity of those cells. Sometimes they need to examine the effects of abnormal experiences on the development of vision. Such experiments are ordinarily not possible with humans. The most popular laboratory animals for studies of visual development are cats. Like primates, but unlike most other mammals, cats have both eyes at the front of the head. Therefore, they have binocular vision and depth perception. Studies on the development of the visual cortex in cats and other species have led to results with great theoretical significance for understanding how the brain develops; they also have implications for alleviating certain human abnormalities.

## DEVELOPMENT OF BINOCULAR INTERACTION

Most neurons in the visual cortex of an adult cat or primate respond to stimuli in both eyes, producing **binocular vision.** Furthermore, they respond to approximately corresponding areas in the two retinas. For example, if a neuron responds to a stimulus 10 degrees above the center of vision in the left eye, it also responds

Development
of the Visual System

# Seeing While the Eye Grows

*Haplochromis burtoni*, an African fish, grows enormously over the course of its life. As its body grows, its eyes grow as well. Its eyes may triple in size during the first two months; eventually each eye may be larger than the whole fish used to be (see Figure 8.12b). Its neural connections were set up back when the eye was tiny. What readjustments does the fish have to make as the eye grows larger?

As Figure 8.13 shows, a large eye sees the same amount of the world as a smaller eye does. As the retina expands, the original receptors grow only a little and they become separated over a wider area. So a receptor that originally occupied a certain arc of the radius of the infant eye occupies a much smaller arc of the adult eye—and consequently sees a smaller arc of the visual field (Figure 8.13b). If no new receptors formed, the fish's retina would have large gaps with no receptors and therefore large blind spots in its visual field.

In fact, new receptors do fill in the gaps. But most of these receptors are rods, not cones. Why does the proportion of receptors change?

Vision in bright light depends almost entirely on cones, and the acuity (precision) of vision depends on the number of cones per degree of visual angle. If the

a

## Figure 8.12
### The African fish *Haplochromis burtoni*
*(**a**) A pair of adult fish. (**b**) Size comparison between adult and infant. Note that the eye of the adult is larger than the whole fish once was. (Photo courtesy of Russell D. Fernald.)*

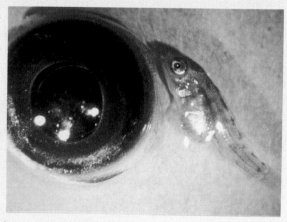

b

to a stimulus 10 degrees above the center of vision in the right eye (Figure 8.15). In infancy, most neurons are about equally responsive to the two eyes, although later in life many of them become more responsive to one eye than to the other (LeVay, Stryker, & Shatz, 1978).

The cortical neurons of kittens have properties surprisingly similar to those of adult cats. Ordinarily, kittens open their eyes for the first time at about age 9 days. At that time, these visually inexperienced kittens have cortical neurons that respond to stimuli in both eyes.

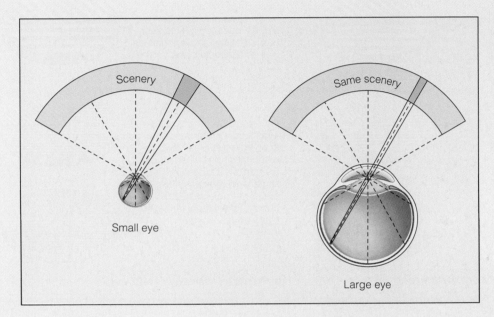

**Figure 8.13
Vision through a
growing eye**
*As the retina expands,
the receptors spread
out over a larger
area. Each receptor
becomes sensitive to a
smaller degree of vi-
sual arc.*

Scenery

Small eye

Same scenery

Large eye

fish added many new cones, its visual acuity might improve, but only if all the synapses in its tectum were
reorganized to take advantage of the new information.
That reorganization could conceivably happen, but the
evidence says it does not (Fernald, 1989). As the retina
expands, the number of cones grows only slightly, and
acuity stays about the same as it was. The cones do
widen, so each one takes in more light than before.

Rods contribute little to the perception of detailed patterns. Their main function is to detect dim
light. Many rods funnel their input into each ganglion
cell; the more rods attached to a given ganglion cell,

the greater the capacity of that cell to detect dim light.
As the retina expands, newly formed rods fill the gaps
in the retina. These new rods funnel their input into
the same ganglion cells as the old rods (Fernald, 1989).

In summary, as the retina grows, the fish maintains the same acuity as before (because of the constant
number of cones), but its ability to see in dim light improves (because of the increased number of rods fun-
neling into each ganglion cell). In the retina of a newly
hatched fish, about 50 percent of the receptors are
rods; in a full-grown adult the percentage rises to almost 95 percent.

## Effects of Early Lack of Stimulation of One Eye

Although the cortical neurons are responsive to both eyes from the time the kitten's eyes open, visual experience is necessary, not only to fine-tune the neurons'
properties but even to maintain them. Suppose an experimenter sutures shut one
eyelid of a kitten for the first 4 to 6 weeks of life, so that the kitten sees with the
other eye only (see Figure 8.16a). At the end of that period the kitten's cortical
neurons are responsive only to the active eye; they have lost their ability to respond to stimuli in the inactive eye (Wiesel, 1982; Wiesel & Hubel, 1963). The

Development
of the Visual System

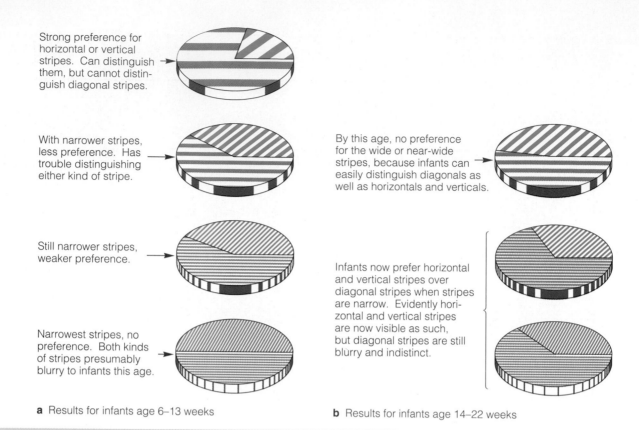

Strong preference for horizontal or vertical stripes. Can distinguish them, but cannot distinguish diagonal stripes.

With narrower stripes, less preference. Has trouble distinguishing either kind of stripe.

By this age, no preference for the wide or near-wide stripes, because infants can easily distinguish diagonals as well as horizontals and verticals.

Still narrower stripes, weaker preference.

Infants now prefer horizontal and vertical stripes over diagonal stripes when stripes are narrow. Evidently horizontal and vertical stripes are now visible as such, but diagonal stripes are still blurry and indistinct.

Narrowest stripes, no preference. Both kinds of stripes presumably blurry to infants this age.

**a** Results for infants age 6–13 weeks    **b** Results for infants age 14–22 weeks

## Figure 8.14

*(a) The youngest infants look more at wide horizontal or vertical stripes than they look at wide diagonal stripes, suggesting that they see the horizontals and verticals more clearly than they see the diagonals. As the stripes become narrower, their preference becomes weaker, presumably because all kinds of stripes look blurry or indistinct. (b) At ages 14 to 22 weeks, infants show an equal preference for wide horizontal, vertical, and diagonal stripes, suggesting that they can see all types well. However, they now show a preference for narrow horizontal or vertical stripes over diagonal stripes, suggesting that they can see some narrow stripes clearly, but not diagonal stripes. These pie charts show the relative amounts of time that infants look at horizontal and diagonal stripes of various widths. (Based on data of Leehy et al., 1975.)*

cat becomes nearly blind in the inactive eye. This effect occurs only if the kitten is deprived of normal experience in one eye during the first few weeks of life. A similar abnormal experience in adulthood has no effect on the cortex. Thus, we say that the first part of the kitten's life—about the first three months—constitutes a **sensitive period** or **critical period** for the development of the cat's visual cortex, because experiences at this time produce major, lasting effects. The concept of a sensitive or critical period is important for many other aspects of development also, not just for vision. We encountered sensitive periods for learning bird song in Chapter 1; we shall study sensitive periods for sexual development in Chapter 12.

### The Role of Competition Among Axons

If one of a kitten's eyes remains shut throughout its entire sensitive period, the cortical neurons become unresponsive to stimulation in that eye. What do you

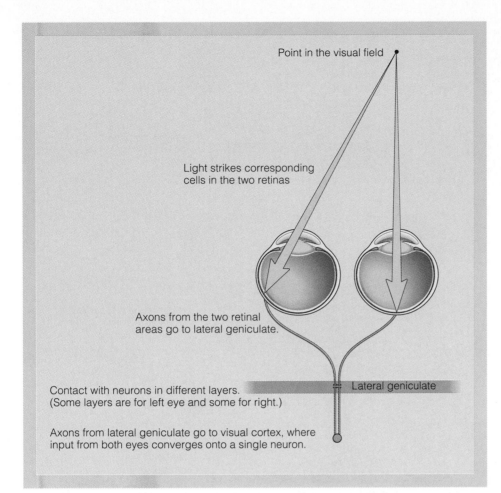

Point in the visual field

Light strikes corresponding cells in the two retinas

Axons from the two retinal areas go to lateral geniculate.

Contact with neurons in different layers. (Some layers are for left eye and some for right.)

Lateral geniculate

Axons from lateral geniculate go to visual cortex, where input from both eyes converges onto a single neuron.

**Figure 8.15**
**The anatomical basis for binocular vision in cats and primates**
*Light from a point in the visual field strikes one point in the left retina and another point in the right retina. Then those two retinal areas send their axons to separate layers of the lateral geniculate. In turn, neurons in the lateral geniculate send axons to the visual cortex, where at last the inputs from the two eyes converge onto a single cell. That cell is connected (via the lateral geniculate) with corresponding areas of the two retinas.*

suppose happens if *both* eyes remain shut throughout the sensitive period? We might guess that the cortex will become unresponsive to both eyes, yet it remains somewhat responsive to both. Granted, many of the cells respond rather sluggishly, but they do continue to respond to both eyes (Figure 8.16b). Evidently, when one eye remains shut during the sensitive period, the cells of the visual cortex become insensitive to axons from that eye not just because they are inactive but also because axons from the other eye are *more* active. In short, the establishment of synapses in the cerebral cortex depends on competition among axons. The more active synapses displace the less active synapses.

To further explore the role of competition, R. W. Guillery (1972) sutured one of a kitten's eyes shut and then surgically damaged a small spot on the retina of the active eye (Figure 8.16c). Nearly all the visual cortex cells became unresponsive to the closed eye. However, cells that were connected to the damaged area of the open eye remained responsive to the closed eye. That is, cells lost responsiveness to the sutured, inactive eye only if they received input from a healthy part of the active eye.

## Restoration of Response After Early Deprivation of Vision

After the cortical neurons have become insensitive to the inactive eye, can experience restore their sensitivity? Yes and no. No, *normal* experience cannot restore

**Figure 8.16**

*Reduced activity in either or both eyes affects the responsiveness of neurons in the visual cortex. Visual cortex neurons lose responsiveness to an inactive input only if there is competition from a more active input.*

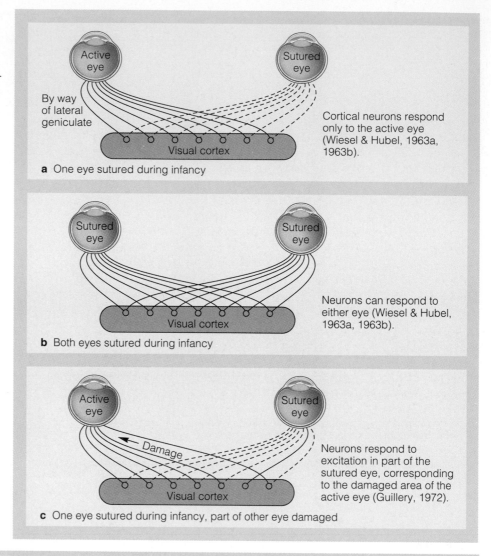

**a** One eye sutured during infancy

By way of lateral geniculate

Cortical neurons respond only to the active eye (Wiesel & Hubel, 1963a, 1963b).

**b** Both eyes sutured during infancy

Neurons can respond to either eye (Wiesel & Hubel, 1963a, 1963b).

**c** One eye sutured during infancy, part of other eye damaged

Neurons respond to excitation in part of the sutured eye, corresponding to the damaged area of the active eye (Guillery, 1972).

sensitivity to stimuli in the formerly deprived eye. If the cat simply lives its normal life with both eyes open, the deprived eye remains functionally blind. However, if the previously active eye is covered or sutured shut for a few months, the cortical cells do regain some responsiveness to the previously deprived eye (Smith, 1981).

This animal research has clear relevance to a human condition. Some children suffer from **lazy eye,** also known by the fancier term **amblyopia ex anopsia,** a condition in which the child uses just one eye for vision, while ignoring the other eye, sometimes not even focusing it in the same direction. Based on the animal work, we can predict that the best way to facilitate normal vision in the ignored eye would be to prevent use of the active eye. The results, in fact, confirm this expectation: If the lazy eye condition goes unchecked, the child becomes nearly blind in the ignored eye, just as if an experimenter had sutured it shut. To correct the condition, the physician puts a patch over the active eye, forcing the child to use the other eye. The child gradually increases his or her attention to vision in the previously ignored eye. Eventually the child is permitted to use both eyes together. The results of animal studies strongly suggest that children with "lazy eye" should undergo the eyepatch procedure as early as possible. We are not sure how long the sensitive period lasts in humans, but wearing an eyepatch is likely to be most effective if it begins during that sensitive period.

## Deprivation of the Simultaneous Use of Both Eyes

As mentioned earlier, in animals with binocular vision, cortical neurons that respond to both eyes generally respond to approximately corresponding portions of the two eyes. This arrangement enables the development of **stereoscopic depth perception,** the perception of depth by comparing the slightly different inputs from the two eyes.

Stereoscopic depth perception requires the brain to detect the discrepancy between what the left eye sees and what the right eye sees. For example, Figure 8.17 shows how two stimuli at different distances may both excite the same receptors in one eye but different receptors in the other eye. The difference between the excited areas of the two eyes is called **retinal disparity.** The greater the retinal disparity, the closer the stimulus must be. This is not our only mechanism of depth perception, but it is an important and versatile one.

Many neurons in the visual cortex respond best to stimuli that produce a small amount of retinal disparity. Different cortical neurons have receptive fields responsive to different amounts of retinal disparity (Ohzawa, DeAngelis, & Freeman, 1990). Presumably, we perceive depth because some cortical cells respond best to one degree of retinal disparity, indicating one distance, while other cortical cells respond best to some other degree of retinal disparity.

But how do we fine-tune those neurons so they will be sensitive to just the right amount of retinal disparity? Somehow a neuron with a receptive field in a

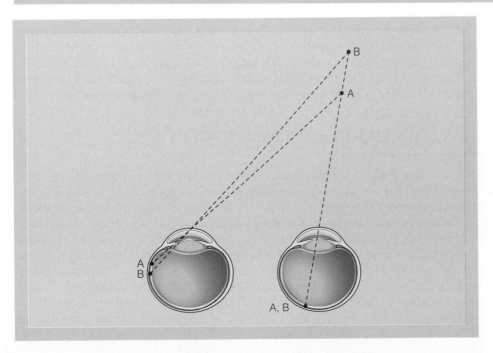

**Figure 8.17**

*Stimuli A and B both excite the same receptors in the right eye but different receptors in the left eye. An object at an extreme distance (such as a star) stimulates exactly corresponding receptors in the two eyes. Close stimuli stimulate decidedly different areas in the two eyes. The amount of discrepancy between the two eyes is the cue for stereoscopic depth perception.*

particular area of the right eye has to pick out axons from an appropriate part of the left eye. The genetic instructions by themselves could not be sufficient; different individuals have slightly different head sizes, and the genes cannot know exactly how far apart the two eyes will be. The fine-tuning of binocular vision must depend on experience.

And indeed it does. Suppose an experimenter sets up a procedure in which a kitten can see with only one eye at a time but in an alternating pattern: the left eye one day, the right eye the next day, and so forth. The kitten therefore receives the same amount of stimulation in both eyes, but it never sees with both eyes at the same time. After several weeks of this, almost every neuron in the visual cortex responds to one eye or the other, but almost none respond to both.

Similarly, suppose a kitten has defective or damaged eye muscles, so that its two eyes cannot focus in the same direction at the same time. In this case, both eyes are active simultaneously, but no neuron in the visual cortex gets *the same message* from both eyes at the same time. Again, the result is that each neuron in the visual cortex chooses one eye or the other and becomes fully responsive to it (Blake & Hirsch, 1975; Hubel & Wiesel, 1965).

The mechanism behind these results is probably that a postsynaptic cell identifies groups of axons with synchronized activity and somehow increases its responsiveness to those axons (Singer, 1986). For example, if a portion of the left retina frequently focuses on the same object as some portion of the right eye, then axons from those two retinal areas frequently carry synchronous messages. A cortical cell would be likely to establish strong synapses with both of them. However, if the eye muscles are damaged, or if one eye at a time is always covered, the cortical cell does not receive simultaneous inputs from the two eyes. Consequently, it establishes strong synapses with axons from one eye and weakens those with axons from the other eye.

Again, a similar phenomenon occurs in humans. Certain children are born cross-eyed or wall-eyed; that is, their eyes never look in the same direction at the same time. This condition is known as **strabismus.** Although children with strabismus continue to see with each eye, each neuron in the visual cortex becomes responsive to just one eye or the other. Consequently, the children do not develop stereoscopic depth perception; they perceive depth no better with two eyes than they do with one. A surgical operation in adulthood to correct the strabismus does not improve their depth perception (Banks, Aslin, & Letson, 1975; D. E. Mitchell, 1980). Presumably the sensitive period for cortical development is long over by then; a much earlier operation might improve binocular vision.

## DEVELOPMENT OF PATTERN PERCEPTION

How does a cell in the visual cortex develop its property of responding only to, say, a vertical line, or to an object moving toward the eyes? Although such properties are present in rough form at birth, visual experience helps to sharpen them.

Kittens normally open their eyes for the first time at age 9 days. Hubel and Wiesel (1963) opened the eyes of an 8-day-old kitten and recorded the response of cortical cells to light stimulation of the retina. They found simple and complex cells with receptive fields similar to those of a normal adult cat. However, many of the kitten's cells responded sluggishly or lacked the clearly defined bar-shaped receptive fields found in adults' simple and complex cells. If a kitten is reared in a normal environment, one-fourth of the total cells are mature at age 2 weeks and three-fourths at age 5 weeks. If a kitten is reared in the dark, however, only 2 percent of the total cells are mature at age 5 weeks (Buisseret & Imbert, 1976). Evidently, visual experience is necessary to promote development of the visual cortex.

A young animal that is exposed to abnormal visual experience develops visual cortex cells with abnormal properties. For example, if a kitten spends its early sensitive period in an environment with only horizontal lines, then nearly all its simple and complex cortical cells become responsive primarily to horizontal lines (Blakemore, 1974; Stryker, Sherk, Leventhal, & Hirsch, 1978). A few months later, when the cat is exposed to vertical lines and objects, it virtually ignores them and continues to do so even after years of living in a normal environment (D. E. Mitchell, 1980). We cannot be sure what happened to the neurons that would have been responsive mostly to vertical lines. Did they switch their responsiveness to horizontal lines? Or did they degenerate and die? One way or the other, the abnormal visual experience early in life altered the properties of cells in the visual cortex in such a way that they became most sensitive to the visual patterns present in the kitten's environment.

Cortical neurons responsive to diagonal lines are evidently more vulnerable to the effects of experience than are neurons responsive to horizontal or vertical lines. In one experiment, a group of kittens wore goggles so that they saw only horizontal and vertical lines during their sensitive period (Figure 8.18). All their cortical neurons became sensitive to horizontal or vertical lines, none of them to diagonal lines. Kittens in a second group saw only diagonal lines; in these kittens, some cortical neurons became responsive to diagonal lines, but others were responsive to horizontal or vertical lines (Leventhal & Hirsch, 1975). Evidently it is easier to abolish responsiveness to diagonal lines than to abolish responsiveness to horizontal and vertical lines.

What would happen to human vision if infants were deprived of normal vision during the sensitive period? The results are largely similar to those in kittens. Occasionally infants are born blind for some reason that can be corrected surgically at a later age. That is, they have no visual experience in early infancy but they begin to see later. Such children do respond to visual stimuli after the operation; for example, they can identify the brightness of light and the direction

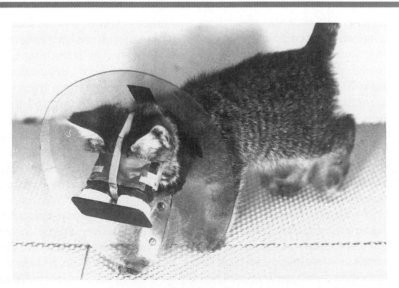

**Figure 8.18**
**Procedure for restricting a kitten's visual experience during early development**
*For a few hours a day the kitten wears goggles that show just one stimulus, such as horizontal stripes or diagonal stripes. For the rest of the day the kitten stays with its mother in a dark room without any mask. (Photo courtesy of Helmut V. Hirsch.)*

**Figure 8.19
An informal test for astigmatism**

*Do the lines in one direction look darker or sharper than the other lines do? If so, notice what happens when you rotate the page or rotate your head. The lines really are identical; certain lines appear darker or sharper because of the shape of your eye. If you wear corrective lenses, try this demonstration both with and without your lenses.*

from which it is coming. However, they find it difficult to identify objects just by looking at them, or even to describe the shapes of the objects they see. They also have trouble using vision to find their way around (Valvo, 1971). In some cases they may even choose to close their eyes and rely on touch and sound cues to maneuver through a hallway or down the stairs.

And what would happen if infants, like the kittens in the experiments, were exposed mainly to vertical lines or to horizontal lines, and not to both equally? You might wonder under what circumstances such a bizarre thing could happen to any child. No parents would let an experimenter subject their child to such a procedure, and it would never happen accidentally in nature. Right?

Wrong. In fact, there is a greater than 50-50 chance that it happened to you! About 70 percent of all infants have **astigmatism,** a blurring of vision for lines in one direction (such as horizontal, vertical, or one of the diagonals). Astigmatism is caused by an asymmetric curvature of the eyes (Howland & Sayles, 1984). The prevalence of astigmatism declines to about 10 percent in 4-year-old children, as a result of normal growth.

You can informally test yourself for astigmatism with Figure 8.19. Do the lines in one direction look darker or sharper, while those in another direction look fainter or blurrier? If so, rotate the page. You will notice that the faintness or blurriness of certain lines depends on how you hold the page, not on how the lines were drawn. If you wear corrective lenses, try this demonstration with and without your lenses. If you see a difference in the lines only when looking without your lenses, then your lenses have corrected your astigmatism.

If your eyes had strong astigmatism during the first year or so of your life (that is, during the sensitive period for development of your visual cortex), you saw lines in one direction more clearly than you saw lines in another direction. If your astigmatism was not corrected during the first 5 to 7 years of your life, then the cells of your visual cortex probably became more responsive to the kind of lines you saw more clearly (D. E. Mitchell, 1980). In that case, you will continue to see lines in one direction or another as slightly faint or blurry, even if your eyes later became completely spherical (Freedman & Thibos, 1975).

## DEVELOPMENT OF OTHER ASPECTS OF VISION

Experience molds the visual cortex in other respects as well. For example, consider what happens if cats see patterns but never see anything move. You can imagine the difficulty of arranging such a world; even if nothing else in the world moved, the kitten's head would be sure to move. Max Cynader and Garry Chernenko (1976) found an ingenious way to prevent an animal from seeing anything in motion: They raised kittens in an environment illuminated only by a strobe light, which flashed eight times a second for 10 microseconds each—hardly enough time to see anything move. In effect, the kittens' visual world was a series of still photographs. After 4 to 6 months in this odd environment, each kitten's visual cortex had neurons that responded normally to shapes but few neurons that responded strongly to moving stimuli. In short, the kittens had become motion-blind.

What if an animal had no opportunity to develop paw-eye coordination during an early sensitive period? Ordinarily, the posterior parietal cortex is an important contributor to hand-eye or paw-eye coordination; cells in that part of the cortex usually respond to both visual and somatic stimuli. In one study, monkeys were reared with their eyes closed for their first 7 to 11 months. Many cells in the posterior parietal cortex became responsive only to somatic information (Hyvärinen, Hyvärinen, & Linnankoski, 1981). Presumably the cells developed active synapses with the axons of the somatic system but rejected the axons from the visual system. After their eyes were opened, the monkeys failed to use visual information to guide their movement. They had to feel their way around, and they frequently bumped into objects or fell off tables.

Still, early experience does not modify all aspects of vision. One monkey was kept for its first three months in an environment with only a narrow bandwidth of red light. Humans in that environment found themselves unable to distinguish the colors of objects. At the end of this period, the monkey was given normal visual experience and was tested for color vision. It learned color discriminations about as well as a monkey did that had normal color experience from the start (Brenner, Cornelisson, & Nuboer, 1990).

## COMPETITION AMONG AXONS AS A GENERAL PRINCIPLE OF NEURAL FUNCTIONING

To some theorists, the principles we have considered so far in this chapter suggest a possible general principle of brain functioning, a principle that Gerald Edelman (1987) calls **neural Darwinism.** The basic principle of Darwinian evolution is that during reproduction, gene mutations and gene reassortment produce individuals with variations in structure and function (see Appendix A). Natural selection favors some variations while weeding out the rest.

Similarly, in the development of the nervous system, we start with more neurons and synapses than we shall keep. Synapses form somewhat randomly at first, and then a selection process keeps some and rejects others. Postsynaptic cells establish synapses with axons that combine forces to produce high levels of stimulation. If two or more axons generally have well-synchronized signals, the postsynaptic cell is likely to accept both of them; it is unlikely to accept pairs of axons that are usually out of synchrony. We have seen this principle clearly in the development of the visual cortex; it probably applies to the development of many other areas of the brain as well. For example, if one nostril of a rat is kept shut early in life, the olfactory bulb that gets its input from that nostril degenerates (Meisami, 1978).

The principle of competition among axons is an important one, although we should handle the analogy with Darwinian evolution cautiously. So far as we know, mutations in the genes occur completely at random. The growth of axonal branches and new synapses is partly random but partly controlled by chemical guidance and trophic factors. Still, in both cases we can talk about the most successful types proliferating at the expense of the less successful. And in both cases a change in the environment can cause a different type of individual to thrive.

### SUMMARY

1. Human infants have nearly normal peripheral vision at birth, although their foveal vision matures later. In mammals, the eyes approach their full size earlier than the rest of the head does. (p. 286)

2. Human infants perceive horizontal and vertical lines more clearly than they perceive diagonal lines. (p. 287)

3. The cells in the visual cortex of infant kittens have nearly normal properties. However, visual experience is necessary to maintain and fine-tune those properties. For example, if a kitten has visual experience in one eye and not in the other during an early sensitive period, its cortical neurons become responsive only to the open eye. (p. 289)

4. Cortical neurons become unresponsive to axons from the inactive eye mainly because of competition from

axons from the active eye. If both eyes are closed, cortical cells remain responsive to axons from them both. If one eye is closed and part of the other eye is damaged, the cortical cells connected to the damaged part of the open eye will remain responsive to the corresponding cells of the closed eye. (p. 290)

5. If cortical cells have become unresponsive to an eye because it was inactive during the early sensitive period, normal visual experience later does not restore normal responsiveness. However, prolonged closure of the previously active eye can increase the response to the previously inactive eye. (p. 291)

6. Ordinarily, most cortical neurons of cats and primates respond to approximately the same portion of both retinas. However, if the two eyes are seldom open at the same time during the sensitive period, or if they consistently focus in different directions, then each cortical neuron becomes responsive to the axons from just one eye and unresponsive to the axons from the other. (p. 293)

7. If a kitten sees only horizontal or only vertical lines during its sensitive period, most of the neurons in its visual cortex become responsive to the kind of lines it saw. For the same reason, children who have a strong astigmatism early in life may develop a permanently decreased responsiveness to one or another kind of lines. (p. 295)

8. Other aspects of vision, such as motion perception and visual coordination of movement, also depend on early experience for their proper development. (p. 296)

9. The principles of development of the visual system suggest possible mechanisms for the development and functioning of the entire nervous system. (p. 297)

## REVIEW QUESTIONS

1. The retina of the fish *Haplochromis burtoni* grows enormously from hatching to adulthood. How does the fish deal with the additional receptors without establishing a huge number of new synapses in the brain? (p. 288)

2. What behavioral evidence supports the conclusion that cortical neurons responsive to diagonal lines are slow to mature? (p. 287)

3. What happens to neurons in a kitten's visual cortex if one of its eyes is closed throughout its early development? What if both eyes are closed? (p. 289)

4. How could an investigator determine the duration of the sensitive period for development of the visual cortex? (p. 290)

5. What is "lazy eye"? How can it be treated? (p. 292)

6. What is retinal disparity? How does it contribute to stereoscopic depth perception? (p. 293)

7. What experience is necessary in early life to maintain binocular input to the neurons of the visual cortex? (p. 294)

8. What is strabismus, and how does it affect the development of the visual cortex? (p. 294)

9. What is astigmatism, and how does early childhood astigmatism sometimes affect the development of the nervous system? (p. 296)

10. What evidence indicates that perception of movement depends on having early experience in watching movement? (p. 296)

11. What does the term *neural Darwinism* mean? (p. 297)

## THOUGHT QUESTIONS

1. A rabbit has eyes on the sides of its head instead of in front. Would you expect rabbits to have many cells with binocular receptive fields—that is, cells that respond to both eyes? Why or why not?

2. Would you expect the cortical cells of a rabbit to be just as sensitive to the effects of experience as are the cells of cats and primates? Why or why not?

## SUGGESTIONS FOR FURTHER READING

**Greenough, W. T., & Jusaska, J. M.** (Eds.), (1986). *Developmental neuropsychobiology.* Orlando, FL: Academic Press. A collection of 16 articles on the development of brain and behavior. Four of them deal with the development of vision.

**Hubel, D. H.** (1988). *Eye, brain, and vision.* New York: Scientific American Library. Excellent source by co-winner of the Nobel Prize. See especially Chapter 9.

# Abnormalities
# of Development

Putting together a brain is a little like preparing an extremely complicated soufflé: It must have the right ingredients in just the right amounts, added at just the right times. Brain development can go wrong in similar ways that a soufflé can: First, the recipe book might contain a misprint or an error, or a page might be missing so that the cook cannot read it. Similarly, a mutated gene or a damaged chromosome can lead to aberrant brain development. Second, a cook can damage a soufflé by adding too much of an ingredient or by spilling some unwanted ingredient into the pan. By the same token, a developing brain that is exposed to alcohol or other toxins may develop abnormally. Third, dropping a soufflé on the floor has an effect similar to a sharp blow on a person's head.

Countless cooks have ruined soufflés. Amazingly, most brains come out reasonably normal, despite their great complexity. But not always: All the processes we have considered so far—the formation of neurons, their migration to appropriate parts of the brain, and their formation of synapses—are subject to error and interference. Let's examine a few of the ways in which a brain can develop abnormally.

## MENTAL RETARDATION

The term **mental retardation** refers to impaired intellectual development, ranging from mild to severe. The causes can be either biological or experiential (relating to inadequate stimulation or emotional distress). Among the biological causes are genetic abnormalities, infection, exposure to toxic substances, poor nutrition, and head injury. We shall concentrate here on the biological causes, but please bear in mind that the biological causes do not operate in a vacuum. Even children with biological abnormalities make intellectual progress, depending on the experiences available to them.

## Genetic Causes

A hundred or so known genes are capable of impairing intellectual development. Most of these genes are rare recessives that produce metabolic disorders in which the body fails to develop adequate amounts of some needed chemical or develops excessive levels of a potentially harmful chemical. The chance of inheriting the same rare recessive gene from both parents is low, and few people suffer retardation because of those genes.

A rare recessive located on the X chromosome produces more problems than does a similar gene located on any other chromosome. Genes located on an X or Y chromosome control what are called sex-linked traits (see Appendix A). A recessive gene on the X chromosome affects males and females differently. Because females have two X chromosomes, an X-linked recessive gene has no more effect on them than a recessive gene on any other chromosome does. However, because males have only one X chromosome, every X-linked gene acts without opposition in males. Color blindness and hemophilia are two examples of traits controlled by genes on the X chromosome; these traits are far more common in males than in females.

**Phenylketonuria** One genetic basis for mental retardation is **phenylketonuria** (FEE-nil-KEET-uhn-YOOR-ee-uh), or **PKU.** Even though PKU is caused by a recessive gene not on the X chromosome, the condition is fairly widespread because the gene itself is common in people of European or Asian ancestry. About 1 percent of Europeans and Asians are carriers for PKU; very few people of African ancestry have the gene (Wang et al., 1989).

The gene for PKU prevents the body from metabolizing **phenylalanine,** an amino acid found in a variety of foods. Normally, some phenylalanine is incorporated into proteins; the liver converts most of the rest to another important amino acid, **tyrosine** (Figure 8.20). A small amount of phenylalanine is converted to other products, including **phenylpyruvate.** Children with PKU lack the enzyme that converts phenylalanine to tyrosine (Kaufman, 1975). As a result, such children accumulate excessive levels of both phenylalanine and phenylpyruvate, which lead to structural malformations of the brain, including a deficit of myelin and a surplus of glia cells. Children with PKU become mentally retarded, restless, irritable, and sometimes prone to temper tantrums.

Physicians can determine whether a newborn baby has PKU by measuring the level of phenylalanine or phenylpyruvate in the blood or urine. This test is routinely performed on nearly all babies born in the United States. If the level is excessively high, indicating PKU, the condition can be controlled by diet. The child is put on a strict, rather difficult diet containing very low levels of phenylalanine. If the parents enforce this diet conscientiously, the child's brain can develop nearly normally and he or she will escape mental retardation. The diet is particularly important while the brain is still developing, over the first 10 years or so. After a child reaches maturity, it is no longer necessary to stick closely to the diet. (The exception to this rule is that a woman with PKU should return to the diet during pregnancy and nursing. Even if her baby is normal, the baby's enzymes cannot handle the enormous levels of phenylalanine that accumulate in the mother's bloodstream on a normal diet.)

You may have noticed on beverages containing NutraSweet this advisory: "Phenylketonurics: Contains Phenylalanine." The reason is that NutraSweet is a compound of two amino acids, one of them being phenylalanine. Anyone with PKU must be certain to avoid NutraSweet.

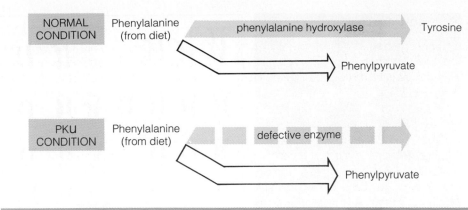

**Figure 8.20** **Metabolism of phenyl-alanine in normal individuals and in those with phenylketonuria (PKU)**

Rats also suffer mental retardation if they are exposed to high levels of phenylalanine while the brain is still developing. They are not impaired at the simplest kinds of learning, such as learning always to approach one stimulus and never another. However, once they have learned to respond to one stimulus, they have trouble shifting to respond to a different stimulus. Also, they have trouble focusing their attention in the face of distraction. For example, rats in one experiment had to choose which of two boxes to open. The correct box had a different kind of lid than the other box. When no other distracting cues were present, the rats that had been exposed to high levels of phenylalanine performed normally. But when irrelevant cues were present (such as sandpaper on the side of one box or the other), these rats learned very slowly (Strupp, Himmelstein, Bunsey, Levitsky, & Kesler, 1990). Such results suggest that PKU children might learn more effectively in situations that minimize distraction and confusion.

**Down's Syndrome** **Down's syndrome** is the most common form of mental retardation with a genetic basis. A person with Down's syndrome has an extra copy of chromosome 21 (Figure 8.21). Most people have exactly two of each chromosome, except for the X and Y chromosomes. However, occasionally an error occurs during reproduction and a fertilized cell has more or fewer than two of a particular chromosome. Embryos with too many or too few of most chromosomes simply do not survive. Those with three copies of chromosome 21 do survive, but the infant is mentally retarded. The brain anomalies generally include low brain weight, reduced numbers of certain kinds of cells, reduced number and depth of sulci in the cerebral cortex, and shorter-than-normal dendrites (Coyle, Oster-Granite, & Gearhart, 1986). By age 40, people with Down's syndrome develop further brain abnormalities of the types also seen in Alzheimer's disease (see Chapter 14).

Down's syndrome is rare in children of young mothers but becomes increasingly common in children born to mothers older than 35. The incidence of Down's syndrome may or may not be related to the father's age; at this point, the data are inconsistent. At most, the father's age is a minor factor in comparison to the mother's age (Erickson & Bjerkedal, 1981; Regal, Cross, Lamson, & Hook, 1980).

Abnormalities
of Development

**Figure 8.21**
(*a*) *A child with Down's syndrome. (Courtesy of PARCA, San Mateo Special Olympics.)* (*b*) *Chromosomes of a girl with Down's syndrome. Arrows indicate the three copies of chromosome 21. Note that this is the smallest of the human chromosomes; an extra copy of one of the larger chromosomes is more likely to be fatal. (Cytogenetics Laboratory, UCSF.)* (*c*) *Increase in frequency of Down's syndrome as a function of the mother's age. For mothers over age 35, the probability of giving birth to a Down's syndrome child increases. Each line represents the results of a different study. (Based on Lilienfeld, 1969.)*

a

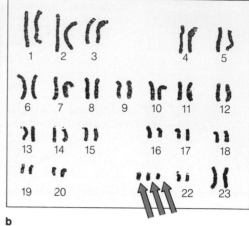

b

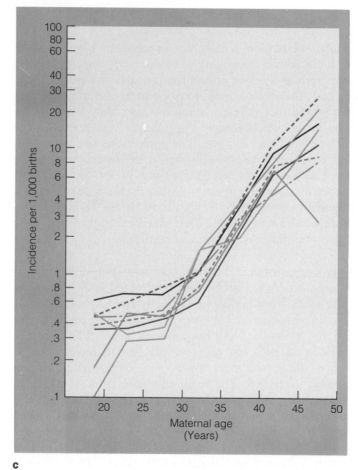

c

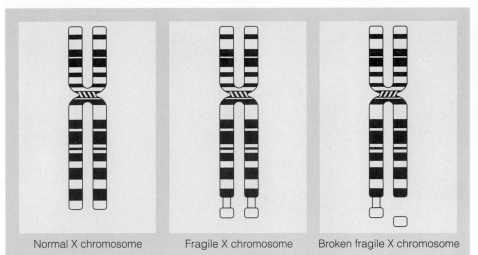

**Figure 8.22**
**The fragile X chromosome**
*Unlike the normal X chromosome, the fragile X chromosome has a portion that can easily break off.*

Normal X chromosome   Fragile X chromosome   Broken fragile X chromosome

**Fragile X Chromosome** The **fragile X chromosome** is the second most common genetic cause of mental retardation, after Down's syndrome (Brown & Jenkins, 1989). A fragile X chromosome has a segment that can literally snap off (Figure 8.22). In people who have a fragile X chromosome, that segment snaps off in some of the body's cells and not in others. In females, a fragile X chromosome generally has no apparent effects, because each cell also has a normal X chromosome. For males, if the fragile X chromosome snaps off in many cells, especially brain cells, the individual will be moderately to severely retarded, with poorly formed dendrites and fewer synapses than normal (Rudelli et al., 1985). If the chromosome segment snaps off in fewer cells, the individual may be mildly retarded or normal. About one male in a thousand develops mental retardation because of the fragile X chromosome (Brown & Jenkins, 1989).

A woman with a fragile X chromosome is called a "carrier." She does not show any symptoms, but she can pass the chromosome to her sons. However, a woman may not know or even suspect that she is a carrier. She may have inherited the chromosome from her mother, who in turn inherited it from her mother, or perhaps even from a father who showed no symptoms. She might suspect she carries a fragile X if she has brothers or uncles who are mentally retarded. If so, she could consult a physician for genetic counseling.

## Exposure to Toxic Substances

The developing brain is more vulnerable to the effects of toxic chemicals and infections than is the mature brain. For example, as noted earlier, high levels of phenylalanine are toxic for children with PKU, while the same levels are less dangerous to the same people in adulthood. Similarly, if a pregnant woman suffers from syphilis or rubella (German measles) during pregnancy, her baby's developing brain may be seriously damaged (Berg, 1986). Exposure to the same infections in adulthood does not cause immediate brain damage. (Long-term, untreated syphilis does produce brain damage, even in adults.)

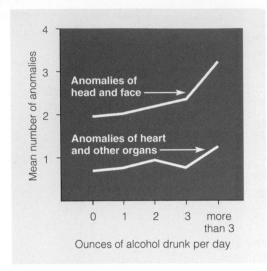

a

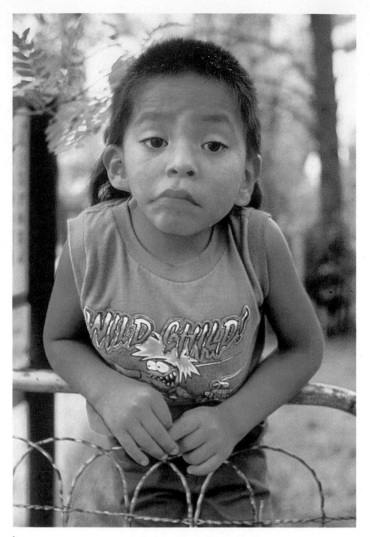

b

**Figure 8.23**
*(a) Mean number of anomalies in children born to mothers who drank different amounts of alcohol during pregnancy. Examples of anomalies are small head, folds around the eyes, malformed ears, and heart murmurs. (Based on data of Ernhart et al., 1987.) (b) Child with fetal alcohol syndrome. (Ted Wood/ Picture Group, Inc.)*

Within the chart (a):
- Mean number of anomalies (y-axis: 1, 2, 3, 4)
- Anomalies of head and face →
- Anomalies of heart and other organs →
- Ounces of alcohol drunk per day (x-axis: 0, 1, 2, 3, more than 3)

Exposure to alcohol also impairs the developing brain much more than it does the mature brain. The children of mothers who drink heavily during pregnancy may be born with **fetal alcohol syndrome,** a condition marked by decreased alertness, hyperactivity, varying degrees of mental retardation, motor problems, heart defects, and facial abnormalities (Streissguth, Barr, & Martin, 1983). Dendrites tend to be short, with less branching than in most other people. The more alcohol the mother drinks, the greater the risk (Figure 8.23), but researchers are not sure whether there is a threshold for the effect of alcohol on the brain. That is, no one knows whether a small amount of alcohol is safe or whether even small amounts may be dangerous. Studies with nonhuman animals suggest that small amounts can have detectable effects on the brain (Jones, 1988). To play it safe, pregnant women should avoid alcohol (and other drugs) during pregnancy. However, this does not mean that one little glass of wine with a holiday meal dooms a woman's baby to mental retardation.

## Malnutrition

A baby who is born much smaller than normal, especially one who weighs less than 2,000 grams (about $4\frac{1}{2}$ pounds), has an increased risk of mental retardation (Morgan & Winick, 1989). This does not mean that all small babies have brain impairments, only that the percentage risk of retardation is higher in such babies.

One possible explanation for this trend is that the mother may have had inadequate nutrition during pregnancy and that her baby did not get enough nutrition for normal development of either body or brain. In cases of severe malnutrition that is probably true, but in mild cases it is hard to be sure. Investigators find a small, inconsistent tendency toward mental retardation in the infants of mothers who had little to eat during pregnancy, especially if they did not get enough protein in their diet. However, such data are difficult to interpret. Many of the mothers with inadequate diets were teenagers; most were poor; many consumed alcohol or other drugs during pregnancy; and many provided poor nutrition for their babies after birth as well as before. Under those circumstances, it is difficult to determine how much of the retardation is due to poor nutrition during pregnancy (Berg, 1985).

A more certain conclusion is that a deficiency of particular vitamins or minerals can seriously impair brain development. For example, a deficiency of iodine in the diet leads to inadequate production of thyroid hormones, and inadequate thyroid hormones early in life lead to **cretinism,** a type of mental retardation characterized by fairly normal appearance at birth but slow mental and physical development (Pollitt, 1988). (Thyroid deficiency in adulthood produces other disorders but not mental retardation.) Iodine deficiency was more common long ago than it is today. Table salt today is nearly always fortified with iodine, so it would be difficult to consume a diet deficient in iodine. However, certain other vitamin and mineral deficiencies, such as iron deficiency, remain moderately common, and pregnant mothers with such deficiencies have an increased risk of bearing mentally retarded babies.

## Head Injury

Birth is an especially vulnerable time for the human brain. While in the uterus, the child derives oxygen from the mother's blood. After birth, the baby breathes. But during passage through the birth canal the baby may have trouble getting enough oxygen, especially if the birth is slow. Without oxygen, neurons die. Birth can also be a time of head injury, especially if the physician has to use instruments to pull the baby's head through the birth canal.

**Cerebral palsy** is movement disability resulting from trauma to the brain at or around the time of birth, or from a defect in the development of the brain. Besides impaired movement, cerebral palsy is sometimes, but not always, associated with mental retardation. Advances in medical care have made cerebral palsy much less common than it used to be.

## SUMMARY

1. Among the more common genetic causes of mental retardation are phenylketonuria, Down's syndrome, and the fragile X syndrome. Each of these disorders is associated with a variety of brain abnormalities, including an overall decrease in the number of neurons and a tendency for neurons to have short dendrites with few branches. (p. 300)

2. Mental retardation can also result from infection, exposure to toxic substances during pregnancy or around the time of birth, or head injury. Because developing neurons are vulnerable to the effects of alco-

hol, mothers who drink alcohol during pregnancy have an increased risk of having a baby with brain impairments. (p. 305)

3. Inadequate diet during pregnancy is another possible cause of mental retardation, especially if the diet is deficient in certain vitamins and minerals. (p. 305)

## REVIEW QUESTIONS

1. What is the relationship between Down's syndrome and the age of the child's parents at the time of the child's birth? (p. 301)

2. Why does the fragile X chromosome produce mental retardation in more males than females? (p. 303)

3. What are the symptoms of fetal alcohol syndrome? (p. 304)

4. Why is iodine deficiency a less common cause of mental retardation than it used to be? (p. 305)

5. What is cerebral palsy and what causes it? (p. 305)

## SUGGESTION FOR FURTHER READING

Spreen, O., Tupper, D., Risser, A., Tuokko, H., & Edgell, D. (1984). *Human developmental neuropsychology.* New York: Oxford University Press. An overview of how the human brain develops and a survey of all major types of brain disorders in childhood.

## GLOSSARY

**amblyopia ex anopsia** reduced vision resulting from disuse of an eye, usually associated with failure of the two eyes to point in the same direction

**astigmatism** blurring of vision for lines in one direction because of the nonspherical shape of the eye

**binocular vision** sight based on simultaneous stimulation of two eyes

**brain-derived neurotrophic factor** chemical related to NGF that promotes growth of certain populations of acetylcholine-containing axons in the hippocampus, amygdala, cerebral cortex, and olfactory areas of the brain

**cell adhesion molecule (CAM)** glycoprotein on the surface of cells that identifies one type of cell from another

**cerebral palsy** movement disability resulting from trauma to the brain at or around the time of birth or from a defect in brain development

**cretinism** a type of mental retardation characterized by fairly normal appearance at birth, but slow mental and physical development

**critical period** time of development when experiences produce major, lasting effects

**differentiation** formation of the axon and dendrites that gives a neuron its distinctive shape

**Down's syndrome** condition marked by mental retardation, caused by having an extra copy of chromosome 21

**fetal alcohol syndrome** condition resulting from prenatal exposure to alcohol and marked by decreased alertness, hyperactivity, varying degrees of mental retardation, motor problems, heart defects, and facial abnormalities

**fragile X chromosome** condition in which an X chromosome has a segment that can snap off; a common cause of mental retardation in males

**lazy eye** a condition in which a child uses just one eye for vision, while ignoring the other eye

**mental retardation** impaired intellectual development

**migration** movement of neurons toward their eventual destinations in the brain

**nerve growth factor** protein that promotes the survival and growth of axons in the sympathetic nervous system and certain axons in the brain

**neural Darwinism** principle that, in the development of the nervous system, synapses form somewhat randomly at first, and then a selection process keeps some and rejects others

**phenylalanine** an amino acid

**phenylketonuria (PKU)** inherited inability to metabolize phenylalanine, leading to mental retardation unless the afflicted person stays on a strict low-phenylalanine diet throughout childhood

**phenylpyruvate** a metabolite of phenylalanine

**PKU** phenylketonuria

**proliferation** the production of new cells

**retinal disparity** difference in locations of the two retinas stimulated by a single item

**sensitive period** time of development when experiences produce major, lasting effects

**stereoscopic depth perception** sensation of depth by comparing the slightly different inputs from the two eyes

**strabismus** condition of the two eyes pointing in different directions

**subplate cell** temporary neuron that forms just below the area where the cerebral cortex is developing

**tectum** part of the midbrain, the main visual area of fish, amphibians, reptiles, and birds

**trophic factor** chemical that promotes survival and activity

**tyrosine** an amino acid, precursor to dopamine and norepinephrine

# CHAPTER NINE

# Movement

## MAIN IDEAS

**1.** An individual can recruit different muscles at different times for a similar task, depending on how difficult the task is at a given moment.

**2.** Movements vary in their sensitivity to feedback, their skill, and their variability in the face of obstacles.

**3.** Different parts of the brain control different aspects of movement, such as fast movements versus slow movements and fine movements versus cruder movements.

**4.** Neurological disorders impair people's control of the coordination and planning of movement.

Imagine that you are a limpet, a small shellfish that lives on a rock at the edge of the ocean. When the tide is out, you cling tightly to the rock. When the tide is in, you loosen your grip enough to capture and eat algae and other tiny plants that float in on the waves. Your main enemies are shorebirds such as oystercatchers. Whenever you loosen your grip on the rock, a shorebird can rip you right out of your shell and swallow you whole. You are almost defenseless against this attack; the birds can see exactly where you are, while your vision is barely capable of distinguishing light from dark. Even if you could see them, you would be unable to defend yourself; the shorebirds are bigger, stronger, faster, and smarter than you are. Under the circumstances, what hope do you have?

You do have one chance: You might happen to be in a rock crevice or some other location where the shorebirds cannot reach you. They gobble up every limpet they can easily reach and then move on. You have no way of knowing whether you are in a safe location, but the longer you have been in one place without getting eaten, the better your chances. If you start moving around, sooner or later you are going to wander into a dangerous spot, and then the birds will probably get you. So your best bet is to stay right where you are. Most limpets do exactly that (Frank, 1981). The moral of the story: If your enemies are bigger and stronger and smarter than you are, you might as well stay in one place and hope they don't find you.

(*Superstock, Inc.*)

In other words, if you have little in the way of brains, you should not move much. The reverse is also true: If you are not going to move much, you do not need an elaborate nervous system. To take the extreme case, most plants do not move at all, and they have no nervous system. Animals need a nervous system to coordinate movements with one another and with sensory stimuli.

Although the ultimate function of the nervous system is to control movement, most psychologists pay little attention to movement. Compared to the study of visual perception, learning, social interactions, motivation, or emotion, the study of muscle contractions seems somehow less impressive, less glamorous, less "psychological."

And yet, consider: Although it takes a typist at least one-fourth of a second to type a single letter in response to a stimulus, many skilled typists type an average of eight or more characters per second (Salthouse, 1984). (Evidently they start each character well before finishing the previous one.) Sometimes a professional baseball player hits a ball thrown at 90 miles per hour, even though his eyes cannot move fast enough to maintain focus on the ball for the last 5 or 6 feet of its travel (Bahill & LaRitz, 1984). Highly skilled movements have to be planned ahead and executed as a coordinated unit, with little margin for error. To understand how such movements occur is a significant challenge for psychology as well as biology.

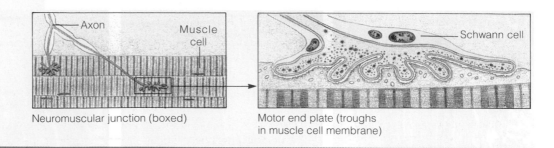

Neuromuscular junction (boxed)    Motor end plate (troughs in muscle cell membrane)

**Figure 9.3**
**A neuromuscular junction, the synapse between a motor neuron and a muscle**
*The terminal of the axon forms many branches, each of which enters a trough in the membrane of the muscle cell. (After Starr & Taggart, 1989.)*

**Figure 9.4**
**A pair of antagonistic muscles**
*The biceps of the arm is a flexor; the triceps is an extensor. (After Starr & Taggart, 1989.)*

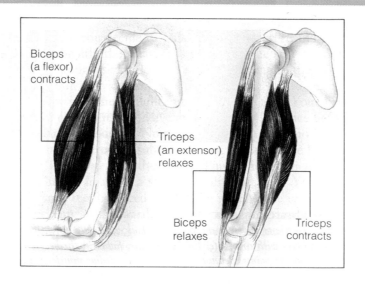

Biceps (a flexor) contracts

Triceps (an extensor) relaxes

Biceps relaxes

Triceps contracts

per three muscle fibers, while the biceps muscles of the arm have a ratio of one axon for more than a hundred fibers (Evarts, 1979). Generally, when an axon innervates relatively few muscle fibers, as in the eye muscles, movements can be more precise than when a single axon innervates many fibers.

A **neuromuscular junction** is a synapse where a motor neuron's axon meets a muscle fiber (Figure 9.3). In skeletal muscles, every axon releases acetylcholine at the neuromuscular junction, and the acetylcholine always has an excitatory effect; that is, the transmitter always causes the muscle to contract.

Each muscle has just one movement — contraction — and so just one direction of movement. In the absence of excitation it relaxes, but it never moves actively in the opposite direction. Moving a leg or arm in two directions requires opposing sets of muscles, called **antagonistic muscles**. An arm, for example, has a **flexor** muscle that flexes or raises it and an **extensor** muscle that extends or straightens it (Figure 9.4). Walking, clapping hands, or any other coordinated sequence of

## Table 9.1 Some Disorders of the Spinal Cord

| Disorder | Description | Cause |
|---|---|---|
| Paralysis | Lack of voluntary movement in part of the body. | Damage to motor neurons in the spinal cord or their axons in the periphery. |
| Flaccid paralysis | Inability to move one part of the body voluntarily, accompanied by low muscle tone and weak reflexive movements. | Damage to motor neurons in the spinal cord. Can be temporary result of damage to axons from brain to spinal cord. |
| Spastic paralysis | Inability to move one part of the body voluntarily, although reflexive movements and tremors remain. Muscles are stiff and muscle tone is higher than normal. Reflexes are strong and jerky. | Damage to axons from the brain to the spinal cord. (Such damage initially causes flaccid paralysis, which eventually gives way to spastic paralysis.) |
| Paraplegia | Loss of sensation and voluntary muscle control in both legs. Reflexes remain in legs. Although no messages pass between the brain and the genitals, the genitals still respond reflexively to touch. Paraplegics feel nothing in their own genitals, but they can function sexually, satisfy their partners, and still experience orgasm (Money, 1967). | Cut through the spinal cord above the segments attached to the legs. |
| Quadriplegia | Loss of sensation and muscle control in all four extremities. | Cut through the spinal cord above the level controlling the arms. |
| Hemiplegia | Loss of sensation and muscle control in the arm and leg on one side. | Cut halfway through the spinal cord or (more commonly) damage to one of the hemispheres of the cerebral cortex. |
| Tabes dorsalis | Impaired sensation in the legs and pelvic region, impaired leg reflexes and walking, loss of bladder and bowel control. | Late stage of syphilis. Dorsal roots of the spinal cord deteriorate gradually. |
| Poliomyelitis | Paralysis. | Virus that damages cell bodies of motor neurons. |
| Amyotrophic lateral sclerosis (Lou Gehrig's disease) | Gradual weakness and paralysis, starting with the arms and later spreading to the legs. Both motor neurons and axons from the brain to the motor neurons are destroyed. | Unknown. |

movements requires a regular alternation between contraction of one set of muscles and contraction of another.

The motor nerves of mammals originate from neurons in the spinal cord or the medulla. All sensory neurons enter the dorsal side of the spinal cord, and all motor neurons leave through the ventral side (see Figure 4.5). The axon of a motor neuron extends all the way from the spinal cord or medulla to the muscle it innervates. Diseases of the spinal cord can impair the control of movement in various ways (see Table 9.1).

The Control
of Movement

313

## Fast and Slow Muscles

At the start of this chapter I asked you to imagine you were a limpet. Now imagine that you are a small fish. You are in constant danger of attack by larger fish, turtles, and birds; your only defense is your ability to get away (Figure 9.5). Are you in any special danger when the water is cold? Remember, as a fish, you cannot maintain a constant body temperature. If the water temperature is 20° C, your body temperature is 20° C; if the water temperature drops to 5°, your body temperature drops to 5° as well.

Any muscle fiber contracts more vigorously at high temperatures than it does at low temperatures. Therefore, you should be able to swim faster at high temperatures; at low temperatures your sluggish movements should leave you extremely vulnerable to attack, especially by warm-blooded animals such as birds. Right?

Strangely, that is not so. A fish swims just as fast at low temperatures as it does at high temperatures, even though every muscle fiber contracts more vigorously at higher temperatures than it does at lower temperatures. The fish maintains its swimming speed by recruiting more muscles at low temperatures than it does at high temperatures (Rome, Loughna, & Goldspink, 1984).

A fish has three kinds of muscles—red, pink, and white. Red muscles produce rather slow movements, but they can continue to respond almost indefinitely without fatigue. White muscles produce the fastest movements, but they can act only for brief periods before becoming fatigued. Pink muscles are intermediate in both speed and fatigue. At high temperatures, a fish relies mostly on its red muscles and uses its pink muscles slightly, because these muscles contract rapidly enough for most purposes. It uses its white muscles only for occasional brief bursts of speed. At colder temperatures, the red and pink muscles produce only slow and weak contractions, and the fish relies more and more on its white muscles. By recruiting enough white muscles, the fish can maintain its usual swimming speed in all water temperatures. However, the fish fatigues faster at low temperatures because of its increased dependence on white muscles.

All right, you can stop imagining that you are a fish. What is the message here for humans? Mammals have **fast-twitch muscles** that produce fast contractions but fatigue rapidly (corresponding to the fish's white muscles) and **slow-twitch muscles** that produce less vigorous contractions without fatiguing (corresponding to the fish's red muscles). We also have a wide variety of intermediate muscles. Unlike fish, our fast-twitch, intermediate, and slow-twitch muscles are all mixed together (Hennig & Lømo, 1985). The fish's muscles are distinctly separated. (Take a look the next time you go to the grocery store.) Although we mammals do not need to concern ourselves much with varying temperatures, we call mostly on fast-twitch muscles for some situations and mostly on slow-twitch muscles for others. For standing, walking, and nonstrenuous aerobic exercise, we rely mostly or entirely on our slow-twitch and intermediate muscles. For running up six flights of stairs at full speed, we use our fast-twitch muscles.

Under extreme conditions we may build up mostly one kind of muscles or another. For example, the Swedish ultramarathon runner Bertil Järlaker once ran 3,520 km (2,188 miles) from Finland to Sweden in 50 days—an average of 1.7 marathons per day. By the end of that time he had built up an enormous amount of nonfatiguing slow-twitch and intermediate-speed muscles in his legs, which made it possible for him to run these enormous distances without pain or fatigue (Sjöström, Friden, & Ekblom, 1987). However, he had built up these slow-twitch and intermediate muscles at the expense of his fast-twitch muscles. So although

**Figure 9.5**
*Fish are "cold blooded", but many of their predators (such as this pelican) are not. At cold temperatures a fish must maintain its normal swimming speed, even though every muscle in its body contracts more slowly than usual. To do so, a fish calls upon white muscles that it would otherwise use only for brief bursts of speed. (Bill Curtsinger/The National Audubon Society Collection/ Photo Researchers, Inc.)*

he could run farther than probably any other human being, his speed for short-distance races fell to a mediocre 6 minutes per kilometer (more than 9 minutes per mile).

## Muscle Control by Proprioceptors

You are walking along on a slightly bumpy road. What happens if the messages your spinal cord sends to your leg muscles are not exactly correct? You might set your foot down a little too hard or not quite hard enough, depending on whether you step onto a bump or into a little dent in the road, and on whether you have recently gained weight or lost weight, and on whether the wind is with you or against you. Nevertheless, you adjust your posture almost immediately and maintain your balance without even thinking about it. How do you do that?

A baby is lying on its back. You playfully tug on one of its feet and then let go. At once the leg bounces back to its original position. How did that happen?

In both cases, the mechanism is under the control of proprioceptors (see Figure 9.6). A **proprioceptor** is a receptor sensitive to the position and movement of a part of the body—in these cases, a muscle. Proprioceptors detect the stretch and tension of a muscle and send messages that enable the spinal cord to adjust its signals. When a muscle is stretched, the spinal cord sends a reflexive signal to contract the muscle. This **stretch reflex** is *caused* by a stretch; it does not *result* in a stretch.

One kind of proprioceptor is the **muscle spindle,** a stretch receptor parallel to the muscle (Merton, 1972; Miles & Evarts, 1979). Whenever the muscle spindle is stretched, its sensory nerve sends a message to a motor neuron in the spinal

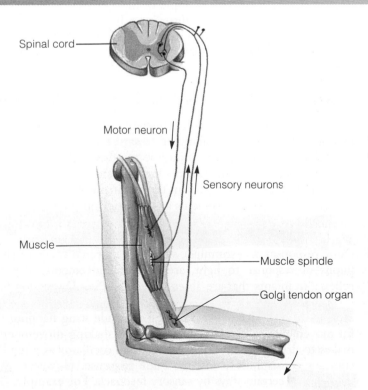

Spinal cord

Motor neuron

Sensory neurons

Muscle

Muscle spindle

Golgi tendon organ

**Figure 9.6
Two kinds of proprio-ceptors regulate the contraction of a muscle**
*When a muscle is stretched, the nerves from the muscle spindles transmit an increased frequency of impulses, resulting in a contraction of the surrounding muscle. Contraction of the muscle stimulates the Golgi tendon organs, which act as a brake or shock absorber to prevent a too-quick or too-extreme contraction.*

315

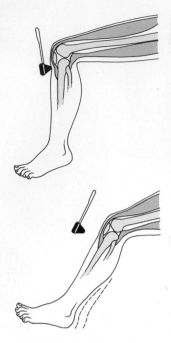

Knee-jerk reaction.

cord, which in turn sends a message back to the muscles surrounding the spindle, causing those muscles to contract. Note that this reflex provides for negative feedback: When the muscle and its spindle are stretched, the spindle sends a message that results in a muscle contraction.

For example, you set your foot down on a slight bump on the road. Your knee bends a bit, stretching the extensor muscles of that leg. The sensory nerves of the spindles send action potentials to the motor neuron in the spinal cord, and the motor neuron sends action potentials to the extensor muscle. Contraction of the extensor muscle straightens the leg, adjusting for the bump on the road.

A physician who asks you to cross your legs and then taps you just below the knee (left) is testing your stretch reflexes. The tap below the knee stretches the extensor muscles and their spindles, resulting in a message that jerks the lower leg upward.

Another proprioceptor, the **Golgi tendon organ,** responds to increases in muscle tension. Located in the tendons at both ends of a muscle, it acts as a brake against an excessively vigorous contraction. Some muscles are so strong that they could damage themselves if too high a percentage of fibers contracted at once. Golgi tendon organs detect the contraction of the muscle. The more vigorously the muscle contracts, the greater the response of the Golgi tendon organs. Their impulses travel to the spinal cord, where they inhibit the motor neurons via messages from interneurons. In short, a vigorous muscle contraction activates the Golgi tendon organs, inhibiting further contraction.

## UNITS OF MOVEMENT

The stretch reflex is one example of movement. Others include speaking, walking, threading a needle, and throwing a basketball through a hoop while off balance and trying to evade two defenders. In many ways these movements are different from one another, and they depend on different kinds of control by the nervous system.

### Movements with High or Low Sensitivity to Feedback

The military uses two kinds of missiles: ballistic missiles and guided missiles. A ballistic missile is simply launched toward the target, much as someone throws a ball. Once launched, there is no way to correct the missile's aim. A guided missile, however, detects the target's location and shifts its trajectory one way or the other to correct for any error in the original aim.

Similarly, some movements are ballistic and others are corrected by feedback. A **ballistic movement** is executed as a whole; once someone has initiated a ballistic movement, he or she cannot alter it or correct its aim. Reflexes (simple, automatic responses to a stimulus), such as the stretch reflex or the contraction of the pupils in response to light, are ballistic movements. We can observe certain reflexes in infants that are absent in adults. (See Digression 9.1.)

**Oscillators,** repetitive alternations of movements, are another type of more or less ballistic movements. Examples include wing flapping in birds and insects, fin movements in fish, and the repetitive shaking movements that a wet animal makes to dry itself off. We may regard an oscillator as a kind of reflex, because a stimulus consistently elicits the same response. However, that response can be modified in certain ways by sensory feedback. For example, the wings of a flying locust oscillate at a fixed rate, and yet the locust makes reflexive adjustments in its flight to correct for displacement by the wind (Gallistel, 1980).

# Infant Reflexes

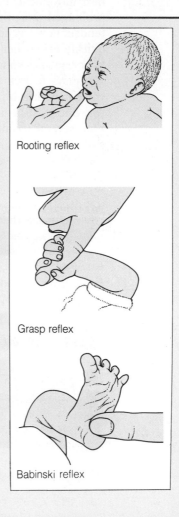

Rooting reflex

Grasp reflex

Babinski reflex

Certain reflexes are present in infants but not in older children or adults. For example, if you place an object firmly in an infant's hand, the infant will reflexively grasp it tightly (the **grasp reflex**). If you touch the cheek of an awake infant, the head will turn toward the stimulated cheek and the infant will begin to suck (the **rooting reflex**). If you stroke the sole of the foot, the infant will reflexively extend the big toe and fan the others (the **Babinski reflex**). As a rule, healthy adults do not display these reflexes.

Although such reflexes fade away over age, the reflexive connections behind them remain intact. They are not lost but rather suppressed by axons from the maturing brain. If the cerebral cortex is damaged, the infant reflexes are released from inhibition. In fact, neurologists and other physicians frequently test for infant reflexes. If a physician has ever stroked the sole of your foot during a physical exam, he or she was probably looking for evidence of brain damage. This is hardly the most dependable test, but it is probably the easiest. If a stroke on the sole of your foot makes you fan your toes as a baby does, you may be suffering from some impairment of your cerebral cortex.

The infant reflexes sometimes also return temporarily if activity of the cerebral cortex is depressed by alcohol, carbon dioxide, or other chemicals. (You might try testing for infant reflexes in a friend who has consumed too much alcohol.)

Although sensory feedback can modify oscillator movements in certain ways, it does not control the frequency of repetition of the alternating movements. For example, consider the **scratch reflex.** C. S. Sherrington found that when he lightly irritated a dog's skin, the dog would raise a limb and scratch the irritated area repetitively. The scratching movement, a well-timed alternation of extensor and flexor muscles, occurred at a constant rate of four to five scratches per second. If the amount of irritation increased, the length and strength of each scratching movement increased, but the rhythm stayed the same. Even if the experimenter tickled the skin rapidly or slowly, the muscles still produced four or five scratches per second. Therefore, Sherrington reasoned, the scratching rhythm is generated by some set of cells in the spinal cord, not by the sensory input.

Many other movements depend to a greater extent on moment-by-moment feedback. For example, when you thread a needle, you make a slight movement

The Control
of Movement

and then observe the new positions of the thread and the needle. If your aim was slightly off in one direction or another, you try to correct that error with your next movement. For another example, when a soprano holds a single note for a prolonged time, the pitch of her voice will inevitably waver slightly from the intended note. When she hears a slight change of pitch, she compensates and quickly brings her voice back to the original note. The importance of the feedback becomes apparent if we distort it. If a device records the soprano's singing and plays it back to her through earphones after a delay of a few seconds, her voice may drift off the intended note for several seconds before she hears her error. She then begins to correct the error, but by the time she hears her correction, several seconds later, she has already overcorrected. Her voice swings back and forth widely around the intended note. This procedure, called *delayed auditory feedback*, disturbs anyone's speech patterns, although one can learn to minimize the effect.

## Movement After Removal of Feedback

Certain sequences of coordinated behavior can proceed remarkably well even after the removal of most sensory feedback. For example, it is possible by surgery to eliminate most of the normal touch feedback from arm and leg movements. Recall that sensory nerves enter the spinal cord via the dorsal root, while motor nerves leave the spinal cord through the ventral root. Because of this anatomical segregation, it is possible to cut all the sensory nerves for a part of the body without harming the motor nerves (see Figure 9.7). Although the animal loses all sensation in the affected part of the body, it suffers no paralysis.

Edward Taub and A. J. Berman (1968) cut all the afferent nerves from one arm of a monkey. Such a limb is referred to as **deafferented.** After the operation, the monkey did not spontaneously use the limb for walking, for picking up objects, or for any other voluntary behaviors. The investigators initially assumed that the monkey could not use the limb because of the lack of sensory feedback. In a later experiment, however, they cut the afferent nerves of both forelimbs; a

**Figure 9.7**
**Cross section through the spinal cord**
*A cut through the dorsal root (as shown) deprives the animal of touch sensations from part of the body, while leaving the motor nerves intact.*

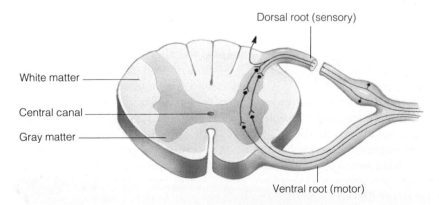

Dorsal root (sensory)

White matter

Central canal

Gray matter

Ventral root (motor)

monkey with this more extensive damage recovered use of both deafferented limbs. Coordination of the limbs recovered gradually over 2 to 6 months, not completely to normal but to a fair approximation. The monkey could walk moderately fast, it could climb upward or sideways on the walls of metal cages, and it could even pick up a raisin between its thumb and forefinger.

Apparently, a monkey with one deafferented forelimb fails to use it only because it is easier to rely on the normal limb. When both limbs are deafferented, the monkey is forced to use both. Evidently, walking is possible without touch feedback from the limbs.

We should not conclude, however, that sensory feedback is unimportant for walking or similar behaviors. Deafferented monkeys are slower and less precise in their movements than normal monkeys. Also, such monkeys have at least indirect feedback; they can feel their body move forward after certain movements and feel it fall after others.

## Skilled and Unskilled Movements

In general, an unskilled sequence of movements is slow and requires moment-by-moment feedback. If you ever learned to play a musical instrument, you began by learning to play one note. You had to make sure you got that note right before you tried another one. After more practice, you could play a long sequence of notes as a familiar "chunk." Similarly, an expert gymnast plans and performs a complex series of movements as a unit, although he or she will pause momentarily between large units to make corrections in aim and balance. In other words, the development of movement skills is mainly a matter of stringing together many individual movements into larger, more or less ballistic units.

A large coordinated chunk of movements depends on a nervous-system mechanism called a **motor program**. A motor program can be either learned or built into the nervous system, but once established, it may be fairly inflexible. A species-specific motor program that develops almost automatically in any normal environment is called a **fixed action pattern**. One example is the grooming behavior of mice (Fentress, 1973). Periodically during the day, a mouse sits up, licks its paws, wipes its paws over its face, closes its eyes as the paws pass over them, licks the paws again, and so forth. The mouse begins with a series of rapid rubs on the nose and then follows with longer, slower strokes. Even mice that lack forelimbs assume the typical posture for grooming and then wiggle their stumps back and forth. Periodically they extend their tongues and close their eyes in synchrony with the movements of the limb stumps, just as if intact paws were passing back and forth over the face. Moreover, they begin with rapid stump movements and then shift to slower movements, like normal mice. In short, once the motor program (or fixed action pattern) for this complex sequence of movements is triggered, it runs to completion.

By comparing species, we can gain some insight into how a motor program can be gained or lost through evolution. For example, if you hold almost any bird several feet above the ground and then drop it, the bird will stretch its wings and flap them. Provine (1979, 1981) found that chickens with featherless wings or amputated wings made the same movements, even though they failed to break their fall. On the other hand, penguins, emus, and rheas, which have not used their wings for flight in countless generations, do not extend or flap their wings when they are dropped (Provine, 1984). Although their ancient ancestors presumably had this motor program, it has been lost over the course of evolution.

Do humans have any built-in motor programs? Yawning is one example (Provine, 1986). A yawn is composed of the opening of the mouth, a prolonged inhalation, often accompanied by stretching, and a shorter exhalation. Yawns are very consistent in duration, with a mean of just less than 6 seconds.

It is sometimes difficult to determine whether some movement does or does not depend on a motor program, mainly because the definition of motor program is rather loose. For example, an outstanding basketball player may shoot every free throw with exactly the same motion. We are tempted to say the player has developed a motor program for that movement. But then we watch the same player shoot field goals from all over the court, altering the shot to compensate for changes in distance and angle. Is there a different motor program for each spot on the floor, or does a player learn systematic rules for modifying a single motor program? Some observers think that the whole concept of motor program breaks down if we apply it to such flexible movements (Gentner, 1987).

## SUMMARY

1. An overall movement may depend on a great many muscle contractions. We attend to the individual contractions only when a task is particularly difficult. (p. 310)

2. Vertebrates have skeletal, cardiac, and smooth muscles. (p. 310)

3. The neuromuscular junction is a specialized type of synapse. (p. 312)

4. Skeletal muscles range from slow muscles that do not fatigue to fast muscles that fatigue quickly. We rely on the slow muscles at most times, but we recruit the fast muscles for brief periods of strenuous activity. (p. 314)

5. Proprioceptors are receptors sensitive to the position and movement of a part of the body. Two kinds of proprioceptors—muscle spindles and Golgi tendon organs—help to regulate muscle movements. (p. 315)

6. Some movements, especially reflexes, proceed as a unit, with little if any guidance from sensory feedback. Other movements, such as threading a needle, are constantly guided and redirected by sensory feedback. (p. 316)

7. Many movements, including walking, can proceed surprisingly well even after the removal of most forms of sensory feedback. (p. 318)

8. Someone who develops skill at a movement comes to execute large chunks of the movement as a whole, with little dependence on moment-by-moment feedback. (p. 319)

## REVIEW QUESTIONS

1. Why can the eye muscles be moved with greater precision than the biceps muscles? (p. 310)

2. What transmitter is released at the neuromuscular junction of skeletal muscles? (p. 312)

3. How does a fish manage to swim at the same speed in water of different temperatures, even though temperature affects the vigor of contraction of each muscle? (p. 314)

4. Someone who runs extraordinary distances builds up muscles that enable long-distance running without fatigue. What disadvantage is likely? Why? (p. 314)

5. While you are holding your arm straight out, someone pulls it down slightly. Immediately it bounces back to its original position. What proprioceptor is responsible? (p. 315)

6. What is the function of Golgi tendon organs? (p. 316)

7. Give an example of a movement that is highly sensitive to feedback and one that is relatively insensitive. (p. 316)

8. What is the evidence that the rhythm of the scratch reflex is generated within the animal's own nervous system? (p. 317)

9. What are the effects of deafferenting a limb on its movement? What are the effects of deafferenting two limbs? (p. 318)

10. Give an example of a motor program or a fixed action pattern. (p. 319)

## THOUGHT QUESTIONS

1. Would you expect jaguars, cheetahs, and other great cats to have mostly slow-twitch, nonfatiguing muscles in their legs or mostly fast-twitch, quickly fatiguing muscles? What kinds of animals might have mostly the opposite kind of muscles?

2. A person with damage to the afferent nerves from one arm does not use that arm. The physician's advice is to tie the other arm behind the person's back. Why?

## SUGGESTIONS FOR FURTHER READING

**Brooks, V. B.** (1986). *The neural basis of motor control.* Oxford, England: Oxford University Press. Detailed description of research on how the nervous system controls the muscles; not easy reading but highly informative.

**Gallistel, C. R.** (1980). *The organization of action: A new synthesis.* Hillsdale, NJ: Erlbaum. Provocative analysis of the units of movement; includes reprints of some classic articles.

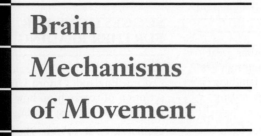

# Brain
# Mechanisms
# of Movement

$S$uppose you go through a sequence of actions: You stand up, walk across the room, sit at the piano, place your hands in position, and start to play. So far as you are consciously aware, you merely decide to perform these actions and then they happen. However, much of your nervous system devotes its time to making them happen. Furthermore, different parts of your brain are responsible for different kinds of movement. Figure 9.8 outlines the major motor areas of the mammalian central nervous system. Don't get too bogged down in their details at this point; we shall attend to each of these areas in due course.

## THE ROLE OF THE SPINAL CORD

Have you ever heard the expression "running around like a chicken with its head cut off"? A rather gruesome image, but a chicken with its head cut off *can* run around . . . for a little while. Naturally, it does not run toward anything or away from anything; it just runs. Nevertheless, it maintains its balance even while running on bumpy ground or up or down a slope. In short, the spinal cord can control walking and running.

In fact, the spinal cord largely controls walking and running even when the brain is intact and even in humans. That is, the motor program for walking is located in the spinal cord. The spinal cord and medulla also have motor programs for chewing, swallowing, breathing, scratching, and a number of other common behaviors (Shik & Orlovsky, 1976). The cerebral cortex does not direct the individual muscle contractions necessary for such movements; it merely turns on the appropriate motor programs.

The spinal cord's motor program for the scratch reflex has received considerable research attention. In cats, the reflex has a rhythm of three or four scratches per second. Cells in the third through fifth lumbar segments of the spinal cord generate that rhythm (Deliagina, Orlovsky, & Pavlova, 1983). A stroking of the skin stimulates certain neurons in that area of the spinal cord to produce impulses at a rate of three or four per second. The rate of scratching remains the same

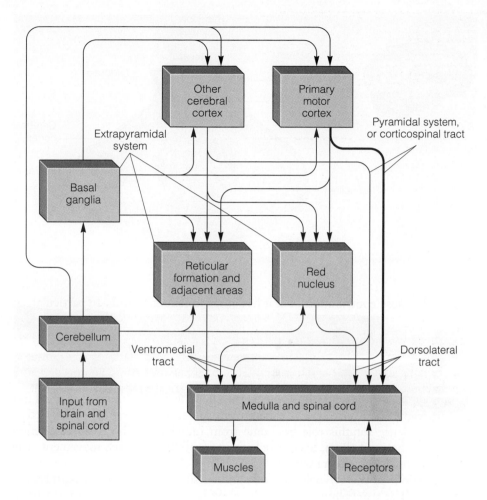

**Figure 9.8**
**Outline of the major motor areas of the mammalian central nervous system**
*The cerebral cortex, especially the primary motor cortex, sends axons directly to the medulla and spinal cord; it also sends axons to the red nucleus, reticular formation, and other brain-stem areas, which in turn send axons to the medulla and spinal cord. The medulla and spinal cord control all muscle movements. The basal ganglia and cerebellum influence movement indirectly through their communication back and forth with the cerebral cortex and brain stem.*

even if those neurons are isolated from all cerebral input, so it appears that the rhythm originates in the spinal cord. Furthermore, those cells generate the rhythm even if the muscles themselves are paralyzed, so the rhythm does not require feedback from muscle movements.

## THE ROLE OF THE CEREBELLUM

The cerebellum, as we noted in Chapter 4, is important for motor control and possibly for certain cognitive functions as well (Leiner, Leiner, & Dow, 1986). The term *cerebellum* is Latin for *little brain*. Although it is smaller than the rest of the brain, the cerebellum contains so many neurons and so many connections that its potential for information processing is comparable to that of the cerebral cortex.

Physiologists long believed that the role of the cerebellum was merely to improve the coordination of muscles and to maintain equilibrium. The cerebellum

Brain Mechanisms
of Movement

**Figure 9.9**
**Cross section through the cerebellum and medulla, showing the location of the cerebellar nuclei relative to the cerebellar cortex**

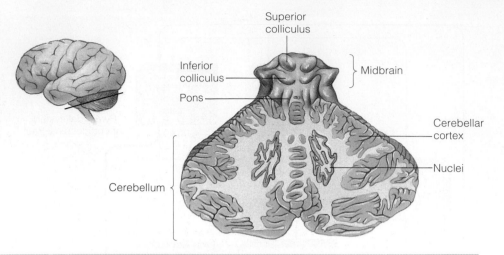

does make those contributions, but it has other functions as well. In particular, we now know that cerebellar neurons are active before movements begin, not just during and after them. Thus, the cerebellum seems to generate and plan movements as well as coordinate them.

Hans Kornhuber (1971, 1974) proposed that the cerebellum plays a key role in all voluntary ballistic movements—that is, those not dependent on moment-by-moment sensory feedback. This role includes the development of learned motor programs that turn slow, deliberate movements into rapid, well-practiced habits. Evidence for this role has come from individuals who have experienced damage to the cerebellum. Such people must carefully plan each movement, even those that used to come automatically.

Variations in the cerebellum across animal species also support Kornhuber's viewpoint. The cerebellum is proportionately larger in birds than in most mammals; birds certainly make a great many rapid, ballistic movements in flight and when landing on perches. The sloth, on the other extreme, is a mammal proverbial for its slowness. When M. G. Murphy and J. L. O'Leary (1973) made cerebellar lesions in sloths, they could detect no change in the animals' movement patterns.

## Cellular Organization of the Cerebellum

The cerebellum receives input from the spinal cord, from each of the sensory systems by way of the cranial nerve nuclei, and from the cerebral cortex. Thus, it is well suited to relate movement to sensory information. That information eventually reaches the **cerebellar cortex,** the surface of the cerebellum (see Figure 9.9). The cerebellar cortex regulates the activity of the nuclei (cell body clusters) in the center of the cerebellum, which in turn send output fibers to the thalamus and to midbrain structures, including the **red nucleus.** From the thalamus, information from the cerebellum is conveyed to the motor areas of the cerebral cortex.

The cerebellar cortex has an extremely regular arrangement of neurons, as Figure 9.10 shows. All the output from the cerebellar cortex is controlled by the **Purkinje cells,** each of which branches extremely widely within one plane, like a flattened leaf. The output of the Purkinje cells inhibits their target cells in the nuclei of the cerebellum.

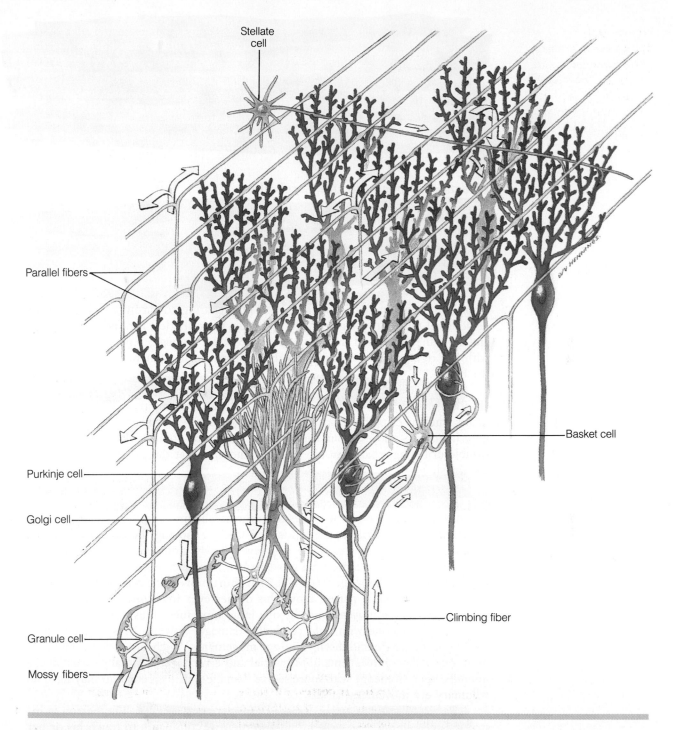

**Figure 9.10**
**Cellular organization of the cerebellum**
*Parallel fibers activate one Purkinje cell after another. Purkinje cells inhibit a target cell in one of the nuclei of the cerebellum. The more Purkinje cells respond, the longer the target cell is inhibited. In this way, the cerebellum controls the duration of a movement.*

The Purkinje cells receive a major part of their input from **parallel fibers** that run perpendicular to the planes of the Purkinje cells. Note how a single parallel fiber can activate a long string of Purkinje cells, one after the other. If all those Purkinje cells send their output to the same target cell, then one after another of them inhibits that cell, producing a prolonged effect. The greater the number of Purkinje cells responding, the longer they will collectively inhibit their target cell. By controlling the target cell for varying periods, the Purkinje cells control the duration (and therefore distance) of ballistic motor responses (Kornhuber, 1974; Llinas, 1975).

## Effects of Damage to the Cerebellum

In humans, damage to the cerebellum causes difficulty with a variety of rapid movements, including speaking, writing, typing, playing a musical instrument, and athletic skills. Affected people make errors in the direction, intensity, velocity, aim, and timing of movements. Although they can still perform the necessary motions individually, they cannot link them together smoothly (Brooks, 1984; Dichgans, 1984). Ordinarily, certain movements accompany one another. For example, when pulling the right arm back in preparing to throw a ball, a normal person will put more weight on the right leg, raise the left leg and the left arm, and shift the pelvis and the neck. After cerebellar damage, a person may throw with the right arm without making the appropriate movements with the rest of the body.

A consistent deficit after cerebellar damage is **dysdiadochokinesia** (dis-die-ah-doe-koh-kih-NEE-zhuh), an inability to perform rapid alternating movements, such as clapping hands. (You might want to learn this bit of medical jargon, if only to impress your friends. The next time some basketball player has trouble dribbling a ball, you can smugly announce that the problem is dysdiadochokinesia.)

The cerebellum is particularly important for the control of **saccades** (sa-KAHDS), ballistic eye movements from one fixation point to another. Saccadic eye movements depend on impulses from the cerebellum and the frontal cortex to the cranial nerves. Only one speed is available for moving the eyes over a given distance. If you attempt to move your eyes slowly from one point to another, your eye muscles divide the total movement into a large number of short movements with pauses between them. But each short movement is rapid and ballistic.

A normal, healthy person moves his or her eyes from one fixation point to another by a single movement or by one large movement plus a small correction at the end. Someone with mild cerebellar damage, however, has difficulty programming the angle and distance of eye movements (Dichgans, 1984). The eyes make many short movements until by trial and error they eventually focus on the intended spot. Someone with more severe damage to the cerebellum may have no voluntary eye movements at all.

Another test of cerebellar damage is the *finger-to-nose test*. The person is instructed to hold one arm straight out and then, at command, to touch his or her nose as quickly as possible. A normal person does so in three steps: First, the finger moves ballistically to a point just in front of the nose. This *move* function depends on the cerebellar cortex, which sends messages to the nuclei (see Figure 9.9). Second, the finger remains steady at that spot for a fraction of a second. This *hold* function depends on the nuclei alone (Kornhuber, 1974). Finally, the finger moves to the nose by a slower movement that does not depend on the cerebellum.

After damage to the cerebellar cortex, a person has trouble with the initial, rapid movement. Either the finger does not go far enough or it goes too far, striking the person in the face. If certain nuclei of the cerebellum have been damaged, the person may have difficulty with the hold segment; after the finger reaches a point just in front of the nose, it wavers wildly.

The symptoms of cerebellar damage markedly resemble those of alcohol intoxication. Drunken individuals as a rule are clumsy, their speech is slurred, and their eye movements are inaccurate. A police officer testing someone for possible drunkenness may use the finger-to-nose test or other tests that are also used for diagnosing damage to the cerebellum because it is one of the first areas of the brain to show the effects of alcohol intoxication.

## THE ROLE OF THE BASAL GANGLIA

The term *basal ganglia* applies collectively to a group of large subcortical structures in the forebrain (see Figure 9.11): the **caudate nucleus,** the **putamen,** the **globus pallidus,** the **substantia nigra,** and the **subthalamic nucleus** (DeLong et al., 1984). Each of these areas exchanges information with the others. The main receptive areas are the caudate nucleus and the putamen, which receive sensory input from parts of the thalamus and from nearly all parts of the cerebral cortex. The main output areas are the globus pallidus and substantia nigra, which send most of their axons to the motor areas of the cerebral cortex and to the midbrain (Carpenter, 1986).

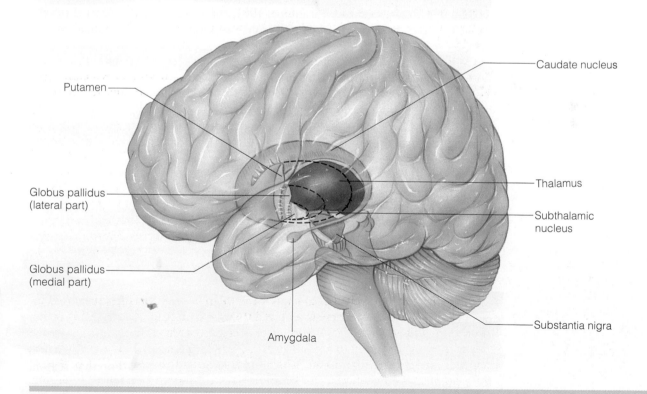

**Figure 9.11**
**Location of the basal ganglia**

The basal ganglia contribute to both movement and cognitive functions. In the control of movement, they are apparently not responsible for selecting which muscles will be active at a given time. Rather, they control the direction and distance of movements, especially postural movements. Cells in the basal ganglia become active before movements begin; for that reason we believe they participate in planning and organizing the movements, not just in coordinating them. Unlike cells of the cerebellum, most basal ganglia cells are especially active prior to gradual movements rather than fast, ballistic movements (DeLong, 1974).

After damage to the basal ganglia, people can still make all the movements they could before the damage, but the movements are weak and poorly coordinated (DeLong et al., 1984; Marsden, 1984). They have difficulty initiating movements; for example, they may have trouble standing up or starting to walk. Once they start walking, they may be able to continue.

Two medical disorders associated with damage to the basal ganglia are Parkinson's disease and Huntington's disease, which we shall consider later in this chapter.

# THE ROLE OF THE CEREBRAL CORTEX

Since the pioneering work of Gustav Fritsch and Eduard Hitzig (1870), neuroscientists have known that direct electrical stimulation of the motor cortex can elicit movements. Electrical stimulation generally leads to a coordinated movement that includes at least a few muscles. It is difficult, in fact, to induce an isolated movement of a single muscle (Asanuma, 1981). In other words, the cortex (unlike the spinal cord) is in charge of overall plans of movement, not individual muscle contractions.

The cerebral cortex is particularly important for the control of complex and varied actions. It contributes little to the control of coughing, sneezing, gagging, laughing, or crying (Rinn, 1984). (Perhaps this lack of control by the cerebral cortex has something to do with why it is hard to perform those actions voluntarily.) We distinguish two major systems in the mammalian cerebral cortex that control the motor neurons of the spinal cord and the medulla: the pyramidal system and the extrapyramidal system.

## The Pyramidal System

The **pyramidal system** consists of a set of cells, most of whose axons cross between the left and right sides of the nervous system in distinctive swellings in the medulla called **pyramids**, as Figure 9.12a shows. About 50 to 60 percent of those axons originate in the precentral gyrus of the frontal lobe (see Chapter 4), which is also known as the **primary motor cortex**. Of the remaining pyramidal axons, many originate either in the postcentral gyrus (the primary somatosensory cortex) or in the prefrontal cortex (Wiesendanger, 1984). However, nearly all parts of the cortex contribute at least a few axons to this system. The axons of the pyramidal system extend directly, without synaptic interruption, from the cerebral cortex to interneurons or motor neurons in the medulla and spinal cord. For that reason, the pyramidal system is also called the corticospinal tract.

At the pyramids of the medulla, most of the pyramidal system axons cross to the contralateral side of the spinal cord, forming the **dorsolateral tract** of the spinal cord. The dorsolateral tract is primarily responsible for movements in the periphery of the body, such as precise control of the fingers. Those pyramidal system axons that remain on the ipsilateral side of the spinal cord join the **ventromedial tract** of the spinal cord. The ventromedial tract controls movements near the midline of the body, such as bending and turning of the trunk.

After damage to the pyramidal system, a person suffers a complete but temporary paralysis. Over the following weeks, reflexes return, followed by voluntary movements. Although the control of fine movements may never recover completely, it sometimes returns to a surprising degree (Wiesendanger, 1984). The recovered movements may depend on undamaged portions of the pyramidal system or on the extrapyramidal system, the other major motor system of the cortex.

The **premotor cortex** and the **supplementary motor cortex,** two areas anterior to the primary motor cortex (see Figure 9.13), integrate movement with sensory information (Roland, 1984). These areas become active, for example, if someone has to move a finger around in a maze in response to someone else's directions. They show specific patterns of activity depending on whether the movement is guided by visual, auditory, or tactile stimuli (Kurata & Tanji, 1986). They are active during the planning of a movement, even if the movement itself is never carried out.

## The Extrapyramidal System

The **extrapyramidal system** is composed of the movement-controlling areas other than the pyramidal system. As Figure 9.12b illustrates, axons from the basal ganglia and diffuse areas of the cerebral cortex converge onto the red nucleus, the reticular formation, the **vestibular nucleus,** and some adjacent areas. Axons from the red nucleus join the dorsolateral tract of the spinal cord (along with most of the axons of the pyramidal system), controlling distal muscles of the body such as those in the hands and feet. In humans, the red nucleus contributes relatively few axons; most of the dorsolateral tract comes from the pyramidal system. All axons in the dorsolateral tract cross from one side of the brain to the contralateral side of the spinal cord; thus, each half of the brain controls distal muscles on the opposite side of the body.

Axons from the reticular formation and vestibular nucleus form the major part of the ventromedial tract, controlling muscles of the neck, back, and trunk (Kuypers, 1989). Here the proportions are reversed; the extrapyramidal axons outnumber the pyramidal axons in the ventromedial tract. Some of the axons in the ventromedial tract cross to the contralateral side, but others remain on the ipsilateral side. Consequently this tract and, in general, the extrapyramidal system control muscles on both sides of the trunk.

In contrast to the pyramidal system, the extrapyramidal system generally controls less precise movements, including postures and overall body movements. For example, damage to the basal ganglia or reticular formation impairs walking, turning, bending, standing up, and sitting down. Extrapyramidal movements generally coordinate both sides of the body, not just the left or the right.

The extrapyramidal system receives input from the basal ganglia and vast areas of the cerebral cortex (Selemon & Goldman-Rakic, 1985). Consequently, while localized cortical damage can obliterate a significant portion of the pyramidal system, a similar amount of cortical damage would not destroy much of the extrapyramidal system.

Ordinarily, most movements rely on both pyramidal and extrapyramidal influences, and both dorsomedial and ventrolateral tracts. The motor systems work in cooperation with each other, not independently.

Brain Mechanisms
of Movement

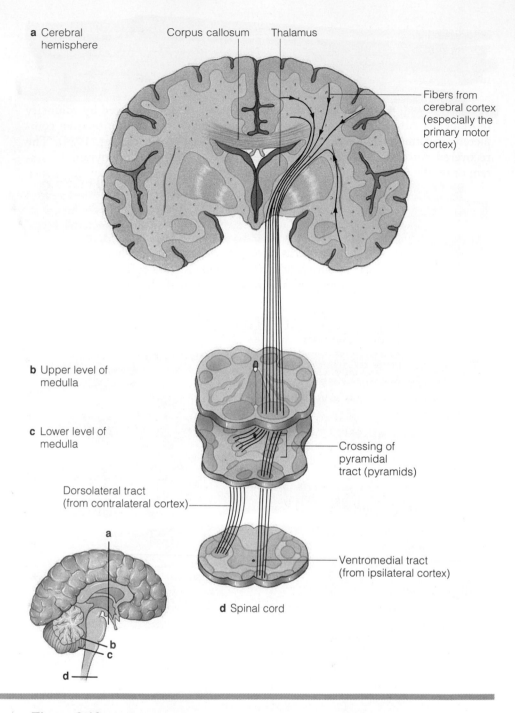

**a** Cerebral hemisphere

Corpus callosum

Thalamus

Fibers from cerebral cortex (especially the primary motor cortex)

**b** Upper level of medulla

**c** Lower level of medulla

Crossing of pyramidal tract (pyramids)

Dorsolateral tract (from contralateral cortex)

Ventromedial tract (from ipsilateral cortex)

**d** Spinal cord

a
b
c
d

### Figure 9.12
### The pyramidal system and the extrapyramidal system

*(a) The pyramidal system, which controls the most precise and most discrete movements, such as movements of a single finger.*

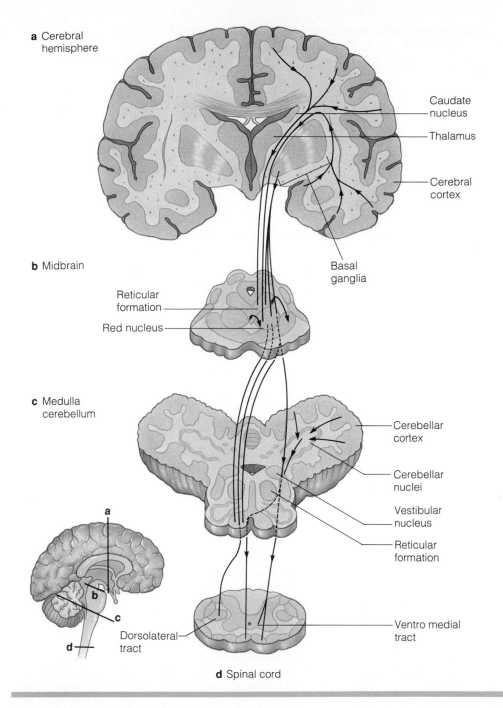

**a** Cerebral hemisphere

Caudate nucleus

Thalamus

Cerebral cortex

Basal ganglia

**b** Midbrain

Reticular formation

Red nucleus

**c** Medulla cerebellum

Cerebellar cortex

Cerebellar nuclei

Vestibular nucleus

Reticular formation

a

b

c

d

Dorsolateral tract

Ventro medial tract

**d** Spinal cord

# Figure 9.12 (continued)

*(b) The extrapyramidal system, which controls more general and bilateral movements, including standing, walking, and adjusting posture. The basal ganglia and cerebellum contribute to both systems. They send input to the primary motor cortex via the thalamus. They also send input directly to the red nucleus and the reticular formation.*

**Figure 9.13**
**Principal areas of the motor cortex in the human brain**
*Cells in the premotor cortex and supplementary motor cortex are active during the planning of movements, even if the movements are never actually executed.*

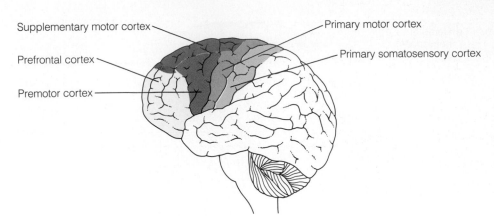

Supplementary motor cortex

Prefrontal cortex

Premotor cortex

Primary motor cortex

Primary somatosensory cortex

## SUMMARY

1. The spinal cord contains the mechanisms for many motor programs such as walking, running, and scratching. It can generate rhythmic movements on its own. (p. 322)

2. The cerebellum helps to generate ballistic movements and to link individual movements into rapid, coordinated sequences. (p. 323)

3. The cells of the cerebellum are arranged in a very regular pattern that enables them to produce outputs of well-controlled duration. (p. 324)

4. After damage to the cerebellum, people have trouble with rapid alternating movements, saccadic eye movements, and rapid movements requiring accurate aim. (p. 326)

5. The basal ganglia are a group of large subcortical structures that control the direction and amplitude of movements, especially postural movements. (p. 327)

6. The pyramidal system is a set of neurons, located mostly in the primary motor cortex and adjacent areas, whose axons extend directly to the medulla and spinal cord. The pyramidal system controls fine movements, especially of the extremities. (p. 328)

7. The extrapyramidal system includes cortical and other neurons that send information to the red nucleus, the reticular formation, and other structures in the midbrain. Those structures in turn send their output to the medulla and spinal cord, controlling less precise movements than the pyramidal system does. The extrapyramidal system is especially important for postural movements. (p. 329)

8. Pyramidal and extrapyramidal axons controlling the distal muscles (the hands, for instance) cross from the brain to the contralateral side of the spinal cord. Axons controlling the trunk muscles are partly ipsilateral, partly contralateral. (p. 329)

## REVIEW QUESTIONS

1. What evidence supports the conclusion that the spinal cord directly controls certain motor programs? (p. 322)

2. Do cells in the cerebellum and basal ganglia become active before a movement or only during and after the movement? (pp. 324, 328)

3. From what structures does the cerebellum receive input? To which structures does it send output? (p. 324)

4. What kind of brain damage produces motor effects that resemble those of alcoholic intoxication and why? (p. 327)

5. Name the structures that compose the basal ganglia. (p. 327)

6. List the main differences between the pyramidal system and the extrapyramidal system. (p. 328)

7. What is the difference in function between the dorsolateral and ventromedial tracts of the spinal cord? (p. 328)

## THOUGHT QUESTION

1. Human infants are at first limited to gross movements of the trunk, arms, and legs. The ability to move one finger at a time matures gradually over more than the first year. What hypothesis would you suggest about which brain areas controlling movement mature early and which ones mature later?

## SUGGESTION FOR FURTHER READING

**Evarts, E. V.** (1979). Brain mechanisms of movement. *Scientific American, 241* (3), 164–179. A good overview of brain mechanisms, written for a general audience.

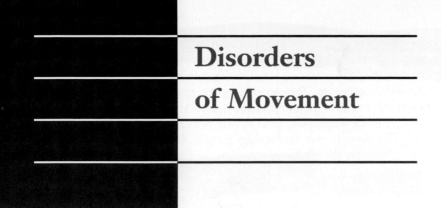

# Disorders
# of Movement

Even if your nervous system and muscles are completely healthy, you may sometimes find it difficult to move in the way you would like. For example, if you have just finished a bout of unusually strenuous exercise, your muscles may be so fatigued that you can hardly move them voluntarily, even though they constantly twitch. Or if your legs "fall asleep" while you are sitting in an awkward position, you may stumble and fall when you try to walk.

A different kind of movement limitation: Suppose you watch an Olympic competitor execute an impressive gymnastic routine. You would like to perform the same movements. You have all the same nerves and muscles, and yet you find yourself unable to copy the Olympian's actions.

Certain neurological disorders produce exaggerated and lasting movement limitations. Some people suffer permanent fatigue and constant twitching. Others lose the ability to perform even simple, everyday movements, such as stirring a cup of coffee, although their muscles are intact. We shall consider a few examples of such disorders.

The cause of a movement disorder can lie anywhere from the muscles to the cerebral cortex. Myasthenia gravis is caused by a problem in the muscles; Parkinson's disease and Huntington's disease are disorders of the extrapyramidal system; apraxia is caused by damage to the cerebral cortex.

## MYASTHENIA GRAVIS

**Myasthenia gravis** (MY-us-THEE-nee-uh GRAHV-iss) is an autoimmune disease — that is, a disease in which the immune system forms antibodies against part of itself. In myasthenia gravis, the immune system attacks the acetylcholine receptors at neuromuscular junctions (Lindstrom, 1979). Most patients have measurable blood levels of antibodies that will destroy those receptors (Drachman, Adams, & Josifer, 1982). A rare condition, myasthenia gravis is responsible each year for the deaths of about 2 or 3 people per 100,000 over the age of 75 and an occasional younger person (Chandra, Bharucha, & Schoenberg, 1984).

The symptoms of myasthenia gravis are progressive weakness and rapid fatigue of the striated muscles. Any repeated movement rapidly gets weaker unless the person pauses to rest. Because the muscles have fewer than the normal number of acetylcholine receptors, the remaining receptors need the maximum amount of transmitter to move the muscles normally. After any motor neuron has fired a few times in quick succession, later action potentials release fewer quanta of acetylcholine. The same is true for healthy people, but they notice no change in their movement because they have an abundance of acetylcholine receptors. In people with myasthenia gravis, transmission at the neuromuscular junction is precarious at best, and even a slight decline in acetylcholine availability has powerful effects (Drachman, 1978).

Myasthenia gravis can be treated with drugs that suppress the immune system (Niakan, Harati, & Rolak, 1986). That approach has its limitations, of course, because suppression of the immune system leaves the patient vulnerable to other illnesses. Many patients are also given drugs that inhibit the enzyme acetylcholinesterase, which breaks down acetylcholine. The result prolongs the action of acetylcholine at the neuromuscular junction. A physician must monitor the dose carefully, however, as an excess can impair the muscles just as badly as myasthenia gravis does.

## PARKINSON'S DISEASE

Parkinson's disease and Huntington's disease are called **extrapyramidal disorders** because they result from a disorder somewhere in the extrapyramidal system. Both are characterized by abnormal movements, not by paralysis.

**Parkinson's disease** is an affliction that occurs mostly in the elderly. The main symptoms are slow movements, difficulty initiating movements, rigidity of the muscles, tremors, and sometimes intellectual impairment and depressed mood (Miller & DeLong, 1988). Investigators are not sure how much of the depression is an understandable reaction to a serious illness and how much of it is a symptom of the illness itself (Dakof & Mendelsohn, 1986). The nature of the symptoms varies a bit from one person to another; for example, some people have mostly tremors and others have mostly rigidity and slowness of movement (Huber, Paulson, & Shuttleworth, 1988). Among people over age 75, Parkinson's disease is responsible for the death of about 1 person per 1,000, with a higher rate among whites than blacks in the United States (Chandra, Bharucha, & Schoenberg, 1984). (See Figure 9.14.)

The immediate cause of Parkinson's disease is the degeneration of various parts of the brain, especially a path of dopamine-containing axons from the substantia nigra to the caudate nucleus and putamen (see Figure 9.15). (What causes this path to degenerate is another story, to be discussed shortly.) Without treatment, the axons continue to degenerate, the condition worsens, and ultimately the person dies.

### L-DOPA Treatment for Parkinson's Disease

The traditional goal of therapy has been to replace the missing dopamine. A patient cannot simply take dopamine pills or injections, because dopamine does not cross the blood-brain barrier. **L-DOPA**, a precursor to dopamine (see Figure 3.8), does cross the barrier, however. Most people with Parkinson's disease take

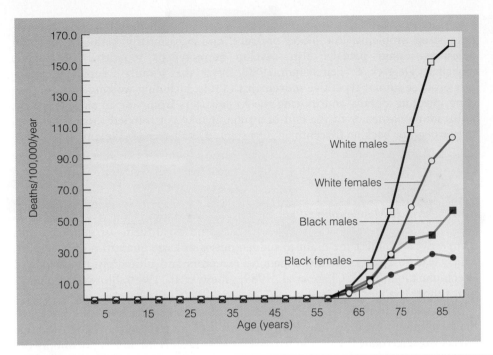

**Figure 9.14**
**The number of people who die from causes related to Parkinson's disease**
*Note that the number increases rapidly after age 65 and that the disorder affects more white than nonwhite people. (Based on Chandra et al., 1984.)*

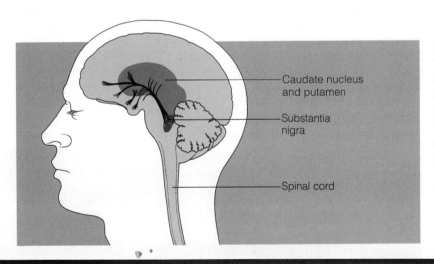

**Figure 9.15**
**The pathway from the substantia nigra to the caudate nucleus and putamen**
*This is the location of the most severe brain damage in Parkinson's disease.*

L-DOPA pills daily, often in conjunction with other drugs. After reaching the brain, the L-DOPA is converted into dopamine. It relieves the symptoms of Parkinson's disease and may return the person to years of active life. It does not cure the problem, however, and the gradual destruction of dopamine-containing axons continues.

Disorders
of Movement

Moreover, L-DOPA produces harmful side effects, including nausea, restlessness, sleep problems, low blood pressure, and occasionally hallucinations and delusions. Some patients also develop stereotyped, repetitive movements (Schallert, DeRyck, & Teitelbaum, 1980). Drugs that stimulate dopamine receptors produce similar repetitive movements in rats, including walking forward, circling, pivoting tightly, and moving the forequarters from side to side. If the rat walks into a corner or to the end of a tube, it may get trapped there, unable to turn around or back up (Szechtman, Ornstein, Teitelbaum, & Golani, 1985). Evidently, while L-DOPA relieves the symptoms of dopamine deficiency, it occasionally overstimulates certain dopamine synapses.

The side effects of L-DOPA can be relieved somewhat by additional drugs that prevent L-DOPA from being converted to dopamine before it enters the brain (Dakof & Mendelsohn, 1986). They can also be minimized by delivering L-DOPA through various slow-release devices. The usual forms of delivery—pills or injections—subject the brain to sudden pulses of large quantities of L-DOPA, which lead to changes in the dopamine receptors and ultimately to periods of overstimulation (T. N. Chase et al., 1989; Obeso et al., 1989). Slow release minimizes those changes.

The side effects of L-DOPA generally grow worse after someone has taken the medication for a long time. However, it is difficult to be sure whether the side effects worsen *because* the person has taken the L-DOPA for so long or simply because the underlying disease has grown worse in the meantime. Due to this uncertainty, it remains controversial whether physicians should prescribe L-DOPA at once for Parkinson's patients or whether they should delay giving the medication and interrupt it for "drug holidays," in hopes of minimizing the side effects.

## Possible Causes of Parkinson's Disease

Parkinson's disease is one of the few neurological or psychological disorders that do not run in families to any significant degree. Even having an identical twin with Parkinson's disease does not increase an individual's risk of contracting the disease (Duvoisin, Eldridge, Williams, Nutt, & Calne, 1981). It would seem, then, that something in the environment causes it.

Parkinson's disease probably has a variety of causes, differing from one person to another. Among the likely causes are an interruption of blood flow to certain parts of the brain, exposure to toxic substances, prolonged exposure to certain drugs, and a history of encephalitis or other viral infections (Jenner, 1990).

The possibility of a toxic cause for Parkinson's disease was discovered by accident (Ballard, Tetrud, & Langston, 1985). In 1982, several young adults (ages 22 to 42) in northern California developed symptoms of Parkinson's disease after using a heroin substitute, which all of them had bought from the same dealer. (See Digression 9.2.) At first, physicians resisted diagnosing their condition as Parkinson's disease, because that disorder usually develops slowly in old age, while these patients had developed it rapidly at a young age. Eventually, however, it became clear that the symptoms matched Parkinson's disease exactly. Before the investigators had a chance to alert the community to the danger of the heroin substitute, a number of other people had used it. Some of them developed severe, eventually fatal Parkinson's disease. Others developed milder symptoms (Tetrud, Langston, Garbe, & Ruttenber, 1989). Still others have developed no symptoms so far, although their substantia nigras have suffered some damage (Calne et al., 1985). These people are probably at serious risk for developing Parkinson's disease later in life.

## "Designer Drugs"

The United States enforces laws against the manufacture, sale, or use of many drugs believed to be harmful. Heroin is one such drug. One way to evade the law is to sell a drug that produces similar effects but is chemically different, even if the difference is as minor as, say, substituting a methyl group for a single hydrogen ion. The laws apply to heroin and other drugs that the federal government has chemically identified and listed. They do not apply to new drugs that have never been sold before, that the government may not even have heard of.

Because of this enormous loophole in the legal system, certain drug dealers manufacture "designer drugs"—drugs that may produce effects similar to heroin (or whatever) and that remain technically legal until the government obtains enough of them to determine what they are and pass a law against them. Although the risk to the drug dealer is low, the risk to the user is unknown and may in certain cases be severe.

The heroin substitute these people used was a mixture of two chemicals: MPPP and MPTP. The body converts MPTP to a related chemical, $MPP^+$, which is selectively toxic to the substantia nigra. A number of studies have confirmed that injections of MPTP can produce symptoms of Parkinson's disease in monkeys and other animals (Snyder & D'Amato, 1986). MPTP damages mostly those neurons that release dopamine as their neurotransmitter; postsynaptic neurons compensate for the loss of their usual dopamine input by increasing their number of dopamine receptors (Chiueh, 1988; see Figure 9.16). The symptoms of Parkinson's disease result partly from the decrease in dopamine input and partly from the jumpy overresponsiveness of the extra receptors (Miller & De-Long, 1988).

Why does MPTP attack mostly the substantia nigra? Latin for *black substance*, *substantia nigra* gets its dark appearance from two chemicals, melatonin and neuromelatonin, which are abundant in this area. MPTP binds tightly to melatonin and neuromelatonin; as it gradually separates from those chemicals, it produces progressive damage in nearby neurons (D'Amato, Lipman, & Snyder, 1986).

No one supposes that illegal drug use is responsible for most cases of Parkinson's disease. A more likely hypothesis is that MPTP and similar chemicals are present in the environment as air or water pollutants. Perhaps certain people accumulate enough of such chemicals to damage their substantia nigra. When they grow old, they lose some of their remaining dopamine neurons and receptors, as most people do (Morgan & Finch, 1988). The combination of early damage with natural deterioration in old age may lead to Parkinson's disease.

What are some possible sources of MPTP in the environment? A number of herbicides and pesticides, including *paraquat*, have a chemical structure similar to that of MPTP and $MPP^+$ (see Figure 9.17). In a survey of the region around Montreal, Quebec, Andre Barbeau (as described by Snyder & D'Amato, 1986) found that the areas where people had used the largest amounts of paraquat had rates of Parkinson's disease seven times higher than the areas that had used it least. A study of Hong Kong residents found that Parkinson's disease was most

Disorders
of Movement

337

**Figure 9.16**
**The results of injecting MPP+ into one hemisphere of the rat brain, as revealed by autoradiography (see p. 139)**

*The upper part shows $D_2$ dopamine receptors; the lower part shows axon terminals that contain dopamine. Red indicates the highest level of activity, followed by yellow, green, and blue. Note that the MPP+ greatly depleted the number of dopamine axons and that the number of $D_2$ receptors increased in response to this lack of input. However, the net result is a great decrease in dopamine activity. (From Chiueh, 1988.)*

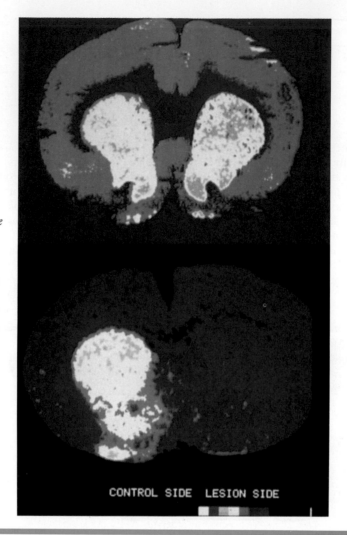

CONTROL SIDE   LESION SIDE

common among people who had worked on farms, especially if they had used herbicides and pesticides, and among people who frequently ate raw vegetables (Ho, Woo, & Lee, 1989).

We should not jump to the conclusion that herbicides and pesticides are the main cause of Parkinson's disease; the worldwide distribution of the disease does not suggest any single or simple cause. Still, exposure to toxins is likely to be a contributing factor in certain cases.

One special reason to be concerned about paraquat is that in 1978 the U.S. government financed a program of spraying Mexican marijuana fields with paraquat in an effort to eradicate the plant. Many of the marijuana leaves were sold in spite of the contamination, however, and were presumably smoked. An estimated 9,000 people in the United States may have been exposed to at least 100 µg of paraquat through the marijuana (Landrigan, Powell, James, & Taylor, 1983).

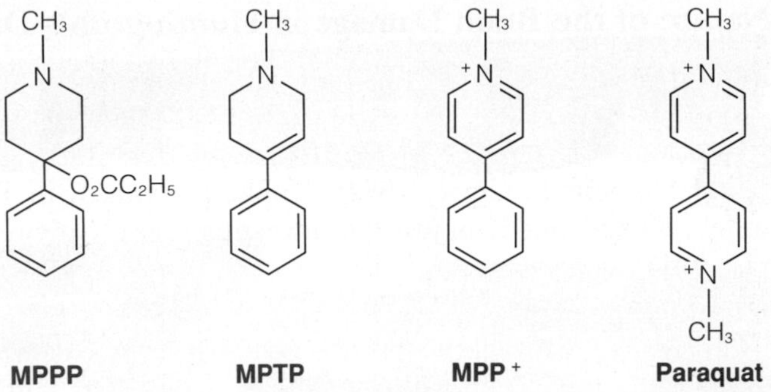

**Figure 9.17**
**The chemical structures of MPPP, MPTP, MPP$^+$, and paraquat**

MPPP          MPTP          MPP$^+$          Paraquat

## New Therapies for Parkinson's Disease

The research on MPTP has led to a new treatment for Parkinson's disease. MPTP itself is harmless; it becomes dangerous after an enzyme called *monoamine oxidase B* converts it to MPP$^+$. Consequently, any drug that blocks monoamine oxidase B prevents the damage caused by MPTP. Research on squirrel monkeys found that MPTP damages the substantia nigra and produces the symptoms of Parkinson's disease; MPTP plus an inhibitor of monoamine oxidase B produces little or no damage (Langston, Irwin, Langston, & Forno, 1984).

Even if MPTP itself is not ordinarily the cause of Parkinson's disease, other similar chemicals might be. With that in mind, investigators tested the effect of **deprenyl** (an inhibitor of monoamine oxidase B) on Parkinson's disease. Two groups of human patients with mild Parkinson's disease were randomly assigned to receive either deprenyl or a placebo. Those receiving the placebo deteriorated more rapidly (Tetrud & Langston, 1989). In other words, deprenyl actually slowed the progress of the disease. In contrast, L-DOPA merely decreases the symptoms, while the underlying disease continues at its own pace.

## HUNTINGTON'S DISEASE

**Huntington's disease,** also known as *Huntington's chorea*, is a severe neurological disorder related to damage in the caudate nucleus and putamen. The motor symptoms usually begin with a facial twitch; later, tremors spread to other parts of the body. Walking, speech, and other voluntary movements become slow and clumsy at first; eventually they become impossible (McHugh, 1989).

In addition, people with Huntington's disease suffer psychological disorders, which may be noticed before the motor symptoms. Among the psychological symptoms are depression, memory impairment, anxiety, hallucinations and delusions, poor judgment, alcohol and drug abuse, and anything from a total lack of sexual responsiveness to indiscriminate sexual promiscuity (Shoulson, 1990).

The most common age of onset is 30 to 50, although cases are known with onset in childhood or in old age. Once the symptoms emerge, both the psychological and the motor symptoms grow progressively worse over a period of about 15 years, culminating in death (Chase, Wexler, & Barbeau, 1979). About 50 people per million in the United States eventually develop Huntington's disease.

Disorders
of Movement

## Nature of the Brain Damage in Huntington's Disease

Huntington's disease is characterized by a progressive loss of neurons especially in the caudate nucleus, putamen, and globus pallidus, with some loss in the cerebral cortex. The overall brain weight may decline by 15 to 20 percent before death (Sanberg & Coyle, 1984). Unlike patients with Parkinson's disease, who suffer damage mostly in just the substantia nigra, patients with Huntington's disease suffer more widespread damage. They especially lose cells with glutamate receptors in the basal ganglia (Young et al., 1988).

An injection of **kainic acid** or **quinolinic acid** into the caudate nucleus and putamen of rats produces both movement disorders and a pattern of brain damage that mimic Huntington's disease (Beal et al., 1986; Sanberg & Johnston, 1981). Both kainic acid and quinolinic acid resemble the neurotransmitter *glutamate*; they damage neurons by overstimulating them. The body itself normally produces small amounts of quinolinic acid. Thus, the brain damage of Huntington's disease might be caused by overstimulation by this or similar chemicals.

## Heredity and Presymptomatic Testing for Huntington's Disease

Huntington's disease is controlled by an autosomal dominant gene. That is, a person who has the gene will eventually develop the disease and will transmit the gene to about half of his or her children, on the average.

Imagine that at the age of 20 you learn that one of your parents has Huntington's disease. You now know that you have a 50 percent chance of developing it yourself, probably in about 20 years. In addition to your grief about your parent's agony, your life will change in two ways. First, you will constantly worry about your own health. Whenever you do something clumsy or experience a slight tremor anywhere in your body, you will fear that it is the start of Huntington's disease. Second, you may have trouble deciding whether to have children. You may decide that you would not want to have children if you have the gene for Huntington's disease. But you do not know whether you have the gene, and you may not find out until you are 40 or older. In fact, because the disease sometimes begins in old age, you may never be confident that you are safe.

For these reasons genetic researchers worked for many years to discover an accurate **presymptomatic test**—a test of whether someone is likely to develop the disease, conducted before any symptoms appear. After trying several tests, they developed one based on direct examination of the chromosomes. The gene for Huntington's disease is located on human chromosome number 4; investigators know its position approximately but not exactly. They do know that it is close to a marker called G8 (Folstein et al., 1985; Gusella et al., 1983). G8 is a gene with four forms—*A*, *B*, *C*, and *D*—that can be distinguished under a microscope. Although the G8 gene itself has nothing to do with Huntington's disease, it is generally inherited along with any Huntington's disease gene that is near it.

The logic of the test is as follows: Suppose a few close relatives who developed Huntington's disease all have at least one copy of the *C* form of the G8 gene. (Because everyone has two copies of chromosome 4 per cell, each of these people will have a second form of G8 as well, which may or may not be a *C*.) We can presume that the gene for Huntington's disease is on the same chromosome with the *C* form in this family. (It will be associated with different markers in different families.) Next suppose that one of these people, who has a *C* and a *B* form, has children with someone else who has two *A* forms. We can now examine their

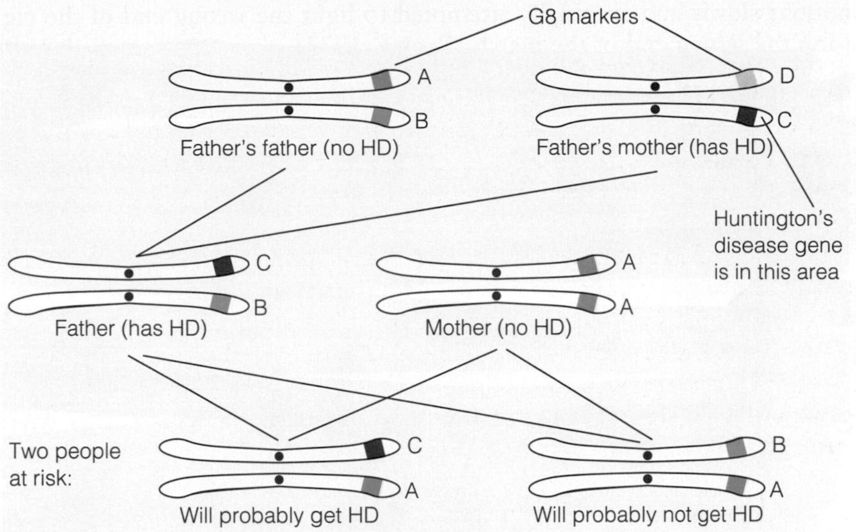
G8 markers
A
B
D
C
Father's father (no HD)
Father's mother (has HD)
Huntington's
disease gene
is in this area
C
B
A
A
Father (has HD)
Mother (no HD)
Two people
at risk:
C
A
B
A
Will probably get HD
Will probably not get HD

**Figure 9.18**
**Example of how medical workers can use the G8 chromosome marker in presymptomatic detection of Huntington's disease**
*In this family, the father inherited a gene for Huntington's disease from his mother. Because both of them have a type-C marker, and the father's father did not, the Huntington's disease gene in this family must be linked to the C marker. (It is linked to different markers in different families.) In the youngest generation, each child with a C marker is likely to develop Huntington's disease.*

children's chromosomes. Those who have a *C* and an *A* probably have the gene for Huntington's disease. Those with a *B* and an *A* should be safe. Figure 9.18 illustrates the testing strategy.

This test works only if investigators can examine the chromosomes of a number of related people with Huntington's disease. Even under the best circumstances, it cannot be 100 percent accurate because of the possibility of *crossing over* of the genes (see Appendix A). That is, the two number 4 chromosomes may exchange pieces. Researchers hope to be able to improve the test and eventually to locate the gene for Huntington's disease itself.

The use of the presymptomatic test raises some serious ethical issues. If you knew that one of your parents had Huntington's disease, would you want to know whether you will get it, too? Some people volunteer to take the test; others decline. When people take the test, they should be offered counseling to help them deal with the results.

## APRAXIA

In certain cases, damage in the cerebral cortex can lead to complex deficits known as **apraxia,** a difficulty in organizing movements purposively. A person with apraxia may, for example, perform some action spontaneously and then prove unable to do the same thing in response to verbal instructions. Frequently apraxic movements stop in the middle of a sequence. Certain patients say they know what to do but cannot organize the movements to do it (Faglioni & Basso, 1985). For example, one patient was told to put a letter into an envelope. He spent a long time trying many unusual ways of folding the letter and never did get it inside the envelope. Then he was told to dial the operator on the telephone. He picked up the receiver and rotated it in his hand, apparently uncertain about which end should go to his ear. Later he was told to light a cigarette. He went through the motions slowly and eventually attempted to light the wrong end of the cigarette, using the wrong end of the match (Brown, 1972).

Different instances of apraxia may be associated with a great many types of brain damage, generally including parts of the cerebral cortex. A patient with damage in the right hemisphere generally has trouble dealing with geometrical relationships or arranging items in visual space. For example, when attempting to copy a drawing, such a person may start too close to one side of the paper and thus be unable to fit the picture on the page. Such a person also has trouble assembling a puzzle or arranging a set of blocks to match a pattern someone else had made.

People with damage in the left hemisphere have trouble coordinating their own body, especially in response to verbal instructions. For example, one brain-damaged man could not follow verbal instructions to use either arm or either leg in isolation or any other single set of muscles by itself (Geschwind, 1975). He could make all the same movements spontaneously, however, and he could follow instructions to stand, walk, bow, kneel, or to make other postural movements of the whole body. He could follow instructions to assume a boxer's position but not to punch with one hand.

His brain damage had disconnected the language areas in his left cerebral cortex from his pyramidal system but not from his extrapyramidal system. That is, the damage interrupted fibers from the language areas to the primary motor cortex. Because the primary motor cortex and the entire pyramidal system were intact, his spontaneous movements were normal. The language areas could not send messages to the pyramidal system, so he could not move individual limbs in response to verbal instructions, but the language areas could communicate with the extrapyramidal system to initiate gross movements and postures.

A few comments in conclusion: The control of movement is an important topic for psychology as well as for biology. The inability to make certain movements may mean that the muscles are paralyzed, but it can also mean that the brain has difficulty planning the movements or conveying the plan from one part of the brain to another. Disorders such as Parkinson's disease and Huntington's disease are known mostly for their effect on movement, but they are also linked to abnormalities of thought and mood. In short, the brain mechanisms that control movement are not tacked on at the end of all the "psychological" processes; they are an integral part of everything the brain does.

## SUMMARY

1. In myasthenia gravis, the body's immune system attacks the neuromuscular junctions. The disease is treated by suppressing the immune system and by prolonging the actions of acetylcholine at the neuromuscular junction. (p. 333)

2. Parkinson's disease is characterized by slow movements, tremor, rigidity, and in most cases depression. It is associated with degeneration of dopamine-containing axons from the substantia nigra to the caudate nucleus and putamen. Generally, it is treated with L-DOPA, which the brain can convert into dopamine, or with deprenyl, which inhibits the enzyme monoamine oxidase B. (pp. 334, 339)

3. The chemical MPTP selectively damages neurons in the substantia nigra and leads to the symptoms of Parkinson's disease. Certain herbicides and pesticides are chemically similar to MPTP. Drugs that prevent the breakdown of MPTP into $MPP^+$ appear to be useful in slowing the progress of Parkinson's disease. (p. 336)

4. Huntington's disease is a hereditary condition marked by deterioration of motor control, plus depression, memory impairment, and other cognitive disorders. It generally has its onset at age 30 to 50. (p. 339)

5. In Huntington's disease, numerous brain cells, especially in the basal ganglia, die. It is possible to mimic the disease in animals by injections of kainic acid or quinolinic acid. (p. 340)

6. By examining chromosome 4 of people at risk for Huntington's disease and their affected and unaffected relatives, physicians can sometimes determine which people are likely to develop Huntington's disease later in life. (p. 340)

7. Apraxia is an inability to organize certain movements purposively or to make them in response to instructions. In some cases, it relates to damage that disconnects one part of the brain from another. (p. 341)

## REVIEW QUESTIONS

1. What causes myasthenia gravis? How can the condition be treated? (p. 333)

2. Which two drugs are used in the treatment of Parkinson's disease? How does each of them work? (pp. 334, 339)

3. Why does MPTP damage neurons in the substantia nigra more than it damages neurons in other parts of the brain? (p. 337)

4. What are the symptoms of Huntington's disease? What is the usual age of onset? (p. 339)

5. What chemicals can produce brain damage that mimics the damage found in Huntington's disease? How do they do so? (p. 340)

6. What procedure enables physicians to determine which people are most likely to get Huntington's disease? (p. 340)

7. Describe an example of apraxia and relate it to brain damage. (p. 342)

## THOUGHT QUESTIONS

1. What effect would haloperidol probably have for someone suffering from Parkinson's disease?

2. The presymptomatic test for Huntington's disease that uses the G8 marker is useless if the parent with Huntington's disease has two G8 markers that are alike—for example, two $D$s. Why is that?

3. In Figure 9.18, suppose the father (who has Huntington's disease) still has a $C$ and a $B$ marker, as in the figure, but the mother (who does not have Huntington's disease) has a $B$ and a $C$ marker, instead of two $A$ markers. They have three children: The first has two $B$ markers; the second has two $C$s, and the third has a $B$ and a $C$. What (if anything) can we say about each child's likelihood of developing Huntington's disease?

## SUGGESTION FOR FURTHER READING

Geschwind, N. (1975). The apraxias. *American Scientist*, *63*, 188–195. Discusses movement disorders in relationship to localized human brain damage.

## GLOSSARY

**amyotrophic lateral sclerosis (Lou Gehrig's disease)** disease that produces gradual weakness and paralysis, due to loss of motor neurons in the spinal cord and loss of axons from the brain to the spinal cord

**antagonistic muscle** muscle that moves a limb in opposite directions (for example, extensor and flexor)

**apraxia** inability to organize movements purposefully

**Babinski reflex** reflexive flexion of the big toe when the sole of the foot is stimulated

**ballistic movement** motion that proceeds as a single organized unit that cannot be redirected once it begins

**cardiac muscle** muscle of the heart

**caudate nucleus** one of the structures of the basal ganglia

**cerebellar cortex** outer covering of the cerebellum

**deafferent** to remove the afferent connections to a structure

**deprenyl** drug that inhibits the enzyme monoamine oxidase B; found to slow the progress of Parkinson's disease

**dorsolateral tract** a path of axons in the spinal cord from the ipsilateral hemisphere of the brain, controlling movements of peripheral muscles

**dysdiadochokinesia** impairment of the ability to make rapid alternating movements such as clapping hands

**extensor** muscle that extends a limb

**extrapyramidal disorder** disruption of movement resulting from damage to part of the extrapyramidal system

**extrapyramidal system** movement-controlling areas other than the pyramidal system; especially the basal ganglia, red nucleus, reticular formation, vestibular nucleus, and adjacent areas

**fast-twitch muscle** muscle that produces fast contractions but fatigues rapidly

**fixed action pattern** motor program that develops almost automatically in any normal environment

**flaccid paralysis** inability to move one part of the body voluntarily, accompanied by weak reflexes

**flexor** muscle that flexes a limb

**globus pallidus** one of the structures of the basal ganglia

**Golgi tendon organ** receptor that responds to the contraction of a muscle

**grasp reflex** reflexive grasp of an object placed firmly in the hand

**hemiplegia** paralysis of the muscles on one side of the body

**Huntington's disease** an inherited disorder characterized by tremor, movement disorder, and psychological symptoms, including depression, memory impairment, hallucinations, and delusions

**kainic acid** chemical similar to glutamate that destroys cell bodies in contact with it but does not destroy passing axons

**L-DOPA** chemical precursor of dopamine and other catecholamines

**motor program** fixed sequence of movements that occur as a single unit

**muscle spindle** receptor that responds to the stretch of a muscle

**myasthenia gravis** autoimmune disease in which the body forms antibodies against the acetylcholine receptors at neuromuscular junctions

**neuromuscular junction** synapse where a motor neuron's axon meets a muscle fiber

**oscillator** repetitive alternation between two movements

**parallel fiber** axon that runs perpendicular to the planes of the Purkinje cells in the cerebellum

**paralysis** total lack of movement in one part of the body

**paraplegia** loss of sensation and voluntary muscle control in both legs, with retention of reflexes

**Parkinson's disease** malady caused by damage to a dopamine pathway, resulting in slow movements, difficulty initiating movements, rigidity of the muscles, and tremors

**poliomyelitis** paralysis caused by a virus that damages cell bodies of the motor neurons

**premotor cortex** area of the frontal cortex, just anterior to the primary motor cortex, active during the planning of a movement

**presymptomatic test** exam to predict the onset of a disease, conducted before any symptoms appear

**primary motor cortex** area of the frontal cortex just anterior to the central sulcus; a primary point of origin for axons of the pyramidal system of motor control

**proprioceptor** receptor that is sensitive to the position and movement of a part of the body

**Purkinje cell** a neuron type in the cerebellum; the type of neuron responsible for all the output from the cerebellar cortex to the cerebellar nuclei

**putamen** one of the structures of the basal ganglia

**pyramid** swelling in the medulla where pyramidal system axons cross from one side of the brain to the opposite side of the spinal cord

**pyramidal system** structure originating mostly in the precentral and postcentral gyri whose axons cross in the pyramids of the medulla and extend to neurons in the medulla or spinal cord; important for control of discrete movements

**quadriplegia** loss of sensation and muscle control in all four extremities, due to a cut through the spinal cord above the level controlling the arms

**quinolinic acid** chemical resembling glutamate that kills certain neurons by overstimulating them

**red nucleus** nucleus midbrain structure whose axons join the dorsolateral tract of the spinal cord, controlling distal muscles of the body such as those in the hands and feet

**rooting reflex** reflexive head turning and sucking after a touch on the cheek

**saccade** rapid movement of the eyes from one fixation point to another

**scratch reflex** reflexive alternation of extension and flexion of a limb in response to irritation of the skin

**skeletal muscle** muscle that controls movement of the body with respect to the environment (such as arm and leg muscles)

**slow-twitch muscle** muscle that produces less vigorous contractions without fatiguing

**smooth muscle** muscle that controls movements of internal organs

**spastic paralysis** inability to move one part of the body voluntarily because of damage to axons from the brain to the spinal cord

**stretch reflex** reflexive contraction of a muscle in response to a stretch of that muscle

**striated muscle** muscle that controls movement of the body with respect to the environment (such as arm and leg movements)

**substantia nigra** midbrain structure with a path of dopamine-containing axons to the caudate nucleus and putamen

**subthalamic nucleus** one of the structures of the basal ganglia

**supplementary motor cortex** area of the frontal cortex active during the planning of a movement

**tabes dorsalis** paralysis caused by a virus that damages cell bodies of motor neurons

**ventromedial tract** a path of axons in the spinal cord providing bilateral control of the trunk muscles

**vestibular nucleus** cluster of neurons in the brain stem, primarily responsible for motor responses to vestibular sensation

# CHAPTER TEN

# Wakefulness and Sleep

## MAIN IDEAS

1. Wakefulness and sleep, as well as temperature and other body activities, vary on a cycle of approximately 24 hours. The body itself generates this cycle.

2. People can suffer insomnia if their biological rhythm is out of phase with the prescribed time for sleeping.

3. Sleep progresses through four stages, which differ in brain activity, heart rate, and other signs of arousal.

4. A special type of stage 1 sleep, known as paradoxical sleep or REM sleep, is light sleep in some ways and deep sleep in others. It is associated with dreaming, especially with vivid dreaming.

5. The reticular formation is important for arousal of the brain. Certain areas of the brain are believed to be important for the control of sleep, although the exact nature of their contribution is not yet clear.

6. For a variety of reasons, many people do not sleep well enough to feel rested the following day.

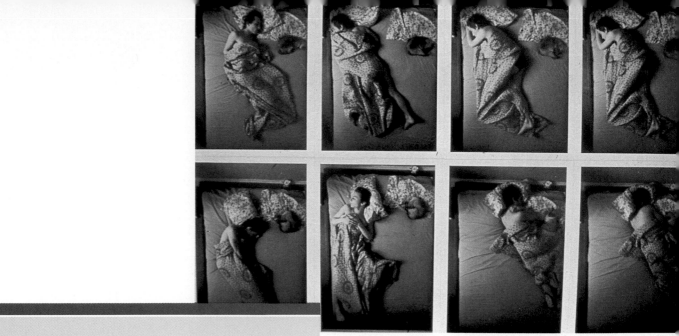

(Ted Spagna/Photo Researchers, Inc.)

Suppose you are an astronaut who has just made the flight to Daynite, a planet in another solar system. Daynite rotates on its axis only once a year; that is, it always keeps the same side facing its sun, and no part of the planet alternates between day and night. Nearly all animals and plants live in a "twilight zone" around the border between light and dark. The animals, having had a very different evolutionary history than any species on Earth, exhibit numerous peculiarities. One is that none of them ever sleeps.

Although you may be surprised to find animals that never sleep, your reaction hardly compares to the reaction of the Daynitian astronauts who simultaneously make their first visit to Earth. They marvel that about once every 365th of a year each animal lies down and stops moving. After these strange Earthlings appear to have been dead for a few hours, they spontaneously come back to life again! The Daynitians wonder, "What on Earth is going on?"

For the purposes of this chapter, let us adopt the perspective of the Daynitians and ask why animals as active as we are spend one-third of our lives doing so little.

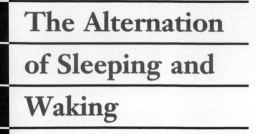

# The Alternation
# of Sleeping and
# Waking

Because the light and temperature at any point on the Earth vary from day to night and from one season to another, each animal becomes more active at certain times and less active at others. Animals do more than just respond to changes in their environment, however; they anticipate the changes. Migratory birds start flying south in the fall even if the weather has remained unseasonably warm in their northern home. Squirrels begin storing nuts and putting on extra layers of fat in preparation for winter long before food becomes scarce. Animals that mate during only one season of the year go through extensive changes in both their anatomy and their behavior as the reproductive season approaches. Humans begin to awaken from a night's sleep before the alarm sounds and before the room becomes light. Somehow the body generates its own rhythms in preparation for changes in the environment.

## ENDOGENOUS RHYTHMS IN BEHAVIOR

How do animals know what time of day or what time of year it is? In the pioneering work on this topic, Curt Richter found that the activity level of rats increases for a while every 2 to 4 hours, coincident with an increase in stomach contractions, even in an unchanging environment (Richter, 1922). He later found that female rats greatly increase their activity every fourth or fifth day, at the fertile period of their estrous cycle. These were the first demonstrations that the body could generate long rhythms independent of rhythmic sensory input.

Even the year-long rhythms underlying migration, hibernation, and similar behavior are governed partly by internal mechanisms. A migratory bird prepares to fly south when the period of light each day declines to a certain level. (Temperature has nothing to do with the timing of migration, as indeed it should not. A sudden cold spell in July or a warm spell in September is a poor predictor of the weather to come.) But although the duration of light is a powerful factor in the timing of migration, it is not the only one. After a bird has wintered in the tropics, how does it know when to return north? In the tropics, the daily duration

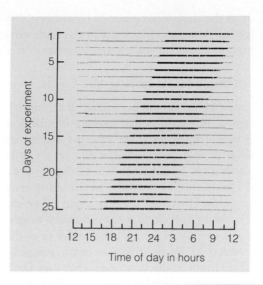

**Figure 10.1
Activity record of a
flying squirrel kept in
constant darkness**
*The thickened segments indi-
cate periods of activity as
measured by a running wheel.
Note that the free-running
rhythm of activity and rest in
this animal under conditions
of constant darkness lasts
slightly less than 24 hours.
(From DeCoursey, 1960.)*

of daylight varies only slightly from season to season. Many birds have an internal timing mechanism that readies them for the approximate time of migration. In one experiment, willow warblers (a European species) were captured from the wild and kept in cages in which 12 hours of light alternated with 12 hours of darkness each day (Gwinner, 1986). For the next three years, the birds showed a characteristic *migratory restlessness* every fall and every spring. Their self-generated "years" ran faster than the true calendar, however, and the birds gradually drifted out of phase with the seasons in the real world.

Evidently, a mechanism somewhere in the bird's body generates a rhythm that prepares the bird for seasonal changes. We refer to that rhythm as an **endogenous circannual rhythm**. (*Endogenous* means *generated from within. Circannual* comes from the Latin words *circum*, for *about*, and *annum*, for *year*. An endogenous circannual rhythm is thus a self-generated rhythm that lasts about a year.) Similar mechanisms underlie a mammal's seasonal changes in reproduction, body fat, and hibernation. In nature, the daily onset of light and darkness fine-tunes such mechanisms to prevent them from running too fast or too slow.

Similarly, animals produce **endogenous circadian rhythms**—rhythms that last about a day. (*Circadian* comes from *circum*, for *about*, and *dies*, for *day*.) Our most familiar endogenous circadian rhythm is the one that controls wakefulness and sleepiness. If you go without sleep all night—as most college students do, sooner or later—you feel sleepier and sleepier as the night goes on, until early morning. But as morning arrives, you actually begin to feel less sleepy. Evidently, your urge to sleep depends on the time of day, separately from how recently you have slept.

Figure 10.1 represents the activity of an animal (in this case, a flying squirrel) kept in total darkness for 25 days. Each horizontal line represents one 24-hour day. A thickening in the line represents a period of activity by the animal. Even in this unchanging environment, animals generate a regular rhythm of activity and sleep. The self-generated cycle may be slightly shorter than 24 hours, as in Figure 10.1, or slightly longer, depending on whether the environment is constantly light or constantly dark and on whether the species is normally active in the light or in the dark (Carpenter & Grossberg, 1984). The cycle may also vary from one individual to another, even in the same environment. Nevertheless, the rhythm is highly consistent for a given individual in a given environment.

## Setting and Resetting the Cycle

Although an animal's circadian rhythm can persist in the absence of light, light is critical for periodically resetting the **biological clock** that underlies the rhythm. A biological clock is the internal mechanism for controlling a behavior—such as sleep or migration—that recurs on a regular schedule. As an analogy, consider a wristwatch. I used to have a windup wristwatch that lost about 2 minutes per day. If I continued to wind the watch but never reset it, it would be an hour slow after a month. We could say that it had a **free-running rhythm** of 24 hours 2 minutes. The biological clock is similar to my wristwatch. Because its free-running rhythm is not exactly 24 hours, it has to be reset daily. The stimulus that resets it is often referred to by the German term **zeitgeber** (TSITE-gay-behr), meaning *time-giver*. Light is the dominant zeitgeber for land animals (Rusak & Zucker, 1979); temperature, social stimuli, and other events may help to reset the clock, but the influence of light generally overrules all else. (The tides are a more important zeitgeber for certain marine animals.)

Humans, too, can generate circadian activity rhythms different from 24 hours, if they stay in caves or other artificial environments that isolate them from sunlight and other cues to time. In fact, even if other time cues are present, the absence of light may free the endogenous rhythms to drift out of phase with real time. One blind person reported that he could sometimes sleep and wake normally, but at other times felt sleepy all day and wakeful all night. Investigators found that he had a free-running rhythm of 24.9 hours for body temperature, alertness, and other functions (Miles, Raynal, & Wilson, 1977). Although he could wake and sleep on schedule whenever his endogenous rhythm was in phase with the outside world, he experienced severe troubles when it was out of phase.

## Attempts to Alter the Biological Clock

Is it possible to change a person's biological clock so that it will produce a different endogenous rhythm? If humans moved to a planet with, say, 20-hour days or 30-hour days, would they adjust easily, or would they have to undergo countless generations of evolutionary change before they felt really at home? In an effort to answer such questions, two volunteers spent a month deep in an isolated part of Mammoth Cave in Kentucky (Kleitman, 1963). The temperature (12° C) and relative humidity (100 percent) were constant at all times, and the only light they saw was the artificial light controlled by a fixed schedule.

Throughout the month in the cave, the set schedule was a 28-hour day, with 19 hours of activity alternating with 9 hours of sleep. One subject (R in Figure 10.2) adjusted reasonably well to the new schedule; his body temperature cycle matched his activity cycle, with low body temperature occurring while he slept. However, he was always sleepy well before the scheduled bedtime, and he had trouble awakening at the scheduled times. The other subject (K in Figure 10.2) was much less successful. He continued to feel sleepy only at his usual bedtime, once every 24 hours, and his body temperature continued to fluctuate on a 24-hour cycle. He had great trouble getting to sleep when the artificial cycle was out of phase with his original cycle. Even by the end of the month, he showed no sign of adjusting to the 28-hour schedule.

Other experimenters have also attempted to train people or laboratory ani-

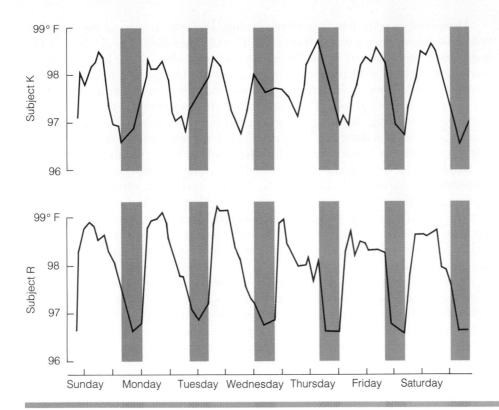

**Figure 10.2
Curves of weekly body temperature of two men under an artificial routine of 19 hours of wakefulness and 9 hours of sleep**
*Shaded areas represent time in bed. K's weekly record has seven 24-hour curves, but R adapted fairly well to the 28-hour schedule; the shaded areas show his temperature minima. (From Kleitman, 1963.)*

mals to follow a cycle other than 24 hours. As a rule, the adjustment is more successful if the imposed cycle is close to 24 hours. In one experiment, a group of 12 young people lived in a cavelike environment, isolated from natural light and other time cues, for 3 weeks. They agreed to go to bed when the clock said 11:45 P.M. and to awaken when it said 7:45 A.M. Although they did not know it, the clock initially ran normally and then gradually ran faster, until it was completing a day in only 22 normal-length hours. When the clock was completing a day in 23 hours, the people were alert during their wakeful periods and reported no trouble awakening on schedule or falling asleep on schedule. On a 22-hour schedule, however, only one subject kept pace with the clock. For the others, alertness rose and fell on a free-running 24-hour cycle that quickly drifted out of phase with the waking-sleeping schedule (Folkard, Hume, Minors, Waterhouse, & Watson, 1985). Evidently, humans find it difficult to adjust to a waking-sleeping cycle much different from 24 hours per day.

## One Biological Clock or More?

Mammals, including humans, have circadian rhythms in their waking and sleeping, frequency of eating and drinking, body temperature, secretion of certain hormones, volume of urination, sensitivity to certain drugs (Moore-Ede, Czeisler, & Richardson, 1983b), frequency of yawning (Anías, Holmgren, Urbá Holmgren, & Equíbar, 1984), and many other variables. Does a single clock underlie all the separate rhythms? Or does the body have more?

The Alternation
of Sleeping and
Waking

Humans appear to have at least two biological clocks. In several experiments, people who have been isolated from sunlight and other contact with the outside world have been allowed to sleep and awaken whenever they choose, neither knowing nor caring what time it is outside. Most of these people maintain a consistent 24- to 25-hour cycle, but an occasional individual starts living on a peculiar cycle, such as 29 hours of wakefulness alternating with 21 hours of sleep. Their cycles of eating, drinking, urination, and hormone secretions stay in phase with their cycles of waking and sleeping. Their body temperature does not, however. Ordinarily, the temperature in the interior of the body (not the skin) rises in the middle of the day to just over 37° C and falls at night to just over 36° C. Body temperature continues to follow a 24- to 25-hour cycle even when the person is following an idiosyncratic cycle for waking and sleeping (Aschoff, Gerecke, & Wever, 1967; Aschoff & Wever, 1976; Czeisler, Weitzman, Moore-Ede, Zimmerman, & Knauer, 1980). Evidently, humans have at least two mechanisms underlying circadian rhythms, one that controls activity levels and one that controls body temperature.

The brain seems to have a primary or "master" clock that drives both the activity level clock and the body temperature clock, keeping them in phase with each other. However, under certain circumstances they can get out of phase (Johnson & Hastings, 1986). Furthermore, it is possible to disrupt one clock without disrupting the other. For example, certain kinds of brain damage in animals can disrupt the circadian rhythm of drinking (which is highly correlated with the activity cycle) without disrupting the circadian rhythm of temperature (Fuller et al., 1981).

## RESETTING THE BIOLOGICAL CLOCK

When evolution built in humans' biological clock, it missed. Instead of giving us a 24-hour clock, it gave us a clock of about 24½ or 24¾ hours. We have to readjust our internal workings every day to stay in phase with the outside world. On weekends, when most of us are freer to follow the dictates of our nature, we tend to stay awake later than usual and awaken later than usual. By Monday morning, when the electric clock says the time is 7 A.M., the biological clock says it is about 5 A.M. (Moore-Ede, Czeisler, & Richardson, 1983a).

### Jet Lag

Because the human biological clock tends to run slower than 24 hours, most of us find it easier to adjust to crossing time zones going west than going east. Going west, we stay awake later at night and awaken later in the morning than we would have at home. Going east, we go to sleep earlier and awaken earlier. In one study, a group of healthy young men reported psychological discomfort and unsatisfactory sleep after crossing seven time zones going east; they took 11 days to return to normal. Such a disruption of biological rhythms is known as **jet lag** (Figure 10.3). A trip west over seven time zones produced no serious complaints (Désir et al., 1981).

### Shift Work and Night Shifts

People who have to sleep irregularly—such as pilots and truck drivers, medical interns, and shift workers in certain factories—find that their duration of sleep depends on their time of going to sleep. When they go to sleep in the morning or early afternoon, after working all night, they sleep only briefly (Frese & Harwich,

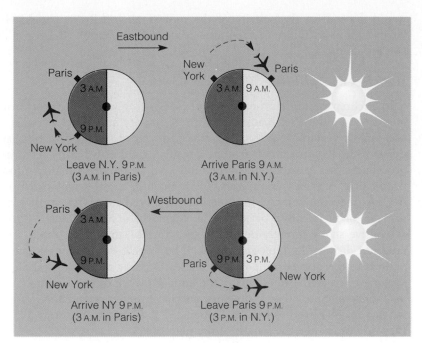

**Figure 10.3**
**Jet lag**
*When people travel east, their new time is later than their home time. People who travel six time zones east must wake up when their biological clocks say it is the middle of the night; they must go to bed when their biological clocks say it is just late afternoon. Most people adjust more easily when they travel west; they stay up later at night and sleep later in the morning.*

1984). They sleep the longest when they go to sleep in the early or middle part of the night. If they do not get to sleep until very late at night or early in the morning, they do not sleep for long (Winfree, 1983).

Some people work in factories or other jobs on a night shift, such as midnight to 8 A.M., and then sleep during the day. Even after working months or years on such a schedule, many workers fail to adjust fully. They continue to feel a little groggy while on the job, they do not sleep soundly during the day, and their body temperature continues to peak during the day, like that of most people, instead of peaking at night while they are working. In general, night-shift workers perform less well and have more accidents than day workers. In short, working at night does not reliably shift the circadian rhythm.

However, exposure to bright lights does. In one study, two groups of young men were active all night and slept during the day. One group was exposed to very bright lights (7,000 to 12,000 lux) during their night activity periods; the other was not. Within 6 days, the men who were exposed to the bright lights had readjusted. They were alert at night, they slept well during the day, and their body temperature reached its peak at night. The other group showed no signs of adjusting to the new schedule (Czeisler et al., 1990). The moral: Night-shift workers should be exposed to bright lights during their work period.

## LOCATION AND NATURE OF THE BIOLOGICAL CLOCK

Given that our biological cycles are generated within the body, we must have a clock somewhere—a physical mechanism that produces 24-hour rhythms. The biological clock might depend on any number of possible mechanisms. We might imagine a device that counts heartbeats or breaths, for example, as an indication of the passage of time. Such a mechanism would be inaccurate, however; its speed would depend on the activity of the individual. Ideally, it should be like your wristwatch in its ability to keep time accurately no matter where you are or what you are doing.

## Interference with the Biological Clock

Curt Richter found that the biological clock is insensitive to most forms of interference. An animal's circadian rhythm of activity and sleep remains intact after blinding or deafening, although it may drift out of phase with the real world because of the loss of zeitgebers. The circadian rhythm is hardly disturbed at all by procedures that greatly modify the total level of activity, including food or water deprivation, X rays, tranquilizers, LSD, alcohol, anesthesia, lack of oxygen, long periods of forced activity, long periods of forced inactivity, most kinds of brain damage, or the removal of any of the hormonal organs (Richter, 1967). Electroconvulsive shock severely depresses an animal's activity for about a week, but it does not disrupt the biological clock. The animal eventually resumes its activity periods at the normal time of day, indicating that the biological clock has been keeping track of the time during the animal's week of just sitting. Certain drugs, including caffeine, other stimulants, and barbiturates, can act as zeitgebers to reset the clock (Ehret, Potter, & Dobra, 1975; Mayer & Scherer, 1975), although they do not change the length of the period.

In one experiment, Curt Richter (1975) put some rats and hamsters in a refrigerated jar for 1 to 4 hours, lowering their breathing rate, heart rate, and brain activity almost to a standstill. He wanted to find out whether the biological clock in some manner monitored heartbeats, brain waves, or anything else that depended on temperature or body activity. The next day some of the animals — 6 of the 15 rats and 13 of the 27 hamsters — awakened 1 to 4 hours later than usual. In other words, their biological clocks had "lost" the hours spent at a lower temperature. However, an additional 8 rats and 14 hamsters awakened *at the normal time* the following day. (One rat became permanently inactive.) Figure 10.4 shows the activity record for one of these hamsters. In other words, the circadian rhythm in this group proceeded normally, despite a 1- to 4-hour depression of their heart rate and overall brain activity.

In a later experiment, Finley Gibbs (1983) confirmed Richter's finding that lowering a hamster's body temperature for 3 hours did not slow its biological clock much. However, Gibbs found that lowering it for longer periods slowed the clock substantially. That is, the biological clock could operate at a near-normal rate in the cold, but only for a limited time. Still, the conclusion remains that only major interference can disrupt the biological clock.

According to Richter (1965, 1970), the interventions that most seriously disturbed the biological clock were substitution of heavy water ($D_2O$) for normal water in the diet and damage to the hypothalamus. Exposure to heavy water can impair the ability of the biological clock to generate 24-hour rhythms; the basis for this effect is not well understood.

## Role of the Suprachiasmatic Nucleus

Later researchers determined more precisely the area of the hypothalamus where damage disrupts the biological clock: the **suprachiasmatic** (soo-pruh-kie-as-MAT-ik) **nucleus,** abbreviated **SCN.** It gets its name from the fact that it is located just above the optic chiasm (see Figure 10.5). The optic nerve sends some branches directly from the retina to the SCN. If the connections from those axons to the SCN are damaged, light can no longer reset the biological clock, even

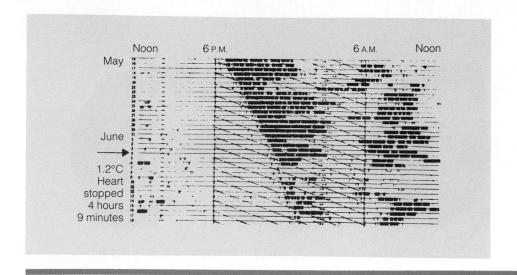

**Figure 10.4**
**The activity record for a hamster whose body temperature was reduced to about 1° C for just over 4 hours**
*Each horizontal line represents the activity for one day. A thickening in the line represents a period of activity. In an unchanging environment, this hamster was producing an endogenous activity rhythm lasting a little more than 24 hours. After the day of refrigeration, this hamster shows an overall depression of activity, but the activity it does show occurs at the normal time. That is, refrigeration did not stop the timing mechanism in this hamster. (From Richter, 1975.)*

though the individual can still see (Rusak, 1977). However, after damage to the axons supplying input to the lateral geniculate, an animal loses all pattern vision, and yet light continues to reset the biological clock (Moore & Eichler, 1972). In short, the visual pathway to the SCN is independent of the pathways responsible for pattern vision. Therefore, animals that become blind because of brain damage still synchronize their activity to periods of light and darkness.

The SCN generates rhythms itself. If neurons of the SCN are removed from an animal's brain, or if they are left in place but are disconnected by cuts from the rest of the brain, the SCN neurons nevertheless produce a pattern of impulses that follows a circadian rhythm (Green & Gillette, 1982; Inouye & Kawamura, 1979).

The SCN alone is responsible for an animal's circadian rhythm of waking and sleeping. One group of experimenters discovered some hamsters bearing a mutant gene that caused them to produce not a 24-hour rhythm, but a 20-hour rhythm (Ralph & Menaker, 1988). They surgically removed the SCN from adult hamsters and then transplanted SCN tissue from hamster fetuses into the adults. When they transplanted SCNs from fetuses with a 20-hour rhythm, the recipients produced a 20-hour rhythm. When they transplanted SCNs from fetuses with a 24-hour rhythm, the recipients produced a 24-hour rhythm. The recipients' rhythm no longer matched their own genes, but only the genes of the SCN donor (Ralph, Foster, Davis, & Menaker, 1990).

After damage to the SCN, animals lose their circadian rhythms of activity but not necessarily their rhythms of body temperature (Turek, 1985). In certain cases, damage to the SCN causes a temporary loss of the temperature cycle, or a

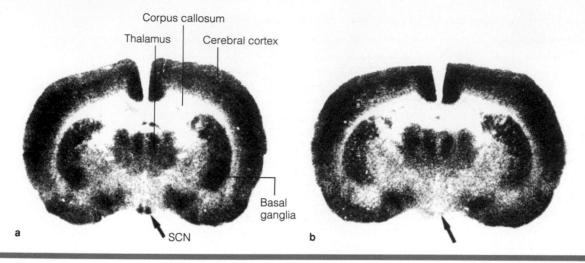

Corpus callosum
Thalamus        Cerebral cortex
Basal
ganglia
a        SCN        b

**Figure 10.5
The suprachiasmatic
nucleus (SCN) of rats,
studied by auto-
radiography**

*The SCN is located at the
base of the brain, just above
the optic chiasm, which has
torn off in these coronal sections through the plane of the
anterior hypothalamus. Each
rat was injected with radioactive 2-deoxyglucose, which is
absorbed by the most active
neurons. A high level of absorption of this chemical produces a dark appearance on
the slide. Note that the level
of activity in SCN neurons is
much higher in section (a), in
which the rat was injected
during the day, than it is in
section (b), in which the rat
received the injection at night.
(From Schwartz & Gainer,
1977.)*

weakening of it, or a change in its speed (Prosser, Kittrell, & Satinoff, 1984). Evidently, the SCN contains the biological clock for activity, while a second biological clock, responsible for temperature variations, lies partly outside the SCN but
is heavily influenced by a healthy SCN.

Knowing that the suprachiasmatic nucleus generates a circadian rhythm does
not tell us *how* it does so, however. The mechanism remains obscure.

## THE FUNCTIONS OF SLEEP

The suprachiasmatic nucleus and other mechanisms of the biological clock control the timing of sleep, but they are not responsible for sleep itself, any more
than they are responsible for eating, drinking, urinating, or any other activity that
follows a circadian rhythm.

Presumably, animals would not have evolved mechanisms that provide alternating periods of activity and sleep unless sleep serves some important function.
But exactly what is that function?

### The Repair and Restoration Theory of Sleep

According to the **repair and restoration theory of sleep,** the function of sleep is
to enable the body to repair itself after the exertions of the day. Many restorative
processes—such as digestion, removal of waste products, and protein synthesis—
occur during sleep (Adam, 1980). However, these same processes also occur during the waking state, and some of them actually occur more during the waking
state than they do during sleep. James Horne's (1988) extensive review of the literature led him to conclude that sleep does not provide any special repair or
restoration functions in humans, except in the brain. That is, the organs outside
the brain get just as much repair during a relaxed wakeful state as they do during
sleep.

The brain, however, is another story. You can rest your muscles while you
are awake, but not your brain. A certain amount of sleep may be necessary to restore the brain to full functioning (Horne, 1988).

One way to examine how sleep restores the brain is to observe the effects of sleep deprivation. People who have gone without sleep for a week or more, either as an experiment or as a publicity stunt, report dizziness, impaired concentration, irritability, hand tremors, and hallucinations (Dement, 1972; Johnson, 1969). Prolonged sleep deprivation in animals (mostly rats) generally produces much more severe consequences, including death (Rechtschaffen, Gilliland, Bergmann, & Winter, 1983). There are good reasons for this apparent difference in species: First, the humans who went without sleep did so voluntarily; they knew how long the study would last, and they knew they could quit if they found the strain unbearable. The rats had no way to predict or control their situation. (Stressors take a greater toll when they are unpredictable and uncontrollable.) Second, because the rats were not participating voluntarily, the experimenters constantly had to prod them and stimulate them in various ways to keep them awake. The rats' health deteriorated not only from sleep deprivation but also from continuous stimulation (Horne, 1988).

Still, the behavioral impairments that humans experience after sleep deprivation confirm that sleep does serve restorative functions. Sleep is not analogous to stopping to catch your breath after running a race, however. If sleep were restorative in that simple sense, we should expect people to sleep significantly more after a day of great physical or mental exertion than after an uneventful day. Great exertion does increase sleep duration, but only slightly. People who ran a 92 km marathon slept poorly on the night after the race, because of multiple aches and pains, but they slept longer than usual the next three nights (Shapiro, Bortz, Mitchell, Bartel, & Jooste, 1981). People in one experiment spent a day visiting an exhibition, a shopping center, a museum, an amusement park, a zoo, and a movie and taking several scenic drives. After this most active and stimulating day, they fell asleep faster than usual but slept no longer than usual (Horne & Minard, 1985). Apparently, how much sleep we need does not depend strongly on how active we were during the day.

Moreover, a few people manage to satisfy their restorative needs in far less than the customary 7 to 8 hours. Two men have been reported to average only 3 hours of sleep per night and to awaken feeling refreshed (Jones & Oswald, 1968). A 70-year-old woman was reported to average only 1 hour of sleep per night; many nights she felt no need to sleep at all (Meddis, Pearson, & Langford, 1973).

## The Evolutionary Theory of the Need for Sleep

Given that the duration of sleep bears little relationship to the activity of the previous day, several theorists have offered an alternative explanation of why we sleep. According to the **evolutionary theory of sleep** (Kleitman, 1963; Webb, 1974), the function of sleep is similar to that of **hibernation,** a special adaptation of certain mammalian species to a season when food is scarce (see Digression 10.1). Hibernating animals' heart rate, breathing, brain activity, and metabolism decrease greatly; they generate only enough body heat to prevent themselves from freezing.

Hibernation is a true need; a ground squirrel that is prevented from hibernating can get as disturbed as a person who is prevented from sleeping. However, the function of hibernation is not to recover from a busy summer; it is simply to conserve energy when the environment is hostile. Similarly, according to the evolutionary theory, the primary function of sleep is to force us to conserve energy when we would be relatively inefficient. The evolutionary theory does not deny that we need to sleep; it merely asserts that evolution built that need into us for a special reason.

## Some Facts About Hibernation

1. Hibernation occurs in certain small mammals such as ground squirrels and bats. It is a matter of definition whether we can say that bears hibernate. Bears sleep most of the winter, but they do not lower their body temperatures the way smaller animals do. *Microcebus*, a primate that lives in Madagascar, sleeps 4 to 6 hours more per day in the winter than it does in the summer (Barre & Petter-Rousseaux, 1988).

2. Hamsters sometimes hibernate. If you keep your pet hamster in a cold, poorly lit place during the winter, and it appears to die, make sure it is not just hibernating before you bury it!

3. Hibernation retards the aging process. Hamsters that spend longer times hibernating have proportionately longer life expectancies than other hamsters do (Lyman, O'Brien, Greene, & Papafrangos, 1981).

4. Hibernating animals produce a chemical that suppresses metabolism and temperature regulation. H. Swan and C. Schätte (1977) injected extracts from the brains of hibernating ground squirrels into the brains of rats, a nonhibernating species. The rats decreased their metabolism and body temperature. Similar brain extracts from nonhibernating ground squirrels had no apparent effect on the rats.

5. Hibernating animals awaken in the spring around the time when food becomes available. Male ground squirrels awaken a few days earlier than the females. Their early awakening is presumably an evolutionary adaptation to the fact that the males compete with one another for mates and that mating occurs as soon as the females awaken. (Males who awaken early are sure to be ready as soon as the females are. Males who awaken at about the same time as the females might miss a chance at any female who awakened a bit early.) Because the males awaken before the females, who awaken at about the time that food becomes available, the males must survive several days without food. They have to gain an enormous amount of weight in the fall to get through both the winter and a few days of full activity in the spring before they can find any food (French, 1988).

The evolutionary theory predicts that animal species should vary in how much sleep they need depending on how much time each day they must devote to the search for food, how safe they are from predators when they sleep, and other aspects of their way of life. In general, the data support these predictions (Allison & Cicchetti, 1976; Campbell & Tobler, 1984).

Horses, cows, and other animals that graze most of the day sleep relatively few hours. Cats and other predators that usually eat just one meal per day sleep much longer. Species that are frequently attacked by predators and whose only defense is their ability to run away (for example, rabbits, sheep, and goats) sleep relatively few hours per night and awaken at slight noises. Cats, dogs, and other species that are seldom attacked spend more hours sleeping and are not awakened easily by stray sounds. Bats, which live in caves that offer excellent protection against predators, are also heavy sleepers (see Figure 10.6).

Although the evolutionary theory of sleep has considerable appeal, it also has its critics (for example, Hauri, 1979). In particular, they argue, the theory seems to predict that sheep, goats, and similar species should not sleep at all, since they are vulnerable to attack when they sleep. The fact that they do sleep suggests that every animal needs some sleep to survive.

The evolutionary theory makes one prediction that has not been tested: A species that has evolved in an environment that does not change during the day

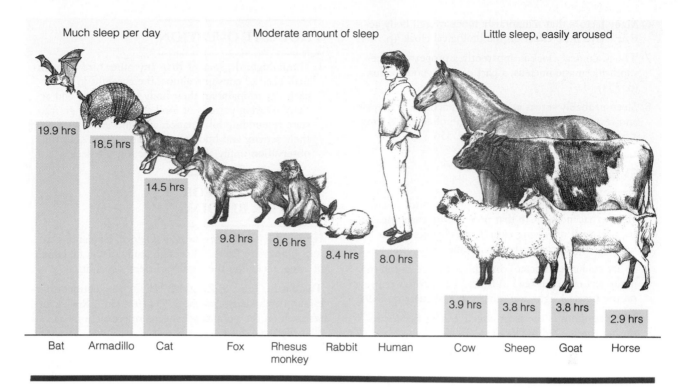

| Much sleep per day | | | Moderate amount of sleep | | | | Little sleep, easily aroused | | | |

19.9 hrs
18.5 hrs
14.5 hrs
9.8 hrs
9.6 hrs
8.4 hrs
8.0 hrs
3.9 hrs
3.8 hrs
3.8 hrs
2.9 hrs

| Bat | Armadillo | Cat | Fox | Rhesus monkey | Rabbit | Human | Cow | Sheep | Goat | Horse |

**Figure 10.6**
**Hours of sleep per day for various animal species**
*Generally, predators and others that are safe when they sleep tend to sleep a great deal; animals in danger of being attacked while they sleep spend less time asleep.*

should not sleep at any consistent time of day, if indeed it sleeps at all. For example, deep-sea fish and cave-dwelling fish live in an environment with no light and almost no changes in temperature. Little is known about the sleep habits of such species. In fact, little is known about the sleep of fish in general (Karmanova, 1982).

Which theory of sleep is right? Actually, adherents of each theory concede that the other is partly right. Suppose you believe that the main function of sleep is to repair and restore the brain. Surely you will grant that each species confines its sleep to those hours when it is least efficient at doing anything else and, furthermore, that species that can afford long periods of inactivity (predators) will evolve a tendency to sleep longer than species that must remain constantly vigilant (prey). Now suppose you believe that the main function of sleep is to conserve energy. Surely you will agree that while an animal is lying around doing nothing else anyway, sleep might be a good time for some repair and restoration functions. In short, the two theories do not directly conflict with each other.

## SUMMARY

1. Animals, including humans, have internally generated rhythms of activity and other functions, approximating both a 24-hour cycle and a 1-year cycle. (p. 348)

2. Although the biological clock can continue to operate in constant light or constant darkness, the onset of light at a particular time can reset the clock. (p. 350)

3. The biological clock can keep pace with an external

rhythm of light and darkness slightly different from 24 hours, but it ignores the external rhythm if the discrepancy is more than 1 or 2 hours. (p. 350)

4. Under certain circumstances, the circadian rhythm of temperature may get out of phase with the activity-sleep rhythm; the two rhythms may even follow different periods. (p. 352)

5. It is easier for people to follow a cycle longer than 24 hours than to follow a cycle shorter than 24 hours. (p. 352)

6. Many factors that temporarily block overall body activity have little effect on the biological clock. (p. 354)

7. The biological clock is apparently a property of the suprachiasmatic nucleus, a part of the hypothalamus. (p. 354)

8. Sleep probably serves at least two functions: (1) repair and restoration and (2) conservation of energy during a period of relative inefficiency. (p. 356)

## REVIEW QUESTIONS

1. Why is it advantageous for a migratory bird to have an internal mechanism that predicts the changing seasons, instead of relying entirely on changes in the light/dark patterns in the environment? (p. 348)

2. What evidence indicates that the body has an internal biological clock, instead of timing its activities entirely on the basis of light and other external cues? (p. 349)

3. What stimulus is the most effective zeitgeber for resetting the biological clock? (p. 350)

4. Which direction of travel is most likely to produce jet lag? (p. 352)

5. What are some factors that do and do not interfere with the biological clock? (p. 354)

6. What is the evidence that the suprachiasmatic nucleus generates circadian rhythms of activity? (p. 354)

7. State the strengths and weaknesses of the repair and restoration theory and the evolutionary theory of the need for sleep. (p. 356)

## THOUGHT QUESTION

1. Hummingbirds, smaller than any other bird or mammal, need to consume almost their weight in nectar each day to maintain their body temperature and activity. During periods of food shortage, they go into a state resembling hibernation at night, greatly lowering their activity and body temperature. What does this observation imply about the functions of sleep?

## SUGGESTIONS FOR FURTHER READING

**Horne, J.** (1988). *Why we sleep.* Oxford, England: Oxford University Press. Thorough study of the functions of sleep, including the results of sleep deprivation.

**Takahashi, J. S., & Zatz, M.** (1982). Regulation of circadian rhythmicity. *Science, 217,* 1104–1111. Review of research on the brain mechanisms responsible for circadian rhythms.

# Sleeping and Dreaming

Advances in scientific research usually result from improvements in our ability to measure something. Sleep research is no exception. The electroencephalograph (EEG), mentioned in Chapter 4, records a gross average of the electrical potentials of the cells and fibers in a particular part of the brain by means of an electrode attached to the scalp (see Figure 10.7). It displays a net average of all the neurons' potentials. That is, if half the cells increase their electrical potentials while the other half decrease, the EEG recording is a flat line. The EEG record rises or falls only when a number of cells fire in synchrony—doing the same thing at the same time. You might compare it to a record of the noise in a crowded football stadium: It shows only slight fluctuations from time to time until some event gets everyone yelling at once.

The EEG provides an objective way for brain researchers to determine whether people are awake or asleep without relying on the people's self-reports. The EEG also enables researchers to compare brain activity at one time of night to activity at a different time of night. Such research has led to the identification of several distinct stages of sleep.

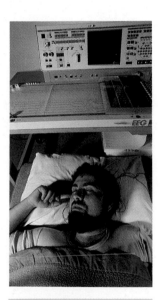

**Figure 10.7**
**Sleeping person with electrodes in place on the scalp for recording brain activity**
*The printout above his head shows the readings from each electrode. (Photo from Richard Nowitz.)*

## THE STAGES OF SLEEP

Figure 10.8 shows the EEG and eye movement records from a male college student during the various stages of sleep. Figure 10.8a begins with a period of relaxed wakefulness for comparison. Note the steady series of waves at a frequency of about 10 per second, known as **alpha waves.** Alpha waves are characteristic of the relaxed state, not of all wakefulness.

In Figure 10.8b the young man has just fallen asleep. During this period, called stage 1 sleep, brain activity is said to be desynchronized; the neurons are not all doing the same thing at the same time. The EEG in stage 1 is dominated by **theta waves,** which are irregular, jagged, and low in voltage.

As Figure 10.8c shows, the most prominent characteristics of stage 2 are sleep spindles and K-complexes. A **sleep spindle** is a burst of 12 to 14 Hz waves lasting at least half a second. A **K-complex** is a sharp high-amplitude negative

**Figure 10.8
Polysomnograph
records from a male
college student**
*A polysomnograph includes
records of EEG, eye move-
ments, and sometimes other
data, such as muscle tension
or head movements. For each
of these records, the top line is
the EEG from one electrode
on the scalp; the middle line is
a record of eye movements;
and the bottom line is a time
marker, indicating 1-second
units. Note the abundance of
slow waves in stages 3 and 4.
(Records provided by T. E.
LeVere.)*

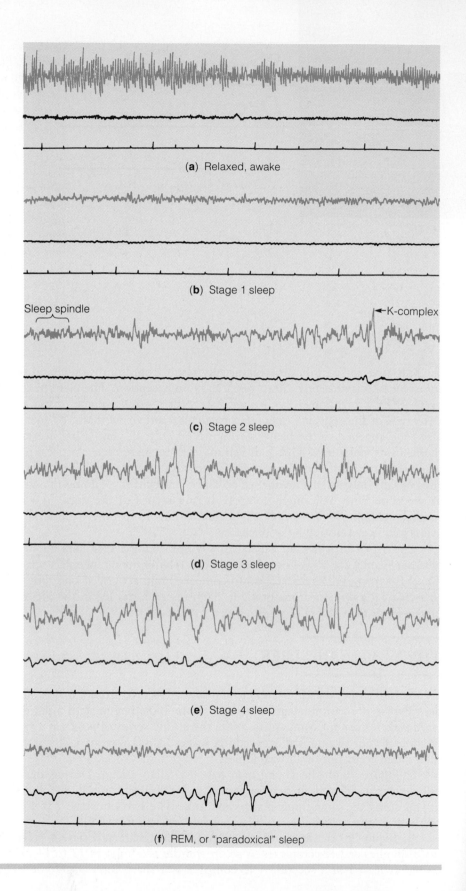

(**a**)  Relaxed, awake

(**b**)  Stage 1 sleep

Sleep spindle

←K-complex

(**c**)  Stage 2 sleep

(**d**)  Stage 3 sleep

(**e**)  Stage 4 sleep

(**f**)  REM, or "paradoxical" sleep

wave followed by a smaller, slower positive wave. Sudden stimuli can evoke K-complexes during other stages of sleep, but they are most common in stage 2.

In each succeeding stage of sleep, heart rate, breathing rate, and brain activity are slower than in the previous stage, and the percentage of slow, large-amplitude waves increases (see Figure 10.8d and e). By stage 4, more than half the record includes large waves of at least a half-second duration. Stages 3 and 4 are known together as **slow-wave sleep (SWS).**

Slow waves indicate that neuronal activity is highly synchronized. In stage 1 or in wakefulness, the cortex receives much input, so various cells are rapidly excited and inhibited out of phase with one another. By stage 4, however, sensory input to the cerebral cortex has been greatly reduced, and the few remaining sources of input can synchronize many cells. As an analogy, imagine the barrage of stimuli arriving at the brain of an alert person as being like dropping hundreds of rocks into a pond over the course of a minute; the resulting waves will largely cancel one another out. Although the surface of the pond will be choppy, it will have few large waves. Contrast that to the effect of dropping just one rock: The surface will have larger waves, like those seen in stage 4 sleep.

## PARADOXICAL, OR REM, SLEEP

A person who has just fallen asleep enters stage 1 sleep. Later in the night people may or may not return to stage 1; more commonly they enter a related but very special stage. Michel Jouvet has called this stage **paradoxical sleep** because it is in some ways the deepest sleep and in other ways the lightest. (The term *paradoxical* means *apparently self-contradictory.*) During paradoxical sleep, the EEG shows irregular, low-voltage fast waves, which suggest a considerable amount of brain activity. Heart rate and breathing rate are higher and more variable than in stages 2 through 4. In those regards paradoxical sleep is light. However, a person in this stage is more difficult to awaken than in any other stage. Furthermore, the postural muscles of the body, such as those that support the head, are more relaxed than in any other stage. In these regards paradoxical sleep is deep. This stage of sleep is also associated with erections in males and vaginal moistening in females. It is not obvious whether we should consider erections and vaginal secretions as indications of deep or light sleep. In short, paradoxical sleep combines deep sleep, light sleep, and ambiguous features. Consequently, most investigators now avoid using the terms *deep* and *light* sleep.

In addition to these steady characteristics, paradoxical sleep has certain intermittent characteristics, including facial and finger twitches. Because the eyes move back and forth under the closed lids (Figure 10.9), this stage has become widely known as **rapid eye movement (REM) sleep** (Aserinsky & Kleitman, 1955; Dement & Kleitman, 1957a). Researchers more commonly use the term *REM sleep* than *paradoxical sleep* when referring to humans. The term *paradoxical sleep* is preferred when dealing with certain animals, especially those without eye movements. This stage is also sometimes known as *desynchronized sleep, D sleep,* or *active sleep.*

Figure 10.8f provides the EEG and eye-movement records for a period of REM sleep. The EEG record is similar to that for stage 1 sleep, but notice how different the eye-movement records are. REM sleep is associated with many eye movements; eye movements are uncommon during other stages of sleep. For this reason the other stages are sometimes known as **non-REM sleep,** abbreviated NREM. They are also sometimes known as *synchronized sleep, S sleep,* or *quiet sleep.*

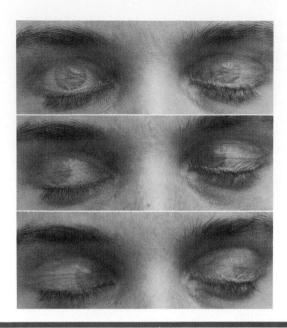

## Sleep Cycles

A person who falls asleep enters stage 1 and slowly progresses through stages 2, 3, and 4 in order. External stimuli can halt this progression, however. For example, noises during stage 3 can prolong this stage or cause a reversion to stage 2, stage 1, or even wakefulness.

About 60 to 90 minutes after going to sleep, the person begins gradually to cycle from stage 4 back through stage 3, stage 2, and then REM sleep. After a period of REM sleep, the sequence repeats, with each complete cycle lasting about 90 to 100 minutes. Early in the night, stages 3 and 4 predominate. Toward morning, the duration of stage 4 grows shorter and the duration of REM sleep grows longer. Figure 10.10 shows typical sequences.

## REM Sleep and Dreaming

REM sleep is associated with dreaming, although the relationship is not perfect. Researchers can determine the sleep stage of a person by monitoring EEG records and eye movements. William Dement and Nathaniel Kleitman (1957b) awakened adult volunteers during various stages of sleep. They found that people awakened during REM sleep reported dreams about 80 to 90 percent of the time. Those dreams often included elaborate visual imagery and complicated plots. People awakened during slow-wave sleep reported dreams less frequently. The percentage of reported dreams in non-REM sleep varies from one investigation to another, from less than 10 percent to more than 70 percent. Much of this discrepancy depends on whether investigators include vague, thoughtlike experiences as dreams or whether they limit dreams to complex experiences with well-defined visual imagery (Foulkes, 1967).

By awakening people during REM sleep, investigators have been able to answer questions that were previously a matter for speculation. For example, as far as we can determine, all normal humans dream. Everyone studied in the labora-

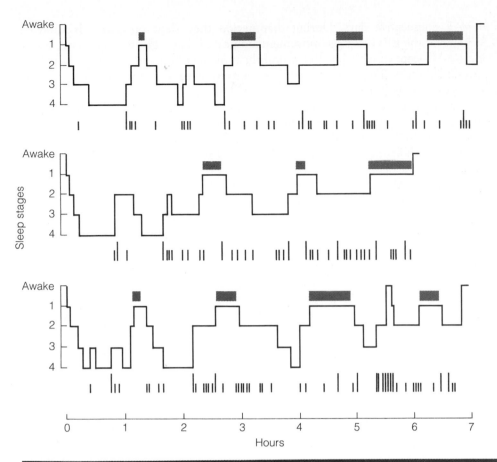

**Figure 10.10
Sequence of sleep stages on three representative nights**
*The horizontal color bars indicate periods of rapid eye movements. The vertical lines indicate body movements; the short lines are minor movements, and the long lines are changes in body position. (From Dement & Kleitman, 1957a.)*

tory has had periods of REM sleep. When people who claim they never dream are awakened during an REM period, they generally report dreams. Most of their dreams are less vivid than those of other people, however. Apparently, they believe they do not dream only because their dreams are not very memorable.

Furthermore, we now know that dreams last about as long as they seem to last, contrary to a once-popular belief that a dream lasts only a second or two. Dement and E. A. Wolpert (1958) awakened people after they had been in REM sleep for varying periods of time. The length of the dreams they reported corresponded closely to the length of the REM period prior to awakening, up to a limit of about 15 minutes. Beyond 15 minutes the volunteers did not report still longer dreams, perhaps because they had already forgotten the beginning of the dream by the time they got to the end of it.

## The Effects of REM Sleep Deprivation

On the average, we humans spend about one-third of our lives asleep and about one-fifth of our sleep in REM sleep. In other words, we spend almost 600 hours per year in REM sleep. What function does REM sleep serve? Dement (1960) observed the behavior of eight men who agreed to be deprived of REM sleep for

Sleeping and
Dreaming

4 to 7 consecutive days. During that period they slept only in a laboratory. Whenever the EEG and eye movements indicated that a given subject was entering REM sleep, an experimenter promptly awakened him and kept him awake for several minutes. The subject was then permitted to go back to sleep until he started REM sleep again.

Over the course of the 4 to 7 nights, the experimenters found that they had to awaken the subjects more and more frequently. On the first night, an average subject had to be awakened 12 times. By the final night, this figure had increased to 26 times. That is, the subjects had increased their "attempts" at REM sleep.

During the deprivation period, the subjects reported mild, temporary personality changes. Most reported increased anxiety, irritability, and impaired concentration. Five of the eight experienced increased appetite and weight gain. Control studies found that a similar number of awakenings not linked to REM sleep did not produce similar effects. The disturbances were therefore due to REM deprivation, not just to the total number of awakenings.

After the deprivation period, seven subjects continued to sleep in the laboratory. During their first uninterrupted night, five of the seven spent more time than usual in REM sleep; 29 percent of the night was devoted to REM sleep, as compared with 19 percent before the deprivation. One of the seven showed no increase. (The investigators discarded the results from the seventh subject, who came to the laboratory drunk that night. Alcohol suppresses REM sleep, so results from this subject would be unreliable.)

Similar experiments have been done with laboratory animals, for which it is possible to impose much longer periods of REM deprivation. Cats have been deprived of REM sleep for up to 70 consecutive days (see Dement, Ferguson, Cohen, & Barchas, 1969). Do not imagine shifts of experimenters monitoring cats 24 hours a day and prodding them whenever they enter REM sleep. Rather, they kept each cat on a tiny island surrounded by water. Although the cat could maintain its balance when awake or in non-REM sleep, as soon as it entered REM sleep its postural muscles relaxed, and it lost its balance and fell into the water. It could have no more than a few seconds of REM sleep at a time before awakening. Over the course of days, the cats placed in this situation made progressively more attempts to enter REM sleep. At the end of the deprivation period, they showed a rebound increase in the time spent in REM sleep. The greater the deprivation, up to about 25 to 30 days, the greater the rebound. Deprivation beyond 30 days did not increase the rebound further, possibly because at that point the cat was making so many attempts at REM sleep that it was getting in a great many very short REM periods prior to all the interruptions. During REM deprivation, a cat's behavior is abnormal in several regards. For example, many male cats will sexually mount almost anything that moves.

These and similar studies indicate a specific need for REM sleep in addition to the need for sleep in general. Exactly why animals need REM sleep is unclear, however. Before we speculate on that point, let us consider how individuals and species differ in the time they devote to REM sleep.

## Individual and Species Differences in REM Sleep

One way to shed light on the function of REM sleep is to see whether there are any consistent differences between animals that get a lot of REM sleep and those that get little. Nearly all mammals and birds show at least a small amount of

# On the Evolutionary Origins of REM Sleep

Nearly all mammals and birds show at least some REM sleep and so do a few reptiles such as the desert tortoise *Gopherus flavomarginatus* (Ayala-Guerrero, Caldéron, & Pérez, 1988). Apparently the capacity for REM sleep evolved long ago in ancient reptiles.

One species of mammal does not have REM sleep—the spiny anteater, or echidna. Spiny anteaters have long periods of slow-wave sleep but no periods with eye movements or aroused EEG or total relaxation of the postural muscles (Allison & Goff, 1968). Because spiny anteaters are among the most primitive of surviving mammals, we naturally wonder whether the original mammals (the ancestors of all of today's mammals) also lacked REM sleep. Maybe, but maybe not. Opossums, which are also very primitive mammals, have REM periods like those of other mammals (Van Twyver & Allison, 1970). Perhaps spiny anteaters have lost a trait their ancient ancestors had.

Fish and amphibians have periods of behavioral inactivity (sleep), although stimuli can arouse them fairly easily during these periods (Karmanova, 1982). They do not have two separate sleep rates, corresponding to REM and NREM, but only one sleep

*(Tom McHugh/PR.)*

state, generally considered to correspond to our non-REM sleep. Unfortunately, our usual definitions of REM sleep do not apply readily to fish or amphibians (Meddis, 1979). They do not produce EEG waves comparable to those of mammals, and they have few eye movements even while awake. And we can hardly ask them about their dreams.

REM sleep, indicating that the capacity for REM sleep is part of our ancient evolutionary heritage. (See Digression 10.2.)

If we compare species, the only pattern that stands out is that the percentage of REM sleep is greatest in those species that have the greatest total amount of sleep. Cats, which spend up to 16 hours a day sleeping, have a great deal of REM sleep. Rabbits, guinea pigs, and sheep, which sleep much less, have very little REM sleep.

Within a species, infants have a higher percentage of REM sleep than adults do. Figure 10.11 demonstrates this relationship for humans. The general trend is the same for most other mammalian species. REM sleep occupies an even greater percentage of total sleep time in premature infants (Astic, Sastre, & Brandon, 1973; Dreyfus-Brisac, 1970). We must admit some difficulty distinguishing between an infant in REM sleep and an infant who is awake but has his or her eyes closed (Lynch & Aserinsky, 1986). For that reason, the data on infants may not be entirely accurate.

The adult humans who get the most sleep per night (9 or more hours) have the highest percentage of REM sleep. Those who get the least total sleep (5 hours or less) spend the lowest percentage of their sleep on REM. From all these

Sleeping and
Dreaming

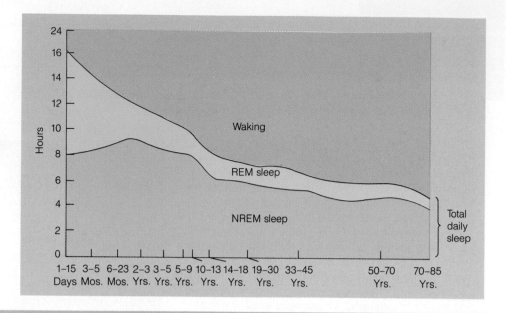

data, a pattern emerges: Across species, across ages, and across individuals, the greater the total amount of sleep, the greater the percentage of REM sleep.

In short, the amount of REM sleep varies more than the amount of non-REM sleep from one individual to another and from one time to another. Perhaps the need for non-REM sleep is greater than the need for REM sleep. After people or other species have been selectively deprived of REM sleep, their recovery sleep on the next night includes an increased proportion of REM sleep. But if they have been deprived of all sleep, their recovery sleep on the first uninterrupted night has an increased proportion of non-REM sleep (Borbély, 1982). Horne (1988) has therefore suggested that much of our REM sleep, perhaps as much as half of it, is "optional." That is, we could survive without it.

## What Is the Function of REM Sleep?

REM sleep appears to be paradoxical in yet another sense: Although deprivation studies indicate a need for REM sleep, the body apparently adds extra REM sleep time only after it has first satisfied its need for non-REM sleep.

Speculations on why we need REM sleep have been numerous. It has been linked to the consolidation of memory, brain growth, the need for periodic arousal of the brain during the night, suppression of inappropriate associations in the brain, and the dampening of excessively strong motivations. According to one suggestion, REM sleep is a method of clearing overloaded circuits (Crick & Mitchison, 1986). During the day, we store an enormous number of memories, distributing them widely over the brain and superimposing them on other memories already stored in the same places. Many of these new memories are useless, however. So REM sleep may be the result of a special kind of arousal that produces "reverse learning," the undoing of useless storage during the day.

At this point, we have no solid evidence for any of these interpretations. The function of REM sleep remains uncertain and a subject for continuing research.

# A BIOLOGICAL PERSPECTIVE ON DREAMING

For decades psychologists have been heavily influenced by Sigmund Freud's theory of dreams, which was based on the assumption that hidden and often unconscious wishes cause dreams. Although Freud was certainly correct in asserting that dreams reflect the dreamer's personality and recent experiences, his theory of the mechanism of dreams depended on a now-obsolete view of the nervous system (McCarley & Hobson, 1977). He believed, for example, that brain cells were inactive except when nerves from the periphery brought them energy. Freud was also hampered by relying on dream reports that his patients gave him hours or days after the dream occurred.

Given a more modern understanding of the brain and the capacity to awaken someone during REM sleep and get an almost immediate dream report, contemporary investigators have offered new interpretations of dream phenomena. According to one influential idea, the **activation-synthesis hypothesis,** during sleep various parts of the brain are activated—either spontaneously or by stimuli in the room—and the brain synthesizes some sort of story to make sense of all the activity (Hobson & McCarley, 1977; McCarley & Hoffman, 1981). According to a slightly different version of this hypothesis, the brain is aroused and ready to process information during REM sleep, but the environment provides few stimuli. Therefore, the individual begins processing information stored in memory, treating the stream of thought and imagery as if it were the real world (Antrobus, 1986).

While we sleep, we do not completely lose contact with external stimuli. (For example, except in early childhood we seldom roll out of the bed.) We incorporate many of the external stimuli into our dreams, at least in some modified form. If water is dripping on your foot, you may dream about swimming or about walking in the rain. In addition to the external stimuli, bursts of activity occur spontaneously in certain parts of the cerebral cortex, including the visual, auditory, and motor cortexes, plus various subcortical areas that contribute to motivation and emotion. According to the activation-synthesis hypothesis, your brain tries to make sense of that spontaneous activity, and the result is a dream. Not surprisingly, almost all dreams include visual imagery, and more than half include hearing or movement. Because the spontaneous activity of the brain shifts from moment to moment, dreams also contain sudden, sometimes bizarre, shifts in the action.

Occasional bursts of vestibular sensation are also common during REM sleep, perhaps because a sleeping person is generally lying prone instead of maintaining the usual upright position. According to the activation-synthesis hypothesis, the brain incorporates those vestibular sensations into the common dreams of falling, flying, or spinning.

Many people dream that they are trying to move but cannot. It is tempting to relate this dream to the fact that the major postural muscles are virtually paralyzed during REM sleep. That is, when you are dreaming, you really *can't* move. However, that explanation becomes less convincing when we realize how often people dream that they *are* moving. (The muscles are relaxed during both kinds of dreams.)

In short, during REM sleep the brain receives occasional external stimuli and is subject to spontaneous activation of various cortical areas. A dream may be the brain's attempt to make sense of that shifting array of stimuli.

*Dreams are real while they last. Can we say more of life?*

Havelock Ellis

Does this explanation conflict with psychotherapists' attempts to interpret the hidden, underlying meanings of dreams? Not necessarily. Different people create different stories out of the more-or-less random stimuli activating their brains during REM sleep; presumably each person relates those stimuli to his or her own recent experiences, hopes, and fears.

## SUMMARY

1. Sleep is composed of distinct stages that EEG records can identify. Stage 1 is a transition from wakefulness to sleep; stage 4 has the least brain activity. (p. 361)

2. One special stage of sleep is rapid eye movement (REM) sleep. During REM sleep an individual has much brain activity, very relaxed postural muscles, and many eye movements. Sleepers are generally difficult to arouse during REM sleep. (p. 363)

3. During a night's sleep, people cycle from stage 1 or REM sleep down to stage 4 and then back to REM or stage 1 again. A complete cycle lasts about 90 to 100 minutes. (p. 364)

4. People are more likely to report dreams, especially their more vivid dreams, when they are awakened from REM sleep than when they are awakened from other stages of sleep. (p. 364)

5. People who are deprived of REM sleep become irritable and report trouble in concentrating. After the end of a period of REM deprivation, people compensate for the loss by spending more time than usual in REM sleep. (p. 365)

6. REM sleep is most common in those individuals and species that spend the most total hours asleep. (p. 366)

7. According to the activation-synthesis hypothesis, dreams are the brain's attempts to make sense of limited, shifting, and somewhat random stimuli when the brain is aroused and ready to process information. (p. 369)

## REVIEW QUESTIONS

1. What is the EEG pattern when neuronal activity is synchronized? What is the pattern when activity is desynchronized? (p. 361)

2. How can an investigator determine whether a person is in sleep stage 1, 2, 3, 4, or REM? (p. 361)

3. Why do many sleep researchers avoid the terms *light sleep* and *deep sleep*? (p. 363)

4. Which sleep stages are most common early in the night? Which ones predominate later in the night? (p. 364)

5. What kinds of dreams (if any) occur during non-REM sleep? (p. 364)

6. Do all people dream? If so, why do some people believe that they do not? (p. 364)

7. What are the effects of REM sleep deprivation? (p. 365)

8. Which animal species have the largest amount of REM sleep? (p. 367)

9. When people are deprived of all sleep for more than 24 hours and then permitted to sleep uninterrupted, is their recovery sleep mostly REM sleep or non-REM sleep? (p. 368)

10. According to the activation-synthesis hypothesis of dreams, what determines the content of our dreams? (p. 369)

11. Offer a biological explanation for the sudden shifts that sometimes occur in dreams. (p. 369)

## THOUGHT QUESTION

1. Can you think of an adaptive explanation for why certain species spend more time in REM sleep than others do? (Hint: Think about which species get the least REM sleep. Think also about the relationship between REM and ease of arousal.)

## SUGGESTIONS FOR FURTHER READING

**Dement, W. C.** (1972). *Some must watch while some must sleep.* New York: Freeman. Highly engaging review of pioneering work on sleep and sleep stages.

**Moorcroft, W. H.** (1989). *Sleep, dreaming, & sleep disorders.* New York: Lanham. Review of later work on sleep and its disorders, clearly presented.

**Winson, J.** (1990, November). The meaning of dreams. *Scientific American, 263* (5), 86–96. Discusses theories of the function of REM sleep and the meaning of dreams.

# Brain Mechanisms in Sleep and Its Disorders

Suppose I buy a new radio. After I play it for 4 hours, it suddenly stops. To explain why it stopped, I would try to discover whether the batteries were dead or whether it needed repair. Suppose I discover that the radio will operate again a few hours later even without repairs or a battery change. I also discover that the radio always stops whenever I play it for 4 hours. I begin to suspect that the manufacturer designed it this way on purpose, perhaps to prevent me from wearing it out too fast or to prevent me from listening to the radio all day. I might then try to find the device in the radio that turns it off whenever I play it for 4 hours. Notice that I am now asking a new question. When I thought that the radio stopped because it needed repairs or new batteries, I would not have thought to ask which device turned the radio off. I ask that question only when I think of the stoppage as something other than an accidental, passive process.

The same is true for sleep. If we think of sleep only as a passive cessation of activity, similar to catching one's breath after running a race, we do not ask which part of the brain is responsible for sleep. But if we think of sleep as a specialized state evolved to serve particular functions, we may look for the devices that control it.

## WAKEFULNESS AND THE RETICULAR ACTIVATING SYSTEM

Making a cut through the midbrain, separating the forebrain and part of the midbrain from the rest of the midbrain, pons, medulla, and spinal cord (line A in Figure 10.12) produces the **cerveau isolé** (SEHR-voh EE-so-lay) preparation (French for *isolated forebrain*). The cerveau isolé animal goes into a prolonged state of sleep. The brain shows no signs of wakefulness in the EEG for the next week or so, and only brief periods of wakefulness later.

Most sensory information enters the nervous system at levels below the cut; thus, the cut isolates the brain from most sources of sensory stimulation. It may seem obvious, therefore, that the cut produces prolonged sleep by isolating the

**Figure 10.12**
**Location of systems in the cat brain that play critical parts in wakefulness and sleep**
*A cut at line A leads to prolonged sleep; a cut at line B leads to prolonged wakefulness. Axons from the ARAS and the raphe system project to widespread areas of the forebrain.*

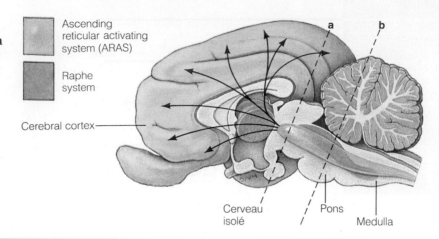

Ascending reticular activating system (ARAS)

Raphe system

Cerebral cortex

Cerveau isolé

Pons

Medulla

a    b

brain from the sensory stimuli that normally activate it. However, the effect of this cut is very different from the effect of cutting off each sensory source individually. Because each sensory tract enters the brain through a well-defined path, it is possible to cut the individual tracts while sparing the rest of the spinal cord and brain stem. As more and more sensory tracts are cut, the animal becomes responsive to fewer and fewer sensory stimuli. Nevertheless, it continues to have normal periods of sleep and wakefulness. Apparently the cerveau isolé cut decreases wakefulness by some means other than just reducing sensory input.

In 1949 Giuseppe Moruzzi and H. W. Magoun found that wakefulness depends not on the sensory tracts themselves but on a system of heavily interconnected neurons extending from the medulla into the forebrain, called the **ascending reticular activating system (ARAS),** which is part of the reticular formation. It is called the ascending reticular formation to distinguish it from the axons of the reticular formation that descend toward the spinal cord. Although the ARAS depends on the sensory tracts for much of its input, it also can generate activity on its own. High-frequency stimulation of the ARAS awakens a sleeping individual or increases alertness in one already awake. It also desynchronizes the EEG. Damage to the ARAS or a cut that separates it from the anterior parts of the brain leads to prolonged sleep or inactivity. Clearly it is critical for wakefulness and alertness.

Figure 10.12 shows the position of the ARAS in a cat brain. The borders shown are only approximate. The term *reticular* (based on the Latin word *rete*, meaning *net*) describes the widespread, diffuse reach of the ARAS. It extends forward at least into parts of the thalamus and hypothalamus; some authorities maintain that it extends all the way into the cerebral cortex. (For more information, see Morgane & Stern, 1974.)

The individual neurons of the ARAS are heavily interconnected, as in parts of a net. Its neurons are characterized by long dendrites that branch diffusely. The connections among neurons do not form straight chains but include multisynaptic paths and looping axon branches. On close inspection the ARAS looks more irregular and disorderly than most of the rest of the brain.

The input and output of the ARAS are diffuse also. The cranial nerves send input to the ascending reticular formation in addition to their primary targets. Thus, the ARAS can be activated by practically any stimulus. The ARAS also generates spontaneous activity of its own. Cells in the ARAS, in turn, send impulses diffusely throughout the cerebral cortex.

The ARAS differs in an important way from the sensory systems. The lateral geniculate nucleus of the thalamus, for example, receives input mostly from the retina and sends its output mostly to the occipital cortex. Similarly, structures in other sensory systems receive limited kinds of input and project their axons to limited targets. The widespread projections of the ARAS to other parts of the brain make it well adapted for serving an energizing function, for controlling arousal and wakefulness. Any strong stimulation—sound, touch, pain, whatever—activates the ARAS, thereby diffusely activating the entire cerebral cortex.

## SLEEP-INDUCING AREAS OF THE BRAIN

We discussed the effects of a cut through the midbrain of a cat at line A in Figure 10.12. If, however, we make the cut at line B, we still isolate the brain from most sensory input, but instead of increasing sleep, this cut increases wakefulness! A cat with such a cut stays awake 70 to 90 percent of the time, about twice as long as a normal cat (Batini, Magni, Palestini, Rossi, & Zanchetti, 1959; Batini, Moruzzi, Palestini, Rossi, & Zanchetti, 1958, 1959; Batini, Palestini, Rossi, & Zanchetti, 1959). Evidently the cut at B spares enough of the ARAS to permit wakefulness but damages a system that promotes sleep; that is, a sleep-promoting area must exist mostly below the cut.

One area that has attracted particular attention is the **raphe system*** (see Figure 10.12). *Raphe* is a Greek word meaning *seam* or *stitching*. The seam referred to here is the line joining the halves of the hindbrain. The raphe system, located medially in the brain stem near the ARAS, includes several distinct nuclei arrayed from the posterior medulla to the anterior midbrain. Many raphe system neurons become most active around the time of sleep onset.

After damage to certain parts of the raphe system, a cat or rat remains awake for a day or more (Jouvet & Renault, 1966; Żernicki, Gandolfo, Glin, & Gottesmann, 1984). Sleep gradually returns, although the animal may never again sleep as much as it used to. Damage to other parts of the raphe system can lead to increased REM sleep, decreased non-REM sleep, or other effects.

If the raphe system is responsible for sleep, we should expect stimulating it to make an animal sleep. Such stimulation does sometimes induce sleep, but it does so only under a narrow range of conditions, such as low-frequency stimulation of a limited area (Kostowski, Giacalone, Garattini, & Valzelli, 1969).

Besides the raphe system, a number of cells in the forebrain are more active during sleep than during wakefulness, including cells in the ventral globus pallidus and several adjacent areas (Szymusiak & McGinty, 1986). Stimulation of those cells can promote sleep; damage to them can suppress sleep. In other words, these cells probably contribute to sleep in the rest of the forebrain. It is not yet clear, however, whether they initiate sleep patterns on their own or whether they merely relay sleep-initiating messages from the raphe system or other areas.

*The *American Heritage Dictionary of Science* and *Webster's Ninth New Collegiate Dictionary* specify the pronunciation RAY-fee. After I suggested this pronunciation in an earlier edition of this text, a reader from Greece wrote to say that the correct Greek pronunciation is ruff-EE. A professor from another university wrote to say that the proper pronunciation is rah-FAY. Be prepared to hear this term pronounced several ways.

## Brain Areas That May Trigger REM Sleep

Michel Jouvet (1960) was the first to suggest that a particular area of the brain, probably in the brain stem, might trigger the events that produce REM sleep. REM sleep begins with a distinctive pattern of high-amplitude electrical potentials that can be detected first in the ARAS of the pons, then in the lateral geniculate of the thalamus, and finally in the occipital cortex (Brooks & Bizzi, 1963; Laurent, Cespuglio, & Jouvet, 1974). Those potentials are known as **PGO waves**—for pons-geniculate-occipital (see Figure 10.13). The PGO waves begin at or just before the start of REM sleep; they continue during REM sleep. Each PGO wave is synchronized with an eye movement (Cespuglio, Laurent, & Jouvet, 1975).

When an animal compensates for a loss of REM sleep, it compensates for the lost PGO waves more precisely than it compensates for the lost REM time (Dement, Ferguson, Cohen, & Barchas, 1969). During a prolonged period of REM deprivation, PGO waves begin to emerge during stages 2 to 4 sleep—when they do not normally occur—and even during wakefulness, often in association with strange behaviors, as if the animal were hallucinating. At the end of the deprivation period, when the animal is permitted to sleep without interruption, the REM periods have an unusually high density of PGO waves.

Where in the brain stem are the cells that trigger the PGO waves and with them REM sleep? One possibility is the dorsal raphe nucleus. Neurons in that area consistently become active just before PGO waves and REM sleep begin (Lydic, McCarley, & Hobson, 1987). Another possibility is the section of the ARAS located in the medial pons. Those cells too are more active during REM sleep than during either wakefulness or non-REM sleep (Ito & McCarley, 1984). A third possibility is the **FTG neurons**—cells of the *gigantocellular tegmental field*. Many FTG neurons become highly active just before and during REM sleep. Their diffusely branching axons would be well placed to control activity throughout the cortex (Hobson, 1977; Hobson, McCarley, & Wyzinski, 1975). However,

**Figure 10.13**

*PGO waves start in the pons (P), then show up in the lateral geniculate (G) and the occipital cortex (O). Each PGO wave is synchronized with an eye movement in REM sleep.*

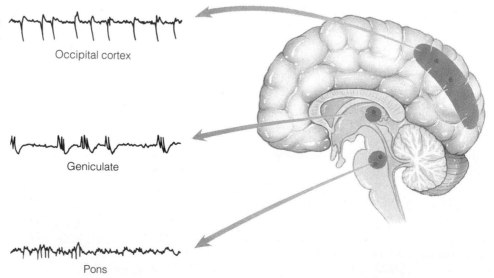

Occipital cortex

Geniculate

Pons

the FTG neurons are not limited specifically to the control of REM sleep. They are just as active or more active during wakeful movements (Siegel, McGinty, & Breedlove, 1977; Siegel, Wheeler, & McGinty, 1979). Apparently their primary function has something to do with movement or perhaps the inhibition of movement (Chase, 1983).

In short, several areas in the brain stem contribute to REM sleep, becoming active before and during REM sleep. Presumably one of these areas or some other area near them is the source of PGO waves. What we do not yet know is what causes these areas to start producing PGO waves or what determines when those waves start and stop.

## The Biochemistry of Sleep

Each of the brain areas we have considered has its own characteristic neurotransmitters, so it is natural to ask whether particular transmitters promote or inhibit certain aspects of wakefulness and sleep. Norepinephrine and dopamine contribute to wakefulness and arousal, so drugs that promote the release of norepinephrine or dopamine tend to keep people awake. A number of sleeping pills operate in part by decreasing norepinephrine or dopamine stimulation.

The primary neurotransmitter of the raphe system is serotonin. After damage to cells of the raphe system, or after chemical depletion of the transmitter serotonin, a number of investigators have reported decreases in the duration of sleep (Laguzzi & Adrien, 1980; Pujol, Buguet, Froment, Jones, & Jouvet, 1971). However, it would be wrong to say that serotonin is necessary for sleep. Even an animal with severely depleted serotonin levels eventually begins to sleep again, for nearly normal amounts of time (Morgane, 1981). But in such animals, REM sleep intrudes into periods normally occupied by non-REM sleep or wakefulness (Jacobs, Henriksen, & Dement, 1972). That is, serotonin activity may suppress REM at inappropriate times.

The possible relationship of serotonin to sleep has prompted some investigators to try precursors to serotonin as possible sleeping pills. The amino acid **L-tryptophan,** after entering the brain, is converted to serotonin. Tryptophan pills were at one time popular as sleep inducers; later the U.S. government banned their use because a batch of pills from one manufacturer had induced serious health hazards (Belongia et al., 1990). Presumably they will be available again someday under closer supervision.

Acetylcholine can promote REM sleep. Injecting drugs that stimulate acetylcholine synapses anywhere within a broad region of the pons triggers the immediate onset of REM sleep (Baghdoyan, Rodrigo-Angulo, McCarley, & Hobson, 1987; Shiromani, Siegel, Tomaszewski, & McGinty, 1986). Injecting the same drugs elsewhere in the brain has either no effect or the opposite effect (Baghdoyan, Rodrigo-Angulo, McCarley, & Hobson, 1984).

Chemicals circulating in the blood can also influence waking and sleeping. Prostaglandin $D_2$ binds mostly to forebrain neurons and induces sleep (Hayaishi, 1988). It also lowers body temperature, a factor that can greatly influence sleepiness (Satinoff, 1988). Prostaglandin $E_2$ reduces sleep (Hayaishi, 1988).

A small glycopeptide, designated **Factor S,** which can be isolated from the nervous system or bloodstream of sleeping animals, can induce sleep, mostly slow-wave sleep, when it is injected into other animals (Inoué, Uchizono, & Nagasaki, 1982; Krueger, Pappenheimer, & Karnovsky, 1982). Evidently the neuronal mechanisms of the raphe system or elsewhere are responsible for initiating sleep, but hormonal factors may be important for maintaining it.

# ABNORMALITIES OF SLEEP

Have you ever stayed awake extremely late at night to finish some project and then found yourself making one mistake after another the next morning? If so, you are not alone. An estimated 8 to 15 percent of adults in the United States have chronic sleep complaints (Weitzman, 1981), and a great many more than that have at least occasional or mild complaints. Sleep disorders can occur in conjunction with various psychological and neurological disorders, including depression and substance abuse (Tan, Kales, Kales, Soldatos, & Bixler, 1984); they also commonly occur in people who work long or irregular hours and in people who frequently fly from one time zone to another. Unsatisfactory sleep is a major cause of accidents on the job, comparable to the effects of drugs and alcohol.

## Insomnia

How much sleep is enough? How much is too little? Six hours of sleep per night are plenty for some people. For others, eight hours may not be enough, especially for people who awaken repeatedly during the night. The best gauge of insomnia is whether the person feels well rested the following day. Anyone who consistently feels tired and sleepy during the day is not sleeping well enough at night.

Insomnia can result from many causes, including excessive noise, worries and stress, drugs and medications, uncomfortable temperatures, sleeping in an unfamiliar place, or trying to fall asleep at the wrong time in one's circadian rhythm (Kales & Kales, 1984). A friend of mine suffered insomnia for months until he realized that he dreaded going to sleep at night because he dreaded waking up in the morning and doing his daily jogging. After he switched his jogging time to late afternoon, he no longer had any trouble sleeping. Before trying sleeping pills or any other method of combating insomnia, a person should carefully identify the reasons for his or her sleep troubles.

It is convenient to distinguish three categories of insomnia: onset insomnia, maintenance insomnia, and termination insomnia. People with **onset insomnia** have trouble falling asleep. Those with **maintenance insomnia** awaken frequently during the night. And those with **termination insomnia** wake up too early and cannot get back to sleep. It is possible to have more than one of the three types.

Certain cases of insomnia are related to abnormalities of biological rhythms (MacFarlane, Cleghorn, & Brown, 1985a, 1985b). As mentioned earlier in this chapter, the circadian rhythm of temperature can get out of phase with the circadian rhythm of waking and sleeping. Ordinarily, people fall asleep while their temperature is declining and awaken while it is rising, as in Figure 10.14a. Some people's body temperature rhythm is *phase delayed*, as in Figure 10.14b. If they try to fall asleep at the normal time, their body temperature is higher than normal for going to sleep. Such people are likely to experience onset insomnia (Morris, Lack, & Dawson, 1990). Other people's body temperature rhythm is *phase advanced*, as in Figure 10.14c. They are likely to suffer termination insomnia. Those who suffer from maintenance insomnia may have major irregularities of their circadian rhythms.

REM sleep occurs mostly during the rising phase of the temperature cycle. For most people, this is the second half of the night's sleep, as Figure 10.14a shows. For people with termination insomnia, or anyone else who falls asleep after the temperature cycle has already hit bottom, REM sleep may start shortly af-

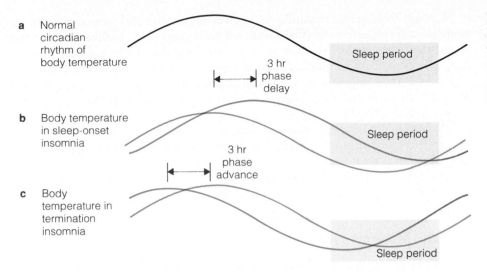

**a** Normal circadian rhythm of body temperature

Sleep period

3 hr phase delay

**b** Body temperature in sleep-onset insomnia

Sleep period

3 hr phase advance

**c** Body temperature in termination insomnia

Sleep period

**Figure 10.14
How a delay or advance in the circadian rhythm of body temperature can relate to insomnia**

ter the person falls asleep (Czeisler, Weitzman, Moore-Ede, Zimmerman, & Knauer, 1980). Because depression is often associated with termination insomnia, many depressed people enter REM sleep earlier in the night than nondepressed people do.

## Sleep Apnea

One special cause of insomnia is **sleep apnea,** an inability to breathe while sleeping (Weitzman, 1981). Many people breathe irregularly during REM sleep, and about 10 to 15 percent of all adults have occasional periods of at least 10 seconds without breathing. Sleep apnea to that degree is considered normal and has no relationship to insomnia (Kales & Kales, 1984). A few people, however, may go a minute or more without breathing and then awaken, gasping for breath (Weitzman, 1981). Such people may stay in bed more than 8 hours per night but sleep only about half that time. In many cases the person does not remember awakening repeatedly during the night; he or she is aware only of feeling poorly rested the next morning.

Obesity is one of several possible causes of sleep apnea. Some obese people, especially men, have trouble finding a sleeping position that enables them to breathe easily. More frequently, however, the origin of sleep apnea lies within the central nervous system.

## Overuse of Sleeping Pills

Another cause of insomnia is, paradoxically, sleeping pills. Although barbiturates and tranquilizers may help a person fall asleep, someone who has taken such drugs a few times may come to depend on them for getting to sleep. Such a person who tries going to sleep without the drug may go into a withdrawal state that prevents sleep (Kales, Scharf, & Kales, 1978). He or she may react to the sleeplessness by taking the sleeping pills again, setting up a cycle from which it is difficult to escape.

Brain Mechanisms in
Sleep and Its
Disorders

Certain short-acting tranquilizers, such as midazolam and triazolam, have become popular because their effects wear off before morning. Unlike certain other drugs, they do not leave the person sleepy the next day. Unfortunately, because their effects wear off so quickly, they may produce withdrawal effects during the night. As a result, someone who takes such drugs may awaken very early as a side effect of the drug and find it impossible to get back to sleep (Kales, Soldatos, Bixler, & Kales, 1983).

A final point regarding tranquilizers as sleeping pills: Certain tranquilizers may either phase-advance the biological clock or phase-delay it, depending on when a person takes them (Turek & Losee-Olson, 1986). Especially if such pills are taken to combat the sleep disorders of jet lag, they may aggravate the problem instead of relieving it, depending on when the person takes the pills and which direction the person has flown.

## Periodic Movements in Sleep

Another factor occasionally linked to insomnia is **periodic movements in sleep,** a repeated involuntary movement of the legs and sometimes arms (Weitzman, 1981). The legs may kick once every 20 to 30 seconds for a period of minutes or even hours, mostly during non-REM sleep. Periodic movements are more common in older people than in younger people and are particularly rare before age 30. If they become extremely frequent or severe, they may awaken the person. They may also cause the person to fall out of bed. Many normal people experience a mild to moderate degree of periodic movements (Kales & Kales, 1984). Such movements may not be a problem unless they annoy the person's sleeping partner.

## Narcolepsy

**Narcolepsy** is a condition characterized by unexpected periods of sleep in the middle of the day (Dement, 1972; Kellerman, 1981; Mahowald & Schenck, 1989; Weitzman, 1981). The condition strikes about one person in a thousand, generally running in families. Four symptoms are generally associated with narcolepsy, although most patients do not report all four:

1. Gradual or sudden attacks of extreme sleepiness during the day.
2. Occasional **cataplexy**—an attack of muscle weakness while the person remains awake. Cataplexy is generally triggered by strong emotions, such as anger or great excitement.
3. Sleep paralysis—a complete inability to move just as the person is falling asleep or waking up. Other people may experience sleep paralysis occasionally, but people with narcolepsy experience it more frequently.
4. *Hypnagogic hallucinations*—dreamlike experiences that the person has trouble distinguishing from reality, often occurring at the onset of sleep.

All these symptoms can be interpreted as intrusions of REM sleep into wakefulness: REM sleep is associated with muscle weakness (cataplexy), paralysis, and dreams (Mahowald & Schenck, 1989). For some unknown reason, certain areas of the brain seem to be active at the wrong times of day in people with narcolepsy. Their brain stem areas responsible for arousal are less active than normal during a waking state but more active than normal at the onset of sleep (Meyer, Ishikawa, Hata, & Karacan, 1987). The low arousal during wakefulness may enable REM states to occur. Various drugs help to suppress narcolepsy; most of them also suppress REM sleep (Mahowald & Schenck, 1989).

## Night Terrors, Sleep Talking, and Sleepwalking

**Night terrors** are experiences of intense anxiety from which a person generally awakens screaming in terror. A night terror should be distinguished from a *nightmare*, which is simply an unpleasant dream that occurs during REM sleep in people of any age. Night terrors occur during non-REM sleep and are far more common in children than in adults.

Many people talk in their sleep occasionally, often unaware that they do. *Sleep talking* has about the same chance of occurring during REM sleep as during non-REM sleep (Arkin, Toth, Baker, & Hastey, 1970).

*Sleepwalking* occurs mostly in children, especially ages 2 to 5, and is most common early in the night, during stage 3 or stage 4 sleep. Its causes are not known, other than the fact that it runs in families. Sleepwalking is generally harmless, both to the sleepwalker and to others. No doubt you have heard people say, "You should never waken someone who is sleepwalking." In fact, it is not harmful or dangerous to awaken a sleepwalker, although the person is likely to feel very confused (Moorcroft, 1989).

## REM Behavior Disorder

For most people the major postural muscles are relaxed and inactive during REM sleep. However, a few people move around vigorously during their REM periods, apparently acting out their dreams. This condition is known as **REM behavior disorder.** Many of their dreams are violent, and they may punch, kick, and leap about, often damaging property and injuring themselves or other people. Their dreams correspond to their movements; that is, they dream they are kicking when they are actually kicking.

A possible explanation for such behavior is damage to the brain areas responsible for inhibiting muscles during REM sleep. For example, after cats have received damage to various areas of the pons and midbrain, their muscles do not relax during REM sleep. Evidently those areas send inhibitory messages to the motor neurons during REM sleep, probably by the release of the neurotransmitter glycine (M. H. Chase, Soja, & Morales, 1989). After damage to those areas, the cats' motor neurons are released from inhibition. During their REM periods, the cats occasionally walk, chase, attack, and perform other actions as if they were acting out dreams (Henley & Morrison, 1974; Jouvet & Delorme, 1965). Similarly, one study of people with REM sleep disorder found multiple areas of damage in the pons and midbrain (Culebras & Moore, 1989). Although the data do not point to a single critical area of the brain, they do suggest that REM sleep disorder is associated with impaired inhibition of the motor neurons.

## SUMMARY

1. The ascending reticular activating system (ARAS) sends diffuse messages throughout the cerebral cortex, regulating general arousal. A person whose forebrain is cut off from the ARAS sleeps most of the day. (p. 372)

2. Other brain areas, including parts of the raphe system and certain areas at the base of the forebrain, promote sleep. Damage to these areas can suppress sleep, at least temporarily. (p. 373)

3. REM sleep begins with PGO waves—waves of brain activity transmitted from the pons to the lateral geniculate to the occipital lobe. (p. 374)

4. The exact point where PGO waves originate is unknown, but the likeliest candidates are the dorsal raphe nucleus, one section of the ARAS in the medial pons, and the FTG neurons. (p. 374)

5. Norepinephrine and dopamine neurons tend to promote wakefulness. Serotonin neurons tend to promote sleep and to suppress REM. Acetylcholine neurons in the pons trigger REM episodes. After sleep has be-

gun, certain circulating chemicals help to maintain it. (p. 375)

6. Insomnia sometimes results from a shift in phase of the circadian rhythm of temperature relative to the circadian rhythm of sleep and wakefulness. It can also result from a difficulty in breathing while asleep, overuse of tranquilizers, and numerous other causes. (p. 376)

7. People with narcolepsy grow very sleepy in the middle of the day. (p. 378)

8. Among other sleep disorders are night terrors, sleep talking, sleepwalking, and REM behavior disorder. (p. 379)

## REVIEW QUESTIONS

1. A cut through one level of the brain stem leads to constant sleeping; a cut through a more posterior level leads to constant wakefulness. Why? (p. 371)

2. How does the structure of the ARAS make it well suited to control the brain's arousal? (p. 372)

3. Which areas of the brain are active just before sleep and probably induce sleep for the rest of the brain? (p. 373)

4. What are PGO waves? Where do they originate? (p. 374)

5. What is the apparent role of serotonin in sleep? What is the role of acetylcholine? (p. 375)

6. Describe some of the possible causes of insomnia. (p. 376)

7. What are the disadvantages of using sleeping pills to combat insomnia? (p. 377)

8. Describe the characteristics of narcolepsy. (p. 378)

9. Are night terrors more common in REM sleep or non-REM sleep? What about sleep talking? Sleepwalking? (p. 379)

## THOUGHT QUESTION

1. When cats are deprived of REM sleep for various periods, the amount of rebound increases for the first 25 to 30 days but does not increase further with a longer deprivation. What prevents the need from accumulating beyond that point? Use PGO waves in your answer.

## SUGGESTION FOR FURTHER READING

**Moorcroft, W. H.** (1989). *Sleep, dreaming, & sleep disorders.* Lanham, MD: University Press of America. Chapter 4 discusses the functions of various brain areas in sleep. Chapter 8 provides a good description of sleep disorders.

## GLOSSARY

**activation-synthesis hypothesis** hypothesis that the brain synthesizes dreams from spontaneous brain activity occurring during sleep

**alpha wave** rhythm of 8 to 12 brain waves per second, generally associated with relaxation

**ascending reticular activating system (ARAS)** system of heavily interconnected neurons extending from the medulla into the forebrain

**biological clock** internal mechanism for controlling rhythmic variations in a behavior

**cataplexy** attack of muscle weakness while a person remains awake

**cerveau isolé** preparation in which the forebrain and part of the midbrain are separated from the rest of the midbrain, hindbrain, and spinal cord

**endogenous circadian rhythm** self-generated rhythm that lasts about a day

**endogenous circannual rhythm** self-generated rhythm that lasts about a year

**evolutionary theory of sleep** concept that the function of sleep is to conserve energy at times of relative inefficiency

**Factor S** small glycopeptide found in the nervous system and bloodstream of sleeping animals

**free-running rhythm** circadian or circannual rhythm that is not being periodically reset by light or other cues

**FTG neuron** neuron of the gigantocellular tegmental field of the brain stem

**hibernation** condition in which heart rate, breathing, brain activity, and metabolism greatly decrease as an adaptation to conserve energy during winter

**insomnia** lack of sleep, leaving the person feeling poorly rested the following day

**jet lag** disruption of biological rhythms caused by travel across time zones

**K-complex** sharp high-amplitude negative wave followed by a smaller, slower positive wave

**L-tryptophan** *see* **tryptophan**

**maintenance insomnia** frequent awakening during the night

**narcolepsy** condition characterized by unexpected periods of sleep in the middle of the day

**night terror** experience of intense anxiety during sleep, from which a person awakens screaming in terror

**non-REM sleep** sleep stages other than REM sleep

**onset insomnia** difficulty falling asleep

**paradoxical sleep** stage of sleep characterized by complete relaxation of the large muscles but high activity in the brain

**periodic movement in sleep** repeated involuntary movement of the legs and sometimes arms during sleep

**PGO wave** pattern of high-amplitude electrical potentials that occurs first in the pons, then in the lateral geniculate, and finally in the occipital cortex

**raphe system** set of neurons in the medial brain stem, many of which become active around the time of sleep onset

**rapid eye movement (REM) sleep** sleep stage with rapid eye movements, high brain activity, and relaxation of the large muscles

**REM behavior disorder** condition in which people move around vigorously during REM sleep

**repair and restoration theory of sleep** concept that the function of sleep is to enable the body to repair itself after the exertions of the day

**reticular formation** *see* **ascending reticular activating system**

**sleep apnea** inability to breathe while sleeping

**sleep spindle** burst of 12 to 14 Hz brain waves lasting at least half a second

**slow-wave sleep (SWS)** stages 3 and 4 of sleep that are occupied largely by slow, large-amplitude brain waves

**suprachiasmatic nucleus (SCN)** area of the hypothalamus where damage disrupts the biological clock

**termination insomnia** tendency to awaken early and to be unable to get back to sleep

**theta wave** irregular, jagged, low-voltage brain wave at a rhythm of 4 to 7 cycles per second

**tryptophan** amino acid, a precursor in the synthesis of serotonin

**zeitgeber** stimulus that resets a biological clock

# The Regulation of Internal Body States

## MAIN IDEAS

**1.** Many physiological and behavioral processes act to maintain a near-constancy of certain body variables, although they often anticipate a need rather than react to a need.

**2.** Mammals regulate body temperature by such physiological processes as shivering and by such behavioral processes as selecting an appropriate environment. Brain areas that control body temperature respond both to their own temperature and to the temperature of the skin and spinal cord.

**3.** Thirst may act to anticipate and prevent water need. Thirst also responds to the osmotic pressure of the blood and the total volume of blood.

**4.** Hunger and satiety are regulated by several factors, including taste, stomach distention, and glucose availability to the cells.

(Ed Reschke.)

W hat is life? Life is many things and can be defined in different ways depending on whether our interest is medical, legal, philosophical, or poetic.

At the most basic biological level we can say that *life is a coordinated set of chemical reactions*. Not every coordinated set of chemical reactions is alive, but life cannot exist without a coordinated set of chemical reactions.

Every chemical reaction in the body takes place in a water medium at a rate that depends on the concentration of molecules in the water, the identity of those molecules, the temperature of the solution, and the presence of any contaminants. To continue the chemical reactions we call "life," we need to prepare the ingredients according to a most precise recipe. Much of our behavior is organized to keep those ingredients present in the right proportions and at the right temperature.

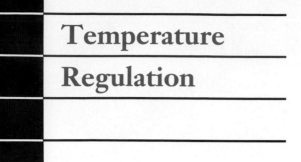

# Temperature Regulation

In an average day, you will probably burn more than 2,000 kilocalories of energy. Where do you suppose all your energy goes? To running, walking, and other physical activity? Not likely. In general, we spend most of our energy simply maintaining our body temperature. Contrast a mammal like yourself with an animal that does not maintain a constant body temperature—such as a snake. A snake can go days, weeks, sometimes even months between meals. You need frequent meals because of all the energy you expend to maintain your body temperature.

Your body has a variety of mechanisms for keeping its temperature almost constant. In many ways temperature regulation is the perfect example of the body's tendency to maintain stability.

## HOMEOSTASIS

Physiologist Walter B. Cannon (1929) introduced the term **homeostasis** (HO-mee-oh-STAY-sis) to refer to temperature regulation and other biological processes that work to keep certain body variables within a fixed range. To understand how a homeostatic process works, we can use the analogy of the thermostat in a house. Someone fixes a set range of temperatures on the thermostat. When the temperature in the house drops below that range, the thermostat triggers the furnace to provide heat until the house temperature returns to the set range. If the house also has an air-conditioning system, the set range for temperature has a maximum as well as a minimum. When the temperature rises above the maximum, the thermostat triggers the air conditioner to cool the house until the temperature returns to the set range.

Similarly, homeostatic processes in animals trigger certain physiological and behavioral activities when some variable passes beyond the limits of its set range. In many cases the range is so narrow that we refer to it as a **set point.** For example, if calcium is deficient in your diet and its concentration in the blood begins to fall below the set point of 0.16 g/l (grams per liter), storage deposits in your bones will release additional calcium into the blood. If the calcium level in the blood rises above 0.16 g/l, part of the excess is stored in the bones and part is ex-

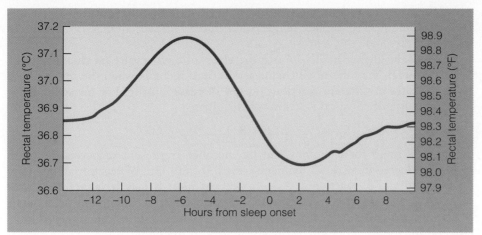

**Figure 11.1
Mean rectal temperatures for nine adults**
*Body temperature reaches its low for the day about two hours after sleep onset; it reaches its peak about six hours before sleep onset. (Based on data of Morris, Lack, & Dawson, 1990.)*

creted in the urine and feces. Analogous mechanisms maintain constant blood levels of water, oxygen, glucose, sodium chloride, protein, fat, and acidity (Cannon, 1929).

Temperature regulation in the mammalian body can be regarded as a homeostatic process, although it does not operate like the thermostat that controls the temperature of a house (Hogan, 1980; Satinoff, 1983). A thermostat compares the temperature at a single point in the house to the set range; if it finds a discrepancy, it turns on the heating system or the cooling system. The body monitors several variables in different parts of the body to determine its need for heat or cold, and it triggers several responses, each partly independent of the others. Also, the set point for temperature varies according to a circadian rhythm; as we discussed in Chapter 10, human body temperature varies between about 36.6° C and 37.2° C daily, with the lowest temperature occurring at night, when activity level also tends to be low (Figure 11.1). Nevertheless, at any given moment the mammalian body maintains a nearly constant temperature.

Although most of the body is adapted for survival at a fairly high body temperature—about 37° C in mammals, 40° or more in birds—reproductive cells require a somewhat cooler environment. The scrotum hangs outside the male body because sperm production requires a temperature a bit cooler than the rest of the body. Similarly, birds sit on eggs instead of keeping them inside the body because the birds' internal temperature of 40° C is too hot for the embryo to survive, at least in the early stages.

## MECHANISMS OF CONTROLLING BODY TEMPERATURE

Fish, amphibians, and reptiles are **poikilothermic;** their body temperature is the same as the temperature of their environment. Mammals and birds are **homeothermic;** they maintain an almost constant body temperature despite large variations in the environmental temperature. Every mammal and bird keeps its body temperature close to the set point under normal circumstances.

Temperature
Regulation

Why have we evolved mechanisms to control body temperature? What difference would it make if body temperature fluctuated over a range of 20 degrees or so each day?

Part of the answer has to do with the effect of temperature on chemical reactions. Although the rates of all chemical reactions increase when the temperature rises, the rates of different reactions do not increase equally. For instance, imagine a sequence of chemical reactions of this form:

$$A \xrightarrow{\;\;1\;\;} B \xrightarrow{\;\;2\;\;} C$$

The letters stand for chemicals and the numbers represent reactions. Suppose that a 10-degree increase in temperature triples the rate of reaction 1 but only doubles the rate of reaction 2. As a result, chemical B may be generated faster than it can be converted to chemical C. The resulting accumulation of B might be harmful. In short, a constant body temperature makes it possible to evolve precise coordinations among the various reactions in the body.

A constant body temperature also makes it easier for the animal to stay active when the environment turns cold. Recall from Chapter 9 that a fish has trouble maintaining a high activity level at a low temperature. To move at a normal speed, it must recruit muscle fibers that fatigue rapidly. By maintaining a constant internal temperature, birds and mammals can be ready for action at any temperature, without needing to recruit different sets of muscles.

## Brain Mechanisms of Temperature Regulation

The body defends the temperature at its core—including the brain and the other internal organs—more carefully than it defends the temperature of the skin. When the body cools below the set point, the blood vessels to the skin constrict, preventing the blood from being cooled by the cold air around the skin. Although the skin may grow very cold, the brain, heart, and other internal organs remain warm. To generate more heat, the muscles contract rhythmically (shivering), or the animal runs about. The fur of a mammal becomes erect, increasing insulation from the cold environment.

If the body begins to overheat, more blood than usual flows to the skin, where it can be cooled by contact with the air (which is almost always cooler than the body). An animal may decrease its heat production by decreasing body activity. Depending on the species, animals sweat, pant heavily, or lick themselves; evaporation of the saliva cools the body.

All these physiological changes depend predominantly on certain areas within the hypothalamus, a small structure at the base of the brain (see Figure 11.2). The hypothalamus contains a number of nuclei, each of which apparently serves a different function. The most critical area for temperature control is the **preoptic area,** a nucleus adjacent to the anterior hypothalamus. (It is called *preoptic* because it is located next to the optic chiasm, where the optic nerves cross.)

The preoptic area monitors body temperature partly by monitoring its own temperature (Nelson & Prosser, 1981). When an experimenter heats the preoptic area, an animal pants or sweats, even in a cool environment. If the same area is cooled, the animal shivers, even in a warm room. These responses are not simply reflexive. When an experimenter heats or cools the preoptic area, an animal will learn to press a lever or to do other work for cold air or hot air reinforcements (Laudenslager, 1976; Satinoff, 1964).

Besides monitoring their own temperature, the cells of the preoptic area also receive input from temperature-sensitive receptors in the skin and spinal cord. The animal shivers most vigorously when both the preoptic area and the other receptors are cold; it sweats or pants most vigorously when both are hot.

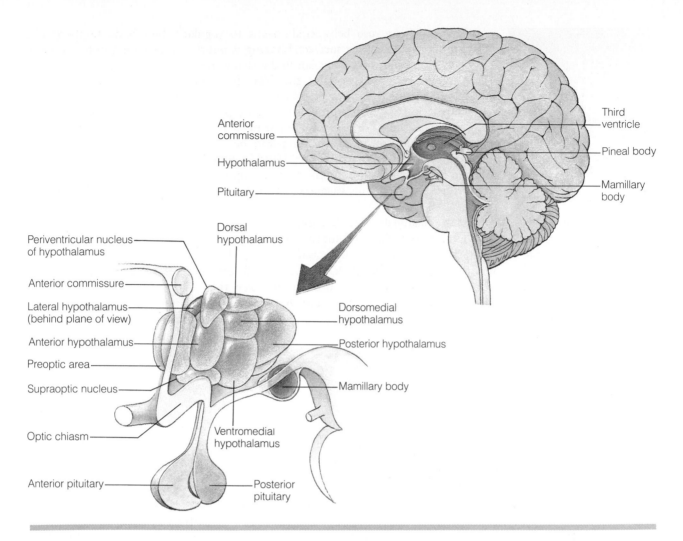

Labels on figure (top brain diagram):
Anterior commissure
Hypothalamus
Pituitary
Third ventricle
Pineal body
Mamillary body

Labels on figure (bottom detail):
Periventricular nucleus of hypothalamus
Anterior commissure
Lateral hypothalamus (behind plane of view)
Anterior hypothalamus
Preoptic area
Supraoptic nucleus
Optic chiasm
Anterior pituitary
Dorsal hypothalamus
Dorsomedial hypothalamus
Posterior hypothalamus
Mamillary body
Ventromedial hypothalamus
Posterior pituitary

**Figure 11.2
Major subdivisions of the hypothalamus and pituitary**
*(After Nieuwenhuys et al., 1988.)*

Damage to the preoptic area impairs a mammal's temperature regulation. It can no longer shiver, so its body temperature plummets in a cold environment (Satinoff, Valentino, & Teitelbaum, 1976). Moreover, even in an environment with a steady temperature, the animal's body temperature fluctuates over a range of 10 degrees or more (Satinoff, Liran, & Clapman, 1982).

The preoptic area is the dominant area for temperature control, but temperature-sensitive cells also exist in other parts of the hypothalamus, elsewhere in the brain, and in the spinal cord. At least fragmentary shivering and sweating can occur after preoptic area damage.

## Behavioral Mechanisms of Temperature Regulation

Although the body temperature of fish, amphibians, and reptiles matches that of their environment, their temperature seldom fluctuates wildly. They regulate their temperature by choosing their environment (Crawshaw, Moffitt, Lemons, & Downey, 1981). A desert lizard burrows into the ground in the middle of the day, when the surface is too hot, and again in the middle of the night, when the surface is too cold. While on the surface, it will choose a spot in the sun or in the shade to keep its body temperature fairly constant.

*Infant rats regulate body temperature by burrowing into the pile of other infant rats to keep warm and by passively floating to the top when they are already warm enough. (A. Cosmos Blank/NAS/Photo Researchers, Inc.)*

Mammals, too, use behavioral means to regulate their body temperature. They do not sit on an icy surface shivering when they can build a nest, or sweat and pant in the sun when they can find a shady spot. The more they can regulate their temperature behaviorally, the less they need to rely on physiological changes (Refinetti & Carlisle, 1986a).

During infancy, behavioral mechanisms compensate for inadequate physiological mechanisms. For example, infant rats have no fur for insulation. An infant rat isolated in a cold room cannot generate heat nearly as fast as it loses it. A litter of 10 to 12 infant rats, however, can huddle together and collectively maintain a normal body temperature. As the ones on top cool off, they burrow into the center of the mass, while the warm ones near the center passively float to the top (Alberts, 1978).

Adult mammals, after damage to the preoptic area, can also regulate their temperature by behavioral means. In a cold environment, they will press a lever to keep a heat lamp on long enough to keep their body temperature near normal (Satinoff & Rutstein, 1970; Van Zoeren & Stricker, 1977). Their temperature regulation is not as good as normal, however; their temperature gets higher than normal during the day and colder than normal during the night (Szymusiak, DeMory, Kittrell, & Satinoff, 1985). Behavioral regulation of temperature is partly under the control of the preoptic area, partly under the control of the posterior hypothalamus (Refinetti & Carlisle, 1986b), and partly under the control of other parts of the brain.

## Fever

People with bacterial and viral infections generally have a fever—an increase in body temperature. As a rule, the fever is not part of the illness; it is part of the body's defense against the illness.

When the body is invaded by bacteria, viruses, fungi, or other foreign bodies, it mobilizes, among other things, its *leukocytes* (white blood cells) to attack them. The leukocytes release a protein, called *endogenous pyrogen* or *leukocytic pyrogen*, which in turn causes the production of **prostaglandin $E_1$.** By unknown means, prostaglandin $E_1$ then causes cells in the preoptic area to raise body temperature (Dascombe, 1986; Dinarello & Wolff, 1982). Prostaglandin $E_1$ elevates body temperature even in animals not suffering any infection; rats injected with the chemical also show an increased preference for the warmer areas in the environment (Marques, Spencer, Burks, & McDougal, 1984). All these effects depend on the preoptic area.

Newborn rabbits, whose hypothalamus is immature, do not get fevers in response to infections. If they are given a choice of environments, however, they will select an unusually warm environment and thereby raise their body temperature (Satinoff, McEwen, & Williams, 1976). That is, they will develop a fever by behavioral rather than physiological means. Fish and reptiles do the same, if they can find a warm enough environment (Kluger, 1978).

Does a fever do the animal any good? Certain types of bacteria grow less vigorously at high temperatures than at normal mammalian body temperatures (Kluger & Rothenburg, 1979). Animals that develop moderate fevers, up to about 2.25 degrees above normal temperature, have a better chance of surviving a bacterial infection than do animals that fail to develop a fever (Kluger & Vaughn, 1978). If the fever goes higher than that, the animal's probability of survival declines.

# HOMEOSTASIS REVISITED

In many regards, temperature regulation is a reasonable example of a homeostatic process. The body reacts to increases in temperature by cooling itself and to decreases in temperature by warming itself. Nevertheless, temperature regulation is not entirely a reaction to a current need. The body sometimes cools or warms itself in preparation for an anticipated need. For example, in response to a frightening stimulus, the sympathetic nervous system activates the sweat glands. The sweat starts to cool the body, not in reaction to current body temperature but in preparation for the overheating that may result from the vigorous activity that may be necessary. In short, temperature regulation in the body is not entirely analogous to the way a thermostat controls the temperature of a house.

Similarly, as we shall see in the remainder of this chapter, thirst and hunger anticipate future needs as much as they react to current needs, and both are subject to wide fluctuations, depending on whether the available water and food taste good. We do not have to throw away the concept of homeostasis; after all, much of our behavior does react to disturbances of the internal environment. But we must remember that our behavior both prepares for future problems and reacts to current problems.

## SUMMARY

1. Homeostasis is a tendency to maintain a body variable near a set point. Temperature, hunger, and thirst are not exactly homeostatic, because the set point varies from time to time. (p. 384)

2. A constant body temperature enables an animal to evolve chemical reactions that are precisely coordinated. It also enables the animal to be equally active and equally resistant to fatigue at all environmental temperatures. (p. 386)

3. The preoptic area of the hypothalamus is critical for temperature control. It monitors both its own temperature and that of the skin and spinal cord. (p. 386)

4. Even homeothermic animals rely partly on behavioral mechanisms for temperature regulation, especially in infancy and after damage to the preoptic area. (p. 387)

5. Fever is caused by the release of prostaglandin $E_1$, which stimulates cells in the preoptic area. A moderate fever may help an animal combat an infection. (p. 388)

## REVIEW QUESTIONS

1. In what ways are certain motivations homeostatic and in what ways are they unlike the thermostat that controls temperature in a house? (p. 384)

2. What evidence do we have that the preoptic area controls body temperature? (p. 386)

3. In what way can an animal continue to regulate body temperature after damage to the preoptic area? (p. 388)

4. What processes in the brain are responsible for fevers? (p. 388)

## THOUGHT QUESTION

1. Speculate on why human body temperature is 37° C. Is that figure just an accident? Would it have been as easy to evolve temperature regulation around a body temperature of 21° or 47°? Why do birds have higher body temperatures than mammals have? If you were asked to predict the body temperature of beings on some other planet, what would you want to know about conditions on that planet before making your prediction?

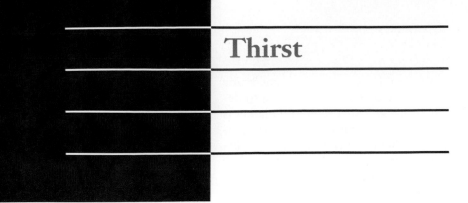

# Thirst

**W**ater constitutes an estimated 70 percent of the mammalian body. Because the rate of all chemical reactions in the body depends on the concentration of the chemicals in water, the body's water must be regulated within narrow limits. The body also needs enough fluid in the circulatory system to maintain normal blood pressure.

## MECHANISMS OF MAINTAINING WATER BALANCE

To maintain a constant amount of water in the body, we have to balance the water we take in and the water we excrete. We take in water by drinking, of course, but also by eating. Nearly all foods contain some water, and certain foods, such as lettuce, contain a great deal. Even dry foods yield some water during digestion. We lose water by urinating, defecating, and sweating. We also lose a little in every breath we exhale and a little by evaporation from the eyes, the mouth, and other moist body surfaces.

Different species have adopted different strategies for balancing water intake and loss. Beavers and other species that live in or near the water drink plenty of water and eat foods with a high water content; they can afford to excrete copious amounts of dilute urine and moist feces. However, gerbils and other desert animals may go through their entire lives without ever drinking water; they gain a little by eating, but they cannot afford to lose much. They have evolved ways of excreting very dry feces and very concentrated urine. They do not sweat; to keep cool, they enter deep burrows during the heat of the day. Their highly convoluted nasal passages minimize the amount of water lost when they exhale.

Humans can use either the beavers' strategy or the gerbils' strategy, depending on circumstances. If you have access to ample supplies of highly palatable beverages, you will probably drink much and urinate much, as beavers do. If you cannot find anything good to drink, or if you have already lost a fair amount of water by sweating or other means, you will conserve your water, as gerbils do. You conserve fluid mainly by decreasing the amount of water in your urine. When body fluids are low, the posterior pituitary (see Figure 11.2) releases a hormone called **antidiuretic hormone (ADH)**, meaning anti-urination hormone, or **vasopressin**, because it raises blood pressure by constricting the blood vessels. ADH causes the kidneys to reabsorb water and secrete highly concentrated urine. So you can maintain your water balance either by increasing your water intake or by decreasing your loss.

## THE MULTIPLE CAUSES OF DRINKING

Sometimes you drink because you are thirsty: You just finished a grueling tennis match; your body is low on water and you need to replenish the supply. At other times you drink to prevent yourself from becoming thirsty: You are going for a long walk on a hot day and you know that you will have only a small canteen of water to drink until you get home, so you take a good drink in advance. That is, drinking is not just a reaction to deficits; it also anticipates and prevents them.

We drink the greatest amount during meals. Drinking with meals is adaptive because food increases the concentration of solutes in the body and thus the need for water. But we do not wait until those solutes enter our cells; we drink long before the food is digested. Although the exact mechanisms are not well understood, apparently food in the stomach stimulates the vagus nerve (a cranial nerve connected to the stomach) and causes the release of histamine. Both the vagus stimulation and the histamine lead to an increase in drinking (Kraly, 1990). But people also drink before the start of a meal. That drinking may reflect classical conditioning of effects previously evoked by the vagus nerve.

People also drink when their throats are dry. At one time physiologists, influenced heavily by Walter B. Cannon, believed that *all* drinking was a response to a dry throat (Fitzsimons, 1973). Cannon pointed out that thirst usually occurs when salivation is at a minimum and that anesthesia of the throat blocks thirst. Today, we regard dryness of the throat as only a minor contributor to thirst. Although someone with inactive salivary glands does drink more than usual during a meal just to wash down the food, such a person drinks only a normal amount over the course of a day. If an animal's esophagus is cut and connected to a tube that empties outside the body, the water that moistens its throat fails to replenish body water supplies, and the animal drinks vastly more than a normal animal does (Blass & Hall, 1976).

In addition, people sometimes drink just because a beverage tastes good or because they like to socialize with friends over a drink or two. In a way, thirst is almost a back-up system, a way of ensuring that we drink enough even when taste, socializing, and eating-related drinking do not supply enough water to the system.

For the most part, thirst depends on the depletion of water from the body. There are actually two components to body water: the concentration of water in the body's cells and the total volume of fluid in the blood. Correspondingly, we experience two kinds of thirst: osmotic thirst and hypovolemic thirst.

## OSMOTIC THIRST

The concentration of all solutes combined in the body fluids remains at a nearly constant level, about 0.15 M (molar) in mammals. (A concentration of 1.0 M has a number of grams of solute equal to the molecular weight of that solute, dissolved in 1 liter of solution.) This fixed concentration of solutes can be regarded as a set point, similar to the set point for temperature. Any deviation from the set point activates mechanisms that act to restore the concentration of solutes to the set point.

The solutes produce an **osmotic pressure,** the force exerted by the concentration of a solute in a water solution toward other solutions separated from it by a semipermeable membrane (a membrane through which water, but not solutes, can pass). Loosely speaking, osmotic pressure is the force with which a solution holds its water and attracts water from an adjacent solution. The osmotic pressure of a solution is proportional to the total number of molecules in the solution per unit volume. In osmosis, water diffuses across a membrane from the side with low solute concentration to the side with high solute concentration. That is, water flows from the area of high water concentration to the area of low water concentration, until the concentration of solutes in water is equal on both sides (see Figure 11.3).

If the concentration of solutes increases in the body, then the osmotic pressure of its fluids increases. This can occur either because the body has lost water or because it has gained solutes. Generally, the body compensates by excreting a concentrated urine, to rid the body of excess solutes, and by drinking, to increase water. The resulting thirst is known as **osmotic thirst.**

Osmotic thirst occurs when a high concentration of solutes outside the cells causes water to flow out of the cells. For example, if concentrated sodium chloride is injected into the blood, the sodium does not readily cross the membranes of cells. Water flows out of the cells and into the blood, shrinking the volume of the cells. The result is increased thirst (Fitzsimons, 1961). An injection of concentrated glucose does not have the same effect because glucose readily crosses the membrane. Therefore, no gradient of osmotic pressure withdraws water from the cell.

Osmotic thirst depends largely on the **lateral preoptic area** of the hypothalamus (Blass & Epstein, 1971; Peck & Novin, 1971), which overlaps the brain area responsible for temperature regulation. If an investigator applies a drop of concentrated salt solution directly to the lateral preoptic area, the animal soon begins to drink. An application of distilled water to the same area causes the animal to stop drinking. Evidently, cells in the lateral preoptic area sense their own state of hydration and osmotic pressure, just as the cells that control temperature monitor their own temperature.

A lesion in the lateral preoptic area decreases a rat's drinking response to an injection of sodium chloride into the blood (Blass & Epstein, 1971; Peck & Novin, 1971). We cannot say that the rat fails to respond to the sodium chloride, however; it merely responds differently from normal rats. After a normal rat is injected with concentrated sodium chloride, it first drinks copious quantities of water. Minutes or even hours later, it excretes great quantities of fairly dilute urine, relieving itself of both the sodium chloride and the excess water. After a rat with lateral preoptic area damage receives a similar injection of sodium chloride, it becomes inactive. It excretes small quantities of highly concentrated urine, removing much of the sodium chloride and only a little body water. Hours later, it drinks a modest amount of water, restoring the normal balance (Stricker, 1976; Stricker & Coburn, 1978). It has achieved the same result as a normal rat by using a different strategy.

If the water tastes bad, a normal, healthy rat resorts to the same strategy as that of the lesioned rat. A rat that is offered only a quinine solution reacts to an injection of sodium chloride by excreting a highly concentrated urine and then,

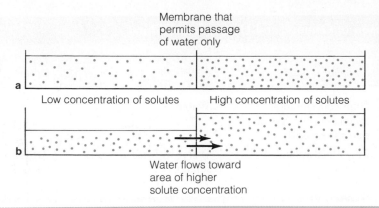

**Figure 11.3**
**Two dishes of solution separated by a semi-permeable membrane**
(*a*) *Two solutions of unequal solute concentration are introduced.* (*b*) *Water flows by osmosis toward the area with a higher concentration of solutes.*

hours later, drinking a little of the quinine solution (Rowland & Flamm, 1977). In other words, an animal with damage to its lateral preoptic area acts as if it dislikes the taste of water.

## HYPOVOLEMIC THIRST

The body needs to maintain an adequate blood pressure. If blood volume, and therefore pressure, is too low, the blood cannot carry enough water and nutrients to the cells. Blood volume may drop sharply after a deep cut or after internal hemorrhaging. The body then needs to replenish not only its water but also the salts and other solutes that have been lost. The result is **hypovolemic** (HI-po-vo-LEE-mik) **thirst,** which is thirst based on low volume.

To study hypovolemic thirst simply by withdrawing blood from an animal is unsatisfactory. An animal that rapidly loses a large amount of blood may go into a state of shock. Two ways to withdraw blood gradually are by injecting polyethylene glycol or dilute formaldehyde just under the skin (Stricker & Macarthur, 1974). Either solution stays where it is injected for hours and causes fluid from the blood to accumulate temporarily in that area.

After a reduction in blood volume, an animal increases its drinking. It will drink only a little pure water, however, because a large amount of water would dilute its body fluids. Instead, it will drink large amounts of a saltwater solution at a concentration similar to that of its blood (Stricker, 1969). If offered one container of pure water and another of highly concentrated salt water, it will alternate between the two to produce a mixture that matches the content of its blood.

Hypovolemic thirst differs from osmotic thirst in several ways, which Table 11.1 summarizes. Besides the fact that it is caused by a loss of blood volume instead of a change in solute concentration, and that it can be satisfied better by salt water than by pure water, hypovolemic thirst apparently depends on cells in the **subfornical organ** and other areas surrounding the third ventricle of the brain, rather than the lateral preoptic area. Because those areas lie outside the usual blood-brain barrier, they are in a good position to monitor all the contents of the blood (Buggy, Fisher, Hoffman, Johnson, & Phillips, 1975; Mangiapane, Thrasher, Keil, Simpson, & Ganong, 1983; Miselis, Shapiro, & Hand, 1979).

| Table 11.1 Comparison of Osmotic and Hypovolemic Thirst | | | |
|---|---|---|---|
| *Type of Thirst* | *Stimulus* | *Best Relieved by Drinking* | *Brain Areas Implicated* |
| Osmotic thirst | High concentration of solutes in cells; loss of water from cells | Water | Lateral preoptic area of the hypothalamus |
| Hypovolemic thirst | Low blood volume | Water with salt or other solutes | Areas surrounding third ventricle |

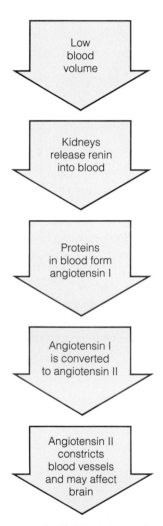

**Figure 11.4
Hormonal response to
hypovolemia**

The flowchart reads: Low blood volume → Kidneys release renin into blood → Proteins in blood form angiotensin I → Angiotensin I is converted to angiotensin II → Angiotensin II constricts blood vessels and may affect brain

## Possible Hormonal Triggers of Hypovolemic Thirst

Hypovolemic thirst depends on at least one, and probably two, stimuli. One stimulus is signals from the **baroreceptors**—receptors on the largest blood vessels that detect their blood pressure. When these receptors report a decrease in blood pressure, thirst increases (Rettig, Ganten, & Johnson, 1981; Zimmerman, Blaine, & Stricker, 1981).

The other possible mechanism is hormones released by the kidneys. When blood volume drops, the kidneys detect the change and respond by releasing *renin*, a hormone. Renin splits a portion off angiotensinogen, a large protein that circulates in the blood, to form angiotensin I, which is quickly converted to angiotensin II. The hormone **angiotensin II** then causes the blood vessels to constrict, compensating for the drop in blood pressure (see Figure 11.4).

When angiotensin reaches the brain, it may directly excite the cells in areas around the third cerebral ventricle, known to be critical for hypovolemic thirst (Fitzsimons, 1971). Injections of angiotensin to those areas can prompt drinking, while injections to other areas have no effect on drinking (Mangiapane & Simpson, 1980). An injection of angiotensin II antiserum (an immunological substance that inactivates angiotensin II) directly into the third ventricle reduces drinking. The effect is not immediate, perhaps because the antiserum takes some time to diffuse from the ventricle into surrounding cells. But one to three hours after the injection, animals drink significantly less than usual (Franci, Kozlowski, & McCann, 1989). This finding supports the conclusion that angiotensin in the brain promotes certain types of thirst. However, it is apparently not critical for the kind of drinking that accompanies eating.

Angiotensin and baroreceptors may have a **synergistic effect** (Epstein, 1983; N. Rowland, 1980). If two effects are synergistic, their combined effect is more than twice the effect of either one acting separately. That is, it may take less angiotensin to stimulate thirst if the baroreceptors are also indicating low blood pressure than if they are indicating normal blood pressure.

## Sodium-Specific Cravings

Many people today have to limit their salt intake to control high blood pressure. However, although excessive salt is harmful, a certain amount of sodium chloride and other salts is necessary for life. When sodium intake is low, the adrenal glands produce the hormone **aldosterone,** which causes the kidneys to conserve sodium when excreting urine.

Individuals who have lost sodium and other solutes by bleeding or other means often experience a craving for salty tastes along with their hypovolemic thirst. That increased preference develops automatically, apparently without any trial-and-error learning (Richter, 1936). In fact, sodium-deficient animals have an increased preference for many salty-tasting solutions, including those containing lithium salts, which are poisonous (Nachman, 1962). Oddly, sodium-deficient rats show a strong preference for salty fluids, but only a mild increase in their preference for salty foods (Bertino & Tordoff, 1988). Sodium-specific cravings are the only known specific hunger that emerges as soon as the need exists; specific hungers for other vitamins and minerals have to be learned by trial and error (Rozin & Kalat, 1971). Even after an animal has recovered from sodium deficiency, it continues to show an increased preference for solutions containing sodium (Sakai, Frankmann, Fine, & Epstein, 1989).

The aldosterone evoked by the sodium deficiency is one major contributor to the salt craving (Stricker, 1983); angiotensin II is another (Dalhouse, Langford, Walsh, & Barnes, 1986). Angiotensin produces different effects in different parts of the brain; in some areas it induces both thirst and sodium preference; in other areas it induces only thirst (Fitts & Masson, 1990). The effects of aldosterone and angiotensin are strongly synergistic; together, they produce a greater effect than either one can alone (Sakai & Epstein, 1990; Stricker, 1983).

## SUMMARY

1. Drinking occurs for many reasons, often in anticipation of a need and not just in response to a current need. Most drinking occurs around mealtime, stimulated by food in the stomach. (p. 391)

2. An increase in the osmotic pressure of the blood, which draws water out of cells, causes osmotic thirst. After damage to the lateral preoptic area of the hypothalamus, an animal drinks less in response to osmotic thirst, although it still maintains a normal osmotic pressure. (p. 391)

3. A loss of blood volume causes hypovolemic thirst. Animals with hypovolemic thirst drink more water containing solutes than pure water. Hypovolemic thirst depends on brain areas surrounding the third ventricle. (p. 393)

4. Two stimuli have been identified for hypovolemic thirst: signals from the baroreceptors and the hormone angiotensin II, which increases when blood pressure falls. The two stimuli may act synergistically. (p. 394)

5. A loss of sodium salts from the body triggers sodium-specific cravings. The hormones aldosterone and angiotensin II synergistically stimulate such cravings. (p. 394)

## REVIEW QUESTIONS

1. By what mechanisms may eating lead to drinking? (p. 391)

2. Why does an injection of sodium chloride produce thirst, while an injection of an equal amount of glucose does not? (p. 392)

3. In what way does an animal with damage to the lateral preoptic area of the hypothalamus resemble an animal that has access only to bad-tasting water? (p. 392)

4. What is the difference between osmotic and hypovolemic thirst? (p. 393)

5. Which hormones synergistically promote a craving for salty tastes? (p. 395)

## THOUGHT QUESTION

1. Certain women during menstruation or pregnancy crave salt. Why?

## SUGGESTION FOR FURTHER READING

Stellar, J. R., & Stellar, E. (1985). *The neurobiology of motivation and reward.* New York: Springer-Verlag. A general treatment emphasizing hunger and thirst.

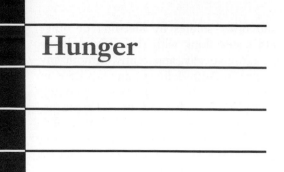

# Hunger

Imagine that your automobile needed a balanced diet, including varying proportions of 20 or more different kinds of fuel, and that the particular balance it needed varied from time to time. Imagine further that you never knew exactly what you were getting at any fuel station. The pumps contain varying combinations of gasoline, kerosene, alcohol, and other ingredients. To say the least, you would have trouble judging how much fuel to add at any time.

Regulating human food intake is even more complicated. Besides needing a balanced diet and never knowing exactly what is in our food, we need different amounts of any one nutrient depending on what other nutrients we are getting. For example, the more carbohydrates we eat, the more thiamine (vitamin $B_1$) we need. Considering all the complexities, it is amazing that anyone ever gets the right amount and balance of foods.

## THE DIGESTIVE SYSTEM AND FOOD SELECTION

Before discussing hunger, let's quickly look at the digestive system, diagrammed in Figure 11.5. Most foods consist of large molecules that cannot be used directly by the cells. The function of the digestive system is to break down the food into smaller, more easily used molecules.

Digestion begins in the mouth, where food is mixed with saliva, which contains enzymes that help break down carbohydrates. When swallowed, the food travels down the esophagus to the stomach. There, it is mixed with hydrochloric acid and several enzymes, which are mostly effective for the digestion of proteins. Between the stomach and the intestines is a round sphincter muscle that closes off the entrance to the intestines. This muscle periodically opens to allow food to enter the intestines, a bit at a time. Thus, the stomach serves as a storage place for food as well as a digestive organ.

Food then passes to the small intestine, which contains enzymes that help to digest proteins, fats, and carbohydrates. It is also the main site for the absorption

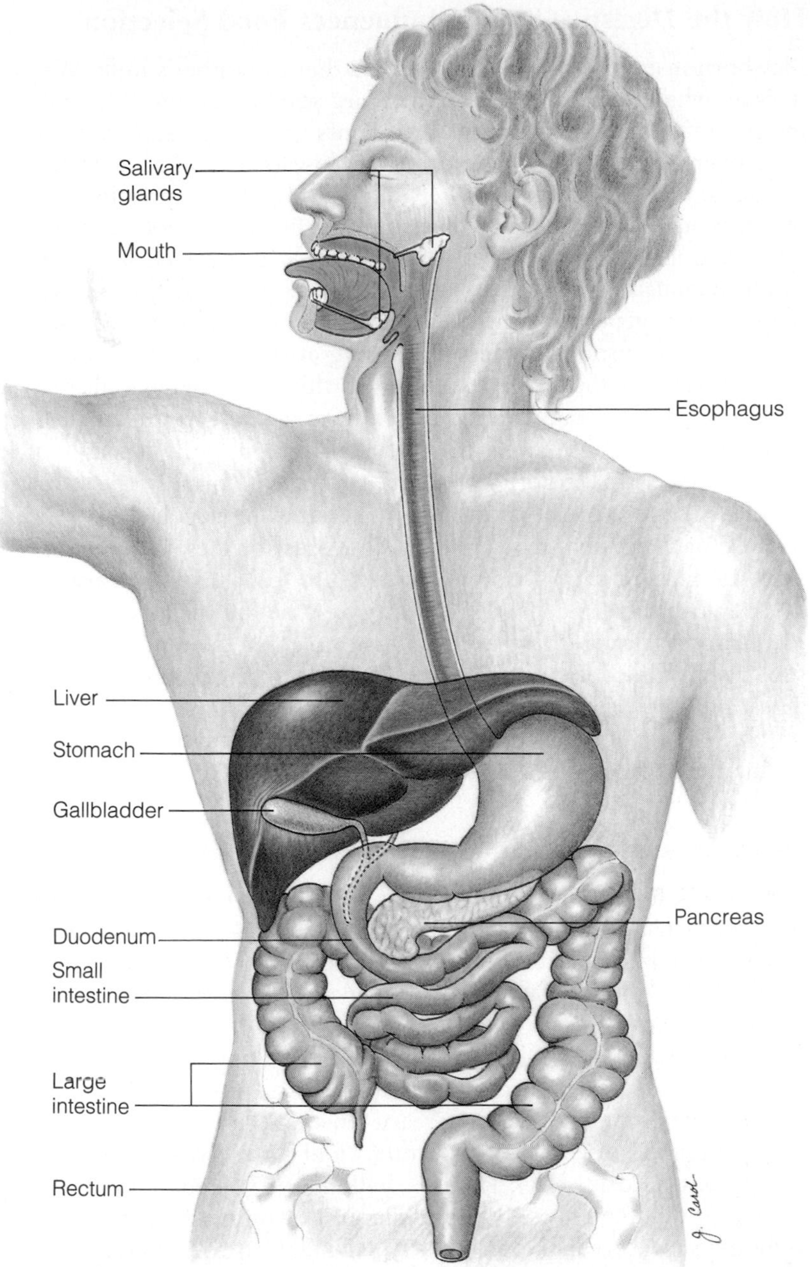

Figure 11.5
The human digestive
system

Figure 11.5 The human digestive system

of digested foodstuffs into the bloodstream; little is absorbed through the walls of the esophagus or stomach. The large intestine absorbs water and minerals and lubricates the remaining materials to pass them as feces.

Digested materials absorbed through the small intestine are carried throughout the body by the blood. If more carbohydrates, proteins, and fats are absorbed than the body can use at one time, the excess is stored as fat. Later, when the body needs additional nutrients, fat reserves are converted into glucose, the body's primary fuel, which is mobilized into the bloodstream.

Hunger

## How the Digestive System Influences Food Selection

Newborn mammals survive entirely on a diet of mother's milk. Why do they stop nursing when they grow older? There are several reasons: The milk dries up, the mother pushes the infants away, the infants grow large enough to try other foods. Moreover, after a certain age, mammals lose their ability to metabolize **lactose,** the sugar in milk, because of declining levels of the intestinal enzyme **lactase,** which is necessary for lactose metabolism. From then on, consumption of milk can cause nausea, vomiting, or other signs of distress (Rozin & Pelchat, 1988). Adult mammals can drink a *little* milk, as you may have noticed with a pet cat or dog, but they generally limit the amount. The declining level of lactase may be an evolved mechanism to encourage weaning at the appropriate time.

Humans are the partial exception to this rule. Many adult humans consume milk, cheese, ice cream, and other products derived from cow or goat milk. And their intestinal lactase levels remain at fairly high levels throughout life. Worldwide, however, the majority of adults cannot comfortably tolerate large amounts of milk products. About two-thirds of all adult humans have low levels of lactase, because of a recessive gene (Flatz, 1987). Most of these people can tolerate moderate amounts of dairy products but begin to feel ill if they consume too much. A smaller number of people can hardly consume any dairy products at all. Figure 11.6 shows the worldwide distribution of lactose tolerance. Note that most Europeans and European-Americans tolerate lactose and therefore have no trouble digesting dairy products. Most Africans and Asians have much lower tolerance for lactose. For that reason, Chinese, Japanese, Thai, and other Asian cuisines do not ordinarily use cheese or any other dairy product.

## Other Influences on Food Selection

For some animal species, selecting a suitable diet is easy; for others it can be rather difficult. A **carnivore** (meat eater) has a relatively simple task; it eats whatever animal it can catch. However, **herbivores** (plant eaters) and **omnivores** (those that eat both meat and plants) must distinguish between edible and inedible substances.

Humans, being omnivores, have to select among many possible foods. To a large extent, our culture accomplishes the task for us. Children who grow up in the United States or Canada learn that peanut butter is "food," grass is "inappropriate," insects are "disgusting," and three-day-old unrefrigerated meat is "dangerous" (Rozin, 1984; Rozin & Fallon, 1987). People in other cultures learn somewhat different rules. For example, in certain parts of the world people willingly eat sheep eyeballs, ant eggs, or rat meat. Mexicans flavor their foods with jalapeños and other hot peppers that many other people reject (Rozin, 1990).

But remove the effects of culture and then what? If you parachuted onto an island with many unfamiliar plants and no other people to guide your choices, could you figure out which ones were edible? Probably so, although you might make occasional mistakes.

You would use a variety of behavioral strategies (Rozin & Vollmecke, 1986). First, you would let taste be your guide. People and other animals have an innate preference for sweet tastes; most naturally occurring sweet substances contain carbohydrates, an important part of our diet. If we need more salt, the need triggers an increased preference for salty tastes, as described earlier (p. 395). We also have an innate dislike for bitter tastes; most bitter substances are harmful to our health (Richter, 1950).

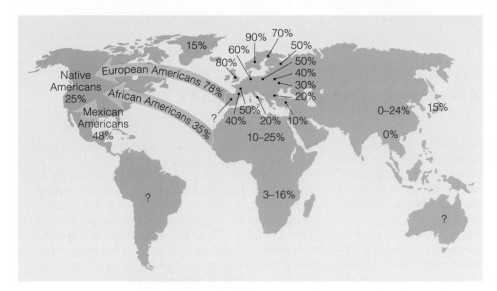

**Figure 11.6**
**The distribution of adult lactose tolerance in different parts of the world**

*People in areas with high lactose tolerance (such as Scandinavia) are likely to enjoy milk, cheese, and other dairy products throughout their lives. People in areas with low tolerance (such as much of Asia) do not ordinarily consume milk or dairy products as adults. (Based on Flatz, 1987, and Rozin & Pelchat, 1988.)*

Second, you would probably seek something that seemed familiar. Even when we try something new it is likely to be similar to an old food; if not, we tend to feel uneasy about it. The first time you tried something new, not just a rearrangement of familiar ingredients, but something with a really unfamiliar flavor—coffee, for example—you probably did not like it as much as you did later. After all, familiar foods are safe, and new foods may or may not be.

Third, you could learn about the consequences of eating various foods. When you feel nausea or similar illness, you are likely to associate the illness with foods you have eaten in the past hour or so, especially any unfamiliar foods (Rozin & Kalat, 1971; Rozin & Zellner, 1985). Thus, by rejecting foods that make you ill, you can determine which foods are acceptable. The learning of aversion to foods that are followed by illness is automatic and sometimes irrational. That is, even if you "know" you got sick from riding the roller coaster, something in your brain may blame the illness on the cotton candy you ate just before climbing aboard. (See Digression 11.1.)

## PHYSIOLOGICAL MECHANISMS OF HUNGER AND SATIETY

Newborn rats, which grow very rapidly, follow a simple rule on the consumption of mother's milk: They nurse as long as milk is available and consume as much as possible (Blass & Teicher, 1980). They stop nursing only if the milk backs up from their stomach into the esophagus so that they cannot breathe!

Bears, even as adults, tend to eat as much as they can (Herrero, 1985). Although bears will eat almost anything, most of them survive largely on nuts and berries, which are in season for only a few days or weeks at a time. When the nuts and berries are available, bears stuff them down nonstop all day long, gaining enough weight to hold them through weeks or months of little food.

Hunger

## Conditioned Taste Aversions and Cancer

When a human or other animal eats something and then gets sick, it generally learns an aversion to eating that substance. This happens even if the substance itself was harmless and the individual became ill for an unrelated reason. We call the food avoidance a **conditioned taste aversion**.

Taste aversion conditioning is ordinarily adaptive, but for cancer patients it can cause a serious problem. Certain kinds of cancer cause frequent bouts of nausea. Furthermore, many patients receive chemotherapy or X-irradiation therapy, both of which also cause nausea. Each time they become ill, they associate the illness with the last food they ate and thereby form an aversion to it. The same is true of animals with cancer (Bernstein, 1985). Many cancer patients gradually lose

their appetite; one reason is that they have learned aversions to so many foods.

Psychologists recommend several strategies to minimize the learned aversions. One is to eat nothing in the hours before chemotherapy or X-irradiation therapy. Another is to pick one "scapegoat" food — a single food that the patient deliberately eats prior to each therapy session so that the brain will always associate illness with that food, sparing all the others (Mattes, 1988). A person who learns aversions in spite of these precautions should eat one food for a while until it becomes aversive and then shift to some other food that has not already become aversive (Bernstein, Treneer, Goehler, & Murowchick, 1985).

In contrast, humans generally eat discrete meals, instead of grazing gradually, like horses, or eating until the food backs up into the esophagus, like infant rats. Something within us tells us when to start eating and when to stop. In fact, we have a number of such mechanisms; if one mechanism fails for any reason, others can do the job.

Those mechanisms work well enough for most of us. However, the enormous market for diet books, diet products, and diet aids attests to the fact that many people fail to adjust their intake to match their need. The diet aids often fail or produce problems of their own. (See Digression 11.2.)

### Oral Factors

People eat partly for the sake of taste. In one experiment, college students consumed lunch five days a week without tasting it. Each swallowed one end of a rubber tube and then pushed a button to pump a liquid diet into his or her stomach (Jordan, 1969; Spiegel, 1973). After a few days of practice, each subject established a consistent pattern, pumping in a constant volume of the liquid each day and maintaining a constant body weight. Most subjects found the untasted meals unsatisfying, however. Many reported a desire to taste or chew something. Moreover, when they were allowed to drink the liquid diet in the normal manner while also receiving it through the stomach tube, they drank almost as much as if they were receiving nothing through the tube (Jordan, 1969).

Eating is also sustained by other facial sensations. A rat explores a potential food with its mouth and whiskers before it starts to eat. The tactile sensations are conveyed to the brain via the fifth cranial nerve (the trigeminal nerve). After that nerve is cut, a rat decreases its exploration of foods and its biting of them. It can still eat moist, soft foods, using its jaw as a scoop, but it loses weight. It not only

# Amphetamine as an Appetite Suppressant

Many people who wish to lose weight resort to extreme strategies such as surgically removing fat, implanting a balloon in the stomach to occupy space, or wiring their jaws shut. Some also turn to appetite-suppressant pills, most of which contain amphetamine or related compounds.

Amphetamine does suppress appetite, at least briefly, at least the first time someone uses it. Both people and laboratory animals lose weight after taking amphetamine the first day, perhaps the first few days, but before long they stop losing and may even regain part of what they had lost, generally leveling off at almost their original weight (see, for example, Wolgin & Salisbury, 1985). That is, they develop a **drug tolerance,** a decreased response to the drug after repeated use. Why?

In two experiments, rats were given amphetamine or similar drugs 15 to 20 minutes before being offered access to milk for 15 or 30 minutes (Carlton & Wolgin, 1971; Woolverton, Kandel, & Schuster, 1978). The rats were given only a little food the rest of the day, so they were hungry enough to nibble at the food in spite of the amphetamine. The following day they were again injected with amphetamine prior to a meal; this time they nibbled a bit more. By the end of the week they were eating as much after the amphetamine injections as they had been eating previously. These rats developed tolerance because they practiced eating while under the drug's influence.

In both experiments another group received an amphetamine injection each day *after* the meal. By the end of a week, they had received as many amphetamine injections as the first group, but they had never tried to eat while under the effects of the drug. On the next day the experimenters injected both groups with amphetamine before a meal. The group that had been receiving amphetamine before meals showed strong tolerance. The group that had been re-

ceiving amphetamine after meals showed no tolerance. They just nibbled a little, as the other group had done on the first day.

The general point is that drug tolerance is based largely on learning. Several experiments with both alcohol and amphetamine confirm this conclusion: If animals are repeatedly given an opportunity to practice some behavior while under the influence of the drug, the animals eventually develop a tolerance to the drug's effect on that behavior. If animals are injected with a drug the same number of times without practicing the behavior, they develop no tolerance. The first time they try the behavior under the influence of the drug, it disrupts their performance greatly (see, for example, Campbell & Seiden, 1973; Wenger, Berlin, & Woods, 1980; Wenger, Tiffany, Bombardier, Nicholls, & Woods, 1981).

These results suggest a way to avoid developing a tolerance to appetite suppressants: Use the pill when you plan to skip a meal altogether, not when you want to eat a very small meal.

But even if this strategy reduced the effect of tolerance, amphetamine probably would not help people lose much weight in the long run, for a different reason: Someone who has skipped a meal (with or without the use of amphetamine) tends to be extra-hungry for the next meal. In another rat experiment, subjects in one group were injected with amphetamine at the start of each day's dark period (the time when rats generally eat the most). Subjects in a control group were injected with salt water at the same time. The rats that got amphetamine ate less than the control group during the first hour, but by the end of the day, both groups had eaten the same amount (Caul, Jones, & Barrett, 1988). The amphetamine had suppressed appetite temporarily, yet appetite had rebounded afterward. A person who uses amphetamine to skip one meal is likely to overeat at the next meal or two.

fails to eat properly but it also will not press a bar as much as normal for food reinforcement. Evidently, a loss of sensation from the mouth leads to a drop in food-related motivation (Zeigler, Jacquin, & Miller, 1985).

Although taste and other mouth sensations contribute to the regulation of eating, they are not sufficient by themselves to end a meal. In **sham-feeding** experiments, an animal is denied nutrition because everything it swallows leaks out

Hunger

a tube connected to the esophagus or stomach. Under such conditions, animals swallow several times as much as normal during each meal (Antin, Gibbs, Holt, Young, & Smith, 1975).

## Stomach Distention

At the end of a meal, little nutrition from the food has entered the blood or the cells. Most of the food is still in the stomach, although some may have entered the small intestine. Accumulating evidence points to **distention** (filling up) of the stomach as the primary mechanism determining the size of a meal under normal conditions.

In one experiment, researchers attached an inflatable cuff at the connection between the stomach and the small intestine (Deutsch, Young, & Kalogeris, 1978). When they inflated the cuff, it closed off the passage of food from the stomach to the duodenum. They carefully demonstrated that the cuff was not traumatic to the animal and did not interfere with feeding, even when inflated. Then they showed that with the cuff inflated, an animal would eat a normal-size meal and then stop; that is, it could become satisfied even though the food did not go beyond the stomach. Those results imply that satiety signals can arise from the stomach, perhaps in conjunction with the mouth and esophagus. They also imply that stimulation of later parts of the digestive system is not necessary for satiety.

If the experimenters withdrew 10 ml of food from the stomach, the animal ate an extra 8 ml in compensation (Deutsch et al., 1978). Apparently, an animal eats until its stomach is full, and it can eat again to return the stomach to full. The term *full* does not refer simply to bulk, however. A rat will eat a larger quantity of low-calorie food than of high-calorie food, partly because high-energy foods of any kind—carbohydrate, protein, or fat—delay emptying of the stomach (McHugh & Moran, 1985).

The stomach conveys satiety messages to the brain via the vagus nerve and the splanchnic nerves. The **vagus nerve** (cranial nerve 10) conveys information about the stretching of the stomach walls. Animals with a damaged vagus nerve eat until they overfill the stomach (Gonzalez & Deutsch, 1981). The **splanchnic** (SPLANK-nik) **nerves** (from the thoracic and lumbar parts of the spinal cord and the ganglia of the sympathetic nervous system to the digestive organs) may convey information about the nutrient contents of the stomach (Deutsch & Ahn, 1986).

Could we trigger satiety messages by artificially distending the stomach? In one study, rats were offered a high-fat diet, on which they gained weight. Then the experimenters implanted water-filled balloons to occupy about one-third of each rat's stomach. The rats ate smaller meals than before and lost weight over a period of weeks (Geliebter, Westreich, Hashim, & Gage, 1987). Whether such a procedure would be safe or effective with obese humans is unclear. (One reason for caution is that the rats' stomachs grew as a result of the balloon implants.)

## The Duodenum and the Hormone CCK

The **duodenum** (DYOU-oh-DEE-num or dyuh-ODD-ehn-uhm) is the part of the small intestine adjoining the stomach; it is the first structure of the digestive system to absorb a significant amount of nutrients. When a bulk substance (nutrient or nonnutrient) enters the duodenum, the animal decreases or stops its eating (Ehman, Albert, & Jamieson, 1971; Vanderweele, Novin, Rezek, & Sanderson, 1974).

**Cholecystokinin** (ko-leh-SIS-teh-KI-nehn) (**CCK**) — which the duodenum releases as a hormone and the brain uses as a neurotransmitter — may play an important role in satiety (Gibbs, Young, & Smith, 1973). For example, introducing food into the duodenum causes the duodenum to release CCK. When CCK is injected into a rat before a meal, the rat will eat less than normal. The more CCK injected, the smaller the meal (Antin, Gibbs, & Smith, 1978). After a large enough dose, a rat that has not fed will go through a sequence of grooming itself and then resting or sleeping, just as it would after a normal meal (Antin et al., 1975). Furthermore, researchers have found obese mice to be deficient in CCK (Straus & Yalow, 1978).

Nevertheless, the route by which CCK contributes to satiety is uncertain. We need not immediately assume that CCK travels directly to receptors in the brain to trigger satiety. One possibility is that CCK has little to do with satiety under normal circumstances. By this interpretation, injections of CCK decrease meal size only by making an animal nauseous. Studies disagree as to whether CCK induces nausea — specifically, whether rats learn an aversion to tastes that are followed by an injection of CCK (Holt, Antin, Gibbs, Young, & Smith, 1974; B. O. Moore & Deutsch, 1985; Verbalis, McCann, McHale, & Stricker, 1986).

Another possibility is that CCK does contribute to satiety under normal conditions, but by influencing the stomach rather than the brain. The effects of CCK on meal size are reduced or abolished by cutting the vagus nerve to the stomach (Hommer, Palkovits, Crawley, Paul, & Skirboll, 1985; G. P. Smith, Jerome, Cushin, Eterno, & Simansky, 1981). Perhaps CCK acts primarily as a short-term signal from the duodenum to inhibit opening the sphincter muscle between the stomach and the duodenum. That is, food entering the duodenum triggers the release of CCK, which delays further emptying of the stomach (McHugh & Moran, 1985). Thus, CCK increases satiety by promoting stomach distention.

In support of that interpretation, one study found that an injection of CCK had no effect on human appetite at the start of a meal. It did, however, shorten the meal (Pi-Sunyer, Kissileff, Thornton, & Smith, 1982). In other words, CCK magnifies the satiety-producing effect of food in the stomach.

## Blood Glucose

Digested food enters the bloodstream, much of it in the form of glucose. An important source of energy for all parts of the body, glucose is by far the most important fuel of the brain. Jean Mayer (1953) proposed that the supply of glucose to the cells is the primary basis for hunger and satiety. When the cells have too little glucose, the individual gets hungry. When they have enough, the individual becomes satiated.

An artificially produced rise in blood glucose decreases feeding (J. D. Davis, Wirtshafter, Asin, & Brief, 1981; Tordoff, Novin, & Russek, 1982), whereas a drug that prevents glucose from entering the cells leads to increased feeding (Thompson & Campbell, 1977). These results support the theory that eating is controlled partly by the availability of glucose to the cells. On the other hand, glucose is certainly not the only factor. Even fructose, a sugar that does not cross the blood-brain barrier and that cannot be converted to glucose, can suppress hunger (Stricker, Rowland, Saller, & Friedman, 1977). So can various other nutrients. Thus, hunger and satiety must be based not on glucose alone but on the availability of all types of nutrients combined (Friedman & Stricker, 1976).

The level of glucose in the blood varies little under normal conditions (Le-Magnen, 1981). Even during a period of prolonged fasting, the liver converts stored glycogen, fats, and proteins into glucose to maintain blood glucose levels.

**Figure 11.7**

*Insulin and glucagon provide a feedback system to control food intake and use. When glucose levels rise, the pancreas releases the hormone insulin, which causes cells to store the excess glucose as fats and glycogen. The entry of glucose into cells suppresses hunger. Lack of hunger leads to decreased eating, which lowers the glucose level; the pancreas releases glucagon, which stimulates the liver to convert stored glycogen into glucose, which enters the blood. The high ratio of glucagon to insulin also stimulates hunger, and the cycle repeats.*

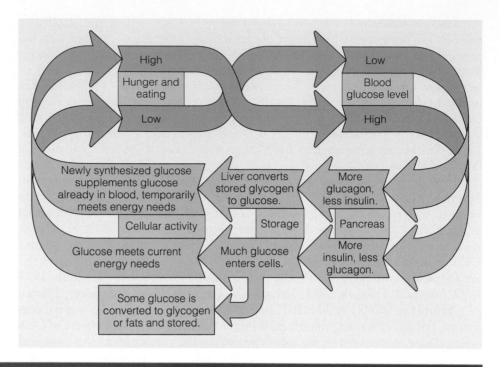

However, the availability of glucose to the cells can vary significantly as a function of changes in blood levels of two pancreatic hormones, insulin and glucagon. The hormone **insulin** facilitates the entry of glucose into the cells, which may either use the glucose for current energy needs or store it as fat or glycogen. **Glucagon,** a hormone released by the pancreas, has the reverse effect: It stimulates the liver to convert stored glycogen to glucose, thus raising blood glucose levels. After a meal, insulin levels rise, much glucose enters the cells, and appetite falls. As time passes, the blood glucose level falls, the pancreas starts releasing more glucagon and less insulin, and hunger returns (Figure 11.7).

Generally, when insulin levels are high, hunger is low. However, if the insulin level remains high and the glucagon level remains low well after the last meal, the body continues to move blood glucose into the cells, and liver cells and fat cells continue to store it as glycogen and fats. Consequently, the blood glucose available for use begins to decline. For example, in late autumn, migratory and hibernating species have high insulin levels and low glucagon levels. They rapidly deposit a large percentage of each meal as fat and glycogen and then grow hungry again (Figure 11.8). Consequently they gain much weight, which is adaptive as a preparation for a period without food. Similarly, people who have chronically high insulin levels tend to eat much and to gain weight.

When the insulin level is extremely low, as in people with diabetes, blood glucose levels may reach three times the normal level, or even more. However, little of the glucose can enter the cells (Figure 11.9). People and animals suffering from diabetes eat more food than normal because their cells are starving (Lindberg, Coburn, & Stricker, 1984), but they lose weight because they excrete most of their glucose unused. (Note the paradox that both high and very low levels of insulin can lead to increased eating, although they do so for different reasons. To maintain normal body weight, it is best to have an intermediate level of insulin.)

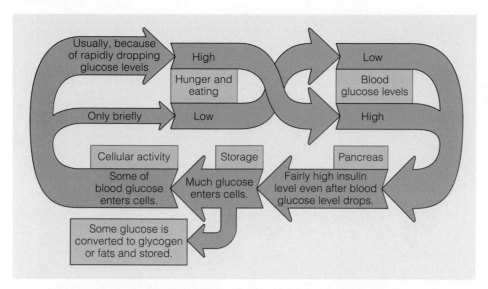

**Figure 11.8**
**Effects of steadily high insulin levels on feeding**
*Even when the glucose level is low, insulin remains high and much of the blood glucose is stored as fats and glycogen. Consequently, the blood's supply of glucose quickly drops and hunger returns.*

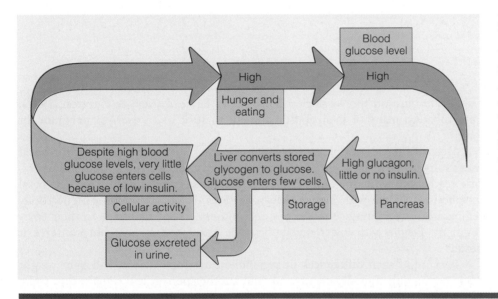

**Figure 11.9**
**Why people with untreated diabetes eat much but lose weight**
*Because of their low insulin levels, the glucose in their blood cannot enter the cells, either to be stored or to be used. Consequently, they excrete glucose in their urine while their cells are starving.*

People produce more insulin when they eat and even when they are getting ready to eat. Up to a point, that is useful, because it prepares the body to let more glucose enter the cells and to store the excess part of the meal as fats. However, obese people produce more insulin than do people of normal weight (Johnson & Wildman, 1983). Their high levels of insulin cause more of their food than normal to be stored as fat, and therefore their appetite returns sooner than normal after a meal (see Figure 11.10).

## Metabolic Rate

Weight is the outcome of both the amount of food consumed and the amount of energy used. Most obese people could lose weight by following habits of regular

**Figure 11.10
Effects of insulin on
glucose, appetite, and
weight**

*People with high insulin levels
eat much and gain weight;
people with very low levels
also eat a great deal but excrete much of what they eat.*

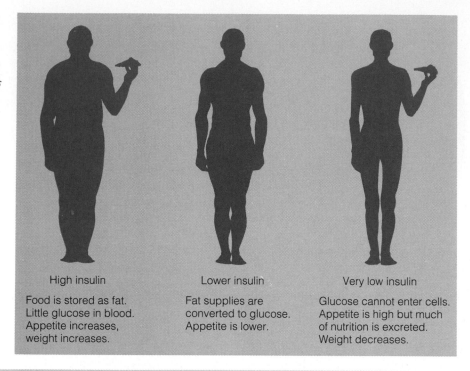

High insulin
Food is stored as fat.
Little glucose in blood.
Appetite increases,
weight increases.

Lower insulin
Fat supplies are
converted to glucose.
Appetite is lower.

Very low insulin
Glucose cannot enter cells.
Appetite is high but much
of nutrition is excreted.
Weight decreases.

exercise to burn off more calories (Thompson, Jarvie, Lahey, & Cureton, 1982); unfortunately, many of them find it difficult to stick to an exercise program for long.

Most of the calories people consume are used not for exercise but for **basal metabolism,** the processes that maintain necessary functions (including temperature regulation) while the body is at rest. People differ significantly in their basal metabolism. People with higher metabolic rates do not maintain a higher body temperature; they produce more heat than others do but radiate it to their environment. People with lower metabolic rates generate less heat but conserve it better.

Because of such differences in metabolic rates, one person will gain weight while eating only a moderate amount, and another person will remain thin while eating much more. Metabolic rates vary depending on many factors, probably including genetics (Bogardus et al., 1986). Similarly, genetic differences strongly influence body weight. According to a Danish study of 540 adopted children who had reached adulthood, their weight correlated strongly with that of their biological relatives, not with that of their adoptive relatives (Stunkard et al., 1986). The implication is that genetic differences in metabolic rate are the primary reason behind differences in adult body weight. We cannot draw a firm conclusion until someone conducts a longitudinal study linking early onset differences in metabolic rate with later-developing differences in body weight. Still, a relationship between the two seems likely.

Unfortunately for those interested in losing weight, lowering food intake leads to a compensatory decrease in metabolic rate (McMinn, 1984). That is, if you adhere to a low-calorie diet, your metabolic rate will decrease and you will burn fewer calories. So after the first few pounds, losing weight becomes more difficult.

## Food-Specific Mechanisms of Satiety

Imagine that a food-deprived, water-deprived rat comes upon a tube full of liquid. At first it does not know what is in the tube; how will it know how much to drink? Until it tastes the liquid, it does *not* know how much it will drink (Mook, 1990).

It tastes the liquid. If the liquid is plain water, the rat drinks a certain amount based on how long it has been deprived of water. If the liquid is sugar water, the rat's intake depends on its need for food, not its need for water. If the liquid contains saccharin, a nonnutritive sweetener, again the rat's intake depends on its need for food. (That is, the rat treats the solution as food, even though it is not.) In short, taste tells the rat whether to use its thirst system or its hunger system to determine satiety. If the rat were salt-deficient as well, a salty-tasting liquid could turn on yet another mechanism.

To some extent, different foods also activate different satiety mechanisms. Suppose you sit down to a meal of baked potatoes. After you eat two or three, your host asks whether you would like another. "No," you reply, "I'm full." You may be too polite to explain, "I'm full *of baked potatoes*. If you had something else, I might be interested in eating again."

The same is true of other animals. A rat that seems fully satiated after eating one substance may begin eating again if it encounters another food (Mook, 1990). (This tendency increases the probability that the rat will eat a varied diet.) Furthermore, taste tells the rat which satiety mechanism to rely on. With most foods, a rat eats more if this is its first meal in 24 hours than if the last meal was just 2 or 3 hours ago. That is, most foods prompt the rat to use satiety mechanisms sensitive to stomach distention, intestinal distention, and blood sugar. However, when the rat finds a concentrated sugar solution, it suddenly relies almost entirely on oral factors to determine satiety. It takes a certain number of licks and then stops, almost independently of how long it has been since the last meal. (For people, certain tasty snacks may be analogous. Would you eat an ice cream cone even when you are not hungry?) Satiety is no simple matter. The conditions for stopping a meal vary depending on the meal.

# BRAIN MECHANISMS IN HUNGER AND SATIETY

In the 1940s and 1950s, investigators discovered that damage to the lateral hypothalamus decreased eating and that damage to the ventromedial hypothalamus increased eating. Their initial interpretation was that the lateral hypothalamus controlled hunger and that the ventromedial hypothalamus controlled satiety. Later it became clear that brain damage can affect feeding in many ways other than simply by controlling hunger and satiety. For example, it can alter activity levels or it can alter the activity of the autonomic nervous system and thus change the activity of the digestive organs. Although most investigators no longer accept the simple idea of a "hunger center" or a "satiety center" in the brain, patterns of activity in certain parts of the hypothalamus can have a powerful effect on feeding.

## The Lateral Hypothalamus

After damage to the **lateral hypothalamus** (Figure 11.11), an animal refuses food and water and starves to death unless it is force-fed, in which case it gradually recovers. Electrical stimulation of the lateral hypothalamus, on the other hand, causes an animal to eat (Brügger, 1943).

**Figure 11.11**
**Three areas of the rat hypothalamus where stimulation or damage produces marked effects on feeding**
*The side view of a rat's head above indicates the plane of the coronal section of the brain below. (After Hart, 1976.)*

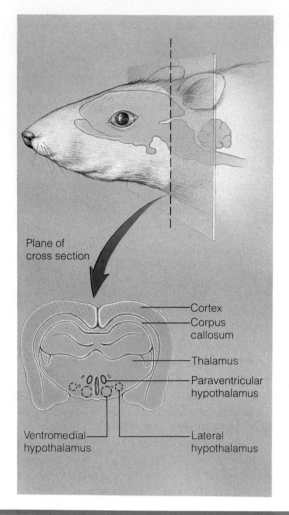

Plane of cross section

Cortex
Corpus callosum
Thalamus
Paraventricular hypothalamus
Ventromedial hypothalamus
Lateral hypothalamus

Damage to the lateral hypothalamus interferes with more than just feeding, however. Animals with lesions are underaroused (Figure 11.12), underresponsive to sensory stimuli (Marshall & Teitelbaum, 1974), and inactive. Such animals, ordinarily unresponsive to food as well as other stimuli, increase their eating in response to a mild pinch of their tail (O'Brien, Chesire, & Teitelbaum, 1985). Evidently lack of arousal is part of the feeding problem.

It is not the whole problem, however, and the mechanisms of arousal are partly separable from the mechanisms of feeding. An ordinary electrode-based lesion of the hypothalamus damages both the neurons there and the dopamine-containing axons passing through the area. The neurons and passing axons apparently have different functions. Using other procedures, an investigator can limit the damage to either the axons or the cells. To destroy the axons alone, investigators inject 6-hydroxydopamine (6-OHDA), which damages only neurons that manufacture dopamine. An injection of 6-OHDA to the lateral hypothalamus damages dopamine-containing axons but spares other neurons. Rats that receive such an injection become very deficient at seeking food (or anything else). However, they react normally to food placed into their mouths (Berridge, Venier, & Robinson, 1989). Evidently those axons are critical for arousal but not directly responsible for hunger.

To destroy neurons, experimenters can inject kainic acid, which destroys cell bodies in the area of the injection but spares axons passing through the area (S. P. Grossman, Dacey, Halaris, Collier, & Routtenberg, 1978; Stricker, Swerdloff, & Zigmond, 1978). They can also make lesions in the lateral hypothalamus of 10-day-old rats, before axons have grown into the area (Almli, Fisher, & Hill, 1979). Either method impairs eating without a significant loss of arousal or responsiveness to stimuli. Evidently the cell bodies of the lateral hypothalamus contribute mainly to feeding, while the passing fibers contribute to overall arousal.

The question remains, *how* does the lateral hypothalamus contribute to feeding? Part of the answer is that activity of the lateral hypothalamus stimulates the release of insulin and digestive juices in the stomach (Morley, Bartness, Gosnell, & Levine, 1985). After damage to this brain area, an animal has low levels of insulin and digestive juices. It has difficulty digesting its foods and little motivation to do so because its fat reserves are being converted into blood glucose, in response to the drop in insulin levels. The animal has fairly high levels of blood sugar even without eating.

## The Ventromedial Hypothalamus

Adjacent to the lateral hypothalamus is the **ventromedial hypothalamus** (Figure 11.11). Damage to that nucleus, including axons passing through and around it, produces effects that are nearly the opposite of those produced by damage to the lateral hypothalamus. The animal eats and drinks excessive amounts and gains weight, sometimes a lot of weight (see Figure 11.13). An adult female rat may double or triple her weight after the lesion. Certain humans with damage in the ventromedial hypothalamus have been known to gain more than 10 kilograms per month (Al-Rashid, 1971; Killeffer & Stern, 1970; Reeves & Plum, 1969). Table 11.2 summarizes the effects of lesions in several areas of the hypothalamus.

Besides eating excessively and gaining weight, rats with ventromedial hypothalamic damage show several other changes in behavior:

1. They drink excessive amounts of water (Wishart & Walls, 1975).

2. They are less responsive than normal rats are to the satiating effects of glucose; introducing large amounts of glucose into their digestive system decreases their food intake less than it does with normal rats (Panksepp, 1973).

3. They are finicky eaters. They overeat on a normal diet and overeat even more on a particularly tasty diet (Ferguson & Keesey, 1975; Teitelbaum, 1955).

4. Although they overeat when food is readily available, they will not work as hard as normal rats will to get food (N. E. Miller, Bailey, & Stevenson, 1950; Teitelbaum, 1957).

Exactly why do animals with damage to the ventromedial hypothalamus overeat? Apparently such animals are not simply deficient in satiety messages. If they were unresponsive to the satiating effects of a meal, each meal should be larger than normal. In fact, however, each meal is about normal in size, but the rats eat *more frequently* than normal—especially during daylight hours, when rats are ordinarily inactive (Duggan & Booth, 1986).

They eat more frequently for two reasons. First, their stomachs empty faster than those of other rats, particularly during daylight hours (Duggan & Booth, 1986). The faster the stomach empties, the sooner an animal is ready for its next meal. Second, damage to the ventromedial hypothalamus leads to a lasting increase in insulin production. (Damage to the lateral hypothalamus produces the opposite effect.) Rats with such damage have higher than normal insulin levels at all times and respond to meals with even larger insulin increases (King, Smith, &

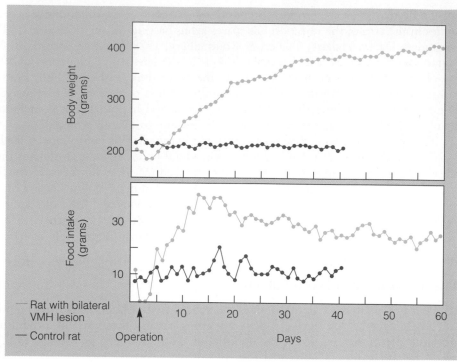

a   b

## Figure 11.13
## The effects of damage to the ventromedial hypothalamus

*(a) On the right, a normal rat. On the left, a rat after damage to the ventromedial hypothalamus. The brain-damaged rat may weigh up to three times as much as a normal rat. (Yoav Levy/Photo-take.) (b) Changes in weight and eating in a rat after damage to the ventromedial hypothalamus. Within a few days after the operation, the rat begins eating much more than normal. As it gains weight, its eating decreases, although it remains above normal. (Adapted from Teitelbaum, 1961.)*

Frohman, 1984). Because of the increased insulin, a larger than normal percentage of each meal is stored as fat. If animals with this kind of damage are kept on a strict diet and are prevented from eating more than they had prior to the lesion, they gain weight anyway! Mark Friedman and Edward Stricker (1976) have therefore proposed that the animal does not gain weight because it overeats; rather, it has to overeat because it stores excessive fat. It has no more usable fuel in its bloodstream than a starving animal has. What it eats is largely converted to fat; to have enough fuel for its current use, it must continue to eat.

## Eating and Neurotransmitters

Advances in our understanding often result from improved technology for conducting experiments or for measuring results. A new technology for studying the effects of neurotransmitters on feeding has facilitated a more detailed investigation of events in the hypothalamus.

**Microdialysis** is a method for extracting minute amounts of chemicals from a brain area. Using stereotaxic procedures, as described in Chapter 4, an investigator implants a tube with a thin membrane, across which chemicals can diffuse. The experimenter withdraws fluid and measures the concentrations of various chemicals. With this procedure, investigators have found that when rats eat something they like, especially if it contains carbohydrates, the lateral hypothalamus and probably other hypothalamic areas release tiny quantities of dopamine and serotonin (Hernandez & Hoebel, 1988; Schwartz, McClane, Hernandez, & Hoebel, 1989; Stanley, Schwartz, Hernandez, Leibowitz, & Hoebel, 1989). The dopamine may be important for the reward value of eating; its release is closely correlated with how hard the animal will work for food. But the serotonin apparently contributes to ending the meal.

| Table 11.2 Effects of Lesions in Certain Areas of the Hypothalamus | |
|---|---|
| *Hypothalamic Area* | *Effect of Lesion* |
| Preoptic area | Deficit in physiological mechanisms of temperature regulation |
| Lateral preoptic area | Deficit in osmotic thirst |
| Areas surrounding third ventricle | Deficit in hypovolemic thirst |
| Lateral hypothalamus | Undereating, weight loss, low insulin level (because of damage to cell bodies); underarousal, underresponsiveness (because of damage to passing axons) |
| Ventromedial hypothalamus | Overeating, weight gain, high insulin level |

Injecting serotonin into any of several locations in the hypothalamus suppresses carbohydrate intake (Weiss, Papadakos, Knudson, & Leibowitz, 1986). If rats (which are nocturnal) have a choice of foods, they generally choose mostly carbohydrates for their first meal after awakening (at the start of the night). Consequently, injecting serotonin into the brain tends to suppress the first meal of the day but has less effect on later meals (Leibowitz, Weiss, Walsh, & Viswanath, 1989).

Injecting norepinephrine or endorphins into the **paraventricular nucleus** (an area of the hypothalamus near the ventromedial nucleus; see Figure 11.11) increases feeding, mostly by increasing meal size rather than meal frequency (Shimazu, Megumi, & Saito, 1986; Shor-Posner, Grinker, Marinescu, & Leibowitz, 1985; Woods & Leibowitz, 1985). How much an animal eats, at least for carbohydrate meals, seems to depend on the balance between competing sets of neurotransmitters: Norepinephrine and endorphins stimulate feeding, and serotonin inhibits it. These are just a few of the many neurotransmitters and hormones that alter various aspects of feeding (Hoebel, 1988).

## INTEGRATION OF MULTIPLE MECHANISMS

We began this chapter with a discussion of homeostasis. Eating has a roughly homeostatic effect; it tends to maintain a fairly constant supply of fuel to the cells and a fairly constant body weight. However, the brain does not simply try to hold a single variable near a set point. Instead, it monitors blood glucose, stomach distention, duodenal distention, body weight, and probably other physiological variables as well. It anticipates future needs as well as responding to current needs. Integrating such diverse and sometimes contradictory information provides a kind of security: If one system provides faulty information, other systems can override that system.

Moreover, people sometimes ignore their physiological signals. They may eat highly attractive foods even when they are satiated and refrain from eating unacceptable foods even when they are hungry. Eating is a complex behavior that depends on an array of cognitive, social, and physiological influences.

## SUMMARY

1. The ability to digest a food is one major determinant of preference for eating that food. For example, people who cannot digest lactose generally do not like to eat dairy products. (p. 398)

2. Other major determinants of food selection include innate preferences for certain tastes, a preference for familiar foods, and the ability to learn about the consequences of foods. (p. 398)

3. People and animals eat partly for the sake of taste. However, a sham-feeding animal, which tastes its foods but does not absorb them, eats far more than normal. (p. 400)

4. The primary factor limiting the size of a meal is stomach distention. Nerves from the stomach report information concerning both mechanical distention and nutrient content. (p. 402)

5. When food reaches the duodenum, it stimulates the release of CCK, which decreases food intake by inhibiting the further release of food from the stomach and possibly by other means. (p. 402)

6. Hunger increases when little glucose and other fuels reach the cells; it decreases when much glucose is available to the cells. Such fluctuations ordinarily depend on the hormones insulin and glucagon, which control the storage of food supplies as fat. (p. 403)

7. People differ in their metabolic rates, partly for genetic reasons. It is likely that a low metabolic rate leads to weight gain. (p. 405)

8. The conditions necessary for achieving satiety vary depending on what the meal contains. Different foods trigger the use of different satiety mechanisms. (p. 407)

9. Damage to cells in the lateral hypothalamus leads to decreased eating and loss of weight, partly because of decreased digestive juices and partly because of a drop in insulin levels. (p. 407)

10. Damage to the ventromedial hypothalamus leads to more frequent meals and weight gain, partly because of more rapid stomach emptying and partly because of an increase in insulin levels. (p. 409)

11. Feeding, at least for carbohydrate meals, depends on competition between norepinephrine and endorphins on the stimulating side and serotonin on the inhibiting side. (p. 410)

## REVIEW QUESTIONS

1. Why do Asian cooks seldom if ever use cheese and other dairy products? (p. 398)

2. What should a cancer patient do to avoid learning aversions to many foods? (p. 400)

3. Why are amphetamine pills generally ineffective as a long-term aid to losing weight? (p. 401)

4. What evidence points to stomach distention as a major contributor to satiety? (p. 402)

5. What causes release of the hormone CCK? By what mechanism does CCK probably act in limiting meal size? (p. 403)

6. Why do high levels of insulin and very low levels of insulin *both* lead to increased eating? (p. 404)

7. Describe several biological reasons why certain people may become overweight. (Refer to stomach emptying speed, CCK, insulin levels, and genetic differences in metabolic rate.) (pp. 402–406)

8. How does damage to the lateral hypothalamus affect eating? (p. 407)

9. How could an investigator destroy axons passing through the lateral hypothalamus without destroying cells in the area? How could he or she destroy cells without damaging the axons? (p. 408)

10. Through what two mechanisms does damage to the ventromedial hypothalamus lead to weight gain? (p. 409)

11. What kind of questions can investigators answer with microdialysis that they could not answer with lesions and electrical stimulation? (p. 410)

## THOUGHT QUESTION

1. For most people, insulin levels tend to be higher during the day than during the night. Use this fact to explain why people grow hungry a few hours after a meal during the day, but not so quickly at night.

## SUGGESTIONS FOR FURTHER READING

**Hoebel, B. G.** (1988). Neuroscience and motivation: Pathways and peptides that define motivational systems. In R. C. Atkinson, R. J. Herrnstein, G. Lindzey, & R. D. Luce (Eds.), *Stevens' handbook of experimental psychology* (2nd ed.) (pp. 547–625). New York: Wiley. Review of brain mechanisms in feeding.

Logue, A. W. (1986). *The psychology of eating and drinking*. New York: Freeman. Discussion includes both normal eating and disorders such as anorexia nervosa and bulimia.

## GLOSSARY

**aldosterone** adrenal hormone that causes the kidneys to conserve sodium when excreting urine

**angiotensin II** hormone that constricts the blood vessels

**antidiuretic hormone (ADH)** pituitary hormone that inhibits urine production

**baroreceptor** receptor that detects the blood pressure in the largest blood vessels

**basal metabolism** rate of energy use while the body is at rest

**carnivore** animal that eats meat

**cholecystokinin (CCK)** hormone released by the duodenum in response to food distention

**conditioned taste aversion** avoidance of tastes that have been followed by illness

**distention** filling up of the stomach or intestines

**drug tolerance** decreased response to a drug after repeated use of it

**duodenum** part of the small intestine adjoining the stomach

**glucagon** pancreatic hormone that stimulates the liver to convert stored glycogen to glucose

**herbivore** animal that eats plants

**homeostasis** tendency to maintain some variable, such as temperature, within a fixed range

**homeothermic** maintaining nearly constant body temperature over a wide range of environmental temperatures

**hypovolemic thirst** thirst provoked by low blood volume

**insulin** hormone that facilitates the entry of glucose into the cells

**lactase** enzyme necessary for lactose metabolism

**lactose** the sugar in milk

**lateral hypothalamus** area of the hypothalamus in which damage impairs eating, drinking, and activity

**lateral preoptic area** portion of the hypothalamus important for osmotic thirst

**microdialysis** method for delivering minute amounts of chemicals to a brain area or extracting minute amounts of chemicals from a brain area

**omnivore** animal that eats both meat and plants

**osmotic pressure** force exerted by the concentration of a solute in water solution toward other solutions separated from it by a semipermeable membrane

**osmotic thirst** thirst that results from an increase in the concentration of solutes in the body

**paraventricular nucleus** area of the hypothalamus in which norepinephrine or endorphin injections increase meal size

**poikilothermic** maintaining the body at the same temperature as the surrounding environment

**preoptic area** nucleus adjacent to the anterior hypothalamus, important for temperature control

**prostaglandin $E_1$** chemical produced during an infection, which stimulates an increase in body temperature

**set point** level at which homeostatic processes maintain some variable

**sham feeding** preparation in which everything an animal swallows leaks out a tube connected to the esophagus or stomach

**splanchnic nerve** nerve from the thoracic and lumbar parts of the spinal cord and the ganglia of the sympathetic nervous system to the digestive organs

**subfornical organ** brain structure adjoining the third ventricle, important for monitoring blood volume and contributing to hypovolemic thirst

**synergistic effect** tendency for two influences acting simultaneously to produce more than twice the effect of either influence acting alone

**vagus nerve** tenth cranial nerve, which sends branches to the stomach and several other organs

**vasopressin** pituitary hormone that raises blood pressure

**ventromedial hypothalamus (VMH)** one of the nuclei of the hypothalamus, in which damage leads to faster stomach emptying and increased secretion of insulin

# CHAPTER TWELVE

# Hormones and Sexual Behavior

## MAIN IDEAS

**1.** Hormones exert effects on behavior either by attaching to receptors on the membrane of a cell or by attaching to receptors within the cell that alter the expression of the genes.

**2.** Sex hormones have organizing and activating effects. Organizing effects are permanent effects on anatomy and the brain, exerted during a critical period of early development. Activating effects are transient effects exerted at any later time.

**3.** In mammals, the presence or absence of testosterone determines whether the gonads and hypothalamus will develop in the male or the female manner, although for certain characteristics testosterone must first be converted to estradiol within the cell.

**4.** Numerous sex hormones, including testosterone and estradiol, can activate specific sexual behaviors, aggressive behaviors, and parental behaviors, depending on the behavior, species, and sex of the individual.

**5.** In nonhuman animals, the organizing effects of hormones can alter many aspects of sexual development including response to male and female partners. Prenatal hormones may also influence human gender identity and sexual orientation; however, convincing evidence is difficult to obtain.

(*Butch Martin/TIB West.*)

At the start of the preceding chapter, I defined life as a coordinated set of chemical reactions. That bare minimum definition omits a critical element: reproduction. Standard biological definitions of life stipulate that a system can be considered alive only if it has the potential to metabolize energy and to reproduce.

We allow for certain exceptions to this definition. Although mules are infertile, no one doubts that they are alive. The same is true for worker bees, the very young and the very old of all species, and various other individuals. Still, for a species to survive, at least certain members of the species must reproduce often enough to replace the individuals that die.

For humans, nearly all other vertebrates, and a large proportion of invertebrates, reproduction occurs sexually. A sperm from the male and an ovum from the female combine to produce a new individual not quite the same as either parent. The constant reshuffling of genes enables the species to adapt evolutionarily to a changing environment. It also provides enough variability among individuals to make it difficult for any one strain of virus or bacterium to wipe out the entire population.

Reproduction is not always easy, however. To reproduce, an individual must find a healthy, sexually mature member of the opposite sex of its own species. It must persuade that partner to accept it as a mate and then synchronize its behavior with that of its partner so that both are ready to engage in the sex act at the same time. Finally, once the young have made their appearance, in most species one or both of the partners must provide care for the young until they are ready to care for themselves.

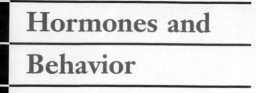

# Hormones and Behavior

In fall, migratory birds prepare for a long flight. The preparation includes changes in eating and metabolism to store enough fat for the journey, a tendency to join into flocks with others of the species, and a preference for flying in a direction somehow identified as "south." In the spring, the same birds fly back north. At that time their feathers change to breeding colors, the birds start looking for appropriate mates, and males start singing. The coordination of widespread changes thoughout the body, such as those that accompany migration and mating, in many cases depends on hormones.

In humans, too, hormones control a wide variety of behaviors; Chapter 11 mentioned the roles of angiotensin, aldosterone, and insulin in drinking and feeding. Hormones are so important to sexual behavior, however, that this is a good context for discussing hormones in general. A **hormone** is a chemical that is secreted by a gland and conveyed by the blood or lymphatic system to other organs, whose activity it influences. Figure 12.1 presents the major **endocrine (hormone-producing) glands.** Table 12.1 lists some important hormones and their principal effects.

## MECHANISMS OF HORMONE ACTIONS

The effects of hormones on behavior overlap greatly with the effects of neurotransmitters. A number of chemicals—including epinephrine, norepinephrine, angiotensin, and CCK—are classed as both neurotransmitters and hormones. The difference between a neurotransmitter and a hormone is that a neurotransmitter is released directly adjacent to the target cell, while a hormone is carried by the blood to targets throughout the body. But even this distinction can be blurry; neurotransmitters sometimes diffuse over a fairly broad area of the brain.

Hormones fall into three major classes with different chemical structures: peptide hormones, thyroid hormones, and steroid hormones (Hadley, 1984). **Peptide hormones** are composed of a chain of amino acids. Insulin is one example of a peptide hormone. *Glycoproteins*, a special kind of peptide hormone, consist

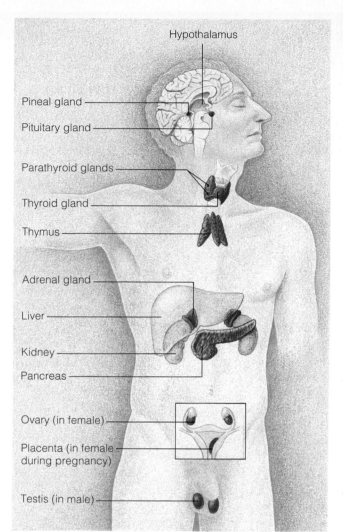

**Figure 12.1**
**Location of some of the major endocrine glands in the human body**
*(From Starr & Taggart, 1989.)*

Hypothalamus

Pineal gland

Pituitary gland

Parathyroid glands

Thyroid gland

Thymus

Adrenal gland

Liver

Kidney

Pancreas

Ovary (in female)

Placenta (in female during pregnancy)

Testis (in male)

of a chain of amino acids attached to a carbohydrate. Peptide hormones attach to receptors on the cell membrane, where they activate an enzyme that produces cyclic AMP, a second messenger. Cyclic AMP then activates a number of enzymes that may alter the metabolism of the cell or the ability of various ions to cross the membrane (Figure 12.2). These changes in the cell may last minutes to hours. Note that peptide hormones affect cells by the same route as peptide neurotransmitters do (Chapter 3).

The thyroid gland produces **thyroid hormones** from the amino acid tyrosine. The two thyroid hormones, triiodothyronine ($T_3$) and thyroxine ($T_4$), both contain iodine. A deficiency of iodine in the diet can impair the thyroid gland's functioning. Thyroid hormones enter the cells, where they bind to receptors in the cytoplasm, mitochondria, and nucleus. They exert their principal effects by increasing or decreasing the expression of certain genes. (In a given cell at a given time, some genes are active and some are not. We say that the active

Hormones and
Behavior

## Table 12.1 Partial List of Hormone-Releasing Glands

| Organ | Hormones | Hormone Functions |
|---|---|---|
| Hypothalamus | Various releasing hormones | Promote or inhibit release of various hormones by pituitary |
| Anterior pituitary | TSH (thyroid-stimulating hormone) | Stimulates thyroid gland |
| | LH (luteinizing hormone) | Increases production of progesterone (female), testosterone (male) |
| | FSH (follicle-stimulating hormone) | Increases production of estrogen and maturation of ovum (female) and production of sperm (male) |
| | ACTH | Increases secretion of steroid hormones by adrenal gland |
| | Prolactin | Increases milk production |
| Posterior pituitary | Oxytocin | Controls uterine contractions and milk production |
| | Vasopressin | Constricts blood vessels, raises blood pressure |
| Pineal | Melatonin | Contributes to regulation of sleep-activity cycles |
| Thyroid | Thyroxine, triiodothyronine | Increase metabolic rate, growth, and maturation |
| Parathyroid | Parathyroid hormone | Increases blood calcium, decreases potassium |
| Adrenal cortex | Aldosterone | Reduces excretion of salts by kidney |
| | Cortisol, corticosterone | Stimulate liver to elevate blood sugar, increase metabolism of proteins and fats |
| Adrenal medulla | Epinephrine, norepinephrine | Similar to effects of sympathetic nervous system |
| Pancreas | Insulin | Increases entry of glucose to cells, increases storage as fats |
| | Glucagon | Increases conversion of stored fats to blood glucose |
| Ovary | Estrogens | Promote ovulation and female sexual characteristics |
| | Progesterone | Maintains pregnancy |
| Testis | Androgens | Promote sperm production, growth of pubic hair, male sexual characteristics |
| Liver | Somatomedins | Stimulate growth |
| Kidney | Angiotensin | Controls blood pressure and aldosterone secretion |
| Thymus | Thymosin (and others) | Promote immune responses |

genes are expressed; the others are not.) In this manner thyroid hormones increase metabolic rate and use of fuel.

**Steroid hormones** contain four carbon rings, as Figure 12.3 shows. Steroid hormones exert their effects through a mechanism similar to that of thyroid hormones: Steroid hormones enter the cell and attach to receptors in the cytoplasm, which then move to the nucleus of the cell where they determine which genes will be expressed (Evans & Arriza, 1989; see Figure 12.4). Steroids can also exert more rapid effects analogous to those of peptide hormones, altering the transmission of ions across the membrane (Nabekura, Oomura, Minami, Mizuno, & Fukuda, 1986).

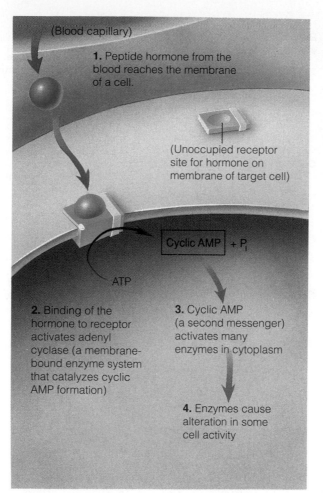

**Figure 12.2**
**Mechanism of action by a peptide hormone**
*When it attaches to its receptor, it activates an enzyme system that releases the second messenger, cyclic AMP, which in turn activates other enzymes that alter the cell's activity. (From Starr & Taggart, 1989.)*

(Blood capillary)

**1.** Peptide hormone from the blood reaches the membrane of a cell.

(Unoccupied receptor site for hormone on membrane of target cell)

Cyclic AMP $+ P_i$

ATP

**2.** Binding of the hormone to receptor activates adenyl cyclase (a membrane-bound enzyme system that catalyzes cyclic AMP formation)

**3.** Cyclic AMP (a second messenger) activates many enzymes in cytoplasm

**4.** Enzymes cause alteration in some cell activity

Cortisol and corticosterone, steroid hormones released by the adrenal cortex, elevate blood sugar and enhance metabolism. They are particularly important in helping the body adapt to prolonged stress.

Two classes of steroid hormones, the **estrogens** (more abundant in females in most species) and the **androgens** (more abundant in males), turn on the genes that contribute to both the physical and behavioral aspects of sexuality. Like other steroid hormones, estrogens and androgens increase the synthesis of certain kinds of RNA and proteins by a factor of 20 to 60 (Shapiro et al., 1989). Some of the genes that sex hormones activate are called **sex-limited genes** because we see their effects much more strongly in one sex than in the other. For example, estrogen activates the genes responsible for breast development in women, and androgens activate the genes responsible for the growth of facial hair in men. Sex hormones can also increase the expression of certain genes in both sexes. For example, androgens stimulate the growth of pubic hair in both sexes. Estrogens increase the number of $5\text{-HT}_1$ receptor sites in the brain (Fischette, Biegon, &

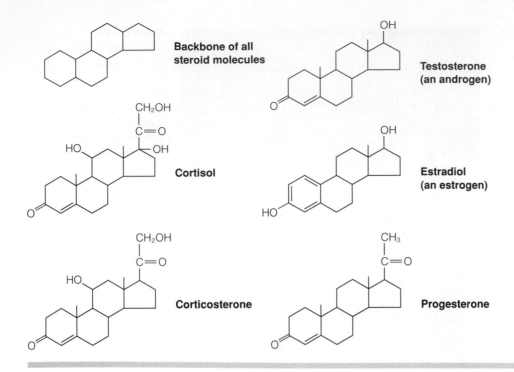

**Figure 12.3**
**Steroid hormones**
*Note the similarity between the sex hormones testosterone and estradiol.*

McEwen, 1983) and the concentration of one protein that contributes to olfaction (Simerly, Young, Capozza, & Swanson, 1989).

Within the brain, estrogen receptors are more abundant in some areas and androgen receptors in others. Thus each hormone affects a different population of neurons and therefore different sets of behaviors (McEwen & Pfaff, 1985).

## Control of Hormone Release

Just as circulating hormones modify brain activity, the brain secretes hormones and controls the secretion of many other hormones. The hypothalamus is attached to the **pituitary gland,** as Figure 12.5 illustrates. The pituitary consists of two distinct glands, the **anterior pituitary** and the **posterior pituitary,** which release different sets of hormones (Table 12.1).

The posterior pituitary, composed of neural tissue, can be considered an extension of the hypothalamus. Cells in the hypothalamus synthesize two hormones, oxytocin and vasopressin (also known as antidiuretic hormone) and then transport them to the posterior hypothalamus, as shown in Figure 12.6. The posterior pituitary stores these hormones until stimulated to release them.

The anterior pituitary, composed of glandular tissue, synthesizes six hormones itself. However, the hypothalamus controls their release (see Figure 12.7). The hypothalamus secretes **releasing hormones,** which flow through the blood to the anterior pituitary. There they stimulate or inhibit the release of six known hormones, five of which control the secretions of other endocrine organs (see Figure 12.8):

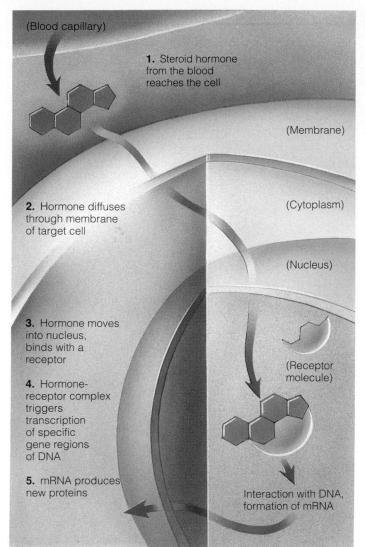

**Figure 12.4**
**Mechanism of action of a steroid hormone**
*The hormone enters a cell, binds with a receptor in the nucleus, and thereby activates particular genes. As a result, the cell increases its production of specific proteins. (From Starr & Taggart, 1989.)*

(Blood capillary)

**1.** Steroid hormone from the blood reaches the cell

(Membrane)

**2.** Hormone diffuses through membrane of target cell

(Cytoplasm)

(Nucleus)

**3.** Hormone moves into nucleus, binds with a receptor

**4.** Hormone-receptor complex triggers transcription of specific gene regions of DNA

**5.** mRNA produces new proteins

(Receptor molecule)

Interaction with DNA, formation of mRNA

| | |
|---|---|
| Adrenocorticotropic hormone (ACTH) | Controls secretions of the adrenal cortex |
| Thyroid-stimulating hormone (TSH) | Controls secretions of the thyroid gland |
| Follicle-stimulating hormone (FSH) } Luteinizing hormone (LH) | Control secretions of the gonads |
| Prolactin | Controls secretions of the mammary glands |
| Somatotropin, also known as growth hormone (GH) | Promotes growth throughout the body |

The hypothalamus maintains fairly constant circulating levels of certain hormones. For example, when the level of thyroid hormone is low, the hypothalamus

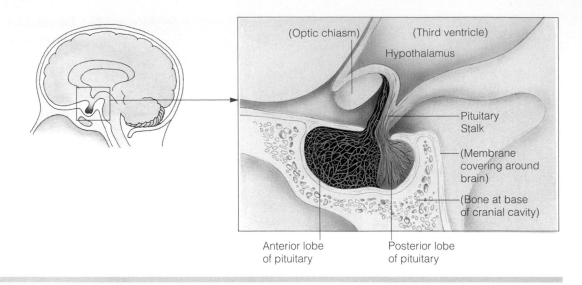

(Optic chiasm)     (Third ventricle)

Hypothalamus

Pituitary Stalk

(Membrane covering around brain)

(Bone at base of cranial cavity)

Anterior lobe of pituitary

Posterior lobe of pituitary

**Figure 12.5**
**Location of the hypothalamus and pituitary gland in the human brain**
*(From Starr & Taggart, 1989.)*

**Figure 12.6**
**Production of oxytocin and vasopressin in the hypothalamus, and their storage and release by the posterior pituitary**
*(From Starr & Taggart, 1989.)*

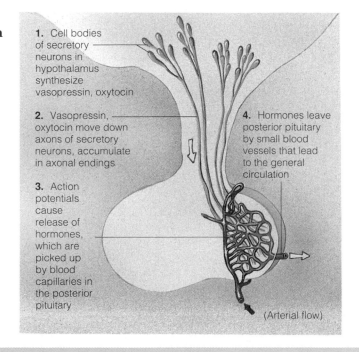

**1.** Cell bodies of secretory neurons in hypothalamus synthesize vasopressin, oxytocin

**2.** Vasopressin, oxytocin move down axons of secretory neurons, accumulate in axonal endings

**3.** Action potentials cause release of hormones, which are picked up by blood capillaries in the posterior pituitary

**4.** Hormones leave posterior pituitary by small blood vessels that lead to the general circulation

(Arterial flow)

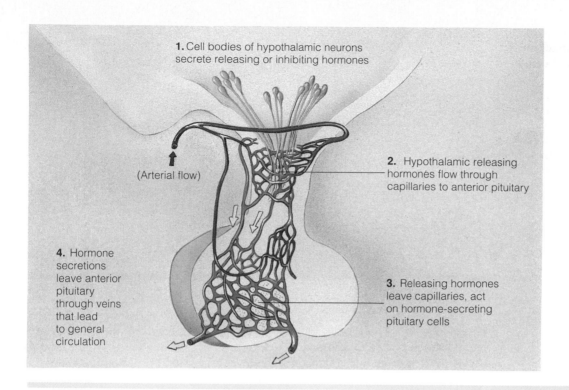

**Figure 12.7**
**How hypothalamic releasing hormones control the activity of the anterior pituitary**
*(From Starr & Taggart, 1989.)*

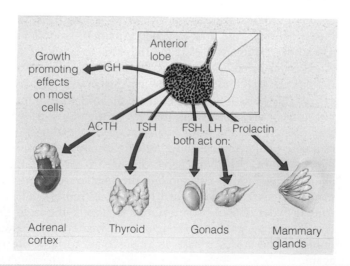

**Figure 12.8**
**Hormones secreted by the anterior pituitary and their primary targets**
*(From Starr & Taggart, 1989.)*

**Figure 12.9
Negative feedback in
the control of thyroid
hormones**

*The hypothalamus secretes a
releasing hormone that stimulates the anterior pituitary to
release TSH, which stimulates
the thyroid gland to release its
hormones. Those hormones in
turn act on the hypothalamus
to decrease its secretion of the
releasing hormone.*

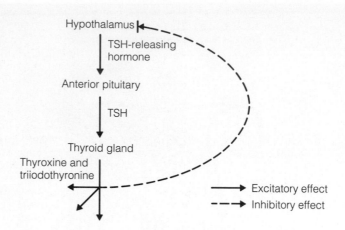

Hypothalamus

TSH-releasing
hormone

Anterior pituitary

TSH

Thyroid gland

Thyroxine and
triiodothyronine

→ Excitatory effect
- - → Inhibitory effect

releases one of its hormones, known as *TSH-releasing hormone,* which stimulates
the anterior pituitary to release TSH, which in turn causes the thyroid gland to
secrete more thyroid hormones. After the level of thyroid hormones has risen, the
hypothalamus decreases its release of TSH-releasing hormone (see Figure 12.9).

## Hormonal Control of the Menstrual Cycle

In women and certain other female primates, the hypothalamus and pituitary interact with the ovaries to produce the **menstrual cycle,** a periodic variation in
hormones and fertility over the course of approximately one month (see Figure
12.10). After the end of a menstrual period, **follicle-stimulating hormone
(FSH)** promotes the growth of follicles in the ovary. Toward the middle of the
menstrual cycle, the follicles produce increasing amounts of one type of estrogen,
**estradiol.** Ordinarily, estradiol inhibits the release of **luteinizing hormone
(LH)** from the pituitary. Near the middle of the menstrual cycle, however, for
reasons not well understood, the increase in estrogen levels causes a sudden surge
of LH release as well as an increase of FSH (top graph in Figure 12.10). These
hormones cause one of the follicles in the ovary to release an *ovum* (egg), and
they prepare the uterus for implantation of a fertilized ovum. They also cause the
remnant of the follicle (now called the *corpus luteum*) to release the hormone
**progesterone,** which prepares the uterus for the implantation of a fertilized
ovum. Progesterone also inhibits the further release of LH. By the end of the
menstrual cycle, the levels of LH, FSH, estradiol, and progesterone have all declined (Feder, 1981). If the ovum is fertilized, the levels of estradiol and progesterone increase gradually thoughout pregnancy. If the ovum is not fertilized, the
lining of the uterus is cast off (menstruation), and the cycle is ready to begin
again.

In real life, the cycle is less predictable than all this may sound. Bright light
can speed up the cycle, darkness can retard it, and various kinds of stress can alter
it in many ways. In some species, social stimuli govern reproductive hormones. A
female rabbit, for example, ovulates only after a male has copulated with her.
Both male and female doves alter their secretion of sex hormones in response to
the behavior of their mates. (See Digression 12.1.) As we saw in Chapter 6, odors
can synchronize women's menstrual cycles.

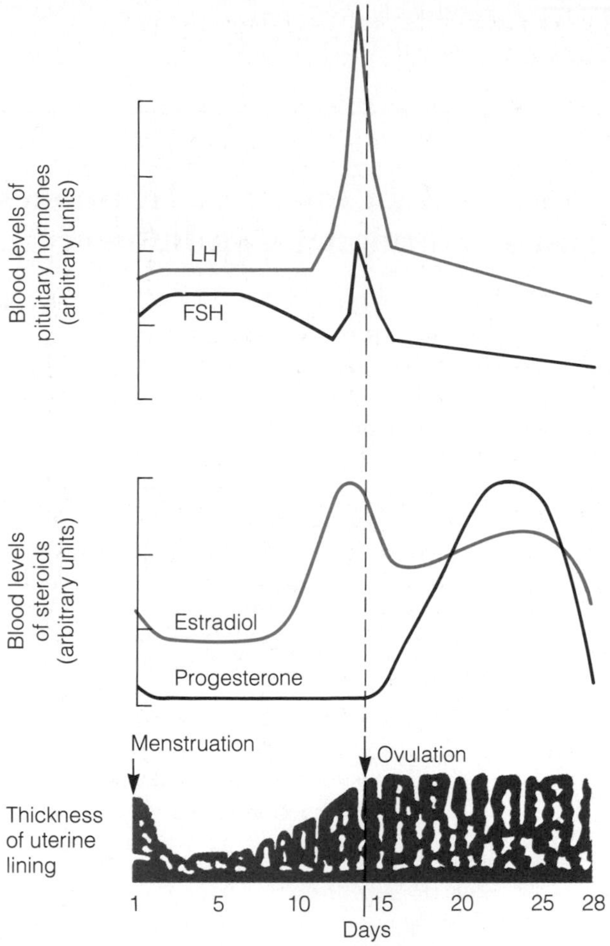

**Figure 12.10
Blood levels of four
hormones over the hu·
man menstrual cycle**

## Birth-Control Pills

Birth-control pills prevent pregnancy by interfering with the usual feedback cycle between the ovaries and the pituitary. The most widely used and most effective birth-control pill is the *combination pill*, containing both estrogen and progesterone. The pill is so effective because it prevents pregnancy in a variety of ways (*Nursing 87 Drug Handbook*, 1987). High levels of estrogen beginning shortly after the end of the menstrual period suppress the release of FSH, thereby blocking the development of the follicle and preventing the release of an ovum. Progesterone blocks the secretion of luteinizing hormone, thus further guaranteeing that an ovum will not be released. Progesterone also thickens mucus that interferes with the movement of sperm.

## ORGANIZING EFFECTS OF SEX HORMONES

We generally refer to the androgens, a group of hormones including testosterone and several others, as "male hormones" and to the estrogens, a group of hormones including estradiol and others, as "female hormones." Those designations

# Behavior Can Influence Hormones,
# Just as Hormones Can Influence Behavior

The mating behavior of the ring-necked dove offers a striking example of how hormones and behavior interact with each other. A newly mated pair of doves goes through a well-synchronized series of behaviors, as outlined in the following table:

| | Male | Female |
|---|---|---|
| Day 1 | Aggressive behavior | Nonaggressive behavior |
| Days 2–6 | Courtship (nest coos) | Courtship (nest coos) |
| | Copulation | Copulation |
| | Nest building (brings twigs) | Nest building (arranges twigs) |
| Day 7 | | Lays two eggs |
| Next 2 weeks | Sits on eggs during middle of the day | Sits on eggs from late afternoon to next morning |
| Next 3 weeks | Tends and feeds chicks | Tends and feeds chicks |

The behaviors of the male and female are tightly synchronized. If the female assumes the receptive posture for copulation too early, the male may copulate but then quickly deserts her (Erickson & Zenone, 1976). But properly timed copulation establishes a "pair bond" that keeps the couple together through the mating season and sometimes even into later years.

Both birds normally ignore nesting materials on day 1, begin to build a nest on day 2 or 3, and, if a nest is not completed by day 6 or 7, work frantically on nest building at that time. Neither pays much attention to a nest with eggs before day 7, but they take turns sitting on eggs after that time. Both produce a "crop milk" that they feed to chicks that hatch 14 days after the eggs are laid, but they do not provide milk if chicks hatch much earlier.

Although certain hormone injections would induce any of the observed behaviors, it is also the case that each change in the birds' behavior induces a change in their hormone secretions. The sequence of behaviors depends on a system in which each behavior causes the production of hormones that prepare a bird for the next stage of behavior. On day 1, the male struts around and makes a cooing display. The male's behavior seems to excite the female; her ovaries increase production of estrogen (Erickson & Lehrman, 1964). By day 2 she is ready for courtship and soon after that for copulation. If a researcher simply injects an isolated female wih estrogen, she is ready for courtship and copulation almost as soon as a male appears. Thus, the function of the male's behavior on the first day is to stimulate the female's hormonal secretions.

Meanwhile, the male seems to be excited by observing the female on day 1; his androgen production increases. By day 2 he is ready for nest building. Based on studies in other bird species (Adkins & Pniewski, 1978), we can assume that different aspects of the male's courtship and nesting behaviors probably depend on different forms of androgen.

A week of courtship and nest building causes the female to produce first estrogen and then a combination of estrogen and progesterone. If we give estrogen injections to an isolated female for a week, with additional progesterone on the last two days, she becomes ready to incubate eggs even if she has neither seen nor heard a male. Evidently, the courting and nesting experiences produce hormonal changes that make her ready for the next behavioral stage.

Similarly, 14 days of sitting on eggs (or of watching through glass another bird sit on eggs) causes either the male or the female to produce the hormone prolactin, which stimulates the production of crop milk and disposes the bird to take care of baby doves. If a dove is isolated from other birds and from nests and eggs, a researcher can still get it to care for baby doves by injecting it repeatedly with prolactin.

In short, one behavior causes a hormonal change, which disposes the bird toward a second behavior, which causes a further hormonal change, and so on to the end of the sequence (Lehrman, 1964; Martinez-Vargas & Erickson, 1973).

are not really correct, however. Both males and females produce both types of hormones. The difference is that in humans and many other species, males secrete more androgens than estrogens, and females secrete more estrogens than androgens.

We distinguish two effects of sex hormones: organizing effects and activating effects. The **organizing effects** of sex hormones, which determine whether the body will develop as a female or as a male, occur at a sensitive stage of development—shortly after birth in rats, well before birth in humans. These organizing effects change the individual's anatomy, more or less permanently. **Activating effects** occur later in life, when a hormone temporarily activates a particular response; activating effects on an organ last only a little longer than the hormone remains in the organ. (We shall say more about activating effects later.)

## Sex Differences in the Gonads and Hypothalamus

During an early stage of prenatal development, the **gonads** (reproductive organs) of every mammalian fetus are the same, and both male and female have a set of Müllerian ducts and a set of Wolffian ducts. The gonads will differentiate into **ovaries** in females and **testes** in males. The **Müllerian ducts** are precursors to female reproductive structures (the oviducts, uterus, and upper vagina); the **Wolffian ducts** are precursors to the male reproductive structures. The fetus also has a set of external structures that differentiate into either female genitals or male genitals (see Figure 12.11). From its initial unisex appearance, the fetus develops in either the female or the male direction, depending on the influence of hormones.

In addition to the obvious differences in the gonads, the sexes differ in the anatomy of several parts of the nervous system, especially the hypothalamus. For example, one portion of the medial preoptic area of the hypothalamus is dependably larger in males than in females—two to three times larger in humans, and even larger in certain other species (Hines, Davis, Coquelin, Goy, & Gorski, 1985; Swaab & Fliers, 1985). These and other differences between the sexes emerge at an early age, presumably organized by early hormones.

The presence of **testosterone,** an androgen, is apparently decisive in the development of the male pattern in both the genitals and the hypothalamus. Ordinarily, during a brief period of early development the male's testes set up a positive feedback cycle: The testes secrete testosterone, which increases the growth of the testes and enables them to produce more testosterone. The testosterone also directs a masculine pattern of development in the hypothalamus.

A female rat that is injected with testosterone during the first 10 days after its birth is partly masculinized, just as if the testosterone had come from her own body. Her clitoris grows larger than normal; her other reproductive structures look intermediate between female and male. At maturity, her pituitary and ovaries produce steady levels of hormones instead of the cycles that are characteristic of females. Anatomically, certain parts of her hypothalamus resemble those of a male more than those of a female. Her behavior is also masculinized: She mounts other females and makes copulatory thrusting movements rather than arching her back and allowing males to mount her. In short, early testosterone promotes the male pattern and inhibits the female pattern (Gorski, 1985; Wilson, George, & Griffin, 1981). With enough testosterone, the individual develops as a male; without testosterone it develops as a female.

Early treatment with estradiol or other estrogens does not have the reverse effect. A male that is injected with small amounts of estrogens still develops as a

**Figure 12.11
Differentiation of human genitals from a single set of precursors**
*(a) At age 6 weeks, male and female look identical. (b) In the second trimester, male and female begin to differentiate. (c) Appearance at birth. (Based on Netter, 1983.)*

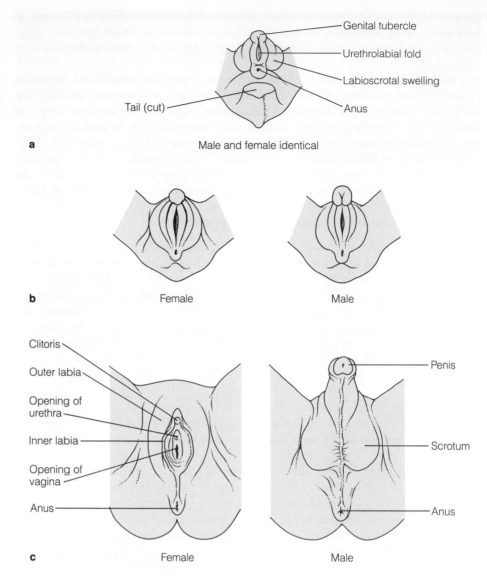

male, although large quantities can interfere with certain aspects of his development (Diamond, Llacuna, & Wong, 1973). Furthermore, if the gonads are removed from either a male or a female rat just after birth, depriving the animal of its own hormones, the young rat develops looking and behaving like a female. (It may need at least a small amount of estrogen to develop a fully normal female pattern, however.)

In short, in the presence of little or no sex hormones, a mammal develops the female pattern of external genitals and hypothalamus. Add estrogens, within normal limits, and the result is still female. Add testosterone and the result is male. Testosterone exerts long-lasting effects only if it is present during an early **critical period**—from birth to 10 days for a rat, about the third and fourth months of pregnancy for a human (Money & Ehrhardt, 1972).

According to studies on rodents, testosterone exerts a major part of its effect on the hypothalamus through a surprising route: After it enters a neuron, it is converted to estradiol! Testosterone and estradiol are chemically very similar, as you can see in Figure 12.3. In organic chemistry, a ring of six carbon atoms containing three double bonds is an **aromatic** compound. An enzyme found in the brain can *aromatize* testosterone into estradiol. Other types of androgens that cannot be aromatized into estrogens are less effective in masculinizing the hypothalamus. Moreover, drugs that prevent testosterone from being aromatized to estradiol block the organizing effects of testosterone on sexual development. Apparently, androgens must be aromatized to estrogens to exert their organizing effects on the hypothalamus.

Why, then, is the female not masculinized by her own estradiol? During the early critical period, immature mammals of most species have in their bloodstream a protein called **alpha-fetoprotein,** which is not present in adults (Gorski, 1980; MacLusky & Naftolin, 1981). Alpha-fetoprotein binds with estrogen and blocks it from leaving the bloodstream and entering the cells that are developing in this early period. Nonrodents have additional mechanisms for inactivating estrogen; for example, it is likely that infant primates break down estrogens into inactive substances. In any event, testosterone is neither bound to alpha-fetoprotein nor metabolized; it is free to enter the cells, where enzymes convert it into estradiol. That is, testosterone is a way of getting estradiol into the cells when estradiol itself cannot leave the blood.

This explanation of testosterone's effects enables us to make sense of an otherwise puzzling fact: Although normal amounts of estradiol have little effect on early development, an injection of a larger amount actually masculinizes a female's development. The reason is that normal amounts are bound to alpha-fetoprotein or metabolized, whereas a larger amount may exceed the body's capacity for inactivation; the excess is thus able to enter the cells and masculinize them.

Testosterone also exerts organizing effects on the nerves and muscles that control the penis. In most mammalian species, a male has certain muscles in or near the penis that are either absent or very small in the area near the female's clitoris. Those muscles receive their neural input from two motor nuclei in the spinal cord; again, those nuclei are present in males and either absent or very small in females. Recall from Chapter 8 that in early development the spinal cord develops more neurons than will survive to maturity. Trophic factors such as nerve growth factor promote the survival of certain neurons; other neurons die. A similar principle applies to the sex-differentiated nuclei of the spinal cord. Early in development, both male and female develop large numbers of neurons in these nuclei. The male's testosterone supports survival of those neurons. In the female the testosterone levels are lower and most of the neurons die. However, if a female receives testosterone injections, both the neurons and the muscles they innervate survive to maturity (Sengelaub & Arnold, 1989; Sengelaub, Nordeen, Nordeen, & Arnold, 1989). Similarly, removal of a male's testes causes degeneration of these spinal neurons (Kurz, Sengelaub, & Arnold, 1986).

## Sex Differences in Nonreproductive Characteristics

Males and females obviously differ in their organs of reproduction and in certain aspects of sexual behavior. But they also differ in many characteristics that have only indirect or nonobvious relationships with reproduction: In most mammalian species, males tend to be larger than females and to fight with one another more than females do (Ellis, 1986). Females tend to live longer and to devote more attention to infant care. (Humans are among the few mammalian species in which the male contributes to care for the young.) In humans, males are more likely to

**Figure 12.12**
**Urination postures of dogs**
*Adult females that had been exposed to androgens shortly before and after birth urinated in the adult male position on 62 percent of occasions. (From Beach, 1974.)*

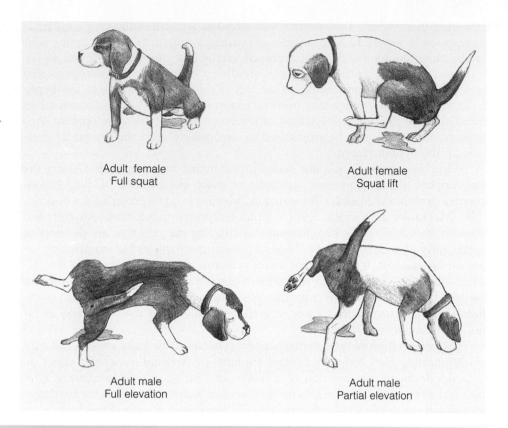

Adult female
Full squat

Adult female
Squat lift

Adult male
Full elevation

Adult male
Partial elevation

be autistic, hyperactive, or alcoholic; females are more likely to be depressed or phobic. No doubt you can think of additional differences between men and women.

Especially with humans, it can be very difficult to find the causes of such differences. Little girls have different experiences from little boys, as well as different genes and different hormones. However, research with animals demonstrates that biological factors *can* contribute strongly to sex differences in nonreproductive behaviors. (How much they *do* contribute to such differences in humans is, of course, another question.)

For one example, consider urination postures in dogs. Ordinarily, male dogs raise one leg against a tree or other prop; female dogs squat. However, female dogs exposed to androgens during the critical period assume the male position for urination (Beach, 1974). (See Figure 12.12.)

Female monkeys exposed to testosterone during their critical period are masculinized in several ways. They attempt to copulate with other females and not with males. They engage in more rough-and-tumble play than other females do during youth, are more aggressive, and make more threatening facial gestures (Quadagno, Briscoe, & Quadagno, 1977; Young, Goy, & Phoenix, 1964). Similar effects on play and aggressive behavior have been noted in dogs (Beach, Buehler, & Dunbar, 1982; Reinisch, 1981) and ferrets (Stockman, Callaghan, Gallagher, & Baum, 1986).

In humans, too, males and females differ in their play patterns and aggressive behavior, even at an early age. It would be consistent with the data on other species to suppose that prenatal hormones predispose humans toward these differences. However, directly relevant data are sparse and hard to interpret because of the consistent cultural influences (Hines, 1982).

The hormones present during the critical period may also be important determinants of life expectancy. It is well known that women live longer than men do, on the average. Many people have suggested that men die earlier because they work harder or worry more. However, females outlive males in most mammalian species, and it is difficult to believe that male bears work harder than females or that male porcupines worry more than females do. Furthermore, prolonged administration of testosterone increases the frequency of injury and death in male cowbirds (Dufty, 1989).

According to the results of one study, females injected with testosterone in the early critical period had lifespans similar to those of males, while males castrated early lived longer than normal males and (in this study) even longer than females (Dörner & Hinz, 1975). Similarly, castrated male cats live longer than intact ones do (Hamilton, Hamilton, & Mestler, 1969). In humans, mentally retarded men who have been castrated survive longer than do similar men who have not been castrated; removal of the ovaries does not affect the life expectancy of women (Hamilton & Mestler, 1969).

## ACTIVATING EFFECTS OF SEX HORMONES

Long after the early hormones have determined the structure of the gonads and the nervous system, current levels of testosterone or estradiol exert activating effects on sexual behaviors. As we have seen, activating effects temporarily modify sexual or other activities; they do not permanently alter anatomy, as organizing effects do.

### Activating Effects on Sexual Behavior

In general, sexual behavior requires at least a minimum level of sex hormones to activate it. Species such as deer mate only in one season of the year, when their sex hormone levels are high. The activating effects of hormones on sexual behavior vary from one species to another.

**Effects on Rats** After removal of the testes from a male rat or the ovaries from a female rat, sexual behavior declines as the sex hormone levels in the blood decline. It may not disappear altogether, partly because the adrenal glands also produce some testosterone and estradiol. An injection of testosterone into a castrated male rat restores sexual behavior, as does an injection of 5-$\alpha$-dihydrotestosterone, which cannot be aromatized into an estrogen (Butera & Czaja, 1989). Evidently androgens activate adult male sexual behavior by themselves and not by conversion into estrogens. Estrogen followed by at least 2 to 4 hours of progesterone is the most effective combination for stimulating sexual behavior in a female rat (Glaser, Etgen, & Barfield, 1987). Oxytocin, a pituitary hormone that probably also serves as a neurotransmitter for some cells, also increases female sexual responsiveness (Caldwell, Jirikowski, Greer, & Pedersen, 1989).

By what mechanism do sex hormones activate sexual behavior? They do so partly by changing sensations. The *pudendal nerve* transmits tactile stimulation from the pubic area to the brain. Estrogens increase the area of skin that excites the pudendal nerve (Komisaruk, Adler, & Hutchison, 1972). Sex hormones probably also facilitate activity at particular synapses in the brain. Drug studies have implicated dopamine and norepinephrine synapses in particular in the stimulation of male sexual activity (Clark, Smith, & Davidson, 1984; Hull et al., 1986; Peters, Koch, & Blythe, 1988).

**Effects on Dogs and Cats** Dogs and cats are less dependent on their levels of sex hormones than rodents are (Beach, 1967, 1970). Male dogs castrated as adults maintain sexual behavior at a somewhat decreased level for several years. Male cats maintain some sexual activity if they have had sexual experience before castration. Female dogs and cats engage in no sexual activity after removal of their ovaries, however.

For an intact female dog, sexual behavior depends largely on estrogen. Frank Beach taught us to distinguish among three aspects of female sexual behavior: attractivity, receptivity, and proceptivity (Beach, 1976). **Attractivity** is a tendency to attract sexual advances from males. **Receptivity** is a tendency to respond favorably to a male's sexual advances and to accept copulation. **Proceptivity** is a tendency to approach a male and actively to seek sexual contact. Just before the start of a dog's **estrus** period (her "heat" period, the time when she is fertile), her estradiol levels increase and she becomes sexually attractive to males. She begins to show proceptive behaviors (approaching males) but not yet receptive behaviors (accepting copulation). During the estrus period itself, her estradiol levels decline while her progesterone levels increase. Here she shows both proceptive and receptive behaviors and copulation occurs. At the end of estrus, estrogen and progesterone levels drop sharply, as do proceptivity, receptivity, and attractivity (Beach, Dunbar, & Buehler, 1982).

**Effects on Nonhuman Primates** Primates (monkeys, apes, and humans) depend even less on current levels of sex hormones than dogs and cats do, although the results differ substantially from one primate species to another. Females of many monkey species are at least moderately receptive to males' sexual advances at all stages of their menstrual cycles (Baum, 1983). Their sex hormones apparently have more influence on their proceptivity than on their receptivity. Estrogen generally increases proceptive behaviors (see, for example, Dixson, 1987). Female rhesus monkeys approach males and make inviting gestures much more frequently just before or during their fertile period (when estrogen levels are high) than they do after the end of the fertile period (Pomerantz & Goy, 1983; Wallen et al., 1984). For female primates, unlike dogs and rodents, progesterone decreases both sexual behavior and attractivity to males (Baum, 1983).

Male monkeys maintain a moderate amount of sexual activity after castration (Phoenix, Slob, & Goy, 1973), although the frequency does decline. After castration, testosterone injections increase sexual activity; estradiol injections do not (Michael, Zumpe, & Bonsall, 1990). Among male rhesus monkeys, those with the highest testosterone levels are not necessarily more active sexually than are those with lower testosterone levels. However, sexual activity does tend to be greater in males with a fairly steady testosterone level throughout the day, as opposed to those that have substantial fluctuations from one time to another (Michael, Zumpe, & Bonsall, 1984).

**Effects on Humans** The dependence of sexual activity on current hormone levels is least in humans, although an influence is certainly demonstrable. Among males, sexual excitement is generally highest at the age when testosterone levels are highest (about ages 15 to 25). Decreases in testosterone levels decrease sexual activity. After castration, for example, most men report a decrease in their sexual interest and activity. As time passes, they first lose their ability to ejaculate, then their ability to have an erection, and finally their sexual interest. However, low testosterone is not the only basis for **impotence** (inability to have an erection). Some men with normal testosterone levels are impotent, and giving them extra testosterone does not alter their condition (Carani et al., 1990).

Typically, sex offenders (exhibitionists, rapists, child molesters, committers of incest, and so forth) have about average testosterone levels (Lang, Flor-Henry, & Frenzel, 1990). They do not have an unusually strong sex drive but rather a sex drive channeled into a socially unacceptable outlet (Earls, 1988). Occasional attempts have been made to control their sexual behavior by administering drugs that lower their testosterone levels. One such drug is *cyproterone*, which blocks the entry of testosterone into cells and the binding of testosterone to receptors within cells. Another drug, *medroxyprogesterone*, blocks testosterone receptor sites in cells and accelerates the breakdown of testosterone into inactive molecules (Bradford, 1988). Most of the treated men cease their offensive behaviors as long as they continue taking the drugs (Berlin & Meinecke, 1981; Money, Wiedeking, Walker, & Gain, 1976). In some cases, psychotherapists attempt to rechannel the men's sexual interests into acceptable outlets while gradually reducing the dosage of the drug.

Women's sexual receptivity has only a slight if any relation to their hormonal cycles. However, at least a minimum level of sex hormones is important. A number of studies show that testosterone contributes to sexual arousal in women as well as men. For example, after **menopause** (a time when middle-aged women stop menstruating), women's levels of sex hormones decline. Some post-menopausal women take low levels of testosterone; the effect is generally an increase in sexual desire and sexual enjoyment (Sherwin, 1988). Estrogen is also important for women's sexual desire. As with nonhuman primates, estrogen appears to be more important for proceptive behaviors than for receptive behaviors. According to two studies, women not taking birth-control pills initiate more sexual activity (either with a partner or by masturbation) about midway between menstrual periods than at other times during the month (Udry & Morris, 1968; Adams, Gold, & Burt, 1978). (See Figure 12.13.) The point midway between the menstrual periods is the time of ovulation and generally the time of the highest estrogen levels.

As with men, women can have low sex interest for reasons unrelated to hormones. One study examined hormone levels in 17 women, age 27 to 39, all either married or living with a man, and all experiencing a consistent lack of sexual desire. On the average, these women had normal levels of sex hormones and normal fluctuations over a month (Schreiner-Engel, Schiavi, White, & Ghizzani, 1989).

## Activating Effects on Aggressive Behavior

Testosterone tends to activate fighting in the males of many species. In species that mate only in one season of the year, males fight with one another mostly during that season, while their testosterone levels are high (Goldstein, 1974; Moyer, 1974). A castrated male fights little; testosterone injections restore aggressive behavior (Brain, 1979). However, hormones produce different effects on different kinds of aggression, such as attacks on males or attacks on females (Haug, Brain, & Kamis, 1986).

Testosterone probably enhances the likelihood of human violence also. Throughout the world, males engage in more violent behavior than females do (Maccoby & Jacklin, 1974; Moyer, 1974). Moreover, the highest incidence of violence, as measured by crime statistics, is in men 15 to 25 years old, who also have the highest levels of testosterone in the blood.

One study of male prisoners found a significant correlation between the testosterone levels of male prisoners and those men's histories of violence prior to imprisonment (Kreuz & Rose, 1972). The five men with the highest testosterone levels had committed a total of two murders, one attempted murder, one assault,

**Figure 12.13
Fluctuation of autosexual activities (masturbation and sexual fantasies) and female-initiated heterosexual activities during the monthly cycle**
*Results are plotted separately for women taking birth-control pills, women using "intrusive" birth-control methods (diaphragm, foam, or condom), and women using "nonintrusive" methods (IUD or vasectomy). Note that women other than pill users increase self-initiated sex activities when their estrogen levels peak. (From Adams, Gold, & Burt, 1978.)*

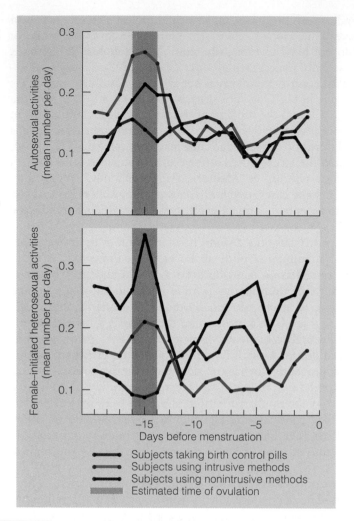

and four armed robberies. The five men with the lowest levels of testosterone had committed larceny or burglary but no murders, assaults, or armed robberies.

A study of more than four thousand male military veterans found that the men with the higher testosterone levels had a greater frequency of assaults on other people, being absent without leave from the military, abusing alcohol and other drugs, and in general getting into trouble (Dabbs & Morris, 1990). However, although these differences were statistically significant, they were fairly small. Testosterone apparently contributes toward violent and impulsive behavior in humans, but it is hardly the only contributor.

### Activating Effects on Activity Levels and Skilled Performance

Female rats become more active than usual on the day before their fertile period (Richter, 1927). That increase in activity corresponds to a surge in circulating estrogens. Might estrogens also enhance arousal and some aspects of performance in women?

According to one study of women age 20 to 39 not taking birth-control pills, women can tap their fingers fastest during the *midluteal phase* of the menstrual cycle, a few days after ovulation. This is when both estrogen and progesterone levels are high. At this same time women generally perform best on other motor tasks and cognitive tasks that require rapid responses (Hampson & Kimura, 1988). High levels of estrogen also enhance women's sensitivity to visual, auditory, and olfactory stimuli (Parlee, 1983).

## PUBERTY

**Puberty,** the onset of sexual maturity, usually begins at about age 12 to 13 for girls and a year later for boys in the United States. Because reproduction requires a great deal of energy, the body does not enter puberty until it has enough energy reserves. On the average, a girl experiences **menarche** (muh-NAR-kee; her first menstruation) when she weighs about 47 kg (see Figure 12.14). Girls who keep their weight very low because of ballet or athletic training or other reasons are slower than others to reach menarche and generally have more irregular menstrual cycles than other girls have. Girls more than 30 percent overweight also have irregular cycles (Frisch, 1983, 1984).

Weight is certainly not the only factor. Short girls may reach menarche at a weight well below 47 kg, tall girls at a greater weight. In several nonhuman species, exposure to bright lights and to males accelerates sexual maturation of females (Garcia & Whitsett, 1983; Steger, 1976). The same may or may not be true of humans; it would be interesting to compare girls in coed schools versus girls in all-girl elementary schools.

Puberty starts when the hypothalamus begins to release bursts of *luteinizing hormone releasing hormone*, at a rate of about one burst per hour. We do not know what stimulates the hypothalamus to do so, but once it begins, it continues

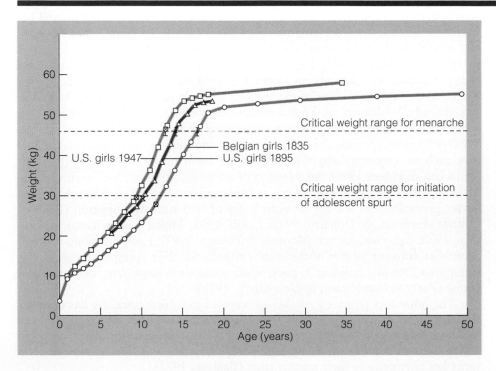

**Figure 12.14
Weight gain and sexual maturation in three samples of girls**
*Girls start their adolescent growth spurt when their weight reaches about 30 kg (66 pounds). They generally reach menarche (the first menstruation) when they weigh about 47 kg (103 pounds). Girls in 1947 reached menarche at a slightly younger age than girls in earlier studies did, presumably because better nutrition and health enabled them to gain weight faster. (After Frisch, 1972.)*

435

throughout the fertile period. This hormone stimulates the pituitary to secrete LH and FSH, which in turn stimulate the gonads to release estradiol or testosterone (B. D. Goldman, 1981). Estradiol causes breast development and broadening of the hips. Testosterone causes lowering of the voice, beard growth, broadening of the shoulders, and growth of hair on the chest, in the underarms, and in the pubic area. Both boys and girls undergo a growth spurt in response to the increase in hormones.

Although a certain amount of variation is normal in the age of puberty, puberty is considered *precocious* if it begins before age 8 in girls, 9 in boys. Although children who begin puberty that early show an immediate growth spurt, their growth stops early and they are generally short as adults. A 6- or 7-year-old child in puberty develops acne and secondary sexual characteristics that often provoke teasing from other children and lead to social awkwardness. If precocious puberty is recognized quickly, the child can be given drugs that inhibit the release of LH and FSH, thus postponing puberty until a more appropriate age (Pescovitz, Cutler, & Loriaux, 1985).

## PARENTAL BEHAVIOR

Sexual behavior has a way of leading to babies. During late pregnancy and just after giving birth, mammalian mothers have high levels of estrogen, progesterone, oxytocin, and prolactin. It is natural to expect that those hormonal changes may predispose her to maternal behavior.

This hypothesis is largely correct for a number of nonhuman mammals. However, humans are a special case. Women who have never been pregnant can be devoted parents; so can men. Hormones are apparently not necessary for human parental behavior, except for the ability of the mother to breast-feed the infant.

In rodents, hormones can strongly influence parental behavior. Late in pregnancy, female rats produce a pattern of hormones incompatible with parental behavior; if infant rats are presented to a pregnant female 2 to 5 days before she is due to give birth, she is actually *less* responsive to them than a virgin female is (Mayer & Rosenblatt, 1984). However, by the day of delivery her hormones have changed (including especially an increase in prolactin and oxytocin) and so has her behavior. The hormones of mother rats strongly promote parental behavior. In one study, 30-day-old rats (just a week or so postweaning themselves) were injected with plasma from mother rats, containing all the mothers' hormones. The 30-day-old rats, especially the females, quickly showed typical rat parental behaviors, such as retrieving baby rats and putting them into a nest (Brunelli, Shindledecker, & Hofer, 1987). An injection of estrogen, progesterone, oxytocin, and prolactin into a virgin female rat can induce maternal behavior, although the behavior generally does not appear until a day or two after the injection (Bridges, DiBiase, Loundes, & Doherty, 1985; Lamb, 1975; Moltz, Lubin, Leon, & Numan, 1970; Pedersen, Ascher, Monroe, & Prange, 1982). Each hormone controls somewhat different aspects of the maternal behavior. For example, progesterone is important for nest building in mice, while prolactin is important for retrieval of young (Zarrow, Gandelman, & Denenberg, 1971).

The hormones prepare a mother to respond to babies; once she has done so, she may be permanently changed. A female rat with just one and a half hours of experience of mothering her young responds in a maternal manner to other young even after a 25-day delay, which stops her from producing milk and returns her hormones to their normal state (Bridges, 1975).

Although hormones facilitate maternal behavior, they are not indispensable for it. If a female rat that has never been pregnant is left with some 5- to 10-day-old babies, her interest in them increases over several days. (Because the babies cannot survive without parental care and food, the experimenter must periodically replace them with new, healthy babies.) After about six days, the adoptive mother builds a nest, assembles the babies in the nest, licks them, and does everything else that a normal mother would, except nurse them. Ovarian hormones aid in this process, but they are not necessary. For example, female rats with or without intact ovaries respond maternally, although those with intact ovaries show more complete parental behavior (Mayer & Rosenblatt, 1979).

Even male rodents can be induced to parental behavior, although their hormonal patterns never resemble those of a new mother. Ordinarily, a male mouse kills babies. If he copulates with a female and stays with her during pregnancy, however, he accepts the young and helps to care for them (Elwood, 1985). A male rat that is caged with infants by himself (with no adult female) may kill them or initially ignore them. Males that ignore the babies gradually come to show parental behavior toward the infants (R. E. Brown, 1986; Rosenblatt, 1967). In this regard the males' behavior is like that of a previously inexperienced female, except that the female shows more parental care.

In short, exposing adult rats to infants for 5 to 10 days can substitute for the hormonal changes that accompany pregnancy and delivery. Would this effect of exposure ever influence behavior in nature? After all, a baby that needed six days to induce an adult to take care of it would die before the adult got mobilized. Rosenblatt's (1970) answer is that maternal behavior goes through two stages. During the first few days after giving birth, hormones facilitate maternal behavior. After those first few days, the mother's familiarity with the young becomes a sufficient basis to maintain maternal care, with or without hormones. The advantage of this system is that maternal care lasts longer than the hormonal changes that accompany giving birth.

Prenatal hormones are also important for parental behavior in many nonhuman primates. In the red-bellied tamarin, a species of monkey that typically gives birth to twins, mothers whose estradiol levels remain stable over the last week before delivery generally become good mothers; they manage to keep one if not two babies alive for at least the first week. Those mothers whose estradiol levels drop sharply in the last week of pregnancy generally fail to keep either baby alive for a week, especially if the mother was giving birth for the first time (Pryce, Abbott, Hodges, & Martin, 1988).

## SUMMARY

1. Three major types of hormones are peptide hormones, thyroid hormones, and steroid hormones. Peptide hormones attach to membrane receptors and exert effects similar to those of neurotransmitters. Thyroid hormones and steroid hormones attach to receptors inside the cell and through those receptors modify the expression of the genes. (p. 416)

2. The hypothalamus controls activity of the pituitary gland by nerve impulses and releasing hormones. The pituitary in turn secretes hormones that alter the activity of other endocrine glands. (p. 420)

3. The organizing effects of a hormone are exerted during an early critical period and bring about relatively permanent alterations in anatomy or in the potential for function. (p. 427)

4. In the absence of sex hormones, or with the addition of small amounts of estrogens, the gonads and hypothalamus of an infant mammal will differentiate like those of a female. In the presence of adequate amounts of testosterone, the infant will develop as a male. (p. 427)

5. At least in rodents, and probably in primates also, testosterone is converted within the cells to estradiol, which actually masculinizes the development of the

hypothalamus. Estradiol in the blood does not masculinize development, either because it is bound to proteins in the blood or because it is metabolized. (p. 428)

6. Sex hormones also exert organizing influences on other aspects of behavior. (p. 429)

7. In adulthood, sex hormones can activate sex behaviors, aggressive behaviors, and increased activity levels. The effects of each hormone differ from male to female, from species to species, and from one behavior to another. (p. 431)

8. Puberty begins when the hypothalamus begins to release bursts of luteinizing hormone releasing hormone. The onset of puberty is controlled by many factors, including weight and social stimuli. (p. 435)

9. Hormones released around the time of giving birth facilitate maternal behavior in females of many mammalian species. Nevertheless, mere prolonged exposure to young is also sufficient to induce parental behavior, even in males of certain species. Hormonal facilitation is apparently not essential to human parental behavior. (p. 436)

## REVIEW QUESTIONS

1. What are the major differences between the anterior pituitary and the posterior pituitary? (p. 420)

2. Describe the hormonal feedback that regulates the menstrual cycle of women. (p. 424)

3. How do combination birth-control pills prevent pregnancy? (p. 425)

4. What is the difference between the organizing and activating effects of a hormone? (p. 427)

5. What are the effects of testosterone in the early critical period on the development of the gonads and the hypothalamus? What are the effects of estradiol? Why does the circulating estradiol in a female fetus have little effect on the cells? (p. 427)

6. Describe the organizing effects of testosterone and estradiol on nonreproductive behaviors. (p. 429)

7. What is the difference between receptivity and proceptivity? (p. 432)

8. What differences exist among mammalian species in their dependence on current hormone levels for sexual behavior? (p. 432)

9. Describe the evidence that sex hormones activate sexual behavior in men and women. (p. 432)

10. What drugs are sometimes used to suppress sexual interest in sex offenders? How do they work? (p. 433)

11. What nonreproductive behaviors do sex hormones activate? (p. 433)

12. What are some of the factors that control the onset of puberty? (p. 435)

13. What is responsible for maternal behavior in the first few days after giving birth? What is responsible for parental behavior later? (p. 436)

## THOUGHT QUESTIONS

1. What would happen to the release of thyroid-stimulating hormone from the pituitary after damage to the thyroid gland? What would happen to pituitary hormones after damage to the ovaries?

2. The presence or absence of testosterone determines whether a mammal will differentiate as a male or a female; estrogens have no effect. In birds, the story is the opposite: The presence or absence of estrogen is critical (Adkins & Adler, 1972). What problems would determination by estrogen create if that were the mechanism for mammals? Why do those problems not arise in birds? (Hint: Think about the difference between live birth and hatching from an egg.)

3. In most mammalian species, females live longer than males do, on the average. Also in most species, females contribute more than males do to infant care. Could these two tendencies be related to one another? (For example, might natural selection have favored a longer lifespan for females because the infants' well-being depends more on the survival of the mother than on the survival of the father?)

## SUGGESTION FOR FURTHER READING

**Adler, N. T.** (Ed.) (1981). *Neuroendocrinology of reproduction.* New York: Plenum. Collection of chapters reviewing many aspects of hormones and sexual behavior.

# Variations in Sexual Development and Sexual Orientation

One species of fish (*Thalassoma duperry*) ordinarily lives in small schools consisting of one male and a few females. If the male dies, a new male may join the school to take his place. If no new male shows up, one of the females changes into a male (Ross, Losey, & Diamond, 1983). (I don't know how they decide which female will become the male.) The converted female not only looks and acts like a male but also produces sperm and fertilizes the eggs of the other females.

Nothing quite like that happens in mammals, but it should alert us to the fact that the categories male and female are not always completely distinct and permanent. Some people develop anatomies that are intermediate between male and female or anatomies that do not match their genetic sex. Some men are sexually interested in other men, some women in other women. These variations in development are interesting to investigate for their own sake and for what they reveal about sexual development in general.

Sexual development is a very sensitive issue, so let us agree from the start: "Different" does not mean "abnormal" (except in the statistical sense). People differ naturally in their sexual development just as they do in their height, weight, emotions, and memory.

## DETERMINANTS OF GENDER IDENTITY

**Gender identity**—the sex with which one identifies and the sex that one calls oneself—is a uniquely human characteristic. Gender identity is closely related to, but not identical with, the concept of **sex role,** the set of activities and dispositions presumed to be common for one sex or the other in a particular society. While someone who adopts the female gender identity is likely to accept the female sex role, for example, it is also possible to reject all or part of that sex role. Someone may say, "Yes, I am a woman, but I like sports and mathematics and I hate housework."

Sex roles are determined to a large extent by one's culture and upbringing. For example, cooking is regarded as women's work by certain societies and as men's work by others. Even within our own society, what we regard as normal behavior for a man or a woman may change sharply from one generation to the next.

Gender identity is undoubtedly also governed heavily by one's upbringing. From an early age, a girl is told, "You are a girl, and later if you decide to marry, you will marry a boy." She is dressed in girl's clothing and placed mostly in the company of other girls. Boys receive the reverse treatment. And yet, a few people are clearly dissatisfied with their assigned sex, a small number of them (transsexuals) to such an extreme degree that they insist on a sex change. Others (homosexuals) have no desire to become a member of the opposite sex, but they direct their sexual interests toward members of their own sex. Might some biological factor, such as prenatal hormones, influence gender identity or homosexual versus heterosexual orientation?

## Intersexes or Pseudohermaphrodites

Recall that testosterone masculinizes the development of the gonads and the hypothalamus during a critical period in early development. If a genetic female is exposed to more testosterone than the average female but less than the average male, she may develop an appearance intermediate between male and female. The same is true of a genetic male who is deprived of some, but not all, of his own testosterone.

Sometimes a female rat fetus is slightly masculinized because she is exposed to a small proportion of the hormones of male fetuses next to her in the uterus. If so, her external genitals grow larger than those of other females (Clemens, Gladue, & Coniglio, 1978). As an adult, she makes sexual approaches toward other females somewhat more often than a normal female rat does (Meisel & Ward, 1981). A male rat fetus that develops between two females grows up to be less aggressive than other males, although this effect may have more to do with increased estradiol levels than decreased testosterone (Vom Saal, Grant, McMullen, & Laves, 1983).

Rarely, human fetuses are exposed to an abnormal hormonal environment before birth. For example, a female fetus or her mother may have an adrenal gland that produces an excess of testosterone and other androgens. Also, certain drugs given to prevent miscarriage, such as diethylstilbestrol (DES), may masculinize the development of a few female fetuses. If, for any reason, a female fetus is exposed to elevated androgen levels, the result is partial masculinization of her external anatomy, as Figure 12.15 illustrates. Note in the figure that the genitals appear intermediate between a clitoris and a penis; swellings near the genitals appear intermediate between normal labia and a normal scrotum.

Individuals whose genitals do not match the normal development for their genetic sex are referred to as **hermaphrodites** (from Hermaphroditus, son of Hermes and Aphrodite, in Greek mythology). There are several types of hermaphrodites. The so-called true hermaphrodite, a rarity, has some normal testicular tissue and some normal ovarian tissue — for example, a testis on one side of the body and an ovary on the other (Simpson, 1976). Individuals whose development is intermediate between male and female, like the one in Figure 12.15, are variously called **intersexes, pseudohermaphrodites,** or simply hermaphrodites.

When a baby is born with a pseudohermaphroditic appearance, a decision must be made: Shall we call it a boy or a girl? Human societies do not recognize *neuter* as an option, and experience has shown that it is harmful to a child's mental health to raise it indecisively, leaving it in doubt about which sex it is.

**Sex Assignment of Human Pseudohermaphrodites** One way to resolve the question might be to do a chromosome test and determine whether the baby is genetically male or female. Most authorities reject that approach. Given that nearly all pseudohermaphrodites are infertile, the important thing is not whether

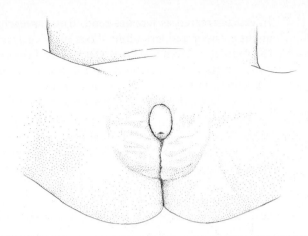

**Figure 12.15
External genitals of a genetic female, age 3 months, masculinized by excess androgens from the adrenal gland before birth (the adrenogenital syndrome)**

the sex one calls oneself matches the chromosomes but whether it matches the external appearance and the behavior.

Another approach is to apply some testosterone directly to the genital region to produce a temporary puberty. The result can give some hint of what will happen later during natural puberty. If the clitoris/penis shows a great deal of growth, the baby can be called a male; otherwise, the infant can be considered a female.

Many authorities favor a much simpler rule: When in doubt, call the child a female. Corrective surgery can reduce the genital growth to clitoral size; a vagina can be either lengthened or constructed artificially; and at puberty, estrogen injections can be given if necessary to stimulate breast growth. Any beard or chest hair that starts to grow can be removed. On the other hand, it is very difficult to alter a hermaphrodite surgically to look like a boy. No one has yet found a satisfactory way to lengthen a penis or to create a new one through surgery.

However, to raise all pseudohermaphrodites as females assumes that gender identity depends entirely on how a child is reared—that is, that the child will accept whichever sex is assigned. Is that true?

**Gender Identity of Human Pseudohermaphrodites** Although most pseudohermaphrodites are reared as females, a number have also been reared as males. Researchers have therefore been able to examine how well various children who started life about the same in appearance adapted to the assignment of male or female. Unfortunately, none of the findings has been scientifically conclusive. Let us examine the existing evidence and some of the difficulties in interpreting it:

1. Many of the pseudohermaphrodites reared as females are tomboyish (Ehrhardt & Money, 1967; Money & Ehrhardt, 1968). During childhood and early adolescence, they show less interest in dolls and more interest in vigorous sports than do most other girls. This tendency parallels the finding that female monkeys exposed to testosterone during the critical period also engage in much aggressive play. We cannot conclude, however, that tomboyishness reflects a direct effect of testosterone on the brain—either in monkeys or in humans. As a result of the early effects of testosterone on the body, pseudohermaphrodites grow taller and more muscular than most females. Thus, they may develop a strong interest in vigorous sports simply because they are bigger and stronger than most other girls.

2. Intersexes reared as females tend, from an early age, to fantasize more often about a career and less often about marriage and family than most other girls (Ehrhardt & Money, 1967; Matheis & Förster, 1980; Money & Ehrhardt, 1968). Again, it is tempting to suggest an explanation in terms of prenatal hormones, but we cannot be sure. Were the girls aware that they were unlikely to have children? Such knowledge could minimize their motherhood fantasies.

3. About 90 to 95 percent of all adult pseudohermaphrodites are satisfied with the sex to which they were assigned at birth; the other 5 to 10 percent express serious dissatisfaction with their assigned sex and may even request a sex reassignment (Money, 1970). Neither the 90 to 95 percent figure nor the 5 to 10 percent figure leads to any unambiguous conclusion about the contributions of genetics and rearing. Most pseudohermaphroditic babies were probably assigned the sex that most nearly matched their appearance at birth, which in turn matched their prenatal hormone pattern. Furthermore, those who eventually rejected their assigned sex could be cases in which the doctor guessed wrong or cases in which the parents reared the child in an inconsistent or unsatisfactory way. If the pseudohermaphrodite eventually accepts the assigned sex, we can explain the agreement either in terms of rearing or in terms of prenatal hormones, as outlined in Figure 12.16.

## Discrepancies of Sexual Appearance by Genetic or Other Accidents

Most of the evidence from pseudohermaphrodites does not tell us anything indisputable about the roles of rearing and hormones in determining gender identity. From a scientific viewpoint, the only decisive way to settle the issue would be to raise a completely normal male baby as a female or to raise a normal female baby as a male. If the process succeeded, we would know that upbringing determines gender identity and that hormones do not. Although no one could perform such an experiment intentionally, it is possible to treat accidental events as natural experiments. Here, we shall consider two examples in which children were (presumably) exposed to the hormonal pattern of one sex and then reared (unambiguously, as far as we know) as the opposite sex.

**Penis Development Delayed Until Puberty** Certain genetic males in the Dominican Republic were born with a gene that prevented penis growth early in life, although their testosterone levels may have been normal. As infants, they were regarded as girls with slightly swollen clitorises and were reared as females. At puberty, their penises suddenly grew, and each was reassigned as a male. Most of them developed clear male gender identities and directed their sexual interest toward females (Imperato-McGinley, Guerrero, Gautier, & Peterson, 1974). One interpretation of these results is that the prenatal hormones favored a male gender identity, even though the children were reared as females. Another possibility is that gender identity is established by social influences around the time of puberty. In either case, the results make it difficult to argue that early rearing experiences are the sole determinant of gender identity, unless we assume that these children were actually recognized as different from the start and were reared in an abnormal way. (We can only speculate about whether it would be equally easy for someone reared as a male to switch to a female identity.)

**Accidental Removal of the Penis** Circumcision is the removal of the foreskin of the penis, a common procedure with newborn boys. One physician, while trying to circumcise a baby boy using an electrical procedure, accidentally used too high

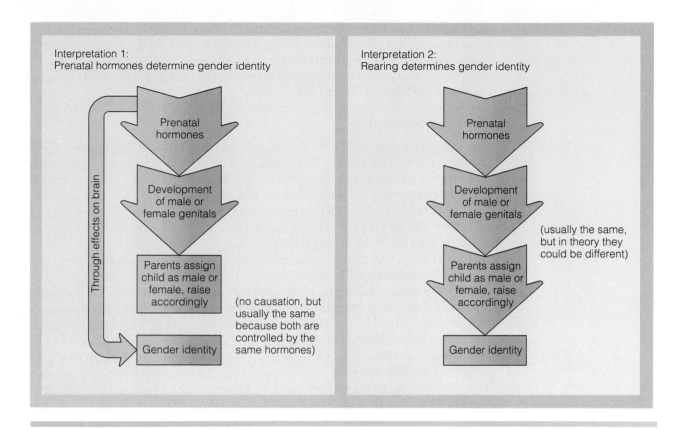

Figure 12.16
Two interpretations of the determinants of gender identity

a current and burned off the entire penis. The parents elected to rear the child as a female, with the appropriate corrective surgery. What makes this a particularly interesting case is that the child has a twin brother (whom the parents did not let the physician try to circumcise). If both twins developed satisfactory gender identities, one as a girl and the other as a boy, we would be likely to conclude that rearing was decisive in gender identity and that prenatal hormones were not.

The child reared as a girl was reported to have a normal female gender identity as a prepubertal child, though she also had strong tomboyish tendencies (Money & Schwartz, 1978). However, as a teenager she was reported to be very unhappy, "beset with problems," and unwilling to discuss sexual matters in any way. When asked to "draw a person," she always drew a man (which is not so unusual) and absolutely refused to draw a woman (which is unusual). She looked and walked like a man; fellow students called her a "cavewoman." No one had told her about her operations or sex reassignment, and no one was sure whether she had remembered or suspected. Rearing this child as a girl was far from a complete success and hardly an endorsement for the idea that rearing is the sole determinant of gender identity (Diamond, 1982). More recent reports have not been published, perhaps to protect the family's privacy.

## POSSIBLE BIOLOGICAL BASES OF HOMOSEXUALITY

While most people seek sex partners of the opposite sex, why do some prefer partners of their own sex? Most people, both homosexual and heterosexual, say that their sexual orientation "just happened," generally at an early age, and that they do not know how or why it developed as it did. Sexual orientation, like left-handedness or right-handedness, is not something that most people voluntarily choose or something they can easily change. In some cases a tendency toward a particular sexual orientation may reveal itself even in patterns of play during childhood (Whitam & Zent, 1984).

## Male Homosexuality

Psychologists at one time attributed male homosexuality to a family pattern that included a dominant mother and a detached father (Van den Aardweg, 1984). That view is no longer so prevalent. In the United States, that family pattern seems to be common for some relatively disturbed or "neurotic" male homosexuals but not common for well-adjusted homosexual men (Siegelman, 1974). In certain other societies, such as Guatemala and Brazil, it is not common for any homosexual men (Whitam & Zent, 1984).

Might some men have a biological predisposition toward homosexuality, specifically a hormonal predisposition? Maybe. Let us examine the evidence.

We can dismiss any explanation based on adult hormone levels, because most homosexual men have hormone levels well within the same range as heterosexual men. A more plausible hypothesis is that some homosexual men may have been exposed to a decreased level of testosterone during some critical period of brain development, perhaps from the middle of the second month of pregnancy until the end of the fifth month (Ellis & Ames, 1987). That temporary, partial decrease in testosterone levels might alter the development of the hypothalamus and other brain structures so that, given certain kinds of experience in childhood or adolescence, these males might have an increased probability of developing a homosexual orientation.

Animal studies suggest that such a hypothesis is plausible, although of course they cannot confirm it. In studies of animals ranging from rats to pigs to zebra finches, males that were exposed to much-decreased levels of testosterone early in life have as adults shown a sexual interest in other males (Adkins-Regan, 1988). That is, early hormones can exert an organizing effect on preference for male or female sexual partners.

However, in many of these animal studies the prolonged deficit of testosterone also led to abnormalities of the genitals. (Homosexual men and heterosexual men are anatomically the same.) A more directly relevant animal study is one in which a treatment altered sexual behavior without much effect on anatomy: Ingeborg Ward (1972, 1977) exposed pregnant rats to a "stressful" experience during the final week of pregnancy by confining them in tight Plexiglas tubes for 135 minutes daily under bright lights. Such stress decreases brain levels of aromatase, the enzyme that converts testosterone into estradiol, which is necessary for masculinization of the hypothalamus (Weisz, Brown, & Ward, 1982). The stress caused the mothers to produce large amounts of adrenal hormones, which crossed into the fetuses' bloodstreams and may have competitively inhibited the actions of testosterone. The stress also caused the male fetuses to produce their peak testosterone levels a day or two earlier than usual, before the critical period for brain differentiation (Ward & Weisz, 1980).

Because the stress took place before birth and rats' genitals differentiate after birth, each male developed a penis and testes of nearly normal size. Behavior was modified, however, presumably because of early effects on the hypothalamus. As adults, the prenatally stressed males responded to injections of either testosterone or estrogen with an increase in female sexual behavior, arching their backs to receive a male partner. Few attempted to copulate with female partners. In a similar study, prenatally stressed males were less likely than other males to fight and more likely than other males to show parental behavior toward infants (McLeod & Brown, 1988).

Although the sexual behavior of prenatally stressed males is altered, their behavior is typically male in certain other regards, such as level of activity in an open [field] (Meisel, Dohanich, & Ward, 1979). Evidently, different aspects of sex-differ[ent] behavior are organized at different times in development or are perha[ps] [by] different types of androgens.

E[...] [e]ffects of the prenatal stress varied, depending on so[...] males reared in isolation or with [...] sexual behavior. Those [...] [nor]mal sexual responsiveness [...] y to other males (Dunl[...]

In [...] [l]ast third of pregnancy [...] [inc]reased responses toward [...] [adu]lt females, slow to eja[c...] [f]emales pregnant (Crum[...]

It i[...] to humans. Hormonal [...] [betw]een rats and primates [...] [and] even between primate and another, see, for example, Baum, [...] Chambers & Phoenix, 198[...] Kendrick [...] [...] 1984; Norman & Spies, 1[...] Relevant human data are difficult to obtain, [...] ly for ethical reasons bu[t] also because it is difficult to study the relationship between prenatal sex hormon[...] and eventual adult outcomes that may not be evident until 20 years or so lat[...] One approach is to inject hormones, such as estrogen, and determine whether they produce different effects on the hypothalamus of homosexual and heterosexual men. So far the results have revealed no consistent difference (Gladue, Green, & Hellman, 1984; Gooren, 1986).

Another approach is to ask the mothers of homosexual men whether they experienced any unusual stress during pregnancy. One such survey contacted 283 mothers of homosexual and heterosexual men, without letting them know why or how they had been chosen. The survey made no mention of sexual orientation; it merely asked about a variety of illnesses and stressors that the woman might have experienced before, during, or after pregnancy. The mothers of homosexual men reported a significantly greater number of stressful events, especially during the second trimester of pregnancy (Ellis, Ames, Peckham, & Burke, 1988). These results are certainly suggestive, although it is problematical to rely on what a woman remembers 20 years after her pregnancy.

## Female Homosexuality

In animals, testosterone injections to female fetuses during the early critical period can exert organizing effects on their adult sexual behavior, increasing their probability of mounting other females and decreasing their receptivity toward males. Dörner (1974) once injected an infant female rat with testosterone and deprived an infant male of his own testosterone by castration. When the rats reached maturity, Dörner placed them together and got the result shown in Figure 12.17. The female mounted the male and the male reacted the way receptive females usually do to the sexual advances of males.

Might the same be true of humans? Some pregnant women take the synthetic estrogen **diethylstilbestrol (DES)** to prevent miscarriage or to deal with other problems. DES can exert masculinizing effects similar to those of testosterone. One study found that of 30 adult women who had been prenatally exposed to

**Figure 12.17
A female rat mounting
a male**

*The female was injected with
androgens during an early
critical period; the male was
castrated at birth and injected
with androgens at adulthood.
(From Dörner, 1974.)*

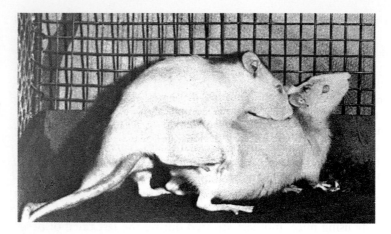

DES, 7 reported some degree of homosexual or bisexual responsiveness. By comparison, only 1 of 30 women not prenatally exposed to DES reported any homosexual or bisexual responsiveness (Ehrhardt et al., 1985). Note that although these results suggest that prenatal hormones may contribute to some instances of female homosexuality or bisexuality, they do not imply a very strong influence.

## GENETIC VARIATIONS OF SEXUAL DEVELOPMENT

Certain individuals with the typical male XY chromosome pattern have the genital appearance of a female. This problem is known as **androgen insensitivity** or **testicular feminization.** Although such individuals produce normal amounts of androgens, their body lacks the mechanism that enables androgens to bind to genes in a cell's nucleus. Consequently, the cells are insensitive to androgens, and the external genitals develop almost like those of a normal female. Two abnormalities appear at puberty: First, in spite of breast development and broadening of the hips, menstruation does not begin, because the body has two internal testes instead of ovaries and a uterus. (The vagina is short and leads to nothing.) Second, pubic hair does not develop, because pubic hair depends on androgens in females as well as males (see Figure 12.18).

A person with androgen insensitivity develops with a fully normal female gender identity. If her condition is medically identified, she is typically given surgery to lengthen the very short vagina and to remove the internal testes, because internal testes are likely to develop tumors and to cause additional health problems.

Abnormal sexual development can also result from abnormalities in the number of sex chromosomes. Normally, a female has two X chromosomes (XX pattern), while a male has an X and a Y chromosome (XY pattern). Occasionally, however, the chromosomes separate improperly during reproduction and a child is born with an unusual chromosome pattern, such as XO, XXY, or XYY.

A female with **Turner's syndrome** has an XO chromosome pattern—one X chromosome and no other sex chromosome. Such females are sterile, short, and immature in appearance. Sometimes, but not always, they have webbed necks and receding chins. Although they do not undergo puberty spontaneously, they do respond to estrogen pills with breast development and other female secondary sexual characteristics. Their overall intelligence is normal, but they are apt to have specific disabilities with map reading and similar spatial orientation tasks (Alexan-

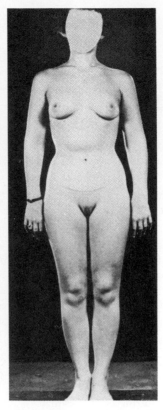

*Two undescended testes produce testosterone and other androgens, to which the body is insensitive. The testes and adrenal glands also produce estrogens that are responsible for the pubertal changes. (From Federman, 1967.)*

der, Ehrhardt, & Money, 1966; Alexander, Walker, & Money, 1964; Steffen, Heinrich, & Kratzer, 1978). Their dreams are so deficient in visual imagery that they resemble those of blind people (Kerr, Foulkes, & Jurkovic, 1978).

A male with **Klinefelter's syndrome** has an **XXY chromosome pattern** (Nielsen, 1969). Most often, such a man has a small penis and testes, breast development during puberty, a high-pitched voice, obesity, and little beard growth. He is generally sterile and has only a low level of interest in sexual activity (Schiavi, Theilgaard, Owen, & White, 1988).

A male with an **XYY chromosome pattern** is generally taller than average. Compared to XY males, XYY males are less likely to establish good relationships with women and less likely to marry. Although they may have sex with many partners, they are less likely than other men to report satisfaction with their sexual activities (Schiavi, Theilgaard, Owen, & White, 1988). Because several reports found more XYY males in prisons than in the rest of the population, some psychologists speculated that the extra Y chromosome had made those men into "super-males"—extra-tall and extra-aggressive. Careful studies of XYY prisoners have revealed, however, that most had been convicted of nonviolent crimes such as car theft, larceny, embezzlement, and reporting false alarms to the police; few had committed violent crimes (Owen, 1972; Witkin et al., 1976). XYY males may have an increased probability of imprisonment not because of high aggressiveness but because of low intelligence (Witkin et al., 1976). Low intelligence may predispose individuals to crime because of social factors, such as decreased employment opportunities. It may also increase the probability that someone who commits a crime gets caught.

# SUMMARY

1. It is difficult to determine the role, if any, of prenatal hormones in the development of gender identity. Because the sex of rearing usually matches the prenatal hormone pattern, the effects of rearing and hormones are hard to separate. (p. 439)

2. Pseudohermaphrodites are people who were subjected to a hormonal pattern intermediate between male and female during their prenatal critical period for sexual development. (p. 440)

3. Although most pseudohermaphrodites accept their assigned sex, 5 to 10 percent are somewhat or greatly dissatisfied. (p. 442)

4. Certain adolescents develop a sexual appearance that does not match their sex of rearing. Observations of such individuals suggest that their sexual orientation may have been influenced, directly or indirectly, by prenatal hormones. (p. 442)

5. In male rats, procedures that prevent testosterone from masculinizing the brain during a prenatal period lead to an adult pattern of sexual responsiveness toward other male rats. The relationship of this finding to human homosexuality is still speculative. (p. 444)

6. Prenatal exposure to masculinizing hormones may contribute to some instances of female homosexuality, although it does not appear to have a strong influence. (p. 445)

7. Abnormal chromosome patterns, such as XO and XXY, lead to sterility and sometimes behavioral abnormalities. (p. 446)

# REVIEW QUESTIONS

1. What are the effects on a female rat fetus if she develops between two male fetuses? What accounts for these effects? (p. 440)

2. What may cause a human to develop as a pseudohermaphrodite, or intersex? (p. 440)

3. Why is each of the observations on gender identity in pseudohermaphrodites scientifically inconclusive? (p. 441)

4. What other kinds of evidence may help to evaluate the possible contribution of prenatal hormones to gender identity? (p. 442)

5. What event in early development can cause a male rat to develop sexual responsiveness to other males and not to females? Through what hormonal mechanism does this event probably work? (p. 444)

6. What evidence pertains to prenatal hormones as a possible contributor to homosexuality in men? What evidence pertains to prenatal hormones as a possible contributor to homosexuality in women? What are the limitations of such evidence? (p. 445)

7. What is testicular feminization, and what are its effects on development? (p. 446)

8. Describe Turner's syndrome, Klinefelter's syndrome, and the XYY chromosome pattern. (p. 446)

# THOUGHT QUESTION

1. On the average, pseudohermaphrodites have IQ scores in the 110 to 125 range, well above the mean for the population (Dalton, 1968; Ehrhardt & Money, 1967; Lewis, Money, & Epstein, 1968). One possible interpretation is that a hormonal pattern intermediate between male and female promotes great intellectual development. Another possibility is that pseudohermaphroditism may be more common in intelligent families than in less intelligent ones or that the more intelligent families are more likely to bring their pseudohermaphroditic children to an investigator's attention. What kind of study would be best for deciding among these hypotheses? (For one answer, see Money & Lewis, 1966.)

# SUGGESTIONS FOR FURTHER READING

**Adkins-Regan, E.** (1988). Sex hormones and sexual orientation in animals. *Psychobiology, 16,* 335–347. A review of research on the effects of prenatal and early postnatal hormones on the adult sexual behavior of nonhuman animals.

**Ellis, L., & Ames, M. A.** (1987). Neurohormonal functioning and sexual orientation: A theory of homosexuality-heterosexuality. *Psychological Bulletin, 101,* 233–258. Provocative article arguing that prenatal hormones are a major contributor to adult sexual orientation.

**Money, J., & Ehrhardt, A. A.** (1972). *Man & woman, boy & girl.* Baltimore: Johns Hopkins University Press. Discusses roles of hormones and social environment in the development of human sexual behavior.

# GLOSSARY

**activating effect** temporary effect of a hormone on behavior or anatomy, occurring only while the hormone is present

**alpha-fetoprotein** protein found in the bloodstream of most immature mammals that binds with estrogen

**androgen** a class of steroid hormones more abundant in males than in females for most species

**androgen insensitivity** condition in which a person lacks the mechanism that enables androgens to bind to genes in a cell's nucleus

**anterior pituitary** portion of the pituitary gland

**aromatic** in chemistry, a chemical containing six carbon atoms with three double bonds

**attractivity** tendency to attract sexual advances

**critical period** time early in development during which some event (such as the presence of a hormone) has a long-lasting effect

**diethylstilbestrol (DES)** a synthetic estrogen

**endocrine gland** organ that produces and releases hormones

**estradiol** one type of estrogen

**estrogen** a class of steroid hormones more abundant in females than in males for most species

**estrus** period when a female animal is fertile

**follicle-stimulating hormone (FSH)** anterior pituitary hormone that promotes the growth of follicles in the ovary

**gender identity** the sex with which a person identifies

**gonad** reproductive organ

**hermaphrodite** individual whose genitals do not match the normal development for his or her genetic sex

**hormone** chemical secreted by a gland and conveyed by the blood or lymphatic system to other organs whose activity it influences

**impotence** inability to have an erection

**intersex** individual whose sexual development is intermediate between male and female

**Klinefelter's syndrome** condition associated with an XXY chromosome pattern

**luteinizing hormone (LH)** anterior pituitary hormone that stimulates the release of an ovum and prepares the uterus for implantation of a fertilized ovum

**menarche** time of a woman's first menstruation

**menopause** time when middle-aged women stop menstruating

**menstrual cycle** periodic variation in hormones and fertility over the course of approximately one month in women

**Müllerian duct** early precursors to female reproductive structures (the oviducts, uterus, and upper vagina)

**organizing effect** long-lasting effect of a hormone that is present during a critical period early in development

**ovary** female gonad that produces eggs

**peptide hormone** hormone composed of a chain of amino acids

**pituitary gland** an endocrine gland attached to the hypothalamus

**posterior pituitary** portion of the pituitary gland

**proceptivity** tendency to approach a partner and actively seek sexual contact

**progesterone** hormone that prepares the uterus for the implantation of a fertilized ovum

**pseudohermaphrodite** individual whose sexual development is intermediate between male and female

**puberty** onset of sexual maturity

**receptivity** tendency to respond favorably to sexual advances

**releasing hormone** hormone that the hypothalamus releases and that flows through the blood to the anterior pituitary

**sex-limited gene** gene that exerts its effects primarily in one sex because of activation by androgens or estrogens

**sex role** the set of activities and dispositions presumed to be common for one sex in a particular society

**steroid hormone** hormone that contains four carbon rings

**testicular feminization** condition in which a person lacks the mechanism that enables androgens to bind to genes in a cell's nucleus

**testis** male gonad that produces testosterone and sperm

**testosterone** one type of androgen

**thyroid hormone** hormone produced by the thyroid gland

**Turner's syndrome** genetic condition of anatomical females with an XO chromosome pattern

**Wolffian duct** early precursors to male reproductive structures

**XXY chromosome pattern** condition of anatomical males with an extra X chromosome, also known as Klinefelter's syndrome

**XYY chromosome pattern** condition of anatomical males with an extra Y chromosome

# CHAPTER THIRTEEN

# Emotional Behaviors and Stress

*If I were tsar, I would make a law that a writer who uses a word whose meaning he can't explain should be deprived of the right to write and receive 100 strokes of the birch.*
Leo Tolstoy
(1878/1978, p. 325)

## MAIN IDEAS

**1.** Emotional states are associated with activation of the autonomic nervous system.

**2.** Several psychosomatic illnesses can be traced to autonomic nervous system activity.

**3.** Chronic stress can suppress activity of the immune system and leave an individual highly vulnerable to various illnesses.

**4.** A set of forebrain structures known as the limbic system is important in emotional behaviors.

**5.** Pleasure is associated with activity of certain brain pathways in areas that are rich in catecholamines and with activity of endorphin synapses.

**6.** Anxiety is linked with high levels of sympathetic nervous system arousal and high levels of norepinephrine activity; GABA synapses can inhibit it.

**7.** Aggressive behavior is associated with activity of the amygdala and with decreased turnover of serotonin.

If Tolstoy's proposed law ever goes into effect, I shall cease at once to use the word *emotion*. In fact, if you have a pen handy, maybe you could do me a favor and cross out the title of this chapter right now. Seriously, suppose we crossed out the word *emotion* every time it appears anywhere in psychology. Would psychology be any poorer for the loss of this word?

Of all the terms psychologists commonly use, *emotion* may be the most difficult to define. To illustrate: Psychologists do not always agree on what memories really are, but they are skilled at detecting and measuring memories in people and animals. Psychologists have even less agreement on what motivation is, but they can generally measure the intensity of a given

(Stephen Dalton/NAS/Photo Researchers, Inc.)

motivation, such as hunger or thirst. But just try to determine how "happy" a rat is, and you will quickly discover how vague our concepts of emotions are.

Even though the term *emotion* is poorly defined, however, the behaviors generally associated with it— such as escape and attack—are too important to ignore. And when we observe that people have become "emotional," their behavior is undeniably different from usual. For example, suppose an experimenter locks you in a room with no windows and challenges you to get out. You systematically (and unemotionally) try to pry the door open or to find a secret passageway. If you fail, you may eventually give up and wait for the experimenter to rescue you. Now suppose that a terrorist has locked you in the same room, but this time with a time bomb. Suddenly your behavior becomes "emotional." Frantically you try climbing the walls, breaking down the door, or prying out the floorboards. You keep on trying even after all efforts fail. In short, emotional behaviors tend to be vigorous and persistent (Tomkins, 1980).

# Emotion, Autonomic Nervous System Arousal, and Health Problems

When driving a car, you have an accelerator to increase speed and a brake pedal to decrease speed. Emotions are a little like that, although I would not push the analogy too far. Some emotional states speed up your actions to deal with an emergency; others slow down your actions to be cautious and to conserve energy.

## ROLE OF THE AUTONOMIC NERVOUS SYSTEM IN EMOTIONAL BEHAVIORS

The two parts of the autonomic nervous system largely govern the vigor of a behavior. The sympathetic nervous system prepares the body for intense, vigorous, emergency activity. The parasympathetic nervous system increases digestion and other processes associated with relaxation. At most times both systems are active, although at a given moment one may be more active than the other. (To review the structure and function of the sympathetic and parasympathetic nervous systems, see p. 104 and especially Figure 4.11.)

The sympathetic nervous system is activated not by stimuli themselves but by how someone interprets those stimuli. In one study, boys who were given a task and told it was a test reacted with increased heart rates. Other boys given the same task but told it was a game reacted with decreased heart rates (Darley & Katz, 1973).

In another study, people who received inescapable shocks and knew the shocks were inescapable had decreased heart rates—a typical parasympathetic response to uncontrollable distress. People who were misled into believing that they might find some way to avoid the shocks had faster heart rates (Malcuit, 1973). In other words, a given task or set of shocks can either increase or decrease sympathetic arousal, depending on what response people think the situation requires.

One way to increase parasympathetic activity is to remove the stimulus that originally excited sympathetic activity. A sudden decrease in sympathetic activity provokes rebound overactivity of the parasympathetic system. For example, if a

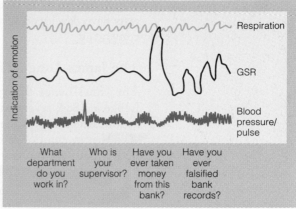

| | | | |
| What department do you work in? | Who is your supervisor? | Have you ever taken money from this bank? | Have you ever falsified bank records? |

serial killer with a chain saw starts chasing you, you will run away, aided by abundant activity of your sympathetic nervous system. Suddenly the police grab the attacker and you realize you are safe. At that point your parasympathetic nervous system takes over, so strongly that you may even faint.

## Measurements of Autonomic Arousal

In everyday life, we generally gauge people's emotions from their self-reports. When people say they are happy, sad, or angry, we believe them. But we need more objective measures for many scientific purposes—certainly when using non-human animals and often with humans as well.

For many purposes, investigators measure sympathetic nervous system responses, such as increased heart rate and rapid breathing. Such measurements provide a crude but sometimes satisfactory indicator of "emotionality" in both humans and nonhumans. However, those measurements do not distinguish among fear, anger, intense happiness, or other emotional states that yield similar autonomic responses. We must also be cautious because some people have consistently greater responses than others. (If my heart rate increases twice as much as yours, I may not be twice as frightened or twice as angry.)

The polygraph test—the so-called lie-detector test—is really a measure of sympathetic nervous system arousal (see Figure 13.1): It typically records heart rate, blood pressure, breathing rate, and **galvanic skin response** (determining the electrical conductance of the skin, a measure of the slight sweating caused by sympathetic nerves to the skin). The theory behind the polygraph test is that people become nervous when they lie and that their nervousness elevates the response of their sympathetic nervous system.

Because lying is only loosely related to nervousness, the polygraph is not a highly reliable indicator of truthfulness. Some people can remain calm while lying about their criminal activities; others become nervous even when they are telling the truth. How would you react if someone strapped you into a polygraph device and then asked whether you had stolen a thousand dollars last Thursday? Ordinarily, about one-third of all innocent people "fail" the lie-detector test (Kleinmuntz & Szucko, 1984).

If someone shows no autonomic arousal, does that mean that the person is experiencing no emotion? And is autonomic arousal just a way of measuring emotion, or is it the cause of emotion? Such questions are difficult to answer because

**Figure 13.1**
**The polygraph test, literally a "many measures test"**
*The examiner asks a series of questions and compares the autonomic responses. One major difficulty is that a heightened response may indicate either nervousness about lying or nervousness about being accused of an offense. (Alon Reiniger/Contact Press Images.)*

Emotion, Autonomic Nervous System Arousal, and Health Problems

of the difficulties in observing and measuring emotional experiences. Psychologists have developed several theories of emotion, although none of them is fully convincing.

## The James-Lange Theory

The James-Lange theory, proposed independently by William James and C. G. Lange in 1884, reverses the commonsense notion that emotions cause arousal and action. According to the **James-Lange theory,** arousal and action lead to emotion; that is, emotion is how we label certain kinds of arousal and action. When I notice that I am running away, I decide that I must be afraid. When I notice that I am attacking, I conclude that I must be angry.

Although it is difficult to test directly, the James-Lange theory does lead to at least two testable predictions: (1) The more intense one's arousal, the greater one's emotion. (2) If a person can discern a difference between emotions, then those emotions must be associated with different types of physiological arousal or overt action.

The first of these predictions is partly, but only partly, correct. Drugs and other treatments that enhance autonomic arousal generally cause people to rate their emotions as more intense (Reisenzein, 1983). On the other hand, many people with spinal cord damage report that their emotions are still as strong as ever, despite reduced sensory input from the viscera (Lowe & Carroll, 1985).

The second prediction is also only partly correct. Different emotions are associated with different physiological changes, but the differences are small (Ekman, Levenson, & Friesen, 1983). For example, galvanic skin response is higher during sadness than during other emotions. Hand temperature increases more during anger than during other emotions. Heart rate increases more with fear and anger than with happiness. Although these differences are statistically reliable, they are not large or consistent or easy to perceive in oneself. It is doubtful that people determine whether they are happy, sad, or angry by observing their skin temperature, heart rate, or skin conductance.

Stanley Schachter and Jerome Singer (1962) offered a theory similar to the James-Lange theory. According to their modification, people (and perhaps other animals, too) seek to understand the source of their autonomic arousal. Different people may experience a given state of arousal as fear, anger, or happiness depending on what they think caused the arousal. If they attribute the arousal to a pill they took, they may not experience the arousal as emotion at all. In other words, autonomic arousal may largely determine the degree of emotion, but cognitive factors determine *which* emotion a person feels.

## The Cannon-Bard Theory

Not everyone agrees that autonomic arousal is indispensable to emotion. According to the **Cannon-Bard theory,** as proposed by Walter Cannon (1927) and modified by Philip Bard (1934), emotions and autonomic changes occur simultaneously but independently. That is, a pattern of sensory information may activate both the autonomic nervous system and the cerebral cortex, so a person could experience an emotion even if he or she received no sensations from the autonomic nervous system.

Which theory is correct: the James-Lange theory, a modification of it, the Cannon-Bard theory, or some other? This question is not a popular topic of current research. It is easier to study the biological factors that increase or decrease a given emotion such as anxiety than to determine what anxiety itself really is.

# EMOTIONS, AUTONOMIC
# RESPONSES, AND HEALTH

Through most of its history, modern medicine has explained diseases in purely physical terms: bacteria, viruses, toxins, or vitamin deficiencies, for example. Researchers saw little merit in the idea of "will to live" or any other relationship between thoughts and health. Such concepts sounded too mystical, too spiritual, too much like the superstitions that medical doctors were trying to replace. To take an extreme case, when soldiers returned from battle with "shell shock," now called **posttraumatic stress disorder,** many physicians rejected any notion that a soldier's fear might have had something to do with the condition. Instead, they suggested "ionized air caused by cannonballs whistling by" and other similarly far-fetched hypotheses (McMahon, 1975).

Today, there is little doubt that stressful experiences and thoughts of despair can increase the risk of many kinds of disease. Likewise, even skeptics are beginning to take seriously the possibility that a hopeful attitude or a sense of humor can help someone overcome cancer or other major illnesses (see, for example, Cousins, 1989).

Appreciating the psychological factors in health is a relatively new idea in Western medicine. It also represents a growing trend in psychology, the focus of **behavioral medicine,** a field that considers the influence of eating and drinking habits, smoking, stress, exercise, and other behaviors on people's health.

Yet it is still rather easy to slip from the enlightened view that experiences can affect health into the old-fashioned idea that blames the victim for illness: In medieval times many people believed that illness was a punishment for sin; today many people seem to assume that victims of deadly diseases are in one way or another responsible for their own misfortune. Psychological factors do have *some* control over health and illness, and it is important to learn more about this control. But they do not have complete control, by any means.

## The Autonomic Nervous System
## and Psychosomatic Illnesses

Most people's autonomic responsiveness is highly consistent over time. Some people show a stronger and quicker sympathetic response to a wide variety of stimuli than other people do. They also tend to show more emotional expression and more overall activity; in addition, they are generally more gregarious, more impulsive, more distractible, and less patient (Shields, 1983). In other words, responsiveness of the sympathetic nervous system is related to much of what we call *personality*.

People with a highly responsive sympathetic nervous system also tend to be relatively vulnerable to heart disease and several other medical disorders. In these **psychosomatic illnesses,** the probability of getting the disease or recovering from it depends in part on the person's personality or experiences. A psychosomatic illness is real, not imaginary or pretended. For example, heart disease is psychosomatic in the sense that it is somewhat more common among tense, hostile, and impatient people than among people who are relaxed and easy going (Booth-Kewley & Friedman, 1987). Perhaps a highly responsive sympathetic nervous system predisposes people to feel tense, while it also overstimulates the heart.

## The Role of the Autonomic Nervous
## System in Ulcer Formation

One illness strongly influenced by autonomic nervous system activity is **ulcers** (open sores on the lining of the stomach or intestines). Ulcers can form in several ways, but people who experience severe work-related stress are believed to be especially vulnerable. Because of the difficulties in studying ulcer formation in humans, experiments have been conducted on animals.

In a pioneering experiment, monkeys were exposed to work-related stress (Brady, Porter, Conrad, & Mason, 1958). Pairs of monkeys were confined to chairs, as Figure 13.2 shows; one foot of each monkey was attached to an electrode that delivered a shock every 20 seconds. One of the monkeys, dubbed the executive monkey of the pair, could forestall the shocks by pressing a lever in front of it. If the executive pressed the lever at least once every 20 seconds, neither monkey received any shocks. But if it waited any longer, both monkeys would receive a shock once every 20 seconds until the executive pressed the lever again. The second, passive monkey had no control over the shocks. The procedure lasted 6 hours at a time, twice a day, every day. Within an hour or two of the first session, each executive monkey had learned the response well and prevented the shocks almost completely from then on.

As the researchers had expected, the executive monkeys got ulcers and the passive monkeys did not. Why? Actually, because the experimental design was imperfect, the results are not easy to interpret. The monkeys were not randomly assigned to the executive and passive roles but rather were assigned on the basis of how well they learned the avoidance response. Conceivably, animals that learn to respond rapidly may also be nervous ones likely to develop ulcers. Regardless of how seriously we worry about that possibility, the experiment does not fully explain why the executives got ulcers and the passives did not. The key factor may have been some combination of emotional strain and physical exertion.

A second experiment sheds important light on the results of the first. E. L. Foltz and F. E. Millett (1964) repeated the executive monkey experiment except that they used the same passive monkey with three different executives. After one executive monkey had served for a few weeks, it was replaced by a second; this new executive, being inexperienced in the apparatus, took a couple of hours to learn what to do. The passive monkey gyrated vigorously in its chair, screaming and gesturing wildly until the new executive started preventing the shocks consistently. Later, when a third untrained executive replaced the second one, the passive monkey went through the same routine and soon developed a severe case of ulcers.

Evidently, the ulcers came not from "being in charge" but from a state of high arousal, whatever its cause. An executive monkey gets ulcers from struggling to avoid shocks; a passive monkey may get ulcers from receiving many unavoidable shocks.

Similar experiments have been conducted on rats. The executive rats never approached 100 percent shock avoidance, as the monkeys did. The passive rats developed more ulcers than the executives, presumably because they could neither control the shocks nor predict their onset (J. M. Weiss, 1968, 1971a, 1971b). Note that the ulcers do not result from the shocks themselves but from the passive rats' lack of an adequate coping response.

Other things being equal, unpredictable shocks cause more ulcers than predictable shocks do (Guile, 1987). When shocks or other stressors are predictable,

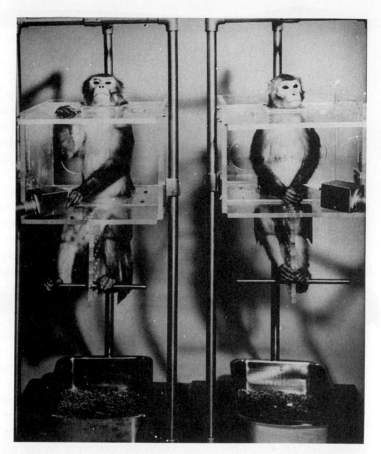

**Figure 13.2
An "executive"
monkey (left) and a
"passive" monkey
(right)**
*When the executive presses
the lever, it temporarily prevents electric shocks for both
monkeys. Note the more relaxed bearing of the passive
monkey. (From Brady et al.,
1958.)*

the individual can be on the alert at the appropriate times. When they are unpredictable, the individual must be alert and tense at all times.

Ulcers do not form during stress periods, while the animals are receiving
shocks or pressing levers to avoid them, but during the rest periods afterward
(Desiderato, MacKinnon, & Hissom, 1974). The shock period greatly activates
the sympathetic nervous system; during the rest period, the parasympathetic system rebounds, releasing an excess of digestive juices that damage the insides of
the stomach and intestines, causing ulcers.

Digestive secretions are not the whole explanation, however. During a stress
period, and especially during the first two hours after the stress period, the stomach makes many slow but intense contractions. These contractions tend to break
up the protective mucus lining of the stomach; they expose parts of the stomach
wall to the digestive secretions (Garrick, 1990; Garrick, Minor, Bauck, Weiner, &
Guth, 1989).

How could a person at high risk for developing ulcers, unable to prevent a
stressful experience, avoid developing ulcers? Eating something just before or after the experience greatly lowers the probability of ulcer formation because food
helps absorb excess digestive secretions. We might well guess that a mild stressor
following the major stressor would also help to reduce ulcer formation by enabling the sympathetic system to "calm down" gradually instead of swinging suddenly to a parasympathetic rebound. However, introducing brief, mild stressors

during the rest period actually increases the probability of ulcers (Murison & Overmier, 1990; Overmier, Murison, Ursin, & Skoglund, 1987). Exactly why is uncertain.

## Voodoo Death and Related Phenomena

Almost everyone knows of someone with a strong will to live who survived well beyond others' expectations or someone who gave up and died of a relatively minor ailment. The extreme case of the latter is *voodoo death*, in which a healthy person dies apparently just because he or she believes that some curse has destined death.

Such phenomena were generally ignored by scientists until Walter Cannon (1942) published a collection of reasonably well-documented reports of voodoo death. A typical example was a woman who ate a fruit and then was told that it had come from a taboo place. Within hours she was dead. The common pattern in such cases was that the intended victim knew about the magic spells and believed that he or she was sure to die from them. The person's friends and relatives also believed in the hex and began to treat the victim as a dying person. Overwhelmed with a feeling of hopelessness, the victim refused food and water and died usually within 24 to 48 hours. In some manner the terror and hopelessness led to death. (For more examples, see Cannon, 1942; Cappannari, Rau, Abram, & Buchanan, 1975; Wintrob, 1973.) Similar examples occur in our own society— not people who die because they believe they are hexed but people who sometimes die quickly because they expect to.

What is the cause of death in such cases? Curt Richter accidentally stumbled on a possible answer while studying the swimming abilities of rats. Ordinarily, rats can swim in turbulent warm water nonstop for 48 hours or more. However, Richter (1957a) found that a rat would die quickly if he cut off its whiskers just before throwing it into the tank. (A rat's whiskers are critical to its ability to find its way around.) The rat would swim frantically for a minute or so and then suddenly sink to the bottom, dead. Richter found that many, but not all, laboratory rats died quickly under these conditions. Wild rats, which are more nervous and emotional than domesticated laboratory rats, all died quickly under the same conditions. Autopsies showed that the rats had not drowned; their hearts had simply stopped beating.

A rat can swim for hours without whiskers if its whiskers are trimmed hours or days in advance. Evidently, the sudden death resulted from combining the de-whiskering operation with immersion in water. That combination greatly stimulated the rat's sympathetic nervous system and greatly elevated its heart rate. After the rat swam frantically for a minute or so and found no escape, its parasympathetic system became highly activated, both as a rebound from the strong sympathetic activation and as the natural response to a terrifying, apparently inescapable situation. The parasympathetic response was so massive that it stopped the rat's heart altogether.

To confirm the role of apparent escapability or inescapability, Richter performed another experiment. First he placed a rat in the water several times, rescuing it each time. Then he cut the rat's whiskers and put it in the water again. The rescues apparently immunized the rat against extreme terror in this situation; the rat swam successfully for many hours. Richter's results suggest that voodoo death and perhaps many other cases of sudden death in a frightening situation may be due to excessive parasympathetic activity, either as a rebound effect or as a response to a frightening, hopeless situation.

# CHRONIC STRESS, THE IMMUNE SYSTEM, AND HEALTH

Up to this point, we have considered the effects of fairly brief stressful periods, lasting from a few seconds to a few hours, that call for vigorous action. We sometimes encounter another kind of stress, however—problems that seem to go on forever, problems that we can do little or nothing about: The government builds a toxic waste dump in your neighborhood. A loved one suddenly dies and you have to live without this person you had depended on. Your business is on the verge of failure and you face the constant worry of whether you will be able to pay the bills. The body's response to chronic stressors differs from its response to temporary emergencies.

Stressors excite both the sympathetic nervous system and an axis composed of the hypothalamus, pituitary gland, and adrenal cortex. With increasingly prolonged stress, the effects of the hypothalamus/pituitary/adrenal axis become more prominent. The hypothalamus induces the anterior pituitary gland to secrete the hormone **ACTH** (adrenocorticotropic hormone), which in turn stimulates the adrenal cortex to secrete **cortisol** and several other hormones; cortisol elevates blood sugar and enhances metabolism (see Figure 13.3). The increased fuel supply to the cells enables them to sustain a high level of activity in the face of stress. It is, however, a steady activity instead of the sudden bursts of "fight or flight" ac-

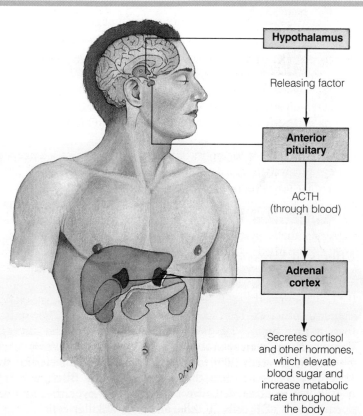

**Figure 13.3 The hypothalamus/anterior pituitary/adrenal cortex axis**

*Prolonged stress leads to the secretion of the adrenal hormone cortisol, which elevates blood sugar and increases metabolism. Those changes help the body to sustain prolonged activity but at the expense of decreased immune system activity.*

Hypothalamus

Releasing factor

Anterior pituitary

ACTH (through blood)

Adrenal cortex

Secretes cortisol and other hormones, which elevate blood sugar and increase metabolic rate throughout the body

459

tivity associated with the sympathetic nervous system. In fact, an individual with elevated cortisol secretion may be withdrawn and inactive much of the time. As cortisol and other hormones shift energy toward increasing blood sugar and metabolism, they shift it away from synthesis of proteins, including the proteins necessary for the immune system. In the short term that shift may not be a problem; however, stress that continues for weeks or months may weaken the immune system and leave the individual vulnerable to a variety of illnesses.

## The Immune System

The **immune system** is a set of structures that protects the body against intruders. To do so, it must distinguish between "self" and "nonself." It must attack all foreign material, such as viruses and bacteria; it should not attack the body's own cells. Sometimes the immune system goes awry and becomes overactive, attacking the body's own cells. The result is an autoimmune disease, such as myasthenia gravis.

The most important elements of the immune system are the **leukocytes,** commonly known as white blood cells (O'Leary, 1990). Leukocytes are produced in the bone marrow; they then migrate to several organs such as the thymus gland, the spleen, and the peripheral lymph nodes. Those organs store the leukocytes and promote their maturation until some foreign body causes their release. When the immune system is functioning properly, its cells identify microorganisms, attach to them, and inactivate them. Each microorganism has surface proteins different from those of the host. Those surface proteins are **antigens** (antibody-generator molecules), which trigger attacks by leukocytes.

Leukocytes are of several types:

**Macrophages** (literally, "big eaters") engulf and attack microorganisms and then display an antigen of the microorganism, as Figure 13.4 illustrates.

**B cells** (so named because they mature in the bone marrow) attach to an intruder and produce a specific antibody to attack the antigen. An **antibody** is a Y-shaped protein that specifically fits onto an antigen and weakens it or marks it for destruction by other cells.

**T cells** (so named because they mature in the thymus) directly attack intruder cells or, as **helper T cells,** stimulate added response by other immune system cells. Helper T cells stimulate B cells to proliferate and to form **B memory cells** that immunize the body against future attacks by the same intruder (see Figure 13.4).

**Natural killer cells** destroy certain kinds of tumor cells and cells infected with viruses.

## Effects of Stress on the Immune System

Certain kinds of chronic stress can suppress the activity of the immune system (O'Leary, 1990). For example, natural killer cells are fewer than normal in women whose husbands are dying of cancer, women whose husbands died within the last six months, and medical students going through their exam period (Glaser, Rice, Speicher, Stout, & Kiecolt-Glaser, 1986; Irwin, Daniels, Risch, Bloom, & Weiner, 1988). In 1979, the Three-Mile-Island nuclear power plant suffered a major accident that was successfully (though barely) contained. The people who continued to live in the vicinity over the next year had lower than normal levels of B cells, T cells, and natural killer cells. They also complained of

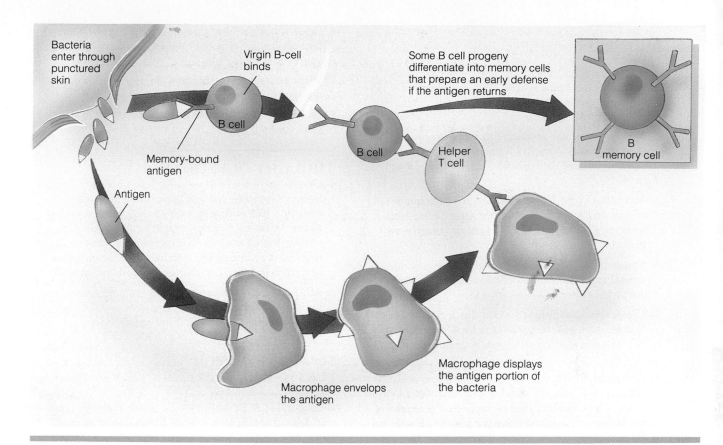

Bacteria enter through punctured skin

Virgin B-cell binds

Some B cell progeny differentiate into memory cells that prepare an early defense if the antigen returns

B cell

B memory cell

Memory-bound antigen

B cell

Helper T cell

Antigen

Macrophage displays the antigen portion of the bacteria

Macrophage envelops the antigen

emotional distress and showed impaired performance on a proofreading task (Baum, Gatchel, & Schaeffer, 1983; McKinnon, Weisse, Reynolds, Bowles, & Baum, 1989).

Prolonged stress can also release endorphins, which decrease pain but also suppress certain immune responses. For example, rats that endure prolonged sessions of inescapable foot shocks have high endorphin levels, low sensitivity to pain, and in many cases depressed levels of natural killer cells. Such animals are highly vulnerable; if they develop a tumor, the tumor grows faster than it does in other animals (Sklar & Anisman, 1981).

In humans, too, certain stressful experiences release endorphins. In one study, eight Vietnam veterans who had suffered particularly traumatic experiences during the war were asked to watch a 15-minute videotape of dramatized combat. As a result, they had elevated endorphin levels and decreased response to pain (Pitman, van der Kolk, Orr, & Greenberg, 1990). However, investigators have not directly tested the effect of such experiences on human vulnerability to cancer and other diseases, and the effects may be fairly small. For example, people suffering from depression and other serious psychological disorders have a virtually normal life expectancy, except for their increased probability of suicide and fatal accidents (Stein, Miller, & Trestman, 1991).

The research on stress suggests that good methods of coping with stress can have health benefits. If people find effective ways to escape from stressful experiences or to fight back against them, they may be able to maintain a strong immune response.

**Figure 13.4**
**Immune system responses to a bacterial infection**
*A macrophage cell engulfs a bacterial cell and displays one of the bacteria's antigens on its surface. Meanwhile, a B cell also binds to the bacteria and produces antibodies against the bacteria. A helper T cell attaches to both the macrophage and the B cell; it stimulates the B cell to generate copies of itself, called B memory cells, which immunize the body against future invasions by the same kind of bacteria.*

Emotion, Autonomic
Nervous System
Arousal, and Health
Problems

## SUMMARY

1. Many emotional stimuli increase the activity of the sympathetic nervous system. Removal of such a stimulus activates the parasympathetic nervous system as a rebound effect. (p. 452)

2. A given event may produce either major sympathetic nervous system arousal, a little, or none at all, depending on how the individual interprets the event. (p. 452)

3. According to the James-Lange theory, autonomic arousal and other body activities come before emotions; an emotion is a label for activity that has already begun. (p. 454)

4. According to the Cannon-Bard theory, autonomic arousal and emotional experiences are caused independently by a given stimulus. (p. 454)

5. Ulcers and possibly also voodoo death result from excessive activity of the parasympathetic nervous system as a rebound after excessive sympathetic activation. (p. 456)

6. Prolonged, inescapable stressful experiences activate the adrenal cortex and increase the release of endorphins. Those changes tend to suppress the activity of the immune system and leave the individual more vulnerable than usual to various illnesses. (p. 459)

## REVIEW QUESTIONS

1. What happens to autonomic nervous system arousal just after removal of a stimulus that excited sympathetic nervous system arousal? (p. 452)

2. Distinguish between the James-Lange theory and the Cannon-Bard theory. (p. 454)

3. What is the evidence, pro and con, concerning the James-Lange theory? (p. 454)

4. If periods of stress alternate with periods of rest, when are ulcers most likely to form? Why? (p. 457)

5. Besides excess digestive juices, what other change in the digestive system contributes to ulcer formation? (p. 457)

6. What activity of the autonomic nervous system may be responsible for certain cases of sudden death, as in voodoo death? (p. 458)

7. What are leukocytes and how do they contribute to the immune response? (p. 460)

8. How does chronic stress affect vulnerability to disease? (p. 460)

## THOUGHT QUESTIONS

1. Suppose someone has just gone through a highly stressful experience and is now at risk for developing ulcers. What kind of drug might be helpful in preventing the ulcers: one that increases or decreases activity of the sympathetic system? One that increases or decreases activity of the parasympathetic system?

2. AIDS is a disease that attacks the immune system, especially T cells. Should the symptoms of AIDS be milder or worse during times of stress? Why?

## SUGGESTIONS FOR FURTHER READING

**Brannon, L., & Feist, J.** (1992). *Health psychology* (2nd ed.). Belmont, CA: Wadsworth. Discussion of relationships among stress, behavior, and health issues.

**Hernandez, D. E., & Glavin, G. B.** (Eds.). (1990). *Neurobiology of stress ulcers* [Special issue]. *Annals of the New York Academy of Sciences, 597.* Collection of contributions on the behavioral and physiological aspects of ulcers.

**Izard, C. E., Kagan, J., & Zajonc, R. B.** (Eds.). (1984). *Emotions, cognition, and behavior.* Cambridge, England: Cambridge University Press. A collection of articles on emotion, including some on nonbiological aspects.

**O'Leary, A.** (1990). Stress, emotion, and human immune function. *Psychological Bulletin, 108,* 363–382. Excellent introduction to how psychological factors affect the immune system and thereby health.

# Reinforcement, Escape and Attack Behaviors, and the Brain

One of the great accomplishments of chemistry is the periodic table of the elements. The periodic table names all the elements that form every compound in existence, every compound that could possibly exist. Moreover, it organizes the elements into a regular, repeating pattern that shows us *why* certain elements are metals, why certain others are gases, and why no chemist is likely to discover some new naturally occurring element that previous scientists had overlooked.

As a psychologist, I envy the chemists' periodic table. I wish we had a periodic table of emotions or motivations. Some psychologists have tried to list all the emotions or all the motivations, but such lists seem haphazard. For example, Carroll Izard (1977) lists ten emotions: interest, joy, surprise, distress, anger, disgust, contempt, fear, shame, and guilt. But why those particular ten? Is each of those states elemental or are some of them compounds? For instance, is disgust a compound of two parts distress and one part contempt? Could we perhaps reduce the list to, say, eight elementary emotions, or five, or even two — approach and avoidance?

Maybe, maybe not. While we are waiting for someone to develop a periodic table of emotions, in this section we shall examine one brain area — the limbic system — regarded as important for all emotional behaviors. We then turn to three important examples of emotional behaviors: reinforcement (an approach behavior), anxiety (an avoidance behavior), and attack (a special kind of approach behavior).

## THE LIMBIC SYSTEM AND EMOTIONS

Emotional behavior depends largely on an area of the forebrain known as the **limbic system;** it includes the hypothalamus, hippocampus, amygdala, olfactory bulb, septum, other small structures, and parts of the thalamus and cerebral cortex. Several investigators have contributed to our understanding of the limbic system. In pioneering studies, Philip Bard (1929, 1934) found that when he removed the entire cerebral cortex of cats, they displayed exaggerated aggressive behaviors

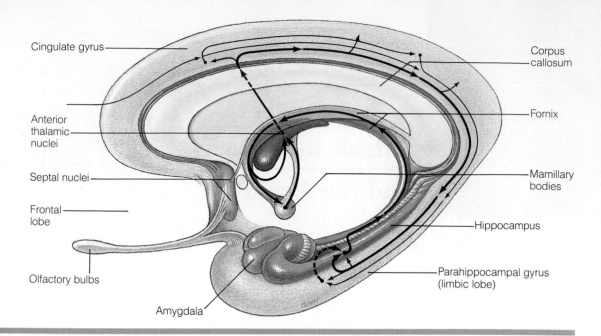

Cingulate gyrus

Anterior thalamic nuclei

Septal nuclei

Frontal lobe

Olfactory bulbs

Amygdala

Corpus callosum

Fornix

Mamillary bodies

Hippocampus

Parahippocampal gyrus (limbic lobe)

**Figure 13.5**
**Some major pathways and connections of the limbic system**
*(Based on MacLean, 1949.)*

and postures in response to various stimuli. Evidently, subcortical areas could generate emotional behaviors; the function of the cerebral cortex was to direct those behaviors toward appropriate targets and, when appropriate, to suppress them.

In 1937, J. W. Papez (rhymes with *grapes*) proposed that the hypothalamus and several other subcortical structures (see Figures 4.14 and 13.5) compose a circuit responsible for emotions. Papez based his theory partly on the fact that cells in much of the limbic system respond to taste, smell, and pain stimuli, all of which evoke strong emotional reactions. These three sensory modalities also have the properties of slow onset, slow offset, and vagueness about location—properties that characterize emotions as well.

Paul MacLean revived and revised Papez's theory on the basis of later studies of brain damage (MacLean, 1949, 1958, 1970), giving Papez's circuit the name *limbic system* because its structures form a border (*limbus*) around certain midline structures. The size of the limbic system is relatively constant across the various mammalian species. By contrast, species vary greatly in the size of their cerebral cortex (see Figure 13.6), an evolutionary trend that suggested to MacLean that the limbic system controls primitive functions that all mammals share in common.

According to MacLean, the strongest evidence that the limbic system is important for emotion comes from observations of people with temporal lobe epilepsy or other abnormalities in the limbic system. Although most people with temporal lobe epilepsy have no particular emotional experiences with their epileptic seizures, a substantial minority experience aggressive impulses, fear, a dissociation of experience similar to multiple personality (Schenk & Bear, 1981), uncontrollable laughter (Swash, 1972), sexual arousal (Rémillard et al., 1983), or a feeling of extreme bliss including a sense of oneness with the universe and the Creator (Cirignotta, Todesco, & Lugaresi, 1980). (The latter experience is named *Dostoyevskian epilepsy* after the Russian novelist who had this type of epilepsy.)

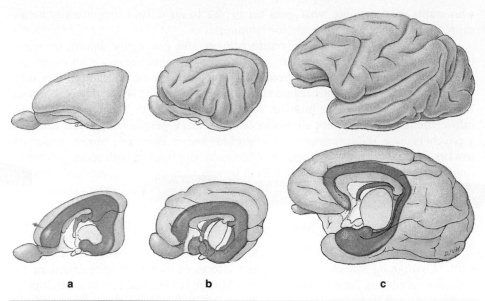

**Figure 13.6**
*Brains of (a) a rabbit, (b) a cat, and (c) a monkey, showing both the lateral surface (top) and the medial surface (bottom). The limbic system (dark areas) shows less variation in size across mammalian species than does the cerebral cortex. (From MacLean, 1954.)*

Within the limbic system, MacLean (1970) distinguished three circuits. One circuit, including the amygdala and the hippocampus, affects behaviors related to self-preservation. Damage to various parts of the amygdala can make an animal excessively tame, unaggressive, and emotionally unresponsive (Zagrodzka & Fonberg, 1979; Aggleton & Passingham, 1981). Monkeys and cats with amygdala damage sometimes attempt to eat feces, burning matches, and other objects that they would ordinarily reject. (However, it is hard to be certain whether they have a loss of emotions or whether they no longer recognize the objects.)

A second circuit in the limbic system includes the cingulate gyrus of the cerebral cortex, the septum, and several other structures. (The septum is a fairly large structure in the rat brain but a much less imposing structure in humans.) This circuit seems to relate to pleasure, especially sexual enjoyment. Electrical or chemical stimulation of this region in rats often causes penile erection, self-grooming, and related behaviors.

A third circuit, according to MacLean, includes parts of the hypothalamus and anterior thalamus. Believed to be important for cooperative social behavior and certain aspects of sexuality, this circuit is larger in primates than in most other mammals.

## BRAIN ACTIVITY AND REINFORCEMENT

Pleasure or happiness is an especially difficult state to study scientifically. Unlike pain, pleasure does not correspond to a particular kind of stimulation. And unlike fear and anger, pleasure does not give rise to any consistent, observable response, such as running away or attacking. Happy people sometimes smile, but not always. (If a friend who is not smiling tells you she is happy, do you disbelieve her?) Dogs wag their tails to display a friendly and presumably happy state, but most other nonhumans have no clear gesture to indicate happiness. So an investigator

Reinforcement, Escape and Attack Behaviors, and the Brain

**Figure 13.7
A rat pressing a lever for self-stimulation of its brain**

who wants to determine what goes on in the brain during happiness is handicapped by not having any gauge for happiness.

We can, however, measure reinforcement and can easily determine which brain processes are associated with reinforcement. *Reinforcement* is an event that increases the probability of the preceding response; for example, food is a reinforcement for a hungry rat because the rat will increase its frequency of whatever response leads to food. For humans, most events that make us happy serve as reinforcements. However, not all reinforcements make people happy. For example, a paycheck is a reinforcement for a worker, but it does not always make the worker *happy*. Some people play video games by the hour; a high score serves as a reinforcement, but it is not necessarily a source of happiness. Even with rats, reinforcement is probably not synonymous with pleasure.

## Self-Stimulation of the Brain in Nonhuman Animals

The brain mechanisms of pleasure and reinforcement were discovered by accident. Two young scientists studying the effects of electrical stimulation of the reticular formation, James Olds and Peter Milner (1954), put rats in a situation in which they had to choose between turning left and turning right. Rats typically hesitate, looking one way and then the other, before choosing. Olds and Milner wanted to test whether stimulation of the reticular formation would cause a rat that was looking in one direction to turn that direction. However, they had implanted the electrode in the rat's septum by mistake. To their surprise, when the rat received the brain stimulation, it would sometimes sit up, look around, and sniff, as rats often react to a favorable stimulus.

Olds and Milner later placed the rat in a Skinner box, where it repeatedly pressed a lever for electrical brain stimulation as a reinforcement (Figure 13.7). That is, it worked for **self-stimulation of the brain.** Olds found that a number of other areas in the limbic system also produce reinforcement; in some cases rats pressed a lever to stimulate certain brain areas as often as 2,000 times per hour, continuing for hours until collapsing from exhaustion (Olds, 1958b). In similar experiments, monkeys pressed a lever as often as 8,000 times per hour (Olds, 1962).

Follow-up experiments indicated that the electricity was not simply stimulating involuntary movements. Animals will press levers to stimulate areas that extend over about one-third of the brain, certain areas much more vigorously than others. They will also work to turn off stimulation in about 5 percent of the brain.

Why is electrical stimulation of certain brain areas reinforcing? Perhaps the stimulation taps into circuits responsible for eating, sexual behaviors, and other natural reinforcers. But we do not know what the animal is experiencing. In some cases, electrical stimulation produces stronger effects than any natural reinforcer does. In one experiment, rats in a T-maze could choose food by turning one direction or electrical stimulation of part of the limbic system by turning the other direction (Spies, 1965). Rats chose the brain stimulation on more than 80 percent of their trials, even though they had been kept on a near-starvation diet for 10 days. In another experiment, rats selected brain stimulation in preference to water and avoidance of shock to the feet (Valenstein & Beer, 1962). Still more impressively, four mother rats abandoned their newborn pups in order to press a lever for brain stimulation (Sonderegger, 1970). Ordinarily, a mother rat will stick with her young at all costs.

In some regards self-stimulation of the brain may be like an addictive behavior. The animal does not rush to the lever as soon as it is available, but once it starts pressing, it persists for long periods. The stimulation may produce a mixture of pleasant and unpleasant feelings; at times the animal withdraws sharply from the stimulation, only to return a few moments later.

## Electrical Stimulation of the Brain and Reinforcement in Humans

Because the brain contains no pain receptors—in fact, no touch receptors of any kind—brain surgery in an awake patient is possible after anesthetizing only the scalp. In certain cases it is desirable to do so, so that the surgeon can test several areas until the patient says, "Yes, that made me feel the way I do right before a seizure." During the 1960s a few surgeons experimented with electrical stimulation of the human brain as a possible therapy for depression or severe pain.

From those medical studies we have learned something about the subjective experience of reinforcing brain stimulation. One 36-year-old epileptic woman received electrical stimulation in the right temporal lobe of her cortex. She reported a pleasant, tingling sensation on the left side of her body. She giggled, said that she enjoyed the sensation very much, and began flirting with the therapist (Delgado, 1969). Electrical stimulation in the temporal lobe of an 11-year-old boy led him to say, "Hey! You can keep me here longer when you give me these; I like those" (Delgado & Hamlin, 1960; Higgins, Mahl, Delgado, & Hamlin, 1956).

On the other hand, a few patients pressed buttons to stimulate their brains electrically yet described the experience as not altogether pleasant. One patient described the result of self-stimulation of the brain as "almost orgasm." He continued pressing, hoping to produce the orgasm, but only prolonged the frustration (Heath, 1963). Other patients have described a feeling of "having something on the tip of my tongue." They continue pressing in hopes of recovering the memory but again are frustrated. In other words, self-stimulation of the brain sometimes produces reinforcement without producing pleasure.

## Pharmacology of the Reinforcement Systems of the Brain

Although an animal will work to self-stimulate numerous points in the brain, these points are largely concentrated along a few pathways (Gallistel, Gomita, Yadin, & Campbell, 1985). Because these pathways are believed to use only a limited number of neurotransmitters, reinforcement (reward) itself may depend on only a few transmitters.

Most of the areas that mediate reinforcement are rich in catecholamine neurotransmitters, especially dopamine (Wise & Rompre, 1989). A particularly reliable area for eliciting self-stimulation is the **medial forebrain bundle** (Figure 13.8), the main ascending dopamine pathway. Drugs known to increase the release of dopamine or to prolong its effectiveness at the synapses also increase self-stimulation of the brain. Conversely, drugs that deplete dopamine supplies or block dopamine synapses decrease self-stimulation.

Dopamine is not the only neurotransmitter of reinforcement, however. By varying the intensity and timing of electrical brain stimulation, researchers have measured the properties of the neurons that an animal works to self-stimulate. Many such neurons have refractory periods, conduction velocities, and other properties that do not match what we know about dopamine neurons (Gallistel, Shizgal, & Yeomans, 1981). That is, reinforcement depends on a chain of neurons; dopamine-containing neurons are part of that chain, but so are other kinds of neurons.

**Figure 13.8**
**The major dopamine pathways of the rat brain, shown in a midsagittal section**
*The medial forebrain bundle is a highly reliable area for eliciting self-stimulation.*

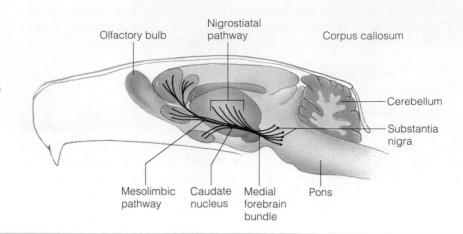

Endorphin synapses may also contribute. Animals will work for injections of opiates that stimulate endorphin synapses (Bozarth & Wise, 1984), and the reinforcing effects of these drugs depend on brain activity, not effects in the periphery of the body (Vaccarino, Pettit, Bloom, & Koob, 1985). Opiates exert their reinforcing effects partly by stimulating dopamine synapses (Wise & Bozarth, 1984; Wise & Rompre, 1989), but also partly by stimulating endorphin synapses.

## FEAR AND ANXIETY

Fear and anxiety feel much the same. We distinguish between them on the basis of when they occur. Fear occurs in a limited situation, such as being out in a small boat in a hurricane. One can escape the fear by escaping the situation. Anxiety is a longer-lasting state that one cannot escape easily. For example, a person can have anxiety about the future, anxiety about interactions with other people, or general "free-floating" anxiety that is not tied to any identifiable stimulus.

Fear serves a useful function; it steers us away from dangers. Mild anxiety may promote cautiousness. But beyond a certain point, anxiety ceases to serve a useful function and begins to interfere with normal activity. A great deal of clinical psychology is devoted to the reduction of anxiety.

Anxiety and fear probably share a similar physiological basis. Much progress has been made toward understanding that basis, partly from the study of drugs that decrease anxiety and partly from the study of abnormally anxious people.

### Anxiety-Reducing Drugs

Decades ago, **barbiturates** (a class of tranquilizers) were the drugs most widely used to combat anxiety. Although barbiturates effectively reduce anxiety, they have two significant drawbacks: They are strongly habit forming, and it is fairly easy to kill oneself with an overdose—either intentionally or accidentally—especially if they are combined with alcohol.

Another class of antianxiety drugs, **benzodiazepines** (BEN-zo-die-AZ-uh-peens), are currently much more widely used than barbiturates because they are

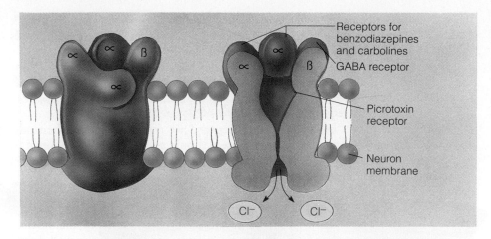

**Figure 13.9
The GABA_A receptor
complex**
*Of its four receptor sites sensitive to GABA, the three α sites are also sensitive to benzodiazepines. (Based on Guidotti, Ferrero, Fujimoto, Santi, & Costa, 1986.)*

less habit forming than barbiturates are and because an overdose is less likely to be fatal. Besides relieving anxiety, benzodiazepines relax the muscles, induce sleep, and decrease the likelihood of convulsions; they are used not only as tranquilizers but also as sleeping pills and as antiepileptic drugs. For decades now, benzodiazepines such as diazepam (trade name Valium), chlordiazepoxide (Librium), and alprazolam (Xanax) have been heavily advertised in medical journals and widely prescribed for people with a variety of complaints (Krupka & Vener, 1985; Robinson, 1987).

Like many other drugs, benzodiazepines were found to be effective long before anyone knew how they worked. And then in the late 1970s and early 1980s, investigators discovered specific benzodiazepine receptors in the CNS to which these drugs bind. The receptors are part of the **GABA_A receptor complex,** shown in Figure 13.9. The complex includes a site that binds the neurotransmitter **GABA** (gamma amino butyric acid) as well as sites that bind other chemicals that modify the sensitivity of the GABA site.

The brain has at least two kinds of receptors for GABA: GABA_A and GABA_B receptors. GABA_A sites apparently decrease anxiety, among other effects. Benzodiazepines facilitate binding of GABA to the GABA_A receptors; in doing so, they help to decrease anxiety.

The heart of the GABA_A receptor complex is a chloride channel. When open, it permits chloride ions ($Cl^-$) to cross the membrane into the neuron, hyperpolarizing the cell. (That is, the synapse is inhibitory.) Surrounding the chloride channel are four units, each containing one or more sites sensitive to GABA. Three of those four units (labeled α in Figure 13.9) also contain a benzodiazepine receptor. Even though it has no effect by itself on the chloride channel, an attached benzodiazepine molecule facilitates the GABA receptor. Presumably it alters the shape of the receptor so that the GABA attaches more easily or binds more tightly (Macdonald, Weddle, & Gross, 1986). The net result is an increased flow of chloride ions across the membrane.

The GABA_A receptor complex has at least two other binding sites. One of those sites is actually inside the chloride channel itself. Certain drugs such as *picrotoxin* can bind to that site; when they do so, they block the passage of chloride ions, regardless of what the GABA or benzodiazepine molecules are doing. The other binding site (not shown in Figure 13.9) is sensitive to barbiturates and to the metabolites of certain hormones (Majewska, Harrison, Schwartz, Barker, & Paul, 1986). Like the benzodiazepine receptor, the barbiturate receptor facilitates the binding of GABA to its own receptor.

Alcohol, a relaxant, also facilitates the binding of GABA and thereby enhances the flow of chloride ions across the membrane (see Digression 13.1). Caffeine, which makes many people feel nervous, displaces benzodiazepines from their receptor and thereby impairs the flow of chloride (Dunwiddie, 1985).

In using the name "benzodiazepine receptor," we do not mean that benzodiazepines are the only chemicals to bind there. (Would evolution have equipped us with receptors waiting around for drug companies to develop benzodiazepines?) As we might expect, these receptors are also sensitive to some chemicals naturally produced by the brain. One such chemical is the brain protein **diazepam-binding inhibitor (DBI),** which blocks the behavioral effects of diazepam and other benzodiazepines (Guidotti et al., 1983). Other chemicals found in mammalian brains, known as **carbolines,** bind to the benzodiazepine receptors as well. Some carbolines excite those receptors; others inhibit them. Injecting certain kinds of carbolines into rats or monkeys produces many indications of increased anxiety, including agitated movement, decreased sleep, increased response to punishment, and avoidance of other animals (Corda, Blaker, Mendelson, Guidotti, & Costa, 1983; File, Pellow, & Braestrup, 1985; Lagarde et al., 1990; Martin, Cook, Hagen, & Mendelson, 1989).

Diazepam-binding inhibitor and the carbolines modify the sensitivity of the GABA$_A$ receptors. Certain experiences, such as familiarity with a situation, apparently release carbolines or other chemicals that facilitate the GABA$_A$ receptors, producing a calming effect (Bodnoff, Suranyi-Cadotte, Quirion, & Meaney, 1989). Other experiences release other kinds of carbolines that increase anxiety.

## Panic Disorder

We may be able to learn more about the physiology of anxiety by studying clinical conditions associated with excess anxiety. One such condition is obsessive-compulsive disorder (see Digression 13.2). Another is **panic disorder,** a psychological condition that afflicts about 1 percent of all adults (Robins et al., 1984). A person with panic disorder suffers occasional attacks of extreme fear, breathlessness, heart palpitations, fatigue, and dizziness.

Why do certain people and not others develop panic disorder? One possibility is that people prone to panic attacks may have too much DBI or too much of the carbolines that impair GABA transmission. No direct evidence is yet available on this point.

A better-documented explanation is that people with panic disorder have chronically high levels of norepinephrine, both at the synapses in the brain and circulating in the blood. Excessive norepinephrine activity in the brain leads to arousal and anxiety. Several drugs that increase the release of norepinephrine at synapses can produce anxiety even in normal people. The same doses produce even greater norepinephrine release—and even greater anxiety—in people susceptible to panic attacks (Charney & Heninger, 1986; Charney, Heninger, & Breier, 1984).

An additional explanation is that many people prone to panic disorder have an overresponsive sympathetic nervous system, one that swings frequently and rapidly between high and low stimulation of the heart and other organs (Nutt, 1989). Such people have a higher than normal heart rate and elevated levels of

# The Relationship Between Alcohol and Tranquilizers

Ethyl alcohol, the type people drink, has behavioral effects similar to those of benzodiazepine tranquilizers. It decreases anxiety and decreases the effects of punishment. Moreover, a combination of alcohol and tranquilizers depresses body activities and brain functioning more severely than either drug alone would. (A combination of alcohol and tranquilizers can be fatal.) Furthermore, alcohol, benzodiazepines, and barbiturates all exhibit the phenomenon of **cross-tolerance:** An individual who has used one of the drugs enough to develop a tolerance to it will show a partial tolerance to other depressant drugs as well.

We now know the reason behind these relationships: Alcohol promotes the flow of chloride ions through the GABA$_A$ receptor complex, just as tranquilizers do (Sudzak et al., 1986). Exactly how alcohol promotes the chloride flow is not known, but it is unlikely that alcohol attaches directly to any of the receptor sites. A more likely hypothesis is that alcohol alters the membrane structure around the GABA and benzodiazepine binding sites in some manner that makes their binding more effective.

Although this is not the only way that alcohol affects the brain, it is apparently how alcohol exerts both its antianxiety effects and its intoxicating effects. Drugs that block the effects of alcohol on the GABA$_A$ receptor complex also block most of alcohol's behavioral effects. One experimental drug, known as Ro15-4513, is particularly effective in this regard (Sudzak et al., 1986). Besides affecting the GABA$_A$ receptor complex, Ro15-4513 blocks the effects of alcohol on motor coordination, its depressant action on the brain, and its ability to reduce anxiety (Becker, 1988; Hoffman, Tabakoff, Szabo, Sudzak, & Paul, 1987; Ticku & Kulkarni, 1988).

Could Ro15-4513 be useful as a "sobering-up" pill, or as a treatment to help people who want to quit

*Two rats that were given the same amount of alcohol. The one on the right was later given the experimental drug Ro15-4513. Within 2 minutes its performance on motor tasks improved significantly. (Photo courtesy of Jules Asher.)*

drinking alcohol? Hoffman-LaRoche, the company that discovered it, eventually concluded that using the drug would be too risky. People who relied on the pill might try to drive home, thinking they were sober when they were still somewhat impaired. Furthermore, giving such a pill to alcoholics could easily backfire. Alcoholics generally drink to get drunk; a pill that decreased their feeling of intoxication would probably lead them to drink even more. Ro15-4513 reverses the behavioral effects of moderate alcohol doses, but a large dose can still be a health hazard, or even fatal (Poling, Schlinger, & Blakely, 1988). For these reasons, Ro15-4513 is used only in experimental laboratories.

# Obsessive-Compulsive Disorder

Although **obsessive-compulsive disorder** is considered an uncommon psychiatric disorder, many people have a mild condition that they never report to a therapist. *Obsessions* are nagging, intrusive thoughts. *Compulsions* are urges to perform repetitive acts such as hand washing or endless double-checking of everything one does (Pollak, 1979).

The causes of obsessive-compulsive disorder are not known in any detail, but several facts point to a biological predisposition of some sort (Turner, Beidel, & Nathan, 1985). The disorder runs in families and is more common among people with type A blood—for unknown reasons. It also tends to run in the same families as Tourette's syndrome, which may be a different expression of the same underlying problem (Pauls, Towbin, Leckman, Zahner, & Cohen, 1986). According to PET scans, obsessive-compulsive people have increased metabolic rates in the caudate nucleus and in parts of the frontal cortex (Baxter et al., 1987). They also have sleep abnormalities, including frequent awakenings, a shortage of stage 4 sleep, and fewer rapid eye movements than normal during REM sleep (Insel et al., 1982).

In many cases obsessive-compulsive disorder responds well to **clomipramine** or **fluvoxamine**, two drugs that inhibit the reuptake of serotonin by the presynaptic neuron (Goodman et al., 1990; Leonard et al., 1989; Yaryura-Tobias, 1977). That is, these drugs prolong the effects of serotonin at the synapse.

Clomipramine is also an effective treatment for *trichotillomania*, compulsive hair pulling. People with this condition habitually pull out their eyelashes, eyebrows, scalp hair, even their pubic hair. Some continue until they become bald. Under the influence of clomipramine, such people decrease their hair pulling to about half of what it used to be (Swedo et al., 1989). The drug's effectiveness suggests that the underlying causes of trichotillomania resemble those of obsessive-compulsive disorder.

Exactly how clomipramine and fluvoxamine relieve obsessive-compulsive disorder and related conditions remains somewhat uncertain. Because they block serotonin reuptake and therefore prolong the availability of serotonin at the synapse, it is easy to suppose that they are simply increasing serotonin stimulation, perhaps overcoming a serotonin deficit. However, a drug that quickly and directly stimulates serotonin receptors makes obsessive-compulsive disorder worse, not better (Zohar, Insel, Zohar-Kadouch, Hill, & Murphy, 1988). Perhaps clomipramine operates indirectly—producing a high but steady level of serotonin stimulation, which in turn decreases the sensitivity of the serotonin receptors.

---

epinephrine (adrenaline) in their blood. Moreover, they respond to even moderate exercise with excessive autonomic arousal (Liebowitz et al., 1985; Nesse, Cameron, Curtis, McCann, & Huber-Smith, 1984). Exercise increases the levels of lactate and carbon dioxide in the blood; a lactate injection or breathing a 5 percent carbon dioxide atmosphere increases autonomic arousal in anyone, but in people prone to panic attacks the response is exaggerated, often including a full-blown panic attack (Gorman et al., 1988; Pitts, 1971).

Many people experiencing a panic attack aggravate their problem by **hyperventilating** (breathing more often or more deeply than they need to). A deep breath or two can often be a good way of calming oneself, but what is good in small doses can be harmful in large doses. Prolonged hyperventilation lowers the levels of carbon dioxide and phosphates in the blood, which in turn decreases parasympathetic nervous system activity (George et al., 1989). Thus, a little exercise, a little stress, an injection of lactate, or anything else that elevates blood $CO_2$ will produce a very large *percentage* increase in $CO_2$, which in turn stimulates a sharp rise in sympathetic nervous system action (Gorman et al., 1986, 1989; Woods et al., 1986).

Some people with panic disorder aggravate their problem by letting themselves get into poor condition physically. Such people experience shortness of breath and rapid heartbeat after moderate exercise or even after a stressful emotional experience (Hull, Young, & Zeigler, 1984). Similarly, mild stress or mildly strenuous activity, which would cause only a little autonomic arousal in most people, may trigger a panic attack in susceptible people.

Several types of therapy are common for panic disorder. First, many people with panic disorder take tranquilizers. Not only are the tranquilizers effective in reducing anxiety (Ballenger et al., 1988) but having them available "just in case" also provides reassurance. Second, psychotherapy can help sufferers to break the cycle of panic attacks leading to worry and hyperventilation that in turn lead to further attacks. Third, a controlled exercise plan may improve physical condition and thereby lessen the autonomic response to mild stressors (Ledwidge, 1980).

What do we learn about anxiety in general from studying victims of panic disorder? We learn that many of the symptoms of anxiety result from autonomic arousal and that anxiety is related to increased norepinephrine activity and decreased GABA activity. Presumably these two transmitters are not independent; GABA may inhibit the effects of norepinephrine synapses, for example.

## AGGRESSIVE BEHAVIORS

Fighting among animals within a species is neither purposeless nor necessarily disadvantageous to the species as a whole. The usual basis for fighting is defense of the animal's territory or of its young. In many species of birds, a male will vigorously attack other males of his own species that approach his nest, his mate, or his young during the mating season. In some species, the female will also attack intruders. The defending bird usually wins in such encounters (like the home team in human sports), driving the intruder out of the territory, generally without inflicting much injury. The winner thereby maintains control over the food supply in its area, removes potential competition for its mate, and avoids a high population density that might attract predators.

Humans also fight under similar circumstances. One of the most common causes of homicide is sexual jealousy, most frequently two men fighting about a woman (Daly, Wilson, & Weghorst, 1982). But some human violent behavior is rather unemotional. Soldiers and police may be forced into a battle without feeling any anger at all, for example, and people sometimes make "cold-blooded" attacks for financial gain.

Similarly, we have to distinguish between at least two kinds of attack behavior in nonhumans. A cat fighting or threatening another cat shrieks, erects its fur, and shows other signs of emotional arousal. This is known as an **affective attack.** (Do not confuse *affective* with *effective*. *Affective* comes from the noun *affect*, meaning emotion.) The same cat may attack and kill a mouse smoothly, swiftly, and calmly; this is a **quiet biting attack.** As we shall see, these two types of attack depend on different systems in the brain.

### Quiet Biting Attack

Electrical stimulation can elicit either a quiet biting (predatory) attack or an affective attack, depending on which brain area is stimulated. Figure 13.10 shows a quiet biting attack in response to stimulation of the perifornical nucleus of the hypothalamus. Similar results follow stimulation of several other areas of the hypothalamus and the midbrain (Siegel & Brutus, 1990; Siegel & Pott, 1988).

**Figure 13.10**
**Quiet biting attack provoked by electrical stimulation of the perifornical nucleus of the hypothalamus in a cat**

*The cat moved swiftly and with little sign of emotion to bite the rat's neck and kill it. (From Siegel & Brutus, 1990.)*

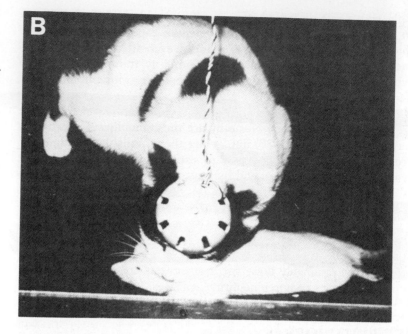

If you have ever watched a cat attack a mouse (or rat), you may have seen it "play" with its prey before killing it. The cat kicks the mouse, bats it with its paws, tosses it in the air, and sometimes picks it up and carries it. Why? Is the cat sadistically tormenting its prey before killing it? That might or might not sound plausible to you, depending on what you think of cats, but it is hardly a scientific explanation. Moreover, considerable evidence indicates that the cat's play is not based on a separate motive; it is a compromise between attack and escape.

When confronted with a prey, some cats swiftly bite it on the neck, killing it in less than 2 minutes. Other cats play with it for 10 minutes or more before either killing it or letting it go. Still others explore it briefly and then withdraw. Those that withdraw tend to be "timid" in a variety of situations; for example, they are slow to explore a new environment. Most cats are highly consistent from one day to the next in how they respond to a potential prey (Adamec, 1975).

Many of the "play" behaviors are defensive movements to avoid the prey's teeth. When the prey faces the cat, the cat is likely to bat, kick, or toss it. When the prey faces away, the cat is more likely to bite at its neck (Pellis et al., 1988). In other words, what appears to be play is actually a combination of attack and defense behaviors.

Various factors can move a cat's behavior one direction or the other along the continuum from withdrawal to attack. When cats become very hungry, those that usually withdraw from the prey start to play with it; those that usually play with it attack more vigorously and kill it. However, if the prey is large or if it fights back vigorously, cats that are usually quick killers start playing with it and those that usually play with it simply withdraw (Adamec, Stark-Adamec, & Livingston, 1980; Biben, 1979). When cats are given benzodiazepine tranquilizers, which presumably lower anxiety and reduce the tendency to withdraw, cats that usually play become quick killers (Pellis et al., 1988). In sum, cats have no separate motive to play; they play when their attack and escape tendencies are about

**Figure 13.11**
**An affective attack expression, evoked by radio stimulation of the medial hypothalamus of a cat**
*Because the cat does not direct its attack toward any target, we regard this as just a fragment of a normal attack. (From Delgado, 1981.)*

equal. If the balance shifts one way or the other, cats move toward quicker attack or toward withdrawal.

## Affective Attack

Facial displays, shrieks, and other signs of autonomic arousal accompany affective attack. In humans, such displays are associated with reports of anger. The physiological basis of affective attacks differs from that of quiet biting attacks.

**Nonhuman Animals** Stimulation of several areas in the hypothalamus, amygdala, and brain stem can elicit an affective attack (Siegel & Pott, 1988). As a result of such stimulation, a cat hisses, growls, arches its back, and bares its teeth. Ordinarily it directs its attack toward any convenient target that is present, but stimulation sometimes elicits just the facial expressions without the rest of the attack sequence (see Figure 13.11).

A full-fledged attack requires sensory cues as well as hypothalamic stimulation. A blindfolded cat shows no signs of attacking in response to brain stimulation. A cat with cortical or thalamic damage hisses and bares its teeth, but generally does not direct its attack toward a target (Flynn, 1973; Flynn, Edwards, & Bandler, 1971). Apparently the thalamus and cortex use the available sensory information to direct attack toward a suitable target; after damage to those areas, the attack is aimless.

Reinforcement, Escape and Attack Behaviors, and the Brain

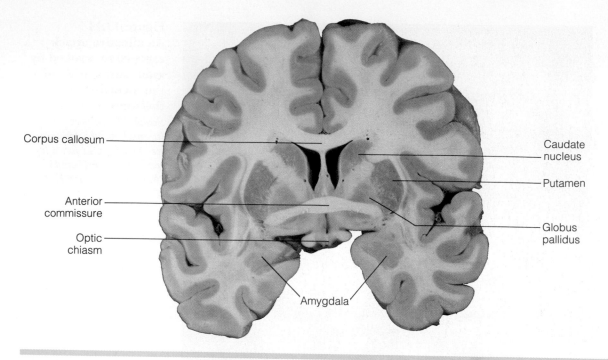

Corpus callosum

Anterior commissure

Optic chiasm

Amygdala

Caudate nucleus

Putamen

Globus pallidus

**Figure 13.12
Coronal section
through the human
brain, showing the
location of the
amygdala**

*(Photo courtesy of Dana
Copeland.)*

Electrical stimulation of the amygdala (see Figure 13.12) can lead to vigorous affective attacks. Damage to the amygdala usually leads to tameness and placidity, although damage in certain nuclei of the amygdala can enhance aggression. Animals with an epileptic focus in the amygdala generally show an increase in aggressive behavior (Pinel, Treit, & Rovner, 1977). **Rabies,** a disease caused by a virus that attacks much of the brain but especially the temporal lobe (including the amygdala), leads to furious, violent behavior (Lentz, Burrage, Smith, Crick, & Tignor, 1982). (*Rabies* is the Latin term for *rage.*)

Damage to the amygdala does not simply cause or prevent a certain emotion, however. Rather, it changes how animals interpret information. For example, male cats with amygdala lesions may sexually mount other males, members of other species, or even inanimate objects (Schreiner & Kling, 1953). (See Figure 13.13.) Their total sexual activity does not increase, but they become indiscriminate in their selection of partners (Aronson & Cooper, 1979). Similarly, certain monkeys with amygdala lesions have trouble interpreting social stimuli from other monkeys; because of their misinterpretations, they may attack inappropriately or fail to defend themselves when attacked.

H. Enger Rosvold, Allan Mirsky, and Karl Pribram (1954) made an amygdala lesion in the most dominant and aggressive monkey of a group of eight. After the lesion, that monkey quickly sank to the lowest status in the dominance hierarchy. Then they made a lesion in the amygdala of the most dominant remaining monkey, who quickly fell to seventh place. When they made a lesion in the third monkey, however, it did not drop significantly in status or in aggressive behavior. One possible explanation is that the lesions had invaded slightly different parts of the brain in the three monkeys. Another possibility is that the effect of the lesions was modified by the social environment. The first two monkeys returned to an environment with aggressive competitors; the third returned to one without aggressive competitors. It may have been harder for the first two monkeys to main-

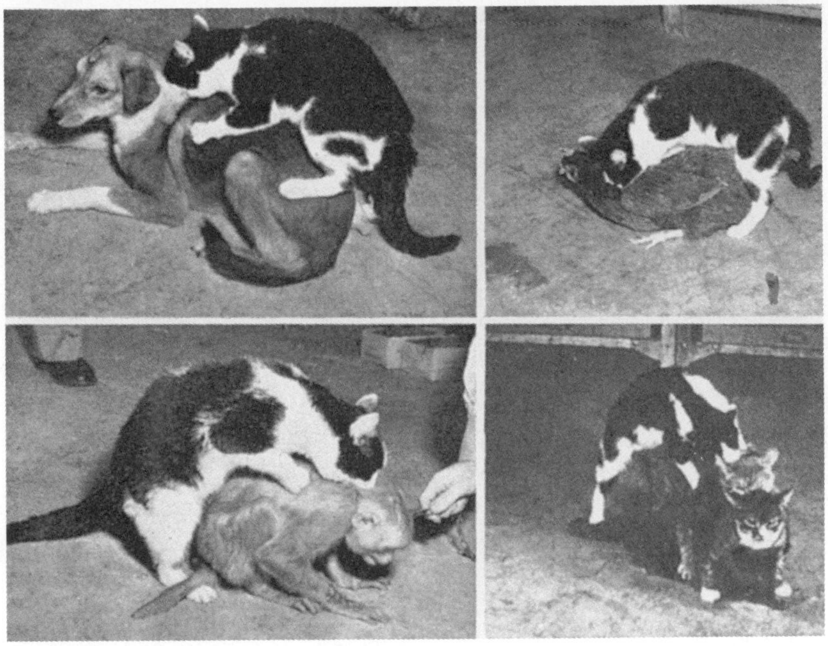

**Figure 13.13**
*Male cats with lesions of the amygdala and surrounding areas sexually mounting a dog (upper left), a hen (upper right), and a monkey (lower left). In the lower right, four male cats with amygdala lesions are simultaneously mounting each other. (From Schreiner & Kling, 1953.)*

tain aggressive behavior in the face of clear competitors than for the third to do so. Figure 13.14 shows the monkeys' dominance hierarchies before and after the three lesions.

**Humans** Can irritation of the temporal lobe provoke violent behavior in humans as well as other species? A number of investigators have looked particularly at temporal lobe epilepsy. An epileptic attack occurs when a large group of neurons suddenly produce synchronous action potentials. The symptoms depend on the location of the epileptic focus. When the focus is in the temporal lobe, the symptoms include hallucinations, lip smacking or other repetitive acts, and in certain cases emotional behaviors.

Here is an example of a patient with temporal lobe epilepsy who had sudden outbursts of unprovoked violent behavior (Mark & Ervin, 1970):

> *Thomas was a 34-year-old engineer, who, at the age of 20, had suffered a ruptured peptic ulcer. He was in a coma for 3 days, which caused some brain damage. Although his intelligence and creativity were unimpaired, there were some serious changes in his behavior, including outbursts of violent rage, sometimes against strangers and sometimes against people he knew. Sometimes his episodes began when he was talking to his wife. He would then interpret something she said as an insult, throw her against the wall and attack her brutally for 5 to 6 minutes. After one of these attacks he would go to sleep for a half hour and wake up feeling refreshed.*
>
> *Eventually he was taken to a hospital, where epileptic activity was found in the temporal lobes of his cerebral cortex. For the next seven months, he was given a combination of tranquilizers, antiepileptic drugs, and other medications. None of these treatments reduced his violent behavior. He had previously been treated by psychiatrists for 7 years without apparent effect. Eventually he agreed to a surgical operation to destroy a small part of the amygdala on both sides of the brain. Afterwards he had no more episodes of rage.*

Reinforcement,
Escape and Attack
Behaviors, and
the Brain

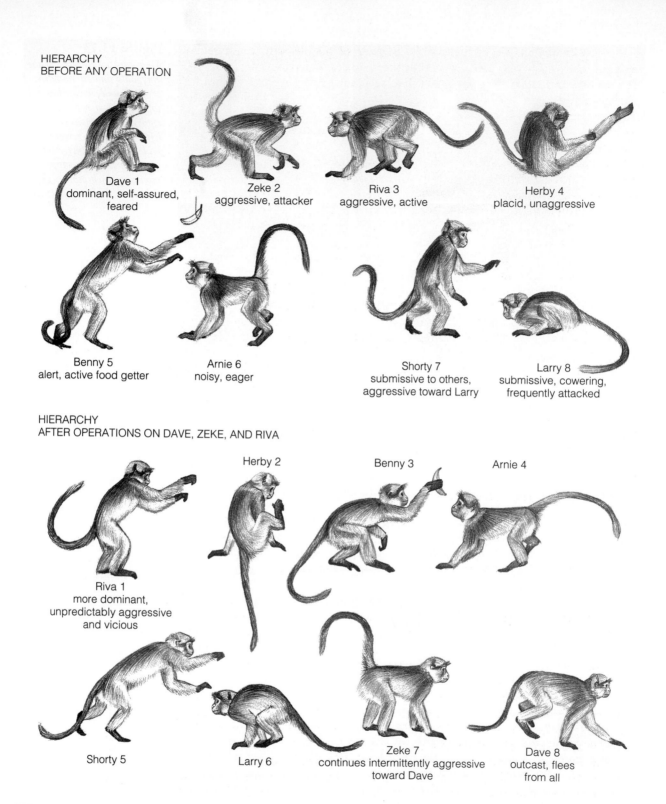

**HIERARCHY BEFORE ANY OPERATION**

Dave 1
dominant, self-assured, feared

Zeke 2
aggressive, attacker

Riva 3
aggressive, active

Herby 4
placid, unaggressive

Benny 5
alert, active food getter

Arnie 6
noisy, eager

Shorty 7
submissive to others, aggressive toward Larry

Larry 8
submissive, cowering, frequently attacked

**HIERARCHY AFTER OPERATIONS ON DAVE, ZEKE, AND RIVA**

Riva 1
more dominant, unpredictably aggressive and vicious

Herby 2

Benny 3

Arnie 4

Shorty 5

Larry 6

Zeke 7
continues intermittently aggressive toward Dave

Dave 8
outcast, flees from all

**Figure 13.14**

*The dominance hierarchy for eight male monkeys before brain operations (top) and after amygdala lesions were made (bottom) in Dave, Zeke, and Riva. (From Rosvold, Mirsky, & Pribram, 1954.)*

According to several reviews, about 10 percent of people with temporal lobe epilepsy have such outbursts of unprovoked violent behavior (Bear & Fedio, 1977; Goldstein, 1974; Pincus, 1980). The accuracy of these estimates has been challenged, however (Volavka, 1990): Temporal lobe epilepsy is difficult to diagnose, violent behavior is not always clearly defined, and in many cases the investigator who diagnosed temporal lobe epilepsy also determined whether the person had a history of violence.

In many instances, antiepileptic drugs have shown promise in controlling episodic violent behavior. In one study, daily doses of Dilantin, a common antiepileptic drug, decreased violent behavior in 19 of 22 men with a history of several unprovoked violent attacks per month (Maletzky, 1973). Other investigators have reported similar results (Neziroglu, 1979; Stephens & Shaffer, 1973; Tunks & Dermer, 1977).

When people with a history of unprovoked violence fail to respond to antiepileptic drugs, a few surgeons have surgically destroyed parts of the amygdala or other brain areas (Balasubramaniam & Kanaka, 1976; Mark & Ervin, 1970; Narabayashi, 1972). They reported success in reducing or eliminating the violent outbursts, with only occasional unwelcome side effects, including overeating or diabetes. But how carefully their patients have been tested for side effects is unclear.

Is brain surgery justifiable when the only goal is to change behavior? Such surgery, known as **psychosurgery,** has a history dating back to lobotomies that hardly inspires confidence. Opponents of psychosurgery object that because it is conducted to protect society, not to help the patient, it can easily be abused. Defenders of psychosurgery reply that a dangerous person's freedom must be restricted, either by the medical profession or by the legal profession. At present, psychosurgery is a rare procedure, but the controversy is likely to continue.

## Serotonin Synapses and Aggressive Behavior

Although it is unlikely that a single neurotransmitter system controls aggressive behavior, or any other behavior, several lines of evidence indicate that serotonin is especially important in the control of aggressive behavior. In particular, a drop in serotonin release is associated with a rise in aggressive behavior.

**Nonhuman Animals** Part of the evidence for this conclusion comes from the work of Luigi Valzelli, studying aggressive behavior in mice. Valzelli (1973) found that four weeks of social isolation induced a drop in serotonin turnover in the brains of the male mice. **Turnover** is the amount of release and resynthesis of a neurotransmitter by presynaptic neurons. That is, a brain with low serotonin turnover may have a normal amount of serotonin, but the neurons fail to release it and synthesize new serotonin to take its place, making it essentially inactive. Turnover can be inferred from the concentration of **5-HIAA** (5-hydroxy-indoleacetic acid), a serotonin metabolite, in the blood, cerebrospinal fluid (CSF), or urine. When 5-HIAA levels are low, serotonin turnover is low.

Valzelli further found that when social isolation lowered a male mouse's serotonin turnover, it also induced increased aggressive behavior toward other males. If he placed two males with low serotonin turnover together, he could count on them to fight. Comparing different genetic strains of mice, he found that the strains with the lowest serotonin turnover fought the most (Valzelli & Bernasconi, 1979). Social isolation does not decrease serotonin turnover in female mice in any genetic strain, and it does not make the females aggressive.

Valzelli also studied interactions between mice and rats. When male rats were socially isolated, some showed increased serotonin turnover, while others showed decreased turnover or no change. When rats that showed a decrease in serotonin turnover were placed with mice, they attacked and killed the mice. Rats that showed no change in serotonin turnover ignored the mice. Those with an increase in serotonin turnover became friendly and almost motherly toward the mice (Valzelli & Garattini, 1972).

Consistent with these results, drugs that block the synthesis or release of serotonin increase aggressive behavior in animals. For example, the drug **PCPA** (para-chloro-phenylalanine) blocks the synthesis of serotonin. After receiving an injection of PCPA that cut their serotonin production in half, male and sometimes even female rats attacked and killed mice (Valzelli, Bernasconi, & Garattini, 1981). Once the aggressive behavior began, it sometimes continued even after the rat's serotonin turnover returned to normal (Valzelli, Bernasconi, & Dalessandro, 1983).

Finally, diets low in tryptophan, a precursor to serotonin, increase aggressive behavior in animals. Administering tryptophan or closely related chemicals decreases aggression (Broderick & Bridger, 1984).

**Humans** Several studies have found that people with a history of violent behavior tend to have lower than normal serotonin turnover (Brown, Goodwin, Ballenger, Goyer, & Major, 1979; Yaryura-Tobias & Neziroglu, 1981). Serotonin turnover is significantly depressed in people who commit suicide and also in those who attempt suicide by violent means. (Nonviolent suicide attempts, often using pills, are generally cries for help more than serious attempts at self-annihilation. People who make such attempts do not show consistent trends in serotonin turnover.)

People who have committed suicide or attempted it by violent means have low levels of 5-HIAA in their CSF or blood, suggesting lower than normal release of serotonin (G. Brown et al., 1982; Edman, Åsberg, Levander, & Schalling, 1986; Mann, Arango, & Underwood, 1990). They also have more 5-HT$_2$ (serotonin$_2$) receptors than usual in the cerebral cortex; the increase in receptors is believed to be the brain's compensation for decreased serotonin release (Arango et al., 1990; Mann, Stanley, McBride, & McEwen, 1986). Serotonin turnover is also depressed in people convicted of arson and other violent crimes (Virkkunen, Nuutila, Goodwin, & Linnoila, 1987).

Diet may affect violent behavior in humans as well as animals. According to Mawson and Jacobs (1978), the murder rate is highest in those countries that consume the most corn. Corn contains very little tryptophan, the precursor to serotonin. That is, eating a lot of corn decreases serotonin synthesis (Lytle, Messing, Fisher, & Phebus, 1975). Needless to say, the relationship between corn in the diet and the murder rate could be explained in many other ways, including a relationship to poverty. This point certainly calls for thorough investigation before we draw any conclusions. In the meantime, it may be prudent for people with a history of violent behavior to be cautious about eating lots of corn or other foods low in tryptophan. Similar caution might be advisable about foods high in phenylalanine (such as NutraSweet) because phenylalanine competes with tryptophan for entry into the brain.

Although we are still far from understanding how a drop in serotonin turnover may increase violent behavior, the relationship may be useful in predicting behavior. For example, in one study of 119 psychiatric patients, 20 percent of those with below-average serotonin turnover levels committed suicide within the

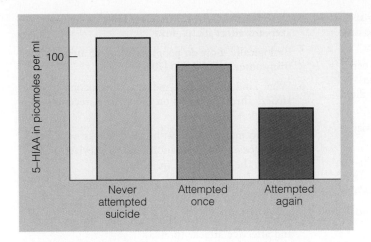

**Figure 13.15**
**Levels of 5-HIAA in the CSF of depressed people who never attempted suicide, those who attempted it once, and those who attempted it again within five years after the first attempt**
*Measurements were taken after the first attempt. Low levels of 5-HIAA indicate low serotonin turnover. (Based on results of Roy, DeJong, & Linnoila, 1989.)*

following year (Träskman, Åsberg, Bertilsson, & Sjöstrand, 1981). A follow-up study of people who had survived suicide attempts found that those with lower serotonin turnover levels were more likely than others to make additional suicide attempts, perhaps fatally, within the next five years (Roy, DeJong, & Linnoila, 1989; see Figure 13.15). A follow-up study on people convicted of manslaughter or arson found that after their release from prison, those with lower serotonin turnover had a greater probability of committing other violent crimes within the next three years. The investigators found that they could have used the serotonin measures to predict violent crime with 84 percent accuracy (Virkkunen, DeJong, Bartko, Goodwin, & Linnoila, 1989).

What do these results tell us about the role of serotonin synapses in behavior? They certainly do *not* indicate that the sole or primary function of serotonin is to suppress violent behavior. Low serotonin turnover has also been reported with depression, sleeplessness, and alcohol abuse. Perhaps one function of serotonin is to inhibit impulsive behavior (Depue & Spoont, 1986). Frequently we feel an impulse—to attack someone or to overindulge in alcohol, for example—that could lead to punishment or some other negative outcome. Serotonin is apparently a key part of the system that suppresses such impulses; when serotonin turnover is low, impulses are expressed despite the risk of punishment (Charney, Woods, Krystal, & Heninger, 1990).

## SUMMARY

1. The brain area most important for emotional behaviors is the limbic system, a circuit that includes the hypothalamus, hippocampus, amygdala, olfactory bulb, septum, other small structures, and parts of the thalamus and cerebral cortex. (p. 463)

2. Animals will work to deliver an electrical stimulation to certain areas of their brains, presumably areas that contribute to natural reinforcements. (p. 466)

3. The reinforcement areas of the brain are generally rich in catecholamines, although the contribution of catecholamine neurons to reinforcement and pleasure may prove to be indirect. (p. 467)

4. Benzodiazepine tranquilizers decrease anxiety by attaching to a receptor next to the GABA$_A$ synapse on the GABA$_A$ receptor complex. (p. 468)

5. The benzodiazepine receptor is also sensitive to certain naturally occurring chemicals in the brain, including carbolines, that modify the sensitivity of the GABA$_A$ synapse. (p. 470)

6. Alcohol relieves anxiety by increasing the sensitivity of the GABA$_A$ synapse. (p. 470)

7. Panic disorder is a clinical condition marked by intense anxiety attacks; people with panic disorder have overresponsive sympathetic nervous systems. (p. 470)

8. Aggressive behavior in animals functions for territorial defense, defense of mates, and self-defense. (p. 473)

9. Stimulation of certain areas of the hypothalamus and midbrain can elicit quiet biting attack; stimulation of parts of the amygdala and hypothalamus can elicit affective attack. (p. 473)

10. Cats "play" with their prey when the tendency toward an affective attack is balanced by a tendency toward withdrawal. Various factors can tilt the balance in one direction or the other. (p. 474)

11. Damage to the amygdala of animals can lead to a decrease in aggressive behavior and a decrease in social rank, partly because the animals misinterpret social stimuli. (p. 476)

12. A small percentage of people with temporal lobe epilepsy have occasional outbursts of violent behavior. Medical treatments to control such violent behavior have shown some promise, but remain controversial. (p. 477)

13. A drop in serotonin release and turnover in the brain is associated with increased aggressive behavior. (p. 479)

14. Lower than normal serotonin turnover has been reported in the brains of people who attempt suicide and people who commit other violent acts. Measures of serotonin turnover may contribute toward prediction of certain kinds of human violence. (p. 480)

## REVIEW QUESTIONS

1. What structures compose the limbic system? What function does that system serve? (p. 463)

2. How did researchers discover that specific areas of the brain are responsible for reinforcement? (p. 466)

3. Which neurotransmitters are believed to be critical for reinforcement? (p. 467)

4. Describe the GABA$_A$ complex. How do benzodiazepines affect it? (p. 469)

5. Biologically, how do people with panic attacks differ from other people? (p. 470)

6. What kind of evidence indicates that alcohol relieves anxiety through effects on the GABA$_A$ receptor complex? (p. 471)

7. Why do many people with panic attacks hyperventilate? Does hyperventilation tend to alleviate or aggravate their problem? (p. 472)

8. What are possible therapies for panic disorder? (p. 473)

9. What is the difference between quiet biting attack and affective attack? (p. 473)

10. Why do some cats "play" with a rat or mouse before killing it? What evidence supports this conclusion? (p. 474)

11. How does amygdala damage alter affective attack? Does the damage affect aggressiveness or perception of stimuli? (p. 476)

12. What behavioral effects sometimes occur in people with temporal lobe epilepsy? (p. 477)

13. What evidence links aggressive behavior with a decrease in serotonin turnover? (p. 479)

14. What dietary habits may alter the likelihood of aggressive behavior? (p. 480)

15. What biological test may identify which violent offenders or suicide attempters are most likely to commit other violent acts? (p. 480)

## THOUGHT QUESTION

1. According to one interpretation of why electrical stimulation of the brain is rewarding, stimulation of different brain areas produces experiences corresponding to different natural reinforcements. That is, stimulation in one area might produce sexual sensations, and stimulation in another area might produce food or drink sensations. How might one test this hypothesis? (For two tests that came to opposite conclusions see Frutiger, 1986, and Olds, 1958b.)

## SUGGESTIONS FOR FURTHER READING

Kidman, A. (1989). Neurochemical and cognitive aspects of anxiety disorders. *Progress in Neurobiology, 32,* 391–402. Excellent review of both biological and behavioral aspects of anxiety.

**Valzelli, L.** (1981). *Psychobiology of aggression and violence.* New York: Raven. A thorough, scholarly review of emotional behavior in general and aggressive behavior in particular.

## GLOSSARY

**ACTH** adrenocorticotropic hormone, which stimulates the adrenal cortex to release cortisol

**affective attack** attack in which an animal shows signs of emotional arousal

**antibody** Y-shaped protein that fits onto an antigen and weakens it or marks it for destruction

**antigen** protein on the surface of a microorganism, in response to which the immune system generates antibodies

**barbiturate** class of drugs used as anticonvulsants, sedatives, and tranquilizers

**B cell** type of leukocyte that matures in the bone marrow

**behavioral medicine** field that considers the influence on people's health of their eating and drinking habits, smoking, stress, exercise, and other behavioral variables

**benzodiazepine** class of widely used antianxiety drugs

**B memory cell** type of cell that immunizes the body against future attacks by a given intruder

**Cannon-Bard theory** concept that autonomic changes and emotions occur simultaneously but independently

**carboline** type of chemical that binds to the same receptors as benzodiazepines

**clomipramine** drug that inhibits the reuptake of serotonin by the presynaptic neuron

**cortisol** hormone released by the adrenal cortex that elevates blood sugar and enhances metabolism

**cross-tolerance** tolerance of a drug because of exposure to a different drug

**diazepam-binding inhibitor (DBI)** brain protein that blocks the behavioral effects of diazepam and other benzodiazepines

**5-HIAA** 5-hydroxyindoleacetic acid, a serotonin metabolite

**fluvoxamine** drug that inhibits the reuptake of serotonin by the presynaptic neuron

**GABA** gamma amino butyric acid, a neurotransmitter

**GABA$_A$ receptor complex** structure that includes a site that binds GABA as well as sites that bind other chemicals that modify the sensitivity of the GABA site

**galvanic skin response** measure of the electrical conductance of the skin

**helper T cell** type of leukocyte that stimulates added response by other immune system cells

**hyperventilation** breathing more often or more deeply than necessary

**immune system** set of structures that protects the body against viruses and bacteria

**James-Lange theory** notion that physiological states cause emotions, not vice versa

**leukocyte** white blood cell, a component of the immune system

**limbic system** area of the forebrain including the hypothalamus, hippocampus, amygdala, olfactory bulb, septum, other small structures, and parts of the thalamus and cerebral cortex

**macrophage** type of leukocyte that engulfs and attacks microorganisms

**medial forebrain bundle** main ascending dopamine pathway in the vertebrate brain

**natural killer cell** type of leukocyte that destroys certain kinds of tumor cells and cells infected with viruses

**obsessive-compulsive disorder** psychological disorder characterized by intrusive thoughts and urges to perform repetitive acts

**panic disorder** condition characterized by occasional attacks of extreme fear, breathlessness, heart palpitations, fatigue, and dizziness

**PCPA** parachlorophenylalanine, a drug that blocks the synthesis of serotonin

**posttraumatic stress disorder** condition characterized by periodic outbursts of anxiety, panic, or depression provoked by reminders of a traumatic experience

**psychosomatic illness** illness for which personality or experience influences onset or recovery

**psychosurgery** brain surgery conducted to change behavior

**quiet biting attack** swift, calm attack with few signs of emotional arousal

**rabies** disease caused by a virus that attacks much of the brain, especially the temporal lobe

**self-stimulation of the brain** response reinforced by direct electrical stimulation of a brain area

**T cell** type of leukocyte that matures in the thymus

**turnover** release and resynthesis of a neurotransmitter

**ulcer** open sore on the lining of the stomach or intestines

# The Biology of Learning and Memory

## MAIN IDEAS

**1.** Understanding the physiology of learning requires answering two questions: What changes occur in a single cell during learning, and how do changed cells work together to produce adaptive behavior?

**2.** People suffering from hippocampal damage, Korsakoff's syndrome, or Alzheimer's disease have great trouble storing lasting memories of specific experiences, although they can still learn new skills and recall old knowledge.

**3.** Damage to the hippocampus, amygdala, or prefrontal cortex impairs memory of specific events, including memory of what one has just done.

**4.** An individual neuron may change in several ways during learning; for example, it may increase its release of transmitter, it may have increased responsiveness to stimulation, or it may change its threshold for an action potential.

**5.** Chemicals and drugs can impair or facilitate learning.

Suppose I type a short program into my computer:

```
10 HOME
20 FOR A=1 TO 100
30 PRINT A∧(0.5)
40 NEXT A
```

I can now leave the computer, come back later, and type "RUN." Provided that the power has not been interrupted, the computer will print out a list of the square roots of the integers 1 to 100. How does the computer remember what to do?

That question is really two questions, which call for two kinds of answers. One is how does the computer store a representation of the keys I type? Somehow, my hitting those keys leads to a physical change in some tiny silicon chips inside the computer. To explain how that happens, we would need to understand the physics of the silicon chip.

But explaining how a silicon chip stores information does not tell us how the computer as a whole works. To explain how the computer can run my program, we would have to answer a second question: How does the computer put to-gether the information stored in numerous silicon chips to make its response? In other words, we would have to understand the wiring diagram.

Similarly, when we try to explain how a person remembers to stop at a red light or to show up for work at 8 A.M., we are really facing two questions. One is how does a pattern of sensory information set up a lasting change in the input-output proper-ties of one or more neurons in the nervous system? That question concerns the biophysics of the neu-ron. The second question is, after the properties of certain neurons have changed, how does the ner-vous system as a whole produce the appropriate behavior? That question concerns the wiring diagram.

We could begin with either question, but in this chapter we shall begin with the second one: How do the various areas of the nervous system work together to produce learned behaviors? Later we turn to the more detailed physiology of how expe-rience changes the properties of the individual cells and synapses.

*(Kevin Forest/TIB West.)*

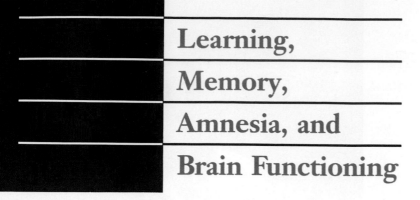

# Learning, Memory, Amnesia, and Brain Functioning

How would you act if you could not remember from one moment to the next what you had just done? For one thing, you would probably repeat yourself many times without even realizing it.

How would you act if you could not remember from one moment to the next what you had just done? For one thing, you would probably repeat yourself many times without even realizing it.

Some people have exactly this problem. Others can remember what they just did and said, but they forget events from a certain period of their past, or they have some other specialized memory loss. A study of the effects of brain damage reveals much about the nature of memory.

## LOCALIZED OR DIFFUSE REPRESENTATIONS OF MEMORY

What is the brain's physical representation of learning and memory? One early, simple idea was that it might be a strengthened connection between two areas. The Russian physiologist Ivan Pavlov discovered the phenomenon we call **classical conditioning** (Figure 14.1a), in which a stimulus comes to elicit a response similar to the response produced by some other stimulus. Ordinarily, the experimenter starts by presenting a **conditioned stimulus (CS)**, which initially elicits no response of note, and then presents the **unconditioned stimulus (US)**, which automatically elicits the **unconditioned response (UR)**. After some pairings of the CS followed by the US (perhaps just one or two pairings, perhaps many), the individual begins responding to the CS, producing a **conditioned response (CR)**. In the original experiments on classical conditioning, Pavlov presented a dog with a sound (CS) followed by meat (US), which stimulated the dog to salivate (UR). After many such pairings, the sound alone would stimulate the dog to salivate (CR).

By contrast, in **operant conditioning** (Figure 14.1b), an individual's response is followed by a reinforcement or punishment. A **reinforcement** is any event that increases the future probability of the response; a **punishment** is an event that

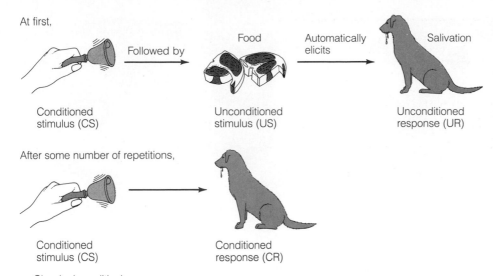

At first,

Conditioned
stimulus (CS) → Followed by → Food → Automatically elicits → Salivation

Unconditioned
stimulus (US)

Unconditioned
response (UR)

After some number of repetitions,

Conditioned
stimulus (CS) →

Conditioned
response (CR)

**a** Classical conditioning

**Figure 14.1**
**The procedures for classical conditioning and operant conditioning**
*In classical conditioning (**a**), two stimuli (CS and US) are presented at certain times, regardless of what the learner does. In operant conditioning (**b**), the learner's behavior controls the presentation of reinforcement or punishment.*

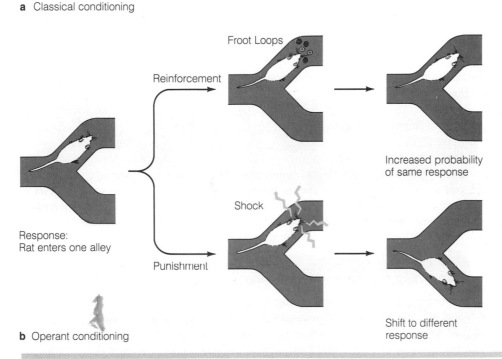

Froot Loops

Reinforcement

Increased probability
of same response

Response:
Rat enters one alley

Shock

Punishment

Shift to different
response

**b** Operant conditioning

decreases the future probability of the response. For example, when a rat enters one arm of a maze and finds Froot Loops cereal (a potent reinforcement for a rat), the probability of entering that arm again increases. If it receives a shock instead, the probability decreases.

Some cases of learning are difficult to label as classical or operant. For example, in bird-song learning (Chapter 1), a male songbird hears the song of his own species during his first spring and summer; he imitates it the following year. During the first year the song he heard was not paired with any other stimulus, so we cannot call this classical conditioning. He made no overt responses and received no reinforcements or punishments, so we cannot call it operant conditioning. That is, classical and operant conditioning do not exhaust all possible kinds of

Learning, Memory,
Amnesia, and Brain
Functioning

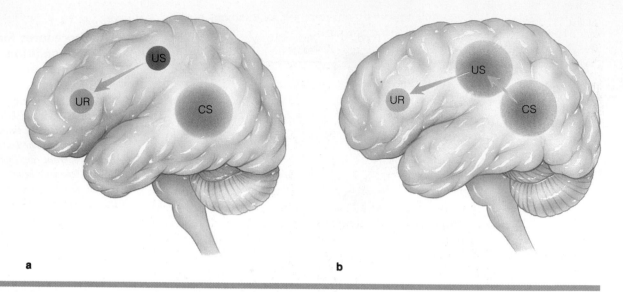

a          b

**Figure 14.2**
**Pavlov's view of the**
**physiology of learning**
*Initially (a), the US excites*
*the US center, which then ex-*
*cites the UR center. The CS*
*excites the CS center, which*
*elicits no response of interest.*
*After training (b), excitation*
*in the CS center flows to the*
*US center, thus eliciting the*
*same response as the US.*

learning; animals have specialized ways of learning in different situations (Rozin & Kalat, 1971).

Both classical conditioning and operant conditioning can be described as an association between two events, and we could imagine that learning requires the growth of a connection between two sets of neurons in the brain. Pavlov believed that classical conditioning reflected a strengthened connection between a brain area that represents CS activity and a brain area that represents US activity. Because of that strengthened connection, any excitation of the CS center flows to the US center, evoking the unconditioned response (Figure 14.2). Pavlov had no direct evidence for this view, but it was highly influential nevertheless.

Karl Lashley set out to test the hypothesis that learning represents a new or strengthened connection between two cortical areas. He said he was searching for the **engram**—the physical representation of learning. (A connection between two brain areas would be one example of an engram but hardly the only possibility.)

Lashley reasoned that if learning depends on connections between a CS center and a US center, as Pavlov asserted, then a knife cut somewhere in the brain should interrupt that connection and abolish the learned response. He trained rats on a variety of mazes and a brightness discrimination task and then made one or more deep cuts in the rats' cerebral cortexes (Lashley, 1929, 1950). For each rat, he made a cut in a different location (Figure 14.3). To his surprise, no cut or combination of cuts seemed to impair a rat's memory. Evidently the types of learning he studied did not depend on strengthened connections across the cortex.

Lashley also tried to find out whether any portion of the cerebral cortex is more important than others for learning. He trained rats on mazes before or after he removed large portions of their cortex. The lesions impaired the rats' performance, but the amount of retardation depended more on the amount of brain damage than on its location.

To summarize his findings, Lashley (1929) suggested two basic principles of brain organization: According to the principle of **mass action,** the neurons of the cortex work together as a whole during learning; the more brain the better. According to the principle of **equipotentiality,** the various parts of the cortex contribute almost equally to complex learned behaviors. No one part of the cortex is more specialized for learning than are other parts.

For years, Lashley's results diminished researchers' interest in localizing memory engrams. However, his studies were limited to the cerebral cortex. Later studies found that damage to certain subcortical structures can drastically impair specific aspects of memory.

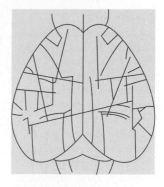

## BRAIN DAMAGE AND HUMAN AMNESIA

People with brain damage sometimes suffer **amnesia** (loss of memory). However, while they show profound impairments in some aspects of memory, other aspects may remain normal. A study of such people can reveal much about how memory is organized and how it relates to brain activity. Observations of both humans and nonhumans indicate that a system of the brain including the hippocampus, the amygdala, and their connections to other structures is particularly important for storing certain kinds of memory.

**Figure 14.3**
**Map of cuts that Lashley made in the brains of various rats to see which one(s) would interfere with memory of a maze**
*None of the cuts interfered with maze memories. (Adapted from Lashley, 1950.)*

### The Story of H. M., a Man with Hippocampal Damage

What gave researchers the idea to focus on the hippocampus? The main impetus was the memory loss of a special individual known to us by his initials H. M., now one of the most famous cases in neurology (Milner, 1959; Penfield & Milner, 1958; Scoville & Milner, 1957).

In 1953, H. M.'s epileptic seizures, which had proved unresponsive to all antiepileptic drugs, became so frequent and incapacitating that he had to quit his job. In desperation, neurosurgeons removed the hippocampus from both sides of his brain (see Figure 14.4), because the seizures seemed to be originating from that structure. They also removed several neighboring structures, including the amygdala. Although the surgeons did not know what to expect from the operation, they acted on the belief that desperate cases call for desperate measures.

The results of the surgery were favorable in some regards. H. M.'s epileptic seizures decreased in frequency and severity, and he was able to take less of the antiepileptic medications. His personality and intellect remained the same; in fact, his IQ score increased slightly after the operation, presumably because of the decreased epileptic interference. However, he suffered moderate **retrograde amnesia** (loss of memory for events that occurred shortly prior to brain damage from trauma or disease). That is, he had some trouble recalling events that happened within the last 1 to 3 years before the operation, but no trouble recalling still older events. He also suffered a massive **anterograde amnesia** (inability to store new memories). He can store new information briefly, but he has great difficulty in recalling it after his attention is distracted.

For example, after the operation he could not learn his way to the hospital bathroom. After reading a story, he was unable to describe what had happened in it. He could read a single magazine over and over without any indication of familiarity or any loss of interest. He lived with his parents, and when they moved to a new address, he had great difficulty finding his way home or locating anything within the house. After eight years, he had finally memorized the floor plan and could find his way from one room to another; however, he still could not find his way home from a distance of more than two blocks (Milner, Corkin, & Teuber, 1968).

In one test of H. M.'s memory, Brenda Milner (1959) asked him to memorize the number "584." After a 15-minute delay without distractions, he was able to

Learning, Memory, Amnesia, and Brain Functioning

**Figure 14.4**

*(a) Location of the hippocampus in the human brain. (b) Photo showing part of the hippocampus, which curves into the interior of each hemisphere. In both parts of the figure, note that the hippocampus curves around over the thalamus and under the cerebral cortex. (Photo courtesy of Dana Copeland.)*

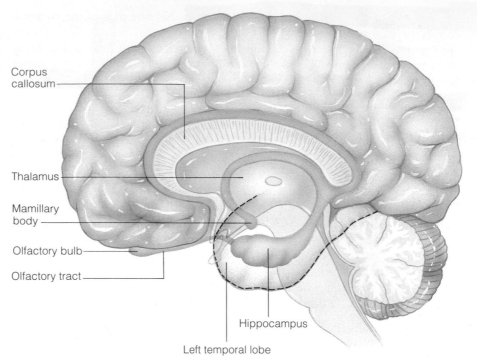

Corpus callosum

Thalamus

Mamillary body

Olfactory bulb

Olfactory tract

Hippocampus

Left temporal lobe

**a**

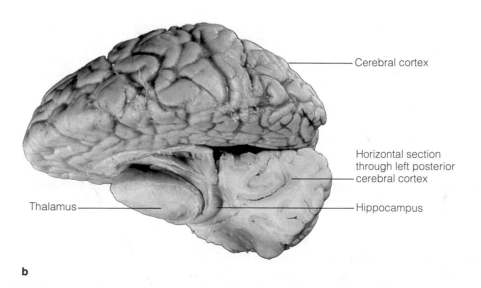

Cerebral cortex

Horizontal section through left posterior cerebral cortex

Thalamus

Hippocampus

**b**

**Figure 14.5**
**The Tower of Hanoi puzzle**
*The task is to transfer all the disks to another peg, moving just one at a time, without ever placing a larger disk on top of a smaller disk. H. M. has learned to solve this problem, although he says he does not remember ever seeing it before.*

recall the number correctly. He explained how he did so. "It's easy. You just remember 8. You see, 5, 8, and 4 add to 17. You remember 8, subtract it from 17, and it leaves 9. Divide 9 in half and you get 5 and 4, and there you are, 584. Easy." A moment later, after H. M.'s attention had been shifted to another subject, he had forgotten both the number and the complicated line of thought he had associated with it.

In 1980, he moved to a nursing home. Four years later, he could not say where he lived or who cared for him. Although he watches the news on television every night, he can recall only a few fragments of events since 1953. For several years after the operation, whenever he was asked his age and the date, he answered "27" and "1953." After a few years, he started guessing wildly, generally underestimating his age by 10 years or more and misestimating the year by as much as 43 years (Corkin, 1984).

Although H. M. has enormous trouble learning new facts and keeping track of current events in his life, he learns new skills without apparent difficulty. For example, he has learned a simple finger maze, he has learned to read material written in mirror fashion, and he has learned the correct solution to the Tower of Hanoi puzzle shown in Figure 14.5 (Cohen, Eichenbaum, Deacedo, & Corkin, 1985). He does not *remember* learning these skills, however. In fact, he says he does not remember seeing the maze or the puzzle before.

## Korsakoff's Syndrome

**Korsakoff's syndrome,** also known as *Wernicke-Korsakoff syndrome*, is a type of brain damage caused by thiamine deficiency. Among its prominent characteristics are apathy, confusion, and a kind of memory impairment similar to H. M.'s.

Ordinarily, the brain uses glucose as its main fuel. For the brain or any other organ to metabolize glucose, it needs thiamine (vitamin $B_1$). Prolonged thiamine deficiency leads to a loss or shrinkage of neurons throughout the brain, especially in the dorsomedial nucleus of the thalamus and the mamillary bodies (part of the hypothalamus) (Squire, Amaral, & Press, 1990; Victor, Adams, & Collins, 1971).

Such severe thiamine deficiency is almost unheard of except in severe alcoholics. Certain extreme alcoholics may go days or weeks at a time eating almost nothing and drinking only alcoholic beverages. In doing so, they become deficient in thiamine and other vitamins and minerals. If they get some thiamine soon enough, they can avoid brain damage, but the longer they remain thiamine deficient, the greater the damage will be. Certain hospitals, especially in large cities, report about one person with Korsakoff's syndrome per 1,000 hospital admissions. Most such patients must be permanently confined to a mental hospital.

Consider an example: A 59-year-old man easily recalls details of his early life and of military experience as a young man, although he can recall almost no recent events. When an interviewer leaves the room after a long conversation and returns a few minutes later, the patient does not recognize the interviewer and does not remember having had a conversation. He does not recognize any doctors or nurses at the hospital and cannot find his way around. He reads the same newspaper repeatedly, showing surprise at the news items each time. When seated at the dinner table with an empty plate in front of him, he does not remember whether he has just finished eating or has not yet started (Barbizet, 1970).

Most Korsakoff's syndrome patients have both retrograde and anterograde amnesia. Generally, the more severe the patients' anterograde amnesia is, the worse their memory for the last 10 years is (Shimamura & Squire, 1986). Their retrograde amnesia is generally more severe than H. M's, covering about the last 15 years before the onset of their illness (Squire, Haist, & Shimamura, 1989). Some suffer a nearly complete loss of memory for their entire adult lives. The anterograde amnesia, characterized by slow learning, impulsive answering, and poor reconstruction of events, resembles that seen in patients with damage to the prefrontal cortex (Oscar-Berman, 1980; Squire, 1982). Most Korsakoff's patients have some atrophy in the prefrontal cortex and extensive damage in the **dorsomedial thalamus,** a nucleus that projects to the prefrontal cortex. Prefrontal cortical damage has been linked to impaired memory of when and where something occurred (Schacter, 1987). For example, a person with prefrontal damage might remember two events but forget which one happened today and which one happened yesterday.

Patients with Korsakoff's syndrome often show indirect signs of memory even when they say that they remember nothing. Psychologists distinguish between **explicit memory,** one that you recognize as a memory, and **implicit memory,** one that influences your behavior without your awareness. Korsakoff's patients often show signs of implicit memory without explicit memory. For example, after patients in one study read a list of words—such as DEFEND, HELIUM, CONVEY, MODIFY, SINKER, BELFRY—they had no explicit memory of the words on the list. When asked to write as many words as they could remember from the list, some replied, "What list?" But then the experimenter gave them a list of word fragments and asked them to fill in complete words:

DEF＿＿  HEL＿＿  CON＿＿  MOD＿＿  SIN＿＿  BEL＿＿

Each of these fragments can be completed in several ways; for example, DEF＿＿ can become DEFEAT, DEFECT, DEFACE, DEFINE, DEFROST, and so on. However, Korsakoff's syndrome patients generally filled in the blanks to form the words they had seen on the list, thus showing implicit memory, even though they insisted that they did not remember the list (Schacter, 1985).

Another example of implicit memory: In one study, normal people and people with Korsakoff's syndrome were asked to hold a set of weights, one at a time, and rate how heavy each one felt on a 1-to-9 scale. About 20 to 25 minutes later, they repeated the procedure with a new set of weights. If the first weights were relatively light, subjects gave the new weights fairly high ratings; if the first weights were relatively heavy, they gave the new weights lower ratings (see Figure 14.6). Evidently they compared the new weights to the old weights, indicating a

**Figure 14.6**
**Experiment on implicit memory (simplified)**
*Subjects rated the heaviness of one set of weights; 20 to 25 minutes later they rated other weights. If they had become accustomed to lighter weights, they rated the new weights fairly high. If they were accustomed to heavier weights, they gave the new weights a low rating. Normal subjects and Korsakoff's syndrome patients responded in the same way, indicating an implicit memory of the weights that lasted at least 20 to 25 minutes. (Based on results of Benzing & Squire, 1989.)*

memory of the old weights (Benzing & Squire, 1989). The Korsakoff's syndrome patients responded in the same way as the normal subjects, although after 20 to 25 minutes most of the Korsakoff's patients did not remember lifting or rating any weights before. In fact, the experimenters had to repeat the instructions for some of them.

## Alzheimer's Disease

Another cause of severe memory loss is **Alzheimer's disease**, a condition that becomes more prevalent with advancing age. According to one estimate, about 20 percent of all people develop Alzheimer's disease by age 80 (Mortimer, Schuman, & French, 1981). The symptoms start with minor forgetfulness, similar to that found in many older people, but they progress to more serious memory loss, confusion, depression, restlessness, hallucinations, delusions, and disturbances of eating, sleeping, and other daily activities (Cummings & Victoroff, 1990).

People with a moderate case of Alzheimer's disease typically have trouble keeping track of what they have just done and what has been going on around them. For example, Schacter (1983) reported playing golf with an Alzheimer's patient who, although he remembered the rules and jargon of the game correctly,

Learning, Memory, Amnesia, and Brain Functioning

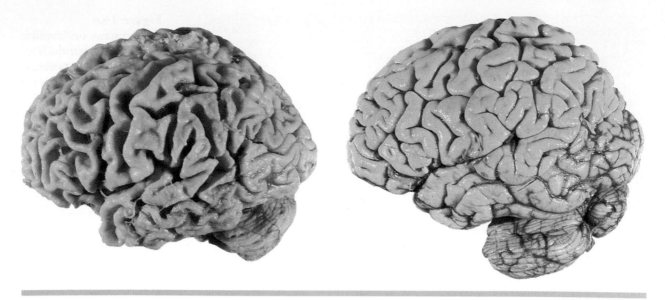

**Figure 14.7**
**Brain atrophy in Alzheimer's disease**

*The cerebral cortex of an Alzheimer's patient (left) has gyri that are clearly shrunken in comparison with those of a normal person (right). (Photos courtesy of Dr. Robert D. Terry.)*

could not remember how many strokes he took on any hole. Five times he teed off, waited for the other player to tee off, and then teed off again, having forgotten his first shot. Even when he remembered not to tee off again, he could not remember where he had hit his ball. He could not say what label was on his ball, although when he picked up a ball he could recognize whether it was his.

As with H. M. and Korsakoff's patients, Alzheimer's patients learn new skills more easily than they learn new facts. In one study, Alzheimer's patients were unable to learn a list of words and were unable to learn to recognize new faces. However, they had little trouble learning the skill of maintaining contact between a hand-held pointer and a moving object (Eslinger & Damasio, 1986).

Alzheimer's disease is associated with a widespread atrophy (wasting away) of the cerebral cortex, hippocampus, and other areas, as Figure 14.7 shows (Hyman, Van Hoesen, Damasio, & Barnes, 1984). The most heavily damaged area is the entorhinal cortex, the portion of the cerebral cortex that conducts the greatest amount of communication with the hippocampus (Van Hoesen, Hyman, & Damasio, 1991). A number of neurons degenerate (see Figure 14.8), especially those that release acetylcholine (Mash, Flynn, & Potter, 1985) and to a lesser extent those that release norepinephrine and other neurotransmitters (Morrison, Rogers, Scherr, Benoit, & Bloom, 1985; Winblad, Hardy, Bäckman, & Nilsson, 1985). Large numbers of **plaques** (formed from degenerating axons and dendrites) appear in the damaged areas, as Figure 14.9 illustrates (Rogers & Morrison, 1985). **Tangles** of axons and dendrites are also common.

Alzheimer's disease runs in certain families, suggesting a genetic basis. The son or daughter of a person with Alzheimer's disease has almost a 50 percent probability of eventually developing Alzheimer's disease (Mohs, Breitner, Silverman, & Davis, 1987). Some people with no family history of Alzheimer's disease also develop the condition (Hardy, 1990); however, they generally develop it later in life, after about age 80. Evidently Alzheimer's disease has both genetic and nongenetic causes.

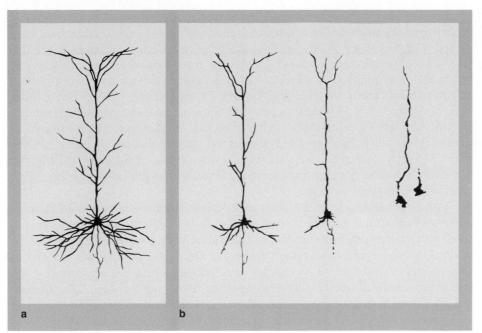

**Figure 14.8**
**Progressive degeneration of neurons in the prefrontal cortex during Alzheimer's disease**
(*a*) *A cell in a normal human;* (*b*) *cells from the same area of cortex in Alzheimer's disease patients at three stages of deterioration. Note the shrinkage of the dendritic tree. (After Scheibel, 1983.)*

a

b

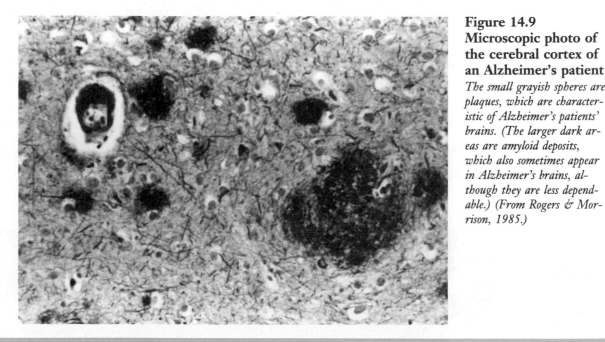

**Figure 14.9**
**Microscopic photo of the cerebral cortex of an Alzheimer's patient**
*The small grayish spheres are plaques, which are characteristic of Alzheimer's patients' brains. (The larger dark areas are amyloid deposits, which also sometimes appear in Alzheimer's brains, although they are less dependable.) (From Rogers & Morrison, 1985.)*

Because people with *Down's syndrome* (a type of mental retardation) invariably get Alzheimer's disease if they survive into middle age, many researchers have looked to chromosome 21 in search of the gene responsible for Alzheimer's disease. Down's syndrome is caused by having three copies of chromosome 21 rather than the usual two copies. Alzheimer's patients do not have a duplication of any part of chromosome 21 (St. George-Hyslop et al., 1987b; Tanzi, Bird, Latt, & Neve, 1987). However, in some families, people who inherit a tendency toward Alzheimer's disease also inherit certain markers on chromosome 21 (Goate et al., 1991; St. George-Hyslop et al., 1987a). People in other families show no such tendency (Schellenberg et al., 1988). Evidently a gene for Alzheimer's disease is on chromosome 21 in some families and on some other chromosome in other families.

The brains of people with Alzheimer's disease often contain elevated concentrations of aluminum, but the role of aluminum is still uncertain. People are exposed to aluminum through aluminum cans, aluminum cookware, and aluminum in drinking water and toothpaste (Verbeeck, Driessens, & Rotgans, 1990). At present, the evidence shows no conclusive relationship between amount of exposure to aluminum and probability of developing Alzheimer's disease. The alternative possibility is that aluminum and other metals enter the brain *after* the onset of Alzheimer's disease because of a breakdown of the blood-brain barrier (Wisniewski & Kozlowski, 1982).

## What Amnesic Patients Teach Us: Different Types of Memory

The study of amnesic patients reveals that when people "lose their memory," they do not lose all aspects of memory equally. H. M. remembers events from long ago although he has forgotten almost everything that has happened since his operation. He and other patients who have great trouble memorizing facts can learn new skills and retain them indefinitely. Evidently people have several kinds of memory, which depend on different parts of the brain and perhaps different mechanisms of storage.

What is the best way to describe the different kinds of memory—specifically, what kind of memory do H. M., Korsakoff's patients and Alzheimer's patients lose, and what kind do they retain? The noted psychologist Donald Hebb (1949) proposed a distinction between short-term memory and long-term memory. **Short-term memory** is memory for events that have just occurred. **Long-term memory** is memory for events that do not currently occupy your attention; to recall them you must retrieve them from storage. Hebb could not imagine how any chemical in your brain could change rapidly enough for you to recall an event immediately yet remain stable enough for you to recall the same event years later. He therefore proposed that short-term memories depend on a quickly developing pattern of electrical activity in the brain, while long-term memories depend on the slower growth of new structures. According to this point of view, H. M. and other patients' problem is that, although they can still form short-term memories and recall long-term memories that they formed many years ago, they cannot establish new long-term memories.

Although the distinction between short-term and long-term memory is useful, other distinctions seem more appropriate for certain situations. For example, suppose you play for a basketball team; your coach calls a time-out to discuss strategy. When you return to the court after the one-minute time-out, you still remember the score, the time remaining, how many fouls you have committed, and who you are guarding. Was all that information in short-term memory? Not likely; a one-minute distraction almost invariably erases short-term memories. But the information wasn't exactly in long-term memory either; you probably won't be able to recall it half a minute later—mainly because it is no longer *true* half a minute later. For situations like this, psychologists distinguish between **reference memory,** which is memory for general principles (such as the rules of basketball), and **working memory,** which is memory for temporary information (such as the current score of the game). Patients with amnesia generally have trouble with working memory, forgetting what they have been doing and what has been going on around them. They have less trouble with reference memory, especially if they had formed the reference memories long ago.

Finally, recall that the amnesic patients we discussed have much trouble learning facts but little trouble learning new skills. That is, they have impairments in their **declarative memory**—memory for facts, what is going on right now, and what happened in the past. They are unimpaired in their **procedural memory**—memory of how to perform acquired skills such as tying shoelaces, driving a stick-shift car, or swinging a tennis racket. Procedural memories are often difficult to put into words.

Which of these distinctions is best—short-term versus long-term, working versus reference, or declarative versus procedural? Or is some other distinction better yet? However we draw the distinction, the important point is that we have more than one kind of memory, and brain damage that greatly impairs one kind may leave another kind intact.

## MEMORY CONSOLIDATION

Suppose we tentatively accept the distinction between short-term and long-term memory. The question then arises, how do memories get from short-term storage into long-term storage? Is it simply a matter of time, such that any memory held in short-term storage for long enough will enter long-term storage? And if not, then what factors facilitate long-term storage?

No doubt you have noticed that you store some of your experiences as long-term memories, but not others. Even among your long-term memories, some are much more available than others. For example, someone asks you the capital of Indonesia. You knew it once but you cannot recall it now. Perhaps you will remember it if someone gives you a hint or a few choices. (It's Jakarta.) So the establishment of a long-term memory is not an all-or-none process. Somehow, some memories become very strong while others remain weak. **Consolidation** is the formation and gradual strengthening of long-term memories.

### Head-Trauma Interference with Consolidation

In Hebb's (1949) original theory, the formation of a long-term memory depended primarily if not entirely on time. Any short-term memory would be gradually converted into a long-term memory if it stayed in short-term storage long enough. Hebb guessed that a short-term memory might be represented by a *reverberating circuit* of neuronal activity in the brain, with a self-exciting loop of neurons. If the reverberating circuit remained active long enough, some chemical or structural change would occur that stored the memory permanently.

Although some time is necessary for the formation of long-term memories, psychologists no longer believe that simply holding something in short-term memory is sufficient to form a long-term memory. If you want to remember forever that Jakarta is the capital of Indonesia, do not spend the next few minutes repeating "Jakarta is the capital of Indonesia." Rather, think about it from as many angles as possible. Find Jakarta on a map of Indonesia, draw a map and fill in Jakarta, make up a little story about where the word *Jakarta* came from, and so

**Figure 14.10
Apparatus for testing passive-avoidance learning**
*When the rat steps off the platform, it gets a shock to its feet. Rats ordinarily learn to avoid stepping down off the platform.*

forth. In short, forming a long-term memory depends on building up lots of meaningful links, not just on waiting for time to pass. Furthermore, you form some long-term memories faster than others. When you read about one of your favorite topics, you form many meaningful links quickly. If you know little about a topic and care less, storing long-term memories is a slow, difficult process. Memories do consolidate over time (as Hebb proposed), but the amount of time necessary varies considerably.

The same is true for the formation of long-term memories in animals. Shortly after Hebb first distinguished between short-term and long-term memory, psychologists thought they could find out how long a memory took to get from short-term to long-term by finding out how long the memory of an event remained vulnerable to destruction. Their idea was that a disruption of brain activity would destroy a short-term memory but not a long-term memory. By controlling the time between an event and the disruption of an animal's brain activity, investigators hoped to discover how long it takes for a vulnerable short-term memory to become a protected long-term memory.

In a typical experiment, experimenters placed rats one at a time on a wooden platform above a metal floor (Figure 14.10). Ordinarily, rats step down to the floor within a few seconds. However, when rats in one group stepped down, they got a shock to their feet. A day later, placed again on the platform, each of these rats stayed on the platform for 5 minutes or more, showing a learned avoidance of stepping down. (This is an example of *passive-avoidance learning*.) Each rat in another group got the same foot shock but also received an electroconvulsive shock (ECS) through the head a second or two after the foot shock. When placed on the platform on a later day, these rats stepped down as quickly as rats that had never received a foot shock. Apparently, the ECS had erased the memory of both the foot shock and the ECS.

Numerous experiments found that increasing the delay between the shock and the ECS decreased the amnesia produced by ECS. Presumably, as time passed the short-term memory of foot shock was consolidated into less vulnerable long-term storage. However, the data did not point to a particular amount of time as necessary for the transfer. In some experiments a memory became consolidated and protected from disruption by ECS within seconds; in others, it took minutes, hours, or even days (Squire & Spanis, 1984). Evidently consolidation requires various kinds of brain activity that no doubt vary from one situation to another.

A complicating factor is that ECS can interfere with both long-term and short-term memories. In several experiments, rats were trained on a task and then, after a few days' delay, given a stimulus similar to the training trials followed by ECS. The ECS produced amnesia for the training, even though that training should have been well established in long-term memory (Lewis, Bregman, & Mahan, 1972; Robbins & Meyer, 1970; Schneider & Sherman, 1968). Apparently ECS interferes with memories that are *active* at the time of the ECS, regardless of whether they were formed recently or long ago (D. J. Lewis, 1979). Because ECS can impair both long-term and short-term memories, it must impair memory by doing something other than just blocking the transfer from short-term to long-term memory.

## Chemical Enhancement and Impairment of Consolidation

Why do you remember some experiences better than others? Sometimes you remember an event because of the way you interpreted it after it was over. You said to yourself, "That was exciting. That was important." Just as a shock or blow to the head can impair the consolidation of a recent memory, your evaluation of something as exciting or important can enhance its consolidation.

But how does that happen physiologically? For the answers, investigators turn to animal studies where they can control the events. An important or exciting experience arouses an animal's sympathetic nervous system; in particular, the adrenal medulla increases its secretion of epinephrine (adrenaline) into the bloodstream. Most learning experiments, especially most of those in which animals learn rapidly, use stimuli such as food, water, sexual opportunities, or electric shock that are important to the animal and likely to excite epinephrine release. Substantial evidence now indicates that increased epinephrine secretion enhances consolidation of a memory (McGaugh, 1990). Injected epinephrine can also enhance memory, even in individuals who would otherwise have forgotten the experience. This conclusion holds for epinephrine injections up to an optimum level; beyond a certain point, excessive epinephrine has a less beneficial effect, and sometimes even a harmful effect. (The same probably holds for humans. People in a panic often have trouble remembering details of the situation later.)

How does epinephrine enhance memory? Chances are, it does not directly stimulate brain synapses; little epinephrine from the periphery crosses the blood-brain barrier. Epinephrine converts stored glycogen to glucose and therefore raises the level of glucose in the blood and available to the brain. Paul Gold and his colleagues have demonstrated that when a high epinephrine level raises the level of blood glucose, the high glucose level facilitates memory. In fact, injecting glucose (to bypass the epinephrine stage) shortly after an experience enhances future memory of it (Gold, 1987; Hall & Gold, 1990; Lee, Graham, & Gold, 1988). Furthermore, animals that eat immediately after a learning trial tend to learn faster than animals that do not eat (Flood, Smith, & Morley, 1987).

Other neurotransmitters and neuromodulators may affect memory formation by direct effects within the brain. Endorphins and related opiate chemicals, if administered to a rat's or mouse's brain soon after an experience, generally impair the memory. They are particularly effective if injected into the septum or the amygdala (Bostock, Gallagher, & King, 1988; Gallagher & Kapp, 1978). The amygdala plays an important role in the emotional behaviors of all mammals (as we saw in Chapter 13); in learning, that role may be to evaluate the importance of an event (McGaugh, 1990), with norepinephrine synapses voting for "important" and endorphin synapses voting for "unimportant."

## ROLE OF THE HIPPOCAMPUS, AMYGDALA, AND FRONTAL CORTEX

So far we have seen that damage to the hippocampus and other areas impairs the formation of long-term declarative memories; we have also seen that memories go through a vulnerable period while they are being consolidated. Can we put these pieces together? That is, are the hippocampus and related areas necessary for the consolidation of certain kinds of memories? To gain greater control of the situation, neuroscientists turn to animal studies. Patients with Korsakoff's syndrome or Alzheimer's disease have fairly diffuse damage, affecting various brain areas to different degrees in different patients. In animals we can study the effects of more limited types of brain damage.

The discovery of how hippocampal damage impaired memory in H. M. and other patients led psychologists to study the effects of hippocampal lesions on rats. In the early experiments, typically they made the lesions and then tested the rats' ability to learn a simple discrimination, such as to turn left in a T-maze for food, or to approach a white card instead of a black card or a high-frequency tone instead of a low-frequency tone. To the investigators' surprise, the rats generally did pretty well. Psychologists puzzled over why hippocampal damage seemed to impair human memory so much more than it impaired animal memory (Isaacson, 1972).

But that was before investigators were sensitive to the distinctions between different kinds of memory. Learning to make a particular response to a particular stimulus can be regarded as procedural memory, a kind of memory not impaired in H. M. or other brain-damaged amnesic patients. Eventually investigators discovered that rats with hippocampal lesions performed well on some memory tasks and poorly on others. Let's consider what kinds of performance a hippocampal lesion does and does not impair.

## Damage to the Hippocampus in Rats

As with humans, hippocampal damage in rats impairs some kinds of memory and spares other kinds. Figure 14.11 illustrates a **radial maze**. In a typical experiment, a rat is placed in the center of eight or more arms, some of which have a bit of food at the end. For example, the rats might have to learn that the arms with a rough floor never have food or that the arms pointing toward the window never have food. The rat stays in the maze until it has found all the food or until it has gone, say, 2 minutes without finding any more food. After enough training trials,

**Figure 14.11
An eight-arm radial maze**

*Food is in some arms, not in others. To perform well, a rat must maintain a working memory of which arms it has already explored. If it reenters one arm before trying other arms, it makes an error of working memory.*

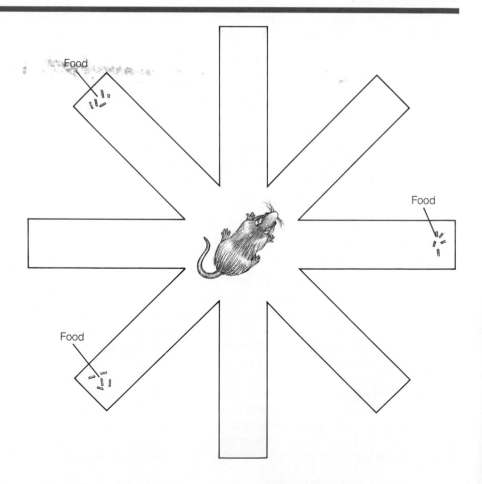

a rat may learn to go down each correct arm once and only once and not to try any of the incorrect arms. A rat can make two types of mistakes: It can go down one of the always incorrect arms, or it can enter one correct arm repeatedly before trying all the other correct arms.

A normal rat makes only a few errors of either kind. Rats with damage to the hippocampus, or with damage to the axons that connect the hippocampus to other structures, seldom enter the arms that are never correct. But they frequently reenter some correct arms while failing to try others. Evidently they lose track of which arms they have already tried (Jarrard, Okaichi, Steward, & Goldschmidt, 1984; Olton & Papas, 1979; Olton, Walker, & Gage, 1978). We could regard their performance as a failure of working memory.

Note that the radial maze is a spatial task. Hippocampal damage did not impair all spatial memories (such as the memory of which arms are never correct), but it greatly impaired the spatial memories that change from time to time. Much evidence points to the hippocampus as particularly important for coding spatial information. In one study, an overhead television camera recorded a rat's location in the environment at each moment, while electrodes recorded activity from neurons in the hippocampus. A computer then correlated the response of the neurons to the rat's location. Many neurons altered their activity sharply as the rat moved from place to place (O'Keefe, 1983). Figure 14.12 illustrates the responses of two neurons as one rat moved around a square platform. One neuron was most active when the rat was anywhere along the southeast edge; the other neuron was most active when the rat was in the northwest portion. Other hippocampal neurons showed still other patterns of activity.

Another study found that the activity of most hippocampal neurons depended not on the rat's position at the moment but on the area that the rat was moving *toward* (Muller & Kubie, 1989). That is, the hippocampal response predicted the rat's future location, representing an intention more than an established fact. Still

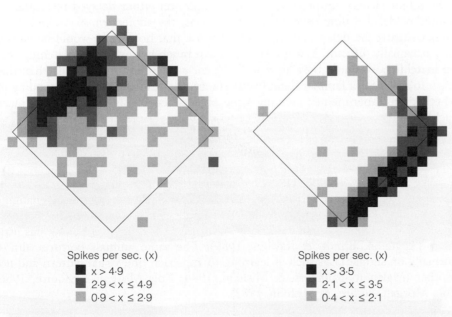

Spikes per sec. (x)
- ■ x > 4.9
- ■ 2.9 < x ≤ 4.9
- ■ 0.9 < x ≤ 2.9

Spikes per sec. (x)
- ■ x > 3.5
- ■ 2.1 < x ≤ 3.5
- ■ 0.4 < x ≤ 2.1

a        b

**Figure 14.12
Responses of two hippocampal neurons as a rat moves from place to place within a square platform**
*Darker areas indicate high activity; lighter areas indicate low activity. (**a**) The response of a less selective neuron, one that is most active when the rat is in the northwest portion of the platform. (**b**) The response of a neuron that is most active when the rat is anywhere along the southeast edge of the platform. (From O'Keefe, 1983.)*

another study found that if a rat was restrained so that it could not move, hippocampal cells became almost unresponsive; what little response they did show was about the same from one location to another (Foster, Castro, & McNaughton, 1989). In other words, hippocampal cells coded for location only if the rat was able to move about on its own.

However, the behavioral meaning of a given neuron's response is not easy to decipher. When a rat explores two environments, each neuron shows high activity in one particular part of each environment, but the spot it responds to in one environment seems unrelated to the spot it responds to in the other environment. For example, a neuron that responds to the southeastern edge of one environment does not necessarily prefer the southeastern portion of a different environment. Nor does a given neuron consistently respond to the area closest to food, the area with the most light, or any other discernible pattern (Kubie & Ranck, 1983). That is, the meaning of each cell's response depends on the overall context, in some as-yet poorly understood manner.

Hippocampal damage also causes spatial deficits in other species (Kesner, 1990). For example, homing pigeons with hippocampal lesions cannot learn to find their way home from an unfamiliar location (Bingman, Ioalé, Casini, & Bagnoli, 1990). Black-capped chickadees with hippocampal lesions hide food in the normal way for their species and later make a normal number of attempts to find food, but they look for it in the wrong places (Sherry & Vaccarino, 1989).

## Damage to the Hippocampus in Primates

Primates are generally tested on some rather complex tasks. In a **delayed matching-to-sample task,** an animal sees an object (the sample) and then, after a delay, gets a choice between two objects, from which it must choose the one that matches the sample. In the **delayed nonmatching-to-sample task** (Figure 14.13), the procedure is the same except that the animal must choose the object that is *different* from the sample. In both cases there may be a spatial component, but the primary task is to recognize which stimulus is familiar and which is new.

An animal's performance on a task like this varies enormously with apparently minor changes in procedure. For example, on either delayed matching-to-sample or delayed nonmatching-to-sample tests, the subject must remember the sample during the delay, and we might suppose that both tasks would be equally easy or equally difficult. Yet monkeys perform much better on nonmatching than on matching; evidently they learn to reach for a new item more easily than they learn to reach for a familiar item. Furthermore, the results can vary depending on whether the experimenter uses the same objects repeatedly or uses new objects each time. For example, if a monkey always has to choose between a red triangle and a blue square, damage to the prefrontal cortex impairs performance. If a monkey has to choose between different objects every time, damage to the hippocampus and amygdala greatly impairs performance.

We shall focus on the latter case: Animals with hippocampal damage make numerous errors on the delayed nonmatching-to-sample task with ever-changing pairs of stimuli. A combined lesion of the hippocampus and amygdala impairs their performance still further, although damage to the amygdala alone has little effect (Aggleton, Blindt, & Rawlins, 1989). The same animals perform almost normally on simple tasks such as learning to approach one visual pattern and not another (Malamut, Saunders, & Mishkin, 1984; Zola-Morgan & Squire, 1986; Zola-Morgan, Squire, & Mishkin, 1982).

Exactly how does the hippocampus contribute to memory? Clearly, we do not store memories *in* the hippocampus itself. Hippocampal damage makes it

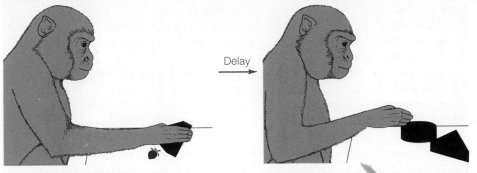

Delayed Nonmatching-to-Sample Test

Delay

Monkey lifts sample object
to get food.

Food is under the new object.

**Figure 14.13**
**The procedure for delayed nonmatching to sample with a monkey**

difficult to store new memories, but it does not impair old memories. Investigators have offered many interpretations of what the hippocampus does. Here are two: One hypothesis is that the hippocampus develops a map of where memories are stored in the cerebral cortex—analogous to a library's card catalog (Teyler & DiScenna, 1986). After damage to the hippocampus, an individual has trouble locating the memory that is correct at this moment, distinguishing it from similar memories stored in the past.

A second hypothesis is that hippocampal neurons maintain a temporary store of sensory information through their own continuous activity. In one experiment, rats heard one tone and then after a 3-second delay heard a second tone. If the two tones were different, then the rats could receive food for pressing a lever; if the tones were the same, lever pressing was ineffective. About 40 percent of the cells in the hippocampus responded strongly to one tone and not the other, maintaining that response during the delay (Sakurai, 1990). Their activity may have been a means of holding onto the sensory information during the delay.

## Contributions of the Prefrontal Cortex

Damage to the prefrontal cortex produces effects similar in some regards to those of hippocampal damage. The hippocampus and amygdala send part of their output to the prefrontal area of the cerebral cortex, so the three areas are closely related. When monkeys perform the delayed matching-to-sample task, neuronal activity increases sharply in their prefrontal cortex (Yamatani, Ono, Nishijo, & Takaku, 1990).

Damage to the prefrontal cortex impairs performance on a variety of tasks, with the results depending on the location of damage within the prefrontal cortex. After damage in a dorsal area called the *principal sulcus*, monkeys have trouble with a variety of spatial problems, similar to the troubles animals often show after hippocampal lesions. After damage limited to a more ventral area, **perseveration** on a wide variety of tasks is typical—that is, once the monkeys have made a particular response, such as choosing a blue square, they tend to make the same response repeatedly, even when they should suppress that response and choose something else (Mishkin & Manning, 1978).

Humans with prefrontal damage face similar difficulties. They are impaired on a **delayed alternation task,** in which they have to alternate between picking

**Figure 14.14**
**The Wisconsin card-sorting task**

*First people sort the cards by one rule, in this case shape. Then they sort them by some other rule, such as color, and then by another rule, such as number. People with prefrontal cortex damage are highly impaired on this task. After they have sorted by one rule, they find it difficult to ignore that rule and follow a different rule.*

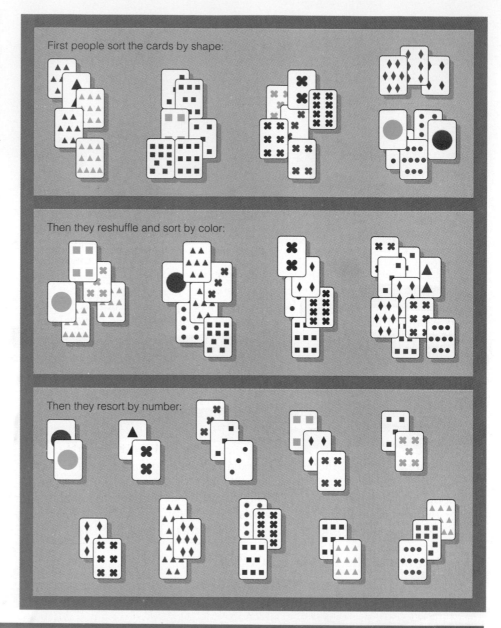

First people sort the cards by shape:

Then they reshuffle and sort by color:

Then they resort by number:

up an object on their left and picking it up on their right, with a delay between responses (Freedman & Oscar-Berman, 1986). Good performance on that task requires memory for what one has just done; it also requires suppressing one's previous response and substituting a new one.

Humans with prefrontal damage are also severely impaired on the **Wisconsin card-sorting task** (see Figure 14.14). This task requires a person first to sort cards into stacks according to one rule (for example, by shape), then reshuffle them and sort by a different rule (for example, color or number). People with prefrontal damage generally have little trouble sorting according to the first rule, whatever it may be. But they have great trouble shifting to a new rule. For example, they may start sorting by color and then quickly revert to sorting by shape (Janowsky, Shimamura, Kritchevsky, & Squire, 1989).

## Comparison Between Human Tasks and Nonhuman Tasks

Rats and monkeys with damage to their hippocampus or prefrontal cortex show specific memory impairments. How similar are those deficits to the memory impairments shown by human amnesic patients with damage in the same general areas of the brain?

Comparing human amnesic patients with brain-damaged animals using the same tasks would be helpful. Although we cannot test monkeys or rats on some of the tasks designed to study human memory, we can study humans on tasks designed for nonhumans. In one study, patients with Korsakoff's syndrome showed a clear impairment on delayed matching-to-sample and delayed nonmatching-to-sample tasks (Squire, Zola-Morgan, & Chen, 1988). Evidently the hippocampus and prefrontal cortex play similar roles in humans and nonhumans.

## SUMMARY

1. Ivan Pavlov suggested that learning depends on the growth of a connection between two brain areas. Karl Lashley showed that learning does *not* depend on new connections across the cerebral cortex. He further demonstrated that damage almost anywhere in the cerebral cortex can impair performance of complex learned behaviors. (p. 486)

2. H. M., a patient with surgical damage to the hippocampus, has a severe impairment in forming new long-term memories. He can still recall memories established before his surgery and has little difficulty learning new skills. (p. 489)

3. Korsakoff's syndrome and Alzheimer's disease result from progressive brain damage affecting parts of the cerebral cortex and subcortical areas. Like H. M., patients with these conditions learn new skills and show normal memory in certain regards but greatly impaired memory in other regards. (p. 491)

4. It is unclear how best to describe the memory loss of brain-damaged patients. They have trouble establishing new long-term memories, they often have trouble with working memories, and they are more impaired in their declarative memories than in their procedural memories. (p. 496)

5. Sometimes the memory of an event is consolidated afterward and sometimes it is not. Electroconvulsive shock or other head trauma can interfere with consolidation. (p. 497)

6. Events evaluated as highly significant generally increase the secretion of epinephrine, which increases blood glucose levels. A high blood glucose level facilitates the consolidation of recent memories. (p. 499)

7. Endorphins impede memory consolidation, apparently through effects within the brain itself. (p. 499)

8. Rats with hippocampal damage are impaired in their memory of recent events, especially if the spatial layout of stimuli is critical. (p. 500)

9. Monkeys with damage to the hippocampus and amygdala have trouble with recent memories, as the delayed nonmatching-to-sample task reveals. (p. 502)

10. Damage to the prefrontal cortex also impairs memory, especially the ability to shift from following one rule to following a different rule. (p. 503)

## REVIEW QUESTIONS

1. What is the procedure for producing classical conditioning? What is the procedure for producing operant conditioning? (p. 486)

2. What does the term *engram* mean? What kind of engram did Karl Lashley expect to find? (p. 488)

3. What kind of learning or memory is least impaired in the patient H. M.? (p. 491)

4. Why is Korsakoff's syndrome more common among alcoholics than among other people? (p. 491)

5. Describe an example of implicit memory that is intact in patients with Korsakoff's syndrome. (p. 492)

6. What observation first led to the suspicion that chromosome 21 in some people contains a gene that causes Alzheimer's disease? (p. 496)

7. What do the observations of brain-damaged amnesic patients tell us about memory? (p. 496)

8. Why did Donald Hebb originally assume that short-term memory must differ from long-term memory? (p. 496)

9. Human head injury that leads to loss of consciousness blots out memories of events just before the trauma (Crovitz, Horn, & Daniel, 1983). How could one describe this observation in terms of consolidation? (p. 497)

10. How does epinephrine enhance consolidation? What neurotransmitter impairs consolidation? (p. 499)

11. After damage to the hippocampus of a rat, what kinds of memory are most impaired? What kinds are least impaired? What evidence points to the importance of the hippocampus for spatial memories? (p. 500)

12. Why are the effects of prefrontal cortex damage similar to those of damage to the hippocampus and amygdala? (p. 503)

13. What are the effects of prefrontal cortex damage on a person's performance of the Wisconsin card-sorting task? (p. 504)

## THOUGHT QUESTIONS

1. Lashley sought to find the engram, the physiological representation of learning. In general terms, how would you recognize an engram if you saw one? That is, what would someone have to demonstrate before you could conclude that a particular change in the nervous system was really an engram?

2. Morphine and heroin users often have trouble remembering events that happened just before or during a period of drug intoxication. There are several possible explanations for this memory impairment; suggest one based on the material you have just read.

## SUGGESTIONS FOR FURTHER READING

**Olton, D. S.; Gamzu, E.; & Corkin, S.** (Eds.) (1985). Memory dysfunctions. *Annals of the New York Academy of Sciences, 444.* A collection of articles on memory loss in humans and nonhumans.

**Squire, L. R.** (1987). *Memory and Brain.* New York: Oxford University Press. Reviews all aspects of the physiology of memory from synapses to brain systems.

# Mechanisms of Storing Information in the Nervous System

Whoen you see something, hear something, or do something, your experience probably leaves several traces in your nervous system. But which of these traces are important for memory?

If I walk through a field, are the footprints that I leave "memories"? How about the mud that I pick up on my shoes? In a sense, both are memories. That is, if the police wanted to know who had walked across that field, a forensics expert could compare the footprints to my shoes and the mud on my shoes to the mud on the field.

Similarly, when a pattern of activity passes through my brain or yours, it leaves a path of physical changes. Any or all of those changes could be memories if something in the brain can use them appropriately, like the forensics expert who knows how to examine footprints. Investigators of the physiology of learning and memory try to determine how an experience lays down lasting traces in the brain and which of those traces the brain uses later. The task is a little like searching for the proverbial needle in the haystack, and researchers have explored many avenues that seemed promising for a while but now seem fruitless (see Digression 14.1).

## LEARNING AND THE HEBBIAN SYNAPSE

Ivan Pavlov's concept of classical conditioning lent itself very well to theorizing about the physiological basis of learning. As we have already seen, Pavlov's theories provoked Karl Lashley's unsuccessful search for new connections across the cerebral cortex. Pavlov's theories also stimulated Donald Hebb to propose a mechanism for change at a synapse.

Hebb suggested that when the axon of neuron A "repeatedly or persistently takes part in firing [cell B], some growth process or metabolic change takes place in one or both cells" that increases the subsequent ability of axon A to excite cell B (Hebb, 1949, p. 62). In other words, an axon that has successfully stimulated cell B in the past becomes even more successful in the future.

# Dead Ends, Blind Alleys, and Abandoned Mines in Research

Textbooks, this one included, talk mostly about "successful" research, the studies that led to our current understanding of a field. You may get the impression that science progresses in a smooth fashion, that each study leads to the next and that each investigator simply contributes to an ever-accumulating body of knowledge. However, if you ever look at the old journals or old textbooks in a field, you will find discussions of various "promising" or "exciting" findings that we disregard today. Scientific research does not progress in a straight line from ignorance to enlightenment; it explores one direction after another, a little like a rat in a complex maze, abandoning the arms that lead nowhere and pursuing those that lead further. Many "promising" lines of research turn out to be blind alleys.

The problem with the maze analogy is that an investigator seldom runs into a "wall" that clearly identifies the end of a route. Perhaps a better analogy is a prospector digging in one location after another, never entirely certain whether to abandon an unprofitable spot or whether to keep digging just a little longer. Many once exciting lines of research in the physiology of learning are now of little more than historical interest. Here are three examples:

1. Wilder Penfield sometimes performed brain surgery for severe epilepsy on conscious patients who had only scalp anesthesia. When he applied a brief, weak electrical stimulus to part of the brain, the patient could describe the experience the stimulation evoked. Stimulation of the temporal cortex sometimes evoked vivid descriptions:

*I feel as though I were in the bathroom at school.*

*I see myself at the corner of Jacob and Washington in South Bend, Indiana.*

*I remember myself at the railroad station in Vanceburg, Kentucky; it is winter and the wind is blowing outside, and I am waiting for a train.*

Penfield (1955; Penfield & Perot, 1963) suggested that each neuron in the temporal cortex stores a particular memory, almost like a videotape of one's life. However, we have several reasons to doubt that the brain stimulation actually evoked old memories. For example, stimulation very rarely evoked a memory of a specific event. More often patients reported vague sights and sounds, or repeated experiences such as "seeing a bed" or "hearing a choir sing 'White Christmas.'" Stimulation almost never elicited memories of doing anything—just seeing and hearing. Also, some patients reported events they had never actually experienced, such as being chased by a robber or seeing Christ descend from the sky. In short, the stimulation produced something more like a dream than an accurate memory.

2. G. A. Horridge (1962) apparently demonstrated that decapitated cockroaches can learn. First he cut the connections between a cockroach's head and the rest of its body. Then he suspended the cockroach so that its legs dangled just above a surface of water. An electrical circuit was arranged as Figure 14.15 shows, so that the roach's leg would get a shock whenever it touched the water. Each experimental roach was paired with a control roach that got a leg shock whenever the first roach did; only the experimental roach had any control over the shock, however. (This kind of experiment is known as a "yoked-control" design.)

Over a period of 5 to 10 minutes, roaches in the experimental group "learned" a response of tucking the leg under the body to avoid shocks. Roaches in the control group did not, on the average, change their leg position during the training period. Thus, the changed response apparently qualifies as learning and not as some accidental by-product of the shocks.

These experiments initially seemed like a promising way of studying anatomical and chemical changes after learning has occurred in a very simple nervous

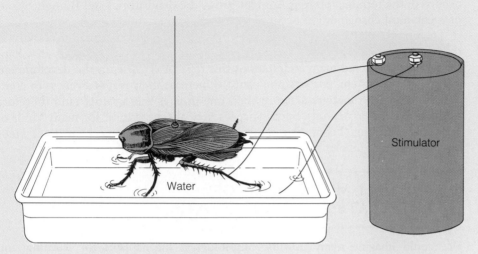

**Figure 14.15 Apparatus for shocking a cockroach leg whenever it enters the water**

*A cockroach in the control group gets a shock whenever this roach does, regardless of the position of the control group roach's leg. (After Horridge, 1962.)*

Stimulator

Water

system—in this case, a single cockroach ganglion (Eisenstein & Cohen, 1965). This is a case of looking for a needle in a very small haystack. Unfortunately, decapitated cockroaches learn slowly, and the results vary sharply from one individual to another, limiting the usefulness of the results. After a few studies in the 1960s and early 1970s, interest in this line of research faded.

3. In the 1960s and early 1970s, several investigators proposed that each memory is coded as a specific molecule, probably RNA or protein. The boldest test of that hypothesis was an attempt to transfer memories chemically from one individual to another. James McConnell (1962) reported that when planaria (flatworms) cannibalized other planaria that had been classically conditioned to respond to a light, they apparently "remembered" what the cannibalized planaria had learned. (At least they learned the response faster than planaria generally do.)

Inspired by that report, other investigators

trained rats to approach a clicking sound for food (Babich, Jacobson, Bubash, & Jacobson, 1965). After the rats were well trained, the experimenters ground up the rats' brains, extracted RNA, and injected it into some untrained rats. The recipient rats learned to approach the clicking sound faster than rats in the control group did.

That report led to a sudden flurry of experiments on the transfer of training by brain extracts. In *some* of these experiments, rats that received brain extracts from a trained group showed apparent memory of the task while those that received extracts from an untrained group did not (Dyal, 1971; Fjerdingstad, 1973).

The results were inconsistent and unreplicable, however, even within a single laboratory (L. T. Smith, 1975). Many laboratories failed to find any hint of a transfer effect. By the mid-1970s most biological psychologists saw no point in continuing research in this area (Gaito, 1976).

Consider how this relates to classical conditioning: Suppose that initially axon A excites cell B only slightly. However, if axon A often fires at the same time as some other axon, say axon C, the combined effect on B may be great, perhaps even producing an action potential. You might think of axon A as the CS and axon C as the US. The pairing of activity in axons A and C causes cell B to increase its responsiveness to A. Hebb was noncommittal about where the change occurred; the terminal of axon A might grow, the dendrites of cell B might grow, or a chemical change might occur in one or the other.

A synapse that increases in effectiveness because of simultaneous activity in the presynaptic and postsynaptic neurons is called a **Hebbian synapse.** In Chapter 8 we encountered many examples of this type of synapse; in the development of the nervous system, postsynaptic neurons increase their responsiveness to combinations of axons that are active at the same time as one another (and therefore as the postsynaptic neuron). Such synapses may also be critical for many kinds of associative learning. Today we can say much more about the mechanisms of Hebbian (or almost-Hebbian) synapses than Hebb himself could have guessed.

## SINGLE-CELL MECHANISMS OF INVERTEBRATE BEHAVIOR CHANGE

We could imagine many possible physiological mechanisms for learning and memory: changes in dendritic branching, changes in glia, increased or decreased release of some neurotransmitter, or development of new proteins within neurons, for example. If we are going to look for the proverbial needle in a haystack, a good strategy might be to look for a small haystack.

By that reasoning, many researchers have turned to studies of invertebrates. Certainly the nervous system of an invertebrate is organized differently from that of a vertebrate; for example, many invertebrates have several widely separated ganglia instead of a single structure we could call a "brain." But the general chemistry of the neuron is the same, the principles of the action potential are the same, even many of the neurotransmitters are the same. (Many key neurotransmitters can be found in one-celled animals, although we do not know what they are doing there.) If we identify the physical basis of learning and memory in some invertebrate, we cannot assume that vertebrates use the same mechanism, but at least we have a good hypothesis of what *might* work. (Biologists have long used this strategy for studying genetics, embryology, and other biological processes.)

### *Aplysia* as an Experimental Animal

*Aplysia*, a marine invertebrate related to the common slug, has become a particularly popular animal for studies of the physiology of learning (see Figure 14.16). *Aplysia* has fewer neurons than any vertebrate, and many of its neurons are rather large (up to 1 mm in diameter) and therefore easy to study. Moreover, unlike vertebrates, *Aplysia* has a nervous system that is practically identical from one individual to another. Many neurons are easy to recognize. For example, after an experimenter identifies the properties of the *R2* cell in one specimen, other experimenters can find the same cell in their own animals and can carry the studies further or relate that neuron to other identified neurons. By contrast, investigators who work with a vertebrate species can describe a neuron *type* that is recognizable from one individual to another individual, but they cannot identify single neurons.

**Figure 14.16**
***Aplysia*, a marine mollusc sometimes known as the sea hare**
*A full-grown animal is a little larger than the human hand. (H. Chaumeton/ Nature.)*

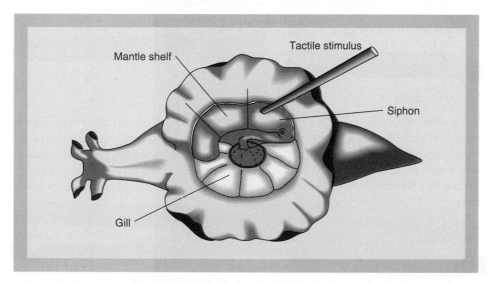

Mantle shelf

Tactile stimulus

Siphon

Gill

**Figure 14.17**
*Touch stimulation of an* Aplysia's *mantle, siphon, or gill causes a withdrawal response. The sensory and motor neurons controlling this reaction have been identified and studied.*

Much of the research on *Aplysia* deals with changes in behavior as a result of experience. Some of those changes may seem simple, and it is a matter of definition whether we call these changes *learning* or use the broader term *plasticity*. One commonly studied behavior is the withdrawal response: If someone touches the siphon, mantle, or gill of an *Aplysia* (Figure 14.17), the animal vigorously withdraws. Investigators have traced the neural path from the touch receptors through various identifiable interneurons to the motor neurons that direct this withdrawal response. The response goes through three experience-based phenomena: habituation, sensitization, and classical conditioning.

## Habituation in *Aplysia*

**Habituation** is a decrease in response to a stimulus that is presented repeatedly and that is accompanied by no change in other stimuli. That is, the animal learns to ignore an irrelevant stimulus. Habituation can be demonstrated in an *Aplysia* by repeatedly stimulating its gills with a brief jet of seawater. At first it withdraws the gills, but after many repetitions it stops responding.

Several possible mechanisms of habituation can be eliminated. First, muscle fatigue can be ruled out because, even after habituation has occurred, direct stimulation of the motor neuron produces a full-sized muscle contraction (Kupfermann, Castellucci, Pinsker, & Kandel, 1970). Second, habituation does not depend on a change in the firing rate of the sensory neuron. After repeated stimulation, the sensory neuron still gives a full, normal response to stimulation; it merely fails to excite the motor neuron as much as before (Kupfermann et al., 1970).

By process of elimination, we are left with the conclusion that habituation in *Aplysia* depends on a change in the synapse between the sensory neuron and the motor neuron (Figure 14.18). To determine the nature of that change, V. Castellucci and Eric Kandel (1974) measured the excitatory postsynaptic potentials (EPSPs) in the motor neuron during habituation. As habituation proceeded, the average size of the EPSP decreased, but each EPSP was still an integral multiple of the quantum of membrane response (as described in Chapter 3), which is presumably based on a quantum of neurotransmitter release. From this evidence, Castellucci and Kandel inferred that habituation reflects a decrease in transmitter release by the presynaptic cell.

## Sensitization in *Aplysia*

After a strong electrical shock or any other intense stimulus, a person undergoes **sensitization,** becoming overresponsive to mild stimuli. Similarly, a strong noxious stimulus almost anywhere on *Aplysia*'s surface can intensify later withdrawal responses to a touch on the siphon, mantle, or gill. Sensitization may last as briefly as a few seconds or as long as days, depending on the strength and repetition of the sensitizing stimulus.

As with habituation, sensitization in *Aplysia* depends on a change in the number of quanta that the presynaptic neuron releases (Dale, Schacher, & Kandel, 1988). The difference is that habituation reflects decreased release while sensitization reflects increased release. Figure 14.19 diagrams the two relevant synapses — one between the sensory neuron and an interneuron and one between the sensory neuron and the motor neuron. Researchers have described the mechanism of that change in some detail (Cleary, Hammer, & Byrne, 1989; Kandel & Schwartz, 1982).

Strong stimulation (of the head, tail, or elsewhere) excites a particular facilitating interneuron, which can be identified in any *Aplysia*. The facilitating interneuron has presynaptic synapses that release serotonin (5-HT) onto the synapses of many sensory neurons. Serotonin interacts with a receptor in each sensory neuron to produce the second messenger cyclic AMP within the cell. An enzyme dependent on cyclic AMP is thereby activated, blocking potassium channels in the membrane. As you will recall from Chapter 2, potassium flows out of the neuron after the peak of the action potential; the exit of potassium restores the neuron to its usual polarization. When the cyclic AMP–dependent enzyme blocks the potassium channels, the net effect is to prolong the action potential and therefore to prolong transmitter release by the presynaptic cell.

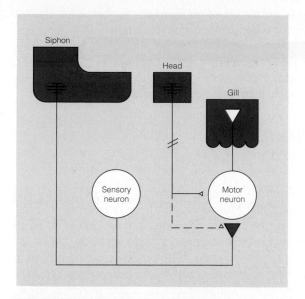

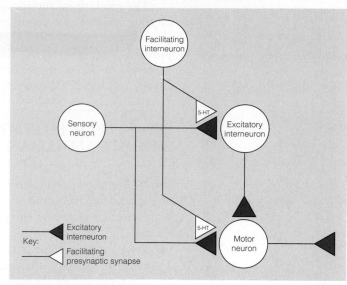

**Figure 14.18**
**Habituation of the gill-withdrawal reflex in *Aplysia* apparently depends on decreased transmission at the synapse between the sensory neuron and the motor neuron**
*Stimulation at other locations, such as the head, can temporarily reexcite a habituated synapse. (After Castellucci et al., 1970.)*

**Figure 14.19**
**Sensitization of the withdrawal response in *Aplysia* depends on the release of serotonin (5-HT) at pre-synaptic synapses.** *(After Kandel & Schwartz, 1982.)*

If the sensitizing stimulus is repeated, the prolonged elevation of cyclic AMP in the sensory neuron leads to the production of new proteins responsible for long-term sensitization. Unlike the short-term variety, long-term potentiation depends on protein synthesis. Drugs that block protein synthesis can prevent it (Schacher, Castellucci, & Kandel, 1988).

## Classical Conditioning in *Aplysia*

Sensitization may sound remote from the complex types of learning that interest us most. However, the mechanisms of complex learning may be simply an elaboration of those for sensitization. In sensitization, a single synapse onto a neuron is repeatedly active; in classical conditioning, two or more synapses are active at the same time. In both cases, a change in the cell enhances synaptic transmission.

Here is one example of classical conditioning in *Aplysia*: Ordinarily, an *Aplysia* responds weakly or not at all to a mild touch on its siphon; it responds vigorously to an electrical stimulation of its tail. If a mild touch on the siphon (CS) is repeatedly paired with electrical stimulation of the tail (US), the animal gradually develops a conditioned response of vigorous withdrawal to the siphon touch. The mechanism of classical conditioning in *Aplysia* is similar to that of sensitization, except that it is more specific: After repeated pairings of CS with US, the sensory neuron (the one responsive to the CS) releases more of its neuro-transmitter than before (Kandel & Schwartz, 1982).

The research on *Aplysia* shows us one set of mechanisms for behavior plasticity and therefore one hypothesis for what mechanisms we might find with vertebrates. It shows us that learning can be based on presynaptic changes. Learning probably does not rely on the same mechanisms in all situations in all species, however. At this point, anyone who investigates a particular example of behavior change can hope to discover *a* mechanism but not *the* mechanism of learning.

# LONG-TERM POTENTIATION IN THE MAMMALIAN BRAIN

Are the cellular mechanisms of vertebrate learning similar to those of molluscs? If not, what other mechanisms can we find? Moreover, are the mechanisms of vertebrate learning primarily changes in presynaptic neurons, as they appear to be in *Aplysia*? Or are some of the mechanisms postsynaptic? Theoretically, there are good reasons to look for postsynaptic mechanisms. The postsynaptic neuron is in a position to compare the responses of several synapses, to note which synapses are active just before the postsynaptic neuron produces an action potential (Bear, Cooper, & Ebner, 1987).

Within the mammalian nervous system, the best candidate for a cellular basis of learning is a phenomenon known as long-term potentiation. In **long-term potentiation (LTP)**, a neuron is bombarded with a brief but rapid series of stimuli—typically, 100 synaptic excitations per second for about 1 to 4 seconds. This burst of intense stimulation leaves the neuron "potentiated" (highly responsive to new input of the same type) for minutes, days, or weeks. LTP can result from repeated stimulation of a single synapse (like sensitization) or from nearly simultaneous stimulation of two or more synapses (more like conditioning). Generally, simultaneous stimulation of different synapses produces a stronger and more lasting effect than stimulation of a single synapse does; this is one reason why LTP is considered promising as a single-cell basis for associative learning.

LTP was first discovered in studies of hippocampal neurons (Bliss & Lømo, 1973). It can also occur in other parts of the nervous system (see, for example, Iriki, Pavlides, Keller, & Asanuma, 1989), although the effect seems especially large and easy to demonstrate in the hippocampus. Many LTP experiments use **hippocampal slices,** sections of the hippocampus removed from the animal and maintained in a culture medium with various nutrients. Such a procedure makes it easier for investigators to stimulate and record from cells and test the effects of various chemicals.

At many hippocampal synapses, LTP depends on the activation of **NMDA receptors** (Cotman, Monaghan, & Ganong, 1988). NMDA (*N*-methyl-D-aspartate) is an artificial chemical, not a neurotransmitter. NMDA receptors are one of three known kinds of glutamate receptors; all glutamate receptors respond to glutamate, but different kinds respond to NMDA, kainate, or quisqualate. Glutamate at its kainate or quisqualate receptors is an excitatory neurotransmitter; at its NMDA receptors it produces little excitation under most circumstances. However, LTP occurs only where NMDA receptors are present. That is, activation of NMDA receptors produces a prolonged facilitation of transmission at the kainate or quisqualate receptors.

As Figure 14.20a shows, magnesium ions block NMDA receptors under most circumstances. However, rapidly repeated stimulation by one or more axons greatly depolarizes the membrane and thereby changes the NMDA receptors, enabling glutamate to stimulate them and open calcium channels (Figure 14.20b). The entry of calcium evidently sets in motion a series of events that produce

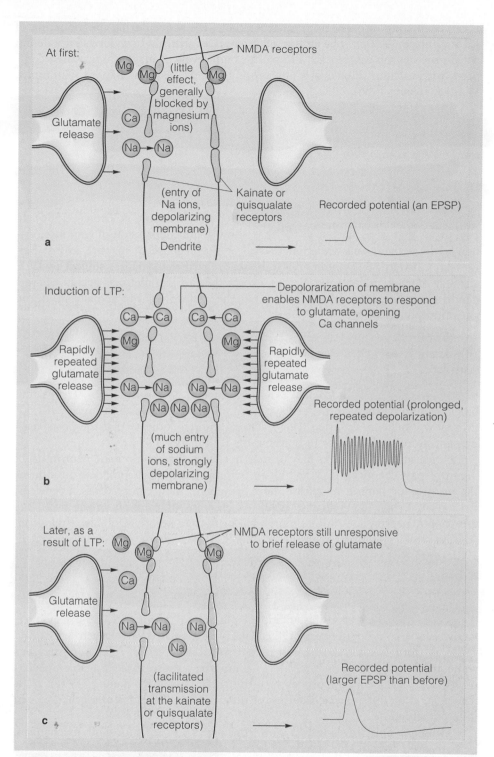

**Figure 14.20**
**One possible arrangement for LTP**

*(a) At first, glutamate stimulation moderately excites the postsynaptic neuron through the kainate or quisqualate receptors. The nearby NMDA receptor is unresponsive.*
*(b) Then LTP is induced by rapidly repeated stimulation; stimulation by two glutamate axons produces more effect than one. This stimulation strongly depolarizes the membrane. Depolarization of the membrane alters the NMDA receptor, enabling glutamate to stimulate it. Thus the NMDA receptor is effective only when the membrane is strongly depolarized. (c) After induction of LTP, transmission at kainate and quisqualate receptors is facilitated. The exact mechanism of facilitation is not yet clear, but it probably includes increased release of glutamate, at least in many cases. Although the NMDA receptor was necessary for inducing LTP, it is not necessary for maintaining it. Once LTP is established, drug blockage of the NMDA receptors does not interfere with the facilitated response by the kainate or quisqualate receptors.*

LTP, facilitating response in those axons that were active during the induction of LTP (Figure 14.20c). The inflow of calcium is critical: Low levels of calcium within the neuron can block LTP; so can high levels of magnesium, which competes with calcium (Hopkins & Johnston, 1984; M. Kessler, Baudry, Cummins, Way, & Lynch, 1986).

Once LTP has been established, it no longer depends on NMDA synapses. Drugs that block NMDA synapses prevent the *establishment* of LTP, but they do not interfere with the *maintenance* of LTP that was already established (Gustafsson & Wigström, 1990).

LTP displays the property of **cooperativity:** Nearly simultaneous stimulation by two or more axons produces more LTP than stimulation by just one. This observation makes LTP an attractive model of learning. Furthermore, only those axons that "cooperated" become facilitated (Kelso, Ganong, & Brown, 1986). In fact, axons that were inactive at the time show a later depression of response; evidently the active axons are strengthened at the expense of inactive axons (Sejnowski, Chattarji, & Stanton, 1990). In this regard the synapses subject to LTP are very much like Hebbian synapses, except that LTP sometimes occurs where a dendrite has been greatly depolarized but the neuron has not actually produced an action potential.

The phenomenon of cooperativity implies that some event in the postsynaptic neuron is necessary to trigger LTP because only the postsynaptic neuron is in a position to detect the fact that two axons have delivered simultaneous input. Furthermore, LTP requires an influx of calcium ions and synthesis of proteins in the postsynaptic neuron (Malenka, Kauer, Zucker, & Nicoll, 1988). Drugs that block protein synthesis in the postsynaptic cell prevent the establishment of LTP (Malinow, Shulman, & Tsien, 1989). These findings indicate that the postsynaptic neuron initiates changes responsible for LTP.

However, those changes may or may not be in the postsynaptic neuron itself. Neurons pass chemicals back and forth; perhaps the postsynaptic neuron induces the presynaptic neuron to release more glutamate than before (Bliss, Clements, Errington, Lynch, & Williams, 1990). At least in some hippocampal areas, the presynaptic neuron does release more glutamate than before (Dolphin, Errington, & Bliss, 1982; Malenka, Madison, & Nicoll, 1986; Skrede & Mathe-Sørenssen, 1981). In other cases the postsynaptic cells change the structure of their dendrites. The burst of stimulation to the hippocampus increases the concentration of calcium in the dendrites, activating **calpain,** a protein that breaks a network of molecules normally found in the dendrites. With that network broken, the dendrites change shape, exposing additional glutamate receptors (Akers, Lovinger, Colly, Linden, & Routtenberg, 1986; Baudry & Lynch, 1980; Lynch & Baudry, 1984). A third possible mechanism is that previously "silent" receptors may become more responsive. Figure 14.21 summarizes these three possible mechanisms; some evidence supports each of the three (Lynch & Baudry, 1991). LTP may depend on different mechanisms or different combinations of mechanisms in different situations.

Although most investigators now consider LTP an important mechanism, perhaps even essential for vertebrate learning, we still do not know how it relates to learned behavior. So far, investigators have focused on one synapse at a time, but facilitation of a single synapse hardly explains an integrated learned behavior. Still, investigators of LTP are probably on the right track; drugs that block NMDA synapses also block LTP in the rat hippocampus, and those same drugs block the kind of learning that depends on the hippocampus (Morris, 1989).

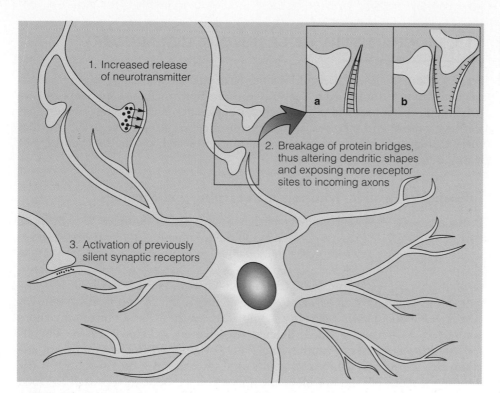

Figure 14.21
Three possible mecha-
nisms of long-term
potentiation

1. Increased release
of neurotransmitter

2. Breakage of protein bridges,
thus altering dendritic shapes
and exposing more receptor
sites to incoming axons

3. Activation of previously
silent synaptic receptors

a

b

## LEARNING ELSEWHERE IN THE NERVOUS SYSTEM

The fact that hippocampal or cortical damage impairs some kinds of learning and not others implies that other parts of the nervous system are essential for certain types of learning. In some cases learning may depend on a change in a very small area of the brain, quite unlike the examples of learning that Lashley studied.

Richard F. Thompson (1986) and his colleagues studied a type of classical conditioning in rabbits. They paired a tone (CS) with a puff of air (US) to the cornea. At first, the rabbits blinked at the air puff but not at the tone; after repeated pairings, they blinked at the tone by itself. That is, classical conditioning took place. At various points in this procedure the investigators recorded the activity from different brain cells. They found changes in cells in one nucleus of the cerebellum, the **lateral interpositus nucleus.** Moreover, they found that damage to the lateral interpositus nucleus caused a permanent loss of the conditioned response (McCormick & Thompson, 1984; Woodruf-Pak, Lavond, & Thompson, 1985). If the tone is presented on just one side of the head and the air puff is presented to just one eye, the conditioning depends on the lateral interpositus nucleus on just one side of the brain (Sears & Steinmetz, 1990). Apparently, this instance of learning depends on changes in one brain area, not in widely scattered spots. Various parts of the cerebellum may be critical for other kinds of learning, especially learning motor skills (Glickstein & Yeo, 1990).

# THE BIOCHEMISTRY OF LEARNING AND MEMORY

Studies of the single-cell basis of learning have attributed learning to increases in calcium within neurons, decreases in potassium flow, increased numbers of certain synaptic receptors, and other biochemical changes. Such findings suggest that learning impairments may result from chemical deficiencies in the brain and that certain drugs may impair or improve learning. Research on the biochemistry of learning has followed several routes.

## Influence of Protein Synthesis on Learning and Memory

Proteins are an important building block of the body; to produce growth of an axon or dendrite, an increase or decrease in the production of a neurotransmitter, or an alteration of any receptor, protein synthesis is a necessary step. Studies of *Aplysia* and LTP suggest that protein synthesis is critical in the formation of long-term memories. Furthermore, drugs that inhibit protein synthesis impair the long-term storage of memory, although they do not impair short-term retention (Davis & Squire, 1984). The more completely synthesis is inhibited, the more completely learning is retarded (Bennett, Rosenzweig, & Flood, 1979). The effects vary from one task to another, however. For example, in one experiment **anisomycin,** a drug that inhibits protein synthesis, blocked a rat's memory of the location of shock but did not block memory of which odor to approach for food (Stäubli, Faraday, & Lynch, 1985).

How does protein synthesis contribute to learning and memory? One hypothesis is that protein synthesis modifies the properties of neurons to store information. Another hypothesis is that its function is merely to keep the brain healthy in general. One way to evaluate these two hypotheses is to test the effects of anisomycin on learning (Davis, Rosenzweig, Bennett, & Squire, 1980). Researchers gave one group of rats a large dose 5 hours before training and a second group a small dose 20 minutes before training. At the time of training, the rats that had received the smaller but more recent dose of anisomycin had greater impairments of both protein synthesis and learning, even though the animals that had received the larger, less recent dose were still suffering greater side effects, including diarrhea, inactivity, and watery eyes. Apparently, inhibiting protein synthesis impairs learning directly, not just by making the animal sick.

## Acetylcholine Synapses and Memory

Ultimately, the outcome of increased protein synthesis, hormonal stimulation, or whatever mechanism is at work must be either a change in the resting activity of certain neurons or a change in the responsiveness at certain synapses. Much evidence indicates that some of the changes occur at acetylcholine synapses.

In normal aging, some memory impairment is common; the degree of memory loss correlates with a decline in brain acetylcholine levels (Bartus, Dean, Beer, & Lippa, 1982; Davies, 1985). People suffering from Alzheimer's disease suffer more severe memory dysfunctions and a striking decline in brain acetylcholine content.

In several experiments, young adult volunteers received injections of **scopolamine,** a drug that blocks acetylcholine synapses. While under the influence of the drug, they showed clear deficiencies on a variety of memory tasks. Their general pattern of performance resembled that of senile people—that is, they were impaired on the same memory tasks on which senile people have the greatest troubles (Beatty, Butters, & Janowsky, 1986; Drachman & Leavitt, 1974).

Given these results, the question arises, could we improve human memory by using **physostigmine** or other drugs that prolong the effects of acetylcholine at the synapses? Several studies have found that physostigmine does improve memory, especially in older people and others with poor memories (Davis, Mohs, Tinklenberg, Pfefferbaum, Hollister, & Kopell, 1978; Sitaram, Weingartner, & Gillin, 1978). Unfortunately, the required doses produce prominent, unwelcome side effects such as restlessness, sweating, diarrhea, and excessive salivation (Bartus et al., 1982). So such drug treatments are not clinically useful.

Researchers have also tried to increase acetylcholine production in the brain by providing dietary precursors, such as choline and lecithin. In numerous studies, these substances have been given to senile or brain-damaged people with serious memory failures. Unfortunately, they apparently produce no significant benefits (Bartus, Dean, Pontecorvo, & Flicker, 1985). Perhaps senility and other memory failures are associated with such a massive depletion of acetylcholine synapses that a slight rise in the availability of the neurotransmitter is ineffective.

Although dietary enrichment does not reverse a memory loss, long-term enrichment may prevent such a loss. In one study, mice that were fed a high-choline diet over 4 1/2 months had better than normal memory in old age (Bartus, Dean, Goas, & Lippa, 1980).

## Other Synapses and Memory

Earlier we considered the role of glutamate synapses in LTP. Besides glutamate and acetylcholine, several other neurotransmitters may be necessary for the expression of learned behaviors. In old age the brain commonly suffers a decline in its supply of norepinephrine, serotonin, and dopamine as well as acetylcholine (Wong et al., 1984). Old monkeys also suffer a variety of memory deficits. Young monkeys suffer the same deficits after depletion of the norepinephrine and dopamine input to their prefrontal cortex. *Clonidine*, a drug that stimulates norepinephrine receptors, reverses these deficits (Arnsten & Goldman-Rakic, 1985a). Norepinephrine and dopamine synapses in the prefrontal cortex apparently are major contributors to memory. Similarly, drugs that enhance the activity of norepinephrine-releasing neurons improve memory performance in aged mice (Zornetzer, 1985).

## Chemical Modulators of Attention

Other neurotransmitters and neuromodulators may play a role in attention. The hormones ACTH and vasopressin improve the performance of rats on numerous learning tasks (Edelstein, 1981; Martinez, Jensen, & McGaugh, 1981; Messing & Sparber, 1985). Vasopressin also enhances the memory performance of senile people (Delwaide, Devoitille, & Ylieff, 1980). The brain metabolizes vasopressin to form the chemical **AVP$_{4-9}$**, which is more effective than vasopressin itself. AVP$_{4-9}$ focuses the brain's attention on the dominant cues in the environment, as the following experiment illustrates (Bunsey, Kramer, Kesler, & Strupp, 1990):

Rats were confronted with two boxes; on each trial one box contained some Froot Loops. One group of rats had to learn to choose the box with the correct covering on its sides; the box lid also varied but was irrelevant. Another group of rats had to choose the box with the correct lid; the side covering also varied but was irrelevant. So each rat had to pay attention to the correct stimulus (either sides or lids) and ignore the other stimulus. Figure 14.22 illustrates the situation.

Mechanisms of
Storing Information
in the Nervous
System

## Figure 14.22
## Procedure for an experiment on attention (Bunsey, Kramer, Kesler, & Strupp, 1990)

*For rats in one group, the side of the box is the relevant cue for where to find food, and the type of lid is irrelevant. For rats in the other group, the type of lid is the relevant cue, and the side of the box is irrelevant. The brain chemical $AVP_{4-9}$ enhanced performance when the side was the relevant cue but impaired performance when the lid was relevant.*

Group 1
Box sides relevant, lids irrelevant (easier)

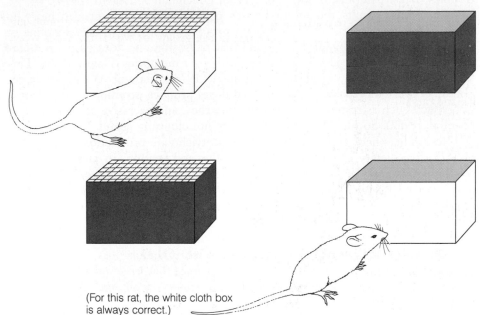

(For this rat, the white cloth box is always correct.)

Group 2
Box sides irrelevant, lids relevant (more difficult)

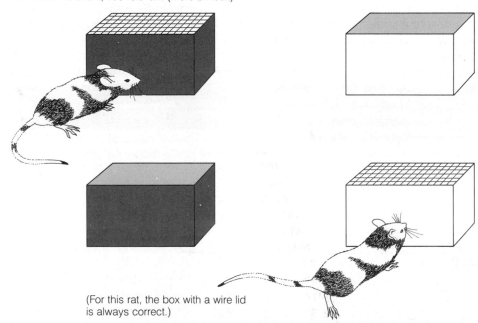

(For this rat, the box with a wire lid is always correct.)

Ordinarily, without drugs or any other treatments, rats learn this task faster when the sides are relevant than when the lids are relevant. That is, they evidently find it easier to pay attention to sides than to lids. In this experiment, an injection of AVP$_{4-9}$ facilitated performance in the group for which the sides were relevant; it impaired performance in the group for which the lids were relevant. That is, AVP$_{4-9}$ evidently focused the rats' attention even more strongly on the stimulus they would have paid attention to anyway. If that was the relevant stimulus, the rats did well; if it was a distraction, the rats did poorly.

At this point we can only speculate on the possible implications for humans. Note, however, that ideal performance requires a balance between the ability to focus attention and the ability to shift one's focus from time to time. Some people (such as autistic children) tend to focus their attention on a single stimulus and ignore other stimuli that might be important. Other people (such as those with schizophrenia or attention deficit disorder) are distracted too easily by extraneous ideas and stimuli.

## BRAIN AND MEMORY IN YOUNG AND OLD

Ideally, investigation of the physiology of learning and memory should lead to insights about why people remember some things better than others or why some people have better memories than other people do. For example, why do infants and old people sometimes have memory difficulties?

A possible key to answering this question is that both infants and old people perform well on some memory tasks and poorly on others. For example, psychologists have long puzzled over **infant amnesia,** the phenomenon that most of us remember very few events from the first four or five years of our lives. Nevertheless, children less than four years old learn to walk, to put on clothing, to eat with fork and spoon (or chopsticks), and to perform other skills that will last a lifetime. That is, in our first four or five years we establish many procedural memories, even if we do not form factual memories that will last long.

In that regard, infant memory resembles that of people with hippocampal damage. Perhaps infants have memory problems because the hippocampus is slow to mature, and old people have troubles because the hippocampus and related structures are deteriorating (Moscovitch, 1985). Studies of monkeys support a parallel between infant memory impairments and the effects of hippocampal damage. For example, monkeys completely fail the nonmatching-to-sample task until age 4 months, and they do not reach adult levels of performance until age 2 years (Bachevalier & Mishkin, 1984).

Many old people and aged animals have memory problems, although one individual may differ sharply from another. Many old people who have great troubles with recent factual memories manage to learn new skills (such as walking with a cane) or adjust old skills. That is, they also share certain similarities with individuals who have a damaged hippocampus.

Again, animal studies support this parallel. On a variety of memory tasks, old rats show deficits similar to those of rats with damage to the hippocampus or prefrontal cortex (Winocur & Moscovitch, 1990). The hippocampus of old rats includes many dead or dying neurons and axons (Greene & Naranjo, 1987); many of the surviving neurons are less active than they are in younger rats (Barnes & McNaughton, 1985). Hippocampal deterioration is probably responsible for the mild memory deficits typical of normal (non-Alzheimer's) aging (Gallagher & Pelleymounter, 1988).

The loss of neurons is hastened by exposure to high levels of *corticosterone*, a hormone the adrenal glands release during stressful periods (Sapolsky, Krey, & McEwen, 1985). Corticosterone does not damage the neurons, but it increases the metabolic activity of the cells, making them more vulnerable to damage by any toxic substances that may be present (Sapolsky, 1985). In other words, corticosterone magnifies the brain damage caused by toxins and thereby accelerates the aging process in the brain.

The prefrontal cortex also deteriorates in old age. Aged monkeys perform poorly on many of the same tasks as do monkeys with prefrontal damage. The deficits of old age may be due in part to a declining number of dopamine and norepinephrine synapses in the prefrontal cortex (Arnsten & Goldman-Rakic, 1985a, 1985b).

Memory may also vary from one age to another because of the rise and fall of levels of glutamate, acetylcholine, and other crucial chemicals. For example, recall from Chapter 8 that special kinds of visual experience can alter connections in the visual system only during a critical period of development. What ends that critical period? Apparently the critical period depends on NMDA receptors, the same receptors necessary for LTP. In one study, injecting a drug that blocks NMDA receptors blocked all effects of visual experience during the critical period (Kleinschmidt, Bear, & Singer, 1987). In another study, prolonged application of NMDA to an amphibian's brain toward the end of the critical period lengthened that period (Udin & Scherer, 1990). These results imply that the modification of synapses during the critical period depends on NMDA synapses; one can shorten the critical period by blocking those synapses or extend it by stimulating those synapses. Presumably, the normal critical period corresponds to a time when NMDA synapses are ordinarily easiest to stimulate.

A second example: Long-term potentiation depends on the entry of calcium ions into postsynaptic neurons. In aged mammals (presumably including humans), calcium channels apparently become somewhat "leaky," resulting in higher than normal resting levels of calcium within neurons. For that reason, calcium that enters during a train of stimuli may produce less effect than it would for a younger individual. In aged mammals, injections of magnesium (which competes with calcium) or of drugs that block calcium channels can enhance learning and memory (Deyo, Straube, & Disterhoft, 1989). Presumably, such treatments lower the resting calcium levels and therefore enhance the effects of calcium entering the cell during stimulation.

A third and final example: Earlier in this chapter we considered the finding that endorphins impair consolidation of memories. Presumably, endorphins block the formation of LTP or interact with the effects of glutamate, acetylcholine, or other neurotransmitters. Endorphin levels have been found to increase in the hippocampus of many aging rats; the greater the rise in endorphin levels, the more a rat's performance was impaired when it had to find an escape platform in a tank of cloudy water (Jiang, Owyang, Hong, & Gallagher, 1989). In short, learning and memory can be impaired by various chemical changes in old age, perhaps through their effects on LTP and related phenomena.

As you have seen in this chapter, an investigator of the physiology of learning must deal with processes ranging from molecular changes to behavior. We cannot say simply that a particular drug or physiological change improves or impairs memory; we must specify the type of memory affected and the way it is affected. In the process, we stand to clarify our understanding not only of the physiology but also of memory itself.

## SUMMARY

1. Donald Hebb proposed that learning occurs because of an increase in effectiveness at any synapse between a presynaptic neuron and postsynaptic neuron that have frequently been active at the same time. (p. 507)

2. Habituation of the gill-withdrawal reflex in *Aplysia* depends on a mechanism that decreases the release of transmitter from a particular presynaptic neuron. (p. 512)

3. Sensitization of the gill-withdrawal reflex in *Aplysia* depends on the release of an enzyme that blocks potassium channels in a presynaptic neuron and thereby prolongs the release of transmitter from that neuron. (p. 512)

4. At the single-cell level, classical conditioning may depend on an elaboration of the same mechanisms responsible for habituation and sensitization. (p. 513)

5. Long-term potentiation (LTP) is an enhancement of response at certain synapses because of a brief but intense series of stimuli delivered to a neuron. The effect is greatest when two or more axons stimulate a postsynaptic neuron simultaneously. Those two axons then become more effective in stimulating that neuron, while other axons become less effective than before. (p. 514)

6. LTP is triggered when great depolarization of a dendrite alters NMDA synapses, enabling them to respond to their transmitter, glutamate. The glutamate opens the NMDA receptor to calcium ions, which in some manner facilitate transmission at other nearby receptors of the kainate or quisqualate type. (p. 514)

7. The mechanisms of LTP may vary from one neuron to another; likely mechanisms include increased glutamate release, changes in dendritic structure, and activation of previously silent receptors. (p. 516)

8. Most complex types of learning depend on changes in many parts of the nervous system. In certain cases, however, such as eyelid conditioning in rabbits, the critical changes are localized to a small brain area. (p. 517)

9. Long-term learning and memory depend on protein synthesis; they can be impaired by drugs that block protein synthesis in the brain. (p. 518)

10. Decreased activity at acetylcholine synapses impairs memory. However, drugs and diets designed to elevate acetylcholine levels do not appear to be clinically useful for improving memory. (p. 518)

11. Certain other chemicals, including one derivative of the hormone vasopressin, alter the division of attention between the more prominent and less prominent stimuli in the environment. (p. 519)

12. Infant amnesia may be due to slow maturation of the hippocampus; memory impairments in old age can be related to gradual loss of neurons and synapses in the hippocampus and prefrontal cortex. (p. 521)

13. Developmental changes in learning and memory may also depend on the rise and fall of chemicals necessary for LTP or transmitters that modulate LTP. (p. 522)

## REVIEW QUESTIONS

1. How can a Hebbian synapse account for the basic phenomena of classical conditioning? (p. 507)

2. What are the advantages of research with *Aplysia* and other molluscs as compared to vertebrates? (p. 510)

3. Why do researchers believe that habituation and sensitization in *Aplysia* depend on presynaptic rather than postsynaptic changes? (p. 512)

4. How do the mechanisms of classical conditioning in *Aplysia* compare to those of sensitization? (p. 513)

5. What procedures produce LTP in the mammalian brain? How does cooperativity contribute to LTP? (p. 514)

6. What is an NMDA synapse? Are NMDA synapses responsible for maintaining LTP after it is established? (p. 514)

7. What are the possible mechanisms of LTP? (p. 516)

8. Why do researchers believe that inhibition of protein synthesis blocks learning and memory directly, not just by making an animal sick? (p. 518)

9. What are the effects of scopolamine and physostigmine on animal learning and memory? (p. 518)

10. Why did some researchers believe that choline and lecithin might improve memory? What was the result of research on that question? (p. 519)

11. What is the effect of the vasopressin derivative $AVP_{4-9}$ on attention? (p. 519)

12. Describe changes in the hippocampus from infancy to old age. How do these changes relate to changes in memory? (p. 521)

13. What procedure can lengthen the critical period for development of the visual system in amphibians? How does that procedure relate to LTP? (p. 522)

14. What chemical injection can improve learning and memory in aged mammals? How does that procedure relate to the mechanisms of LTP? (p. 522)

## THOUGHT QUESTION

1. In one experiment (Castellucci & Kandel, 1974), habituation was attributed to a presynaptic change because the size of the quantum remained the same even though the size of the EPSP decreased. What conclusion, if any, could you draw if the size of the quantum decreased during habituation? Can you think of any other way to decide whether an alteration in EPSP size was due to presynaptic or postsynaptic changes?

## SUGGESTIONS FOR FURTHER READING

**Gustafsson, B., & Wigström, H.** (1990). Basic features of long-term potentiation in the hippocampus. *Seminars in the Neurosciences, 2,* 321–333. Review of the main findings on LTP.

**Lynch, G.; McGaugh, J. L.; & Weinberger, N. M.** (1984). *Neurobiology of learning and memory.* New York: Guilford. Collection of 34 chapters by prominent investigators, covering most aspects of current research.

**Thompson, R. F.** (1986). The neurobiology of learning and memory. *Science, 233,* 941–947. A brief treatment of current research issues.

## GLOSSARY

**Alzheimer's disease** condition characterized by memory loss, confusion, depression, restlessness, hallucinations, delusions, and disturbances of eating, sleeping, and other daily activities

**amnesia** memory loss

**anisomycin** drug that inhibits protein synthesis

**anterograde amnesia** inability to store new memories after a certain event

**AVP$_{4-9}$** metabolite of vasopressin that has been found to enhance attention toward the dominant cues in the environment

**calpain** protein that breaks a network of molecules normally found in the dendrites

**classical conditioning** type of conditioning produced by the pairing of two stimuli, one of which evokes an automatic response

**conditioned response (CR)** response evoked by a conditioned stimulus as a result of the pairing of that stimulus with an unconditioned stimulus

**conditioned stimulus (CS)** stimulus that comes to evoke a particular response only after the pairing of that stimulus with an unconditioned stimulus

**consolidation** formation and strengthening of long-term memories

**cooperativity** tendency for nearly simultaneous stimulation by two or more axons to produce more LTP than stimulation by just one

**declarative memory** memory of factual information

**delayed alternation task** task in which animals have to alternate between two responses with a delay between responses

**delayed matching-to-sample task** task in which an animal sees an object and then after a delay must choose the object matching the sample

**delayed nonmatching-to-sample task** task in which an animal sees an object and then after a delay must choose the object not matching the sample

**dorsomedial thalamus** area of the thalamus that sends axons mostly to the frontal cortex; damaged in Korsakoff's syndrome

**engram** the physical representation of learning

**equipotentiality** principle that neurons in various cortical areas contribute almost equally to complex learned behaviors

**explicit memory** memory that one can identify as a memory

**habituation** decrease in response to a stimulus that is presented repeatedly and that is accompanied by no change in other stimuli

**Hebbian synapse** synapse that increases in effectiveness because of simultaneous activity in the presynaptic and postsynaptic neurons

**hippocampal slice** section of hippocampus removed from an animal and maintained in a culture medium

**implicit memory** memory that influences behavior without one's awareness that it refers to a past event

**infant amnesia** tendency for people to recall few specific events that occurred before about age 4 or 5 years

**Korsakoff's syndrome** type of brain damage caused by thiamine deficiency, characterized by apathy, confusion, and memory impairment

**lateral interpositus nucleus** a nucleus of the cerebellum critical for classical conditioning of the eyeblink response in rabbits

**long-term memory** memory for an event that was not currently in one's attention

**long-term potentiation (LTP)** increased responsiveness to axonal input as a result of a previous period of rapidly repeated stimulation

**mass action** principle that all cortical neurons work together during learning; the more neurons, the better the performance

**NMDA receptor** glutamate receptor that also responds to *N*-methyl-D-aspartate

**operant conditioning** type of conditioning in which reinforcement or punishment changes the future probabilities of a given behavior

**perseveration** tendency to make the same response repeatedly, even when it would be appropriate to suppress that response and substitute a different one

**physostigmine** drug that blocks the effects of the enzyme acetylcholinesterase

**plaque** structure formed from degenerating axons and dendrites in the brains of people with Alzheimer's disease

**procedural memory** memory of how to do something

**punishment** event that decreases the future probability of the preceding response

**radial maze** apparatus with many arms radiating from a central point, generally with food at the end of some or all of the arms

**reference memory** memory for general principles

**reinforcement** event that increases the future probability of the preceding response

**retrograde amnesia** loss of memory for events that occurred before brain damage

**scopolamine** drug that blocks acetylcholine synapses

**sensitization** increase in response to mild stimuli as a result of previous exposure to more intense stimuli

**sensory store** extremely brief storage of sensory information

**short-term memory** memory for an event that just happened

**tangle** collection of disrupted axons and dendrites found in the brains of people with Alzheimer's disease

**unconditioned response (UR)** response automatically evoked by an unconditioned stimulus

**unconditioned stimulus (US)** stimulus that automatically evokes an unconditioned response

**Wisconsin card-sorting task** task in which a person first sorts cards according to one rule and then reshuffles them and sorts them according to a different rule

**working memory** memory for current but temporary information

# Recovery from Brain Damage

## MAIN IDEAS

**1.** The human brain can be damaged by a sharp blow, an interruption of blood flow, or several other types of injury. Batteries of tests are available for estimating the location and extent of damage.

**2.** Although both humans and animals typically recover in part from brain damage, behavior is never as securely established as it would be if the brain had never been damaged. Behavior is likely to deteriorate again as a result of stress or fatigue and in old age.

**3.** Many mechanisms contribute to recovery from brain damage, including restoration of undamaged neurons to full activity, regrowth of axons, readjustment of surviving synapses, and behavioral adjustments.

**4.** The degree of recovery from brain damage is sometimes better and sometimes worse if the damage occurs in infancy.

**5.** Several forms of therapy are available for helping people recover from brain damage. At present, most people rely on behavioral and reeducational strategies instead of drugs or other medical interventions.

An American soldier who suffered a wound to the left hemisphere of his brain during the Korean War was at first unable to speak at all. Three months later he was able to speak in short fragments. When he was shown a letterhead, "New York University College of Medicine," and asked to read it, all he could say was, "Doctors—little doctors." Eight years later, when someone asked him again to read the letterhead, he replied, "Is there a catch? It says 'New York University College of Medicine'" (Eidelberg & Stein, 1974).

People with brain damage typically show some behavioral recovery; they are most impaired shortly after the damage and less impaired later on. And yet their recovery is seldom if ever complete. For example, people who recover their speech, like the soldier just described, generally show lasting impairments in finding the right words, expressing themselves clearly, or understanding complex speech by others.

Given that the mammalian nervous system cannot replace lost neurons (with the few exceptions mentioned in Chapter 2), we face the theoretical question of how people recover from brain damage at all. From a practical standpoint, we wonder what therapists could do to facilitate recovery. A further reason to study recovery is that an understanding of recovery may yield new insights into the functioning of the healthy brain.

(Stephen Marks/TIB West.)

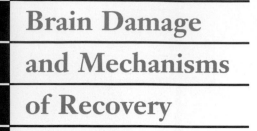

# Brain Damage and Mechanisms of Recovery

Your body is a partially self-repairing machine. You get a cut, it heals; you lose some skin cells, you grow new ones. When you lose neurons, however, you cannot replace them — with a few exceptions such as olfactory receptors. How, then, does recovery take place?

## CAUSES OF HUMAN BRAIN DAMAGE

The human brain can incur damage in many ways. In young adults the most common cause is a sharp blow to the head from a fall, an automobile or motorcycle accident, a violent assault, or other traumas. About 8 million people receive such closed-head injuries each year in the United States; some 400,000 of them suffer a coma and probable brain damage (Peterson, 1980). Head injuries cause damage partly by subjecting the brain to rotational forces that drive brain tissue against the inside of the skull (see Digression 15.1).

In a **stroke,** also known as a **cerebrovascular accident,** a blood clot or other obstruction closes an artery, or an artery ruptures, interrupting the blood flow — and thus the oxygen supply — to an area of the brain. Deprived of oxygen, the neurons die within a few minutes. **Hypertension** (high blood pressure) greatly increases the probability of a stroke, and it is noteworthy that most strokes occur between 10:00 A.M. and noon — when blood pressure is usually highest (J. Marler et al., 1989). Stroke damage may be limited to a fairly sharply defined region; neurons outside that region survive without permanent impairment. Figure 15.1 shows the brain of a person who died immediately after a stroke, the brain of a person who survived for a long time after a stroke, and the brain of a victim of a bullet wound.

Strokes vary in their severity from barely noticeable to immediately fatal. About 30 percent of stroke victims die within the first month after the stroke. Survivors experience various behavioral symptoms, depending on the extent and location of the damage; most experience substantial recovery within the first 2 to

## Why Don't Woodpeckers Give Themselves Concussions?

When a woodpecker strikes its bill against a tree, it repeatedly bangs its head against an unyielding object at a velocity of 6 to 7 meters per second (about 15 miles per hour). How does it escape brain injury?

P. R. A. May and associates (May, Fuster, Haber, & Hirschman, 1979) used slow-motion photography to observe the behavior of woodpeckers. They found that a woodpecker often makes a pair of quick, preliminary taps against the wood before a hard strike, much like a carpenter lining up a hammer with a nail. When it makes the hard strike, it does so in an almost perfectly straight line, keeping its neck rigid. The result is a near absence of rotational forces and whiplash. The fact that woodpeckers are so careful to avoid rotating their heads during impact is one line of evidence (among several others) that rotational forces are a major factor in traumatic brain injuries.

The researchers suggested several implications for football players, race car drivers, and others who wear protective helmets. One implication is that the helmet would give more protection if it extended down to the shoulders, like the metal helmets that medieval knights wore. The advice for non-helmet-wearers: If you see a potential automobile accident or similar trauma on the way, tuck your chin to your chest and tighten your neck muscles.

*A male hairy woodpecker. (Superstock, Inc.)*

3 months and moderate but gradual improvement continuing long after that (Dombovy & Bach-y-Rita, 1988). Many people who survive one stroke have one or more later attacks.

Strokes are rare in young people but become increasingly common beyond age 60 (Kurtzke, 1976). The reported incidence of strokes in the United States declined for a number of years and then rose again, as Figure 15.2 shows. Note that the *reported* incidence is not the same as *actual* incidence, however. The initial decline began with the introduction of treatments to combat hypertension; the later increase probably represents improved reporting of mild strokes after the introduction of CAT scans (Broderick, Phillips, Whisnant, O'Fallon, & Bergstralh, 1989).

A stroke kills neurons in two ways. First, cells that lose their source of oxygen suffocate and die. Second, a ruptured blood vessel may flood nearby neurons with excessive calcium, which can damage and even kill them. That is, many of the neurons actually die from *overstimulation*. Even the cells cut off from oxygen are,

Brain Damage and Mechanisms of Recovery

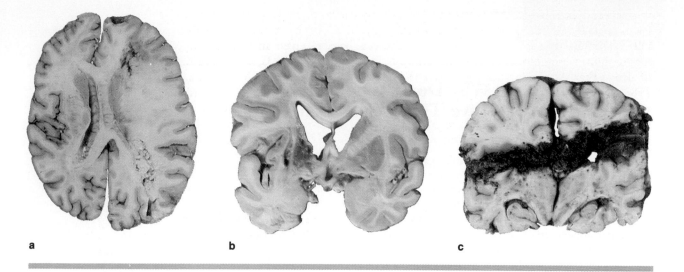

**Figure 15.1**
**Three damaged human brains**
*(a) Brain of a person who died immediately after a stroke. Note the swelling on the right side. (b) Brain of a person who survived for a long time after a stroke. Note the cavities on the left side, where many cells were lost. (c) Brain of a person who suffered a gunshot wound and died immediately. (Photos courtesy of Dana Copeland.)*

**Figure 15.2**
**Reported incidence of strokes in the United States**
*Incidence declined for a number of years because of treatments for hypertension; the later rise is probably due to improved accuracy at detecting mild strokes. (From Broderick, Phillips, Whisnant, O'Fallon, & Bergstralh, 1989.)*

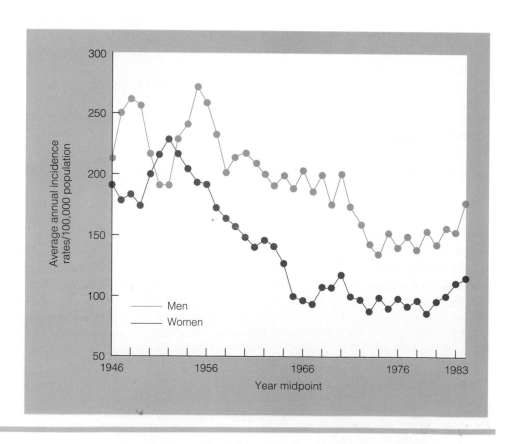

in a sense, dying from overstimulation: Any activity causes them to burn their fuel faster than it can be resupplied. An artificially produced stroke in rats ordinarily kills many neurons, but it kills few cells if the rats have received an injection of magnesium, which blocks all synaptic transmission (Rothman, 1983); an injection of drugs that block glutamate synapses (Kochhar, Zivin, Lyden, & Mazzarella, 1988; Simon, Swan, Griffiths, & Meldrum, 1984); or an injection of insulin, which decreases all neuronal activity (Voll, Whishaw, & Auer, 1989). A temporary reduction in body temperature also decreases the stroke damage, again by decreasing neuronal activity during the interruption of blood flow (Strachan, Whittle, & Miller, 1989).

Besides closed-head injuries and strokes, other sources of brain damage include tumors in the brain, certain bacteria and viruses, drugs and toxic substances, bullet wounds, and exposure of the head to radiation. Huntington's disease and Korsakoff's syndrome cause gradual, diffuse damage to many brain areas. In this chapter we focus mainly on the outcome of strokes and other sudden, localized brain damage.

## DIAGNOSIS OF BRAIN DAMAGE

If neuropsychologists know or suspect that a person has suffered brain damage, they administer certain tests to determine the nature of the behavioral deficits and to infer the location of the damage. Of greater practical importance, they use the results to plan a program of physical therapy, occupational therapy, or speech therapy to help the person regain control over the activities of daily living. Some behavioral deficits—such as impairments of memory, attention, and abstract thinking—signal brain damage without specifying the type or location of the damage (Goodglass & Kaplan, 1979). Other deficits suggest a particular type of damage.

One battery of tests designed to identify the type and extent of brain damage is the **Halstead-Reitan test.** It consists of a series of measurements ranging from speed of finger tapping to comprehension of language, each of which is especially sensitive to a particular type of brain damage. Other items on the test include placing blocks into the correct holes in a board with one's eyes closed, identifying whether two rhythms are the same or different, and connecting 25 numbered circles in order from 1 to 25 (Golden, 1981). The Halstead-Reitan test is lengthy, taking about 8 hours to complete.

Another examination used to test for brain damage is the **Luria-Nebraska neuropsychological battery,** pioneered by the Russian psychologist A. R. Luria and revised by researchers at the University of Nebraska (Golden, 1984). The test consists of 269 items divided into 14 scales. Here are a few examples of items:

- Touch your thumb to each of the other four fingers, one at a time.
- Count the number of tones in a musical sequence.
- Localize where you have been touched on the arm.
- Copy drawings of a circle, square, and triangle.
- Memorize a list of seven words.
- Tap a rhythm to copy one you have heard.

The Luria-Nebraska test can be completed in about 2.5 hours (Golden, 1981). However, many psychologists are not convinced that it provides information as reliable or useful as the Halstead-Reitan test does.

Brain Damage and
Mechanisms of
Recovery

The reason that both batteries include so many items is that a person may fail a given item for any of several reasons. Interpreting the result on one item requires comparing it with results on other items. For example, someone might fail to copy drawings of circles, squares, and triangles because of poor vision, poor coordination of the hand muscles, or inability to remember the instructions. To evaluate the results of this item, it helps to know whether the person has also failed other visual items, other hand coordination items, or all items in general.

## THE PRECARIOUS NATURE OF RECOVERY FROM BRAIN DAMAGE

A person or animal that has recovered from brain damage is never fully the same as before the damage. For analogy, someone with a sore foot may be able to walk just about normally under most conditions. The same person carrying a heavy load uphill, however, may slow down greatly, stumble frequently, or even have to quit altogether. Similarly, people and animals that have recovered from brain damage may perform almost normally under most conditions, but their behavior deteriorates under mildly difficult conditions that would scarcely bother a person without brain damage. Further, even after they have recovered, brain-damaged individuals make more frequent errors than uninjured individuals do (Chappell & LeVere, 1988).

### How Stress Impairs Recovered Behavior

Someone who loses the ability to speak after a stroke and then gradually regains it may lose it again, temporarily, after a couple of beers or at the end of a tiring day. The behavior of brain-damaged rats also deteriorates under stress or fatigue. For example, in a cool room, both normal rats and rats that have recovered from lateral hypothalamic lesions increase their food intake. (Eating and digesting food generate body heat.) If the room gets colder, a normal rat eats even more, but the animal recovered from brain damage may fail to eat altogether, especially if only dry food and water are available (Snyder & Stricker, 1985).

A second example: A normal rat reacts to hypovolemia (decreased blood volume) by drinking and reacts to decreased blood glucose by eating. By contrast, a rat recovered from lateral hypothalamic damage temporarily acts the way it did just after the damage: It ignores food and water, does not react to sensory stimuli, and hardly moves (Stricker, Cooper, Marshall, & Zigmond, 1979).

A third example: After damage to one side of the cerebral cortex, especially the parietal cortex, both humans and rats pay less attention to stimuli on the opposite side of the body. At first they may ignore stimuli on the opposite side altogether. This reaction is known as **sensory neglect** (see Figure 15.3). In milder cases or after partial recovery, they respond to stimuli on the side opposite the brain damage *if* those stimuli are presented alone. If a competing stimulus is present on the normal side of the body, they respond to that stimulus first. Human patients say that the stimulus on the normal side feels stronger. This reaction is known as **sensory extinction.**

Eventually, both people and rats respond to stimuli on both sides equally. For example, a rat with strings tied to both forelimbs works equally hard at trying to remove one as the other. However, under mild stress or after a slight change in the environment, the rat loses its recovered behavior. If the experimenter simply

Figure 15.3
Behavior of a rat after
damage to one side of
the cerebral cortex

Immediate effect: Sensory neglect. Rat ignores sensory stimulus on opposite side of body.

Later effect: Sensory extinction. Rat responds first on the normal side. It responds to the string on the opposite side later.

Still later: Rat responds to both sides equally *unless* the environment is changed or the rat is stressed.

turns on the lights or opens the cage door, the rat temporarily goes back to paying more attention to the normal side (Schallert & Whishaw, 1984). Presumably, humans also revert to sensory neglect or sensory extinction under conditions of stress or an altered environment that would scarcely affect a normal individual.

## The Loss of Recovered Behavior in Old Age

A recovered rat also deteriorates more in old age than normal rats do. In rats as in humans, a certain number of neurons die in old age. If the brain is initially intact, the loss of neurons may not impair behavior noticeably. A brain-damaged animal cannot afford to lose any additional neurons, however. By the time a rat that has recovered from lateral hypothalamic damage is 2 years old (old age for a rat), it begins to lose its recovered feeding and drinking behaviors and its responsiveness to sensory stimuli. Eventually the rat returns to a condition approximating its behavior just after the lesion (Schallert, 1983).

The same principle may hold for humans, Timothy Schallert (1983) speculates. For example, Parkinson's disease may be the result of brain damage suffered early in life, probably not even noticed at the time if it was due to the gradual effects of toxins. When the person reaches old age, losing a small number of additional neurons greatly impairs behavior.

## POSSIBLE MECHANISMS OF RECOVERY FROM BRAIN DAMAGE

When the behavior of a human or any other mammal recovers, even slightly, from the effects of brain damage, it is a challenge to try to understand how the recovery took place. Unlike the skin, which can make new cells to replace any that are lost, the brain cannot recover by making new neurons.

A simple, popular assumption is that some other area of the brain takes over the functions of the damaged area. That assumption is valid only in a limited sense. Someone who has injured her left leg may learn to walk on her right leg and crutches. In a sense we may say that the right leg and the two arms have taken over the function of the damaged leg, although they certainly are not transformed into a left leg. In a similar way, a blind person learns to pay more attention to auditory and somatic stimuli; if an animal is blinded throughout infancy, the nonvisual areas of its cortex may grow larger than usual (Burnstine, Greenough, & Tees, 1984). But such changes simply make better use of the nonvisual information available; nonvisual areas of the brain do not take over visual functions.

A brain-damaged individual can recover lost functions by structural changes in the surviving neurons or by learning new ways to solve old problems. Let us consider some of the ways the brain reacts to damage.

## Diaschisis and Its Reduction

An individual's behavioral deficit after brain damage reflects more than just the loss of cells. Ordinarily, axons from each neuron provide stimulation that helps to keep other neurons active. When a neuron dies, the other neurons that depended on it for input become less active, and the total behavioral disturbance includes the results from inactivating distant cells. **Diaschisis** (di-AS-ki-sis, from a Greek term meaning "to shock throughout") refers to the decreased activity of neurons after they have lost part of their input because other neurons were damaged (Feeney & Baron, 1986).

If diaschisis is an important contributor to behavioral deficits following brain damage, then stimulant drugs should promote recovery from the damage. In a series of experiments, D. M. Feeney and colleagues measured the behavioral effects of cortical damage in rats and cats. Depending on the location of the damage, the animals showed impairments in coordinated movement or depth perception. Injecting amphetamine (which stimulates dopamine and norepinephrine synapses) significantly enhanced the behaviors, and animals that practiced the behaviors under the influence of amphetamine showed long-lasting benefits. Injecting the drug haloperidol (which blocks those synapses) impaired the recovery of behavior (Feeney & Sutton, 1988; Feeney, Sutton, Boyeson, Hovda, & Dail, 1985; Hovda & Feeney, 1989; Sutton, Hovda, & Feeney, 1989).

Similarly, damage to cells in the lateral hypothalamus decreases the activity in certain areas of the cerebral cortex where lateral hypothalamic neurons send their axons (Kolb & Whishaw, 1977). The suppression of cortical activity contributes to the loss of feeding, drinking, and responsiveness to sensory stimuli ordinarily observed after lateral hypothalamic lesions. Behavioral recovery depends partly on a gradual increase in activity by cortical cells.

Reduction of diaschisis also contributes to the recovery of spinal reflexes after a cut through the spinal cord. After such a cut, the neurons below the cut lose their input from long axons from the brain and upper levels of the spinal cord. Consequently, the neurons below the cut temporarily become unresponsive to all stimulation; even though they continue to receive input from skin receptors, they produce no reflexive responses. Days later, chemical changes in the lower spinal neurons compensate for the loss, and the excitability returns.

## Recovery by the Regrowth of Axons

Although a destroyed cell body cannot be replaced, damaged axons do grow back under certain circumstances. A neuron of the peripheral nervous system has its cell body in the spinal cord and an axon that extends into the periphery. When such an axon is crushed, the degenerated portion grows back toward the periph-

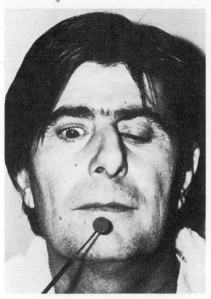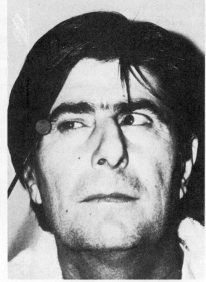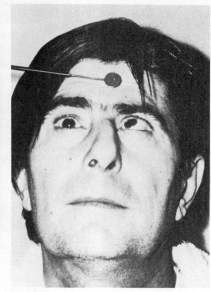

**Figure 15.4**
**Example of what can happen if damaged axons regenerate
to incorrect muscles**
*Damaged axons to the muscles of the patient's right eye regenerated but attached incorrectly.
When he looks down, his right eyelid opens wide instead of closing, as the other eyelid does. His
eye movements are frequently misaimed and he has trouble moving his right eye upward or to the
left. (From P. Thomas, 1988.)*

ery at a rate of about 1 mm per day. If it is a myelinated axon, the regenerating
axon follows the myelin path back to its original target, whether muscle, gland, or
sensory receptor. If the axon was cut instead of crushed, the myelin on the two
sides of the cut does not line up correctly, and the regenerating axon may not
have a path to follow. Then, although each axon will grow back to *some* target, it
may not be the correct target, as Figure 15.4 illustrates.

Within the mammalian brain or spinal cord, a damaged axon regenerates
only briefly over an insignificant distance, if at all. That is why the paralysis
caused by spinal cord injury is permanent. However, after a cut through the optic
nerve or the spinal cord of certain species of fish, enough axons regenerate across
the cut to restore fairly normal functioning, even though the connections are not
the same as before (Bernstein & Gelderd, 1970; Rovainen, 1976; Scherer, 1986;
Selzer, 1978). Why do damaged axons regenerate in the central and peripheral
nervous systems of fish and in the peripheral nervous system of mammals, but not
in the central nervous system of mammals? If we find the answer, perhaps we can
find some way to make such regeneration possible in mammals, including humans.

**Inhibiting the Growth of Scar Tissue** One impediment to regeneration of axons in the mammalian central nervous system is that astroglia form a thick layer
of scar tissue at the point of injury in mammals. (Much less scar tissue forms in
fish.) A regenerating axon stops growing when it reaches an astroglial layer, partly

because the scar tissue forms a mechanical barrier but mostly because the astroglia secrete chemicals that interfere with axonal growth (Liuzzi & Lasek, 1987).

Several attempts have been made to promote recovery in the mammalian spinal cord by trying to reduce the formation of scar tissue. In the 1950s and early 1960s, several investigators followed up on reports that a bacterial infection inhibits the growth of scar tissue, for unknown reasons. A number of animals were given daily injections of bacteria after spinal cord injury. Even when the bacteria slightly reduced the formation of scar tissue, however, very few axons regenerated across the cut, and most of those failed to make lasting synapses (McMasters, 1962; Scott & Clemente, 1955; Windle, Littrell, Smart, & Joralemon, 1956).

**Bridging a Cut in the Spinal Cord** During development, the bones of the spinal column continue to grow after the nervous tissue of the spinal cord has stopped (see Figure 4.7). Consequently, the spinal cord is under a slight mechanical tension. When the spinal cord is cut, the lower half may pull away from the upper half (Gearhart, Oster-Granite, & Guth, 1979). Thus, even if an axon regenerated, it would have to traverse a substantial distance to reach the other half of the cord.

One attempt to deal with this difficulty was to construct a bridge made of peripheral nerve and to attach it to the two ends of a cut spinal cord, as S. David and A. J. Aguayo (1981) did with rats. Axons that entered the bridge did not have to cross scar tissue; furthermore, they had myelin sheaths as guides between the two ends of the cord. Axons in the bridge regenerated substantial distances, up to 3 cm, until they reached the other half of the cut spinal cord. When they reached that point, however, the growth stopped.

One implication of these results is that axons in the central nervous system *can* regenerate over significant distances. Another implication is that simply getting across the cut is not enough.

**Chemicals That Promote Regeneration** The regeneration of an axon may depend on promotion by certain chemicals, produced either in the axon itself or by surrounding cells. Perhaps such chemicals are present in fish and in the mammalian peripheral nervous system but absent in the mammalian central nervous system. In David and Aguayo's axon bridge experiment, axons in the mammalian central nervous system regenerated much more than normal because they grew through a bridge of peripheral nerve, which provided the chemical environment that promotes regeneration. Several other experiments have confirmed that CNS axons will regenerate along a transplanted segment of peripheral nerve but not along a segment of transplanted axons from the brain (Friedman & Aguayo, 1985; Schwab & Thoenen, 1985).

Researchers may be able to identify chemicals that increase regeneration. For example, while a rat's damaged peripheral nerve is regenerating, protein synthesis and modification increase tenfold; protein synthesis does not increase in a damaged optic nerve, which does not regenerate (Shyne-Athwal, Riccio, Chakraborty, & Ingoglia, 1986). Large quantities of a particular protein accumulate in regenerating peripheral axons. The same protein has also been found in high concentration in the developing neurons of infant rats, but it does not accumulate in damaged axons of the central nervous system (Müller, Gebicke-Härter, Hangen, & Shooter, 1985). Although the function of this protein is not known, such a protein could easily play an important role in regeneration.

In fish, the nonneuronal cells that surround a damaged axon of either the central or peripheral nervous system release chemicals that promote regrowth. One group of experimenters cut the optic nerves of fish and of rabbits. The optic nerve of the fish regenerated; that of the rabbits did not. Then they took a segment of regenerating fish nerve and placed it near an injured rabbit optic nerve. The fish tissues apparently released a chemical that promotes regeneration, because the optic nerve of the rabbit regenerated in part (Schwartz et al., 1985).

These results suggest that fish nerves regenerate more than mammalian nerves in the central nervous system because the fish axons themselves or the surrounding cells release chemicals that make regrowth possible. Perhaps if we can find ways to produce large amounts of the right chemical, we may enable axons of the mammalian central nervous system to regenerate, too.

## Sprouting

After damage to one set of axons, uninjured axons in the surrounding area may form new branches, or **collateral sprouts,** that attach to vacant synapses (see Figure 15.5). Gradually, over several months, the sprouts fill in most but not all of the vacated synapses (Matthews, Cotman, & Lynch, 1976). An axon sprouts to occupy such synapses only if it previously terminated in the same general area as the damaged axon (Cotman & Nieto-Sampedro, 1982; Finger & Stein, 1982). In certain cases, however, axons may sprout to make functional synapses at sites that previously responded to a different neurotransmitter (Moore, 1974; Moore, Björklund, & Stenevi, 1971; Raisman, 1969; Raisman & Field, 1973). We must assume that the sprouted axons induce the postsynaptic cells to manufacture different synaptic receptors.

Sprouting is probably a normal condition, not one that occurs only in response to brain damage (Cotman & Nieto-Sampedro, 1984). Periodically old synapses break and new ones replace them via sprouting; in time, some of these new ones may be broken and replaced themselves.

Sprouting will be most useful in combating the effects of brain damage if the sprouting axon is similar to the damaged one; in that case, it provides a good sub-

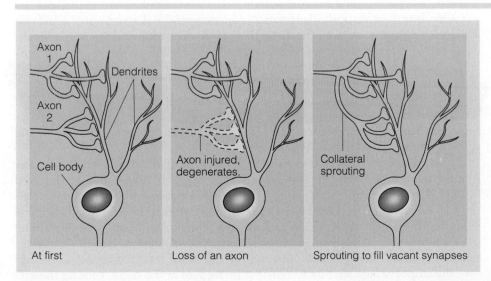

**Figure 15.5
Collateral sprouting**

stitute. However, when an axon sprouts to occupy the synapses previously occupied by an unrelated axon, the usefulness of sprouting is less certain. Perhaps the individual learns to use the new connections appropriately, or perhaps the new connections interfere with normal behavior.

Evidence exists that sprouting is at least sometimes beneficial, although that evidence is largely indirect. For example, **gangliosides** (a class of glycolipids — that is, combined carbohydrate and fat molecules) are believed to enhance collateral sprouting, among other effects. Gangliosides, which are found on the membranes of neurons, reduce the behavioral deficits caused by damage to the caudate nucleus (Sabel, Slavin, & Stein, 1984). Moreover, the time course of behavioral recovery after brain damage matches the time course of sprouting.

In one experiment using rats, connections from one side of the cerebral cortex to one side of the hippocampus were destroyed. Over the next 2 weeks, axons from the opposite side of the cerebral cortex formed collateral sprouts onto the hippocampus on the damaged side. The behaviors that were initially impaired after the lesion recovered over the same two weeks (Scheff & Cotman, 1977). In a follow-up study, researchers measured the degree of behavioral recovery and the amount of electrical activity in the hippocampus. As the electrical activity increased (apparently reflecting collateral sprouting), the behavior recovered proportionately. The animals with the most rapid collateral sprouting had the most rapid behavioral recovery (Reeves & Smith, 1987).

## Denervation Supersensitivity

A postsynaptic cell that is deprived of synaptic input for a long time becomes more sensitive to the neurotransmitter. For example, a normal muscle cell responds to the neurotransmitter acetylcholine only at the neuromuscular junction. If the axon is cut, or if it is inactive for days, the muscle cell builds additional receptors, becoming sensitive to acetylcholine over a wider area of its surface (Johns & Thesleff, 1961; Levitt-Gilmour & Salpeter, 1986). The same process occurs in neurons. Heightened sensitivity to the neurotransmitter after the destruction of incoming axons is known as **denervation supersensitivity** (Glick, 1974). Heightened sensitivity as a result of inactivity by incoming axons is called **disuse supersensitivity.** Both kinds of supersensitivity can result from increased numbers of receptors on the surface of the cell or from changes within the cell.

One way to investigate denervation supersensitivity is to remove dopamine synapses selectively by injecting **6-OHDA (6-hydroxydopamine)** into relevant parts of the brain. Because 6-OHDA is chemically similar to dopamine and norepinephrine, the neurons that release these neurotransmitters recognize 6-OHDA and absorb it. After entering the neurons, it is oxidized into toxic chemicals that destroy those neurons. As Figure 15.6 shows, injecting 6-OHDA on one side of the brain increases the number of dopamine receptors on that side (LaHoste & Marshall, 1989). Sometimes it also increases the metabolic rate of the cells (Kozlowski & Marshall, 1981).

These changes contribute to recovery by increasing neurons' responses to the limited amount of dopamine that remains. In one study, experimenters injected 6-OHDA on one side of rats' brains, damaging dopamine neurons on that side only (see Figure 15.7). They waited weeks for postsynaptic neurons to become supersensitive to dopamine. Then they injected the rats with either amphetamine or apomorphine. Amphetamine causes dopamine-containing axons to release more neurotransmitter. Because one side of the brain was lacking dopamine axons, the amphetamine stimulated only the intact side of the brain, causing the rats

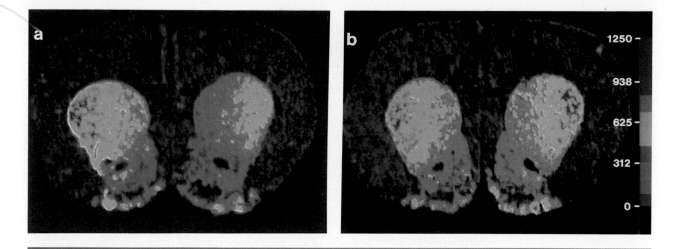

## Figure 15.6
## Responses of dopamine receptors to decreased input

*In these autoradiography slides, red indicates the highest amount of radioactive binding, followed by yellow, green, and blue. (a) An injection of 6-OHDA destroyed dopamine axons in the hemisphere on the left. In response, that hemisphere developed an increased number of $D_2$ receptors, as indicated by increased binding of a radioactive drug that attaches to those receptors. (b) Rats in another group also received a 6-OHDA lesion to one hemisphere, but then they received daily injections of a drug that blocks $D_2$ receptors. Here, $D_2$ receptors increased equally in both hemispheres. (From LaHoste & Marshall, 1989.)*

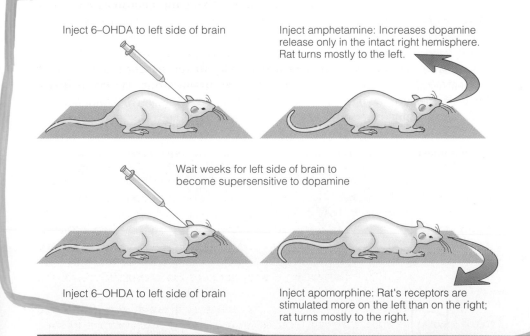

Inject 6–OHDA to left side of brain

Inject amphetamine: Increases dopamine release only in the intact right hemisphere. Rat turns mostly to the left.

Wait weeks for left side of brain to become supersensitive to dopamine

Inject 6–OHDA to left side of brain

Inject apomorphine: Rat's receptors are stimulated more on the left than on the right; rat turns mostly to the right.

## Figure 15.7
## Results of an experiment demonstrating denervation supersensitivity

*Injecting 6-OHDA destroys axons releasing dopamine on one side of the brain. Later, amphetamine stimulates only the intact side of the brain because it cannot cause axons to release dopamine on the damaged side. Apomorphine stimulates the damaged side more strongly because it directly stimulates dopamine receptors and the dopamine receptors have become supersensitive on that side. (Based on data from Marshall, Drew, & Neve, 1983.)*

to turn in one direction (toward the brain-injured side). **Apomorphine** is a morphine derivative that directly stimulates dopamine receptors. Because of denervation supersensitivity, apomorphine strongly stimulates the damaged side of the brain, causing the rats to turn in the opposite direction (Marshall, Drew, & Neve, 1983). These results (shown in Figure 15.7) indicate that the denervated side of the brain has become supersensitive to dopamine and to drugs that stimulate dopamine receptors.

## Activation of Previously Ineffective Synapses

As we saw in Chapter 8, during development many axons form tentative connections with a given postsynaptic neuron. Through a competitive process the postsynaptic neuron strengthens the synapses with one or more of those axons. The rejected axons, however, may remain attached to the cell, even though their synapses are ineffective, or silent. If an axon with active synapses is destroyed, the competition reopens and one of the previously rejected axons may form effective synapses (Wall, 1988).

For example, one section in the primary somatosensory cortex of a monkey is responsive to touch stimuli from the five fingers of one hand, as Figure 15.8a shows. Although each set of neurons responds to synapses representing a given finger, it probably has silent synapses representing the adjacent fingers. In one study, experimenters amputated finger 3 in an owl monkey. The neurons that had previously responded to it became temporarily inactive. As time passed, more and more of them became responsive to finger 2, finger 4, or part of the palm, until eventually the cortex had the pattern of responsiveness we see in Figure 15.8b (Kaas, Merzenich, & Killackey, 1983; Merzenich et al., 1984). Such reorganization does not cause fingers 2 and 4 to feel like the lost finger. When humans lose a finger, they become more sensitive in the neighboring fingers, better able to localize a sensation on one of them.

The general point here is that the connections from the sensory receptors to the brain are not permanently fixed. Synapses that once were silent may become functional when other synapses become inactive. Exactly how they do so is another matter; one possibility is sprouting by a previously inactive axon, and another is denervation supersensitivity in the postsynaptic neuron.

**Figure 15.8
Changes in the representation of the fingers in the somatosensory cortex of an owl monkey after amputation of the third finger**

*Note that the cortical area previously responsive to the third finger ($D_3$) becomes responsive to the second and fourth fingers ($D_2$ and $D_4$) and part of the palm ($P_3$). (Based on Kaas, Merzenich, & Killackey, 1983.)*

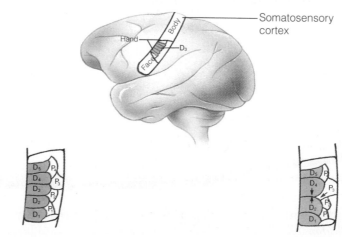

**a** Normal (before amputation)

**b** After amputation of 3rd digit

**Table 15.1 Summary of Possible Mechanisms of Recovery from Brain Damage**

1. Return to normal function by undamaged neurons: Reduction of diaschisis

2. Regeneration of damaged axons (occurs in the central and peripheral nervous systems of fish; occurs only in the peripheral nervous system for mammals)

3. Changes at synapses in the brain:
   Sprouting
   Denervation supersensitivity
   Activation of previously ineffective synapses

4. Learned adjustments in behavior

## Learned Adjustments in Behavior

Much of the recovery that takes place after brain damage is learned; the brain-damaged individual makes better use of abilities unaffected by the damage. For example, someone who has lost vision in all but the center of the visual field may at first fail to see some of the environment. Later, the person moves his or her head back and forth to compensate for the loss in peripheral vision (Marshall, 1985).

A brain-damaged person or animal may also learn to use abilities that appear to be lost but actually are just impaired. For example, as discussed in Chapter 9, a monkey that receives no sensation from one arm does not use it in walking. The monkey is clearly capable of using it, however, because if sensation from the other arm is cut off as well, the monkey will use both arms. When it has one normal arm and one with no sensation, the monkey apparently finds it easier to use the normal one than to use both.

Similarly, many victims of brain damage find it easier, especially at first, to struggle along without using some ability that has been partly impaired by the damage. Many of them are capable of doing more than they are doing and more than they realize they can do. Therapy for brain-damaged people sometimes focuses on showing them how much they are already capable of doing and encouraging them to practice those skills.

Table 15.1 summarizes the mechanisms we have discussed that may contribute to recovery from brain damage.

## SUMMARY

1. Strokes, rare in young people, are a common cause of brain damage in old age. A sudden blow to the head is a more common cause of brain damage in young people. (p. 528)

2. The Halstead-Reitan and Luria-Nebraska batteries assess brain damage. Because performance on a given item may be impaired for many reasons, these tests compare a person's performance across a variety of items. (p. 531)

3. People and animals that have recovered from brain damage are more likely than normal individuals are to deteriorate under conditions of stress or in old age. (p. 532)

4. After brain damage, neurons remote from the site of damage may become inactive because they receive less input than usual. Behavioral recovery from brain damage depends partly on increased activity by these remote neurons; stimulant drugs promote recovery by facilitating activity in surviving cells. (p. 534)

5. A cut axon may regenerate in the peripheral nervous system of a mammal and in either the central or peripheral nervous system of certain fish. Several explanations have been proposed for why cut axons do not regenerate in the mammalian central nervous system. (p. 534)

6. When one set of axons dies, neighboring axons may under certain conditions sprout new branches to innervate the vacant synapses. (p. 537)

7. If many of the axons innervating a given postsynaptic neuron die or become inactive, that neuron's sensitivity to its remaining synaptic inputs may increase. (p. 538)

8. After brain damage, some of the synapses that had previously been silent in the brain may become active, causing certain neurons to respond to stimuli that had not activated them previously. (p. 540)

9. Much of the recovery that takes place after brain damage does not require structural changes in the brain; it depends on learned changes in behavior to take advantage of the skills that remain, even if they are impaired. (p. 541)

## REVIEW QUESTIONS

1. What is a stroke? (p. 528)

2. Besides stroke, what are some other causes of human brain damage? (p. 528)

3. Why do the Halstead-Reitan and Luria-Nebraska tests assess many separate behaviors? (p. 532)

4. In what ways is a person or animal that has recovered from brain damage different from one that has never suffered brain damage? (p. 532)

5. The drug haloperidol is given to many patients suffering from schizophrenia and several other psychological disorders. Why would it be unwise to administer haloperidol to a patient who had recently suffered a stroke? (p. 534)

6. Give three reasons why axons may fail to regenerate across a cut through the mammalian spinal cord. (p. 535)

7. What is the evidence that collateral sprouting sometimes aids in recovery from brain damage? (p. 537)

8. Why does 6-OHDA destroy only the neurons that release dopamine or norepinephrine as their neurotransmitters? (p. 538)

9. How may the functions of a part of the brain change when previously silent synapses become active? (p. 540)

10. What shows that brain-damaged animals are sometimes capable of behaviors they do not spontaneously engage in? Describe one example. (p. 541)

## THOUGHT QUESTION

1. Ordinarily patients with Parkinson's disease move very slowly, if at all. However, during an emergency (such as a fire in the building), some such patients move rapidly and vigorously. Suggest a possible explanation.

## SUGGESTIONS FOR FURTHER READING

**DeMille, A.** (1981). *Reprieve: A memoir.* Garden City, NY: Doubleday. A stroke victim's own account of her stroke and recovery from it, with interpolated commentary by a neurologist, Fred Plum.

**Freed, W. J.; Medinaceli, L.; & Wyatt, R. M.** (1985). Promoting functional plasticity in the damaged nervous system. *Science, 227,* 1544–1552. A review article that focuses largely on the regeneration of nerves in both the central and peripheral nervous systems.

**Marshall, J. F.** (1985). Neural plasticity and recovery of function after brain injury. *International Review of Neurobiology, 26,* 201–247. A general review of mechanisms of recovery.

# Factors Influencing Recovery from Brain Damage

If two individuals suffer the same brain damage, one of them may show more severe symptoms than the other does. Why? Sometimes it is because they were different ages at the time of the injury. In other cases it is because one suffered the damage suddenly and the other gradually. Still another possibility is that one received therapy after the damage.

## EFFECTS OF AGE AT THE TIME OF THE DAMAGE

According to the **Kennard principle,** named after Margaret Kennard, who first offered this generalization (Kennard, 1938), recovery from brain damage early in life will be more complete than recovery from damage later in life. A child whose left hemisphere is damaged eventually gains or regains a greater ability to speak than an adult with similar damage. A child with damage to the sensory or motor cortex also shows greater gains than an adult with similar damage (Hécaen, Perenin, & Jeannerod, 1984).

The Kennard principle is no more than partly correct, however. Depending on the location of the damage and the behavioral deficits studied, the effects of early brain damage may be greater than, less than, or the same as the effects of adult brain damage (Kolb & Whishaw, 1989; Stein, Finger, & Hart, 1983). For example, although damage limited to, say, the motor cortex of a young child may only moderately impair motor control, it is likely to produce other, more generalized difficulties not found after adult brain damage, such as slow learning and a low IQ score (Taylor, 1984).

Moreover, the effect of age on recovery from brain damage depends on the cause of damage. Although children may recover better than adults from the destruction of a limited area of the brain, they recover less from infection, poor nutrition, inadequate oxygen, or exposure of the brain to alcohol or other drugs (O'Leary & Boll, 1984). Such factors disrupt the organization of developing neurons without killing them, so the neurons may make abnormal connections. The result is a generalized loss of sensory and motor functions and intelligence.

Why might the effects of infant brain damage be different from those of adult brain damage? We can identify several possible reasons.

## Effects on Other, Still Developing Neurons

In normal development, the immature brain produces many more neurons and synapses than will survive to adulthood, as we saw in Chapter 8. As development proceeds, many of the extra neurons and extra connections are lost. If damage strikes during this early stage of development, the brain can react in ways that would be impossible later in life. When one set of neurons dies, a second set that might otherwise have perished may survive instead. Alternatively, when one set dies, a second set may die, too, if it depends on the first set as a source of input or as a primary target of output.

Both of those possibilities do occur. First, after complete removal of one hemisphere of a rat brain in infancy, the other hemisphere increases in thickness (Kolb, Sutherland, & Whishaw, 1983). No such increase occurs after removal of a hemisphere in adult rats. Evidently, neurons of each hemisphere compete with neurons of the other hemisphere for the chance to survive; if one hemisphere is damaged, a greater percentage of cells in the opposite hemisphere can survive.

Second, after removal of the anterior portion of the cortex in infant rats, the posterior portion of the cortex develops less than normal (Kolb & Holmes, 1983). Apparently neurons in the posterior cortex require interaction with neurons in the anterior cortex to survive. The same is not true in adulthood. For that reason, damage to the anterior cortex affects the behavior of infant rats more than it does the behavior of adults, even though damage to an entire hemisphere produces *weaker* effects in infants.

## Effects on Axons

Damage to any structure in the adult brain destroys not only the neurons with cell bodies in that area but also neurons whose axons go into or through that structure. However, if a structure is damaged early in infancy, before a certain set of axons has entered the area, those axons may grow around the damaged area and still reach their target (Bregman & Goldberger, 1982). Thus, brain damage in infancy may spare axons that would have been destroyed by similar damage in adulthood. Even if axons are destroyed, infant axons have some potential to regenerate, but adult axons in the CNS do not (Kalil, 1988).

If a structure is damaged before the axons that ordinarily innervate it have reached it, those axons may innervate a neighboring structure. For example, suppose the superior colliculus on the left side of an infant hamster's brain is damaged before the optic nerve reaches it. When axons of the optic nerve do reach the damaged area, they cross to attach to the superior colliculus on the right side instead (see Figure 15.9). The hamsters then show some spatial orientation toward what they see in the right visual field. Unfortunately, they orient in the wrong direction, however. That is, a hamster that sees something on the right turns to the left. It is as if the right superior colliculus interprets all the input it receives as coming from the left visual field as usual (Schneider & Jhaveri, 1974). Although this odd recovery may not do the animal any good, it provides an example of how early brain damage can lead to a different pattern of connections than adult damage — possibly better, possibly worse.

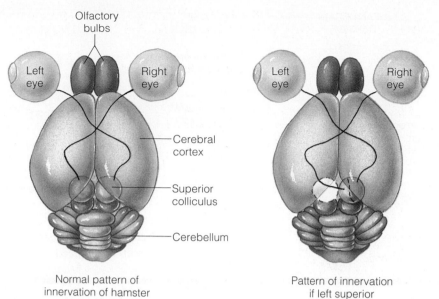

**Figure 15.9**

*If the superior colliculus of a newborn hamster is destroyed on one side, the axons that normally innervate the damaged side go to the opposite superior colliculus. (Based on results of Schneider & Jhaveri, 1974.)*

Olfactory bulbs

Left eye

Right eye

Cerebral cortex

Superior colliculus

Cerebellum

Normal pattern of innervation of hamster superior colliculus

Left eye

Right eye

Pattern of innervation if left superior colliculus is destroyed in newborn

## Effects on Sprouting and Denervation Supersensitivity

Various types of brain damage elicit more vigorous collateral sprouting in young animals than in adults. After damage to one source of input to the hippocampus, axons from the other sources sprout to fill the vacant synapses. The sprouting takes place more rapidly in young rats than in adults, and it reinnervates a higher percentage of the vacant synapses (McWilliams & Lynch, 1983, 1984).

After partial damage to dopamine pathways in the brain, many neurons increase their sensitivity to the remaining dopamine — that is, they display denervation supersensitivity. In one study, aging mice (24 to 26 months old) failed to show denervation supersensitivity after loss of dopamine input (Randall, Severson, & Finch, 1981). Yet in a different study, 27- to 28-month-old rats showed just as much denervation supersensitivity as younger rats and just as much behavioral recovery after damage to axons containing dopamine (Marshall, Drew, & Neve, 1983). Perhaps sprouting and denervation supersensitivity deteriorate in old age under some circumstances but not others.

## Effects on Development of Other Structures

Injury at an early age may damage a structure before it is mature enough to contribute to behavior. Patricia Goldman found that monkeys whose **dorsolateral prefrontal cortex** (an area of the prefrontal cortex) had been injured in infancy showed only a moderate deficit on a delayed alternation task, in which they had to alternate between choosing an object on the left and choosing an object on the right. A year after the injury, they performed surprisingly well, almost as well as other 1-year-old monkeys without brain damage. When tested 2 years after the

Factors Influencing Recovery from Brain Damage

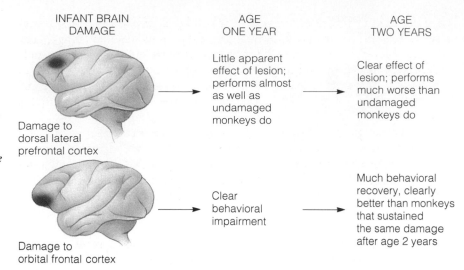

**Figure 15.10
Summary of
Patricia Goldman's
experiments on brain
damage in infant
monkeys**
*After damage to the dorsolateral prefrontal cortex, monkeys seem relatively unimpaired at age 1 year but more severely impaired later, when this area ordinarily matures. After damage to the orbital frontal cortex, monkeys show a clear behavioral impairment at first but substantial recovery later.*

INFANT BRAIN
DAMAGE

AGE
ONE YEAR

AGE
TWO YEARS

Damage to
dorsal lateral
prefrontal cortex

Little apparent
effect of lesion;
performs almost
as well as
undamaged
monkeys do

Clear effect of
lesion; performs
much worse than
undamaged
monkeys do

Damage to
orbital frontal cortex

Clear
behavioral
impairment

Much behavioral
recovery, clearly
better than monkeys
that sustained
the same damage
after age 2 years

lesion, however, the monkeys that had received the damage in infancy showed clear behavioral deficits (Goldman, 1971). Apparently, the dorsolateral cortex does not mature until a monkey is about 2 years old. The monkeys tested at 1 year of age were unimpaired because this structure did not contribute much to behavior at that age anyway. The effects of the lesion became apparent when the structure would normally have matured (see Figure 15.10).

In other cases the deficit caused by a lesion in one area may *decrease* when another area matures. If infant monkeys receive damage to the **orbital frontal cortex** (an anterior area of the prefrontal cortex), they show deficits at age 1 year on the delayed alternation task. By age 2 years, the behavior improves considerably. If the damage occurs at age 2 or later, however, the monkeys show no such improvement (Goldman, 1976; Miller, Goldman, & Rosvold, 1973). Early damage to the orbital frontal cortex apparently leads other, later developing brain areas — probably including the dorsolateral cortex — to change their organization in a way that compensates for the damage. By age 2, the normal functions of these other areas are already established, and they cannot reorganize in response to brain damage elsewhere. (See Figure 15.10.)

## DIFFERENCES BETWEEN SLOW-ONSET AND RAPID-ONSET LESIONS

After sudden damage to the motor cortex on both sides of its brain, a monkey suffers a total and permanent loss of fine movements. However, if the damage occurs in several stages, with a couple of weeks to recover from one small brain injury before the next one occurs, the monkey may continue to walk and to carry on other activities even though the entire motor cortex is ultimately destroyed (Travis & Woolsey, 1956). The **serial-lesion effect** refers to better recovery after a series of small lesions than after a single lesion of the same total size.

The serial-lesion effect does not occur with all kinds of brain damage; sometimes a series of small lesions produces just as great an effect as one large lesion. When the serial-lesion effect does occur, two explanations are possible: (1) Gradual brain damage may allow for collateral sprouting or other structural changes that cannot occur after sudden, complete damage, or (2) gradual damage may enable the individual to learn new ways of coping and better ways to use the abilities spared by the lesion.

Here is an experiment that supports the second interpretation: After bilateral damage to their somatosensory and motor cortex, rats display a variety of sensory and motor impairments from which they recover only slightly. After unilateral damage to the same areas, rats display unilateral impairments from which they make substantial recovery—but only if they are allowed to practice the behaviors. If they then sustain damage on the opposite side of the brain, the behaviors that recovered after the first damage remain intact (deCastro & Zrull, 1988). Evidently the rats recovered from the first damage largely through some learning process. The learned behaviors survived after damage to the opposite side of the brain.

## THERAPIES FOR BRAIN DAMAGE

After someone suffers brain damage, physicians, physical therapists, and others try to help the person recover. Although therapy at this time consists almost entirely of supervised practice of the impaired behaviors, direct intervention in the brain may become possible in the future.

### Behavioral Interventions

You may fail to find a book that you know the library used to have, either because the library has lost or misplaced the book or because it has lost the card that records the book's location. Similarly, a brain-damaged person or animal may seem to have forgotten a particular skill either because it completely lost the skill or because it "cannot find" it. Therapists help brain-damaged people find their lost skills or learn to use their remaining abilities more effectively.

For example, some people with frontal lobe damage behave in socially inappropriate ways, such as using obscene language, failing to wash and bathe, and making lewd sexual overtures to strangers. Although they seem to have lost their social skills, they remain capable of acceptable behaviors. Therapists work with them, perhaps providing positive reinforcement for polite speech, good grooming, and self-restraint. The brain-damaged people gradually recover the social skills they appeared to have lost (McGlynn, 1990).

Similarly, a brain-damaged animal that seems to have forgotten a learned skill may still retain it in a way that is difficult to assess. After damage to its visual cortex, a rat that had previously learned to approach a white card instead of a black card for food chose randomly between the two cards. Had the rat forgotten the discrimination completely? Evidently not, since it can learn again to approach the white card significantly more easily than it can learn to approach the black card (LeVere & Morlock, 1973). Apparently some trace of the original learning remained after the brain damage. (See Figure 15.11.)

Thomas LeVere (1975) proposed that such a lesion does not destroy the memory representation but merely impairs the rat's ability to find the memory. When the rat relearns the task, it is refinding or reaccessing the memory, which

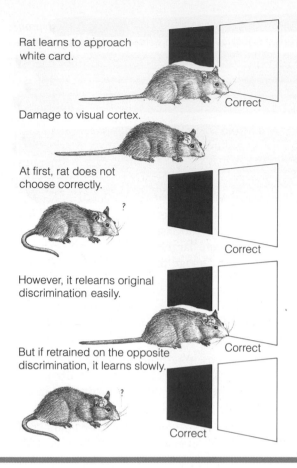

**Figure 15.11
Results of an
experiment by
LeVere and Morlock
(1973)**

*Brain damage impairs
retrieval of a memory but
does not destroy it com-
pletely.*

Rat learns to approach
white card.

Correct

Damage to visual cortex.

At first, rat does not
choose correctly.

?

Correct

However, it relearns original
discrimination easily.

Correct

But if retrained on the opposite
discrimination, it learns slowly.

?

Correct

is different from original learning. Moreover, the reaccessing process is not impaired by a drug that greatly impedes the learning of new tasks (Davis & LeVere,
1979).

Similarly, humans who have suffered brain damage may have trouble access-
ing certain skills and memories. Further, just as a monkey that has no sensation in
one arm may try to get by without using it, a person who has an impaired sensory
system may try to get by without using it at all (LeVere, 1980). The task of
physical therapists, occupational therapists, and speech therapists is to prod
brain-damaged patients to practice their impaired skills instead of ignoring them
altogether.

In an experiment that supports this approach to therapy, N. D. LeVere and
T. E. LeVere (1982) trained rats with visual cortex lesions on a brightness discrimination task, in which tactile stimuli were also present. For one group of rats
the tactile stimuli were redundant with the brightness cues; the rats could solve
the problem by responding to either stimulus. This group solved the task rapidly
but paid attention only to the tactile stimuli. If the tactile stimuli were removed,
the rats responded randomly. For a second group of rats the tactile stimuli were
irrelevant; they could solve the problem only on the basis of brightness. This
group took much longer than normal rats to solve the problem—their attention
to the tactile stimuli distracted them from the relevant visual cues—but they did
eventually solve it. In short, rats with visual cortex lesions can learn about visual
stimuli, but they are unlikely to do so if other stimuli are available to which they

can respond (Davis & LeVere, 1982). To help such rats, or to help humans with similar brain damage, it would be useful either to simplify the problem by removing distracting stimuli or to teach the individual to concentrate on the relevant stimuli.

## Drug Therapies

Several drugs have shown signs of aiding recovery from brain damage in animals. So far no evidence is available concerning their effect on humans.

**Nimodipine,** a drug that prevents calcium from entering cells, aids memory in aged animals. It also improves memory for visual learning tasks in rats with visual cortex lesions (LeVere, Brugler, Sandin, & Gray-Silva, 1989). Presumably it acts not by facilitating anything specific to brain damage but simply by enhancing memory.

Several studies indicate that gangliosides (which, as we have seen, may enhance collateral sprouting) promote the restoration of damaged brains. Their location on the membranes of neurons suggests that they contribute to the recognition of one neuron by another in early development, guiding axons to the correct locations to form synapses. Daily injections of gangliosides aid the recovery of behavior after several kinds of brain damage (Cahn, Borziex, Aldinio, Toffano, & Cahn, 1989; Ramirez et al., 1987a, 1987b; Sabel, Slavin, & Stein, 1984). Exactly how they do so is unknown.

## The Prospects for Therapy by Brain Grafts

Therapy for brain damage concentrates on molding behavior, not on trying to induce structural changes. In the future, neuropsychologists may develop drug therapies to encourage or regulate collateral sprouting, denervation supersensitivity, and the like (Sabel, Slavin, & Stein, 1984). A more exotic possibility is to promote recovery by grafting brain tissue to replace dead neurons.

Surgeons can graft brain tissue from one individual to another with little problem of tissue rejection. Perhaps because the blood-brain barrier protects the brain from foreign substances, the immune system is relatively inactive in the brain. The grafted brain tissue may not be functional, however. When transplanted from one adult brain to another, its axons and dendrites do not grow and have no apparent effect on the host brain. On the other hand, if neurons from a fetal brain are transplanted into the appropriate portion of an adult brain, the axons and dendrites grow and develop, possibly forming synapses with the host brain.

In a pioneering study, M. J. Perlow and colleagues (1979) injected the chemical 6-OHDA to make lesions in the substantia nigra on one side of the brain in rats. (The substantia nigra is the part of the brain that Parkinson's disease damages.) Each rat developed movement abnormalities resembling Parkinson's disease, although the abnormalities were limited to one side of the body. After the movement abnormalities had stabilized, the experimenters transplanted the substantia nigra from rat fetuses to locations where those cells would normally make synapses in the adult rat brains. The grafts survived in 29 of the 30 rats that received them, making synapses in varying numbers. Four weeks after the grafts were implanted, most recipients had recovered much of their normal movement. Control animals that suffered the same brain damage without receiving the brain grafts showed little or no behavioral recovery.

Inspired by this report, other investigators have tried transplanting fetal tissue to reverse the effects of many types of brain damage (Gash, Collier, & Sladek,

1985; Kimble, 1990). An implant of hypothalamic neurons from one strain of rats to another alleviated genetically determined diabetes in the second strain (Gash, Sladek, & Sladek, 1980). Similarly, grafts of acetylcholine-rich neurons into the hippocampus improved the memory of aged rats (Gage, Björklund, Stenevi, Dunnett, & Kelly, 1984). Grafting embryonic caudate nucleus tissue into damaged rat caudate nuclei improved the rats' motor control (Valoušková et al., 1990). Many researchers refer to these studies as "Frankenstein research" or as science fiction come to life.

Is tissue grafting the therapy of the future for Parkinson's disease, Alzheimer's disease, or other human disorders? Maybe, maybe not. To perform such surgery with humans raises a variety of ethical and practical issues.

The ethical problem is where to find donors. One possible but problematic source is aborted human fetuses. Abortion itself is ethically controversial, but even some people who accept the idea of abortion are troubled by the idea of taking brain tissue from fetuses to help brain-damaged adults.

Fetal tissue transplant presents a difficult practical problem as well: Fetal brain tissue is suitable for transplantation only for a brief period during development. After it is removed, it must be transplanted rapidly into the recipient's brain or the cells will not survive. Human fetuses can be a suitable source for neural transplants only if the abortion takes place at exactly the right time in fetal development and if the tissue is rushed almost instantly into transplantation surgery. Even then, the cells will die unless they receive adequate blood supply at once. Whether this can ever be achieved reliably is uncertain. Surgeons have made a few attempts to transplant fetal tissue into the brain of Parkinson's disease patients, but they report only slight benefits to the recipients (Lindvall et al., 1989), and in many cases no benefit at all.

An alternative is to transplant tissue from a fetal monkey into a human brain. Transplants from mouse brain to rat brain have succeeded (Björklund, Stenevi, Dunnett, & Gage, 1982; Daniloff, Wells, & Ellis, 1984). Perhaps transplants from monkey to human would succeed as well, although it is difficult to guess what the result might be.

Still another possibility—limited in its potential application—is to transplant tissue from a person's own adrenal medulla into the brain. Cells of the adrenal medulla, part of the adrenal gland, produce and release epinephrine, norepinephrine, and dopamine. If such cells are transplanted into the brain, they continue to release those chemicals, which may substitute for the neurotransmitters previously released by now-destroyed neurons. Operations of this type have been tried on human patients suffering from severe Parkinson's disease, with varying but mostly unencouraging outcomes (see, for example, Backlund et al., 1985). At this point the results call for more research, not for large-scale clinical implementation.

One of the main questions researchers must address is *how* fetal tissue transplants benefit behavior (when they do so at all). The simplest assumption—that the transplanted neurons form synaptic contacts that replace the damaged ones—is probably incorrect. Several studies with rats have found that the grafting procedure aids behavioral recovery from brain damage *even if* few of the grafted cells survive or make synaptic contacts with the host brain (Bohn, Cupit, Marciano, & Gash, 1987; Dunnett, Ryan, Levin, Reynolds, & Bunch, 1987; review by Kimble, 1990). Evidently the graft operates (in some if not all cases) by releasing neurotrophic factors that enhance the growth of axons and dendrites in the host brain. If neuroscientists can identify and synthesize those neurotrophic factors, perhaps injecting such chemicals would be more effective than transplanting brain tissue.

## SUMMARY

1. Recovery from brain damage may be better or worse in infants than in adults, depending on a number of circumstances. (p. 543)

2. Recovery is sometimes better if the damage develops in several stages, instead of all at once, or if the damaged individual had certain experiences before the damage. (p. 546)

3. At present, therapy for brain damage consists mostly of helping the person practice the abilities that have been impaired but not destroyed. (p. 547)

4. Drugs that enhance memory or guide axonal growth promote recovery after certain kinds of brain damage. (p. 549)

5. Animal experiments suggest the possibility of transplanting brain grafts from fetal donors as a therapy for brain damage. (p. 549)

## REVIEW QUESTIONS

1. Why might the effects of infant brain damage differ from those of adult brain damage? Give more than one reason and evidence for each. (p. 543)

2. What are the usual methods and goals of therapy for people with brain damage? (p. 547)

3. What kind of donor must be used in brain graft experiments if the transplanted tissue is to survive and make connections? (p. 550)

4. If brain graft transplants are to be used in humans, what are the possible sources of brain tissue? (p. 550)

## THOUGHT QUESTION

1. If brain grafts could be made successfully from fetal monkeys to adult humans, how should we decide whether it is right to conduct such surgery?

## SUGGESTIONS FOR FURTHER READING

**Kolb, B., & Whishaw, I. Q.** (1989). Plasticity in the neocortex: Mechanisms underlying recovery from early brain damage. *Progress in Neurobiology, 32,* 235–276. Review of research on differences between young and old in recovery from brain damage.

**Sladek, J. R., Jr., & Gash, D. M.** (1984). *Neural transplants.* New York: Plenum. Discussion of the use of brain grafts.

## GLOSSARY

**apomorphine** morphine derivative that stimulates dopamine receptors

**cerebrovascular accident** commonly called a **stroke**

**collateral sprout** newly formed branch from an uninjured axon that forms a synapse vacated when another axon was destroyed

**denervation supersensitivity** increased sensitivity by a postsynaptic cell after removal of an axon that formerly innervated it

**diaschisis** decreased activity in neurons that have lost part of their input

**disuse supersensitivity** increased sensitivity by a postsynaptic cell after a period of decreased input by incoming axons

**dorsolateral prefrontal cortex** area of the prefrontal cortex

**ganglioside** molecule composed of combinations of carbohydrates and fats

**Halstead-Reitan test** set of behavioral tests designed to identify the type and extent of brain damage

**hypertension** high blood pressure

**Kennard principle** generalization (not always correct) that it is easier to recover from brain damage early in life than later in life

**Luria-Nebraska neuropsychological battery** set of behavioral tests designed to identify the type and extent of brain damage

**nimodipine** drug that prevents calcium from entering cells; found to enhance memory in aged or brain-damaged animals

**orbital frontal cortex** an anterior area of the prefrontal cortex

**sensory extinction** tendency to respond first and more strongly to stimuli on the same side of the body as brain damage, as opposed to stimuli on the opposite side

**sensory neglect** ignoring of stimuli on the side of the body opposite an area of brain damage

**serial-lesion effect** tendency for recovery to be more complete after a series of small lesions than after a single, large lesion

**6-hydroxydopamine** chemical that destroys neurons that release dopamine or norepinephrine

**6-OHDA** abbreviation for 6-hydroxydopamine

**stroke** brain damage caused when a blood clot or other obstruction interrupts the flow of blood and therefore oxygen to a brain area

# CHAPTER SIXTEEN

# Biology of Mood Disorders, Schizophrenia, and Autism

## MAIN IDEAS

**1.** Mood disorders and schizophrenia are the product of numerous biological and environmental influences.

**2.** Various drugs used for treating depression and schizophrenia alter transmission at certain types of synapses. The drugs' effectiveness suggests that the underlying causes of the disorders may include some problem affecting particular neurotransmitters.

**3.** A number of nondrug biological treatments are also effective against certain cases of depression, including electroconvulsive shock, changes in sleep patterns, exposure to bright light, and the use of lithium salts.

**4.** Autism is a rare childhood disorder that resembles schizophrenia in certain regards, although the underlying causes differ.

Until the late 1860s, people with aphasia were considered mentally ill. After physicians discovered that aphasia was caused by localized brain damage, those patients were treated by neurologists instead of psychiatrists. Similarly, after physicians discovered that general paresis, a type of intellectual deterioration, was a symptom of the third stage of syphilis infection (see Figure 16.1), people with this problem were classified as neurological instead of psychiatric patients. Apparently, as soon as we find a neurological basis for a psychiatric disorder, people hesitate to call it a mental illness.

If we found neurological bases for all psychological disorders, would psychiatrists and clinical psychologists go out of business? No. Talking with a psychotherapist can be helpful for people suffering from aphasia, general paresis, or even a broken leg. Evidence accumulating since about 1950 indicates that anxiety, obsessive-compulsive disorder, sleep disorders, violent behavior, and many other psychological

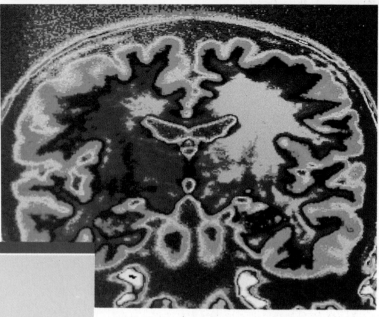

*(E. F. Torrey & M. F. Casanova/NIMH.)*

disorders have biological aspects. Psychotherapists
have learned to coordinate talk therapy with biological therapy, but they still find ample demand for talk
therapy. The presence of biological contributors to a
disorder does not deny the importance of experiential
contributors.

In this chapter we deal with depression, schizophrenia, and related disorders — disorders that in
many cases become so severe that they absolutely
dominate a person's life. Researchers disagree, sometimes sharply, about the relative importance of biological and environmental causes for these disorders; they
also disagree about the relative advantages and disadvantages of biological therapies, talk therapies, and
combinations of the two. Here we emphasize the biological components of depression, schizophrenia, and
autism; *Biological Psychology* is, after all, the title of this
book. But this emphasis does not imply that other aspects are unimportant.

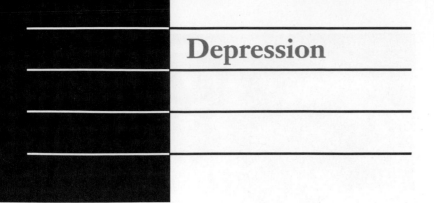

# Depression

Why do people live in a particular city? Some were born there. Some chose the city because of some attraction, a job offer, or a college or hospital or other institution that fits their needs. If the city has a prison, a few people were brought there without any choice. Although all these people have ended up in about the same place, their reasons for being there are diverse.

The same is true for many psychological conditions, including depression. Some people are depressed because of extremely unpleasant events that would make almost anyone depressed. Others are depressed because of a chemical imbalance that developed gradually in their brains for genetic or hormonal reasons. Others may have had their depression triggered by poor dietary or sleeping habits. Most have become depressed for a combination of reasons. People reach the same final destination, depression, through many routes.

## TYPES OF DEPRESSION

A depressed person feels fearful and gloomy, helpless and hopeless. Depressed people are generally inactive; when they do anything at all, it is unproductive, such as pacing back and forth, wringing their hands. They say they feel unhappy, and their facial expressions indicate unhappiness.

Depressed people almost invariably have trouble sleeping. On the average, they take longer than most normal people to fall asleep. After sleeping not very restfully, they awaken earlier than they wanted and cannot get back to sleep. During the day they feel drowsy.

The opposite of depression is **mania**. A manic person is bursting with restless activity, excitement, laughter, a mostly happy mood, and few inhibitions. The manic person's speech rambles from one idea to another. Some of the ideas may be good ones, but the manic person does not distinguish between the good and the bad. He or she is also impulsive, investing money recklessly and engaging in aggressive or sexual behavior that a normal person would restrain. In extreme

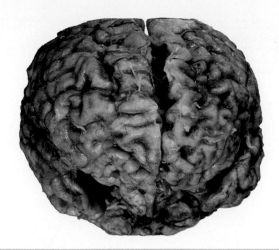

**Figure 16.1
The brain of a person with general paresis (the final stage of syphilis)**
*Many of the gyri in the cerebral cortex are shrunken. (Photo courtesy of Dana Copeland.)*

cases, manic people are dangerous to themselves and others. Figure 16.2 represents the rise and fall of a manic episode in one hospitalized patient. In mild cases, known as **hypomania,** people are energetic, outgoing, and sometimes highly successful.

## Difficulties in Diagnosing Depression

If you feel sad and gloomy today, are you suffering from a psychological disorder, is your brain chemistry out of balance, and should you arrange to see a therapist? Probably not. You may have good reasons for feeling low today, and you may start feeling better soon. A clinician would consider you depressed only if your distress is persistent and disabling, if your mood seriously interferes with your everyday life for a long time, generally months.

Even then, depression may not be your main problem. Many people who complain of depression also suffer from alcohol or drug abuse, and often it is not clear whether depression led to substance abuse problems or whether substance abuse led to depression. Certain hormonal disorders produce symptoms that closely resemble depression (P. W. Gold et al., 1986). One study of patients in the California mental health system found that more than one-third had serious, undiagnosed physical illnesses that could cause or at least aggravate their psychological distress (Koran et al., 1989). Ideally, a therapist should find out what other problems a person might have before beginning to treat depression.

## Unipolar Versus Bipolar Disorder

Depression can occur as either a unipolar or a bipolar disorder. **Unipolar disorder** has only one pole, or extreme, of mood. That is, a person varies between normal mood and depression. About 5 percent of all people suffer an episode of major depression at some time in their lives (Robins et al., 1984). Depression is diagnosed more frequently in women than in men (Murphy, Sobol, Neff, Olivier, & Leighton, 1984), and the mean age of onset is about 40.

Depression

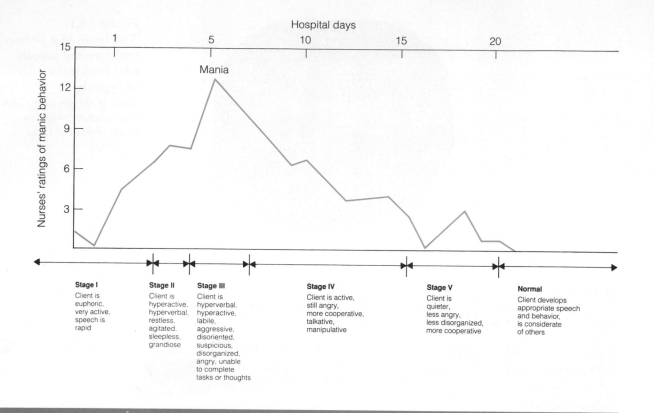

**Figure 16.2**
**Stages of a manic episode of a hospitalized patient over three weeks**
*(After Janosik and Davies, 1986.)*

**Bipolar disorder**—also known as **manic-depressive disorder**—has two poles, mania and depression. Someone suffering from bipolar disorder alternates between periods of mania and depression, passing through a normal mood on the way. Although hypomania may occur as a unipolar condition—indeed, as a permanent personality characteristic—extreme mania is almost unheard of as a unipolar condition. That is, extreme mania occurs almost exclusively as a condition that alternates with depression.

A depressed person may become less depressed, gradually pass through normality and into a manic state, and then return toward normality and depression again. The entire cycle may last a year or only a few days (Bunney, Murphy, Goodwin, & Borge, 1972). Some people follow such a regular cycle that one can predict their manic and depressive episodes long in advance (Richter, 1938, 1957b, 1957c), as Figure 16.3 shows. About one person in a thousand is diagnosed with bipolar disorder, but many more have mild, undiagnosed, and untreated cases. The mean age of onset is the late 20s.

## POSSIBLE BIOLOGICAL CAUSES OF DEPRESSION

The causes of depression may differ from one person to another. Further, a given individual may become depressed for more than one reason. We discuss here a few of the possible biological causes.

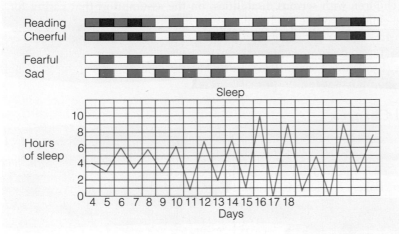

**Figure 16.3**
**One example of bipolar disorder: records for a woman who had one-day manic periods alternating with one-day depressed periods**
*Blue means definitely, red means somewhat, and white means no. Note that days of cheerfulness and reading alternated with days of fearfulness and sadness. Note also that she slept well on her cheerful days and poorly on her sad days. (Based on Richter, 1938.)*

## Stressful Events

Yes, a stressful event can be a biological cause. Stressful events activate the sympathetic nervous system, the reticular formation, and other parts of the nervous system, increasing the release of norepinephrine, dopamine, and other neurotransmitters. Particularly intense stress may release these transmitters faster than they can be resynthesized, thus decreasing their availability. The postsynaptic neurons might decrease their sensitivity in response to the great release of neurotransmitters during the stress period and the reduction afterward. Through such changes, severe stress might trigger a bout of depression (Anisman & Zacharko, 1982).

One impediment to evaluating this hypothesis is the difficulty of measuring stress. The death of a loved one is an incapacitating stress for many people, yet for someone who has nursed a suffering relative through years of painful decline, death may be a relief. Similarly, divorce, pregnancy, or the loss of a job may be highly stressful, unstressful, or even a cause for celebration, depending on a multitude of circumstances. For this reason we must be cautious in interpreting studies that ask depressed and undepressed individuals to report how many stressful experiences they have undergone recently.

A better way to study the effects of stress on depression is to examine people who have been exposed to undeniable stress and then to find out how many of them became depressed. One such study compared mothers of normal children to

Depression

mothers of children with serious disabilities, on the assumption that caring for a handicapped child is a source of chronic stress. The mothers of handicapped children had no greater probability than the other women of becoming depressed, although if they did become depressed, their depression was in certain regards more severe (Breslau & Davis, 1986). In other words, in this study, stress aggravated depression but was not its primary cause.

## Hormonal Changes

Several lines of evidence link depression to fluctuations in sex hormones, particularly in women. Of all women admitted to one psychiatric hospital for depression, 41 percent were admitted on the day before or the first day of menstruation (Abramowitz, Baker, & Fleischer, 1982). Certainly this does not mean that menstruation causes depression; it suggests that the hormonal changes preceding menstruation may slightly aggravate a preexisting depression, making it severe enough to require treatment.

Similarly, a certain amount of depression is common just after giving birth. Most women experience "the blues" for a day or two after delivery, because of pain, the inconvenience of hospital care, and possibly the hormonal changes occurring at this time. About 20 percent experience a more serious **postpartum depression**—that is, a depression after giving birth—though it is still within their ability to cope. About one woman in a thousand enters a severe, long-lasting depression (Hopkins, Marcus, & Campbell, 1984). Even in these cases, however, it is doubtful that giving birth caused the depression, because many such women will have one or more other episodes of major depression at other times (Schöpf, Bryois, Jonquière, & Le, 1984). A reasonable interpretation is that giving birth triggered an episode of depression in women who were already predisposed to depression.

Thyroid hormones may also play a role in depression. Most depressed and manic-depressive patients have at least mild thyroid hormone deficiencies (Lipton, Breese, Prange, Wilson, & Cooper, 1976; Fieve & Platman, 1969).

## Genetics

Both depression and bipolar disorder run in families. About 10 to 20 percent of the parents, brothers, and sisters of depressed and bipolar patients suffer from these same disorders themselves (Smeraldi, Kidd, Negri, Heimbuch, & Melica, 1979; Weissman et al., 1984). Children of depressed individuals have a high risk of developing either depression or substance abuse (Weissman et al., 1987).

The fact that depressed people have depressed relatives tells us only that we cannot rule out genetics as a contributing factor. Stronger evidence for a genetic basis of depression is that adopted children who become depressed have, on the average, more depressed biological relatives than depressed adoptive relatives (Wender et al., 1986).

At one time, researchers thought they had located a gene for bipolar disorder on chromosome 11. Within one genetically isolated population, the Old Order Amish of Pennsylvania, relatives who resembled one another with regard to bipolar disorder also resembled one another with regard to certain genes known to be on chromosome 11 (Egeland et al., 1987). However, a follow-up study on a larger sample of the Old Order Amish population and two studies on other populations found no evidence linking bipolar disorder to chromosome 11 (Detera-Wadleigh et al., 1987; Hodgkinson et al., 1987; Kelsoe et al., 1989). Because so many factors are involved in depression, probably many genes predispose people to depression. Consequently, it may prove difficult to isolate any single gene.

| Table 16.1 Borna Disease Virus and Depression | | |
|---|---|---|
| | Tested Positive for Borna Virus | Total People Tested |
| Depressed and bipolar | 12 | 265 |
| Nondepressed | 0 | 105 |

## Viruses

Preliminary evidence suggests that some cases of depression may be linked to a little-known viral infection called **Borna disease.** Borna disease infects the nervous systems of animals, mostly horses and sheep. Its symptoms vary from one species to another, but one common effect is an alternation between periods of frantic activity and periods of inactivity.

Although no humans are known to suffer from Borna disease, one group of investigators wondered whether any humans might carry the virus. (Many viruses are passed between humans and other species, even if the effects on humans are quite different from the effects on other species.) In 1985, they reported the results of a blood test given to several hundred humans (Amsterdam et al., 1985). Only 12 people tested positive for Borna disease virus, but *all 12 were suffering from major depression or bipolar disorder.* These 12 were a small percentage of the depressed people tested in the study; still, it is significant that *no* undepressed people tested positive for the virus. (See Table 16.1.)

After the 1985 report, little research was reported on the possible role of Borna disease virus in depression because researchers had no rapid, accurate test for the presence of the virus. In 1990, investigators improved their methods of testing for the virus; we can expect to see more research on this topic (Vande-Woude et al., 1990).

## Abnormalities of Hemispheric Dominance

The rate of glucose metabolism, a good indicator of overall brain activity, varies as a function of mania and depression, as Figure 16.4 shows. During mania, activity is higher than normal. During depression, it is lower than normal, especially in the left frontal lobe (Baxter et al., 1985) and parts of the temporal and parietal lobes (Sackeim et al., 1990).

Several other lines of evidence suggest that most depressed people have depressed activity in the left hemisphere, especially the left frontal cortex. The EEG and other measures show more activation in the right hemisphere than in the left hemisphere (Davidson, 1984; Starkstein & Robinson, 1986). In response to an arousing stimulus, depressed people have less than the normal increase in electrical conduction of the skin on the right hand. When dealing with a cognitive problem, their eyes gaze to the left, not to the right as in most people (Lenhart & Katkin, 1986).

Many people with left-hemisphere damage become seriously depressed; fewer people with right-hemisphere damage become depressed (Bolla-Wilson, Robinson, Starkstein, Boston, & Price, 1989). Depending on the exact location of the damage, many people with right-hemisphere damage become emotionally unresponsive; they even have difficulty deciding whether two faces are showing the same or different emotional expressions (Kolb & Taylor, 1981). In rare cases,

Depression

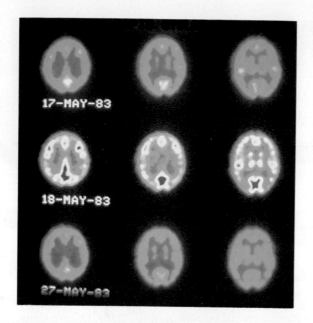

**Figure 16.4**
*PET scans taken on three different days for a patient who went through rapid and enormous changes in mood. Three separate horizontal planes are shown for each day. On May 17 and May 27, when the patient was depressed, brain metabolic rates were low. On May 18, when the patient was in a cheerful, hypomanic mood, the brain metabolic rate was high. Red indicates the highest metabolic rate, followed by yellow, green, and blue. (Courtesy of L. R. Baxter, Jr.)*

people with right-hemisphere damage become manic. Nearly all of those who develop mania after a stroke had some predisposition to mania either because of previous subcortical brain damage or a family history of psychiatric disorders (Robinson, Boston, Starkstein, & Price, 1988).

Overall, the evidence suggests that left-hemisphere damage or inactivity is associated with depression. We shall return to this point when we discuss the effects of electroconvulsive shock to the left or right hemisphere.

## ANIMAL MODELS OF DEPRESSION AND BIPOLAR DISORDER

One way to form or test a hypothesis about the cause of some human disorder is to find out what causes a similar disorder in animals. Curt Richter offered the first serious animal model of a major psychiatric disorder when he studied activity cycles in rats.

Richter kept rats in cages with running wheels; mechanical counters recorded the number of wheel turns for each rat each day. During a wide-ranging investigation of the variables that control a rat's running activity, Richter found that partial damage to the thyroid gland causes a rat to show unusual cycles of activity and inactivity (Richter, 1933a, 1955, 1957b, 1957c, 1957d; Richter, Jones, & Biswanger, 1959; Richter & Rice, 1956). Figure 16.5 shows the effects of chemically induced damage to the thyroid on the activity of one rat. Note that periods of 8 to 13 days of almost complete inactivity alternated with periods of high activity.

On the basis of such results, Richter proposed that an impairment somewhere in the endocrine system might predispose people to bipolar disorder or might at least influence the speed of cycling between mania and depression. Although his hypothesis received little attention at the time, it remains a viable pos-

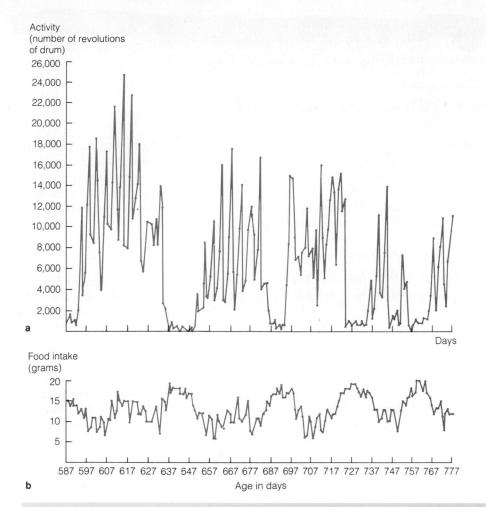

Activity
(number of revolutions
of drum)

**a** Days

Food intake
(grams)

587 597 607 617 627 637 647 657 667 677 687 697 707 717 727 737 747 757 767 777

**b** Age in days

**Figure 16.5
Record of (a) daily
activity in running
wheel and (b) food
intake by a rat
treated with the
drug sulfamerazine,
which damages
the thyroid**
*Notches on the horizontal axis
represent blocks of 10 days.
(From Richter, 1957d.)*

sibility. One study of 30 patients with rapid-cycling bipolar disorder found thyroid problems in 18 cases (Bauer, Whybrow, & Winokur, 1990).

A more influential animal model emerged in the early 1960s. Several investigators independently and almost simultaneously suggested that depression could result from a deficiency of activity at catecholamine synapses (Garattini & Valzelli, 1960; MacLean, 1962; Stein, 1962). Larry Stein offered the clearest and most explicit of these models; he found that antidepressant drugs increase rats' self-stimulation of the brain, apparently by increasing catecholamine activity. Stein inferred that depressed people have deficient stimulation of the reward areas of their brains because of low catecholamine activity. Later studies with animal models indicated that depletion of norepinephrine could lead to inactivity and a lack of hunger and exploration; depletion of serotonin as well added an element of fearfulness (Ellison, 1977).

Another animal model, more behavioral than physiological, is the **learned helplessness** model. An animal that receives a series of inescapable shocks on one day will act helpless in the face of escapable, avoidable shocks the following day (Maier, Seligman, & Solomon, 1969). Both the animal's general demeanor and its failure to engage in productive behavior resemble human depression. Perhaps certain cases of depression begin when someone fails repeatedly on an important

Depression

task, particularly if the person attributes the failure to his or her own shortcomings, as opposed to something about the task or to some temporary interference with performance (Abramson, Seligman, & Teasdale, 1978).

# MONOAMINES AND DEPRESSION

Logically, we might imagine that investigators would first figure out the causes of a psychological disorder and then develop a treatment to address that cause. The sequence in real life has generally been the opposite: First investigators find a drug or other therapy that appears to be helpful, and then they infer what the underlying cause must have been. Antidepressant drugs were discovered by accident; they led to new hypotheses about the biology of depression.

## Antidepressant Drugs and Their Effects

Antidepressant drugs fall into three major categories: MAOIs, tricyclics, and serotonin reuptake blockers. The **monoamine oxidase inhibitors (MAOIs)** (such as phenelzine, trade name Nardil) block the enzyme *monoamine oxidase (MAO)*, which metabolizes catecholamines and serotonin into inactive forms. When MAOIs block this enzyme, released neurotransmitter molecules remain longer than usual at the synapse without being inactivated; they therefore stimulate the postsynaptic cell more than usual. The **tricyclics** (such as imipramine, trade name Tofranil) operate by preventing the presynaptic neuron from reabsorbing catecholamines or serotonin after releasing them; thus, the neurotransmitters remain longer in the synaptic cleft and continue stimulating the postsynaptic cell. The **serotonin reuptake blockers** resemble the tricyclics in their mode of action, but they are more selective, blocking the reuptake of serotonin but not the catecholamines. The serotonin reuptake blockers were developed later than the others, and as of the early 1990s only one such drug is in wide use: fluoxetine, trade name Prozac.

Before the 1980s, a physician prescribing an antidepressant drug would almost always start with a tricyclic, because tricyclics are more effective than MAOIs for most patients. If the drug did not work, the physician might increase the dose or try a different drug, perhaps an MAOI. About two-thirds of depressed patients experience significant relief by taking one or another drug. However, each drug produces unwanted side effects that vary from one person to another. Common side effects from tricyclics include dizziness, drowsiness, blurred vision, rapid heartbeat, dry mouth, and excessive sweating. Many people experience such severe side effects that they have to quit taking the drug or reduce the dose to a level where it becomes ineffective.

Since the mid-1980s, fluoxetine has rapidly risen in popularity because it produces much less dizziness, drowsiness, sweating, and rapid heartbeat than tricyclics do. Its most common side effects are nausea and headache, but these are usually not severe. Most depressed people can better tolerate the side effects of fluoxetine than those of other antidepressant drugs; consequently they can take a large enough dose to alleviate their depression (Burrows, McIntyre, Judd, & Norman, 1988; Stark & Hardison, 1985). An additional benefit is that fluoxetine leaves the body very slowly, so a patient can easily maintain a steady level of the drug. The use of fluoxetine has become controversial because of reports that it occasionally provokes suicidal thoughts. Researchers may need to identify certain kinds of patients who should avoid the drug for this reason.

## Implications for the Physiology of Depression

Now that we know what kinds of drugs relieve depression, we can infer what brain abnormalities are responsible for depression, right? Unfortunately, it is not that simple. We can say with some confidence that serotonin synapses are somehow involved in depression because of the antidepressant effect of fluoxetine, which is highly selective for serotonin reuptake. That conclusion is confirmed by studies in which the rapid depletion of serotonin has led to a sudden episode of depression (P. Delgado et al., 1990). We are less certain about the role of catecholamines; many antidepressant drugs alter both catecholamine and serotonin transmission, but none of them alters catecholamine transmission alone.

A further problem is to explain the time course of the drugs' effectiveness. Antidepressant drugs elevate the concentration of serotonin (or both serotonin and catecholamines) at the synapses within hours after someone takes the first pill. However, most patients must take the medication for 2 or 3 weeks before they experience antidepressant effects. Obviously, the effects of the drugs must change in some way over the course of several weeks. But how?

Apparently two processes develop gradually over that 2- to 3-week period. One is the opposite of denervation supersensitivity (discussed in Chapter 15). Just as a period of low stimulation at a synapse leads to increased receptor density, a prolonged rise in neurotransmitter release can lead to decreased receptor density. Prolonged use of antidepressant drugs decreases the number of serotonin and catecholamine receptors.

The second process is a gradual decrease in the responsiveness of **autoreceptors,** receptors that respond to the transmitter that the presynaptic neuron releases (Starke, 1981). Most autoreceptors probably serve as negative feedback. When the presynaptic cell releases its neurotransmitter, some of that transmitter comes back to stimulate the autoreceptors, which then inhibit the cell from releasing more of the transmitter. (See Figure 3.13.)

Most antidepressant drugs decrease the sensitivity of the autoreceptors (Antelman, Chiodo, & DeGiovanni, 1982; Sulser, Gillespie, Mishra, & Manier, 1984). The consequence of decreased autoreceptor sensitivity is decreased inhibition of neurotransmitter release; that is, transmitter release is prolonged. The neurons of someone taking an antidepressant release substantially more catecholamines and serotonin after three weeks of drug use than after one day (Crews & Smith, 1978).

You are excused if you feel confused at this point. Prolonged use of antidepressant drugs produces effects in opposite directions: It increases the amount of neurotransmitter released while decreasing receptor sensitivity to the neurotransmitter. Perhaps one of those effects is more important than the other; perhaps both are necessary in some way for antidepressant drugs to be effective.

What does all this tell us about the underlying causes of depression? Primarily they imply that the mechanisms are more complex than simply having "too much" or "too little" of a particular neurotransmitter.

## OTHER BIOLOGICAL THERAPIES FOR DEPRESSION AND BIPOLAR DISORDER

Antidepressant drugs are effective for about two-thirds of all seriously depressed patients, but because of their unpleasant side effects, they are not a perfect treatment. Other biological treatments are beneficial under certain circumstances.

## Electroconvulsive Therapy

**Electroconvulsive therapy (ECT)** has had a stormy history (Fink, 1985). Its use originated with the observation that among certain people who suffer from both epilepsy and schizophrenia, an increase in the symptoms of one disorder is associated with a decrease in the symptoms of the other (Trimble & Thompson, 1986). In the 1930s, a Hungarian physician, Ladislas Meduna, intentionally induced a convulsive seizure in schizophrenic patients to see whether it would relieve the symptoms of schizophrenia. Soon other physicians were doing the same, generally inducing the seizures by a large dose of insulin. Insulin shock is a dreadful experience, however, and very difficult to control. An Italian physician, Ugo Cerletti, after years of experimentation with animals, developed a method of inducing seizures by an electric shock across the head (Cerletti & Bini, 1938). Electroconvulsive shock was quicker than insulin; more important, most patients awakened from it calmly and did not remember the shock.

Although ECT proved to be only occasionally beneficial in treating schizophrenia, psychiatrists began experimenting with it for other disorders. They discovered that it did seem to help many people suffering from major depression. ECT became a common treatment for depression, even though its use for this disorder was based on no theory at all. It developed a bad reputation, however, because of overuse and misuse, especially during the 1950s. Certain patients were given ECT a hundred times or more, without their consent, even if it seemed to be doing them no good.

When antidepressant drugs became available in the late 1950s, the use of ECT declined rapidly. All states now have laws that permit the use of ECT only after a patient has given informed consent. Many states have also imposed laws restricting the ages of people who can receive ECT and the disorders for which it can be used (Winslade, Liston, Ross, & Weber, 1984).

Beginning in the 1970s, ECT has made a partial comeback, with many modifications. It is now used almost exclusively for depression, rarely for schizophrenia or other disorders. It is applied on alternate days for usually about two weeks. Patients are given muscle relaxants or anesthetics to minimize discomfort and the possibility of injury (Figure 16.6). To minimize the side effects, the intensity of the shock is much lower than in earlier years. In some cases physicians administer the shock over just the right hemisphere instead of the whole head. Right-hemisphere ECT can be just as effective as bilateral ECT for relieving depression *if* the right-side-only ECT is intense enough to induce a seizure (Horne, Pettinati, Sugerman, & Varga, 1985; Miller, Small, Milstein, Malloy, & Stout, 1981). Because depression is associated with decreased activity of the left hemisphere, right-hemisphere ECT may promote a better balance of activity between the two hemispheres or it may somehow enhance activity in the left hemisphere.

ECT is used primarily for three kinds of depressed patients (Scovern & Kilmann, 1980; Weiner, 1979). First, it is given to patients who have not responded to any of the antidepressant drugs; ECT produces good results in most such patients (Paul et al., 1981). Second, it is used for patients with suicidal tendencies because it takes effect in about a week, whereas antidepressant drugs usually take 2 to 3 weeks. For a patient likely to attempt suicide, a delay of effect may be fatal. Third, ECT has proved particularly effective for depressed patients who suffer from delusions.

Medical commissions in both the United States and Great Britain have concluded that ECT is both safe and effective (Fink, 1985). According to one extensive review of the literature, 80 percent of all severely depressed patients respond

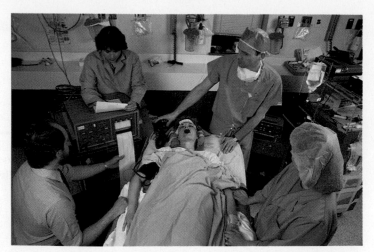

**Figure 16.6 Electroconvulsive therapy (ECT)**

*In contrast to the practices of an earlier era, ECT today is administered with muscle relaxants or anesthetics to minimize discomfort. It can be given only if the patient gives informed consent. (James D. Wilson/Woodfin Camp & Associates.)*

well to ECT, while only 64 percent respond well to tricyclic drugs and even fewer respond to MAOIs (Janicak et al., 1985). The benefits of ECT are not permanent, however; many patients will relapse into depression unless they are given drugs or other therapies to prevent it.

Many people today distrust ECT, partly because it seems barbaric and partly because they believe, rightly or wrongly, that it produces serious side effects. For most patients the side effects are minor and temporary, including a period of confusion and both retrograde and anterograde amnesia during the first 1 to 6 months after the end of treatment (Squire, Wetzel, & Slater, 1979). However, a few patients experience long-term memory deficits and other health risks (Weiner, 1984). Memory loss is most severe in patients with a long history of psychiatric or neurological problems (Summers, Robins, & Reich, 1979). Applying ECT to only the right hemisphere minimizes memory impairment (Squire & Zouzounis, 1986).

Half a century after the introduction of ECT, no one yet is sure how it relieves depression. We know that it does not act as a punishment, and it need not impair memory to be effective. It must induce a seizure, however. ECT that produces a seizure affects the brain in many ways, such as increasing the release of hormones from the hypothalamus and pituitary (Fink, 1980). It decreases the number of norepinephrine receptors at postsynaptic cells (Kellar & Stockmeier, 1986; Lerer & Shapira, 1986). Conflicting results have been reported about whether it increases or decreases receptor sensitivity at autoreceptors (Chiodo & Antelman, 1980; Reches et al., 1984).

## Alterations of Sleep Patterns

Most depressed people, especially those middle aged or older, experience sleep abnormalities that suggest a disorder of their biological rhythms. Recall from Chapter 10 that a normal undepressed person who goes to bed at the normal time first enters REM sleep about 80 minutes after falling asleep. The normal person has little REM sleep during the first half of the night and an increasing percentage in the second half. That trend is controlled by the time of day, not by how long the person has been asleep. If someone who usually falls asleep at 11 P.M.

Depression

**Figure 16.7**
**Relationship of sleep and REM to the circadian cycle of body temperature**

*The circadian rhythm is shifted for most depressed people. Depressed people going to bed at their normal time enter REM sleep quickly, as do normal people going to bed several hours later than usual. (Bottom graphs adapted from Hobson, 1989.)*

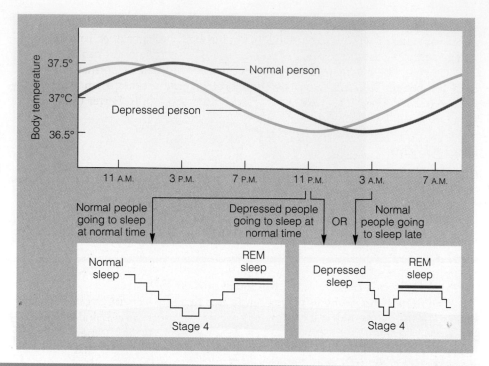

waits until 3 A.M. to go to sleep, that person is likely to enter REM sleep rapidly and to have a lot of REM sleep per hour. The reason is that REM sleep is related to circadian rhythms, as reflected by changes in body temperature (see Figure 16.7). REM sleep occupies a small percentage of total sleep while body temperature is declining and a larger percentage while body temperature is rising (Czeisler, Weitzman, Moore-Ede, Zimmerman, & Knauer, 1980).

Most depressed people enter REM sleep within 45 minutes after going to bed at their normal time. When the depressed person goes to sleep, body temperature may already be starting to rise, as Figure 16.7 illustrates. For that reason, REM sleep begins early and may occupy a great deal of sleep time throughout the night. Curiously, manic patients also have quick onset of REM sleep (Hudson, Lipinki, Frankenburg, Grochocinski, & Kupfer, 1988).

Several means of adjusting sleep habits can alleviate depression (Gillin, 1983). One promising method is to have the person go to sleep earlier than usual, in phase with his or her temperature cycle. The person goes to sleep at, say, 6 P.M., when the temperature cycle is at about the point it is in undepressed people at 11 P.M.; he or she sleeps 8 hours and awakens at 2 A.M. On each succeeding night the person goes to sleep half an hour later, until the bedtime reaches 11 P.M. or some other satisfactory point. In short, therapists treat the depressed patient like someone who is having trouble adjusting to a change in time zones. The result is a relief from depression that lasts for months (Sack, Nurnberger, Rosenthal, Ashburn, & Wehr, 1985).

Another approach is to keep the person awake all night. Doing so produces a rapid relief from depression (Pflug, 1973). Why this procedure is effective is not known; furthermore, its benefits last only a day or two, and depressed patients frankly hate to go through this treatment. It is also possible to relieve depression by depriving the depressed person of REM sleep by awakening him or her whenever signs of REM appear (Vogel, Thompson, Thurmond, & Rivers, 1973). The benefits of REM deprivation develop gradually over days but can last days to weeks. Again, the mechanism of the effect is not known. For normal people, or even for people suffering from psychological disorders other than depression, sleep deprivation or REM deprivation makes mood worse, not better (Roy-Byrne, Uhde, & Post, 1986).

## Bright Lights

One uncommon form of depression is **seasonal affective disorder,** conveniently abbreviated **SAD.** People who suffer from seasonal affective disorder become depressed, sometimes seriously depressed, every winter. Most of them become at least slightly manic in the summer. The disorder is more common and more severe in regions closer to the poles, where the nights are extra long in winter and short in summer. Some patients who suffer depression every winter in their far northern homes experience no such depression if they spend the winter in, say, southern California (Pande, 1985; Rosenthal et al., 1984).

The underlying problem is apparently not the cold of winter but the darkness. Most people feel more cheerful on a sunny day than on a dark day. According to the results of one survey, more than 90 percent of people experience some seasonal variation in mood, generally feeling happier in summer than in winter (Kasper, Wehr, Bartko, Gaist, & Rosenthal, 1989). For some people these mood swings are exaggerated, with a small minority reaching levels that qualify as depression and mania (Lewy et al., 1985).

It is possible to relieve SAD by exposing the person to very bright lights (for example, 2,500 lux). The person sits in front of the lights for about 6 hours a day before the sun rises. A similar period of exposure in the evening is less effective (Sack et al., 1990). The lights, acting as an artificial sun, relieve SAD for people who follow this plan daily (Wehr et al., 1986). A similar period of exposure to dim lights has no effect on mood (Rosenthal et al., 1985).

Researchers are not agreed on what causes seasonal affective disorder or on how bright light alleviates it (Blehar & Rosenthal, 1989). In many ways SAD differs from other types of depression; for example, SAD patients have phase-delayed sleep and temperature rhythms, unlike most other depressed patients, who have phase-advanced rhythms (Figure 16.8). One hypothesis is that bright lights in the morning alleviate depression by resetting the circadian rhythms (Lewy, Sack, Miller, & Hoban, 1987); however, other explanations are possible.

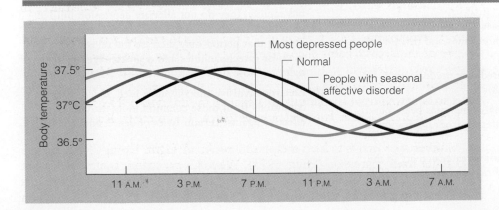

**Figure 16.8**
**Typical sleep and temperature cycles for normal people, depressed patients, and SAD patients**
*Note that SAD patients are phase delayed while most other depressed patients are phase advanced.*

567

## Lithium

The most effective known therapy for bipolar disorder, and for certain cases in which a person alternates regularly between depression and normal mood, is the use of **lithium** salts. The effectiveness of lithium was discovered by accident. An Australian investigator, J. F. Cade, believing that uric acid would be therapeutically useful for treating mania and depression, mixed uric acid with a lithium salt to help it dissolve and then gave the solution to patients. It was indeed helpful, although investigators eventually realized that the lithium was the effective agent.

Lithium levels out the mood of a bipolar patient. With continued use, it prevents a relapse into either mania or depression. The use of lithium must be regulated carefully, however. The therapeutic dose is not much less than the dose that begins to produce toxic effects. Also, lithium sometimes causes serious medical harm if combined with ECT or with the drug haloperidol (Gottfried & Frankel, 1981; Small, Kellams, Milstein, & Small, 1980).

Because lithium is chemically similar to sodium, it may partly take the place of sodium in crossing the membrane and in various other body functions. It produces a great many effects on the brain, the blood, and other systems (Tosteson, 1981). How it relieves bipolar disorder is not known. Because it alleviates both mania and depression—opposite states—its effects cannot be explained simply in terms of increasing or decreasing the activity at a particular type of synapse. It may act by stabilizing both dopamine and serotonin synapses, preventing alternations between increased and decreased receptor density (Pert, Rosenblatt, Sivit, Pert, & Bunney, 1978; Treiser et al., 1981). In the rat hippocampus, lithium elevates serotonin release but decreases serotonin binding to the receptors (Treiser et al., 1981). Perhaps these competing effects generate stability. Lithium may also lengthen the circadian rhythms of temperature and sleep (Wirz-Justice et al., 1982). Finally, lithium blocks the synthesis of a widespread second messenger, phosphoinositide (Worley, Heller, Snyder, & Baraban, 1988). Because so many neurotransmitters exert their effects through this second messenger, it is difficult to determine lithium's overall effect on brain activity.

## SUMMARY

1. A person with a unipolar disorder has periods of depression; someone with a bipolar disorder has periods of both depression and mania. (p. 556)

2. Intense stress may aggravate depression by provoking release of certain transmitters faster than they can be resynthesized. (p. 557)

3. Many depressed people have abnormalities in their hormones, especially sex hormones and thyroid hormones. (p. 558)

4. It is possible to have a hereditary predisposition toward depression. (p. 558)

5. The Borna disease virus has sometimes been found in the blood of people suffering from depression or bipolar disorder. (p. 559)

6. Most depressed people show greater activity in the right than in the left cerebral hemisphere. (p. 559)

7. Studies of the effects of antidepressants on animals led to the initial hypothesis that depression and mania relate to abnormalities at the catecholamine synapses. (p. 560)

8. Three kinds of drugs are useful as antidepressants: tricyclics, monoamine oxidase inhibitors, and serotonin reuptake blockers. (p. 562)

9. Although antidepressant drugs alter synaptic activities rapidly, they do not alleviate depression until a person has taken the drugs for 2 weeks or more. During that period they increase the release of serotonin or catecholamines and decrease receptor sensitivity to those neurotransmitters. (p. 563)

10. Electroconvulsive therapy, now used under different conditions from those common in its early days, is effective against certain types of depression. (p. 564)

11. Most depressed people have sleep troubles related to a shift of their circadian rhythms. Shifting their time of sleep or temporarily depriving them of sleep can relieve their depression. (p. 565)

12. Certain people become depressed every winter; their depression can be relieved by bright light that extends the apparent daylight period. (p. 567)

13. The most effective known therapy for bipolar disorder is lithium. (p. 568)

## REVIEW QUESTIONS

1. What are the symptoms of depression and of mania? (p. 554)

2. What is the difference between unipolar disorder and bipolar disorder? (p. 555)

3. What evidence indicates that stress and hormonal fluctuations trigger episodes of depression, even if they may not be the ultimate cause of depression? (p. 557)

4. By what means do tricyclic drugs and MAOIs prolong the effects of catecholamines and serotonin at the synapses? (p. 562)

5. Why has fluoxetine become popular as an antidepressant? Why are some people still skeptical about using it? (p. 562)

6. How long after someone starts taking antidepressant drugs is the person likely to experience relief from depression? What happens in the brain during that delay? (p. 563)

7. How are the procedures for delivering ECT different today from what they were in the 1950s? (p. 564)

8. What modification of the procedure for ECT reduces the impairment it causes in memory? (p. 565)

9. What kind of sleep abnormality is most characteristic of depressed people? (p. 565)

10. What change in sleep timing can relieve depression? (p. 566)

11. What treatment is effective for seasonal affective disorder? (p. 567)

12. What is the most common treatment for bipolar disorder? (p. 568)

## THOUGHT QUESTIONS

1. Certain people suffer from what they describe as "post-Christmas depression." They claim that they feel depressed as a letdown after all the excitement of the holiday season. What other explanation could you offer?

2. ECT applied over the right hemisphere only can relieve depression with minimum impairment of memory. What result would you expect from ECT applied over just the left hemisphere? Why?

## SUGGESTIONS FOR FURTHER READING

**Galton, L.** (1979). *You may not need a psychiatrist.* New York: Simon & Schuster. Discusses how vitamin deficiencies, sleep abnormalities, brain damage, and a variety of other problems can lead to depression and other disorders.

**McNeal, E. T., & Cimbolic, P.** (1986). Antidepressants and biochemical theories of depression. *Psychological Bulletin, 99,* 361–374. A good overview of evidence linking depression to abnormalities of transmission at the synapses.

# Schizophrenia and Autism

Here is a conversation between two people diagnosed with schizophrenia (Haley, 1959):

**A:** Do you work at the air base?

**B:** You know what I think of work. I'm 33 in June, do you mind?

**A:** June?

**B:** 33 years old in June. This stuff goes out the window after I live this, uh—leave this hospital. So I can't get my vocal cords back. So I lay off cigarettes. I'm in a spatial condition, from outer space myself. . . .

**A:** I'm a real spaceship from across.

**B:** A lot of people talk that way, like crazy, but Believe it or not, by Ripley, take it or leave it—alone—it's in the *Examiner*, it's in the comic section, Believe it or not, by Ripley, Robert E. Ripley, Believe it or not, but we don't have to believe anything, unless I feel like it. Every little rosette—too much alone.

**A:** Yeah, it could be possible.

**B:** I'm a civilian seaman.

**A:** Could be possible. I take my bath in the ocean.

**B:** Bathing stinks. You know why? Cause you can't quit when you feel like it. You're in the service.

People with schizophrenia say and do things that other people (including most other people with schizophrenia) find difficult to understand. The reasons behind the disorder are still not well understood, but they apparently include a large biological component.

## THE CHARACTERISTICS OF SCHIZOPHRENIA

**Schizophrenia** is a generally severe disorder characterized by deteriorating ability to function in everyday life and some combination of hallucinations, delusions, thought disorder, movement disorder, and inappropriate emotional expressions. The *Diagnostic and Statistical Manual of Mental Disorders, Third Edition Revised* (DSM-III-R), provides a more formal and complete description (American Psychiatric Association, 1987). Its diagnosis is difficult; many people show some

570

symptoms of both schizophrenia and other disorders, especially bipolar disorder or depression. Therapists try very hard to maintain the same standards of diagnosis, but inevitably some apply the standards differently from others. This difficulty of diagnosis is one reason why different studies of the physiology of schizophrenia sometimes come to different conclusions.

Schizophrenia was originally known as *dementia praecox*, which is Latin for "premature deterioration of the mind." In 1911 Eugen Bleuler introduced the term *schizophrenia*, which has been preferred ever since. Although schizophrenia is Greek for "split mind," it is *not* the same thing as *multiple personality*, a condition in which a person alternates between one personality and another. A schizophrenic person has only one personality. The split in the schizophrenic mind is between the emotional and intellectual sides of the person. That is, what the person expresses emotionally—or fails to express emotionally—is often at odds with what the person is saying.

## Behavioral Symptoms

Most people with schizophrenia have either hallucinations, delusions, or a characteristic thought disorder. **Hallucinations** are sensory experiences that do not correspond to reality, such as hearing voices. Few people with schizophrenia have visual hallucinations, which are more characteristic of drug abusers. **Delusions** are beliefs that other people regard as unfounded, such as the belief that one is severely persecuted or the belief that invaders from outer space are trying to control one's behavior.

The most typical **thought disorder** of schizophrenia is a difficulty understanding and using abstract concepts. For example, a schizophrenic person has trouble understanding such proverbs as "When the cat is away, the mice will play," interpreting them literally. Schizophrenic people also show a lack of organizing purpose in their stream of thoughts and have loose associations among ideas, as in a dream.

Hallucinations, delusions, and thought disorder are sometimes known as **positive symptoms** of schizophrenia because they represent the presence of certain behaviors. In contrast, **negative symptoms** represent the absence of certain behaviors: Many schizophrenic people lack emotional expression, fail to interact socially with others, and speak very little. Some researchers find that patients with mostly negative symptoms are more likely to have brain atrophy (Goetz & van Kammen, 1986); however, patients with either kind of symptoms respond to the same kinds of treatment (Kay & Singh, 1989).

Before antischizophrenic drugs first became available in the mid-1950s, most schizophrenic people were confined to a mental hospital for life. Today, about one-third of all people with schizophrenia manage to live normally with the aid of drugs and outpatient treatment. About 10 percent enter a mental hospital once and then leave, never to return (Pokorny, 1978). The others are alternately in and out of mental hospitals all their lives. Because schizophrenia lasts so many years, its economic and human costs are almost as great as those of more common ailments, such as heart attacks (Andrews et al., 1985).

## Demographic Data

Because of borderline cases and disagreements about diagnosis, it is difficult to state the exact incidence of schizophrenia. A common estimate is that 1 to 2 percent of the population will be afflicted with the disorder at some point (Robins et al., 1984). Schizophrenia occurs in all ethnic groups and in all parts of the world, although it is rare in the tropics. It is reported 10 to 100 times more often in the United States and Europe than in most Third World countries (Torrey, 1986). Within the United States, it is more common in impoverished areas than in wealthy areas. It is about equally common in men and women, although it is generally diagnosed at an earlier age in men (Lewine, 1981).

Schizophrenia may have either an **acute** (sudden) or **chronic** (gradual) onset. Generally, people with an acute onset have a greater probability of recovery (Crow, 1980). Schizophrenia is generally first diagnosed in people between the ages of 15 and 30, less commonly in people 30 to 45, and almost never at later ages. Once a person has the disorder, however, it is likely to continue for years, perhaps for life.

## BRAIN ATROPHY OR DYSFUNCTION

Many but not all schizophrenic patients show signs of mild brain damage or atrophy (shrinkage) in parts of the thalamus, cerebral cortex, and hippocampus. Brain damage or atrophy is not typically found in patients suffering from other psychological disorders.

Several lines of evidence point to brain damage in schizophrenia. First, examinations after death reveal that the forebrains of schizophrenic people are about 6 percent lighter than those of other mental patients (R. Brown et al., 1986).

**Figure 16.9**
**The hippocampus of two normal people (left) and two people with schizophrenia (right)**
*Notice the atrophy of the brains on the right. (From Bogerts, Meertz, & Schönfeldt-Bausch, 1985; photos courtesy of B. Bogerts.)*

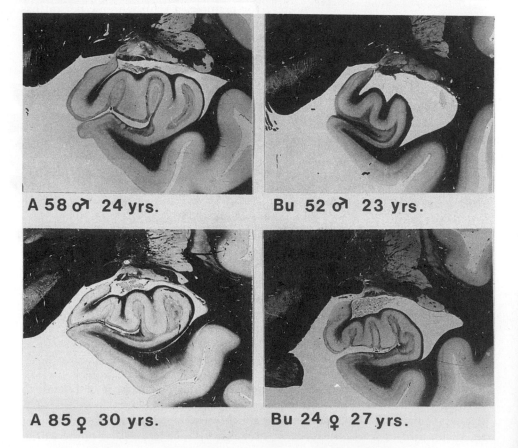

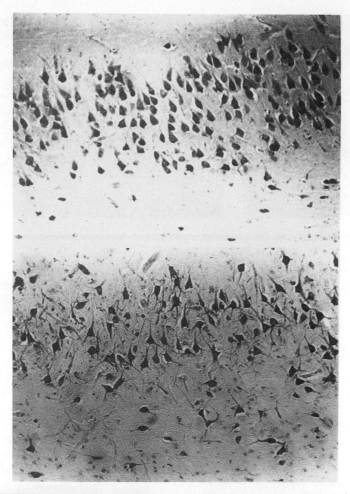

**Figure 16.10
Cells of the hippocampus in a normal person (top) and a person with schizophrenia (bottom)**
*The cells on the bottom are arranged in a more haphazard, disorganized manner. (Photos courtesy of Arnold Scheibel.)*

Schizophrenic brains have fewer neurons in the cerebral cortex (Benes, Davidson, & Bird, 1986), the dorsomedial nucleus of the thalamus (Pakkenberg, 1990), the amygdala, and the hippocampus (Altshuler, Casanova, Goldberg, & Kleinman, 1990; Bogerts, Meertz, & Schönfeldt-Bausch, 1985). Neurons in parts of the hippocampus and cerebral cortex are more scattered or less neatly arranged than those of nonschizophrenic brains (Benes & Bird, 1987). (See Figures 16.9 and 16.10.)

Through such techniques as PET scans, CAT scans, and regional cerebral blood flow (see Chapter 4), we can determine the size and activity of various structures in living people. The results indicate that many schizophrenic people have larger than normal ventricles (Andreasen et al., 1990a; DeLisi et al., 1986; Luchins, Lewine, & Meltzer, 1984; Pearlson et al., 1989). The ventricles are fluid-filled spaces; enlarged ventricles mean that neurons occupy less space. (See Figure 16.11.) Researchers are not sure why the ventricles are enlarged in some patients and not others. Scattered reports suggest that enlargement occurs most commonly in males (Andreasen et al., 1990b) or in those with a long history of poor social behavior (Pandurangi, Bilder, Rieder, Mukherjee, & Hamer, 1988). Enlarged ventricles are about as common in young patients as in old patients (Andreasen et al., 1990b), suggesting that the cell loss occurs early in life rather than accumulating over the life span.

Schizophrenia and
Autism

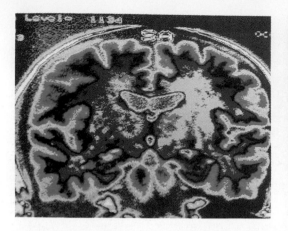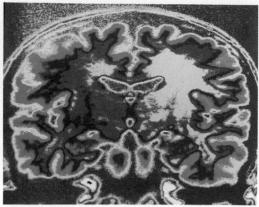

**Figure 16.11
Coronal sections
through the brains
of identical twins**
*The twin on the left has
schizophrenia; the twin on the
right does not. Note that the
ventricles (near the center of
each brain) are larger in the
twin with schizophrenia.
(Photos courtesy of E. F.
Torrey & M. F. Casanova/
NIMH.)*

According to most studies, schizophrenic people also have lower than average levels of brain metabolism. Many studies find that the metabolism is especially low in the temporal and frontal areas of the cortex (Andreasen et al., 1986; Farkas et al., 1984; Wolkin et al., 1985), but some studies find the metabolism equally depressed in all areas (Gur et al., 1987). One study found a normal metabolic rate in the frontal cortex but an *elevated* metabolic rate in posterior areas of the cortex (Mathew, Wilson, Tant, Robinson, & Prakash, 1988). Although the pattern of results seems inconsistent, there does seem to be a trend toward greater posterior than anterior metabolic rate. (See Figure 16.12.)

Schizophrenic people fail to recruit extra activity in parts of the frontal cortex when necessary. For example, when healthy people sort cards according to complex or changing rules, they recruit metabolic activity in the dorsolateral part of their prefrontal cortex. Generally, the greater the increase in metabolic activity, the better they perform the task. Schizophrenic people fail to show such a rise in metabolic activity when they attempt these tasks (Berman, Zec, & Weinberger, 1986; Weinberger, Berman, & Zec, 1986), and they perform the tasks poorly (Goldberg, Weinberger, Berman, Pliskin, & Podd, 1987).

People with schizophrenia also show signs of impaired transfer of information across the corpus callosum. For example, an experimenter points at one of the patient's fingers, say the ring finger of the left hand, and asks the patient to raise the same finger on the opposite hand. In general, schizophrenic patients perform poorly on such tasks (Craft, Willerman, & Bigler, 1987). They also show deficits implying a left-hemisphere impairment, such as being slow to shift their attention from an object on their left to an object on their right (Posner, Early, Reiman, Pardo, & Dhawan, 1988). These results suggest that the lateralization of function between the two hemispheres fails to take place properly in the brains of people who eventually become schizophrenic.

## POSSIBLE CAUSES OF SCHIZOPHRENIA

The results just discussed indicate that *something* causes brain damage in schizophrenic people. What might that something be?

Over the years, a great many hypotheses have been proposed and considered. A few examples: Schizophrenia may be due to the accumulation of copper or

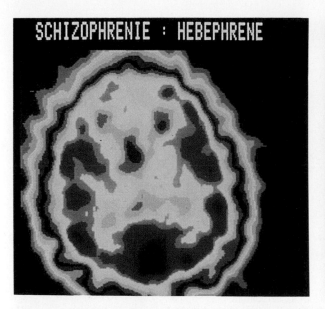
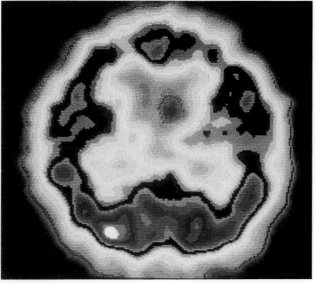

Figure 16.12
PET scans of
(a) a person with
schizophrenia and
(b) a person without
schizophrenia
*Red indicates the highest level
of metabolism, followed by
yellow, green, and blue. Several studies find that people
with schizophrenia have lower
than normal activity in their
frontal cortex (toward the top
in each figure). (SPL/Photo
Researchers, Inc.)*

other heavy metal ions in the brain (Bowman & Lewis, 1982). The schizophrenic brain may produce certain chemicals, such as bufotenine, that can induce hallucinations (Kety, 1975; Potkin et al., 1979; Wyatt, Termini, & Davis, 1971). The schizophrenic brain may produce 6-hydroxydopamine, which would destroy norepinephrine synapses, lead to a loss of pleasure and motivated behavior, and sometimes impair movement (Stein & Wise, 1971).

Support for all of those hypotheses, as well as several others, has faded, although we are not in a position to rule them out altogether. Now let us consider some of the possibilities that current investigators take most seriously.

## Genetics

According to most studies, schizophrenia runs in families (Figure 16.13). That is, people with schizophrenia are more likely than others to have schizophrenic relatives (Gottesman, 1991). Furthermore, even among the unschizophrenic relatives of a schizophrenic patient, many show indications of minor brain damage or dysfunction, just as the schizophrenic patients do (Kinney, Woods, & Yurgelun-Todd, 1986; Marcus, Hans, Mednick, Schulsinger, & Michelsen, 1985).

Similarity within a family indicates only that genetics is a possible factor, however. Members of a family may resemble one another because of either genetics or similar environment. We must look further to distinguish between these two possibilities.

**Twin Studies** One line of evidence is a comparison of monozygotic (identical) twins and dizygotic (fraternal) twins. (See Appendix A for a review of genetics.) When one monozygotic twin is schizophrenic, the other twin of the pair has about a 50 percent probability of becoming schizophrenic also. Even those who do not become schizophrenic are likely to develop other serious disturbances, including borderline schizophrenia (Kendler & Robinette, 1983). On the other

Schizophrenia and
Autism

575

Figure 16.13
Probability of
developing
schizophrenia for
people with various
relationships to a
schizophrenic person
*The probability is highest for*
*people who are close relatives.*
*(Based on data from I. I.*
*Gottesman, 1991.)*

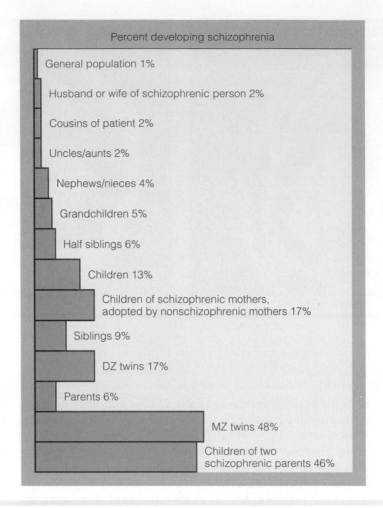

Percent developing schizophrenia

General population 1%

Husband or wife of schizophrenic person 2%

Cousins of patient 2%

Uncles/aunts 2%

Nephews/nieces 4%

Grandchildren 5%

Half siblings 6%

Children 13%

Children of schizophrenic mothers,
adopted by nonschizophrenic mothers 17%

Siblings 9%

DZ twins 17%

Parents 6%

MZ twins 48%

Children of two
schizophrenic parents 46%

hand, if one dizygotic twin is schizophrenic, the other twin has only about a 15 percent probability of schizophrenia (Kendler, 1983; McGuffin, Farmer, Gottesman, Murray, & Reveley, 1984). That is, monozygotic twins have a 50 percent **concordance** (similarity) for schizophrenia, and dizygotic twins have a 15 percent concordance. Presumably, the monozygotic twins have a greater concordance because they share more genes. Furthermore, those twin pairs who mistakenly thought they were monozygotic (identical) but who are really dizygotic are less concordant for schizophrenia than those twin pairs who always thought they were dizygotic but who are really monozygotic (Kendler, 1983). That is, *being* monozygotic has a greater effect on a pair of twins than *being treated as* monozygotic.

Curiously, the concordance rate for schizophrenia between monozygotic twins is related to the concordance rate for handedness. Some monozygotic twins are mirror images of one another: One is right handed, the other is left handed, and the two are mirror images in physical appearance (Segal, 1984). Among pairs of monozygotic twins that are both right handed, the schizophrenia concordance rate is 92 percent. That is, if one is schizophrenic, the other has a 92 percent probability of being schizophrenic as well. But among pairs in which one is right handed and the other is left handed, the concordance rate is only 25 percent (Boklage, 1977).

**Adopted Children Who Become Schizophrenic** A second line of evidence supporting a genetic basis for schizophrenia is an examination of adopted children who become schizophrenic. More of the biological relatives than the adoptive relatives of such children suffer from schizophrenia themselves (Kessler, 1980; Kety, Rosenthal, Wender, Schulsinger, & Jacobsen, 1975; Lowing, Mirsky, & Pereira, 1983). A child of a schizophrenic parent adopted by a normal couple is more likely to become schizophrenic than is a child of normal parents adopted by a couple that includes one schizophrenic (Wender, Rosenthal, Kety, Schulsinger, & Welner, 1974). These data point to either genetics or prenatal environment as a determining factor in schizophrenia.

Finally, in rare cases an adopted child has a **paternal half-sibling** who was also adopted. Paternal half-siblings have the same father but different mothers; they are more closely related than cousins but less closely related than brother and sister. One study in Denmark found sixty-three adopted schizophrenics who had a paternal half-sibling adopted by another family. Eight of the sixty-three half-siblings were schizophrenic also—a concordance well above the approximately 1 percent prevalence of schizophrenia in the population. Note that because these children had different mothers, they did not share a common environment even before birth.

**Children of Schizophrenic Parents and Their Twins** Suppose a schizophrenic person has a twin who does not become schizophrenic and that both twins eventually become parents. What risk of schizophrenia do their children have?

Researchers have tested this question by going through the medical records of Norway and Denmark. (The Scandinavian countries have kept amazingly thorough records on their citizens throughout the twentieth century.) Those records indicate that the children of the unschizophrenic twin have almost the same risk of schizophrenia as the children of the schizophrenic twin (Gottesman & Bertelson, 1989; Kringlen & Cramer, 1989).

What do these data mean? Apparently both twins inherited genes that predispose a person to schizophrenia. Some unknown influence caused those genes to produce schizophrenia in one twin and not in the other, but both twins were capable of passing the genes to their children. These data indicate that genes are not the whole explanation of schizophrenia; clearly someone with genes for schizophrenia may avoid becoming schizophrenic. They also suggest that people without genes for schizophrenia seldom become schizophrenic. (If purely environmental factors caused schizophrenia in a twin with no genes for schizophrenia, the other twin would not be likely to have schizophrenic children.)

**The Search for Schizophrenic Genes** Data of the types just discussed make a convincing case that genetic predisposition plays an important role in schizophrenia. Most researchers believe that further research of the same type will not tell us much that we do not already know (Holzman & Matthysse, 1990). The next step is to find out whether schizophrenia depends on one gene or many, and how the gene or genes produce their effects on the brain.

In 1988, one group of researchers reported evidence that a gene for schizophrenia is located on human chromosome 5 (R. Sherrington et al., 1988). In the same issue of the same journal, another group of researchers reported evidence that there is *not* a gene for schizophrenia on chromosome 5 (Kennedy et al., 1988). Paradoxically, both research groups may have been right. Schizophrenia is a complex disorder that probably results from somewhat different causes in different people. It may well be that several genes on different chromosomes can lead to schizophrenia and therefore that researchers working with different population samples will get different results.

**Beyond Simple Genetic Determinism** Clearly, heredity is a major contributor to schizophrenia but not the only contributor. Occasionally someone with no known schizophrenic relatives becomes schizophrenic. Conversely, the monozygotic twin of a schizophrenic person may develop normally.

Paul Meehl (1989) has proposed that the effect of the gene or genes is to produce a defect of neural activity he calls "schizotypy," characterized by altered sensory and thought processes. A variety of environmental factors determine whether schizotypy eventually develops into schizophrenia. These environmental factors may include stressful experiences in the family, at school, or in other social settings. But they can also include infections and diseases, dietary insufficiencies, a blow to the head, and other biological influences. At this point we do not know which environmental factors are most crucial.

## Stress as a Possible Trigger for Schizophrenia

Many psychologists once believed that schizophrenia was caused by the parents' behavior. The parents of certain schizophrenics were reported to give confusing "come here, go away" messages, for example. This hypothesis is now considered obsolete. The main reason for its downfall was the results of adoption studies. The probability of schizophrenia relates more to the genes that the biological parents provide than to the environment that the adopting parents provide. Furthermore, the time course of the disorder does not fit the hypothesis; schizophrenia is usually first diagnosed at ages 20 to 30, when parental influence should be lessening.

Other types of experience may have something to do with the onset of schizophrenia, however. Stressful experiences may aggravate the condition, even if they are not the original cause. Curt Richter (1956, 1958a, 1958b) offered an animal model of schizophrenia. He exposed rats to the highly stressful experience of swimming in turbulent water nonstop for 60 hours. The survivors held abnormal positions rigidly for long times and occasionally leaped suddenly, as if they were responding to a hallucinated sight or sound. Promising as this demonstration may have been, however, it was not pursued further.

In humans, surveys indicate that people with schizophrenia are no more likely than other psychiatric patients—and only slightly more likely than normal, healthy people—to report stressful events during the months just before their first diagnosis of schizophrenia (Rabkin, 1980). A reasonable hypothesis is that extreme stress may provoke a sudden onset of schizophrenia in very rare cases, which might not be evident in the group averages. In more cases, stress may accelerate a schizophrenic deterioration or trigger it to start earlier than it would have otherwise. In most cases, however, stressful events are probably not responsible for the onset of schizophrenia.

## A Virus?

One peculiarity sets schizophrenia apart from other psychological disorders: More schizophrenic people are born during the winter months than during any other season (Bradbury & Miller, 1985). No such tendency is found in the birth dates of people suffering from depression, alcoholism, or other psychological disturbances (Watson, Tilleskjor, Kucala, & Jacobs, 1984). This **season-of-birth effect** for schizophrenia is stronger in the northern United States than in the south;

# Effects of the AIDS Virus on the Brain

Acquired immune deficiency syndrome (AIDS) is a fatal condition caused by a retrovirus known as HTLV-III (human T-lymphotropic virus III). Unlike the influenza virus and other viruses that can be transmitted by casual contact between two people, the AIDS virus can be transmitted only if it enters the blood of the recipient. It enters the blood if one receives a blood transfusion from a person with the virus or if one takes an injection with a needle previously used by an infected person. The virus can also be transmitted along with the sperm during sex if the sex partner has a break in the skin where the virus can enter. It has spread widely among homosexuals in the United States. Among heterosexuals, men can transmit it to women more easily than women can transmit it to men (Kaplan, 1988).

Because the AIDS virus resembles a virus common in African monkeys, humans probably got the virus from those monkeys, perhaps as recently as the 1950s. From its point of origin it spread slowly at first, then more rapidly. The virus has an incubation period of 5 years or more. That is, a person may have the virus for years before showing any symptoms.

The virus most often infects T4 lymphocytes, cells of the immune system (Gallo, 1987). With these cells inactivated, the body becomes more vulnerable to all infections; the person has no defense against any of the viruses and bacteria that it could otherwise fight off without any trouble.

The AIDS virus can cause brain damage in two ways. First, because the virus has weakened the body's immune system, the brain is vulnerable to infections, just as the other organs are. Various patients suffer from encephalitis, meningitis, bacterial infections, brain tumors, and hemorrhage of the blood vessels in the brain (Levy, Bredesen, & Rosenblum, 1985). Second, in many patients the virus enters the brain, where it infects microglial cells in particular (Watkins et al., 1990). The viral infection of the brain may lead to intellectual deterioration and a loss of coordinated movement (Price et al., 1988).

worldwide, the tendency disappears in the tropics. It is particularly pronounced for schizophrenics who have no schizophrenic relatives. That is, a family with several close schizophrenic relatives has a fairly high probability that any given child will become schizophrenic, regardless of when that child is born. A family with no history of schizophrenia ordinarily has very little probability of having a child who will become schizophrenic, but that probability increases if the child is born in the winter (Bradbury & Miller, 1985).

What might account for the season-of-birth effect? One possibility, though not the only one, is viral infection. A number of viruses, such as the rabies virus and the AIDS virus (Digression 16.1), selectively damage the brain. Perhaps an infant who is exposed to a virus at some critical stage of development would suffer certain kinds of brain damage (such as cortical and hippocampal atrophy) and eventually develop schizophrenia.

Viral epidemics are more common in fall than in winter, especially in northern climates. Therefore, the reasoning goes that during a fall epidemic, many pregnant women become infected with a virus. The second trimester of pregnancy is important for brain development; a woman who is in her second trimester of pregnancy during the fall gives birth in the winter. In short, according to this hypothesis, babies born in the winter have an increased risk of schizophrenia because their mothers may have had a viral infection in the preceding fall.

Schizophrenia and Autism

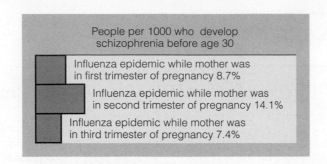

People per 1000 who develop
schizophrenia before age 30

Influenza epidemic while mother was
in first trimester of pregnancy 8.7%

Influenza epidemic while mother was
in second trimester of pregnancy 14.1%

Influenza epidemic while mother was
in third trimester of pregnancy 7.4%

**Figure 16.14
Probability of
developing schizophre-
nia by people who
were in various stages
of gestation during an
influenza epidemic**
*The probability of schizophre-
nia is greatest if the epidemic
occurred during the second
trimester. (Based on data of
Mednick, Machon, & Hut-
tunen, 1990.)*

To test this hypothesis, we can ask several questions. First, is the season-of-birth effect particularly strong in years of a major fall epidemic of some viral disease? The answer is apparently yes. For example, Europe had a major influenza epidemic in the fall of 1957. Women who were in their second trimester of pregnancy that fall gave birth in January to March of 1958. The schizophrenia rate for Finnish children born in January to March of 1958 was almost twice as high as the rate for children born before January or after March (Mednick, Machon, & Huttunen, 1990). (See Figure 16.14.) Data for children born in Edinburgh, Scotland, in 1958 showed a trend in the same direction, although it was not statistically significant (Kendell & Kemp, 1989).

Second, if the incidence of viral disease is greater than usual in a month not in the fall, will the incidence of schizophrenia be greater than usual for the babies born three months later? Studies in both Denmark and the northeastern United States have reported that the answer is yes (Barr, Mednick, & Munk-Jorgensen, 1990; Torrey, Rawlings, & Waldman, 1988). Those studies suggest that almost any viral infection is dangerous; the risk of schizophrenia increased after epidemics of influenza, measles, polio, and chicken pox.

Because all the reported effects are small, we need to examine more data before drawing any firm conclusions. At this point we can note only a "possible" relationship between viral epidemics and the season-of-birth effect.

If the relationship is genuine, it is still uncertain how to explain it. Ordinarily, viruses do not cross from a mother's blood into her fetus's blood. Perhaps the mother's fever affects the brain development of the fetus, or the activation of the mother's immune system may directly or indirectly affect the fetus.

One more point about the viral hypothesis: It assumes that the virus damages brain development prior to birth, yet schizophrenia generally develops gradually, with symptoms becoming pronounced by age 20 to 30. Why would the symptoms take so long to emerge?

The time course may not be so puzzling as it seems at first (Weinberger, 1987). One of the primary areas of impairment in schizophrenia is the dorsolateral prefrontal cortex. Schizophrenic people generally perform poorly on tasks known to depend on that area, and they fail to recruit extra metabolic activity in that area when performing such tasks. As we saw in Chapter 15, the dorsolateral prefrontal cortex is one of the last brain areas to reach maturity. Infant monkeys with damage in that area behave normally at first and gradually become *more* impaired at a later age when the dorsolateral prefrontal cortex would ordinarily become mature. Similarly, we can imagine that the same kind of damage in human infants might produce more serious behavioral problems in late adolescence and young adulthood than it did in early childhood. Thus, particular kinds of early brain damage may lead to delayed effects on psychological well-being.

# THE BIOCHEMISTRY OF SCHIZOPHRENIA

Whatever the actual cause of schizophrenia may be—genetics, stress, virus—it must act through changes in the brain's structure and chemistry. Since the discovery of antischizophrenic drugs in the 1950s, much research has made it clear that schizophrenia is associated with an abnormality related to the dopamine synapses of the brain. Still, the exact nature of that abnormality remains elusive.

## Chemicals That Can Provoke a State Similar to Schizophrenia

Large doses of amphetamine, especially if repeated often within a few days, can induce **amphetamine psychosis,** a condition that includes hallucinations, delusions, and other symptoms similar to schizophrenia. Large doses of cocaine, LSD, or Antabuse sometimes also induce a state similar to schizophrenia. The main differences between drug-induced psychosis and schizophrenia are that victims of the drug-induced states often report visual hallucinations, while schizophrenic people seldom do, and that a drug-induced psychosis is generally temporary (Ellinwood, 1969; Sloviter, Damiano, & Connor, 1980).

The drugs that can produce psychosis all increase the stimulation of dopamine synapses. For example, amphetamine increases the release of dopamine from the presynaptic endings. The drug L-DOPA, which is often given as a treatment for Parkinson's disease, also stimulates dopamine synapses. Among the typical side effects of L-DOPA are delusions, such as delusions of persecution, and other behaviors characteristic of schizophrenia (Gershon, Angrist, & Shopsin, 1977). Moreover, L-DOPA aggravates the symptoms of schizophrenic patients. In short, overstimulation of dopamine synapses can produce the symptoms of schizophrenia.

## Neuroleptics and the Dopamine Hypothesis of Schizophrenia

The strongest link between dopamine synapses and schizophrenia comes from studies of drugs that alleviate schizophrenia. In the 1950s researchers discovered that the drug **chlorpromazine** (trade name Thorazine) helps to relieve schizophrenia. Before the introduction of chlorpromazine, few schizophrenic patients who entered a mental hospital ever left. Chlorpromazine and related drugs can halt the course of the disease, especially when treatment begins at an early stage. The drugs do not actually cure schizophrenia; rather, they control it, somewhat as insulin controls diabetes. A schizophrenic person must continue to take the drug—daily or monthly, depending on the drug—or the symptoms are likely to return (Davis, 1976).

If chlorpromazine were the only drug useful in treating schizophrenia, we would have no easy way to determine how it works because it affects brain chemistry in so many ways. The best way to determine how it works is to find what it has in common with other effective drugs.

Researchers have discovered many antischizophrenic or **neuroleptic drugs.** Most of them belong to two chemical families, the **phenothiazines,** which include chlorpromazine, and the **butyrophenones,** which include **haloperidol** (trade name Haldol). All these drugs share two properties: They block the postsynaptic dopamine receptors (Snyder, Banerjee, Yamamura, & Greenberg, 1974; van Praag, 1977) and they block the release of dopamine from the presynaptic neuron (Pickar et al., 1986; Seeman & Lee, 1975).

Figure 16.15 illustrates the relationship between the antischizophrenic effect of a drug and its ability to block postsynaptic dopamine receptors. For each drug,

## Figure 16.15
## Antidopamine effects of neuroleptic drugs

*Drugs are arranged along the horizontal axis in terms of the average daily dose prescribed for schizophrenic patients. (Horizontal lines indicate common ranges of dosage.) Along the vertical axis is a measurement of the amount of each drug required to achieve a certain degree of blockage of postsynaptic dopamine receptors. A drug's effectiveness in blocking dopamine synapses is almost perfectly correlated with its ability to control schizophrenia. (From Seeman, Lee, Chau-Wong, & Wong, 1976.)*

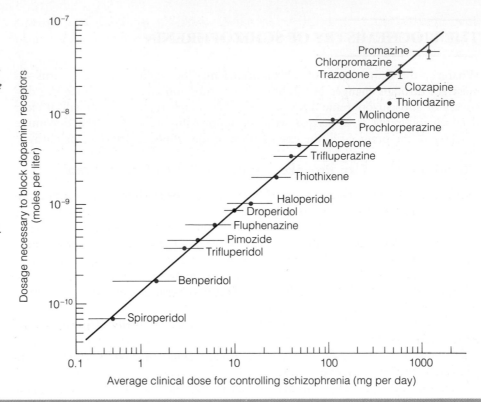

researchers determined the mean dose prescribed for schizophrenic patients (displayed along the horizontal axis). Presumably, drugs such as spiroperidol (at the lower left in the figure) are prescribed in the lowest doses because they are effective in these low doses; drugs such as chlorpromazine are prescribed in larger doses because such doses are necessary to achieve the desired effect. The investigators also determined what dose of each drug is necessary to block dopamine receptors (displayed along the vertical axis). As the figure shows, the more effective a given drug is for blocking dopamine receptors, the more effective it is for relieving schizophrenia (Seeman, Lee, Chau-Wong, & Wong, 1976).

These results give rise to the **dopamine hypothesis of schizophrenia.** According to this hypothesis, schizophrenia results from excess activity at dopamine synapses; neuroleptic drugs relieve schizophrenia by decreasing that activity.

### Strengths and Weaknesses of the Dopamine Hypothesis

The fact that dopamine-blocking drugs relieve schizophrenia is certainly strong evidence that the causes of schizophrenia have something to do with dopamine synapses. Furthermore, most schizophrenic patients blink more frequently than normal, a behavior that probably reflects excessive dopamine stimulation (Kleinman et al., 1984). Also, drugs that stimulate dopamine synapses can temporarily induce attention disorders in normal people that resemble the disorders of schizophrenic patients (Braff & Huey, 1988).

Despite the attractiveness of the dopamine hypothesis, some important questions remain concerning the role of dopamine in schizophrenia. First, people with schizophrenia do not have enormously elevated concentrations of dopamine or its metabolites in their blood or cerebrospinal fluid. Some studies have found normal concentrations, and others have found slightly elevated concentrations (Bacopoulous, Spokes, Bird, & Roth, 1979; Davis et al., 1985; Haracz, 1982; Rao, Gross, & Huber, 1984). But no studies have reported concentrations far from the normal range.

If the dopamine concentrations are approximately normal, what about the dopamine receptors? Several studies have reported substantial increases in the number of dopamine receptors in schizophrenic brains (for example, Seeman et al., 1984). However, nearly all the patients in those studies had been taking neuroleptic drugs, and it is likely that the drugs themselves elevated the number of dopamine receptors. Other studies have carefully limited their scope to young schizophrenic patients who had never taken neuroleptic drugs. Unfortunately, the data are in conflict; some studies have found an elevated concentration of dopamine receptors in these patients (Wong et al., 1986), while other studies have found normal concentrations (Farde et al., 1990).

A further difficulty for the dopamine hypothesis is the time course for the effects of neuroleptic drugs. Although such drugs block dopamine receptors almost at once and reach their full effectiveness within a few days, their effects on behavior build up gradually over 2 or 3 weeks (Lipton & Nemeroff, 1978). As with the similar pattern for antidepressant drugs, neuroleptic drugs probably induce gradual changes in both the pattern of release by the presynaptic neuron and the sensitivity of the postsynaptic neuron. Changes in the postsynaptic neuron may include changes in the proteins within the cell (Okada, Crow, & Roberts, 1990).

One possibility is that prolonged use of neuroleptic drugs decreases the number of spontaneously active dopamine neurons in the **mesolimbic system,** a set of neurons that project from the midbrain tegmentum to the limbic system (White & Wang, 1983). Another possibility is that the underlying problem in schizophrenia is not an excess of dopamine activity but a deficit of glutamate activity (Kornhuber, 1983). Glutamate is a neurotransmitter released by axons extending from the cerebral cortex to the limbic system; dopamine synapses are known to inhibit the release of glutamate in that area. One study reported that schizophrenics have only about half as much glutamate as normal in their brain (Kim & Kornhuber, 1982). If glutamate levels are low, one way to increase them would be to block the dopamine synapses that inhibit the glutamate synapses. One attraction of the decreased-glutamate hypothesis is that it fits with the evidence of damage to the cerebral cortex.

## Side Effects of Neuroleptic Drugs and the Search for Improved Drugs

Neuroleptic drugs produce a variety of unpleasant side effects. Some effects, such as impotence in males, develop quickly and cease as soon as the person stops taking the drug (Mitchell & Popkin, 1982). A more serious side effect is **tardive dyskinesia** (TARD-eev dis-kih-NEE-zhee-uh), tremors and other involuntary movements that develop gradually over years of drug use in many but not all people who take neuroleptics (Chouinard & Jones, 1980). It is most common in older patients who have been socially withdrawn for a long time (Waddington, Youssef, Dolphin, & Kinsella, 1987; Wegner, Catalano, Gibralter, & Kane, 1985). These, incidentally, are the patients for whom the drugs are generally least effective (Cseransky, Kaplan, & Hollister, 1985).

A simple, appealing theory is that tardive dyskinesia results from denervation supersensitivity (Chapter 15): Because of prolonged blockage of transmission at dopamine synapses, the postsynaptic neurons develop more receptors and begin to respond vigorously to even small amounts of dopamine. Slight stimulation of these highly responsive synapses leads to bursts of involuntary movements. (As we saw in Chapter 9, dopamine synapses in the basal ganglia stimulate movement.)

**Figure 16.16**
**Two major dopa-mine pathways**
*The mesolimbic system is apparently responsible for the symptoms of schizophrenia; the path to the basal ganglia is responsible for tardive dyskinesia, which sometimes results from use of neuroleptic drugs. (Adapted from Valzelli, 1980.)*

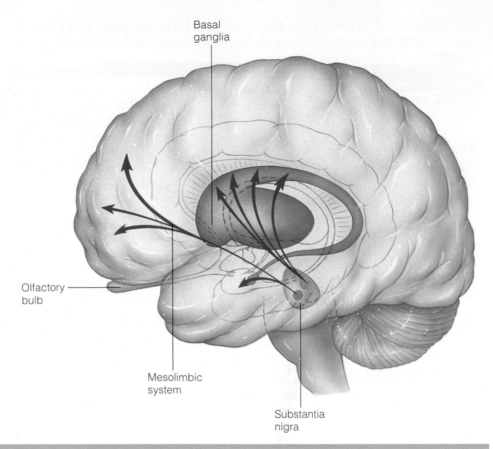

Basal ganglia

Olfactory bulb

Mesolimbic system

Substantia nigra

However, this simple theory appears to be wrong. In one study, investigators labeled dopamine receptors with a radioactive drug and then examined the brain with a PET scan. They found the same concentration of dopamine receptors in patients with and without tardive dyskinesia (Andersson et al., 1990). Evidently tardive dyskinesia is not linked to an excess of dopamine receptors, although the actual cause is unknown.

Once tardive dyskinesia emerges, it is apparently permanent, even after the patient stops taking the drug. In fact, without the drug, the dopamine receptors are no longer blocked, and the symptoms of tardive dyskinesia grow *worse*. Various drugs are in use for relieving tardive dyskinesia (Thaker et al., 1987).

Given the difficulties of combating tardive dyskinesia after it starts, the best solution is to prevent it from starting. Certain new drugs, called *atypical antipsychotic drugs*, show much promise for alleviating schizophrenia without causing tardive dyskinesia. The brain has several types of dopamine receptors and several dopamine pathways, each with somewhat different drug sensitivities (Albanese, Altavista, & Rossi, 1986). The neuroleptic drugs that produce tardive dyskinesia inhibit both the mesolimbic system and the dopamine path from the substantia nigra to the basal ganglia. Apparently the mesolimbic system has the most to do with the symptoms of schizophrenia; the path to the basal ganglia is responsible for tardive dyskinesia (see Figure 16.16). The new atypical antipsychotic drugs, such as clozapine and thioridazine, block dopamine activity in the mesolimbic system and thereby alleviate schizophrenia. Because they have less effect on the dopamine receptors in the basal ganglia, they are less likely to produce tardive dyskinesia (White & Wang, 1983).

# PROSPECTS FOR PREDICTION OR EARLY DIAGNOSIS OF SCHIZOPHRENIA

Suppose you are a psychiatrist with a patient who may be in the early stages of schizophrenia. Do you start the patient on neuroleptic drugs? If you do and the patient does not have schizophrenia, you do no good and you run the risk of causing tardive dyskinesia and other side effects. Yet, if the patient is suffering from schizophrenia, the longer you wait before starting the drugs, the more the patient will deteriorate and the less chance the patient will have for the drugs to help.

It would be beneficial to identify as quickly and as accurately as possible which people are on their way to becoming schizophrenic. Several kinds of studies have attempted to determine what distinguishes people who are likely to become schizophrenic.

## The Behavior of Children at Risk for Schizophrenia

One way to study the characteristics of people who will later become schizophrenic is to collect voluminous data on children or adolescents and then to conduct a follow-up study when they reach the age of 40, to determine which of them became schizophrenic and which did not. This kind of study faces two practical difficulties: It requires about 30 years to complete, and it requires an enormous sample of children or adolescents, since only about 1 percent will become schizophrenic. In spite of these difficulties, one such study has been conducted (Hartmann et al., 1984). It started with extensive interviews of 1,000 teenage boys. Many years later, after all these boys had passed the age of 40, investigators reexamined them. The 24 boys who eventually became schizophrenic (a higher number than we would expect from a sample of 1,000) had been different from the others in several regards: They had high levels of anxiety, difficulty in interpersonal relationships, a lack of ambition, a fear of trying anything new, and a negative attitude toward school. Most of them felt no affection for their fathers, and most rarely participated in group activities. They reported a lack of pleasure and a lack of a "sense of self continuing over time." We may regard these as characteristics of boys who are more likely than others to develop schizophrenia.

It is possible to simplify such a study, at the expense of losing part of the accuracy. An experimenter may compare a large number of children of schizophrenic mothers to children of other mothers. We can safely assume that a larger percentage of the children of schizophrenic mothers will eventually become schizophrenic themselves. Anything that is more common among these children than among children of normal mothers is presumably a characteristic of children *at risk* for schizophrenia.

Two such studies found that children at risk for schizophrenia (1) are relatively passive as babies, with a short attention span; (2) make few friends in school and often disrupt class (Parnas, Schulsinger, Schulsinger, Mednick, & Teasdale, 1982); and (3) have mild versions of the same thought disorders found in adult schizophrenics (Arboleda & Holzman, 1985).

## Biological Markers of Schizophrenia

Another approach to early diagnosis of schizophrenia is to identify biological markers—that is, biological characteristics found in schizophrenics, including both young, never-medicated schizophrenics and those whose behavior has been restored to normal by neuroleptic drugs. Such markers might help us to diagnose someone whose behavior has not yet deteriorated badly.

One promising marker is an impairment of smooth pursuit eye movements. There are two kinds of eye movements, saccadic movements and pursuit movements. A **saccadic eye movement** is a sudden shift from one target to another. When you read this page, your eyes jump from one fixation point to another by a saccadic movement. A **pursuit eye movement** is a movement to focus on a moving target, as when you watch another person walk by. Most schizophrenic people have deficits in their pursuit eye movements; either the eyes stop moving while the target continues or the eyes make a saccadic movement that takes them off the target. They have such difficulties both when their symptoms are severe and after drugs have relieved them. Patients with greater thought disorders tend to have greater impairments of their pursuit eye movements (Solomon, Holzman, Levin, & Gale, 1987). Almost half of their close relatives also have dysfunctions of pursuit eye movements (Holzman, 1985). Furthermore, college students with the least accurate pursuit eye movements have the highest incidence of *schizotypal personality*, a mild personality disorder related to schizophrenia (Siever, Coursey, Alterman, Buchsbaum, & Murphy, 1984). All these results support the hypothesis that impaired pursuit eye movements may indicate vulnerability to schizophrenia.

## INFANTILE AUTISM

**Figure 16.17**
*An autistic boy with two stereotyped behaviors: pulling on his ears and biting his hand. His right hand is covered with welts and calluses.*

**Infantile autism** is a rare condition, affecting about one child in 2,500. It resembles schizophrenia in certain regards, although the underlying causes differ. Like other kinds of abnormal behavior, autism comes in all degrees, from mild to severe. In full-blown cases the following behaviors are characteristic (Creak, 1961; Kanner, 1943; Ornitz & Ritvo, 1976):

1. *Social isolation.* The autistic child largely ignores other people, shows little attachment to parents or other relatives, and retreats into a world of his or her own. Many parents remark that their autistic child was an unresponsive infant from the start, failing to orient to adult faces or to "mold" to the parent's body when held.

2. *Stereotyped behaviors.* An autistic child rocks back and forth, bites his or her hands, stares at something, rotates an object, or engages in other repetitive behaviors for long, uninterrupted periods. Each autistic child has a special repertoire of preferred stereotyped behaviors. (See Figure 16.17.)

3. *Resistance to any change in routine.* The child establishes strong habits and becomes upset if the routine is changed.

4. *Abnormal responses to sensory stimuli.* The autistic child may ignore visual stimuli and sounds, especially speech, sometimes to such an extent that others assume the child is deaf. At other times the child may show an excessive startle reaction to a mild stimulus.

5. *Insensitivity to pain.* At least some of the time, autistic children fail to react to cuts, burns, extreme hot or cold, and other pain.

6. *Inappropriate emotional expressions.* Autistic children have sudden bouts of fear and crying for no obvious reason; at other times they display utter fearlessness and unprovoked laughter. Their emotions seem to spring from spontaneous internal sources rather than from any event.

7. *Disturbances of movement.* Certain autistic children may be hyperactive or inactive for prolonged periods.

8. *Poor use of speech.* Some autistic children never speak. A larger number learn the names of many common objects and develop good pronunciation but seldom use language to ask for anything or to enhance social relationships. Although they often repeat what they hear, they seldom initiate a conversation. Autistic children do not resemble deaf children or children with brain damage in the left hemisphere, however (Fein, Humes, Kaplan, Lucci, & Waterhouse, 1984). Although autistic children use language poorly, language impairment does not appear to be the root of their problems.

9. *Specific, limited intellectual abnormalities.* Many autistic children do well, even unusually well, on certain intellectual tasks but very poorly on others. The exact pattern of impairment varies from child to child. It is difficult to estimate their overall intelligence because they often fail to follow the instructions for a standard IQ test.

Autism has often been compared to schizophrenia because social isolation is a prominent characteristic of both. The two conditions differ in many regards, however. (See Table 16.2.) Autistic children rarely become schizophrenic adults (Petty, Ornitz, Michelman, & Zimmerman, 1984).

One mildly autistic boy who largely recovered from the disorder described his experiences as follows (White & White, 1987, pp. 224–225):

*At the age of about two I could say a fair number of words but hardly any full sentences. I was rarely able to hear sentences because my hearing distorted them. I was sometimes able to hear a word or two at the start and understand it and then the next lot of words sort of merged into one another and I could not make head or tail of it. . . . I did not get on very well at nursery school. . . . Sometimes when other kids spoke to me I could scarcely hear them and sometimes they sounded like bullets. I thought I was going to go deaf. . . . I was also frightened of the vacuum cleaner, the food mixer and the liquidizer because they sounded about five times as loud as they actually were. . . . Now off to school. . . . Shortly after the start of the [second year] the class went off on a trip to Bristol Zoo. The bus started with a clap of thunder, the*

## Table 16.2 Distinctions Between Schizophrenia and Autism

| Characteristics | Schizophrenia | Autism |
|---|---|---|
| Usual age at first diagnosis | 15 to 30 years old | A few months to 3 years old |
| Sex ratio | Equal numbers of males and females | Mostly males |
| Genetics | Clear genetic tendency | Uncertain; usually does not appear in same family with other autistics or schizophrenics |
| Response to neuroleptic drugs | Symptoms generally reduced | Little effect other than sedation |

*engine sounding almost four times as loud as normal and I had my hands in my ears for most of the journey. We finally arrived there. It was a very bright day and very hot. My eyesight blurred several times that day and once I could see no more than a yard in front. I jumped out of my skin when the animals made noises.*

Given these sensory distortions, we can begin to understand why an autistic child retreats into his or her own world.

## Biological Abnormalities in Autistic Children

Autistic children demonstrate such a wide variety of biological abnormalities that it is difficult to specify which of their many abnormalities is the primary problem. Autistic children give no indication of gross brain atrophy, damage, or malformation (Creasey et al., 1986). However, they do show signs of neurological impairment (Gillberg & Gillberg, 1983), including a very high metabolic rate in some brain regions and a very low rate in others (Rumsey et al., 1985). Many autistic children suffer from various other abnormalities, including deficient response to vestibular sensation (Ornitz, Atwell, Kaplan, & Westlake, 1985), EEG abnormalities, irregular waking-sleeping cycles, presence of potentially hallucinogenic chemicals in their blood, and many minor physical anomalies. One striking and puzzling characteristic, which no theory to date has even attempted to explain, is that most autistic children are unusually good looking. Also surprising is the report that many autistic children huddle around radiators or other heat sources in a room at normal temperature, as if they feel cold (Jeddi, 1970). Moreover, many parents have reported that whenever their autistic children have a fever, they behave almost normally, with better than usual communication with other people and more attention to their surroundings (Sullivan, 1980).

## Possible Causes of Autism

Autism, like most other psychological disorders, is probably the product of several causes. At this time, the most likely factors are biological.

**Parental Behavior?** The early accounts of autistic children described their parents as well-educated, upper-middle-class, intellectual people who displayed little emotion (Kanner, 1943). Certain theorists suggested that the parents' lack of emotional warmth actually caused the children to become autistic. Virtually all authorities now dismiss this hypothesis for several reasons. One is that later studies have failed to confirm the supposed overrepresentation of autism in intellectual or upper-middle-class families (Koegel, Schreibman, O'Neill, & Burke, 1983; Tsai, Stewart, & August, 1981). Second, providing a great deal of extra warmth and love does not alleviate autism significantly. Third, nearly all the brothers and sisters of autistic children develop normally. If the parents were bad enough to make one child behave so strangely, we would expect the other children in the family to be a bit odd as well. The normal behavior of the brothers and sisters argues strongly against the bad-parent theory.

**Genetics** Given how early the condition develops, it is natural to look for indications of a genetic basis. Twin studies do support a hereditary contribution. It is not easy to find many autistic children who have a twin, considering how rare autism is and how few people have twins. The most extensive study examined 40 pairs of twins that included at least one autistic child. Of 23 monozygotic pairs,

22 were concordant for autism; of 17 dizygotic pairs, 4 were concordant (Ritvo, Freeman, Mason-Brothers, Mo, & Ritvo, 1985). Autism is unlikely to depend on a single gene, however; only about 2 percent of the brothers and sisters of autistic children are themselves autistic.

One possible way to reconcile the high concordance in identical twins to the much lower concordance in brothers and sisters is to assume that autism depends on a large number of genes, many of which must be present to produce the condition. The greater frequency of autism in males than in females could mean that females need a greater "dose" of the abnormal genes than males do to become autistic. Indeed, female autistic children have more EEG abnormalities, more movement disturbances, poorer bladder and bowel control, and more evidence of brain dysfunction than equally autistic males have (Tsai, Stewart, & August, 1981).

One interesting development in genetic research on autism is the discovery that a large number of autistic children have a fragile X chromosome, a weak spot on an X chromosome that is vulnerable to breakage under certain conditions (see Chapter 8). The fragile X syndrome has also been noted in many mentally retarded people and in the relatives of autistic and mentally retarded children (August & Lockhart, 1984; Gillberg, Wahlström, & Hagberg, 1984). An explanation in terms of a fragile X chromosome would help to make sense of the disproportionate number of boys with autism: Girls have a second X chromosome that can compete with the effects of a defective one.

**Endorphins** Autistic children sometimes fail to react to painful stimuli. One of the most reliable ways to decrease sensitivity to pain is an injection of morphine or other opiate drugs. Consider some other symptoms of morphine intoxication (Desmond & Wilson, 1975; Glass, Evans, & Rajegowda, 1975; Ream, Robinson, Richter, Hegge, & Holloway, 1975): (1) social withdrawal, (2) repetitive and sometimes stereotyped behaviors, (3) ignoring most sensory stimuli but hallucinating others, (4) sedation under most circumstances but sometimes a driven hyperactivity, and (5) happiness and fearlessness. During withdrawal from morphine, the symptoms include restlessness, fear and anxiety, crying, and a jumpy overresponsiveness to stimulation. In short, a person who alternately took morphine injections and then went through withdrawal would show many of the same behaviors as autism.

Children who are born to narcotic-addicted mothers suffer many effects on their brain development and behavior (Householder, Hatcher, Burns, & Chasnoff, 1982). A few of these effects resemble the behavior of autistic children: The children of addicts have delayed learning and language development, and they are less responsive to their care givers in infancy.

Obviously, autistic children are not morphine addicts, and few of their mothers were narcotics users. But the body does have its own opiates, the endorphins. Perhaps for some unknown reason an autistic child's brain sometimes releases excessive amounts of endorphins and at other times releases very low amounts (Kalat, 1978; Panksepp, Herman, & Vilberg, 1978).

Do autistic children have some anomaly in their endorphins? One study measured endorphin levels in the CSF of autistic children and normal children. Of 20 autistic children, 11 had higher endorphin levels than the highest of the 8 normal children (Gillberg, Terenius, & Lönnerholm, 1985). Other studies have found elevated endorphin levels in autistic children with high frequencies of self-injurious behaviors (Sandman et al., 1990).

## Therapies for Autism

Autism is generally a lifelong condition, although some individuals become more or less self-sufficient adults. If we take the endorphin hypothesis seriously, we might expect that an opiate-blocking drug, such as naloxone or naltrexone, could help to relieve autism. Several early studies have found that such drugs reduce self-injurious behaviors such as handbiting (Sahley & Panksepp, 1987; Sandman et al., 1990); more data are needed, especially on the effects of such drugs at early ages.

Other drug therapies have been tried, but so far none has proved to be reliably helpful. Chlorpromazine, amphetamine, Ritalin, Valium, and several other drugs seem to do as much harm as good. A combination of vitamins and minerals, including vitamin $B_6$ and magnesium, helps some autistic children to use more words, show more interest in learning, and sometimes decrease self-mutilating behavior (Lelord, Muh, Barthelemy, Martineau, & Garreau, 1981; Rimland, Callaway, & Dreyfus, 1978). In general, however, the most successful treatments for autism concentrate on special education rather than on any biological intervention (Schopler, 1987).

## SUMMARY

1. The positive symptoms of schizophrenia are hallucinations, delusions, and thought disorder. The negative symptoms are the absence of emotional expression, social interactions, and speech. (p. 571)

2. Many schizophrenic patients have a moderate atrophy of the cerebral cortex, thalamus, and hippocampus. Some studies also indicate decreased metabolic activity in the frontal cortex. (p. 572)

3. Studies of twins and adopted children indicate that schizophrenia has a genetic basis, although not everyone with the gene(s) develops schizophrenia. (p. 575)

4. More schizophrenic patients were born in winter than in other seasons. One possible explanation is that their mothers may have been exposed to a viral infection in the fall before giving birth, when the fetus's brain was at a critical stage of development. (p. 578)

5. Large doses of amphetamine and certain other chemicals can induce a temporary state that resembles schizophrenia. (p. 581)

6. Neuroleptics, the drugs that relieve schizophrenia, block dopamine synapses and block the release of dopamine. Consequently, many investigators believe overactivity of dopamine synapses is part of the cause of schizophrenia. (p. 581)

7. Neuroleptic drugs induce tardive dyskinesia as a side effect in certain patients. Researchers are seeking drugs that can produce the antischizophrenic effects without tardive dyskinesia. (p. 583)

8. Children at risk for schizophrenia have mild thought disorders, poor social interactions, a lack of pleasure, and other behavioral abnormalities. (p. 585)

9. Impairment of pursuit eye movements may be a biological marker indicating vulnerability to schizophrenia. (p. 586)

10. Infantile autism, a rare condition that begins in early childhood, is characterized by social isolation, stereotyped behaviors, and insensitivity to pain. It resembles schizophrenia in certain regards, although the underlying causes are almost certainly different. (p. 586)

11. Autistic children differ from normal children in many biological regards; which of these differences relates most directly to the causes of autism is unknown. (p. 588)

12. Monozygotic twins are almost always concordant for autism; however, most brothers and sisters of autistic children are normal. Autism may have a genetic basis, but if so, it cannot be a simple effect of a single gene. (p. 588)

13. Certain symptoms of autism suggest a possible disorder of endorphin synapses. (p. 589)

## REVIEW QUESTIONS

1. What are the symptoms of schizophrenia? (p. 571)

2. What evidence of brain damage is found in many schizophrenic patients? (p. 572)

3. If a schizophrenic person has a nonschizophrenic twin, is the nonschizophrenic twin likely to have

children who eventually develop schizophrenia? What conclusions follow from this answer? (p. 577)

4. Is stress a likely cause of schizophrenia? (p. 578)

5. What is the season-of-birth effect and what is a promising hypothesis to explain it? (p. 578)

6. What is the main behavioral difference between schizophrenia and amphetamine psychosis? (p. 581)

7. What synaptic effects do neuroleptic drugs have? (p. 581)

8. Describe the strengths and weaknesses of the dopamine hypothesis of schizophrenia. (p. 582)

9. What is usually the most troublesome side effect of neuroleptic drugs? (p. 583)

10. What behaviors are characteristic of children at risk for schizophrenia? (p. 585)

11. What biological marker may indicate vulnerability to schizophrenia? (p. 586)

12. What are the symptoms of infantile autism? (p. 586)

13. Why is it unlikely that autism depends on a single gene? (p. 589)

14. Why might one suspect a link between endorphins and autism? What evidence supports this hypothesis? (p. 589)

## THOUGHT QUESTIONS

1. One problem for any genetic hypothesis of schizophrenia is to explain how the genes responsible for schizophrenia could become as common as they seem to be. Schizophrenic people have a higher than normal probability of dying young (Allebeck & Wistedt, 1986) and a lower than normal probability of having children. Evolution, it certainly seems, should select strongly against a gene for schizophrenia. How could we account for the apparently high prevalence of this gene in spite of the apparently strong selection against it?

2. Schizophrenics are reported to have fewer dreams than other people and to have some PGO spikes (see p. 374) during wakefulness. Speculate on what this might mean in relation to the causes of schizophrenia.

3. According to available evidence, the concordance rate for autism is higher for dizygotic twins than for brother and sister, even though the genetic similarity is no greater for one relationship than the other. What possible explanation might you offer?

## SUGGESTIONS FOR FURTHER READING

**Carson, R. C., & Sanislow, C. A., III** (in press). The schizophrenias. In H. E. Adams & P. B. Sutker (Eds.), *Comprehensive handbook of psychopathology.* New York: Plenum. A systematic treatment of schizophrenia with a somewhat skeptical review of the literature on its biological bases.

**Gottesman, I. I.** (1991). *Schizophrenia genesis.* New York: W. H. Freeman. Discussion of the causes of schizophrenia with emphasis on genetics.

**Namba, N., & Kaiya, H.** (Eds.) (1982). *Psychobiology of schizophrenia.* Oxford: Pergamon. A collection of articles covering research on the biology of schizophrenia.

**Rutter, M., & Schopler, E.** (1978). *Autism.* New York: Plenum. Good introduction to research on autistic children.

## GLOSSARY

**acute** having a sudden onset

**amphetamine psychosis** condition resembling schizophrenia provoked by a large dose of amphetamine

**autoreceptor** presynaptic receptor that responds to the neurotransmitter released by the presynaptic cell itself

**bipolar disorder** condition in which a person alternates between two poles, mania and depression

**Borna disease** viral disease that affects the nervous system of farm animals, possibly also humans, causing behavioral changes

**butyrophenone** class of neuroleptic drugs including haloperidol

**chlorpromazine** first drug found to relieve schizophrenia

**chronic** having a gradual onset and long duration

**concordance** agreement (A pair of twins is concordant for a trait if both of them have it or if neither has it.)

**delusion** belief that other people regard as unfounded, such as the belief that one is severely persecuted

**dopamine hypothesis of schizophrenia** hypothesis that schizophrenia is due to excess activity at dopamine synapses

**electroconvulsive therapy (ECT)** attempt to relieve depression or other disorders by an electrically induced convulsion

**hallucination** sensory experience that does not correspond to reality

**haloperidol** a common neuroleptic drug

**hypomania** condition in which people are highly energetic but not quite manic

**infantile autism** condition characterized by social isolation, stereotyped behaviors, abnormal responses to sensory stimuli, inappropriate emotional expressions, and abnormal development of speech and intellect

**learned helplessness** inactivity, helplessness, and possible depression resulting from a series of inescapable unpleasant experiences

**lithium** an element whose salts are often used as a therapy for bipolar disorder

**mania** condition of restless activity, excitement, laughter, mostly happy mood, and few inhibitions

**manic-depressive disorder** condition in which a person alternates between mania and depression; also called bipolar disorder

**mesolimbic system** set of neurons that project from the midbrain tegmentum to the limbic system

**monoamine oxidase inhibitor (MAOI)** drug that blocks the enzyme monoamine oxidase

**negative symptom** absence of a behavior ordinarily seen in normal people

**neuroleptic drug** drug that relieves schizophrenia

**paternal half-sibling** a person who has the same father as someone else but a different mother

**phenothiazine** a class of neuroleptic drugs including chlorpromazine

**positive symptom** presence of a behavior not seen in normal people

**postpartum depression** depression after giving birth

**pursuit eye movement** eye movement that follows a moving target

**saccadic eye movement** sudden shift of the eyes from one target to another

**schizophrenia** disorder characterized by deteriorating ability to function in everyday life and some combination of hallucinations, delusions, thought disorder, movement disorder, and inappropriate emotional expressions

**season-of-birth effect** tendency for people born in winter to have a greater probability of becoming schizophrenic than people born in other seasons have

**seasonal affective disorder (SAD)** period of depression that reoccurs each winter

**serotonin reuptake blocker** drug that blocks reuptake of serotonin by the presynaptic neuron that released it

**tardive dyskinesia** side effect of neuroleptic drugs characterized by tremors and other involuntary movements

**thought disorder** impaired thinking, such as difficulty understanding and using abstract concepts

**tricyclic** drug that prevents the presynaptic neuron from reabsorbing catecholamine or serotonin molecules after releasing them

**unipolar disorder** mood disorder with only one extreme (or pole), generally depression

APPENDIX A

# Genetics and Evolution

**MAIN IDEAS**

**1.** The expression of a given gene depends on the environment and on interactions with other genes.

**2.** Genes are located on chromosomes, which are composed of the chemical DNA. DNA chains determine the structure of RNA chains, which in turn determine the structure of proteins.

**3.** It is difficult to measure the contribution of heredity to the variations in human behavior, although several methods are in common use.

**4.** Although it is often difficult to determine exactly how a species has evolved from its ancestors, the basic process of evolution through natural selection is a logical necessity.

This appendix is not intended to be comprehensive. It presents only those aspects of genetics and evolution that one needs to know in order to deal with biological psychology. Readers with a strong previous background should just skim over the parts familiar to them.

## MENDELIAN GENETICS

Prior to the work of Gregor Mendel, a late-nineteenth-century monk, scientists thought that inheritance was a blending process, in which the properties of the sperm and the egg simply mixed, much as one might mix red paint and yellow paint.

Mendel demonstrated that inheritance occurs through **genes,** units of heredity that maintain their structural identity from one generation to another and do not blend with one another. Suppose, as in one of Mendel's experiments, we breed a pea plant with yellow seeds and one with white seeds. (Most plants reproduce sexually just as animals do.) All the offspring of this cross have yellow seeds. Now we breed two of these offspring with each other. In the next generation, about three-fourths have yellow seeds and one-fourth have white seeds. Thus, although the second generation had only yellow seeds, the genes for white seeds have not been lost.

To account for results like these, Mendel proposed that inheritance depends on structural particles (later called genes) that come in pairs. In the example of the pea plants, one parent has a pair of genes for yellow seeds, which we could represent as *AA*. The other parent has a pair of genes for white seeds, which we could designate *aa*. (Each parent also has millions of other genes controlling a wide variety of characteristics.) During reproduction, each parent contributes one gene from each pair. So the first parent contributes an *A* gene (for yellow seeds) and the second parent contributes an *a* gene (for white seeds). The offspring therefore have an *Aa* gene combination. In this case the gene for yellow seeds, *A*, is **dominant** over the gene for white seeds, *a*, which is **recessive.** If an individual has one of each gene, it shows the trait corresponding to the dominant gene.

Although all members of the second generation produce yellow seeds, they carry both an *A* and an *a* gene. Thus, during reproduction, each individual can contribute either gene to offspring. If both parents contribute an *a* gene, they will produce a white-seed offspring, even though both parents have yellow seeds. (On the other hand, if both parents produce only white seeds, none of their offspring can produce yellow seeds. Do you see why?)

Statistically, an *Aa* individual contributes an *A* gene to 50 percent of its offspring and an *a* gene to the other 50 percent. Therefore, an *Aa* and *Aa* mating produces 25 percent *AA* offspring, 50 percent *Aa*, and 25 percent *aa*. (See Figure A.1.)

Many human traits depend on a single gene that follows these simple Mendelian ratios. Examples include eye color (brown dominant, blue recessive), ability to taste the chemical phenylthiocarbamide (ability to taste dominant, inability recessive), and ability to curl one's tongue lengthwise (ability dominant, inability recessive).

An individual who has two identical genes for some trait (either *AA* or *aa*) is **homozygous** for that gene. One who has different genes (*Aa*) is **heterozygous.**

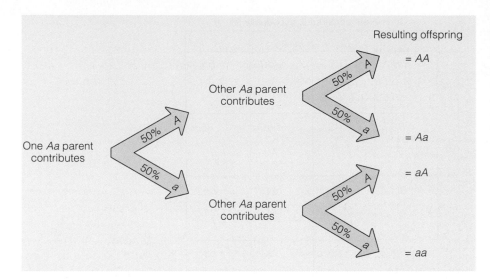

**Figure A.1**
**Results of an *Aa* by *Aa* mating**
*Each offspring has a 25 percent chance of receiving the* AA *combination, a 25 percent chance of* aa, *and a 50 percent chance of* Aa.

In many cases, neither gene is dominant; the heterozygous individual is then intermediate between the two homozygous conditions. In the preceding example, if neither gene were dominant, the *Aa* individuals might produce light yellow seeds. A cross between two *Aa* individuals would then yield about 25 percent yellow-seed individuals (*AA*), 50 percent light yellow (*Aa*), and 25 percent white (*aa*).

Many characteristics depend on more than one gene pair. Suppose, for example, that the length of a worm depends on two gene pairs. Genes *B* and *C* are dominant genes for long body; genes *b* and *c* are recessive for short body. If we cross a long worm with *BBCC* **genotype** (gene pattern) and a short worm with *bbcc* genotype, the first worm contributes a *B* and a *C*; the second contributes a *b* and a *c*. Therefore, the offspring will have a *BbCc* genotype and will have long bodies.

Now, let us cross a *BbCc* with another *BbCc*. Assume that the *B* and *C* genes arrange themselves independently of each other. That is, a parent that contributes a *B* gene can contribute either a *C* or a *c*; it has an equal chance of contributing any of the combinations *BC*, *Bc*, *bC*, and *bc*. The same goes for the other parent. Thus, the possibilities for offspring are as Figure A.2 shows.

In 9 of the 16 possibilities, the offspring has at least one *B* gene and at least one *C* gene. Because *B* and *C* are dominant genes, all these offspring are long. Only one of the possible offspring types has both a *bb* and a *cc* combination; only the individuals of this type are short. The other six possibilities have at least one dominant gene at either the *B* or the *C* locus, and two recessive genes at the other (for example, *Bbcc* or *bbCC*); these worms are intermediate in length between the two original types.

Things can get more complicated. Perhaps *B* makes more of a difference than *C*, so that a *Bbcc* worm is longer than a *bbCc*. Or perhaps more than two gene pairs contribute to body length (or any other characteristic). Furthermore, the effects of a gene may depend on the environment or on what other genes the individual has.

Genetics and
Evolution

**Figure A.2**
**Results of a *BbCc*
(long) by *BbCc* (long)
cross**
*Of the offspring, 9/16 are
long, 6/16 are intermediate,
and 1/16 are short.*

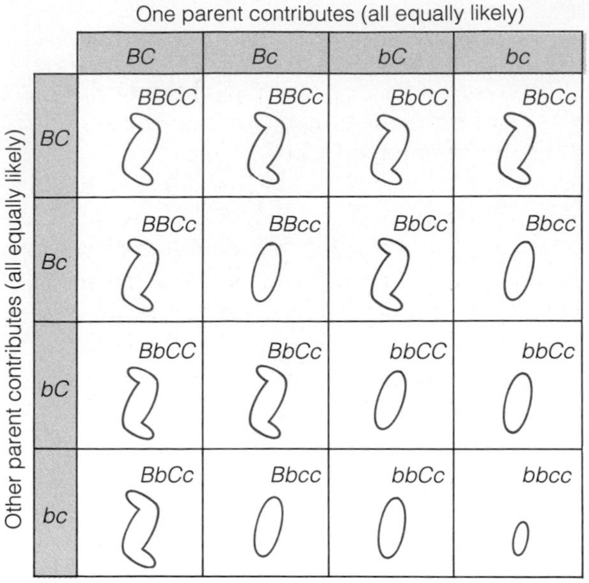

Chromosome Linkage

Up to this point we have dealt with genes that are inherited independently of one another. Genes can be physically linked so that someone who inherits one gene is likely to inherit a second one, too.

Genes are located on strands of DNA called **chromosomes.** Each chromosome participates in reproduction independently of the others, and each species has a certain number of chromosomes (23 pairs in humans, 4 pairs in fruit flies). Thus, if an individual has a *BbCc* genotype, and if the *B* and *C* genes are on different chromosomes, its contribution of a *B* or *b* gene has nothing to do with whether it contributes a *C* or a *c*. But suppose they are on the same chromosome. If one chromosome has the *BC* combination and the other has *bc*, then an individual who contributes a *B* gene will probably also contribute a *C*.

The exception to this statement comes about as a result of **crossing over.** During reproduction, a pair of chromosomes may break apart and reconnect such that part of one chromosome attaches to the other part of the second chromosome. If one chromosome has the *BC* combination and the other chromosome has the *bc* combination, crossing over between the *B* locus and the *C* locus leaves new chromosomes with the combinations *Bc* and *bC*. The closer the *B* locus is to the *C* locus, the less often crossing over will occur between them.

The phenomenon of crossing over can be used to determine the location of a particular gene on the chromosomes. For example, human chromosome number 4 has a marker known as "G8," which is visible on the chromosome although no one knows what contribution it makes to heredity. The G8 marker has four identifiable forms. The gene for Huntington's disease (see Chapter 9) is believed to lie close to the G8 marker. When a parent and child both have Huntington's disease, about 98 percent of the time they have the same form of the G8 marker (Gusella et al., 1984). That is, the gene for Huntington's disease and the G8 marker lie so close together on the chromosome that crossing over occurs between them in only 2 percent of all matings.

## Sex-Linked and Sex-Limited Genes

Each individual has a certain number of chromosomes. All but one pair are known as autosomal chromosomes; all genes located on these chromosomes are referred to as **autosomal genes.** The other two chromosomes are the sex chromosomes; genes located on them are known as **sex-linked genes.**

In mammals, the two sex chromosomes are designated X and Y. (Unlike the symbols *A*, *B*, and *C* introduced to illustrate gene pairs, X and Y are standard symbols for sex chromosomes used by all geneticists.) A female mammal has two X chromosomes; a male has an X and a Y. During reproduction, the female necessarily contributes an X chromosome, and the male contributes either an X or a Y. If he contributes an X, the offspring will be female; if he contributes a Y, the offspring will be male. (Birds are different. Male birds have two sex chromosomes alike, designated ZZ; the female has two different sex chromosomes, designated ZW.)

The **Y chromosome** is small and carries few if any genes other than the gene that causes the individual to develop as a male instead of a female. The **X chromosome,** however, carries many genes. Thus, when biologists speak of sex-linked genes, they ordinarily mean X-linked genes.

Characteristics controlled by sex-linked genes occur more often in one sex than in the other. If a gene is a sex-linked dominant, the characteristic it controls occurs more often in females than in males because females, with two X chromosomes, have twice the chance males have of getting the sex-linked gene.

On the other hand, a characteristic that is controlled by a sex-linked recessive gene produces its effects only if the dominant gene is not present. Thus, for a female to show the effects of a sex-linked recessive, she would have to have two such genes. A male, however, has only one X chromosome; if he has an X-linked recessive gene, he cannot have a dominant gene to overrule it. Color blindness is controlled by a sex-linked recessive gene in humans. Most color-blind people are male. For a female to be color blind, she would have to have a color-blind father and a mother with at least one gene for color blindness. Other examples of sex-linked recessive genes are those for hemophilia ("bleeder's disease") and albinism.

Distinct from sex-linked genes are the **sex-limited genes.** A sex-limited gene has an effect in one sex only, or at least it has a much stronger effect in one sex than the other. For instance, genes control the amount of chest hair in men, breast size in women, the amount of crowing in roosters, and the rate of egg production in hens. Such genes need not be on the sex chromosomes; both sexes have the genes, but the genes exert their effects more strongly under the influence of either testosterone or estrogen.

## Sources of Variation

If reproduction always produced offspring that were exact copies of the parents, evolution would not be possible. One source of variation is **recombination.** The effects of a gene depend on what other genes are present. An offspring, in receiving some genes from one parent and some from the other, may have a new combination of genes that together yield characteristics not found in either parent.

Another source of variation is a **mutation,** or change, in a single gene. For instance, a gene for brown eyes might mutate into a gene for blue eyes. Mutation of a given gene is a rare event, but because each of us has millions of genes, mutations provide a constant source of variation.

A mutation is a random event; that is, the needs of the organism do not guide it. A mutation is analogous to having an untrained person add, remove, or distort something on the blueprints for your new house. The likely result is to make the house less desirable than it would have been, perhaps even to make it collapse; only rarely would the random change improve the house.

A third source of variation—almost always disadvantageous—is for one parent to contribute something other than exactly one copy of each chromosome. Occasionally one parent contributes two or zero copies of a given chromosome. For example, if one human parent contributes two copies of chromosome 21, the child has a total of three copies, counting the one obtained from the other parent. The consequence is **Down's syndrome,** a genetic disorder characterized by mental retardation. An extra or absent sex chromosome can cause the XXY pattern, the XXX pattern, or the XO pattern, all of which cause sterility and various abnormalities of appearance.

## Penetrance

When we refer to, say, "a gene for brown eyes," we mean that the gene makes a difference between having brown eyes and some other color of eyes *under the usual environmental conditions.* Some genes have observable effects only if the individual experiences a certain climate, a particular pattern of light and darkness, a specific diet, a given social setting, or some other environmental condition. A gene may also have effects that emerge only in individuals who have certain other genes. A gene that affects some individuals but not others has partial **penetrance.** That is, its effects "penetrate" into observable characteristics only under certain conditions.

Because of the phenomenon of partial penetrance, it is sometimes possible to reduce the undesirable effects of a gene by changing the environment. One clear example is a condition known as phenylketonuria (PKU), discussed in more detail in Chapter 8. The gene for PKU prevents the body from metabolizing phenylalanine. The consequent buildup of phenylalanine interferes with normal brain development and causes mental retardation. However, if a child with this gene stays on a low-phenylalanine diet at least until about age 12, the brain can develop normally. In short, a controlled diet prevents penetrance of the gene.

## THE BIOCHEMISTRY OF GENETICS

A chromosome is actually a molecule of the double-stranded chemical deoxyribonucleic acid, or **DNA** (with some proteins attached). Each strand of DNA is composed of four bases in varying orders—guanine, cytosine, adenine, and thymine—attached to a skeleton made of phosphate and a sugar, deoxyribose. The order of these four bases along the chromosome determines all the genetic information. A gene is a small segment of the DNA molecule.

A strand of DNA serves as a **template,** or model, for the synthesis of **RNA** (ribonucleic acid) molecules. RNA is a single strand composed of a sequence of bases—guanine, cytosine, adenine, and uracil—attached to a skeleton made of phosphate and the sugar ribose. The RNA bases are arranged in a manner complementary to those of DNA: Where a DNA chain has guanine, the RNA chain has cytosine; similarly, DNA's cytosine, adenine, and thymine pair up with RNA's guanine, uracil, and adenine, respectively, as Figure A.3 illustrates.

After being synthesized from the DNA template, RNA molecules disperse to various places in the cell. Different kinds of RNA serve different functions. One kind, tRNA (transfer RNA), transports amino acids to the ribosomes of the cell. Another kind, mRNA (messenger RNA), serves as a template for the formation of

RNA strand G—C—U—A—C—A—G—U—U

DNA strand C—G—A—T—G—T—C—A—A

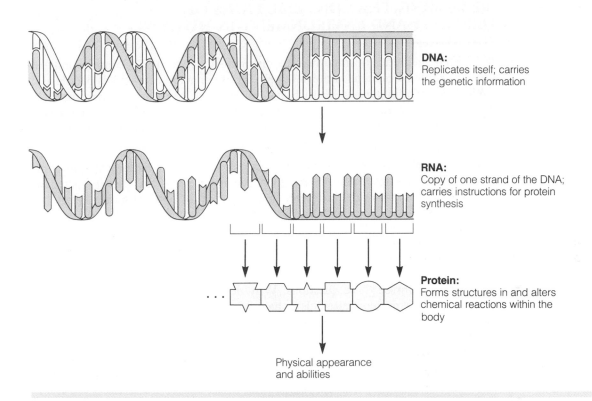

DNA:
Replicates itself; carries the genetic information

RNA:
Copy of one strand of the DNA; carries instructions for protein synthesis

Protein:
Forms structures in and alters chemical reactions within the body

Physical appearance and abilities

**Figure A.4**
**How DNA controls development of the organism**

*The sequence of bases along a strand of DNA determines the order of bases along a strand of RNA; RNA in turn controls the sequence of amino acids in a protein molecule.*

proteins. An mRNA chain determines the amino-acid structure of a protein by a code: Each sequence of three RNA bases codes for one amino acid. For instance, the RNA sequence guanine-cytosine-guanine codes for the amino acid arginine. The order of RNA bases determines the order of the protein's amino acids. Figure A.4 summarizes the main steps in translating DNA information into proteins.

The proteins then determine the development and properties of the organism. Some proteins form part of the structure of the body; others serve as **enzymes,** or biological catalysts that regulate chemical reactions in the body.

**Retroviruses** reverse the classical sequence of DNA producing RNA. Viruses are infectious agents composed of RNA. Like any other kind of RNA, they serve as templates for the formation of proteins. One of the proteins produced by a retrovirus, however, causes the formation of a new segment of DNA

Genetics and
Evolution

complementary to the RNA. If that segment of DNA becomes incorporated into one of the chromosomes, it will continue producing more of the retrovirus, in the standard DNA-to-RNA direction. A retrovirus is therefore extremely difficult to attack medically. AIDS and some forms of leukemia are caused by retroviruses.

## MEASURING THE CONTRIBUTIONS OF HEREDITY AND ENVIRONMENT IN HUMANS

It is often theoretically important to distinguish between the contributions of heredity and environment in the development of behavior. Sometimes people ask, "Which is more important for such-and-so behavior, heredity or environment?" The question is meaningless in that form, although we can rephrase it in a meaningful way. To see what is wrong with the phrasing of the question, consider two analogies:

1. Why does your computer do the things it does? Is it because of the computer's hardware or its software? (You see at once that the question is meaningless. Everything the computer does depends on both its hardware and its software.)

2. Which is more important for the area of a rectangle, its height or its width? (Again, the question is meaningless; neither height nor width contributes anything independently of the other.)

Now let us rephrase these questions: Why does your computer do some tricks differently from my computer? Is it because the two computers have different hardware or because we are running different software?

The rectangles in Figure A.5 differ in area. Is that *difference* in area due mostly to differences in height or to differences in width?

Similarly, the proper way to phrase the heredity-environment question is: This group differs from that group in such-and-so behavior; do they differ because of differences in their heredity or because of differences in their environment? This question may be difficult to answer in practice, but at least it makes sense in principle. Note that the answer will depend not only on which behavior we examine but also on which groups we compare. For the rectangles in Figure

**Figure A.5**
*It is pointless to ask whether the area of a rectangle depends more on height or width, but it is meaningful to ask whether the differences in area for a given group of rectangles depend more on differences in height or in width. The same is true for the roles of heredity and environment in determining behavior.*

A.5, the differences in area depend mostly on differences in width; for some other set of rectangles, the answer might be different. Similarly, the differences in behavior between red lizards and green lizards might be mostly due to genetic differences, while the differences between green lizards and blue lizards might be due mostly to environmental differences. We have to examine each case separately.

The standard measurement of the contributions of heredity and environment is **heritability.** Heritability is a mathematical construct designed to measure how closely the variations in some characteristic correlate with differences in heredity as opposed to differences in environment. Heritability can vary from zero to 1.0. A heritability of zero means that none of the observed variation is due to differences in heredity; a heritability of 1.0 means that all the observed differences are due to differences in heredity.

It is difficult to get adequate data about heritability in humans. Investigators have no control over who mates with whom or what environment their children grow up in. The time between generations is long, and we are often uncertain which aspects of the environment are critical.

In many cases the goal of research is merely to determine whether heredity contributes at all to the differences in behavior. The following types of evidence can be used in studies of the heritability of human behavior, beginning with the *least* convincing and working up from there.

## Similarities Among Relatives

Does the similarity in behavior between individuals correspond to their degree of genetic relationship? If we designate the genetic relationship between a person and himself or herself as 1.0, then other relationships are as follows:

| Relationship | Degree of Relationship |
|---|---|
| Identical twin | 1.0 |
| Fraternal twin | 0.5 |
| Brother or sister | 0.5 |
| Father, mother, son, daughter | 0.5 |
| Grandparent, grandchild | 0.25 |
| Uncle, aunt, nephew, niece | 0.25 |
| Half-brother, half-sister | 0.25 |
| First cousin | 0.125 |
| Second cousin | 0.0625 |
| Unrelated person | 0.0 |

(These figures assume that people mate randomly rather than choosing genetically similar individuals as mates. Because that assumption is false for humans, the correct numerical coefficients should be somewhat higher.)

If some variation in behavior depends partly on genetics, then the closer the genetic relationship between people, the greater should be the similarity in their behavior. For example, identical twins should resemble each other more than siblings, who should resemble each other more than cousins, and so on.

When this is *not* true—if identical twins resemble each other no more than two unrelated people, for example—we may confidently reject genetics as a significant reason for the variation in behavior. On the other hand, this type of information is never strong evidence *in favor* of a genetic explanation. Identical

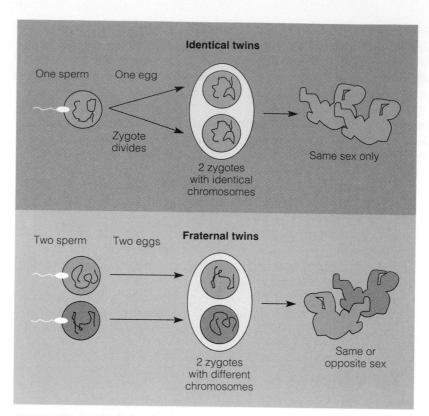

**Figure A.6**
*Identical (monozygotic) twins are produced from the same fertilized egg. Fraternal (dizygotic) twins grow from two eggs fertilized by two different sperm.*

twins share more of their environment in common than brother and sister, who in turn share more than cousins. Thus, strong similarity between closely related people does not distinguish between genetic and environmental explanations.

### Similarities Between Identical Twins and Fraternal Twins

Is the similarity greater between identical twins than between fraternal twins? Fraternal, or nonidentical, twins are also known as **dizygotic** ("two-egg") twins (see Figure A.6). Although they are born at the same time, they are no more closely related genetically than brother and sister. Identical twins, also known as **monozygotic** ("one-egg") twins, begin as a single fertilized egg; they have identical genetics.

A pair of twins of either kind grows up sharing a common environment. Identical twins, however, share more genetics in common. Therefore, if some behavior shows greater similarity between identical twins than between fraternal twins, we can suspect that this added similarity reflects a genetic influence.

This kind of evidence does not support a firm conclusion, however. Identical twins are more likely to be treated alike than are fraternal twins by their families and by other people. Thus, identical twins may have greater environmental similarity than fraternal twins as well as greater genetic similarity.

### Behavior of Twins Reared in Separate Environments

Do twins reared in separate environments resemble each other? Occasionally twins are adopted by different families. If we examine a large number of twin pairs who were reared in separate adoptive homes and find that some behavior shows marked similarity within most pairs, one likely interpretation is that the genetic similarity is responsible for the behavioral similarity. Two other interpretations are possible: One is that pairs of twins have been adopted by similar families, providing similar environments. (This is a reasonable possibility. Adoption agencies do not place children at random.) The other is that something in the **prenatal** (before-birth) environment strongly influenced development.

## Behavior of Adopted Children

Does the behavior of an adopted child more closely resemble that of the genetic relatives or that of the adopted relatives? If a child is adopted at an early age, the people who provide the child's environment are different from those who provided the genes. In some cases it can be demonstrated that a child's probability of developing some behavior corresponds more closely to the incidence of that behavior among the genetic relatives than to its incidence among the adopted relatives. The most likely interpretation then would be a genetic influence on the behavior or an influence by the prenatal environment.

Although evidence of this type can be fairly strong, it is not without its complications (Kamin, 1974). For example, most adoption agencies try to place a child in an adoptive family that resembles the child's biological family. In some cases a child may come to resemble his or her biological family because of environmental influences that the adoptive family provides. Still, selective placement in adoptive homes cannot explain cases in which children resemble their biological parents *more* than they resemble their adoptive parents.

Adoption data indicate some role of genetics in IQ scores, activity level, emotionality, sociability versus shyness, schizophrenia, and several other behavioral characteristics (Plomin, 1990). In each of these cases, however, the data suggest that the behavioral outcome depends on a large number of genes (not just one) and on the influences of the environment.

## Paternal Half-siblings

How much do adopted paternal half-siblings resemble each other? A sibling is a brother or sister. Half-siblings have one parent in common but not the other. **Paternal half-siblings** have the same father but different mothers.

Occasionally two paternal half-siblings are adopted at early ages by different families—generally because the same man has fathered illegitimate children by more than one mother. Such children have been reared in different environments and did not even share a common prenatal environment, because they had different mothers. Therefore, any strong resemblance between adopted paternal half-siblings is almost certainly due to genetics.

Evidence of this type is potentially about as convincing as any evidence we can get about human heritability. The only problem is that such evidence is scarce. Adopted paternal half-siblings are not easy to locate.

# EVOLUTION

**Evolution** is a change in the gene frequencies for a population over generations. It is important to distinguish two questions concerning evolution: How *did* species evolve, and how *do* species evolve? To ask how species did evolve is to ask what evolved from what. To answer this question, biologists have to reconstruct a history based on fossils and other kinds of evidence. Their inferences are always subject to revision if new evidence becomes available.

How species *do* evolve is a question of how the process works. To a large extent we could establish the process of evolution as a logical necessity, even if we had no fossil evidence at all, using the following argument: The study of genetics has established that offspring generally resemble their parents. We also know, however, that mutations and recombinations lead to a steady supply of new variations within the population and that these new variations are themselves passed on to later generations. If individuals with some genetic variation have an advantage, in the sense that they reproduce more often and more successfully, then their genes will become more common in the population; that is, evolution will occur.

This general principle has long been familiar to animal and plant breeders as **artificial selection.** By selectively breeding only the most productive egg-laying chickens, or the dogs that are the best at herding sheep, breeders can develop a new strain of chickens or dogs with a high degree of the desired characteristic. Darwin's (1859) theory of evolution merely extended this idea, saying that nature acts like a selective breeder. If individuals with a particular new gene combination are more successful than others in finding food, or escaping enemies, or attracting mates, or protecting their offspring, the result will be a gradual increase in the frequency of that gene combination, just as surely as if some breeder had been selecting for that gene.

## SUMMARY

1. In a normal environment, every individual with a dominant gene will show its effects. A recessive gene's effects are fully expressed only if no dominant gene is present. (p. 594)

2. If two genes are on the same chromosome, someone who inherits one of those genes is likely to inherit the other as well. (p. 596)

3. Because sex-linked genes are on the X chromosome, sex-linked recessive genes show their effects more in males than in females, whereas sex-linked dominant genes show their effects more frequently in females. Although a sex-limited gene may be on any chromosome, its effects occur only in one sex. (p. 597)

4. A gene is said to have partial penetrance if its effects depend on variations in the environment. (p. 598)

5. Chromosomes are composed of the molecule DNA, which makes RNA copies of itself that, in turn, determine the formation of proteins. (p. 598)

6. It is difficult to estimate the heritability of most significant human behaviors because the available evidence is subject to alternative explanations. (p. 600)

7. Although it is difficult to be certain about which species evolved from which and how, the fundamental process of evolution is a logical necessity. (p. 603)

## REVIEW QUESTIONS

1. Distinguish between dominant and recessive, homozygous and heterozygous. (p. 594)

2. How can a researcher determine the approximate location of a given gene on the human chromosomes? (p. 596)

3. Why do sex-linked dominant genes show their effects more in women than in men? (p. 597)

4. Why do sex-linked recessive genes show their effects mostly in men? (p. 597)

5. What is a sex-limited gene? (p. 597)

6. What is a mutation? (p. 597)

7. Describe an example of a gene whose effects can be modified or eliminated by a change in the environment. (p. 598)

8. What are chromosomes composed of? (p. 598)

9. What is the route by which DNA controls the production of proteins? (p. 598)

10. How does a retrovirus reproduce? (p. 599)

11. What is the best way to phrase the heredity-environment question? (p. 600)

12. Describe the strengths and weaknesses of the various lines of evidence used to determine the role of heredity in the development of human behavior. (p. 601)

## THOUGHT QUESTION

1. How can we study the evolution of behavior? Behavior leaves no fossils, with the exception of occasional footprints. (Hint: How might you study the evolution of the heart, kidney, or other internal organs, which also leave few fossils?)

## SUGGESTION FOR FURTHER READING

Plomin, R. (1990). The role of inheritance in behavior. *Science, 248,* 183–188. A brief summary of methods for studying the genetics of behavior in humans and other species.

## GLOSSARY

**artificial selection** change in the gene pool of a population by a breeder's selection of desired individuals for mating purposes

**autosomal gene** gene on any of the chromosomes other than the sex chromosomes (X and Y)

**chromosome** strand of DNA bearing the genes

**crossing over** exchange of parts between two chromosomes during replication

**dizygotic twin** fraternal (nonidentical) twin

**DNA** deoxyribonucleic acid, the chemical that composes the chromosomes

**dominant gene** gene that exerts noticeable effects even in an individual who has only one copy of the gene per cell

**Down's syndrome** condition caused by having three strands of chromosome 21 per cell instead of two, resulting in mental retardation

**enzyme** any protein that catalyzes biological reactions

**evolution** change in the gene pool of a population over generations

**gene** a physical particle that determines some aspect of inheritance

**genotype** the total collection of an individual's genes

**heritability** a correlation coefficient, ranging from zero to 1.0, indicating the degree to which variations in some characteristic depend on variations in heredity for a given population

**heterozygous** having two unlike genes for a given trait

**homozygous** having two identical genes for a given characteristic

**monozygotic twin** identical twin

**mutation** change in a gene during reproduction

**paternal half-sibling** individual with the same father as someone else but a different mother

**penetrance** the degree of expression of a gene

**prenatal** before birth

**recessive** a gene that exerts noticeable effects only in an individual who has two copies of the gene per cell

**recombination** a reassortment of genes during reproduction, sometimes leading to a characteristic that is not apparent in either parent

**retrovirus** virus made of RNA that makes a DNA copy of itself

**RNA** ribonucleic acid, a chemical whose structure is determined by DNA and that in turn determines the structure of proteins

**sex-limited gene** gene whose effects are seen only in one sex, although members of both sexes may have the gene

**sex-linked gene** gene on either the X or the Y chromosome

**template** model from which copies are made

**tyrosine** an amino acid that serves as the precursor to several neurotransmitters

**X chromosome** a chromosome of which female mammals have two and males have one

**Y chromosome** a chromosome of which female mammals have none and males one

# Brief, Basic Chemistry

**MAIN IDEAS**

**1.** All matter is composed of a limited number of elements that combine in endless ways.

**2.** The component parts of an element— the atoms—consist of protons, neutrons, and electrons. Most atoms can either gain, lose, or share electrons with other atoms.

**3.** The chemistry of life is predominantly the chemistry of carbon compounds.

To understand certain aspects of biological psychology, particularly the action potential and the molecular mechanisms of synaptic transmission, you need to know a little about chemistry. If you have taken a high school or college course in chemistry and remember the material reasonably well, you should have no trouble with the chemistry in this text. If your knowledge of chemistry is pretty hazy, perhaps this appendix will help. (If you plan to take other courses in biological psychology, you should study as much biology and chemistry as possible.)

## ELEMENTS AND COMPOUNDS

If you look around, you will see an enormous variety of materials — dirt, water, wood, plastic, metal, cloth, glass, your own body. All those countless types of objects are composed of a small number of basic building blocks. For example, if a piece of wood catches fire, it breaks down into ashes, gases, and some water vapor. The same is true of your body. In turn, an investigator could take those ashes, gases, and water and break them down by chemical and electrical means into carbon, oxygen, hydrogen, nitrogen, and a few other materials. Eventually, however, the investigator arrives at a set of materials that cannot be broken down further: Pure carbon or pure oxygen, for example, cannot be converted into anything simpler — at least not by ordinary chemical means. (High-power bombardment with subatomic particles is another story.) Evidently the matter we see is composed of **elements** — materials that cannot be broken down into other materials — and **compounds** — materials made up by combining elements.

Chemists have found 92 elements in nature, and they have constructed some more in the laboratory. (Actually, one of the 92 — technetium — is so rare as to be virtually unknown in nature.) Figure B.1, the periodic table, lists each of these elements. Of these, only a few are important for life on Earth. Table B.1 shows the elements that compose nearly all of the human body.

Note that each element has a one- or two-letter abbreviation, such as O for oxygen, H for hydrogen, and Ca for calcium. These are internationally accepted symbols that facilitate communication among chemists who speak different languages. For example, element number 19 is called potassium in English, potassio in Italian, kālijs in Latvian, and draslík in Czech. But chemists in all countries use the symbol K (from *kalium*, the Latin word for *potassium*). Similarly, the symbol for sodium is Na (from *natrium*, the Latin word for *sodium*), and the symbol for iron is Fe (from the Latin word *ferrum*).

A compound is represented by the symbols for the elements that compose it. For example, NaCl represents sodium chloride (common table salt). $H_2O$, the symbol for water, indicates that water is formed by combining two parts of hydrogen with one part of oxygen.

### Atoms and Molecules

A block of iron can be chopped into finer and finer pieces until a certain point. Eventually it is divided into tiny pieces that cannot be divided any further. Those pieces are called **atoms.** Every element is composed of atoms.

Similarly, a compound such as water can be divided into tinier and tinier pieces until a certain point. The smallest possible piece of a compound is called a **molecule.** A molecule of water can be decomposed into two atoms of hydrogen

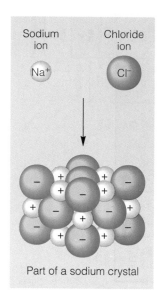

Sodium
ion

Chloride
ion

Na⁺

Cl⁻

Part of a sodium crystal

**Figure B.2**
**The crystal structure
of sodium chloride**
*Each sodium ion is sur-
rounded by chloride ions, and
each chloride ion is sur-
rounded by sodium ions; no
ion is bound to any other single ion in particular.*

a weight just trivially greater than zero. The atomic weight of the element is the number of protons in the atom plus the average number of neutrons. For example, most hydrogen atoms have one proton and no neutrons; a few atoms per thousand have one or two neutrons, giving an average atomic weight of 1.008. Sodium ions have 11 protons; most also have 12 neutrons, and the atomic weight is slightly less than 23. (Can you figure out the number of neutrons in the average potassium atom? Refer to Figure B.1.)

### Ions and Chemical Bonds

When an atom gains or loses one or more electrons, it is then called an **ion.** For example, if sodium and chloride come together, the sodium atoms readily lose one electron each and the chloride atoms gain one each. The result is a set of positively charged sodium ions (indicated Na⁺) and negatively charged chloride ions (Cl⁻). Potassium atoms, like sodium atoms, tend to lose an electron and to become positively charged ions (K⁺); calcium ions tend to lose two electrons and to gain a double positive charge (Ca⁺⁺).

Because positive charges attract negative charges, sodium ions attract chloride ions. When dry, sodium and chloride form a crystal structure, as Figure B.2 shows. (In water solution, the two kinds of ion move about haphazardly, occasionally attracting one another but then pulling apart.) The attraction of sodium ions for chloride ions is an **ionic bond.**

In contrast, some pairs of atoms may share electrons with each other, instead of transferring an electron from one atom to another. For example, two hydrogen atoms bind as shown in Figure B.3. Two hydrogen atoms bind with an oxygen atom as shown in Figure B.4. In such cases the atoms are bound by a **covalent bond**—a bond that shares electrons. When a covalent bond forms, an atom is bound to another particular atom. Until that bond is broken, neither atom can move independently of the other.

### REACTIONS OF CARBON COMPOUNDS

Living organisms depend on the enormously versatile compounds of carbon. Carbon forms covalent bonds with other carbon atoms as well as with hydrogen, oxygen, and a number of other elements. Because of the importance of carbon compounds for life, the chemistry of carbon is known as organic chemistry.

Carbon forms covalent bonds with other carbon atoms. Two carbon atoms may share one pair of electrons, two pairs, or three pairs. Such bonds can be indicated as shown below:

$C-C$     Two atoms share one pair of electrons.

$C=C$     Two atoms share two pairs of electrons.

$C\equiv C$     Two atoms share three pairs of electrons.

Each carbon atom typically forms a total of four covalent bonds, either with other carbon atoms, with hydrogen atoms, or with other atoms. Many biologically important compounds include long chains of carbon compounds linked to one another, such as:

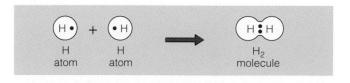

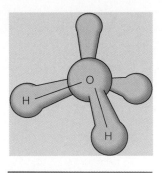

## Figure B.3
## Structure of a hydrogen molecule
*A hydrogen atom has one electron; in the compound, the two atoms share the two electrons equally.*

## Figure B.4
## Structure of a water molecule
*The oxygen atom shares a pair of electrons with each hydrogen atom, although it does not share them equally. Oxygen holds the electrons more tightly, making the oxygen part of the molecule more negatively charged than the hydrogen part of the molecule.*

$$\begin{array}{ccc} \text{H} & \text{H} & \text{H} \\ | & | & | \\ \text{H---C---C---C---OH} \\ | & | & | \\ \text{H} & \text{H} & \text{H} \end{array} \qquad \text{H---C=C---C=C---C=C---H}$$

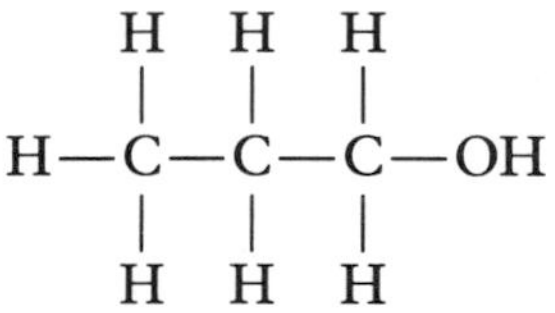

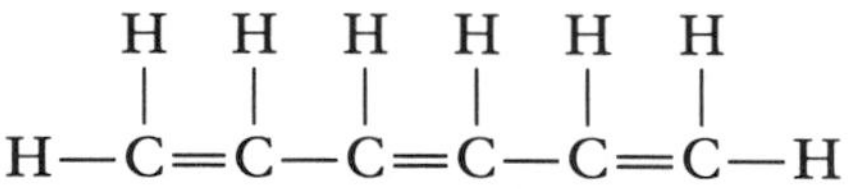

Note that each carbon atom has a total of four bonds, counting each double bond as two. In some molecules, the carbon chain may loop around to form a ring:

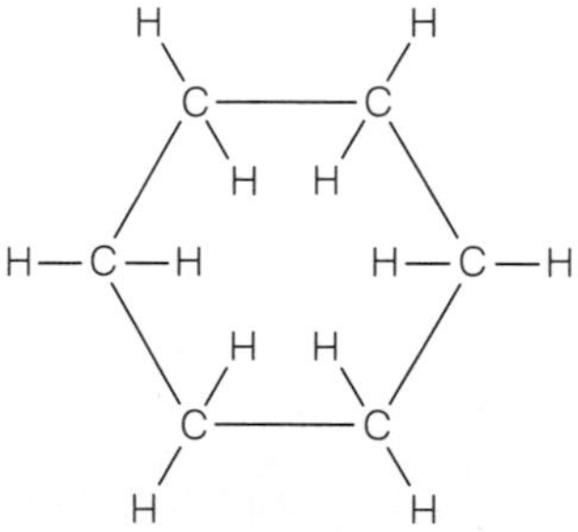

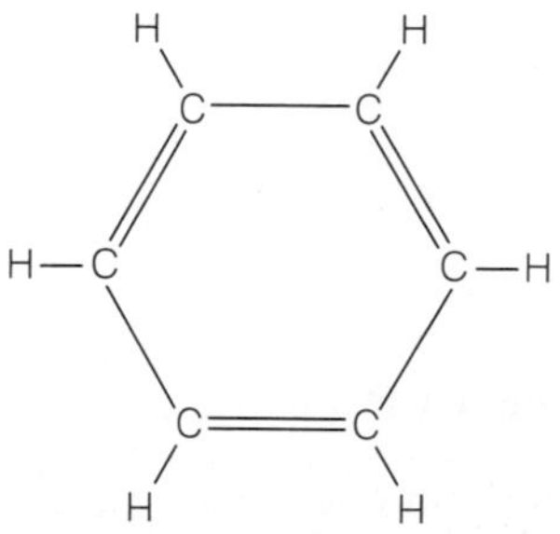

Structures like these are common in organic chemistry. To simplify the diagrams, chemists often omit the hydrogen atoms. The reader can simply assume that each carbon atom in the diagram has four covalent bonds and that all the bonds not shown are bonds with hydrogen atoms. To further simplify the diagrams, chemists often omit the carbon atoms themselves, showing only the carbon-to-carbon bonds. For example, the two molecules shown above might be rendered as follows:

Brief, Basic
Chemistry

**611**

If a particular carbon atom has a bond with some atom other than hydrogen, the diagram shows the exception. For example, in each of the two molecules diagrammed below, one carbon has a bond with an oxygen atom, which in turn has a bond with a hydrogen atom. All the bonds that are not shown are carbon-hydrogen bonds.

Figure B.5 illustrates some carbon compounds that are critical for animal life. Purines and pyrimidines form the central structure of DNA and RNA, the chemicals responsible for heredity. Proteins, fats, and carbohydrates are the primary types of fuel that the body uses.

The body also manufactures its own proteins, fats, and carbohydrates. Proteins form an important part of most body structures. Hemoglobin, the compound in the blood that transports oxygen and carbon dioxide, is a protein. So are actin and myosin, the compounds responsible for the contraction of muscles. Fats and carbohydrates are stored as a source of energy.

## Chemical Reactions in the Body

A living organism is an immensely complicated, coordinated set of chemical reactions. Life requires that the rate of each reaction be carefully regulated. In many cases one reaction produces a chemical that enters into another reaction, which produces another chemical that enters into another reaction, and so forth. If any one of those reactions proceeds too rapidly, its product will accumulate to levels that might be harmful. If a reaction proceeds too slowly, it will not produce enough of some needed product at the right time, stalling the reaction that uses that product.

**Enzymes** are proteins that control the rate of chemical reactions in the body. Each reaction is controlled by its own particular enzyme. (Enzymes are a type of catalyst. A catalyst is any chemical that facilitates a reaction among other chemicals, without being altered itself in the process.)

## The Role of ATP

The body relies on one chemical, **ATP** (adenosine triphosphate), as its main way of delivering energy where it is needed (Figure B.6). When food is digested, much of the energy it releases goes into forming ATP molecules. Those ATP molecules travel to the muscles and other parts of the body that use energy.

ATP consists of the chemical adenosine bound to ribose and three phosphate groups ($PO_3$). Phosphates form high-energy covalent bonds. That is, a large amount of energy is required to form those bonds and a large amount of energy is released when they break. ATP can break off one or two of its three phosphates to provide energy to the muscles or other body parts.

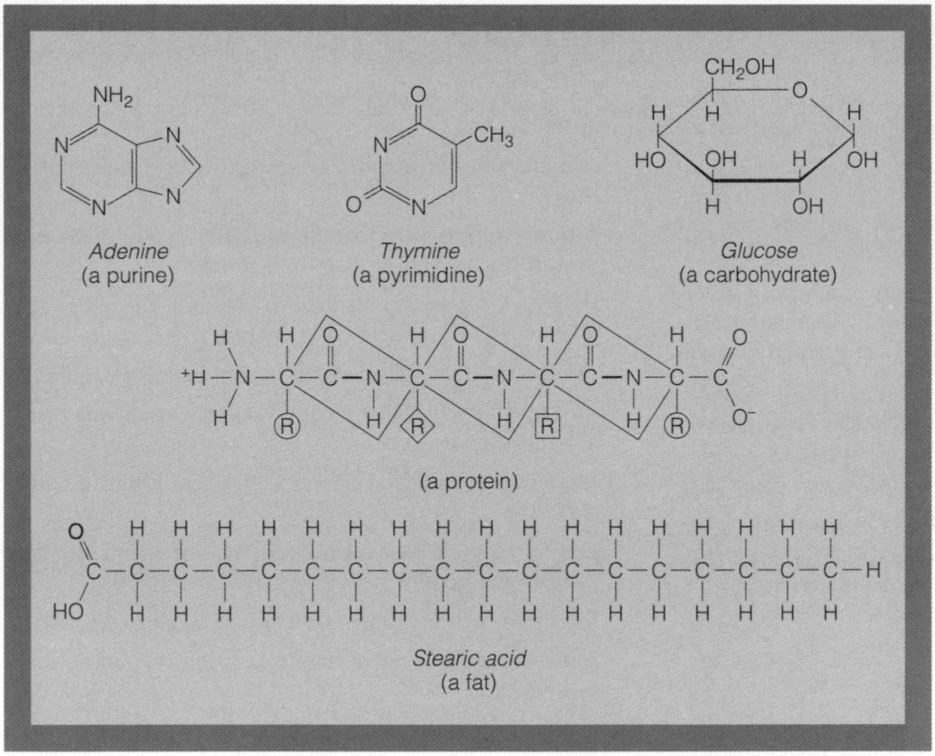

**Figure B.5**
**Structure of some important biological molecules**
*The "R" in the protein represents a point of attachment for various chains that differ from one amino acid to another.*

Adenine
(a purine)

Thymine
(a pyrimidine)

Glucose
(a carbohydrate)

(a protein)

Stearic acid
(a fat)

**Figure B.6**
**ATP, composed of adenosine, ribose, and three phosphates**
*ATP can lose one phosphate group to form ADP (adenosine diphosphate) and then lose another one to form AMP (adenosine monophosphate). Each time it breaks off a phosphate group it releases energy.*

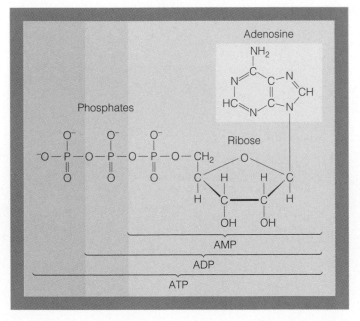

Adenosine

Phosphates

Ribose

AMP

ADP

ATP

## SUMMARY

1. All naturally occurring matter is composed of 92 elements that combine to form an endless variety of compounds. (p. 607)

2. The smallest piece of an element is an atom. The smallest piece of a compound that maintains the properties of the compound is a molecule. (p. 607)

3. The atoms of some elements can gain or lose an electron, thus becoming ions. Positively charged ions attract negatively charged ions. That attraction is called an ionic bond. (p. 610)

4. In some cases two or more atoms may share electrons, thus forming a covalent bond. (p. 610)

5. Enzymes are proteins that promote and control certain chemical reactions in the body. (p. 612)

6. The principal carrier of energy in the body is a chemical called ATP. (p. 612)

## REVIEW QUESTIONS

1. What is the difference between an atom and a molecule? What is the difference between an atom and an ion? (p. 607)

2. What are the most abundant elements in the human body? (p. 609)

3. What does the atomic number of an element represent? What does the atomic weight represent? (p. 609)

4. What kind of bonds do carbon atoms form—ionic or covalent? (p. 610)

## GLOSSARY

**atom** piece of an element that cannot be divided any further

**atomic number** number of protons in the nucleus of an atom

**atomic weight** number indicating the weight of an atom relative to a weight of one for a proton

**ATP** (adenosine triphosphate) a chemical the body uses as its main way of delivering energy where it is needed

**compound** material made up by combining elements

**covalent bond** chemical bond between two atoms that share electrons

**element** material that cannot be broken down into other materials

**enzyme** protein that controls the rate of chemical reactions in the body

**ion** atom that has gained or lost one or more electrons

**ionic bond** chemical attraction between two ions of opposite charge

**molecule** smallest possible piece of a compound

# Society for Neuroscience Guidelines for Animal Research

## INTRODUCTION

Research in the neurosciences contributes to the quality of life by expanding knowledge about living organisms. This improvement in quality of life stems in part from progress toward ameliorating human disease and disability, in part from advances in animal welfare and veterinary medicine, and in part from the steady increase in knowledge of the abilities and potentialities of human and animal life. Continued progress in many areas of biomedical research requires the use of living animals in order to investigate complex systems and functions because, in such cases, no adequate alternatives exist. Progress in both basic and clinical research in such areas cannot continue without the use of living animals as experimental subjects. The use of living animals in properly designed scientific research is therefore both ethical and appropriate. Nevertheless, our concern for the humane treatment of animals dictates that we weigh carefully the benefits to human knowledge and welfare whenever animal research is undertaken. The investigator using research animals assumes responsibility for proper experimental design, including ethical as well as scientific aspects.

The scientific community shares the concern of society at large that the use of animals in research should conform to standards that are consonant with those applied to other uses of animals by humans. While it is unlikely that any particular set of standards will satisfy everyone, it is appropriate for scientific societies to formulate guidelines that apply to the humane use of laboratory animals in particular areas of research. Ideally, such guidelines should also be acceptable to society at large as reasonable and prudent.

Most of the more specific sections of this document were formulated with respect to research using warm-blooded vertebrates. As a general principle, however, ethical issues involved in the use of any species, whether vertebrate or invertebrate, are best considered in relation to the complexity of that species' nervous system and its apparent awareness of the environment, rather than physical appearance or evolutionary proximity to humans.

## FACTORS THAT RELATE TO THE DESIGN OF EXPERIMENTS

The primary factor used to evaluate humane treatment in animal research is degree of distress or discomfort assessed by anthropomorphic judgments made by reasonable and prudent human observers. *The fundamental principle of ethical animal research is that experimental animals must not be subjected to avoidable distress or discomfort.* This principle must be observed when designing any experiment that uses living animals.

Although most animal research involves minimal distress or discomfort, certain valid scientific questions may require experimental designs that inevitably produce these effects. Such situations, while uncommon, are extremely diverse and must be evaluated individually. It is critical that distress and discomfort be minimized by careful experimental design. It is also important to recognize that there is no difference between distress and discomfort that may be inherent in a valid experimental design and that which may occur as an unintended side effect. It is therefore incumbent on the investigator to recognize and to eliminate all *avoidable* sources of distress and discomfort in animal subjects. This goal often requires attention to specifics of animal husbandry and to experimental design.

Invasive procedures and paralytic drugs should never be employed without benefit of anesthetic agents unless there is a very strong scientific justification and careful consideration is given to possible alternatives. Advances in experimental techniques, such as the use of devices chronically implanted under anesthesia, can offer alternative approaches. If these are not feasible, it is essential to monitor nociceptive responses (for example, recordings of EEG, blood pressure, and pupillary responses) that may indicate distress in the animal subject, and to use these as signals of the need to alleviate pain, to modify the experimental design, or to terminate the experiment.

When designing research projects, investigators should carefully consider the species and numbers of animals necessary to provide valid information, as well as the question whether living subjects are required to answer the scientific question. As a general rule, experiments should be designed so as to minimize the number of animals used and to avoid the depletion of endangered species. Advances in experimental methods, more efficient use of animals, within-subject designs, and modern statistical techniques all provide possible ways to minimize the numbers of animals used in research. This goal is completely consistent with the critical importance of replication and validation of results to true progress in science.

# FACTORS THAT RELATE TO THE
# CONDUCT OF EXPERIMENTS

Research animals must be acquired and cared for in accordance with the guidelines published in the *NIH Guide for the Care and Use of Laboratory Animals* (National Institutes of Health Publications, No. 85-23, Revised 1985). Investigators must also be aware of the relevant local, state, and federal laws. The quality of research data depends in no small measure on health and general condition of the animals used, as well as on the specifics of experimental design. Thus, proper animal husbandry is integral to the success of any research effort using living animal subjects. General standards for animal husbandry (housing, food quality, ventilation, etc.) are detailed in the *NIH Guide*. The experienced investigator can contribute additional specifics for optimum care for particular experimental situations, or for species not commonly encountered in laboratory settings.

Surgery performed with the intent that the animal will survive (for example, on animals intended for chronic study) should be carried out, or directly supervised, by persons with appropriate levels of experience and training, and with attention to asepsis and prevention of infection. Major surgical procedures should be done using an appropriate method of anesthesia to render the animal insensitive to pain. Muscle relaxants and paralytics have no anesthetic action and should not be used alone for surgical restraint. Postoperative care must include attention to minimize discomfort and the risk of infection.

Many experimental designs call for surgical preparation under anesthetic agents with no intent that the animal should survive. In such cases, the animals ordinarily should be maintained unconscious for the duration of the experiment. At the conclusion of the experiment, the animal should be killed without regaining consciousness and death ensured before final disposition.

Certain experiments may require physical restraint, and/or withholding of food or water, as methodological procedures rather than experimental paradigms. In such cases, careful attention must be paid to minimize discomfort or distress and to ensure that general health is maintained. Immobilization or restraint to which the animals cannot be readily adapted should not be imposed when alternative procedures are practical. Reasonable periods of rest and readjustment should be included in the experimental schedule unless these would be absolutely inconsistent with valid scientific objectives.

When distress and discomfort are unavoidable attributes of a valid experimental design, it is mandatory to conduct such experiments so as to minimize these effects, to minimize the duration of the procedure, and to minimize the numbers of animals used, consistent with the scientific objectives of the study.

# References

Numbers or letters in parentheses following citations indicate the chapter or appendix in which a reference is cited.

Abraham, H.D. (1983). Visual phenomenology of the LSD flashback. *Archives of General Psychiatry, 40*, 884–889. (3)

Abramowitz, E.S., Baker, A.H., & Fleischer, S.F. (1982). Onset of depressive psychiatric crises and the menstrual cycle. *American Journal of Psychiatry, 139*, 475–478. (16)

Abramowitz, I., Gordon, J., Hendrickson, A., Hainline, L., Dobson, V., & La-Bossiere, E. (1982). The retina of the newborn human infant. *Science, 217*, 265–267. (8)

Abramson, L.Y., Seligman, M.E.P., & Teasdale, J.D. (1978). Learned helplessness in humans: Critique and reformulation. *Journal of Abnormal Psychology, 87*, 49–74. (16)

Adam, K. (1980). Sleep as a restorative process and a theory to explain why. *Progress in Brain Research, 53*, 289–305. (10)

Adamec, R. (1975). The behavioral basis of prolonged suppression of predatory attack in cats. *Aggressive Behavior, 1*, 297–314. (13)

Adamec, R.E., Stark-Adamec, C., & Livingston, K.E. (1980). The development of predatory aggression and defense in the domestic cat (*Felis catus*): 3. Effects on development of behavior between 180 and 365 days of age. *Behavioral and Neural Biology, 30*, 435–447. (13)

Adams, D.B., Gold, A.R., & Burt, A.D. (1978). Rise in female-initiated sexual activity at ovulation and its suppression by oral contraceptives. *New England Journal of Medicine, 299*, 1145–1150. (12)

Adkins, E.K., & Adler, N.T. (1972). Hormonal control of behavior in the Japanese quail. *Journal of Comparative and Physiological Psychology, 81*, 27–36. (12)

Adkins, E.K., & Pniewski, E.E. (1978). Control of reproductive behavior by sex steroids in male quail. *Journal of Comparative and Physiological Psychology, 92*, 1169–1178. (12)

Adkins-Regan, E. (1988). Sex hormones and sexual orientation in animals. *Psychobiology, 16*, 335–347. (12)

Aggleton, J.P., Blindt, H.S., & Rawlins, J.N.P. (1989). Effects of amygdaloid and amygdaloid-hippocampal lesions on object recognition and spatial working memory in rats. *Behavioral Neuroscience, 103*, 962–974. (14)

Aggleton, J.P., & Passingham, R.E. (1981). Syndrome produced by lesions of the amygdala in monkeys (*Macaca mulatta*). *Journal of Comparative and Physiological Psychology, 95*, 961–977. (13)

Akers, R.F., Lovinger, D.M., Colley, P.A., Linden, D.J., & Routtenberg, A. (1986). Translocation of protein kinase C activity may mediate hippocampal long-term potentiation. *Science, 231*, 587–589. (14)

Albanese, A., Altavista, M.C., & Rossi, P. (1986). Organization of central nervous system dopaminergic pathways. *Journal of Neural Transmission, Supplementum 22*, 3–17. (16)

Alberts, J.R. (1978). Huddling by rat pups: Group behavioral mechanisms of temperature regulation and energy conservation. *Journal of Comparative and Physiological Psychology, 92*, 231–245. (11)

Alexander, D., Ehrhardt, A.A., & Money, J. (1966). Defective figure drawing, geometric and human, in Turner's syndrome. *Journal of Nervous and Mental Disease, 142*, 161–167. (12)

Alexander, D., Walker, H.T., Jr., & Money, J. (1964). Studies in direction sense. *Archives of General Psychiatry, 10*, 337–339. (12)

Alexander, M.P., Benson, D.F., & Stuss, D.T. (1989). Frontal lobes and language. *Brain and Language, 37*, 656–691. (5)

Allebeck, P., & Wistedt, B. (1986). Mortality in schizophrenia. *Archives of General Psychiatry, 43*, 650–653. (16)

Allison, T., & Cicchetti, D.V. (1976). Sleep in mammals: Ecological and constitutional correlates. *Science, 194*, 732–734. (10)

Allison, T., & Goff, W.R. (1968). Sleep in a primitive mammal, the spiny anteater. *Psychophysiology, 5*, 200–201. (10)

Almli, C.R., Fisher, R.S., & Hill, D.L. (1979). Lateral hypothalamus destruction in infant rats produces consummatory deficits without sensory neglect or attenuated arousal. *Experimental Neurology, 66*, 146–157. (11)

Al-Rashid, R.A. (1971). Hypothalamic syndrome in acute childhood leukemia. *Clinical Pediatrics, 10*, 53–54. (11)

Altner, H. (1978). Physiology of taste. In R.F. Schmidt (Ed.), *Fundamentals of sensory physiology* (pp. 218–227). New York: Springer-Verlag. (6)

Altshuler, L.L., Casanova, M.F., Goldberg, T.E., & Kleinman, J.E. (1990). The hippocampus and parahippocampus in schizophrenic, suicide, and control brains. *Archives of General Psychiatry, 47*, 1029–1034. (16)

American Medical Association. (1988). *Use of animals in biomedical research*. (1)

American Psychiatric Association. (1987). *Diagnostic and statistical manual of mental disorders* (3rd ed., rev.). Washington, DC: Author. (16)

Amoore, J.E. (1963). Stereochemical theory of olfaction. *Nature, 198*, 271–272. (6)

Amoore, J.E. (1967). Specific anosmia: A clue to the olfactory code. *Nature, 214*, 1095–1098. (6)

Amoore, J.E. (1977). Specific anosmia and the concept of primary odors. *Chemical Senses and Flavor, 2*, 267–281. (6)

Amsterdam, J.D., Winokur, A., Dyson, W., Herzog, S., Gonzalez, F., Rott, R., & Koprowski, H. (1985). Borna disease virus. *Archives of General Psychiatry, 42*, 1093–1096. (16)

Anders, J.J., Dorovini-Zis, K., & Brightman, M.W. (1980). Endothelial and astrocytic cell membranes in relation to the composition of cerebral extracellular fluid. In H.M. Eisenberg & R.L. Suddith (Eds.), *The cerebral microvasculature* (pp. 193–209). New York: Plenum. (2)

Andersen, R.A., Essick, G.K., & Siegel, R.M. (1985). Encoding of spatial location by posterior parietal neurons. *Science, 230,* 456–458. (4)

Anderson, W.J., & Altman, J. (1972). Retardation of cerebellar and motor development in rats by focal x-irradiation beginning at four days. *Physiology & Behavior, 8,* 57–67. (4)

Andersson, U., Eckernäs, S.-Å., Hartvig, P., Ulin, J., Långström, B., & Häggström, J.-E. (1990). Striatal binding of ¹¹C-NMSP studied with positron emission tomography in patients with persistent tardive dyskinesia: No evidence for altered dopamine $D_2$ receptor binding. *Journal of Neural Transmission, 79,* 215–226. (16)

Andreasen, N.C. (1988). Brain imaging: Applications in psychiatry. *Science, 239,* 1381–1388. (4)

Andreasen, N.C., Ehrhardt, J.C., Swayze, V.W., Alliger, R.J., Yuh, W.T.C., Cohen, G., & Ziebell, S. (1990a). Magnetic resonance imaging of the brain in schizophrenia. *Archives of General Psychiatry, 47,* 35–44. (16)

Andreasen, N.C., Nasrallah, H.A., Dunn, V., Olson, S.C., Grove, W.M., Ehrhardt, J.C., Coffman, J.A., & Crossett, J.H.W. (1986). Structural abnormalities in the frontal system in schizophrenia. *Archives of General Psychiatry, 43,* 136–144. (16)

Andreasen, N.C., Swayze, V.W., II, Flaum, M., Yates, W.R., Arndt, S., & McChesney, C. (1990b). Ventricular enlargement in schizophrenia evaluated with computed tomographic scanning. *Archives of General Psychiatry, 47,* 1008–1015. (16)

Andrews, G., Hall, W., Goldstein, G., Lapsley, H., Bartels, R., & Silove, D. (1985). The economic costs of schizophrenia. *Archives of General Psychiatry, 42,* 537–543. (16)

Anías, J., Holmgren, B., Urbá Holmgren, R., & Eguíbar, J.R. (1984). Circadian rhythm of yawning behavior. *Acta Neurobiologiae Experimentalis, 44,* 179–186. (10)

Anisman, H., & Zacharko, R.M. (1982). Depression: The predisposing influence of stress. *The Behavioral and Brain Sciences, 5,* 89–137. (16)

Antelman, S.M., Chiodo, L.A., & DeGiovanni, L.A. (1982). Antidepressants and dopamine autoreceptors: Implications for both a novel means of treating depression and understanding bipolar illness. *Advances in Biochemical Psychopharmacology, 31,* 121–132. (16)

Antin, J., Gibbs, J., Holt, J., Young, R.C., & Smith, G.P. (1975). Cholecystokinin elicits the complete behavioral sequence of satiety in rats. *Journal of Comparative and Physiological Psychology, 89,* 784–790. (11)

Antin, J., Gibbs, J., & Smith, G.P. (1978). Intestinal satiety requires pregastric food stimulation. *Physiology & Behavior, 20,* 67–70. (11)

Antrobus, J.S. (1986). Dreaming: Cortical activation and perceptual thresholds. *Journal of Mind and Behavior, 7,* 193–211. (10)

Aram, D.M., & Ekelman, B.L. (1986). Spoken syntax in children with acquired unilateral hemispheric lesions. *Brain and Language, 27,* 75–100. (5)

Arango, V., Ernsberger, P., Marzuk, P.M., Chen, J.-S., Tierney, H., Stanley, M., Reis, D.J., & Mann, J.J. (1990). Autoradiographic demonstration of increased serotonin 5-HT₂ and beta-adrenergic receptor binding sites in the brain of suicide victims. *Archives of General Psychiatry, 47,* 1038–1047. (13)

Arboleda, C., & Holzman, P.S. (1985). Thought disorder in children at risk for psychosis. *Archives of General Psychiatry, 42,* 1004–1013. (16)

Arkin, A.M., Toth, M.F., Baker, J., & Hastey, J.M. (1970). The frequency of sleep talking in the laboratory among chronic sleep talkers and good dream recallers. *Journal of Nervous and Mental Disease, 151,* 369–374. (10)

Arnold, A.P. (1980). Sexual differences in the brain. *American Scientist, 68,* 165–173. (1)

Arnold, A.P. (1982). Neural control of passerine song. In D.E. Kroodsma & E.H. Miller (Eds.), *Acoustic communication in birds* (Vol. 1, pp. 75–94). New York: Academic Press. (1)

Arnsten, A.F.T., & Goldman-Rakic, P.S. (1985a). Alpha₂-adrenergic mechanisms in prefrontal cortex associated with cognitive decline in aged nonhuman primates. *Science, 230,* 1273–1276. (14)

Arnsten, A.F.T., & Goldman-Rakic, P.S. (1985b). Catecholamines and cognitive decline in aged nonhuman primates. *Annals of the New York Academy of Sciences, 444,* 218–234. (14)

Aronson, L.R., & Cooper, M.L. (1979). Amygdaloid hypersexuality in male cats reexamined. *Physiology & Behavior, 22,* 257–265. (13)

Arvidson, K., & Friberg, U. (1980). Human taste: Response and taste bud number in fungiform papillae. *Science, 209,* 807–808. (6)

Asanuma, H. (1981). The pyramidal tract. In V.B. Brooks (Ed.), *Handbook of physiology: Section 1: The nervous system, Volume 2. Motor control* (Pt. 1, pp. 703–733). Bethesda, MD: American Physiological Society. (9)

Aschoff, J., Gerecke, U., & Wever, R. (1967). Desynchronization of human circadian rhythms. *Japanese Journal of Physiology, 17,* 450–457. (10)

Aschoff, J., & Wever, R. (1976). Human circadian rhythms: A multioscillatory system. *Federation Proceedings, 35,* 2326–2332. (10)

Aserinsky, E., & Kleitman, N. (1955). Two types of ocular motility occurring in sleep. *Journal of Applied Physiology, 8,* 1–10. (10)

Ashmore, J., & Saibil, H. (1990). Introduction: Ears, eyes, noses, and tongues—cellular mechanisms for sensory transduction. *Seminars in the Neurosciences, 2,* 1–2. (6)

Astic, L., Sastre, J.-P., & Brandon, A.-M. (1973). Etude polygraphique des états de vigilance chez le foetus de cobaye [Polygraphic study of the states of arousal of the guinea pig fetus]. *Physiology & Behavior, 11,* 647–654. (10)

Attardi, D.G., & Sperry, R.W. (1963). Preferential selection of central pathways by regenerating optic fibers. *Experimental Neurology, 7,* 46–64. (8)

August, G.J., & Lockhart, L.H. (1984). Familial autism and the fragile-X chromosome. *Journal of Autism and Developmental Disorders, 14,* 197–204. (16)

Augustine, G.J., Charlton, M.P., & Smith, S.J. (1987). Calcium action in synaptic transmitter release. *Annual Review of Neuroscience, 10,* 633–693. (3)

Ayala-Guerrero, F., Calderón, A., & Pérez, M.C. (1988). Sleep patterns in a chelonian reptile (*Gopherus flavomarginatus*). *Physiology & Behavior, 44,* 333–337. (10)

Babich, F.R., Jacobson, A.L., Bubash, S., & Jacobson, A. (1965). Transfer of a response to naive rats by injection of ribonucleic acid extracted from trained rats. *Science, 149,* 656–657. (14)

Bachevalier, J., & Mishkin, M. (1986). Visual recognition impairment follows ventromedial but not dorsolateral prefrontal lesions in monkeys. *Behavioral Brain Research, 20,* 249–261. (14)

Backlund, E.-O., Granberg, P.-O., Hamberger, B., Sedvall, G., Seiger, A., & Olson, L. (1985). Transplantation of adrenal medullary tissue to striatum in Parkinsonism. In A. Björklund & U. Stenevi (Eds.), *Neural grafting in the mammalian CNS* (pp. 551–556). Amsterdam: Elsevier. (15)

Bacopoulos, N.C., Spokes, E.G., Bird, E.D., & Roth, R.H. (1979). Antipsychotic drug action in schizophrenic patients: Effect on cortical dopamine metabolism after long-term treatment. *Science, 205,* 1405–1407. (16)

Baghdoyan, H.A., Rodrigo-Angulo, M.L., McCarley, R.W., & Hobson, J.A. (1984). Site-specific enhancement and suppression of desynchronized sleep signs following cholinergic stimulation of three brainstem regions. *Brain Research, 306,* 39–52. (10)

Baghdoyan, H.A., Rodrigo-Angulo, M.L., McCarley, R.W., & Hobson, J.A. (1987). A neuroanatomical gradient in the pontine tegmentum for the cholinoceptive induction of desynchronized sleep signs. *Brain Research, 414,* 245–261. (10)

Bahill, A.T., & LaRitz, T. (1984). Why can't batters keep their eyes on the ball? *American Scientist, 72,* 249–253. (9)

Balasubramaniam, V., & Kanaka, T.S. (1976). Hypothalamotomy in the management of aggressive behavior. In T.P. Morley (Ed.), *Current controversies in neurosurgery* (pp. 768–777). Philadelphia: Saunders. (13)

Ballard, P.A., Tetrud, J.W., & Langston, J.W. (1985). Permanent human parkinsonism due to 1-methyl-4-phenyl-1,2,3,6-tetrahydropyridine (MPTP). *Neurology, 35,* 949–956. (9)

Ballenger, J.C., Burrows, G.D., DuPont, R.L., Jr., Lesser, I.M., Noyes, R., Jr.,

Pecknold, J.C., Rifkin, A., & Swinson, R. P. (1988). Alprazolam in panic disorder and agoraphobia: Results from a multicenter trial. *Archives of General Psychiatry, 45,* 413–422. (13)

Banks, M.S., Aslin, R.N., & Letson, R.D. (1975). Sensitive period for the development of human binocular vision. *Science, 190,* 675–677. (8)

Baptista, L.F. (1985). The functional significance of song sharing in the white-crowned sparrow. *Canadian Journal of Zoology, 63,* 1741–1752. (1)

Baptista, L.F., & Petrinovich, L. (1984). Social interaction, sensitive phases and the song template hypothesis in the white-crowned sparrow. *Animal Behaviour, 32,* 172–181. (1)

Barbaro, N.M. (1988). Studies of PAG/PVG stimulation for pain relief in humans. In H.L. Fields & J.-M. Besson (Eds.), *Progress in brain research* (vol. 77, pp. 165–173). Amsterdam: Elsevier. (6)

Barbizet, J. (1970). *Human memory and its pathology.* San Francisco: W. H. Freeman. (14)

Bard, P. (1929). The central representation of the sympathetic system. *Archives of Neurology and Psychiatry, 22,* 230–246. (13)

Bard, P. (1934). On emotional expression after decortication with some remarks on certain theoretical views. *Psychological Review, 41,* 309–329. (13)

Bardach, J.E., & Villars, T. (1974). The chemical senses of fishes. In P.T. Grant & A.M. Mackie (Eds.), *Chemoreception in marine organisms* (pp. 49–104). New York: Academic. (6)

Barde, Y.-A. (1989). Trophic factors and neuronal survival. *Neuron, 2,* 1525–1534. (8)

Barnes, C.A., & McNaughton, B.L. (1985). An age comparison of the rates of acquisition and forgetting of spatial information in relation to long-term enhancement of hippocampal synapses. *Behavioral Neuroscience, 99,* 1040–1048. (14)

Barr, C.E., Mednick, S.A., & Munk-Jorgensen, P. (1990). Exposure to influenza epidemics during gestation and adult schizophrenia. *Archives of General Psychiatry, 47,* 869–874. (16)

Barre, V., & Petter-Rousseaux, A. (1988). Seasonal variations in sleep-wake cycle in *Microcebus murinus. Primates, 19,* 53–64. (10)

Bartoshuk, L.M., Gentile, R.L., Moskowitz, H.R., & Meiselman, H.L. (1974). Sweet taste induced by miracle fruit (*Synsephalum dulcificum*). *Physiology & Behavior, 12,* 449–456. (6)

Bartoshuk, L.M., Lee, C.-H., & Scarpellino, R. (1972). Sweet taste of water induced by artichoke (*Cynara scolymus*). *Science, 178,* 988–990. (6)

Bartus, R.T., Dean, R.L., III, Beer, B., & Lippa, A.S. (1982). The cholinergic hypothesis of geriatric memory dysfunction. *Science, 217,* 408–417. (14)

Bartus, R.T., Dean, R.L., Goas, J.A., & Lippa, A.S. (1980). Age-related changes in passive avoidance retention: Modulation with dietary choline. *Science, 209,* 301–303. (14)

Bartus, R.T., Dean, R.L., Pontecorvo, M.J., & Flicker, C. (1985). The cholinergic hypothesis: A historical overview, current perspective, and future directions. *Annals of the New York Academy of Sciences, 444,* 332–358. (14)

Batini, C., Magni, F., Palestini, M., Rossi, G.F., & Zanchetti, A. (1959). Neural mechanisms underlying the enduring EEG and behavioral activation in the midpontine pretrigeminal cat. *Archives Italiennes de Biologie, 97,* 13–25. (10)

Batini, C., Moruzzi, G., Palestini, M., Rossi, G.F., & Zanchetti, A. (1958). Persistent patterns of wakefulness in the pretrigeminal midpontine preparation. *Science, 128,* 30–32. (10)

Batini, C., Moruzzi, G., Palestini, M., Rossi, G.F., & Zanchetti, A. (1959). Effects of complete pontine transections on the sleep-wakefulness rhythm: The midpontine pretrigeminal preparation. *Archives Italiennes de Biologie, 97,* 1–12. (10)

Batini, C., Palestini, M., Rossi, G.F., & Zanchetti, A. (1959). EEG activation patterns in the midpontine pretrigeminal cat following sensory deafferentation. *Archives Italiennes de Biologie, 97,* 26–32. (10)

Baudry, M., & Lynch, G. (1980). Hypothesis regarding the cellular mechanisms responsible for long-term synaptic potentiation in the hippocampus. *Experimental Neurology, 68,* 202–204. (14)

Bauer, M.S., Whybrow, P.C., & Winokur, A. (1990). Rapid cycling bipolar affective disorder. *Archives of General Psychiatry, 47,* 427–432. (16)

Baum, A., Gatchel, R.J., & Schaeffer, M.A. (1983). Emotional, behavioral, and physiological effects of chronic stress at Three Mile Island. *Journal of Consulting & Clinical Psychology, 51,* 565–572. (13)

Baum, M.J. (1983). Hormonal modulation of sexuality in female primates. *BioScience, 33,* 578–582. (12)

Baxter, L.R., Phelps, M.E., Mazziotta, J.C., Guze, B.H., Schwartz, J.M., & Selin, C.E. (1987). Local cerebral glucose metabolic rates in obsessive-compulsive disorder. *Archives of General Psychiatry, 44,* 211–218. (13)

Baxter, L.R., Phelps, M.E., Mazziotta, J.C., Schwartz, J.M., Gerner, R.H., Selin, C.E., & Sumida, R.M. (1985). Cerebral metabolic rates for glucose in mood disorders. *Archives of General Psychiatry, 42,* 441–447. (16)

Bayer, S.A. (1985). Neuron production in the hippocampus and olfactory bulb of the adult rat brain: Addition or replacement? *Annals of the New York Academy of Sciences, 457,* 163–172. (2)

Beach, F.A. (1967). Cerebral and hormonal control of reflexive mechanisms involved in copulatory behavior. *Physiological Reviews, 47,* 289–316. (12)

Beach, F.A. (1970). Hormonal effects on socio-sexual behavior in dogs. In M. Gibian & E.J. Plotz (Eds.), *Mammalian reproduction* (pp. 437–466). Berlin: Springer-Verlag. (12)

Beach, F.A. (1974). Effects of gonadal hormones on urinary behavior in dogs. *Physiology & Behavior, 12,* 1005–1013. (12)

Beach, F.A. (1976). Sexual attractivity, proceptivity, and receptivity in female animals. *Hormones and Behavior, 7,* 105–138. (12)

Beach, F.A., Buehler, M.G., & Dunbar, I.F. (1982). Competitive behavior in male, female, and pseudohermaphroditic female dogs. *Journal of Comparative and Physiological Psychology, 96,* 855–874. (12)

Beach, F.A., Dunbar, I.F., & Buehler, M.G. (1982). Sexual characteristics of female dogs during successive phases of the ovarian cycle. *Hormones and Behavior, 16,* 414–462. (12)

Beal, M.F., Kowall, N.W., Ellison, D.W., Mazurek, M.F., Swartz, K.J., & Martin, J.B. (1986). Replication of the neurochemical characteristics of Huntington's disease by quinolinic acid. *Nature, 321,* 168–171. (9)

Bear, D.M., & Fedio, P. (1977). Quantitative analysis of interictal behavior in temporal lobe epilepsy. *Archives of Neurology, 34,* 454–467. (13)

Bear, M.F., Cooper, L.N., & Ebner, F.F. (1987). A physiological basis for a theory of synapse modification. *Science, 237,* 42–48. (14)

Beatty, W.W., Butters, N., & Janowsky, D.S. (1986). Patterns of memory failure after scopolamine treatment: Implications for cholinergic hypotheses of dementia. *Behavioral and Neural Biology, 45,* 196–211. (14)

Bechara, A., & van der Kooy, D. (1985). Opposite motivational effects of endogenous opioids in brain and periphery. *Nature, 314,* 533–534. (6)

Becker, H.C. (1988). Effects of the imidazobenzodiazepine Ro15-4513 on the stimulant and depressant actions of ethanol on spontaneous locomotor activity. *Life Sciences, 43,* 643–650. (13)

Begleiter, H., Porjesz, B., Bihari, B., & Kissin, B. (1984). Event-related brain potentials in boys at risk for alcoholism. *Science, 225,* 1493–1496. (3)

Békésy, G. — See von Békésy, G.

Belongia, E.A., Hedberg, C.W., Gleich, G.J., White, K.E., Mayeno, A.N., Loegering, D.A., Dunnette, S.L., Pirie, P.L., MacDonald, K.L., & Osterholm, M.T. (1990). An investigation of the cause of the eosinophilia-myalgia syndrome associated with tryptophan use. *New England Journal of Medicine, 323,* 357–365. (10)

Bellugi, U., Poizner, H., & Klima, E.S. (1983). Brain organization for language: Clues from sign aphasia. *Human Neurobiology, 2,* 155–170. (5)

Benes, F.M., & Bird, E.D. (1987). An analysis of the arrangement of neurons in the cingulate cortex of schizophrenic patients. *Archives of General Psychiatry, 44,* 608–616. (16)

Benes, F.M., Davidson, J., & Bird, E.D. (1986). Quantitative cytoarchitectural studies of the cerebral cortex of schizophrenics. *Archives of General Psychiatry, 43,* 31–35. (16)

Bennett, E.L., Rosenzweig, M.R., & Flood, J.F. (1979). Role of neurotransmitters and protein synthesis in short- and long-term memory. In J. Obiols, C. Ballús, E. González Monclús, & J. Pujol (Eds.), *Biological psychiatry today* (pp. 211–219).

Amsterdam: Elsevier/North Holland Biomedical Press. (14)

Benzing, W.C., & Squire, L.R. (1989). Preserved learning and memory in amnesia: Intact adaptation-level effects and learning of stereoscopic depth. *Behavioral Neuroscience, 103,* 538–547. (14)

Berg, J.M. (1985). Physical determinants of environmental origin. In A.M. Clarke, A.D.B. Clarke, & J.M. Berg (Eds.), *Mental deficiency: The changing outlook* (4th ed.) (pp. 99–134). New York: Free Press. (8)

Berg, J.M. (1986). Etiology update and review. I. Biomedical factors. In J. Wortis (Ed.), *Mental retardation and developmental disabilities* (vol.14, pp. 20–35). New York: Elsevier. (8)

Berlin, F.S., & Meinecke, C.F. (1981). Treatment of sex offenders with antiandrogenic medication: Conceptualization, review of treatment modalities, and preliminary findings. *American Journal of Psychiatry, 138,* 601–607. (12)

Berman, K.F., Zec, R.F., & Weinberger, D.R. (1986). Physiologic dysfunction of dorsolateral prefrontal cortex in schizophrenia: II. Role of neuroleptic treatment, attention, and mental effort. *Archives of General Psychiatry, 43,* 126–135. (4, 16)

Bernstein, I.L. (1985). Learned food aversions in the progression of cancer and its treatment. *Annals of the New York Academy of Sciences, 443,* 365–380. (11)

Bernstein, I.L., Treneer, C.M., Goehler, L.E., & Murowchick, E. (1985). Tumor growth in rats: Conditioned suppression of food intake and preference. *Behavioral Neuroscience, 99,* 818–830. (11)

Bernstein, J.J., & Gelderd, J.B. (1970). Regeneration of the long spinal tracts in the goldfish. *Brain Research, 20,* 33–38. (15)

Berridge, K.C., Venier, I.L., & Robinson, T.E. (1989). Taste reactivity analysis of 6-hydroxydopamine-induced aphagia: Implications for arousal and anhedonia hypotheses of dopamine function. *Behavioral Neuroscience, 103,* 36–45. (11)

Bertino, M., & Tordoff, M.G. (1988). Sodium depletion increases rats' preferences for salted food. *Behavioral Neuroscience, 102,* 565–573. (11)

Biben, M. (1979). Predation and predatory play behaviour of domestic cats. *Animal Behaviour, 27,* 81–94. (13)

Bickford, R.G., Dodge, H.W., Jr., & Uihlein, A. (1960). Electrographic and behavioral effects related to depth stimulation in human patients. In E.R. Ramey & D.S. O'Doherty (Eds.), *Electrical stimulation in the unanesthetized brain* (pp. 248–261). New York: P.B. Hoeber. (1)

Bingman, V.P., Ioalé, P., Casini, G., & Bagnoli, P. (1990). The avian hippocampus: Evidence for a role in the development of the homing pigeon navigational map. *Behavioral Neuroscience, 104,* 906–911. (14)

Birch, G.G., & Mylvaganam, A.R. (1976). Evidence for the proximity of sweet and bitter receptor sites. *Nature, 260,* 632–634. (6)

Bisiach, E., & Luzzatti, C. (1978). Unilateral neglect of representational space. *Cortex, 14,* 129–133. (4)

Björklund, A., Stenevi, U., Dunnett, S.B., & Gage, F.H. (1982). Cross-species neural grafting in a rat model of Parkinson's disease. *Nature, 298,* 652–654. (15)

Black, I.B., Adler, J.E., & LaGamma, E.F. (1986). Impulse activity differentially regulates colocalized transmitters by altering messenger RNA levels. In T. Hökfelt, K. Fuxe, & B. Pernow (Eds.), *Progress in brain research* (vol. 68, pp. 121–127). Amsterdam: Elsevier. (3)

Blake, R., & Hirsch, H.V.B. (1975). Deficits in binocular depth perception in cats after alternating monocular deprivation. *Science, 190,* 1114–1116. (8)

Blakemore, C. (1974). Developmental factors in the formation of feature extracting neurons. In F.O. Schmitt & F.G. Worden (Eds.), *The neurosciences: Third study program* (pp. 105–113). Cambridge, MA: MIT Press. (8)

Blakemore, C., & Sutton, P. (1969). Size adaptation: A new aftereffect. *Science, 166,* 245–247. (7)

Blass, E.M., & Epstein, A.N. (1971). A lateral preoptic osmosensitive zone for thirst in the rat. *Journal of Comparative and Physiological Psychology, 76,* 378–394. (11)

Blass, E.M., & Hall, W.G. (1976). Drinking termination: Interactions among hydrational, orogastric, and behavioral controls in rats. *Psychological Review, 83,* 356–374. (11)

Blass, E.M., & Teicher, H.M. (1980). Suckling. *Science, 210,* 15–22. (11)

Blehar, M.C., & Rosenthal, N.E. (1989). Seasonal affective disorders and phototherapy. *Archives of General Psychiatry, 46,* 469–474. (16)

Bleuler, E. (1950). *Dementia praecox; or the group of schizophrenias.* New York: International Universities Press. (Original work published 1911). (16)

Bliss, T.V.P., Clements, M.P., Erington, M.L., Lynch, M.A., & Williams, J.H. (1990). Presynaptic changes associated with long-term potentiation in the dentate gyrus. *Seminars in the Neurosciences, 2,* 345–354. (14)

Bliss, T.V.P., & Lømo, T. (1973). Long-lasting potentiation of synaptic transmission in the dentate area of the anaesthetized rabbit following stimulation of the perforant path. *Journal of Physiology* (London), *232,* 331–356. (14)

Bloom, F.E. (1987). Molecular diversity and cellular functions of neuropeptides. In E.R. deKloet, V.M. Wiegant, & D. deWied (Eds.), *Progress in brain research* (Vol. 72, pp. 213–220). Amsterdam: Elsevier. (3)

Blumstein, S.E., Katz, B., Goodglass, H., Shrier, R., & Dworetsky, B. (1985). The effects of slowed speech on auditory comprehension in aphasia. *Brain and Language, 24,* 246–265. (5)

Bodnoff, S.R., Suranyi-Cadotte, B.E., Quirion, R., & Meaney, M.J. (1989). Role of the central benzodiazepine receptor system in behavioral habituation to novelty. *Behavioral Neuroscience, 103,* 209–212. (13)

Bogardus, C., Lillioja, S., Ravussin, E., Abbott, W., Zawadzki, J.K., Young, A., Knowler, W.C., Jacobowitz, R., & Moll, P.P. (1986). Familial dependence of the resting metabolic rate. *New England Journal of Medicine, 315,* 96–100. (11)

Bogen, J.E., Schultz, D.H., & Vogel, P.J. (1988). Completeness of callosotomy shown by magnetic resonance imaging in the long term. *Archives of Neurology, 45,* 1203–1205. (5)

Bogerts, B., Meertz, E., & Schönfeldt-Bausch, R. (1985). Basal ganglia and limbic system pathology in schizophrenia. *Archives of General Psychiatry, 42,* 784–791. (16)

Bohn, M.C., Cupit, L., Marciano, F., & Gash, D.M. (1987). Adrenal medulla grafts enhance recovery of striatal dopaminergic fibers. *Science, 237,* 913–916. (15)

Boklage, C.E. (1977). Schizophrenia, brain asymmetry development, and twinning: Cellular relationship with etiological and possibly prognostic implications. *Biological Psychiatry, 12,* 19–35. (16)

Bolla-Wilson, K., Robinson, R.G., Starkstein, S.E., Boston, J., & Price, T.R. (1989). Lateralization of dementia of depression in stroke patients. *American Journal of Psychiatry, 146,* 627–634. (13)

Booth-Kewley, S., & Friedman, H.S. (1987). Psychological predictors of heart disease: A quantitative review. *Psychological Bulletin, 101,* 343–362. (13)

Borbély, A.A. (1982). Circadian and sleep-dependent processes in sleep regulation. In J. Aschoff, S. Daan, & G.A. Groos (Eds.), *Vertebrate circadian rhythms* (pp. 237–242). Berlin: Springer-Verlag. (10)

Boring, E.G. (1950). *A history of experimental psychology* (2nd ed.). New York: Appleton-Century-Crofts. (5)

Borod, J.C., Koff, E., Lorch, M., & Nicholas, M. (1986). The expression and perception of facial emotion in brain-damaged patients. *Neuropsychologia, 24,* 169–180. (5)

Bostock, E., Gallagher, M., & King, R.A. (1988). Effects of opioid microinjections into the medial septal area on spatial memory in rats. *Behavioral Neuroscience, 102,* 643–652. (14)

Bowman, M.B., & Lewis, M.S. (1982). The copper hypothesis of schizophrenia: A review. *Neuroscience & Biobehavioral Reviews, 6,* 321–328. (16)

Bozarth, M.A., & Wise, R.A. (1984). Anatomically distinct opiate receptor fields mediate reward and physical dependence. *Science, 224,* 516–517. (13)

Bradbury, M. (1979). Why a blood-brain barrier? *Trends in Neurosciences, 2,* 36–38. (2)

Bradbury, T.N., & Miller, G.A. (1985). Season of birth in schizophrenia: A review of evidence, methodology, and etiology. *Psychological Bulletin, 98,* 569–594. (16)

Bradford, J.M.W. (1988). Organic treatment for the male sexual offender. *Annals of the New York Academy of Sciences, 528,* 193–202. (12)

Bradshaw, J.L., & Nettleton, N.C. (1981). The nature of hemispheric specialization in man. *Behavioral and Brain Sciences, 4,* 51–91. (5)

Brady, J.V., Porter, R.W., Conrad, D.G., & Mason, J.W. (1958). Avoidance behavior and the development of gastroduodenal ulcers. *Journal of the Experimental Analysis of Behavior, 1,* 69–72. (13)

Braff, D.L., & Huey, L. (1988). Methylphenidate-induced information processing dysfunction in non-schizophrenic patients. *Archives of General Psychiatry, 45,* 827–832. (16)

Brain, P.F. (1979). Steroidal influences on aggressiveness. In J. Obiols, C. Ballús, E. González Monclús, & J. Pujol (Eds.), *Biological psychiatry today* (pp. 1204–1208). Amsterdam: Elsevier/North Holland Biomedical Press. (12)

Braus, H. (1960). *Anatomie des Menschen, 3. Band: Periphere Leistungsbahnen II. Centrales Nervensystem, Sinnesorgane. 2.Auflage* [Human anatomy: Vol. 3. Peripheral pathways II. Central nervous system, sensory organs (2nd ed.)]. Berlin: Springer-Verlag. (4, 6)

Bregman, B.S., & Goldberger, M.E. (1982). Anatomical plasticity and sparing of function after spinal cord damage in neonatal cats. *Science, 217,* 553–555. (15)

Brenner, E., Cornelissen, F., & Nuboer, W. (1990). Striking absence of long-lasting effects of early color deprivation on monkey vision. *Developmental Psychobiology, 23,* 441–448. (8)

Breslau, N., & Davis, G.C. (1986). Chronic stress and major depression. *Archives of General Psychiatry, 43,* 309–314. (16)

Bridgeman, B., & Staggs, D. (1982). Plasticity in human blindsight. *Vision Research, 22,* 1199–1203. (7)

Bridges, R.S. (1975). Long-term effects of pregnancy and parturition upon maternal responsiveness in the rat. *Physiology & Behavior, 14,* 245–249. (12)

Bridges, R.S., DiBiase, R., Loundes, D.D., & Doherty, P.C. (1985). Prolactin stimulation of maternal behavior in female rats. *Science, 227,* 782–784. (12)

Broderick, J.P., Phillips, S.J., Whisnant, J.P., O'Fallon, W.M., & Bergstralh, E.J. (1989). Incidence rates of stroke in the eighties: The end of the decline in stroke? *Stroke, 20,* 577–582. (15)

Broderick, P.A., Bridger, W.H. (1984). A comparative study of the effect of L-tryptophan and its acetylated derivative N-acetyl-L-tryptophan on rat muricidal behavior. *Biological Psychiatry, 19,* 89–94. (13)

Bronson, F.H. (1974). Pheromonal influences on reproductive activities in rodents. In M.C. Birch (Ed.), *Pheromones* (pp. 344–365). Amsterdam: North Holland. (6)

Brooks, D.C., & Bizzi, E. (1963). Brain stem electrical activity during deep sleep. *Archives Italiennes de Biologie, 101,* 648–665. (10)

Brooks, V.B. (1984). Cerebellar functions in motor control. *Human Neurobiology, 2,* 251–260. (9)

Brown, G.L., Ebert, M.H., Goyer, P.F., Jimerson, D.C., Klein, W.J., Bunney, W.E., & Goodwin, F.K. (1982). Aggression, suicide, and serotonin: Relationships of CSF amine metabolites. *American Journal of Psychiatry, 139,* 741–746. (13)

Brown, G.L., Goodwin, F.K., Ballenger, J.C., Goyer, P.F., & Major, L.F. (1979). Aggression in humans correlates with cerebrospinal fluid amine metabolites. *Psychiatry Research, 1,* 131–139. (13)

Brown, J.W. (1972). *Aphasia, apraxia, and agnosia.* Springfield, IL: Charles C. Thomas. (9)

Brown, R., Colter, N., Corsellis, N., Crow, T.J., Frith, C., Jagoe, R., Johnstone, E.C., & Marsh, L. (1986). Postmortem evidence of structural brain changes in schizophrenia. *Archives of General Psychiatry, 43,* 36–42. (16)

Brown, R.E. (1986). Paternal behavior in the male Long-Evans rat (*Rattus norvegicus*). *Journal of Comparative Psychology, 100,* 162–172. (12)

Brown, W.T., & Jenkins, E.C. (1989). Mental retardation, Fragile X syndrome. In G. Adelman (Ed.), *Neuroscience year* (pp. 102–104). Boston: Birkhäuser. (8)

Bruce, C., Desimone, R., & Gross, C.G. (1981). Visual properties of neurons in a polysensory area in superior temporal sulcus of the macaque. *Journal of Neurophysiology, 46,* 369–384. (7)

Brügger, M. (1943). Fresstrieb als hypothalamisches Symptom [Feeding drive as a hypothalamic syndrome]. *Helvetica Physiologica et Pharmacologica Acta, 1,* 183–198. (11)

Brunelli, S.A., Shindledecker, R.D., & Hofer, M.A. (1987). Behavioral responses of juvenile rats (*Rattus norvegicus*) to neonates after infusion of maternal blood plasma. *Journal of Comparative Psychology, 101,* 47–59. (12)

Bruyer, R., Dupuis, M., Ophoven, E., Rectem, D., & Reynaert, C. (1985). Anatomical and behavioral study of a case of asymptomatic callosal agenesis. *Cortex, 21,* 417–430. (5)

Bryan, A.L. (1963). The essential basis for human culture. *Current Anthropology, 4,* 297–306. (5)

Buell, S.J., & Coleman, P.D. (1981). Quantitative evidence for selective dendritic growth in normal human aging but not in senile dementia. *Brain Research, 214,* 23–41. (2)

Buggy, J., Fisher, A.E., Hoffman, W.E., Johnson, A.K., & Phillips, M.I. (1975). Ventricular obstruction: Effect on drinking induced by intracranial injection of angiotensin. *Science, 190,* 72–74. (11)

Buisseret, P., & Imbert, M. (1976). Visual cortical cells: Their developmental properties in normal and dark reared kittens. *Journal of Physiology, 255,* 511–525. (8)

Bullock, T.H. (1979). Evolving concepts of local integrative operations in neurons. In F.O. Schmitt & F.G. Worden (Eds.), *The neurosciences: Fourth study program* (pp. 43–49). Cambridge, MA: MIT Press. (2)

Bungaard, M. (1986). Pathways across the vertebrate blood-brain barrier: Morphological viewpoints. *Annals of the New York Academy of Sciences, 481,* 7–19. (2)

Bunney, W.E., Jr., Murphy, D.L., Goodwin, F.K., & Borge, G.F. (1972). The "switch process" in manic-depressive illness. *Archives of General Psychiatry, 27,* 295–302. (16)

Bunsey, M., Kramer, D., Kesler, M., & Strupp, B.J. (1990). A vasopressin metabolite increases attentional selectivity. *Behavioral Neuroscience, 104,* 277–287. (14)

Burnstine, T.H., Greenough, W.T., & Tees, R.C. (1984). Intermodal compensation following damage or deprivation: A review of behavioral and neural evidence. In C.R. Almli & S. Finger (Eds.), *Early brain damage* (vol. 1, pp. 3–34). Orlando, FL: Academic Press. (15)

Burrows, G.D., McIntyre, I.M., Judd, F.K., & Norman, T.R. (1988, August). Clinical effects of serotonin reuptake inhibitors in the treatment of depressive illness. *Journal of Clinical Psychiatry, 49* (Suppl. 8), 18–22. (16)

Butera, P.C., & Czaja, J.A. (1989). Activation of sexual behavior in male rats by combined subcutaneous and intracranial treaments of 5-alpha-dihydrotestosterone. *Hormones and Behavior, 23,* 92–105. (12)

Byne, W., Bleier, R., & Houston, L. (1988). Variations in human corpus callosum do not predict gender: A study using magnetic resonance imaging. *Behavioral Neuroscience, 102,* 222–227. (5)

Cahn, R., Borziex, M.-G., Aldinio, C., Tofano, G., & Cahn, J. (1989). Influence of monosialoganglioside inner ester on neurologic recovery after global cerebral ischemia in monkeys. *Stroke, 20,* 652–656. (15)

Caldwell, J.D., Jirikowski, G.F., Greer, E.R., & Pedersen, C.A. (1989). Medial preoptic area oxytocin and female sexual receptivity. *Behavioral Neuroscience, 103,* 655–662. (12)

Calford, M.B., Graydon, M.L., Huerta, M.F., Kaas, J.H., & Pettigrew, J.D. (1985). A variant of the mammalian somatotopic map in a bat. *Nature, 313,* 477–479. (4)

Calne, D.B., Langston, J.W., Martin, W.R.W., Stoessl, A.J., Ruth, T.J., Adam, M.J., Pate, B.D., & Schulzer, M. (1985). Positron emission tomography after MPTP: Observations relating to the cause of Parkinson's disease. *Nature, 317,* 246–248. (9)

Camel, J.E., Withers, G.S., & Greenough, W.T. (1986). Persistence of visual cortex dendritic alterations induced by postweaning exposure to a "superenriched" environment in rats. *Behavioral Neuroscience, 100,* 810–813. (2)

Campbell, J.C., & Seiden, L.S. (1973). Performance influence on the development of tolerance to amphetamine. *Pharmacology, Biochemistry, and Behavior, 1,* 703–708. (11)

Campbell, S.S., & Tobler, I. (1984). Animal sleep: A review of sleep duration across phylogeny. *Neuroscience & Biobehavioral Reviews, 8,* 269–300. (10)

Campion, J., Latto, R., & Smith, Y.M. (1983). Is blindsight an effect of scattered light, spared cortex, and near-threshold vision? *The Behavioral and Brain Sciences, 6,* 423–486. (7)

Cannon, W.B. (1927). The James-Lange theory of emotion. *American Journal of Psychology, 39,* 106–124. (13)

Cannon, W.B. (1929). Organization for physiological homeostasis. *Physiological Reviews, 9,* 399–431. (11)

Cannon, W.B. (1942). "Voodoo" death. *American Anthropologist, 44,* 169–181. (13)

Caplan, P.J., & Kinsbourne, M. (1976). Baby drops the rattle: Asymmetry of duration of grasp by infants. *Child Development, 47,* 532–534. (5)

Caporael, L.R. (1976). Ergotism: The Satan loosed in Salem? *Science, 192,* 21–26. (3)

Cappannari, S.C., Rau, B., Abram, W.S., & Buchanan, D.C. (1975). Voodoo in the general hospital. *Journal of the American Medical Association, 232,* 938–940. (13)

Capranica, R.R., & Frishkopf, L.S. (1966). Responses of auditory units in the medulla of the cricket frog. *Journal of the Acoustical Society of America, 40,* 1263. (6)

Capranica, R.R., Frishkopf, L.S., & Nevo, E. (1973). Encoding of geographic dialects in the auditory system of the cricket frog. *Science, 182,* 1272–1275. (6)

Caramazza, A. (1988). Some aspects of language processing revealed through the analysis of acquired aphasia: The lexical system. *Annual Review of Neuroscience, 11,* 395–421. (5)

Carani, C., Zini, D., Baldini, A., Della Casa, L., Ghizzani, A., & Marrama, P. (1990). Effects of androgen treatment in impotent men with normal and low levels of free testosterone. *Archives of Sexual Behavior, 19,* 223–234. (12)

Carlsson, A. (1987). Perspectives on the discovery of central monoaminergic neurotransmission. *Annual Review of Neuroscience, 10,* 19–40. (3)

Carlton, P.L., & Wolgin, D.L. (1971). Contingent tolerance to the anorexigenic effects of amphetamine. *Physiology & Behavior, 7,* 221–223. (11)

Carpenter, G.A., & Grossberg, S. (1984). A neural theory of circadian rhythms: Aschoff's rule in diurnal and nocturnal mammals. *American Journal of Physiology, 247,* R1067–R1082. (10)

Carpenter, M.B. (1986). Anatomy of the basal ganglia. In P.J. Vinken, G.W. Bruyn, & H.L. Klawans (Eds.), *Handbook of clinical neurology* (vol. 49, pp. 1–18). Amsterdam: Elsevier. (9)

Casagrande, V.A., Harting, J.K., Hall, W.C., Diamond, I.T., & Martin, G.F. (1972). Superior colliculus of the tree shrew: A structural and functional division into superficial and deep layers. *Science, 177,* 444–447. (7)

Castellucci, V.F., & Kandel, E.R. (1974). A quantal analysis of the synaptic depression underlying habituation of the gill-withdrawal reflex in *Aplysia. Proceedings of the National Academy of Sciences, U.S.A., 71,* 5004–5008. (14)

Castellucci, V.F., Pinsker, H., Kupfermann, I., & Kandel, E. (1970). Neuronal mechanisms of habituation and dishabituation of the gill-withdrawal reflex in *Aplysia. Science, 167,* 1745–1748. (14)

Catterall, W.A. (1984). The molecular basis of neuronal excitability. *Science, 223,* 653–661. (2)

Caul, W.F., Jones, J.R., & Barrett, R.J. (1988). Amphetamine's effects on food consumption and body weight: The role of adaptive processes. *Behavioral Neuroscience, 102,* 441–450. (11)

Cerletti, U. & Bini, L. (1938). L'Elettroshock [Electroshock]. *Archivio Generale di Neurologia e Psichiatria e Psicoanalisi, 19,* 266–268. (16)

Cespuglio, R., Laurent, J.P., & Jouvet, M. (1975). Étude des relations entre l'activité ponto-géniculo-occipitale (PGO) et la motricité oculaire chez le chat sous reserpine [Study of the relations between ponto-geniculo-occipital activity (PGO) and ocular motility in the cat under reserpine]. *Brain Research, 83,* 319–335. (10)

Chambers, K.C., & Phoenix, C.H. (1989). Apomorphine, deprenyl, and yohimbine fail to increase sexual behavior in rhesus monkeys. *Behavioral Neuroscience, 103,* 816–823. (12)

Chandra, V., Bharucha, N.E., & Schoenberg, B.S. (1984). Mortality data for the U.S. for deaths due to and related to twenty neurologic diseases. *Neuroepidemiology, 3,* 149–168. (9)

Changeux, J.-P. (1986). Coexistence of neuronal messengers and molecular selection. In T. Hökfelt, K. Fuxe, & B. Pernow (Eds.), *Progress in brain research* (vol. 68, pp. 373–403). Amsterdam: Elsevier. (3)

Changeux, J.-P., Devillers-Thiéry, A., & Chemouilli, P. (1984). Acetylcholine receptor: An allosteric protein. *Science, 225,* 1335–1345. (3)

Chappell, E.T., & LeVere, T.E. (1988). Recovery of function after brain damage: The chronic consequence of large neocortical injuries. *Behavioral Neuroscience, 102,* 778–783. (15)

Charney, D.S., & Heninger, G.R. (1986). Abnormal regulation of noradrenergic function in panic disorder. *Archives of General Psychiatry, 43,* 1042–1054. (13)

Charney, D.S., Heninger, G.R., & Breier, A. (1984). Noradrenergic function in panic anxiety. *Archives of General Psychiatry, 41,* 751–763. (13)

Charney, D.S., Woods, S.W., Krystal, J.H., & Heninger, G.R. (1990). Serotonin function and human anxiety disorders. *Annals of the New York Academy of Sciences, 600,* 558–573. (13)

Chase, M.H. (1983). Synaptic mechanisms and circuitry involved in motoneuron control during sleep. *International Review of Neurobiology, 24,* 213–258. (10)

Chase, M.H., Soja, P.J., & Morales, F.R. (1989). Evidence that glycine mediates the postsynaptic potentials that inhibit lumbar motoneurons during the atonia of active sleep. *Journal of Neuroscience, 9,* 743–751. (10)

Chase, T.N., Baronti, F., Fabbrini, G., Heuser, I.J., Juncos, J.L., & Mouradian, M.M. (1989). Rationale for continuous dopaminomimetic therapy of Parkinson's disease. *Neurology, 39*(Suppl. 2), 7–10. (9)

Chase, T.N., Wexler, N.S., & Barbeau, A. (1979). *Advances in neurology: Vol. 23. Huntington's disease.* New York: Raven. (9)

Chiarello, C. (1980). A house divided? Cognitive functioning with callosal agenesis. *Brain and Language, 11,* 128–158. (5)

Chiodo, L.A., & Antelman, S.M. (1980). Electroconvulsive shock: Progressive dopamine autoreceptor subsensitivity independent of repeated treatment. *Science, 210,* 799–801. (16)

Chiueh, C.C. (1988). Dopamine in the extrapyramidal motor function: A study based upon the MPTP-induced primate model of Parkinsonism. *Annals of the New York Academy of Sciences, 515,* 226–248. (9)

Chouinard, G., & Jones, B.D. (1980). Neuroleptic-induced supersensitivity psychosis: Clinical and pharmacological characteristics. *American Journal of Psychiatry, 137,* 16–21. (16)

Chugani, H.T., & Phelps, M.E. (1986). Maturational changes in cerebral function in infants determined by $^{18}$FDG positron emission tomography. *Science, 231,* 840–843. (4, 8)

Cicone, N., Wapner, W., Foldi, N.S., Zurif, E., & Gardner, H. (1979). The relation between gesture and language in aphasic communication. *Brain and Language, 8,* 324–349. (5)

Cirignotta, F., Todesco, C.V., & Lugaresi, E. (1980). Temporal lobe epilepsy with ecstatic seizures (so-called Dostoevsky epilepsy). *Epilepsia, 21,* 705–710. (13)

Clark, J.T., Smith, E.R., & Davidson, J.M. (1984). Enhancement of sexual motivation in male rats by yohimbine. *Science, 225,* 847–849. (12)

Cleary, L.J., Hammer, M., & Byrne, J.H. (1989). Insights into the cellular mechanisms of short-term sensitization in *Aplysia.* In T.J. Carew & D.B. Kelley (Eds.), *Perspectives in neural systems and behavior* (pp. 105–119). New York: Alan R. Liss. (14)

Clemens, L.G., Gladue, B.A., & Coniglio, L.P. (1978). Prenatal endogenous androgenic influences on masculine sexual behavior and genital morphology in male and female rats. *Hormones and Behavior, 10,* 40–53. (12)

Cohen, N.J., Eichenbaum, H., Deacedo, B.S., & Corkin, S. (1985). Different memory systems underlying acquisition of procedural and declarative knowledge. *Annals of the New York Academy of Sciences, 444,* 54–71. (14)

Cohen, R.M., Semple, W.E., Gross, M., Holcomb, H.H., Dowling, M.S., & Nordahl, T.E. (1988). Functional localization of sustained attention: Comparison to sensory stimulation in the absence of instruction. *Neuropsychiatry, Neuropsychology, and Behavioral Neurology, 1,* 3–20. (4)

Coile, D.C., & Miller, N.E. (1984). How radical animal activists try to mislead humane people. *American Psychologist, 39,* 700–701. (1)

Comings, D.E., & Amromin, G.D. (1974). Autosomal dominant insensitivity to pain with hyperplastic myelinopathy and autosomal dominant indifference to pain. *Neurology, 24,* 838–848. (6)

Coons, E.E., Levak, M., & Miller, N.E. (1965). Lateral hypothalamus: Learning of food-seeking response motivated by electrical stimulation. *Science, 150,* 1320–1321. (1)

Coopersmith, R., & Leon, M. (1987). Glycogen phosphorylase activity in the olfactory bulb of the young rat. *Journal of Comparative Neurology, 261,* 148–154. (2)

Corda, M.G., Blaker, W.D., Mendelson, W.B., Guidotti, A., & Costa, E. (1983).

Beta-carbolines enhance shock-induced suppression of drinking in rats. *Proceedings of the National Academy of Sciences, U.S.A., 80,* 2072–2076. (13)

Coren, S., & Porac, C. (1977). Fifty centuries of right-handedness: The historical record. *Science, 198,* 631–632. (5)

Corkin, S. (1984). Lasting consequences of bilateral medial temporal lobectomy: Clinical course and experimental findings in H.M. *Seminars in Neurology, 4,* 249–259. (14)

Corso, J.F. (1973). Hearing. In B.B. Wolman (Ed.), *Handbook of general psychology* (pp. 348–381). Englewood Cliffs, NJ: Prentice-Hall. (6)

Corso, J.F. (1985). Communication, presbycusis, and technological aids. In H.K. Ulatowska (Ed.), *The aging brain: Communication in the elderly* (pp. 33–51). San Diego, CA: College Hill. (6)

Coss, R.G., Brandon, J.G., & Globus, A. (1980). Changes in morphology of dendritic spines on honeybee calycal interneurons associated with cumulative nursing and foraging experiences. *Brain Research, 192,* 49–59. (2)

Coss, R.G., & Globus, A. (1979). Social experience affects the development of dendritic spines and branches on tectal interneurons in the Jewel fish. *Developmental Psychobiology, 12,* 347–358. (2)

Cotman, C.W., Monaghan, D.T., & Ganong, A.H. (1988). Excitatory amino acid neurotransmission: NMDA receptors and Hebb-type synaptic transmission. *Annual Review of Neuroscience, 11,* 61–80. (14)

Cotman, C.W., & Nieto-Sampedro, M. (1982). Brain function, synapse renewal, and plasticity. *Annual Review of Psychology, 33,* 371–401. (2)

Cousins, N. (1989). *Head first: The biology of hope.* New York: E.P. Dutton. (13)

Cowan, J.D. (1983). Testing the escape hypotheses: Alcohol helps users to forget their feelings. *Journal of Nervous and Mental Disease, 171,* 40–48. (3)

Coyle, J.T., Oster-Franite, M.L., & Gearhart, J.D. (1986). The neurobiologic consequences of Down syndrome. *Brain Research Bulletin, 16,* 773–787. (8)

Craft, S., Willerman, L., & Bigler, E.D. (1987). Callosal dysfunction in schizophrenia and schizo-affective disorder. *Journal of Abnormal Psychology, 96,* 205–213. (16)

Crawley, J.N. (1990). Coexistence of neuropeptides and "classical" neurotransmitters. *Annals of the New York Academy of Sciences, 579,* 233–245. (3)

Crawshaw, L.I., Moffitt, B.P., Lemons, D.E., & Downey, J.A. (1981). The evolutionary development of vertebrate thermoregulation. *American Scientist, 69,* 543–550. (11)

Creak, M. (1961). Schizophrenic syndrome in childhood. *British Medical Journal, 2,* 889–890. (16)

Creasey, H., Rumsey, J.M., Schwartz, M., Duara, R., Rapoport, J.L., & Rapoport, S.I. (1986). Brain morphometry in autistic men as measured by volumetric computed tomography. *Archives of Neurology, 43,* 669–672. (16)

Crews, F., & Smith, C.B. (1978). Presynaptic alpha-receptor subsensitivity after long-term antidepressant treatment. *Science, 202,* 322–324. (16)

Crick, F., & Mitchison, G. (1986). REM sleep and neural nets. *Journal of Mind and Behavior, 7,* 229–249. (10)

Crovitz, H.F., Horn, R.W., & Daniel, W.F. (1983) Interrelationships among retrograde amnesia, post-traumatic amnesia, and time since head injury: A retrospective study. *Cortex, 19,* 407–412. (14)

Crow, T.J. (1980). Molecular pathology of schizophrenia: More than one disease process? *British Medical Journal, 280,* 66–68. (16)

Crump, C.J., & Chevins, P.F.D. (1989). Prenatal stress reduces fertility of male offspring in mice, without affecting their adult testosterone levels. *Hormones and Behavior, 23,* 333–343. (12)

Csernansky, J.G., Kaplan, J., & Hollister, L.E. (1985). Problems in classification of schizophrenics as neuroleptic responders and nonresponders. *Journal of Nervous and Mental Disease, 173,* 325–331. (16)

Cserr, H.F., & Bundgaard, M. (1986). The neuronal microenvironment: A comparative view. *Annals of the New York Academy of Sciences, 481,* 1–6. (2)

Culebras, A., & Moore, J.T. (1989). Magnetic resonance findings in REM sleep behavior disorder. *Neurology, 39,* 1519–1523. (10)

Cummings, J.L., & Victoroff, J.I. (1990). Noncognitive neuropsychiatric syndromes in Alzheimer's disease. *Neuropsychiatry, Neuropsychology, & Behavioral Neurology, 3,* 140–158. (14)

Cummins, C.J., Lust, W.D., & Passonneau, J.V. (1983). Regulation of glycogen metabolism in primary and transformed astrocytes *in vitro. Journal of Neurochemistry, 40,* 128–136. (2)

Cusick, C.G., Wall, J.T., & Kaas, J.H. (1986). Representations of the face, teeth and oral cavity in areas 3b and 1 of somatosensory cortex in squirrel monkeys. *Brain Research, 370,* 359–364. (4)

Cynader, M., & Chernenko, G. (1976). Abolition of direction selectivity in the visual cortex of the cat. *Science, 193,* 504–505. (8)

Czeisler, C.A., Johnson, M.P., Duffy, J.F., Brown, E.N., Ronda, J.M., & Kronauer, R.E. (1990). Exposure to bright light and darkness to treat physiologic maladaptation to night work. *New England Journal of Medicine, 322,* 1353–1359. (10)

Czeisler, C.A., Weitzman, E.D., Moore-Ede, M.C., Zimmerman, J.C., & Knauer, R.S. (1980). Human sleep: Its duration and organization depend on its circadian phase. *Science, 210,* 1264–1267. (10, 16)

Dabbs, J.M., & Morris, R. (1990). Testosterone, social class, and antisocial behavior in a sample of 4,462 men. *Psychological Science, 1,* 209–211. (13)

Dabrowska, B., Harmata, W., Lenkiewicz, Z., Schiffer, Z., & Wojtusiak, R.J. (1981). Colour perception in cows. *Behavioural Processes, 6,* 1–10. (7)

Dakof, G.A., & Mendelsohn, G.A. (1986). Parkinson's disease: The psychological aspects of a chronic illness. *Psychological Bulletin, 99,* 375–387. (9)

Dalby, J.T., Arboleda-Florez, J., & Seland, T.P. (1989). Somatic delusions following left parietal lobe injury. *Neuropsychiatry, Neuropsychology, and Behavioral Neurology, 2,* 306–311. (4)

Dale, N., Schacher, S., & Kandel, E.R. (1988). Long-term facilitation in *Aplysia* involves increase in transmitter release. *Science, 239,* 282–285. (14)

Dalhouse, A.D., Langford, H.G., Walsh, D., & Barnes, T. (1986). Angiotensin and salt appetite: Physiological amounts of angiotensin given peripherally increase salt appetite in the rat. *Behavioral Neuroscience, 100,* 597–602. (11)

Dalton, K. (1968). Ante-natal progesterone and intelligence. *British Journal of Psychiatry, 114,* 1377–1382. (12)

Daly, M., Wilson, M., & Weghorst, S.J. (1982). Male sexual jealousy. *Ethology & Sociobiology, 3,* 11–27. (13)

Damasio, A. (1979). The frontal lobes. In K.M. Heilman & E. Valenstein (Eds.), *Clinical neuropsychology* (pp. 360–412). New York: Oxford University Press. (4)

Damasio, A.R. (1983). Language and the basal ganglia. *Trends in Neurosciences, 6,* 442–444. (4)

Damasio, A.R., & Geschwind, N. (1984). The neural basis of language. *Annual Review of Neuroscience, 7,* 127–147. (5)

Damasio, H., & Damasio, A.R. (1980). The anatomical basis of conduction aphasia. *Brain, 103,* 337–350. (5)

D'Amato, R.J., Lipman, Z.P., & Snyder, S.H. (1986). Selectivity of the Parkinsonian neurotoxin MPTP: Toxic metabolite MPP$^+$ binds to neuromelanin. *Science, 231,* 987–989. (9)

Daniloff, J.K., Wells, J., & Ellis, J. (1984). Cross-species septal transplants: Recovery of choline acetyltransferase activity. *Brain Research, 324,* 151–154. (15)

Darley, S.A., & Katz, I. (1973). Heart rate changes in children as a function of test versus game instructions and test anxiety. *Child Development, 44,* 784–789. (13)

Darwin, C. (1859). *On the origin of species.* Reprinted by various publishers. (A)

Dascombe, M.J. (1986). The pharmacology of fever. *Progress in Neurobiology, 25,* 327–373. (11)

David, S., & Aguayo, A.J. (1981). Axonal elongation into peripheral nervous system "bridges" after central nervous system injury in adult rats. *Science, 214,* 931–933. (15)

Davidson, R.J. (1984). Affect, cognition, and hemispheric specialization. In C.E. Izard, J. Kagan, & R.B. Zajonc (Eds.), *Emotions, cognition, & behavior* (pp. 320–365). Cambridge, England: Cambridge University Press. (16)

Davies, P. (1985). A critical review of the role of the cholinergic system in human memory and cognition. *Annals of the New York Academy of Sciences, 444,* 212–217. (14)

Davis, J.D., Wirtshafter, D., Asin, K.E., & Brief, D. (1981). Sustained intracerebroventricular infusion of brain fuels reduces body weight and food intake in rats. *Science, 212,* 81–83. (11)

Davis, J.M. (1976). Recent developments in the drug treatment of schizophrenia. *American Journal of Psychiatry, 133,* 208–214. (16)

Davis, H.P., Rosenzweig, M.R., Bennett, E.L., & Squire, L.R. (1980). Inhibition of cerebral protein synthesis: Dissociation of nonspecific effects and amnesic effects. *Behavioral and Neural Biology, 28,* 99–104. (14)

Davis, H.P., & Squire, L.R. (1984). Protein synthesis and memory: A review. *Psychological Bulletin, 96,* 518–559. (14)

Davis, K.L., Davidson, M., Mohs, R.C., Kendler, K.S., Davis, B.M., Johns, C.A., DeNigris, Y., & Horvath, T.B. (1985). Plasma homovanillic acid concentration and the severity of schizophrenic illness. *Science, 227,* 1601–1602. (16)

Davis, K.L., Mohs, R.C., Tinklenberg, J.R., Pfefferbaum, A., Hollister, L.E., & Kopell, B.S. (1978). Physostigmine: Improvement of long-term memory processes in normal humans. *Science, 201,* 272–274. (14)

Davis, N., & LeVere, T.E. (1979). Recovery of function after brain damage: Different processes and the facilitation of one. *Physiological Psychology, 7,* 233–240. (15)

Davis, N., & LeVere, T.E. (1982). Recovery of function after brain damage: The question of individual behaviors or functionality. *Experimental Neurology, 75,* 68–78. (15)

deCastro, J.M., & Zrull, M.C. (1988). Recovery of sensorimotor function after frontal cortex damage in rats: Evidence that the serial lesion effect is due to serial recovery. *Behavioral Neuroscience, 102,* 843–851. (15)

DeCoursey, P. (1960). Phase control of activity in a rodent. *Cold Spring Harbor symposia on quantitative biology, 25,* 49–55. (10)

Delgado, J.M.R. (1969). *Physical control of the mind.* New York: Harper & Row. (1, 12)

Delgado, J.M.R. (1981). Neuronal constellations in aggressive behavior. In L. Valzelli & L. Morgese (Eds.), *Aggression and violence: A psycho/biological and clinical approach* (pp. 82–98). Milan, Italy: Edizioni Saint Vincent. (13)

Delgado, J.M.R., & Hamlin, H. (1960). Spontaneous and evoked electrical seizures in animals and in humans. In E.R. Ramey & D.S. O'Doherty (Eds.), *Electrical studies on the unanesthetized brain* (pp. 133–158). New York: P.B. Hoeber. (13)

Delgado, P.L., Charney, D.S., Price, L.H., Aghajanian, G.K., Landis, H., & Heninger, G.R. (1990). Serotonin function and the mechanism of antidepressant action. *Archives of General Psychiatry, 47,* 411–418. (16)

Deliagina, T.G., Orlovsky, G.N., & Pavlova, G.A. (1983). The capacity for generation of rhythmic oscillations is distributed in the lumbosacral spinal cord of the cat. *Experimental Brain Research, 53,* 81–90. (9)

DeLisi, L.E., Goldin, L.R., Hamovit, J.R., Maxwell, E., Kurtz, D., & Gershon, E.S. (1986). A family study of the association of increased ventricular size with schizophrenia. *Archives of General Psychiatry, 43,* 148–153. (16)

DeLong, M.R. (1974). Motor functions of the basal ganglia: Single-unit activity during movement. In F.O. Schmitt & F.G. Worden (Eds.), *The neurosciences, third study program* (pp. 319–325). Cambridge, MA: MIT Press. (9)

DeLong, M.R., Alexander, G.E., Georgopoulos, A.P., Crutcher, M.D., Mitchell, S.J., & Richardson, R.T. (1984). Role of basal ganglia in limb movements. *Human Neurobiology, 2,* 235–244. (9)

Delwaide, P.J., Devoitille, J.M., & Ylieff, M. (1980). Acute effect of drugs upon memory of patients with senile dementia. *Acta Psychiatrica Belgica, 80,* 748–754. (14)

Dement, W. (1960). The effect of dream deprivation. *Science, 131,* 1705–1707. (10)

Dement, W. (1972). *Some must watch while some must sleep.* San Francisco: W.H. Freeman. (10)

Dement, W., Ferguson, J., Cohen, H., & Barchas, J. (1969). Non-chemical methods and data using a biochemical model: The REM quanta. In A.J. Mandell & M.P. Mandell (Eds.), *Psychochemical research in man* (pp. 275–325). New York: Academic Press. (10)

Dement, W., & Kleitman, N. (1957a). Cyclic variations in EEG during sleep and their relation to eye movements, body motility, and dreaming. *Electroencephalography and Clinical Neurophysiology, 9,* 673–690. (10)

Dement, W., & Kleitman, N. (1957b). The relation of eye movements during sleep to dream activity: An objective method for the study of dreaming. *Journal of Experimental Psychology, 53,* 339–346. (10)

Dement, W., & Wolpert, E.A. (1958). The relation of eye movements, body motility, and external stimuli to dream content. *Journal of Experimental Psychology, 55,* 543–553. (10)

Depue, R.A., & Spoont, M.R. (1986). Conceptualizing a serotonin trait: A behavioral dimension of restraint. *Annals of the New York Academy of Sciences, 487,* 47–62. (13)

Desiderato, O., MacKinnon, J.R., & Hissom, H. (1974). Development of gastric ulcers in rats following stress termination. *Journal of Comparative and Physiological Psychology, 87,* 208–214. (13)

DeSimone, J.A., Heck, G.L., & Bartoshuk, L.M. (1980). Surface active taste modifiers: A comparison of the physical and psychophysical properties of gymnemic acid and sodium lauryl sulfate. *Chemical Senses, 5,* 317–330. (6)

Desimone, J.A., Heck, G.L., Mierson, S., & Desimone, S.K. (1984). The active ion transport properties of canine lingual epithelia in vitro. *Journal of General Physiology, 83,* 633–656. (6)

Desimone, R. (1991). Face-selective cells in the temporal cortex of monkeys. *Journal of Cognitive Neuroscience, 3,* 1–8. (7)

Desimone, R., Albright, T.D., Gross, C.G., & Bruce, C. (1984). Stimulus-selective properties of inferior temporal neurons in the macaque. *Journal of Neuroscience, 4,* 2051–2062. (7)

Desimone, R., & Gross, C.G. (1979). Visual areas in the temporal cortex of the macaque. *Brain Research, 178,* 363–380. (7)

Désir, D., van Cauter, E., Fang, V.S., Martino, E., Jadot, C., Spire, J.-P., Noël, P., Refetoff, S., Copinschi, G., & Golstein, J. (1981). Effects of "jet lag" on hormonal patterns. I. Procedure variations in total plasma proteins, and disruption of adrenocorticotropin-cortisol periodicity. *Journal of Clinical Endocrinology and Metabolism, 52,* 628–641. (10)

Desmond, M.M., & Wilson, G.S. (1975). Neonatal abstinence syndrome: Recognition and diagnosis. *Addictive Diseases, 2,* 113–121. (16)

Desor, J.A., & Beauchamp, G.K. (1974). The human capacity to transmit olfactory information. *Perception & Psychophysics, 16,* 551–556. (6)

Detera-Wadleigh, S.D., Berrettini, W.H., Goldin, L.R., Boorman, D., Anderson, S., & Gershon, E.S. (1987). Close linkage of c-Harvey-*ras*-1 and the insulin gene to affective disorder is ruled out in three North American pedigrees. *Nature, 325,* 806–808. (16)

Deutsch, J.A., & Ahn, S.J. (1986). The splanchnic nerve and food intake regulation. *Behavioral and Neural Biology, 45,* 43–47. (11)

Deutsch, J.A., Young, W.G., & Kalogeris, T.J. (1978). The stomach signals satiety. *Science, 201,* 165–167. (11)

DeValois, R.L., Albrecht, D.G., & Thorell, L.G. (1982). Spatial frequency selectivity of cells in macaque visual cortex. *Vision Research, 22,* 545–559. (7)

DeValois, R.L., & Jacobs, G.H. (1968). Primate color vision. *Science, 162,* 533–540. (7)

Devane, W.A., Dysarz, F.A., III, Johnson, M.R., Melvin, L.S., & Howlett, A.C. (1988). Determination and characterization of a cannabinoid receptor in rat brain. *Molecular Pharmacology, 34,* 605–613. (3)

Deyo, R., Straube, K.T., & Disterhoft, J.F. (1989). Nimodipine facilitates associative learning in aging rabbits. *Science, 243,* 809–811. (14)

Diamond, I.T. (1979). The subdivisions of neocortex: A proposal to revise the traditional view of sensory, motor, and association areas. *Progress in Psychobiology and Physiological Psychology, 8,* 1–43. (4)

Diamond, I.T. (1983). Parallel pathways in the auditory, visual, and somatic systems. In G. Macchi, A. Rustioni, & R. Spreafico (Eds.), *Somatosensory integration in the thalamus* (pp. 251–272). Amsterdam: Elsevier. (4)

Diamond, M. (1982). Sexual identity, monozygotic twins reared in discordant sex roles and a BBC follow-up. *Archives of Sexual Behavior, 11,* 181–186. (12)

Diamond, M., Llacuna, A., & Wong, C.L. (1973). Sex behavior after neonatal progesterone, testosterone, estrogen, or antiandrogens. *Hormones and Behavior, 4,* 73–88. (12)

Dichgans, J. (1984). Clinical symptoms of cerebellar dysfunction and their topodiagnostic significance. *Human Neurobiology, 2,* 269–279. (9)

Dimond, S.J. (1979). Symmetry and asymmetry in the vertebrate brain. In D.A. Oakley & H.C. Plotkin (Eds.), *Brain, behaviour, and evolution* (pp. 189–218). London: Methuen. (5)

Dinarello, C.A., & Wolff, S.M. (1982). Molecular basis of fever in humans. *American Journal of Medicine, 72,* 799–819. (11)

Dixon, A.F. (1987). Effects of adrenalectomy upon proceptivity, receptivity, and sexual attractiveness in ovariectomized marmosets (*Callithrix jacchus*). *Physiology & Behavior, 39,* 495–499. (12)

Dolphin, A.C., Errington, M.L., & Bliss, T.V.P. (1982). Long-term potentiation of the perforant path in vivo is associated with increased glutamate release. *Nature, 297,* 496–498. (14)

Dombovy, M.L., & Bach-y-Rita, P. (1988). Clinical observations on recovery from stroke. In S.G. Waxman (Ed.), *Advances in neurology* (vol. 47, pp. 265–276). New York: Raven Press. (15)

Dörner, G. (1967). Tierexperimentelle Untersuchungen zur Frage einer hormonellen Pathogenese der Homosexualität [Animal experimentation on the question of a hormonal pathogenesis of homosexuality]. *Acta Biologica et Medica Germanica, 19,* 569–584. (12)

Dörner, G. (1974). Sex-hormone-dependent brain differentiation and sexual functions. In G. Dörner (Ed.), *Endocrinology of sex* (pp. 30–37). Leipzig: J.A. Barth. (12)

Dörner, G., & Hinz, G. (1975). Androgen-dependent brain differentiation and life span. *Endokrinologie, 65,* 378–380. (12)

Dowling, J.E. (1987). *The retina.* Cambridge, MA: Harvard University Press. (7)

Dowling, J.E., & Boycott, B.B. (1966). Organization of the primate retina. *Proceedings of the Royal Society of London,* B, *166,* 80–111. (7)

Drachman, D.A., & Leavitt, J. (1974). Human memory and the cholinergic system. *Archives of Neurology, 30,* 113–121. (14)

Drachman, D.B. (1978). Myasthenia gravis. *New England Journal of Medicine, 298,* 136–142, 186–193. (9)

Drachman, D.B., Adams, R.N., & Josifer, L.F. (1982). Functional activities of autoantibodies to acetylcholine receptors and the clinical severity of myasthenia gravis. *New England Journal of Medicine, 307,* 769–775. (9)

Drager, U.C., & Hubel, D.H. (1975). Physiology of visual cells in mouse superior colliculus and correlation with somatosensory and auditory input. *Nature, 253,* 203–204. (7)

Dreyfus-Brisac, C. (1970). Ontogenesis of sleep in human prematures after 32 weeks of conceptional age. *Developmental Psychobiology, 3,* 91–121. (10)

Dubocovich, M.L. (1984). Presynaptic alpha-adrenoceptors in the central nervous system. *Annals of the New York Academy of Sciences, 430,* 7–25. (3)

Dufty, A.M. Jr. (1989). Testosterone and survival: A cost of aggressiveness? *Hormones and Behavior, 23,* 185–193. (12)

Duggan, J.P., & Booth, D.A. (1986). Obesity, overeating, and rapid gastric emptying in rats with ventromedial hypothalamic lesions. *Science, 231,* 609–611. (11)

Dunlap, J.L., Zadina, J.E., & Gougis, G. (1978). Prenatal stress interacts with prepubertal social isolation to reduce male copulatory behavior. *Physiology and Behavior, 21,* 873–875. (12)

Dunnett, S.B., Ryan, C.N., Levin, P.D., Reynolds, M., & Bunch, S.T. (1987). Functional consequences of embryonic

neocortex transplanted to rats with prefrontal cortex lesions. *Behavioral Neuroscience, 101,* 489–503. (15)

Dunwiddie, T.V. (1985). The physiological role of adenosine in the central nervous system. *International Journal of Neurobiology, 27,* 63–139. (13)

Duvoisin, R.C., Eldridge, R., Williams, A., Nutt, J., & Calne, D. (1981). Twin study of Parkinson disease. *Neurology, 31,* 77–80. (9)

Dyal, J.A. (1971). Transfer of behavioral bias: Reality and specificity. In E.J. Fjerdingstad (Ed.), *Chemical transfer of learned information* (pp. 219–263). New York: American Elsevier. (14)

Dykes, R.W., Sur, M., Merzenich, M.M., Kaas, J.H., & Nelson, R.J. (1981). Regional segregation of neurons responding to quickly adapting, slowly adapting, deep and Pacinian receptors within thalamic ventroposterior lateral and ventroposterior inferior nuclei in the squirrel monkey (*Saimiri sciureus*). *Neuroscience, 6,* 1687–1692. (6)

Earls, C.M. (1988). Aberrant sexual arousal in sexual offenders. *Annals of the New York Academy of Sciences, 528,* 41–48. (12)

Easter, S.S. Jr., Purves, D., Rakic, P., & Spitzer, N.C. (1985). The changing view of neural specificity. *Science, 230,* 507–511. (8)

Eccles, J.C. (1964). *The physiology of synapses.* Berlin: Springer-Verlag. (3)

Eccles, J.C. (1986). Chemical transmission and Dale's principle. In T. Hökfelt, K. Fuxe, & B. Pernow (Eds.), *Progress in brain research* (Vol. 68, pp. 3–13). Amsterdam: Elsevier. (3)

Edelman, G.M. (1987). *Neural Darwinism.* New York: Basic Books. (8)

Edelstein, E.L. (1981). Vasopressins and other neuropeptides as CNS mental modulators: A review. *Israel Journal of Psychiatry & Related Sciences, 18,* 229–236. (14)

Edman, G., Åsberg, M., Levander, S., & Schalling, D. (1986). Skin conductance habituation and cerebrospinal fluid 5-hydroxyindoleacetic acid in suicidal patients. *Archives of General Psychiatry, 43,* 586–592. (13)

Egeland, J.A., Gerhard, D.S., Pauls, D.L., Sussex, J.N., Kidd, K.K., Allen, C.R., Hostetter, A.M., & Housman, D.E. (1987). Bipolar affective disorders linked to DNA markers on chromosome 11. *Nature, 325,* 783–787. (16)

Ehman, G.K., Albert, D.J., & Jamieson, J.L. (1971). Injections into the duodenum and the induction of satiety in the rat. *Canadian Journal of Psychology, 25,* 147–166. (11)

Ehret, C.F., Potter, V.R., & Dobra, K.W. (1975). Chronotypic action of theophylline and of pentobarbital as circadian Zeitgebers in the rat. *Science, 188,* 1212–1215. (10)

Ehrhardt, A.A., Meyer-Bahlburg, H.F.L., Rosen, L.R., Feldman, J.F., Veridiano, N.P., Zimmerman, I., & McEwen, B.S. (1985). Sexual orientation after prenatal exposure to exogenous estrogen. *Archives of Sexual Behavior, 14,* 57–77. (12)

Ehrhardt, A.A., & Money, J. (1967). Progestin-induced hermaphroditism: IQ

and psychosexual identity in a study of ten girls. *Journal of Sex Research, 3,* 83–100. (12)

Ehrlichmann, H., & Weinberger, A. (1978). Lateral eye movements and hemispheric asymmetry: A critical review. *Psychological Bulletin, 85,* 1080–1101. (5)

Eidelberg, E., & Stein, D.G. (1974). Functional recovery after lesions of the nervous system. *Neurosciences Research Program Bulletin, 12,* 191–303. (15)

Eisenstein, E.M., & Cohen, M.J. (1965). Learning in an isolated prothoracic insect ganglion. *Animal Behaviour, 13,* 104–108. (14)

Ekman, P., Levenson, R.W., & Friesen, W.V. (1983). Autonomic nervous system activity distinguishes among emotions. *Science, 221,* 1208–1210. (13)

Ellinwood, E.H., Jr. (1969). Amphetamine psychosis: A multi-dimensional process. *Seminars in Psychiatry, 1,* 208–226. (16)

Elliott, T.R. (1905). The action of adrenalin. *Journal of Physiology* (London), *32,* 401–467. (3)

Ellis, L. (1986). Evidence of neuroandrogenic etiology of sex roles from a combined analysis of human, nonhuman primate and nonprimate mammalian studies. *Personality and Individual Differences, 7,* 519–552. (12)

Ellis, L., & Ames, M.A. (1987). Neurohormonal functioning and sexual orientation: A theory of homosexuality-heterosexuality. *Psychological Bulletin, 101,* 233–258. (12)

Ellis, L., Ames, M.A., Peckham, W., & Burke, D. (1988). Sexual orientation of human offspring may be altered by severe maternal stress during pregnancy. *Journal of Sex Research, 25,* 152–157. (12)

Ellison, G.D. (1977). Animal models of psychopathology: The low-norepinephrine and low-serotonin rat. *American Psychologist, 32,* 1036–1045. (16)

Elwood, R.W. (1985). Inhibition of infanticide and onset of paternal care in male mice (*Mus musculus*). *Journal of Comparative Psychology, 99,* 457–467. (12)

Epstein, A.N. (1983). The neuropsychology of drinking behavior. In E. Satinoff & P. Teitelbaum (Eds.), *Handbook of behavioral neurobiology: Vol. 6. Motivation* (pp. 367–423). New York: Plenum. (11)

Erickson, C., & Lehrman, D. (1964). Effect of castration of male ring doves upon ovarian activity of females. *Journal of Comparative and Physiological Psychology, 58,* 164–160. (12)

Erickson, C.J., & Zenone, P.G. (1976). Courtship differences in male ring doves: Avoidance of cuckoldry? *Science, 192,* 1353–1354. (12)

Erickson, J.D., & Bjerkedal, T.O. (1981). Down syndome associated with father's age in Norway. *Journal of Medical Genetics, 18,* 22–28. (8)

Ernhart, C.B., Sokol, R.J., Martier, S., Moron, P., Nadler, D., Ager, J.W., & Wolf, A. (1987). Alcohol teratogenicity in the human: A detailed assessment of specificity, critical period, and threshold. *American Journal of Obstetrics and Gynecology, 156,* 33–39. (8)

Eslinger, P.J., & Damasio, A.R. (1986). Preserved motor learning in Alzheimer's disease: Implications for anatomy and behavior. *Journal of Neuroscience, 6,* 3006–3009. (14)

Evans, R.M., & Arriza, J.L. (1989). A molecular framework for the actions of glucocorticoid hormones in the nervous system. *Neuron, 2,* 1105–1112. (12)

Evarts, E.V. (1979). Brain mechanisms of movement. *Scientific American, 241* (3), 164–179. (9)

Faglioni, P., & Basso, A. (1985). Historical perspectives on neuroanatomical correlates of limb apraxia. In E.A. Roy (Ed.), *Neuropsychological studies of apraxia and related disorders* (pp. 3–44). Amsterdam: North Holland. (9)

Fantz, R.L. (1963). Pattern vision in newborn infants. *Science, 140,* 296–279. (8)

Farde, L., Wiesel, F.-A., Stone-Elander, S., Halldin, C., Nordström, A.-L., Hall, H., & Sedvall, G. (1990). D₂ dopamine receptors in neuroleptic-naive schizophrenic patients. *Archives of General Psychiatry, 47,* 213–219. (16)

Farkas, T., Wolf, A.P., Jaeger, J., Brodie, J.D., Christman, D.R., & Fowler, J.S. (1984). Regional brain glucose metabolism in chronic schizophrenia. *Archives of General Psychiatry, 41,* 293–300. (16)

Farwell, L.A., & Donchin, E. (1988). Talking off the top of your head: Toward a mental prosthesis utilizing event-related brain potentials. *Electroencephalography and Clinical Neurophysiology, 70,* 510–523. (4)

Feder, H.H. (1981). Estrous cyclicity in mammals. In N.T. Adler (Ed.), *Neuroendocrinology of reproduction* (pp. 279–348). New York: Plenum. (12)

Federman, D.D. (1967). *Abnormal sexual development.* Philadelphia, PA: W.B. Saunders. (12)

Feeney, D.M. (1987). Human rights and animal welfare. *American Psychologist, 42,* 593–599. (1)

Feeney, D.M., & Baron, J.-C. (1986). Diaschisis. *Stroke, 17,* 817–830. (15)

Feeney, D.M., & Sutton, R.L. (1988). Catecholamines and recovery of function after brain damage. In D.G. Stein & B.A. Sabel (Eds.), *Pharmacological approaches to the treatment of brain and spinal cord injury* (pp. 121–142). New York: Plenum. (15)

Feeney, D.M., Sutton, R.L., Boyeson, M.G., Hovda, D.A., & Dail, W.G. (1985). The locus coeruleus and cerebral metabolism: Recovery of function after cerebral injury. *Physiological Psychology, 13,* 197–203. (15)

Fein, D., Humes, M., Kaplan, E., Lucci, D., & Waterhouse, L. (1984). The question of left hemisphere dysfunction in infantile autism. *Psychological Bulletin, 95,* 258–281. (16)

Fentress, J.C. (1973). Development of grooming in mice with amputated forelimbs. *Science, 179,* 704–705. (9)

Ferguson, N.B.L., & Keesey, R.E. (1975). Effect of a quinine-adulterated diet upon body weight maintenance in male rats with ventromedial hypothalamic lesions. *Journal of Comparative and Physiological Psychology, 89,* 478–488. (11)

Fernald, R.D. (1989). Seeing through a growing eye. In T.J. Carew & D.B. Kelley (Eds.), *Perspectives in Neural Systems and Behavior* (pp. 151–174). New York: Alan R. Liss. (8)

Fettiplace, R. (1990). Transduction and tuning in auditory hair cells. *Seminars in the Neurosciences, 2,* 33–40. (6)

Fieve, R.R., & Platman, S.R. (1969). Follow-up studies of lithium and thyroid function in manic-depressive illness. *American Journal of Psychiatry, 125,* 1443–1445. (16)

File, S.E., Pellow, S., & Braestrup, C. (1985). Effects of the beta-carboline, FG7142, in the social interaction test of anxiety and the holeboard: Correlations between behaviour and plasma concentrations. *Pharmacology Biochemistry & Behavior, 22,* 941–944. (13)

Finger, S., & Stein, D.G. (1982). *Brain damage and recovery.* New York: Academic. (15)

Fink, M. (1980). A neuroendocrine theory of convulsive therapy. *Trends in Neurosciences, 3,* 25–27. (16)

Fink, M. (1985). Convulsive therapy: Fifty years of progress. *Convulsive Therapy, 1,* 204–216. (16)

Finlay, B.L., & Pallas, S.L. (1989). Control of cell number in the developing mammalian visual system. *Progress in Neurobiology, 32,* 207–234. (8)

Fischette, C.T., Biegon, A., & McEwen, B.S. (1983). Sex differences in serotonin 1 receptor binding in rat brain. *Science, 222,* 333–335. (12)

Fitts, D.A., & Masson, D.B. (1990). Preoptic angiotensin and salt appetite. *Behavioral Neuroscience, 104,* 643–650. (11)

Fitzsimons, J.T. (1961). Drinking by nephrectomized rats injected with various substances. *Journal of Physiology, 155,* 563–579. (11)

Fitzsimons, J.T. (1971). The hormonal control of water and sodium appetite. In L. Martini & W.F. Ganong (Eds.), *Frontiers in neuroendocrinology, 1971* (pp. 103–128). New York: Oxford University Press. (11)

Fitzsimons, J.T. (1973). Some historical perspectives in the physiology of thirst. In A.N. Epstein, H.R. Kissileff, & E. Stellar (Eds.), *The neurophysiology of thirst* (pp. 3–33). Washington, DC: Winston. (11)

Fjerdingstad, E.J. (1973). Transfer of learning in rodents and fish. In W.B. Essman & S. Nakajima (Eds.), *Current biochemical approaches to learning and memory* (pp. 73–98). Flushing, NY: Spectrum. (14)

Flatz, G. (1987). Genetics of lactose digestion in humans. *Advances in Human Genetics, 16,* 1–77. (11)

Fletcher, R., & Voke, J. (1985). *Defective colour vision.* Bristol, England: Adam Hilger. (7)

Flood, J.F., Smith, G.E., & Morley, J.E. (1987). Modulation of memory processing by cholecystokinin: Dependence on the vagus nerve. *Science, 236,* 832–834. (14)

Flynn, J.P. (1973). Patterning mechanisms, patterned reflexes, and attack behavior in cats. *Nebraska Symposium on Motivation 1972,* 125–153. (13)

Flynn, J.P., Edwards, S.B., & Bandler, R.J., Jr. (1971). Changes in sensory and motor systems during centrally elicited attack. *Behavioral Science, 16,* 1–19. (13)

Folkard, S., Hume, K.I., Minors, D.S., Waterhouse, J.M., & Watson, F.L. (1985). Independence of the circadian rhythm in alertness from the sleep/wake cycle. *Nature, 313,* 678–679. (10)

Folstein, S.E., Phillips, J.A., III, Meyers, D.A., Chase, G.A., Abbott, M.H., Franz, M.L., Waber, P.G., Kazazian, H.H., Jr., Conneally, P.M., Hobbs, W., Tanzi, R., Faryniarz, A., Gibbons, K., & Gusella, J. (1985). Huntington's disease: Two families with differing clinical features show linkage to the G8 probe. *Science, 229,* 776–779. (9)

Foltz, E.L., & Millett, F.E. (1964). Experimental psychosomatic disease states in monkeys. I. Peptic ulcer — "executive monkeys." *Journal of Surgical Research, 4,* 445–453. (13)

Foote, S.L., & Morrison, J.H. (1987). Extrathalamic modulation of cortical function. *Annual Review of Neuroscience, 10,* 67–95. (4)

Forger, N.G., & Breedlove, S.M. (1987). Motoneuronal death during human fetal development. *Journal of Comparative Neurology, 264,* 118–122. (8)

Foster, T.C., Castro, C.A., & McNaughton, B.L. (1989). Spatial selectivity of rat hippocampal neurons: Dependence on preparedness for movement. *Science, 244,* 1580–1582. (14)

Foulkes, D. (1967). Nonrapid eye movement mentation. *Experimental Neurology* (Suppl. 4), 28–38. (10)

Franci, C.R., Kozlowski, G.P., & McCane, S.M. (1989). Water intake in rats subjected to hypothalamic immunoneutralization of angiotensin II, atrial natriuretic peptide, vasopressin, or oxytocin. *Proceedings of the National Academy of Sciences, U.S.A., 86,* 2952–2956. (11)

Frank, P.W. (1981). A condition for a sessile strategy. *American Naturalist, 118,* 288–290. (9)

Freedman, M., & Oscar-Berman, M. (1986). Bilateral frontal lobe disease and selective delayed response deficits in humans. *Behavioral Neuroscience, 100,* 337–342. (14)

Freedman, R.D., & Thibos, L.N. (1975). Contrast sensitivity in humans with abnormal visual experience. *Journal of Physiology, 247,* 687–710. (8)

French, A.R. (1988). The patterns of mammalian hibernation. *American Scientist, 76,* 568–575. (10)

Frese, M., & Harwich, C. (1984). Shiftwork and the length and quality of sleep. *Journal of Occupational Medicine, 26,* 561–566. (10)

Friedlander, W.J. (1986). Who was "the father of bromide treatment of epilepsy"? *Archives of Neurology, 43,* 505–507. (3)

Friedman, B., & Aguayo, A.J. (1985). Injured neurons in the olfactory bulb of the adult rat grow axons along grafts of peripheral nerve. *Journal of Neuroscience, 5,* 1616–1625. (15)

Friedman, M.I., & Stricker, E.M. (1976). The physiological psychology of hunger: A physiological perspective. *Psychological Review, 83,* 409–431. (11)

Frisch, R.E. (1972). Weight at menarche: Similarity for well nourished and undernourished girls at differing ages, and evidence for historical constancy. *Pediatrics, 50,* 445–450. (12)

Frisch, R.E. (1983). Fatness, puberty, and fertility: The effects of nutrition and physical training on menarche and ovulation. In J. Brooks-Gunn & A.C. Petersen (Eds.), *Girls at puberty* (pp. 29–49). New York: Plenum. (12)

Frisch, R.E. (1984). Body fat, puberty, and fertility. *Biological Reviews, 59,* 161–188. (12)

Fritsch, G., & Hitzig, E. (1870). Über die elektrische Erregbarkeit des Grosshirns [Concerning the electical stimulability of the cerebrum]. *Archiv fur Anatomie Physiologie und Wissenschaftliche Medicin,* 300–332. (1, 9)

Frutiger, S.A. (1986). Changes in self-stimulation at stimulation-bound eating and drinking sites in the lateral hypothalamus during food or water deprivation, glucoprivation, and intracellular or extracellular dehydration. *Behavioral Neuroscience, 100,* 221–229. (13)

Fukuda, Y., Hsiao, C.-F., & Watanabe, M. (1985). Morphological correlates of Y, X, and W type ganglion cells in the cat's retina. *Vision Research, 25,* 319–327. (7)

Fuller, C.A., Lydic, R., Sulzman, F.M., Albers, H.E., Tepper, B., & Moore-Ede, M.C. (1981). Circadian rhythm of body temperature persists after suprachiasmatic lesions in the squirrel monkey. *American Journal of Physiology, 241,* R385–R391. (10)

Fuller, R.K., & Roth, H.P. (1979). Disulfiram for the treatment of alcoholism: An evaluation in 128 men. *Annals of Internal Medicine, 90,* 901–904. (3)

Fuster, J.M. (1989). *The prefrontal cortex* (2nd ed.). New York: Raven Press. (4)

Gage, F.H., Björklund, A., Stenevi, U., Dunnett, S.B., & Kelly, P.A.T. (1984). Intrahippocampal septal grafts ameliorate learning impairments in aged rats. *Science, 225,* 533–536. (15)

Gaito, J. (1976). Molecular psychobiology of memory: Its appearance, contributions, and decline. *Physiological Psychology, 4,* 476–484. (14)

Galin, D., Johnstone, J., Nakell, L., & Herron, J. (1979). Development of the capacity for tactile information transfer between hemispheres in normal children. *Science, 204,* 1330–1332. (5)

Gallagher, M., & Kapp, B.S. (1978). Manipulation of opiate activity in the amygdala alters memory processes. *Life Sciences, 23,* 1973–1977. (14)

Gallagher, M., & Pelleymounter, M.A. (1988). Spatial learning deficits in old rats: A model for memory decline in the aged. *Neurobiology of Aging, 9,* 549–556. (14)

Gallistel, C.R. (1980). *The organization of action: A new synthesis.* Hillsdale, NJ: Erlbaum. (9)

Gallistel, C.R. (1981). Bell, Magendie, and the proposals to restrict the use of animals in neurobehavioral research. *American Psychologist, 36,* 357–360. (1)

Gallistel, C.R., Gomita, Y., Yadin, E., & Campbell, K.A. (1985). Forebrain origins and terminations of the medial forebrain bundle metabolically activated by rewarding stimulation or by reward-blocking doses of pimozide. *Journal of Neuroscience, 5,* 1246–1261. (13)

Gallistel, C.R., Shizgal, P., & Yeomans, J.S. (1981). A portrait of the substrate for self-stimulation. *Psychological Review, 88,* 228–273. (13)

Gallo, R.C. (1987, January). The AIDS virus. *Scientific American, 256* (1), 46–56. (16)

Gallup, G.G., Jr., & Suarez, S.D. (1980). On the use of animals in psychological research. *Psychological Record, 30,* 211–218. (1)

Gallup, G.G., Jr., & Suarez, S.D. (1985). Alternatives to the use of animals in psychological research. *American Psychologist, 40,* 1104–1111. (1)

Gamse, R., Leeman, S.E., Holzer, P., & Lembeck, F. (1981). Differential effects of capsaicin on the content of somatostatin, substance P, and neurotensin in the nervous system of the rat. *Naunyn-Schmiedeberg's Archives of Pharmacology, 317,* 140–148. (6)

Garattini, S., & Valzelli, L. (1960). Sulla valutazione farmacologica delle sostanze antidepressive [On the pharmacological validation of antidepressive substances]. In *Le sindromi depressive* (pp. 7–30.) (16)

Garcia, I.M.P.S., & Whitsett, J.M. (1983). Influence of photoperiod and social environment on sexual maturation in female deer mice *(Peromyscus maniculatus bairdii). Journal of Comparative Psychology, 97,* 127–134. (12)

Garcia, J. (1981). Tilting at the pater mills of academe. *American Psychologist, 36,* 149–158. (inside cover)

Gardner, B.T., & Gardner, R.A. (1975). Evidence for sentence constituents in the early utterances of child and chimpanzee. *Journal of Experimental Psychology: General, 104,* 244–267. (5)

Gardner, H., & Zurif, E.B. (1975). *Bee* but not *be:* Oral reading of single words in aphasia and alexia. *Neuropsychologia, 13,* 181–190. (5)

Gardner, H., Zurif, E.B., Berry, T., & Baker, E. (1976). Visual communication in aphasia. *Neuropsychologia, 14,* 275–292. (5)

Garrick, T. (1990). The role of gastric contractility and brain thyrotropin-releasing hormone in cold restraint-induced gastric mucosal injury. *Annals of the New York Academy of Sciences, 597,* 51–70. (13)

Garrick, T., Minor, T.R., Bauck, S., Weiner, H., & Guth, P. (1989). Predictable and unpredictable shock stimulates gastric contractility and causes mucosal injury in rats. *Behavioral Neuroscience, 103,* 124–130. (13)

Gash, D.M., Collier, T.J., & Sladek, J.R., Jr. (1985). Neural transplantation: A review of recent developments and potential applications to the aged brain. *Neurobiology of Aging, 6,* 131–150. (15)

Gash, D.M., Sladek, J.R., Jr., & Sladek, C.D. (1980). Functional development of grafted vasopressin neurons. *Science, 210,* 1367–1369. (15)

Gattass, R., Sousa, A.P.B., & Gross, C.G. (1988). Visuotopic organization and extent of V3 and V4 of the macaque. *Journal of Neuroscience, 8,* 1831–1845. (7)

Gaze, R.M., & Sharma, S.C. (1970). Axial differences in the reinnervation of the goldfish optic tectum by regenerating optic fibers. *Experimental Brain Research, 10,* 171–181. (8)

Gazzaniga, M.S., LeDoux, J.E., & Wilson, D.H. (1977). Language, praxis, and the right hemisphere: Clues to some mechanisms of consciousness. *Neurology, 27,* 1144–1147. (5)

Gearhart, J., Oster-Granite, M.L., & Guth, L. (1979). Histological changes after transection of the spinal cord of fetal and neonatal mice. *Experimental Neurology, 66,* 1–15. (15)

Geliebter, A., Westreich, S., Hashim, S.A., & Gage, D. (1987). Gastric balloon reduces food intake and body weight in obese rats. *Physiology & Behavior, 39,* 399–402. (11)

Gentner, D.R. (1987). Timing of skilled motor performance: Tests of the proportional duration model. *Psychological Review, 94,* 255–276. (9)

George, D.T., Nutt, D.J., Walker, W.V., Porges, S.W., Adinoff, B., & Linnoila, M. (1989). Lactate and hyperventilation substantially attenuate vagal tone in normal volunteers. *Archives of General Psychiatry, 46,* 153–156. (13)

Gershon, S., Angrist, B., & Shopsin, B. (1977). Pharmacological agents as tools in psychiatric research. In E.S. Gershon, R.H. Belmaker, S.S. Kety, & M. Rosenbaum (Eds.), *The impact of biology on modern psychiatry* (pp. 65–93). New York: Spectrum. (16)

Geschwind, N. (1970). The organization of language and the brain. *Science, 170,* 940–944. (5)

Geschwind, N. (1972). Language and the brain. *Scientific American, 226* (4), 76–83. (5)

Geschwind, N. (1975). The apraxias: Neural mechanisms of disorders of learned movements. *American Scientist, 63,* 188–195. (5, 9)

Geschwind, N., & Galaburda, A.M. (1985). Cerebral lateralization: Biological mechanisms, associations, and pathology: I. A hypothesis and a program for research. *Archives of Neurology, 42,* 428–459. (5)

Geschwind, N., & Levitsky, W. (1968). Human brain: left-right asymmetries in temporal speech region. *Science, 161,* 186–187. (5)

Getchell, T.V., & Getchell, M.L. (1987). Peripheral mechanisms of olfaction: Biochemistry and neurophysiology. In T.E. Finger & W.L. Silver (Eds.), *Neurobiology of taste and smell* (pp. 91–123). New York: John Wiley. (6)

Getchell, T.V., Margolis, F.L., & Getchell, M.L. (1984). Perireceptor and receptor events in vertebrate olfaction. *Progress in Neurobiology, 23,* 317–345. (6)

Gibbs, F.P. (1983). Temperature dependence of the hamster circadian pacemaker. *American Journal of Physiology, 244,* R607–R610. (10)

Gibbs, J., Young, R.C., & Smith, G.P. (1973). Cholecystokinin decreases food intake in rats. *Journal of Comparative and Physiological Psychology, 84,* 488–495. (11)

Gillberg, C., & Gillberg, I.C. (1983). Infantile autism: A total population study of reduced optimality in the pre-, peri-, and neonatal period. *Journal of Autism and Developmental Disorders, 13,* 153–166. (16)

Gillberg, C., Terenius, L., & Lönnerholm, G. (1985). Endorphin activity in childhood psychosis. *Archives of General Psychiatry, 42,* 780–783. (16)

Gillberg, C., Wahlström, J., & Hagberg, B. (1984). Infantile autism and Rett's syndrome: Common chromosomal denominator? *Lancet, 2*(8411), 1094–1095. (16)

Gillin, J.C. (1983). The sleep therapies of depression. *Progress in Neuro-Psychopharmacology & Biological Psychiatry, 7,* 351–364. (16)

Giraudat, J., & Changeux, J.-P. (1981). The acetylcholine receptor. In J.W. Lamble (Ed.), *Towards understanding receptors* (pp. 34–43). Amsterdam: Elsevier/North Holland Biomedical Press. (3)

Gjedde, A. (1984). Blood-brain transfer of galactose in experimental galactosemia, with special reference to the competitive interaction between galactose and glucose. *Journal of Neurochemistry, 43,* 1654–1662. (2)

Gladue, B.A., Green, R., & Hellman, R.E. (1984). Neuroendocrine response to estrogen and sexual orientation. *Science, 225,* 1496–1499. (12)

Glaser, J.H., Etgen, A.M., & Barfield, R.J. (1987). Temporal aspects of ventromedial hypothalamic progesterone action in the facilitation of estrous behavior in the female rat. *Behavioral Neuroscience, 101,* 534–545. (12)

Glaser, R., Rice, J., Speicher, C.E., Stout, J.C., & Kiecolt-Glaser, J.K. (1986). Stress depresses interferon production by leukocytes concomitant with a decrease in natural killer cell activity. *Behavioral Neuroscience, 100,* 675–678. (13)

Glass, A.V., Gazzaniga, M.S., & Premack, D. (1973). Artificial language training in global aphasics. *Neuropsychologia, 11,* 95–103. (5)

Glass, L., Evans, H.E., & Rajegowda, B.K. (1975). Neonatal narcotic withdrawal. In R.W. Richter (Ed.), *Medical aspects of drug abuse* (pp. 124–133). Hagerstown, MD: Harper & Row. (16)

Glick, S.D. (1974). Changes in drug sensitivity and mechanisms of functional recovery following brain damage. In D.G. Stein, J.J. Rosen, & N. Butters (Eds.), *Plasticity and recovery of function in the central nervous system* (pp. 339–372). New York: Academic. (15)

Glickstein, M., & Yeo, C. (1990). The cerebellum and motor learning. *Journal of Cognitive Neuroscience, 2,* 69–80. (14)

Gloning, I., Gloning, K., Weingarten, K., & Berner, P. (1954). Über einen Fall mit Alexie der BRAILLEschrift [On a case with alexia for Braille writing]. *Wiener Zeitschrift für Nervenheilkunde, 10,* 260–273. (5)

Goate, A., Chartier-Harlin, M.-C., Mullan, M., Brown, J., Crawford, F., Fidani, L., Giuffra, L., Haynes, A., Irving, N., James, L., Mant, R., Newton, P., Rooke, K., Roques, P., Talbot, C., Pericak-Vance, M., Roses, A., Williamson, R., Rossor, M., Owen, M., & Hardy, J. (1991). Segregation of a missense mutation in the amyloid precursor protein gene with familial Alzheimer's disease. *Nature, 349,* 704–706. (14)

Goetz, K.L., & vanKammen, D.P. (1986). Computerized axial tomography scans and subtypes of schizophrenia. *Journal of*
Nervous and Mental Disease, 174, 31–41. (16)

Gold, P.E. (1987). Sweet memories. *American Scientist, 75,* 151–155. (14)

Gold, P.W., Loriaux, L., Roy, A., Kling, M.A., Calabrese, J.R., Kellner, C.H., Nieman, L.K., Post, R.M., Pickar, D., Gallucci, W., Avgerinos, P., Paul, S., Oldfield, E.H., Cutler, G.B., Jr., & Chrousos, G.P. (1986). Responses to corticotropin-releasing hormone in the hypercortisolism of depression and Cushing's disease. *New England Journal of Medicine, 314,* 1329–1335. (16)

Goldberg, T.E., Weinberger, D.R., Berman, K.F., Pliskin, N.H., & Podd, M.H. (1987). Further evidence for dementia of the prefrontal type in schizophrenia? *Archives of General Psychiatry, 44,* 1008–1014. (16)

Golden, C.J. (1981). *Diagnosis and rehabilitation in clinical neuropsychology* (2nd ed.). Springfield, IL: Charles C. Thomas. (15)

Golden, C.J. (1984). Rehabilitation and the Luria-Nebraska neuropsychological battery. In B.A. Edelstein & E.T. Couture (Eds.), *Behavioral assessment and rehabilitation of the traumatically brain-damaged* (pp. 83–120). New York: Plenum. (15)

Goldman, B.D. (1981). Puberty. In N.T. Adler (Ed.), *Neuroendocrinology of reproduction* (pp. 229–239). New York: Plenum. (12)

Goldman, M.S. (1983). Cognitive impairment in chronic alcoholics: Some cause for optimism. *American Psychologist, 38,* 1045–1054. (3)

Goldman, P.S. (1971). Functional development of the prefrontal cortex in early life and the problem of neuronal plasticity. *Experimental Neurology, 32,* 366–387. (15)

Goldman, P.S. (1976). The role of experience in recovery of function following orbital prefrontal lesions in infant monkeys. *Neuropsychologia, 14,* 401–412. (15)

Goldman-Rakic, P.S. (1987). Development of cortical circuitry and cognitive function. *Child Development, 58,* 601–622. (4)

Goldman-Rakic, P.S. (1988). Topography of cognition: Parallel distributed networks in primate association cortex. *Annual Review of Neuroscience, 11,* 137–156. (inside cover, 4)

Goldstein, A. (1980). Thrills in response to music and other stimuli. *Physiological Psychology, 8,* 126–129. (6)

Goldstein, M. (1974). Brain research and violent behavior. *Archives of Neurology, 30,* 1–35. (12, 13)

Gonzalez, M.F., & Deutsch, J.A. (1981). Vagotomy abolishes cues of satiety produced by gastric distension. *Science, 212,* 1283–1284. (11)

Goodglass, H., & Kaplan, E. (1979). Assessment of cognitive deficit in the brain-injured patient. In M.S. Gazzaniga (Ed.), *Handbook of behavioral neurology* (vol. 2, pp. 3–22). New York: Plenum. (15)

Goodman, W.K., Price, L.H., Delgado, P.L., Palumbo, J., Krystal, J.H., Nagy, L.M., Rasmussen, S.A., Heninger, G.R., & Charney, D.S. (1990). Specificity of serotonin reuptake inhibitors in the treatment of obsessive-compulsive disorder. *Archives of General Psychiatry, 47,* 577–585. (13)
Gooren, L. (1986). The neuroendocrine response of luteinizing hormone to estrogen administration in heterosexual, homosexual, and transsexual subjects. *Journal of Clinical Endocrinology and Metabolism, 63,* 583–588. (12)

Gorman, J.M., Battista, D., Goetz, R.R., Dillon, D.J., Liebowitz, M.R., Fyer, A.J., Kahn, J.P., Sandberg, D., & Klein, D.F. (1989). A comparison of sodium bicarbonate and sodium lactate infusion in the induction of panic attacks. *Archives of General Psychiatry, 46,* 145–150. (13)

Gorman, J.M., Cohen, B.S., Liebowitz, M.R., Fyer, A.J., Ross, D., Davies, S.O., & Klein, D.F. (1986). Blood gas changes and hypophosphatemia in lactate-induced panic. *Archives of General Psychiatry, 43,* 1067–1071. (13)

Gorman, J.M., Fyer, M.R., Goetz, R., Askanazi, J., Liebowitz, M.R., Fyer, A.J., Kinney, J., & Klein, D.F. (1988). Ventilatory physiology of patients with panic disorder. *Archives of General Psychiatry, 45,* 31–39. (13)

Gorski, R.A. (1980). Sexual differentiation of the brain. In D.T. Krieger & J.C. Hughes (Eds.), *Neuroendocrinology* (pp. 215–222). Sunderland, MA: Sinauer. (12)

Gorski, R.A. (1985). The 13th J.A.F. Stevenson memorial lecture. Sexual differentiation of the brain: Possible mechanisms and implications. *Canadian Journal of Physiology and Pharmacology, 63,* 577–594. (12)

Gottesman, I.I. (1991). *Schizophrenia genesis.* New York: W.H. Freeman. (16)

Gottesman, I.I., & Bertelson, A. (1989). Confirming unexpressed genotypes for schizophrenia. *Archives of General Psychiatry, 46,* 867–872. (16)

Gottfried, S., & Frankel, M. (1981). New data on lithium and haloperidol incompatibility. *American Journal of Psychiatry, 138,* 818–821. (16)

Graziadei, P.P.C., & deHan, R.S. (1973). Neuronal regeneration in frog olfactory system. *Journal of Cell Biology, 59,* 525–530. (2)

Graziadei, P.P.C., & Monti Graziadei, G.A. (1985). Neurogenesis and plasticity of the olfactory sensory neurons. *Annals of the New York Academy of Sciences, 457,* 127–142. (2)

Green, D.J., & Gillette, R. (1982). Circadian rhythm of firing rate recorded from single cells in the rat suprachiasmatic brain slice. *Brain Research, 245,* 198–200. (10)

Greene, E., & Naranjo, J.N. (1987). Degeneration of hippocampal fibers and spatial memory deficit in the aged rat. *Neurobiology of Aging, 8,* 35–43. (14)

Greenblatt, S.H. (1973). Alexia without agraphia or hemianopsia: Anatomical analysis of an autopsied case. *Brain, 96,* 307–316. (5)

Greenfield, P.M., & Savage-Rumbaugh, E.S. (1990). Grammatical combination in *Pan paniscus:* Processes of learning and invention in the evolution and development of language. In S.T. Parker & K.R. Gibson (Eds.), *Language and intelligence in monkeys and apes* (pp. 540–578). New York: Cambridge University Press. (5)

Greenough, W.T. (1975). Experiential modification of the developing brain. *American Scientist, 63,* 37–46. (2)

Griffin, D.R., Webster, F.A., & Michael, C.R. (1960). The echolocation of flying insects by bats. *Animal Behaviour, 8,* 141–154. (6)

Gross, C.G., Bruce, C.J., Desimone, R., Fleming, J., & Gattass, R. (1981). Cortical visual areas of the temporal lobe: Three areas in the macaque. In C.N. Woolsey (Ed.), *Cortical sensory organization: Multiple visual areas* (pp. 187–216). Clifton, NJ: Humana. (7)

Grossman, M., Carey, S., Zurif, E., & Diller, L. (1986). Proper and common nouns: Form class judgments in Broca's aphasia. *Brain and Language, 28,* 114–125. (5)

Grossman, S.P., Dacey, D., Halaris, A.E., Collier, T., & Routtenberg, A. (1978). Aphagia and adipsia after preferential destruction of nerve cell bodies in hypothalamus. *Science, 202,* 537–539. (11)

Guidotti, A., Ferrero, P., Fujimoto, M., Santi, R.M., & Costa, E. (1986). Studies on endogenous ligands (endocoids) for the benzodiazepine/beta carboline binding sites. *Advances in Biochemical Pharmacology, 41,* 137–148. (13)

Guidotti, A., Forchetti, C.M., Corda, M.G., Konkel, D., Bennett, C.D., & Costa, E. (1983). Isolation, characterization, and purification to homogeneity of an endogenous polypeptide with agonistic action on benzodiazepine receptors. *Proceedings of the National Academy of Sciences, U.S.A., 80,* 3531–3535. (13)

Guile, M.N. (1987). Differential gastric ulceration in rats receiving shocks on either fixed-time or variable-time schedules. *Behavioral Neuroscience, 101,* 139–140. (13)

Guillery, R.W. (1972). Binocular competition in the control of geniculate cell growth. *Journal of Comparative Neurology, 144,* 117–130. (8)

Gulick, W.L. (1971). *Hearing: physiology and psychophysics.* New York: Oxford University Press. (6)

Gur, R.E., Resnick, S.M., Alavi, A., Gur, R.C., Caroff, S., Dann, R., Silver, F.L., Saykin, A.J., Chawluk, J.B., Kushner, M., & Reivich, M. (1987). Regional brain function in schizophrenia. I. A positron emission tomography study. *Archives of General Psychiatry, 44,* 119–125. (16)

Gusella, J.F., Tanzi, R.E., Anderson, M.A., Hobbs, W., Gibbons, K., Raschtchian, R., Gilliam, T.C., Wallace, M.R., Wexler, N.S., & Conneally, P.M. (1984). DNA markers for nervous system diseases. *Science, 225,* 1320–1326. (A)

Gusella, J.F., Wexler, N.S., Conneally, P.M., Naylor, S.L., Anderson, M.A., Tanzi, R.E., Watkins, P.C., Ottina, K., Wallace, M.R., Sakachi, A.Y., Young, A.B., Shoulson, I., Bonilla, E., & Martin, J.B. (1983). A polymorphic DNA marker genetically linked to Huntington's disease. *Nature, 306,* 234–238. (9)

Gustafsson, B., & Wigström, H. (1990). Basic features of long-term potentiation in the hippocampus. *Seminars in the Neurosciences, 2,* 321–333. (14)

Guyton, A.C. (1974). *Function of the human body* (4th ed.). Philadelphia: Saunders. (2)

Gwinner, E. (1986). Circannual rhythms in the control of avian rhythms. *Advances in the Study of Behavior, 16,* 191–228. (10)

Hadley, M.E. (1984). *Endocrinology.* Englewood Cliffs, NJ: Prentice-Hall. (12)

Haley, J. (1959). An interactional description of schizophrenia. *Psychiatry, 22,* 321–332. (16)

Hall, J.L., & Gold, P.E. (1990). Adrenalectomy-induced memory deficits: Role of plasma glucose levels. *Physiology & Behavior, 47,* 27–33. (14)

Hall, M.J., Bartoshuk, L.M., Cain, W.S., & Stevens, J.C. (1975). PTC taste blindness and the taste of caffeine. *Nature, 253,* 442–443. (6)

Hamilton, J.B., Hamilton, R.S., & Mestler, G.E. (1969). Duration of life and causes of death in domestic cats: Influence of sex, gonadectomy, and inbreeding. *Journal of Gerontology, 24,* 427–437. (12)

Hamilton, J.B., & Mestler, G.E. (1969). Mortality and survival: Comparison of eunuchs with intact men and women in a mentally retarded population. *Journal of Gerontology, 24,* 395–411. (12)

Hampson, E., & Kimura, D. (1984). Hand movement asymmetries during verbal and nonverbal tasks. *Canadian Journal of Psychology, 38,* 102–125. (5)

Hampson, E., & Kimura, D. (1988). Reciprocal effects of hormonal fluctuations on human motor and perceptual-spatial skills. *Behavioral Neuroscience, 102,* 456–459. (12)

Haracz, J.L. (1982). The dopamine hypothesis: An overview of studies with schizophrenic patients. *Schizophrenia Bulletin, 8,* 438–469. (16)

Harada, S., Agarwal, D.P., Goedde, H.W., Tagaki, S., & Ishikawa, B. (1982). Possible protective role against alcoholism for aldehyde dehydrogenase isozyme deficiency in Japan. *Lancet, ii*(8302), 827. (3)

Hardy, J. (1990). Molecular genetics of the dementias. *Seminars in the Neurosciences, 2,* 109–115. (14)

Harrison, J.M., & Irving, R. (1966). Visual and nonvisual auditory systems in mammals. *Science, 154,* 738–743. (4)

Hart, B.L. (Ed.). *Experimental psychobiology.* San Francisco: W.H. Freeman. (11)

Hartline, H.K. (1949). Inhibition of activity of visual receptors by illuminating nearby retinal areas in the Limulus eye. *Federation Proceedings, 8,* 69. (7)

Hartmann, E., Milofsky, E., Vaillant, G., Oldfield, M., Falke, R., & Ducey, C. (1984). Vulnerability to schizophrenia. *Archives of General Psychiatry, 41,* 1050–1056. (16)

Harvey, P.H., & Krebs, J.R. (1990). Comparing brains. *Science, 249,* 140–146. (4)

Haug, M., Brain, P.F., Kamis, A.B. (1986). A brief review comparing the effects of sex steroids on two forms of aggression in laboratory mice. *Neuroscience & Biobehavioral Reviews, 10,* 463–468. (12)

Hauri, P. (1979). What can insomniacs teach us about the functions of sleep? In R. Drucker-Colín, M. Shkurovich, & M.B. Sterman (Eds.), *The functions of sleep* (pp. 251–271). New York: Academic Press. (10)

Hawkins, R.A., & Biebuyck, J.F. (1979). Ketone bodies are selectively used by individual brain regions. *Science, 205,* 325–327. (2)

Hayaishi, O. (1988). Sleep-wake regulation by prostaglandins $D_2$ and $E_2$. *Journal of Biological Chemistry, 263,* 14593–14596. (10)

Heath, R.G. (1963). Electrical self-stimulation of the brain in man. *American Journal of Psychiatry, 120,* 571–577. (13)

Heath, R.G. (1964). Pleasure response of human subjects to direct stimulation of the brain: Physiologic and psychodynamic considerations. In R.G. Heath (Ed.), *Role of pleasure in behavior* (pp. 219–243). New York: Harper. (1)

Hebb, D.O. (1949). *Organization of behavior.* New York: Wiley. (inside cover, 14)

Hécaen, H., & Kremin, H. (1976). Neurolinguistic research on reading disorders resulting from left hemisphere lesions: Aphasic and "pure" alexias. In H. Whitaker & H.A. Whitaker (Eds.), *Studies in neurolinguistics* (Vol. 2, pp. 269–329). New York: Academic Press. (5)

Hécaen, H., Perenin, M.T., & Jeannerod, M. (1984). The effects of cortical lesions in children: Language and visual functions. In C.R. Almli & S. Finger (Eds.), *Early brain damage* (pp. 277–298). Orlando, FL: Academic Press. (15)

Heffner, R.S., & Heffner, H.E. (1982). Hearing in the elephant (*Elephas maximus*): Absolute sensitivity, frequency discrimination, and sound localization. *Journal of Comparative and Physiological Psychology, 96,* 926–944. (6)

Heller, W., & Levy, J. (1981). Perception and expression of emotion in righthanders and left-handers. *Neuropsychologia, 19,* 263–272. (5)

Helm-Estabrooks, N., & Ramsberger, G. (1986). Treatment of agrammatism in long-term Broca's aphasia. *British Journal of Disorders of Communication, 21,* 39–45. (5)

Helzer, J.E., Canino, G.J., Yeh, E.-K., Bland, R.C., Lee, C.K., Hwu, H.-G., & Newman, S. (1990). Alcoholism—North America and Asia. *Archives of General Psychiatry, 47,* 313–319. (3)

Henley, K., & Morrison, A.R. (1974). A reevaluation of the effects of lesions of the pontine tegmentum and locus coeruleus on phenomena of paradoxical sleep in the cat. *Acta Neurobiologiae Experimentalis, 34,* 215–232. (10)

Hennig, R., & Lømo, T. (1985). Firing patterns of motor units in normal rats. *Nature, 314,* 164–166. (9)

Herkenham, M., Lynn, A.B., Little, M.D., Johnson, M.R., Melvin, L.S., deCosta, B.R., & Rice, K.C. (1990). Cannabinoid receptor localization in brain. *Proceedings of the National Academy of Sciences, U.S.A., 87,* 1932–1936. (14)

Herman, L.M., Richards, D.G., & Wolz, J.P. (1984). Comprehension of sentences by bottlenosed dolphins. *Cognition, 16,* 129–219. (5)

Hernandez, L., & Hoebel, B.G. (1988). Feeding and hypothalamic stimulation increase dopamine turnover in the accumbens. *Physiology & Behavior, 44,* 599–606. (11)

Herrero, S. (1985). *Bear attacks: Their causes and avoidance*. Piscataway, NJ: Winchester. (6, 11)

Hess, W.R. (1944). Das Schlafsyndrom als Folge dienzephaler Reizung [Sleep syndrome as a consequence of diencephalic stimulation]. *Helvetica Physiologica Acta, 2*, 305–344. (1)

Hibbard, L.S., McGlone, J.S., Davis, D.W., & Hawkins, R.A. (1987). Three-dimensional representation and analysis of brain energy metabolism. *Science, 236*, 1641–1646. (4)

Hicks, R.E. (1975). Intrahemispheric response competition between vocal and unimanual performance in normal adult human males. *Journal of Comparative and Physiological Psychology, 89*, 50–60. (5)

Higgins, J.W., Mahl, G.F., Delgado, J.M.R., & Hamlin, H. (1956). Behavioral changes during intracerebral electrical stimulation. *Archives of neurology and psychiatry, 76*, 399–419. (13)

Hikosaka, O., & Wurtz, R.H. (1986). Saccadic eye movements following injection of lidocaine into the superior colliculus. *Experimental Brain Research, 61*, 531–539. (7)

Hines, M. (1982). Prenatal gonadal hormones and sex differences in human behavior. *Psychological Bulletin, 92*, 56–80. (12)

Hines, M., Davis, F.C., Coquelin, A., Goy, R.W., & Gorski, R.A. (1985). Sexually dimorphic regions in the medial preoptic area and the bed nucleus of the stria terminalis of the guinea pig brain: A description and an investigation of their relationship to gonadal steroids in adulthood. *Journal of Neuroscience, 5*, 40–47. (12)

Ho, S.C., Woo, J., & Lee, C.M. (1989). Epidemiologic study of Parkinson's disease in Hong Kong. *Neurology, 39*, 1314–1318. (9)

Hobson, J.A. (1977). The reciprocal interaction model of sleep cycle control: Implications for PGO wave generation and dream amnesia. In R.R. Drucker-Colín & J.L. McGaugh (Eds.), *Neurobiology of sleep and memory* (pp. 159–183). New York: Academic Press. (10)

Hobson, J.A., & McCarley, R.W. (1977). The brain as a dream state generator: An activation-synthesis hypothesis of the dream process. *American Journal of Psychiatry, 134*, 1335–1348. (10)

Hobson, J.A., McCarley, R.W., & Wyzinski, P.W. (1975). Sleep cycle oscillation: Reciprocal discharge by two brainstem neuronal groups. *Science, 189*, 55–58. (10)

Hodgkinson, S., Sherrington, R., Gurling, H. Marchbanks, R., Reeders, S., Mallet, J., McInnis, M., Petursson, H., & Brynjolfsson, J. (1987). Molecular genetic evidence for heterogeneity in manic depression. *Nature, 325*, 805–806. (16)

Hoebel, B.G. (1988). Neuroscience and motivation: Pathways and peptides that define motivational systems. In R.C. Atkinson, R.J. Herrnstein, G. Lindzey, & R.D. Luce (Eds.), *Stevens' Handbook of Experimental Psychology* (2nd ed.) (pp. 547–625). New York: John Wiley. (11)

Hoffman, P.L., Tabakoff, B., Szabó, G., Suzdak, P.D., & Paul, S.M. (1987). Effect of an imidazobenzodiazepine, Ro15-4513, on the incoordination and hypothermia produced by ethanol and pentobarbital. *Life Sciences, 41*, 611–619. (13)

Hogan, J.A. (1980). Homeostasis and behaviour. In F.M. Toates & T.R. Halliday (Eds.), *Analysis of motivational processes* (pp. 3–21). London: Academic. (11)

Hökfelt, T., Holets, V.R., Staines, W., Meister, B., Melander, T., Schalling, M., Schultzberg, M., Freedman, J., Björklund, H., Olson, L., Lindh, B., Elfvin, L.-G., Lundberg, J.M., Lindgren, J.A., Samuelsson, B., Pernow, B., Terenius, L., Post, C., Everitt, B., & Goldstein, M. (1986). Coexistence of neuronal messengers—an overview. *Progress in brain research* (vol. 68, pp. 33–70). Amsterdam: Elsevier. (3)

Holst—see von Holst

Holt, J., Antin, J., Gibbs, J., Young, R.C., & Smith, G.P. (1974). Cholecystokinin does not produce bait shyness in rats. *Physiology & Behavior, 12*, 497–498. (11)

Holtzman, J.D., & Gazzaniga, M.S. (1985). Enhanced dual task performance following corpus commissurotomy in humans. *Neuropsychologia, 23*, 315–321. (5)

Holzman, P.S. (1985). Eye movement dysfunctions and psychosis. *International Review of Neurobiology, 27*, 179–205. (16)

Holzman, P.S., & Matthysse, S. (1990). The genetics of schizophrenia: A review. *Psychological Science, 1*, 279–286. (16)

Hommer, D.W., Palkovits, M., Crawley, J.N., Paul, S.M., & Skirboll, L.R. (1985). Cholecystokinin-induced excitation in the substantia nigra: Evidence for peripheral and central components. *Journal of Neuroscience, 5*, 1387–1392. (11)

Hopkins, J., Marcus, M., & Campbell, S.B. (1984). Postpartum depression: A critical review. *Psychological Bulletin, 95*, 498–515. (16)

Hopkins, W.F., & Johnston, D. (1984). Frequency-dependent noradrenergic modulation of long-term potentiation in the hippocampus. *Science, 226*, 350–351. (14)

Hoptman, M.J., & Levy, J. (1988). Perceptual asymmetries in left- and right-handers for cartoon and real faces. *Brain & Cognition, 8*, 178–188. (5)

Horne, J.A. (1988). *Why we sleep*. Oxford, England: Oxford University Press. (10)

Horne, J.A., & Minard, A. (1985). Sleep and sleepiness following a behaviourally "active" day. *Ergonomics, 28*, 567–575. (10)

Horne, R.L., Pettinati, H.M., Sugerman, A., & Varga, E. (1985). Comparing bilateral to unilateral electroconvulsive therapy in a randomized study with EEG monitoring. *Archives of General Psychiatry, 42*, 1087–1092. (16)

Horowitz, G.P., & Whitney, G. (1975). Alcohol-induced conditioned aversion: Genotype specificity in mice (*Mus musculus*). *Journal of Comparative and Physiological Psychology, 89*, 340–346. (3)

Horridge, G.A. (1962). Learning of leg position by the ventral nerve cord in headless insects. *Proceedings of the Royal Society of London, B, 157*, 33–52. (14)

Householder, J., Hatcher, R., Burns, W., & Chasnoff, I. (1982). Infants born to narcotic-addicted mothers. *Psychological Bulletin, 92*, 453–468. (16)

Hovda, D.A., & Feeney, D.M. (1989). Amphetamine-induced recovery of visual cliff performance after bilateral visual cortex ablation in cats: Measurements of depth perception thresholds. *Behavioral Neuroscience, 103*, 574–584. (15)

Howland, H.C., & Sayles, N. (1984). Photorefractive measurements of astigmatism in infants and young children. *Investigative Ophthalmology and Visual Science, 25*, 93–102. (8)

Hubel, D.H. (1963, November). The visual cortex of the brain. *Scientific American, 209* (5), 54–62. (7)

Hubel, D.H., & Wiesel, T.N. (1959). Receptive fields of single neurons in the cat's striate cortex. *Journal of Physiology, 148*, 574–591. (7)

Hubel, D.H., & Wiesel, T.N. (1963). Receptive fields of cells in striate cortex of very young, visually inexperienced kittens. *Journal of Neurophysiology, 26*, 944–1002. (8)

Hubel, D.H., & Wiesel, T.N. (1965). Binocular interaction in striate cortex of kittens reared with artificial squint. *Journal of Neurophysiology, 28*, 1041–1059. (8)

Hubel, D.H., & Wiesel, T.N. (1977). Functional architecture of macaque monkey visual cortex. *Proceedings of the Royal Society of London, B, 198*, 1–59. (7)

Huber, S., Paulson, G.W., & Shuttleworth, E.C. (1988). Depression in Parkinson's disease. *Neuropsychiatry, Neuropsychology, and Behavioral Neurology, 1*, 47–51. (9)

Hudson, J.I., Lipinski, J.F., Frankenburg, F.R., Grochocinski, V.J., & Kupfer, D.J. (1988). Electroencephalographic sleep in mania. *Archives of General Psychiatry, 45*, 267–273. (16)

Hudspeth, A.J. (1985). The cellular basis of hearing: The biophysics of hair cells. *Science, 230*, 745–752. (6)

Hughes, J., Smith, T.W., Kosterlitz, H.W., Fothergill, L.A., Morgan, B.A., & Morris, H.R. (1975). Identification of two related pentapeptides from the brain with potent opiate agonist activity. *Nature, 258*, 577–579. (6)

Hull, E.M., Bitran, D., Pehek, E.A., Warner, R.K., Band, L.C., & Holmes, G.M. (1986). Dopaminergic control of male sex behavior in rats: Effects of an intracerebrally-infused agonist. *Brain Research, 370*, 73–81. (12)

Hull, E.M., Young, S.H., & Zeigler, M.G. (1984). Aerobic fitness affects cardiovascular and catecholamine responses to stressors. *Psychophysiology, 21*, 353–360. (13)

Hurvich, L.M., & Jameson, D. (1957). An opponent-process theory of color vision. *Psychological Review, 64*, 384–404. (7)

Hyman, B.T., van Hoesen, G.W., Damasio, A.R., & Barnes, C.L. (1984). Alzheimer's disease: Cell-specific pathology isolates the hippocampal formation. *Science, 225*, 1168–1170. (14)

Hyvärinen, J., Hyvärinen, L., & Linnankoski, I. (1981). Modification of parietal association cortex and functional blindness after binocular deprivation in young monkeys. *Experimental Brain Research, 42*, 1–8. (8)

Iggo, A., & Andres, K.H. (1982). Morphology of cutaneous receptors. *Annual Review of Neuroscience, 5,* 1–31. (6)

Imperato-McGinley, J., Guerrero, L., Gautier, T., & Peterson, R.E. (1974). Steroid 5 alpha-reductase deficiency in man: An inherited form of male pseudohermaphroditism. *Science, 186,* 1213–1215. (12)

Innocenti, G.M. (1980). The primary visual pathway through the corpus callosum: Morphological and functional aspects in the cat. *Archives Italiennes de Biologie, 118,* 124–188. (5)

Innocenti, G.M., & Caminiti, R. (1980). Postnatal shaping of callosal connections from sensory areas. *Experimental Brain Research, 38,* 381–394. (5)

Innocenti, G.M., Frost, D.O., & Illes, J. (1985). Maturation of visual callosal connections in visually deprived kittens: A challenging critical period. *Journal of Neuroscience, 5,* 255–267. (5)

Inoué, S., Uchizono, K., & Nagasaki, H. (1982). Endogenous sleep-promoting factors. *Trends in Neurosciences, 5,* 218–220. (10)

Inouye, S.T., & Kawamura, H. (1979). Persistence of circadian rhythmicity in a mammalian hypothalamic "island" containing the suprachiasmatic nucleus. *Proceedings of the National Academy of Sciences, U.S.A., 76,* 5962–5966. (10)

Insel, T.R., Gillin, J.C., Moore, A., Mendelson, W.B., Loewenstein, R.J., & Murphy, D.L. (1982). The sleep of patients with obsessive-compulsive disorder. *Archives of General Psychiatry, 39,* 1372–1377. (13)

Iriki, A., Pavlides, C., Keller, A., & Asanuma, H. (1989). Long-term potentiation in the motor cortex. *Science, 245,* 1385–1387. (14)

Irwin, M., Daniels, M., Risch, S.C., Bloom, E., & Weiner, H. (1988). Plasma cortisol and natural killer cell activity during bereavement. *Biological Psychiatry, 24,* 173–178. (13)

Isaacson, R.L. (1972). Hippocampal destruction in man and other animals. *Neuropsychologia, 10,* 47–64. (14)

Ito, K., & McCarley, R.W. (1984). Alterations in membrane potential and excitability of cat medial pontine reticular formation neurons during changes in naturally occurring sleep-wake states. *Brain Research, 292,* 169–175. (10)

Ivy, G.O., & Killackey, H.P. (1981). The ontogeny of the distribution of callosal projection neurons in the rat parietal cortex. *Journal of Comparative Neurology, 195,* 367–389. (5)

Izard, C. (1977). *Human emotions.* New York: Plenum. (13)

Jacobs, B.L. (1987). How hallucinogenic drugs work. *American Scientist, 75,* 386–392. (3)

Jacobs, B.L., Henriksen, S.J., & Dement, W.C. (1972). Neurochemical bases of the PGO wave. *Brain Research, 48,* 406–411. (10)

Jancsó, G., Kiraly, E., & Jancsó-Gábor, A. (1977). Pharmacologically induced selective degeneration of chemosensitive primary sensory neurones. *Nature, 270,* 741–743. (6)

Janicak, P.G., Davis, J.M., Gibbons, R.D., Ericksen, S., Chang, S., & Gallagher, P. (1985). Efficacy of ECT: A meta-analysis. *American Journal of Psychiatry, 142,* 297–302. (15)

Janosik, E.H., & Davies, J.L. (1987). *Psychiatric mental health nursing.* Boston: Jones & Bartlett. (16)

Janowsky, J.S., Shimamura, A.P., Kritchevsky, M., & Squire, L.R. (1989). Cognitive impairment following frontal lobe damage and its relevance to human amnesia. *Behavioral Neuroscience, 103,* 548–560. (14)

Jarrard, L.E., Okaichi, H., Steward, O., & Goldschmidt, R.B. (1984). On the role of hippocampal connections in the performance of place and cue tasks: Comparisons with damage to hippocampus. *Behavioral Neuroscience, 98,* 946–954. (14)

Jeddi, E. (1970). Confort du contact et thermoregulation comportementale [Contact comfort and behavioral thermoregulation]. *Physiology & Behavior, 5,* 1487–1493. (16)

Jeeves, M.A., & Silver, P.H. (1988). The formation of finger grip during prehension in an acallosal patient. *Neuropsychologia, 26,* 153–159. (5)

Jeeves, M.A., & Temple, C.M. (1987). A further study of language function in callosal agenesis. *Brain and Language, 32,* 325–335. (5)

Jenner, P. (1990). Parkinson's disease: Clues to the cause of cell death in the substantia nigra. *Seminars in the Neurosciences, 2,* 117–126. (9)

Jerison, H.J. (1985). Animal intelligence as encephalization. *Philosophical Transactions of the Royal Society of London, B, 308,* 21–35. (4)

Jiang, H.-K., Owyang, V., Hong, J.-S., & Gallagher, M. (1989). Elevated dynorphin in the hippocampal formation of aged rats: Relation to cognitive impairment on a spatial learning task. *Proceedings of the National Academy of Sciences, U.S.A., 86,* 2948–2951. (14)

Johns, T.R., & Thesleff, S. (1961). Effects of motor inactivation on the chemical sensitivity of skeletal muscle. *Acta Physiologica Scandinavica, 51,* 136–141. (15)

Johnson, C.H., & Hastings, J.W. (1986). The elusive mechanism of the circadian clock. *American Scientist, 74,* 29–36. (10)

Johnson, D. (1990). Animal rights and human lives: Time for scientists to right the balance. *Psychological Science, 1,* 213–214. (1)

Johnson, E.M., Jr., Gorin, P.D., Brandeis, L.D., & Pearson, J. (1980). Dorsal root ganglion neurons are destroyed by exposure in utero to maternal antibody to nerve growth factor. *Science, 210,* 916–918. (8)

Johnson, L.C. (1969). Physiological and psychological changes following total sleep deprivation. In A. Kales (Ed.), *Sleep: Physiology & pathology* (pp. 206–220). Philadelphia: Lippincott. (10)

Johnson, W.G., & Wildman, H.E. (1983). Influence of external and covert food stimuli on insulin secretion in obese and normal subjects. *Behavioral Neuroscience, 97,* 1025–1028. (11)

Jones, D.G. (1988). Influence of ethanol on neuronal and synaptic maturation in the

central nervous system—morphological investigations. *Progress in Neurobiology, 31,* 171–197. (8)

Jones, E.G. (1985). *The thalamus.* New York: Plenum. (4)

Jones, H.S., & Oswald, I. (1968). Two cases of healthy insomnia. *Electroencephalography and Clinical Neurophysiology, 24,* 378–380. (10)

Jordan, H.A. (1969). Voluntary intragastric feeding. *Journal of Comparative and Physiological Psychology, 68,* 498–506. (11)

Jouvet, M. (1960). Telencephalic and rhombencephalic sleep in the cat. In G.E.W. Wolstenholme & M. O'Connor (Eds.), *CIBA foundation symposium on the nature of sleep* (pp. 188–208). Boston: Little, Brown. (10)

Jouvet, M., & Delorme, F. (1965). Locus coeruleus et sommeil paradoxal [Locus coeruleus and paradoxical sleep]. *Comptes Rendus des Séances de la Société de Biologie, 159,* 895–899. (10)

Jouvet, M., & Renault, J. (1966). Insomnie persistante après lésions des noyaux du raphe chez le chat [Persistent insomnia after lesions of the raphe nuclei in the cat]. *Comptes Rendus des Séances de la Société de Biologie, 160,* 1461–1465. (10)

Juhler, M., Barry, D.I., Offner, H., Konat, G., Klinken, L., & Paulson, O.B. (1984). Blood-brain and blood-spinal cord barrier permeability during the course of experimental allergic encephalomyelitis in the rat. *Brain Research, 302,* 347–355. (2)

Kaas, J.H. (1983). What, if anything, is SI? Organization of first somatosensory area of cortex. *Physiological Reviews, 63,* 206–231. (6)

Kaas, J.H. (1989). Why does the brain have so many visual areas? *Journal of Cognitive Neuroscience, 1,* 121–135. (7, 8)

Kaas, J.H., Merzenich, M.M., & Killackey, H.P. (1983). The reorganization of somatosensory cortex following peripheral nerve damage in adult and developing mammals. *Annual Review of Neuroscience, 6,* 325–356. (15)

Kaas, J.H., Nelson, R.J., Sur, M., Lin, C.-S., & Merzenich, M.M. (1979). Multiple representations of the body within the primary somatosensory cortex of primates. *Science, 204,* 521–523. (4)

Kalat, J.W. (1978). Letter to the editor: Speculations on similarities between autism and opiate addiction. *Journal of Autism and Childhood Schizophrenia, 8,* 477–479. (16)

Kales, A., & Kales, J.D. (1984). *Evaluation and treatment of insomnia.* New York: Oxford. (10)

Kales, A., Scharf, M.B., & Kales, J.D. (1978). Rebound insomnia: A new clinical syndrome. *Science, 201,* 1039–1041. (10)

Kales, A., Soldatos, C.R., Bixler, E.O., & Kales, J.D. (1983). Early morning insomnia with rapidly eliminated benzodiazepines. *Science, 220,* 95–97. (10)

Kalil, K. (1988). Regeneration of pyramidal tract axons. In S.G. Waxman (Ed.), *Advances in Neurology* (Vol. 47, pp. 67–85). New York: Raven Press. (14)

Kalsner, S. (1990). Heteroreceptors, autoreceptors, and other terminal sites. *Annals*

*of the New York Academy of Sciences, 604,*
1–6. (3)

Kamin, L.J. (1974). *The science and politics of IQ.* New York: Wiley. (A)

Kandel, E.R., & Schwartz, J.H. (1982). Molecular biology of learning: Modulation of transmitter release. *Science, 218,* 433–443. (14)

Kanner, L. (1943). Autistic disturbances of affective contact. *Nervous Child, 2,* 217–250. (16)

Kaplan, E.H. (1988). Crisis? A brief critique of Masters, Johnson, and Kolodny. *Journal of Sex Research, 25,* 317–322. (16)

Kaplan, M.S. (1985). Formation and turnover of neurons in young and senescent animals: An electromicroscopic and morphometric analysis. *Annals of the New York Academy of Sciences, 457,* 173–192. (2)

Karmanova, I.G. (1982). *Evolution of sleep.* Basel: Karger. (10)

Kasper, S., Wehr, T.A., Bartko, J.J., Gaist, P.A., & Rosenthal, N.E. (1989). Epidemiological findings of seasonal changes in mood and behavior. *Archives of General Psychiatry, 46,* 823–833. (16)

Kauer, J.S. (1987). Coding in the olfactory system. In T.E. Finger & W.L. Silver (Eds.), *Neurobiology of taste and smell* (pp. 205–231). New York: John Wiley. (6)

Kaufman, S. (1975). Hepatic phenylalanine hydroxylase and PKU. In N.A. Buchwald & M.A.B. Brazier (Eds.), *Brain mechanisms in mental retardation* (pp. 445–458). New York: Academic Press. (8)

Kay, S.R., & Singh, M.M. (1989). The positive-negative distinction in drug-free schizophrenic patients. *Archives of General Psychiatry, 46,* 711–718. (16)

Kellar, K.J., & Stockmeier, C.A. (1986). Effects of electroconvulsive shock and serotonin axon lesions on beta-adrenergic and serotonin-2 receptors in rat brain. *Annals of the New York Academy of Sciences, 462,* 76–90. (16)

Kellerman, H. (1981). *Sleep disorders: Insomnia and narcolepsy.* New York: Brunner/Mazel. (10)

Kelso, S.R., Ganong, A.H., & Brown, T.H. (1986). Hebbian synapses in hippocampus. *Proceedings of the National Academy of Sciences, U.S.A., 83,* 5326–5330. (14)

Kelsoe, J.R., Ginns, E.I., Egeland, J.A., Gerhard, D.S., Goldstein, A.M., Bale, S.J., Pauls, D.L., Long, R.T., Kidd, K.K., Conte, G., Housman, D.E., & Paul, S.M. (1989). Re-evaluation of the linkage relationship between chromosome 11p loci and the gene for bipolar affective disorder in the Old Order Amish. *Nature, 342,* 238–243. (16)

Kempler, D., Metter, E.J., Jackson, C.A., Hanson, W.R., Riege, W.H., Mazziotta, J.C., & Phelps, M.E. (1988). Disconnection and cerebral metabolism: The case of conduction aphasia. *Archives of Neurology, 45,* 275–279. (5)

Kendell, R.W., & Kemp, I.W. (1989). Maternal influenza in the etiology of schizophrenia. *Archives of General Psychiatry, 46,* 878–882. (16)

Kendler, K.S. (1983). Overview: A current perspective on twin studies of schizophrenia. *American Journal of Psychiatry, 140,* 1413–1425. (16)

Kendler, K.S., & Robinette, C.D. (1983). Schizophrenia in the National Academy of Sciences–National Research Council twin registry—A 16-year update. *American Journal of Psychiatry, 140,* 1551–1563. (16)

Kendrick, K.M., & Dixson, A.F. (1984). A quantitative description of copulatory and associated behaviors of captive marmosets. *International Journal of Primatology, 5,* 199–212. (12)

Kennard, M.A. (1938). Reorganization of motor function in the cerebral cortex of monkeys deprived of motor and premotor areas in infancy. *Journal of Neurophysiology, 1,* 477–496. (15)

Kennedy, J.L., Giuffra, L.A., Moises, H.W., Cavalli-Sforza, L.L., Pakstis, A.J., Kidd, J.R., Castiglione, C.M., Sjogren, B., Wetterberg, L., & Kidd, K.K. (1988). Evidence against linkage of schizophrenia to markers on chromosome 5 in a northern Swedish pedigree. *Nature, 336,* 167–170. (16)

Kerr, N.H., Foulkes, D., & Jurkovic, G.J. (1978). Reported absence of visual dream imagery in a normally sighted subject with Turner's syndrome. *Journal of Mental Imagery, 2,* 247–264. (12)

Kesner, R.P. (1990). Learning and memory in rats with an emphasis on the role of the hippocampal formation. In R.P. Kesner & D.S. Olton (Eds.), *Neurobiology of comparative cognition* (pp. 179–204). Hillsdale, NJ: Lawrence Erlbaum. (14)

Kessler, M., Baudry, M., Cummins, J.T., Way, S., & Lynch, G. (1986). Induction of glutamate binding sites in hippocampal membranes by transient exposure to high concentrations of glutamate or glutamate analogs. *Journal of Neuroscience, 6,* 355–363. (14)

Kessler, S. (1980). The genetics of schizophrenia: A review. *Schizophrenia Bulletin, 6,* 404–416. (16)

Kety, S.S. (1975). Progress toward an understanding of the biological substrates of schizophrenia. In R.R. Fieve, D. Rosenthal, & H. Brill (Eds.), *Genetic research in psychiatry* (pp. 15–26). Baltimore, MD: Johns Hopkins University Press. (16)

Kety, S.S., Rosenthal, D., Wender, P.H., Schulsinger, F., & Jacobsen, B. (1975). Mental illness in the biological and adoptive families of adopted individuals who have become schizophrenic. In R.R. Fieve, D. Rosenthal, & H. Brill (Eds.), *Genetic research in psychiatry* (pp. 147–165). Baltimore, MD: Johns Hopkins University Press. (16)

Killackey, H.P. (1990). Neocortical expansion: An attempt toward relating phylogeny and ontogeny. *Journal of Cognitive Neuroscience, 2,* 1–17. (4, 8)

Killackey, H.P., & Chalupa, L.M. (1986). Ontogenetic change in the distribution of callosal projection neurons in the postcentral gyrus of the fetal rhesus monkey. *Journal of Comparative Neurology, 244,* 331–348. (5)

Killeffer, F.A., & Stern, W.E. (1970). Chronic effects of hypothalamic injury. *Archives of Neurology, 22,* 419–429. (11)

Kim, J.S., & Kornhuber, H.H. (1982). The glutamate theory in schizophrenia: Clinical and experimental evidence. In N.

Namba & H. Kaiya (Eds.), *Psychobiology of schizophrenia* (pp. 221–234). Oxford, England: Pergamon. (16)

Kimble, D.P. (1990). Functional effects of neural grafting in the mammalian central nervous system. *Psychological Bulletin, 108,* 462–479. (15)

Kimelberg, H.K., & Norenberg, M.D. (1989, April). Astrocytes. *Scientific American, 260*(4), 66–76. (2)

Kimura, D. (1973a). Manual activity during speaking—I. Right handers. *Neuropsychologia, 11,* 45–50. (5)

Kimura, D. (1973b). Manual activity during speaking—II. Left handers. *Neuropsychologia, 11,* 51–55. (5)

Kimura, D., & Watson, N. (1989). The relation between oral movement control and speech. *Brain and Language, 37,* 565–590. (5)

King, B.M., Smith, R.L., & Frohman, L.A. (1984). Hyperinsulinemia in rats with ventromedial hypothalamic lesions: Role of hyperphagia. *Behavioral Neuroscience, 98,* 152–155. (11)

Kinnamon, J.C. (1987). Organization and innervation of taste buds. In T.E. Finger and W.L. Silver (Eds.) *Neurobiology of taste and smell* (pp. 277–297). New York: John Wiley. (6)

Kinney, D.K., Woods, B.T., & Yurgelun-Todd, D. (1986). Neurologic abnormalities in schizophrenic patients and their families. *Archives of General Psychiatry, 43,* 665–668. (16)

Kinsbourne, M. (1972). Eye and head turning indicates cerebral lateralization. *Science, 176,* 539–541. (5)

Kinsbourne, M., & McMurray, J. (1975). The effect of cerebral dominance on time sharing between speaking and tapping by preschool children. *Child Development, 46,* 240–242. (5)

Kleinman, J.E., Karson, C.N., Weinberger, D.R., Freed, W.J., Berman, K.F., & Wyatt, R.J. (1984). Eye-blinking and cerebral ventricular size in chronic schizophrenic patients. *American Journal of Psychiatry, 141,* 1430–1432. (16)

Kleinmuntz, Z.B., & Szucko, J.J. (1984). Lie detection in ancient and modern times. *American Psychologist, 39,* 766–776. (13)

Kleinschmidt, A., Bear, M.F., & Singer, W. (1987). Blockade of "NMDA" receptors disrupts experience-dependent plasticity of kitten striate cortex. *Science, 238,* 355–358. (14)

Kleitman, N. (1963). *Sleep and wakefulness* (rev. ed.). Chicago: University of Chicago Press. (10)

Klerman, G.L. (1975). Relationships between preclinical testing and therapeutic evaluation of antidepressive drugs: The importance of new animal models for theory and practice. In A. Sudilovsky, S. Gershon, & B. Beer (Eds.), *Predictability in psychopharmacology* (pp. 159–178). New York: Raven. (3)

Kluger, M.J. (1978). The evolution and adaptive value of fever. *American Scientist, 66,* 38–43. (11)

Kluger, M.J., & Rothenburg, B.A. (1979). Fever and reduced iron: Their interaction as a host defense response to bacterial infection. *Science, 203,* 374–376. (11)

Kluger, M.J., & Vaughn, L.K. (1978). Fever and survival in rabbits infected with *Pas-*

teurella multocida. *Journal of Physiology, 282,* 243–251. (11)

Klüver, H., & Bucy, P.C. (1939). Preliminary analysis of functions of the temporal lobes in monkeys. *Archives of Neurology and Psychiatry, 42,* 979–1000. (4)

Knudsen, E.I., & Konishi, M. (1978). Space and frequency are represented separately in the auditory midbrain of the owl. *Journal of Neurophysiology, 41,* 870–884. (6)

Kochhar, A., Zivin, J.A., Lyden, P.D., & Mazzarella, V. (1988). Glutamate antagonist therapy reduces neurologic deficits produced by focal central nervous system ischemia. *Archives of Neurology, 45,* 148–153. (15)

Kodama, J., Fukushima, M., & Sakata, T. (1978). Impaired taste discrimination against quinine following chronic administration of theophylline in rats. *Physiology & Behavior, 20,* 151–155. (6)

Koegel, R.L., Schreibman, L., O'Neill, R.E., & Burke, J.C. (1983). The personality and family-interaction characteristics of parents of autistic children. *Journal of Consulting & Clinical Psychology, 51,* 683–692. (16)

Kolb, B., & Holmes, C. (1983). Neonatal motor cortex lesions in the rat: Absence of sparing of motor behaviors and impaired spatial learning concurrent with abnormal cerebral morphogenesis. *Behavioral Neuroscience, 97,* 697–709. (15)

Kolb, B., Sutherland, R.J., & Whishaw, I.Q. (1983). Abnormalities in cortical and subcortical morphology after neonatal neocortical lesions in rats. *Experimental Neurology, 79,* 223–244. (15)

Kolb, B., & Taylor, L. (1981). Affective behavior in patients with localized cortical excisions: Role of lesion site and side. *Science, 214,* 89–90. (5, 16)

Kolb, B., & Whishaw, I.Q. (1977). Effects of brain lesions and atropine on hippocampal and neocortical electroencephalograms in the rat. *Experimental Neurology, 56,* 1–22. (9)

Kolb, B., & Whishaw, I.Q. (1989). Plasticity in the neocortex: Mechanisms underlying recovery from early brain damage. *Progress in Neurobiology, 32,* 235–276. (15)

Komisaruk, B.R., Adler, N.T., & Hutchison, J. (1972). Genital sensory field: Enlargement by estrogen treatment in female rats. *Science, 178,* 1295–1298. (12)

Konishi, M. (1969). Hearing, single-unit analysis, and vocalizations in songbirds. *Science, 166,* 1178–1181. (1)

Koran, L.M., Sox, H.C., Jr., Marton, K.I., Moltzen, S., Sox, C.H., Kraemer, H.C., Imai, K., Kelsey, T.G., Rose, T.G., Jr., Levin, L.C., & Chandra, S. (1989). Medical evaluation of psychiatric patients. *Archives of General Psychiatry, 46,* 733–740. (16)

Kornhuber, H.H. (1971). Motor functions of cerebellum and basal ganglia. *Kybernetik, 8,* 157–162. (9)

Kornhuber, H.H. (1974). Cerebral cortex, cerebellum, and basal ganglia: An introduction to their motor functions. In F.O. Schmitt & F.G. Worden (Eds.), *The neurosciences: Third study program* (pp. 267–280). Cambridge, MA: MIT Press. (9)

Kornhuber, H.H. (1983). Chemistry, physiology and neuropsychology of schizophrenia: Towards an earlier diagnosis of schizophrenia I. *Archiv für Psychiatrie und Nervenkrankheiten, 233,* 415–422. (16)

Kostowski, W., Giacalone, E., Garattini, S., & Valzelli, L. (1969). Electrical stimulation of midbrain raphe: Biochemical, behavioral, and bioelectrical effects. *European Journal of Pharmacology, 7,* 170–175. (10)

Kozlowski, M.R., & Marshall, J.F. (1981). Plasticity of neostriatal metabolic activity and behavioral recovery from nigrostriatal injury. *Experimental Neurology, 74,* 318–323. (15)

Kraly, F.S. (1990). Drinking elicited by eating. *Progress in Psychobiology and Physiological Psychology, 14,* 67–133. (11)

Kreuz, L.E., & Rose, R.M. (1972). Assessment of aggressive behavior and plasma testosterone in a young criminal population. *Psychosomatic Medicine, 34,* 321–332. (12)

Kringlen, E., & Cramer, G. (1989). Offspring of monozygotic twins discordant for schizophrenia. *Archives of General Psychiatry, 46,* 873–877. (16)

Krnjević, K., & Reinhardt, W. (1979). Choline excites cortical neurons. *Science, 206,* 1321–1323. (3)

Kroodsma, D.E. (1976). Reproductive development in a female songbird: Differential stimulation by quality of male song. *Science, 192,* 574–575. (1)

Kroodsma, D.E., & Miller, E.H. (1982). Introduction. In D.E. Kroodsma & E.H. Miller (Eds.), *Acoustic communication in birds* (Vol. 1, pp. xxi–xxxvi). New York: Academic Press. (1)

Krueger, J.M., Pappenheimer, J.R., & Karnovsky, M.L. (1982). The composition of sleep-promoting factor isolated from human urine. *Journal of Biological Chemistry, 257,* 1664–1669. (10)

Krupka, L.R., & Vener, A.M. (1985). Prescription drug advertising: Trends and implications. *Social Science & Medicine, 20,* 191–197. (13)

Kubie, J.L., & Ranck, J.B., Jr. (1983). Sensory-behavioral correlates in individual hippocampus neurons in three situations: Space and context. In W. Seifert (Ed.), *Neurobiology of the hippocampus* (pp. 433–447). London: Academic Press. (14)

Kuffler, S.W. (1953). Discharge patterns and functional organization of the mammalian retina. *Journal of Neurophysiology, 16,* 37–68. (7)

Kupfermann, I., Castellucci, V., Pinsker, H., & Kandel, E. (1970). Neuronal correlates of habituation and dishabituation of the gill withdrawal reflex in *Aplysia. Science, 167,* 1743–1745. (14)

Kurata, K., & Tanji, J. (1986). Premotor cortex neurons in macaques: Activity before distal and proximal forelimb movements. *Journal of Neuroscience, 6,* 403–411. (9)

Kurtzke, J.R. (1976). An introduction to the epidemiology of cerebrovascular disease. In F. Scheinberg (Ed.), *Cerebrovascular diseases* (pp. 239–253). New York: Raven. (15)

Kurz, E.M., Sengelaub, D.R., & Arnold, A.P. (1986). Androgens regulate the dendritic length of mammalian motoneurons in adulthood. *Science, 232,* 395–398. (12)

Kuypers, H.G.J.M. (1989). Motor system organization. In G. Adelman (Ed.), *Neuroscience year* (pp. 107–110). Boston: Birkhäuser. (9)

Lagarde, D., Laurent, J., Milhaud, C., Andre, E., Aubin, H.J., & Anton, G. (1990). Behavioral effects induced by beta CCE in free or restrained rhesus monkeys (*Macaca mulatta*). *Pharmacology Biochemistry & Behavior, 35,* 713–719. (13)

Laguzzi, R.F., & Adrien, J. (1980). Inversion de l'insomnie produite par la parachlorophenylalanine chez le rat [Relief from insomnia produced by parachlorophenylalanine in the rat]. *Archives Italiennes de Biologie, 118,* 109–123. (10)

LaHoste, G.J., & Marshall, J.F. (1989). Non-additivity of $D_2$ receptor proliferation induced by dopamine denervation and chronic selective antagonist administration: Evidence from quantitative autoradiography indicates a single mechanism of action. *Brain Research, 502,* 223–232. (15)

LaMantia, A.-S., & Purves, D. (1989). Development of glomerular pattern visualized in the olfactory bulbs of living mice. *Nature, 341,* 646–649. (8)

Lamb, M.E. (1975). Physiological mechanisms in the control of maternal behavior in rats: A review. *Psychological Review, 82,* 104–119. (12)

Lamb, T.D., & Pugh, E.N., Jr. (1990). Physiology of transduction and adaptation in rod and cone photoreceptors. *Seminars in the Neurosciences, 2,* 3–13. (4)

LaMotte, C.C., & Collins, W.F. (1982). Physiological anatomy of pain. In J.R. Youmans (Ed.), *Neurological surgery* (2nd ed.) (Vol. 6, pp. 3461–3479). Philadelphia: Saunders. (6)

Land, E.H., Hubel, D.H., Livingstone, M.S., Perry, S.H., & Burns, M.M. (1983). Colour-generating interactions across the corpus callosum. *Nature, 303,* 616–618. (7)

Land, E.H., & McCann, J.J. (1971). Lightness and retinex theory. *Journal of the Optical Society of America, 61,* 1–11. (7)

Landrigan, P.J., Powell, K.E., James, L.M., & Taylor, P.R. (1983). Paraquat and marijuana: Epidemiologic risk assessment. *American Journal of Public Health, 73,* 784–788. (9)

Lang, R.A., Flor-Henry, P., & Frenzel, R.R. (1990). Sex hormone profiles in pedophilic and incestuous men. *Archives of Sex Research, 3,* 59–74. (12)

Langston, J.W., Irwin, I., Langston, E.B., & Forno, L.S. (1984). Pargyline prevents MPTP-induced Parkinsonism in primates. *Science, 225,* 1480–1482. (9)

Lansdell, H. (1969). Verbal and nonverbal factors in right-hemisphere speech: Relation to early neurological history. *Journal of Comparative and Physiological Psychology, 69,* 734–738. (5)

Lashley, K.S. (1929). Brain mechanisms and intelligence. Chicago: University of Chicago Press. (4, 14)

Lashley, K.S. (1930). Basic neural mechanisms in behavior. *Psychological Review, 37*, 1–24. (inside cover)

Lashley, K.S. (1950). In search of the engram. *Symposia of the Society for Experimental Biology, 4*, 454–482. (14)

Lassonde, M., Bryden, M.P., & Demers, P. (1990). The corpus callosum and cerebral speech lateralization. *Brain and Language, 38*, 195–206. (5)

Laudenslager, M.L. (1976). Proportional hypothalamic control of behavioral thermoregulation in the squirrel monkey. *Physiology & Behavior, 17*, 383–390. (11)

Laurent, J.-P., Cespuglio, R., & Jouvet, M. (1974). Délimitation des voies ascendantes de l'activité ponto-géniculo-occipitale chez le chat [Demarcation of the ascending paths of ponto-geniculo-occipital activity in the cat]. *Brain Research, 65*, 29–52. (10)

Lavau, M., Fornari, V., & Hashim, S.A. (1978). Ketone metabolism in brain slices from rats with diet induced hyperketonemia. *Journal of Nutrition, 108*, 621–639. (2)

Ledwidge, B. (1980). Run for your mind: Aerobic exercise as a means of alleviating anxiety and depression. *Canadian Journal of Behavioral Science, 12*, 126–140. (13)

Lee, M.K., Graham, S.N., & Gold, P.E. (1988). Memory enhancement with post-training intraventricular glucose injections in rats. *Behavioral Neuroscience, 102*, 591–595. (14)

Leehy, S.C., Moskowitz-Cook, A., Brill, S., & Held, R. (1975). Orientational anisotropy in infant vision. *Science, 190*, 900–902. (8)

Lehrman, D.S. (1964). The reproductive behavior of ring doves. *Scientific American, 211*(5), 48–54. (12)

Leibowitz, S.F., Weiss, G.F., Walsh, U.A., & Viswanath, D. (1989). Medial hypothalamic serotonin: Role in circadian patterns of feeding and macronutrient selection. *Brain Research, 503*, 132–140. (11)

Leiner, H.C., Leiner, A.L., & Dow, R.S. (1986). Does the cerebellum contribute to mental skills? *Behavioral Neuroscience, 100*, 443–454. (9)

Leiner, H.C., Leiner, A.L., & Dow, R.S. (1989). Reappraising the cerebellum: What does the hindbrain contribute to the forebrain? *Behavioral Neuroscience, 103*, 998–1008. (4)

Lelord, G., Muh, J.P., Barthelemy, C., Martineau, J., & Garreau, B. (1981). Effects of pyridoxine and magnesium on autistic symptoms—initial observations. *Journal of Autism and Developmental Disorders, 11*, 219–230. (16)

LeMagnen, J. (1981). The metabolic basis of dual periodicity of feeding in rats. *Behavioral and Brain Sciences, 4*, 561–607. (11)

Lenhart, R.E., & Katkin, E.S. (1986). Psychophysiological evidence for cerebral laterality effects in a high-risk sample of students with subsyndromal bipolar depressive disorder. *American Journal of Psychiatry, 143*, 602–607. (16)

Lentz, T.L., Burrage, T.G., Smith, A.L., Crick, J., & Tignor, G.H. (1981). Is the acetylcholine receptor a rabies virus receptor? *Science, 215*, 182–184. (13)

Leonard, H.L., Swedo, S.E., Rapoport, J.L., Koby, E.V., Lenane, M.C., Cheslow, D.L., & Hamburger, S.D. (1989). Treatment of obsessive-compulsive disorder with clomipramine and desipramine in children and adolescents. *Archives of General Psychiatry, 46*, 1088–1092. (13)

Lerer, B., & Shapira, B. (1986). Neurochemical mechanisms of mood stabilization. *Annals of the New York Academy of Sciences, 462*, 367–375. (16)

Lesse, S. (1984). Psychosurgery. *American Journal of Psychotherapy, 38*, 224–228. (4)

Lester, L.S., & Fanselow, M.S. (1985). Exposure to a cat produces opioid analgesia in rats. *Behavioral Neuroscience, 99*, 756–759. (6)

Lettvin, J.Y., Maturana, H.R., McCulloch, W.S., & Pitts, W.H. (1959). What the frog's eye tells the frog's brain. *Proceedings of the Institute of Radio Engineers, 47*, 1940–1951. (6)

LeVay, S., Stryker, M.P., & Shatz, C.J. (1978). Ocular dominance columns and their development in layer IV of the cat's visual cortex: A quantitative study. *Journal of Comparative Neurology, 179*, 223–244. (8)

Levenson, R.W., Oyama, O.N., & Meek, P.S. (1987). Greater reinforcement from alcohol for those at risk: Parental risk, personality risk, and sex. *Journal of Abnormal Psychology, 96*, 242–253. (3)

Leventhal, A.G., & Hirsch, H.V.B. (1975). Cortical effect of early selective exposure to diagonal lines. *Science, 190*, 902–904. (8)

LeVere, N.D., & LeVere, T.E. (1982). Recovery of function after brain damage: Support for the compensation theory of the behavioral deficit. *Physiological Psychology, 10*, 165–174. (15)

LeVere, T.E. (1975). Neural stability, sparing and behavioral recovery following brain damage. *Psychological Review, 82*, 344–358. (15)

LeVere, T.E. (1980). Recovery of function after brain damage: A theory of the behavioral deficit. *Physiological Psychology, 8*, 297–308. (15)

LeVere, T.E., Brugler, T., Sandin, M., & Gray-Silva, S. (1989). Recovery of function after brain damage: Facilitation by the calcium entry blocker nimodipine. *Behavioral Neuroscience, 103*, 561–565. (15)

LeVere, T.E., & Morlock, G.W. (1973). Nature of visual recovery following posterior neodecortication in the hooded rat. *Journal of Comparative and Physiological Psychology, 83*, 62–67. (15)

Levi-Montalcini, R. (1987). The nerve growth factor 35 years later. *Science, 237*, 1154–1162. (8)

Levine, D.N., Warach, J.D., Benowitz, L., & Calvanio, R. (1986). Left spatial neglect: Effects of lesion size and premorbid brain atrophy on severity and recovery following right cerebral infarction. *Neurology, 36*, 362–366. (4)

Levine, J.S., & MacNichol, E.F., Jr. (1982). Color vision in fishes. *Scientific American, 246*(2), 140–149. (7)

Levitt, R.A. (1975). *Psychopharmacology.* Washington, DC: Hemisphere. (3)

Levitt-Gilmour, T.A., & Salpeter, M.M. (1986). Gradient of extrajunctional

acetylcholine receptors early after denervation of mammalian muscle. *Journal of Neuroscience, 6*, 1606–1612. (15)

Levitzki, A. (1988). From epinephrine to cyclic AMP. *Science, 241*, 800–806. (3)

Levy, J. (1982). Handwriting posture and cerebral organization: How are they related? *Psychological Bulletin, 91*, 589–608. (5)

Levy, J. (1983). Language, cognition, and the right hemisphere: A response to Gazzaniga. *American Psychologist, 38*, 538–541. (5)

Levy, J., Nebes, R.D., & Sperry, R.W. (1971). Expressive language in the surgically separated minor hemisphere. *Cortex, 7*, 49–58. (5)

Levy, R.M., Bredesen, D.E., & Rosenblum, M.L. (1985). Neurological manifestations of the acquired immunodeficiency syndrome (AIDS): Experience at UCSF and review of the literature. *Journal of Neurosurgery, 62*, 475–495. (16)

Levy-Agresti, J., & Sperry, R.W. (1968). Differential perceptual capacities in major and minor hemispheres. *Proceedings of the National Academy of Sciences U.S.A., 61*, 1151. (5)

Lewine, R.R.J. (1981). Sex differences in schizophrenia: Timing or subtypes? *Psychological Bulletin, 90*, 432–444. (16)

Lewis, D.J. (1979). Psychobiology of active and inactive memory. *Psychological Bulletin, 86*, 1054–1083. (14)

Lewis, D.J., Bregman, N.J., & Mahan, J.J., Jr. (1972). Cue-dependent amnesia in rats. *Journal of Comparative and Physiological Psychology, 81*, 243–247. (14)

Lewis, E.R., Everhart, T.E., & Zeevi, Y.Y. (1969). Studying neural organization in *Aplysia* with the scanning electron microscope. *Science, 165*, 1140–1143. (3)

Lewis, V.G., Money, J., & Epstein, R. (1968). Concordance of verbal and nonverbal ability in the adrenogenital syndrome. *Johns Hopkins Medical Journal, 122*, 192–195. (12)

Lewy, A.J., Nurnberger, J.I., Jr., Wehr, T.A., Pack, D., Becker, L.E., Powell, R.-L., Newsome, D.A. (1985). Supersensitivity to light: Possible trait marker for manic-depressive illness. *American Journal of Psychiatry, 142*, 725–727. (16)

Lewy, A.J., Sack, R.L., Miller, S., & Hoben, T.M. (1987). Antidepressant and circadian phase-shifting effects of light. *Science, 235*, 352–354. (16)

Liebeskind, J.C., & Paul, L.A. (1977). Psychological and physiological mechanisms of pain. *Annual Review of Psychology, 28*, 41–60. (6)

Liebowitz, M.R., Gorman, J.M., Fyer, A.J., Levitt, M., Dillon, D., Levy, G., Appleby, I.L., Anderson, S., Palij, M., Davies, S.O., & Klein, D.F. (1985). Lactate provocation of panic attacks: II. Biochemical and physiological findings. *Archives of General Psychiatry, 42*, 709–719. (13)

Lilienfeld, A. (1969). *Epidemiology of mongolism.* Baltimore, MD: Johns Hopkins University Press.

Lindberg, N.O., Coburn, C., & Stricker, E.M. (1984). Increased feeding by rats after subdiabetogenic streptozotocin treatment: A role for insulin in satiety. *Behavioral Neuroscience, 98*, 138–145. (11)

Lindsay, P.H., & Norman, D.A. (1972). *Hu-Human information processing*. New York: Academic Press. (6)

Lindstrom, J. (1979). Autoimmune response to acetylcholine receptors in myasthenia gravis and its animal model. *Advances in Immunology, 27*, 1–50. (3, 9)

Lindvall, O., Rehncrona, S., Brundin, P., Gustavii, B., Åstedt, B., Widner, H., Lindholm, T., Björklund, A., Leenders, K.L., Rothwell, J.C., Frackowiak, R., Marsden, D., Johnels, B., Steg, G., Freedman, R., Hoffer, B.J., Seiger, A., Bygdeman, M., Strömberg, I., & Olsen, L. (1989). Human fetal dopamine neurons grafted into the striatum in two patients with severe Parkinson's disease. *Archives of Neurology, 46*, 615–631. (15)

Lipton, M.A., Breese, G.R., Prange, A.J., Jr., Wilson, I.C., & Cooper, B.R. (1976). Behavioral effects of hypothalamic polypeptide hormones in animals and man. In E.J. Sachar (Ed.), *Hormones, behavior, and psychopathology* (pp. 15–29). New York: Raven. (16)

Lipton, M.A., & Nemeroff, C.B. (1978). An overview of the biogenic amine hypothesis of schizophrenia. In W.E. Fann, I. Karacan, A. Pokorny, & R.L. Williams (Eds.), *Phenomenology and treatment of schizophrenia* (pp. 431–453). New York: Spectrum. (16)

Liuzzi, F.J., & Lasek, R.J. (1987). Astrocytes block axonal regeneration in mammals by activating the physiological stop pathway. *Science, 237*, 642–645. (15)

Livingstone, M.S. (1988, January). Art, illusion and the visual system. *Scientific American, 258*(1), 78–85. (7)

Livingstone, M.S., & Hubel, D. (1988). Segregation of form, color, movement, and depth: Anatomy, physiology, and perception. *Science, 240*, 740–749. (7)

Llinás, R.R. (1975, January). The cortex of the cerebellum. *Scientific American, 232*(1), 56–71. (9)

Loewenstein, W.R. (1960, August). Biological transducers. *Scientific American, 203*(2), 98–108. (6)

Loewi, O. (1960). An autobiographical sketch. *Perspectives in Biology, 4*, 3–25. (3)

London, E.D., Cascella, N.G., Wong, D.F., Phillips, R.L., Dannals, R.F., Links, J.M., Herning, R., Grayson, R., Jaffe, J.H., & Wagner, H.N. (1990). Cocaine-induced reduction of glucose utilization in human brain. *Archives of General Psychiatry, 47*, 567–574. (3)

Lowe, J., & Carroll, D. (1985). The effects of spinal injury on the intensity of emotional experience. *British Journal of Clinical Psychology, 24*, 135–136. (13)

Lowing, P.A., Mirsky, A.F., & Pereira, R. (1983). The inheritance of schizophrenia spectrum disorders: A reanalysis of the Danish adoptee study plan. *American Journal of Psychiatry, 140*, 1167–1171. (16)

Luchins, D.J., Lewine, R.R.J., & Meltzer, H.Y. (1984). Lateral ventricular size, psychopathology, and medication response in the psychoses. *Biological Psychiatry, 19*, 29–44. (16)

Lydic, R., McCarley, R.W., & Hobson, J.A. (1987). Serotonin neurons and sleep: II. Time course of dorsal raphe discharge, PGO waves, and behavioral states.

*Archives Italiennes de Biologie, 126*, 1–28. (10)

Lyman, C.P., O'Brien, R.C., Greene, G.C., & Papafrangos, E.D. (1981). Hibernation and longevity in the Turkish hamster *Mesocricetus brandti*. *Science, 212*, 668–670. (10)

Lynch, G., & Baudry, M. (1984). The biochemistry of memory: A new and specific hypothesis. *Science, 224*, 1057–1063. (14)

Lynch, G., & Baudry, M. (1991). Reevaluating the constraints on hypotheses regarding LTP expression. *Hippocampus, 1*, 9–14. (14)

Lynch, J.A., & Aserinsky, E. (1986). Developmental changes of oculomotor characteristics in infants when awake and in the "active state of sleep." *Behavioural Brain Research, 20*, 175–183. (10)

Lynch, J.C. (1980). The functional organization of posterior parietal association cortex. *The Behavioral and Brain Sciences, 3*, 485–534. (4)

Lynch, J.C. (1989). Columnar organization of the cerebral cortex (cortical columns). In G. Adelman (Ed.), *Neuroscience Year* (pp. 37–40). Boston: Birkhäuser. (7)

Lytle, L.D., Messing, R.B., Fisher, L., & Phebus, L. (1975). Effects of long-term corn consumption on brain serotonin and the response to electric shock. *Science, 190*, 692–694. (13)

Maccoby, E.E., & Jacklin, C.N. (1974). *The psychology of sex differences*. Stanford, CA: Stanford University Press. (12)

Macdonald, R.L., Weddle, M.G., & Gross, R.A. (1986). Benzodiazepine, β-carboline, and barbiturate actions on GABA responses. *Advances in Biochemical Psychopharmacology, 41*, 67–78. (13)

MacFarlane, J.G., Cleghorn, J.M., & Brown, G.M. (1985a). Melatonin and core temperature rhythms in chronic insomnia. In G.M. Brown & S.D. Wainwright (Eds.), *The pineal gland: Endocrine aspects* (pp. 301–306). New York: Pergamon. (10)

MacFarlane, J.G., Cleghorn, J.M., & Brown, G.M. (1985b, September). *Circadian rhythms in chronic insomnia*. Paper presented at the 4th World Congress of Biological Psychiatry, Philadelphia. (10)

MacLean, P.D. (1949). Psychosomatic disease and the "visceral brain": Recent developments bearing on the Papez theory of emotion. *Psychosomatic Medicine, 11*, 338–353. (13)

MacLean, P.D. (1954). Studies on limbic system ("visceral brain") and their bearing on psychosomatic problems. In E.D. Wittkower & R.A. Cleghorn (Eds.), *Recent developments in psychosomatic medicine* (pp. 101–125). Philadelphia: Lippincott. (13)

MacLean, P.D. (1958). Contrasting functions of limbic and neocortical systems of the brain and their relevance to psychophysiological aspects of medicine. *American Journal of Medicine, 25*, 611–626. (13)

MacLean, P.D. (1962). Neurophysiologie. In *Monoamines et système nerveux central* (pp. 269–276). Geneva: Georg a Cie, 1962. (16)

MacLean, P.D. (1970). The limbic brain in relation to the psychoses. In P. Black (Ed.), *Physiological correlates of emotion* (pp. 129–146). New York: Academic Press. (13)

MacLusky, N.J., & Naftolin, F. (1981). Sexual differentiation of the central nervous system. *Science, 211*, 1294–1303. (12)

MacPhail, E.M. (1985). Vertebrate intelligence: The null hypothesis. *Philosophical Transactions of the Royal Society of London, B, 308*, 37–51. (4)

Maffei, L., & Fiorentini, A. (1973). The visual cortex as a spatial frequency analyser. *Vision Research, 13*, 1255–1267. (7)

Mahowald, M.W., & Schenck, C.H. (1989). Narcolepsy. In G. Adelman (Ed.), *Neuroscience year* (pp. 114–116). Boston: Birkhäuser. (10)

Maier, S.F., Seligman, M.E.P., & Solomon, R.L. (1969). Pavlovian fear conditioning and learned helplessness: Effects on escape and avoidance behavior of (a) the CS-US contingency and (b) the independence of the US and voluntary responding. In B.A. Campbell & R.M. Church (Eds.), *Punishment and aversive behavior* (pp. 299–342). New York: Appleton-Century-Crofts. (16)

Maier, S.F., Sherman, J.E., Lewis, J.W., Terman, G.W., & Liebeskind, J.C. (1983). The opioid/nonopioid nature of stress-induced analgesia and learned helplessness. *Journal of Experimental Psychology: Animal Behavior Processes, 9*, 80–90. (6)

Majewska, M.D., Harrison, N.L., Schwartz, R.D., Barker, J.L., & Paul, S.M. (1986). Steroid hormone metabolites are barbiturate-like modulators of the GABA receptors. *Science, 232*, 1004–1007. (13)

Malamut, B.L., Saunders, R.C., & Mishkin, M. (1984). Monkeys with combined amygdalo-hippocampal lesions succeed in object discrimination learning despite 24-hour intertrial intervals. *Behavioral Neuroscience, 98*, 759–769. (14)

Malcuit, G. (1973). Cardiac responses in aversive situation with and without avoidance possibility. *Psychophysiology, 10*, 295–306. (13)

Malenka, R.C., Kauer, J.A., Zucker, R.S., & Nicoll, R.A. (1988). Postsynaptic calcium is sufficient for potentiation of hippocampal synaptic transmission. *Science, 242*, 81–83. (14)

Malenka, R.C., Madison, D.V., & Nicholl, R.A. (1986). Potentiation of synaptic transmission in the hippocampus by phorbol esters. *Nature, 321*, 175–177. (14)

Maletzky, B.M. (1973). The episodic dyscontrol syndrome. *Diseases of the Nervous System, 34*, 178–185. (13)

Malinow, R., Schulman, H., & Tsien, R.W. (1989). Inhibition of postsynaptic PKC or Ca MKII blocks induction but not expression of LTP. *Science, 245*, 862–866. (14)

Mangiapane, M.L., & Simpson, J.B. (1980). Subfornical organ: Forebrain site of pressor and dipsogenic action of angiotensin II. *American Journal of Physiology, 239*, R382–R389. (11)

Mangiapane, M.L., Thrasher, T.N., Keil, L.C., Simpson, J.B., & Ganong, W.F.

(1983). Deficits in drinking and vasopressin secretion after lesions of the nucleus medianus. *Neuroendocrinology, 37,* 73–77. (11)

Mann, J.J., Arango, V., & Underwood, M.D. (1990). Serotonin and suicidal behavior. *Annals of the New York Academy of Sciences, 600,* 476–485. (13)

Mann, J.J., Stanley, M., McBride, A., & McEwen, B.S. (1986). Increased serotonin₂ and $\beta$-adrenergic receptor binding in the frontal cortices of suicide victims. *Archives of General Psychiatry, 43,* 954–959. (13)

Marcus, J., Hans, S.L., Mednick, S.A., Schulsinger, F., & Michelsen, N. (1985). Neurological dysfunctioning in offspring of schizophrenics in Israel and Denmark. *Archives of General Psychiatry, 42,* 753–761. (16)

Mark, V.H., & Ervin, F.R. (1970). *Violence and the brain.* New York: Harper & Row. (13)

Marler, J.R., Price, T.R., Clark, G.L., Muller, J.E., Robertson, T., Mohr, J.P., Hier, D.B., Wolf, P.A., Caplan, L.R., & Foulkes, M.A. (1989). Morning increase in onset of ischemic stroke. *Stroke, 20,* 473–476. (15)

Marler, P. (1970). A comparative approach to vocal learning: Song development in white-crowned sparrows. *Journal of Comparative and Physiogical Psychology, 71* (No. 2, Pt. 2), 1–25. (1)

Marler, P., & Peters, S. (1977). Selective vocal learning in a sparrow. *Science, 198,* 519–521. (1)

Marler, P., & Peters, S. (1981). Sparrows learn adult song and more from memory. *Science, 213,* 780–782. (1)

Marler, P., & Peters, S. (1982). Long-term storage of learned birdsongs prior to production. *Animal Behaviour, 30,* 479–482. (1)

Marler, P., & Peters, S. (1987). A sensitive period for song acquisition in the song sparrow, *Melospiza melodia:* A case of age-limited learning. *Ethology, 76,* 89–100. (1)

Marler, P., & Peters, S. (1988). Sensitive periods for song acquisition from tape recordings and live tutors in the swamp sparrow, *Melospiza georgiana. Ethology, 77,* 76–84. (1)

Marques, P.R., Spencer, R.L., Burks, T.F., & McDougal, J.N. (1984). Behavioral thermoregulation, core temperature, and motor activity: Simultaneous quantitative assessment in rats after dopamine and prostaglandin E1. *Behavioral Neuroscience, 98,* 858–867. (11)

Marsden, C.D. (1984). Motor disorders in basal ganglia disease. *Human Neurobiology, 2,* 245–250. (9)

Marshall, J.C., & Halligan, P.W. (1990). Line bisection in a case of visual neglect: Psychophysical studies with implications for theory. *Cognitive Neuropsychology, 7,* 107–130. (4)

Marshall, J.F. (1985). Neural plasticity and recovery of function after brain injury. *International Review of Neurobiology, 26,* 201–247. (15)

Marshall, J.F., Drew, M.C., & Neve, K.A. (1983). Recovery of function after mesotelencephalic dopaminergic injury

in senescence. *Brain Research, 259,* 249–260. (15)

Marshall, J.F., & Teitelbaum, P. (1974). Further analysis of sensory inattention following lateral hypothalamic damage in rats. *Journal of Comparative and Physiological Psychology, 86,* 375–395. (11)

Martin, A.R. (1977). Junctional transmission. II. Presynaptic mechanisms. In E.R. Kandel (Ed.), *Handbook of physiology* (Sect. 1, Vol. 1, Pt. 1, pp. 329–355). Bethesda, MD: American Physiological Society. (3)

Martin, J.V., Cook, J.M., Hagen, T.J., & Mendelson, W.B. (1989). Inhibition of sleep and benzodiazepine receptor binding by a beta-carboline derivative. *Pharmacology Biochemistry & Behavior, 34,* 37–42. (13)

Martin, R.C., & Blossom-Stach, C. (1986). Evidence of syntactic deficits in a fluent aphasic. *Brain and Language, 28,* 196–234. (5)

Martinez, J.L., Jr., Jensen, R.A., & McGaugh, J.L. (1981). Attenuation of experimentally induced amnesia. *Progress in Neurobiology, 16,* 155–186. (14)

Martinez-Vargas, M.C., & Erickson, C.J. (1973). Some social and hormonal determinants of nest-building behaviour in the ring dove (*Streptopelia risoria*). *Behaviour, 45,* 12–37. (12)

Mash, D.C., Flynn, D.D., & Potter, L.T. (1985). Loss of M2 muscarine receptors in the cerebral cortex in Alzheimer's disease and experimental cholinergic denervation. *Science, 228,* 1115–1117. (14)

Masterton, R.B. (1974). Adaptation for sound localization in the ear and brainstem of mammals. *Federation Proceedings, 33,* 1904–1910. (6)

Matheis, M., & Förster, C. (1980). Zur psychosexuellen Entwicklung von Mädchen mit adrenogenitalem Syndrom [On the psychosexual development of girls with adrenogenital syndrome]. *Zeitschrift für Kinder- und Jugend-Psychiatrie, 8,* 5–17. (12)

Mathew, R.J., Wilson, W.H., Tant, S.R., Robinson, L., & Prakash, R. (1988). Abnormal resting regional cerebral blood flow patterns and their correlates in schizophrenia. *Archives of General Psychiatry, 45,* 542–549. (16)

Matossian, M.K. (1982). Ergot and the Salem witchcraft affair. *American Scientist, 70,* 355–357. (3)

Matsuda, L.A., Lolait, S.J., Brownstein, M.J., Young, A.C., & Bonner, T.I. (1990). Structure of a cannabinoid receptor and functional expression of the cloned cDNA. *Nature, 346,* 561–564. (3)

Mattes, R.D. (1988). Blocking learned food aversions in cancer patients receiving chemotherapy. *Annals of the New York Academy of Sciences, 510,* 478–479. (11)

Matthews, D.A., Cotman, C., & Lynch, G. (1976). An electron microscopic study of lesion-induced synaptogenesis in the dentate gyrus of the adult rat. II. Reappearance of morphologically normal synaptic contacts. *Brain Research, 115,* 23–41. (15)

Mawson, A.R., & Jacobs, K.W. (1978). Corn, tryptophan, and homicide. *Journal of Orthomolecular Psychiatry, 7,* 227–230. (13)

May, P.R.A., Fuster, J.M., Haber, J., & Hirschman, A. (1979). Woodpecker drilling behavior: An endorsement of the rotational theory of impact brain injury. *Archives of Neurology, 36,* 370–373. (15)

Mayer, A.D., & Rosenblatt, J.S. (1979). Hormonal influences during the ontogeny of maternal behavior in female rats. *Journal of Comparative and Physiological Psychology, 93,* 879–898. (12)

Mayer, A.D., & Rosenblatt, J.S. (1984). Postpartum changes in maternal responsiveness and nest defense in *Rattus norvegicus. Journal of Comparative Psychology, 98,* 177–188. (12)

Mayer, J. (1953). Glucostatic mechanism of regulation of food intake. *New England Journal of Medicine, 249,* 13–16. (11)

Mayer, W., & Scherer, I. (1975). Phase shifting effect of caffeine in the circadian rhythm of *Phaseolus coccineus* L. *Zeitschrift für Naturforschung, C, 30,* 855–856. (10)

McCarley, R.W., & Hobson, J.A. (1977). The neurobiological origins of psychoanalytic dream theory. *American Journal of Psychiatry, 134,* 1211–1221. (10)

McCarley, R.W., & Hoffman, E. (1981). REM sleep, dreams, and the activation-synthesis hypothesis. *American Journal of Psychiatry, 138,* 904–912. (10)

McConnell, J.V. (1962). Memory transfer through cannibalism in planarians. *Journal of Neuropsychiatry, 3* (Suppl. 1), 42–48. (14)

McConnell, S.K., Ghosh, A., & Shatz, C.J. (1989). Subplate neurons pioneer the first axon pathway from the cerebral cortex. *Science, 245,* 978–982. (8)

McCormick, D.A. (1989). Acetylcholine: Distribution, receptors, and actions. *Seminars in the Neurosciences, 1,* 91–101. (3)

McCormick, D.A., & Thompson, R.F. (1984). Cerebellum: Essential involvement in the classically conditioned eyelid response. *Science, 223,* 296–299. (14)

McEwen, B.S., & Pfaff, D.W. (1985). Hormone effects on hypothalamic neurons: Analysing gene expression and neuromodulator action. *Trends in Neurosciences, 8,* 105–110. (12)

McGaugh, J.L. (1990). Significance and remembrance: The role of neuromodulatory systems. *Psychological Science, 1,* 15–25. (14)

McGlynn, S.M. (1990). Behavioral approaches to neuropsychological rehabilitation. *Psychological Bulletin, 108,* 420–441. (15)

McGuffin, P., Farmer, A.E., Gottesman, I.I., Murray, R.M., & Reveley, A.M. (1984). Twin concordance for operationally defined schizophrenia. *Archives of General Psychiatry, 41,* 541–545. (16)

McHugh, P.R. (1989). The neuropsychology of basal ganglia disorders. *Neuropsychiatry, Neuropsychology, and Behavioral Neurology, 2,* 239–247. (9)

McHugh, P.R., & Moran, T.H. (1985). The stomach: A conception of its dynamic role in satiety. *Progress in Psychobiology and Physiological Psychology, 11,* 197–232. (11)

McKinnon, W., Weisse, C.S., Reynolds, C.P., Bowles, C.A., & Baum, A. (1989). Chronic stress, leukocyte-subpopulations, and humoral response to latent viruses. *Health Psychology, 8,* 389–402. (13)

McLean, S., Skirboll, L.R., & Pert, C.B. (1985). Comparison of substance P and enkephalin distribution in rat brain: An overview using radioimmunocytochemistry. *Neuroscience, 14,* 837–852. (6)

McLeod, P.J., & Brown, R.E. (1988). The effects of prenatal stress and postweaning housing conditions on parental and sexual behavior of male Long-Evans rats. *Psychobiology, 16,* 372–380. (12)

McMahon, C.E. (1975). The wind of the cannon ball: An informative anecdote from medical history. *Psychotherapy & Psychosomatics, 26,* 125–131. (13)

McMasters, R.E. (1962). Regeneration of the spinal cord in the rat: Effects of Piromen and ACTH upon the regenerative capacity. *Journal of Comparative Neurology, 119,* 113–121. (15)

McMinn, M.R. (1984). Mechanisms of energy balance in obesity. *Behavioral Neuroscience, 98,* 375–393. (11)

McWilliams, J.R., & Lynch, G. (1983). Rate of synaptic replacement in denervated rat hippocampus declines precipitously from the juvenile period to adulthood. *Science, 221,* 572–574. (15)

McWilliams, J.R., & Lynch, G. (1984). Synaptic density and axonal sprouting in rat hippocampus: Stability in adulthood and decline in late adulthood. *Brain Research, 294,* 152–156. (15)

Meagher, M.W., Grau, J.W., & King, R.A. (1990). Role of supraspinal systems in environmentally induced antinociception: Effect of spinalization and decerebration on brief shock-induced and long shock-induced antinociception. *Behavioral Neuroscience, 104,* 328–338. (6)

Meddis, R. (1979). The evolution and function of sleep. In D.A. Oakley & H.C. Plotkin (Eds.), *Brain, behaviour and evolution* (pp. 99–125). London: Methuen. (10)

Meddis, R., Pearson, A.J.D., & Langford, G. (1973). An extreme case of healthy insomnia. *EEG and Clinical Neurophysiology, 35,* 213–214. (10)

Mednick, S.A., Machon, R.A., & Huttunen, M.O. (1990). An update on the Helsinki influenza project. *Archives of General Psychiatry, 47,* 292. (16)

Meehl, P.E. (1989). Schizotaxia revisited. *Archives of General Psychiatry, 46,* 935–944. (16)

Meisami, E. (1978). Influence of early anosmia on the developing olfactory bulb. *Progress in Brain Research, 48,* 211–230. (8)

Meisel, R.L., Dohanich, G.P., & Ward, I.L. (1979). Effects of prenatal stress on avoidance acquisition, open-field performance and lordotic behavior in male rats. *Physiology & Behavior, 22,* 527–530. (12)

Meisel, R.L., & Ward, I.L. (1981). Fetal female rats are masculinized by male littermates located caudally in the uterus. *Science, 213,* 239–242. (12)

Melzack, R., & Wall, P.D. (1965). Pain mechanisms: A new theory. *Science, 150,* 971–979. (6)

Merton, P.A. (1972). How we control the contraction of our muscles. *Scientific American, 226*(5), 30–37. (9)

Merzenich, M.M., Nelson, R.J., Stryker, M.P., Cynader, M.S., Schoppman, A., & Zook, J.M. (1984). Somatosensory cortical map changes following digit amputation in adult monkeys. *Journal of Comparative Neurology, 224,* 591–605. (15)

Messing, R.B., & Sparber, S.B. (1985). Greater task difficulty amplifies the facilitatory effect of des-glycinamide arginine vasopressin on appetitively motivated learning. *Behavioral Neuroscience, 99,* 1114–1119. (14)

Meyer, J.S., Ishikawa, Y., Hata, T., & Karacan, I. (1987). Cerebral blood flow in normal and abnormal sleep and dreaming. *Brain and Cognition, 6,* 266–294. (10)

Michael, R.P., Zumpe, D., & Bonsall, R.W. (1984). Sexual behavior correlates with the diurnal plasma testosterone range in intact male rhesus monkeys. *Biology of Reproduction, 30,* 652–657. (12)

Michael, R.P., Zumpe, D., & Bonsall, R.W. (1990). Estradiol administration and the sexual activity of castrated male rhesus monkeys (*Macaca mulatta*). *Hormones and Behavior, 24,* 71–88. (12)

Miczek, K.A., Thompson, M.L., & Shuster, L. (1986). Analgesia following defeat in an aggressive encounter: Development of tolerance and changes in opioid receptors. *Annals of the New York Academy of Sciences, 467,* 14–29. (6)

Miles, F.A., & Evarts, E.V. (1979). Concepts of motor organization. *Annual Review of Psychology, 30,* 327–362. (9)

Miles, L.E.M., Raynal, D.M., & Wilson, M.A. (1977). Blind man living in normal society has circadian rhythms of 24.9 hours. *Science, 198,* 421–423. (10)

Miller, E.A., Goldman, P.S., & Rosvold, H.E. (1973). Delayed recovery of function following orbital prefrontal lesions in infant monkeys. *Science, 182,* 304–306. (15)

Miller, E.H. (1982). Character and variance shift in acoustic signals of birds. In D.E. Kroodsma & E.H. Miller (Eds.), *Acoustic communication in birds,* (Vol. 1, pp. 253–295). New York: Academic Press. (1)

Miller, K.W. (1985). The nature of the site of general anesthesia. *International Review of Neurobiology, 27,* 1–61. (2)

Miller, M.J., Small, I.F., Milstein, V., Malloy, F., & Stout, J.R. (1981). Electrode placement and cognitive change with ECT: Male and female response. *American Journal of Psychiatry, 138,* 384–386. (16)

Miller, N.E. (1985). The value of behavioral research on animals. *American Psychologist, 40,* 423–440. (1)

Miller, N.E., Bailey, C.J., & Stevenson, J.A.F. (1950). Decreased "hunger" but increased food intake resulting from hypothalamic lesions. *Science, 112,* 256–259. (11)

Miller, W.C., & DeLong, M.R. (1988). Parkinsonian symptomatology: An anatomical and physiological analysis. *Annals of the New York Academy of Sciences, 515,* 287–302. (9)

Millhorn, D.E., Bayliss, D.A., Erickson, J.T., Gallman, E.A., Szymeczek, C.L., Czyzyk-Krzeska, M., & Dean, J.B. (1989). Cellular and molecular mecha-

nisms of chemical synaptic transmission. *American Journal of Physiology, 257*(6 Part 1), L289–L310. (3)

Milner, B. (1959). The memory defect in bilateral hippocampal lesions. *Psychiatric Research Reports, 11,* 43–58. (14)

Miselis, R.R., Shapiro, R.E., & Hand, P.J. (1979). Subfornical organ efferents to neural systems for control of body water. *Science, 205,* 1022–1025. (11)

Mishkin, M., & Manning, F.J. (1978). Nonspatial memory after selective prefrontal lesions in monkeys. *Brain Research, 143,* 313–323. (14)

Mitchell, D.E. (1980). The influence of early visual experience on visual perception. In C.S. Harris (Ed.), *Visual coding and adaptability* (pp. 1–50). Hillsdale, NJ: Erlbaum. (8)

Mitchell, J.E., & Popkin, M.K. (1982). Antipsychotic drug therapy and sexual dysfunction in men. *American Journal of Psychiatry, 139,* 633–637. (16)

Mohr, J.P., Weiss, G.H., Caveness, W.F., Dillon, J.D., Kistler, J.P., Meirowsky, A.M., & Rish, B.L. (1980). Language and motor disorders after penetrating head injury in Viet Nam. *Neurology, 30,* 1273–1279. (5)

Mohs, R.C., Breitner, J.C.S., Silverman, J.M., & Davis, K.L. (1987). Alzheimer's disease: Morbid risk among first-degree relatives approximates 50% by 90 years of age. *Archives of General Psychiatry, 44,* 405–408. (14)

Moltz, H., Lubin, M., Leon, M., & Numan, M. (1970). Hormonal induction of maternal behavior in the ovariectomized nulliparous rat. *Physiology & Behavior, 5,* 1373–1377. (12)

Money, J. (1967). Sexual problems of the chronically ill. In C.W. Wahl (Ed.), *Sexual problems: Diagnosis and treatment in medical practice* (pp. 266–287). New York: Free Press. (9)

Money, J. (1970). Matched pairs of hermaphrodites: Behavioral biology of sexual differentiation from chromosomes to gender identity. *Engineering and Science (Cal. Tech.), 33,* 34–39. (12)

Money, J., & Ehrhardt, A.A. (1968). Prenatal hormonal exposure: Possible effects on behaviour in man. In R.P. Michael (Ed.), *Endocrinology and human behaviour* (pp. 32–48). London: Oxford University Press. (12)

Money, J., & Ehrhardt, A.A. (1972). *Man & woman, boy & girl.* Baltimore, MD: Johns Hopkins University Press. (12)

Money, J., & Lewis, V. (1966). IQ, genetics and accelerated growth: Adrenogenital syndrome. *Bulletin of the Johns Hopkins Hospital, 118,* 365–373. (12)

Money, J., & Schwartz, M. (1978). Biosocial determinants of gender identity differentiation and development. In J.B. Hutchison (Ed.), *Biological determinants of sexual behaviour* (pp. 765–784). Chichester, England: John Wiley. (12)

Money, J., Wiedeking, C., Walker, P.A., & Gain, D. (1976). Combined antiandrogenic and counseling program for treatment of 46,XY and 47,XYY sex offenders. In E.J. Sachar (Ed.), *Hormones, behavior, and psychopathology* (pp. 105–120). New York: Raven. (12)

Mook, D.G. (1990). Satiety, specifications, and stop rules: Feeding as voluntary action. *Progress in Psychobiology and Physiological Psychology, 14,* 1–65. (11)

Moonen, C.T.W., van Zijl, P.C.M., Frank, J.A., LeBihan, D., & Becker, E.D. (1990). Functional magnetic resonance imaging in medicine and physiology. *Science, 250,* 53–61. (4)

Moorcroft, W.J. (1989). *Sleep, dreaming, & sleep disorders.* Lanham, MD: University Press of America. (10)

Moore, B.O., & Deutsch, J.A. (1985). An antiemetic is antidotal to the satiety effects of cholecystokinin. *Nature, 315,* 321–322. (11)

Moore, R.Y. (1974). Central regeneration and recovery of function: The problem of collateral reinnervation. In D.G. Stein, J.J. Rosen, & N. Butters (Eds.), *Plasticity and recovery of function in the central nervous system* (pp. 111–128). New York: Academic Press. (15)

Moore, R.Y., Bjorklund, A., & Stenevi, U. (1971). Plastic changes in the adrenergic innervation of the rat septal area in response to denervation. *Brain Research, 33,* 13–35. (15)

Moore, R.Y., & Eichler, V.B. (1972). Loss of a circadian adrenal corticosterone rhythm following suprachiasmatic lesions in the rat. *Brain Research, 42,* 201–206. (10)

Moore-Ede, M.C., Czeisler, C.A., & Richardson, G.S. (1983a). Circadian timekeeping in health and disease. *New England Journal of Medicine, 309,* 469–476. (10)

Moore-Ede, M.C., Czeisler, C.A., & Richardson, G.S. (1983b). Circadian timekeeping in health and disease. Part 2. Clinical implications of circadian rhythmicity. *New England Journal of Medicine, 309,* 530–536. (10)

Morgan, B.L.G., & Winick, M. (1989). Malnutrition, central nervous system effects. In G. Adelman (Ed.), *Neuroscience year* (pp. 97–99). Boston: Birkhäuser. (8)

Morgan, D.G., & Finch, C.E. (1988). Dopaminergic changes in the basal ganglia: A generalized phenomenon of aging in mammals. *Annals of the New York Academy of Sciences, 515,* 145–159. (9)

Morgane, P.J. (1981). Serotonin: Twenty-five years later. *Psychopharmacology Bulletin, 17,* 13–17. (10)

Morgane, P.J., & Stern, W.C. (1974). Chemical anatomy of brain circuits in relation to sleep and wakefulness. In E.D. Weitzman (Ed.), *Advances in sleep research* (Vol. 1, pp. 1–131). Flushing, NY: Spectrum. (10)

Morley, J.E., Bartness, T.J., Gosnell, B.A., & Levine, A.S. (1985). Peptidergic regulation of feeding. *International Review of Neurobiology, 27,* 207–298. (11)

Morris, M., Lack, L., & Dawson, D. (1990). Sleep-onset insomniacs have delayed temperature rhythms. *Sleep, 13,* 1–14. (10, 11)

Morris, R.G.M. (1989). Synaptic plasticity and learning: Selective impairment of learning in rats and blockade of long-term potentiation *in vivo* by the N-methyl-D-aspartate receptor antagonist AP5. *Journal of Neuroscience, 9,* 3040–3057. (14)

Morrison, J.H., Rogers, J., Scherr, S., Benoit, R., & Bloom, F.E. (1985). So-matostatin immunoreactivity in neuritic plaques of Alzheimer's patients. *Nature, 314,* 90–92. (14)

Morrow, L., Ratcliff, G., & Johnston, C.S. (1986). Externalising spatial knowledge in patients with right hemispheric lesions. *Cognitive Neuropsychology, 2,* 265–273. (5)

Mortimer, J.A., Schuman, L.M., & French, L.R. (1981). Epidemiology of dementing illness. In J.A. Mortimer & L.M. Schuman (Eds.), *Epidemiology of Dementia* (pp. 3–23). New York: Oxford University Press. (14)

Moruzzi, G., & Magoun, H.W. (1949). Brain stem reticular formation and activation of the EEG. *Electroencephalography and Clinical Neurophysiology, 1,* 455–473. (10)

Moscovitch, M. (1985). Memory from infancy to old age: Implications for theories of normal and pathological memory. *Annals of the New York Academy of Sciences, 444,* 78–96. (14)

Moulton, D.G. (1976). Spatial patterning of response to odors in the peripheral olfactory system. *Physiological Reviews, 56,* 578–593. (6)

Mountcastle, V.B. (1957). Modality and topographic properties of single neurons of cat's somatic sensory cortex. *Journal of Neurophysiology, 20,* 408–434. (4)

Moyer, K.E. (1974). Sex differences in aggression. In R.C. Friedman, R.M. Richart, & R.L. VandeWiele (Eds.), *Sex differences in behavior* (pp. 335–372). New York: Wiley. (12)

Müller, H.W., Gebicke-Härter, P.J., Hangen, D.H., & Shooter, E.M. (1985). A specific 37,000-Dalton protein that accumulates in regenerating but not in nonregenerating mammalian nerves. *Science, 228,* 499–501. (15)

Muller, R.U., & Kubie, J.L. (1989). The firing of hippocampal place cells predicts the future position of freely moving rats. *Journal of Neuroscience, 9,* 4101–4110. (14)

Murison, R., & Overmier, J.B. (1990). Proactive actions of psychological stress on gastric ulceration in rats—Real psychobiology. *Annals of the New York Academy of Sciences, 597,* 191–200. (13)

Murphy, J.M., Sobol, A.M., Neff, R.K., Olivier, D.C., & Leighton, A.H. (1984). Stability of prevalence. *Archives of General Psychiatry, 41,* 990–997. (16)

Murphy, M.G., & O'Leary, J.L. (1973). Hanging and climbing functions in raccoon and sloth after total cerebellectomy. *Archives of Neurology, 28,* 111–117. (9)

Myers, J.J., & Sperry, R.W. (1985). Interhemispheric communication after section of the forebrain commissures. *Cortex, 21,* 249–260. (5)

Nabekura, J. Oomura, Y., Minami, T., Mizuno, Y., & Fukuda, A. (1986). Mechanism of the rapid effect of 17-β-estradiol on medial amygdala neurons. *Science, 233,* 226–228. (12)

Nachman, M. (1962). Taste preferences for sodium salts by adrenalectomized rats. *Journal of Comparative and Physiological Psychology, 55,* 1124–1129. (11)

Narabayashi, H. (1972). Stereotaxic amygdalotomy. In B.E. Eleftheriou (Ed.), *The neurobiology of the amygdala* (pp. 459–483). New York: Plenum. (13)

Nathans, J. Piantanida, T.P., Eddy, R.L., Shows, T.B., & Hogness, D.S. (1986). Molecular genetics of inherited variations in human color vision. *Science, 232,* 203–210. (7)

Nathans, J., Thomas, D., & Hogness, D.S. (1986). Molecular genetics of human color vision: The genes encoding blue, green, and red pigments. *Science, 232,* 193–202. (7)

Nebes, R.D. (1974). Hemispheric specialization in commissurotomized man. *Psychological Bulletin, 81,* 1–14. (5)

Neitz, J., & Jacobs, G.H. (1986). Reexamination of spectral mechanisms in the rat (*Rattus norvegicus*). *Journal of Comparative Psychology, 100,* 21–29. (7)

Nelson, D.O., & Prosser, C.L. (1981). Intracellular recordings from thermosensitive preoptic neurons. *Science, 213,* 787–789. (11)

Nelson, T.O., McSpadden, M., Fromme, K., & Marlatt, G.A. (1986). Effects of alcohol intoxication on metamemory and on retrieval from long-term memory. *Journal of Experimental Psychology: General, 115,* 247–254. (3)

Nesse, R.M., Cameron, O.G., Curtis, G.C., McCann, D.S., & Huber-Smith, M.J. (1984). Adrenergic function in patients with panic anxiety. *Archives of General Psychiatry, 41,* 771–776. (13)

Netter, F.H. (1983). *CIBA collection of medical illustrations: Vol. 1. Nervous system.* New York: CIBA. (12)

Newsome, W.T., & Paré, E.B. (1988). A selective impairment of motion perception following lesions of the middle temporal visual area (MT). *Journal of Neuroscience, 8,* 2201–2211. (7)

Nezirogĺu, F. (1979). Behavioral and organic aspects of aggression. In J. Obiols, C. Ballús, E. González Monclús, & J. Pujol (Eds.), *Biological psychiatry today* (pp. 1215–1222). Amsterdam: Elsevier/North Holland Biomedical. (13)

Niakan, E., Harati, Y., & Rolak, L.A. (1986). Immunosuppressive drug therapy in myasthenia gravis. *Archives of Neurology, 43,* 155–156. (9)

Nicholson, C., & Rice, M.E. (1986). The migration of substances in the neuronal microenvironment. *Annals of the New York Academy of Sciences, 481,* 55–71. (2)

Nicoll, R.A., & Madison, D.V. (1982). General anesthetics hyperpolarize neurons in the vertebrate central nervous system. *Science, 217,* 1055–1057. (2)

Nielsen, J. (1969). Klinefelter's syndrome and the XYY syndrome. *Acta Psychiatrica Scandinavica, 45* (Suppl. 209), 1–353. (12)

Norman, R.L., & Spies, H.G. (1986). Cyclic ovarian function in a male macaque: Additional evidence for a lack of sexual differentiation in the physiological mechanisms that regulate the cyclic release of gonadotropins in primates. *Endocrinology, 118,* 2608–2610. (12)

North, R.A. (1989). Neurotransmitters and their receptors: From the clone to the clinic. *Seminars in the Neurosciences, 1,* 81–90. (3)

Nottebohm, F. (1980a). Testosterone triggers growth of brain vocal control nuclei in adult female canaries. *Brain Research, 189,* 429–436. (1)

Nottebohm, F. (1980b). Brain pathways for vocal learning in birds: A review of the first 10 years. *Progress in Psychobiology and Physiological Psychology, 9,* 85–124. (1)

*Nursing 87 Drug Handbook* (1987). Springhouse, PA: Springhouse Corporation.

Nutt, D.J. (1989). Altered central alpha2-adrenoceptor sensitivity in panic disorder. *Archives of General Psychiatry, 46,* 165–169. (13)

Obeso, J.A., Grandas, F., Vaamonde, J., Luquin, M.R., Artieda, J., Lera, G., Rodriguez, M.E., & Martinez-Lage, J.M. (1989). Motor complications associated with chronic levodopa therapy in Parkinson's disease. *Neurology, 39*(Suppl. 2), 11–19. (9)

O'Brien, D.P., Chesire, R.M., & Teitelbaum, P. (1985). Vestibular versus tail-pinch activation in cats with lateral hypothalamic lesions. *Physiology & Behavior, 34,* 811–814. (11)

O'Dowd, B.F., Lefkowitz, R.J., & Caron, M.G. (1989). Structure of the adrenergic and related receptors. *Annual Review of Neuroscience, 12,* 67–83. (3)

Ohzawa, I., DeAngelis, G.C., & Freeman, R.D. (1990). Stereoscopic depth discrimination in the visual cortex: Neurons ideally suited as disparity detectors. *Science, 249,* 1037–1041. (8)

Okada, F., Crow, T.J., & Roberts, G.W. (1990). G-proteins (Gi, Go) in the basal ganglia of control and schizophrenic brain. *Journal of Neural Transmission, 79,* 227–234. (16)

O'Keefe, J. (1983). Spatial memory within and without the hippocampal system. In W. Seifert (Ed.), *Neurobiology of the hippocampus* (pp. 375–403). London: Academic Press. (14)

Olds, J. (1958a). Effects of hunger and male sex hormone on self-stimulation of the brain. *Journal of Comparative and Physiological Psychology, 51,* 320–324. (13)

Olds, J. (1958b). Satiation effects in self-stimulation of the brain. *Journal of Comparative and Physiological Psychology, 51,* 675–678. (13)

Olds, J. (1962). Hypothalamic substrates of reward. *Physiological Reviews, 42,* 554–604. (13)

Olds, J., & Milner, P. (1954). Positive reinforcement produced by electrical stimulation of the septal area and other regions of the rat brain. *Journal of Comparative and Physiological Psychology, 47,* 419–428. (13)

O'Leary, A. (1990). Stress, emotion, and human immune function. *Psychological Bulletin, 108,* 363–382. (13)

O'Leary, D.S., & Boll, T.J. (1984). Neuropsychological correlates of early generalized brain dysfunction in children. In C.R. Almli & S. Finger (Eds.), *Early brain damage* (pp. 215–229). Orlando, FL: Academic Press. (15)

Olsen, T.S., Bruhn, P., & Öberg, R.G.E. (1986). Cortical hypoperfusion as a possible cause of "subcortical aphasia." *Brain, 109,* 393–410. (5)

Olton, D.S., & Papas, B.C. (1979). Spatial memory and hippocampal function. *Neuropsychologia, 17,* 669–682. (14)

Olton, D.S., Walker, J.A., & Gage, F.H. (1978). Hippocampal connections and spatial discrimination. *Brain Research, 139,* 295–308. (14)

O'Malley, S.S., & Maisto, S.A. (1985). Effects of family drinking history and expectancies on responses to alcohol in men. *Journal of Studies on Alcohol, 46,* 289–297. (3)

Oppenheim, R.W., Haverkamp, L.J., Prevette, D., McManaman, J.L., & Appel, S.H. (1988). Reduction of naturally occurring motoneuron death in vivo by a target-derived neurotrophic factor. *Science, 240,* 919–922. (8)

Ornitz, E.M., Atwell, C.W., Kaplan, A.R., & Westlake, J.R. (1985). Brain-stem dysfunction in autism. *Archives of General Psychiatry, 42,* 1018–1025. (16)

Ornitz, E.M., & Ritvo, E.R. (1976). Medical assessment. In E.R. Ritvo (Ed.), *Autism* (pp. 7–23). New York: Spectrum. (16)

Oscar-Berman, M. (1980). Neuropsychological consequences of long-term chronic alcoholism. *American Scientist, 68,* 410–419. (14)

Ostrin, R.K., & Schwartz, M.F. (1986). Reconstructing from a degraded trace: A study of sentence repetition in agrammatism. *Brain and Language, 28,* 328–345. (5)

Overmier, J.B., Murison, R., Ursin, H., & Skoglund, E.J. (1987). Quality of post-stressor rest influences the ulcerative process. *Behavioral Neuroscience, 101,* 246–253. (13)

Owen, D.R. (1972). The 47,XYY male: A review. *Psychological Bulletin, 78,* 209–233. (12)

Owren, M.J., Hopp, S.L., Sinnott, J.M., & Petersen, M.R. (1988). Absolute auditory thresholds in three old world monkey species (*Cercopithecus aethiops, C. neglectus, Macaca fuscata*) and humans (*Homo sapiens*). *Journal of Comparative Psychology, 102,* 99–107. (6)

Pakkenberg, B. (1990). Pronounced reduction of total neuron number in mediodorsal thalamic nucleus and nucleus accumbens in schizophrenics. *Archives of General Psychiatry, 47,* 1023–1028. (16)

Palay, S.L., & Chan-Palay, V. (1977). General morphology of neurons and neuroglia. In J.M. Brookhart & V.M. Mountcastle (Eds.), *Handbook of physiology: Section 1. The nervous system* (Vol. 1, Pt. 1, pp. 5–37). Bethesda, MD: American Physiological Society. (2)

Pande, A.C. (1985). Light-induced hypomania. *American Journal of Psychiatry, 142,* 1126. (14)

Pandurangi, A.K., Bilder, R.M., Rieder, R.O., Mukherjee, S., & Hamer, R.M. (1988). Schizophrenic symptoms and deterioration. *Journal of Nervous and Mental Disease, 176,* 200–206. (16)

Panksepp, J. (1973). The ventromedial hypothalamus and metabolic adjustments of feeding behavior. *Behavioral Biology, 9,* 65–78. (11)

Panksepp, J., Herman, B., & Vilberg, T. (1978). An opiate excess model of childhood autism. *Neuroscience Abstracts, 4*(Abstract 1601), 500. (16)

Papanicolaou, A.C., Moore, B.D., Deutsch, G., Levin, H.S., & Eisenberg, H.M. (1988). Evidence for right-hemisphere involvement in recovery from aphasia. *Archives of Neurology, 45,* 1025–1029. (5)

Papez, J.W. (1937). A proposed mechanism of emotion. *Archives of Neurology and Psychiatry, 38,* 725–743. (13)

Pappone, P.A., & Cahalan, M.D. (1987). *Pandinus imperator* scorpion venom blocks voltage-gated potassium channels in nerve fibers. *Journal of Neuroscience, 7,* 3300–3305. (2)

Parker, D.E. (1980). The vestibular apparatus. *Scientific American, 243*(5), 118–135. (6)

Parker, G.H. (1922). *Smell, taste, and allied senses in the vertebrates.* Philadelphia: Lippincott. (6)

Parlee, M.B. (1983). Menstrual rhythms in sensory processes: A review of fluctuations in vision, olfaction, audition, taste, and touch. *Psychological Bulletin, 93,* 539–548. (12)

Parnas, J., Schulsinger, F., Schulsinger, H., Mednick, S.A., & Teasdale, T.W. (1982). Behavioral precursors of schizophrenia spectrum. *Archives of General Psychiatry, 39,* 658–664. (16)

Paul, S.M., Extein, I., Calil, H.M., Potter, W.Z., Chodoff, P., & Goodwin, F.K. (1981). Use of ECT with treatment-resistant depressed patients at the National Institute of Mental Health. *American Journal of Psychiatry, 138,* 486–489. (16)

Pauls, D.L., Towbin, K.E., Leckman, J.F., Zahner, G.E.P., & Cohen, D.J. (1986). Gilles de la Tourette's syndrome and obsessive-compulsive disorder. *Archives of General Psychiatry, 43,* 1180–1182. (13)

Paulson, O.B., & Newman, E.A. (1987). Does the release of potassium from astrocyte endfeet regulate cerebral blood flow? *Science, 237,* 896–898. (2)

Peachey, J.E., & Naranjo, C.A. (1983). The use of disulfiram and other alcohol-sensitizing drugs in the treatment of alcoholism. *Research Advances in Alcohol and Drug Problems, 7,* 397–431. (3)

Pearlson, G.D., Kim, W.S., Kubos, K.L., Moberg, P.J., Jayaram, G., Bascom, M.J., Chase, G.A., Goldfinger, A.D., & Tune, L.E. (1989). Ventricle-brain ratio, computed tomographic density and brain area in 50 schizophrenics. *Archives of General Psychiatry, 46,* 690–697. (16)

Pearson, K.G. (1979). Local neurons and local interactions in the nervous system of invertebrates. In F.O. Schmitt & F.G. Worden (Eds.), *The Neurosciences: Fourth study program* (pp. 145–157). Cambridge, MA: MIT Press. (2)

Peck, J.W., & Novin, D. (1971). Evidence that osmoreceptors mediating drinking in rabbits are in the lateral preoptic area. *Journal of Comparative and Physiological Psychology, 74,* 134–147. (11)

Pedersen, C.A., Ascher, J.A., Monroe, Y.L., & Prange, A.J., Jr. (1982). Oxytocin induces maternal behavior in virgin female rats. *Science, 216,* 648–650. (12)

Pellegrino, L.J., & Cushman, A.J. (1967). *A stereotaxic atlas of the rat brain.* New York: Appleton-Century-Crofts. (4)

Pellis, S.M., O'Brien, D.P., Pellis, V.C., Teitelbaum, P., Wolgin, D.L., &

Kennedy, S. (1988). Escalation of feline predation along a gradient from avoidance through "play" to killing. *Behavioral Neuroscience, 102,* 760–777. (13)

Penfield, W. (1955). The permanent record of the stream of consciousness. *Acta Psychologica, 11,* 47–69. (14)

Penfield, W., & Milner, B. (1958). Memory deficit produced by bilateral lesions in the hippocampal zone. *Archives of Neurology and Psychiatry, 79,* 475–497. (14)

Penfield, W., & Perot, P. (1963). The brain's record of auditory and visual experience. *Brain, 86,* 595–696. (14)

Penfield, W., & Rasmussen, T. (1950). *The cerebral cortex of man.* New York: Macmillan. (4)

Penfield, W., & Roberts, L. (1959). *Speech and brain mechanisms.* Princeton, NJ: Princeton University Press. (1)

Pepperberg, I.M. (1981). Functional vocalizations by an African grey parrot. *Zeitschrift für Tierpsychologie, 55,* 139–160. (5)

Pepperberg, I.M. (1990). Cognition in an African gray parrot (*Psittacus erithacus*): Further evidence for comprehension of categories and labels. *Journal of Comparative Psychology, 104,* 41–52. (5)

Perenin, M.T., & Jeannerod, M. (1978). Visual function within the hemianopic field following early cerebral hemidecortication in man—I. Spatial localization. *Neuropsychologia, 16,* 1–13. (7)

Perlow, M.J., Freed, W.J., Hoffer, B.J., Seiger, A., Olson, L., & Wyatt, R.J. (1979). Brain grafts reduce motor abnormalities produced by destruction of nigrostriatal dopamine system. *Science, 204,* 643–647. (15)

Pert, A., Rosenblatt, J.E., Sivit, C., Pert, C.B., & Bunney, W.E., Jr. (1978). Long-term treatment with lithium prevents the development of dopamine receptor supersensitivity. *Science, 201,* 171–173. (16)

Pert, C.B., & Snyder, S.H. (1973). The opiate receptor: Demonstration in nervous tissue. *Science, 179,* 1011–1014. (6)

Pescovitz, O.H., Cutler, G.B., Jr., & Loriaux, D.L. (1985). Precocious puberty. *Neuroendocrine Perspectives, 4,* 73–93. (12)

Peters, R.H., Koch, P.C., & Blythe, B.L. (1988). Differential effects of yohimbine and naloxone on copulatory behaviors of male rats. *Behavioral Neuroscience, 102,* 559–564. (12)

Petersen, S.E., Fox, P.T., Posner, M.I., Mintun, M., & Raichle, M.E. (1988). Positron emission tomographic studies of the cortical anatomy of single-word processing. *Nature, 331,* 585–589. (5)

Peterson, G.C. (1980). Organic mental disorders associated with brain trauma. In H.I. Kaplan, A.M. Freedman, & B.J. Sadlock (Eds.), *Comprehensive textbook of psychiatry* (3rd ed.), (Vol. 2, pp. 1422–1437). Baltimore, MD: Williams & Wilkins. (15)

Petty, L.K., Ornitz, E.M., Michelman, J.D., & Zimmerman, E.G. (1984). Autistic children who become schizophrenic. *Archives of General Psychiatry, 41,* 129–135. (16)

Pfaffmann, C., Frank, M., & Norgren, R. (1979). Neural mechanisms and behavioral aspects of taste. *Annual Review of Psychology, 30,* 283–325. (6)

Pflug, B. (1973). Therapeutic aspects of sleep deprivation. In W.P. Koella & P. Levin (Eds.), *Sleep: Physiology, biochemistry, psychology, pharmacology, clinical implications* (pp. 185–191). Basel: Karger. (16)

Phelps, M.E., & Mazziotta, J.C. (1985). Positron emission tomography: Human brain function and biochemistry. *Science, 228,* 799–809. (4)

Phillips, H.S., Hains, J.M., Laramee, G.R., Rosenthal, A., & Winslow, J.W. (1990). Widespread expression of BDNF but not NT3 by target areas of basal forebrain cholinergic neurons. *Science, 250,* 290–294. (8)

Phoenix, C.H., Slob, A.K., & Goy, R.W. (1973). Effects of castration and replacement therapy on sexual behavior of adult male rhesuses. *Journal of Comparative and Physiological Psychology, 84,* 472–481. (12)

Pickar, D., Labarca, R., Doran, A.R., Wolkowitz, O.M., Roy, A., Breier, A., Linnoila, M., & Paul, S.M. (1986). Longitudinal measurement of plasma homovanillic acid levels in schizophrenic patients. *Archives of General Psychiatry, 43,* 669–676. (16)

Pierce, P.A., & Peroutka, S.J. (1989). The 5-hydroxytryptamine receptor families. *Seminars in the Neurosciences, 1,* 145–153. (3)

Piercey, M.F., Schroeder, L.A., Folkers, K., Xu, J.-C., & Horig, J. (1981). Sensory and motor functions of spinal cord substance P. *Science, 214,* 1361–1363. (6)

Pincus, J.H. (1980). Can violence be a manifestation of epilepsy? *Neurology, 30,* 304–307. (13)

Pincus, J.H., & Tucker, G.J. (1978). *Behavioral neurology* (2nd ed.). New York: Oxford University Press. (3)

Pinel, J.P.J., Treit, D., & Rovner, L.I. (1977). Temporal lobe aggression in rats. *Science, 197,* 1088–1089. (13)

Pi-Sunyer, X., Kissileff, H.R., Thornton, J., & Smith, G.P. (1982). C-terminal octapeptide of cholecystokinin decreases food intake in obese men. *Physiology & Behavior, 29,* 627–630. (11)

Pitman, R.K., van der Kolk, B.A., Orr, S.P., & Greenberg, M.S. (1990). Naloxone-reversible analgesic response to combat-related stimuli in posttraumatic stress disorder. *Archives of General Psychiatry, 47,* 541–544. (13)

Pitts, F.N., Jr. (1971). Biochemical factors in anxiety neurosis. *Behavioral Science, 16,* 82–91. (13)

Plomin, R. (1990). The role of inheritance in behavior. *Science, 248,* 183–188. (A)

Pokorny, A.D. (1978). The course and progress of schizophrenia. In W.E. Fann, I. Karacan, A.D. Pokorny, & R.L. Williams (Eds.), *Phenomenology and treatment of schizoprenia* (pp. 21–37). New York: Spectrum. (16)

Poling, A., Schlinger, H., & Blakely, E. (1988). Failure of the partial inverse benzodiazepine agonist Ro15-4513 to block the lethal effects of ethanol in rats. *Pharmacology Biochemistry & Behavior, 31,* 945–947. (13)

Pollak, J.M. (1979). Obsessive-compulsive personality: A review. *Psychological Bulletin, 86,* 225–241. (13)

Pollitt, E. (1988). Developmental impact of nutrition on pregnancy, infancy, and childhood: Public health issues in the United States. In N.W. Bray (Ed.), *International Review of Research in Mental Retardation* (Vol. 15, pp. 33–80). San Diego: Academic Press. (8)

Pomerantz, S.M., & Goy, R.W. (1983). Proceptive behavior of female rhesus monkeys during tests with tethered males. *Hormones and Behavior, 17,* 237–248. (12)

Pomeranz, B., & Chung, S.H. (1970). Dendritic-tree anatomy codes form-vision physiology in tadpole retina. *Science, 170,* 983–984. (4)

Pomeranz, B.H. (1989). Transcutaneous electrical nerve stimulation (TENS). In G. Adelman (Ed.), *Neuroscience year* (pp. 161–164). Boston: Birkhäuser. (6)

Porter, R.H., Balogh, R.D., Cernoch, J.M., & Franchi, C. (1986). Recognition of kin through characteristic body odors. *Chemical Senses, 11,* 389–395. (6)

Posner, M.I., Early, T.S., Reiman, E., Pardo, P.J., & Dhawan, M. (1988). Asymmetries in hemispheric control of attention in schizophrenia. *Archives of General Psychiatry, 45,* 814–821. (16)

Posner, M.I., Petersen, S.E., Fox, P.T., & Raichle, M.E. (1988). Localization of cognitive operations in the human brain. *Science, 240,* 1627–1631. (5)

Potkin, S.G., Karoum, F., Chuang, L.-W., Cannon-Spoor, H.E., Phillips, I., & Wyatt, R.J. (1979). Phenylethylamine in paranoid chronic schizophrenia. *Science, 206,* 470–471. (16)

Preilowski, B. (1975). Bilateral motor interaction: Perceptual-motor performance of partial and complete split-brain patients. In K.J. Zülch, O. Creutzfeldt, & G.C. Galbraith (Eds.), *Cerebral localization* (pp. 115–132). New York: Springer-Verlag. (5)

Premack, A.J. (1976). *Why chimps can read.* New York: Harper & Row. (5)

Premack, A.J., & Premack, D. (1972). Teaching language to an ape. *Scientific American, 227*(4), 92–99. (5)

Price, R.W., Brew, B., Sidtis, J., Rosenblum, M., Scheck, A.C., & Cleary, P. (1988). The brain in AIDS: Central nervous system HIV-1 infection and AIDS dementia complex. *Science, 239,* 586–592. (16)

Pritchard, T.C., Hamilton, R.B., Morse, J.R., & Norgren, R. (1986). Projections of thalamic gustatory and lingual areas in the monkey, *Macaca fascicularis. Journal of Comparative Neurology, 244,* 213–228. (6)

Prosser, R., Kittrell, E.M.W., & Satinoff, E. (1984). Circadian body temperature rhythms in rats with suprachiasmatic nuclear lesions. In J.R.S. Hales (Ed.), *Thermal physiology* (pp. 67–70). New York: Raven. (10)

Provine, R.R. (1979). "Wing-flapping" develops in wingless chicks. *Behavioral and Neural Biology, 27,* 233–237. (9)

Provine, R.R. (1981). Wing-flapping develops in chickens made flightless by feather mutations. *Developmental Psychobiology, 14,* 481–486. (9)

Provine, R.R. (1984). Wing-flapping during development and evolution. *American Scientist, 72,* 448–455. (9)

Provine, R.R. (1986). Yawning as a stereotyped action pattern and releasing stimulus. *Ethology, 72,* 109–122. (9)

Provine, R.R., & Westerman, J.A. (1979). Crossing the midline: Limits of early eye-hand behavior. *Child Development, 50,* 437–441. (5)

Pryce, C.R., Abbott, D.H., Hodges, J.K., & Martin, R.D. (1988). Maternal behavior is related to prepartum urinary levels in red-bellied tamarin monkeys. *Physiology & Behavior, 44,* 717–726. (12)

Pujol, J.F., Buguet, A., Froment, J.L., Jones, B., & Jouvet, M. (1971). The central metabolism of serotonin in the cat during insomnia: A neurophysiological and biochemical study after administration of *p*-chlorophenylalanine or destruction of the raphe system. *Brain Research, 29,* 195–212. (10)

Purves, D., & Hadley, R.D. (1985). Changes in the dendritic branching of adult mammalian neurones revealed by repeated imaging *in situ. Nature, 315,* 404–406. (2)

Purves, D., & Lichtman, J.W. (1980). Elimination of synapses in the developing nervous system. *Science, 210,* 153–157. (8)

Purves, D., & Lichtman, J.W. (1985). Geometrical differences among homologous neurons in mammals. *Science, 228,* 298–302. (2)

Quadagno, D.M., Briscoe, R., & Quadagno, J.S. (1977). Effect of perinatal gonadal hormones on selected nonsexual behavior patterns: A critical assessment of the non-human and human literature. *Psychological Bulletin, 84,* 62–80. (12)

Rabkin, J.G. (1980). Stressful life events and schizophrenia: A review of the research literature. *Psychological Bulletin, 87,* 408–425. (16)

Raczkowski, D., Hamos, J.E., & Sherman, S.M. (1988). Synaptic circuitry of physiologically identified W-cells in the cat's dorsal lateral geniculate nucleus. *Journal of Neuroscience, 8,* 31–48. (7)

Rafal, R., Smith, J., Krantz, J., Cohen, A., & Brennan, C. (1990). Extrageniculate vision in hemianopic humans: Saccade inhibition by signals in the blind field. *Science, 250,* 118–121. (7)

Raisman, G. (1969). Neuronal plasticity in the septal nuclei of the adult rat. *Brain Research, 14,* 25–48. (15)

Raisman, G., & Field, P.M. (1973). A quantitative investigation of the development of collateral reinnervation after partial deafferentation of the septal nuclei. *Brain Research, 50,* 241–264. (15)

Rakic, P. (1978). Neuronal migration and contact guidance in the primate telencephalon. *Postgraduate Medical Journal, 54*(Suppl. 1), 25–37. (8)

Rakic, P. (1985). DNA synthesis and cell division in the adult primate brain. *Annals of the New York Academy of Sciences, 457,* 193–211. (2)

Rakic, P. (1988). Specification of cerebral cortical areas. *Science, 241,* 170–176. (4)

Ralph, M.R., Foster, R.G., Davis, F.C., & Menaker, M. (1990). Transplanted suprachiasmatic nucleus determines circadian period. *Science, 247,* 975–978. (10)

Ralph, M.R., & Menaker, M. (1988). A mutation of the circadian system in golden hamsters. *Science, 241,* 1225–1227. (10)

Ramirez, J.J., Fass, B., Karpiak, S.E., & Steward, O. (1987a). Ganglioside treatments reduce locomotor hyperactivity after bilateral lesions of the entorhinal cortex. *Neuroscience Letters, 75,* 283–287. (15)

Ramirez, J.J., Fass, B., Kilfoil, T., Henschel, B., Grones, W., & Karpiak, S.E. (1987b). Ganglioside-induced enhancement of behavioral recovery after bilateral lesions of the entorhinal cortex. *Brain Research, 414,* 85–90. (15)

Randall, P.K., Severson, J.A., & Finch, C.E. (1981). Aging and the regulation of striatal dopaminergic mechanisms in mice. *Journal of Pharmacology and Experimental Therapeutics, 219,* 695–700. (15)

Rao, M.L., Gross, G., & Huber, G. (1984). Altered interrelationship of dopamine, prolactin, thyrotropin and thyroid hormone in schizophrenic patients. *European Archives of Psychiatry and Neurological Sciences, 234,* 8–12. (16)

Rapoport, S.I., & Robinson, P.J. (1986). Tight-junctional modification as the basis of osmotic opening of the blood-brain barrier. *Annals of the New York Academy of Sciences, 481,* 250–267. (2)

Ream, N.W., Robinson, M.G., Richter, R.W., Hegge, F.W., & Holloway, H.C. (1975). Opiate dependence and acute abstinence. In R.W. Richter (Ed.), *Medical aspects of drug abuse* (pp. 81–123). Hagerstown, MD: Harper & Row. (16)

Reches, A., Wagner, H.R., Barkai, A.I., Jackson, V., Yablonskaya-Alter, E., & Fahn, S. (1984). Electroconvulsive treatment and haloperidol: Effects on pre- and postsynaptic dopamine receptors in rat brain. *Psychopharmacology, 83,* 155–158. (16)

Rechtschaffen, A., Gilliland, M.A., Bergmann, B.M., & Winter, J.B. (1983). Physiological correlates of prolonged sleep deprivation in rats. *Science, 221,* 182–184. (10)

Reed, T.E. (1985). Ethnic differences in alcohol use, abuse, and sensitivity: A review with genetic interpretation. *Social Biology, 32,* 195–209. (3)

Reeves, A.G., & Plum, F. (1969). Hyperphagia, rage, and dementia accompanying a ventromedial hypothalamic neoplasm. *Archives of Neurology, 20,* 616–624. (11)

Reeves, T.M., & Smith, D.C. (1987). Reinnervation of the dentate gyrus and recovery of alternation behavior following entorhinal cortex lesions. *Behavioral Neuroscience, 101,* 179–186. (15)

Refinetti, R., & Carlisle, H.J. (1986a). Complementary nature of heat production and heat intake during behavioral thermoregulation in the rat. *Behavioral and Neural Biology, 46,* 64–70. (11)

Refinetti, R., & Carlisle, H.J. (1986b). Effects of anterior and posterior hypothalamic temperature changes on thermoregulation in the rat. *Physiology & Behavior, 36,* 1099–1103. (11)

Regal, R.R., Cross, P.K., Lamson, S.H., & Hook, E.B.U. (1980). A search for evidence for a paternal age effect independent of a maternal age in birth certificate reports of Down's syndome in New York state. *American Journal of Epidemiology, 112,* 650–655. (8)

Regan, T. (1986). The rights of humans and other animals. *Acta Physiologica Scandinavica, 128*(Suppl. 554), 33–40. (1)

Reichling, D.B., Kwiat, G.C., & Basbaum, A.I. (1988). Anatomy, physiology, and pharmacology of the periaqueductal gray contribution to antinociceptive controls. In H.L. Fields & J.-M. Besson (Eds.), *Progress in brain research* (Vol. 77, pp. 31–46). Amsterdam: Elsevier. (6)

Reinisch, J.M. (1981). Prenatal exposure to synthetic progestins increases potential for aggression in humans. *Science, 211,* 1171–1173. (12)

Reisenzein, R. (1983). The Schachter theory of emotion: Two decades later. *Psychological Bulletin, 94,* 239–264. (13)

Rémillard, G.M., Andermann, F., Testa, G.F., Gloor, P., Aubé, M., Martin, J.B. Feindel, W., Guberman, A., & Simpson, C. (1983). Sexual ictal manifestations predominate in women with temporal lobe epilepsy: A finding suggesting sexual dimorphism in the human brain. *Neurology, 33,* 323–330. (13)

Rensch, B. (1971). *Biophilosophy.* New York: Columbia University Press. (1)

Rensch, B., & Dücker, G. (1963). Haptisches Lern- und Unterscheidungs-Vermögen bei einem Waschbären [Haptic learning and discrimination abilities of a raccoon]. *Zeitschrift für Tierpsychologie, 20,* 608–615. (4)

Rettig, R., Ganten, D., & Johnson, A.K. (1981). Isoproterenol-induced thirst: Renal and extrarenal mechanisms. *American Journal of Physiology, 241,* R152–R157. (11)

Reuter-Lorenz, P.A., Kinsbourne, M., & Moscovitch, M. (1990). Hemispheric control of spatial attention. *Brain and Cognition, 12,* 240–266. (5)

Richter, C.P. (1922). A behavioristic study of the activity of the rat. *Comparative Psychology Monographs, 1,* 1–55. (10)

Richter, C.P. (1927). Animal behavior and internal drives. *Quarterly Review of Biology, 2,* 307–343. (12)

Richter, C.P. (1933). The role played by the thyroid gland in the production of gross body activity. *Endocrinology, 17,* 73–87. (16)

Richter, C.P. (1936). Increased salt appetite in adrenalectomized rats. *American Journal of Physiology, 115,* 155–161. (11)

Richter, C.P. (1938). Two-day cycles of alternating good and bad behavior in psychotic patients. *Archives of Neurology and Psychiatry, 39,* 587–598. (16)

Richter, C.P. (1950). Taste and solubility of toxic compounds in poisoning of rats and humans. *Journal of Comparative and Physiological Psychology, 43,* 358–374. (6, 11)

Richter, C.P. (1955). Experimental production of cycles in behaviour and physiology in animals. *Acta Medica Scandinavica, 152*(Suppl. 307), 36–37. (16)

Richter, C.P. (1956). Ovulation cycles and stress. In C.A. Villee (Ed.), *Gestation — Transactions of the third conference* (pp. 53–70). New York: Josiah Macy, Jr. Foundation. (16)

Richter, C.P. (1957a). On the phenomenon of sudden death in animals and man. *Psychosomatic Medicine, 19,* 191–198. (13)

Richter, C.P. (1957b). Behavior and metabolic cycles in animals and man. In P.H. Hoch & J. Zubin (Eds.), *Experimental psychopathology* (pp. 34–54). New York: Grune & Stratton. (16)

Richter, C.P. (1957c). Hormones and rhythms in man and animals. In G. Pincus (Ed.), *Recent progress in hormone research* (Vol. 13, pp. 105–159). New York: Academic Press. (16)

Richter, C.P. (1957d). Abnormal but regular cycles in behaviour and metabolism in rats and catatonic-schizophrenics. *Second International Congress for Psychiatry,* 4th report, 326–327. (16)

Richter, C.P. (1958a). Neurological basis of responses to stress. In G.E.W. Wolstenholme & C.M. O'Connor (Eds.), *CIBA foundation symposium on the neurological basis of behaviour* (pp. 204–217). Boston: Little, Brown. (16)

Richter, C.P. (1958b). Abnormal but regular cycles in behavior and metabolism in rats and catatonic-schizophrenics. In M. Reiss (Ed.), *Psychoendocrinology* (pp. 168–181). New York: Grune & Stratton. (16)

Richter, C.P. (1965). Sleep and activity: Their relation to the 24-hour clock. *Association for Research in Nervous and Mental Disease, 45,* 8–29. (10)

Richter, C.P. (1967). Psychopathology of periodic behavior in animals and man. In J. Zubin & H.F. Hunt (Eds.), *Comparative psychopathology* (pp. 205–227). New York: Grune & Stratton. (10)

Richter, C.P. (1970). Blood-clock barrier: Its penetration by heavy water. *Proceedings of the National Academy of Sciences, 66,* 244. (10)

Richter, C.P. (1975). Deep hypothermia and its effect on the 24-hour clock of rats and hamsters. *Johns Hopkins Medical Journal, 136,* 1–10. (10)

Richter, C.P., Jones, G.S., & Biswanger, L. (1959). Periodic phenomena and the thyroid. *Archives of Neurology and Psychiatry, 81,* 233–255. (16)

Richter, C.P., & Langworthy, O.R. (1933). The quill mechanism of the porcupine. *Journal für Psychologie und Neurologie, 45,* 143–153. (4)

Richter, C.P., & Rice, K.K. (1956). Experimental production in rats of abnormal cycles in behavior and metabolism. *Journal of Nervous and Mental Disease, 124,* 393–395. (16)

Riley, J.N., & Walker, D.W. (1978). Morphological alterations in hippocampus after long-term alcohol consumption in mice. *Science, 201,* 646–648. (2)

Rimland, B., Callaway, E., & Dreyfus, P. (1978). The effect of high doses of vitamin B$_6$ on autistic children: A double-blind crossover study. *American Journal of Psychiatry, 135,* 472–475. (16)

Rinn, W.E. (1984). The neuropsychology of facial expression: A review of the neurological and psychological mechanisms for producing facial expressions. *Psychological Bulletin, 95,* 52–77. (5, 9)

Riska, B., & Atchley, W.R. (1985). Genetics of growth predict patterns of brain-size evolution. *Science, 229,* 668–671. (8)

Ritvo, E.R., Freeman, B.J., Mason-Brothers, A., Mo, A., & Ritvo, A.M. (1985). Concordance for the syndrome of autism in 40 pairs of afflicted twins. *American Journal of Psychiatry, 142,* 74–77. (16)

Ritvo, E.R., Spence, M.A., Freeman, B.J., Mason-Brothers, A., Mo, A., & Marazita, M.L. (1985). Evidence for autosomal recessive inheritance in 46 families with multiple incidences of autism. *American Journal of Psychiatry, 142,* 187–192. (16)

Robbins, M.J., & Meyer, D.R. (1970). Motivational control of retrograde amnesia. *Journal of Experimental Psychology, 84,* 220–225. (14)

Robillard, T.A.J., & Gersdorff, M.C.H. (1986). Prevention of pre- and perinatal acquired hearing defects, Part I: Study of causes. *Journal of Auditory Research, 26,* 207–237. (6)

Robins, L.N., Helzer, J.E., Weissman, M.M., Orvaschel, H., Gruenberg, E., Burke, J.D., Jr., & Regier, D.A. (1984). Lifetime prevalence of specific psychiatric disorders in three sites. *Archives of General Psychiatry, 41,* 949–958. (13, 16)

Robinson, B. (1987, Feb. 16). Major classes of drugs continue on comeback trail. *Drug Topics, 131*(4), 67. (13)

Robinson, R.G., Boston, J.D., Starkstein, S.E., & Price, T.R. (1988). Comparison of mania and depression after brain injury: Causal factors. *American Journal of Psychiatry, 145,* 172–178. (13)

Rogers, J., & Morrison, J.H. (1985). Quantitative morphology and regional and laminar distributions of senile plaques in Alzheimer's disease. *Journal of Neuroscience, 5,* 2801–2808. (14)

Roland, P.E. (1984). Organization of motor control by the normal human brain. *Human Neurobiology, 2,* 205–216. (9)

Rome, L.C., Loughna, P.T., & Goldspink, G. (1984). Muscle fiber activity in carp as a function of swimming speed and muscle temperature. *American Journal of Physiology, 247,* R272–R279. (9)

Rose, J.E., Brugge, J.F., Anderson, D.J., & Hind, J.E. (1967). Phase-locked response to low-frequency tones in single auditory nerve fibers of the squirrel monkey. *Journal of Neurophysiology, 30,* 769–793. (6)

Rose, J.E., & Woolsey, C.N. (1949). Organization of the mammalian thalamus and its relationships to the cerebral cortex. *Electroencephalography and Clinical Neurophysiology, 1,* 391–404. (4)

Rosenblatt, J.S. (1967). Nonhormonal basis of maternal behavior in the rat. *Science, 156,* 1512–1514. (12)

Rosenblatt, J.S. (1970). Views on the onset and maintenance of maternal behavior in the rat. In L.R. Aronson, E. Tobach, D.S. Lehrman, & J.S. Rosenblatt (Eds.), *Development and evolution of behavior* (pp. 489–515). San Francisco: W.H. Freeman. (12)

Rosenthal, N.E., Sack, D.A., Carpenter, C.J., Parry, B.L., Mendelson, W.B., & Wehr, T.A. (1985). Antidepressant effects of light in seasonal affective disorder. *American Journal of Psychiatry, 142,* 163–170. (16)

Rosenthal, N.E., Sack, D.A., Gillin, C.J., Lewy, A.J., Goodwin, F.K., Davenport, Y., Mueller, P.S., Newsome, D.A., &

Wehr, T.A. (1984). Seasonal affective disorder. *Archives of General Psychiatry, 41,* 72–80. (16)

Ross, R.M., Losey, G.S., & Diamond, M. (1983). Sex change in a coral-reef fish: Dependence of stimulation and inhibition on relative size. *Science, 217,* 574–576. (12)

Rosvold, H.E., Mirsky, A.F., & Pribram, K.H. (1954). Influence of amygdalectomy on social behavior in monkeys. *Journal of Comparative and Physiological Psychology, 47,* 173–178. (13)

Roth, R.H. (1984). CNS dopamine autoreceptors: Distribution, pharmacology, and function. *Annals of the New York Academy of Sciences, 430,* 27–53. (3)

Rothman, S.M. (1983). Synaptic activity mediates death of hypoxic neurons. *Science, 220,* 536–537. (15)

Rovainen, C.M. (1976). Regeneration of Müller and Mauthner axons after spinal transection in larval lampreys. *Journal of Comparative Neurology, 168,* 545–554. (15)

Rowland, N. (1980). Drinking behavior: Physiological, neurological, and environmental factors. In T.M. Toates & T.R. Halliday (Eds.), *Analysis of motivational processes* (pp. 39–59). London: Academic Press. (11)

Rowland, N., & Flamm, C. (1977). Quinine drinking: More regulatory puzzles. *Physiology & Behavior, 18,* 1165–1170. (11)

Roy, A., DeJong, J., & Linnoila, M. (1989). Cerebrospinal fluid monoamine metabolites and suicidal behavior in depressed patients. *Archives of General Psychiatry, 46,* 609–612. (13)

Roy-Byrne, P.P., Uhde, T.W., & Post, R.M. (1986). Effects of one night's sleep deprivation on mood and behavior in panic disorder. *Archives of General Psychiatry, 43,* 895–899. (16)

Rozin, P. (1984). The acquisition of food habits and preferences. In J.D. Matarazzo, S.M. Weiss, J.A. Herd, N.E. Miller, & S.M. Weiss (Eds.), *Behavioral health: A handbook of health enhancement and disease prevention* (pp. 590–607). New York: John Wiley. (11)

Rozin, P. (1990). Getting to like the burn of chili pepper. In B.G. Green, J.R. Mason, & M.R. Kare (Eds.), *Chemical senses,* (Vol. 2, pp. 231–269). New York: Marcel Dekker. (11)

Rozin, P., & Fallon, A.E. (1987). A perspective on disgust. *Psychological Review, 94,* 23–41. (11)

Rozin, P., & Jonides, J. (1977). Mass reaction time measurement of the speed of the nerve impulse and the duration of mental processes in class. *Teaching of Psychology, 4,* 91–94. (2)

Rozin, P., & Kalat, J.W. (1971). Specific hungers and poison avoidance as adaptive specializations of learning. *Psychological Review, 78,* 459–486. (11, 14)

Rozin, P., & Pelchat, M.L. (1988). Memories of mammaries: Adaptations to weaning from milk. *Progress in Psychobiology and Physiological Psychology, 13,* 1–29. (11)

Rozin, P., & Vollmecke, T.A. (1986). Food likes and dislikes. *Annual Review of Nutrition, 6,* 433–456. (11)

Rozin, P., & Zellner, D. (1985). The role of Pavlovian conditioning in the acquisition of food likes and dislikes. *Annals of the New York Academy of Sciences, 443*, 189–202. (11)

Rudelli, R.D., Brown, W.T., Wisniewski, K., Jenkins, E.C., Laure-Kamionowska, M., Connell, F., & Wisniewski, H.M. (1985). Adult fragile X syndrome. Clinico-neuropathologic findings. *Acta Neuropathologica, 67*, 289–295. (8)

Rumbaugh, D.M. (Ed.). (1977). *Language learning by a chimpanzee: The Lana project.* New York: Academic Press. (5)

Rumbaugh, D.M. (1990). Comparative psychology and the great apes: Their competency in learning, language, and numbers. *Psychological Record, 40*, 15–39. (5)

Rumsey, J.M., Duara, R., Grady, C., Rapoport, J.L., Margolin, R.A., Rapoport, S.I., & Cutler, N.R. (1985). Brain metabolism in autism. *Archives of General Psychiatry, 42*, 448–455. (16)

Rusak, B. (1977). The role of the suprachiasmatic nuclei in the generation of circadian rhythms in the golden hamster, *Mesocricetus auratus. Journal of Comparative Physiology* A, *118*, 145–164. (10)

Rusak, B., & Zucker, I. (1979). Neural regulation of circadian rhythms. *Physiological Reviews, 59*, 449–526. (10)

Russell, M.J., Switz, G.M., & Thompson, K. (1980). Olfactory influences on the human menstrual cycle. *Pharmacology, Biochemistry, and Behavior, 13*, 737–738. (6)

Sabel, B.A., Slavin, M.D., & Stein, D.G. (1984). GM1 ganglioside treatment facilitates behavioral recovery from bilateral brain damage. *Science, 225*, 340–342. (15)

Sack, D.A., Nurnberger, J., Rosenthal, N.E., Ashburn, E., & Wehr, T.A. (1985). Potentiation of antidepressant medications by phase advance of the sleep-wake cycle. *American Journal of Psychiatry, 142*, 606–608. (16)

Sack, R.L., Lewy, A.J., White, D.M., Singer, C.M., Fireman, M.J., & Vandiver, R. (1990). Morning vs. evening light treatment for winter depression. *Archives of General Psychiatry, 47*, 343–351. (16)

Sackeim, H.A., Prohovnik, I., Moeller, J.R., Brown, R.P., Apter, S., Prudic, J., Devanand, D.P., & Mukherjee, S. (1990). Regional cerebral blood flow in mood disorders. I. Comparison of major depressives and normal controls at rest. *Archives of General Psychiatry, 47*, 60–70. (16)

Sackeim, H.A., Putz, E., Vingiano, W., Coleman, E., & McElhiney, M. (1988). Lateralization in the processing of emotionally laden information, I. Normal functioning. *Neuropsychiatry, Neuropsychology, and Behavioral Neurology, 1*, 97–110. (5)

Sahley, T.L., & Panksepp, J. (1987). Brain opioids and autism: An updated analysis of possible linkages. *Journal of Autism and Developmental Disorders, 17*, 201–216. (16)

Saito, H., Yukie, M., Tanaka, K., Hikosaka, K., Fukada, Y., & Iwai, E. (1986). Integration of direction signals of image motion in the superior temporal sulcus of the macaque monkey. *Journal of Neuroscience, 6*, 145–157. (7)

Sakai, R.R., & Epstein, A.N. (1990). Dependence of adrenalectomy-induced sodium appetite on the action of angiotensin II in the brain of the rat. *Behavioral Neuroscience, 104*, 167–176. (11)

Sakai, R.R., Frankmann, S.P., Fine, W.B., & Epstein, A.N. (1989). Prior episodes of sodium depletion increase the need-free sodium intake of the rat. *Behavioral Neuroscience, 103*, 186–192. (11)

Sakurai, Y. (1990). Cells in the rat auditory system have sensory-delay correlates during the performance of an auditory working memory task. *Behavioral Neuroscience, 104*, 856–868. (14)

Salthouse, T.A. (1984, February). The skill of typing. *Scientific American, 250*(2), 128–135. (9)

Sanberg, P.R., & Coyle, J.T. (1984). Scientific approaches to Huntington's disease. *CRC Critical Reviews in Clinical Neurobiology, 1*, 1–44. (9)

Sanberg, P.R., & Johnston, G.A. (1981). Glutamate and Huntington's disease. *Medical Journal of Australia, 2*, 460–465. (9)

Sanberg, P.R., Pevsner, J., Autuono, P.G., & Coyle, J.T. (1985). Fetal methylazoxymethanol acetate-induced lesions cause reductions in dopamine receptor-mediated catalepsy and stereotypy. *Neuropharmacology, 24*, 1057–1062. (4)

Sanders, R.J. (1989). Sentence comprehension following agenesis of the corpus callosum. *Brain and Language, 37*, 59–72. (5)

Sandman, C.A., Barron, J.L., Demet, E.M., Chicz-Demet, A., Rothenberg, S.J., & Zea, F.J. (1990). Opioid peptides and perinatal development: Is beta-endorphin a natural teratogen? *Annals of the New York Academy of Sciences, 579*, 91–108. (16)

Sapolsky, R.M. (1985). A mechanism for glucocorticoid toxicity in the hippocampus: Increased neuronal vulnerability to metabolic insults. *Journal of Neuroscience, 5*, 1228–1232. (14)

Sapolsky, R.M., Krey, L.C., & McEwen, B.S. (1985). Prolonged glucocorticoid exposure reduces hippocampal neuron number: Implications for aging. *Journal of Neuroscience, 5*, 1222–1227. (14)

Sarnat, H.B., & Netsky, M.G. (1981). *Evolution of the nervous system* (2nd ed.). New York: Oxford University Press. (4)

Saron, C.D., & Davidson, R.J. (1989). Visual evoked potential measures of interhemispheric transfer time in humans. *Behavioral Neuroscience, 103*, 1115–1138. (5)

Sastre, J.-P., Sakai, K., & Jouvet, M. (1979). Persistance du sommeil paradoxal chez le chat après destruction de l'aire gigantocellulaire du tegmentum pontique par l'acide kaïnique [Persistence of paradoxical sleep in the cat after destruction of the gigantocellular field of the pontine tegmentum by Kainic acid]. *Comptes Rendus des Séances de l'Académie des Sciences, Série D, 289*, 959–964. (9)

Satinoff, E. (1964). Behavioral thermoregulation in response to local cooling of the rat brain. *American Journal of Physiology, 206*, 1389–1394. (11)

Satinoff, E. (1983). A reevaluation of the concept of the homeostatic organization of temperature regulation. In E. Satinoff & P. Teitelbaum (Eds.), *Handbook of behavioral neurobiology: Vol. 6. Motivation* (pp. 443–472). New York: Plenum. (11)

Satinoff, E. (1988). Thermal influences on REM sleep. In R. Lydic & J.F. Biebuyck (Eds.), *Clinical physiology of sleep* (pp. 135–144). Bethesda, MD: American Physiological Society. (10)

Satinoff, E., Liran, J., & Clapman, R. (1982). Aberrations of circadian body temperature rhythms in rats with medial preoptic lesions. *American Journal of Physiology, 242*, R352–R357. (11)

Satinoff, E., McEwen, G.N., Jr., & Williams, B.A. (1976). Behavioral fever in newborn rabbits. *Science, 193*, 1139–1140. (11)

Satinoff, E., & Rutstein, J. (1970). Behavioral thermoregulation in rats with anterior hypothalamic lesions. *Journal of Comparative and Physiological Psychology, 71*, 77–82. (11)

Satinoff, E., Valentino, D., & Teitelbaum, P. (1976). Thermoregulatory cold-defense deficits in rats with preoptic/anterior hypothalamic lesions. *Brain Research Bulletin, 1*, 553–565. (11)

Satz, P. (1979). A test of some models of hemispheric speech organization in the left- and right-handed. *Science, 203*, 1131–1133. (5)

Sauerwein, H.C., Lassonde, M.C., Cardu, B., & Geoffroy, G. (1981). Interhemispheric integration of sensory and motor functions in agenesis of the corpus callosum. *Neuropsychologia, 19*, 445–454. (5)

Savage-Rumbaugh, E.S. (1990). Language acquisition in a nonhuman species: Implications for the innateness debate. *Developmental Psychobiology, 23*, 599–620. (5)

Savage-Rumbaugh, E.S., Sevcik, R.A., Brakke, K.E., & Rumbaugh, D.M. (in press). Symbols: Their communicative use, communication, and combination by bonobos (*Pan paniscus*). In L.P. Lipsitt & C. Rovee-Collier (Eds.), *Advances in Infancy Research* (Vol. 7, pp. 221–278). Norwood, NJ: Ablex. (5)

Scalia, F., & Winans, S.S. (1976). New perspectives on the morphology of the olfactory system: Olfactory and vomeronasal pathways in mammals. In R.L. Doty (Ed.), *Mammalian olfaction, reproductive processes and behavior* (pp. 7–28). New York: Academic Press. (6)

Schacher, S., Castellucci, V.F., & Kandel, E.R. (1988). cAMP evokes long-term facilitation in *Aplysia* sensory neurons that requires new protein synthesis. *Science, 240*, 1667–1669. (14)

Schacter, D.L. (1983). Amnesia observed: Remembering and forgetting in a natural environment. *Journal of Abnormal Psychology, 92*, 236–242. (14)

Schacter, D.L. (1985). Priming of old and new knowledge in amnesic patients and normal subjects. *Annals of the New York Academy of Sciences, 444*, 41–53. (14)

Schacter, D.L. (1987). Memory, amnesia, and frontal lobe dysfunction. *Psychobiology, 15*, 21–36. (14)

Schachter, S., & Singer, J.E. (1962). Cognitive, social and physiological determinants of emotional state. *Psychological Review, 69*, 379–399. (13)

Schall, J.D., Vitek, D.J., & Leventhal, A.G. (1986). Retinal constraints on orientation specificity in cat visual cortex. *Journal of Neuroscience, 6*, 823–836. (7)

Schallert, T. (1983). Sensorimotor impairment and recovery of function in brain-damaged rats: Reappearance of symptoms during old age. *Behavioral Neuroscience, 97*, 159–164. (15)

Schallert, T., & Whishaw, I.Q. (1984). Bilateral cutaneous stimulation of the somatosensory system in hemidecorticate rats. *Behavioral Neuroscience, 98*, 518–540. (15)

Scheff, S.W., & Cotman, C.W. (1977). Recovery of spontaneous alternation following lesions of the entorhinal cortex in adult rats: Possible correlation to axon sprouting. *Behavioral Biology, 21*, 286–293. (15)

Scheibel, A.B. (1983). Dendritic changes. In B. Reisberg (Ed.), *Alzheimer's disease* (pp. 69–73). New York: Free Press. (14)

Scheibel, A.B. (1984). A dendritic correlate of human speech. In N. Geschwind & A.M. Galaburda (Eds.), *Cerebral Dominance* (pp. 43–52). Cambridge, MA: Harvard University Press. (4)

Scheibel, M.E., & Scheibel, A.R. (1963). Some structure-functional correlates of development in young cats. *Electroencephalography and Clinical Neurophysiology, 15*(Suppl. 24), 235–246. (4)

Schellenberg, G.D., Bird, T.D., Wijsman, E.M., Moore, D.K., Boehnke, M., Bryant, E.M., Lampe, T.H., Nochlin, D., Sumi, S.M., Deeb, S.S., Beyreuther, K., & Martin, G.M. (1988). Absence of linkage of chromosome 21q21 markers to familial Alzheimer's disease. *Science, 241*, 1507–1510. (14)

Schenk, L., & Bear, D. (1981). Multiple personality and related dissociative phenomena in patients with temporal lobe epilepsy. *American Journal of Psychiatry, 138*, 1311–1316. (13)

Scherer, S.S. (1986). Reinnervation of the extraocular muscles in goldfish is nonselective. *Journal of Neuroscience, 6*, 764–773. (15)

Schiavi, R.C., Theilgaard, A., Owen, D.R., & White, D. (1988). Sex chromosome anomalies, hormones, and sexuality. *Archives of General Psychiatry, 45*, 19–24. (12)

Schiffman, S.S. (1983). Taste and smell in disease. *New England Journal of Medicine, 308*, 1275–1279, 1337–1343. (6)

Schiffman, S.S., Diaz, C., & Beeker, T.G. (1986). Caffeine intensifies taste of certain sweeteners: Role of adenosine receptor. *Pharmacology, Biochemistry & Behavior, 24*, 429–432. (6)

Schiffman, S.S., & Erickson, R.P. (1971). A psychophysical model for gustatory quality. *Physiology & Behavior, 7*, 617–633. (6)

Schiffman, S.S., & Erickson, R.P. (1980). The issue of primary tastes versus a taste continuum. *Neuroscience & Biobehavioral Reviews, 4*, 109–117. (6)

Schiffman, S.S., Lockhead, E., & Maes, F.W. (1983). Amiloride reduces the taste intensity of Na$^+$ and Li$^+$ salts and sweeteners. *Proceedings of the National Academy of Sciences, U.S.A., 80*, 6136–6140. (6)

Schiffman, S.S., McElroy, A.E., & Erickson, R.P. (1980). The range of taste quality

of sodium salts. *Physiology & Behavior, 24*, 217–224. (6)

Schiffman, S.S., Simon, S.A., Gill, J.M., & Beeker, T.G. (1986). Bretylium tosylate enhances salt taste. *Physiology & Behavior, 36*, 1129–1137. (6)

Schiller, F. (1979). *Paul Broca.* Berkeley: University of California Press. (5)

Schiller, P.H., & Lee, K. (1991). The role of the primate extrastriate area V4 in vision. *Science, 251*, 1251–1253. (7)

Schmidt, J.T., Cicerone, C.M., & Easter, S.S. (1977). Expansion of the half retinal projection to the tectum in goldfish: An electrophysiological and anatomical study. *Journal of Comparative Neurology, 177*, 257–278. (8)

Schneider, A.M., & Sherman, W. (1968). Amnesia: A function of the temporal relation of footshock to electroconvulsive shock. *Science, 159*, 219–221. (14)

Schneider, B.A., Trehub, S.E., Morrongiello, B.A., & Thorpe, L.A. (1986). Auditory sensitivity in preschool children. *Journal of the Acoustical Society of America, 79*, 447–452. (6)

Schneider, G.E. (1969). Two visual systems. *Science, 163*, 895–902. (7)

Schneider, G.E., & Jhaveri, S.R. (1974). Neuroanatomical correlates of spared or altered function after brain lesions in the newborn hamster. In D.G. Stein, J.J. Rosen, & N. Butters (Eds.), *Plasticity and recovery of function in the central nervous system* (pp. 65–109). New York: Academic Press. (15)

Schnur, P., Martinez, Y., & Hang, D. (1988). Effects of stress on morphine-elicited locomotor activity in hamsters. *Behavioral Neuroscience, 102*, 254–259. (6)

Schöpf, J., Bryois, C., Jonquière, M., & Le, P.K. (1984). On the nosology of severe psychiatric post-partum disorders. *European Archives of Psychiatry and Neurological Sciences, 234*, 54–63. (16)

Schopler, E. (1987). Specific and nonspecific factors in the effectiveness of a treatment system. *American Psychologist, 42*, 376–383. (16)

Schreiner, L., & Kling, A. (1953). Behavioral changes following rhinencephalic injury in cat. *Journal of Neurophysiology, 16*, 643–659. (13)

Schreiner-Engel, P., Schiavi, R.C., White, D., & Ghizzani, A. (1989). Low sexual desire in women: The role of reproductive hormones. *Hormones and Behavior, 23*, 221–234. (12)

Schuckit, M.A. (1984). Subjective responses to alcohol in sons of alcoholics and control subjects. *Archives of General Psychiatry, 41*, 879–884. (3)

Schusterman, R.J., & Krieger, K. (1986). Artificial language comprehension and size transposition by a California sea lion (*Zalophus californianus*). *Journal of Comparative Psychology, 100*, 348–355. (5)

Schwab, M.E., & Thoenen, H. (1985). Dissociated neurons regenerate into sciatic but not optic nerve explants in culture irrespective of neurotrophic factors. *Journal of Neuroscience, 5*, 2415–2423. (15)

Schwartz, D.H., McClane, S., Hernandez, L., & Hoebel, B. (1989). Feeding increases extracellular serotonin in the lateral hypothalamus of the rat as measured

by microdialysis. *Brain Research, 479*, 349–354. (11)

Schwartz, M., Belkin, M., Harel, A., Solomon, A., Lavie, V., Hadani, M., Rachailovich, I., & Stein-Izsak, C. (1985). Regenerating fish optic nerves and a regeneration-like response in injured optic nerves of adult rabbits. *Science, 228*, 600–603. (15)

Schwartz, W.J., & Gainer, H. (1977). Suprachiasmatic nucleus: Use of $^{14}$C-labeled deoxyglucose uptake as a functional marker. *Science, 197*, 1089–1091. (10)

Schweiger, A., Zaidel, E., Field, T., & Dobkin, B. (1989). Right hemispheric contribution to lexical access in an aphasic with deep dyslexia. *Brain and Language, 37*, 73–89. (5)

Scott, D., Jr., & Clemente, C.D. (1955). Regeneration of spinal cord fibers in the cat. *Journal of Comparative Neurology, 102*, 633–669. (15)

Scott, T.R. (1987). Coding in the gustatory system. In T.E. Finger & W.L. Silver (Eds.), *Neurobiology of taste and smell* (pp. 355–378). New York: John Wiley. (6)

Scott, T.R., & Chang, F.-C.T. (1984). The state of gustatory neural coding. *Chemical Senses, 8*, 297–314. (6)

Scott, T.R., & Perrotto, R.S. (1980). Intensity coding in pontine taste area: Gustatory information is processed similarly throughout rat's brain stem. *Journal of Neurophysiology, 44*, 739–750. (6)

Scovern, A.W., & Kilmann, P.R. (1980). Status of electroconvulsive therapy: Review of the outcome literature. *Psychological Bulletin, 87*, 260–303. (16)

Scoville, W.B., & Milner, B. (1957). Loss of recent memory after bilateral hippocampal lesions. *Journal of Neurology, Neurosurgery, and Psychiatry, 20*, 11–21. (14)

Sears, L.L., & Steinmetz, J.E. (1990). Acquisition of classically conditioned-related activity in the hippocampus is affected by lesions of the cerebellar interpositus nucleus. *Behavioral Neuroscience, 104*, 681–692. (14)

Seeman, P., & Lee, T. (1975). Antipsychotic drugs: Direct correlation between clinical potency and presynaptic action on dopamine neurons. *Science, 188*, 1217–1219. (16)

Seeman, P., Lee, T., Chau-Wong, M., & Wong, K. (1976). Antipsychotic drug doses and neuroleptic/dopamine receptors. *Nature, 261*, 717–719. (16)

Seeman, P., Ulpian, C., Bergeron, C., Riederer, P., Jellinger, K., Gabriel, E., Reynolds, G.P., & Tourtellotte, W.W. (1984). Bimodal distribution of dopamine receptor densities in brains of schizophrenics. *Science, 225*, 728–731. (16)

Segal, N. (1984). Asymmetries in monozygotic twins. *American Journal of Psychiatry, 141*, 1638. (16)

Sejnowski, T.J., Chattarji, S., & Stanton, P.K. (1990). Homosynaptic long-term depression in hippocampus and neocortex. *Seminars in the Neurosciences, 2*, 355–363. (14)

Selemon, L.D., & Goldman-Rakic, P.S. (1985). Longitudinal topography and interdigitation of corticostriatal projections in the rhesus monkey. *Journal of Neuroscience, 5*, 776–794. (9)

Selzer, M.E. (1978). Mechanisms of functional recovery and regeneration after spinal cord transection in larval sea lamprey. *Journal of Physiology, 277,* 395–408. (15)

Sengelaub, D.R., & Arnold, A.P. (1989). Hormonal control of neuron number in sexually dimorphic spinal nuclei of the rat: I. Testosterone-regulated death in the dorsolateral nucleus. *Journal of Comparative Neurology, 280,* 622–629. (12)

Sengelaub, D.R., Nordeen, E.J., Nordeen, K.W., & Arnold, A.P. (1989). Hormonal control of neuron number in sexually dimorphic spinal nuclei of the rat: III. Differential effects of the androgen dihydrotestosterone. *Journal of Comparative Neurology, 280,* 637–644. (12)

Sergent, J. (1986). Subcortical coordination of hemisphere activity in commissurotomized patients. *Brain, 109,* 357–369. (5)

Shanon, B. (1980). Lateralization effects in musical decision tasks. *Neuropsychologia, 18,* 21–31. (5)

Shapiro, B.E., & Danly, M. (1985). The role of the right hemisphere in the control of speech prosody in propositional and affective contexts. *Brain and Language, 25,* 19–36. (5)

Shapiro, C.M., Bortz, R., Mitchell, D., Bartel, P., & Jooste, P. (1981). Slow-wave sleep: A recovery period after exercise. *Science, 214,* 1253–1254. (10)

Shapiro, D.J., Barton, M.C., McKearin, D.M., Chang, T.-C., Lew, D., Blume, J., Nielsen, D.A., & Gould, L. (1989). Estrogen regulation of gene transcription and mRNA stability. *Recent Advances in Hormone Research, 45,* 29–64. (12)

Shavit, Y., Terman, G.W., Martin, F.C., Lewis, J.W., Liebeskind, J.C., & Gale, R.P. (1985). Stress, opioid peptides, the immune system, and cancer. *Journal of Immunology, 135,* 834S–837S. (6)

Shepherd, G.M. (1988). *Neurobiology* (2nd ed.). New York: Oxford University Press. (3)

Sherman, S.M., & Spear, P.D. (1982). Organization of visual pathways in normal and visually deprived cats. *Physiological Reviews, 62,* 738–855. (7)

Sherrington, C.S. (1906). *The integrative action of the nervous system.* New York: Scribner's. (2nd ed.). New Haven, CT: Yale University Press, 1947. (3)

Sherrington, R. Brynjolfsson, J., Petursson, H., Potter, M., Dudleston, K., Barraclough, B., Wasmuth, J., Dobbs, M., & Gurling, H. (1988). Localization of a susceptibility locus for schizophrenia on chromosome 5. *Nature, 336,* 164–170. (16)

Sherry, D.F., & Vaccarino, A.L. (1989). Hippocampus and memory for food caches in black-capped chickadees. *Behavioral Neuroscience, 103,* 308–318. (14)

Sherwin, B.B. (1988). A comparative analysis of the role of androgen in human male and female sexual behavior: Behavioral specificity, critical thresholds, and sensitivity. *Psychobiology, 16,* 416–425. (12)

Shields, S.A. (1983). Development of autonomic nervous system responsivity in children: A review of the literature. *International Journal of Behavioral Development, 6,* 291–319. (13)

Shik, M.L., & Orlovsky, G.N. (1976). Neurophysiology of locomotor automatism. *Physiological Reviews, 56,* 465–501. (9)

Shimamura, A.P., & Squire, L.R. (1986). Korsakoff's syndrome: A study of the relation between anterograde amnesia and remote memory impairment. *Behavioral Neuroscience, 100,* 165–170. (14)

Shimazu, T., Megumi, N., & Saito, M. (1986). Chronic infusion of norepinephrine into the ventromedial hypothalamus induces obesity in rats. *Brain Research, 369,* 215–223. (11)

Shirley, S.G., & Persaud, K.C. (1990). The biochemistry of vertebrate olfaction and taste. *Seminars in the Neurosciences, 2,* 59–68. (6)

Shiromani, P.J., Siegel, J.M., Tomaszewski, K.S., & McGinty, D.J. (1986). Alterations in blood pressure and REM sleep after pontine carbachol microinfusion. *Experimental Neurology, 91,* 285–292. (10)

Shor-Posner, G., Grinker, J.A., Marinescu, C., & Leibowitz, S.F. (1985). Role of hypothalamic norepinephrine in control of meal patterns. *Physiology & Behavior, 35,* 209–214. (11)

Shoulson, I. (1990). Huntington's disease: Cognitive and psychiatric features. *Neuropsychiatry, Neuropsychology, and Behavioral Neurology, 3,* 15–22. (9)

Shutts, D. (1982). *Lobotomy: Resort to the knife.* New York: Van Nostrand Reinhold. (4)

Shyne-Athwal, S., Riccio, R.V., Chakraborty, G., & Ingoglia, N.A. (1986). Protein modification by amino acid addition is increased in crushed sciatic but not optic nerves. *Science, 231,* 603–605. (15)

Sidman, R.L., Green, M.C., & Appel, S.H. (1965). *Catalog of the neurological mutants of the mouse.* Cambridge, MA: Harvard University Press. (4)

Sidtis, J.J., Volpe, B.T., Holtzman, J.D., Wilson, D.H., & Gazzaniga, M.S. (1981). Cognitive interaction after staged callosal section: Evidence for transfer of semantic activation. *Science, 212,* 344–346. (5)

Siegel, A., & Brutus, M. (1990). Neural substrates of aggression and rage in the cat. *Progress in Psychobiology and Physiological Psychology, 14,* 135–233. (13)

Siegel, A., & Pott, C.B. (1988). Neural substrates of aggression and flight in the cat. *Progress in Neurobiology, 31,* 261–283. (13)

Siegel, J.M., McGinty, D.J., & Breedlove, S.M. (1977). Sleep and waking activity of pontine gigantocellular field neurons. *Experimental Neurology, 56,* 553–573. (10)

Siegel, J.M., Wheeler, R.L., & McGinty, D.J. (1979). Activity of medullary reticular formation neurons in the unrestrained cat during waking and sleep. *Brain Research, 179,* 49–60. (10)

Siegelman, M. (1974). Parental background of male homosexuals and heterosexuals. *Archives of Sexual Behavior, 3,* 3–18. (12)

Siever, L.J., Coursey, R.D., Alterman, I.S., Buchsbaum, M.S., & Murphy, D.L. (1984). Impaired smooth pursuit eye movement: Vulnerability marker for schizotypal personality disorder in a normal volunteer population. *American Journal of Psychiatry, 141,* 1560–1566. (16)

Silinsky, E.M. (1989). Adenosine derivatives and neuronal function. *Seminars in the Neurosciences, 1,* 155–165. (3)

Simerly, R.B., Young, B.J., Capozza, M.A., & Swanson, L.W. (1989). Estrogen differentially regulates neuropeptide gene expression in a sexually dimorphic olfactory pathway. *Proceedings of the National Academy of Sciences, U.S.A., 86,* 4766–4770. (12)

Simmons, J.A., Wever, E.G., & Pylka, J.M. (1971). Periodical cicada: Sound production and hearing. *Science, 171,* 212–213. (6)

Simon, R.P., Swan, J.H., Griffiths, T., & Meldrum, B.S. (1984). Blockade of N-methyl-D-aspartate receptors may protect against ischemic damage in the brain. *Science, 226,* 850–852. (15)

Simpson, J.L. (1976). *Disorders of sexual differentiation.* New York: Academic Press. (12)

Singer, W. (1986). Neuronal activity as a shaping factor in postnatal development of visual cortex. In W.T. Greenough & J.M. Jusaska (Eds.), *Developmental neuropsychobiology* (pp. 271–293). Orlando, FL: Academic Press. (8)

Sitaram, N., Weingartner, H., & Gillin, J.C. (1978). Human serial learning: Enhancement with arecholine and choline and impairment with scopolamine. *Science, 201,* 274–276. (14)

Sjöström, M., Friden, J., & Ekblom, B. (1987). Endurance, what is it? Muscle morphology after an extremely long distance run. *Acta Physiologica Scandinavica, 130,* 513–520. (9)

Sklar, L.S., & Anisman, H. (1981). Stress and cancer. *Psychological Bulletin, 89,* 369–406. (13)

Skrede, K.K., & Mathe-Sørenssen, D. (1981). Increased resting and evoked release of transmitter following repetitive electrical tetanization in hippocampus: A biochemical correlate to long-lasting synaptic potentiation. *Brain Research, 208,* 436–441. (14)

Sloviter, R.S., Damiano, B.P., & Connor, J.D. (1980). Relative potency of amphetamine isomers in causing the serotonin behavioral syndrome in rats. *Biological Psychiatry, 15,* 789–796. (16)

Small, J.G., Kellams, J.J., Milstein, V., & Small, I.F. (1980). Complications with electroconvulsive treatment combined with lithium. *Biological Psychiatry, 15,* 103–112. (16)

Smeraldi, E., Kidd, K.K., Negri, F., Heimbuch, R., & Melica, A.M. (1979). Genetic studies of affective disorders. In J. Obiols, C. Ballús, E. González Monclús, & J. Pujol (Eds.), *Biological psychiatry today* (pp. 60–65). Amsterdam: Elsevier/North Holland Biomedical Press. (16)

Smith, D.C. (1981). Functional restoration of vision in the cat after long-term monocular deprivation. *Science, 213,* 1137–1139. (8)

Smith, D.V., VanBuskirk, R.L., Travers, J.B., & Bieber, S.L. (1983a). Gustatory neuron types in hamster brain stem. *Journal of Neurophysiology, 50,* 522–540. (6)

Smith, D.V., VanBuskirk, R.L., Travers, J.B., & Bieber, S.L. (1983b). Coding of taste stimuli by hamster brain stem neurons. *Journal of Neurophysiology, 50,* 541–558. (6)

Smith, G.P., Jerome, C., Cushin, B.J., Eterno, R., & Simansky, K.J. (1981). Abdominal vagotomy blocks the satiety effect of cholecystokinin in the rat. *Science, 213,* 1036–1037. (11)

Smith, L.T. (1975). The interanimal transfer phenomenon: A review. *Psychological Bulletin, 81,* 1078–1095. (14)

Snyder, G.L., & Stricker, E.M. (1985). Effects of lateral hypothalamic lesions on food intake of rats during exposure to cold. *Behavioral Neuroscience, 99,* 310–322. (15)

Snyder, S.H. (1984). Drug and neurotransmitter receptors in the brain. *Science, 224,* 22–31. (3)

Snyder, S.H., Banerjee, S.P., Yamamura, H.I., & Greenberg, D. (1974). Drugs, neurotransmitters, and schizophrenia. *Science, 184,* 1243–1253. (16)

Snyder, S.H., & D'Amato, R.J. (1986). MPTP: A neurotoxin relevant to the pathophysiology of Parkinson's disease. *Neurology, 36,* 250–258. (9)

Snyder, S.H., Sklar, P.B., Hwang, P.M., & Pevsner, J. (1989). Molecular mechanisms of olfaction. *Trends in Neuroscience, 12,* 35–38. (6)

Solomon, C.M., Holzman, P.S., Levin, S., & Gale, H.J. (1987). The association between eye-tracking dysfunctions and thought disorder in psychosis. *Archives of General Psychiatry, 44,* 31–35. (16)

Somjen, G.G. (1988). Nervenkitt: Notes on the history of the concept of neuroglia. *Glia, 1,* 2–9. (2)

Sonderegger, T.B. (1970). Intracranial stimulation and maternal behavior. *APA Convention Proceedings,* 78th meeting, 245–246. (13)

Sperry, R.W. (1943). Visuomotor coordination in the newt (*Triturus viridescens*) after regeneration of the optic nerve. *Journal of Comparative Neurology, 79,* 33–55. (8)

Sperry, R.W. (1961). Cerebral organization and behavior. *Science, 133,* 1749–1757. (5)

Sperry, R.W. (1988). Psychology's mentalist paradigm and the religion/science tension. *American Psychologist, 43,* 607–613. (1)

Spiegel, T.A. (1973). Caloric regulation of food intake in man. *Journal of Comparative and Physiological Psychology, 84,* 24–37. (11)

Spies, G. (1965). Food versus intra-cranial self-stimulation reinforcement in food-deprived rats. *Journal of Comparative and Physiological Psychology, 60,* 153–157. (13)

Spurzheim, J.G. (1908). *Phrenology* (rev. ed.). Philadelphia: Lippincott. (4)

Squire, L.R. (1982). The neuropsychology of human memory. *Annual Review of Neuroscience, 5,* 241–273. (14)

Squire, L.R., Amaral, D.G., & Press, G.A. (1990). Magnetic resonance imaging of the hippocampal formation and mammillary nuclei distinguish medial temporal lobe and diencephalic amnesia. *Journal of Neuroscience, 10,* 3106–3117. (14)

Squire, L.R., Haist, F., & Shimamura, A.P. (1989). The neurology of memory: Quantitative assessment of retrograde amnesia in two groups of amnesic pa-

tients. *Journal of Neuroscience, 9,* 828–839. (14)

Squire, L.R., & Spanis, C.W. (1984). Long gradient of retrograde amnesia in mice: Continuity with the findings in humans. *Behavioral Neuroscience, 98,* 345–348. (14)

Squire, L.R., Wetzel, C.D., & Slater, P.C. (1979). Memory complaint after electroconvulsive therapy: Assessment with a new self-rating instrument. *Biological Psychiatry, 14,* 791–801. (16)

Squire, L.R., Zola-Morgan, S., & Chen, K.S. (1988). Human amnesia and animal models of amnesia: Performance of amnesic patients on tests designed for the monkey. *Behavioral Neuroscience, 102,* 210–221. (14)

Squire, L.R., & Zouzounis, J.A. (1986). FCT and memory: Brief pulse versus sine wave. *American Journal of Psychiatry, 143,* 596–601. (16)

Staller, J., Buchanan, D., Singer, M., Lappin, J., & Webb, W. (1978). Alexia without agraphia: An experimental case study. *Brain and Language, 5,* 378–387. (5)

Stanford, L.R. (1987). Conduction velocity variations minimize conduction time differences among retinal ganglion cell axons. *Science, 238,* 358–360. (7)

Stanley, B.G., Schwartz, D.H., Hernandez, L., Leibowitz, S.F., & Hoebel, B.G. (1989). Patterns of extracellular 5-hydroxyindoleacetic acid (5-HIAA) in the paraventricular hypothalamus (PVN): Relation to circadian rhythm and deprivation-induced eating behavior. *Pharmacology, Biochemistry, & Behavior, 33,* 257–260. (11)

Stark, P., & Hardison, C.D. (1985, March). A review of multicenter controlled studies of fluoxeine vs. imipramine and placebo in outpatients with major depressive disorders. *Journal of Clinical Psychiatry, 46*(3, Sec. 2), 53–58. (16)

Starke, K. (1981). Presynaptic receptors. *Annual Review of Pharmacology and Toxicology, 21,* 7–30. (3, 16)

Starkstein, S.E., & Robinson, R.G. (1986). Cerebral lateralization in depression. *American Journal of Psychiatry, 143,* 1631. (16)

Stäubli, U., Faraday, R., & Lynch, G. (1985). Pharmacological dissociation of memory: Anisomycin, a protein synthesis inhibitor, and leupeptin, a protease inhibitor, block different learning tasks. *Behavioral and Neural Biology, 43,* 287–297. (14)

Steffen, H., Heinrich, U., & Kratzer, W. (1978). Raumorientierungsstörung und Körperschemairritation bei Turner-Syndrom-Patienten. Ein Syndrom der rechtshemisphärischen Hirnreifungsverzögerung [Disturbance of spatial orientation and body image in Turner's syndrome patients. A syndrome of impaired maturation of the right hemisphere of the brain]. *Zeitschrift für Kinder- und Jugendpsychiatrie, 6,* 131–141. (12)

Steger, R.W. (1976). Extrahypothalamic neural influences affecting the onset of puberty in the female. In E.S.E. Hafez & J.J. Peluso (Eds.), *Sexual maturity* (pp. 53–69). Ann Arbor, MI: Ann Arbor Science. (12)

Stein, D.G., Finger, S., & Hart, T. (1983). Brain damage and recovery: Problems and perspectives. *Behavioral and Neural Biology, 37,* 185–222. (15)

Stein, L. (1962). Effects and interactions of imipramine, chlorpromazine, reserpine, and amphetamine on self-stimulation: Possible neurophysiological basis of depression. In J. Wortis (Ed.), *Recent advances in biological psychiatry* (Vol. 4, pp. 288–308). New York: Plenum. (16)

Stein, L., & Wise, C.D. (1971). Possible etiology of schizophrenia: Progressive damage to the noradrenergic reward system by 6-hydroxydopamine. *Science, 171,* 1032–1036. (16)

Stein, M., Miller, A.H., & Trestman, R.L. (1991). Depression, the immune system, and health and illness. *Archives of General Psychiatry, 48,* 171–177. (13)

Stephens, J.H., & Shaffer, J.W. (1973). A controlled replication of the effectiveness of diphenylhydantoin in reducing irritability and anxiety in selected neurotic outpatients. *Journal of Clinical Pharmacology, 13,* 351–356. (13)

Stephenson, F.A., & Dolphin, A.C. (1989). GABA and glycine neurotransmission. *Seminars in the Neurosciences, 1,* 115–123. (3)

St. George-Hyslop, P.H., Tanzi, R.E., Polinsky, R.J., Haines, J.L., Nee, L., Watkins, P.C., Myers, R.H., Feldman, R.G., Pollen, D., Drachman, D., Growdon, J., Bruni, A., Foncin, J.-F., Salmon, D., Frommelt, P., Amaducci, L., Sorbi, S., Piacentini, S., Stewart, G.D., Hobbs, W.J., Conneally, M., & Gusella, J.F. (1987a). The genetic defect causing familial Alzheimer's disease maps on chromosome 21. *Science, 235,* 885–890. (14)

St. George-Hyslop, P.H., Tanzi, R.E., Polinsky, R.J., Neve, R.L., Pollen, D., Drachman, D., Growdon, J., Cupples, L.A., Nee, L., Myers, R.H., O'Sullivan, D., Watkins, P.C., Amos, J.A., Deutsch, C.K., Bodfish, J.W., Kinsbourne, M., Feldman, R.G., Bruni, A., Amaducci, L., Foncin, J.-F., & Gusella, J.F. (1987b). Absence of duplication of chromosome 21 genes in familial and sporadic Alzheimer's disease. *Science, 238,* 664–666. (14)

Stockman, E.R., Callaghan, R.S., Gallagher, C.A., & Baum, M.J. (1986). Sexual differentiation of play behavior in the ferret. *Behavioral Neuroscience, 100,* 563–568. (12)

Strachan, R.D., Whittle, I.R., & Miller, J.D. (1989). Hypothermia and severe head injury. *Brain Injury, 3,* 51–55. (15)

Straus, E., & Yalow, R.S. (1978). Cholecystokinin in the brains of obese and nonobese mice. *Science, 203,* 68–69. (11)

Streissguth, A.P., Barr, H.M., & Martin, D.C. (1983). Maternal alcohol use and neonatal habituation assessed with the Brazelton scale. *Child Development, 54,* 1109–1118. (8)

Strichartz, G., Rando, T., & Wang, G.K. (1987). An integrated view of the molecular toxinology of sodium channel gating in excitable cells. *Annual Review of Neuroscience, 10,* 237–267. (2)

Stricker, E.M. (1969). Osmoregulation and volume regulation in rats: Inhibition of hypovolemic thirst by water. *American Journal of Physiology, 217,* 98–105. (11)

Stricker, E.M. (1976). Drinking by rats after lateral hypothalamic lesions: A new look at the lateral hypothalamic syndrome. *Journal of Comparative and Physiological Psychology, 90,* 127–143. (11)

Stricker, E.M. (1983). Thirst and sodium appetite after colloid treatment in rats: Role of the renin-angiotensin-aldosterone system. *Behavioral Neuroscience, 97,* 725–737. (11)

Stricker, E.M., & Coburn, P.C. (1978). Osmoregulatory thirst in rats after lateral preoptic lesions. *Journal of Comparative and Physiological Psychology, 92,* 350–361. (11)

Stricker, E.M., Cooper, P.H., Marshall, J.F., & Zigmond, M.J. (1979). Acute homeostatic imbalances reinstate sensorimotor dysfunctions in rats with lateral hypothalamic lesions. *Journal of Comparative and Physiological Psychology, 93,* 512–521. (15)

Stricker, E.M., & Macarthur, J.P. (1974). Physiological bases for different effects of extravascular colloid treatments on water and NaCl solution drinking by rats. *Physiology & Behavior, 13,* 389–394. (11)

Stricker, E.M., Rowland, N., Saller, C.F., & Friedman, M.I. (1977). Homeostasis during hypoglycemia: Central control of adrenal secretion and peripheral control of feeding. *Science, 196,* 79–81. (11)

Stricker, E.M., Swerdloff, A.F., & Zigmond, M.J. (1978). Intrahypothalamic injections of kainic acid produce feeding and drinking deficits in rats. *Brain Research, 158,* 470–473. (11)

Strupp, B.J., Himmelstein, S., Bunsey, M., Levitsky, D.A., & Kesler, M. (1990). Cognitive profile of rats exposed to lactational hyperphenylalaninemia: Correspondence with human mental retardation. *Developmental Psychobiology, 23,* 195–214. (8)

Stryker, M.P., Sherk, H., Leventhal, A.G., & Hirsch, H.V.B. (1978). Physiological consequences for the cat's visual cortex of effectively restricting early visual experience with oriented contours. *Journal of Neurophysiology, 41,* 896–909. (8)

Stunkard, A.J., Sørensen, T.I.A., Hanis, C., Teasdale, T.W., Chakraborty, R., Schull, W.J., & Schulsinger, F. (1986). An adoption study of human obesity. *New England Journal of Medicine, 314,* 193–198. (11)

Stuss, D.T., & Benson, D.F. (1984). Neuropsychological studies of the frontal lobes. *Psychological Bulletin, 95,* 3–28. (4)

Sudzak, P.D., Glowa, J.R., Crawley, J.N., Schwartz, R.D., Skolnick, P., & Paul, S.M. (1986). A selective imidazobenzodiazepine antagonist of ethanol in the rat. *Science, 234,* 1243–1247. (13)

Sullivan, R.C. (1980). Why do autistic children?... *Journal of Autism and Developmental Disorders, 10,* 231–241. (16)

Sulser, F., Gillespie, D.D., Mishra, R., & Manier, D.H. (1984). Desensitization by antidepressants of central norepinephrine receptor systems coupled to adenylate cyclase. *Annals of the New York Academy of Sciences, 430,* 91–101. (16)

Summers, W.K., Robins, E., & Reich, T. (1979). The natural history of acute organic mental syndrome after bilateral electroconvulsive therapy. *Biological Psychiatry, 14,* 905–912. (16)

Surprenant, A. (1989). The neurotransmitter noradrenaline and its receptors. *Seminars in the Neurosciences, 1,* 125–136. (3)

Sutton, R.L., Hovda, D.A., & Feeney, D.M. (1989). Amphetamine accelerates recovery of locomotor function following bilateral frontal cortex ablation in rats. *Behavioral Neuroscience, 103,* 837–841. (15)

Swaab, D.F., & Fliers, E. (1985). A sexually dimorphic nucleus in the human brain. *Science, 228,* 1112–1115. (12)

Swan, H., & Schätte, C. (1977). Antimetabolic extract from the brain of the hibernating ground squirrel *Citellus tridecemlineatus. Science, 195,* 84–85. (10)

Swash, M. (1972). Released involuntary laughter after temporal lobe infarction. *Journal of Neurology, Neurosurgery, and Psychiatry, 35,* 108–113. (13)

Swedo, S.E., Leonard, H.L., Rapoport, J.L., Lenane, M.C., Goldberger, E.L., & Cheslow, D.L. (1989). A double-blind comparison of clomipramine and desipramine in the treatment of trichotillomania (hair-pulling). *New England Journal of Medicine, 321,* 497–501. (13)

Szymusiak, R., DeMory, A., Kittrell, M.W., & Satinoff, E. (1985). Diurnal changes in thermoregulatory behavior in rats with medial preoptic lesions. *American Journal of Physiology, 249,* R219–R227. (11)

Szymusiak, R., & McGinty, D. (1986). Sleep-related neuronal discharge in the basal forebrain of cats. *Brain Research, 370,* 82–92. (10)

Takeuchi, A. (1977). Junctional transmission: I. Postsynaptic mechanisms. In E.R. Kandel (Ed.), *Handbook of physiology Section 1: Neurophysiology, Vol. 1. Cellular biology of neurons* (Pt. 1, pp. 295–327). Bethesda, MD: American Physiological Society. (3)

Tan, T.-L., Kales, J.D., Kales, A., Soldatos, C.R., & Bixler, E.O. (1984). Biopsychobehavioral correlates of insomnia, IV: Diagnosis based on DSM-III. *American Journal of Psychiatry, 141,* 357–362. (10)

Tanabe, T., Iino, M., & Takagi, S.F. (1975). Discrimination of odors in olfactory bulb, pyriform-amygdaloid areas, and orbitofrontal cortex of the monkey. *Journal of Neurophysiology, 38,* 1284–1296. (6)

Tanzi, R.E., Bird, E.D., Latt, S.A., & Neve, R.L. (1987). The amyloid beta protein gene is not duplicated in brains from patients with Alzheimer's disease. *Science, 238,* 666–669. (14)

Tasker, R.R. (1976). Somatotopographic representation in the human thalamus, midbrain, and spinal cord. In T.P. Morley (Ed.), *Current controversies in neurosurgery* (pp. 485–495). Philadelphia: Saunders. (6)

Taub, E., & Berman, A.J. (1968). Movement and learning in the absence of sensory feedback. In S.J. Freedman (Ed.), *The neuropsychology of spatially oriented behavior* (pp. 173–192). Homewood, IL: Dorsey. (9)

Tauc, L. (1982). Nonvesicular release of neurotransmitter. *Physiological Reviews, 62,* 857–893. (3)

Taylor, H.G. (1984). Early brain injury and cognitive development. In C.R. Almli &

S. Finger (Eds.), *Early brain damage* (pp. 325–345). Orlando, FL: Academic Press. (15)

Teitelbaum, P. (1955). Sensory control of hypothalamic hyperphagia. *Journal of Comparative and Physiological Psychology, 48,* 156–163. (11)

Teitelbaum, P. (1957). Random and food-directed activity in hyperphagic and normal rats. *Journal of Comparative and Physiological Psychology, 50,* 486–490. (11)

Teitelbaum, P. (1961). Disturbances in feeding and drinking behavior after hypothalamic lesions. In M.R. Jones (Ed.), *Nebraska Symposia on Motivation 1961* (pp. 39–69). Lincoln, NE: University of Nebraska Press. (11)

Temple, C.M., Jeeves, M.A., & Vilarroya, O. (1989). Ten pen men: Rhyming skills in two children with callosal agenesis. *Brain and Language, 37,* 548–564. (5)

Terman, G.W., & Liebeskind, J.C. (1986). Relation of stress-induced analgesia to stimulation-produced analgesia. *Annals of the New York Academy of Sciences, 467,* 300–308. (6)

Terman, G.W., Shavitt, Y., Lewis, J.W., Cannon, J.T., & Liebeskind, J.C. (1984). Intrinsic mechanisms of pain inhibition: Activation by stress. *Science, 226,* 1270–1277. (6)

Terrace, H.S., Petitto, L.A., Sanders, R.J., & Bever, T.G. (1979). Can an ape create a sentence? *Science, 206,* 891–902. (5)

Tetrud, J.W., & Langston, J.W. (1989). The effect of deprenyl (Selegiline) on the natural history of Parkinson's disease. *Science, 245,* 519–522. (9)

Tetrud, J.W., Langston, J.W., Garbe, P.L., & Ruttenber, A.J. (1989). Mild parkinsonism in persons exposed to 1-methyl-4-phenyl-1,2,3,6-tetrahydropyridine (MPTP). *Neurology, 39,* 1483–1487. (9)

Teyler, T.J., & DiScenna, P. (1986). The hippocampal memory indexing theory. *Behavioral Neuroscience, 100,* 147–154. (14)

Thaker, G.K., Tamminga, C.A., Alphs, L.D., Lafferman, J., Ferraro, T.N., & Hare, T.A. (1987). Brain gamma-aminobutyric acid abnormality in tardive dyskinesia. *Archives of General Psychiatry, 44,* 522–529. (16)

Thomas, P.K. (1988). Clinical aspects of PNS regeneration. In S.G. Waxman (Ed.), *Advances in Neurology* (Vol. 47, pp. 9–29). New York: Raven Press. (15)

Thomas, R.K. (1980). Evolution of intelligence: An approach to its assessment. *Brain Behavior and Evolution, 17,* 454–472. (4)

Thompson, D.A., & Campbell, R.G. (1977). Hunger in humans induced by 2-deoxy-D-glucose: Glucoprivic control of taste preference and food intake. *Science, 198,* 1065–1068. (11)

Thompson, J.K., Jarvie, G.J., Lahey, B.B., & Cureton, K.J. (1982). Exercise and obesity: Etiology, physiology, and intervention. *Psychological Bulletin, 91,* 55–79. (11)

Thompson, R.F. (1986). The neurobiology of learning and memory. *Science, 233,* 941–947. (14)

Ticku, M.K., & Kulkarni, S.K. (1988). Molecular interactions of ethanol with GABAergic system and potential of

Ro15-4513 as an ethanol antagonist. *Pharmacology Biochemistry & Behavior, 30,* 501–510. (13)

Tinbergen, N. (1951). *The study of instinct.* Oxford, England: Oxford University Press. (1)

Tinbergen, N. (1973). The search for animal roots of human behavior. In N. Tinbergen, *The animal in its world* (Vol. 2, pp. 161–174). Cambridge, MA: Harvard University Press. (1)

Tippin, J., & Henn, F.A. (1982). Modified leukotomy in the treatment of intractable obsessional neurosis. *American Journal of Psychiatry, 139,* 1601–1603. (4)

Tolstoy, L. (1978). *Tolstoy's letters: Vol. 1. 1828–1879.* New York: Scribner's. (13)

Tomkins, S. (1980). Affect as amplification: Some modifications in theory. In R. Plutchik & H. Kellerman (Eds.), *Emotion: Theory, research, and experience* (Vol. 1, pp. 141–164). New York: Academic Press. (13)

Tong, L., Spear, P.D., Kalil, R.E., & Callahan, E.C. (1982). Loss of retinal X-cells in cats with neonatal or adult visual cortex damage. *Science, 217,* 72–75. (8)

Tordoff, M.G., Novin, D., & Russek, M. (1982). Effects of hepatic denervation on the anorexic response to epinephrine, amphetamine, and lithium chloride: A behavioral identification of glucostatic afferents. *Journal of Comparative and Physiological Psychology, 96,* 361–375. (11)

Torrey, E.F. (1986). Geographic variations in schizophrenia. In C. Shagass, R.C. Josiassen, W.H. Bridger, K.J. Weiss, D. Stoff, & G.M. Simpson (Ed.), *Biological Psychiatry 1985* (pp. 1080–1082). New York: Elsevier. (16)

Torrey, E.F., Rawlings, R., & Waldman, I.N. (1988). Schizophrenic births and viral diseases in two states. *Schizophrenia Research, 1,* 73–77. (16)

Tosteson, D.C. (April 1981). Lithium and mania. *Scientific American, 244*(4), 164–174. (16)

Träskman, L., Åsberg, M., Bertilsson, L., & Sjöstrand, L. (1981). Monoamine metabolites in CSF and suicidal behavior. *Archives of General Psychiatry, 38,* 631–636. (12)

Travers, S.P., Pfaffmann, C., & Norgren, R. (1986). Convergence of lingual and palatal gustatory neural activity in the nucleus of the solitary tract. *Brain Research, 365,* 305–320. (6)

Traverse, J., & Latto, R. (1986). Impairments in route negotiation through a maze after dorsolateral frontal, inferior parietal or premotor lesions in cynomolgus monkeys. *Behavioural Brain Research, 20,* 203–215. (4)

Travis, A.M., & Woolsey, C.N. (1956). Motor performance of monkeys after bilateral partial and total cerebral decortications. *American Journal of Physical Medicine, 35,* 273–310. (15)

Treiser, S.L., Cascio, C.S., O'Donohue, T.L., Thoa, N.B., Jacobowitz, D.M., & Kellar, K.J. (1981). Lithium increases serotonin release and decreases serotonin receptors in the hippocampus. *Science, 213,* 1529–1532. (16)

Trevarthen, C. (1974). Cerebral embryology and the split brain. In M. Kinsbourne & W.L. Smith (Eds.), *Hemispheric disconnec-*

tion and cerebral function (pp. 208–236). Springfield, IL: Charles C. Thomas. (5)

Trimble, M.R., & Thompson, P.J. (1986). Neuropsychological and behavioral sequelae of spontaneous seizures. *Annals of the New York Academy of Sciences, 462,* 284–292. (16)

Tsai, L., Stewart, M.A., & August, G. (1981). Implication of sex differences in the familial transmission of infantile autism. *Journal of Autism and Developmental Disorders, 11,* 165–173. (16)

Ts'o, D.Y., & Gilbert, C.D. (1988). The organization of chromatic and spatial interactions in the primate striate cortex. *Journal of Neuroscience, 8,* 1712–1727. (7)

Tucker, D.M. (1981). Lateral brain function, emotion, and conceptualization. *Psychological Bulletin, 89,* 19–46. (5)

Tunks, E.R., & Dermer, S.W. (1977). Carbamezepine in the dyscontrol syndrome associated with limbic system dysfunction. *Journal of Nervous and Mental Disease, 164,* 56–63. (13)

Turek, F.W. (1985). Circadian neural rhythms in mammals. *Annual Review of Physiology, 47,* 49–64. (10)

Turek, F.W., & Losee-Olson, S. (1986). A benzodiazepine used in the treatment of insomnia phase-shifts the mammalian circadian clock. *Nature, 321,* 167–168. (10)

Turner, S.M., Beidel, D.C., & Nathan, R.S. (1985). Biological factors in obsessive-compulsive disorders. *Psychological Disorders, 97,* 430–450. (13)

Udin, S.B., & Scherer, W.J. (1990). Restoration of the plasticity of binocular maps by NMDA after the critical period in *Xenopus. Science, 249,* 669–672. (14)

Udry, J.R., & Morris, N.M. (1968). Distribution of coitus in the menstrual cycle. *Nature, 220,* 593–596. (12)

Ungerleider, L.G., & Pribram, K.H. (1977). Inferotemporal versus combined pulvinar-prestriate lesions in the rhesus monkey: Effects on color, object, and pattern discrimination. *Neuropsychologia, 15,* 481–498. (7)

Uphouse, L. (1980). Reevaluation of mechanisms that mediate brain differences between enriched and impoverished animals. *Psychological Bulletin, 88,* 215–232. (2)

Vaccarino, F.J., Pettit, H.O., Bloom, F.E., & Koob, G.F. (1985). Effects of intracerebroventricular administration of methyl naloxonium chloride on heroin self-administration in the rat. *Pharmacology Biochemistry & Behavior, 23,* 495–498. (13)

Vaillant, G.E., & Milofsky, E.S. (1982). The etiology of alcoholism. *American Psychologist, 37,* 494–503. (3)

Valenstein, E.S., & Beer, B. (1962). Reinforcing brain stimulation in competition with water reward and shock avoidance. *Science, 137,* 1052–1054. (13)

Valenstein, E.S., Cox, V.C., & Kakolewski, J.W. (1970). Reexamination of the role of the hypothalamus in motivation. *Psychological Review, 77,* 16–31. (1)

Vallacher, R.R., & Wegner, D.M. (1987). What do people think they're doing? Action identification and human behavior. *Psychological Review, 94,* 3–15. (9)

Valousková, V., Brácha, V., Bures, J., Hernandez-Mesa, N., Macias-Gonzales, R., Mazurová, Y., & Nemecek, S. (1990). Unilateral striatal grafts induce behavioral and electrophysiological asymmetry in rats with bilateral kainate lesions of the caudate nucleus. *Behavioral Neuroscience, 104,* 671–680. (15)

Valvo, A. (1971). *Sight restoration after long-term blindness.* New York: American Foundation for the Blind. (8)

Valzelli, L. (1973). The "isolation syndrome" in mice. *Psychopharmacologia, 31,* 305–320. (13)

Valzelli, L., & Bernasconi, S. (1979). Aggressiveness by isolation and brain serotonin turnover changes in different strains of mice. *Neuropsychobiology, 5,* 129–135. (13)

Valzelli, L., Bernasconi, S., & Dalessandro, M. (1983). Time-courses of P-CPA-induced depletion of brain serotonin and muricidal aggression in the rat. *Pharmacological Research Communications, 15,* 387–395. (13)

Valzelli, L., Bernasconi, S., & Garattini, S. (1981). p-Chlorophenylalanine-induced muricidal aggression in male and female laboratory rats. *Neuropsychobiology, 7,* 315–320. (13)

Valzelli, L., & Garattini, S. (1972). Biochemical and behavioural changes induced by isolation in rats. *Neuropharmacology, 11,* 17–22. (13)

Van den Aardweg, G.J. (1984). Parents of homosexuals—not guilty? Interpretation of childhood psychological data. *American Journal of Psychiatry, 38,* 180–189. (12)

Vanderweele, D.A., Novin, D., Rezek, M., & Sanderson, J.D. (1974). Duodenal or hepatic-portal glucose perfusion: Evidence for duodenally based satiety. *Physiology & Behavior, 12,* 467–473. (11)

VandeWoude, S., Richt, J.A., Zink, M.C., Rott, R., Narayan, O., & Clements, J.E. (1990). A Borna virus cDNA encoding a protein recognized by antibodies in humans with behavioral diseases. *Science, 250,* 1278–1281. (16)

Van Hoesen, G.W., Human, B.T., & Damasio, A.R. (1991). Entorhinal cortex pathology in Alzheimer's disease. *Hippocampus, 1,* 1–8. (14)

van Praag, H.M. (1977). The significance of the cerebral dopamine metabolism in the pathogenesis and treatment of psychotic disorders. In E.S. Gershon, R.H. Belmaker, S.S. Kety, & M. Rosenbaum (Eds.), *The impact of biology on modern psychiatry* (pp. 1–26). New York: Plenum. (16)

VanTwyver, H., & Allison, T. (1970). Sleep in the opossum *Didelphis marsupialis. Electroencephalography and Clinical Neurophysiology, 29,* 181–189. (10)

Van Zoeren, J.G., & Stricker, E.M. (1977). Effects of preoptic, lateral hypothalamic, or dopamine-depleting lesions on behavioral thermoregulation in rats exposed to the cold. *Journal of Comparative and Physiological Psychology, 91,* 989–999. (11)

Varon, S.S., & Somjen, G.G. (1979). Neuron-glia interactions. *Neurosciences Research Program Bulletin, 17,* 1–239. (2)

Verbalis, J.G., McCann, M.J., McHale, C.M., & Stricker, E.M. (1986). Oxytocin secretion in response to cholecystokinin and food: Differentiation of nausea from satiety. *Science, 232,* 1417–1419. (11)

Verbeeck, R.M.H., Driessens, F.C.M., & Rotgans, J. (1990). Aluminum in tooth pastes and Alzheimer's disease. *Acta Stomatologica Belgica, 87,* 141–144. (14)

Victor, M., Adams, R.D., & Collins, G.H. (1971). *The Wernicke-Korsakoff syndrome.* Philadelphia: F.A. Davis. (14)

Virkkunen, M., DeJong, J., Bartko, J., Goodwin, F.K., & Linnoila, M. (1989). Relationship of psychobiological variables to recidivism in violent offenders and impulsive fire setters. *Archives of General Psychiatry, 46,* 600–603. (13)

Virkkunen, M., Nuutila, A., Goodwin, F.K., & Linnoila, M. (1987). Cerebrospinal fluid monoamine metabolite levels in male arsonists. *Archives of General Psychiatry, 44,* 241–247. (13)

Vizi, E.S. (1984). *Non-synaptic interactions between neurons: Modulation of neurochemical transmission.* Chichester, England: John Wiley. (3)

Vogel, G.W., Thompson, F.C., Jr., Thurmond, A., & Rivers, B. (1973). The effect of REM deprivation on depression. In W.P. Koella & P. Levin (Eds.), *Sleep: Physiology, biochemistry, psychology, pharmacology, clinical implications* (pp. 191–195). Basel: Karger. (16)

Volavka, J. (1990). Aggression, electroencephalography, and evoked potentials: A critical review. *Neuropsychiatry, Neuropsychology, and Behavioral Neurology, 3,* 249–259. (13)

Voll, C.L., Whishaw, I.Q., & Auer, R.N. (1989). Postischemic insulin reduces spatial learning deficit following transient forebrain ischemia in rats. *Stroke, 20,* 646–651. (15)

vom Saal, F.S., Grant, W.M., McMullen, C.W., & Laves, K.S. (1983). High fetal estrogen concentrations: Correlation with increased adult sexual activity and decreased aggression in male mice. *Science, 220,* 1306–1309. (12)

von Békésy, G. (1956). Current status of theories of hearing. *Science, 123,* 779–783. (6)

von Békésy, G. (1957). The ear. *Scientific American, 197*(2), 66–78. (6)

von Bonin, G. (1950). *Essay on the cerebral cortex.* Springfield, IL: Charles C. Thomas. (4)

von Holst, E., & von St. Paul, U. (1960). Vom Wirkungsgefüge der Triebe [Concerning the stratification of drives]. *Naturwissenschaften, 47,* 409–422. (1)

von Uexküll, J. (1957). A stroll through the worlds of animals and men. In C.H. Schiller (Ed.), *Instinctive Behavior* (pp. 5–80). New York: International Universities Press. (Original work published 1934) (4)

Waddington, J.L., Youssef, H.A., Dolphin, C., & Kinsella, A. (1987). Cognitive dysfunction, negative symptoms, and tardive dyskinesia in schizophrenia. *Archives of General Psychiatry, 44,* 907–912. (16)

Wald, G. (1968). Molecular basis of visual excitation. *Science, 162,* 230–239. (7)

Waldvogel, J.A. (1990). The bird's eye view. *American Scientist, 78,* 342–353. (7)

Wall, P.D. (1988). Recruitment of ineffective synapses after injury. In S.G. Wax-

man (Ed.), *Advances in neurology* (Vol 47, pp. 387–400). New York: Raven Press. (15)

Wallen, K., Winston, L.A., Gaventa, S., Davis-DaSilva, M., & Collins, D.C. (1984). Periovulatory changes in female sexual behavior and patterns of ovarian steroid secretion in group-living rhesus monkeys. *Hormones and Behavior, 18,* 431–450. (12)

Wallesch, C.-W., Henriksen, L., Kornhuber, H.-H., & Paulson, O.B. (1985). Observations on regional cerebral blood flow in cortical and subcortical structures during language production in normal man. *Brain and Language, 25,* 224–233. (5)

Wallman, J., & Pettigrew, J.D. (1985). Conjugate and disjunctive saccades in two avian species with contrasting oculomotor strategies. *Journal of Neuroscience, 5,* 1418–1428. (7)

Wang, T., Okano, Y., Eisensmith, R., Huang, S.Z., Zeng, Y.T., Wilson, H.Y.L., & Woo, S.L. (1989). Molecular genetics of phenylketonuria in Orientals: Linkage disequilibrium between a termination mutation and haplotype 4 of the phenylalanine hydroxylase gene. *American Journal of Human Genetics, 45,* 675–680. (8)

Ward, I.L. (1972). Prenatal stress feminizes and demasculinizes the behavior of males. *Science, 175,* 82–84. (12)

Ward, I.L. (1977). Exogenous androgen activates female behavior in noncopulating, prenatally stressed male rats. *Journal of Comparative and Physiological Psychology, 91,* 465–471. (12)

Ward, I.L., & Reed, J. (1985). Prenatal stress and prepubertal social rearing conditions interact to determine sexual behavior in male rats. *Behavioral Neuroscience, 99,* 301–309. (12)

Ward, I.L., & Weisz, J. (1980). Maternal stress alters plasma testosterone in fetal males. *Science, 207,* 328–329. (12)

Watkins, B.A., Dorn, H.H., Kelly, W.B., Armstrong, R.C., Totts, B.J., Michaels, F., Kufta, C.V., & Dubois-Dalcq, M. (1990). Specific tropism of HIV-1 for microglial cells in primary human brain cultures. *Science, 249,* 549–553. (16)

Watson, C.G., Tilleskjor, C., Kucala, T., & Jacobs, L. (1984). The birth seasonality effect in nonschizophrenic psychiatric patients. *Journal of Clinical Psychology, 40,* 884–888. (16)

Webb, W.B. (1974). Sleep as an adaptive response. *Perceptual and Motor Skills, 38,* 1023–1027. (10)

Wegner, J.T., Catalano, F., Gibralter, J., & Kane, J.M. (1985). Schizophrenics with tardive dyskinesia. *Archives of General Psychiatry, 42,* 860–865. (16)

Wehr, T.A., Jacobsen, F.M., Sack, D.A., Arendt, J., Tamarkin, L., & Rosenthal, N.E. (1986). Phototherapy of seasonal affective disorder. *Archives of General Psychiatry, 43,* 870–875. (16)

Weinberger, D.R. (1987). Implications of normal brain development for the pathogenesis of schizophrenia. *Archives of General Psychiatry, 44,* 660–669. (16)

Weinberger, D.R., Berman, K.F., & Zec, R.F. (1986). Physiologic dysfunction of dorsolateral prefrontal cortex in schizo-

phrenia. I. Regional cerebral blood flow evidence. *Archives of General Psychiatry, 43,* 114–124. (16)

Weiner, R.D. (1979). The psychiatric use of electrically induced seizures. *American Journal of Psychiatry, 136,* 1507–1517. (16)

Weiner, R.D. (1984). Does electroconvulsive therapy cause brain damage? *Behavioral and Brain Sciences, 7,* 1–53. (16)

Weiskrantz, L., Warrington, E.K., Sanders, M.D., & Marshall, J. (1974). Visual capacity in the hemianopic field following a restricted occipital ablation. *Brain, 97,* 709–728. (7)

Weiss, G.F., Papadakos, P., Knudson, K., & Leibowitz, S.F. (1986). Medial hypothalamic serotonin: Effects on deprivation and norepinephrine-induced eating. *Pharmacology, Biochemistry, and Behavior, 25,* 1223–1230. (11)

Weiss, J.M. (1968). Effects of coping responses on stress. *Journal of Comparative and Physiological Psychology, 65,* 251–260. (13)

Weiss, J.M. (1971a). Effects of coping behavior in different warning signal conditions on stress pathology in rats. *Journal of Comparative and Physiological Psychology, 77,* 1–13. (13)

Weiss, J.M. (1971b). Effects of punishing the coping response (conflict) on stress pathology in rats. *Journal of Comparative and Physiological Psychology, 77,* 14–21. (13)

Weiss, P. (1924). Die funktion transplantierter amphibienextremitäten. Aufstellung einer resonanztheorie der motorischen nerventätigkeit auf grund abstimmter endorgane [The function of transplanted amphibian limbs. Presentation of a resonance theory of motor nerve action upon tuned end organs]. *Archiv für Mikroskopische Anatomie und Entwicklungsmechanik, 102,* 635–672. (8)

Weissman, M.M., Gammon, G.D., John, K., Merikangas, K.R., Warner, V., Prusoff, B.A., Sholomskas, D. (1987). Children of depressed parents: Increased psychopathology and early onset of major depression. *Archives of General Psychiatry, 44,* 847–853. (16)

Weissman, M.M., Gershon, E.S., Kidd, K.K., Prusoff, B.A., Leckman, J.F., Dibble, E., Hamovit, J., Thompson, D., Pauls, D.L., & Guroff, J.J. (1984). Psychiatric disorders in the relatives of probands with affective disorders. *Archives of General Psychiatry, 41,* 13–21. (16)

Weisz, J., Brown, B.L., & Ward, I.L. (1982). Maternal stress decreases steroid aromatase activity in brains of male and female rat fetuses. *Neuroendocrinology, 35,* 374–379. (12)

Weitzman, E.D. (1981). Sleep and its disorders. *Annual Review of Neurosciences, 4,* 381–417. (10)

Wender, P.H., Kety, S.S., Rosenthal, D., Schulsinger, F., Ortmann, J., & Lunde, I. (1986). Psychiatric disorders in the biological and adoptive families of adopted individuals with affective disorders. *Archives of General Psychiatry, 43,* 923–929. (16)

Wender, P.H., Rosenthal, D., Kety, S.S., Schulsinger, F., & Welner, J. (1974).

Crossfostering: A research strategy for clarifying the role of genetic and experiential factors in the etiology of schizophrenia. *Archives of General Psychiatry, 30,* 121–128. (16)

Wenger, J.R., Berlin, V., & Woods, S.C. (1980). Learned tolerance of the behaviorally disruptive effects of ethanol. *Behavioral and Neural Biology, 28,* 418–430. (11)

Wenger, J.R., Tiffany, T.M., Bombardier, C., Nicholls, K., & Woods, S.C. (1981). Ethanol tolerance in the rat is learned. *Science, 213,* 575–577. (11)

West, J.R., Hodges, C.A., & Black, A.C., Jr. (1981). Prenatal exposure to ethanol alters the organization of hippocampal mossy fibers in rats. *Science, 211,* 957–959. (2)

Westbrook, G.L., & Jahr, C.E. (1989). Glutamate receptors in excitatory neurotransmission. *Seminars in the Neurosciences, 1,* 103–114. (3)

Whitam, F.L., & Zent, M. (1984). A cross-cultural assessment of early cross-gender behavior and familial factors in male homosexuality. *Archives of Sexual Behavior, 13,* 427–439. (12)

White, B.B., & White, M.S. (1987). Autism from the inside. *Medical Hypotheses, 24,* 223–229. (16)

White, F.J., & Wong, R.Y. (1983). Differential effects of classical and atypical antipsychotic drugs on A9 and A10 dopamine neurons. *Science, 221,* 1054–1057. (16)

Wiesel, T.N. (1982). Postnatal development of the visual cortex and the influence of environment. *Nature, 299,* 583–591. (8)

Wiesel, T.N., & Hubel, D.H. (1963). Single-cell responses in striate cortex of kittens deprived of vision in one eye. *Journal of Neurophysiology, 26,* 1003–1017. (8)

Wiesendanger, M. (1984). Pyramidal tract function and the clinical "pyramidal syndrome." *Human Neurobiology, 2,* 227–234. (9)

Wild, H.M., Butler, S.R., Carden, D., & Kulikowski, J.J. (1985). Primate cortical area V4 important for colour constancy but not wavelength discrimination. *Nature, 313,* 133–135. (7)

Williams, R.W., & Herrup, K. (1988). The control of neuron number. *Annual Review of Neuroscience, 11,* 423–453. (2)

Wilson, J.D., George, F.W., & Griffin, J.E. (1981). The hormonal control of sexual development. *Science, 211,* 1278–1284. (12)

Winblad, B., Hardy, J., Bäckman, L., & Nilsson, L.-G. (1985). Memory function and brain biochemistry in normal aging and in senile dementia. *Annals of the New York Academy of Sciences, 444,* 255–268. (14)

Windle, W.F., Littrell, J.L., Smart, J.O., & Joralemon, J. (1956). Regeneration in the cord of spinal monkeys. *Neurology, 6,* 420–428. (15)

Winfree, A.T. (1983). Impact of a circadian clock on the timing of human sleep. *American Journal of Physiology, 245,* R497–R504. (10)

Winocur, G., & Moscovitch, M. (1990). Hippocampal and prefrontal cortex contributions to learning and memory:

Analysis of lesion and aging effects on maze learning in rats. *Behavioral Neuroscience, 104,* 544–551. (14)

Winslade, W.J., Liston, E.H., Ross, J.W., & Weber, K.D. (1984). Medical, judicial, and statutory regulation of ECT in the United States. *American Journal of Psychiatry, 141,* 1349–1355. (16)

Wintrob, R.M. (1973). The influence of others: Witchcraft and rootwork as explanations of behavior disturbances. *Journal of Nervous and Mental Disease, 156,* 318–326. (13)

Wirz-Justice, A., Groos, G.A., & Wehr, T.A. (1982). The neuropharmacology of circadian timekeeping in mammals. In J. Aschoff, S. Daan, & G.A. Groos (Eds.), *Vertebrate circadian rhythms* (pp. 183–193). Berlin: Springer-Verlag. (16)

Wise, R.A., & Bozarth, M.A. (1984). Brain reward circuitry: Four circuit elements "wired" in apparent series. *Brain Research Bulletin, 12,* 203–208. (13)

Wise, R.A., & Rompre, P.-P. (1989). Brain dopamine and reward. *Annual Review of Psychology, 40,* 191–225. (13)

Wishart, T.B., & Walls, E.K. (1975). Water intoxication death following hypothalamic lesions in the rat. *Physiology & Behavior, 15,* 377–379. (11)

Wisniewski, H.M., & Kozlowski, P.B. (1982). Evidence for blood-brain barrier changes in senile dementia of the Alzheimer type (SDAT). *Annals of the New York Academy of Sciences, 396,* 119–129. (14)

Witelson, S.F. (1985). The brain connection: The corpus callosum is larger in left-handers. *Science, 229,* 665–668. (5)

Witelson, S.F., & Pallie, W. (1973). Left hemisphere specialization for language in the newborn: Neuroanatomical evidence of asymmetry. *Brain, 96,* 641–646. (5)

Witkin, H.A., Mednick, S.A., Schulsinger, F., Bakkestrom, E., Christiansen, K.O., Goodenough, D.R., Hirschhorn, K., Lundesteen, C., Owen, D.R., Philip, J., Rubin, D.B., & Stocking, M. (1976). Criminality in XYY and XXY men. *Science, 193,* 547–555. (12)

Wolgin, D.L., Cytawa, J., & Teitelbaum, P. (1976). The role of activation in the regulation of food intake. In D. Novin, W. Wyrwicka, & G. Bray (Eds.), *Hunger: Basic mechanisms and clinical implications* (pp. 179–191). New York: Raven. (11)

Wolgin, D.L., & Salisbury, J.J. (1985). Amphetamine tolerance and body weight set point: A dose-response analysis. *Behavioral Neuroscience, 99,* 175–185. (11)

Wolkin, A., Jaeger, J., Brodie, J.D., Wolf, A.P., Fowler, J., Rotrosen, J., Gomez-Mont, F., & Cancro, R. (1985). Persistence of cerebral metabolic abnormalities in chronic schizophrenia as determined by positron emission tomography. *American Journal of Psychiatry, 142,* 564–571. (16)

Wong, D.F., Wagner, H.N., Jr., Dannals, R.F., Links, J.M., Frost, J.J., Ravert, H.T., Wilson, A.A., Rosenbaum, A.E., Gjedde, A., Douglass, K.H., Petronis, J.D., Folstein, M.F., Toung, J.K.T., Burns, H.D., & Kuhar, M.J. (1984). Effects of age on dopamine and serotonin receptors measured by positron tomog-

raphy in the living human brain. *Science, 226,* 1393–1396. (14)

Wong, D.F., Wagner, H.N., Jr., Tune, L.E., Dannals, R.F., Pearlson, G.D., Links, J.M., Tamminga, C.A., Broussolle, E.P., Ravert, H.T., Wilson, A.A., Toung, J.K.T., Malat, J., Williams, J.A., O'Touma, L.A., Snyder, S.H., Kuhar, M.J., & Gjedde, A. (1986). Positron emission tomography reveals elevated $D_2$ dopamine receptors in drug-naive schizophrenics. *Science, 234,* 1558–1563. (16)

Wong-Riley, M.T.T. (1989). Cytochrome oxidase: An endogenous metabolic marker for neuronal activity. *Trends in Neurosciences, 12,* 94–101. (2)

Woodruf-Pak, D.S., Lavond, D.G., & Thompson, R.F. (1985). Trace conditioning: Abolished by cerebellar nuclear lesions but not lateral cerebellar cortex aspirations. *Brain Research, 348,* 249–260. (14)

Woods, J.S., & Leibowitz, S.F. (1985). Hypothalamic sites sensitive to morphine and naloxone: Effects on feeding behavior. *Pharmacology, Biochemistry, & Behavior, 23,* 431–438. (11)

Woods, S.W., Charney, D.S., Loke, J., Goodman, W.K., Redmond, D.E., Jr., & Heninger, G.R. (1986). Carbon dioxide sensitivity in panic anxiety. *Archives of General Psychiatry, 43,* 900–909. (13)

Woolverton, W.L., Kandel, D., & Schuster, C.R. (1978). Tolerance and cross-tolerance to cocaine and d-amphetamine. *Journal of Pharmacology and Experimental Therapeutics, 205,* 525–535. (11)

Worley, P.F., Heller, W.A., Snyder, S.H., & Baraban, J.M. (1988). Lithium blocks a phosphoinositide-mediated cholinergic response in hippocampal slices. *Science, 239,* 1428–1429. (16)

Wurtman, J.J. (1985). Neurotransmitter control of carbohydrate consumption. *Annals of the New York Academy of Sciences, 443,* 145–151. (3)

Wurtman, R.J. (1982). Nutrients that modify brain function. *Scientific American, 246*(4), 50–59. (3)

Wurtman, R.J. (1983). Behavioural effects of nutrients. *Lancet, 1*(8334), 1145–1147. (3)

Wurtman, R.J., Hefti, F., & Melamed, E. (1981). Precursor control of neurotransmitter synthesis. *Pharmacological Reviews, 32,* 315–335. (3)

Wurtz, R.H., & Albano, J.E. (1980). Visual-motor function of the primate superior colliculus. *Annual Review of Neuroscience, 3,* 189–226. (7)

Wyatt, R.J., Termini, B.A., & Davis, J. (1971). Biochemical and sleep studies of schizophrenia: A review of the literature 1960–1970: Part I. Biochemical studies. *Schizophrenia Bulletin, 4,* 10–66. (16)

Yamamoto, T. (1984). Taste responses of cortical neurons. *Progress in Neurobiology, 23,* 273–315. (6)

Yamamoto, T., Yuyama, N., Kato, T., & Kawamura, Y. (1985). Gustatory responses of cortical neurons in rats. II. Information processing of taste quality. *Journal of Neuroscience, 53,* 1356–1369. (6)

Yamatani, K., Ono, T., Nishijo, H., & Takaku, A. (1990). Activity and distribution of learning-related neurons in monkey *(Macaca fuscata)* prefrontal cortex. *Behavioral Neuroscience, 104,* 503–531. (14)

Yarsh, T.L., Farb, D.H., Leeman, S.E., & Jessell, T.M. (1979). Intrathecal capsaicin depletes substance P in the rat spinal cord and produces prolonged thermal analgesia. *Science, 206,* 481–483. (6)

Yaryura-Tobias, J.A. (1977). Obsessive-compulsive disorders: A serotoninergic hypothesis. *Journal of Orthomolecular Psychiatry, 6,* 317–326. (13)

Yaryura-Tobias, J.A., & Neziroglu, F.A. (1981). Aggressive behavior, clinical interfaces. In L. Valzelli & L. Morgese (Eds.), *Aggression and violence: A psycho/biological and clinical approach* (pp. 195–210). Milan, Italy: Edizioni Saint Vincent. (13)

Yau, K.-W., Matthews, G., & Baylor, D.A. (1979). Thermal activation of the visual transduction mechanism in retinal rods. *Nature, 279,* 806–807. (7)

Yeni-Komshian, G.H., & Benson, D.A. (1976). Anatomical study of cerebral asymmetry in the temporal lobe of humans, chimpanzees, and rhesus monkeys. *Science, 192,* 387–389. (5)

Yoon, M. (1971). Reorganization of retinotectal projection following surgical operations on the optic tectum in goldfish. *Experimental Neurology, 33,* 395–411. (8)

Yost, W.A., & Nielsen, D.W. (1977). *Fundamentals of hearing.* New York: Holt, Rinehart, & Winston. (6)

Young, A.B., Greenamyre, J.T., Hollingsworth, Z., Albin, R., D'Amato, C., Shoulson, I., & Penney, J.B. (1988). NMDA receptor losses in putamen from patients with Huntington's disease. *Science, 241,* 981–983. (9)

Young, W.C., Goy, R.W., & Phoenix, C.H. (1964). Hormones and sexual behavior. *Science, 143,* 212–218. (12)

Zagrodzka, J., & Fonberg, E. (1979). Alimentary instrumental responses and neurological reflexes in amygdalar cats. *Acta Neurobiologiae Experimentalis, 39,* 143–156. (13)

Zaidel, D., & Sperry, R.W. (1977). Some long-term motor effects of cerebral commissurotomy in man. *Neuropsychologia, 15,* 193–204. (5)

Zaidel, E. (1983). Advances and retreats in laterality research. *Behavioral and Brain Sciences, 6,* 523–528. (5)

Zarrow, M.X., Gandelman, R., & Denenberg, V.H. (1971). Prolactin: Is it an essential hormone for maternal behavior in the mammal? *Hormones and Behavior, 2,* 343–354. (12)

Zeigler, H.P., Jacquin, M.F., & Miller, M.G. (1985). Trigeminal orosensation and ingestive behavior in the rat. *Progress in Psychobiology and Physiological Psychology, 11,* 63–196. (11)

Zeki, S. (1980). The representation of colours in the cerebral cortex. *Nature, 284,* 412–418. (7)

Zeki, S. (1983). Colour coding in the cerebral cortex: The responses of wavelength-selective and colour-coded cells in monkey visual cortex to changes in wavelength composition. *Neuroscience, 9,* 767–781. (7)

Zeki, S., & Shipp, S. (1988). The functional logic of cortical connections. *Nature, 335,* 311–317. (7)

Zernicki, B., Gandolfo, G., Glin, L., & Gottesmann, C. (1984). Cerveau isolé and pretrigeminal rats. *Acta Neurobiologiae Experimentalis, 44,* 159–177. (10)

Zihl, J. (1980). "Blindsight": Improvement of visually guided eye movements by systematic practice in patients with cerebral blindness. *Neuropsychologia, 18,* 71–77. (7)

Zilles, K., Armstrong, E., Moser, K.H., Schleicher, A., & Stephan, H. (1989). Gyrification in the cerebral cortex of primates. *Brain, Behavior, and Evolution, 34,* 143–150. (4)

Zimmerman, M.B., Blaine, E.H., & Stricker, E.M. (1981). Water intake in hypovolemic sheep: Effects of crushing the left atrial appendage. *Science, 211,* 489–491. (11)

Zohar, J., Insel, T.R., Zohar-Kadouch, R.C., Hill, J.L., & Murphy, D.L. (1988). Serotonergic responsivity in obsessive-compulsive disorder. *Archives of General Psychiatry, 45,* 167–172. (13)

Zola-Morgan, S., & Squire, L.R. (1986). Memory impairment in monkeys following lesions limited to the hippocampus. *Behavioral Neuroscience, 100,* 155–160. (14)

Zola-Morgan, S., Squire, L.R., & Mishkin, M. (1982). The neuroanatomy of amnesia: Amygdala-hippocampus versus temporal stem. *Science, 218,* 1337–1339. (14)

Zornetzer, S.F. (1985). Catecholamine system involvement in age-related memory dysfunction. *Annals of the New York Academy of Sciences, 444,* 242–254. (14)

Zurif, E.B. (1980). Language mechanisms: A neuropsychological perspective. *American Scientist, 68,* 305–311. (5)

Zwislocki, J.J. (1981). Sound analysis in the ear: A history of discoveries. *American Scientist, 69,* 184–192. (6)

# Acknowledgments

**Page 1:** Photo courtesy of the Cincinnati Zoo.
**Page 6:** Figure 1.1 from "Sexual differences in the brain" by A. P. Arnold, *American Scientist*, 1980, 68:165–173. Photos courtesy of A. P. Arnold.
**Page 7:** Top photo © Ed Reschke. Bottom photo © Russell Fieber/FPG International Corp.
**Page 13:** Figure 1.2 redrawn from "Vom Wirkungsgefüge der Triebe" by E. von Holst and U. von St. Paul in *Naturwissenschaften*, 1960, 47:409–422. Used by permission of Springer-Verlag.
**Page 18:** Figure 1.5 courtesy of the Foundation for Biomedical Research.

**Page 23:** Photo © Ed Reschke.
**Page 26:** Figure 2.2: photo courtesy of Glenn L. Decker.
**Page 27:** Figure 2.3: photo © Dan McCoy/Scheibel/Rainbow.
**Page 31:** Figure 2.7(f) from R. G. Coss, *Brain Research*, 1982. Used by permission of R. G. Coss.
**Page 32:** Figure 2.8: photo © Manfred Kage/Peter Arnold, Inc.
**Page 35:** Figure 2.10 from "Spine stems on tectal interneurons in Jewel fish are shortened by social stimulation" by R. G. Coss and A. Globus, *Science*, 1978, 200:787–790. Copyright 1978 by the AAAS. Reprinted by permission of AAAS and R. G. Coss.
**Page 36:** Figure 2.11 from "Changes in the dendritic branching of adult mammalian neurons revealed by repeated imaging in situ" by D. Purves and R. D. Hadley, *Nature*, 315: 404–406. Copyright © 1985 Macmillan Magazines. Reprinted by permission. Photos provided by D. Purves.
**Page 41:** Figure 2.13(b): photo by Fritz Goro.

**Page 57:** Photo from Lennart Nilsson, *The Incredible Machine*, National Geographic Society.
**Page 74:** Figure 3.9: (b) Photo by D. D. Kunkel, University of Washington/BPS. (c) From "Studying neural organization in

*Aplysia* with the scanning electron microscope" by E. R. Lewis et al., *Science*, 1969, 165:1142. Copyright 1969 by the AAAS. Reprinted by permission of AAAS and E. R. Lewis.
**Page 76:** Figure 3.11 redrawn from "Autoimmune response to acetylcholine receptors in myasthenia gravis and its animal model" by J. Lindstrom, in H. G. Kunkel and F. J. Dixon (eds.), *Advances in Immunology*, 1979, 27:1–50. Used by permission of Academic Press, Inc. and J. Lindstrom.
**Page 87:** Figure 3.15 from "Cocaine-induced reduction of glucose utilization in human brain" by E. D. London et al., *Archives of General Psychiatry*, 1990, 47:567–574. Copyright 1990, American Medical Association. Used by permission of AMA and E. D. London.
**Page 91:** Figure 3.17 redrawn from "Event-related brain potentials in boys at risk for alcoholism" by H. Begleiter, *Science*, 1984, 225: 1493–1496. Copyright 1984 by the AAAS. Reprinted by permission of AAAS and H. Begleiter.

**Page 95:** Photo © Dan McCoy/Rainbow.
**Page 96:** Figure 4.1: photo © Neil G. McDaniel/The National Audubon Society Collection/Photo Researchers, Inc.
**Page 98:** Figure 4.3 modified after *The Vertebrate Body* by A. S. Romer, 1962, W. B. Saunders, Philadelphia.
**Page 101:** Figure 4.6: photo © Manfred Kage/Peter Arnold, Inc.
**Page 103:** Figure 4.8 from *Biology: The Unity and Diversity of Life*, 5th Edition, by Cecie Starr and Ralph Taggart, 1989, Wadsworth Publishing Company.
**Page 105:** Figure 4.10: photo © Manfred Kage/Peter Arnold, Inc.
**Page 106:** Figure 4.11 from *Biology: The Unity and Diversity of Life*, 5th Edition, by Cecie Starr and Ralph Taggart, 1989, Wadsworth Publishing Company.
**Page 111:** Figure 4.13 modified after *The Human Central Nervous System*, 3rd Edition, by R. Nieuwenhuys et al., 1988, Springer-Verlag, Berlin.

**Page 113:** Figure 4.15: Two left photos courtesy of Dr. Dana Copeland. Right photo © Dan McCoy/Rainbow.
**Pages 114, 115, 116:** Figures 4.16, 4.17, and 4.18 modified after *The Human Central Nervous System*, 3rd Edition, by R. Nieuwenhuys et al., 1989, Springer-Verlag, Berlin.
**Pages 117, 120:** Figures 4.19 and 4.20: photos courtesy of Dr. Dana Copeland.
**Page 121:** Figure 4.21 from *The Anatomy of the Nervous System* by S. W. Ranson and S. L. Clark, 1959. Reprinted by permission of W. B. Saunders Co.
**Page 124:** Figure 4.24 after *The Cerebral Cortex of Man* by W. Penfield and R. Rasmussen, 1950. Used by permission of Macmillan Publishing Co.
**Page 127:** Figure 4.26 after *The Prefrontal Cortex* by J. M. Fuster, 1989, Raven Press. Used by permission of Raven Press and J. M. Fuster.
**Page 128:** Photo courtesy of Dr. Dana Copeland.
**Page 129:** Figure 4.27: photo by Doug Goodman/Monkmeyer Press.
**Page 131:** Figure 4.29 adapted from "Animal intelligence as encephalization" by H. J. Jerison, *Philosophical Transactions of the Royal Society of London*, 1985, B 308: 21–35. Used by permission of The Royal Society and H. J. Jerison.
**Page 135:** Figure 4.31: photo provided by James W. Kalat.
**Page 136:** Figure 4.33 from *A Stereotaxic Atlas of the Rat Brain*, 2nd Edition, by L. J. Pellegrino, A. S. Pellegrino, and A. J. Cushman, 1979. Reprinted by permission of Plenum Publishing Corp. and Louis Pellegrino.
**Page 141:** Figure 4.34 from "Dendritic-tree anatomy codes form vision physiology in tadpole retina" by B. Pomeranz and S. H. Chung, *Science*, 1970, 170:983–984. Copyright 1970 by the AAAS. Reprinted by permission of AAAS and B. Pomeranz. Photos provided courtesy of B. Pomeranz.
**Page 142:** Figure 4.35: photo © Dan McCoy/Rainbow.

**Page 143:** Figure 4.36: photo © Dan McCoy/Rainbow.

**Page 145:** Figure 4.37 (Above) from "Brain electrical correlates of pattern recognition" by E. Donchin in G. F. Inbar (ed.), *Signal Analysis and Pattern Recognition in Biomedical Engineering* © 1975 Keter Publishing House Ltd., Jerusalem. Used by permission. (Below) from L. A. Farwell and E. Donchin, *Electroencephalography and Clinical Neurophysiology*, 1988, 70:510–553. Used by permission of L. A. Farwell.

**Page 145:** Figure 4.38: photo © Burt Glinn/Magnum.

**Page 146:** Figure 4.39: photo courtesy of Karen Berman and Daniel Weinberger, National Institute of Mental Health.

**Page 146:** Figure 4.40: photos courtesy of Michael E. Phelps and John C. Mazziotta, University of California, Los Angeles, School of Medicine.

**Page 151:** Photo courtesy of Irene Pepperberg.

**Page 155:** Photo courtesy of Dr. Dana Copeland.

**Page 160:** Figure 5.6 from "Asymmetry of perception in free viewing of chimeric faces" by J. Levy, W. Heller, M. T. Banich, and L. A. Burton, *Brain and Cognition*, 1983, 2:404–419. Used by permission of Academic Press.

**Page 164:** Figure 5.8: From "Human brain: Left-right asymmetries in temporal speech region" by N. Geschwind and W. Levitsky, *Science*, 1968, 161:186–187. Copyright 1968 by the AAAS. Reprinted by permission of AAAS and N. Geschwind.

**Page 171:** Figure 5.11: Photo courtesy of Ann Premack.

**Page 173:** Figure 5.12: Photo courtesy of Duane Rumbaugh from Georgia State University's Language Research Center, operated with the Yerkes Primate Center of Emory.

**Page 174:** Figure 5.13: Photo courtesy of David Carter.

**Page 176:** Figure 5.15 from "Observations on regional cerebral blood flow in cortical and subcortical structures during language production in normal man" by C. W. Wallesch, L. Henriksen, H. H. Kornhuber, and O. B. Paulson, 1985, *Brain and Language*, 25:224–233. Used by permission of Academic Press and O. B. Paulson.

**Pages 179–180:** Quote from tape recording by Nancy Kaplan, provided courtesy of the Duke University Department of Speech Pathology and Audiology.

**Page 181:** Figure 5.16 from "Localization of cognitive operations in the human brain" by M. Posner, S. E. Petersen, P. T. Fox, and M. E. Raichle, *Science*, 1988, 240:1627–1631. Copyright 1988 by the AAAS. Reprinted by permission of AAAS and M. I. Posner.

**Page 182:** Figure 5.17 from "Positron emission tomographic studies of the cortical anatomy of single-word processing" by S. E. Petersen, P. T. Fox, M. I. Posner, M. Mintun, and M. E. Raichle. Reprinted by permission from *Nature*, 1988, 331:585–589. Copyright © 1988 Macmillan Magazines Ltd. Photos provided by S. E. Petersen.

**Page 187:** Photo © Blair Seitz/Photo Researchers, Inc.

**Page 196:** Figure 6.4 by permission of A. J. Hudspeth. Photos courtesy of A. J. Hudspeth, R. Jacobs, P. Leake, and M. Miller.

**Page 201:** Figure 6.8 after *Human Information Processing* by P. H. Lindsay and D. A. Norman, 1972. Used by permission of Academic Press and P. H. Lindsay.

**Page 207:** Figure 6.13: photo © Ed Reschke.

**Page 216:** Figure 6.17 after "A psychophysical model for gustatory quality" by S. S. Schiffman and R. P. Erickson, in *Physiology and Behavior*, 1971, 7:617–633. Used by permission of Pergamon Press, Inc., and S. S. Schiffman.

**Page 217:** Figure 6.18: photo © SIU/Peter Arnold, Inc.

**Page 229:** Photo © Tom McHugh/The National Audubon Society Collection/Photo Researchers, Inc.

**Page 232:** Figure 7.2: photo © Chase Swift.

**Pages 233, 249:** Figures 7.3(a) and 7.17: After "Organization of the primate retina" by J. E. Dowling and B. B. Boycott, *Proceedings of the Royal Society of London*, B, 1966, 166:80–111. Used by permission of the Royal Society of London and John Dowling.

**Page 233:** Figure 7.3(b): photo © Ed Reschke.

**Page 234:** Figure 7.4 from *The Retina* by John E. Dowling, 1987, Belknap Press of Harvard University Press. Micrograph by M. Tachibana and A. Kaneko. Reprinted by permission of John E. Dowling.

**Page 235:** Figure 7.6: micrograph courtesy of E. R. Lewis, F. S. Werblin, and Y. Y. Zeevi.

**Page 250:** Figure 7.18: photo © Don Wong/Science Source/Photo Researchers, Inc.

**Page 256:** Figure 7.22 from "Segregation of form, color, movement, and depth: Anatomy, physiology, and perception" by M. Livingstone and D. Hubel, *Science*, 1988, 240:740–749. Copyright 1988 by the AAAS. Reprinted by permission of AAAS and Margaret Livingstone.

**Page 257:** Figure 7.23: photo Tate Gallery, London/Art Resource, N.Y. Copyright 1991 ARS, N.Y./ADAGP.

**Pages 258, 259:** Figures 7.24 and 7.25: Based on "Receptive fields of single neurons in the cat's striate cortex" by D. H. Hubel and T. N. Wiesel, in *Journal of Physiology*, 1959, 148:574–591. Used by permission of the *Journal of Physiology* and David Hubel.

**Page 264:** Figure 7.31 adapted from "The visual cortex of the brain" by David H. Hubel, *Scientific American*, November 1963, Vol. 209, No. 5, pp. 54–63. Copyright © 1963 by Scientific American, Inc. All rights reserved. Reprinted by permission.

**Page 271:** Photo © William Munoz/Photo Researchers, Inc.

**Page 274:** Figure 8.2: photo courtesy of Dr. Dana Copeland.

**Page 275:** Figure 8.3 from "Development of glomerular pattern visualized in the olfactory bulbs of living mice" by A. S. LaMantia and D. Purves. Reprinted by permission from *Nature*, 1989, 341:646–649. Copyright © 1989 Macmillan Magazines Ltd. Photo courtesy of Dale Purves.

**Page 277:** Figure 8.4 modified after *The Vertebrate Body* by A. S. Romer, 1962, W. B. Saunders, Philadelphia.

**Page 279:** Figure 8.6 from "Preferential selection of central pathways by regenerating optic fibers" by D. G. Attardi and R. W. Sperry, *Experimental Neurology*, 1963, 7:46–64. Used by permission of Academic Press and R. W. Sperry.

**Page 282:** Figure 8.9 after "Elimination of synapses in the developing nervous system" by D. Purves and J. W. Lichtman, *Science*, 1980, 210:153–157. Copyright 1980 by the AAAS. Used by permission of AAAS and Dale Purves.

**Page 282:** Figure 8.10 from "Motoneuronal death in the human fetus" by N. G. Forger and S. M. Breedlove, *Journal of Comparative Neurology*, 1987, 264:118–122. Copyright 1987 Alan R. Liss, Inc. Used by permission of Nancy G. Forger.

**Page 288:** Figure 8.12: photos courtesy of Russell D. Fernald.

**Page 295:** Figure 8.18: photo courtesy of Helmut V. Hirsch.

**Page 302:** Figure 8.21(a): photo courtesy of San Mateo County Special Olympics, sponsored by the Peninsula Association for Retarded Children and Adults. Figure 8.21 (b): photo courtesy of Cytogenetics Laboratory, University of California, San Francisco. Figure 8.21(c) based on *Epidemiology of Mongolism* by Abraham Lilienfeld, 1969, The Johns Hopkins University Press. Used by permission.

**Page 304:** Figure 8.23: photo © Ted Wood/Picture Group, Inc.

**Page 309:** Photo © Superstock, Inc.

**Page 311:** Figure 9.1 art after Cecie Starr and Ralph Taggart, *Biology: The Unity and Diversity of Life*, 5th Edition, 1989, Wadsworth Publishing Company.

**Page 311:** Figures 9.1 and 9.2: photos © Ed Reschke.

**Page 312:** Figures 9.3 and 9.4 after Cecie Starr and Ralph Taggart, *Biology: The Unity and Diversity of Life*, 5th Edition, 1989, Wadsworth Publishing Company.

**Page 314:** Figure 9.5: photo © Bill Curtsinger/The National Audubon Society Collection/Photo Researchers, Inc.

**Page 335:** Figure 9.14 from "Mortality data for the U.S. for deaths due to and related to twenty neurologic diseases" by V. Chandra, N. E. Bharucha, and B. S. Shoenberg, *Neuroepidemiology*, 1984, 3:149–168. Used by permission of S. Karger AG, Basel and V. Chandra.

**Page 338:** Figure 9.16 from "Dopamine in the extrapyramidal motor function: A study based upon the MPTP-induced primate model of Parkinsonism" by C. C. Chiueh, 1988, *Annals of The New York Academy of Sciences*, 515:226–248. Reprinted by permission of the New York Academy of Sciences and C. C. Chiueh.

**Page 347:** Photo © Ted Spagna/Photo Researchers, Inc.

**Page 349:** Figure 10.1 from "Phase control of activity in a rodent" by P. J. DeCoursey, *Cold Spring Harbor Symposia on Quantitative Biology*, 1960, 25:49–55. Used by permission of Cold Spring Harbor Laboratory and P. J. DeCoursey.

**Page 351:** Figure 10.2 from *Sleep and Wakefulness* by N. Kleitman. Used by permission of The University of Chicago Press and N. Kleitman. Copyright 1963 by the University of Chicago. All rights reserved.

**Page 355:** Figure 10.4 from "Deep hypothermia and its effect on the 24-hour clock of rats and hamsters" by C. P. Richter, *Johns Hopkins Medical Journal*, 1975, 136:1–10. Copyright 1975 The Johns Hopkins University Press. Used by permission. Photo courtesy of C. P. Richter.

**Page 356:** Figure 10.5 from "Suprachiasmatic nucleus: Use of 14-C-labeled deoxyglucose uptake as a functional marker" by W. J. Schwartz and H. Gainer, *Science*, 1977, 197:1089–1091.

**Page 361:** Figure 10.7: photo by Richard Nowitz.

**Page 362:** Figure 10.8: records provided by T. E. LeVere.

**Page 364:** Figure 10.9: photo from Dr. J. Allan Hobson.

**Page 365:** Figure 10.10 from "Cyclic variations in EEG during sleep and their relation to eye movements, body motility, and dreaming" by W. Dement and N. Kleitman, *Electroencephalography and Clinical Neuropsychology*, 1957, 9:673–690. Reproduced by permission of Elsevier/North Holland Biomedical Press and W. C. Dement.

**Page 367:** Photo © Tom McHugh/The National Audubon Society Collection/Photo Researchers, Inc.

**Page 368:** Figure 10.11 from "Ontogenetic Development of Human Sleep-Dream Cycle" by H. P. Roffwarg, J. N. Muzio, and W. C. Dement, *Science*, 1966, 152:604–609. Copyright 1966 by the AAAS. Used by permission of AAAS and W. C. Dement.

**Page 383:** Photo © Ed Reschke.

**Page 385:** Figure 11.1 from "Sleep-onset insomniacs have delayed temperature rhythms" by M. Morris, L. Lack, and D. Dawson, *Sleep*, 1990, 13:1–14. Reprinted by permission of Raven Press and Leon Lack.

**Page 387:** Figure 11.2 modified after *The Human Central Nervous System* by R. Nieuwenhuys et al., 1988, Springer-Verlag.

**Page 388:** Photo © A. Cosmos Blank/The National Audubon Collection/Photo Researchers, Inc.

**Page 409:** Figure 11.12 from "The role of activation in the regulation of food intake" by D. L. Wolgin, J. Cytawa, and P. Teitelbaum in D. Novin, W. Wyrwicka, and G. Bray (eds.), *Hunger: Basic Mechanisms and Clinical Implications*, 1976. Copyright 1976 by Raven Press. Reprinted by permission of Raven Press. Photo courtesy of P. Teitelbaum.

**Page 410:** Figure 11.13: (a) photo © Yoav Levy/Phototake; (b) from "Disturbances in feeding and drinking behavior after hypothalamic lesions" by P. Teitelbaum in M. R. Jones (ed.), *1961 Nebraska Symposium on Motivation*, pp. 39–69. Copyright 1961 by University of Nebraska Press. Used by permission.

**Page 415:** Photo © 1991 Butch Martin/The Image Bank, West.

**Pages 417, 419, 421, 423:** Figures 12.1, 12.2, 12.4, 12.5–12.8 from Cecie Starr and Ralph Taggart, *Biology: The Unity and Diversity of Life*, 5th Edition, 1989. Wadsworth Publishing Company.

**Page 430:** Figure 12.12 redrawn from "Effects of gonadal hormones on urinary behavior in dogs" by F. A. Beach, in *Physiology and Behavior*, 1974, 12:1005–1013. Used by permission of Brain Research Publications, Inc. and F. A. Beach.

**Page 434:** Figure 12.13 from "Rise in female-initiated sexual activity at ovulation and its suppression by oral contraceptives" by D. B. Adams, A. R. Gold, and A. D. Burt, in *New England Journal of Medicine*, 1978, 299: 1145–1150. Reprinted by permission from *The New England Journal of Medicine*.

**Page 435:** Figure 12.14 adapted from "Weight at menarche: Similarity for well-nourished girls at differing ages, and evidence for historical

constancy" by R. E. Frisch, *Pediatrics*, 1972, 50: 445–450. Copyright 1972 by Pediatrics. Reprinted by permission.

**Page 446:** Figure 12.17 from "Sex-hormone-dependent brain differentiation and sexual functions" by G. Dörner, in G. Dörner (ed.), *Endocrinology of Sex*. Copyright 1975 by Johann Ambrosius Barth. Reprinted by permission of Johann Ambrosius Barth.

**Page 447:** Figure 12.18 from *Abnormal Sexual Development* by D. D. Federman, 1967. Used by permission of W. B. Saunders Company.

**Page 451:** Photo © Stephen Dalton/The National Audubon Collection/Photo Researchers, Inc.

**Page 453:** Figure 13.1: photo © Alon Reiniger/Contact Press Images.

**Page 457:** Figure 13.2 from "Avoidance behavior and the development of gastroduodenal ulcers" by J. V. Brady, R. W. Porter, D. G. Conrad, and J. W. Mason, *Journal of the Experimental Analysis of Behavior*, 1958, 1:69–72. Copyright 1958 by the Society for the Experimental Analysis of Behavior, Inc. Reprinted by permission of the Society for the Experimental Analysis of Behavior and J. V. Brady.

**Page 464:** Figure 13.5 based on "Psychosomatic disease and the 'visceral brain': Recent developments bearing on the Papez theory of emotion" by P. D. MacLean, *Psychosomatic Medicine*, 1949, 11:338–353. Used by permission of the American Psychosomatic Society.

**Page 465:** Figure 13.6 redrawn from "Studies on limbic systems ('visceral brain') and their bearing on psychosomatic problems" by P. D. MacLean in E. D. Wittkower and R. A. Cleghorn (eds.), *Recent Developments in Psychosomatic Medicine*, 1954. Copyright Sir Isaac Pitman & Sons, Ltd. Used by permission of J. B. Lippincott Co. and Sir Isaac Pitman & Sons, Ltd.

**Page 469:** Figure 13.9 based on "Studies on endogenous ligands (endacoids) for the benzodiazepine/beta-carboline binding sites" by A. Guidotti, P. Ferrero, M. Fujimoto, R. M. Santi, and E. Costa, 1986, *Advances in Biochemical Psychopharmacology*, 41:137–148. Used by permission from Raven Press, New York.

**Page 471:** Photo courtesy of Jules Asher. From "New Drug Counters Alcohol Intoxication" by G. Kolata, 1986, *Science*, 234:1199. Copyright 1986 by the AAAS. Used by permission of AAAS.

**Page 474:** Figure 13.10 from "Neural substrates of aggression and rage in the cat" by A. Siegel and M. Brutus, *Progress in Psychobiology and Physiological Psychology*, 1990, 14:135–233. Reprinted by permission of Academic Press and A. Siegel.

**Page 475:** Figure 13.11 from "Neuronal constellations in aggressive behavior" by José Delgado, in L. Valzelli and L. Morgese (eds.), *Aggression and Violence: A Psycho/biological and Clinical Approach*, Edizioni Saint Vincent, 1981. Used by permission of José Delgado.

**Page 476:** Figure 13.12: photo courtesy of Dr. Dana Copeland.

**Page 477:** Figure 13.13 from "Behavioral changes following rhinencephalic injury in cat" by L. Schreiner and A. Kling, *Journal of Neurophysiology*, 1953, 16:643–659. Reprinted by permission of the American Physiological Society.

**Page 485:** Photo © Kevin Forest/The Image Bank, West.

**Page 490:** Figure 14.4: photo courtesy of Dr. Dana Copeland.

**Page 494:** Figure 14.7: photos courtesy of Dr. Robert D. Terry, Department of Neurosciences, School of Medicine, University of California at San Diego.

**Page 495:** Figure 14.8 after "Dendritic Changes" by A. B. Scheibel, Figure 8-1, p. 70, in B. Reisberg (ed.), *Alzheimer's Disease*, 1983, Free Press.

**Page 495:** Figure 14.9 from "Quantitative morphology and regional and laminar distributions of senile plaques in Alzheimer's disease" by J. Rogers and J. H. Morrison, *Journal of Neuroscience*, 1985, 5:2801–2808. Copyright 1985 by the Society for Neuroscience. Photo courtesy of Dr. Joseph Rogers. Reprinted by permission of Dr. Joseph Rogers.

**Page 501:** Figure 14.12 from "Spatial memory within and without the hippocampal system" by J. O'Keefe in W. Seifert (ed.), *Neurobiology of the Hippocampus*, 1983. Reprinted by permission of Academic Press and J. O'Keefe.

**Page 509:** Figure 14.15 based on "Learning of leg position by the ventral nerve cord in headless insects" by G. A. Horridge, in *Proceedings of the Royal Society of London*, B, 1962, 157: 33–52. Used by permission of the Royal Society of London and G. A. Horridge.

**Page 511:** Figure 14.16: photo from H. Chaumeton/Nature.

**Page 513:** Figure 14.18 redrawn from "Neuronal mechanisms of habituation and dishabituation of the gill-withdrawal reflex in *Aplysia*" by V. Castellucci, H. Pinsker, I. Kupfermann, and E. R. Kandel, *Science*, 1970, 167:1745–1748. Copyright 1970 by the AAAS. Used by permission of AAAS and V. Castellucci.

**Page 527:** Photo © 1991 Stephen Marks/The Image Bank, West.

**Page 529:** Photo from Superstock, Inc.

**Page 530:** Figure 15.1: photos courtesy of Dr. Dana Copeland.

**Page 530:** Figure 15.2 from "Incidence rates of stroke in the eighties: The end of the decline in stroke?" by J. P. Broderick, S. J. Phillips, J. P. Whisnant, W. M. O'Fallon, and E. J. Bergstrahl, *Stroke*, 1989, 20:577–582. Used by permission of the American Heart Association and J. P. Whisnant.

**Page 535:** Figure 15.4 from "Clinical aspects of PNS regeneration" by P. K. Thomas in S. G. Waxman (ed.), *Advances in Neurology, Vol. 47: Functional Recovery in Neurological Disease*, 1988, Raven Press. Reprinted by permission of Raven Press and P. K. Thomas. Photo by Michael D. Sanders.

**Page 539:** Figure 15.6 from "Non-additivity of D2 receptor proliferation induced by dopamine denervation and chronic selective antagonist administration" by G. J. LaHoste and J. F. Marshall, *Brain Research*, 1989, 502:223–232. Reprinted by permission of Elsevier Science Publishers. Photos courtesy of G. J. LaHoste.

**Page 540:** Figure 15.8: Redrawn by permission from *The Annual Review of Neuroscience*, Volume 6, copyright 1983 by Annual Reviews, Inc. Used by permission of Annual Reviews, Inc. and Jon H. Kaas.

**Page 553:** Photo courtesy E. F. Torrey and M. F. Casanova/NIMH.

**Page 555:** Figure 16.1: photo courtesy of Dr. Dana Copeland.

**Page 556:** Figure 16.2 redrawn from E. Janosik and J. Davies, *Psychiatric Mental Health Nursing*, p. 173. © 1986 Jones and Bartlett Publishers: Boston. Used by permission.

Page 557: Figure 16.3 from "Two-day cycles of alternating good and bad behavior in psychotic patients" by C. P. Richter, *Archives of Neurology and Psychiatry*, 1938, 39:587–598. Copyright 1938, American Medical Association. Used by permission.

Page 560: Figure 16.4 reprinted by permission of L. R. Baxter Jr. Photo courtesy of L. R. Baxter Jr.

Page 561: Figure 16.5 from "Hormones and rhythms in man and animals" by C. P. Richter in G. Pincus (ed.), *Recent Progress in Hormone Research* (vol. 13), 1957. Used by permission of Academic Press and C. P. Richter.

Page 565: Figure 16.6: photo by James D. Wilson/Woodfin Camp and Associates.

Page 566: Figure 16.7 adapted from *Sleep* by J. Allan Hobson, Scientific American Library, 1989. Reprinted by permission of W. H. Freeman and Company.

Page 572: Figure 16.9: photos courtesy of B. Bogerts.

Page 573: Figure 16.10: photos courtesy of Arnold Scheibel.

Page 574: Figure 16.11: photos courtesy of E. F. Torrey and M. F. Casanova/NIMH.

Page 575: Figure 16.12: photos © CEA-Orsay/CNRI/SPL/Photo Researchers, Inc.

Page 582: Figure 16.15 from "Antipsychotic drug doses and neuroleptic/dopamine receptors" by P. Seeman, T. Lee, M. Chau-Wong, and K. Wong, *Nature*, 261, (1976), 717–719. Copyright 1976 Macmillan Magazines Limited. Reprinted by permission of *Nature* and Phillip Seeman.

## Sources for Endsheet Quotations

**Ramón y Cajal, S.** (1937). Recollections of my life. *Memoirs of the American Philosophical Society*, 8, parts 1 and 2. (Photo from Bettman Archive.)

**Sherrington, C. S.** (1941). *Man on his nature.* New York: Macmillan, p. 104.

**Goldman-Rakic, P. S.** (1988). Topography of cognition: Parallel distributed networks in primate association cortex. *Annual Review of Neuroscience, 11,* 137–156. (p. 152)

**Sperry, R. W.** (1975). In search of psyche. In **F. G. Worden, J. P. Swazey, & G. Adelman** (Eds.), *The neurosciences: Paths of discovery* (pp. 424–434). Cambridge, MA: MIT Press.

**Jerre Levy:** personal communication.

**Geschwind, N.** (1965). Disconnexion syndromes in animals and man. *Brain, 88,* 237–294, 585–644.

**Susan S. Schiffman:** personal communication.

**Candace Pert:** personal communication.

**David Hubel:** personal communication.

**Wiesel, T. N.** (1982). Postnatal development of the visual cortex and the influence of environment. *Nature, 299,* 583–591.

**Levi-Montalcini, R.** (1988). *In praise of imperfection.* New York: Basic Books, p. 94

**Dement, W.** (1972). *Some must watch while some must sleep.* San Francisco: W. H. Freeman.

**Cannon, W. B.** (1945). *The way of an investigator.* New York: Norton.

**Edward Stricker:** personal communication. "In memoriam: Frank A. Beach." (1988). *Hormones and Behavior, 22,* 419–443; and personal communication.

**Curt P. Richter:** personal communication.

**Paul MacLean:** personal communication.

**Luigi Valzelli:** personal communication.

**Lashley, K. S.** (1930). Basic neural mechanisms in behavior. *Psychological Review, 37,* 1–24.

**Hebb, D. O.** (1949). *Organization of behavior.* New York: John Wiley & Sons. (p. xiii.)

**Garcia, J.** (1981). Tilting at the paper mills of Academe. *American Psychologist, 36,* 149–158. (p. 151.)

**Eric R. Kandel:** personal communication.

# Name Index

Llacuna, A., 428
Llinás, R.R., 326
Lockhart, L.H., 589
Lockhead, E., 218
Loegering, D.A. See Belongia, E.A.
Loewenstein, W.R., 207
Loewi, O., studies of, 66–67
Loke, J. See Woods, S.W.
Lolait, S.J., 85
Lomo, T., 314, 514
London, E.D., 86, 87
Lönnerholm, G., 589
Lorch, M., 159
Loriaux, D.L., 436
Loriaux, L. See Gold, P.W.
Losee-Olson, S., 378
Losey, G.S., 439
Loughna, P.T., 314
Loundes, D.D., 436
Lovinger, D.M., 516
Lowe, J., 454
Lowing, P.A., 577
Lubin, M., 436
Lucci, D., 587
Luchins, D.J., 573
Lugaresi, E., 464
Lunde, I. See Wender, P.H.
Luria, A.R., 531
Lust, W.D., 34
Luzzatti, C., 125
Lyden, P.D., 531
Lydic, R., 374
Lyman, C.P., 358
Lynch, G., 516, 518, 537, 545
Lynch, J.A., 367
Lynch, J.C., 125, 126, 264
Lynch, M.A., 516
Lynn, A.B. See Herkenham, M.
Lytle, L.D., 480

Macarthur, J.P., 393
Maccoby, E.E., 433
MacDonald, K.L. See
  Belongia, E.A.
Macdonald, R.L., 469
MacFarlane, J.G., 376
Machon, R.A., 580
MacKinnon, J.R., 457
MacLean, P.D., 464, 465, 561
MacLusky, N.J., 429
MacNichol, E.F., Jr., 237
MacPhail, E.M., 131
Madison, D.V., 48, 516. See also
  Malcuit, G.
Maes, F.W., 218
Maffei, L., 263
Magendie, F., 102
Magni, F., 373
Magoun, H.W., 372
Mahan, J.J., Jr., 498
Mahl, G.F., 467
Mahowald, M.W., 378
Maier, S.F., 213, 561
Maisto, S.A., 91
Majewska, M.D., 470
Major, L.F., 480
Malamut, B.L., 502
Malcuit, G., 452
Malenka, R.C., 516
Maletzky, B.M., 479
Malinow, R., 516
Malloy, F., 564
Mangiapane, M.L., 393, 394
Manier, D.H., 563
Mann, J.J., 480. See also Arango, V.
Manning, F.J., 503

Mant, R. See Goate, A.
Marazita, M.L. See Ritvo, E.R.
March, L. See Brown, R.
Marciano, F., 550
Marcus, J., 575
Marcus, M., 558
Margolis, F.L., 222
Marinescu, C., 411
Mark, V.H., 477, 479
Marlatt, G.A., 89
Marler, J.R., 528
Marler, P., 7
Marques, P.R., 388
Marrama, P. See Carani, C.
Marsden, C.D., 328
Marshall, J., 265
Marshall, J.C., 125
Marshall, J.F., 408, 532, 538, 539,
  540, 541, 545
Marthelemy, C. See Lelord, G.
Martier, S. See Ernhart, C.B.
Martin, A.R., 73
Martin, D.C., 304
Martin, F.C. See Shavit, Y.
Martin, G.F., 265
Martin, J.B. See Beal, M.F.
Martin, J.V., 470
Martin, R.C., 179
Martin, R.D., 437
Martin, W.R.W. See Calne, D.B.
Martineau, J., 590
Martinez, J.L., Jr., 519
Martinez, Y., 213
Martinez-Vargas, M.C., 426
Martino, E. See Désir, D.
Marton, K.I. See Koran, L.M.
Marzuk, P.M. See Arango, V.
Mash, D.C., 494
Mason, J.W., 456
Mason-Brothers, A., 589
Masson, D.B. See Fitts, D.A., 395
Masterson, R.B., 202
Matheis, M., 442
Mathe-Sørenssen, D., 516
Mathew, R.J., 574
Matisse, Henri, 257
Matossian, M.K., 88
Matsuda, L.A., 85
Mattes, R.D., 400
Matthews, D.A., 537
Matthews, G., 237
Matthysse, S., 577
Maturana, H.R., 186
Mawson, A.R., 480
Maxwell, E. See DeLisi, L.E.
May, P.R.A., 529
Mayeno, A.N. See Belongia, E.A.
Mayer, A.D., 436, 437
Mayer, J., 403
Mayer, W., 354
Mazurek, M.F. See Beal, M.F.
Mazzarella, V., 531
Mazziotta, J.C., 144, 146. See also
  Baxter, L.R.
McBride, A., 480
McCane, S.M., 394
McCann, D.S., 472
McCann, J.J., 243
McCann, M.J., 403
McCarley, R.W., 369, 374, 375
McChesney, C. See
  Andreasen, N.C.
McClane, S., 410
McConnell, J.V., 509
McConnell, S.K., 284
McCormick, D.A., 80, 517
McCulloch, W.S., 186

McDougal, J.N., 388
McElhiney, M., 160
McElroy, A.E., 215
McEwen, B.S., 420, 480, 522. See
  also Ehrhardt, A.A.
McEwen, G.N., Jr., 388
McGaugh, J.L., 499, 519
McGinty, D., 373
McGinty, D.J., 375
McGlone, J.S., 139
McGlynn, S.M., 547
McGuffin, P., 576
McHale, C.M., 403
McHugh, P.R., 339, 402, 403
McIntyre, I.M., 562
McKearin, D.M. See Shapiro, D.J.
McKinnon, W., 461
McLean, S., 210
McLeod, P.J., 445
McMahon, C.E., 455
McManaman, J.L., 283
McMasters, R.E., 536
McMinn, M.R., 446
McMullen, C.W., 440
McMurray, J., 162
McNaughton, B.L., 502, 521
McSpadden, M., 89
McWilliams, J.R., 545
Meagher, M.W., 213
Meaney, M.J., 470
Meddis, R., 357, 367
Mednick, S.A., 575, 580, 585. See
  also Witkin, H.A.
Meduna, L., 564
Meehl, P.E., 578
Meek, P.S., 91
Meertz, E., 573
Megumi, N., 411
Meinecke, C.F., 433
Meisami, E., 297
Meisel, R.L., 440, 445
Meiselman, H.L., 219
Melamed, E., 58
Melica, A.M., 558
Meltzer, H.Y., 573
Melvin, L.S., 85
Melzack, R., 208
Menaker, M., 355
Mendel, G., 594
Mendelsohn, G.A., 334, 336
Mendelson, W.B., 470
Merton, P.A., 315
Merzenich, M.M., 124, 208, 540
Messing, R.B., 480, 519
Mestler, G.E., 431
Metter, E.J. See Kempler, D.
Meyer, D.R., 498
Meyer, J.S., 378
Meyer-Bahlburg, H.F.L. See
  Ehrhardt, A.A.
Meyers, D.A. See Folstein, S.E.
Michael, C.R., 186
Michael, R.P., 432
Michelman, J.D., 587
Michelsen, N., 575
Miczek, K.A., 213
Mierson, S., 218
Miles, F.A., 315
Miles, L.E.M., 350
Milhaud, C. See Lagarde, D.
Miller, A.H., 461
Miller, E.A., 546
Miller, E.H., 7, 8
Miller, G.A., 578, 579
Miller, J.D., 531
Miller, K.W., 46

Miller, M.G., 401
Miller, M.J., 564
Miller, N.E., 12, 19, 409
Miller, S., 567
Miller, W.C., 334, 337
Millett, F.E., 456
Millhorn, D.E., 78, 79
Milner, B., 489–491. See also
  Penfield, W.
Milner, P., 466
Milofsky, E. See Hartmann, E.
Milofsky, E.S., 90
Milstein, V., 564, 568
Minami, T., 418
Minard, A., 357
Minor, T.R., 457
Minors, D.S., 351
Mintun, M., 181
Mirsky, A.F., 476, 478, 577
Miselis, R.R., 393
Mishkin, M., 502, 503, 521
Mishra, R., 563
Mitchell, D., 357
Mitchell, D.E., 294, 295, 296
Mitchell, J.E., 583
Mitchell, S.J. See DeLong, M.R.
Mitchison, G., 368
Mizuno, Y., 418
Mo, A., 589
Moeller, J.R. See Sackeim, H.A.
Moffitt, B.P., 387
Mohr, J.P., 184
Mohs, R.C., 494, 519
Moises, H.W. See Kennedy, J.L.
Moll, P.P. See Bogardus, C.
Moltz, H., 436
Monaghan, D.T., 514
Money, J., 428, 433, 441, 442, 443,
  447, 448
Monroe, Y.L., 436
Monti Graziadei, G.A., 35
Mook, D.G., 407
Moonen, C.T.W., 142
Moorcroft, W.J., 379
Moore, A. See Insel, T.R.
Moore, B.D., 159
Moore, B.O., 403
Moore, J.T., 379
Moore, R.Y., 355, 537
Moore-Ede, M.C., 351, 352, 377,
  566
Morales, F.R., 379
Moran, T.H., 402, 403
Morgan, B.L.G., 305
Morgan, D.G., 337
Morgane, P.J., 372, 375
Morley, J.E., 409, 499
Morlock, G.W., 547
Moron, P. See Ernhart, C.B.
Morris, M., 376, 385
Morris, N.M., 433
Morris, R., 434
Morris, R.G.M., 516
Morrison, A.R., 379
Morrison, J.H., 114, 494, 495
Morrongiello, B.A., 194
Morrow, L., 161
Morse, J.R., 218
Mortimer, J.A., 493
Moruzzi, G., 372, 373
Moscovitch, M., 162, 521
Moser, K.H., 130
Moskowitz, H.R., 219
Moskowitz-Cook, A., 287, 290
Moulton, D.G., 224
Mountcastle, V.B., 120
Mouradian, M.M. See Chase, T.N.

# Subject Index

sodium succinate, 216
soma, **55**. *See also* cell body
somatic nervous system, 97–98, **149**
somatomedins, 418
somatosensory cortex, 208
somatosensory system, 124, 206–208, **226**
somatotropin, 421
sound recognition, 161
sounds
  localizing, 200–203
  tasks requiring attention to, 126
sound shadows, 200, 202
sound waves, 193–194
  in localizing sound, 200, 202, 203
sour tastes, 215–216, 218, 220–221
spastic paralysis, 313
spatial perceptions, 126, 160, 161
  parietal lobe damage and, 125
spatial summation, 61–62, **93**
  temporal summation and, 63
speaking ability, 156–157
species differences, 15–17
  in axon growth, 276–277
  in brains, 98, 273
  in color vision, 237
  in columns in cerebral cortex, 120
  in development of eyes, 286
  in evolution of brain, 129–131
  in hibernation, 358
  in intelligence, 131
  in language abilities, 170–174
  in localizing sound, 202
  in maintaining water balance, 390
  in menstrual cycles, 424
  in numbers of rods and cones, 236
  in prefrontal cortex development, 129
  in regrowth of axons, 535
  in REM sleep needs, 366–368
  in representation of body in, 125
  in sensitive periods, 7
  in sensory information, 186
  in size of cerebellum, 324
  in sleeping habits, 358–359
specific anosmia, 224, **226**
speech. *See also* language
  basal ganglia, 113
  hemispheres and, 159
  loss of, 532
speech therapy, 184
speed of diffusion, 73
speed perception, 254
spinal cord, 97, 101–104, **149**
  cross section, 101
  development of, 102
  disorders of, 313
  injuries to, 534–535, 536
  reflexes and, 58, 59, 62
  role of, in movement, 322–323
  segments of, 102–103
  sensory neurons of, 30, 31
  spinal pathways, 103–104
spinal nerves, 102, **149**
spiny anteater, 367
splanchnic nerves, 402, **413**
splenium, 182
split-brain people, 156–158, 159, 160, 165
spontaneous firing rate, 63, **93**, 190
squid, 27
squirrel monkeys, 339

squirrels. *See also* flying squirrels
  hibernation and, 357–358
S sleep. *See* non-REM sleep
standing up, 329
stapes (stirrup), 194, 196
statoacoustic nerve, 110
stereoscopic depth perception, 252, **268**, 293–294, **307**
stereotaxic atlas, 134, **149**
stereotaxic instrument, 134–136, **149**
stereotaxic procedures, for measuring brain chemicals, 410
steroid hormones, 416, 418–420, **449**
stimulants, biological clocks and, 354
stimuli, synapses and, 58–59
stirrup (stapes), 194, 196
strabismus, 294, **307**
stress
  alcohol and, 91
  as biological cause of depression, 557–558
  chronic, 459–461
  endorphin release during, 213
  illness and, 456–457
  menstrual cycle and, 424
  recovered behavior and, 532–533
  schizophrenia and, 578
  unpredictable and uncontrollable, 357
stretch reflex, 315
striate cortex. *See* visual cortex (primary or V1)
striated muscles. *See* skeletal muscles
stroke patients, 160–161
  recovery from aphasia, 184
strokes, 528–531, **551**
  mania following, 560
stuttering, 167
subarachnoid space, 115, **149**
subfornical organ, 393, **413**
subplate cell, **307**
substance abuse. *See also* alcohol use/abuse
  genetic factors in, 558
  sleep disorders and, 376
substance P, 71, 210, **227**
substantia nigra, 110, **149**, 327, 334, 335, 336, 549
  MPTP and, 337
subthalamic nucleus, 327
sucrose (cane sugar), 219
sugar, 219
suicide
  ECT to prevent, 564
  fluoxetine (Prozac) and, 562
  serotonin levels and, 480–481
sulcus (sulci), 100
superior colliculus, 108, 109, **149**, 234, 265–266
  effects of damage to, 544–545
  lesions on, 265
superior (direction), 99–100
supplementary motor cortex, 329
suprachiasmatic nucleus (SCN), 354–356, **381**
swallowing, 322
sweat rate, 105
sweet tastes, 187, 215–216, 218, 219, 220–221
  preferences for, 398
sweet-bitter taste, 219
Sylvian fissure, 163, **185**
symbols, patients with aphasia and, 184

sympathetic nervous system, 104–106, **149**. *See also* autonomic nervous system
  behavior and, 452–453
  measuring, 453
  nerve growth factor and, 283
  stress and, 459
synapses, 28, 57, **93**. *See also* neuromuscular junctions
  activating previously ineffective, 540
  chemical events at, 66–80
  concept of, 58–64
  decision process and, 64
  diagram of, 74
  displacing the less active, 291
  effect of drugs on, 83–91
  electrical versus chemical theory of, 66–67
  elimination of, 282
  formation of, 280
  inhibitory, 62–63
  ionic effects at, 76
  metabotropic effects at, 76–77
  properties of, 58–63
  of Purkinje cell, 30, 31
  size of cleft, 73
  spatial summation at, 61–62
  in spinal cord, 103
  sprouting of, 537–538
  temporal summation at, 59–61
synchronized sleep. *See* non-REM sleep
synergistic effect, 394–395, **413**
syphilis, 199, 303

tabes dorsalis, 313
tangles, 494, **525**
tardive dyskinesia, 583–584, **592**
target cells, 276–283
taste, 215–221
  preferences, 394, 395, 398, 399
  satiety mechanisms and, 407
taste buds, 217, **227**
taste receptors, 188, 216–220
T cells, 460, **483**
tectum, 108, **149**, 277, **307**
  experiments on, 277–281
tegmentum, 110, **149**
temperature regulation, 385–388. *See also* body temperature
templates, 7, **21**, **605**
  of DNA, 598
  mRNA (messenger RNA), 598–599
  viruses as, 599
temporal lobes, 126, **149**
  effect of reading on, 181
temporal summation, 59–61, **93**
  spatial summation and, 63
TENS. *See* transcutaneous electrical nerve stimulation
termination insomnia, 376, **381**
testes, 427
  pituitary gland and, 112
testicular feminization, 446, **449**
testis, **449**
  hormones and functions, 418
testis cells, 33–34
testosterone, 420, 427–429, 433–434, **449**
  in birds, 5–7
  homosexuality and, 444
  left-handedness and, 167
thalamus, 109, 110, 114, **149**
  intrinsic nuclei of, 121
  role in conveying information to cerebral cortex, 324

in somatosensory system, 208
  visual information and, 234
therapy
  for aphasia, 184
  for brain damage, 547–550
  for depression, 562–568
  for schizophrenia, 581–584
theophylline, 219
theta waves, 361, **381**
thiamine (vitamin B1), **55**
  ability to use glucose and, 35
  deficiency, 89, 491–492
third ventricle, 411
thirst, 390–395
thoracic nerves, 102
Thorazine (chlorpromazine), 581, 590, **591**
thought disorder, 571, **592**
Three Mile Island nuclear power plant, 460–461
threshold, **55**
  opening gates at, 46
  of stimulation in cells, 44
throxine, 417
thymosin, 418
thymus gland, 167
  hormones and functions, 418
thyroid gland
  deafness and, 200
  pituitary gland and, 112
thyroid gland, hormones and functions, 418
thyroid hormones, 416, 417, **449**
  as biological cause of depression, 558
  deficiency, 305
thyroid-stimulating hormone (TSH), 418, 421–424
thyroxine, 418
tides, 350
tingling sensations, 124
Tofranil (imipramine), 562
tongue receptors, 218
toothpaste, 219
touch receptors, 206–207
touch sensations, 124, 125. *See also* mechanical senses
Tourette's syndrome, 472
Tower of Hanoi puzzle, 491
toxic substances. *See also* alcohol
  effects of, on the brain, 303–304
  exposure to, 336
  infant reflexes and, 317
tract, 100
tranquilizers
  alcohol and, 89, 471
  biological clocks and, 354
  for insomnia, 377–378
  for panic disorder, 473
  withdrawal, 377–378
transcutaneous electrical nerve stimulation (TENS), 213, **227**
transduction, 188, **227**, 237
transsexuals, 440
transverse plane. *See* horizontal plane
traveling waves, 199
triazolam, 378
trichotillomania, 472
trichromatic (Young-Helmholtz) theory, 238–239, **269**
tricyclic drugs, 86, 562, 565, **592**
trigeminal nerve, 110
triiodothyronine, 417, 418
trochlear nerve, 110
trophic factor, 283, **307**
tryptophan, **93**, **381**
  aggressive behavior and, 480

tryptophan (*continued*)
  as sleep inducer, 375
  transport system of, 69
TSH (thyroid-stimulating hormone), 418, 421–424
tuberculosis, drugs for, 84
Turner's syndrome, 446–447, **449**
turnover, 479, **483**
turtles, 103
tympanic membrane, 194–196, **227**
tyrosine, 300–301, **307**, 417, **605**
  conversion of, 86
  effect of AMPT on, 84
  in synthesis, 68, 72

ulcers, 456–458, **483**
ultraviolet light (short-wavelength), 186
unconditioned response (UR), 486, **525**
unconditioned stimulus (US), 486, **525**
unipolar disorder, 555, **592**
urea, permeability of, 40
urination, biological clock and, 351, 352
urine, 390–391, 392

V1. *See* visual cortex (primary or V1)
V2. *See* visual cortex (secondary or V2)
V3, 254, **269**
V4, 243, 254, **269**
vagus nerve, 110, 217, 390–391, 402, **413**
Valium (diazepam), 469
vasoactive intestinal protein (VIP), 71
vasopressin, 71, 391, **413**, 418, 420, 519
ventral (direction), 98, 99–100

ventricles, 115, 117, **149**, 573
ventromedial hypothalamus (VMH), 409–410, 411, **413**
ventromedial tract, 329, 345
vertebrates, 96–98
  eye of, 247
  muscle categories of, 310
vesicles, 73, **93**
  networks of, 27
vestibular nucleus, 329
vestibular organs, 126, 205, **227**
vestibular sensations, 205–206. *See also* mechanical senses
  during dreaming, 369
Vietnam veterans, 461
violence, 433–434. *See also* aggressive behavior
viral infections
  and depression, 559
  and schizophrenia, 578–580
vision, 123–124
  color coding, 237–243
visual cortex, 119, 251, **268**
  damage to, 182–183
  lesions on, 265
  shape perception and, 256–265
visual cortex (primary or V1), 123, 243, 251, 254, **268**
  cells in, 261
  complex cells in, 258
visual cortex (secondary or V2), 252, 254, **268, 269**
  cells in, 261
  complex cells in, 258
visual fatigue, 260, 262
visual field, 154, **185**
visual perceptions, 126
visual receptors, 188, 190, 234–237
visual stimulation, 76
visual system
  binocular interaction, 287–294
  development in infants, 286–287, 290

development of, 286–297
  early lack of stimulation and, 289–294
  lack of visual experience and, 289–290
  motion perception, 296
  neural basis of perception, 245–266
  pathways in, 250–256
  pattern perception, 294–296
  processing at higher levels, 252–254
  relationship of pathways to perception, 254–256
  shape perception in, 256–265
visual tasks/information, 160, 161
vitamins
  for autism, 590
  B1 (thiamine), 35, **55**, 89, 396, 491–492
  B12, 222
  deficiencies, 89, 222, 305
volley principle, 198–199, **227**
voltage-activated gates, 46, **55**
vomiting, 107
voodoo death, 458

wakefulness, 372–373, 375
walking, 322, 328, 329
wall-eye. *See* strabismus
war. *See* combat disorders
warmth perception, 206
waste materials, 32
water balance, 390–395
waterfall illusion, 262
water permeability, 40
W cells, 250, **269**
Weigert stain, 138
weight. *See* body weight
Wernicke-Korsakoff syndrome, 491–493

Wernicke's aphasia, 150, 178–180, 183
Wernicke's area, 126, 178, **185**
  Broca's area and, 181–182
white matter, 104, **149**
Wisconsin card-sorting task, 504, **525**
withdrawal, 377–378
Wolffian ducts, 427, **449**
women. *See* females; sex differences
woodpeckers, 529
word blindness, 182–183, **185**
working memory, 497, **525**
writing. *See* language

Xanax (alprazolam), 469
X cells, 250–251, **269**
X chromosome, 243, 300, 597, **605**
xenon, 143
XO chromosome pattern, 446–447
X rays
  biological clocks and, 354
  brain maturation and, 140
  CT scan and, 141
XXY chromosome pattern, 447, **449**
XY chromosome pattern, 446
Xylocaine, 46, 86
XYY chromosome pattern, 447, **449**

yawning
  biological clock and, 351
  as fixed action pattern, 319–320
Y cells, 250–251, **269**
Y chromosome, 597, **605**
Young-Helmholtz theory, 238–239, **269**

zeitgebers, 350, **381**
  effective and ineffective, 354

### Patricia S. Goldman-Rakic

*The question of how the brain organizes its subsystems to produce integrated behavior is perhaps the most challenging that can be posed.*

### Paul MacLean

*I am often ashamed of myself because of the name I chose for our laboratory, Laboratory of Brain Evolution and Behavior. I mean, anybody in science talks as though behavior is the only thing that counts, whereas we all know that the only thing that counts is what we are feeling inside ourselves and how we relate to other individuals.*

### Roger W. Sperry

*When subjective values have objective consequences . . . they become part of the content of science. . . . Science would become the final determinant of what is right and true, the best source and authority available to the human brain for finding ultimate axioms and guideline beliefs to live by, and for reaching an intimate understanding and rapport with the forces that control the universe and created man.*

### Santiago Ramón y Cajal (1852–1934)

*How many interesting facts fail to be converted into fertile discoveries because their first observers regard them as natural and ordinary things! . . . It is strange to see how the populace, which nourishes its imagination with tales of witches or saints, mysterious events and extraordinary occurrences, disdains the world around it as commonplace, monotonous and prosaic, without suspecting that at bottom it is all secret, mystery, and marvel.*

### Edward Stricker

*I believe that by studying the biochemistry of the catecholaminergic neurons that are so importantly involved in motivation, we are essentially studying the biochemistry of motivation, including human behavior. I foresee a time when we will be discussing motivation in terms of the underlying biochemistry just as we now can discuss movement of a limb in terms of its underlying anatomy.*

### William C. Dement

*The average person would not, at first blush, pick watching people sleep as the most apparent theme for a spine-tingling scientific adventure thriller. However, there is a subtle sense of awe and mystery surrounding the "short death" we call sleep.*